D0742398

ROTH FAMILY FOUNDATION

Music in America Imprint

Michael P. Roth

and Sukey Garcetti

have endowed this

imprint to honor the

memory of their parents,

Julia and Harry Roth,

whose deep love of music

they wish to share

with others.

The publisher gratefully acknowledges the generous contribution toward the publication of this book provided by the Chairman's Circle of the University of California Press Foundation, whose members are:

Anonymous
Jeanne & Michael Adams
Carol & John Field
Jean E. Gold
Adele M. Hayutin
Barbara S. Isgur
Beth & Fred Karren
John Lescroart & Lisa Sawyer
Fred Levin & Nancy Livingston / Shenson Foundation,
in memory of Ben & A. Jess Shenson
Michael McCone
Thormund A. & Barbara Miller
James & Carlin Naify
Eric Papenfuse & Catherine Lawrence
Loren & Frances Rothschild
Lisa See & Richard Kendall
Meryl Selig
Ralph & Shirley Shapiro
Susan Stone
John & Donna Sussman
Judy & Bill Timken

Publication of this book was supported by grants from the H. Earle Johnson Fund of the Society of American Music and the Dragan Plamenac Publication Endowment Fund of the American Musicological Society.

GEORGE GERSHWIN

Other books by Howard Pollack:

Aaron Copland: The Life and Work of an Uncommon Man

John Alden Carpenter: A Chicago Composer

*Harvard Composers: Walter Piston and His Students,
from Elliott Carter to Frederic Rzewski*

Walter Piston

Howard Pollack

GEORGE GERSHWIN

His Life and Work

University of California Press   Berkeley · Los Angeles · London

University of California Press, one of the most
distinguished university presses in the United States,
enriches lives around the world by advancing
scholarship in the humanities, social sciences, and
natural sciences. Its activities are supported by the UC
Press Foundation and by philanthropic contributions
from individuals and institutions. For more information, visit www.ucpress.edu.

University of California Press
Berkeley and Los Angeles, California

University of California Press, Ltd.
London, England

Library of Congress Cataloging-in-Publication Data

Pollack, Howard.
George Gershwin : his life and work / Howard Pollack.
p.   cm.
Includes bibliographical references (p.   ) and index.
ISBN-13: 978-0-520-24864-9 (cloth : alk. paper)
ISBN-10: 0-520-24864-3 (cloth : alk. paper)
1. Gershwin, George, 1898–1937.   2. Composers—
United States—Biography.   I. Title.
ML410.G288P65   2007
780.92—dc22
[B]   2006017926

Manufactured in the United States of America

15   14   13   12   11   10   09   08   07   06
      10   9   8   7   6   5   4   3   2   1

This book is printed on Natures Book, which contains
50% post-consumer waste and meets the minimum
requirements of ANSI/NISO Z39.48–1992 (R 1997)
(*Permanence of Paper*).♾

To the memory of

Darryl Marcus Wexler

Where had he got it?—from the sounds of the streets? the taxis creak-
ing to a stop? the interrogatory squeak of a streetcar? some distant and
obscure city sound in which a plaintive high note, bitten sharp, follows
a lower note, strongly clanged and solidly based? Or had he got it from
Schoenberg or Stravinsky?—or simply from his own nostalgia, among
the dark cells and the raspings of New York, for those orchestras and
open squares which his parents had left behind?—or from the cadences,
half-chanted and despairing, of the tongue which the father had known,
but which the child had now forgotten and was never to know again?

But the relations between Schoenberg and the taxi brakes and the synagogue resisted further speculation. And, in any case, what charmed and
surprised one, in this as in all works of art, was no mere combination of
elements, however picturesque or novel, but some distinctive individual
quality which the artist himself supplied. Of all the young Jews in New
York who had listened to the service in the synagogue or who had been
kept awake at night by taxis, how many had written good music, even
good popular music?

EDMUND WILSON, *I Thought of Daisy*

Contents

This book builds upon the work of the main chroniclers of George Gershwin's life and work, including Isaac Goldberg, Merle Armitage, David Ewen, Edward Jablonski, Lawrence Stewart, Robert Payne, Robert Kimball, Alfred Simon, Charles Schwartz, Deena Rosenberg, Joan Peyser, and William Hyland. These writers had the advantage of knowing members of Gershwin's intimate circle—and in some cases, Gershwin himself—and any investigation of the composer has no choice but to take stock of their collective and in many ways notable achievement. However, their writings largely predated not only the appearance of a number of important publications, dissertations, recordings, and performances, but the availability of a variety of archival materials, including a large cache of Gershwin manuscripts discovered in a Warner Brothers warehouse in Secaucus, New Jersey, in 1982. Accordingly, the time seems ripe for a broad reexamination of Gershwin's life and work.

The current study is organized along partly thematic, partly chronological lines. Part I contains chapters devoted to Gershwin's childhood and family, musical education, early relation to popular music, achievement as a pianist, youthful activities on Broadway, friendships and love affairs, continuing study of music, involvement with serious music, mature thoughts on popular music and jazz, creative process, and lifestyle and character.

Part II surveys Gershwin's output from his earliest compositions to those pieces brought forth posthumously by his brother Ira. Unlike most other books on Gershwin, this one pays close attention to music, shows, films, recordings, and critical writings from both the composer's own time and after his death. Again, the coverage is not strictly chronological. The chapter on *Girl Crazy* (1930), for instance, includes some discussion of that musical's various revivals and film adaptations, as well as the importance of one of its songs, "I Got Rhythm," to the history of jazz; while the chapter on Gershwin's *Song-Book* (1932) considers some of the wide uses of the Gershwin songbook on record, on film, and in theaters.

In light of the book's organization, a few chronological markers might be helpful to keep in mind. Born in New York on September 26, 1898,

Gershwin began piano lessons about 1910 and started to compose around the same time as well. He left high school in 1914 at age fifteen to work as a song plugger for Remick, a popular music publishing house, though he continued to study and compose on his own. In early1917 he quit Remick and in early 1918 he landed a position as a songwriter for T. B. Harms, forthwith his principal publisher. In 1919 he wrote his first Broadway show—*La-La-Lucille!*—as well as a song, "Swanee," whose immense popularity brought him international recognition. He became that much better known in 1924 with the introduction of his *Rhapsody in Blue* for piano and jazz band and hit shows on both the West End *(Primrose)* and Broadway *(Lady, Be Good!)*. In the ensuing years, he continued to compose both concert works—including the Concerto in F (1925) and *An American in Paris* (1928)—and musical comedies—including *Girl Crazy* (1930) and *Of Thee I Sing* (1931), the first musical comedy to win a Pulitzer Prize—largely with great success. Having long resided with his parents and three siblings, he moved into an apartment of his own in 1929, living the rest of his short life as a bachelor, but never far from brother Ira, his primary lyricist since 1924. He traveled frequently, especially to London, and spent some of 1930–1931 and 1936–1937 in Hollywood working on musical pictures. His career climaxed with the opera *Porgy and Bess,* which had its world premiere in Boston on September 30, 1935, before moving to Broadway. He died of an undiagnosed brain tumor in Los Angeles on July 11, 1937, at age thirty-eight.

Recognizing Gershwin as fundamentally a man of the theater, this study surveys his work on Broadway and Hollywood in some depth, providing for each of his shows a synopsis of the story (if a book musical— that is, a musical with a plot), details about the cast and other aspects of its first production, and reportage of the work's critical reception and performance history. This emphasis challenges the common notion of Gershwin's musical comedies as so much window dressing for hit songs, while underscoring the deep connection between his music and the popular theatrical genres of his time, including farce, parody, romantic comedy, and melodrama.

Most of the capsule plot summaries found here—many of which can be found nowhere else—at least provide the original dramatic contexts for Gershwin's songs on stage and screen. At the same time, they are typically quite convoluted, and readers can skim or skip them without losing the basic thread of the book. In any case, they generally endeavor to reflect Gershwin's shows as they debuted on Broadway, providing they made it there, which nearly all of them did (though note that in the case of *Strike Up the Band* and *Pardon My English,* synopses of their pre-liminary Philadelphia versions appear in the body of the text, whereas those of their considerably altered Broadway versions appear in the notes). However, musical comedies of this period existed in a state of flux, sometimes wildly so, and those scripts that survive do not always, if ever, indicate exactly what opening night audiences actually saw and heard. A broad brush—along with some scrutiny of programs and re-views—can help circumvent such difficulties, but even so, these synopses cannot be considered definitive.

A few stylistic inconsistencies and irregularities might be mentioned here as well. The book, which generally designates adults by their full or surnames, reserves "Gershwin" for the composer, and often refers to Ira and the rest of his family by just their first names. The use of nicknames generally depends on their familiarity as such. For songs whose listing in programs differs from their published titles, preference is given to the latter. If not specified, "the *Rhapsody*" typically refers to Gershwin's *Rhapsody in Blue* as opposed to his *Second Rhapsody.* The years given for concert pieces generally indicate their date of completion; those for shows and films, their official premiere; and those for books and recordings, their published copyright date. In the context of the prewar musical com-edy, the term *choreographer* is anachronistic, and might be thought of as synonymous with the more historically precise *dance director.* Songs and shows are sometimes identified only by their composer (that is, with-out mention of lyricists or librettists, as customary). Note numbers refer back to entire paragraphs.

One can roughly convert stated dollar amounts to today's prices by multiplying by twenty for the time period from Gershwin's birth in 1898 to about 1916; by fourteen for the years 1917 and 1918; by eleven for the years from 1919 to 1931; and by fourteen for the years from 1932 to Gershwin's death in 1937.

The book assumes some knowledge of basic musical terms (with more technical observations often appearing in parentheses). For those unfa-miliar with popular song jargon, the main part of a song is the "chorus" or "refrain"; the introductory portion is known as the "verse"; and the couplet that frequently serves as a transition between the verse and the chorus is called the "vest." During Gershwin's working years, popular song refrains typically—though by no means invariably—comprised four eight-measure phrases that either involved a return of the principal theme at the midpoint (*abab*) or, after some contrasting material (the "bridge"), toward the end (*aaba*). However, the labels *abab* and *aaba* should not be taken too literally, as few of these *a*s and *b*s tended to be identical; a more accurate, if more cumbersome, shorthand might read *aba¹b¹* (or *aba¹c*) and *aba¹a²*.

Unless otherwise indicated, the unpublished Gershwin manuscripts mentioned in this book, including sketches, drafts, and completed works, are from either the Gershwin Collection at the Music Division of the Library of Congress, or the Ira and Leonore Gershwin Trusts in San Francisco. (Beginning in 1939, the Gershwin family and subsequently members of their circle donated archival materials related to the composer—including the aforementioned treasure trove found in 1982—to the Music Division of the Library of Congress, which over the years supplemented this collection with various purchases of its own. The Gershwin Collection now comprises an estimated 15,000 items, including scrapbooks that themselves contain hundreds of clippings, though other relevant documents remain in the possession of the Ira and Leonore Gershwin Trusts.)

Gershwin's extraordinary fame perhaps is not quite what it was for much of the twentieth century. Even so, people around the globe still enjoy some contact with his work—whether heard on the radio or in concert, in department stores or hotels, in restaurants and nightclubs, on television or at the movies, onstage or at home. This book, it is hoped, will lead to an enhanced understanding of not only the man and his music, but also the world from which he emerged and the world that he helped to create.

I am deeply appreciative of the generous help I received on this project. Raymond White of the Library of Congress proved especially invaluable, answering innumerable questions and requests promptly and graciously. Farhad Moshiri, Joan O'Connor, Tammy Ravas, and others on staff at the University of Houston also provided excellent assistance. Mark Goldberg Trent and Michael Owen of the Ira and Leonore Gershwin Trusts, Samuel Brylawski and Stephanie Poxon of the Library of Congress, George Boziwick at the New York Public Library, and Gershwin's nephews, Marc Gershwin and Leopold Godowsky III, fielded many inquiries as well, as did scores of other librarians, archivists, scholars, friends, and students, including Thomas Rigney. In addition, a number of experts and enthusiasts supplied rare materials, and in this respect I am particularly indebted to Michael Feinstein.

My parents, Adele and Walter Pollack, and friends, including Thomas Sattler, John Reynolds, Philip Silverman, and Steven Tulin, facilitated research trips to New York, San Francisco, and Washington, D.C. I received support as well from the University of Houston and the National Endowment for the Humanities.

Michael Feinstein, Alex Jeschke, Robert Kimball, Andrew Lamb, and Tony Sessions read drafts of the entire manuscript and helped enormously by correcting mistakes and offering valuable suggestions. Edward Berlin, Steven Cassedy, Andrew Davis, George Ferencz, Philip Furia, Miles Kreuger, Jeffrey Morgan, Don Rayno, Wayne Shirley, Lawrence Stewart, Darryl Wexler, and many others similarly commented on various portions of the book, which also benefited greatly from the expertise of Mary Francis, Mary Severance, and others at the University of California Press.

Part One

LIFE

Chapter One

Gershwin and His Family

George Gershwin's father, Morris, was born Moishe Gershovitz (Gershowitz) in St. Petersburg around January 1872. Moishe's father, Yakov, an inventor and mechanic, had served in the Russian artillery, which gave him dispensation as a Jew to move to St. Petersburg from the Pale of Settlement along Russia's western border, an area to which the country's Jews were largely confined in the nineteenth century. By some accounts, Yakov's father was a rabbi, but little else is known about the Gershovitzes, even the name of Yakov's wife (George's paternal grandmother), in part because whereas Morris immigrated to New York, most of his family apparently remained in Russia.[1]

Gershwin's mother, Rose, was born Rosa Bruskin (Brushkin) around January 1875, also in St. Petersburg. Her father, Gershon (b. approximately 1852), a furrier, similarly hailed from the Pale—specifically Vilna (that is, Vilnius, the capital of Lithuania). Gershon married Mariaska (Mary) Dechinik (b. approximately 1858) about 1878, and the two had nine children, only three of whom survived: Rose, Bernard (Barney, b. 1888), and Katiel (Kate, b. 1890). Why the Bruskins were allowed residence in the Russian capital remains unknown, though Kate recalled something about their having more latitude than other Jews because Gershon "worked for important people in the fur business."[2]

Family lore holds that Morris and Rose knew each other before they left for America, and that an enamored Morris followed Rose across the seas. But the record suggests that Morris arrived in New York—by himself, though preceded by an uncle—in 1890, and that Rose and her immediate family arrived in 1892. Some commentators also have suggested that Morris emigrated to avoid military service, though by this point the rise of anti-Semitism in Russia had accelerated to the point that millions of Jews needed little special incentive for leaving that country behind.[3]

On July 21, 1895, within a few years of their arrival in the States, Rose married Morris (by this time Gershvin, though by 1920 Gershwin, a name apparently first adopted by his son George as a nom de plume about 1913). Four children followed: Israel (called Isidore or Izzy, later Ira; December 6, 1896–August 17, 1983); Jacob (Yakov), named after Morris's father (though called George as early as his second year; September 26, 1898–July 11, 1937); Arthur (March 14, 1900–November 20, 1981); and Frances ("Frankie"; December 6, 1906–January 18, 1999). Morris and Rose learned English—they had grown up speaking both Russian and Yiddish, the family mother tongue—and became naturalized citizens in 1898. Still, they had been in the country a mere five years or so when George was born.[4]

In the first twenty-odd years of their marriage, the Gershwins resided, by Ira's later estimate, at as many as twenty-eight different New York locations, with Morris pursuing nearly as many occupations, including leather worker, shoemaker, bookie, and proprietor (sometimes in league with Abraham Wolpin, the husband of Rose's sister, Kate) of a stationery store, a cigar store (with billiard parlor), a summer hotel, Turkish baths, and numerous eateries, including a chain of bakeries called Wolpin and Gershv/win (W & G). The scant evidence suggests steadily increasing prosperity. In 1900, for instance, Morris earned his living making "uppers" for women's shoes; by 1909 he had acquired two "eating houses"; and in 1914 the Manhattan telephone directory listed no fewer than four Wolpin and Gershwin bakeries, perhaps the four "stores" alluded to by Ira in 1915. In still later years, George typically referred to his father as "a successful restaurant owner" or a "businessman."[5]

The fortunes of the Gershwin household may have fluctuated, but Morris "always made enough money to take care of the family," according to Rose, who, *Time* magazine reported, was "pretty scornful" of the "rags-to-riches theme" underpinning *Rhapsody in Blue,* the 1945 film biography of her son George. "There was always enough money for Georgie's lessons," she asserted. "Poppa had twelve restaurants." When their children were still young, the Gershwins employed a maid and obtained a piano and a record player, all signs of middle-class comfort. Ira's lifelong friend and fellow lyricist Edgar Y. ("Yip") Harburg (originally Irwin Hochberg) recalled a visit to the Gershwins' "swank" apartment on Second Avenue, adding, "Compared to most of us, the Gershwins were affluent; Ira had an allowance and money to buy magazines, books and records." The

Gershwins similarly provided Frances with dancing and elocution lessons and sent her to summer camp. Rose claimed that although they could have afforded to live in a better neighborhood, they resided largely on the Lower East Side—an overcrowded and generally poor area—because she wanted her children to be "regular kids" and see "how life begins."[6]

Little given to displays of emotion, Morris and Rose were a well-liked couple who enjoyed entertaining friends at home with a game of pinochle or poker, or going out to the theater or the races. Morris, who liked opera and purchased recordings, was the more musical of the two. "He could sing fairly," stated George, "and could whistle even better. He used to give excellent imitations of a cornet, and could wax music out of the silliest contraptions, such as combs and clothespins and pencils. But this was the extent of his musicality." George's further description of his father as "a very easy-going, humorous philosopher, who takes things as they come" conformed with his sister's recollection of him as "a real shnook," a "darling person," a gentle, kindly man who refused to honk his car at cyclists and who always gave money to panhandlers "for fear of missing someone who really needed aid." Composer Vernon Duke remembered George "arguing violently" with Morris, with whom he was "habitually rather snappy," but added, "they loved each other and the arguments were food of their love."[7]

As the film biography suggests, Morris enjoyed tinkering with mechanical contraptions. A 1941 article also referred to this side interest, as well as to his many businesses and residences: "A craftsman himself, he [Morris] imparted into his sons two principles: the importance of design and technique and an abiding passion for moving" (at least as concerned George, for Ira became quite the homebody in his later years). Morris's whimsical humor provided, meanwhile, a source of amusement for George, Ira, and their friends, though the charm of some reported anecdotes in part depended on his accent, including one in which *George* sounded like *judge*. (Vernon Duke enjoyed recalling how "Pops," on being asked by Russel Crouse, at an opening-night reception that followed one of his son's shows, how he had liked it, answered, "What you mean how I like it? I *have* to like it.") One wonders how the esteemed actor Morris Carnovsky prepared for his film portrayal of Morris, who died of leukemia in 1932. Perhaps he remembered the man—much of New York's theater community came to know Morris and Rose.[8]

Slightly taller than Morris, Rose was a formidable housewife. "Mrs. Gershwin is level-headed and practical," wrote playwright S. N. Behrman; "I imagine it was she who steered the family through the early years and

who helped Gershwin père to the eminence of a restaurant proprietor."
"When she wanted," added Yip Harburg, "she had the strength of a bull-dozer along with her playfulness." The 1945 biopic emphasized Rose's more workaday side, showing her cooking dinner, mending clothes, and worrying about money, as opposed to her penchant for playing poker, gambling at the racetracks, attending the Yiddish theater, and designing hats and dresses. "There was creativity in her family," recalled her daughter, Frances. In her later years, after her husband's death, she dined out nearly every night at Lindy's, a Manhattan haunt popular with theater crowds, and dated some men as well.[9]

A surviving 1935 letter from Rose to Ira, written in a heavily inflected English on stationery from Miami's Blackstone Hotel, also reveals her as extremely attentive to family matters: she tells Ira that she has just reminded George to write to him; she urges Ira to call Arthur; she complains that while George is attentive when he's with her, he forgets about her afterward (" . . . and soon hea lives you hea forget you"); and she wishes she had Ira or someone else with her "from home." She frets, too, about health matters—her own and Ira's—and hopes Ira's "getting busy on the show."[10]

This letter exemplifies George's description of his mother as "nervous, ambitious, and purposeful," to which he added, "She was never the doting type. Although very loving, she never watched every move we made. She was set on having us completely educated, her idea being that if everything else failed we could always become school-teachers." Such descriptions—along with George's 1933 oil painting of his mother, in which she looms over an isolated house with an almost fierce strength—helped fuel those depictions of her as manipulative and unaffectionate (though Gershwin plainly describes her as "very loving") and his father, conversely, as naive and warm, that characterize most Gershwin biographies. Such interpretations found additional grist when one biographer quoted George's psychiatrist, Gregory Zilboorg, as saying, "had Gershwin adored his mother and only respected his father, he would have become a hopeless psychoneurotic. Gershwin's adjustment to his work and to his life . . . was made possible only because his relations to his mother and father were exactly what they were."[11]

Whatever this quote actually betokens, and whatever its accuracy, the evidence points to a particularly close bond between Rose and George. "His mother," stated his first biographer, Isaac Goldberg, in 1929, "who is of intense importance to him psychologically, is the ideal mother in Israel,—the miracle of devotion that is too often forgotten by sons and daughters when they have acquired a sufficiently thick veneer of the new culture to make them ashamed of a culture more ancient." In 1944, publisher Bennett Cerf wrote, "Mrs. Gershwin was adored by everybody. 'You must meet my mother,' George would tell anybody who called. 'She's the most wonderful mother in the world.' On further reflection, he would frequently add, 'and so modest about *me*.'" "She's what the mammy writers write about," George told a reporter, "and what the mammy singers sing about. But they don't mean it and I do." Late in life, Kate Wolpin, after noting that her sister Rose had a "nice figure" and "dressed very well," added, "George was very proud of her."[12]

George's affection for his mother could be inferred further from his letters to her, with their ever-present concern about her health, and from family photographs taken in Beverly Hills in 1937, in which mother and son tenderly embrace. Frances confirmed that George "was very sweet to my mother." Significantly, when George described his mother as "nervous, ambitious and purposeful," as "never the doting type," as someone surprisingly "modest" about her famous son, he could have been describing himself for he, too, was nervous, ambitious, and purposeful, far from the doting type, and in his own way modest. He even told Isaac Goldberg, "I believe I have more of my mother's qualities than my father's."[13]

After Gershwin's death, his biographers depicted Rose in an increasingly harsh light. David Ewen's seminal writings registered such changing attitudes, from his portrayal of Rose as the "soft-eyed, little gentle woman whose entire life rotated about George's many triumphs as a composer" (1938), to the "wise, gentle woman, with a heart that continually overflowed with affection" (1943), to, finally, the "proud and self-centered woman whose driving ambition for herself and her family made her continually restless" (1956). This trend peaked with Joan Peyser's monograph (1993), which delineated Rose as unrelentingly vain and rapacious. Such disparagement reflected at least to some extent the perspectives of Ira and Frances, neither of whom had the kind of warm relationship with Rose that George seems to have had. Ira and Rose even engaged in something of a tussle for control of Gershwin's estate after the latter died intestate; and after Rose died of a heart attack in 1948, Ira further disputed her will, which left him only 20 percent of her estate as opposed to Arthur's and Frances's 40 percent each, an inequity amicably resolved among the siblings. Meanwhile, Frances harbored resentments toward her mother, attributing the problems that she and her brothers had in developing "real" relationships to her mother's neglect and narcissism (she felt further that thanks to psychotherapy, she alone among her siblings succeeded in having a mature and loving marriage).[14]

Neither Morris nor Rose, it is true, provided much support for George's early artistic ambitions, though whether this left him more defiant or regretful is difficult to say. "There is no such thing as tradition for me," he stated in 1929. "Whatever I know about music, I've wrenched out for myself. I had no parents to stand over me and encourage me in the little tunes that I used to make up. No one ever urged me on by telling me that Mozart was a great composer when he was eleven." Such lack of parental guidance made him concerned about the arts education of young people and reinforced his belief "that parents should encourage children in whatever they may want to do."[15]

On the other hand, at least in later years, his parents took obvious pleasure in his work, in particular Morris, whom observers often described as "beaming" through performances of his son's music (though proud of his son Izzy as well, the man who referred to "Fascinating Rhythm" as "Fashion on the River" was obviously less equipped to appreciate Ira's talents). The Gershwin lore includes amusing stories about Morris whistling or humming to assist George in the act of composing—inspiring one such episode in the 1945 film—and singer Eva Gauthier was somewhat taken aback when George turned up to a rehearsal at her apartment in 1923 with Morris in tow—apparently as a chaperon, or so Gauthier thought, but more likely just for the company.[16]

Rose also involved herself in George's musical career, certainly more so than sometimes suggested. Although she hoped that he would become a businessman or a lawyer or, after he started working on Broadway, at least the manager of a theater (she was concerned he'd "wind up in an orchestra" and preferred to see him "make enough money to know and enjoy music on the side"), she urged her children to "keep up their interest in music," taking them to hear violinist Mischa Elman's 1908 New York debut. According to Gershwin's close collaborator in his early years, lyricist Irving Caesar, Rose—whom Caesar remembered as "a very wonderful woman, very bright"—"insisted that George should start writing [songs] with Ira." Ewen mentioned, too, "She was always to be found in a prominent seat at important first performances of Gershwin's work, and at the end of the performance she was traditionally the first from whom he accepted congratulations." Rose also invested money in some of George's shows and, like other members of the family, rendered opinions about his music that he at least accepted graciously. After Gershwin privately auditioned Anne Brown for *Porgy and Bess* (dedicated, incidentally, to his parents), he asked that she return a week later to audition for Ira and Rose, whom Brown thought "rather arrogant, a doting mother who was interested only in her son, not even her *two* sons. I didn't like her very much." The costume designs for the opera's first production so displeased Rose that she went to the Lower East Side to procure for the cast shabbier garments.[17]

George was, in any case, a devoted son, who from early adulthood supported his parents financially and who lived with them until he was thirty-one, that is, for most of his short life. Frances confirmed that he was "a good son to his parents. After he had his own place, he would visit often. He always brought ice cream. He loved ice cream which he brought for everybody, although he would sit down and eat most of it himself."[18]

George remained close to his entire family, thoughtfully returning from trips with gifts for relatives. In 1936 he gave his uncle Abraham a $1,500 loan (with Rose's approval) so that he could invest in a restaurant; the loan, his aunt Kate wrote to him, "thrilled me to tears," not only because of the money "but the way you did it, your quick and sweet reply, the way you expressed your best wishes." Years later, Kate recalled how George expected family members, including herself, to attend the opening of his shows and the premieres of his concert works, and to see him off when he sailed for Europe. On one occasion, when his grandmother, Mary, demurred about going down to the ship, he insisted, saying, "Bubby ['Grandmother' in Yiddish], if you don't come, I'm not going to Europe." Commented Kate: "He made you feel so important. . . . He made everybody that he cared for feel good about themselves. That's a gift that nobody I know has." When he commissioned David Alfaro Siqueiros in 1936 to paint the large *George in an Imaginary Concert Hall*, he asked the Mexican painter, in Siqueiros's fanciful telling, to include in the first row "all of the members of my family—my father, now deceased, my favorite uncle, my father's brother, also deceased, the wife of my favorite uncle, also deceased, and also my mother, who is alive, and my brother the wastrel and my cousin the cheater, and another cousin who started by studying for the priesthood and ended up being a gigolo."[19]

This extended family, including his maternal grandparents, Gershon and Mary Bruskin, barely surfaces in the Gershwin literature—a surprising lacuna, considering that even in the 1930s George was drawing and painting their portraits, including one of his most accomplished oils, a Chagall-like portrait of his grandfather, who remained a furrier until his death in 1917 (and whose son, Bernard, entered the fur business as well before becoming a photographer). As late as 1910, neither Gershon nor Mary apparently spoke English, conversing rather in Yiddish. Kate recalled that Gershon nonetheless knew American history better than she did. After Gershon's death, Mary moved in with her daughter Kate's family. In 1924 Ira wrote to George, then in London, "Grandma wants you to get her something when you return, says no matter how inexpensive so long as you remember her," a request that sounds very much like Rose.[20]

Gershwin also had some contact with Morris's family in the form of his father's younger half-brother, Aaron (b. 1889), who arrived in New York in 1913 and who, like Morris, went into the restaurant business. Aaron—who also changed his name from Gershvin to Gershwin—was as debonair and sophisticated as Morris was unassuming and ingenuous. Aaron and his wife, Zena, had one child, Emil, who became a noted illustrator of *Tarzan* and *Flash Gordon* comic strips.[21]

Morris and Rose began their married life on Manhattan's Lower East Side, the epicenter of the city's Jewish immigrant population, but after Ira's birth they moved to 242 Snedicker Avenue, near Pitkin Avenue, a two-story brick building—large enough to board a Mr. Taffelstein of the Singer Sewing Machine Company and his family—in the then semisuburban East New York section of Brooklyn, where George was born in September 1898. The family returned to the Lower East Side, first to 425 Third Avenue in 1899 and then to 21 Second Avenue, where Arthur was born in March 1900, though by June of that year they were back in Brooklyn at 1310 8th Avenue, near Prospect Park, where the census takers caught up with them and where Rosie Fabalin, a seamstress from Russia, resided as well. About 1904 the peripatetic Gershwins moved to 126th Street in Harlem, another largely Jewish neighborhood, and about 1906 they again returned to the Lower East Side, where they lived at various residences on Second Avenue, Grand Street, Forsyth Street, and Chrystie Street, including a fairly large apartment complex at 253 Grand in 1910. In February 1915 they moved to 108 West 111th Street, just north of Central Park off Seventh Avenue, leaving the Lower East Side behind them for good. And in September 1917 they returned to Harlem, moving to 520 West 144th Street, just east of Broadway.[22]

Thus, the popular moniker of Gershwin as a "Brooklyn composer"—as when borough president Abe Stark declared him a "native Brooklynite" on the occasion of George Gershwin Day on September 26, 1963—was rather misleading. George spent nearly all of his childhood and adolescence in Manhattan, no doubt attending a school in Harlem when very young, then Public Schools 20 and 25 on the Lower East Side, followed by nearly two years at the High School of Commerce (1912–1914) at 155 West 65th Street before cutting short his sophomore year in order to pursue a musical career (Commerce High, incidentally, was largely demolished in 1965 to make room for the Juilliard School at Lincoln Center). He spent the remainder of his life primarily in Manhattan as well.[23]

Although Morris and Rose lived mostly in neighborhoods with a high percentage of Jewish immigrants, they presided over a rather assimilated household. At the same time, they spoke Russian and Yiddish as well as English at home. Stravinsky remembered George knowing some Russian words, while actor Edward G. Robinson (born Emanuel Goldenberg in Bucharest, though also a child of the Lower East Side) recalled conversations with Ira and George in Yiddish.[24]

As for the role of religion in the home, the evidence is somewhat contradictory. Most sources state that Ira was the only son to become a bar mitzvah and that the family rarely attended synagogue or observed religious holidays. According to Michael Feinstein, who worked for Ira for nearly a decade, George and Ira would even ask their parents "to pull down the curtains so the neighbors wouldn't see that they were not observing the holidays." On the other hand, interviewed in 1938, Rose claimed that although she had put religious orthodoxy—other than a "devout belief in the Ten Commandments"—behind her, when her children were young the family "adhered rigidly to the Jewish faith. The home was strictly orthodox. They [Ira, George, and Arthur] were taught by rabbis, and were all bar mitzvah." And Aunt Kate remembered that Morris and Rose regularly hosted Passover seders.[25]

How seriously George took his Jewish heritage in later years is similarly difficult to ascertain. He at least aspired to find a Jewish wife, and in a number of letters, he thanked or blessed God for one thing or another (Gershwin once wrote to Irving Caesar, as the latter recalled, "I pray to God that he will send me a good blues for my concerto," to which Yip Harburg, hearing this, responded, "Well, he may have [prayed to God] inside—but he was on a very special, playful relationship with God"). Moreover, anti-Semitism at home and abroad would have made him that much more aware of his ethnicity; he reportedly kidded his friend Kay Swift about living on East 86th Street in the heart of Manhattan's German American Yorkville neighborhood, a hotbed of pro-Nazi sentiment, by saying, "This little Jewish boy has a hard time walking through the German section!" During his later years, he also supported various Jewish causes.[26]

At the same time, writer Carl Van Vechten stated, "It's absurd to talk about Jewish tradition in George Gershwin. There was nothing notably Jewish in him at all. Why, we never thought of it." And although actress Kitty Carlisle remembered attending a Passover seder with the Gershwins in the mid-1930s in which pianist Oscar Levant, assisted by George, presided over the service "in a kind of mad jazz rhythm," she added that it was "all a big joke." The entertainment world was certainly highly assimilationist, as evidenced by the widespread practice—as in Gershwin's case—of changing names that sounded too ethnic. And aside from his aborted opera *The Dybbuk,* he showed little interest in working with explicitly Jewish themes or materials. "My people are Americans," he famously stated in 1927. "My time is to-day."[27]

The relative secularism of the Gershwins in part may have reflected Morris's and Rose's roots in St. Petersburg as opposed to the more insular towns and shtetls of the Pale. But secularized Jewish households, bolstered by the prominence of socialist and other progressive movements of the time, were actually a commonplace on the Lower East Side, where Gershwin spent most of his adolescent years. "The fixed rituals that had bound the east European Jews broke down under the weight of American freedom," observes Irving Howe. "The patterns of social existence had to be remade each day. The comedy of social dislocation gave edge and abundance to life." Those Jews overhauling traditional religious mores were inclined to question inherited American ones as well, and many challenging voices emerged from this milieu.[28]

A colorful neighborhood, and one of the world's densest in terms of population, the Lower East Side teemed with pushcarts, horse-drawn wagons, and throngs of men, women, and children. The general area contained scores of churches and synagogues, factories and shops, schools and theaters, bars and brothels, squalid tenements and middle-class flats. Delinquency, gambling, prostitution, disease, and labor unrest were common. "No child raised in the immigrant quarter would lack for moral realism," writes Howe; "just to walk through Hester Street was an education in the hardness of life."[29]

The area harbored not only a large Jewish community but Irish, Italian, and German enclaves as well. Jewish children ventured into these other neighborhoods at their own risk; the young George reportedly suffered a brain concussion attempting to flee an Irish gang. But it was too tempting for most Jewish children not to explore these nearby sections or, for that matter, Chinatown farther south. "Venturing into gentile streets," states Howe, "became a strategy for testing the reality of the external world and for discovering that it was attractive in ways no Jewish voice had told him." Nor were the various neighborhoods as segregated as all that. For example, the Gershwins' apartment building at 253 Grand, though predominantly Jewish, housed a number of Irish, Italian, and Greek families. Meanwhile, the Gershwins' intermittent residences in Harlem brought them into contact with a burgeoning African American population there.[30]

George was an active if not hyperactive child, haunting the busy thoroughfares of the Lower East Side, playing stickball, and diving into the East River. His early heroes included superathlete Jim Thorpe and baseball star Christy Mathewson, and he himself became a local roller-skating champion. In contrast to his reserved older brother, he regularly got into scrapes and scuffles, engaging in fisticuffs, breaking glass, setting fires, and stealing food from pushcarts. Once, after urinating behind a wagon, he had his ear twisted by a policeman. On another occasion, a horse kicked him on the bridge of his nose. A deep scar by his right eye bore witness to such rough play. Some neighbors thought him a "fresh kid" and even his adoring aunt Kate remembered him as a "wild boy," like her own son Arnold. "He was the one," she added, "that used to get punished by the father [Morris]," who predicted that George would "grow up to be a bum."[31]

Nathaniel Phillips, one of Gershwin's teachers at Public School 20, remembered him, on the other hand, as "a nice lad—modest and retiring." Located at Rivington and Forsyth Streets, Public School 20 during these years included among its student body not only George and Ira but such future notables as Irving Caesar, Harry Golden, Jacob Javits, Paul Muni, and Edward G. Robinson. Phillips attributed the school's success to its emphasis on discipline, noting that during a three-day absence on his part, his class carried on without him. "It was shoes shined, nails clean . . . every day," he remembered. "No coming to class without a tie." (Ira once credited a sixth-grade lesson at the school about varying pronunciations of the word *neither* as planting the seed for the song "Let's Call the Whole Thing Off.")[32]

And although Ira explicitly referred to his brother as "a poor student at school," Gershwin's aptitude for mathematics at least led to admittance to the High School of Commerce, where it was thought he might train to become an accountant. In a 1936 letter to a friend, Gershwin himself wrote, "In public school I was considered pretty good at composition, but for some reason or other (I'm not bothering much with reasons lately) I never kept it up." His surviving letters indeed reveal a good command of language and a bold, clear penmanship. He no doubt honed such skills in the public schools of the Lower East Side, where teaching English to immigrant children took high priority. Yip Harburg, for example, warmly recalled the "terrific" education he received at the neighborhood's public schools, with their "inspiring teachers" who introduced him to English lyric poetry and the dramatic arts.[33]

Gershwin even evidenced some attraction to academic life in a 1930 letter to Rosamund Walling, a young friend then at Swarthmore: "The picture you painted of college life (*your* college life) in your last letter seemed so wonderful that I shall never misunderstand you[r] preference for that life to all others. The books you read, the fact you could walk the woods alone and think, the fact that you were very happy doing it made me realize how attractive it really was. None of the sordidness of the outside world. And constantly learning. How lucky you are." "I think he was very sorry he never finished school," reflected his sister. "He had a great feeling for learning. He was very bright and he wrote wonderful letters that were just to the point."[34]

Ira, who would play a crucial role in George's life, was the true scholar of the family, however. As early as 1908, the studious twelve-year-old began compiling a remarkable scrapbook of newspaper and journal articles on everything from "How Phrases Originate" and "Points of Constitutional Law" to "The First Taxicab" and "Saturn the Great Celestial Wonder." He read voraciously, and by the time he finished grade school, he had devoured the popular classics of Horatio Alger, James Fenimore Cooper, Arthur Conan Doyle, Alexandre Dumas père, Anna Sewell, Harriet Beecher Stowe, and Jules Verne, among others.[35]

While at Townsend Harris Hall (1910–1914), City College's preparatory high school for exceptional students located on the Lower East Side, Ira contributed cartoons and light verse to the school newspaper, the *Academic Herald,* sometimes in collaboration with his classmate Yip Harburg. "Ira was the shyest, most diffident boy we had ever known," recalled Harburg. "In a class of lower east side rapscallions, his soft-spoken gentleness and low-keyed personality made him a lovable incongruity. He spoke in murmurs, hiding behind a pair of steel-rimmed spectacles." He also continued reading novels—he was reading Arnold Bennett and John Galsworthy in 1912—but he and Harburg shared a special interest in a long line of light, satirical poetry from Renaissance parodists and W. S. Gilbert to the latest newspaper verse of Franklin P. Adams, Bert

Taylor, and the young Dorothy Parker. Carolyn Wells's anthology of society verse in particular became an indispensable resource as the two boys experimented with such classic forms as the ballad, limerick, ode, rondeau, and triolet. In time, these two friends—along with such like-minded colleagues as Lorenz Hart and Cole Porter—would help usher in the so-called golden age of American popular song by applying the traditions of sophisticated light verse to modern lyric writing.[36]

Although Ira's musical interests were not nearly as deep or far-ranging as George's, his abilities in that area naturally enhanced his eventual career as a lyricist. Taking some piano lessons with Aunt Kate about 1910, he acquired enough skill to play a duet, "The Fairy Waltz," with her, and to entertain friends in 1917, writing with characteristic self-deprecation in his diary, "I divinely played with 1 finger of the right hand & three of the left and almost my entire repertoire consisting of Pink Lady waltz, a Spanish waltz (introducing a trill herenthere) and a few simple old songs like 'Singing Polly woodywoodle all the Way,' 'Annie Laurie,' and such in the simplest keys." The possessor of a capable singing voice—he sang better than George did, by most accounts—he made a number of home recordings, including one of the score for *The Firebrand of Florence* (for which he had written the lyrics) with its composer, Kurt Weill, at the piano, in a voice that reminded one listener of Groucho Marx. And his extraordinary memory extended to his recall of tunes, no small advantage when his collaborations often entailed setting words to finished melodies.[37]

Ira entered City College in the fall of 1914 as an English major, happily immersing himself in the novels of Theodore Dreiser and Henry James and the plays of James Barrie, Henrik Ibsen, and G. B. Shaw. He also continued publishing light verse in a variety of journals, sometimes with Harburg as "Yip and Gersh." In the spring of 1916, either during or after his sophomore year, he quit City College as a full-time student, to his mother's dismay. Over the next three years, he worked as a cashier and bookkeeper for his father's bathhouses, B. Altman's department store, and even a traveling circus while pursuing some night classes (possibly with the idea of becoming an accountant or a doctor, as Rose hoped) and writing and sometimes publishing light verse along with stories in the tradition of Guy de Maupassant and O. Henry. He especially valued the counsel of journalist-playwright Paul Potter, who after reading one of his stories suggested that he learn "American slang" and become "an attentive listener and observer."[38]

During these years, Ira was drawn gradually into the world of musical theater, in part because of George's activities in that arena. In 1916 he began to keep record of his attendance at plays and musical shows, and during the 1917–1918 season he wrote vaudeville reviews for the *New York Clipper.* He was particularly charmed by the work of P. G. Wodehouse, who, along with Gilbert, became an inspiration for his own increasing preoccupation with lyric writing, which by 1920 had reached the point that he gave his profession as "lyric writer."[39]

George and Ira began to collaborate on some songs in the late 1910s, and though they did not work exclusively with each other, especially at first, by the mid-1920s they had become a famous songwriting team, Ira establishing himself as one of the finest lyricists of the age. Lorenz Hart, when asked about his fellow lyricists, for example, stated, "First there is Ira, then me; then nobody." Similarly, Wodehouse, who thought the lyrics of Cole Porter "terribly uneven" and those of Hart without "charm," considered Ira the "best of the whole bunch" and the "greatest lyricist of them all" (after reading Hart's lyrics to *Pal Joey,* Wodehouse wrote to his friend, Guy Bolton, "Ira is worth ten of him"). George himself stated that the "wistfulness" and "whimsicality" of his brother's lyrics placed him "among the foremost of lyric writers in America."[40]

In later years, such insightful observers as Lawrence Stewart (1959), Deena Rosenberg (1991), and Philip Furia (1996) helped chart Ira's great achievement. In a helpful summation, distinguished writer and impresario Lincoln Kirstein wrote, "Without condescension or parody he [Ira] created a new prosody, a new means for lyric-writing which incorporated the season's slang, references to local events, echoes of the vernacular rhythms of ordinary speech in a frame of casual thrown-away elegance which was never false, insistent or self-conscious. He seemed to have stumbled on what was right, fitting, appropriate, surprising and charming, as if such had been coins tossed in his path." Ned Rorem, another admirer, thought Ira's verse "less bathetic and a good deal tighter than some of the poetasting used by, say, Schubert and Fauré. Witty too, and ingeniously confected." They "make you glad of whatever education you have," stated John O'Hara in 1941, "but sad that you didn't stay around for a little more."[41]

In the course of their fruitful collaboration, Ira helped supervise George's career, while George galvanized and prodded Ira, who claimed that had it not been for George, he would have been "contented to be a bookkeeper." Ira's great admiration for his brother became one of his most remarked-upon characteristics. When George played through his opera *Porgy and Bess* for director Rouben Mamoulian for the first time, the latter noticed Ira looking back and forth between his brother and himself "with half-open eyes and pantomime with a soft gesture of his hand, as if saying, '*He* did it. Isn't it wonderful? Isn't *he* wonderful?'" S. N. Behrman similarly observed, "At the Gershwin parties, with everyone spellbound around the piano, while George was playing and singing Ira's lyrics, I would steal a look at Ira, standing on the outskirts of the crowd, a small, benignant smile on his face, stirred to happiness by the effect his brother was creating." (When Behrman suggested to Ira that he was "every bit as good as George," the latter responded, "No, George was more original.") Such affection was mutual; commented Ira's wife, Leonore: "I never saw a greater love than the love George and Ira had for each other."[42]

In September 1926, Ira married Leonore Strunsky (1900–1991), who in Merle Armitage's phrase "moved smoothly into the picture." George and Ira had known the vivacious and attractive "Lee" for some years; she was the sister of one of George's dearest friends, Emily Paley (1897–1990), at whose 1920 wedding she and Ira first met. Born in San Francisco to a Jewish family of Russian heritage, Emily and Leonore relocated to New York with their parents, Albert and Mascha Strunsky, after the 1906 earthquake. "Papa" Strunsky, who acquired a fair amount of Greenwich Village property, became known for his charitable behavior on behalf of artists unable to pay rent (he's depicted with other local notables on a mural in Manhattan's Christopher Street subway station). George enjoyed entertaining friends at one of Strunsky's establishments, Three Steps Down, on West 8th Street. Leonore and Emily also had a brother, William English ("English"), named after their uncle, William English Walling, a dedicated socialist well known for his activities on behalf of trade unions and civil rights, and the husband of Albert's sister Anna, a radical writer who enjoyed a lifelong friendship with Jack London.[43]

Leonore, by some accounts, was originally in love with George and married Ira as a second-best alternative. Ira himself admitted that the Gershwin name meant much more to her than to him. Or perhaps she was emulating her sister Emily, who also married a lyricist, Lou Paley. In any case, Leonore proposed to Ira a number of times before he accepted. According to Michael Feinstein, "Ira was impressed with Leonore because she was a real flapper." Aunt Kate added that he thought highly of her intelligence.[44]

Leonore skillfully helped arrange Ira's and George's busy social lives, in the process gaining a reputation for hospitality that surpassed Rose's. "There is no more gracious hostess in the world," opined Behrman; her management of the Gershwin ménage, according to Oscar Levant, revealed "qualities of feminine tact, sensibility and patience which existed, as far as my experience is a criterion, only in her." At the same time, she had an imperious side that revealed itself more and more with the passing years, perhaps related to her increasing reliance on prescription drugs; even as early as the 1945 biopic, Julie Bishop played her with a kind of arch sangfroid. Describing their experiences with Leonore on tour with *Porgy and Bess* in the 1950s, Maya Angelou remembered her face as "sour with propriety" and found her "maternalistic attitude" infuriating, while Truman Capote portrayed her as a haughty grande-dame who, on seeing the imperial Russian jewels at the Hermitage, said, "I feel so dissatisfied, I'd like to go home and crack my husband on the head." Michael Feinstein found it "extraordinary" that Emily—whom he thought "the most delightful, gentle, and kind person" that he had ever met—and Leonore "came from the same family." In discussing his two sisters, English himself remarked that although both were strong women, "Emily was interested in the world, while Lee was interested in herself." George was solicitous toward but reportedly somewhat critical of Leonore, at least according to Aunt Kate, who remembered him feeling that "every woman—particularly without children—should do something."[45]

George also maintained—more so than did Ira and Leonore—a warm relationship with younger brother Arthur, described by Frances as "the funny one of the family. He had a great sense of humor." "I used to be George's pal," remarked Arthur. "We used to go to ballgames together and all the fights together." However, the two saw less of each other after Gershwin's first trip to Hollywood in 1930, a development that represented one of a number of disappointments in Arthur's life. Another concerned his floundering musical career. He briefly studied violin, learned to play the piano by ear, and composed his own songs. A salesman of motion pictures early in life, he gave up his later vocation as a stockbroker in the 1930s in order to pursue music full-time. George featured two of Arthur's songs, "Slowly but Surely" and "Home James" (lyrics, Eddie Heyman), on his 1934 radio show; and in 1945 Arthur enjoyed a modest success with a musical comedy, *The Lady Says Yes* (lyrics, Fred Spielman). But his career never got off the ground. After hearing some of Arthur's songs in 1968, Ira found them—to his surprise—"very good in 'a Sigmund Romberg operetta' kind of way," according to Michael Feinstein, who expressed his own particular liking for "After All These Years." Another of Arthur's songs, "Invitation to the Blues," turned up in the film comedy *Tootsie* (1982).[46]

Though the baby of the family, Frances helped pioneer the Gershwins' break into show business. By age ten, perhaps coached by George, at the time a song plugger, she was singing and dancing on the vaudeville circuit, assisted by Rose in the perhaps unexpected role of stage mother. Frances—described by Vernon Duke as "a chubby chestnut-haired flapper"—continued performing in vaudeville and musical comedy, including the unsuccessful 1928 edition of the hit 1926 show *Americana*. Also in 1928, while traveling in Europe with George and Ira, she consented, at Cole Porter's behest, to sing a set of Gershwin songs in a lavish Parisian revue for two weeks—the climax of her short-lived stage career. Frances remembered George as lovingly if prudishly overprotective, while George expressed "great fondness for her as a person as well as the usual brotherly love."[47]

In 1928 Frances began dating her future husband, Leopold Godowsky Jr. ("Leo"), a violinist and personal assistant to his father, the celebrated pianist. (Though an archconservative, the senior Godowsky, who attended the premiere of the *Rhapsody in Blue,* regarded Gershwin's talent highly, as his son remembered, and was personally "very fond of him.") George and the younger Godowsky had known each other since the early 1920s through their frequent visits to the Palais Royal to hear the Paul Whiteman Orchestra; and both studied composition with Rubin Goldmark about this time as well.[48]

After Frances married Leopold in 1930, she gave up her singing career but continued to perform in a voice variously described as "small, somewhat husky," "a light soprano," and "sweet but unexceptional." George, who admired her renditions of his songs, featured her singing his "Oh Gee!–Oh Joy!" on the same 1934 radio broadcast on which he programmed Arthur's music. In 1973, well into her sixties, Frances released a recording of Gershwin songs she had been singing all her life. Like Ira and George, she took up painting as well, her art teachers including her cousin, Henry Botkin, and Morris Davidson. Meanwhile, Leopold, with his old friend pianist-composer Leopold Mannes (the son of famed violinist David Mannes and the nephew of conductor Walter Damrosch), remained passionately involved not only with music but with photography, the two coinventing the Kodachrome and other color-photography processes for Eastman Kodak in the 1930s.[49]

George's death on July 11, 1937, devastated his family. "For the last two weeks the loss has hit me harder than ever," wrote Ira to his mother on August 17. "An hour doesn't go by but that some memory doesn't suddenly hit me. I know it's the same with you, Mom, and we've just got to be brave about it. Maybe time will smooth off the edges of our pain. Let's hope so." Ira eventually resumed work, and in later years successfully collaborated with Jerome Kern, Kurt Weill, Aaron Copland, Arthur Schwartz, Burton Lane, and Harold Arlen. But by the mid-1950s he had essentially put lyric writing behind him and devoted himself to overseeing the Gershwin estate, answering fan mail, and annotating an anthology of his verse, *Lyrics on Several Occasions* (1959). When Michael Feinstein went to work for him in the late 1970s, the young pianist-singer discovered that Ira's home had become a veritable shrine to his brother's memory and that he talked to George in his sleep, carrying on conversations "filled with anger, centering around Ira's desire not to stay here on earth and George's insistence that he stay."[50]

Though generous to favored friends and family and utterly bound by their devotion to George's memory, Ira and Leonore maintained what was taken to be a cold, unhappy marriage by many, including actress Lotte Lenya, who in 1944 told her husband Kurt Weill that it would be a "blessing" if they had the decency to separate. For their parts, both Arthur and Frances faced the similarly heavy burden of caring for their famous brother's legacy and even artifacts, which played some part in Arthur's rocky marriage to singer Judy Lane (b. 1917) and Frances's decision to enter psychotherapy. Gershwin clearly had been something of the glue that had kept his family together, and without his presence, family ties, though cordial, began to unravel.[51]

Whereas Ira and Leonore had no children, Arthur and Judy had one child, Marc George (b. 1943); and Leopold and Frances Godowsky, four: Sandra ("Alexis") (b. 1934), Leopold III (b. 1938), and the twins, Nadia and Georgia (b. 1945). In 1980, shortly before Arthur's and Ira's demise, Marc and Leopold became trustees of the George Gershwin estate; while over time, Ira's nephew and English's son, Michael Strunsky, assumed responsibility for the Ira Gershwin estate (with musical theater historian and Gershwin scholar Robert Kimball becoming the estate's artistic advisor in 1982). These assorted cousins in many ways followed paths forged by their forebears. Like English, Michael Strunsky was a businessman; like Arthur, Marc Gershwin became a stockbroker; like his paternal grandfather, father, and uncle George, composer-pianist Leopold Godowsky III emerged an accomplished musician, the *Chicago Tribune* deeming his 1998 recording of Gershwin's Concerto in F under José Serebrier "one of the most romantic and heartful . . . in the last three decades";[52] and like their mother Frances, Sandra—who adopted the name Alexis Gershwin— performed popular songs on the stage; Georgia Keidan, after some early involvement in musical comedy, turned to painting (though she thought her art more playful and lyrical than her mother's); and Nadia Natali became a dancer, eventually working as a dance therapist and pursuing a doctorate in somatic psychology. Meanwhile, two of Marc's sons, Adam (b. 1971) and Todd (b. 1975), who along with their brother Alex (b. 1986) alone among their generation of cousins inherited the Gershwin name, assisted in the running of the Gershwin music business.

Although Gershwin never married, he may have fathered a child. So, at any rate, claimed Alan Gershwin, who in 1959 announced in *Confidential* magazine, "I Am George Gershwin's Illegitimate Son." Alan Gershwin was born Albert Schneider in Brooklyn on May 18, 1926 (Alan was his nickname, and he eventually adopted Gershwin as his surname). He asserted that his mother, a married chorus girl named Margaret Manners, had had an affair with Gershwin after meeting him through lyricist Buddy DeSylva, and that he was the child of that liaison. Manners (originally Mollie Charleston of Brooklyn, the Charleston family name having been changed from Charlkovitz) allegedly gave the boy to be raised by her sister, Fanny Schneider, and remarried sometime in the mid-1930s. Alan remembered surreptitious meetings with Gershwin, whom he resembled physically, and recalled, further, that money changed hands between Gershwin and the Schneiders.[53]

Although Ira and other family members rejected Alan as an imposter, Charles Schwartz, in his book on Gershwin (1973), concluded that the case deserved further investigation. In her own biography (1993), Joan Peyser supported Alan's general story after finding corroborative witnesses, notably Gershwin's valet Paul Mueller, who reportedly helped arrange the boy's visits with his presumed father. Reunited with Alan in 1988, Mueller even presented him with a cherished Gershwin self-portrait in his possession, saying that he thought the composer's son should have it. (Peyser reproduced this 1934 drawing, inspired by Edward Steichen's celebrated 1927 photograph of the composer, in her monograph.)

Peyser's allegations did not go uncontested, however. Reviewing her biography, Laurie Winer opined, for instance, that the author's factual unreliability and questionable journalistic practices cast serious doubt on her credibility. That Alan Gershwin's remembrances contained some implausibilities and inconsistencies, and that Mueller, who died before the book's publication, could not confirm or amplify statements made on his behalf raised additional uncertainty. Moreover, Alan apparently never submitted a request to either George's or Ira's estate for DNA samples to help bolster his claim. In short, the evidence remained circumstantial, and the matter, unresolved.[54]

Chapter Two

Gershwin's Musical Education to
the *Rhapsody in Blue* (1924)

$\mathcal{G}$ershwin encountered classical music at an early age. His father played recordings of the great Enrico Caruso—and presumably other opera singers—on the family Victrola. (In 1910, about the time the family acquired a piano, they conveniently lived upstairs from a Second Avenue record store, Birns Brothers Phonographs.) And the young George attended some concerts at the Educational Alliance, a Lower East Side settlement house, located at 197 East Broadway, that sponsored a string orchestra of mostly Jewish adolescents under the leadership of Sam Franko.[1]

Two youthful musical experiences proved especially memorable. The first occurred when he was about six, as he recalled: "I stood outside a penny arcade listening to an automatic piano leaping through [Anton] Rubinstein's *Melody in F.* The peculiar jumps in the music held me rooted. To this very day I can't hear the tune without picturing myself outside that arcade on One Hundred and Twenty-fifth Street, standing there barefoot and in overalls, drinking it all in avidly." He had a more decisive revelation about 1908 when he was ten or so, as he stood outside his Lower East Side public school and heard within a schoolmate, a violin prodigy two years his junior, Max ("Maxie") Rosenzweig (later Rosen), perform Antonín Dvořák's *Humoresque* during recess. "It was, to me," he said, "a flashing revelation of beauty."[2]

These recollections help underscore the connection between the popular classics of the nineteenth century—or what Peter Van der Merwe calls "the nineteenth-century vernacular"—and that repertoire with which Gershwin would become most associated: popular music of the early twentieth century. Pieces like the *Melody in F* and the *Humoresque* even could be said to anticipate popular music, not only in terms of style and structure (including the thirty-two-bar *aaba* form that was coming to typify popular song) but in their tone, the former leaning more toward the sentimental, the latter toward the ironic. Significantly, during the 1910s popular composers frequently co-opted such chestnuts for their own purposes: Felix Arndt, for instance, parodied the *Humoresque* in his *Desecration Rag* no. 1 (1914); Philip Braham, the *Melody in F* in "Oh, Mister Rubinstein!" (1915). (As late as 1941, a team of songwriters turned another Rubinstein favorite, *Romance,* into "If You Are but a Dream.")[3]

Moreover, certain details of the *Melody in F* and *Humoresque* prefigured Gershwin's work to the extent that Hans Keller concluded "that the structural outlines of the Rubinstein and the Dvořák are remembered in virtually every Gershwin song." Regarding the *Humoresque,* this included Gershwin's predilection for pentatonic melodies, dotted rhythms, and even blue notes—as in his *Short Story* for violin and piano, described by Paul Bowles as "'Humoresque' brought partially up to date." Van der Merwe, who considered Dvořák "the bluesiest" of his contemporaries, similarly thought Gershwin's "Summertime" closer to Dvořák than to blues singer Bessie Smith. Meanwhile, echoes of the *Melody in F* could be heard in Gershwin's own "leaping" melodies, as in the similarly titled Concerto in F or in some of his more romantic songs. One can even superimpose the main phrases of the *Melody* with that of Gershwin's "He Loves and She Loves," though doing so only heightens the humor of the latter. Some irony may even have hovered about from the start, considering that Gershwin associated Rubinstein's sentimental tune with a player piano in a penny arcade. Perhaps the incongruity grabbed him as much as anything.[4]

Born in Romania, Max Rosen (1900–1956) grew up on the Lower East Side, where his father, a former bandmaster, had a barbershop. On the day George heard *Humoresque,* after waiting in the rain for more than an hour in the hopes of meeting Max, he "trekked" to the young violinist's home, dripping wet, where he "unceremoniously" presented himself "as an admirer" of Max's. The Rosenzweigs, amused, arranged a meeting between the two boys. "From the first moment we became the closest of friends," remembered Gershwin. "We chummed about arm in arm; we lavished childish affection upon one another in true Jean Christophe fashion; we exchanged letters even when only a week-end and some hundred blocks lay between us." Max "opened the world of music up to me," added Gershwin, who recalled discussing music with him when the two weren't wrestling; according to brother Arthur, the two also eventually made music together. Previously, George had regarded music students as "Maggies," that is, sissies (the similarity between "Maggie" and "Maxie" seems, in this context, rather striking). Now he aimed to pursue the piano and outdo Max.[5]

About the time he became friends with Gershwin, Max also attracted the attention of various philanthropists, who sponsored his education at home and later abroad. Before leaving for Europe in 1912 to study with Leopold Auer, he allegedly wounded Gershwin by saying that the latter hadn't "any talent at all," a story enough like a known exchange between Gershwin and the young pianist Abram Chasins to suggest that during these early years, George's musical friends viewed his ambitions as greater than his abilities. In any case, on Rosen's triumphant return to the States in 1917—he made a smashing Carnegie Hall debut with the New York Philharmonic on January 12, 1918—he resumed his friendship with the Gershwin family, eventually serving as an honorary pallbearer at George's funeral (1937) and best man at Arthur's wedding (1940). He never quite had the career for which he seemed destined, but he left behind some sensitive recordings featuring a relatively small but particularly sweet tone. Moreover, he provided some inspiration for Fannie Hurst's story "Humoresque" (1918), adapted twice for the screen (1920, 1946). (The lives of Gershwin and Rosen intertwined once again when Warner Brothers used, for the 1946 *Humoresque* film, a Clifford Odets screenplay that had been intended for a film biography of Gershwin.)[6]

About 1910 the Gershwins acquired an upright piano—"to be in style," as the composer once recalled, though the purchase may have been made at least partly at his instigation—with the intention that Ira, who already had taken a few piano lessons with Aunt Kate and who had succeeded in making his way through about thirty-two pages of Ferdinand Beyer's popular *Elementary Instruction Book,* would become the family musician. "But the upright had scarcely been put in place," remembered Ira, "when George twirled the stool down to size, sat, lifted the keyboard cover, and played an accomplished version of a then popular song. I remember being particularly impressed by his swinging left hand and by harmonic and rhythmic effects I thought as proficient as those of most of the pianists I'd heard in vaudeville." The astonished Gershwins discovered that George not only had learned to play by experimenting on a player piano at the home of a friend, but had begun his lifelong habit of jotting down musical ideas in a notebook. Yip Harburg, who corroborated this story, added that by running errands for a local piano store, Gershwin also had been able to practice on some of their instruments.[7]

The piano installed in the living room, George began to take piano lessons himself. "Studying the piano made a good boy out of a bad one," he later stated. "It took the piano to tone me down. It made me more serious. I was a changed person six months after I took it up." Psychiatrist and pianist Richard Kogan, who suggested that music indeed had a curative effect on the impulsive George, further wondered how the composer's life and career might have unfolded had he been treated rather, as common with hyperactive youngsters today, with psychotropic medications.[8]

According to one of his earliest piano teachers, Mrs. Louis A. Greene, Gershwin started studying first with a neighborhood teacher who charged fifty cents a lesson, and then for three years with Greene, who traveled from her home on East 116th Street to the Lower East Side to teach him, and who assigned him various exercises and such easy pieces as Robert Schumann's "The Jolly Farmer." He might have had Greene in mind when he told Rose, "Mom, if I could read the notes, I could play better than she does." In any case, Greene recalled that in later years Gershwin "always introduced me as his piano teacher . . . always extended himself to make me feel important."[9]

Gershwin subsequently met a young pianist by the name of Goldfarb, whose "gusto" and "barrel of gestures" so impressed him that he sought out the boy's teacher, a "former leader of a Hungarian band and of operetta" named Von Zerly. Von Zerly, who charged, as Gershwin further recalled, the "stiff" price of $1.50 per lesson, started him on a book of operatic excerpts. After about six months, he could play the overture to Rossini's *William Tell*.[10]

About the same time—that is, sometime in his freshman year of high school (1912–1913)—Gershwin befriended another young musician, Jack Miller, who played piano with the Beethoven Musical Society Orchestra, a community orchestra composed largely of Jewish youth from the Lower East Side and conducted by Henry Lefkowitz. Recalled Gershwin:

> Miller spoke to me of his teacher, a certain Charles Hambitzer, and took me along with him one eventful day. Hambitzer, whose memory I revere, for he was the first great musical influence in my life, asked me to play something. I rubbed my fingers and dived into the Overture to William Tell. Hambitzer said nothing until I had finished. "Listen," he finally spoke, getting up from his chair. "Let's hunt out that guy [Von Zerly] and shoot him—and not with an apple on his head, either!"

Gershwin proceeded to study with Hambitzer, whom he once described as not only his "first great musical influence," as above, but also "the greatest musical influence in my life."[11]

Charles Hambitzer (1878–1918) grew up in Milwaukee, where he studied piano with Julius Albert Jahn and harmony, counterpoint, and orchestration with German opera composer Hugo Kaun (1863–1932), who in 1902 returned to his native Berlin and an eventual position with the Berlin Conservatory. In 1908 or perhaps earlier, Hambitzer moved to New York, where he taught piano privately and played piano and other instruments in the Waldorf-Astoria Orchestra under Joseph Knecht. This hotel orchestra, comprising a highly trained group of mostly Italian and Jewish musicians, regularly gave serious concerts, including one that Gershwin attended on April 13, 1913, at which Hambitzer performed the first movement of Anton Rubinstein's Piano Concerto in D Minor. Hambitzer is also said to have been one of the first Americans to play Schoenberg's *Six Little Piano Pieces,* op. 19 (1911), in public. Another student, conductor Nathaniel Shilkret, whose extraordinary career with the Victor company brought him into frequent contact with many of the day's finest musicians, thought Hambitzer "one of the greatest pianists I ever heard. And I would say he was a genius." Shilkret and Mabel Schirmer, who on Gershwin's recommendation also studied with Hambitzer, further remembered him as an extremely sweet man.[12]

Hambitzer was furthermore a composer of unpublished orchestral tone-poems and incidental music, art songs, and light operas, including *Kadja, The Love Wager,* and *The Amethyst Ring,* the latter left unfinished at the time of his death in 1918, apparently of tuberculosis, a disease that had claimed his wife in 1914. In 1931 a Milwaukee journalist, Walter Monfried, reported that the composer's daughter had "trunks full" of her father's manuscripts and that Gershwin, who considered Hambitzer's operettas "the finest light music of the day," hoped to complete *The Amethyst Ring* for Broadway. Conductor Louis Kroll, who toured with *The Love Wager* in 1913, seconded Gershwin's assessment, remembering the piece as "a beautiful work, full of lovely melodies and stirring choruses." But by the time Kroll sought out the score in 1945, all of Hambitzer's papers had mysteriously disappeared.[13]

However, decades letter, Arthur Gershwin's widow, Judy, discovered a small collection of Hambitzer manuscripts in the storage room of her Central Park West apartment, the same apartment previously occupied by her mother-in-law, Rose, who presumably inherited this material along with the rest of Gershwin's estate; a page from *Porgy and Bess* found among these papers suggests that Gershwin acquired these papers sometime in the 1930s, confirming his long-standing regard for his former teacher. Considering the aforementioned reference to "trunks" of music and the fragmentary nature of the material represented here, Gershwin possibly acquired other manuscripts, including the full operetta scores. In any case, the preserved music (donated to the Library of Congress in 1991) suggests that Hambitzer served Gershwin as a compositional model, not only in terms of the delicacy and elegance of the music (Gershwin struck an especially Hambitzer-like note, for instance, in his ballet music for *Primrose*), but, as in the case of the comparable Victor Herbert, more generally in his ability to write for both the concert hall and the popular stage.[14]

The actual time Gershwin spent with Hambitzer remains somewhat uncertain. In 1925 Gershwin stated, "I stopped taking [piano] lessons because my teacher [Hambitzer] died," and there's no reason to doubt this, though some sources assert that these lessons ended earlier. At the same time, Gershwin often claimed that he studied piano for only four or five years, telling one interviewer, for instance, "My technique is not like that of so-called great pianists. I developed an original method, for altogether I have studied only about five years." If he started studying piano about 1910, and worked with Hambitzer from 1913 to 1918, that would total eight or nine years. Perhaps he discounted his piano studies prior to working with Hambitzer.[15]

Further uncertainty surrounds this oft-quoted excerpt from a letter that Hambitzer allegedly wrote to his sister in Milwaukee: "I have a new pupil who will make his mark in music if anybody will. The boy is a genius, without a doubt; he's just crazy about music and can't wait until it's time to take his lesson. No watching the clock for this boy! He wants to go in for this modern stuff, jazz and what not. But I'm not going to let him for a while. I'll see that he gets a firm foundation in the standard music first." Unfortunately, this familiar quote cannot be dated, as the letter, which appears lost, was never cited. Hambitzer presumably wrote it about 1913, when Gershwin apparently began working with him; but the word *jazz* came into common use only late in 1916. Unless Hambitzer would refer to Gershwin as a "new pupil" after four or five years of study, the accuracy of this source seems seriously compromised.[16]

This letter also gave rise to the dubious notion of Hambitzer as antipathetic toward Gershwin's interest in popular music, a view that looms large in some biographies, not to mention the 1945 biopic (assuming that the film's Professor Frank is a fictionalized projection of Hambitzer). Even if authentic, the letter reveals only that Hambitzer sought uppermost to provide Gershwin with a "firm foundation in the standard music," while his own career would suggest some sympathy for Gershwin's more popular aspirations.

It would be interesting to know more about what Hambitzer meant by a "firm foundation." At the least, Gershwin, who developed a superb piano technique, credited Hambitzer with teaching him to play with a flexible wrist. Recalled Mabel Schirmer: "He [Hambitzer] was an extraordinary teacher, unlike any I had ever had before. . . . He had two pianos in his studio on the ground floor of a building, I think, but I'm not sure, on 125th Street, near or on Central Park West. He was not a typical teacher who sat at your side while you played. On his piano he would demonstrate the piece . . . then you would take it home and learn it. He would then listen to you play it on one piano while he just listened from his piano." Nathaniel Shilkret further recollected Hambitzer telling him with regard to Gershwin, "He is a tremendous talent. I have listened to him playing classics with great rhythmic extemporizing, and I have not discouraged him."[17]

As for specific repertory, Schirmer remembered "a lot of Chopin." Carl Van Vechten confirmed that Gershwin had been working on the Chopin preludes when Hambitzer died, and Oscar Levant noted that some Chopin preludes were among the few solo classical pieces that Gershwin would play in his later years, aside from those Czerny exercises used as a preconcert warm-up. Meanwhile, Shilkret mentioned Hambitzer's knowledge of Bach, Mozart, Beethoven, Schubert, Schumann, Chopin, and Liszt, adding, "Pieces just poured out of him flawlessly."[18]

In view of the latter recollection, Van Vechten's claim that Gershwin "was as yet unfamiliar with the work of Bach, Beethoven, Schumann, Schubert, or Brahms" during his time with Hambitzer seems implausible, not to mention the young George's attendance at concerts that featured these very composers. Moreover, Gershwin was discovered practicing a prelude and fugue from Bach's *Well-Tempered Clavier* while working for the music publisher Remick in the mid-teens, indicating that he studied Bach with Hambitzer.[19]

For his part, Gershwin denied ever playing "very serious things" as a piano student, though he told Monfried, "Hambitzer familiarized me with the music and the composers who have shaped my career—Liszt, Chopin and Debussy." Certainly Gershwin's structural thinking—not to mention his piano writing—often recalled Liszt, while his projected plan for a set of twenty-four preludes fell in the tradition of Chopin and Debussy (and, of course, Bach, another admired composer). Chopin seems further to have helped inspire Gershwin's ideal of a popular serious music. "I think many things are made classic by time that were not classic when they were written," he said in 1924. "For instance the polkas and the mazurkas of Chopin's time; they were popular music in that period, but he has made them live."[20]

Gershwin's even closer ties with Debussy involved not only the appropriation of parallel harmonies, mixed orchestral colors, and other stylistic devices, but his basic working method of allowing melody free rein, supported by unconventional harmonies; the clarinet melody that opens the *Rhapsody in Blue* is a child—albeit a saucy American one—of the flute solo that begins Debussy's *Afternoon of a Faun.* This close affinity survived the *antidebussyste* reaction of the 1920s, as represented by Jean Cocteau and *les Six.* In 1928 Gershwin, on the contrary, was thrilled to return home from Paris with an eight-volume bound set of Debussy's works. When he said that *An American in Paris,* composed the same year, was "in typical French style, in the manner of Debussy and 'The Six,'" this did not signify, as sometimes claimed, a naive understanding of the complex relations between Debussy and *les Six* as much as it indicated his own absorption of both currents. If anything, his indebtedness to Debussy grew more marked and profound in the 1930s.[21]

Hambitzer also allegedly introduced Gershwin to Grieg's Piano Sonata and the music of Ravel as well. Although Gershwin never cited Grieg as a formative influence, some of his early music—such as *Rialto Ripples* (1916)—pointed in that direction. In a 1944 foreword to his arrangement of "The Man I Love," pianist-composer Percy Grainger tellingly located correspondences, too, between Grieg's Violin Sonata no. 3 and Gershwin's "The Man I Love," as well as Grieg's Piano Concerto in A Minor and Gershwin's *Rhapsody in Blue.* "None of this detracts from Gershwin's immense and indisputable originality," argued Grainger, who suggested nonetheless that such connections demonstrated Grieg's "life-giving inspiration" to "almost all truly progressive composers that came after him," while proving "how deeply Gershwin's genius . . . was rooted in the traditions of classical cosmopolitan music."[22]

Probably in the early years of their association, Gershwin played for Hambitzer a song he had written, "Since I Found You" (ca. 1913), in which he found himself stumped after moving from one key to another a full step away. Hambitzer reportedly responded, "You are to study composition, my boy, and harmony, before you can hope to write music properly." Whether Hambitzer taught Gershwin harmony per se (the evidence is contradictory), he at least made him "harmony-conscious," and for theory instruction eventually pointed him, as with other pupils, in the direction of a friend with whom he played in the Waldorf-Astoria Orchestra, composer-violinist-theorist Edward Kilenyi.[23]

Born in Hungary, Kilenyi (1884–1968) studied with Pietro Mascagni in Rome and, after immigrating to the States, with Daniel Gregory Mason in New York. Most of his known compositions, including the opera *The Cry of the Wolf* (1916), date from the 1910s, during which time he also collaborated on an anthology of Latin American folk songs (1914), providing lovely accompaniments to tunes collected by Eleanor Hague. Meanwhile, his scholarly work included an incomplete English translation of Arnold Schoenberg's theory text, *Harmonielehre* (1911), which he appreciatively if cautiously reviewed in 1915. Citing musical examples by Béla Bartók, Alban Berg, Franz Shrecker, and Anton Webern as well as by Schoenberg, this review showed an expert and sympathetic understanding—probably quite rare in America at that time—of the technical and aesthetic aims of Schoenberg and other avant-garde Austro-Hungarian composers. Kilenyi also wrote an article for *Musical Quarterly* (1919) arguing that Hungarian folk music derived not from Gypsy sources, as commonly thought, but from rhythmic and modal formulas associated with the music of Bach's era and before. In 1919 he began producing and supervising music for film, a pursuit that in the late 1920s took him to Hollywood, where he settled in 1931, and where he worked for RKO and Twentieth Century–Fox. Late in life, he published an article about his mentorship of Gershwin, as well as writing an unpublished monograph along these lines, *Gershwiniana: Recollections and Reminiscences of Times Spent with My Student George Gershwin.*[24]

According to David Ewen, Gershwin began studying with Kilenyi at Hambitzer's recommendation in 1915, but subsequent biographers, citing a theory notebook dating from August 1919 through September 1921, claimed rather that he worked with Kilenyi exclusively during that two-year period, an argument supported by Osborne Osgood's 1926 statement that Gershwin studied with Kilenyi "on and off for two years, more off than on." However, it seems doubtful that Gershwin (whom Hambitzer described to Kilenyi as someone "uncommonly serious in his search for knowledge of music") could have completed all his work with Kilenyi—the study of scales, harmony (including textbooks by Percy Goetschius and Benjamin Cutter that drew on examples from Bach through Scriabin), part-writing, figured bass, movable clefs, modulation, transposition, analysis (including the study of such works as Beethoven's "Spring" Sonata and Eighth Symphony as well as, according to Ira, the music of Schoenberg), instrumentation (including having professionals demonstrate their instruments), orchestration (including some consideration of Broadway arrangements), and free composition—within a two-year period, especially considering that during the time in question Gershwin, preoccupied with shows, needed to stop lessons for months at a stretch. Moreover, Susan Neimoyer notes that although Gershwin and Kilenyi reportedly went through the Goetschius text cover to cover, the 1919–1921 notebook begins with the study of dominant seventh chords as found on page 77 of that text.[25]

Indeed, even the most elementary work in the Gershwin notebook reveals a command of voice-leading and harmony beyond that of a rank beginner. The more modest assignments involve realizing a particular melody or bass line from Goetschius into a four-voiced setting in two staves, with harmonies identified by traditional Roman-numeral notation. The more advanced work shows increased attention to modulation, in particular the rapid cycling through keys and the use of secondary-dominant harmonies. Although these exercises represent nothing extraordinary in themselves, they not only suggest that Gershwin began his work with Kilenyi prior to August 1919 but also support claims of his seriousness, for they show considerable attention to detail. They additionally help explain the adroit voice-leading of Gershwin's work, which made it possible for expert arrangers like Robert Russell Bennett to orchestrate his show music without having to rewrite any of the parts, including the bass lines.[26]

Ira provided an additional clue to when Gershwin may have started lessons with Kilenyi, for he mentions in his diary that George left his full-time job at Remick in March 1917 in order to have more time to study. In light of all the evidence, it seems that Gershwin began theory lessons (for a while, two times a week) with Kilenyi sometime between 1915 and 1917. Nor do we know that Gershwin ended his lessons in the fall of 1921. Ewen, in fact, reports that he stopped working with Kilenyi in 1922, while Neimoyer argues for lessons as late as 1923, pointing to a second theory notebook from 1922–1923 that contains annotations in a hand virtually identical to Kilenyi's. (This later notebook focused on chromatic modulations, sometimes as distant as a tritone away.) If so, his lessons with Kilenyi and Rubin Goldmark would have overlapped; but in any case, Gershwin seems to have studied with Kilenyi for four years or more.[27]

Kilenyi claimed that he weaned Gershwin away from an overdependence on the deceptive cadence, but he cited as perhaps his most important contribution his transmission of Schoenberg's teachings as exemplified by the *Harmonielehre,* in particular, the concept of *Stufen-reichtum* (or what he called, after Percy Goetschius, the "law of propinquity"), defined as expressing "smoothness, richness of stepwise progressions, part writing of voices to create fresh, new, lush or strange chromatic harmonies." Kilenyi even deemed the law of propinquity one of Gershwin's guiding compositional principles—an assessment supported by Neimoyer, who further credited Kilenyi with encouraging Gershwin to apply such principles in an individual way. Meanwhile, how Kilenyi's study of folk music may have influenced Gershwin's thoughts on music and culture can only be imagined.[28]

Kilenyi guided Gershwin in career matters as well. As the latter won fame as a popular composer in the early 1920s and "often spoke of his desire to quit writing popular music and retire somewhere far away so that he could devote himself to serious music," Kilenyi told him, "In a few years, you would be forgotten as a Broadway writer. You would face the same difficulty all young Americans have to face when trying to have their works performed. You would come nearer to your goal if you were to continue your studies and become even a bigger success that [*sic*] you are today. You should attain such fame that conductors in due time would ask you for serious compositions to be performed by them." Gershwin apparently took such counsel to heart, and, moreover, passed on similar advice to composers younger than himself. In any case, he once cited Kilenyi as "the man to whom I owe everything" and his most important teacher (at least according to Kilenyi, for Gershwin, as mentioned, singled out Hambitzer for that distinction). For his part, Kilenyi thought Gershwin "never . . . anything but the eager, ambitious, respectful and serious musician I have known him to be."[29]

Even before Gershwin completed his work with Kilenyi, he took two music courses at Columbia University in the summer of 1921: Elementary Orchestration and Nineteenth-Century Romanticism in Music, both taught by Rossetter G. Cole (1866–1952), the Chicago composer who taught at Columbia's summer program from 1908 to 1939. These classes met for one hour each day, five days a week, for six weeks beginning in early July. For students not pursuing a degree, like Gershwin, admission into these classes depended on the approval of the instructor.

According to the course description, Elementary Orchestration covered "the historical development of the orchestra, the study of the technical possibilities and tonal qualities of each instrument of the modern orchestra, the principles of tone combination, and the arranging of particular compositions for various groups of instruments and for full orchestra." On July 25, 1921, while taking the course, Gershwin sketched out an incomplete "figured choral," a setting of the first two phrases of the German hymn "Freu dich sehr, o meine Seele," scored, in an immaculate hand, for clarinet, two bassoons, two horns, viola, cello, and bass. Whether written for Cole or Kilenyi, this exercise shows Gershwin, according to Wayne Shirley, "already comfortable with those two bugaboos of the beginning orchestrator, Transposition and The Alto Clef." Although the received wisdom states that Gershwin acquired Cecil Forsyth's *Orchestration* in 1925 as an aid in the writing of the Concerto in F, he more likely acquired this classic 1914 text while taking Cole's course, or perhaps for his work with Kilenyi, whose handwriting Shirley discovered on a page in Gershwin's copy. Whenever acquired, the Forsyth text became, according to Oscar Levant, his "bible."[30]

Romanticism in Music, meanwhile, surveyed music from Berlioz and Schumann through Richard Strauss and Debussy, including "the rise and development of nationalism in music, especially in such countries as Russia, Scandinavia, and Bohemia." Gershwin may have taken this course in part because it met directly after Elementary Orchestration in the same room, but he had a lively interest in music history, collecting a wide assortment of books about music, and surprising friends with his knowledge of little-known musical facts. And this particular study of nineteenth-century music may well have helped shape his developing aesthetics.[31]

Although Gershwin did some free composition with Kilenyi, including writing a string quartet movement that became his *Lullaby* (1919), by the early 1920s he felt the need to work with a prominent composition teacher. He showed some interest, apparently spurred by Kilenyi, in studying with Jewish-Swiss émigré Ernst Bloch (1880–1959), probably the time's most distinguished American composition teacher, and one whose students over time included Douglas Moore, Quincy Porter, Roger Sessions, and Randall Thompson; but this would not have been feasible, as during the period 1920–1925 Bloch taught at the Cleveland Institute. Instead, Gershwin took some lessons with Rubin Goldmark (1872–1936), another prominent composer-teacher with a similarly impressive student roster, including Aaron Copland, Vittorio Giannini, Alexei Haieff, and Frederick Jacobi. Grandson of a Hungarian cantor, nephew of Viennese composer Karl Goldmark, and a student of Johann Nepomuk Fuchs in Vienna and Antonín Dvořák and pianist Rafael Joseffy in New York, Goldmark—a native New Yorker—was so highly regarded that when Juilliard was established in 1924, he was named head of its theory and composition department.

The circumstances surrounding Gershwin's study with Goldmark remain characteristically vague. These lessons are said to have taken place in 1923, and in fact, on January 12, 1923, Ira wrote to a cousin that George was "studying form and composition with Goldmark." Although most sources state that Gershwin took a mere three lessons with Goldmark, Ewen claimed that he studied with Goldmark for "several months." In any case, these lessons presumably transpired, at least in part, in the interim between the December 4 opening of Gershwin's show *Our Nell* and his February departure for England to work on *The Rainbow*.[32]

Composer-arranger Ferde Grofé, meanwhile, stated that Gershwin was studying orchestration with Goldmark about the time he composed the *Rhapsody* in early 1924, so he presumably resumed lessons on his return from Europe. Yet another surviving music notebook contains a number of short studies, composed in March and April 1924, that may have been written under Goldmark as well. Written in eight-measure, sixteen-measure, twenty-four-measure, and larger forms, these sketches suggest pedagogical intentions, though Gershwin possibly intended them as drafts for a set of piano preludes that he spoke about during these years. Indeed, the "Moderato" (in G Minor) and "Lento" (in F♯ Minor) stand on their own as appealing little pieces, while another of these sketches, the more bluesy "Moderato" (E♭ Major), provided the main theme to Gershwin's celebrated song, "The Man I Love."[33]

Accordingly, Gershwin might have studied with Goldmark intermittently from late 1922 or early 1923 to the spring of 1924, if not later (Kay Swift recalled accompanying Gershwin to two lessons with Goldmark, which would extend such study at least to 1925). Whatever the length and nature of Gershwin's studies with Goldmark, commentators have dismissed them too readily. Isaac Goldberg set the tone early on, reporting that in the "early weeks" of his study with Goldmark, Gershwin brought into a lesson his *Lullaby* for string quartet composed a few years earlier, to which Goldmark responded: "It's good. Yes, very good. . . . It's plain to be seen that you have already learned a great deal of harmony from me!" The story may well be true, but need not be taken as evidence that Gershwin learned nothing from Goldmark. On the contrary, Gershwin "assured" Carl Van Vechten that "he received invaluable suggestions" from Goldmark, "especially in regard to form."[34]

Moreover, in 1929 Gershwin, citing Goldmark as "my teacher and friend," described him as "a prominent and significant Jewish composer" whose *Negro Rhapsody* (1922), composed about the time of their closest association, helped pave the way to a distinctively American music. Although the piece, wrote Gershwin, might seem "pretty feeble stuff" to modern listeners, "as a pioneer 'work, its importance cannot be overestimated. Overlooking the fact that this is, at best, pretty thin music; that it resembles Dvořák more closely than it does anything American; that its fragmentary moments of beauty are as far removed from the American spirit as Rubin Goldmark himself was—overlooking these things, the fact remains that Goldmark was among the very first to turn his eye towards the negro and to attempt to interpret America through the poignant strains of the spiritual." Attending a performance of the *Negro Rhapsody* in 1960, Ross Parmenter wrote that the piece "at times suggested sketches for Gershwin's *Porgy and Bess.*"[35]

Nor should Gershwin's however-long tenure with Goldmark be taken as indicating some incapacity for sustained study. On the contrary, Gershwin showed considerable determination in pursuing the study of music theory and composition while juggling a hectic schedule of writing show music and recording piano rolls. In the early 1920s, he also studied piano with Herman Wasserman as well as with Ernest Hutcheson, who eventually became president of the Juilliard School. Exactly when he studied with them—let alone the repertory and techniques learned—remains unknown, but signed photographs (Wasserman's inscribed, "To my dear pal George Gershwin—the most remarkable talent I have met in America") at least reveal that Gershwin knew Wasserman and Hutcheson no later than 1921 and 1922, respectively. Pianist Lester Donahue noted, in any case, that when they met shortly before the premiere of the *Rhapsody,* Gershwin was "tremendously acquisitive about all phases of music and impressed me by delving into Bach at a time when he was still regarded only as a brilliant and promising composer of Broadway shows."[36]

Gershwin had also been reading about classical music by age twelve, and by age fourteen had been regularly attending concerts as well. A record of some of these activities survives, thanks to a scrapbook of music-related clippings that George began in 1910, about the time the family acquired a piano. Most of these little articles, largely culled, as Ira remembered, from *Etude* magazine, concerned the lives of famous composers and pianists (some of the latter grouped under the charmingly redundant heading "Great Pianists of the Keyboard"). Gershwin showed a special interest in Russian composers, especially Anton Rubinstein, perhaps in part because he could now associate him with the *Melody* that had so transported him as a child, or because of Hambitzer's involvement with the composer. Gershwin would have read that Rubinstein "was of Jewish ancestry," and that, according to César Cui, although "he often wished to write Russian music," he produced "only more or less clever counterfeits," a statement whose anti-Semitic implications probably were not entirely lost on the young George. The scrapbook even included a bibliography for Rubinstein; Ira was not the only member of the family with a scholarly bent.

From 1912 through essentially 1917, Gershwin also occasionally pasted concert programs into this scrapbook, preserving a partial record of his attendance at concerts. Most of these programs date from 1913, with a gap from 1914 through 1916. Ira himself described the scrapbook as merely "representative" of Gershwin's concertgoing activities. John Jackson Totten, who started ushering for Carnegie Hall in 1903 and who eventually became the theater's manager, confirmed that Gershwin was "a music-hungry youngster" to whom he occasionally gave free passes.[37]

These programs reveal that Gershwin heard many of the time's most celebrated pianists, including Ossip Gabrilowitsch, Leopold Godowsky, Josef Hofmann (in a 1914 all-Chopin concert "For the Relief of the Poles"), Josef Lhévinne, Leo Ornstein, and Sigismund Stojowski. Most of these pianists were Russian Jews, and as a group they comprised as important an aspect of Gershwin's Russian-Jewish heritage as popular Yiddish music. He also heard violinist Efrem Zimbalist (and in earlier years Mischa Elman, as mentioned), the Kneisel String Quartet, and conductor Pierre Monteux, as well as the Musical Art Society in a concert of choral music by Palestrina, Arcadelt, Mozart, and Brahms. Moreover, he attended the concerts of such associates as Max Rosen, Jack Miller (and the Beethoven Musical Society Orchestra), and Charles Hambitzer (and the Waldorf-Astoria Orchestra), and, in 1913 and 1914, attended enough recitals by organist Alexander Russell (including some at the great Wanamaker Organ) to suggest some hitherto undisclosed relationship with either Russell or one of his students.[38]

These concerts generally featured such nineteenth-century masters as Beethoven, Schubert, Chopin, Liszt, Wagner, Brahms, and Dvořák, with more recent developments represented by Rimsky-Korsakov, MacDowell, Rakhmaninov, and lesser names now forgotten. Nothing particularly new or daring stands out. Even the April 3, 1913, recital by America's soon-to-be enfant terrible, Leo Ornstein, which included the pianist-composer's pastiche "In modo Scarlatti" (1911), was rather conventional. Still, Gershwin clearly had ample exposure to much standard repertory performed to the highest standards. Moreover, the inclusion of lighthearted fare on many of these programs may have provided an impetus toward a more popular-oriented concert style. In any case, Gershwin placed great importance on these early concert experiences. In 1927, he attributed his musical "facility" to his "habit of intensive listening," which he had "consciously cultivated" since his early teens. "I had gone to concerts and listened not only with my ears," he wrote, "but with my nerves, my mind, my heart. I had listened so earnestly that I became saturated with the music. Then I went home and listened in memory. I sat at the piano and repeated the *motifs*."[39]

In late 1917, at age nineteen, Gershwin essentially stopped keeping a scrapbook, though he continued to attend classical concerts throughout his life. With his entry into society in the 1920s, he also had the opportunity to hear many distinguished artists, including pianist Arthur Rubinstein, perform in more casual settings. Gershwin's song "Mischa, Jascha, Toscha, Sascha," composed with Ira around 1921, derived from such informal socializing with the four virtuoso violinists alluded to in the song's title: Mischa Elman, Jascha Heifetz, Toscha Seidel, and Sascha Jacobsen.[40]

Gershwin saved only a few later programs, including that to a January 1, 1920, Metropolitan Opera performance of Italo Montemezzi's 1913 opera *L'Amore dei tre re* ("The Love of Three Kings") with a legendary cast, including Claudia Muzio, Giovanni Martinelli, and Pasquale Amato as the ill-fated love triangle. This opera of adulterous love set in tenth-century Italy possibly served as one model, among others, for Gershwin's first operatic attempt, *Blue Monday Blues,* and perhaps even for *Porgy and Bess.* That the opera's librettist, Italian playwright Sam Benelli, had scored a Broadway hit in 1919 with *The Jest* (an English adaptation of his 1910 play *La cena delle beffe*), illustrates the kind of interaction between classical and popular traditions characteristic of Italian opera, as evident, too, from Puccini's adaptations of David Belasco, namely, *Madama Butterfly* (1904) and *The Girl of the Golden West* (1910). Gershwin surely grasped these connections.

Gershwin also preserved the program for a February 4, 1923, concert sponsored by New York's International Composers' Guild that featured the American premiere of Arnold Schoenberg's *Pierrot lunaire* (1912) along with Charles Koechlin's Sonata for Two Flutes, Erik Satie's *Sports et divertissements,* and excerpts from Darius Milhaud's *Saudades do Brasil.* Although by this point *Pierrot* had been around for a while, worldwide performances of the work in the early 1920s, states David Metzer, "served as a lightning rod for the growing and vehement dispute surrounding new music." Considering that Gershwin saved the program, and remembering, too, the deep respect Hambitzer and Kilenyi held for Schoenberg, one can easily guess on which side he came down.[41]

Gershwin had more exposure to Schoenberg later in the year, when on November 1, 1923, he collaborated with Eva Gauthier on what was billed as a "Recital of Ancient and Modern Music for Voice" at New York's Aeolian Hall. In addition to a set of popular songs for which Gershwin played the piano, Gauthier, accompanied by pianist Max Jaffe, performed a sophisticated mix of Bellini, Perucchini, Purcell, Byrd, Bartók, Hindemith, Schoenberg, Bliss, Milhaud, Maurice Delage (a student of Ravel's), and Swan Hennessy (an Irish American composer living in Paris). The Schoenberg selection consisted of the American premiere of "Song of the Wood Dove" from *Gurrelieder,* arranged for voice and piano by Alban Berg. Gershwin had the opportunity to hear some of this and other music while collaborating with Gauthier on subsequent concerts in Boston (1924), London (1925), and Derby, Connecticut (1926).[42]

Gershwin witnessed not only the American premiere of *Pierrot* in 1923, but very likely another landmark event in New York's musical life: the city's first hearing of Stravinsky's *Rite of Spring* on January 31, 1924, with Pierre Monteux and the Boston Symphony Orchestra. Assuming he attended the concert, Gershwin presumably would have recognized some shared aims and ideals, as did early listeners to the *Rhapsody in Blue*—unveiled a mere two weeks after the Stravinsky premiere. In any case, the work, which "exercised a very great influence on him," as he told Merle Armitage, became one of his favorite compositions.[43]

In the fourteen years or so from the time he began piano lessons to the time he composed the *Rhapsody in Blue,* his first extended concert work, Gershwin remained actively involved in the practice and study of classical music. This included at least five years of piano instruction (including work with Hambitzer on music from Bach through Debussy); probably four years or more of lessons in harmony, figured bass, analysis, and orchestration with Kilenyi; courses at Columbia in orchestration and music history; and the study of form, composition, and orchestration with Goldmark. During the same years, he read widely about classical music and attended many concerts featuring eminent artists performing music from Palestrina to Schoenberg.

These facts challenge the common notion of Gershwin as an untrained composer who, after the *Rhapsody,* attempted to redress his lack of schooling through some serious, if fitful, study. In fact, even as a young man Gershwin acquired a much more extensive musical education than typically allowed, and though he continued his studies after the *Rhapsody*, that only extended long-standing goals. Discussing his association with Gershwin in the early 1920s, Vernon Duke, himself the product of a Russian conservatory education, wrote, "Gershwin impressed me as a superbly equipped and highly skilled composer."[44]

Aside from the technical weaknesses inferred from the *Rhapsody*—a rather subjective criterion—two factors, among others, help explain the widespread deprecation of Gershwin's musical education: the unlikeliness that a busy composer of musical comedies who had dropped out of high school would have either the time or the inclination to study music seriously; and the fact that he never worked with an internationally renowned composition teacher. Furthermore, Ferde Grofé's orchestration of the *Rhapsody* misleadingly suggested an inability in that particular area. But more decisive than any of these, perhaps, was Gershwin's own tendency to downplay his education, including his protests that he took piano lessons for only four or five years; that he never played "very serious things"; that he studied harmony "on and off for two years, more off than on"; that he learned nothing (or so he once implied) from Goldmark; that he acquired his "facility" from his "habit of intensive listening"; and that, as he told Duke, he "didn't study much," he was "a natural born composer." Whatever the truth of these remarks, Gershwin at the least exaggerated his lack of training. For instance, Isaac Goldberg, who knew him personally, wrote, "Up to the time that he began work on the famous *Rhapsody* . . . he knew—formally—about as much harmony as could be found in a ten-cent manual"—this about someone who had spent years studying harmony and who had maneuvered his way through two formidable harmony textbooks.[45]

Gershwin's elusiveness, which now makes it difficult simply to chronicle his musical education, seemed a function of the extreme ingenuousness and modesty—even that sense of inferiority—that marked his personality. Or perhaps it reflected, equally characteristically, his bravado: the same impulse that led him to tell interviewers about the boy who played hooky from school and who thought music was for girls and sissies, as opposed to the boy who kept a scrapbook filled with concert programs and who "lavished childish affection" on Maxie Rosenzweig.

This bravado surfaced in a reminiscence by pianist Abram Chasins (1903–1987), another young friend. In 1919, Chasins suggested that Gershwin study with Goldmark, saying, "Nobody can do what you want to do without basic training," to which Gershwin angrily "shouted and stamped," retorting, "You're just the kind of person who's keeping me from doing my great work." Chasins thought that this "explosive rejection of formal study . . . may have been a piece of wisdom," but it might have indicated more simply a disdain for academic smugness.[46]

This is not to deny the shortcomings of Gershwin's early formal education, including limited work in counterpoint and orchestration (which helps explain his determination to master those skills in later years). In addition, New York was still somewhat provincial compared to such European capitals as Paris or Vienna—though this was rapidly changing—and, partly for that reason, at the time of the *Rhapsody* Gershwin's knowledge of the newer trends was accordingly more circumscribed than that of some American musicians studying abroad. [47]

Moreover, Gershwin composed mostly popular theater music during his formative years of study. "My serious music," he once said, "was an outgrowth of light music. I had written light music for ten or fifteen shows before I composed my *Rhapsody in Blue*." Even so, it seems imprecise to refer to Gershwin as someone from the other side of the tracks who came to the classical tradition relatively late in life. From his early years, Gershwin's involvement with concert music paralleled his activities in popular music. He did not so much cross over as from the very beginning plant one foot on each side of the tracks and attempt to straddle them as firmly as he could.[48]

Chapter Three

Gershwin and the New Popular Music

$\mathscr{G}$rowing up in New York, Gershwin heard a wide range of popular musics, some mainstream, others emanating from the city's many ethnic communities. Among the tunes learned at school, including "Annie Laurie" (1838; music adapted by Lady John Scott), he remembered being "especially haunted" by the Scottish folk song "Loch Lomond," with its refrain, "You'll take the high road and I'll take the low road"; and Arthur Sullivan's "The Lost Chord" (1877). (Melodies with repeated notes, as found in the latter song, would emerge as a basic impulse for Gershwin, whether in the percussive *Second Rhapsody* or the tuneful "They Can't Take That Away from Me.") Morris Gershwin's recording of Sullivan's *H.M.S. Pinafore* also made a lasting impression. Ira in particular became an avid Gilbert and Sullivan enthusiast, acquiring recordings of some of the other operettas, whose wit and sophistication set a lifelong standard for both him and George.[1]

These recollections suggest an early absorption of British popular music, an inheritance displayed in various Gershwin scores, especially those composed for the West End *(Primrose)*, those that smacked of Savoyard satire *(Strike Up the Band),* or those that involved Scottish or English characters *(A Damsel in Distress).* More generally, Gershwin's penchant for pentatonic and other gapped scales may have owed a debt to British music, though Walter Rubsamen argued that he developed this orientation not so much through "English-Irish-Scotch modal folk-song" as through "Negro spirituals and jazz" on the one hand and "Russian-Jewish folk song and synagogical chant" on the other (to which one might add Asian or quasi-Asian sources).[2]

Gershwin's pentatonic leanings may have derived as well from traditional American songs, such as a professed favorite, "He's Gone Away," a tune whose mix of pentatonic inflections and blue notes prefigured his own melodies. He naturally was also familiar with the pentatonic-flavored tunes of Stephen Foster, and even exploded onto the music scene on Foster's coattails, as it were, with a vigorous two-step, "Swanee" (1919), drenched in daffy references to "Old Folks at Home" (1851). This Foster tune appeared as well in Gershwin's show *Of Thee I Sing* as sung by Senator Robert E. Lyons, whose constituency includes "Aunt Jemima" and "Uncle Joe"; while in the show's sequel, *Let 'Em Eat Cake*, the melody cast a shadow over "Union Square," a pastoral chorus (described Ira as "schottischey") ironically interrupted by the ravings of a radical agitator. Such mocking appropriations of Foster constituted a complex but genuine inheritance.[3]

True to the melting-pot ideal of which he often spoke, Gershwin assimilated other musics, including those associated with Hispanic, Asian, and African American populations. In 1927 he recalled, in Whitmanesque fashion, "the chorus of city sounds" of his childhood:

> Wherever I went I heard a concourse of sounds. Many of them were not audible to my companions, for I was hearing them in memory. Strains from the latest concert, the cracked tones of a hurdy gurdy, the wail of a street singer to the obligato of a broken violin, past or present music, I was hearing within me.
>
> Old music and new music, forgotten melodies and the craze of the moment, bits of opera, Russian folk songs, Spanish ballads, chanson's [*sic*], rag-time ditties, combined in a mighty chorus in my inner ear. And through and over it all I heard, faint at first, loud at last, the soul of this great America of ours.[4]

As this discussion might suggest, Gershwin rarely dwelled on his Jewish-Russian background. Indeed, despite his mention here of "Russian folk songs"—or his reference in the same article to his "Russian parentage"—he denied any special "sensitiveness" to Russian music (though he successfully evoked popular Russian idioms in his operetta *Song of the Flame*). At most, he once vaguely attributed his closeness to "Negro music" to his Russian "ancestry."[5]

Gershwin proved similarly elusive about Jewish music—a repertoire notably absent from the "concourse of sounds" enumerated above. In his most extensive statement on the subject, a 1925 interview in the *American Hebrew*, he noted that "the traditional Hebrew religious melodies have had a marked influence upon modern music" and that "the Hebrew chants possess a peculiarly plaintive wail which give them a universal appeal." Discussing Jewish prominence in the field of music, he added, "To write good music one must have feeling. This quality is possessed to a great degree by the Jewish people. Perhaps the fact that through the centuries the Jews have been an oppressed race, has helped to intensify this feeling. As a result we have had many great Jewish composers." He further attributed the success of Al Jolson and Eddie Cantor to "the intense Jewish feeling they possess for melody." [6]

On a more personal note, he reportedly told composer Lazare Saminsky, "While I actually do not know much about Jewish folksong, I think that many of my themes are Jewish in feeling although they are purely American in style," a statement congruent not only with the *American Hebrew* article, but with a quote reported by Nathan Ausubel. Gershwin apparently believed that "the internal, deep emotional element" of his melodies—though nothing stylistic—derived from varied Jewish sources, including Hebrew chant and Yiddish folk song. Isaac Goldberg also recalled conversations with the composer "about the Jewish element in his music," discussed "from the standpoint of psychology and of art—not of religious creeds." [7]

Although Ira once stated that "there was no Jewish religious music at home—in fact, no music at all," the aforesaid sources indicate that George nonetheless acquired some knowledge of synagogue melodies as well as the kinds of popular Jewish music played at weddings and such. But of the distinctively Jewish musics with which he came into contact, he probably had the greatest familiarity with that of the Yiddish theater of the Lower East Side. In his youth, he even ran errands for members of the Yiddish theater and appeared onstage as an extra. He continued to attend such shows while working for Remick in the mid-teens, by which time the Lower East Side had established itself as the world's center for Yiddish theater, boasting such legendary actors as Jacob P. Adler, David Kessler, and Boris Thomashevsky; a large cluster of theaters, including Thomashevsky's National Theatre on Houston Street and Kessler's Second Avenue Theatre; and a repertoire that embraced European and Yiddish classics as well as new American creations. [8]

The American Yiddish theater had a profound impact on Gershwin's generation, particularly—but not only—on Jews from the Lower East Side like himself. Drama critic Harold Clurman cited gentile writer Hutchins Hapgood's claim that in the early decades of the twentieth century, the Yiddish theater was "about the best in New York at that time both in stuff and acting." Clurman himself described the Yiddish theater as "in every sense a *people*'s or a *community* theatre, that is to say, a *true* theatre, the like of which was rarely if ever to be achieved again in our country," and "a beacon light, a symbol of striving toward spirituality and human meaning." And Yip Harburg wrote, "Everything in the Yiddish theater set me afire. The funny plays had me guffawing; they were broad and boisterous. And the tragedies were devastating." The Yiddish language, opined Harburg, "had more onomatopoetic, satiric, and metaphoric nuances ready-made for comedy than any other language I know of."[9]

Music played an important part in the Yiddish theater, as incidental music for plays, to be sure, but even more so in its hallmark musicals, which Clurman referred to as "charming folk operettas." Abraham Goldfaden (1840–1908), credited with establishing the modern Yiddish theater in the 1870s in Romania (though he worked elsewhere, including New York), helped formulate its musical language, creating a synthesis, with the aid of assistants, that drew on Yiddish folk song, Hebrew cantillation, and European operetta. Some of his most popular numbers, like "Rozshinkes mit Mandlen" from *Shulamis* (1880), became in essence Jewish folk tunes, comparable to certain songs by Stephen Foster.[10]

Goldfaden's most important successors worked in New York, including Lithuanian Joseph Rumshinsky (1881–1956), who arrived there in 1904 and who dominated Yiddish musical theater in the 1910s; and Ukrainian Sholom Secunda (1894–1974), who arrived in 1908. Rumshinsky, dubbed the "Jewish Victor Herbert," helped introduce popular American and British musical styles into the mix. In an early song like "Dos Lid der Libe" from *Shir ha-Shirim* (1911), he approximated such American operetta composers as Rudolf Friml and Sigmund Romberg. In later years, perhaps more than Friml or Romberg, he accommodated the influence of Irving Berlin as well. In such ways, the Yiddish theater served as a mediator between Jewish and American musics for the great migration of Eastern European Jews and their immediate descendants in the early twentieth century, a confluence embodied by the appearance, in 1932, of both Jay Gorney's hit from *Americana,* "Brother, Can You Spare a Dime?" (lyrics, Harburg), a song strongly redolent of the Yiddish theater; and Secunda's "Bay mir bistu sheyn," from *M'ken lebn nor m'lozt nit,* widely popularized later in the decade as a swing staple.

George and Ira knew Rumshinsky early on through their father, who played pinochle with him when the Gershwins lived on the Lower East Side; Rumshinsky retained memories of George's "quiet determination." By 1917 George and Ira also had become friendly with Boris Thomashevsky and his family, especially with his sons Harry (1895–1993), a writer and producer in his own right and director of the film *The Yid-*

dish King Lear (1934); and Milton (1897–1936), who became a doctor (another son, Ted, fathered Michael Tilson Thomas, a noted Gershwin interpreter). Two years earlier, in 1915, Boris Thomashevsky had invited Gershwin to collaborate with Secunda on a musical for the National Theatre, but Secunda rejected the idea, citing Gershwin's lack of formal schooling.[11]

During these years, Gershwin performed songs from the Yiddish theater at the piano. Visiting a private home in Brooklyn with Boris Thomashevsky in the 1910s, Rumshinsky heard Gershwin play excerpts from his operettas *Shir Hashirim* and *Dos tsebrokehene fidele.* And in 1916 Gershwin recorded a piano-roll medley of two popular Yiddish songs on the Perfection label of "Hebrew music": "Dos Pintele Yid" ("The Little Spark of Jewishness"), music by Arnold Perlmutter (1859–1953) and Herman Wohl (1877–1936), from the 1909 play of the same name by Thomashevsky; and "Got un zayn mishpet iz gerekht" ("God and His Judgment Are Just"), music by David Meyrowitz (1867–1943), from Z. Libin's 1903 play *Di gebrokhene Herster* ("The Broken Hearts"). Both numbers had lyrics by Louis Gilrod that concerned Jewish endurance in the face of oppression. The modal irregularities of the music, including some cross-relations in "Dos Pintele Yid" not unlike those found in the blues, presumably helped expand Gershwin's musical horizons.[12]

Gershwin remained interested in the Yiddish theater. Rumshinsky recalled seeing him at a performance of his show *Oy, iz dos a Meydl* in 1927. And in April 1928, while in Berlin, George and Ira attended a musical comedy adapted from Mendele Mokher Seforim's classic 1862 Yiddish novel *The Travels of Benjamin III,* produced by the Moscow Jewish Academy. Noted Ira in his diary: "the direction was absolutely sensational, and never have I seen such acting on the stage. . . . The music, while Yiddish, was absolutely different from the Yiddish music of Rumshinsky . . . who obviously emulates the style of the Broadway tinpan alley scriveners." In London that June, the Gershwins attended another Jewish Academy production, *200,000,* an adaptation of Sholem Aleichem's *The Big Win,* with music by Leib Pulver.[13]

As for how various Jewish musics may have influenced Gershwin, one biographer, Robert Payne, emphasized, much like the composer himself, correspondences of feeling and emotion. "Somewhere below the surface of nearly all the music he ever wrote can be discerned a plaintive lament or a Jewish lullaby," wrote Payne, who concluded his study with the thought that Gershwin would be remembered as "a musician who at his best either consciously or unconsciously drew his inspiration from the deep wells of Jewish lamentation." Lazare Saminsky similarly found in the piano concerto (presumably the opening solo theme) "something which might adorn the mystic dreams of the young *Talmudist*-student from the *Dibbuk*-legend."[14]

Some commentators noted stylistic connections as well. Saminsky, for instance, heard "the gait and the hue of a Balkan-Jewish wedding tune" in the opening theme of the *Rhapsody*. Walter Rubsamen, as mentioned, attributed Gershwin's pentatonic impulses in part to Jewish sources, while Charles Schwartz cited some other melodic traits possibly related to Jewish music, including the use of falling thirds (the second of the *Three Preludes*), stepwise sighs ("Seventeen and Twenty-One"), and declamatory rhythms ("My One and Only"). Maurice Peress thought the unmeasured counterpoint in "Oh, Hev'nly Father" from *Porgy and Bess* reminiscent of a "davenning minyan." Both Secunda and singer Molly Picon further asserted that Gershwin—who, according to Bernard Herrmann, worried that "Summertime" sounded more "Yiddish" than "colored"—never hid his debt to Abraham Goldfaden. Picon remembered Gershwin saying in particular that he modeled "My One and Only" after Goldfaden's lullaby "Shlof in Freydn" ("Sleep in Joy"); Secunda pondered the connection between "'S Wonderful" and Goldfaden's "Noyakhs Teyve" ("Noah's Ark") from *Akeidas Itzkhok* ("The Sacrifice of Isaac," 1887).[15]

In the most ample inquiry along these lines, Jack Gottlieb locates correspondences between some Gershwin tunes and not only Yiddish song, but such Hebrew chants as "Hashkiveinu" (verse to "Swanee"), "Mah nishtano" ("Mornin' time an' evenin' time" from "Bess, You Is My Woman"), and "Bor'chu es adoshem ham'vorach" ("It Ain't Necessarily So"). Gottlieb further discerns certain Jewish modes that seem to inform a number of the composer's melodies, in particular, the "Adonai malakh" mode (akin to the mixolydian mode, though with a flatted third in its upper range) and the "Ukrainian Dorian" mode (similar to the dorian mode, but with a tritone and variable sixth and seventh degrees). Gottlieb concludes that Gershwin, like Irving Berlin, wore his Jewishness more "comfortably" than did Jerome Kern and Richard Rodgers.[16]

At the same time, many of the typical signifiers of Hebrew and Russian-Jewish music—minor modes, melodic augmented seconds, and hora and slow waltz rhythms—assumed no special prominence in Gershwin's music. Ira even thought the lack of "Hebraic influence" a point of distinction between his brother's music and that of Harold Arlen, whose father was a cantor. Gershwin surely made more direct use of blues and jazz scales than the "Adonai malakh" or "Ukrainian Dorian" modes (though similarities among all these modes help explain the widespread confluence of black and Jewish musics during this period); and if a few songs recalled the outlines of some Jewish melodies, their rhythms and harmonies often made such resemblances moot. The intentions behind Gershwin's most Jewish-sounding music warranted consideration as well. That "Wintergreen for President," for instance, satirized political pandering to a Jewish constituency, and that "It Ain't Necessarily So" parodied religious fundamentalism only complicated their apparent connections to Jewish styles, and in a way somewhat comparable to Gershwin's appropriation of Foster in "Swanee" and *Of Thee I Sing*.[17]

In any case, the young George presumably developed greater affinity for contemporary American popular music—including the work of Charles Harris ("After the Ball," 1892), Paul Dresser ("On the Banks of the Wabash," 1897), Harry Von Tilzer ("A Bird in a Gilded Cage," 1900), Charles B. Ward ("Strike Up the Band, Here Comes a Sailor," 1900), Theodore F. Morse ("Dear Old Girl," 1903), George M. Cohan ("Give My Regards to Broadway," 1904), Egbert Van Alstyne ("In the Shade of the Old Apple Tree," 1905), and Albert Von Tilzer ("Take Me Out to the Ball Game," 1908)—than with any specifically Jewish music (for Harris and the Tilzers were Jewish). Gershwin remembered these songs with a respect that bespoke more than collegial solidarity: "You can compare the sentimental songs of Dresser, Harris and von Tilzer with the romantic period of classic music which came in with Schubert, Schumann and Chopin. They are a bit old-fashioned in this unromantic, mechanical age of ours." Some of these songwriters also evoked various ethnic styles, usually for comic effect, thus creating a whole subgenre of novelty songs especially popular with vaudeville entertainers, in and out of blackface and other disguises. Meanwhile, Irish American vaudevillian George M. Cohan (1878–1942) carved his own niche by celebrating America in songs indebted to the "march king," John Philip Sousa (1854–1932).[18]

By the 1910s, however, Irving Berlin (1888–1989) had superseded all the rest, at least as far as Gershwin was concerned. Born Israel Baline in a small Russian town where his father was a cantor, Berlin arrived in New York at age five, a refugee from a pogrom that saw his family's home burned to the ground. He grew up in a working-class area of the Lower East Side and at age fourteen left school in order to pursue a career in popular music, first as a singer, then as a lyricist, then as a composer and publisher, and eventually as a producer and theater owner.

Berlin helped initiate a new era in American music with three hit songs from 1911 for which he also wrote the lyrics: "That Mysterious Rag" (with Ted Snyder), "Everybody's Doin' It," and, above all, "Alexander's Ragtime Band," a song that, in the words of Alexander Woollcott, "stamped a new character on American music." Some of Berlin's rivals anticipated and almost duplicated this achievement, including Shelton Brooks (1888–1959), an African American songwriter whose "Some of These Days" (1910), as popularized by Jewish vaudevillian Sophie Tucker, became the archetypal torch song; and Lewis F. Muir (1884–1950), whose "Play That Barber Shop Chord" (1910), introduced by black vaudevillian Bert Williams, and "Waiting for the Robert E. Lee" (1912) vied with "Alexander's Ragtime Band" as landmarks of their kind. Gershwin, who in his teens enjoyed Muir's counsel and encouragement, and who described "Waiting for the Robert E. Lee" as "a glorious tune," told Isaac Goldberg, "Muir was in his way a glorious, a remarkable fellow. He could play only in one key, F-sharp, just like that master melodist, Berlin. But he was a thorough musician none the less. He deserves to be mentioned in any complete history of our popular songs during the early days of the twentieth century."[19]

But Berlin's importance to Gershwin, as with many other Americans, remained preeminent, not only because of Berlin's later work but because of the germinal role played specifically by "Alexander's Ragtime Band" (which quickly turned up in John Alden Carpenter's 1914 tone-poem *Adventures in a Perambulator,* much as "That Mysterious Rag" found its way into Erik Satie's 1917 ballet *Parade*). A "passionate admirer" of the song, Gershwin allegedly used it to demonstrate the virtues of popular music to his piano teacher Charles Hambitzer. Years later, in 1929, Gershwin held up the song, in contrast to both ragtime songs of the 1890s and the serious work of Edward MacDowell and others, as "the first real American musical work. . . . Berlin had shown us the way; it was now easier to attain our ideal."[20]

The common dismissal of "Alexander's Ragtime Band" as both exploitative and devoid of real ragtime largely misses the point; the song's significance resides precisely in its distance from ragtime songs of the turn of the twentieth century. Berlin simply used the word *ragtime* in this song for something that by 1917 would be referred to as "jazz"; indeed, discussions of jazz in the 1920s, including Gershwin's own, frequently took "Alexander's Ragtime Band" as their starting point. That listeners after 1930 increasingly realized that jazz constituted a distinct performing tradition does not minimize the importance of the song, which helped inaugurate what might be called, more simply, the new popular music.[21]

The song's chorus especially explored novel territory in its bluesy slurring of its main motive, fused to Berlin's entreaty, "Come on and hear"; in its ironic quotations of such disparate materials as bugle calls and "Old Folks at Home," the latter used, as William Austin observes, "precisely as a climax, marvelously absorbed into its own continuity"; in its whimsical lyric, redolent of black dialect ("That's just the bestest band what am, honey lamb"); in its expanded thirty-bar form and large vocal range; and especially in its rhythmic energy, which evoked the atmosphere of something like jazz and which over time recommended itself especially to Dixieland jazz musicians. For Alec Wilder, "Alexander's Ragtime Band" and "Waiting for the Robert E. Lee" were among the first popular songs to swing.[22]

That some blackface vaudevillians helped popularize "Alexander's Ragtime Band" underscored its connections to the coon songs of earlier years; the name Alexander itself had minstrel associations, as in Berlin's more conventionally raggy "Alexander and His Clarionet" (1910, with Ted Snyder). But Berlin's sardonic quotation of "Old Folks" in "Alexander's Ragtime Band" marked a change from that tradition, as did other features of the song, including not only its rhythmic swing but, according to Charles Hamm, its "complete absence of racial stereotyping and 'comical' demeaning." Late in life, Berlin suggested that "the idea of inviting every receptive auditor within shouting distance" to become "a part of the happy ruction" was "the secret of the song's tremendous success"; and although he did not place this in a racial context, the call to join in a black-related revelry surely formed a part of the song's modernity, bringing the song to the threshold of the Harlem Renaissance and anticipating not only Shelton Brooks's "Darktown Strutter's Ball" (1917) but also a wealth of similar invocations in the postwar years, including Gershwin's "Sweet and Low-Down" (1925) and Berlin's own "Puttin' On the Ritz" (1930).[23]

Because Berlin was Jewish as were other leading songwriters of his time—including Louis Hirsch and Jerome Kern among contemporaries, and Gershwin, Rodgers, Harry Ruby, and Arthur Schwartz among a slightly younger generation—the notion arose that the new popular song as epitomized by "Alexander's Ragtime Band"—or "jazz," as many called such music during the 1920s—was something of an Africanized Jewish music, a claim that sometimes registered anti-Semitic overtones but often appeared largely as a given. Henry Cowell, for instance, defined *jazz* in 1931 as "Negro minstrel music as interpreted by 'Tin-Pan-Alley' New Yorkers of Hebrew origin," while as late as 1941, John Tasker Howard wrote that jazz "in a very real sense . . . has become a Jewish interpretation of the Negro" (adding, "And what could be more American than such a combination, even though it does ignore those of us who have Puritan ancestors?"). That such famous singers of the new popular song as Eddie Cantor, George Jessel, Al Jolson, and Sophie Tucker were also Jewish and at least occasionally appeared in blackface supported such notions.[24]

At the same time, many important composers and lyricists associated with the new popular song, including Vincent Youmans, Cole Porter, Harry Warren, Hoagy Carmichael, and, among lyricists, P. G. Wodehouse and Buddy DeSylva, were white gentiles, while Eubie Blake, Shelton Brooks, Maceo Pinkard, Noble Sissle, Fats Waller, Duke Ellington, and others were black. In short, the new popular song, which also absorbed Asian and Hispanic currents, could not be identified exclusively with any particular ethnicity—or even nationality, as America's music houses published contemporary popular music from Europe and Latin America in addition to homegrown material.

And although Jewish Americans clearly contributed significantly to the development of popular music in the early twentieth century, this phenomenon remains subject to widely varying interpretations. Evidently Jews around the world took part in a whole range of musical and theatrical activities in part because gentile majorities tolerated their participation in that area as opposed to many others. Irving Howe proposed further that immigrant life nurtured certain dramatic and comic sensibilities, while Andrea Most argues that the musical comedy in particular allowed Jews "to invent themselves anew." Moreover, a heightened ability to acculturate may have helped some Jews participate in the remarkable hybridization, especially the absorption of African American styles, that girded the development of the modern popular song, though this matter has proved particularly controversial.[25]

At the least, "Alexander's Ragtime Band" appeared in New York about the same time as did important new forms of African American music, including the blues (first published in the years around 1910) and early jazz. Ragtime authority Edward Berlin points out that with the introduction of tied syncopations, polyrhythms, dotted and triplet rhythms, and blue notes, ragtime itself had begun to evolve—or erode, as the author would have it—in the years after 1907 and especially after 1910. "Alexander's Ragtime Band," significantly, contained some of these new features, including blue notes and dotted rhythms, suggesting that Berlin absorbed something from emerging styles associated with African Americans. In turn, the success of "Alexander's Ragtime Band" helped further the popularity of the same features in late ragtime.[26]

Stung by rumors that he paid black assistants to provide him with tunes and allegations that Scott Joplin had composed "Alexander's Ragtime Band," Berlin in his later years vehemently denied any indebtedness to black sources. But Berlin certainly knew a number of black ragtime pianists, including not only Joplin but Lukie Johnson and Eubie Blake, who remembered playing for Berlin in the years just prior to "Alexander's Ragtime Band." "He always used to like the way I play," recalled Blake. (After Berlin composed "Alexander's Ragtime Band," Blake found himself playing the song "about twenty times a night," adding, "There was no question it would be one of the greatest hits of all time.") And Berlin reportedly knew a black "jazz" bandleader, Jack Alexander, a possibly fictitious figure whose name he allegedly adopted for this song. In any case, by 1910 he probably had some familiarity as well with a black musician widely associated with the transition from ragtime to jazz, namely, James Reese Europe, a musician who not only seems yet another possible model for Berlin's Alexander, but also exerted a strong influence on the young George Gershwin.[27]

James Reese Europe (1880–1919) was born in Mobile, Alabama, and grew up in Washington, D.C., where his father, who had been born into slavery, worked for the post office. A pianist and violinist, Europe moved to New York about 1903 and quickly established himself as a leading conductor of dance bands and theater orchestras; his work with Bob Cole and J. Rosamond Johnson during these years helped shape the sound of Broadway. He also found time to further his music studies with black composer Harry Burleigh, who had studied with Dvořák. In the early 1910s, Europe enjoyed considerable success as the leader of the Clef Club Orchestra (founded 1910) and his Society Orchestra (founded 1913), two groups for which he also wrote music. In 1917 Europe joined the National Guard with the rank of lieutenant, leading such black military bands as the famed Hellfighters to glory. After returning to civilian life in 1919, he was fatally stabbed backstage by a disgruntled drummer. The loss felt was so great that he became the first African American in New York City history to receive a public funeral.[28]

Berlin would have known about Europe at the latest by 1914, when they almost collaborated on the show *Watch Your Step*. But he likely encountered Europe earlier, even before "Alexander's Ragtime Band," either by way of Europe's participation in dance bands or perhaps through his work in the pit for such Cole-Johnson musicals as *The Shoo-Fly Regi-*

ment (1907) and *The Red Moon* (1909), or for Bert Williams's vehicle *Mr. Lode of Koal* (1909). A similar uncertainty attends Gershwin's acquaintance with Europe, though David Ewen suggests that at least here the contact was seminal:

> One day, during the same period [ca. 1905], while roller-skating in Harlem, he [Gershwin] heard jazz music outside the Baron Wilkins Club [*sic*] where Jim Europe and his band performed regularly. The exciting rhythms and raucous tunes made such an impression on him that he never forgot them. From then on he often skated up to the club and sat down on the sidewalk outside to listen to the music. He later told a friend that his lifelong fascination for Negro rags, blues, and spirituals undoubtedly began at this time; that Jim Europe's music was partially responsible for his writing works like *135th Street* and parts of *Porgy and Bess*.

Known for its gambling, women, and music, Barron Wilkins, located on Seventh Avenue and 134th Street in the heart of Harlem, was a private club that catered to an affluent white crowd. Ewen's account accords with the fact that the Gershwins lived on 126th Street for a few years around 1905, but Barron Wilkins apparently opened in the early 1910s. Joan Peyser claims that the forecited incident actually postdates the Gershwins' move to 111th Street in 1915. Whether Ewen's version is entirely accurate or a conflation of different stories, it would appear that Gershwin heard some dance music in Harlem in his early years and that he developed considerable admiration, even gratitude, for James Reese Europe in particular.[29]

Europe's bands typically comprised six to eleven players: one or two violins, one or more clarinets, a trumpet, a banjo or mandolin, a piano, drums, perhaps a cello, and often a bass instrument like a trombone, double bass, or tuba. They played the hits of the day as well as arrangements of some popular classics. But was it jazz? Notwithstanding the appearance of such jazz musicians as trumpeter Freddie Keppard (1889–1933) and pianist Jelly Roll Morton (ca. 1890–1941) in New York as early as 1911, New Orleans jazz did not make that much of a dent there until the appearance of the black Creole Band in 1915 and even more so the white Original Dixieland Jazz Band in 1917. Jazz historians further agree that Europe's bands differed from their New Orleans counterparts in that their improvisations tended to be more restrained and their sound less brassy, with an emphasis on violins and strummed instruments like banjo and mandolin, as opposed to cornet and trombone.

Europe's recordings with the Society Orchestra from 1913 and 1914 have impressed jazz critics, nonetheless. "It is hard to imagine that any music of the period could have been more viscerally stimulating," observed Gunther Schuller. "The music had a rough excitement and rhythmic momentum that simply carried its audience along physically . . . Europe could take a polite salon piece and make it swing—in a rudimentary sort of way." Samuel Charters and Leonard Kunstadt similarly thought these recordings to feature "lusty, noisy instrumental music with definite Afro-American musical characteristics" and, in contrast to ragtime, "a looser melodic line and a greater rhythmic excitement." At least from the perspective of the late 1910s, this was certainly jazz and unquestionably new. Recalling a 1912 concert by Europe, James Weldon Johnson wrote, "New York had not yet become accustomed to jazz; so when the Clef Club opened its concert with a syncopated march, playing it with a biting attack and an infectious rhythm, and on the finale bursting into singing, the effect can be imagined. The applause became a tumult!"[30]

This particular concert was no ordinary one, but a performance at Carnegie Hall with an orchestra of 125 players, including ten pianos and eighty-five mandolins, bandores, harp-guitars, and banjos, so that the sound somewhat resembled a Russian balalaika orchestra. Throughout his career, Europe balanced workaday obligations with such ambitious undertakings, at one point stating, "We have developed a kind of symphony music that, no matter what else you think, is different and distinctive, and that lends itself to the playing of the peculiar compositions of our race." By 1919 he thought of his bands as potential vehicles for such black composers as Will Marion Cook, Samuel Coleridge-Taylor, and his teacher, Harry Burleigh, adding, "The music of our race springs from the soil, and this is true today with no other race, except possibly the Russians." In all this, he helped set the stage for the *Rhapsody in Blue*.[31]

During the years that Berlin wrote "Alexander's Ragtime Band" and Europe formed the Clef Club Orchestra, W. C. Handy (1873–1958) made another epochal contribution with the publication of "Memphis Blues" in 1912. For although they were not the first published works of their kind, "Memphis Blues" and an even bigger hit by Handy, "St. Louis Blues" (1914), decisively brought certain traits and sensibilities associated with the blues to bear on American music at large.[32]

Like Europe, Handy was born in Alabama the son of a former slave, but he grew up in the northwestern corner of the state. Moreover, his family stayed in the South, where his father was a preacher and his mother a "shouting Methodist." From this background, he came to revere Negro spirituals and the songs of black laborers. Handy learned to play the organ, guitar, and cornet, and aside from a short stint teaching college, worked mostly as an itinerant musician, playing in and leading various minstrel and dance bands. He settled in Memphis in 1905, and in 1918, after the success of "St. Louis Blues," he moved himself, his family, and his publishing company to New York. In his later years, Handy—like Berlin his own lyricist—continued to compose, but he also published various books, including a blues anthology (1926) and an engaging autobiography, *Father of the Blues* (1941).[33]

"The Memphis Blues" began life as a 1911 campaign song for Edward H. Crump, a reformist Memphis mayor up for reelection. In order to help pull in the black vote, Handy decided that what was needed was some "hot-cha music" that was also "mellow," and he composed a song, "Mister Crump," based on a "weird melody" that he had heard strummed by a black guitarist. "Folks went wild about it," recalled Handy, and the song helped elect Crump to a second term. Handy subsequently adapted the song with new lyrics as "The Memphis Blues," as the music contained features of a folk genre, known as the blues, popular with "Negro roustabouts, honky-tonk piano players, wanderers and others of their underprivileged but undaunted class from Missouri to the Gulf." As such it enjoyed enormous success nationwide after its 1912 publication.[34]

Though similar in some respects to ragtime, "The Memphis Blues" distinctively incorporated such aspects of the blues as twelve-bar form, call-and-response gestures, and flatted thirds and sevenths (sometimes in strikingly dissonant contexts). Handy referred to these so-called blue notes as a "slur," writing, "I had never heard this slur used by a more sophisticated Negro, or by a white man." The end result was ironic and earthy, "hot-cha" and "mellow." Handy consolidated and intensified these traits (some of which had surfaced earlier in the century in certain coon songs and ragtime instrumentals) in "St. Louis Blues" by using grace notes in order to depict more accurately the "slur," and "gaps and waits" in order to evoke more explicitly call-and-response patterns.[35]

Handy—who wrote "The Memphis Blues" in the same year that "Alexander's Ragtime Band" appeared, and who spoke of Berlin as "that genius, sane, sympathetic, sincere and unaffected; one of the kind of men who have made America great"—never hid his indebtedness to minstrelsy. On the contrary, by his own admission he "resorted to the humorous spirit of the bygone coon songs" and made use of comic black dialect in writing "St. Louis Blues." He recognized this as "a real problem," but he defended himself nonetheless:

> Negro intellectuals were turning from dialect in poetry as employed by Paul Lawrence [*sic*] Dunbar. I couldn't follow them, for I felt then, as I feel now, that certain words of Negro dialect are more musical and more expressive than pure English. Take the expression "Gonna walk all over God's Heaven." When Negro singers say "Heab'm" with their large nasal cavities serving as resonators and top it off by prolonging the *m*, they produce an effect that it is impossible for any other singers to match. Imagine sacrificing this pure magic for the sake of a properly enunciated "Heaven"!

At the same time, as early as 1926 the white blues enthusiast Abbe Niles recognized in Handy's work an "undertone of dissent." More recently, Adam Gussow similarly argued that "St. Louis Blues" can be read as a "racial protest" against "white southern violence and the dislocations it imposes." "Blues introduced to popular song a new frankness, breadth of subject matter, and assertiveness. . . . " summarizes David Evans. "Blues were distinctly secular and worldly, unsentimental, sexually explicit, and ironic, with an undertone of deep dissatisfaction. All these characteristics were new or unusual within popular American music, often contradicting established rules of Western musical form and performance style as well as popular stereotypes and expectations of black music."[36]

Although Handy doubted that the blues could serve as the basis of a symphonic work, as his friend James Weldon Johnson predicted, he saw this "prophecy" fulfilled when he "heard and enjoyed" George Gershwin performing his *Rhapsody in Blue* with Paul Whiteman at Carnegie Hall. His 1926 anthology paid special tribute to Gershwin, including themes not only from the *Rhapsody* but from the Concerto in F and the song "Half of It, Dearie, Blues." In 1940, listening to "Summertime" and "I Got Rhythm" at a festival of American music, Handy was reminded of "the untimely passing of this youthful genius" as his mind drifted back to a dinner with Gershwin, Whiteman, and composer Charles Wakefield Cadman in which they "discussed the great potentialities and possibilities of American music."[37]

Gershwin probably encountered "Memphis Blues" and "St. Louis Blues" early on, as they quickly influenced national music trends; he himself recorded his first blues—Oscar Gardner's "Chinese Blues"—in 1916. In any case, on August 30, 1926, he presented Handy with an inscribed copy of the solo version of the *Rhapsody* that read, "To Mr. Handy, Whose early 'blue' songs are the forefathers of this work. With admiration + best wishes, George Gershwin," words that reportedly left Handy "deeply touched." Gershwin also featured the "St. Louis Blues" (described as "immortal") and the same composer's "Beale Street Blues" (called "an American classic") on two of his 1934 radio shows. Black composer William Grant Still reported that Gershwin's open acknowledgment of Handy made it "easier for Negroes to understand and appreciate" the latter's work.[38]

In his introduction to Handy's blues anthology, Abbe Niles considered Gershwin's relation to the blues, a subject that tended to get lost amid the question of the composer's connection to jazz. Opining that the *Rhapsody* conveys, "with the help of the blue note as well as by other means for which Gershwin has no one else to thank, a rowdy, troubled humor as marked as that of the best of the old blues," Niles further wrote, "rejecting the tantalizing over-and-over effect of the bob-tailed, twelve-bar strain, which of course would break the long line he would achieve, he has nevertheless made a serious study of the question 'wherein blue;' not content with abject imitation, he has thought out the philosophy for himself, making the old tricks somehow his own where he uses them, and making his own point of view the flavor of his work." In 1970 pianist Henry Levine, who had studied the *Rhapsody* with Gershwin, discussed that work's relation to Handy's music in more specific detail, illustrating its extensive use of motives found in Handy's "St. Louis Blues" and "Beale Street Blues," and arguing that many of the work's rhythmic innovations derived from the "Memphis Blues." Indeed, although commentators have tended to discuss Handy's blues mostly in terms of pitches and harmonies, Levine's article intimated the importance of their polyrhythms, which provided a footing for some of the most characteristic rhythmic devices of American music of the 1920s, including Gershwin's.[39]

With stunning global coincidence, the new popular music emerged alongside not only jazz but also such landmarks of European musical modernism as Stravinsky's *Petrushka* (1911) and *Rite of Spring* (1913), Bartók's *Allegro barbaro* and *Bluebeard's Castle* (both 1911), and Schoenberg's *Pierrot lunaire* (1912). These new musics—which similarly tended toward a revitalized relationship with the vernacular, a preoccupation with new rhythms and scales, and a proclivity toward irony and ambiguity—won many of the same friends, but many of the same enemies as well, especially among reactionaries. In 1925, for instance, American composer Daniel Gregory Mason described the "curious aesthetic kinship" between Berlin and Gershwin on the one hand and Stravinsky on the other as an "atavism by which the traits of savage ancestors reappear in neurotic descendents." Mason's "savage ancestors" and "neurotic descendents" alluded to the widespread association of newer music with blacks, Jews, and Slavs, a line of criticism that had its ugly side.[40]

Paralleling the close relationship between modernist musical trends and bodily movement—as found especially in the Stravinsky ballets—the new popular music of the early 1910s arose largely in the context of dance music composed for an American public that had gone "dance mad." "Alexander's Ragtime Band" was advertised as a two-step; James Reese Europe's orchestras were primarily dance bands; and the public danced to Handy's blues as well.[41]

Many of the popular social dances of the time were themselves new, with the creation of more than one hundred dances in the period 1912–1914 alone. Such groundbreaking developments in dance were clearly related to those in music. In his early biography of Berlin, for instance, Alexander Woollcott claimed that "Alexander's Ragtime Band" represented "the first full free use of the new rhythm which had begun to take form in the honkey-tonks where pianists were dislocating old melodies to make them keep step with the swaying hips and shoulders of the spontaneous darky dancers." The history of "St. Louis Blues" exemplified similar interactions. According to Handy, the song "tricked the dancers" by beginning with a voguish "tango introduction" before breaking "into a low-down blues." When the blues proper arrived, recalled Handy, "suddenly I saw the lightning strike. The dancers seemed electrified. Something within them came suddenly to life. An instinct that wanted so much to live, to fling its arms and to spread joy, took them by the heels. By this I was convinced that my new song was accepted." Such new arm and heel movements naturally led to new dances, which in turn inspired new music, and so on in a symbiotic dance of its own.[42]

Many of the new dances had animal names (which themselves suggested a rebellion against Victorian inhibitions) and many of them derived from the one-step, an energetic dance typically danced to cut time, with one step per beat; or the two-step, a moderately fast dance in duple or quadruple meter with alternating slow and quick steps, often quick-quick-slow. Some popular one-steps of 1912 included the turkey trot, the bunny hug, and the grizzly bear, the last danced in a mock-threatening manner with upraised arms and lumbering torsos. The most important two-step, the fox-trot, had something of a prehistory, but as popularized in 1914 by the dance team of Vernon Castle (born Blyth, 1887–1918) and his wife, Irene (1893–1969), it employed a basic pattern of two slow, gliding steps and three or four quick steps. The Castles also helped advance sundry variations on the one-step, such as the Castle walk, a 1914 craze that involved vigorous steps on one's toes in time to a marchlike pattern of two beats. "It sounds silly and is silly," wrote the Castles in their 1914 dance manual. "That is the explanation of its popularity!" Yet another new sensation was the Texas tommy, which Ethel Williams successfully made her own in Harlem's *Darktown Follies* of 1913, the year, too, of Nat Ayer's "The Original Texas Tommy Dance." This particular dance involved kicks, steps, and hops, including a move wherein partners would break away, thus anticipating the Lindy Hop, the jitterbug, and other swing dances.[43]

The fox-trot merits additional comment because of its centrality to Gershwin's work. The majority of his piano rolls, for instance, were fox-trots, as were many of the numbers from his shows. Even the great "Andantino" theme from the *Rhapsody in Blue* could be described as in fox-trot rhythm. Composers wrote fox-trots in a wide range of tempos (though usually moderately fast) and a diversity of time signatures; but they all shared a gently lilting sense of four pulses per measure. According to Mark Grant, this new rhythmic sensibility not only signaled a historic move away from the popular 2/4, 3/4, and 6/8 dance patterns of the previous century (and a return to the four-beat patterns of the Baroque) but underpinned the development of the modern musical comedy. "The foxtrot's strength as a theater song template," Grant writes, "was its separation of 'top' and 'bottom' rhythm, allowing the melody and lyric space to breathe, to dance, to dramatize."[44]

Meanwhile, some other popular dances arrived from Latin America, most notably the Argentine tango, a sultry dance featuring outstretched arms and suave footwork that enjoyed extraordinary popularity in the States in 1913 and 1914. Another prevalent Latin dance of the period, the Brazilian maxixe, combined polka and Afro-Latin dance steps (Gershwin would quote a popular maxixe in *An American in Paris*). Both the tango and the maxixe diminished in popularity after the war, but they were still danced, and they paved the way for the entry of the rumba, conga, and many other Latin dances into American social dancing.

The new dances of the early 1910s shared a profound debt to African American dance in the larger hemispherical sense. And unlike earlier popular dances associated with black culture, like the cakewalk or buck-and-wing dancing (the latter, at this point, developing into modern tap), the new dances were not so much theatrical entertainments with strong ethnic associations as they were social dances overtaking, though not crowding out entirely, European dances like the polka and the waltz. In other words, the new dances, with amazing rapidity, furthered a black dimension to mainstream social dancing, including a new vocabulary of movements, distinct from the contained motions of the polka and waltz, that involved swaying shoulders, wiggling hips, raised arms, bent torsos, and skipping, hopping, and waddling steps. These movements scandalized many observers, and the new dances came in for more criticism, even outright bans, than the new popular music; it was clearly one thing to tap your foot to Berlin or Handy, but quite another to gyrate your pelvis to them.

Hence the importance of Vernon and Irene Castle: they made the new dancing not only respectable, but the height of chic. Vernon, a tall, skinny Englishman, and Irene, a willowy, androgynous American beauty, both danced independently with modest success before marrying in 1911 and becoming partners. After delighting Paris with their interpretations of the new American dances in 1912, they returned to the States, dancing on Broadway, in cabarets, and in private homes to great acclaim, their entrance into high society smoothed over by Elizabeth ("Bessie") Marbury, the dramatic agent who would also help midwife the new musical comedy. By 1914 they had become one of America's most famous couples, but their careers were cut short by Vernon's death training pilots for combat in Texas during World War I. Harbingers of a new Jazz Age sensibility, they not only taught Americans how to dance; as Irene bobbed her hair, applied lipstick, smoked cigarettes, shortened her hemline, and dispensed with corsets (a requirement for the freer movements associated with the new dances), so did women all across the land.[45]

Part of the success of the Castles lay in criticizing and refining some of the crudities associated with the new dances. But their popularity depended, too, on their shrewd choice of musical collaborators. In 1913 they entered into a close association with James Reese Europe, using his Society Orchestra at every opportunity and dancing to his own music, including his "Castle Walk" of 1914. In the same year, they not only initiated the fox-trot craze after they adapted Handy's "Memphis Blues" for that purpose, but became the toast of Broadway while appearing in Irving Berlin's *Watch Your Step* (whose New York opening George and Ira viewed from the second balcony of the New Amsterdam Theatre). The Castles, in short, epitomized the interconnectedness of the new popular dancing, the new popular music, and new ways of living.[46]

In drawing on the nexus of Irving Berlin's popular songs, James Reese

Europe's ragtime-jazz, and W. C. Handy's blues, the Castles looked ahead to Gershwin's own career. They also proved a "tremendous influence" on their greatest successor, Fred Astaire, who developed an "idolatrous feeling" for the Castles, and who stood in relation to Gershwin somewhat as the Castles did to Berlin, Europe, and Handy. When Gershwin took a job plugging songs in 1914, he arrived not so much as a trailblazer but as someone eager to join in the excitement.[47]

Chapter Four

The Popular Pianist

In 1914 Gershwin heard from a friend, Ben Bloom, who plugged songs for music publisher Jerome H. Remick, that the company needed a pianist who "could read notes readily, to play over songs to be tried out." After an audition in which Gershwin demonstrated his sight-reading and transposition skills, the office manager, songwriter Mose Gumble, offered him a job as a song plugger for fifteen dollars a week. Although his mother opposed his becoming a musician, "she offered very little resistance," recalled Gershwin, when he decided in May, at only fifteen years old, to leave high school to work full-time at Remick (becoming, or so it is said, New York's youngest song plugger).[1]

Originating in Detroit, Remick was one of the most successful music publishers of the time, though it never achieved the prestige later garnered by Harms, the publisher of Jerome Kern. Remick's catalog included such best-selling songs as Jack Norworth and Nora Bayes's "Shine On, Harvest Moon" (1908), Gus Edwards's "By the Light of the Silvery Moon" (1909), Percy Wenrich's "On Moonlight Bay" (1910), Nat Ayer's "Oh, You Beautiful Doll" (1911), and Egbert Van Alstyne's "That Old Girl of Mine" (1912), along with more rags than any other major firm (one reason it may have hired Gershwin, an excellent ragtime player). Working at Remick from 1914 to early 1917, Gershwin was around for some other hit songs, as well as for the Hawaiian craze of 1916, to which Remick contributed Henry Kailimai's "My Honolulu Ukulele Baby" and staff composer Richard Whiting's "Along the Way to Waikiki." But he left the company before the deluge of patriotic songs published by the popular music houses on America's entry into World War I.[2]

After establishing a New York branch in the early 1900s, Remick moved to a brownstone on West 28th Street between Broadway and Sixth Avenue—a street, dubbed Tin Pan Alley, that had been home to many of America's leading music publishers since the 1890s. More than twenty firms could be found in the immediate environs, most of them crowded side by side on this one noisy block. In 1912, Remick relocated to more spacious quarters on West 46th Street that included a two-hundred-seat auditorium and fifteen piano cubicles. Other music publishers similarly moved into the West 40s during these years, but the term *Tin Pan Alley* remained a generic designation for the popular music industry for several decades more.

Tin Pan Alley was big business, in large part spurred by a steep increase in piano sales in the early twentieth century. To supply an almost insatiable demand for music that could be played and sung at home, the Alley published literally millions of pieces of sheet music, primarily songs and piano pieces. Although the price of sheet music during this period ranged from about ten to forty cents, a successful song could make tens of thousands of dollars, while a smash hit could reap a hundred thousand dollars or more simply from sales, without including royalties from theatrical performances, piano rolls, recordings, and eventually radio and the motion pictures. To help promote and manage this enormous enterprise, the major publishers hired, in addition to business personnel, teams of composers, lyricists, arrangers, orchestrators, and song pluggers.[3]

Song pluggers not only demonstrated the company's wares at the home office, but also performed (or arranged performances of) such music in theaters, stores, and restaurants, and at public events like parades. This sometimes involved journeying out of town, with the beach resort, Atlantic City, a popular destination (Gershwin was no exception, traveling to Atlantic City in the summer of 1916). Pluggers were usually pianists or singers or both, and naturally had to be able to put over a song. (Gershwin worked for Remick primarily as a pianist, often teaming up with singer Ben Bloom; but he also performed songs himself, as he would for his entire career.) In addition, pluggers needed to cultivate good relations with the entertainers who frequented the publishing houses in search of new material, because the success of a song often depended on its association with a star performer, an established principle of the music business from Stephen Foster's day to our own.

Song plugging provided a training ground of sorts, and a number of the leading songwriters of the time, including not only Gershwin but Irving Berlin, Jerome Kern, and Vincent Youmans, began their careers as pluggers or staff pianists for music publishers. One got to know, in Isaac

Goldberg's words, "what took, and what didn't." The job also enabled Gershwin to meet and befriend a number of people in show business, not just established names but other young people starting out, like the dance team of Fred and Adele Astaire, as well as fellow pluggers Milton Ager (1893–1979), who later produced such hits as "Hard Hearted Hannah" (1924), "Ain't She Sweet" (1927), and "Happy Days Are Here Again" (1929); and Harry Ruby (1895–1974), whose partnership with lyricist Bert Kalmar eventually yielded "I Wanna Be Loved by You" (1928) and "Three Little Words" (1930) along with successful vehicles for the Marx Brothers, including *Animal Crackers* (1928) and *Duck Soup* (1933).[4]

Gershwin appreciated, too, that Remick exacted a lighter workload than other firms, for which reason he turned down another offer for more money. Still, his recollections of his time at Remick were decidedly ambivalent, at least as reported by Beverly Nichols: "Every day at nine o'clock I was there at the piano, playing popular tunes for anybody who came along. Colored people used to come in and get me to play them 'God Send You Back to Me' in seven keys. Chorus ladies used to breathe down my back. Some of the customers treated one like dirt. Others were charming."[5]

Gershwin quickly became a "much-sought-after accompanist," according to lyricist Irving Caesar, who remembered that people "loved to have George play the new songs for them." A self-described "piano-buff," Caesar would visit Remick just to hear Gershwin play: "His rhythms had the impact of a sledge hammer. His harmonies were years ahead of the time. I had never before heard such playing of popular music." Harry Ruby confirmed, "It was far and beyond better than the piano playing of any of us. As I look back upon it I can say it was a completely different musical world from ours, and we did not completely understand it at the time, though we all reacted to it instinctively. I am also sure we were all jealous of him, too." Gershwin also caught the attention of some outstanding black ragtime pianists. Shortly after arriving in New York in 1916, Eubie Blake heard from pianists James P. Johnson and Charles Luckeyth ("Luckey") Roberts about "this very talented ofay piano player at Remick. They said he was good enough to learn some of those terribly difficult tricks that only a few of us could master."[6]

In time, Gershwin emerged as one of the most celebrated pianists of his age, with many distinguished observers testifying to his achievement in this area (though after 1920 he largely performed only his own music). Oscar Levant, for instance, vividly recalled hearing him onstage, accompanying Nora Bayes, in 1918: "I had never heard such fresh, brisk, unstudied, completely free and inventive playing—all within a consistent frame that set off her singing perfectly." Words like *magic* and *hypnotic* often appeared in accounts of Gershwin's playing. "To anyone who has not heard Gershwin play, his piano magic is hard to describe," said Vernon Duke. "His extraordinary left hand performed miracles in counter-rhythms, shrewd canonic devices, and unexpected harmonic shifts. The facility for abrupt yet felicitous modulations, the economy and logic of the voice-leading, and the over-all sureness of touch were masterly in their inevitability." Abram Chasins thought Gershwin "the only pianist I ever heard who could make a piano laugh, really laugh. . . . His playing, when he was in the mood, was hypnotic and no more to be described than imitated." Pianist Jean Wiéner spoke of "the diabolical independence of his hands." And composer Dimitri Tiomkin wrote, "His whole body moved with his hands and the music, swaying, bending, twisting. There was no suggestion of exhibitionism or showmanship. Rather, you were reminded of some blithesome person who seems to dance as he walks. It was musical magic, Gershwin playing Gershwin."[7]

Pianist Mario Braggiotti offered this even more studied description:

> Gershwin had the light, incisive touch, the poetic melodies and sure sense of rhythm that gave what he wrote its shape, its weight and its color. All the pedagogic pointers in the world were there for anyone who cared to listen. His pedaling was extraordinarily subtle, and he never sacrificed anything at the expense of rhythm. He always had a climax to his phrasing as if he were telling a thought with a convincing punch line. And his singing tone had a nostalgic quality and an unpredictable texture that I have never heard equalled. His playing carried intuitively the great overall secret of all forms of projection—whether they be in music, elocution or athletics—in one word, control.[8]

Other notable musicians extolled Gershwin's talents as a pianist. After conducting the Concerto in F with the composer in 1927, Fritz Reiner stated, "Gershwin has remarkable technical skill as a pianist, too. He does certain things in the way of playing that no other pianist can do—not even the greatest. Gershwin's left-hand playing is quite marvelous and he does certain technical 'stunts' that are amazing." And conductor Serge Koussevitzky, discussing Gershwin's performance of the *Rhapsody,* recalled, "The sweeping brilliance, virtuosity and rhythmic precision of his playing were incredible; his perfect poise and ease beyond belief; his dynamic influence on the orchestra and on the audience electrifying." Even some of the era's greatest keyboard virtuosos lauded Gershwin's pianistic abilities, including Serge Rakhmaninov, who admired his "piano execution," and Josef Hofmann, who described him as "a fine pianistic talent, with a firm, clear, good command of the keyboard."[9]

Such praise was not universal, however. A few critics, for instance, took issue with his performances of his own *Rhapsody in Blue* and Concerto in F on tour with the Leo Reisman Orchestra in 1934, including Herbert Elwell, who suggested that he would "do better to let someone else perform his music, for as a pianist he is a good composer." Earl Wild similarly recalled that Gershwin's "pale" tone made him at times inaudible when performing with orchestra. Still, his reputation as a pianist was such that in 1927 he was asked, along with Josef Hofmann and another esteemed pianist, Ernest Hutcheson, to review for a New York paper (in his case, the *World*) a benefit recital for the MacDowell Foundation by three amateur pianists: Ernest Urchs, manager of Steinway and Sons; John Erskine, novelist and Columbia University professor; and music critic Olin Downes. Gershwin's review preserved, by the way, a relatively rare record of his affable but decidedly ironic wit:

> Although the program consisted of Brahms, Mozart, and Bach, the concert was not altogether devoid of jazz. On several occasions I heard "blue" notes. Perhaps the Downes-Erskine-Urchs combination felt that a concert to-day was incomplete without a few sour ones; or again, it may be that the long lay-off—Mr. Erskine has just taken up the piano after twenty years—made it a bit difficult for the fourth finger of either hand always to hit the note it was aimed for.
>
> But all in all it was a good concert and made me feel that I'd rather hear amateurs play music that I liked rather than professionals play music that they liked. To-night is your last chance to hear a music critic, a college professor and a pillar of the Steinway Company play good music on three pianos. Don't miss it.[10]

Early on, Gershwin found outlets for his pianistic skills besides plugging songs for Remick. Even before joining the firm, he made—thanks to Ira's intervention—his first known public appearance as a pianist on March 21, 1914, at a meeting of City College's literary society, the Finley Club, accompanying a singer and performing a tango he had composed. He also played at a hotel in the Catskills, probably in the summer of 1914 or 1915, with violinist Jack Diamond. And throughout the teens, he performed with groups associated with banjoist Fred Van Eps (1878–1960), with whom he seems to have made some recordings as well. Moreover, on two dates in July 1920, as a member of the Gershwin Trio, he made test recordings for Victor of Norman Spencer's "Cuban Moon"

(1920), Guido Deiro's "Kismet" (1911, pub. 1920), and his own "Chica (Mexican Dance)" (1920, presumably the same "Mexican Dance" associated with the 1920 *Scandals*) with saxophonist Bert Ralton and banjoist Vic King (at the time, both Ralton and King played with the Art Hickman Orchestra, a popular dance band comparable to the Paul Whiteman Orchestra). These varied activities placed Gershwin in the context of inchoate jazz styles.[11]

Gershwin also began making rolls for player pianos in 1915, an activity he pursued intermittently through 1925 or 1926, but primarily in the late 1910s and especially in 1916 and 1917, during which time he made more than half of his 140 known rolls. The many rolls that survive, much like his phonograph recordings, provide an appreciable record of his pianistic style and technique.[12]

An invention of the late nineteenth century, the pneumatically operated or player piano firmly established itself in America in the early 1900s following the Aeolian Company's launching of its trademarked Pianola, a cabinet or "push-up" player (that is, a foot-treadled cabinet positioned over a piano keyboard) that became so popular that its name became a generic term for the player piano—although by 1910, push-up players had largely been superseded by "inner players" (which internally incorporated the player mechanism). The development of hand-played rolls (that is, rolls recorded by live pianists as opposed to those prepared by draftsmen), a new technology widely adopted in the States in the years prior to World War I, further enhanced the popularity of player pianos. As the pièce de résistance, manufacturers brought forth the "reproducing" piano: first the Welte-Mignon, introduced by the German firm M. Welte and Company in 1904, and followed in the States by the American Piano Company's Ampico in 1912 and the Aeolian Company's Duo-Art in 1914. Whereas older player pianos could reproduce phrasing and pedaling (over which performers—pianolists—could superimpose dynamics through hand levers and foot pumps), the reproducing piano could record as well a full range of dynamics and accents. Many of the greatest pianists and composers of the day made rolls for one or another reproducing piano.

By 1914, forty-two companies were manufacturing player pianos nationally, and by 1919, production of pneumatically operated pianos slightly exceeded that of conventional ones. This phenomenon paralleled America's peak of piano ownership generally, but the player and reproducing piano offered the advantage that one needed no greater skill than the ability to control hand levers and foot pumps, if that. However, by the late 1920s, these instruments could no longer compete with improving and less costly phonograph and radio technology, and by the early 1930s they had become rather antiquated.[13]

Although player and reproducing pianos, like conventional pianos, varied in quality, they were generally expensive, especially an upscale brand like Aeolian's Duo-Art reproducing piano, some models of which retailed for more than four thousand dollars in the early 1920s. Moreover, manufacturers produced rolls that were not necessarily interchangeable. Again quality varied as did price, from about twenty-five cents to three dollars or more per roll in the 1910s. During the player piano's heyday, from about 1915 to 1925, companies at home and abroad produced thousands of roll titles, including popular songs, hymn tunes, piano pieces, and symphonic arrangements. As an aid to singers, rolls of songs sometimes included lyrics stenciled along one edge.

In creating hand-played rolls, pianists played on a specially prepared piano electrically hooked up to a mechanical device, which either marked or perforated a master roll. Afterward, while preparing the finished roll, editors could correct mistakes and add notes—sometimes elaborately so, for maximum richness of texture. And at least with popular music, editors frequently regularized the beat with metronomic precision, in part to suit the needs of dancers.

Gershwin cut his first rolls at age seventeen for the Standard Music Roll Company's budget Perfection label late in 1915—rolls issued for sale early the following year. Traveling to the company's recording studio in East Orange, New Jersey, on Saturdays, he made a neat thirty-five dollars for six rolls (more than double his week's salary) or five dollars per roll if he recorded fewer than six. Milton Ager, whom Gershwin encouraged to make rolls, hated the process, saying, "It took about a minute and a half to play a verse and two choruses, then four hours to make the corrections!" Regardless of whether Gershwin similarly participated in the editing process (and performing artists commonly did), one could rely on him not to play too many wrong notes.[14]

Gershwin recorded for Standard's Perfection and SingA label throughout 1916 and 1917, not only under his own name but for a short time under the pseudonyms James Baker, Fred Murtha, and Bert Wynn (reportedly in homage to comedian Ed Wynn); roll companies used pseudonyms to lend the appearance of a large staff of pianists. Thanks to pianist-composer Felix Arndt, in early 1916 Gershwin also began making rolls for a variety of labels issued by the prestigious Aeolian Company, including Universal, Metro-Art, Mel-O-Dee, Duo-Art, Meloto, and

British Duo-Art (Aeolian's affiliate, the Wilcox & White Company of Meriden, Connecticut, further released some of these recordings on the Angelus, Angelus-Voltem, and Artrio-Angelus labels). He recorded more than twenty of these rolls as duets, mostly with Aeolian staff pianists Rudolph O. Erlebach or Edwin E. Wilson but also with Cliff Hess and Muriel Pollock, two notable ragtime pianists.[15]

In addition, in 1919 Gershwin produced the first of his thirteen known rolls for the Welte-Mignon reproducing piano, traveling up to the Bronx to record for the Red T-100 system. Artis Wodehouse, who in the 1990s oversaw recordings and published transcriptions of the Gershwin rolls, suspects that Welte (which also recorded Grieg, Debussy, Bartók, and Milhaud) attempted to capture the composer as he actually played, without any subsequent editing. She adds that "this attempt to represent Gershwin accurately led to rolls that were rhythmically jerky compared to Aeolian's more rhythmically polished but thick-textured rolls of the same period," though Jeffrey Morgan, another expert, suggests that this perceived jerkiness might be attributed to the limitations of the early T-100 system as compared to the more recently developed Duo-Art.[16]

Gershwin recorded the music of such established songwriters as Irving Berlin, Walter Donaldson, Louis Hirsch, Jerome Kern, Harry Von Tilzer, Pete Wendling, and Richard Whiting, along with those of his friends Milton Ager, Herman Paley, and Harry Ruby. With the September 1916 release of his song "When You Want 'Em, You Can't Get 'Em" and his piano rag *Rialto Ripples,* he began cutting his own music as well, an increasing preoccupation by late 1919, though he continued to record other composers' music as late as 1921. Wodehouse cannot discern, in many cases, any particular reason for Gershwin's choice of repertoire, expressing surprise in particular that he did not record more of the Remick catalog while he worked there. On the other hand, after becoming a Broadway rehearsal pianist in 1917, he began recording numbers from the shows with which he was affiliated, in some instances performing the same song with different companies, which suggests that he and the various roll companies agreed on the repertoire together.[17]

Some of Gershwin's rolls, beginning with Henry Lange's "I Gave My Heart to Someone in Dixieland" (released 1916), evoked the mythic South, while his recording of Oscar Gardner's "Chinese Blues" (also released 1916) initiated not only a number of blues recordings but a series of pieces that alluded to the Far East, including two of Gershwin's own songs released in 1920, "Limehouse Nights" and "Idle Dreams." The latter group—which helps explain James P. Johnson's remark that when he first met him at the Aeolian Company in 1920, Gershwin was "cutting 'oriental' numbers"—employed a wide range of stereotypical Chinese musical figures, including pentatonic melodies, repeated notes, grace notes, harmonic clusters, parallel fourths, staccato basses, and high-pitched tremolos. The extent to which Gershwin derived such mannerisms from stock formulas, or from such composers as Debussy and Puccini, as opposed to actual Asian music-making remains unknown (he at least had some acquaintance with Chinese music, perhaps dating back to his early years growing up near Chinatown). But whatever the source, such orientalisms, as Ryan Raul Banagale has pointed out, became a significant feature of his general musical vocabulary.[18]

Typical for the period, Gershwin's renditions of popular songs generally comprised an introduction, alternating statements of verse and chorus (usually *vcvc, vcvcc, cvcvc,* or, more rarely, *cvcc*), and occasionally a coda; while his recordings of ragtime songs and pieces—such as Artie Matthews's *Pastime Rag. no. 3* (released as *A Slow Drag,* 1916), Hugo Frey's "Havanola" (released 1917), and Harry Akst's "Jaz-o-mine" (released 1917), as well as Gershwin's own *Rialto Ripples*—characteristically featured more sectional designs.

Nearly all of Gershwin's rolls were advertised as some kind of dance music, including the waltz and the one-step, but mostly the fox-trot. Accordingly, many of the rolls delivered an emphatic meter of four, with sturdy beats energized by bursts of sixteenth notes. Some of the slower fox-trots, like Con Conrad and J. Russel Robinson's "Singin' the Blues" (released 1920), revealed the closeness between the fox-trot and the blues during these years. Those still rarer releases advertised as "ballads"—including two of his own songs, "I Was So Young (You Were So Beautiful)" (released 1919) and "So Am I" (released 1925)—took even more relaxed tempos.

On some of his rolls, Gershwin seemed particularly respectful toward the written page, especially in instrumental compositions like his *Rialto Ripples* and Matthews's *Pastime Rag,* or in those songs whose sheet-music arrangements were amply conceived, such as his own, or Kern's, or "Wait'n for Me" by Maceo Pinkard (best remembered today for his 1925 hit, "Sweet Georgia Brown"). However, in most instances he took considerable liberties, often swinging—or at least dotting—the notated rhythms. At various juncture points (less often within a phrase itself), he also occasionally interpolated short interludes that, like his introductions, gave fuller scope to his inventiveness. These interpolations sometimes involved the ironic quotation of old favorites: the traditional air "The Girl I Left Behind Me" in Berlin's "For Your Country and My Country" (released 1917), Septimus Winner's "Listen to the Mockingbird" in Kern's "Whip-Poor-Will" (released 1920), Stephen Foster's "Old Black Joe" in Pinkard's "Wait'n for Me" (released as "Waitin' for Me," 1920), Foster's "Old Folks at Home" (in minor) and Joseph K. Emmet's "Lullaby" in Donaldson's "Rock-a-Bye, Lullabye Mammy" (released 1920), and once again "Listen to the Mockingbird" (this time the verse) in his own "Swanee" (released 1920), which as written already incorporated a phrase from "Old Folks at Home." These quotes often appeared—like a concluding gag—shortly before the final cadence, a strategy that became associated with music for animated cartoons.

Gershwin also often fleshed out the music, in ways far removed from the printed page, with added chromatic voices and more active and shapely bass lines. Toward the end of phrases, he also showed a distinct tendency, as in the composition of his own songs, to speed up the harmonic rhythm for extra zest. Of course, not knowing whether and to what degree the roll manufacturers altered his arrangements in the editorial process restricts what can be said about them. Even so, aside from frequent doublings and added tremolos, some commentators probably have exaggerated the degree to which editors fussed with his initial performances, for many passages and even whole pieces are playable by two hands—as evident from transcriptions of some of the rolls by Jack Gibbons and Artis Wodehouse.[19]

In recent years, such record companies as Klavier, Elektra Nonesuch, and Biograph have elicited renewed interest in Gershwin's rolls by releasing anthologies of them on long-playing records and compact discs. The two Nonesuch volumes (1993 and 1995) supervised by Artis Wodehouse enjoyed special popularity, with sales in the hundreds of thousands. The significant differences among these recordings reflected such variables as playback technology, editorial oversight, and interpretative approach. Biograph, for instance, used a 1924 Steinway Baby Grand Duo-Art; Klavier, a 1929 Hamburg Steinway Duo-Art; while for the Nonesuch recording, Wodehouse operated a 1911 Pianola playing a nine-foot Yamaha Disklavier, except for the Duo-Art and Welte rolls, which Richard Tonnesen and Richard Brandle converted directly onto floppy disks.

The Elektra Nonesuch releases proved especially controversial. Michael Montgomery, a notable collector who supplied Wodehouse with a number of rolls, deemed these recordings "the most careful, scholarly, faithful, high-integrity job that has ever been done with piano rolls," whereas Howard Reich, music critic for the *Chicago Tribune,* lambasted them as "blurry, imprecise, overpedaled and rhythmically stodgy." Most of these reviews paid too little attention to differences between those rolls directly scanned into computer files by Tonnesen and Brandle and those realized on a push-up player by Wodehouse, for the former exhibited a particularly veiled quality compared to the more crisp and present sound heard on the other tracks, let alone the Klavier and Biograph releases. Pianist Jack Gibbons expressed particular surprise at how the digitalized rolls smoothed over "the wonderful but extremely subtle rhythmic idiosyncrasies of Gershwin's original roll recordings." Meanwhile, none of these recordings quite captured the delicacy and nuance of Gershwin's phonograph recordings, though whether this reflected the limitations of today's player and reproducing pianos, the electronic transfer process, or more simply the paper-roll medium remains hard to say.[20]

At the least, Gershwin's rolls, some claims to the contrary, were clearly his own and offer plentiful intimations of the rhythmic exuberance, harmonic sophistication, contrapuntal finesse, and sheer technical command that impressed so many in live performance. Moreover, the earliest rolls show such traits in place a mere five or six years after he had begun studying piano, proving the composer a gifted prodigy, while underscoring the relation of his evolving musical style to twentieth-century technology. Some high points include the effervescent "Havanola" and the suave "Whip-Poor-Will," not to mention the authoritative renderings of his own songs. The few rolls cut after 1921, devoted exclusively to his own music, seem particularly masterful, in part perhaps because under the supervision of editor Frank Milne, the Aeolian company strove, writes Wodehouse, "to re-create the now famous Gershwin performance style as accurately as possible for playback on the Duo-Art reproducing piano." These later rolls include recordings of "Kickin' the Clouds Away" and "So Am I" (both released 1925), "Sweet and Low-Down" and "That Certain Feeling" (both released 1926), and a solo version of the *Rhapsody in Blue* (part two ["Andantino and Finale"] released 1925, part one released 1927)—Gershwin's only uncut recording of the work.[21]

Meanwhile, Gershwin made his first phonograph recording in 1924 for Victor, performing the *Rhapsody* with the Paul Whiteman Orchestra. Considering the technology of the time, he and the orchestra presumably huddled about and played into a large acoustical horn that transmitted vibrations, via a diaphragm and a stylus, onto a grooved wax disk. In the following year, 1925, record companies started replacing such horns with microphones and amplifiers, which not only gave recordings added brilliance and volume but allowed sound engineers to record larger groups spaced more or less as they would be in a theater and thereby achieve a more natural balance and spatial atmosphere. Such advances in turn helped spur public interest in phonograph recordings, evidenced by the success of the new machines designed to play them. In 1927 Gershwin duly returned to the Victor studio to rerecord the *Rhapsody,* again with the Paul Whiteman Orchestra, but this time conducted by Nathaniel Shilkret. This recording naturally sounded more vivid than the earlier one, though the exigencies of early electrical recording technology unwittingly cut Gershwin down to size, to the extent that he could hardly be heard in some passages.[22]

In the late 1920s Gershwin also recorded, for Victor's great rival Columbia, his *Three Preludes* (recorded 1928) and the "Andantino" from the *Rhapsody* arranged for solo piano (recorded 1928), as well as fifteen of his show tunes (recorded 1926 and 1928). "One is immediately impressed with, and overwhelmed by, Gershwin's extraordinary pianistic skill, energy and stamina," wrote pianist Richard Dowling regarding these Columbia recordings. "He developed a unique style of playing that combined an orchestral texture with propulsive drive. His left hand and arm were unusually strong, leaping easily between large chords (usually filled-out tenths) on strong beats and full chords on off-beats. Simultaneously, his virtuoso right hand would play a syncopated melodic line in unrelenting passages of octaves and filled-out chords. Presumably, this is how Gershwin played at those legendary parties."[23]

In many ways, these recordings resembled his rolls, as the description above might suggest. Artis Wodehouse tellingly cites a number of pianistic traits found in the recordings that can be said to characterize the rolls as well: a preference for quick tempos, loud dynamics, and detached articulation, as well as the restrained use of the pedal "to enhance sonorities at key structural points in the composition or to suppress for very brief moments the more accented effect of non-pedalled playing." Clearly, in such matters genre played a more decisive role than the recording technology, for Gershwin's pianism in his concert works, as revealed by both rolls and phonograph records, showed greater variety of tempo, dynamics, touch, and pedaling than found in his renditions of songs, however reproduced.[24]

Even so, distinctions between Gershwin's rolls and phonograph recordings of his songs can be made, aside from obvious differences in sound. For instance, the phonograph recordings, with their brilliant modulations and multihued textures, are generally more complex and expansive than the rolls. Consequently, while they seem comparable to the rolls in their suitability as dance music, they presumably served singers less well.

Moreover, lacking the benefit of editing, the phonograph recordings are less polished than the rolls. Indeed, they contain a fair number of apparent wrong notes, as in the songs recorded at a July 6, 1926, session, which seems to have caught Gershwin in less than his best form. He flubbed some passages in his recording of the *Three Preludes* as well. While admiring the "spirit, excitement, and imagination" of Gershwin's recordings, Edward Berlin notes that his playing "could be sloppy and imprecise," though at least some of Gershwin's smears seem intentionally slapdash. In any case, a few wrong notes might be expected in light of the technical difficulties of the song arrangements in particular; were these rolls, one might suspect that extra notes had been added. Gershwin certainly had reams of technique, and his recordings of the *Rhapsody* are virtually note-perfect.[25]

Gershwin recorded very little after 1928. The collapse of the economy along with the rise of commercial radio left the recording industry in the doldrums, not to recover until the late 1930s. However, Gershwin's Depression-era radio broadcasts suggest that his playing reached new heights in his later years.[26]

In 1932, Gershwin published arrangements of eighteen of his show tunes in his *Song-Book* for piano, which provides some further sense of how he performed his songs by this late date. In his preface to this collection, he also offered some recommendations regarding the playing of American popular music generally, including the suggestion that pianists lay aside certain techniques associated with Chopin in favor of "almost a stencilled style. . . . The rhythms of American popular music are more or less brittle; they should be made to snap, and at times to cackle," he wrote. "The more sharply the music is played, the more effective it sounds." Again, in making these remarks, Gershwin ostensibly had arrangements of popular songs in mind as opposed to his concert works, for which, judged by his own playing, he would have qualified such advice.[27]

The same preface included a brief history of the evolution of "our popular pianistic style," which "really began with the introduction of ragtime, just before the Spanish-American War, and came to its culminating point in the jazz era that followed upon the Great War." Gershwin noted the contributions in particular of Mike Bernard (pseudonym of

Mike Barnett), Leslie ("Les") Copeland, Melville Ellis, Luckey Roberts, Edward "Zez" Confrey, and duo-pianists Philmore ("Phil") Ohman and Victor Arden (pseudonym of Lewis Fuiks). He personally knew most of these musicians—he even remembered hearing Les Copeland's "fine rag-time playing" as a youth standing outside a cafe in Coney Island—as well as a number of other popular pianists unmentioned here, including Felix Arndt, Eubie Blake, James P. Johnson, and Willie "The Lion" Smith.[28]

Born between 1879 and 1898, these sundry pianists generally hailed from the East Coast and lived in New York. However, historians tradi-tionally have divided them into two groups: the black "Harlem stride" pianists, including Blake, Johnson, Roberts, Smith, and later Fats Waller; and the white ragtime (or "novelty" or "show-biz–ragtime") pianists, including the other forenamed musicians.

The emergence of Harlem stride piano during World War I ran parallel—geographically as well as temporally—to the rise of jazz. Whereas jazz emerged largely along the Mississippi from New Orleans to Chicago, Harlem stride traveled a similar course along the eastern seaboard, from the coastal Southeast to New York; for although Eubie Blake (1887–1983) came from Baltimore, Luckey Roberts (1893–1968) from Philadelphia, James P. Johnson (1894–1955) from New Jersey, and Willie "The Lion" Smith (1897–1983) from New York, all four had roots in the Southeast.[29]

This shared background informed their music, alternatively described as a late form of ragtime or an early kind of jazz. Like their New Or-leans contemporaries, they infused ragtime with folk and blues elements; but the folk music in question was not that of the Mississippi delta, but rather that of the coastal regions of Georgia and South Carolina, in par-ticular the ring-shouts peculiar to that area. Johnson recalled falling asleep upstairs in his New Brunswick home listening to ring-shouts below, while Willie Smith stated, "Shouts are stride piano—when James P. and Fats and I would get a romp-down shout going, that was playing rocky, just like the Baptist people sing," and added that one could hear such shout-ing in Harlem at the Convent Avenue Baptist Church.[30]

Working in New York's saloons and dance halls, the stride pianists had further contact with black culture of the coastal South. While com-monly associated with Harlem, they came of age during the 1910s play-ing and sometimes living in that section of Manhattan called San Juan Hill—the so-called Jungles, a district, located in the low West 60s west of Columbus Avenue, whose black population (which grew by about two-thirds in the years between 1910 and 1920) featured a large Gullah component. About 1917, Johnson responded to the dancing and music of the area with the creation of his rag "Carolina Shout," one of the landmarks of Harlem stride; while his "Charleston," composed for the 1923 musical *Runnin' Wild*, helped transform the southern ring-dance into a national dance craze. When Gershwin—who had attended high school in the San Juan Hill area during the mid-teens—traveled south to study Gullah music in association with *Porgy and Bess* and proved himself a convincing ring-shouter, he had been prepared for such an adventure by, among other things, his long-standing involvement with the stride pianists.

The stride pianists distinguished themselves from New Orleans jazz musicians in other ways. As more or less classically educated musicians living in New York, they prided themselves on their greater familiarity with opera, symphony, and the great concert pianists (perhaps unfairly, considering the long tradition of opera and concert music in New Orleans). Johnson in time pursued a career, inspired by Gershwin's *Rhapsody* and *Porgy and Bess,* as a composer of serious music, including the symphonic jazz piece *Yamekraw: A Negro Rhapsody* (1927, orchestrated by W. G. Still in 1928) and the recently rediscovered opera *De Organizer* (1940). "The reason the New York [stride piano] boys became such high-class musicians," remarked Johnson, "was because the New York piano was developed by the European method, system and style. The people in New York were used to hearing good piano played in concerts and cafés."[31]

This orientation expressed itself most obviously in the stride pianists' penchant for ragging the classics, a tradition that could be traced back to New York's Ben Harney (1871–1938), a pianist of ambiguous racial identity who helped introduce ragtime to white audiences. But the stride pianists' inclination toward the classics could be seen more generally in their cultivation of more intricate textures and harmonies than often found in ragtime. They particularly esteemed a lively, independent bass line; whereas traditional ragtime often pitted a syncopated melody against a marchlike bass, the stride pianists went a step further by casting the bass into asymmetrical units for added rhythmic interest. "The trouble with most piano players is that they don't play enough Bach. Bach develops the left hand," explained Smith, who, like Gershwin, also cited Chopin and Debussy as influences.[32]

Finally, the stride pianists established closer ties with both Tin Pan Alley and Broadway than was typical for most ragtime or jazz musicians. Eubie Blake, with lyricist Noble Sissle, created the score to *Shuffle Along*

(1921), whose songs included "I'm Just Wild about Harry." Johnson wrote his own Broadway shows, most notably *Runnin' Wild* (1923), which, as mentioned, featured "Charleston"; his later songs included the 1926 hit "If I Could Be with You (One Hour Tonight)." Fats Waller, in collaboration with Madagascar-born lyricist Andy Razaf, enjoyed comparable success on Broadway; Roberts much less so, though he and Smith composed some popular rags nonetheless.

The stride pianists plainly prefigured and influenced Gershwin in a number of ways. After Gershwin's death, Roberts even claimed to have taught the young pianist-composer himself: "Bert Williams and Will Vodery (Ziegfeld's conductor) were the ones that got me to teach George Gershwin. At that time he couldn't play. He didn't have a tune in his head. He was selling orchestrations at Remick and stood behind the counter, and Will Vodery said, 'Son, help him along. He's very ambitious.' He couldn't play jazz, but he had two good hands for the classics." Others similarly reported that Roberts gave Gershwin lessons in "syncopation" and "styling," perhaps in 1917 at Roberts's apartment, where Gershwin went to hear him play. The questionable reliability of these sources, including the accuracy of the years cited, need not preclude the larger point that Roberts made a strong impression on Gershwin, for the former was in the forefront of developing the new popular piano styles of the 1910s.[33]

Although Blake intimated that both Roberts and Johnson had at least heard about Gershwin as early as 1916, Johnson, meanwhile, did not remember actually encountering Gershwin until 1920, when they met cutting rolls for Aeolian, as mentioned. "He had written 'Swanee' and was interested in rhythm and blues," recalled Johnson. "Like myself, he wanted to write them on a higher level. We had lots of talks about our ambitions to do great music on American themes." Gershwin would have been about twenty-two at the time, Johnson, twenty-six. In the spring of 1923, their paths crossed again in London when a revue Gershwin had written for the West End, *The Rainbow,* interpolated an extended excerpt from Johnson's show *Plantation Days* (1922).[34]

Back in New York, Gershwin presumably attended Johnson's *Runnin' Wild,* as he had Blake's *Shuffle Along.* By 1924 he had become acquainted with Smith and Waller as well, for about that time, he arranged for Johnson, Smith, and Waller to perform, as Smith tells it, at "one of those fancy cocktail shindigs" on Park Avenue:

> We all knew Gershwin because he used to come up to Harlem to listen to us and he was the one who got us invited. It looked for a while as

though he was going to stay seated at the piano all night himself and hog all the playing. We three were standing at the bar getting up our courage and the more we imbibed the more anxious we became to get at those keys.

I finally went over and said to Gershwin, "Get up off that piano stool and let the real players take over, you tomato." He was a good-natured fellow and from then on the three of us took over the entertainment.

This party seems to have marked the entry into high society for Waller and Smith, who subsequently saw Gershwin at other Park Avenue "shindigs."[35]

Gershwin's closeness to the stride pianists was underscored by occasional allegations of borrowing that arose within that very community. Eubie Blake, for instance, claimed that Gershwin derived "I Got Rhythm" from a tune William Grant Still created during the days when the latter played oboe in the pit of *Shuffle Along*. Some errors accompanying Blake's charge threw doubt on its credibility—Blake admitted in any case that "Gershwin probably didn't mean to take it or steal it because he didn't have to. The man was a genius!"—and thorough investigation failed to substantiate such claims; the resemblance was apparently coincidental. Moreover, Still's allusion to "I Got Rhythm" in the scherzo of his most famous work, the *Afro-American Symphony* (1931), seemed more a friendly nod than anything else. Still's wife, Verna Arvey, herself concluded that Gershwin's music was ultimately "his own." Even so, the notion that Gershwin appropriated material was itself revealing.[36]

Blake also believed that Gershwin adapted "Swanee Ripples" (that is, presumably, *Rialto Ripples*) from a theme by Luckey Roberts. Roberts asserted, more outspokenly, that he himself wrote "The Man I Love," that Maceo Pinkard wrote "Liza," and that Fats Waller ("for a bottle of gin, or maybe two bottles") wrote "Summertime." Roberts further took credit for some of the themes in the *Rhapsody*, saying, "When you hear *Rhapsody in Blue*, you hear me. He [Gershwin] had all of my tricks in that. He had all of my better themes." Roberts liked to stretch the truth—John Fell and Terkild Vinding suggest that he simply confused Pinkard's "Liza" (1922) with Gershwin's song of the same name—but again, just the supposition that Gershwin derived music from Roberts, Pinkard, and Waller signaled his affinity with these musicians.[37]

In fact, *Rialto Ripples* does sound somewhat like the rags that Blake and Roberts wrote in the mid-1910s, and Gershwin no doubt learned much from the Harlem stride pianists. Nor was Gershwin hesitant about acknowledging artistic debts, as evident from his *Song-Book* preface.

"You can't tell many people that they borrowed, but you could George," commented Harold Arlen, who added, "Of course, George made everything distinctively his own—he never just copied."[38]

Moreover, New York's popular pianists, as epitomized by the city's ragtime competitions and "cutting contests," treated the "ragging" of someone else's material as a sign of sophistication, homage, and perhaps subversion. Johnson explicitly referred to the ability to steal as an accomplishment, as in his reaction to hearing Jelly Roll Morton in 1911: "I was able to appreciate him then, but I couldn't steal his stuff. I wasn't good enough yet." Speaking of Gershwin's alleged borrowings, a younger stride pianist, Johnny Guarnieri (1917–1985), commented in 1977, "Well, it was like the Guarnieri family and the Stradivarius family back in Cremona. They all lived at the same town and they all knew each other. In New York there were great composers."[39]

In contrast to the stride pianists, the white pianists mentioned by Gershwin, though popular in their own time, have largely been forgotten—at least as pianists, for Les Copeland (1887–1942) and Zez Confrey (1898–1971) remain known for their compositions: the former, for his rags of the 1910s; the latter, for such novelty pieces as *Kitten on the Keys* (1921) and *Dizzy Fingers* (1923). Mike Bernard (1881–1936) also stands out because, like his rival Ben Harney, he seems to have pioneered the dissemination of ragtime piano playing in New York's great vaudeville houses. "New York's introduction to ragtime, at the hands of Harney and Bernard, colored the city's idea of the music for decades," write David A. Jasen and Gene Jones. "Manhattan associated rags with vaudeville, because that was the site of its first acquaintance, and ragtime would continue to be seen from a show-business perspective, as a spectator sport." Melville Ellis (1879–1917) and the team of Phil Ohman (1896–1954) and Victor Arden (1893–1962) similarly made their greatest mark in theatrical contexts.[40]

In his *Song-Book* preface, Gershwin specified some influential traits associated with this group: Copeland's gliding from a "blurred group of notes" into a "regular chord"; Bernard's "habit of playing the melody in the left hand," surrounded by filigree in the right; and the "more permanent" contributions of Confrey, whose "piano figures found their way into serious American composition." Indeed, such commentators as Artis Wodehouse and Dick Hyman have noted Gershwin's special indebtedness to Zez Confrey, whose *Modern Course in Novelty Piano Playing* (1923) even served, perhaps, as something of a primer for the *Rhapsody*.[41]

New York–born Felix Arndt (1889–1918), though not cited in the

Song-Book preface, deserves mention as well, for his music, including the extremely popular "Nola" (1916), anticipated Gershwin, Zez Confrey, and a host of later American composers. Gershwin met Arndt no later than 1916, when, as earlier stated, the latter helped get him work with the Aeolian Company. "Gershwin often visited Arndt at his studio in the Aeolian Building on 42nd Street and was a great admirer of his piano music, which the composer played to him by the hour," states Ewen, who concludes that Arndt was "by no means a negligible influence in shaping Gershwin's own style of writing for the piano." Had Arndt not died in 1918 while still in his twenties, his contribution might well have been even more evident.[42]

Although jazz historians have tended to marginalize the Harlem stride pianists and simply to dismiss the popular white ragtime pianists, recent critics have found many of these musicians, judged on their own terms, musically and historically compelling. In any case, the conventional wisdom has tended to exaggerate the difference between these black and white pianists, for they interacted cordially and developed similar styles, including whimsical excursions into foreign keys, colorful use of parallel augmented and ninth-chords, and a marked preference for tenths. Fell and Vinding state, "A combination of Black musicals, the success of popular Black entertainers who finally broke into midtown Manhattan shows, and prohibition combined to ease interchange among pianists of any persuasion."[43]

Dividing New York's popular pianists along racial lines obscures not only commonalities among them but meaningful differences within each group. Blake, for instance, remained closer to ragtime than did the other stride pianists; Confrey fitted the label "novelty pianist" better than other musicians labeled as such; while Ohman and Arden—whose two-piano playing in the pit for four of Gershwin's shows *(Lady Be Good, Tip-Toes, Oh, Kay!* and *Funny Face)* contributed significantly to their success—embodied the concept of "showbiz ragtime."

Gershwin seems to have absorbed—how uniquely is hard to say—aspects of these varying approaches, helping to give his playing a richly textured profile that might be described as some fusion of classical, ragtime, and jazz piano rather than jazz or even ragtime per se. Songwriter Hoagy Carmichael, who often heard Gershwin play in the 1930s, stated point-blank, "George wasn't a real jazzman, and he knew it." But Gershwin's playing was jazzier than that of many contemporary popular pianists, and it became jazzier still in his later years—a point often overlooked because of the scarcity of recordings after 1928. Jazz historian

Martin Williams observed that "anyone who has heard Gershwin the pianist on a piece like his *"I Got Rhythm" Variations* [1933] knows that there was more jazz in him that we generally suppose." And pianist Dick Hyman went so far as to assert, "Gershwin was certainly playing jazz piano, however obsolete our ears perceive his style to have been." More to the point, perhaps, Gershwin created a distinctive performing style indebted, like his music, to varied sources, including some of the outstanding black and white popular pianists of his time.[44]

Chapter Five

Toward a Career in the Theater

*D*uring his nearly three years at Remick, Gershwin became increasingly frustrated with the company's unwillingness to publish any of his songs, and he grew disenchanted with the music business in general, notwithstanding his continued admiration for the likes of Berlin and Muir. Harry Ruby and other friends "thought he was going highfalutin'" when he would speak "of the artistic mission of popular music." "The height of artistic achievement to us was a 'pop' song that sold lots of copies," recalled Ruby, "and we just didn't understand what he was talking about."[1]

"The popular-song racket began to get definitely on my nerves," explained Gershwin. "Its tunes somehow began to offend me. Or, perhaps my ears were becoming attuned to better harmonies. . . . I began to realize that my musical ambitions were slightly above popular song." On March 17, 1917, he quit Remick and turned his attention more decidedly toward operetta and musical comedy.[2]

Gershwin's affinity for operetta—perhaps nurtured by his teacher Charles Hambitzer, whose operettas he admired—dated back to his boyhood fondness for Yiddish musical theater and Gilbert and Sullivan. He also developed over the years a high regard for Viennese operetta. While in Europe in 1928, he welcomed the opportunity to meet, along with the widow of Johann Strauss Jr., Franz Lehár (1870–1948) and Emmerich (Imre) Kálmán (1882–1953), the celebrated Hungarian-born composers of *The Merry Widow* and *Countess Maritza*, respectively. Gershwin spent considerable time especially with Kálmán during his brief week in Vienna: they sat together at a gala luncheon at the Hotel Sacher on April 28; had another meal at the Kálmán home the following day; met at the

Westminster Café on the thirtieth; and reunited for a farewell lunch at the Hotel Bristol (where Gershwin was staying) on May 5. The two possibly saw each other even more often than this; Kálmán later remembered—after he had arrived in the States, a Jewish refugee from Nazi-occupied Austria—that while in Vienna, Gershwin called on him nearly every day.

Kálmán, who "loved" Gershwin "at once," further recalled that they played their own music for each other as well as duets. "He could understand a little German," said Kálmán, "though he could not speak it, and we both knew a little French. We could not talk much in words, so we talked in music." (Kálmán's future wife, Vera, remembered that George and Ira spoke German, though with a Russian-Polish accent.) During this memorable week, Kálmán happily heard the *Rhapsody* played not only by the house bands of the Hotel Sacher and the Westminster Café but by Gershwin at his own home. Astonished to learn that Kálmán was completely familiar with the New York theatrical scene, Gershwin, for his part, attended the Austrian's latest operetta, *The Duchess of Chicago,* on April 28; the score, which included the hit number "A Little Slow Fox with Mary," exhibited the influence of American music, noted Gershwin, who thought the show's scale Ziegfeldian—and its length, Wagnerian. (The operetta's humorous counterposing of American jazz and the Viennese waltz found, incidentally, a playful echo in George and Ira's 1936 Johann Strauss parody, "By Strauss.") Before leaving Vienna, Gershwin presented Kálmán with one of his writing implements—a silver pencil—as well as a photograph signed, "To my great friend Kálmán with ardent esteem. George."[3]

According to Oscar Levant, Gershwin in particular liked, among Viennese operettas, *The Chocolate Soldier* (1908) by Oscar Straus (1870–1954), of whom he saw "a good deal," presumably during Straus's extended stays in Hollywood in the 1930s. By this time Gershwin had become friendly with yet another Viennese operetta composer, violinist Fritz Kreisler (1875–1962). In 1934, Gershwin paid homage to Kreisler on his radio show, programming his *Caprice Viennois,* which he described as "one of the most expressive and lilting waltzes ever to come out of Vienna."[4]

Although Vienna, London, and Paris remained the primary hubs of operetta production at the beginning of the twentieth century, American composers, notably Reginald De Koven (1861–1920) in *Robin Hood* (1890); John Philip Sousa (1854–1932) in *El Capitán* (1896); and, above all, Dublin-born Victor Herbert (1859–1924) in *Babes in Toyland* (1903), *The Red Mill* (1906), *Naughty Marietta* (1910), and *Sweethearts* (1913), had begun to mold international operetta conventions into a vital national art form. Gershwin particularly admired Herbert's work, saying that he was delighted to become a staff composer for Harms in 1917 in part because of Herbert's association with the company. As late as 1934, he twice programmed Herbert's music on his radio show, stating, "I feel very close to this great man, for I have always admired his extraordinary melodic gifts, and also because he was one of the most generous, lovable, and considerate musicians who ever lived. He was always helping and advising young composers, and I was fortunate enough to be one of those." In writing for the popular stage, the concert hall, and the opera house, Herbert arguably anticipated Gershwin even more decisively than had Offenbach, though his one full-length opera, *Natoma* (1911), with its Spanish California setting, enjoyed barely a fraction of the success of *Porgy and Bess*.[5]

By the time Gershwin started working at Remick, American operetta had begun to accommodate more vulgar forms of musical theater, partly in order to help differentiate comic from heroic characters, but more generally to keep the form lively and up-to-date. In the forefront of this development stood Czech-born Rudolf Friml (1879–1972), who settled in New York in 1906, and Hungarian-born Sigmund Romberg (1887–1951), who arrived in 1909. Friml's early Broadway shows—including *The Firefly* (1912), *High Jinks* (1913), and *Katinka* (1915)—helped initiate this new era of operetta. Romberg, for his part, began his Broadway career in 1914 writing songs for various revues, an apprenticeship that served him well, to judge from the smash success of his 1917 operetta, *Maytime*. By the mid-1920s, thanks largely to Friml and Romberg, New York had overtaken virtually all foreign capitals as the center of operetta, as evident from the international success of Friml's *Rose Marie* (1924) and *The Vagabond King* (1925) and Romberg's *The Student Prince* (1924), *The Desert Song* (1926), and *The New Moon* (1928). Gershwin knew and respected both composers. On one of his radio broadcasts, he programmed "Allah's Holiday" from Friml's *Katinka*, which he deemed an outstanding exemplar of "one of the best operetta composers." And in 1928 he collaborated on a Ziegfeld show, *Rosalie*, with Romberg, with whom he and Ira developed an amiable friendship.[6]

Gershwin's theatrical work revealed some absorption of these various operetta traditions. His operetta *Song of the Flame* (1925), for instance, met Friml and Romberg on their own ground, while the impact of Viennese operetta could be heard not only in his many waltzes (including the aforementioned "By Strauss"), but even in "I Wants to Stay Here" from *Porgy and Bess* (1935), at least according to Oscar Levant, who amused the composer by referring to this duet as "Porgy in Vienna."[7]

However, the popular theater music that most impressed him was Jerome Kern's. He left Remick, he said, specifically because he "wanted to be closer to production-music—the kind Jerome Kern was writing," explaining further, "Kern was the first composer who made me conscious that most popular music was of inferior quality and that musical-comedy music was made of better material. I followed Kern's work and studied each song that he composed. I paid him the tribute of frank imitation and many things I wrote at this period sounded as though Kern had written them himself."[8]

Jerome Kern (1885–1945) was not only an outstanding composer but the prime force in the development of American musical comedy. The form essentially arose in the 1890s in London, where composers Ivan Caryll (1861–1921) and Lionel Monckton (1861–1924)—collaborating on a series of shows for the Gaiety Theatre—along with such figures as Paul Rubens (1875–1917) and Leslie Stuart (1863–1928), the latter a favorite of Kern's, enlivened the narrative framework of operetta with the vigor of the music hall and the variety show, including prominent use of singing dancers and comedians. After moving to New York, Caryll wrote such hybrid works for Broadway, including *The Pink Lady* (1911), a landmark effort. Meanwhile, George M. Cohan created his own hit shows, notably *Little Johnny Jones* (1904), along similar but more distinctively American lines.

Kern accomplished a more complete synthesis. A well-trained musician, he had grown up in Manhattan and Newark the son of a prosperous German-Jewish businessman and had worked as a song plugger and rehearsal pianist in the early years of the century before making his mark, both on Broadway and on the West End, as a composer of interpolated songs for musicals of the Caryll-Monckton variety. Two such songs proved especially irresistible: a lilting one-step, "You're Here and I'm Here" (1913; lyrics, Harry B. Smith), used in as many as five separate productions in 1913 and 1914; and the romantic fox-trot "They Didn't Believe Me" (1914; lyrics, Herbert Reynolds, the pseudonym of Michael E. Rourke), featured in *The Girl from Utah*. Gershwin and thousands of others quickly took notice.[9]

Such songs neatly wedded the delicacy of the British musical and the sensuous elegance of Viennese operetta with the composer's own sense of structure and style, including a harmonic language marked by smart progressions, artfully spaced chords, and flavorful dissonance in the melody line. Kern experimented with rhythm as well, even trying his hand with changing meters in the song "Who Cares?" (1916; not to be con-

fused with the Gershwin song of the same name). Some of these innovations pointed to the influence of Debussy; in 1918 Kern himself spoke
of "trying to apply modern art to light music as Debussy and those men
have done to more serious work." Such aspirations brought him in range
of those serious American composers, like John Alden Carpenter, then
engaged in absorbing both Debussy and more popular traditions.[10]

Had Kern gone on simply writing songs like "You're Here and I'm
Here" and "They Didn't Believe Me," his contribution to American mu-
sic would have been assured; they provided a new direction for Gershwin and many others. But in the mid-1910s, Kern collaborated on a series of musical comedies, including *Nobody Home* (1915), *Very Good
Eddie* (1915), *Oh Boy!* (1917), *Leave It to Jane* (1917), and *Oh, Lady!
Lady!!* (1918), that helped advance the musical-comedy genre as a
whole. Part of a series known as the Princess Theatre shows (though
Leave It to Jane played at the Longacre), these musicals owed much to
F. Ray Comstock, their producer, and Elizabeth Marbury, who coproduced the first of the bunch. Marbury, who as mentioned had helped
launch the Castles, had the idea of producing intimate, sophisticated musicals in the 299–seat Princess Theatre at 104 West 39th Street, built in
1913 by brothers Lee and J. J. Shubert to house small plays. Dispensing
with the opulence typical of the Broadway musical, these shows rather
would feature an orchestra of about ten players, a chorus of similar size,
and at most two sets. To economize further, stories would be contemporary, so that the cast could wear inexpensive modern dress; and the
personnel would be largely young and relatively unknown, hence less
costly. Because of its small size, however, the Princess would still have
to charge the high price of one to three dollars a ticket.[11]

Comstock employed various composers, lyricists, and bookwriters for
the Princess shows, but principally Kern, lyricist P. G. ("Plum") Wodehouse (1881–1975), and bookwriter Guy Bolton (1884–1979). A short
story writer, novelist, and lyricist, Wodehouse only recently had moved
to New York from his native England, while Bolton had grown up on both
sides of the Atlantic and had studied architecture before pursuing a career in the theater. Bolton collaborated on all the forenamed musicals and
Wodehouse on all but the very first, *Nobody Home,* which featured the
work of a number of lyricists.

An adaptation of Rubens's *Mr. Popple (of Ippleton)* (1905), a British
musical comedy that anticipated the Princess shows (as did Kern's first
full score, *The Red Petticoat* of 1912), *Nobody Home* established the
"pattern of the Princess shows," writes Lee Davis, by featuring "con-

temporary talk, lightning pace, two sets and two acts, chorus girls with names instead of numbers, the old man chasing the young girls, the love affair resolved on the last page, the comic older woman, the wisecracking girl who ends up with nothing but her fame, the show's title as the last line of dialogue, and the finale . . . that sends everyone out of the theatre feeling personally contacted." Wodehouse added to the mix bright and clever lyrics that helped transmit the tradition of W. S. Gilbert to such younger rhymesters as Ira Gershwin, Yip Harburg, Lorenz Hart, and Cole Porter. (Ironically, the best-remembered Wodehouse-Kern song, "Bill"— a reject from *Oh, Lady! Lady!!*—made a first and somewhat altered appearance on the Broadway stage as an interpolation in Kern's 1927 musical with Oscar Hammerstein, *Show Boat.*)[12]

The Princess Theatre shows garnered critical praise for their realistic settings, their satirical view of American prudery and other national foibles, and their integration of plot, lyric, and music. They also featured stylish production values, often brought together under the expert eye of director Edward Royce. For some of the shows, this included the orchestrations of Frank Saddler (1864–1921), whose "arrangements just sparkled no matter who wrote the tunes," as his eminent successor, Robert Russell Bennett, recalled. "When you went to one of those Kern shows at the old Princess Theatre," remarked Bennett, "you just sat back and wondered what delightful touch [Saddler would] treat the music to next. He'd have two violins playing a duet against the melody, and then some whimsical bass progression, or he'd come up with a low woodwind that was just right for some little looker with a little voice. One fine idea after another."[13]

Bennett, who himself orchestrated many of Kern's later musicals, including *Show Boat,* further cited Saddler, along with Victor Herbert, as the two "indispensable" names in the history of the Broadway orchestra. Among other things, they began the process of liberating second violins and violas from restrictive rhythmic functions. (Ira Gershwin even recalled hearing Saddler and Herbert "having an unheated discussion about the use of second violins in theatre musicals. It was too technical for me so left no impression as to whether they were arguing or agreeing.") But whereas Herbert created a lush sound that suited his operettas, Saddler developed a more delicate sound apropos of Kern. Thus, wrote Bennett, Saddler "established once and for all the position of the orchestrator as a personality quite apart from the composer of the songs. He is responsible for the fact that even composers who can make creditable arrangements for the orchestra decline to do so in view of the great advantage of their melodies of having new and equally inspired brains create the orchestrations."[14]

The Princess Theatre musicals largely enjoyed good runs, but considering the size of the theater, far fewer people saw them than most hit shows of the time. Still, they had an impact disproportionate to their size on an elite audience, including Dorothy Parker, who in reviewing *Oh, Lady! Lady!!* wrote, "I was completely sold on it. . . . But then Bolton and Wodehouse and Kern are my favorite indoor sport, anyway. I like the way they go about a musical comedy. I like the way the action slides casually into the songs. I like the deft rhyming of the song that is always sung in the last act by two comedians and a comedienne. And oh, how I do like Jerome Kern's music." Ira, who described *Leave It to Jane* as "very charming," similarly admired the Princess Theatre musicals. But he also liked such other works by Kern as *Love o' Mike* (1917) and the two shows for which his brother George had been rehearsal pianist: *Miss 1917* (1917) and *Rock-a-Bye Baby* (1918).[15]

When Gershwin left Remick in March 1917, he was still a few months away from working on these shows, however, and had to face the immediate necessity of making a living. In the course of the previous year, he had managed to publish a couple of songs with Harry Von Tilzer and G. Schirmer, but these had yielded little money. So he continued making piano rolls and playing gigs, some with a small combo in a Brooklyn nightclub for a few weeks in 1917.[16]

Upon speaking with his friend, black arranger Will Vodery, about "getting into the musical-comedy field," he learned about an opening for a pianist at Fox's City Theatre, a prominent vaudeville house. Hired to play the supper show (so called because the orchestra members took their dinner break during this time slot, necessitating a pianist in the pit), Gershwin lost his place in the music on his very first day at work and was heckled by one of the performing comedians, to the amusement of the audience. Mortified, Gershwin quit after this one performance, without collecting his pay. Years later, he recalled this incident with unusual vehemence as "the most humiliating moment of my life," one that "left a scar in my memory."[17]

Gershwin's luck improved when he was hired in July as a rehearsal pianist for a high-profile revue, *Miss 1917*. Coproduced by Broadway moguls Charles B. Dillingham and Florenz Ziegfeld, the show drew on some of the best musical-comedy talent around: director Ned Wayburn, composers Victor Herbert and Jerome Kern (among others), lyricist P. G. Wodehouse, bookwriter Guy Bolton, choreographer Adolph Bolm, set designer Joseph Urban, and an all-star cast that included singer Vivienne Segal, the comedy team of Gus Van and Joe Schenck, female impersonator Bert Savoy, comedian Lew Fields, dancer Irene Castle, the dance team of Ann Pennington and George White, and even, in a small role, Marion Davies, not to mention acrobats, performing animals, and the famous Ziegfeld chorus girls. The show was booked for the grand Century Theatre, described by Wodehouse and Bolton as "the last word in theaters," located at Central Park West and West 62nd Street. Will Vodery, who regularly orchestrated for Ziegfeld, may have helped get Gershwin this job, too.[18]

In his journal, Ira noted in October that George was working "hard" on the show and coming into "contact" with a number of "notables." It must have been a thrill especially to work with Herbert and Kern; if they knew nothing about Gershwin previously, they did now. Gershwin also had an opportunity to observe his heroes at their most temperamental: for a crucial spot near the end of the first act, Herbert insisted that Segal sing his popular "Kiss Me Again" while Kern wanted her to perform "They Didn't Believe Me," with Segal's decision to sing the former occasioning angry words and stormy threats from Kern.[19]

The bulk of the score actually fell to Kern, who surpassed himself, writing two numbers—"Land Where the Good Songs Go" and "Go Little Boat"—that approached art song. But despite all the expense and talent expended, *Miss 1917*, described by Wodehouse and Bolton as a "lamentable mishmash" and a "historic floperoo," closed after only forty performances. "There was only one thing about *Miss 1917* that is of historic interest," added Wodehouse and Bolton. "The boy who played the piano at rehearsals was a young fellow named George Gershwin."[20]

On September 3, 1917, while still working on the show, Gershwin appeared at Proctor's 58th Street Theatre in two performances with singer Rita Gould performing the latest from Tin Pan Alley, including "Sweet Emalina, My Gal" (Henry Creamer and J. Turner Layton) and "Send Me Away with a Smile" (Louis Weslyn and Al Piantadosi). Gould—who had a minor career, including eventually a bit part in the Kern film musical *Roberta* (1935)—apparently helped popularize "Send Me Away," judging from her signed photograph on the cover of the sheet music. Advertised as "a war love song with a universal appeal," the number was one of numerous patriotic songs composed that year (the most popular being George M. Cohan's "Over There," written in April after President Wilson declared war). Gershwin presumably gave the song the requisite verve, but he had no intention of taking up arms himself. On the contrary, he began to study saxophone with the intention of joining a military band if he needed to serve.

At each of his two shows on September 3, Gershwin performed a solo: at the first, Felix Arndt's *Desecration Rag* no. 1 (1914), so called because of its jazzy treatment of famous melodies by Liszt, Chopin, and Dvořák (including Gershwin's beloved, but obviously not sacred, *Humoresque*); and at the second, another lively rag, Harry Jentes's *California Sunshine* (1913). Arndt's irreverent treatment of classic melodies was part of a trend that obviously appealed to Gershwin, who wrote his own number in this vein, "Ragging the Traumerei," about 1913.

Soon after, Gershwin also found employment playing in the pit for another revue, *The Land of Joy (La Tierra de la Alegría),* at the Park Theatre, with music by Spain's Joaquín ("Quinito") Valverde Jr. (1875–1918)—not to be confused with his father, an equally acclaimed theater composer. The show opened in New York on November 1, having premiered in Havana the previous month, on October 6. For part of the run, La Argentina (Antonia Mercé, 1888–1936), the fabulous Spanish dancer and castanetist who helped revive her country's traditional dancing, appeared in the revue, stopping the show "with a heel dance, a table dance, and an impassioned tango." Gershwin surely profited from knowing Valverde's richly eclectic score, which featured songs and dances in Spanish, Moroccan, Latin American, and American popular styles.[21]

Meanwhile, after *Miss 1917* opened at the Century Theatre on November 5, Gershwin participated in the theater's Sunday night concerts (like other Broadway theaters, the Century offered entertainment at dead times, especially Sunday nights). The first such concert, on November 11, featured a galaxy of stars, including not only such cast members as Segal, Pennington, White, and Van and Schenck, but Fanny Brice, Eddie Cantor, and Bert Williams. On the eighteenth, Gershwin accompanied Arthur Cunningham, a comic singer; and then on the twenty-fifth, the young star of *Miss 1917,* Vivienne Segal (1897–1992), described by Wodehouse and Bolton as a talented comedian with "a wonderful voice." At the start of a long and versatile career that would see her originate roles as different as Margot Bonvalet in *The Desert Song* and Vera Simpson in *Pal Joey,* Segal programmed two of Gershwin's own songs that evening, "There's More to the Kiss than the X-X-X" and "You-oo Just You."[22]

Impressed with these two numbers, Harry Askins, the company manager of *Miss 1917,* brought Gershwin to the attention of Max Dreyfus (1874–1964), head of the music publishing company T. B. Harms (after its founder, Tom B. Harms). A Jewish violinist and pianist, Dreyfus emigrated from the small German town of Kuppenheim to the States, where for a while, reported Richard Rodgers with some disbelief, he played cornet on a Mississippi showboat. Dreyfus worked his way up in the music business, joining the publishing house of Tom B. Harms as an arranger in 1898 and becoming head of the company (renamed T. B. Harms) in 1904. T. B. Harms merged with the British firm of Francis, Day & Hunter in 1908, but severed this relationship in 1920 and entered instead into an arrangement with British music publisher Chappell (subsequently run by Max's brother Louis, born Ludwig). In 1921, the firm shortened its name to Harms.[23]

Rodgers described Dreyfus as "a shrewd bargainer and a hard man to get along with," whereas Robert Russell Bennett, who often accompanied him to the Metropolitan Opera, remembered him as "a slight, soft-spoken man with his roots in the German Schwarzwald, a man who quietly took over the destinies of the words and music of Broadway. His success, I think . . . was due as much to his general education and capacity for learning as to his music studies." Wrote fellow publishing executive Hans W. Heinsheimer:

> Who will ever forget Mr. Max, frail, small, pale, very soft-spoken, coming into the music room of Chappell in New York for an audition? He sat there, silent, seemingly dreaming, dressed in his celebrated linen jacket, the royal purple of his trade and the symbol of his majestic station. There the great composers and the great writers paraded, not at all great in his presence, ready to accept the verdict of the little man in the linen jacket, and when he leaned a little forward and cupped his hand to his ear and said "I don't hear any music," they hastily scrapped what they had just played for him and turned to the next number, hoping that Mr. Max would just say nothing at all or, perhaps, nod a little or just, quietly, go back to dreaming.

In 1929, Gershwin himself described Dreyfus to a friend as follows: "He is a pretty cold person to play for. And although he is very sincere in what he says, it must be taken with a grain of salt. To Mr. Dreyfus, melody is the one essential thing in music. He is not quite up to liking the new rhythms, although he published many of them."[24]

Dreyfus helped further the practice—pioneered by Tom B. Harms— of publishing sheet music from Broadway shows by persuading stage performers to interpolate Harms songs and Broadway producers to employ Harms composers. Visiting the Harms office at 62 West 45th Street in 1924, Vernon Duke discovered "a political hell, with Boss Dreyfus dispensing patronage to the Faithful and selling producers on commissioning entire musical-comedy scores to the older and better-established 'boys,' or interpolated numbers to promising beginners." In such ways, Dreyfus made Harms the nation's largest and most prestigious publisher of popular music, while nurturing the careers of Kern, Friml, Gershwin, Youmans, Porter, Rodgers, and others. But he took no credit for Gershwin's success, saying, "A man with Gershwin's talent did not need anybody to push him ahead. His talent did all the pushing."[25]

In February 1918, Dreyfus offered Gershwin a salaried position as a staff composer for thirty-five dollars a week (the kind of wage he had been earning as a Broadway rehearsal pianist), with no obligations other than to compose songs. And for every one of his songs that Harms published, he would receive another fifty dollars as an advance and a royalty of three cents on sales. Wrote Ira in his diary on hearing the news: "Some snap."[26]

Gershwin essentially remained with Harms and then Chappell for the rest of his life. In 1927 Harms began publishing Gershwin's music under a subsidiary, the New World Music Company; and in 1929 Dreyfus sold his interest in Harms for eleven million dollars to the Warner Brothers Corporation, which continued to publish Gershwin's music under the New World imprint. Meanwhile, the Dreyfus brothers maintained their association with Chappell, and after 1934, Gershwin began publishing his music under a division of that company—the Gershwin Publishing Corporation—devoted exclusively to his work (Warner Brothers acquired this music as well in the late 1980s). Consequently, Dreyfus, assisted by his secretary Irene Gallagher and his music editor Albert Sirmay, oversaw the publication of nearly all of Gershwin's work, including not only his show music but such serious works as the *Rhapsody* and *Porgy and Bess*.

However, during Gershwin's first year at Harms, the firm published only one of his songs, "Some Wonderful Sort of Something." So at least throughout 1918, he maintained a busy schedule as a rehearsal pianist, probably as much in order to learn more about the theater and to establish contacts as to supplement his income. Even before officially beginning at Harms, in the weeks following Dreyfus's offer, he accompanied vaudeville star Louise Dresser (1878–1965) on an East Coast tour, including a Washington, D.C., performance attended by President Wilson.

Dresser's program included selections by Cohan, Kern, and Herman Paley, as well as her signature song, Paul Dresser's sentimental "My Gal Sal" (1905), composed specifically for her. (Though not related to Paul Dresser, on becoming his protégée she adopted his surname and posed as his sister at his suggestion; Paul Dresser, confusingly enough, was the brother of novelist Theodore Dreiser.) Louise Dresser recalled that although "Georgie" disliked "My Gal Sal," he played it so beautifully that she would "almost forget the lyrics" listening to him. "It wouldn't have surprised me one bit had he banged the piano one day and walked off the stage," added Dresser. "I wouldn't have blamed him too much—but that lovable, shy lad wouldn't have done such a thing."[27]

In the early spring, Gershwin became the rehearsal pianist for another Kern musical, *Rock-a-Bye Baby* (lyrics, Herbert Reynolds), a lighthearted farce that inspired a particularly tinkly score, Kern's own "personal favorite," but one more sweet than lively. After attending its May 22, 1918, premiere, Ira wrote in his diary, "I don't know of any musical comedy that has appealed to me more." However, the show, which starred Louise Dresser and Frank Morgan (best remembered today as MGM's Wizard of Oz), had a disappointingly short run—drowned out, no doubt, by noisier musicals.[28]

Gershwin next worked on the *Ziegfeld Follies of 1918*, which allowed him to participate in one of Broadway's most renowned institutions, that glamorous series of revues bearing the Ziegfeld name since 1913 mounted in the lavish New Amsterdam Theatre on 42nd Street. The show, which opened on June 18, featured comics Eddie Cantor, W. C. Fields, and Will Rogers; famous Ziegfeld beauty Lillian Lorraine; the singing Fairbanks Twins; and dancers Ann Pennington and, making a sensation in her Ziegfeld debut, Marilyn Miller, later to star in Gershwin's *Rosalie* (1928). Ziegfeld regulars Louis Hirsch (1887–1924) and Dave Stamper (1883–1963) provided the music, with additional contributions by, among others, Eubie Blake and Irving Berlin, who provided some patriotic sentiment as the war entered its final months.[29]

Hirsch and Stamper worked extensively together during these years, especially for Ziegfeld. A pianist who had studied in Germany with Rafael Joseffy, Hirsch in particular had become one of the leading songwriters of the 1910s—he was the only composer besides Kern to write a Princess Theatre show—and although he composed no enduring standard, his music, which blended features related to both Berlin and Kern, remains at least historically important. The biggest hit of the *Follies of 1918*, "When I Hear a Syncopated Tune" (lyrics, Gene Buck), for instance, anticipated Gershwin, including "The Real American Folk Song" (1918), which George and Ira began work on just about the time that the show opened. Gershwin paid tribute to Hirsch (whose "The Love Nest" served George Burns and Gracie Allen as their signature tune for decades) by devoting one of his 1934 radio programs to his work.

Although it is generally thought that Gershwin ended his career as a rehearsal pianist with the 1918 *Follies,* he seems to have worked on later shows, including Hirsch's book musical, *Oh, My Dear!* (lyrics, P. G. Wodehouse), which premiered on November 27, 1918. Artis Wodehouse at least surmises as much, noting that Gershwin traditionally cut piano rolls of songs from shows he had helped prepare, and that in 1919 he "produced six single-tune rolls plus an extended medley from the show *[Oh, My Dear!]*—a comprehensive coverage unique in Gershwin's rollography." Wodehouse further wonders whether Gershwin was trying to develop a relationship with Hirsch as a way of getting his songs into the *Follies. Oh, My Dear!* turned out to be the last and least successful of the Princess Theatre musicals; many critics felt the absence of Kern, who, however, permitted (as did composer Jean Schwartz) the interpolation of some of his music into the show.[30]

Gershwin also served as rehearsal pianist for an edition of the *Ziegfeld Midnight Frolic* (and possibly its early show, the *Ziegfeld Nine O'Clock Frolic*) that premiered on December 9, 1918. Begun in 1915, the *Midnight Frolics* were essentially floor shows held on the roof of the New Amsterdam Theatre that gave late-night New Yorkers, including those getting out of the *Follies* below, an after-hours place to drink and dance. *Follies* stars, present and future, often performed in the *Frolics,* with Bert Williams appearing in this second edition of 1918. Ned Wayburn (1871–1942) directed the series (until Prohibition effected its demise) and Dave Stamper typically provided the music. Chorus girl Marcelle Earle recalled Gershwin in rehearsal "wearing an immaculate white shirt with rolled up sleeves," and sitting at the piano "for hours, intent on the music and minding his own business." She also remembered one occasion in which Stamper brought the "shy" Gershwin along for a command performance of the *Frolic* for the sailors aboard the USS *Seattle,* docked in the Hudson.[31]

Some evidence suggests that Gershwin worked in addition for the *Ziegfeld Midnight Frolic* that premiered October 2, 1919; discussing "Swanee," Irving Caesar recalled that Gershwin would sometimes play the song while rehearsing the *Midnight Frolic* "to entertain the girls who happened to be up there," thus attracting the attention of Ned Wayburn, who interpolated the song into a show that opened on October 24 of that year. The proximity of these two October shows, along with the song's apparent 1919 date of composition, imply that the unnamed *Frolic* was the fall 1919 edition, which starred Fanny Brice and W. C. Fields, though it remains best remembered for its tropical-bird scene featuring Dolores dressed in a remarkable peacock outfit. Stamper once again provided music, along with others. This revue may have marked the end of Gershwin's career as a rehearsal pianist—at least for other composers' shows.[32]

Meanwhile, in the early fall of 1918, Gershwin traveled with a new musical comedy, *Look Who's Here* (later, *Ladies First*; music, A. Baldwin Sloane; book and lyrics, Harry B. Smith), on at least most of its six-week tryout tour of the East Coast and Midwest prior to its October 24 Broadway opening. The star of the show, Nora Bayes (born Eleanor Goldberg, 1880–1928), had discovered Gershwin on a visit to Harms, and decided not only to employ him as a pianist but to interpolate three of his songs, including one composed with Ira, "The Real American Folksong." Gershwin was given a few lines in the show as well; after cuts were announced on tour, he cheered up a distraught Bayes by saying, "S'funny, none of my lines have been cut out."[33]

A composer in her own right (she had written "Shine on Harvest Moon" in 1909 with her husband, Jack Norworth, who formerly had been married, incidentally, to Louise Dresser), Bayes was celebrated for her dramatic delivery, and Gershwin liked her rendition of "The Real American Folksong," writing to Max Abramson, "Oh Momma what she does to it." But she was also temperamental, and while on the tour she periodically threatened to fire Gershwin, complaining that his playing distracted her. On one occasion, after Gershwin refused to change the ending of one of his songs, Bayes protested, "You're a mere kid! Why, Irving Berlin or Jerome Kern would make the change for me at the mere suggestion," to which Gershwin responded, "I'd be glad to do it if it were any other song. But this ending cost me plenty of time and effort. Besides, I like it as it stands." Such disagreements allegedly caused Gershwin to return to New York before the completion of the six-week tour, but he and Bayes subsequently became "the best of friends" nonetheless.[34]

Around the time of this tour, Gershwin experienced some tension with Jerome Kern as well. He had become acquainted with Kern while working on the latter's shows, and characteristically turned to him for advice. Kern counseled him against composing a whole show at this point in his career, or something to that effect, because while on tour with *Look Who's Here*, Gershwin wrote to Abramson, "Seriously, I am thinking of writing a show, Max. In spite of what J. K. told me. I am getting confidence and encouragement from this show, and B. Sloane (and his royalties). I'm going to make an attempt when I reach N.Y." Gershwin did so, landing his first Broadway musical in early 1919, in defiance of Kern's advice and without consulting him, which allegedly miffed the older composer. Gershwin, in turn, reportedly resented Kern's preferential treatment of composer Lewis Gensler, as well as a teasing comment he made sometime during this period: "And here's Gershwin, who showed a lot of promise." (Ira, who heard this remark, subsequently wished he had retorted, in reference to Kern's inconstant patronage of Gershwin, "And here's Kern, who promised a lot of shows.") Kern and Gershwin reconciled differences soon enough, Oscar Levant observing, "There was always a little antagonism between them, but nothing serious."[35]

Gershwin also established some contact with Irving Berlin. In early 1919 Berlin, between publishers, visited Harms and offered them a foxtrot, "That Revolutionary Rag," mocking Russia's "tricky slicky Bolsheviki." Dreyfus requested that Gershwin notate the song for Berlin, who usually dictated his songs to musical secretaries. Gershwin duly transcribed the music, and then played it back with his customary flair. "I couldn't hear my own tune," recalled Berlin, "but it was brilliant."[36]

Gershwin had met Berlin before, when he had played some of his own music for the famous songwriter in the hope that his firm might publish them. In later years, Berlin could not recollect that earlier meeting. But now, as Gershwin played not only "That Revolutionary Rag" but some of his own songs destined for his first musical *(La-La-Lucille!),* Berlin was impressed. Depending on who's telling the story, either Berlin turned down Gershwin's offer that he become his secretary, or else Gershwin rejected this proposal from Berlin; in any case, Berlin agreed, saying, "What the hell do you want to work for anybody else for? Work for yourself!"[37]

Berlin was, of course, right. Within six years, the "lovable, shy lad" whose slipup at Fox's City Theatre had occasioned a traumatic humiliation, whose piano playing had annoyed Nora Bayes, and whose ambitions possibly had struck Kern as overreaching, would appear on the cover of *Time* magazine.

Chapter Six

Gershwin among His Friends

*B*efore leaving 111th Street in the fall of 1917, Gershwin befriended an extended family, some of whom occupied a large house around the corner at 112th and Seventh Avenue. This family included brothers Herman and Lou Paley; their niece Mabel Pleshette, whose mother, Anna Paley (sister to Herman and Lou), had married one Louis Pleshette; and their cousins, Max Abramson and his brother, George Pallay. Gershwin apparently met Herman Paley at Remick, where the latter had established himself as one of the firm's more successful songwriters, and where his cousin Max, a drama critic (and later motion picture publicist), enjoyed spending time. Herman and Max quickly recognized that the young George would go far, while the latter found among these assorted Paleys a congenial second family.[1]

Although he had a lot in common with Herman, a fellow songwriter whose teachers also included Hambitzer and Kilenyi, Gershwin developed a special rapport with Herman's younger brother Lou (1885–1952), an elementary school teacher who was, like Ira, an erudite lyricist and W. S. Gilbert enthusiast (in later years, after giving up lyric writing, Paley taught English at Wadleigh High School on West 114th Street and became co-owner of a Greenwich Village bookstore). George's friendship with the "loveable" Lou, as Vernon Duke described him, lasted his entire life, far beyond their few years' collaboration on songs in the late teens. In 1920 Lou married Emily Strunsky, a bright and vivacious woman with whom Gershwin also became particularly close. (In 1926, as mentioned, Ira married Emily's sister, Leonore, whom he had met at Lou and Emily's wedding.) "What a grand person you are, dear Em," Gershwin wrote to her in the last year of his life; "so generous, so understanding, so beautiful." Gershwin often cited Emily as the kind of woman he would like to marry.[2]

Gershwin's friendship with Lou and Emily Paley could only be compared, in terms of warmth and longevity, to that with Mabel Pleshette (later Schirmer, 1897–1994), who also studied with Hambitzer, though she never pursued music all that seriously. In the 1920s she married Robert Schirmer, a Princeton-educated archaeologist whose father, Gustave, had founded Schirmer Music; she kept her husband's name after she and Robert divorced in the early 1930s. Gershwin's letters to Mabel—perhaps the most revealing and sympathetic of all his surviving correspondence—intimated a deep affection. "Perhaps dear Mabel this is our year," he wrote to her at the turn of 1937. "A year that will see both of us finding that elusive something that seems to bring happiness to the lucky." During these final years in Hollywood, he regularly wrote to her in New York, imploring her to visit: "Why don't you come out and loll around our pool with us?" he asked in October 1936. "I'd love to see you again, darling." The "darling" notwithstanding, the two never became romantically involved, though not for Gershwin's "lack of trying," according to Schirmer's niece Mary Pleshette Willis, who asserted that her aunt "feared that their friendship would be jeopardized if they had an affair." In the decades after Gershwin's death, Mabel Schirmer maintained close ties not only with Lou and Emily but with Gershwin's sister, Frances, whose son Leopold remembered Mabel as "enthusiastic" and "vibrant."[3]

After their marriage in 1920, Lou and Emily, who like Mabel never had any children, moved to spacious quarters at 19 West Eighth Street in Greenwich Village, where they regularly entertained on Saturday nights with tea, cookies, charades, and music, with Gershwin often presiding at the piano. In its salad days, this mostly Jewish circle of friends included, besides George and Ira, songwriters Milton Ager, Phil Charig, Vernon Duke, and Vincent Youmans; playwrights S. N. Behrman and Morrie Ryskind; lyricists Irving Caesar, B. G. DeSylva, and Howard Dietz (who lived downstairs from the Paleys); comedians Groucho and Harpo Marx and particularly Fanny Brice, a good friend of the Strunsky sisters; and pianist-critic Samuel Chotzinoff. Conversation naturally inclined toward the arts, and when Oscar Levant started attending these parties in 1925, he found an appreciative audience for such zingers as "[Sigmund Romberg] writes the kind of music you whistle on the way *into* the theater."[4]

Samuel Chotzinoff (1889–1964) provided this "Saturday night gang," as Gershwin termed them, with a vital link to the world of concert music. An immigrant from Vitebsk who had settled on the Lower East Side at a young age and who had studied music with Daniel Gregory Mason at Columbia, he was a noted accompanist. But he also wrote criticism, including a June 1923 piece for *Vanity Fair* titled "Jazz: A Brief History" that traced, as it were, two histories for American music: a largely corrupt and sentimental line that included Stephen Foster, minstrelsy, Victor Herbert, George M. Cohan, and Edward MacDowell; and a more distinctive tradition of "extraordinary rhythmic force," rooted in black spirituals, that included ragtime, Irving Berlin, the blues, the black musical *Shuffle Along* (whose "verve, simplicity and ardor have again rejuvenated the spineless and degenerate American musical-comedy"), and, above all, the modern jazz band, whose complexities have prepared listeners, he argued, for the technical challenges of Debussy and Ravel, if not necessarily the "emotional content" of Beethoven's late quartets or even Brahms's famous "lullaby."[5]

Chotzinoff's idea of the superior jazz band was more along the lines of the Paul Whiteman Orchestra than of, in his own words, those "barbaric, blatant orchestras" associated with improvising black musicians and "dancers engaged in tortuous and unseemly evolutions." But at the same time, he emphasized the cumulative contribution of various black musics to America's "musical speech." "The negro genius," he concluded, "has been chiefly responsible for whatever musical development America can boast."

Gershwin surely knew this 1923 article, which in some ways looked ahead to the *Rhapsody in Blue* premiere less than a year later. However, Chotzinoff himself was wary about the use of popular idioms as the basis for concert works. The success of the *Rhapsody* surprised him without totally winning him over. Even in his enthusiastic review of Gershwin's Concerto in F in 1925, he noted, by way of a caveat, that Gershwin "lacks depth, and it seems that because of his lifelong environment he never will be able to rid himself of jazz, no matter how he sublimates it." Like many elite critics to follow, Chotzinoff remained most fond of the show tunes, though he suspected that *Porgy and Bess* might surpass the composer's concert works, explaining, "The prime essential of opera is melody, and Gershwin is a first-rate melodist by nature."[6]

Another eminent member of the Saturday night gang, and one of Gershwin's most devoted friends, was playwright S. N. Behrman (1893–1973). After graduating from Harvard in 1916, Behrman wrote criticism for the *New Republic*, the *New Yorker*, and other journals and newspapers before securing his first big Broadway success with the play *The Second*

Man (1927). In contrast to the naturalistic tragedies and bedroom farces that dominated American theater at the time, Behrman's comedies explored ethical issues, somewhat in the tradition of Shaw, whom he greatly admired, as he did Max Beerbohm—an orientation shared by Gershwin, who cited both Shaw and Beerbohm as among his favorite writers. Behrman once stated, "I'm interested in what problems affect mature and intelligent people," leaving one wondering how the Paley circle may have shaped his dramatic imagination.

Robert Gross's description of the Behrman plays as marked by "a tension between a tragic substructure and a comic surface" suggests, moreover, some intriguing similarities to Gershwin's work. Harold Clurman further described this "tension" as that between "the somewhat Anglicized gentleman gracing a cosmopolitan salon where deft speech and a twinkling eye will lend him a most engaging personality" and the "sensitive, secretively observing boy nearly always on the verge of sobbing over the spectacle he beholds—of which one of the saddest phenomena is his own discomfort and inability to speak freely," a disguise, thought Clurman, reminiscent of Oscar Wilde, except that Wilde "was more genuinely a worldling" and "really exulted in his mask." Behrman hoped to collaborate with Gershwin on a musical comedy, including possibly an adaptation of Beerbohm's *Zuleika Dobson;* he also expressed his abiding affection for the man by way of the character Vincent Bendix from his play *Let Me Hear the Melody!* (1951).[7]

Gershwin was clearly the star of the Paley circle, however. When Behrman and others traveled to the Paley family's hotel in Belmar, New Jersey, to celebrate Lou and Emily's sixth wedding anniversary in 1926, Gershwin arranged for the assembled friends to pose for a photograph on the front steps of the hotel, with himself lying on his side closer to the camera, "the Young God recumbent," in the words of Shana Alexander (whose parents, Milton and Cecelia Ager, attended the event). At the Paley socials, Gershwin typically played piano and sang songs for hours, as he was wont to do at practically any gathering with a piano in sight. Indeed, he had an almost compulsive need to be at a piano during parties. "This is his conversation," explained Isaac Goldberg; "this is the way he talks to you." Gershwin's ubiquitous piano playing gave rise to humorous anecdotes—"I wonder if my music will be played a hundred years from now," he is reported to have said, prompting humorist Newman Levy to reply, "It certainly will be, if you are still around"—not to mention some genuine annoyance by partygoers who would rather be talking than listening to music; but the Paley circle seems to have been as addicted to his playing as he was. "I felt on the instant, when he sat down to play," recalled Behrman, "the newness, the humor, above all the rush of the great heady surf of vitality. The room became freshly oxygenated; everybody felt it, everybody breathed it." When Cecelia Ager was read this passage years later, she exclaimed, on hearing the word *oxygenated*, "That is the word! For forty years I have been looking for the word that would describe George's effect upon a room, and that is it. You cannot imagine what a party was like when he was expected and he did not appear." Another friend, Kay Swift, noted that when Gershwin began to play, people would leap from their seats and rush to the piano to stand and watch him. "It was extraordinary; it really was," she added. "I've never seen anything like it." Quipped Oscar Levant, "An evening with Gershwin is a Gershwin evening." If Gershwin and Schubert were, as Irving Kolodin argued, "as much alike as any two composers I can think of," then a gathering at the Paleys could be called a Gershwiniade.[8]

By the early 1920s Gershwin had become, thanks to his great talent and charm, one of New York society's most sought-after guests, and while still a mainstay at the Paleys', he began circulating at parties thrown by Cartier executive Jules Glaenzer, writer and photographer Carl Van Vechten, publishers Condé Nast and Alfred Knopf, banker-philanthropist Otto Kahn, and such members of New York's four hundred as Sidney and Olga Fish, Edsel Ford, and Schuyler Parsons. And there was no shortage of parties. "The Twenties were famous for parties," recalled Van Vechten; "everybody both gave and went to them; there was always plenty to eat and drink, lots of talk and certainly a good deal of lewd behavior." The number of eminent people whom Gershwin encountered at such gatherings can only be imagined. At a small party hosted by Schuyler Parsons in 1927, for instance, he met Charles Lindbergh, who sat next to him on the piano bench as he played his *Rhapsody*—a meeting that, as recalled by Dwight Taylor, offered some record of Gershwin as a tactful conversationalist.[9]

Gershwin's associations with Jules Glaenzer and Carl Van Vechten assumed particular significance. An amateur pianist and debonair man-about-town, Glaenzer, one of New York's leading jewelry salesmen, had, noted one commentator, a "Byronic" fortitude for hosting parties, about two hundred in any single year, including dinner, cocktail, and opening-night parties. Although such events, which Glaenzer wrote off as tax deductions, helped him professionally, they seemed motivated by a genuine love of people and music.[10]

Gershwin started to attend Glaenzer's parties no later than 1920, when he performed at a reception for Lord Louis and Lady Edwina Mountbatten. Held mostly at his East 65th Street duplex, Glaenzer's socials featured an unconventional mix of high society, theater folk, famed virtuosos, and celebrated athletes. One guest arriving late for a cocktail party in the 1930s was startled to find Gershwin and Glaenzer at the piano playing a popular Rube Bloom tune, "Truckin'," with Maurice Chevalier singing along and musical-comedy star Gertrude Niesen showing Edsel Ford how to "truck on down."[11]

Glaenzer's soirees, especially his Sunday night "musical parties," often featured performances by some of his guests. Harmonica player Larry Adler recalled how Glaenzer surprised him and Gershwin at a party by announcing that they would perform the *Rhapsody* together; their impromptu rendition brought cheers from, among others, Ethel Merman and Vivienne Segal and immediately established the *Rhapsody* as one of Adler's signature pieces. Glaenzer managed to coax the most intractable musicians to perform and insisted on quiet during performances, leading to such nicknames as "Shush Glaenzer" and "The Great Shusher," and a well-known anecdote in which Glaenzer forced the city's mayor, Jimmy Walker, into another room when he refused to stop talking during a performance. "I'd rather play piano for him than for anybody else," stated Richard Rodgers. "His sincerity and his gratification are tremendous. Often, he'll have tears in his eyes." Indeed, when attending a rehearsal of Gershwin's *Rhapsody,* he reportedly cried on hearing the "Andantino" theme, causing Gershwin to cry in response. In later years, Glaenzer took credit for teaching Gershwin about manners and fine living, but his greater gift, perhaps, was in providing a responsive milieu that allowed the composer to flourish artistically.[12]

Carl Van Vechten proved, in this connection, even more important. Though best remembered today as a Jazz Age purveyor of urban chic, Van Vechten (1890–1964) was also a distinguished novelist, photographer, and music critic. Along with Paul Rosenfeld, he became one of the first Americans to cheer the emergence of Satie, Schoenberg, and Stravinsky. But whereas Rosenfeld was nothing if not earnest, Van Vechten—a transplanted Midwesterner and married homosexual—adopted, like Behrman, a playful style. In one of his novels, a character asks, "How was it possible to read an author who never laughed? For it was only behind laughter that true tragedy could lie concealed, only the ironic author who could awaken the deeper emotions." One biographer grouped him with Elinor Wylie, James Branch Cabell, and other contemporaries who provided the twenties with an "aesthetic, sophisticated, artful diversion concerned with manner as well as message," while historian Ann Douglas thought him "perhaps the first American self-consciously to write 'camp' from a gay perspective, a deft, exhilarating display of wide-eyed enthusiasm and heartfelt cynicism."[13]

Relatedly, Van Vechten—like H. L. Mencken, George Jean Nathan, and Gilbert Seldes—enthusiastically embraced the vernacular; and because of his musical sophistication, his remarks in that area carried special weight. A landmark statement along these lines was a *Vanity Fair* article titled "The Great American Composer: His Grandfathers Are the Present Writers of Our Popular Ragtime Song" (1917). "When some curious critic, a hundred years hence, searches through the available archives in an attempt to discover what was the state of American music at the beginning of the Twentieth Century," asked Van Vechten in a Beerbohm-like gambit, "do you fancy that he will take the trouble to exhume and dig in to the ponderous scores of Henry Hadley, Arthur Foote, Ernest Schelling, George W. Chadwick, Horatio W. (*sic*) Parker, and the rest of the recognizedly 'important' composers of the present day?" No, answered Van Vechten, the "true grandfathers of the Great American Composer of the year 2001" are the men who wrote such ragtime songs as "Waiting for the Robert E. Lee," "Alexander's Ragtime Band," and "Hello, Frisco!" (that is, Lewis Muir, Irving Berlin, and Louis Hirsch, respectively). For in contrast to America's concert music, which has "nothing new to say and no particular reason for saying it," such ragtime songs contain syncopated rhythms that express "the very soul of the epoch" and the "complicated vigor of American life." Thus, ragtime is the "only American music" enjoyed by people around the world, including "lovers of Mozart and Debussy," who prefer it to "the inert classicism of our more serious-minded composers." "I do not mean to suggest," he wrote, "that Edgar Stillman Kelley should write variations on the theme of 'Oh You Beautiful Doll!' or that Arthur Farwell should compose a symphony utilizing 'The Gaby Glide' for the first subject of the 'allegro' and 'Everybody's Doing It' for the second, with the adagio movement based on 'Pretty Baby' in the minor key." Rather, American composers should take a hint from Grainger, Satie, and Stravinsky and create "a new form" for "the rhythms and tunes that dominate the hearts of the people." This *Vanity Fair* article helped popularize what must have been a dubious idea in 1917, and prepared the way for the *Rhapsody in Blue*.[14]

Viewed in light of Van Vechten's later career, this *Vanity Fair* article showed surprisingly little regard for the connection between ragtime and black Americans, aside from the provocative remark, "curiously enough the best ragtime has not been written by negroes." In the 1920s, however, he more than compensated for this oversight by championing African American art to the point that he himself emerged as a central figure of the Harlem Renaissance, a movement associated with such black artists as poets Jean Toomer and Langston Hughes; writers James Weldon Johnson, Zora Neale Hurston, and Alain Locke; painters Aaron Douglas and Archibald Motley Jr.; photographer James VanDerZee; singers Bessie Smith, Ethel Waters, and Paul Robeson; and bandleader Duke Ellington. (A number of these black artists were homosexual, which colored the movement's sensibilities, and which might have helped attract Van Vechten to its cause.) Though not usually associated with the Harlem Renaissance, some white artists also participated in its general goals and activities, including not only Van Vechten but playwright Eugene O'Neill, artist Winold Reiss, photographers Doris Ulmann and Walker Evans, and composers Louis Gruenberg and George Gershwin, all of whom were "passionately engaged in black representational discourses," to use Richard J. Powell's defining phrase.[15]

This movement had been under way for some time prior to Van Vechten's involvement. Ann Douglas dates its beginnings to New York's Silent Protest Parade against racism of 1917 (and traces its demise to the Harlem riot of 1935), while others also cite portrayals of blacks on the Broadway stage by Ridgely Torrence (three one-act plays, 1917) and Eugene O'Neill (*The Emperor Jones*, 1920). But Van Vechten helped bring the movement to its 1925 climax, represented not only by Alain Locke's voluminous compendium, *The New Negro*, but by Van Vechten's own best-selling novel, *Nigger Heaven*, whose sensational portrayal of Harlem life helped promote the area as a fashionable hot spot. He further contributed to the Harlem Renaissance by power-broking behind the scenes, propagandizing in the press, and hosting endless rounds of parties at his West 55th Street apartment, thereby bringing together the movement's leading white and black participants and sympathizers.[16]

Van Vechten first met Gershwin in 1919 and took note of his hit song "Swanee" the following year. After hearing "(I'll Build a) Stairway to Paradise" in the 1922 *Scandals*, he "completely capitulated to his [Gershwin's] amazing talent and nominated him to head my list of jazz composers." In 1923, when a friend, Canadian mezzo-soprano Eva Gauthier, contemplated performing a set of popular American songs in a November 1 concert at New York's Aeolian Hall, Van Vechten suggested that she employ Gershwin as "accompanist and guide," and cheered her decision to program a set of popular songs by Gershwin (including "Innocent Ingenue Baby," a collaboration with William Daly), Berlin, Kern, and Walter Donaldson between selections by Bartók and Schoenberg.[17]

At this historic recital Gershwin, making his debut on the concert stage, accompanied Gauthier only on the popular songs, for which she appeared onstage in a black velvet dress, long black gloves, a large green ostrich-feather fan, and enormous paste diamond earrings. Some were appalled, but others went wild with delight. One observer noted that opera star Ernestine Schumann-Heink and lieder singer Elena Gerhardt broke into "good round Teutonic laughter" as Gauthier launched into "Stairway to Paradise." Comparing the house's response to this popular song set with its reaction to Bartók and Hindemith, music critic Deems Taylor wrote, "Here was music they didn't have to think about, or intellectualize over, or take solemnly. They didn't have to do anything about it, in fact, except listen to it—which was easy—and enjoy it—which was unavoidable." The audience even demanded that Gauthier repeat her encore, Gershwin's "Do It Again," slyly embellished by the composer with a quotation from *Scheherazade*.[18]

Gauthier collaborated with Gershwin again on successful concerts in Boston on January 29, 1924, in London on May 22, 1925, and in Derby, Connecticut, on January 21, 1926, and sang his songs with other pianists on tour as well, thus widening among elite listeners the kind of stature that he held for Van Vechten. Reviewing the Boston concert, a few weeks before the premiere of the *Rhapsody in Blue,* the eminent H. T. Parker thought that the likes of Alfredo Casella and Darius Milhaud "might draw hints and profit" from the young American songwriter.[19]

Van Vechten welcomed the arrival of the *Rhapsody* in 1924; and although he urged Gershwin to go further in the direction of a "new form," suggesting some combination of "jazz and the moving-picture technique," he nonetheless deemed the piece, as he told his friend Gertrude Stein and eventually the readers of *Vanity Fair,* "the very finest piece of serious music that had ever come out of America" and a fulfillment of his 1917 prophecies. The music showed "a gift for rhythmic expression" and "a classical sense of form," he wrote, even if it lacked "tenderness and passion," a shortcoming he noted in Stravinsky as well. When the work's first recording was released later in 1924, Van Vechten played it "constantly." By the end of the year, he and Gershwin started talking about collaborating on an opera with a Negro cast.[20]

About the same time, Van Vechten moved to West 55th Street and began hosting his famous integrated parties, at which he might appear in a "magnificent cerise and gold mandarin robe," reminding Lawrence Langner of "the Dowager Empress of China gone slightly berserk." For a period, Gershwin came nearly every night, as Van Vechten recalled: "There was a wonderful fire in him. The room would light up when he came in. There was an astonishing vitality in him. You were intimate with him the moment you saw him, and he had thousands of intimate friends." At one party, with novelists Elinor Wylie and Theodore Dreiser in attendance, Gershwin played some music from his latest show, Paul Robeson sang spirituals, and James Weldon Johnson recited one of his poems. At another, with Alfred and Blanche Knopf, Deems Taylor, Miguel Covarrubias, and Otto Kahn in attendance, Adele Astaire danced, Marguerite d'Alvarez sang Gershwin, Robeson once again performed spirituals, Johnson once again recited his poetry, and Gershwin played the *Rhapsody*.[21]

Of the black artists associated with Van Vechten, Gershwin established a special closeness with brothers James Weldon Johnson (1871–1938) and J. Rosamond Johnson (1873–1954). In earlier years, the Johnsons had been a songwriting team much like the Gershwins, with attorney James Weldon the scholarly lyricist and New England Conservatory graduate J. Rosamond the well-trained composer. As such, they enjoyed considerable success, especially after they teamed up with Bob Cole to write such hits as "Under the Bamboo Tree." On their own, they also wrote "Lift Every Voice and Sing" (later dubbed the "Negro National Anthem"). After 1906, as J. Rosamond and Cole toured vaudeville together, James Weldon pursued a career as a diplomat, poet, civil rights activist, and eventually professor of literature at Fisk University.

In the spirit of the Harlem Renaissance, the Johnson brothers also cultivated an interest in African American folk music. In 1925 and 1926, at the movement's zenith, they brought forth two volumes of Negro spirituals, arranged by J. Rosamond and Lawrence Brown. Each spiritual bore a dedication to some friend or hero, including Booker T. Washington and W. E. B. Du Bois, dedications that taken together helped chart the social terrain of the Harlem Renaissance. The Johnsons dedicated three spirituals to Van Vechten, more than to anyone else, and one to his wife, Fania Marinoff; and in the second volume, they dedicated the lively spiritual "In dat Great Gittin' Up Mornin'" to Gershwin (who was, along with Percy Grainger and Fritz Kreisler, one of the small number of white composers so honored). A reminiscence of Gershwin by J. Rosamond also proved one of the few that considered him away from the piano: "On such occasions . . . you would find him in some far corner and yet, while remaining as one of the group, he was continually thinking, think-ing, always thinking. It was only through the kindly expression of his eyes and the modest yet captivating smile which sent out the exquisite pleasure he felt in being among friends." For his part, James Weldon, on hearing of Gershwin's death, sent Ira a telegram stating, "America has lost a great composer. Personally I feel his loss as a friend."[22]

The Van Vechten parties provided an opportunity for Gershwin to frat-ernize not only with such prominent black figures as the Johnson broth-ers, Paul Robeson, and Bessie Smith, but with musicologist Ernest New-man and contralto Marguerite d'Alvarez, who, taking her cue from Gauthier, collaborated with Gershwin on a set of popular songs in recital during the 1926–1927 season. Gershwin apparently was not on hand to meet white southern writer DuBose Heyward when the latter visited the Van Vechtens in late 1926, but by then he had already read Heyward's novel *Porgy*, widely known and admired in the Van Vechten circle. Indeed, James Weldon Johnson extended his personal support to Heyward on the occasion of the Broadway premiere of the book's stage adaptation, much as J. Rosamond helped cast Gershwin's operatic version of the same story, and himself created and for many years performed one of its mi-nor roles, that of Lawyer Frazier.[23]

Van Vechten also invited Gershwin to his apartment to meet Gertrude Stein and Alice B. Toklas during their 1934–1935 tour of the States; af-ter Gershwin performed (presumably in early 1935) portions of his new opera, *Porgy and Bess,* Stein, who listened quietly in a chair by the piano, "threw her arms around him," as Bennett Cerf recalled. "'George, it's wonderful!' she cried. 'Now I know it's right,' said Gershwin." Some ob-servers even associated Gershwin's work with that of Stein's. After read-ing Stein's *Wars I Have Seen* in 1945, Van Vechten, for instance, wished that Gershwin were "alive to write music about these pages!" And En-glish novelist Harold Acton thought that the *Rhapsody* "expressed a des-perate modernity entirely un-European" and "cast a twentieth-century spell which dove-tailed into the divagations of Picasso, Mr. Prufrock and Gertrude Stein." In a 1935 letter to Kitty Carlisle, Gershwin himself wrote, "Are you off for the coast from Detroit? Let know, please. Let know please, plans. (It's the Gertrude Stien [*sic*] in me.) Please let know plans, please."[24]

During his travels abroad in the 1920s—to London and Paris in 1923, to London in 1924 and 1925, to London and Paris in 1926, and finally to London, Paris, Berlin, and Vienna in 1928—Gershwin became ac-quainted with not only numerous European musicians but also fashionable society and even royalty. In London, for instance, he became a favorite guest of Lord and Lady Mountbatten as well as of Prince George (King George's fourth son, the Duke of Kent), who presented him with a photograph signed, "From George to George Gershwin." Gershwin also befriended the Sitwells, the extraordinary literary family that included Dame Edith and her brothers Sir Osbert and Sacheverell. "He possessed a fine racial appearance," Osbert recalled in 1948; "nobody could have mistaken him for anything but a Jew." And although he had been "brought up in the poorest quarter of New York," continued Osbert, "his manners were notably excellent, his voice was pleasant, and though the force of his personality was plain in his whole air, he was modest in bearing" without "a trace of the arrogance with which he has been credited." Osbert admitted that he and his contemporaries may have "attributed an exaggerated value" to the *Rhapsody,* but asserted that the composer's show songs remained "altogether typical in their audacity of the age that gave them birth; the Twenties lived and expired to his ingenious tunes, so expert of their kind, and no chronicle of the epoch could fail to mention them and their pervasive influence."[25]

At home, Gershwin began hosting his own parties, especially after he and Ira moved to Riverside Drive in 1929. Ira and Leonore typically entertained on Sunday afternoons, followed by music at George's. In addition to the Paleys and their friends, the Gershwin circle now included playwrights Moss Hart, George S. Kaufman, and Lillian Hellman and her husband from 1925 to 1932, writer Arthur Kober. Later, the Gershwins' California homes became favorite gathering places as well, not only for old pals similarly working in Hollywood but for new friends as well, including members of Los Angeles's growing refugee community. At the latter events, Hellman sometimes appeared with Kober and her lover, Dashiell Hammett, either alternately or together. Throughout, Gershwin often had a dog (usually a terrier) by his side, including Bombo, Tinker, or Tony; Edward G. Robinson once noted that George "made playing with his dog an enviable—lovingly enviable—pastime."[26]

In his later years, Gershwin increasingly showed what Oscar Levant referred to as "a curious partiality for successful, well-to-do people of the stockbrocker type with whom he could play golf and go on week ends." Levant presumably was thinking of such friends as stock promoter George Pallay and financier Emil Mosbacher. In addition to offering Gershwin financial advice, Pallay and Mosbacher assisted him in various romantic pursuits (according to some sources, Pallay helped find women for him, while Mosbacher served as his beard). Mosbacher also generously made his residences available to Gershwin during the composition of *Porgy and Bess,* and both he and Pallay took active roles in trying to save his life at the very end.[27]

Meanwhile, Gershwin's growing interest in the fine arts brought him into friendly contact with Merle Armitage (1893–1975), the impresario, art collector, and author of monographs on Schoenberg and Stravinsky. Armitage began his career arranging bookings for such artists as John McCormack and Pavlova. He eventually settled in Los Angeles, where he founded the Los Angeles Grand Opera Association in 1924 and became manager of the city's Philharmonic Auditorium in 1933, in which capacity he arranged all-Gershwin concerts in February 1937 and, after Gershwin's death, the West Coast premiere of *Porgy and Bess* in 1938. In that same year he edited and contributed to a memorial collection of essays on Gershwin, and in 1958 he published his own book on the composer. The latter publication reported what some of his famous clients had to say about the composer, including Chaliapin ("Gershwin is beginning to convince me that art can come from a mechanized civilization, too"); Mary Garden ("How does he do it?"); Walter Gieseking, who played the music privately for friends ("George was born at the precise moment when America was on the move, when everything was burgeoning with energy and creation. So the forces of the Jew, the Negro, the new land of creation, flowered in a few men, and one of the rare ones was Gershwin"); Fritz Kreisler ("He has introduced something that may very well be the voice of America"); John McCormack ("Gershwin is so courageous that he haunts me"); and even Amelita Galli-Curci, who canceled an engagement so that she could catch the New York premiere of a Gershwin show ("that Gershwin was worth it"). Armitage was also better prepared than most to assess Gershwin's taste in art and achievement as a painter.[28]

Although Gershwin's romantic life largely went undiscussed publicly, he struck a number of observers and friends like English Strunsky as having "quite a sexual appetite." He apparently frequented brothels (where his lovemaking on one occasion disappointed friends spying on him). Strunsky further recalled that he had sexual relations with chorus girls in his shows "who felt it might be a good idea to go to bed with the composer." One date, Carol Koshland, told Michael Feinstein that Gershwin was "one of the most oversexed men she ever met" and that "he was constantly coming on to women and making eyes at them." A few in his circle disapproved of his physical boldness even with mere acquaintances, though when, during his final days and apparently semidelirious, he began to fondle Oscar Levant's girlfriend and future wife, June Gale, Levant was forgiving: "He was horny, as sick as he was. That didn't bother me. I loved George." Robert Payne, who apparently spoke with Gershwin's psychiatrist about such matters, concluded, "Gershwin's attitude to sex was comparable with that of a healthy and irresponsible adolescent. He enjoyed sexual encounters for their own sake and because they stimulated him to compose new musical themes."[29]

Over the years, speculation that Gershwin was homosexual made its way into print as fact, although the scant evidence—including conclusions to that effect purportedly reached by such friends as Simone Simon and Cecelia Ager—ultimately pointed, if anything, to perhaps some latent homosexuality. All commentators at least agreed that Gershwin showed little sustained emotional involvement with any of his girlfriends, artist Al Hirschfeld going so far as to say, "George was so in love with work that he seemed asexual to me. Like [Frank] Crowninshield and [Alexander] Woollcott. Neither was homosexual or interested in women; their passions were all tied up in their work" (though Woollcott—the inspiration for Sheridan Whiteside in the play *The Man Who Came to Dinner*—was, in fact, homosexual). Oscar Levant reported that after a "Don Quixote tilt with a blond windmill in the form of a charming girl" (thought to mean Ginger Rogers), Gershwin remarked, "She has a little love for everyone and not a great deal for anybody," leaving Levant to wonder if Gershwin had not "unconsciously mirrored himself in these words." Frances Gershwin, meanwhile, attributed her brother's emotional reserve to their upbringing, stating, "when you don't have nurturing parents you don't know how to give love."[30]

At the least, Gershwin enjoyed the company of young, attractive, and intelligent women. He started dating perhaps as early as age nine. In maturity, he often had a good-looking date by his side; Van Vechten remembered him showing up at his parties with a different woman practically each time. About five feet ten inches tall and 155 pounds, he was no conventional matinee idol—he had a broad nose and thinning black hair—but with his brilliant talent, elegant manners, snappy dress, athletic build, expressive eyes (described by one observer as "yellow-brown" and "direct in their gaze"), and "lovely luminous smile" (in the words of actress Louise Brooks), he had no trouble attracting women. Moreover, he was, according to Kitty Carlisle and others, "a real flirt," romancing women at the piano with a little waltz reserved for that purpose, in which at certain moments he'd fill in his companion's name.[31]

Gershwin's many dates over the years—some more romantic than others—included (roughly in chronological order from 1919 on) pianists Josepha Rosanska and Pauline Heifetz; Rosamond Walling; the Countess Nadige de Ganny; pianist-composer Kay Swift; Julia Thomas Van Norman; and actresses Marilyn Miller, Ginger Rogers, Aileen Pringle, Roberta Robinson, Kitty Carlisle, Elizabeth Allen, Simone Simon, Luise Rainer, and Paulette Goddard.

The details concerning most of these relationships remain sketchy at best. Mary Ellis—the soprano who starred in Friml's *Rose-Marie,* and who in 1924 attended after-theater supper parties with Gershwin—wrote that although she "adored" the "warm reticent" Gershwin, he was in love with the "beautiful" Pauline Heifetz, sister of the famed violinist. Gershwin came close to proposing to Pauline but hesitated, at least in part over concern that she might have a problem adjusting to his lifestyle, including his habit of working at night. Pauline purportedly agreed to wed Samuel Chotzinoff only after accepting the unlikelihood of marrying Gershwin.[32]

By a number of accounts, Gershwin wanted a Jewish wife, and Rosamond Walling, to whom he proposed in 1929, recalled in fact that although he would say, apropos of her father's British background, that he liked "the English and Southerners and Westerners," he'd add, "But thank God your mother is Jewish." He'd also chastise her by saying, "Don't be so Anglo-Saxon."[33]

The daughter of William English Walling and Anna Strunsky (both related to Ira through marriage, as discussed earlier), Rosamond was only nine when she met George through her cousin, Emily Paley. During her last two years as a history major at Swarthmore (1929–1931), she occasionally dated Gershwin, whose letters to her are among his most romantic to have surfaced. After she graduated and left for Europe, he wrote to her, for instance, "Often when I think of you, I get a desire to fly over to where you are, swoop down like an eagle & steal you & bring you to a big rock on a mountain & there have you all to myself. And I may do it someday." But his letters to her, rarely even this ardent, remained characteristically lighthearted. "Despite his heavenly eyes, he never made me feel needed," recalled Walling, discussing her reason for turning him down. "He didn't need me. . . . I did not like the idea of missing romance." Walling's sister, Anna Walling Hamburger, who accompanied George and Rosamond on some of their dates, recalled that except maybe for "a kiss goodnight on the cheek—a peck—at the door," there was no "physical contact" between them. Hamburger concluded that Gershwin essentially wanted a "trophy wife."[34]

During the same years, Gershwin established a particularly close romantic relationship with a married friend, Katharine ("Kay") Faulkner Swift (1897–1993). The daughter of New York music critic Samuel Swift, Kay grew up in a home steeped in music and opera. She studied piano and composition, and graduated from the Institute of Musical Art (the forerunner of Juilliard) in 1916. Her many eminent teachers included pianist Bertha Fiering Tapper, composer Arthur Johnstone, and theorist Percy Goetschius. While living in Boston (1919–1921), she also worked with composer Charles Martin Loeffler. Her compositions showed the influence of Debussy and sometimes featured aspects of the American vernacular, including black spirituals.[35]

In 1918 Swift married James Warburg, a member of a prominent Jewish banking family, some of whom Warburg scandalized by marrying outside his religion; but he and Kay were representative of a new, rebellious generation, and their town house on East 70th Street and their country estate, Bydale, in Greenwich, Connecticut, quickly became centers for the New York smart set of the 1920s. One commentator described Kay as "vain, childish, witty, delightful—the beautiful flapper who reliably taught guests how to do the Charleston." Her cousin, actor Trader Faulkner, further remarked, "She seemed to be very superficial, but she was au fond very astute."[36]

The Warburgs first met Gershwin at their home on April 17, 1925, at a reception for Jascha Heifetz at which George and Pauline arrived with a group that also included cellist Marie Roemaet Rosanoff, a close friend of Swift's. Over the next few months, Gershwin periodically saw Katharine, whom he took to calling Kay (a nickname that she subsequently adopted as her professional name), and the two soon formed a romantic bond. Although Swift already had some appreciation for popular music, Gershwin made a thorough convert of her, and she became an utterly devoted factotum, editing his music, taking down notation, copying parts, and placing her guest house at Bydale at his disposal. Even as she undertook some more serious projects—including, thanks to Gershwin's intervention, a ballet for Balanchine, *Alma Mater* (1934, orchestrated by Morton Gould, also at Gershwin's recommendation)—she began to write popular theater music strongly influenced by Gershwin. Her biggest hits included the song "Can't We Be Friends?" (1929) and the show *Fine and Dandy* (1930, the first complete Broadway score by a woman), works that were written in collaboration with her husband (who wrote the lyrics under the name Paul James) and that provide a good record of the Warburgs' style and sophistication. ("Some people have a baby to try to save a marriage," commented their granddaughter, Katharine Weber. "My grandparents had a Broadway musical.") After Gershwin's death, Ira found Swift an invaluable consultant on various musical matters, including the creation of the posthumous Gershwin film score, *The Shocking Miss Pilgrim* (1946).[37]

Gershwin's affair with Swift, which by all accounts lasted about ten years, took its toll, not least on Swift's eldest daughter, April, who resented the relationship (as opposed to her younger daughters, Andrea and Kay, who adored Gershwin). "George was a fascinating but disturbing element at Bydale," wrote James Warburg. "His exuberant vitality and many-sided zest for life knew no bounds. . . . Day turned into night and night into day when George was in the throes of creation. I found his visits stimulating but tiring. I liked Gershwin but resented the way in which our whole life was taken over by this completely self-centered but charming genius whose premature death was all too soon to end a brilliant career. I still consider him our most authentically American composer."[38]

After the Warburgs separated in 1934, Swift, who described Gershwin to Michael Feinstein as "the best lover I ever had," hoped to marry Gershwin, but he equivocated. Emil Mosbacher recalled that both Gershwin and Swift spoke with him about marriage, adding, "From George I'd get it every day. He was nuts about her." Oscar Levant had no illusions about that particular prospect; he is said to have once remarked, "Here comes George Gershwin with the future Miss Kay Swift." By the time Gershwin left for Hollywood in 1936, he and Swift had decided to go their own ways romantically. "She has written me about a new relationship which has developed between herself and some fellow I know," Gershwin wrote to Mabel Schirmer in early 1937, "which seems to have done the trick for her. I am very happy for her sake that she was able to adjust herself so soon." Some have wondered, as Swift herself did, whether her having three children might have been an impediment to marriage. Aunt Kate Wolpin believed that Kay simply wasn't "attractive enough" for Gershwin. Others cited his determination to find a Jewish wife. "I would never marry her," he told Kitty Carlisle. "She's not Jewish."[39]

In 1927, Gershwin befriended another married woman, pianist and poet Julia Thomas Van Norman (ca. 1905–1977), who became infatuated with him after hearing a recording of the *Rhapsody* (a gift from her husband, Horace, an aspiring songwriter) and who wrote him worshipful letters for the rest of his life. Gershwin met with her periodically, and although the two apparently did not embark on an affair (an earlier claim that Gershwin fathered Van Norman's daughter, Nancy Bloomer Deussen, born in 1931, has been retracted), the relationship had its erotic side, at least on Van Norman's part: "Don't you suppose I am aware of that warm, living, beautiful body of yours?" she wrote to him in 1933. Concerned about his wife's fragile emotional health, Horace supported the relationship. Gershwin wrote shorter and fewer letters to Van Norman than she to him, but these letters allowed him to vent his frustrations in unique ways and showed, further, an appreciation for her intelligence and empathy.[40]

Gershwin juggled other affairs during these years. According to society hostess Elsa Maxwell, he fell deeply in love, for instance, with the Countess Nadige de Ganny, "a ravishing French beauty," after the two met in Paris in 1928. Gershwin hoped to marry her, wrote Maxwell, but the countess was attached to wealthy art collector Joseph E. Widener, and the doomed relationship left him "haggard and distraught." Maxwell, who saw Gershwin in Paris during this time, remains the only real source for this story, though some correspondence from Gershwin to the countess survives. Ira also mentions "some countess" in his 1928 travel diary, though he may have meant the celebrated Countess Anna de Noailles, who entertained the Gershwins while in Paris. In any case, de Ganny seems to have been the inspiration for the character of Christine Gilbert (played by Alexis Smith) in the Gershwin film biography (1945).[41]

On his first trip to Hollywood in the fall and early winter of 1930–1931, Gershwin also had an affair with Aileen Pringle (1895–1989)—or "Pringie," as he called her. Known in Hollywood as "the darling of the intelligentsia," Pringle, a silent-film star who had successfully made the transition to sound, was less like those starlets with whom his name was sometimes associated than like Kay Swift—a sympathetic and sophisticated older woman. The two probably became acquainted through their mutual friend, Carl Van Vechten. Gershwin maintained a lively correspondence with her for at least a year, telling her, in one letter, to "take care of that gorgeous Basque body."[42]

In the course of the 1930s, as Gershwin established himself as one of America's most eligible bachelors, the press periodically queried him about women and marriage. In answer to a question posed by *Vogue* in 1934, "What feature in a woman do you look at first, and why?" Gershwin answered, "At 40 paces—her shape/At 25 paces—her ankles and shoes/At 10 paces—her face/At 8 paces—her eyes/At 5 paces—her mouth/At no paces—her conversation." And on the occasion of his thirty-sixth birthday, he told gossip columnist Sheilah Graham that he would never marry until he found a "girl" who, "A—Understands him; B—Fulfills a certain need (George isn't quite sure himself what that is); C—Measures up to his ideal conception of woman and D—Resembles Ginger Rogers or Irene Dunne" ("Ginger Rogers is so bubbling with gaiety and vivacity I don't understand any man who can resist her charms," he explained). He further declared marriage "a grand institution—for those who enjoy that sort of thing. I don't." And he wondered why he should take a chance on marriage "when so many of my friends have made a failure of it." "I'm an idealist," he told Graham. "I'd expect too much from a wife. But if ever I find one, and I suppose I've been looking subconsciously for her all my life, I'll get married." Gershwin may have reached the conviction that, as much as he hoped otherwise, he might not be able to sustain a happy marriage. Kay Swift herself imagined that had she and Gershwin wed, the marriage would have ended in divorce—or at least ruined the romance.[43]

Whatever other difficulties Gershwin faced in finding a suitable mate, he had to deal with his mother's feeling that no woman was "good enough" for him, according to Aunt Kate, who claimed that every time he came close to marriage, Rose "cut it off." However, Rose seemed amenable to the notion of Kitty Carlisle (born Catherine Conn, 1910) as a daughter-in-law. After George's death, she even wanted the young actress, as Carlisle recalled, "to act like the bereaved widow" and "sit with the family at the funeral" (Carlisle, who felt that that would be dishonest, attended the funeral with Irving Caesar). Gershwin met Carlisle, still in her early twenties, when they appeared together on a *Fleischmann Hour* radio show, hosted by Rudy Vallee, that aired on November 9, 1933; only a few weeks prior, Carlisle had debuted on Broadway as Prince Orlofsky in *Champagne, Sec,* an adaptation of Johann Strauss's *Die Fledermaus.* Gershwin immediately put her at her ease and, after the radio show, thrilled her by taking her to a party at Elsa Maxwell's. From then to Gershwin's departure to Hollywood in August 1936, the two sporadically dated, Gershwin taking her dancing to El Morocco in midtown and to Small's Paradise and the Cotton Club in Harlem.[44]

Gershwin and Carlisle discussed the possibility of marriage. Carlisle's mother loved the idea ("What mother wouldn't!" remarked Carlisle. "He was rich, famous, and a marvelous catch") and she herself found Gershwin an appealing companion. But she realized that they did not love each other, and after he left for Hollywood, she diplomatically telegrammed to say that she was "too involved" in her career to get married. "He never made me feel as though I were a very important part of his life," recalled Carlisle, who married playwright Moss Hart in 1946. "His letters to me were flip, affectionate, and a little sophomoric except when he wrote about his work. They were hardly of a tone to inspire serious feelings."[45]

During his final year in California, Gershwin "consoled himself rather too quickly," from Carlisle's perspective, by dating a number of prominent film stars, including Ginger Rogers (born McMath, 1911–1995). In her memoirs, Rogers fondly recalled her dates with the composer, which ranged from dancing at the Trocadero to dinners at secluded restaurants along the beach to a football game in Pasadena: "We screamed, yelled, cheered, ate hot dogs, got mustard all over us, and had the best time." Rogers's portrait supports the impression of an affable and impulsively generous man. "I *was* crazy about George Gershwin, and so was everyone who knew him," said Rogers.[46]

Gershwin also saw a fair amount of French "sex kitten" Simone Simon (1911–2005), who would eventually score her greatest Hollywood success with the horror classic *Cat People* (1942). Merle Armitage recalled that she and Gershwin—who first met in Paris in 1928—would talk "interminably" on the telephone, while Levant remembered Gershwin coaching her on a Massenet opera. Simon's own recollections of the affair, at least as related by rival suitor Larry Adler, were less sanguine; she recalled Gershwin's resentment when on one occasion the public made more of a fuss over her than him, and thought him "strange"— that is, possibly homosexual—that he showed no sexual interest in her when they had the opportunity to sleep together. The affair nonetheless took a somewhat scandalous turn in the aftermath of Gershwin's death, when a gold key to Simon's home with the initials G. G., cited in a lawsuit, turned up among Gershwin's possessions.[47]

Gershwin struck a somewhat forlorn note about his dates with Hollywood stars in a letter perhaps calculated to please Julia Van Norman. "They are very interesting," he wrote her in November 1936, "but a movie star is a movie star. They leave you with a sort of emptyness [*sic*] when you say 'good-night.' Your prediction that I would be happily settled soon may come true but so far I have seen no part of it. Maybe this is the storm before the calm. Who knows."[48]

The storm continued in the form of actress Paulette Goddard (born Levy, 1911–1990), whom Gershwin met the following March at a party in honor of Stravinsky at the home of Edward G. Robinson (the other guests included such Hollywood notables as Frank Capra, Marlene Dietrich, Douglas Fairbanks, and Charlie Chaplin, secretly wed to Goddard). Nearing the height of her movie career, Goddard was Gershwin's type: smart, beautiful, and lively—"the most interesting personality I've come across since arriving in Hollywood," he told Mabel Schirmer some months later.[49]

Gershwin started escorting Goddard around town and the two became an item, noted as such by Walter Winchell in his gossip column. His sister, Frances, later stated, "That's the only time I saw him really have a crush on a woman as a woman." That she was of part-Jewish descent no doubt enhanced her potential as a wife in the eyes of the Gershwin circle, and even his mother took an interest; but as Gershwin informed friends and relatives, Goddard had married Charlie Chaplin the year before. According to Goddard, that only heightened her appeal to Gershwin: "If you know his pattern or his story in any way—absolutely unattainable was what excited him." Chaplin allowed Goddard to "go with George" because she'd "always been a one-man woman." In any case, the two apparently broke off their romance a few months before Gershwin's demise.[50]

After his death in 1937, Goddard and Chaplin "mourned George" as did so many friends, though few suffered as keenly as Julia Van Norman, who had a psychotic breakdown and was removed to a state hospital where she remained until her death in 1997. Hundreds of heartfelt letters and telegrams of condolence reached Ira in the days following his brother's demise. Moss Hart was plunged into depression; George S. Kaufman, who described Gershwin's death as "the most tragic thing I have ever known," developed severe headaches; and Lillian Hellman, after sleepless nights haunted by Gershwin's final days, left Hollywood. "No one knows," wrote George Pallay to Irene Gallagher shortly after Gershwin's death, "that my love for George was because I felt uplifted when I was near him. And there is no one left in the world who can give me this one thing that was vital to my very character."[51]

Gershwin's vitality and genius, along with his ingratiating sweetness, remained a vivid, poignant memory—a "frightful and irreparable loss," in the words of film composer Alfred Newman—for his many friends. "When George died a great many people felt not only sad but bored," stated Swift. "He loved every aspect of life, and made every aspect of life loveable. People thought they could never sense that special joy again." Even John O'Hara, who regretted that he "did not like George" and "was not his friend," found it "impossible to inter Gershwin," famously stating, "George died on July 11, 1937, but I don't have to believe it if I don't want to." Wrote Vernon Duke in 1955: "I don't think any of Gershwin's friends who are still living have ever gotten used to the idea of his not being among them."[52]

Chapter Seven

Later Studies

*E*ven after the great success of the *Rhapsody in Blue,* Gershwin continued his musical studies. "To express the richness of [American] life fully a composer must employ melody, harmony and counterpoint as every great composer of the past has employed them," he stated in 1925. "Not, of course, in the same way, but with a full knowledge of their value." To friends concerned that study might jeopardize his freshness and originality, he argued "that every composer of the past who had added anything vital to music had been a well-trained musician and that I was convinced that the native talent which can be killed by study must be too frail to amount to much." As late as 1930 he expressed his determination to "continue to study for a long time."[1]

To this end, he sought an outstanding composer-teacher, although this pursuit largely came to naught. Sometime in the mid-1920s, for instance, he considered studying with the French émigré composer and leader of New York's musical avant-garde Edgard Varèse (1883–1965), whom he would have known not only from mutual acquaintances but from attending concerts sponsored by the International Composers' Guild, which Varèse directed from 1921 to 1927. Varèse acknowledged Gershwin's talent but turned him down as a student, saying, "I can't help you. We're going in different directions. We have nothing in common musically"—though it remains debatable whether Varèse, who used police sirens in his impression of *Amériques* (1921), had "nothing in common" with Gershwin, who used taxi horns in his musical depiction of *An American in Paris* (1928). (Conductor James Levine underscored this kinship by programming these two works back-to-back in concerts with the Met Orchestra and the Boston Symphony Orchestra in 2005.)[2]

In March 1928 Gershwin approached another Frenchman, Maurice Ravel, about lessons. Ravel had arrived in New York earlier that year, participating in a January 15 concert of his music that included his String Quartet (1903), *Sonatine* (1905), *Introduction and Allegro* (1906), and recently completed Violin Sonata (1923–1927). After the recital Gershwin, along with Varèse, Béla Bartók, and Fritz Kreisler, attended a reception at which black dancers and singers performed. In the weeks and months ahead, as Ravel periodically left and returned to New York, he attended Gershwin's new musical, *Funny Face* (which "enchanted" him), and accompanied Gershwin and composer Alexandre Tansman (who helped translate) to the Savoy Ballroom in Harlem to hear jazz.[3]

Gershwin also obliged Ravel by performing a selection of his work, including the *Rhapsody,* at a March 7 dinner party at Eva Gauthier's in honor of the French composer's fifty-third birthday (at Ravel's request, all male, except for the hostess). Gershwin's playing left Ravel "dumbfounded," wrote Gauthier: "The thing that astonished Ravel was the facility with which George scaled the most formidable technical difficulties and his genius for weaving complicated rhythms and his great gift of melody." In an issue of *Musical Digest* published the same month, Ravel counseled Americans to "take jazz seriously," saying, "Personally I find jazz most interesting: the rhythms, the way the melodies are handled, the melodies themselves. I have heard some of George Gershwin's works and I find them intriguing." Ravel's susceptibility to Gershwin might well have predated this trip. David Schiff suggests, for instance, that Ravel possibly modeled the fox-trot from his opera *L'Enfant et les sortilèges* (1925) after Gershwin's "Do It Again" (1922), while the Gershwin style perhaps found its way into the "Blues" movement of the Violin Sonata as well. In any case, Gershwin unquestionably influenced Ravel's later work, in particular the Piano Concerto in G Major, completed in 1931, a work long regarded as a kind of homage to Gershwin, though its debts to Satie and Milhaud are perhaps greater still.[4]

At the March 7 party, Gershwin asked Ravel about studying with him, perhaps in Paris, as the former was preparing to take a working vacation in France. The idea of lessons was somewhat quixotic, as neither knew the other's language very well. But Ravel took the request seriously and declined, telling Gershwin—according to Gauthier, who served as interpreter that evening—"that it would probably cause him to write bad 'Ravel' and lose his great gift of melody and spontaneity." He suggested, rather, that Gershwin consider working with Nadia Boulanger, the brilliant French musician known for her tutelage of young American composers, including Aaron Copland, Virgil Thomson, Walter Piston, and Gershwin's friend Richard Hammond.[5]

On the following day, March 8, Ravel penned a note to Boulanger:

Dear friend,
There is a musician here endowed with the most brilliant, most enchanting, and perhaps the most profound talent: George Gershwin. His worldwide success no longer satisfies him, for he is aiming higher. He knows that he lacks the technical means to achieve his goal. In teaching him those means, one might ruin his talent.

Would you have the courage, which I wouldn't dare have, to undertake this awesome responsibility?

I expect to return home in early May, and will come to see you in order to discuss this matter.

In the meantime, I send you my most cordial regards.
Maurice Ravel

After arriving in Paris in the spring, Gershwin duly arranged to meet Boulanger. In his own letter of introduction, he vaguely remembered meeting her in Paris in 1926 through violinist Paul Kochanski, though he presumably had met her as well at a January 1, 1925, reception at the home of Walter Damrosch on the occasion of her forthcoming American organ debut (performing Aaron Copland's *Organ Symphony*), and again at a January 7, 1925, gathering at Kochanski's in honor of Stravinsky.[6]

By this time, writes Léonie Rosenstiel, Boulanger had become "a fan" of Gershwin's music, "avidly devouring each of his new scores as it was brought to her by her old friend and student Richard Hammond." Nonetheless, she too decided against accepting him as a student. "I had nothing to offer him," she stated in 1938. "He was already quite well known when he came to my house, and I suggested that he was doing all right and should continue. I told him what I could teach him wouldn't help him much . . . and he agreed. Never have I regretted the outcome. He died famous." Mabel Schirmer, who attended this interview, added that Boulanger turned down Gershwin "because he had a natural musical talent that she wouldn't dare disturb for anything."[7]

While in Paris in 1928, Gershwin also visited Jacques Ibert (1890–1962) at his home and surprised him by suggesting that he study orchestration with him, for the French composer had "trouble imagining that a musician of his quality would need advice." When Gershwin further stated his ambition to write "serious" music and Ibert asked him what he meant by that, Gershwin coined a response, as Ibert remembered, in which the words *Bach, fugue,* and *counterpoint* recurred. Discovering that Ibert knew, among his work, only "Swanee" and the *Rhapsody,* Gershwin laughed and launched into some of his more recent compositions at the piano. "It was magic," recalled Ibert. "I was dazzled by his prodigious technique and amazed at his melodic sense, at the boldness of his modulations, and by his audacious and often unexpected harmonic inventions." Ibert agreed to look over Gershwin's scores with him the next day, but advised that he not bother with any more instruction, adding that orchestration couldn't be taught in a few weeks in any case.[8]

About the same time, Gershwin apparently approached Stravinsky about lessons as well. He initially met the Russian at the aforementioned reception given by their mutual friend, Paul Kochanski, on January 7, 1925, on the eve of three all-Stravinsky concerts by the New York Philharmonic at Carnegie Hall with the composer at the podium. The next night, following Stravinsky's performance of, among other works, the *Firebird Suite,* the *Song of the Nightingale,* and *Pulcinella,* they met again at a reception hosted by playwright Mary Hoyt Wiborg. Stravinsky later remembered that at the time, he "hardly knew who he [Gershwin] was and was totally unacquainted with his music." Gershwin entertained at Wiborg's by playing his *Rhapsody* and some of his show tunes. "None of the music interested me," recalled Stravinsky, who was reminded of "one rather bad moment of pure Gershwin" of his own at the end of *The Nightingale.* (Merle Armitage reported, in contrast, that Stravinsky told him with regard to Gershwin's music, "This is fascinating, this is America. This Gershwin is a *very* talented man.")[9]

At the same party, a proposed four-hand improvisation session by the "two great masters of rhythm" was short-circuited by John Hays Hammond Jr. (the inventor of the Hammond organ), who, by disabling Wiborg's piano ("a curious contraption connected with a pipe organ in the same room"), spared them both "probable embarrassment," according to pianist Lester Donahue, who stated that such sensitivity helped set the stage for Hammond's subsequent friendship with both composers. Gershwin probably returned to Carnegie Hall on January 10 to hear Stravinsky conduct *Petrushka,* one of his favorite pieces; and perhaps he attended as well a concert by Stravinsky and members of the New York Philharmonic featuring such chamber works as *Ragtime* and the Octet.[10]

When Gershwin inquired about lessons in 1928, Stravinsky allegedly asked him how much he made, and upon hearing "a hundred thousand dollars a year—maybe two hundred thousand," responded, "Well, then, in that case perhaps it is I who ought to study under you!" Richard Hammond, an eyewitness, corroborated this famous anecdote, though Stravinsky in later years dismissed it as sheer fabrication, saying, "A nice story but I heard it about myself from Ravel before I met Gershwin."[11]

In any event, Gershwin remained heedful of Stravinsky. He attended an all-Stravinsky concert at Town Hall on January 7, 1935, sponsored by the League of Composers (that event featured various songs and chamber pieces, including the *Serenade in A* for piano, played by Beveridge Webster, and the *Three Pieces* for string quartet); he studied the score to *Les noces* (which he heard in Hartford on February 14, 1936, along with the American premiere of Erik Satie's *Socrate*); and he acquired cherished copies of a recording of the *Symphony of Psalms* and the composer's autobiography. Moreover, he turned up at a star-studded soiree at the home of Edward G. Robinson in 1937 at which, wrote Gershwin, Stravinsky and Samuel Dushkin performed "eight pieces, & very interesting too" (these presumably included all or some of the *Duo concertant* and the *Suite italienne*, music that Stravinsky and Dushkin frequently performed during these years).[12]

As in the case of his other would-be composer-teachers, Gershwin apparently received an education of sorts from Stravinsky's music itself. Steven Gilbert observes in particular his use of the "Petrushka chord" (a sonority comprised of two major triads a tritone apart) in *An American in Paris* and *Porgy and Bess*. Hans Keller more generally noted rhythmic similarities between the two composers, especially a shared aversion to upbeat phrases, which imparted, Keller argued, a suspended (or in Theodor Adorno's more critical view, "catatonic") quality that contrasted with the more flowing developmental forms characteristic of central Europe: "Gershwin and Stravinsky beat time with its own weapon: they beat time against time; they do not sing against the dance, but dance on top of it and against it." And yet, Keller opined, unlike Stravinsky, Gershwin's subversion of the upbeat ultimately served a sense of forward motion: "His [Gershwin's] syncopations are either anticipations or anticipatory suspensions: when he stems the flow, the effect is that of a floodgate, in that an all the intenser forward-motion is anticipated." Gershwin thus charted a middle course between Stravinsky and Schoenberg, an achievement, Keller argued, possibly related to his combined Russian-Jewish heritage.[13]

Gershwin's continuing search for guidance led to another well-known encounter with a Russian composer, namely, Alexander Glazounov. On December 14, 1929, Glazounov attended a Young People's Concert in Carnegie Hall with his friend pianist Vladimir Drozdoff, specifically to hear the *Rhapsody* performed by the New York Philharmonic under the baton of Ernest Schelling, with Gershwin at the piano. After deeming the piece "part human and part animal," Glazounov went backstage with Drozdoff, who years later recalled, "I have never seen any man's face become so radiant as Gershwin's did when he was introduced to Glazounov." Gershwin asked Drozdoff to tell Glazounov that it had been "the dream of my life to go to Russia to study orchestration under him." (Gershwin presumably knew Glazounov's popular violin concerto and other works, including the Fifth Symphony, performed at the premiere of his own Concerto in F, and apparently appreciated the orchestral expertise that Glazounov had inherited from his teacher, Rimsky-Korsakov.) Glazounov responded by telling Drozdoff in Russian, "He wants to study orchestration? He hasn't the slightest knowledge of counterpoint," and proceeded to make the same point—a little more graciously one can only hope—to Gershwin in his halting English. Though "crestfallen," Gershwin subsequently visited Glazounov at his hotel to ask him to recommend a counterpoint teacher. This incident says more about Gershwin's modesty and determination than it does about his technical shortcomings.[14]

Meanwhile, in the course of the 1920s, Gershwin took some conducting lessons with the Austrian-born conductor of the Metropolitan Opera, Artur Bodanzky (1877–1939), a renowned Wagner specialist who had served as Mahler's assistant at the Vienna Opera before moving to New York in 1915. According to Robert Russell Bennett, Gershwin's publisher, Max Dreyfus, sent him to Bodanzky so that he could "read scores and study classical, serious music." The lessons lasted about six months. When Dreyfus at one point asked Bodanzky about Gershwin's progress, Bodanzky reportedly answered, "Max, you know even studying requires a certain talent." Bennett concluded from this anecdote that Gershwin was not much of a student (certainly with no disrespect: he cited in this context Jesus and Lincoln as well), an assessment, however, that conflicts with much other evidence. At all events, Gershwin acquired enough skill to start leading orchestras, making his official conducting debut at New York's Lewisohn Stadium with the New York Philharmonic in a performance of *An American in Paris* on August 26, 1929. This successful appearance led to more engagements with the Philharmonic and other orchestras.[15]

When Gershwin emerged in the early 1920s, New York boasted two major orchestras: the New York Symphony Society, under the longtime leadership of Walter Damrosch, and the New York Philharmonic Society, whose principal directors included Willem Mengelberg, Willem van Hoogstraten, Arturo Toscanini, and, toward the end of Gershwin's life,

John Barbirolli and Artur Rodzinski. However, in the 1928–1929 season, the Philharmonic merged with—or, more accurately, cannibalized—
the Symphony Society, leaving Damrosch essentially without an orchestra, though he made a few guest appearances with the Philharmonic in
the months following the merger.

Just prior to its demise, the Symphony Society, known for its support
of American composers, commissioned and premiered Gershwin's Concerto in F (1925) and *An American in Paris* (1928). In contrast, during
the same years, the New York Philharmonic paid notoriously little attention to native composers. When in December 1928 Damrosch conducted Gershwin with the Philharmonic—first *An American in Paris* in
a subscription concert, and then the Concerto in F, with the composer
as soloist, in a Pension Fund benefit concert—the orchestra showed resistance, as Winthrop Sargeant recalled:

> The Philharmonic hated Gershwin with the instinctive loathing that
> most European classical musicians have for American jazz, and Gershwin
> obviously regarded the Philharmonic with the particular truculence that
> characterizes popular musicians who approach the hallowed world of
> classical music from the wrong side of the railroad tracks. To emphasize
> this feeling Gershwin wore a derby hat and smoked a big cigar during
> the entire rehearsal. This breach of good taste did nothing to redeem the
> prestige of Damrosch, who was put in a position of foisting his musical
> barbarian, insultingly, on the touchy Philharmonikers. The Philharmonic
> pretended to regard Gershwin's music humorously, made funny noises, and
> played it, in general, with a complete lack of understanding of the Amer-
> ican idiom. The leisurely baton waving of Damrosch helped not at all.

These performances marked not only the near end of Damrosch's conducting career, but the last time the Philharmonic played Gershwin in
one of its subscription concerts until after his death, when in 1942 Dimitri Mitropoulos conducted the *Rhapsody in Blue*.[16]

Meanwhile, Lewisohn Stadium, a large sports arena built in Greco-
Roman style on the campus of the City University of New York in 1915
(and destroyed in 1973), began hosting symphony concerts each year for
eight weeks in July and August, with the Philharmonic becoming the
official stadium orchestra in 1922 and Hoogstraten its chief conductor
the following year. The stadium seated six thousand, but when its infield
was opened for concerts it could accommodate thousands more; and with
ticket prices as low as twenty-five cents, some popular programs could
attract upwards of fifteen thousand attendants. The arena's superb
acoustics made it possible for listeners to hear a good deal of orchestral

nuance, and straw mats helped make the concrete seats more comfortable (audiences customarily showed appreciation by tossing their straw mats up in the air). In 1924 the Philharmonic, in yet another democratically inspired gesture, established a series of Young People's Concerts, presided over during these years by composer Ernest Schelling.[17]

Although the Lewisohn and the Young People's Concert series presented programs similar to those of the Philharmonic's subscription concerts, they showed a greater openness to contemporary and American music. Schelling, as mentioned in connection with Glazounov, conducted the *Rhapsody* at a Young People's Concert in 1929, nearly fifteen years before the work found its way into the Mitropoulos subscription concert. But it was at Lewisohn Stadium that Gershwin found his venue par excellence. From 1927 to his death, the Philharmonic performed his music there on seven separate occasions, with Gershwin participating in all but one as either conductor or pianist, or both. These programs included two all-Gershwin concerts: the first of its kind (and the first time the Philharmonic ever devoted an entire program to a living composer) on August 16, 1932, at which the composer's *Rumba* (later retitled *Cuban Overture*) received its world premiere; and another on July 9, 1936, that featured selections from *Porgy and Bess* in addition to various instrumental works. All-Gershwin events—Gershwin Nights—remained a staple at Lewisohn Stadium, as at the Hollywood Bowl, for decades after the composer's death.[18]

Huge crowds flocked to Lewisohn Stadium to hear and see Gershwin. When he performed the solo part in the *Rhapsody* and the Concerto in F in his Lewisohn debut on July 23, 1927, an audience of about fifteen thousand turned out, breaking the attendance record previously held by a concert featuring Beethoven's Ninth Symphony. Gershwin continued to attract large audiences, with seventeen thousand jamming into the first all-Gershwin concert in 1932 (another four thousand had to be turned away). That Gershwin's piano playing (particularly of the *Rhapsody*) was a big draw was suggested by the fact that only five thousand came to hear Hoogstraten conduct *An American in Paris* in a July 8, 1929, concert for which the composer simply took a bow. If only seven thousand attended his last appearance at Lewisohn, at an all-Gershwin concert in 1936, this was primarily because the concert took place on the hottest day ever recorded in New York City to that time.

Gershwin showed extraordinary courage in making his 1929 conducting debut leading a world-class orchestra unsympathetic to his music in a performance of the challenging *An American in Paris* before an audience of many thousands. It presumably helped that the Philharmonic had recently performed the work with both Damrosch and Hoogstraten, though it may well have been their somewhat lackluster renditions of the work that prompted Gershwin to conduct the piece in the first place. In any case, Gershwin prepared for this debut by having some coaching sessions with his former teacher Edward Kilenyi and, more than likely, his friend William Daly, whose conducting he particularly admired (as he did Pierre Monteux among symphonic conductors).[19]

Gershwin's conducting debut earned unanimously good press. The *Herald-Tribune* noted his ability to give "a brisk, high-colored performance of his music, with unrestricted spirit and gusto"; the *Times* praised his "clear and admirable sense of rhythm"; and the *Evening Telegram,* while a bit nonplussed by Gershwin's "meteoric flight to fame," asked, "Yet, how could one take to task a young man who led with such genuine authority, such simple and straightforward directness, such smiling seriousness?" Charles Isaacson of the *Telegram* even intimated that Gershwin's rendition of the work was superior to both Damrosch's and Hoogstraten's: "He knew what he wanted, and truth to tell, he got it. Thrice now have these ears listened to 'An American in Paris' . . . and only on this occasion, did the Broadwayic epic mean anything. Gershwin modeled the work into form, and unashamably [sic] exhibited its plebeian soul and its jazz outlook. As a result, the blues were more melancholy and the ragging more vulgar and uproarious. Which proves that George Gershwin is his own best conductor."[20]

On August 28, 1930, Gershwin conducted the work again with the Philharmonic at Lewisohn Stadium before an audience of about twelve thousand. And once more, he garnered good reviews: the *American* reported that "his baton revealed a particular ability to secure from his coworkers whatever effect was intended," while the *Telegram* stated that he "provided a lesson in simplicity and modesty of motion to conductors addicted to the traceries of the manual art." However, in 1932 Allen Lincoln Langley, a Philharmonic violist whose own music regularly appeared in stadium concerts, challenged this consensus with a scathing attack, "The Gershwin Myth," that accused the composer of, among other things, possessing "none of the traditional conductor's accomplishment." Gershwin had no pretensions to being a professional conductor, but Langley's charge that the composer couldn't read a score, let alone his own, was preposterous.[21]

Gershwin not only continued to perform *An American in Paris* with various symphony orchestras, but began conducting as well the opening nights of his Broadway shows, including *Strike Up the Band* (the 1930 version), *Girl Crazy, Of Thee I Sing,* and *Pardon My English.* Isaac Goldberg, who observed Gershwin preparing the Boston premiere of *Strike Up the Band,* left this vivid description of the composer in rehearsal:

> To watch him at rehearsals is to see with what ease he gets the most out of the men under his baton. Baton, did I say? George conducts with a baton, with his cigar, with his shoulders, with his hips, with his eyes, with what not. Yet without any antics for the eyes of the audience. It is, rather, a gentle polyrhythm of his entire body—a quiet dance. He sings with the principals and the chorus; he whistles; he imitates the various instruments of the orchestra; nothing but a sense of propriety, indeed, keeps him from leaping over the footlights and getting right into the show himself.[22]

During these later years, Gershwin continued his studies in music theory with Henry Cowell (1897–1965), Wallingford Riegger (1885–1961), and Joseph Schillinger (1895–1943). The lessons with Cowell took place intermittently over a two-year interval; their exact dates remain fuzzy, though they apparently transpired sometime between 1927 and 1931. Gershwin studied briefly with Riegger during this period as well, probably about the time that the latter joined Cowell on the faculty of the New School for Social Research in 1931; while his more extensive work with Schillinger lasted from 1932 to virtually the end of his life.[23]

By the late 1920s Cowell, as precocious in his own way as Gershwin, had established himself as a leading American composer, admired both at home and abroad especially for his piano music, which involved plucking and scraping the strings of the instrument as well as playing tone clusters on the keyboard with fist, palm, and forearm. He initially met Gershwin, as best he could recall, about 1927 through family connections—one of his mother's closest friends, Anna Strunsky Walling, was aunt to Emily Paley and Leonore Gershwin. Gershwin became intrigued with Cowell's music, presenting him at his home on various occasions, including at a 1931 soiree at which Cowell both played and discussed his music. Ira recalled in particular (because of its title) a performance of *The Banshee.*[24]

Cowell, for his part, invited Gershwin to contribute an essay to his 1933 volume *American Composers on American Music* but stopped short of commissioning an article about him for the same publication. Indeed, his view of the music was somewhat severe. In 1931 he wrote that Gershwin's attempt to fuse classical music and jazz had "failed to create anything worthy in this idiom, because he makes the mistake of removing the jazzy elements when he arranges his jazz for 'classic' works, and the residue is a sticky and commonplace sentimentality." And in 1933 he similarly described Gershwin as one "who is the greatest master of real jazz but who extracts all original qualities from his jazz and puts it into a typically European sentimental style, mixing Liszt, Puccini, Stravinsky, and Wagner when he tries to write 'classical' music." However, his appreciation of Gershwin deepened after the latter took him to a performance of *Porgy and Bess* (1935), which he deemed, especially in light of Gershwin's alleged struggles with orchestration and form, "an astounding achievement." And on hearing of Gershwin's death, Cowell wrote to Nicolas Slonimsky, "It was too bad about Gershwin—I always enjoyed him, and although his music always seemed horridly gushing to me, I recognized its vitality, and believe that he would have improved consistently, as he was doing to the end."[25]

Cowell described his sessions with Gershwin as follows:

> The lessons were to be once a week, but usually something would interfere, so they were nearer once in three weeks. His fertile mind leaped all over the place; he thought the rules of counterpoint were just about the silliest things he had ever come across, and was far too annoyed with them to devote himself to perfecting the counterpoint; it was never more that %90 [*sic*] right. But this was because he was exasperated at the rules, not because he was incapable, of course. With no effort he rattled off the almost perfect exercise, but would get side-tracked into something using juicy 9th and altered chords that he liked better, and would insert these into the Palestrina-style motet.

Intent on mastering counterpoint, Gershwin presumably engaged Cowell with that goal in mind, though the idea of studying sixteenth-century counterpoint, as the mention of Palestrina suggests, was Cowell's, according to his wife, Sidney: "Henry had the quaint notion that sixteenth century counterpoint would teach him what he wanted to know." Cowell possibly shared with Gershwin as well some thoughts about "dissonant counterpoint," a concept developed by Charles Seeger that stood eighteenth-century counterpoint on its head by treating traditional dissonance as the norm and consonances as dissonances needing resolution, though the idea had other applications, including rhythmic ones.[26]

Like Cowell, Wallingford Riegger was a prolific and versatile composer whose output ranged from folk-song arrangements to adventurous forays like *Dichotomy* for orchestra (1931), one of the first notable American adaptations of Schoenberg's twelve-tone method. He came to public attention especially in 1929 with performances of his atonal *Study in Sonority* (1927) in Philadelphia and New York by Stokowski and the Philadelphia Orchestra. Gershwin studied harmony with Riegger, according to Cowell, who doubted that the former "ever felt that there was any value" in his lessons with either Riegger or himself.[27]

Cowell possibly helped steer Gershwin in the direction of yet another New School instructor, Joseph Schillinger, but the decisive recommendation apparently came from Joseph Achron (1886–1943), the Russian émigré violinist-composer known, like Bloch, for his works based on traditional Jewish materials. According to Schillinger, Gershwin felt he was "at a dead end of creative musical experience" and "was ready to leave for Paris, where he contemplated studying with one of the leading composers," when Achron suggested that he work with Schillinger, who helped him through this crisis. Some commentators have dismissed this account as self-serving—Ira went so far as to protest Schillinger's claims in print—but the story at least suggests one reason why Gershwin so assiduously sought instruction: study stimulated his creativity. In any event, he told Charles Previn that his work with Schillinger was "the most rewarding music study I ever engaged in."[28]

Born in Kharkov, Ukraine, Schillinger had studied with Nikolay Tcherepnin at the St. Petersburg Conservatory, and had made a name for himself as a composer and teacher both in the Ukraine and in Russia before arriving in New York in 1928. Trained also as a mathematician, he taught mathematics and music at area institutions, including the New School (1931–1933), but mostly privately. He continued to compose as well, including works for the theremin, an electronic instrument devised by Leon Theremin (Lev Termin) in consultation with Henry Cowell.

Schillinger developed a composition method that involved an encyclopedic catalog of musical resources classified according to mathematical, graphic, and kinetic principles, as found in a series of mostly posthumous publications, most notably the two-volume *Schillinger System of Musical Composition,* coedited by Lyle Dowling and Arnold Shaw (1946). Ilya Levinson places the system—described by Elena Dubinets and Lou Pine as an attempt "to separate the main musical elements from each other; to determine and regulate the mathematical relations in the elements; and to synchronize and combine the elements into a musical composition"—in the tradition of such Russian composers as Sergey Taneyev and Georgy Konyus, and in the context of early Soviet aesthetics and ideals. It's doubtful that many of Schillinger's famous students—including not only Gershwin, Vernon Duke, and Oscar Levant but jazz musicians Eubie Blake, Tommy Dorsey, Benny Goodman, John Lewis, Glenn Miller, and Gerry Mulligan and film composers Carmine Coppola, Charles Previn, and Frank Skinner—mastered the algebraic and geometric concepts underpinning this system; rather, they more likely set their sights on the method's more practical applications.[29]

According to Arnold Shaw, the system's greatest novelty involved establishing rhythm as its foundation, including the translation of hundreds of rhythmic patterns into series that could be applied "to the other elements of tonal art: to the intervals between successive tones in a melody, to the shifting directions of a melody, to the sequence of different types of chords, to the counterpoint and duration of themes, to the successive use of different orchestral choirs, to the relationship between the various segments of a large work, etc." In its emphasis on mathematical relations and its embrace of any and all musical materials, the system anticipated some of the most characteristic trends of the post-1945 avant-garde, including those associated with John Cage and Earle Brown, a Schillinger disciple. Henry and Sidney Cowell spoke warmly of the *System* in 1946, stating that its principles "can be made to cover all styles of music known" and noting its value in offering the composition student "a plan by which he may discover, organize, and use whatever type of material it pleases him to investigate." Elliott Carter, on the other hand, criticized the same treatise as embodying a point of view that came "straight out of middle Europe in the early twenties when the application of a mechanistically conceived scientific method to the arts was all the rage," and one comparable to the pseudo-science of "the Bauhaus books and the prose writings of Eisenstein on the movies." Carter further argued that the method's success depended on its use by composers "who were already well-trained enough to distinguish the musical results from the non-musical ones," though he acknowledged its inclusive scope and its usefulness for "hurried arrangers" needing to fill up "radio time" and "background music of a not too original character." Charles Previn, who started studying with Schillinger in 1937, observed along these lines, "Schillinger's devices for balancing, for expanding and for contracting themes are a film composer's gold mine."[30]

Gershwin worked with Schillinger from early 1932 to his departure for Hollywood in August 1936, after which he studied with him long-distance (he surely would have resumed lessons on his planned return to New York in 1937). When his schedule allowed, he took three ninety-minute lessons each week, studying melody, rhythm, harmony, counterpoint, canon, fugue, and "ostinato" (passacaglia), and doing scores of varied assignments on his own. These exercises not only strengthened his technique but explored such modern resources as polytonality, polymodality, pandiatonicism, and unusual scales, including, on a page with the phrase "Schönberg, Berg, Von Webern and Co." scrawled in its midst, twelve-tone rows.[31]

At least one contrapuntal exercise evolved into an actual composition, namely, "Mine" from *Let 'Em Eat Cake* (1933). But Schillinger's influence went much deeper than this. Steven Gilbert and Wayne Shirley, for instance, have outlined ways in which Gershwin in his late work developed material using Schillingeresque formulas, Gilbert pointing to "geometric expansion" in the *Variations on "I Got Rhythm"* (1933), and Shirley to "rotations" of various themes in *Porgy and Bess* (1935). Paul Nauert similarly detailed Schillinger's influence on the latter work, including the symmetrical chord progressions in the chorus "Gone, Gone, Gone" and the rhythmic canon in the finale to act 1.[32]

In his study of the opera's third act, Ilya Levinson, for his part, located five procedures associated with the Schillinger system: permutation of patterns, synchronization of patterns, "geometric expansion" and "geometric projection," symmetrical pitch groupings (including the octatonic scale), and "coupling" (doubling a melody at a fixed interval). William Rosar further thought the opera's prelude, in which quartal chords in the brass emerge from the surrounding perpetual motion, to embody Schillinger's principle of "rhythmic resultants." Kay Swift, who attended some of Gershwin's lessons with Schillinger, recalled ways in which Schillinger helped him develop his material by saying, for example, "Don't use all this, you could use it later, just use half this, then use it in inversion, and use it in different intervals, use [it] a fourth up instead of a fifth or third."[33]

Vernon Duke paid special attention to Schillinger's influence on Gershwin's orchestral writing, which previously had been "brilliant in spots, adequate in others, but on the whole top-heavy and with too much doubling and padding," and now "shone with a new and dazzling brilliance." Duke himself studied with Schillinger in order to improve his abilities in this area, saying, "whatever their worth as music-creators, Schillinger pupils are without exception peerless and much-sought-after orchestrators. A score by a Schillinger pupil can be recognized not only because of its previously unexplored sonorities but also by reason of the peculiar lucidity of its texture and the effective economy of its orchestral language." Although Duke cited no specific examples, Gershwin's late orchestral works indeed revealed a new "lucidity" and "economy," along with "previously unexplored sonorities."[34]

These observations only intimated the full extent of Schillinger's influence. Earl E. Ferris, the publicist for Gershwin's 1934 radio show, remembered the composer telling him that aside from "Summertime," all of *Porgy and Bess* had been worked out "with algebraic formulas," a notion, to judge from the composer's sketchbooks, less far-fetched than it sounds. At the same time, Gershwin had been moving in this general direction all along. Schillinger even used Gershwin's earlier music—including his manipulation of tetrachords in the *Rhapsody* and the head motive in "I Got Rhythm"—to illustrate points to other students and to Gershwin himself. "I used to do all kinds of things—harmony and counterpoint, I mean—did them correctly, too," Gershwin told Duke, "but didn't even know what I was doing! It was pure instinct and—well, I guess, some talent!" Schillinger clearly helped Gershwin develop such impulses more thoroughly and systematically.[35]

On October 13, 1936, about two months after arriving in California, Gershwin wrote Schillinger that he planned to begin an orchestral work with or without solo piano, and asked about the advisability of continuing lessons with either Arnold Schoenberg (1874–1951) or Ernst Toch (1887–1964), two distinguished Viennese-born Jewish composers who had taken refuge in Los Angeles. Gershwin's knowledge of Schoenberg had deepened since his early encounter with *Pierrot lunaire;* he had acquired the master's *Six Little Piano Pieces,* op. 19, in 1927 and had heard the Kolisch Quartet play the first movement of his Second String Quartet in Paris in 1928. While in Berlin that same year, he had visited Schoenberg, who gave him an inscribed photograph of himself, signed April 24. In 1933, Gershwin welcomed Schoenberg to the States and contributed to a scholarship fund for young composers to study with him at the Malkin School of Music in Boston.[36]

Gershwin similarly met with Toch soon after the latter's arrival in New York in 1934, at which time he "showed himself," as Toch's wife Alice ("Lilly") later recalled, "very fully informed about my husband's activities and even works. He knew a number of his works." Toch encouraged the composition of *Porgy and Bess,* while Gershwin sponsored Toch's membership into the American Society of Composers, Authors, and Publishers (ASCAP) and helped him procure his first Hollywood film assignment, *Peter Ibbetson* (1935). On March 3, 1936, Toch signed his photograph to Gershwin, "Your 'Porgy' gave me the first strong musical impression in this country and one of the strongest of the last years at all. I wish you may produce many more 'Porgy's." Soon after, on April 1, Gershwin presented Toch with a score to his opera, signed, "for Ernst—with keen appreciation of his music and with warm friendliness." George and Ira attended Toch's 1927 opera *The Princess and the Pea* (which opened for a short run at the Biltmore Theater on June 9, 1936) as many as two or three times, according to Lilly, who claimed that the work "charmed" them both.[37]

To the question of whether he should study with Schoenberg or Toch, Schillinger suggested that he work with both. "Why not find out what the well reputed composers have to say on the subject," he wrote. "I think it would be a good idea to work with Schoenberg on four-part fugues and to let Toch supervise your prospective symphonic compositions."[38]

In the end, a grueling Hollywood schedule—and reluctance on at least Toch's side—prevented Gershwin from studying with either, but he maintained friendly ties with both men. In early September he attended a performance of Toch's *Music for Orchestra and Baritone* (1931) conducted by Otto Klemperer in a concert sponsored by the American Guild for German Cultural Freedom, and later in the month he joined Toch at an anti-Nazi demonstration. Lilly recalled that Gershwin confided to Toch his desire to acquire enough craft to write "a really good quartet," but Toch "told him that he thought it was not at all an essential thing for him to do, that he should really stay with what was given him in an extraordinary way and continue there." Toch was impressed, said Lilly, not only with Gershwin's "invention and the highly original—*highly* original—lode of music which he had in his soul," but also with his rhythmic ingenuity, as evidenced by his ability to beat on a table top any two rhythms, say, thirteen against nine. And while Toch, she added, thought Copland a "very gifted" composer as well, he maintained his belief that Gershwin was "really the first and only great composer" that America had "produced up to that time," as "quite elemental and quite outstanding, a real composer," as "number one."[39]

Meanwhile, Schoenberg enjoyed playing tennis with Gershwin at the latter's Beverly Hills home once a week. "He would arrive with an entourage consisting of string-quartet players, conductors and disciples," recalled Oscar Levant, who at the time was studying with Schoenberg, and who was banned from the tennis court "since my tennis costume was identical with my costume for every other occasion—a dark, subtly spotted business suit, suitable for all Fahrenheits from 0 to 212, heavy leather shoes, shirt and tie." Albert Sendrey left a revealing account of one such game between the thirty-eight-year-old Gershwin and the sixty-two-year-old Schoenberg, contrasting the alternately "nervous" and "nonchalant," "relentless" and "chivalrous" Gershwin, "playing to an audience," to an "overly eager" and "choppy" Schoenberg who "has learned to shut his mind against public opinion."[40]

Gershwin also hired Edward Weston to take photographs of Schoenberg (one of which served as the basis for Gershwin's painting of the composer) and underwrote recordings of the four Schoenberg string quartets by the Kolisch Quartet, which had performed these works, along with the late Beethoven quartets, in a concert series sponsored by Elizabeth Sprague Coolidge—performances that "impressed" both George and Ira "deeply." In addition, Gershwin attended a Federal Music Project concert on April 14, 1937, at Trinity Auditorium at which Schoenberg conducted his tone-poem *Pelleas und Melisande* (on a program that also included Gerald Strang conducting some of his own Suite, Adolph Weiss's *American Life,* Levant's *Nocturne,* and Webern's *Passacaglia,* op. 1). According to Levant, Gershwin wanted to commission a work from Schoenberg, "but due to the disparity in their success, status and age, was embarrassed to approach him."[41]

The relationship was not always easy. Following one of the Kolisch Quartet concerts, Gershwin reiterated his desire to write a quartet, adding that it would be "something simple, like Mozart." According to Levant, Schoenberg took this as an implied criticism, and, "nettled," responded, "I'm not a simple man—and, anyway, Mozart was considered far from simple in his day." The defensiveness of both men, as suggested here, must have added an extra edge to their tennis game.[42]

After Gershwin's death, Schoenberg penned two tributes to him, one read as part of a memorial broadcast recorded on July 12, 1937, the other written for Merle Armitage's book of essays. In the first, he stated,

> George Gershwin was one of these rare kinds of musicians to whom music is not a matter of more or less ability. Music to him was the air he breathed, the food which nourished him, the drink that refreshed him. Music was what made him feel and music was the feeling he expressed.
>
> Directness of this kind is given only to great men and there is no doubt that he was a great composer.
>
> What he has achieved was not only to the benefit of a national American music, but also a contribution to the music of the whole world. In this meaning I want to express the deepest grief for the deplorable loss to music; but may I mention that I lose also a friend whose amiable personality was very dear to me.[43]

Schoenberg's more extensive published tribute again stressed Gershwin's naturalness, here compared to an apple tree bearing fruit, which made him a "real composer" and an "innovator," as opposed to the so-called "serious composer" who, drawing from "the fashions and aims current among contemporary composers at certain times," presents a "superficial union of devices applied to a minimum of idea." "His melodies are not products of a combination," Schoenberg wrote, "nor of a mechanical union, but they are units and could therefore not be taken to pieces. Melody, harmony and rhythm are not welded together, but cast." The "impression" the music makes "is that of an improvisation with all the merits and shortcomings appertaining to this kind of production," comparable to an oration, and requiring of the auditor, as in all art, to "get from a work about as much as you are able to give to it yourself." Deferring to posterity the question of whether Gershwin was "a kind of Johann Strauss or Debussy, Offenbach or Brahms, Lehar or Puccini," he concluded, "But I know he is an artist and a composer; he expressed musical ideas; and they were new—as is the way in which he expressed them."[44]

In his book *Style and Idea* (1950), Schoenberg again grouped Gershwin with Offenbach and Strauss, but now in contrast to unnamed artists who in his estimation condescended to the masses. "There are a few composers, like Offenbach, Johann Strauss and Gershwin," he wrote, "whose feelings actually coincide with those of the 'average man in the street.' To them it is no masquerade to express popular feelings in popular terms. They are natural when they talk thus and about that."[45]

For all the naturalness of his music, Gershwin assiduously studied music throughout his life, including, in his formative years, piano with Hambitzer, Wasserman, and Hutcheson; theory and composition with Kilenyi and Goldmark; and orchestration and music history with Cole; as well as, in later years, conducting with Bodanzky and theory with Cowell, Riegger, and Schillinger. He also explored the possibility of taking lessons with Varèse, Ravel, Boulanger, Ibert, Stravinsky, Glazounov, Toch, and Schoenberg, and seriously considered whatever advice he could glean from them. The commonplace notion of Gershwin as naive or ignorant accordingly exasperated Ira, who pointed out "that George from the age of 13 or 14 never let up in his studies of so-called classical foundations and that by the time he was 30 or so could be considered a musicologist (dreadful word) of the first degree besides being a composer." "I can't recall a period in George's life when, despite all his musical creativity, he didn't find time to further his academic studies," added Ira, who remembered that at the very end of his life, his brother was studying Polynesian music. The ingratiating charm and modesty of Gershwin's person and work combined to disguise the extent to which he was an educated composer.[46]

Chapter Eight

Gershwin and the Great Tradition

$\mathcal{C}$oncurrent with his later theoretical studies, Gershwin further investigated the classical repertoire. Merle Armitage presumably overstated the case when he wrote that Gershwin had a knowledge of music's "rich heritage from Palestrina to Bartók," including "the world of Rameau, Pergolesi, Palestrina, and Gluck," along with "almost everything written by Bach and Beethoven." But such claims, however exaggerated, at least offered a corrective to the common view of the composer as uncultivated.[1]

Gershwin especially admired Bach, Mozart, Beethoven, Schubert, Chopin, Wagner, Brahms, Rimsky-Korsakov, Richard Strauss, Debussy, and Stravinsky. He even commissioned artist William Henry Cotton (1880–1958) to paint caricatures of the six of these who probably represented his very favorites: Bach, Mozart, Beethoven, Wagner, Debussy, and Stravinsky. In 1927, for instance, he stated, "My idea of music is Bach, Wagner, Beethoven and Debussy." And in 1928 he similarly singled out Bach, Mozart, Wagner, and Stravinsky. When asked specifically what pieces he would want to hear on a symphony program, he proposed Bach's Passacaglia (and Fugue in C Minor), orchestrated by Stokowski; a Mozart or Beethoven symphony (preferably the latter's fifth or seventh); Stravinsky's *Petrushka* or *Rite of Spring;* and Strauss's *Till Eulenspiegel,* Debussy's *Afternoon of a Faun,* or one of Bach's *Brandenburg Concertos.*[2]

Gershwin not only went to concerts but studied the great classics at home, including the Bach keyboard toccatas, if we can judge from a worn edition of those pieces in his personal library. Discovering the score to Mozart's G Minor Symphony in Gershwin's Boston hotel room in early 1932, Isaac Goldberg concluded that the composer was "evidently studying" the work. Gershwin also enjoyed playing two-piano and four-hand arrangements of classical music—including Bach's organ music, Mozart's string quartets, and various pieces by Schumann, Brahms, Debussy, and Ravel—with such friends as William Daly, Oscar Levant, and Kay Swift, who described him as "a fantastic sight reader" who "would gallop along in the tempo prescribed by the markings without exception—vivace or presto or any time." Regarding their readings of the Brahms string quartets, Levant said, "It was the long line and free development of melodic material in Brahms that particularly attracted him" (Gershwin referred to some of his more expansive melodies, like the slow theme from the *Second Rhapsody*, as "Brahmsian"). And in the early 1930s he became a devotee of Schubert's great String Quintet in C Major, whose influence Levant spotted in the song "Union Square" from *Let 'Em Eat Cake*.[3]

Asked by a journalist in 1929, "Just how do you measure a composer's greatness?" Gershwin spoke about his musical ideals: "To my mind all artists are a combination of two elements—the heart and the brain. Some composers overdo one of the elements in their work. Tchaikowsky (although he was a good technician) was apt to stress the heart too much in his music; Berlioz was all mind. Now Bach was a glorious example of the unity of the two." Queried about Ravel, he said, "I admire Ravel intensely. He is a superb master of technique. But he has never known great inspiration." When his interlocutor suggested that this was "possibly because he's French," Gershwin responded, "Never! Debussy is one of the most profound composers of his time. Look at *Pelléas and Mélisande*."[4]

In 1935 Gershwin returned to the question of "the heart and the brain," stating, "I'm going to try to develop my brains more in music to match my emotional development. Bach, Mozart and Beethoven did that and therefore they are more powerful than such composers as Grieg and Tchaikovsky, who neglected intellect." At the same time, as revealed above, he acknowledged the claims of "the heart," saying on yet another occasion, "to me feeling counts more than anything else. In my belief it eventually determines the greatness of any artistic effort. It means more than technique or knowledge, for either of these without feeling is of no account. Of course feeling by itself, without certain other attributes is not enough, but it is the supreme essential." And in 1934, he advised young composers not only "to study the history of music—for history repeats itself in music as in everything else," but to avoid becoming "too technical . . . because good music combines the two—emotions and technique." (Irving Berlin, he once remarked, knew "nothing of serious music, but then he is a genius.")[5]

After Gershwin's death, Arthur Loesser further reported that the composer had told him that "he was profoundly impressed with those qualities in the works of the great masters of music that gave them their long-lived vitality; the qualities of originality, resourcefulness, workmanship, cohesion and large-scale planning which permit these works to triumph over the changing fashions of centuries." For Loesser, such sensibilities marked Gershwin as an "idealist, possessed of disinterested artistic ambition."[6]

Gershwin took an interest as well in current developments and in meeting other composers both at home and abroad, including England, where he established contact in the early 1920s with such varied figures as Arthur Benjamin, Lord Berners (Gerald Tyrwhitt), Herbert Howells, John Ireland, Poldowski (Irene Wieniawska Paul), Cyril Scott, and William Walton. However, Gershwin often impressed his British colleagues more than they did him. For instance, whereas hearing Walton play some of his music (including *Portsmouth Point* and possibly some of *Façade*) in May 1925 left him rather unenthused, Walton, who had liked Gershwin's "brilliant and captivating tunes" even before meeting him, became a still greater admirer after hearing him play a few songs and some of the piano concerto. "I was hypnotized by his fabulous piano-playing and his melodic gift," recalled Walton, who especially liked the song "I Was So Young (You Were So Beautiful)," and whose receptivity to Gershwin quickly revealed itself in his incidental music to Lytton Strachey's play *The Son of Heaven* (1925). Walton, who in later years opined that the music of Leonard Bernstein "doesn't begin to compare with Gershwin," took pride in comparisons between his music and Gershwin's, "saying that they both belonged to the same tradition."[7]

John Ireland (1879–1962), an esteemed composer of songs and other works, also became a great admirer. Listening to a recording of "The Man I Love" in the 1920s, whiskey in hand, he told a young friend, "That, my boy, is a masterpiece—a *masterpiece*, do you hear? This man Gershwin beats the lot of us. He sits down and composes one of the most original, most perfect, songs of our century. . . . Who wants another symphony if he can write a song like that? Perfect, my boy, perfect. This is the music of America, it will live as long as a Schubert *Lied,* a Brahms *waltz.*" Another source reports that when Gershwin asked Ireland how many performances the latter's own rhapsody (presumably *Mai-Dun*) garnered a year and Ireland answered, "Three," Gershwin commented, "Ah! *Mine* gets played two or three times a *day!*"[8]

Gershwin remained for many years a potent influence on English music, as evidenced by Arthur Benjamin's Concertino for Piano and Orchestra (1927), Constant Lambert's *The Rio Grande* (1929), and Benjamin Britten's *Peter Grimes* (1945). In his 1930 list of the world's "best fifty" musical compositions, British conductor-composer Albert Coates cited only one American work, Gershwin's Concerto in F. These close transatlantic ties survived Lambert's lambasting of Gershwin in his book *Music Ho!* (1934), perhaps best remembered today for its dismissal of the *Rhapsody in Blue* as "neither good jazz nor good Liszt, and in no sense of the word a good concerto," and as, like all of Gershwin's works, "the hybrid child of a hybrid. A rather knowing and unpleasant child too, ashamed of its parents and boasting of its French lessons." Years later, Ralph Vaughan Williams, who treated himself to a performance of *Porgy and Bess* for his eightieth birthday, more temperately wrote, "We must not make the mistake of thinking lightly of the very characteristic art of Gershwin or, to go further back, the beautiful melodies of Stephen Foster. Great things grow out of small beginnings." And Michael Tippett, who first saw *Porgy and Bess* in 1949 (and who quoted "The Man I Love" in his 1952 opera, *The Midsummer Marriage*), wrote in his 1991 memoirs, "I have since come to revere Gershwin: in an age of experimentation with rhythm, percussive and fragmented textures, Gershwin kept song alive. I sometimes wonder now what might have happened to that irrepressible creative spirit, had he lived on through the Second World War and into Vietnam. After all, he was born only seven years before I was."[9]

Whereas Gershwin's annual trips to London during the period 1923–1926 familiarized him with the British scene, during these same years he spent no time on the Continent aside from two short excursions to Paris in April 1923 and April 1926. However, in the spring of 1928, accompanied by Ira and Leonore, he embarked on an extensive three-and-a-half-month European tour specifically "to benefit my technic as much as possible from a study of European orchestral methods." Gershwin spent most of March and April in London and Paris, late April and early May in Berlin and Vienna, the second half of May in Paris, and early June in London again.[10]

The time in Paris happily coincided with acclaimed premieres of the *Rhapsody* and the Concerto in F, and as the toast of the town, Gershwin had ample opportunity to mingle with a number of composers from France (Georges Auric, Jacques Ibert, Darius Milhaud, Francis Poulenc, and Maurice Ravel), Switzerland (Arthur Honegger), Italy (Vittorio Rieti), Poland (Alexandre Tansman), Russia (Vernon Duke, Sergey Prokofiev, Lazare Saminsky, and Igor Stravinsky), and Cuba (Ernesto Lecuona). Although Gershwin had met a number of these composers before, this trip in many instances afforded him an opportunity to get to know them and their music better.

Gershwin's description of his work in progress, *An American in Paris,* as "in the manner of Debussy and the Six" suggests a particularly strong response to such members of *les Six* as Auric, Honegger, Milhaud, and Poulenc. He already had some acquaintance with their music, including Honegger's *Pacific 231;* in August 1925 he wryly wrote to Pauline Heifetz from Chautauqua that conductor Albert Stoessel, in the midst of his six-week season there with the New York Symphony, "tries occasionally to awaken the populace by playing Stravinsky or Honegger, but the church-loving Americans haven't yet emerged from the magic spell of 'The Rosary' or 'Oh Promise Me.' And they tell him in letters they wish he would be forced to conduct 'Pacific 231,' for example, 231 times in succession before foisting it on them once more."[11]

Now in Paris, he heard a work of Honegger's based on American Indian music, *Le chant de Nigamon* (1917), which Ira described in his diary as "good." He further visited Honegger at his home in Montmartre, telling reporters, with typical detachment, that the composer was "very handsome" and "rather shy," adding, "His head is beautifully formed, his hair dark and curly, and though he is not what would be described as slender, neither is he stout." He also observed Honegger's love of horses and engines "both for themselves and their appearance" and "for their grace and fleetness." Privately discussing a "virtuoso piece" by Honegger probably encountered about this time, Gershwin seemed somewhat ambivalent, telling Vernon Duke, "The European boys have small ideas but they sure know how to dress 'em up." At the same time, Oscar Levant mentioned that Gershwin liked Honegger's operetta *Les aventures du roi Pausole* (1930).[12]

According to Levant, Gershwin also was fond of a recording of a "violin concerto" by Milhaud—presumably the *Concertino de Printemps* for violin and orchestra (1935)—but nothing's known about his reaction to the same composer's jazzy ballet, *The Creation of the World*—surprisingly so, considering its resemblances to his own concert work. First performed in Paris in October 1923 but not played in New York until 1933, the Milhaud ballet in particular prefigured the *Rhapsody in Blue,* unveiled only a few months afterward. The received wisdom presumes that both composers, similarly molded by American jazz and Jewish sensibilities, arrived at their related styles independently, but that, to quote Deborah Mawer, "Milhaud got there first."[13]

In fact, Gershwin beat Milhaud to the punch with such pieces as *Blue Monday Blues* (1922). Moreover, while it's unlikely that Milhaud knew that particular work, he had had some exposure to Gershwin's other music prior to 1923, to the point of providing some percussion accompaniment to pianist Jean Wiéner's playing of Gershwin tunes on the opening night of Paris's Bar Gaya in early 1921. Milhaud even briefly cited "Swanee" in *The Creation of the World*, where the quote, played by the piano and trumpets (at rehearsal 27), seamlessly matches the surrounding material. At the same time, Gershwin possibly heard something of Milhaud's in the months leading up to the *Rhapsody*—perhaps some of the pieces that Milhaud himself performed on his 1922–1923 American tour or perhaps *Man and His Desire,* performed by the Swedish Ballet in New York in November 1923. In any case, Gershwin no doubt would have learned about *The Creation* by the time of his 1928 visit to Paris, and, indeed, certain details in *An American in Paris* (such as the creeping, syncopated chromatic melody at the "Calmato" that follows rehearsal 56) suggest the influence of the Milhaud score.[14]

Meanwhile, *An American in Paris* more explicitly appropriated Poulenc's *Mouvements perpetuels,* a copy of which the French composer inscribed to Gershwin in 1928 ("à George Gershwin, source de mélodie, avec ma cordiale amitié, F. Poulenc"). Perhaps Gershwin absorbed something as well from Poulenc's *Promenades,* also found among his possessions. Poulenc, in turn, cited *An American in Paris* as one of his favorite works of the century.[15]

Gershwin's stay in Paris occasioned encounters with other leading composers, including Sergey Prokofiev (1891–1953), whose Third Piano Concerto (1921) he had come to know and admire. Prokofiev apparently did not attend the May 29 European premiere of the Concerto in F, as Vernon Duke later reported, but he at least met with Gershwin and Duke earlier in the season, on April 8. Perhaps Duke had this April meeting in mind—not one on May 30 as he recollected—when he wrote, "George came and played his head off; Prokofiev liked the tunes and the flavorsome embellishments, but thought little of the concerto (repeated by Gershwin), which, he said later, consisted of 32-bar choruses ineptly bridged together. He thought highly of Gershwin's gifts, both as composer and pianist, however, and predicted that he'd go far should he leave 'dollars and dinners' alone." Duke also remembered Prokofiev saying, "His [Gershwin's] piano playing is full of amusing tricks, but the music is amateurish."[16]

Prokofiev met Gershwin again in 1930, attending (thanks once more to Duke) a reception that followed the January 14 premiere of *Strike Up the Band* (though not the show itself). "The operetta God of America," Prokofiev noted in his journal afterward, "Gershwin also attempts to compose serious music, and sometimes he even does that with a certain flair, but not always successfully." At this reception, he was particularly amused by Morris Gershwin, who spoke to him in fractured Russian while George played his "pyanyi" ("drunken") concerto, and whom Prokofiev described as "a Jew who half-belonged to the intelligentsia." Soon after George's death Prokofiev, who by this time had acquired the vocal score to *Porgy and Bess*, memorialized him as a gifted composer, but one whose involvement with "music of dubious taste" compromised his more serious work. Still, he regretted Gershwin's early death and imagined that had he lived, he "might have spread his wings and soared to great heights" (a presumably intentional reference to "Summertime"). Gershwin at least gave the promise of a "new kind of American music."[17]

In discussing Gershwin and Prokofiev, his "two best and most cherished friends in music," Duke noted certain similarities:

> Both were endowed with exceptional pianistic gifts; both were blessed with a great gift of melody, the essential trademark of every first-rate composer; both appealed strongly to the people's imagination; both had pronounced nationalist traits without a trace of chauvinism. . . . Gershwin was as genuinely American (although of Russian antecedents) as Prokofiev was profoundly Russian; neither practiced the synthetic art of pastiche; neither rationalized, preached or issued grandiloquent advance notices of their own work; both were wonderfully generous with their contemporaries and readily embraced music of a cast entirely foreign to their nature, provided it was recognizable as the work of an authentic musician.

Pianist Barbara Nissman, observing resemblances between Prokofiev's *Toccata* and the finale to Gershwin's Concerto in F, compiled her own list of correspondences, whereas William Austin opined that Prokofiev "was not rightly to be classified with . . . Glazunov or Khachaturian, much less with Lehár or Gershwin."[18]

While in Berlin in 1928, Gershwin met with Kurt Weill (1900–1950)— and apparently Schoenberg—on April 24, and with Franz Lehár (1870– 1948) the following day. Two years his junior, the precocious Weill, fast approaching international fame, had written the jazzy *Mahagonny Songspiel* with Bertolt Brecht in 1927, and would launch his greatest triumph, *The Threepenny Opera*, later in 1928. He possibly first met Gershwin at an informal gathering in which the latter addressed a group of German composers about the American music publishing business.

Weill's wife, Lotte Lenya, recalled that Gershwin also called on them at home, while according to Ira Gershwin's travel diary, Weill visited Gershwin at his hotel as well.[19]

Lenya stated that she and her husband knew nothing about Gershwin at the time, but it would have been difficult for Weill to have escaped the hoopla surrounding the Berlin premiere of the *Rhapsody* by the Paul Whiteman Orchestra at the Grosses Schauspielhaus in 1926. He might have known some of the show music as well, for Harms's German affiliates published some vocal selections in translation in the mid-1920s. At the same time, Gershwin himself bemoaned the lack of interest in American musicals in Berlin, citing German antipathy toward anything "light or extreme" and further observing, "Juveniles with good voices in Germany are usually very fat, and those that are handsome and slender have bad voices." At any rate, according to one expert, the jazzy works of Weill and Krenek from the 1920s drew less on Gershwin and his contemporaries than on American popular music of an earlier era.[20]

After the Weills immigrated to the States in 1935, they occasionally socialized with George and Ira. At one such meeting at his Manhattan apartment, Gershwin mentioned that he liked the recording (1930) of *The Threepenny Opera,* except for the leading lady's "squitchadickeh" voice, not realizing that the voice in question belonged to Lenya, who reportedly never forgave him for the remark; Gershwin later tried extricating himself by likening her to a "hillbilly singer," but that may have just added insult to injury. Weill himself developed a contemptuous attitude toward Gershwin. After attending a reception at Gershwin's Beverly Hills home following an all-Gershwin concert, he wrote to Lenya, "The Gershwin party was 'Hollywood at its worst.' There was a bar with Javanese hula-hula girls, another one with American whores, and one jazz and one Russian orchestra, both of which couldn't play because Gershwin insisted on playing his own compositions again, although everybody (except me) already had an entire Gershwin concert behind them" (that he hadn't attended the concert might explain why the "whole Gershwin clan" was "very cool" toward him). On leaving, he at least took satisfaction that the Gershwins saw his "slick" new car. "You should have seen their eyes pop out," he wrote to Lenya. "That made it worth the trouble."[21]

In his correspondence with Lenya, Weill further described Gershwin as "a nebbish" and "stupid," and stated, on the occasion of a Los Angeles performance of his own *Lindbergh Flight,* "Gershwin behaved obnoxiously, but this bumpkin is just too dumb even to bother with." Some commentators have attributed such allegedly "erratic" behavior on Gershwin's part to his declining health, but Weill's scorn might sooner be explained by a sense of professional rivalry: "Gershwin seems to be shitting in his pants because of me," he wrote to Lenya in March 1937. Weill nonetheless admired *Porgy and Bess* as soon as he heard it in 1935, seven years later deeming its songs "still magnificent," even if the rest of the score was "pretty bad." Especially as revised by Cheryl Crawford, the opera served as a model for Weill's own tenement opera, *Street Scene* (1947), and—at least in its prominent use of a black chorus—his musical *Lost in the Stars* (1949, after the novel *Cry, the Beloved Country*). John O'Hara further detected Gershwin's influence on Weill's greatest Broadway success, *Lady in the Dark* (1941), for which Ira provided the lyrics.[22]

Conversely, Donald Jay Grout viewed Weill's work of the 1920s as "the inspiration of many modern American operatic works of a socially critical, satirical, or topical nature," including Gershwin's *Of Thee I Sing* (though the latter's antiwar satire, *Strike Up the Band*, actually preceded *The Threepenny Opera* by a year). Indeed, certain passages in Gershwin's late musical comedies—such as the verse to the title song from *Let 'Em Eat Cake* (1933)—seemed reminiscent of Weill. Hans Keller, meanwhile, discerned a fundamental similarity between both men's work: "Like Gershwin's, Weill's songs create new forms out of eclectic material whose elements of jazz, Blues and cabaret idiom make it easy for the insensitive listener to mistake the style for the stuff. As soon as the stuff is understood, however, the style itself discloses its originality and homogeneity."[23]

During his 1928 stay in Vienna, Gershwin lunched again with Lehár, met playwright Ferenc Molnár, and enjoyed the company of Emmerich Kálmán, as discussed above. On April 29 he and Ira attended Ernst Krenek's jazzy new opera, *Jonny spielt auf* (1927), whose familiar American title, *Johnny Strikes Up the Band*, evoked their own *Strike Up the Band* of the same year. "It was certainly worth seeing if only for its novelty," Gershwin stated. "It was put on like a revue—prodigious and picturesque" (Ira, for his part, liked the music "here and there"). Krenek (1900–1991) was first introduced to the music of Gershwin, along with that of Irving Berlin and Vincent Youmans, by pianist Artur Schnabel in 1921.[24]

Gershwin and his friend Josepha Rosanska also visited Alban Berg at the latter's home on the evening of May 5. Gershwin, who had just heard Rosanska perform Berg's piano sonata in Berlin, showed uncustomary reticence when asked to play for the Austrian composer, but Berg encouraged him, saying, "Music is music." "George big hit with Berg," wrote Ira in his journal, "even Josie impressed." Two days later, Gershwin heard the Kolisch Quartet play Berg's recent *Lyric Suite* (1926) at the home of the quartet's first violinist, Rudolf Kolisch, who was Rosanska's husband as well as Schoenberg's brother-in-law. Gershwin was so taken with the work that he subsequently "went all over Europe talking about Berg."[25]

Returning home with a copy of the *Lyric Suite* and a photograph of Berg inscribed with a quotation from the work, Gershwin deemed his time with Berg "one of the high spots of my visit" and hoped to interest Americans, including Stokowski, in the composer. "Although this quartet is dissonant to the extent of proving disagreeable to the average music-lover's consonant-trained ear," he said of the *Suite*, "it seems to me the work has genuine merit. Its conception and treatment are thoroughly modern in the best sense of the word." Gershwin later acquired the Galimir Quartet's recording of the piece, as well as a "treasured" vocal score to *Wozzeck*, whose 1931 American premiere in Philadelphia under Stokowski left him "thrilled" and "deeply impressed." Encountering Gershwin at this performance, Marc Blitzstein recalled his "grinning" reaction to the opera: "'S wonderful! Wonderful!"[26]

"As Gershwin grew toward complexity," observed Michael Tilson Thomas in this context, "Berg's process was one of greater and greater simplification. It's interesting that they both died at such a young age. If they had lived, I think they would have arrived at a similar style." Allen Forte offered his own "Reflections upon the Gershwin-Berg Connection," speculating that resemblances of harmonic style attracted Gershwin to Berg and suggesting ways in which the *Lyric Suite* and *Wozzeck* possibly influenced Gershwin's later work, including the use of the octatonic scale, though he admitted that Debussy and Stravinsky may have been just as influential in this regard. Discussing some striking parallels between *Wozzeck* and *Porgy and Bess*, Christopher Reynolds further surmised that in the latter work, Gershwin absorbed Berg's "approach to scene construction," including "techniques of unification across great stretches of time" and "even details of counterpoint and rhythm."[27]

Gershwin made additional discoveries in his later years. In 1929 he acquired the score to Alfredo Casella's *Serenata* for five instruments, inscribed by the composer "with admiration and friendship." And he grew partial to a certain string quartet by Paul Hindemith, telling a friend, "I'm the only one in the gang that likes it." He and Levant explored various other scores at the piano, including a Manuel de Falla piece that elicited, "with a slight touch of disparagement," Gershwin's comment, "He's a kind of Spanish Gershwin."[28]

Moreover, on vacation in Havana in 1932, Gershwin renewed his acquaintance with Ernesto Lecuona (1895–1963), whom he had met on June 2, 1928, at the Salle Gaveau in Paris before a gathering that also included Ravel and Varèse (Lecuona presumably played some of his music on this occasion, perhaps including his popular *Malagueña*). Known as "the Gershwin of Cuba," Lecuona periodically performed the *Rhapsody* (a piece that would inspire his own *Rapsodia Negra* for piano and orchestra of 1937), including a 1928 Havana premiere of the work with the Havana Symphony Orchestra under composer-conductor Gonzalo Roig (1890–1970). Andrew Lamb surmises that during the same visit to Havana, Gershwin also met Roig and yet another famed Cuban musician, Amadeo Roldán (1900–1939), if not Alejandro García Caturla (1906–1940), who, like Lecuona, championed the *Rhapsody* in Cuba, but mostly in Remedios. When Gershwin traveled to Mexico in 1935, he similarly spent some time with that country's foremost composer, Carlos Chávez.[29]

As indicated by Merle Armitage, Gershwin also had some familiarity with the music of Béla Bartók, whom he met in New York in 1928. Had he lived to witness Bartók's immigration to the States in 1940, he might well have sought out his guidance, and perhaps made the Hungarian's new life in America more welcoming. In the last volume of his *Mikrokosmos,* published in 1940, Bartók paid Gershwin superb homage in the fourth of his *Six Dances in Bulgarian Rhythm,* which he described as "Very much in the style of Gershwin. Gershwin's tonality, rhythm, and color. American folk song feeling. Moderate tempo but vital, crisp, and accented." Marjory Irvin also discerned a connection between Gershwin and the last of these dances. As Bartók's tastes ran to folk music on the one hand and art music on the other, he presumably thought of Gershwin not so much in the context of popular urban music, which he disdained, but as the composer of a characteristic art music, like Stravinsky and Falla.[30]

Gershwin developed, too, an appreciation of Shostakovich's First Symphony, and he regretted having to miss the 1935 New York premiere of that composer's *Lady Macbeth of Mtsensk,* which Ira attended with Vernon Duke. (Ira, who liked the opera—even if Stravinsky, whom he met during intermission, didn't—wrote to George, "Strangely enough, it reminded me in spots of 'Porgy,' not the music, of course, but the treatment—and definitely of 'Of Thee I Sing' in two scenes.") For his part, Shostakovich, who attended a makeshift performance of the "magnificent" *Porgy and Bess* by the Stanislavsky Players under the direction of Aleksandr Khessin in 1945, deemed the opera a worthy descendant of Borodin and Mussorgsky. In 1954, he further cited Gershwin as the American composer who interested him most.[31]

Many leading foreign and émigré composers, attracted to the charm, vitality, and originality of Gershwin's music, clearly took him more seriously than one might suppose. This sympathetic group included Serge Rakhmaninov (1873–1943), who assiduously attended his performances— a keen interest that has been largely overlooked by most commentators, even if a few have suspected Gershwin's influence on such late works as the Fourth Piano Concerto (1927).

Meanwhile, Gershwin knew more about his own country's composers than he generally made known. Beginning in his youth, when he heard with some regularity the work of Edward MacDowell (1860–1908), he encountered a wide range of American music at concerts, eventually including those sponsored by the International Composers' Guild. He also had some awareness of the Copland-Sessions concerts and possibly attended at least the two (on February 24, 1929, and February 9, 1930) that included his friend Vernon Duke's music. Moreover, he apparently subscribed to Henry Cowell's *New Music Quarterly,* and in 1930 requested as well that Isaac Goldberg tell him "about any new music" played by the Boston Symphony.[32]

In 1929 Gershwin published his most extensive statement on the subject, "Fifty Years of American Music":

> American music means to me something very specific, something very tangible. It is something indigenous, something autochthonous, something deeply rooted in our soil. It is music which must express the feverish tempo of American life. It must express the unique life we lead here—a life of weary activity—and our groping and vain ideals. It must be a voice of the masses, a voice expressing our masses and at the same time immortalizing their strivings. In our music we must be able to catch a glimpse of our skyscrapers, to feel that overwhelming burst of energy which is bottled in our life, to hear that chaos of noises which suffuses the air of our modern American city. This, I feel, must be in every American.

The "profuse and sentimental outpourings" of Charles Wakefield Cadman, Reginald De Koven, Edward Burlingame Hill, and Ethelbert Nevin accordingly constituted "neither American music nor good music and so we may dismiss their efforts with a wave of the hand." And although MacDowell represented America's "first important musical voice," his

music, "a pale shadow of Brahms, an echo of Brahms's intense and hy-
per-sensitive emotion," could not be considered American music either.
The attempt to build a national school on American Indian music was
likewise doomed to fail, as the "pale and fragile tenderness of Indian music can no more express the fret and chaos of our modern American life
than can the music of Brahms or Schubert." Gershwin accorded greater
credit to Rubin Goldmark, who recognized the importance of the Negro spiritual, even if his *Negro Rhapsody* (1922) "seems to be pretty
feeble stuff." "Real American music" began rather with Irving Berlin's
"Alexander's Ragtime Band."[33]

This article further singled out four contemporary composers (all Jewish, incidentally) for praise: Leo Ornstein, the author of "some really felicitous music" ("There is a remarkable force to all of Ornstein's music—
a burst of energy, a frenzy and a passion which are ever refreshing to the
tired musical ear"); Ernest Bloch, whose "sublime" *America* (1926) possesses "a grandeur, a breadth, a healthy vigor" that seems to capture the
"nympholepsy" of the country's pioneers and early statesmen; and Louis
Gruenberg and Aaron Copland, authors of "highly agreeable" jazz-in-
spired music distinguished by "lyrical" melodies and "decorated with
ever original and striking harmonies." However, these "consummate musicians" also have "failed in their attempts at American music" because,
as composers trained abroad, their efforts have been "diluted" by European traditions, Ornstein and Bloch by Brahms and Richard Strauss,
Copland by Stravinsky and Schoenberg. "Fortunately," he stated, "neither Irving Berlin nor I were taught by European masters—and so we
were the free men whereas all others were slaves." Not that he had yet
achieved his aims in his concert works, he more modestly conceded. "But
I shall certainly continue in that direction. And if I do not succeed myself, I shall be happy, indeed, if I know that at least my efforts have inspired other composers to continue with this monumental labor."

Although this essay only cursorily mentioned John Alden Carpenter
(1876–1951) as "the composer of that intriguing jazz-ballet, *Skyscrapers,*" in an article published two years later, Gershwin more explicitly
praised *Skyscrapers* (1924), along with Werner Janssen's *New Year's Eve*
(1928), as "outstanding" American compositions: "Jazz pieces like 'Skyscrapers' and 'New Year's Eve' are proof that music may have the so-
called jazz quality and yet exercise an intellectual as well as musical appeal for the most sophisticated." Carpenter's absorption of ragtime and
popular song in such pieces as the *Concertino* for piano and orchestra
(1915) and the ballet *Krazy Kat* (1921) at the very least prefigured Gersh-

win's own work. Indeed, Gershwin's name was routinely linked with Carpenter's during the 1920s; theirs was also the only concert music included by W. C. Handy in his 1926 blues anthology. Carpenter, who attended the Chicago premiere of *Porgy and Bess* in 1936, plainly held Gershwin in high esteem, if not quite to the level of Irving Berlin.[34]

Gershwin otherwise rarely discussed American art music. One wonders what he thought, for instance, of William Grant Still (1895–1978), a black contemporary whose *Afro-American Symphony* (1930), more than most American musics, anticipated *Porgy and Bess*. Verna Arvey, Still's wife, at least remembered that Gershwin attended the premiere of her husband's *Levee Land* (1925) at a concert of the International Composers' Guild on January 24, 1926, at Aeolian Hall. For his part, Still appreciated *Porgy and Bess* from the first ("I felt all along that Gershwin would achieve splendid results," he wrote to Irving Schwerké in October 1935); and even though in later years he expressed greater ambivalence ("white imitations of Negro music will always be superficial," he wrote in 1944 with *Porgy* partly in mind), he respected Gershwin for acknowledging his indebtedness to black sources.[35]

Gershwin's general disposition—as in his association with Cowell—at least implied a special regard for some of America's more adventurous composers. Indeed, about 1934 he attempted to contact Charles Ives—a great maverick, though still relatively unknown—and told some intermediaries, including Ives's binder and an employee at his insurance firm, that he had long admired the composer, that Ives's *Concord Sonata* and songs (presumably the *114 Songs,* published, like the *Concord,* in the early 1920s at Ives's expense) had been an inspiration to him, and that, as Ives noted in his memos, "he had gotten more out of my music than of any other especially new chords and new rhythms and that he wants to ask about more copies etc." Ives further recalled that Gershwin attended the January 29, 1927, Town Hall performance of the first two movements of his Fourth Symphony by members of the New York Philharmonic under Eugene Goossens. But despite being provided with Gershwin's address and telephone number, he never responded to the younger man's inquiries.[36]

Gershwin took an interest as well in the microtonal endeavors of Hans Barth (1897–1956), the German-born pianist-composer (best remembered for his association with Ives) who attracted considerable attention in the late 1920s and early 1930s for his performances on his own quarter-tone piano (patented in 1931), including a solo recital at Carnegie Hall on February 23, 1930, and a performance of his concerto for quarter-tone piano and strings with Stokowski and the Philadelphia Orchestra on March 28 of the same year. Reviewing his February 23 recital, the *New York Times* marveled at the "whole new world of shadowy effects, pungent and mordant" revealed by Barth's quarter-tone piano, which contained two eighty-eight-note keyboards tuned a quarter-tone apart. In preparation for a Carnegie Hall concert still later in the year, on December 13, 1930, Barth collaborated with Gershwin on a quarter-tone version of the second of the *Three Preludes*.[37]

Gershwin also attended the February 20, 1934, premiere of Virgil Thomson's opera *Four Saints in Three Acts* (libretto, Gertrude Stein) on Broadway, with an all-black cast, similar to his own forthcoming *Porgy and Bess*. "The libretto was entirely in Stein's manner," wrote Gershwin to his own librettist, DuBose Heyward, on February 26, "which means that it has the effect of a 5-year-old prattling on. Musically, it sounded early 19th Century, which was a happy inspiration and made the libretto bearable—in fact, quite entertaining. There may be one or two in the cast that would be useful to us." Another source reported that he thought the opera as "refreshing as a new dessert."[38]

Meanwhile, Oscar Levant facilitated some contact between Copland and Gershwin, who invited the former to a party in 1932, even if the two, as Copland recalled, had "nothing to say to each other." Gershwin may well have revised his opinion of Copland, as expressed above, on the basis of a radio broadcast of the latter's children's opera, *The Second Hurricane* (1937), whose first performance he had helped sponsor; indeed, he liked the work well enough to want a copy of the score, on whose strength he supported Copland's membership into ASCAP.[39]

Although Gershwin fraternized with Copland and other American composers, he counted only a few as friends, including Vernon Duke (1903–1969), Charles Martin Loeffler (1861–1935), Oscar Levant (1906–1972), Alexander Steinert (1900–1982), and George Antheil (1900–1959).

Vernon Duke (born Vladimir Dukelsky, near Pskov) studied with Reyngol'd Glier at the Kiev Conservatory. He left Communist Russia via Constantinople, where an encounter with "Swanee" in 1920 sent him into "ecstasies" and made him an "'early-jazz' fiend" (that such music, as he later learned, was not really jazz did not dampen his enthusiasm; on the contrary, he found in Gershwin's music a "composer's inventiveness . . . missing from the 'real' thing, largely a collectively produced mood, anonymous and crude"). On arrival in New York in 1922, he met Gershwin, and the two were soon "inseparable." After he played, by his own admission, "an extremely cerebral piano sonata" for Gershwin, the latter told him, "There's no money in that kind of stuff, and no heart in it, either. Try to write some real popular tunes—and don't be scared about going low-brow. They will open you up."[40]

Duke's subsequent efforts at lighter music—eventually including "April in Paris" (1932) and "Autumn in New York" (1935)—impressed Gershwin, who introduced him to his publisher, Max Dreyfus, and occasionally lent him money. In 1924 Gershwin also hired Duke to arrange the *Rhapsody in Blue* for solo piano and to assist him on that year's *Scandals* by composing some of its incidental music and preparing some of its songs for publication. "He is just as handsome (and opinionated) as ever," George wrote to Ira in 1926 after visiting Duke in Paris, where the latter had temporarily settled and written a successful ballet, *Zéphyr et Flore* (1925), for the Ballets Russes. Before returning to New York in 1929, Duke agreed, at Boris Asafiev's suggestion, to translate some of Gershwin's musicals into Russian, feeling "that no better anti-Soviet propaganda could be imagined than a big, healthy dose of Gershwin music, and the good American things it stands for," though he got no further than composing Russian lyrics for "Fascinating Rhythm" and "Oh, Lady, Be Good!" Back in New York, he began writing for the Broadway stage—including the *Ziegfeld Follies of 1936* (with Ira) and *Cabin in the Sky* (1940)—under a name suggested by Gershwin, Vernon Duke (eventually adopted for all his works). In his 1955 memoir, *Passport to Paris*, Duke chronicled his friendship with Gershwin, while his 1963 survey of American music *Listen Here!* deemed the premiere of *Rhapsody in Blue* the day "American music came to life—although it would be foolish to claim, as some do, that it came of age."[41]

Nearly forty years Gershwin's senior, German-born Charles Martin Loeffler had studied composition and violin in Berlin and Paris before immigrating to the States in 1881. After almost two decades as a violinist with the Boston Symphony, he resigned in 1903 to devote himself full-time to composition, and moved in 1910 to a farmhouse in Medfield, Massachusetts. Deeply influenced by Debussy, Loeffler proved one of the most sophisticated American composers of his generation. In the 1920s, he also became a jazz enthusiast—"Duke Ellington's trumpeters could throw Loeffler into pardonable ecstasies," wrote Carl Engel—and he toyed with the idiom himself.[42]

For Loeffler, meeting Gershwin and hearing him play and sing some of his music at a party hosted by his former student, Kay Swift, in April 1927 was "a revelation." In a letter to Swift soon after, he praised Gershwin "for his unusual gifts which often touch on genius, and for that rare something indefinably lovable in the man." Gershwin, in turn, was "thrilled" to meet Loeffler. In 1928, Loeffler attended the premiere of *An American in Paris* in Gershwin's box at the composer's invitation. He also attended rehearsals and performances of Gershwin's shows as they came through Boston, as well as two performances of *Girl Crazy* in New York.[43]

In addition, Loeffler wrote Gershwin warmly supportive letters. In one 1927 exchange, he compared Gershwin to such composers as George Antheil and Aaron Copland:

> It is needless to say, that I have pinned my faith on your delightful genius and on your future. You alone seem to express charm, grace and invention amongst the composers of our time. When the Anthland[s] and Coptheils ed tutti quanti will be forgotten, and Janitors, Chorewomen, Dead-heads and Press-reporters no longer will have to sit up (on their la-bemols) at the formers [*sic*] musical antics, you, my dear friend, will be recorded in the Anthologies of coming ages!

And in 1928 he wrote, "There is something Mozartean about your stuff, something beautifully personal and frightfully simple. . . . Your brother Ira has some of a similar quality in him. Dieu Merci, for the two of you!" Of *Girl Crazy,* he stated, "It was a great delight—in the Mozartean sense—to me; it had much charm and amusement in the Debussyan sense (vide. his articles on the mission of Music to be 'amusante')."[44]

Gershwin sent Loeffler scores to his Concerto in F and *An American in Paris* (the latter inscribed "to my dear friend, Charles Martin Loeffler, in greatest admiration & affection"), along with a copy of Isaac Goldberg's 1931 biography, which elicited this response: "If *I* had written it (the book) I dare say the account of you personally, and of your great musical charm and gifts would have been more glowing—but some day I shall take up this matter of writing your portrait; followed by a choice analysis of the essence of your delightful music and genius." Loeffler also offered Gershwin some professional advice, recommending d'Indy, for instance, as a possible teacher of orchestration.[45]

Oscar Levant, a student of pianist Zygmunt Stojowski, came under Gershwin's spell before meeting him, when about age twelve he heard the composer onstage, as discussed earlier. In 1925, as Levant began to establish himself as a preeminent interpreter of the *Rhapsody,* he made his way into the Paley circle (via another Gershwin acolyte, Phil Charig), though he did not establish a close friendship with Gershwin till about 1930. At the Paleys', he sometimes played Gershwin's music when the composer was not around to do so himself, "brilliantly," as Duke recalled, "although with a certain caustic dryness, robbing George's tunes and piano pieces of their romantic lushness." (One 1932 newspaper review similarly thought that Gershwin possessed a "considerably more agreeable" tone than Levant, who conceded that the composer's recording of the *Rhapsody* was superior to his own.) [46]

Like Duke, Levant assisted Gershwin in various musical chores and served as a conduit to the serious musical community, including his two primary mentors, Arnold Schoenberg and Aaron Copland. However, Levant, who similarly wrote for both the concert stage and Broadway, enjoyed less success as a composer than did Duke, let alone Gershwin, who seemed rather cool toward Levant's popular and serious efforts alike. In any case, aside from his career as a Hollywood character actor, Levant became known largely as Gershwin's interpreter and sidekick, playing himself as such in the 1945 film biography. In the chapter "My Life or The Story of George Gershwin" from his 1940 memoir, he even blamed Gershwin, with typically self-deprecating humor, for his own reduction "from industry to inertia," explaining, "I got so much, vicariously, out of his ability and creativeness that whatever latent talents I had were completely submerged."[47]

Such feelings helped fuel a "small element of nastiness" in their friendship, "a fondness for putting the blast on each other" (they quarreled "all the time," stated Levant), which yielded some prized Gershwin anecdotes. Sharing a drawing room on an overnight train, Gershwin, wrote Levant, assumed "with a proprietary air" the lower berth, murmuring later that night, "Upper berth—lower berth. That's the difference between talent and genius." Levant had his revenge later when at a party, after observing Gershwin talk about himself to a mesmerized audience "absorbed with the fascinated attentiveness of a Storm-trooper listening to one of Hitler's well-modulated firehouse chats," asked, "Tell me, George, if you had to do it all over, would you fall in love with yourself again?" After Gershwin's death, Levant, who remained close friends with Ira and Leonore, composed a *Suite for Orchestra* (1937–1938), whose slow movement, "Dirge," he dedicated to Gershwin's memory. And his two published memoirs—*A Smattering of Ignorance* (1940) and *The Memoirs of an Amnesiac* (1965)—provided a wealth of information about Gershwin, though colored by the author's mordant wit.[48]

Gershwin befriended Alexander Steinert only toward the end of his life, after the two met at a January 1935 reception for Stravinsky. Aware of Steinert's reputation and abilities as a vocal coach, Gershwin asked him if he would help prepare the premiere of *Porgy and Bess*. Steinert not only did so, but subsequently conducted the work on tour and in revival. In the process, he developed a friendship with Gershwin that became "one of the most inspiring" of his life, singling out, among Gershwin's other qualities, "his complete belief in what he was doing. . . . He knew he had something to say, and he said it."[49]

The descendant of a Boston family of piano manufacturers, Steinert graduated from Harvard in 1922, after which he studied privately with Loeffler in Boston, and with Koechlin, d'Indy, and Gédalge in Paris. His music, which won him a 1927 Prix de Rome, was admired in its time for its elegance and craft. Gershwin showed some characteristic ambivalence toward Steinert's music, at least as suggested by Levant's recollection of a posh 1936 reception in which out of "sheer politeness" Gershwin "finally suggested that Steinert play something of his own, in the confident belief that the surroundings and his own abashment would dissuade him. However, Steinert responded with the whole of a piano concerto by himself, which George slightly resented as an excess of acquiescence."[50]

Gershwin established cordial ties as well with George Antheil, who, though set in opposition to him by Loeffler, advocated on Gershwin's behalf—at least after the latter's death. During most of the 1920s, Antheil lived in Berlin and Paris, where he gained notoriety for his machine-inspired music, such as the *Airplane Sonata* for piano (1922) and *Ballet mécanique* (1923–1925), scored for an unusual percussion ensemble that included propellers and a siren. Engaged during these years with popular music styles as well, he initially deemed Gershwin's *Rhapsody* "a very mediocre piece" and hoped that his own *Jazz Symphony* (1925) would "put Gershwin in the shade."[51]

Antheil met Gershwin, whom he later described as "an intensely interesting and prepossessing personality," in April 1926 in Paris at the home of Mabel and Robert Schirmer, who were friends of his wife, Boski Markus. At this gathering, Gershwin played his concerto and Antheil demonstrated some of the soon-to-be-premiered *Ballet mécanique* (an encounter that presumably inspired Gershwin's public dismissal, a few months later, of "those compositions of the Dada school, which employ the instrumentation of electric fans or couple fifty synchronized pianos in a riot of noisy cacophony" as "merely delirium"). The two became reacquainted after Antheil returned to the States in 1931. In 1937 Antheil eulogized Gershwin as "one of the greatest American composers of all time" and the *Rhapsody* as "a marvelously flamboyant piece full of breath-taking Americana."[52]

This 1937 tribute helped popularize the dubious idea that Gershwin was spurned by America's serious composers: "George Gershwin has been recognized by everybody except those whose admiration and understanding he most craved—the American Composer. The admiration of the Coplands, the Sessions, the Thomsons, the Jacobies, and the rest of this special contemporaneous group which undoubtedly contains the very best of American creative musical talent. I do not know why George craved this, for he certainly never needed their admiration, but he was hurt by their misunderstandings of his work, and their frequent criticisms wounded him." In view of Antheil's earlier description of the *Rhapsody* as "mediocre" and his references even here to the composer's "occasional crudities" and lack of "a certain amount of technical skill," his indignation arguably said more about his own disenchantment than it did about Gershwin's reputation in his own time. That Antheil projected his own feelings might be inferred further from a letter Gershwin wrote to him in 1936: "It was very kind of you to write me telling me that you liked my opera. I also appreciate your antagonism towards the snobberies of our high-hat confreres." In any case, virtually no evidence supports the notion that the critiques of colleagues "hurt" or "wounded" Gershwin. On the contrary, he maintained an attitude about negative criticism that his sister, Frances, described as "Maybe there's something to it. I'll have to try it out and see for myself."[53]

Moreover, Gershwin's music was, in fact, highly regarded by many prominent American composers, particularly among such relatively conservative artists as Marion Bauer, Walter Damrosch, Ferde Grofé, Henry Hadley, Howard Hanson, E. B. Hill, Douglas Moore, Deems Taylor, and others already mentioned, such as Carpenter, Loeffler, and Still. For instance, Moore (1893–1969), at the start of his own outstanding operatic career, wrote to Gershwin after seeing *Porgy and Bess* in early 1936, "It is a magnificent work full of stimulating musical ideas, and beautifully realized. I don't know when I have heard so much American music at one time that seemed to be of such a consistently high quality." But more modernist composers admired Gershwin as well, including the said Aaron Copland, Roger Sessions, Virgil Thomson, and Frederick Jacobi. And if many of the latter composers entertained some reservations along the lines of Antheil himself, they generally stood impressed with Gershwin and their quibbles were not unlike the sort they leveled at one another.[54]

Copland, for example, included Gershwin along with Antheil, Sessions, and Roy Harris in a 1927 lecture on four promising young American composers, and performed his piano music along with that of Sessions, Harris, Chávez, and his own at a 1929 lecture-recital. Someone further recalled hearing him say "many nice things" about Gershwin in his classes at the New School in the late 1920s. According to David Diamond, Copland did not share the view that Gershwin's work lacked aptitude—he especially admired in this respect, as Diamond recalled, the *Variations on "I Got Rhythm"*—and was not surprised by Boulanger's decision against accepting a student so fully formed. And although Copland began incorporating aspects of jazz into his concert work largely independently of Gershwin, some of his music from the mid-1920s especially—such as the Piano Concerto and the *Two Pieces* for violin and piano (both 1926)—intimated a rather direct response to Gershwin's work. At the same time, Copland observed, like Antheil, "various technical deficiencies" in Gershwin's music, and delimited his achievement by deeming him "the best composer of light music that America has yet had," as "serious up to a point."[55]

Admittedly, many of America's more daring composers preferred Copland to Gershwin, as Carol Oja has shown. And a number of colleagues of all stripes could be condescending. But it was hard for even Gershwin's most exacting or envious rivals not to hold him in some esteem. And as concerned his work in musical comedy, composers—even more than the general public—widely considered him peerless.[56]

For his part, Gershwin, although he kept abreast of serious American music and enjoyed some friendly interaction with a number of composers, did not cultivate the sort of solidarity found among those circles associated with Varèse and Cowell or Copland and Sessions. His greatest affinity and loyalty were always to Broadway's composers, including those, like Duke and Levant, who were like himself active in more serious realms as well. If he remained at the periphery of the American new-music concert scene, he did so at least in part intentionally.

Chapter Nine

Gershwin and Popular Music and Jazz after 1920

$\mathcal{W}$hereas Gershwin stood somewhat apart from his more serious colleagues, from the mid-1920s to the end of his life he reigned as Broadway's indispensably central composer, the epicenter of a circle that included composers Milton Ager, Harold Arlen, Irving Berlin, Rube Bloom, Hoagy Carmichael, Phil Charig, Vernon Duke, Johnny Green, Jerome Kern, Burton Lane, Oscar Levant, Cole Porter, Richard Rodgers, Ann Ronell, Harry Ruby, Arthur Schwartz, Kay Swift, Dana Suesse, Harry Warren, and Vincent Youmans, along with lyricists Irving Caesar, Buddy DeSylva, Howard Dietz, and Yip Harburg.

Popular composers and lyricists flocked to George and Ira in part because of the sympathetic interest they showed toward colleagues. "George was very keen about the progress of the entertainment world," wrote Fred Astaire. "He was always impressed by the growing numbers of talented new young people and their ideas." Harold Arlen commented, "It will come as a surprise to many who know . . . the man's excitement over his own work and his enthusiastic appreciation of every contribution he had to make, to learn that he also had a very eager enthusiasm and wholehearted appreciation for what a great many of us were writing." "I never saw a composer who cared that much about everybody else's music," confirmed Kay Swift. After playing some of his songs for Gershwin in 1925, Arthur Schwartz (1900–1984)—the composer of *The Band Wagon* (1931)—remembered the former's reaction as "the warmest, most encouraging I had yet received." The composer of *Finian's Rainbow* (1947), Burton Lane (born Levy, 1912–1997), similarly recalled the interest the older composer took in his music after the two met in 1929, how they would play Lane's latest tunes together at two pianos, and how Gershwin encouraged him to pursue his music studies.[1]

Gershwin further assisted his songwriting friends by introducing them to lyricists, publishers, and producers, and by sometimes finding work for them as arrangers or rehearsal pianists. He also offered guidance in professional matters, even down to christening Duke and Ronell with their pen names. When composers played their material for him, he balanced enthusiastic support with detached candor, sometimes aiding in a technical difficulty. On one occasion, he helped Hoagy Carmichael complete a song by suggesting a chord progression that the latter had been "looking for all month."[2]

In 1980 Yip Harburg elaborated on the importance that such social interactions, under Gershwin's stewardship, held for popular music during this period:

> All the songwriters got together regularly at the Gershwins in the twenties and thirties. Something like Fleet Street in Samuel Johnson's time—an artistic community where people took fire from each other. We'd hang around George's piano, playing our latest songs to see how they went over with the boys. We were all interested in what the other fellas were up to; we criticized and helped each other. There was great respect for each other's work and the integrity of our own music and lyrics. Sometimes, we would hear a whole great score before a show opened, a new Gershwin show, or Rodgers and Hart. We ate it up, analyzed it, played it over and over. You wouldn't dare write a bad rhyme or a clichéd phrase or an unoriginal or remotely plagiarized tune, because you were afraid of being ripped apart by your peers. This continuous give-and-take added to the creative impulse. It worked as incentive, opened up new ideas, made it necessary to keep working and evolving.
>
> Everyone you could imagine came to the Gershwin parties on weekends, not only songwriters, but all kinds of people—performers, critics, actors, novelists, choreographers—the likes of Moss Hart, Oscar Levant, Harpo Marx. Wherever the Gershwins happened to be living, whether on Riverside Drive or in Beverly Hills, when we all went out west writing for the movies, their house was always crammed with creative people. Those were exciting, inspiring days.

Kay Swift noted that Gershwin's piano playing itself served as a stimulus: "I've known people who rushed away from his playing and painted or rushed away and composed or whatever it was. It made one feel stimulated to go on working."[3]

Gershwin's music likewise influenced his colleagues. "When I met him [Gershwin]," recalled Vernon Duke, "he was leading the American popular composers away from the light operatic genre of Offenbach, Sullivan, Herbert and Kern into a field accentuated by new rhythms. He was also discrediting the old theory that a score should contain two hits and so much incidental music. George lavished care on everything he wrote." Burton Lane—who remembered being "lifted out of my seat" by the originality of Gershwin's shows—placed this shift away from operetta not so much in the context of new rhythms, but more generally in terms of the music's inherent humor, which inspired Lane to try to "get humor" into his music as well.[4]

Gershwin's influence on popular music spread beyond national boundaries, most immediately to England. Billy Mayerl (1902–1959), for instance, who probably met Gershwin on the composer's first trip to England in 1923 and who performed the latter's music onstage in the 1927 revue *Shake Your Feet,* became a devotee, as suggested not only by his jazzy piano pieces but by his strong reaction to the news of Gershwin's death, which left him "weeping copiously." And Noël Coward (1899–1973), who heard Gershwin play the *Rhapsody* at Jules Glaenzer's in 1924, liked the music so much he decided to use some of it in his play *The Vortex* (1924). "I sit down to listen to it a normal healthy Englishman," wrote Coward to Gershwin about the piece, "and by the time the second half is over I could fling myself into the wildest ecstasies of emotional degeneracy. Please be careful what you write in [the] future or I won't be answerable for the consequences!" Gershwin, in turn, admired Coward's work. While in London in March 1928, he attended two nights in a row the Coward revue *This Year of Grace,* which included the hit song "A Room with a View." "Noel Coward's lyrics, of course, are bright and sophisticated," George stated some months later. "You know who Noel Coward is, of course. He's the actor-author who takes a bow everytime he is hissed."[5]

Among American songwriters, Gershwin developed a special interest in Vincent Youmans (1898–1946), his junior by one day (they accordingly took to calling each other "Old Man" and "Junior"). Their careers followed a similar trajectory, from cutting rolls for Aeolian and plugging songs for Remick to rehearsing Broadway shows and securing a contract with Harms. Moreover, about the same time that Gershwin established his international fame with the *Rhapsody* (1924), Youmans scored a worldwide triumph with *No, No, Nanette* (1925), which included "Tea for Two" and "I Want to Be Happy." Like other observers, Ethan Mordden viewed Youmans as a "second Gershwin," noting that "the two had in common a taste for advanced harmony and rhythmic dexterity that distinguished them from their coevals."[6]

Youmans proved not so much a second as a lesser Gershwin; more uneven than Gershwin, his work was less original as well. Moreover, his output suffered from some collaborations with inferior lyricists. As his career floundered in later years, including abortive attempts to write a symphonic work of his own, his long-standing rivalry with Gershwin left him embittered; in one instance, he railed against Gershwin as a "bastard" whose "Looking for a Boy" (1925) plagiarized "Tea for Two." But on balance, it might be argued, no other songwriter came so near to Gershwin's particular achievement, as suggested by a comparison of not only "Looking for a Boy" and "Tea for Two" but Gershwin's "The Man I Love" (1924) and Youmans's "More Than You Know" (1929), Gershwin's "Clap Yo' Hands!" (1926) and Youmans's "Hallelujah!" (1927), or Gershwin's "Funny Face" (1927) and Youmans's "Oh Me! Oh My!" (1921).[7]

Gershwin, who in Harold Arlen's words liked to be "kingpin," was not immune to a sense of rivalry himself, and in the 1930s he attentively observed the ascendancy of Cole Porter (1891–1964) and Richard Rodgers (1902–1979) on Broadway, as well as Harry Warren (1893–1981) in Hollywood. But he thrived on competition, and if at first he had a rather distant relationship with Rodgers, this was perhaps because the latter, especially in the years prior to *A Connecticut Yankee* (1927), envied Gershwin's meteoric rise. It was not until 1928 that a friendly rapport developed between the two, thanks to the intervention of Jules Glaenzer, an avid Rodgers and Hart enthusiast. In December 1929 Gershwin, Glaenzer, and Rodgers even attended one of Elsa Maxwell's "come as somebody else" parties dressed as Groucho, Chico, and Zeppo Marx, respectively, with Justine Johnson as Harpo.[8]

Even so, after Rodgers expressed his admiration for *An American in Paris* to Gershwin, the latter startled him by responding, "I didn't think you'd like anybody's music but your own." Rodgers took no offense, citing Gershwin's ingenuousness; but perhaps he recognized some truth to the statement as well. Publicly, he announced, "Actually, it would have been impossible not to love all of Gershwin's music," but in letters to his wife, although he declared the Hollywood community "damn fools" for detesting Gershwin's score to *Shall We Dance*, he himself thought the music to *Funny Face* "a terrible disappointment" and criticized the recitatives in *Porgy and Bess*. In his earlier years especially, Rodgers showed no small susceptibility to Gershwin's style, though as a whole his career suggested that the taste of Broadway audiences hewed closer to Kern than to the jazzier forms of musical comedy associated with Gershwin. When

Alfred Simon asked Gershwin, for his part, his opinion of Rodgers and Hart's *Spring Is Here* (1929), the latter commented, "It's very nice. It's a very good score."[9]

Gershwin apparently enjoyed an even more congenial relationship with Cole Porter, whom he saw on trips to Paris in the 1920s. On one such occasion in 1928, he and Porter played piano "late into the night." During the same stay, Porter arranged to have Frances Gershwin, as mentioned, perform a set of Gershwin songs in his *Revue des Ambassadeurs*. Gershwin saw still more of Porter after the latter returned to the States and, as Yip Harburg recalled, joined "those people who got together every week, usually at George Gershwin's house" in order to "more or less compare the things we were working on." Ira placed Porter in the august company of Kern, Berlin, and Gershwin in his lyric for "By Strauss" (1936), while Gershwin similarly honored Porter by suggesting that the two of them collaborate on a song. At the same time, though apparently influenced by Gershwin, Porter's music arguably continued more in the tradition of Berlin. Berlin himself recognized in Porter his truest successor, while Porter's song, "You're the Top," declared "a Berlin ballad" tops.[10]

Gershwin found his own heir in Harold Arlen (1905–1986), who became not only a good friend but, along with Vernon Duke, probably as much of a protégé as he ever had. Intrigued by such early Arlen songs as "Get Happy" (1930) and "Stormy Weather" (1933), Gershwin no doubt appreciated the music's striking absorption of the blues and jazz. Though indebted to his own work, this music set a new tone among popular songwriters, one that, as John Andrew Johnson suggests, might have exerted some influence on *Porgy and Bess*. Gershwin nonetheless cautioned Arlen against overcomplexity, commenting, after hearing one song in progress, "Harold, why do you get so complicated? People can't sing these songs." Not so easily dissuaded, Arlen persevered in breaking new ground, especially with regard to harmony and phrase structure. Such daring earned him the affection of connoisseurs—Alec Wilder judged his song output superior to Gershwin's—but at the cost, perhaps, of greater popularity. In this sense, Arlen—who often cited Gershwin as his favorite composer— differed from his mentor, whose theater music, for all its sophistication, imposed greater limits in the interest of accessibility.[11]

Gershwin also became an admirer of a musician often compared to Arlen, namely, Hoagy Carmichael (1899–1981), the composer of "Stardust" (1927/1929). Kay Swift remembered that on discovering Carmichael's "Washboard Blues" (1925), Gershwin played it "seven or eight times right then and there. He loved it." And at a party at Jules Glaenzer's in 1934, Harry Evans overheard Gershwin tell Carmichael (apparently in some reference to African American music), "You've got it, Hoagy." "No person in the room was more interested in Hoagy's playing and singing than George Gershwin," observed Evans, "nor was anyone more appreciative of his work." Gershwin and Carmichael became friends during these years as well; Gershwin played selections from *Porgy and Bess* at Carmichael's wedding on March 14, 1936, and the two subsequently socialized and played tennis together in Los Angeles.[12]

Meanwhile, Gershwin retained the highest regard for the two heroes of his youth, Jerome Kern and Irving Berlin. On a 1932 radio show, he deemed Kern's *Show Boat* (1927) "the finest light opera achievement in the history of American music." And toward the end of his life, he painted Kern's portrait. In contrast, Kern, who had come to resent Gershwin's hogging the piano at social gatherings, seemed somewhat distant on the subject of his younger colleague; in a brief memorial, he mentioned the younger man's "bigness" and "gusto," and singled out his "naïveté" as indicative of his "greatness." Nor did Kern acknowledge Gershwin's influence, even though commentators like Ronald Sanders offered, as an explanation for the "striking difference" between Kern's *Sally* (1920), with its "British sound," and "the utterly American" *Show Boat,* the "appearance of Gershwin in the interval."[13]

Gershwin remained especially "in awe" of Berlin. When asked in 1927 about the music he most admired, after stating his "special reverence for Bach," he remarked, "And to the list of famous B's of music—Bach, Beethoven, Brahms—I add the modern Irving Berlin, whose melodies and harmonies appeal deeply to me." On another occasion, when Kay Swift criticized Berlin's work to Gershwin as less interesting than his own, he played and sang more than an hour's worth of Berlin at the piano to prove "how much versatility and greatness there was to Berlin's writing. 'He's a master,' Gershwin kept on saying, 'and let's make no mistake about *that.*'" In 1929, his public adulation of Berlin reached new heights: "I frankly believe that Irving Berlin is the greatest songwriter who has ever lived. He has that vitality—both rhythmic and melodic—which never seems to lose any of its exuberant freshness; he has that rich, colorful melodic flow which is ever the wonder of all those of us who, too, compose songs; his ideas are endless. His songs are exquisite cameos of perfection." He was, opined Gershwin, America's Franz Schubert.[14]

Berlin, for his part, seemed particularly impressed with Gershwin's more ambitious undertakings—the opposite of those serious composers who preferred his show music—and wrote him a warm telegram on the occasion of the premiere of the Concerto in F, wishing him "the success and glory you so richly deserve." After Gershwin's death, he wrote a short poem in his memory that included the quatrain, "As a writer of serious music, / He could dream for a while in the stars, / And step down from the heights of Grand Opera / To a chorus of thirty-two bars."[15]

Gershwin's interest in popular composers—along with his conviction that radio had "raised the tastes of the average man and woman" and "educated them to a real appreciation and enjoyment of the best that music has to offer"—led to a successful radio show, *Music by Gershwin,* that he hosted throughout 1934 and that paid a hefty two thousand dollars per week. The program aired on NBC Blue from February through May on Mondays and Fridays from 7:30 to 7:45 P.M.; expanded to a half hour, the show resumed in late September, airing each Sunday on CBS from 6:00 to 6:30 P.M. through the farewell show on December 23. Narrated by Don Wilson, these episodes included anecdotes by Gershwin about his music along with selections from his work and that of composers he liked. Louis Katzman presided over the WJZ studio orchestra, and Gershwin often played the piano himself. "I want you to feel as though you had simply dropped in at my house or I at yours, to run over a few tunes that may have given us pleasure," Gershwin told his radio audience on the premiere airing on February 19. The format changed somewhat with the fall season to include brief scripted exchanges between Gershwin and guest composers.[16]

The music presented by Gershwin ranged from ragtime (including that of Felix Arndt, Zez Confrey, Les Copeland, and Edward Claypoole) to popular song (including selections by Milton Ager, Harry Akst, Harold Arlen, Hoagy Carmichael, Vernon Duke, Rudolf Friml, Johnny Green, W. C. Handy, Ray Henderson, Louis Hirsch, Cole Porter, Richard Rodgers, Arthur Schwartz, Kay Swift, and Vincent Youmans, along with the teams of Jimmy McHugh and Dorothy Fields, and Harold Spina and Johnny Burke) to light concert music (including that of Rube Bloom, Ferde Grofé, Thomas Griselle, Fritz Kreisler, and Dana Suesse, also known as "the girl Gershwin"). Some other featured artists included Billy Hill, whose cowboy song "The Last Round-Up" Gershwin considered "an important contribution to American folk music"; Herman Hupfeld, the little-known composer of "As Time Goes By" ("You see," explained Gershwin, "Mr. Hupfeld is not a publicity hound, he just writes fine tunes and sets them to clever lyrics"); and society hostess Elsa Maxwell, "a genuine person and probably the greatest party giver of all time," Gershwin explained, "but few people know that she is also a composer." On his penultimate show, he also presented the songs of his brother Arthur.

Gershwin retained his interest in the blues as well, as suggested by his inclusion of W. C. Handy on his radio show. And thanks to his friendship with Carl Van Vechten, he had the opportunity to hear such outstanding blues singers as Bessie Smith with some regularity. Recalling one such occasion in April 1928 when Smith and her pianist, Porter Grainger, performed for a group that included Gershwin, Van Vechten recalled, "I am quite certain that anybody who was present that night will never forget it. This was no actress; no imitator of woman's woes; there was no pretense. It was the real thing: a woman cutting her heart open with a knife until it was exposed for us all to see, so that we suffered as she suffered, exposed with a rhythmic ferocity, which could hardly be borne. In my own experience, this was Bessie Smith's greatest performance." The same year, Gershwin told an interviewer that, as for the blues, he preferred "the lowest musical form." And in 1931 he singled out the blues as the form of jazz that most approached "tragic expression," even if "the bluest of blue notes" could only "portray tragedy in caricature."[17]

Gershwin's appreciation for jazz proved more ambivalent. The first jazz band he remembered hearing—the Original Dixieland Jazz Band, a white combo that took New York by storm in 1917—struck him as "loud and much too discordant," as did some other early jazz groups. He seems to have been most receptive to jazz pianists, including Edward K. "Duke" Ellington (1899–1974), Earl "Fatha" Hines (1903–1983), Thomas "Fats" Waller (1904–1943), and Art Tatum (1910–1956).[18]

Gershwin developed a particularly close friendship with Waller, whom he knew at least as early as 1924. Waller's son Maurice remembered that Gershwin, who often visited them at their home, would go "anywhere" to hear his father, including Harlem rent parties or "rent shouts," at which pianists, for a few dollars and a meal, performed at the home of someone who would charge a small admission fee and sell food and drink in order to help raise rent money. "George always spoke fondly of those rent-party days," stated Maurice: "'I loved to watch your father eat. I would sit there and feed him and encourage him to drink more. I was determined to see him fall flat on his face, but no matter how much he ate or drank, nothing ever happened.'" Waller's cousin, Herman Shepherd, similarly recalled, "Fats and George Gershwin were great friends and they deeply respected one another. They'd sit for hours, playing tunes for each other and making suggestions to one another. Ira sat there as a kind of judge. When he heard something he liked, he'd just smile and tell them, 'I like that tune.'"[19]

Gershwin kept abreast of Waller's music in other ways, including attending a performance of *Keep Shufflin'* (1928), for which the latter wrote some of the score. In all likelihood, he saw Waller's 1929 revue *Hot Chocolates* as well. As he did with the older Harlem stride pianists, Gershwin arranged for Waller to play at high-toned affairs, crucially abetting his career by presenting him at one such 1934 gathering to William Paley, president and founder of the Columbia Broadcasting System. In addition, Gershwin introduced him to his sister's father-in-law, pianist Leopold Godowsky, with whom Waller reportedly studied for a while.

As Waller increasingly became preoccupied with finding a more serious scope for his music, he "constantly talked about his admiration" for the *Rhapsody in Blue,* the Concerto in F, *An American in Paris,* and *Porgy and Bess.* Moreover, Harry Brooks, who collaborated with Waller on *Hot Chocolates,* admitted that the show's big hit, "Ain't Misbehavin'," "was an attempt to copy the successful formula Gershwin used for 'The Man I Love.' We imitated the opening phrase that began just after the first beat and the minor part of the bridge, too." In turn, some of Gershwin's later music, such as "The Lorelei" and "My Cousin from Milwaukee" from *Pardon My English* (1933), suggested the possible influence of Waller; the instrumental cue "Walking the Dog" from *Shall We Dance* (1937) even began with a motive almost identical to that of "Ain't Misbehavin'." Such correspondences revealed Gershwin's continued rapport with New York's black jazz musicians.[20]

Gershwin knew Duke Ellington, one year his junior, both from the Kentucky Club, where the latter performed after moving to New York in 1923, and from the Cotton Club, where the Ellington band started playing in 1927 (according to drummer Sonny Greer, Gershwin originated the popular term *jungle music* for the band's Cotton Club style). In 1929 the Ellington band appeared in Gershwin's musical comedy *Show Girl,* an engagement the bandleader considered "invaluable in terms of both experience and prestige." And in 1931, with "Sam and Delilah," Ellington started recording Gershwin as well.[21]

A 1946 press release quoted Oscar Levant as saying that Gershwin spent "many hours" in the "company of Ellington's music, sometimes playing Ellington compositions at his piano, but more often sitting quietly, listening to the many Ellington records which he owned and prized so highly that they were kept completely separate from the hundreds of others in his music room." According to Levant's 1940 memoir, Gershwin particularly admired the "rich effects and fine tonal originality" of such Ellington "mood pieces" as "Creole Love Call" (with Bubber Miley, 1927), "Swanee River Rhapsody" (with Irving Mills and Clarence Gaskill, 1930), and "Daybreak Express" (1933), and wished that he had composed the bridge to "Sophisticated Lady" (1932). Ellington deeply valued such praise, though according to clarinetist Barney Bigard he turned down Gershwin's suggestion that they collaborate on some unspecified venture.[22]

Like Waller, Ellington may have influenced Gershwin's later work—something of "Creole Love Call," for instance, possibly made its way into *An American in Paris*—but Gershwin plainly made a decisive impression on Ellington, especially in inspiring him to undertake works longer than the average three-minute number. Ellington's first such attempt, *Creole Rhapsody* (recorded twice, 1931), evoked the *Rhapsody in Blue* not only in name but in style and form; its better, second version even quoted the work's famously dissonant climactic harmony. Described by Gunther Schuller as "rather haphazardly strung together," the *Creole Rhapsody* ultimately revealed less formal control than Johnson's *Yamekraw* (1927), which itself aspired with only partial success to emulate the *Rhapsody*. But it provided a foundation for Ellington's later, more assured concert pieces. Ellington declared that he and Gershwin shared similar aims, that they were among "a number of composers" who had been "experimenting" with popular music and jazz "on a large scale," adding, "I spoke of my own tone poem and opera. Then there's the work of Gershwin which is not the same but moves in the same general direction."[23]

On a more personal note, Ellington took umbrage at Hollywood's 1945 portrayal of Gershwin as "a man and artist of temperament who was somewhat rude at times"—"an aspect of him," retorted Ellington, "I certainly never encountered . . . I never heard of this in his lifetime, and I was very close to many people who were as close to him as they could be, and they could not recall this side of him either." On the contrary, Ellington remembered Gershwin as humble and down-to-earth, as someone who came to the openings of his shows "dressed like a stagehand. . . . If you didn't know him, you would never guess that he was the great George Gershwin."[24]

Ellington's admiration for Gershwin quickly became obscured as such critics as Roger Pryor Dodge (1929), R. D. Darrell (1932), Spike Hughes (1933), and Constant Lambert (1934) extolled the former at the expense of the latter. An article by Edward Morrow, "Duke Ellington on Gershwin's 'Porgy,'" published in *New Theatre* in December 1935, proved particularly divisive in this regard. Peeved by the mostly positive reception of *Porgy and Bess,* Morrow interviewed Ellington about the opera with the intention of discrediting it; he asked leading questions, apparently distorted his replies, and reached his own conclusions:

> It was very evident that here was one colored composer [Ellington] who realized the cramping forces of exploitation which handicap not only him and his colleagues, but the Negro masses as well. That is why their expression is filled with protest. He is also fully conscious that there are imitators and chiselers, always ready to capitalize on specious productions purporting to 'represent' the Negro. They are totally lacking in social vision, and their art is phony. . . .
>
> But the times are here to debunk such tripe as Gershwin's lamp-black Negroisms, and the melodramatic trash of the script of *Porgy.* The Negro artists are becoming socially-conscious and class-conscious, and more courageous.

Ellington repudiated this article in a statement prepared by his publisher's advertising director, Richard Mack, published in a 1936 issue of *Orchestra World* ("Duke was very unhappy over these uncalled-for misquotations," reported Mack, "and feverishly rushed to straighten matters out. Though months have passed since this event, Duke feels the injustice of it to this date and constantly expressed the hope that 'Gershwin didn't take any stock in those things I was supposed to have said'"). But the harm not only had been done, but was made worse by commentators who routinely began attributing some of Morrow's statements to Ellington, in particular the comment about "lamp-black Negroisms."[25]

Even taking Morrow's article at face value, Ellington said nothing that warranted the author's inflammatory conclusion. On the one hand, he thought that the music was "grand" and the play "swell" (hardly "melodramatic trash"), though he opined that the opera's characters needed a more distinctively Negro musical language; hence his preference for the hurricane music to that for the street vendors. Even in his 1936 retraction, he reiterated this basic criticism, telling Richard Mack that he "felt that Gershwin's music, though grand, was not distinctly or definitely negroid in character." Ellington's use of the word *grand,* associated here with eclecticism, evoked the genre of opera itself, and indeed the Morrow article revealed some general ambivalence about opera on Ellington's part. "I do not believe people honestly like, much less understand, things like *Porgy and Bess,*" he replied when asked about his own possible operatic ambitions. "An opera would not express the things I have in mind." At the same time, *Porgy* apparently served as an inspiration in this respect, for soon afterward Ellington reversed himself, stating his intention (never realized) to write an opera of his own. And the Gershwin opera clearly influenced the work of arranger-composer Billy Strayhorn, Ellington's principal collaborator after 1939.[26]

Gershwin first met Earl Hines, the Pittsburgh-born pianist best remembered for his collaborations with Louis Armstrong, at Chicago's Apex Club, possibly in 1928 when Hines played with Jimmie Noone's Apex Orchestra. On that occasion, Gershwin reportedly heard Hines play portions of the *Rhapsody* and, without introducing himself, complimented his performance. Widely regarded as the father of modern jazz piano, Hines made remarkable use of Gershwin's songs over the course of his long career, framing his two-record album of Gershwin (1973) with improvisations on the *Rhapsody* in honor of their first meeting.[27]

In his last years, Gershwin became especially taken with Art Tatum, whose brilliance and elegance earned him the esteem of a wide range of pianists, including such classical virtuosi as Vladimir Horowitz and Arthur Rubinstein. Levant recalled that Gershwin, who heard Tatum at the Onyx Club on West 52nd Street (where the latter regularly performed after the club opened in 1933) and at a similar club in Los Angeles in 1936 and 1937, would listen "with rapture" to the nearly blind Tatum, especially to his playing of Gershwin's own "Liza" and "I Got Rhythm." Gershwin was "so enthused with Tatum's playing," writes Levant, that shortly before leaving for Hollywood in 1936, he had "an evening" at his East 72nd Street apartment at which Tatum performed for an hour and a half. On another occasion, at the club in Los Angeles, Levant and Gershwin "joined the group of enthusiasts clustered around the piano. . . . To George's great joy, Tatum played virtually the equivalent of Beethoven's thirty-two variations on his tune 'Liza.' Then George asked for more."[28]

Gershwin had contacts with other jazz musicians. For the revised *Strike Up the Band* and *Girl Crazy* (both 1930), whose opening nights he conducted, he worked with bandleader-trumpeter Red Nichols in staffing the pit orchestras, and found himself presiding over such outstanding white jazz musicians as clarinetists Benny Goodman, Pee Wee Russell, and Babe Russin; trombonists Glenn Miller and Jack Teagarden; and drummer Gene Krupa. Levant reported Gershwin's special admiration for Goodman, while David Ewen credited him with aiding the careers of bandleaders Artie Shaw and Xavier Cugat.[29]

Meanwhile, Gershwin's contribution to jazz was immense. The songs—sometimes just the chord progressions, but often the melodies as well—

proved particularly useful, as they provided the basis for countless jazz improvisations. Citing their jazzy rhythms, repeated-note and two-note melodies, contrapuntal accompaniments, rich harmonies, and succinct structures, C. André Barbera enumerated certain technical aspects of this repertoire thought especially congenial to jazz musicians. But Gershwin's enormous appeal—Barbera considered him "probably the favorite song-writer of jazz musicians"—no doubt stemmed from the composer's elegance, charm, and originality as well.[30]

Although he generally disliked writing, Gershwin was sometimes motivated or prevailed on to pen a short article about popular music, his working methods, or in one instance *Porgy and Bess*. The result was a slim but helpful collection of published pieces: "Our New National Anthem" (1925) for *Theatre Magazine;* "Does Jazz Belong to Art?" (1926) and "Mr. Gershwin Replies to Mr. Kramer" (1926), both for *Singing;* "Melody Shop Formulas" (1927) for *Musical Digest;* "Jazz Is the Voice of the American Soul" (1927) for *Theatre Magazine;* "Fifty Years of American Music" (1929) for the *American Hebrew;* "Making Music" for the *Sunday World Magazine* (1930); "The Composer in the Machine Age" (1930) for *Revolt in the Arts,* edited by Oliver Sayler; the introduction (1930) to Isaac Goldberg's *Tin Pan Alley;* the introduction (1932) to his own *Song-Book;* "The Relation of Jazz to American Music" (1933) for *American Composers on American Music: A Symposium,* edited by Henry Cowell; and "Rhapsody in Catfish Row: Mr. Gershwin Tells the Origin and Scheme for His Music in That New Folk Opera Called 'Porgy and Bess'" (1935) for the *New York Times.*[31]

These writings, especially those about popular music that concern us here, tend to be lively and engaging, but also elusive and sometimes contradictory. Like many others of his time, Gershwin used the term *jazz,* the core subject of most of these essays, rather vaguely. For although he often spoke of jazz as a kind of style, he eschewed technical explanations (he observed, for instance, that Bach, too, used syncopation), and provided only the sketchiest of historical contexts: he dated its origins to the early 1910s and asserted that it emerged from "plantation songs," coon songs, and ragtime, "improved and transformed into finer, bigger harmonies." Virtually his only cited examples of jazz appeared in his 1926 article for *Singing,* in which he suggested, for the journal's classically oriented readers, "eleven jazz songs suitable for concert use," including songs by himself, Kern, Berlin, Handy, Donaldson, Richard Whiting, and Henry Souvaine (a pianist-composer primarily remembered today for producing the original Texaco Opera Quiz for the Metropolitan Opera's radio broadcasts). As suggested here, he typically thought of jazz at least as much in terms of composition as of performance, though that changed somewhat over time.[32]

In this 1926 article, Gershwin further distinguished "jazz" from "street songs," writing, "It is true that many of the street songs of today are jazz in character, but our best jazz is far too good musically to be popular in the street. Practically none of my own songs can boast of that wide popularity which entitles them to be called 'songs of the street.'" In a subsequent article, he similarly differentiated "popular songs" from "show tunes," which permitted "greater latitude" than the former, though not as much as "classic music."[33]

When A. Walter Kramer challenged Gershwin's description of Kern's "They Didn't Believe Me" as jazz (he thought the music of Berlin and Kern better described as folk songs), Gershwin demurred; he agreed that he did not consider the Kern song jazz either and attributed its inclusion to a stenographic error, adding that he had actually meant to say Berlin's "Everybody Step." He further stated that the term *jazz* was too widely used and claimed a distinction not only between jazz and street songs, as he had previously, but between jazz and jazzy adaptations of the classics, Negro spirituals, popular waltz numbers, and his own concert works. "The word 'jazz,'" he wrote, "ought to be limited to a certain type of dance music."[34]

Gershwin continued to skirt around such taxonomic difficulties until the 1930s, when he avoided them altogether. In 1927 he spoke of jazz as essentially synonymous with popular songs, including street songs. And in 1930 he further called jazz "a conglomeration of many things. It has a little bit of ragtime, the blues, classicism and spirituals." He continued to speak of jazz as something "old," elements of which could be found in folk songs and Stephen Foster, adding in 1932, "There are passages of jazz in Bach and, I understand, in Beethoven." He accordingly settled on this rather nebulous definition: "Basically, it is a matter of rhythm. After rhythm in importance come intervals, music intervals which are peculiar to the rhythm." Meanwhile, discussing "jazz" with a reporter in 1934, he mentioned three recent songs he found particularly appealing: Arthur Schwartz's "Dancing in the Dark" (1931), Harold Arlen's "Stormy Weather" (1933), and Jerome Kern's "Smoke Gets in Your Eyes" (1933).[35]

During these later years, Gershwin clarified matters somewhat by noting that jazz had a distinctive performance style, one that emphasized sharpness of attack, as opposed to the sustained sounds and legato phrasing characteristic of the preceding century. This kinetic sense, he advised classical musicians, would "add a new rhythmic meaning to your whole repertoire, old and new," but he warned that it had to be acquired early in life, and, moreover, needed to be accompanied by a "real musical soul . . . entirely apart from the powerful reaction of its native rhythms." He recommended as paragons singers Marion Harris and Al Jolson, as well as the vocal quartet the Revelers.[36]

Gershwin also consistently and rather ambivalently described jazz as "crude," "vulgar," "ugly," "noisy," "boisterous," full of "animal vigor" and "unthinking vitality," even associated with "evil." He evoked such a lexicon not only, perhaps, to disarm his more genteel critics, but because such phrases underscored one of his central convictions: that jazz reflected American life, which he similarly described as "nervous, hurried, syncopated, ever accelerando, and slightly vulgar." He further viewed jazz as basically a matter of national temperament, as in this 1925 statement: "Europeans cannot write jazz; it belongs peculiarly to America. It is American music, and nothing else." As citizens of other lands recognized, he argued in 1927, jazz gave "voice" to the "soul of the American people." "If critics and would-be reformers would realise that music must change according to the times," he stated in 1929, "and that the jazz of today is no more demoralising than the automobile, which in days gone by was looked upon with suspicion, the world might come to accept jazz for what it is . . . the music of America." Whatever else jazz was, he reiterated in 1930, "one thing is certain. Jazz has contributed an enduring value to America in the sense that it has expressed ourselves."[37]

As for jazz's relation to black culture, Gershwin once again proved somewhat equivocal. In 1925 he dismissed the "superstition" that jazz was "essentially Negro," stating, "Jazz is not Negro but American." In 1927, however, in discussing jazz as "the voice of the American soul," he qualified such pronouncements: "I do not assert that the American soul is negroid. But it is a combination that includes the wail, the whine and the exultant note of the old mamy [*sic*] songs of the South. It is black and white. It is all colors and all souls unified in the great melting-pot of the world. Its dominant note is vibrant syncopation." And in 1929 he more bluntly stated that jazz had its "roots deeply embedded in the negro spiritual," a type of music, he felt, that provided a basic foundation for American serious music as well.[38]

At the heart of nearly all of Gershwin's writings about jazz lay the hope and conviction that such music could form the basis of an enduring art music. Gershwin expounded on this idea in his very first publication, "Our New National Anthem," which hailed jazz as "the germ of a new school of music," predicting that it would be "absorbed into the great musical tradition" and advocating that it take "its proper and subordinate place in music," thereby attaining "lasting value." "It is for the trained musician who is also the creative artist to bring out this vitality," he further wrote, "and to heighten it with the eternal flame of beauty." He himself had attempted to employ jazz "almost incidentally" in his *Rhapsody in Blue*.[39]

In later articles, Gershwin similarly emphasized jazz's role in providing an important "germ" or distinctive "tincture" to a developing American music. In a 1932 interview, he extended this biological metaphor to include the concept of Harlem as a "breeding ground," adding, "You can find new rhythm, ever richer harmonies there, but the germs are left for outsiders to pick up and develop." Gershwin also drew analogies between jazz and skyscrapers, suggesting that the evolution of jazz from its "germinal state" into a work of "beauty" resembled the progress of the skyscraper from its early "ugliness" to structures like the Woolworth Tower and the Hotel Shelton that show "that the skyscraper can be as beautiful as it is original."[40]

Gershwin early identified as a "difficulty" attending the "employment of jazz" (and here he apparently had in mind his musical comedies as well as his concert works) the tendency of performers to take undue liberties with the music. "Once give the musicians their head with jazz," he observed, "and in a short while they will evolve something which the author himself will fail to recognize as his own offspring." Consequently, he advised conductors of jazzy scores to supervise musicians with "an iron hand" and "a check rein, so that the music is not changed beyond recognition by trick effects." "Indeed, when a conductor undertakes to direct a work in which jazz plays an important part," he stated in 1925, "he must be even more jealous of the composer's intention than if he were conducting a classical symphony."[41]

Although Gershwin's writings about music are very much of a piece, his articles from the early 1930s exhibit a few new concerns and perspectives. Although as early as 1925 he happily foresaw music composed specifically for the wireless, in his 1930 essay "The Composer in the Machine Age," he more fully considered the impact of the phonograph and radio on musical composition, arguing that although such technological tools can "bastardize music and give currency to a lot of cheap things," they can only aid and stimulate the composer by making his music potentially available to millions of people. "The composer who writes music for himself," he observed, "and doesn't want it to be heard is generally a bad composer." Had composers of the past, like Schubert, access to such contemporary "means of distribution," they would have enjoyed greater recognition and financial rewards in their lifetime.[42]

Some commentators have regarded this argument, with its seeming unconcern for the relation between such "means of distribution" and musical form and content (a matter that preoccupied Gershwin's contemporary, critic Theodor Adorno), as representing the composer at his most ingenuous or naive—often forgetting that in its early years especially, American radio made some effort to commission and disseminate new works by serious composers. As for the specific reference to Schubert—or for that matter, Gershwin's description of Berlin as "America's Franz Schubert"—the view of Schubert as a prototypical popular song composer had become by this time something of a commonplace (with some of Schubert's melodies even enjoying success on the international operetta circuit, as in Heinrich Berte's 1916 *Das Dreimäderlhaus*, adapted by Sigmund Romberg in 1921 as *Blossom Time*).[43]

"The Composer in the Machine Age" further surmised that quarter-tones, like jazz and bitonality, might provide a viable resource for American composers. Gershwin's interest in microtonality, previously mentioned in the context of his association with Hans Barth, went back as far as 1925 and was presumably related to the use of quarter-tones, or at least bent inflections, in Jewish, black, Chinese, and other ethnic musics close to him (according to Michael Feinstein, he loved the way Hoagy Carmichael "approximated the quarter-tone scale" when he sang "Hong Kong Blues").[44]

Gershwin's last major writing on jazz and American music, commissioned by Henry Cowell and published in 1933, reflected shifting trends: "The best music being written today," he now asserted, "is music which comes from folk-sources." For Americans, this included "jazz, ragtime, negro spirituals and blues, Southern mountain songs, country fiddling, and cowboy songs," with jazz described as a "very powerful" folk music "which is probably in the blood and feeling of the American people more than any other style of folk-music." All these folk musics, he argued, could be "employed in the creation of American art-music," but in what might have been a salvo at Cowell and his readers, he acknowledged that the "highly individualized styles and methods" of some native composers should similarly be considered American "just as an invention is called American if it is made by an American!"[45]

As Gershwin increasingly discussed jazz as but one of a number of American folk musics—though plainly a crucial one—he began to employ such generic terms as *Americana* and *the American idiom* in discussions of his own music. "I want to jot down Americana in music," he stated in 1934, "to develop a nationalistic style. That is what the great composers did with their native folk music." He further minimized the importance of jazz to his own music in another 1934 pronouncement: "I base my work on the American idiom—with a dash of jazz and a suggestion of Negro spirituals." In 1937 he even confessed that he had "always hated" the word *jazz* and expressed a preference for the term *swing*.[46]

On the whole, Gershwin's writings seemed largely preoccupied with classifying and evaluating folk music, popular music, and jazz in terms of their relevance to American art music. (He hardly ever referred, incidentally, to other commentators, although in 1929 he expressed interest in obtaining a copy of R. W. S. Mendl's 1927 *The Appeal of Jazz*.) He ranked the classical tradition especially highly, admiring both its "beauty" and its longevity, the latter virtue shared with folk music as well. Jazz, a distinctive kind of popular music, enjoyed—whatever its limitations—the special advantage of embodying the "soul" of contemporary America. Thanks to its greater scope, show music similarly rated better than common popular music, which at least in Gershwin's early writings hovered relatively low in his estimation, though it was commendable for its popularity, however short-lived. Over time, however, Gershwin drew fewer distinctions among these various categories, until by the 1930s he regarded popular music and jazz simply as varieties of folk music, all of which held his interest primarily as material for serious musical composition. In short, Gershwin advocated a wide range of American musics, a stance that largely distanced him from the many debates about low and high art raging about him.[47]

Chapter Ten

Working Methods

$\mathcal{G}$ershwin was a composer of enormous facility, bursting with ideas. Ira recalled that while on the road with *Funny Face,* George left "two notebooks containing at least forty tunes" in a hotel room in Wilmington, Delaware. "After calling the hotel and learning the notebooks could not be located, he did not seem greatly perturbed," wrote Ira. "His attitude is that he can always write new ones."[1]

At the same time, Gershwin worked enormously hard, prompting Ira to comment, "To me George was a little sad all the time because he had this compulsion to work. He never relaxed." Gershwin himself emphasized the importance of sheer work in the creative process. "I can think of no more nerve-racking, no more mentally arduous task than making music," he stated in 1930. "There are times when a phrase of music will cost many hours of internal sweating." Acknowledging such other factors as "talent," "play," "emotion," and "inspiration," he considered these secondary, describing his work as "little else than a matter of invention, aided and abetted by emotion." "Melodies and rhythms are for the most part manufactured," he explained in 1927, "and I don't exactly wake up in the morning with a sentimental tune or a snappy fox-trot ringing in my ears" (though on one occasion, at least, he woke up at 3:00 A.M. with the song "Fidgety Feet," title and all, in his head; "I got right up and wrote it," he excitedly told his secretary later that morning, "like you read about!"). If he had to rely only on "inspiration," he guessed, he would compose at most three songs a year. Hence he strove to write something every day. "Like the pugilist," he once remarked, "the songwriter must always keep in training."[2]

Gershwin further pointed out that a composer needed to be self-critical so as "to develop his own musical personality" and "to avoid reminiscence." By his own admission, he created a lot of music that he never used, and friends confirmed that he would endlessly improvise themes at the piano, only some of which he might write down and develop. "As fussy about his popular music as about his more serious pieces," reported *News-Week* in 1935, "he completely rewrites almost everything ten to a dozen times." Stated Gershwin the following year: "It's just as difficult to write popular music as it is to write serious music. Well, let me put it this way: I use as much energy in writing popular music as I do in writing the other kind. I work hard to find a good theme for a popular song. I try to get one that doesn't sound like all the others, and then I like to put a little twist into the song that will make it 'different.'" He accordingly kept notebooks filled with musical jottings and even complete songs for possible future use; since the practice of "retrospection and judgment takes time" and "cannot be done effectively when working under pressure," he explained, such activities prepared him for future projects. At the same time, he could produce work extremely quickly, from songs tossed off in a couple of hours to larger scores composed within weeks.[3]

After a seven- or eight-hour sleep and a breakfast of orange juice, toast, eggs, and coffee, Gershwin frequently worked from late morning to past midnight, interrupted only for lunch in midafternoon, some walk or athletic activity in the late afternoon, and dinner about eight. When he and Ira were working on shows, it vexed him that his brother often slept past noon, thus sometimes holding him up. "Once he got started on a piece," recalled Emil Mosbacher, he "would work from seven in the morning until two the next morning." Though capable of writing music at any time, with or without people around, he preferred, like Ira, to work at night, citing the quiet available to him "when people are asleep or out for a good time." It was not unknown for him to return home from a party after midnight and plunge into his work until dawn. He liked devoting afternoons to such "physical chores" as orchestration and music copying, during which time he welcomed the company of such friends as Mabel Schirmer, who obliged him by spending the afternoon at her petit point while he orchestrated *Porgy and Bess*. And he cited a further predilection for working in the fall and winter, saying, "A beautiful spring or summer day is least conducive to making music, for I always prefer the outdoors to the work."[4]

Gershwin ordinarily composed at the piano, partly in order to get into the "proper frame of mind," adding, "Frequently I have to force myself into a mood. Although to write a happy song, for example, I do not actually have to be happy, I must try to feel like one who is happy." While he did not consider composing at the piano "a good practice" as it posed the danger of restricting his imagination, he ameliorated this bad "habit" by allowing his mind "free rein," using the piano "only to try what you can hear mentally" and "to stimulate thought and set an idea aflame. . . . The actual composition must be done in the brain."[5]

Indeed, he sometimes came up with musical ideas, even whole pieces, away from the piano, as the aforementioned story about "Fidgety Feet" reveals. The fifth and final version of the song "Strike Up the Band" similarly came to him after he retired for the night, leading Ira to observe, "Interestingly enough, the earlier four had been written at the piano; the fifth and final came to him while lying in bed." Isaac Goldberg reported that Gershwin traveled with a notepad in order to jot down musical ideas created "in the rattle of the subway, in the din of discussion that rages in publishers' offices, in the auto returning from a midnight drive, and anywhere else that composers snatch airs out of the air." Quoting the composer as saying, "I frequently hear music in the very heart of noise," Goldberg added that Gershwin "heard—and even saw on paper—the complete construction of the rhapsody [*in Blue*], from beginning to end" while riding a train from New York to Boston. Apparently Gershwin wrote much of the *Variations on "I Got Rhythm"* away from the piano as well. And speaking of the first of the *Three Preludes*, Kay Swift remarked, "It was not just an improvisation, he already had it worked out in his head."[6]

If Gershwin used the piano to test his ideas, he also liked trying out his songs in what he referred to as his "small but disagreeable" voice— a voice variously described as an "irresistible falsetto" (Samuel Chotzinoff), "inelastic" (Lester Donahue), "piping" (Arthur Schwartz), "nasal" (Burton Lane), "oddly Negroid" (Vernon Duke), and "awful, rotten, bad" (Todd Duncan, the first Porgy). Anne Brown (the first Bess) further observed, "His voice was like a nutmeg grater—husky—but he got the melody over. The pitch was perfect but the quality of the sound was really not pleasing. And his chin shook, his whole head shook a little when he sang." Nanette Kutner, meanwhile, remembered the time he exuberantly danced the Black Bottom while composing some show music "to see if its steps fitted his rhythms."[7]

From the start of his career, Gershwin, as mentioned above, recorded musical ideas in notebooks of various sizes, some small and horizontal, but most vertical with twelve staves. He often dated these sketches to the day, month, and year, leaving behind clear evidence that he consulted them at a distance of some years; his sketches of 1921 and 1922, for instance, contain music subsequently used in *Lady, Be Good!* (1924), *Oh, Kay!* (1926), and even *Let 'Em Eat Cake* (1933). Moreover, Gershwin typically distinguished ideas for songs ("tunes") from those for more extended pieces ("themes"), to the point of keeping them in separate notebooks, a practice that, as Susan Neimoyer observes, challenges the common notion of the composer's concert works as a collection of tunes.[8]

Gershwin's sketches confirm the primacy of melody in his creative work: they typically feature an unaccompanied single soprano line of some multiple of eight bars, though often accompanied by parallel thirds and sixths below, a habit that suggests the source of much of his harmonic thinking. These sketches show few signs of indecision, suggesting that Gershwin largely arrived at his ideas of whatever length well formed before committing them to paper (which is not to say that he never revised them at some later date). He also sometimes added to his sketched melodies an occasional accompanying chord, notably at beginnings and ends of phrases; to what extent he had other harmonies in mind this early in the compositional process remains an open question. Moreover, bits of accompanying counterpoint, usually consisting of longish notes in the alto voice moving upward or downward by half-step, appear with striking frequency. Such countermelodies often color and animate melodies that feature repeated notes or motives, such as the chorus to "The Man I Love" and the verse to "But Not for Me"; but they also accompany scores of other melodies, a ubiquitous practice that points to the contrapuntal nature of Gershwin's thinking and the influence of Edward Kilenyi's "law of propinquity."

The surviving sketches for the larger concert works and for *Porgy and Bess* present a more complicated picture. Here Gershwin began by notating ideas of varying lengths, from a single measure to a whole page of music or more. And while melody remained of uppermost concern, these sketches, even in their initial phases, showed more attention to harmony and texture. In some of the *Cuban Overture* (1932) sketches, for instance, he drafted melodies, countermelodies, and harmonies spread over two to four staves, even if he ultimately reordered, refined, and sometimes rejected these ideas.

For these larger works, Gershwin also occasionally described his formal intentions in words and charts. With the Concerto in F (1925), such summations ranged from reducing the entire three-movement piece to a handful of words ("Rhythm," "Melody [Blues]," and "More Rhythm") to specifying a projected order of the finale's themes and tonal areas in outline form. Gershwin verbalized his intentions even more thoroughly in such later works as the *Cuban Overture,* whose sketches include, for example, the following: "7 bars—4 bars of rhythmic interlude/ continuation of duet 7 bars/ then 8 bar rhythmic interlude/ then intensify duet/ then to basso ostinato using B theme in bass/ perhaps something new on top leading to stretto using canonic imitation of all rhythms. Stretto on 1 or 2 themes finish." During these later years, under Joseph Schillinger's influence, he began to use graphs as well.

After sketching out ideas for his larger orchestral works, Gershwin would proceed to create a manuscript sketch score for either one or two pianos. These reduced scores occasionally indicated cues to orchestration, sometimes meticulously so. Finally, in all of these works but the *Rhapsody in Blue,* which Ferde Grofé scored for the Paul Whiteman Orchestra, Gershwin prepared a carefully notated orchestral score in his own hand, freely adding, deleting, and altering materials from the reduced sketch score.

Throughout his life and even after, allegations arose that he did not score his own orchestral works. As early as 1926, A. Walter Kramer divulged the allegedly open secret that "someone else" orchestrated the Concerto in F, a charge immediately refuted by the composer in print. An incendiary 1932 article by Alan Lincoln Langley helped spread such rumors; it was not Langley's primary intention, as often suggested, to question the provenance of Gershwin's orchestrations—he was mainly concerned with discrediting the "myth" of Gershwin as a great American composer by arguing that the music was "meretricious," "absurd," and, finally, "disgusting"—but he suggested in passing that Gershwin's orchestrations may not have been entirely his own (that Gershwin's orchestral scores were indubitably in his own hand, he pointed out, proved nothing), and he cast a knowing glance in the direction of Gershwin's friend William Daly. Wrote Langley: "There is no such thing as a characteristically Gershwinian orchestration; no repetitive idiosyncrasies, such as are found in all composers of stature, no recognizable habits."[9]

Daly responded in print by stating that he had not "so much as orchestrated one whole bar of any one of his [Gershwin's] symphonic works," adding, "My only contribution consisted of a few suggestions about reinforcing the scoring here and there, and I'm not sure that Gershwin, probably with good reason, accepted them." Still, even such later experts as Charles Schwartz—who cited Ferde Grofé's assertion that at least at the time of the *Rhapsody in Blue,* Gershwin "could not orchestrate"—questioned the authorship of Gershwin's orchestrations.[10]

In fact, the evidence shows that Gershwin not only scored all his orchestral compositions after the *Rhapsody,* but surely could have orchestrated that work as well. After all, he studied orchestration with Edward Kilenyi and Rossetter Cole about 1920 (during which time he seems to have acquired Cecil Forsyth's *Orchestration*), and in April 1922 arranged and orchestrated the number "Naughty Baby," his earliest surviving orchestral score. Later that year, in September 1922, pianist Beryl Rubinstein stated point-blank, "Gershwin knows orchestration." Gershwin continued his lessons in orchestration with Goldmark about the time of the *Rhapsody,* a work he very likely would have scored were it not for extenuating circumstances later to be discussed.[11]

Gershwin's actual abilities as an orchestrator are another matter. Virgil Thomson, for one, found the "plum-pudding," or as he later put it, "gefiltefish" scoring of *Porgy and Bess* "heavy, over-rich and vulgar." Morton Gould similarly thought that Gershwin's "messy" orchestrations needed some "thinning out," at least according to Joan Peyser, who argued that the deficiencies of the composer's orchestrations proved their authenticity. On the other hand, although Maurice Peress found "many examples of naive, meaningless, and even counterproductive scoring" in Gershwin's earliest orchestral pieces, he noted as well "some fine touches," and further opined that "given a good orchestra, neither the listener nor the average musician is aware of any problem." And Wayne Shirley observed orchestral passages felt to project the composer's "musical thought not only adequately but often brilliantly and sometimes with great sonic beauty." But whatever the case, Gershwin's orchestrations were his own.[12]

Conditioned by his life in the theater, Gershwin sometimes tried out his orchestral works prior to their premieres, including trial runs of at least portions of the Concerto in F, the *Second Rhapsody,* and *Porgy and Bess.* Based on the results, and sometimes in consultation with such friends as William Daly, he would edit his orchestrations. However, whereas he worked mostly on his own in writing concert music, his stage and film work naturally involved a much greater degree of collaboration with a wide range of people, including producers, bookwriters, lyricists (principally his brother Ira), choreographers, arrangers, orchestrators, and sometimes other composers.

Although composers were less marginalized on Broadway than they were in Hollywood, the creation of stage and film musicals in Gershwin's time unfolded similarly. Producers typically would contract one or two bookwriters, a composer, and a lyricist and propose some general ideas, including a possible play or novel for adaptation. They also often lined up at least a few key stars early on, in part so that the material could be tailored to suit them. Producers naturally cast parts later in the process as well, often in consultation with the writers and composers. (Gershwin, who often accompanied singers at auditions, aspired to produce his own shows, telling his friend Emil Mosbacher, "I cast all the shows, why shouldn't I produce them?")[13]

Bookwriters, composers, and lyricists cobbled together their musicals at lightning speed, quite often within two or three months. Theaters around the country had a large audience for musicals, and considering the ephemeral nature of the product—even successful musicals rarely ran for more than 250 performances on Broadway—producers wanted to satisfy demand as quickly as possible. If they owned theaters themselves, as was sometimes the case, they also felt the pressure to keep them up and running. Moreover, producers placed a premium on fashion; a trendy idea or dance might tarnish if not aired promptly.

After a rehearsal period of about four or five weeks, musicals were tried out in regional theaters on the East Coast over a period lasting from one week to two months or longer before the all-important Broadway premiere. Many musicals entered this tryout interval with a barely completed book or score. In any event, bookwriters, composers, and lyricists were expected to be on hand in order to revise material as deemed necessary by directors, actors, choreographers, and others; in dire cases, producers sometimes engaged outsiders to help doctor the show as well. Tryouts could be extremely stressful and tempestuous, with people quitting or getting fired, though both George and Ira consistently won kudos in the theatrical community for their congeniality and for the absence of those displays of temperament that sometimes overtook even their most low-key associates.

The received wisdom asserts that the musical-comedy book of this period served as a mere pretext for the launching of popular tunes fitted to generic lyrics. But at least in the hands of artists like the Gershwins, the early musical comedy had its own dramatic principles and aims. In their joint memoir *Bring on the Girls!* Guy Bolton and P. G. Wodehouse recalled, for instance, their ambition to write "real, coherent, consecutive" stories for the musical stage and their pride in having integrated the book, lyrics, and music for *Have a Heart* (1917) "in a fashion then unknown, the lyrics all fitting into the story and either advancing the action or highlighting a character." That such ideas crystallized in 1917 was further suggested by contemporary statements by Kern ("It is my opinion that the musical numbers should carry the action of the play, and should be representative of the personalities of the characters who sing them") and Bolton ("The intimate form of comedy is becoming more popular. . . . The big ensembles in opening and closing, the kings of mysterious kingdoms, the impossible situations, are no longer desired by amusement seekers. They want real people and real situations—everyday situations, with musical numbers introduced naturally, and with comedy that arises from conditions of universal appeal"). "Whatever fine distinctions are made between the musicals after the great Rodgers and Hammerstein hit [*Oklahoma!*] and those of Irving Berlin, Jerome Kern, George Gershwin, Cole Porter and Vincent Youmans, as well as those of Rodgers himself (in collaboration with Larry Hart) in the twenties and thirties," observed Harold Clurman in 1962, "it is certain that the work of those early days was of the same nature as, and of equal (if not superior) value to, that of our more 'integrated' musicals today."[14]

That newspaper reviews paid attention to matters of plot and character, and that musicals frequently adapted novels and plays (and sometimes even generated novels and straight films), further highlight the extent to which commentators have underappreciated the dramatic integrity of the early musical comedy. Wodehouse, for instance, who found that writing musical comedies in the 1910s and 1920s honed his skills as a writer, based his novel *The Small Bachelor* on one of the Princess shows, *Oh, Lady! Lady!!* The early musical comedy similarly proved instructive to playwright Neil Simon who, in having to adapt older shows for television, found, "by retracing the steps of the former great book writers of Broadway musicals, I was learning form, construction, motivation, and character—that is, as much as was permitted by the constraints of musicals written in the twenties, thirties, and forties." *Show Boat* and *Of Thee I Sing* were not so much aberrations as superior examples of their kind.[15]

The standard working procedure of Gershwin and his contemporaries evidenced such concerns. Bookwriters usually first drafted a scenario, and then provided to songwriters—at least ideally—a full or partial script, including suggested spots for numbers (the Gershwins regularly alluded to lulls in their activity caused by a wayward script). Granted, many bookwriters took their cues from songwriters, even building an entire show around a few selected songs. But however the bookwriters and songwriters worked, the better ones aimed for as close a melding of script and song as possible, unless impeded by star performers who insisted on loosely constructed entertainments suitable for interpolated or improvised routines.[16]

This is not to say that the songwriters, like the bookwriters for that matter, were impervious to the conventions of the time. Ira noted, for example, "In the Twenties it was almost *de rigueur* in the finale of a show to wind up the plot and relationships by setting new lyrics to one of the principal songs." He might have added any number of other conventions, such as the opening chorus, the requisite comedy song, or the rousing eleven o'clock number. As with the constraints imposed by the thirty-two-bar refrain, songwriters worked within and around these accepted practices.[17]

Moreover, like other composers of the period, Gershwin commonly recycled older materials, including songs dropped from a previous show or rescued from a flop. Ira further admitted that between musicals, he and George often composed songs "of a general nature" that could be "introduced into any show." But although the interpolation of such material could be jarring, it could alternatively be dramatically trenchant and apropos; the entire structuring of the early musical comedy depended on just such piecing together of disparate elements.[18]

Ira discussed such matters more explicitly than did George, in large part because he lived long enough to reminisce about them. Lawrence Stewart, for instance, reported that Ira thought of his lyrics in the "larger context" of "the show itself with its plots and turns and situations of confrontation and reconciliation." Philip Furia reasserted that Ira "came to conceive of his lyrics as 'lodgments' for specific dramatic occasions, always integrally related to some situation in the plot or to the personality of a particular character." Added Ira in 1964: "I have always worked on lyrics and on projects that held intellectual excitement."[19]

But George also occasionally spoke about his theatrical work and aspirations. In 1920, for instance, he stated, "Operettas that represent the life and spirit of this country are decidedly my aim." And in 1924 he said, "I love to write musical comedies; I would rather do that than anything else." The following year (and again in 1930), he distinguished songs "of the comedy variety," in which he often needed to write "to the lyric, giving the lyric full scope because the lyric is the important thing in a comedy song," from songs "that you hope people will learn to whistle and dance to," for which he composed the melody first "so as not to be hampered by the lyric writers' rhythms." In 1927 he referred to the musical comedy's accepted "combination" of "a sentimental song, a dance number, and a smart fox-trot," adding, "One cannot very well have two fox-trots fight for first place in the same show." In 1928 he was quoted as saying that, compared to musical comedies, writing symphonic works afforded "more fun and personal satisfaction," explaining, "The songs and music I write for the stage are more or less made to order, but when I write such a score as the *Rhapsody*, I have only myself to consider and can write as I please. I dislike being tied down to a certain situation or set of lyrics when I write musical comedies, and therefore the freedom I have in composing my own symphonic pieces is all the more welcome and pleasing." (He also often pointed out the restrictions posed by having to write songs for dancers and comedians.) And about 1929 he stated, "The American world is waiting for a new style of musical comedy. . . . Oh! for a new, a good, comical book!" These remarks reveal a sensitivity to the dramatic intentions of his shows—along with Ira, he selected from among various book ideas offered him—and an attentiveness to stage conventions and requirements, even if, in later years especially, he seemed somewhat grudging about the limitations they imposed.[20]

Ira confirmed that Gershwin heeded the dramatic needs of their shows. "Once we receive the outline of the plot we really get down to work," he stated in 1930. "We decide that such and such a tune is best for this or that situation." Years later, Ira told Michael Feinstein that because Gershwin "understood the limitations of musical theater of the time and knew how creaky the plots were, he put unifying factors into the songs themselves so that the listener subconsciously felt that the songs came from the same score," a claim borne out by Deena Rosenberg's study of the musicals. According to Ira, Gershwin "sublimated" the notion of the musical comedy as a vehicle for hits "in order to write a structurally perfect show."[21]

Fred Astaire—recalling meetings in 1924 with Gershwin, bookwriter Guy Bolton, and producer Alex Aarons during the early stages of *Lady, Be Good!*—corroborated such claims:

> The four of us used to talk about the vehicle a lot and chip in whatever suggestions we could. We often got together and discussed what kind of number made sense for such and such a spot—or decided *that* would be a place for another kind of number. We were concerned about finding ways to get into a number the right way. The placement of songs and their relationship with plot and characters mattered to George a great deal. He wanted the song to work in context, to have a good reason why a character would break into song at a particular point.

Morrie Ryskind, another collaborator, thought Gershwin's music "particularly noteworthy" for "the graceful way that it could be used to advance a story."[22]

Like most popular theater composers of the time, Gershwin generally wrote the music first, with a number's introductory verse often composed only after he had completed the chorus. His lyricists then fitted words to the music—"mosaically," as described by Ira, who compared his work to that of a "gemsetter."[23]

Although considerable precedent existed for putting words to preexisting tunes, this general practice represented something of a break with traditional light opera and had considerable ramifications, as it allowed composers to take the lead in exploring new rhythmic ideas. In this regard, some have found it instructive to compare Richard Rodgers's work with Lorenz Hart (who typically put words to music) to that with Oscar Hammerstein (who preferred providing lyrics to composers); in the opinion of Alec Wilder and others, setting Hammerstein's poetry deprived Rodgers's music of "that spark and daring flair which existed in the songs he wrote with Hart."[24]

Gershwin actually proved himself adept at working in either fashion, as evidenced by his work with DuBose Heyward and Ira on *Porgy and Bess,* for which Heyward typically wrote the words first, while Ira largely lyricized composed melodies. What impact these different methods may have had on that particular work is hard to say; Ira doubted that listeners would be able to tell the difference. At the same time, the greater variety of compositional method found in *Porgy and Bess*—or, for that matter, in *Of Thee I Sing*—arguably helped broaden their range.[25]

Meanwhile, setting words to music encouraged lyric writers to find original patterns of their own. "The setting of words to a jazz-type melody forces the versifier to follow, in all its twists and turns, a jagged, capricious melodic line, and his ingenuity is kept on the alert, challenged to feats of dexterity," noted Isaac Goldberg. "Seen by themselves, many of the stanzas look more foolish than they are; they do not readily suggest the music to which they have been often skillfully patterned." Wodehouse, who thought one got "the best results by giving the composer his head and having the lyricist follow him," similarly observed, "When you have the melody, you can see which are the musical high-spots in it and can fit the high-spots of the lyric to them." At the same time, Ira cautioned, "It takes years and years of experience to know that such a note cannot take such a syllable, that many a poetic line can be unsingable, that many an ordinary line fitted into the proper musical phrase can sound like a million."[26]

When writing the music first, composers sometimes supplied to lyricists a lead sheet, that is, a melody notated or otherwise diagrammed—a provision that proved largely unnecessary for Ira, who had an extraordinary musical memory. Rather, while working on lyrics, Ira would sing aloud or play the piano with one finger, prompting a new maid to ask his wife, "Don't Mr. Gershwin never go to work?"[27]

The practice of writing the lyric after the music even allowed Ira to lyricize Gershwin's song sketches after the latter's death. But it would be a mistake to assume that the collaboration between the Gershwins, or between most songwriters of the period, occurred at a distance or in clearly defined stages. On the contrary, the accepted practice of composing the music first fostered considerable give-and-take—perhaps because of the fluidity of notes as compared to words. That the Gershwins were brothers, that they lived together or at least nearby, and that they worked almost exclusively with each other only made their interaction that much more intense. "It was," wrote Merle Armitage of the Gershwins, "a partnership, a brotherhood, and a teamwork of the rarest sort."[28]

Ira liked first to select a song title—even prior to any music—and then incorporate it at the very end, sometimes with a twist (as in the pun "And there's no knot for me" that concludes "But Not for Me"). He discussed this and other aspects of his craft in an annotated anthology of his verse, *Lyrics on Several Occasions* (1959), as well as in a 1930 article, "Words and Music," for the *New York Times*:

> There is probably little literary value to the present lyric. With the limited vocabulary permitted us, we know not the bosky dells of the poet, and if we did the audience wouldn't. When people read poetry they can study the printed page, but each song lyric is hurled at them only once or twice in the course of an evening, and the audience has no chance to rehear or reread it. Thus, good lyrics should be simple, colloquial, rhymed, conversational lines. . . . But the song itself is the important thing, not the words or the music as separate entities, and often too great a straining for cleverness in a lyric will make too cerebral an offering that should be light and jingly.[29]

Sometimes Ira simply suggested to George a mood or a fragment of text, culling his ideas from, among other sources, the mannerisms of stage performers and common slang. In one instance, he suggested that they "do something with the sounds of 'do, do' and 'done, done,'" which resulted in "Do, Do, Do." Discussing "A Foggy Day," Ira further recalled, "All I had to say was: 'George, how about an Irish verse?' and he sensed instantly the degree of wistful loneliness I meant. Generally, whatever mood I thought was required, he, through his instinct and inventiveness, could bring my hazy musical vision into focus. Needless to say, this sort of affinity between composer and lyricist comes only after long association between the two." Gershwin worked in similar ways with other lyricists, including Irving Caesar, who remembered making up titles "just to have him [Gershwin] sit down and go up and down the keys and see what he could strike from them, and he could work wonders."[30]

"I hit on a new tune," Gershwin explained further, "play it for Ira, and he hums it all over the place for a while until he gets an idea for the lyric, and then we work the thing out together." During the latter stage, the two often engaged in a complex interplay at the piano, as DuBose Heyward observed during the composition of *Porgy and Bess*:

> The brothers Gershwin, after their extraordinary fashion, would get at the piano, pound, wrangle, swear, burst into weird snatches of song, and eventually emerge with a polished lyric. . . . Each had a profound influence on the other; each completed the other. When they collaborated on popular music, George's understanding of the lyrics equalled his brother's feeling for music. They worked with an amazing rapidity and seemingly without effort, although those close to them knew how often they would struggle over a single phrase.

Morrie Ryskind similarly wrote,

> What I especially remember from our sessions together is being amazed at the telepathy that existed between them. I've never seen anything even remotely like it with other songwriters, certainly not with the composers that I've worked with. Having watched Ira merely nod to get George to play one section from a particular melody from one of a dozen songs in front of him, or when George would play a few bars and exclaim, 'It fits,' before Ira would read the lyric that he was still writing—which did indeed fit—I feel secure in my belief that the genius of their songs was truly the product of one mind.[31]

A remark by Oscar Levant—"Rhythmically and formally the flow of Ira's verse frequently conditioned the turn of George's melodic and harmonic ideas"—underscored the reciprocity of their collaborative work. Specific examples are rare to come by—and surviving manuscripts suggest rather that Gershwin largely composed his tunes on his own—but in his conversations with Ira, Michael Feinstein learned of one revealing instance: Gershwin's main motive for "They Can't Take That Away from Me" ("The way you wear your hat") originally comprised four rather than six notes, with a three-note rather than a five-note upbeat, until Ira asked for "a few more notes" to fit his lyric, resulting in a more speech-like melody. Gershwin also agreed to Ira's suggestion that they omit the second eight-bar phrase from "Bidin' My Time," a revision that gave the song a "more folksy validity."[32]

Moreover, Ira helped choose, from Gershwin's seemingly endless store of tunes, which melodies to develop and for what purposes, proposing, for example, that they adapt a discarded march, "Trumpets of Belgravia," as the opening chorus for *Of Thee I Sing*. "When Ira failed to nod," remembered Harburg, "George would attack the keyboard with renewed dynamic vigor, until he met Ira's intransigent . . . demands." Ira even admitted to occasionally supplying his own musical ideas: "If, once in a great while in deliberations with the composer, a short musical phrase came to me as a possibility and was found acceptable to my collaborator, that didn't make me a composer. More often than not . . . my suggestions arose from some musical phrase of the composer's own, which he had overlooked or whose potentiality he was unaware of."[33]

For his part, Gershwin had some input into the lyrics. Ira remembered asking him what he thought about the phrases "a foggy day in London" and "a foggy day in London Town," to which he answered, "I like it better with town." And while working on "Fascinating Rhythm," Gershwin argued with Ira "for days," insisting on a double rhyme (eventually "quiver" and "flivver") for the fourth and eighth lines of the chorus, whereas Ira preferred rhyming single syllables. "We are both pretty critical and outspoken," said Ira, "George about my lyrics and I about his music. Praise is very faint."[34]

After completing their songs, the Gershwins often performed them together as well, as described by Isaac Goldberg: "George at the piano, sometimes joining in the words, Ira standing at his side, looking up at the ceiling as if he were reading the words and notes there—singing softly to George's equally unobtrusive playing."[35]

Some commentators have regarded the successful collaboration of the Gershwins as strengthened by the differences in their temperaments. Philip Furia, for instance, argued that "the secret" of their art lay in the tension between Gershwin's "sensuous, driving energy" and Ira's "urbanely innocent wit." Joan Peyser even claimed, somewhat dubiously, that Ira's lyrics provided a kind of running commentary on his brother's life. But the outward disparity between the two brothers obscured shared sensibilities, including a distinctively whimsical sense of humor, that no doubt enhanced their collaborative efforts as well.[36]

In readying his musical comedy scores, Gershwin also supplied or at least supervised overtures, entr'actes, incidental music, and scene transitions, as well as orchestrations and dance and choral arrangements. However, less is known about these activities than about virtually any other aspect of his career. Unlike most musical-comedy composers, Gershwin had the ability to do all this work himself, but time restrictions, among other considerations, necessitated professional assistance. Dance arrangements, for instance, arose only in collaboration with the show's choreographer during the few weeks set aside for rehearsal, so they needed to be completed in short order. And because overtures and entr'actes were typically based on the songs of a show, the removal or addition of a song during the tryout period could sometimes require last-minute revisions of these as well. Finally, the entire show had to be scored and parts prepared for an orchestra of about twenty-five musicians, all at a time when a composer might have to revise songs or write new ones.

Nonetheless, Gershwin was more involved in these activities than most if not all of his colleagues—though to what extent is difficult to ascertain, especially since so much of this material failed to survive (producers in these years often threw out scores and parts after the run of a show). Fortunately, existing sketches and manuscripts for the Gershwin musicals, including a trove of arrangements and orchestrations discovered in 1982 in a Warner Brothers warehouse in Secaucus, New Jersey, shed some light on this matter.[37]

Gershwin typically composed the overtures and at least some of the instrumental music for his shows. Overtures actually demanded relatively little work, for the practice of the time involved linking four or five songs with transitions, prefaced by an introduction and wrapped up with a brief coda. Gershwin used the period's shorthand of sketching out the introduction—specifying the first song by name, composing a transition to the second song, and so on. Even within these limits, however, he could effect a neatly turned curtain-raiser, while the overtures to *Of Thee I Sing* (1931) and *Let 'Em Eat Cake* (1933) transcended such conventions altogether, making them, according to Wayne Schneider, "dramatic music-making and surely two of Gershwin's finest compositions."[38]

Gershwin claimed in 1927 that he had "no time" to orchestrate his shows, stating that it took "five men two or three weeks" to prepare such scores. The previous year, he had minimized the importance of orchestration generally, writing, "The ability to orchestrate is a talent apart from the ability to create. The world is full of [the] most competent orchestrators who cannot for the life of them write four bars of original music." However, at the least he generally indicated the desired instrumentation for his shows, including the idea, first introduced in *Lady, Be Good!* (1924), of having two pianos in the pit, a jazzy novelty apparently borrowed from the Paul Whiteman band that came to characterize Gershwin's Broadway sound from the mid-1920s. Otherwise, his musicals typically featured rather standard Broadway instrumentation: two flutes, oboe, two clarinets, bassoon, two horns, two trumpets, one or two trombones, percussion, piano, harp, and strings. By the time of *Show Girl* (1929), the reed players often doubled on saxophone as well, making such personnel as a second flute and second horn unnecessary.[39]

At least as early as *Primrose* (1924), Gershwin also occasionally orchestrated some portions of his shows himself, though to what extent is again hard to determine, not least because orchestrations were often unattributed or misattributed. For instance, although no one but Robert Russell Bennett received official credit for orchestrating *Girl Crazy*, Bennett stated that Gershwin offered "help in the form of an orchestration" that was so accomplished he had "no need to revise or re-do anything." Gershwin also orchestrated some of *Funny Face, Rosalie, Of Thee I Sing,* and no doubt other shows. He also arranged and orchestrated some purely instrumental cues in his movie musicals. At the least, he seems to have supervised all the orchestrations for his shows; during the Philadelphia tryout of *Lady, Be Good!* Ira wrote to friends that George was in New York "attending to some new orchestrations for the show." Moreover, Gershwin expected fidelity to his piano score, insisting that Bennett take out "an undercurrent" that he had added to "Embraceable You" from *Girl Crazy.* "I don't think I ever changed anything else for George," said Bennett.[40]

Bennett further remarked, "Most of his [Gershwin's] plays through the years were orchestrated by Sears & Roebuck, which was our inelegant way of saying he passed out his numbers to four or five arrangers as they were available without type-casting in any way," a statement consistent with Gershwin's mention of "five men." Even so, from virtually the start of his career, Gershwin secured the services of many of Broadway's best orchestrators. For instance, Frank Saddler, whose superb orchestrations set high standards, as already discussed, scored at least portions of *La-La-Lucille!* (1919), the 1920 *Scandals,* and *A Dangerous Maid* (1921); Maurice DePackh claimed that Saddler's "help and advice" helped "speed" Gershwin "on his way to success." And for his 1922 opera *Blue Monday Blues,* Gershwin collaborated with Will Vodery, the distinguished orchestrator whom Duke Ellington credited as a major influence. Other Gershwin shows similarly employed superior arrangers: not only Bennett and DePackh, but William Daly, Adolph Deutsch, Stephen O. Jones, and Max Steiner, who, like most of these men, later had a major Hollywood career.[41]

William Merrigan Daly Jr. (1888–1936) deserves special attention because of his close relationship with Gershwin. Born into a theatrical family in Cincinnati and raised in Boston, he studied piano and music theory while still in high school with Carl Faelton, the former head of the New England Conservatory, and Faelton's brother Reinhold. Daly attended Harvard from 1904 to 1908, getting average grades in nearly all of his classes, none of them music. After graduation he worked for *Everybody's Magazine,* eventually becoming a general manager. But on hearing him conduct a chorus in 1914, pianist Ignacy Paderewski persuaded him to pursue a musical career. He duly played piano with various Broadway orchestras, and in time established himself as a highly sought-after Broadway (and later radio) arranger, orchestrator, and conductor.

Ann Ronell, who studied with Daly at Gershwin's suggestion, remembered him as "a marvelous man and a brilliant musician," and Ira—who collaborated with Daly on an unproduced musical based on Chopin's melodies (1923)—similarly thought him "one of the most erudite men" he had ever met. Charles Schwartz portrayed Daly as Gershwin's very opposite, as "the Harvard gentleman: circumspect, leisurely in gait, spectacled and shy, tall and lanky, fair-complexioned with unruly hair, and . . . usually casually attired with clothes that bordered on the shabby." Such an appearance reminded one observer in 1932 of "a cartoonist's conception of a musician."[42]

Gershwin and Daly met in the late 1910s, and the two subsequently collaborated on the scores to *Piccadilly to Broadway* (1920), *For Goodness Sake* (1922), and *Our Nell* (1923). In the course of his career, Gershwin regularly turned to Daly, his favorite Broadway conductor, for professional advice. Daly—who, according to Dimitri Tiomkin, "worshiped" Gershwin "as the musical genius of the time"—became a good friend as well, "probably my best friend," Gershwin told George Pallay in 1931. (For some unknown reason, they jokingly took to calling each other "Pincus.")[43]

This close friendship even bred, as mentioned, the false rumor that Daly orchestrated Gershwin's concert works, though he did help in other ways, including preparing chamber-orchestra versions of some of these pieces for radio. For a few of his concert appearances with orchestras, including those of the *Rhapsody in Blue* with the New York Philharmonic at Lewisohn Stadium in 1931 and 1932, Gershwin arranged for Daly to conduct. His confidence in Daly's abilities was rewarded with some of the best reviews of his career. After their August 13, 1931, performance of the *Rhapsody,* in which Daly made his debut with the Philharmonic, Gershwin received a full ten-minute ovation, more than half the length of the piece itself; while a review of their August 16, 1932, performance praised Daly's "particularly lively reading" of the work. Regrettably, Gershwin and Daly—who died at home of a heart attack in late 1936 at age forty-eight, just months before Gershwin's own demise—never collaborated on a recording.[44]

Gershwin's principal editor, Albert Sirmay (1880–1967), merits special note as well. Sirmay (Szirmai) studied music at the Academy of Music in his native Budapest, where he enjoyed success as an operetta composer. After arriving in New York in the 1920s, he served for many years as a principal music editor at Harms and later Chappell. Although he never completed a doctorate, the "large, rotund" Sirmay was thought by some to have done so and was widely referred to as "the Doctor" or "Doc." His thick Hungarian accent and professorial dignity made him the butt of numerous jokes among the denizens of Tin Pan Alley, who nonetheless sought his opinions and welcomed his sympathetic support. (He cried on first hearing Gershwin's "Bess, You Is My Woman Now" as well as Porter's "Ev'ry Time We Say Goodbye," which he thought "not less a gem than any immortal song of a Schubert or Schumann.")[45]

At Harms, Sirmay had the responsibility of editing and often arranging the songs of their best composers, including Kern, Porter, Gershwin, Youmans, and Rodgers. Sirmay "excelled at preserving the composer's intention and having, at the same time, a sense of what the average piano player could and could not do," writes Cole Porter's biographer, William McBrien. "He was a superb editor with a superior sense of how to syllabify the lyrics so that the right syllables coincided with the right notes." In the case of Porter, this meant working out the accompaniments with the composer, but Gershwin's music was so expert that Sirmay did little actual arranging. Rather, he made, according to Charles Schwartz, "'pianistic adjustments' where necessary in Gershwin's works to make them more playable and changed or added minor details such as dynamic and metronomic markings where they were called for." And when Sirmay set about preparing the vocal-piano score for *Porgy and Bess*, he and Gershwin agreed on publishing the complex piano reduction as originally conceived, leaving easier arrangements for a later time.[46]

Chapter Eleven

Gershwin the Man

$\mathcal{G}$ershwin's hit song "Swanee" (1919) brought him fame and fortune at age twenty-one, and he remained quite well-off for the rest of his short life, the 1929 stock market crash notwithstanding. Indeed, in 1930 he earned a whopping $70,000 for the film musical *Delicious,* as well as a good portion of the $50,000 paid by Universal Pictures for the right to use the *Rhapsody in Blue* in the picture *King of Jazz;* nor did this include other royalties and fees for a year that also saw the opening of one of his biggest Broadway hits, *Girl Crazy.* Such income more than compensated for some tens of thousands of dollars he lost in the stock market. By the time of his death in 1937, his estate, including the residual value of his compositions but exclusive of his superb art collection, was estimated at approximately $400,000 (that is, about $5.5 million in today's prices); and even this was a gross underestimate (intentionally so, suggests Charles Schwartz, for inheritance-tax purposes), considering that his music was valued at only $50,125, with *Porgy and Bess* appraised for a mere $250.[1]

Gershwin liked the accoutrements of wealth, but he did not care as much about money as his brother Ira, in whose hands he often left business matters, and who assiduously followed the stock market even as a young man. "George had no particular feeling for money per se," observed Oscar Levant. "He was not consumed by wanting to produce hit songs; he was only concerned with creating music of quality." If he felt the need to host radio shows, write movie musicals, or, for that matter, endorse Arrow shirts and Gillette razors, at least partly for financial reasons, it was not only to help maintain his lifestyle—Isaac Goldberg estimated his expenses in 1932 at no less than an astonishing thousand dollars per week—but to help support his family and to sustain such projects as *Porgy and Bess*.[2]

About 1920, in the first flush of George's success, the immediate Gershwin family moved from Harlem to 501 West 110th Street at Amsterdam Avenue, where their relatively modest apartment contained a workroom with two grand pianos for George. In 1925 the family moved again to more spacious quarters at 316 West 103rd Street between West End Avenue and Riverside Drive—a five-story house, complete with elevator, that included a ballroom on the ground floor that the Gershwins transformed into a table tennis room. Rose and Morris resided on the second floor, Arthur and Frances on the third, Ira (and after 1926 his new wife, Leonore) on the fourth, with George at the top. Observers painted a picturesque portrait of this residence, with Morris riding the elevator, Rose cooking borscht in the kitchen, Frances on her way to dance lessons, and George making occasional retreats to the nearby Whitehall Hotel to get some work done—a scene that might have sprung from the pages of the play *You Can't Take It with You* (1936) by two friends of the Gershwins, George S. Kaufman and Moss Hart. Years later, Frances remembered with some amazement how she would sometimes return home and find groups of people independently socializing on each floor of the house.[3]

This ménage lasted only four years, however. In 1929 George and Ira moved into adjoining penthouses (connected by a terrace) at 33 Riverside Drive, between West 75th and 76th Streets. George's penthouse—with its gym, complete with punching bags and fencing foils, and its view of the Hudson and the Palisades—became known for its Moderne decor, including a "weirdly crenellated electric lamp" on the dining room table that reminded S. N. Berhman of the last act of Eugene O'Neill's *Dynamo*. Gershwin clearly took a keen interest in furnishing this, his first apartment, as documented by a letter to a friend: "I've chosen the materials & colors for the apartment & also the silver. All that remains now is to choose the china. It is really exciting all this business. I went to the factory yesterday & saw my furniture being made. The detail of the whole thing amazes me."[4]

In 1933 George and Ira moved again, this time to apartments across the street from each other on the Upper East Side, connected by a private phone line. Needing space to house his expanding art collection, Gershwin chose a duplex at 132 East 72nd Street, between Park and Lexington, that contained an imposing fourteen rooms. More traditional in its decor than the Riverside Drive penthouse, this apartment contained a study with a specially designed desk for oversize orchestral manuscript paper, an art studio, and, once again, a gym, though Oscar Levant thought its most "ingenious" feature was the absence of a guest room, accusing Gershwin "of foreseeing the occasion when I might want to stay over some night" (in fact, the duplex had upstairs guest quarters).[5]

This would be Gershwin's last New York home. While working in Hollywood in 1930–1931, he rented a house with Ira and Leonore located at 1027 Chevy Chase in Beverly Hills, a dwelling glamorous enough to have served at one time as Greta Garbo's address. (Gershwin joked that the fact that he was sleeping in Garbo's bed kept him up some nights.) On their return to Hollywood in 1936–1937, the three Gershwins rented another stately home in Beverly Hills, a Spanish Colonial located at 1019 North Roxbury Drive, complete with tennis court and swimming pool. By this time Ira, unlike George, had no plans to return to New York, and three years after George's death, he and Leonore bought the house next door at 1021 North Roxbury, where they remained for the rest of their lives.[6]

By the mid-1920s, Gershwin's wealth made it possible for him to hire assistants and staff in addition to the maids that his family had long employed. In the mid-1920s Nanette Kutner began working for him as a secretary, eventually replaced in the 1930s by Zenaide ("Zena") Hanenfeldt, a Russian musician associated with Leon Theremin. Kutner's portrait of Gershwin as "self-conscious and studied," "dignified, dependable," "boyish, marveling at everything," and moody and sometimes "thoughtless," remains a unique recollection. Gershwin also hired domestics, at first couples; then in 1929, a Viennese émigré named Frank Dindl (who, Gershwin wrote, "looks more like an M.D. than a servant"); and finally, after 1931, German-born Paul Mueller, who served Gershwin as valet, chauffeur, masseur, and general assistant till the end.[7]

Whereas Ira liked staying home, poring over reference books and poetry anthologies (though brother Arthur recalled that Ira had been a fine swimmer in his youth, once swimming from Coney Island to Brighton Beach), George was an enthusiastic sportsman who took up, with skill and enormous determination, tennis, golfing, skiing, fishing, horseback riding, boxing, wrestling, table tennis, hiking, and swimming. A great fan of prizefights, he cultivated friendships with champion pugilists Jack Dempsey and Georges Carpentier, and postponed a trip to South Carolina in 1934 in order to attend the now-legendary June 14 bout between heavyweights Max Baer and Primo Carnera. He himself worked out at home with weights, sometimes with a personal trainer; commented Oscar Levant, in a reference to the famous Hercules of Hollywood films: "George had more muscles in his forearms than Steve Reeves."[8]

Gershwin was an excellent dancer as well, to the point that he was able to suggest steps to such brilliant dancers as Fred Astaire, Marilyn Miller, and Jack Donahue in rehearsal and in turn demonstrate some of Astaire's routines to his sister Frances. "When we'd dance together," recalled Frances, "he loved to trick me into rhythms by going off beat with his steps, trying to catch me. I had been a dancer and also had a good sense of rhythm, so he didn't trick me very much." Kay Swift recalled many pleasurable evenings of social dancing with him, and remembered, too, how he would tap-dance, sometimes with cane in hand, while waiting for elevators.[9]

Considering the sedentary life of a composer, athletics and dancing helped channel Gershwin's extraordinary physical energy. "I feel that I was meant for hard physical work, to chop down trees, to use my muscles," he told Isaac Goldberg. "This composing is indoor labor, much of it, and it takes it out of a fellow like me." Like many observers, Gershwin made connections between his personal vigor and, as he put it, the "outdoor pep" of his music, once stating, "I'd like my compositions to be so vital that I'd be required by law to dispense sedatives with each score sold."[10]

In other ways, George and Ira were alike. Both inherited from their parents a love for the theater, an interest in horse racing, a fondness for card games—whether hearts, rummy, casino, or poker—usually played for small stakes, and a general love of gambling. They were also both irrepressible doodlers, with Ira, whose earliest watercolor dated back to 1911, at one point even considering a career as an illustrator. Gershwin, for his part, often sketched heads, especially his own (all nose and chin, not unlike caricatures of him by Miguel Covarrubias and William Auerbach-Levy) on letters, musical sketches, canceled checks, telephone pads, or whatever was at hand, and took up watercoloring in 1927. By 1928 he also had begun acquiring art, including five lithographs of George Bellows, among them *Dempsey through the Ropes* and *Prayer Meeting.*[11]

In 1929 Gershwin started to collect art more seriously and took to scouring New York's museums and galleries, sometimes guided by his cousin, painter Henry Botkin (1896–1983). The son of Rose Gershwin's presumed first cousin Anna Dechinek Botkin, Henry and his younger brother Benjamin had grown close to George and Ira after the Botkins moved from Boston to New York in the early years of the century. A graduate of the Massachusetts School of Art, Henry became a somewhat conservative painter of landscapes and still lifes (though he turned toward abstraction in later years), living primarily in Paris in the late 1920s and early 1930s, while Benjamin pursued a career as one of the century's out-standing anthropologists.[12]

Recalling their explorations of the New York art scene, Botkin re-membered that the galleries "had to open the whole place and pull every-thing out. He [Gershwin] just couldn't wait. He wanted more, and more, and more. He had good judgment too." However, Gershwin bought much of his art from Parisian galleries, with Botkin often serving as his agent; familiar with Gershwin's predilections, the latter would send pho-tographs and descriptions of available items in a suitable price range that he thought would interest his cousin. In a mere seven years or so, Gersh-win spent a reported $50,000 acquiring more than 150 works of art, in-cluding paintings by Chagall, Derain, de Segonzac, Dufy, Gauguin, Ja-cob, Kandinsky, Kokoschka, Léger, Masson, Modigliani, Pascin, Picasso, Rouault, Rousseau, Utrillo, Vlaminck, and other European artists, but also African sculpture and the work of such Americans as Thomas Hart Benton, Maurice Sterne, and Max Weber, the last two personal friends.[13]

Gershwin's taste ran to Parisian artists of a slightly older generation, including those colorful painters known as the Fauves ("wild beasts"), though his interests were catholic enough to encompass Kandinsky and Benton as well. Some evidence indicates a subtle appreciation. In one let-ter to Botkin, for instance, he wrote, "*The Suburbs* of Utrillo is painted with a much more vigorous brush than some of the ones I have seen in America. It is a very luminous picture. It seems to throw out its own light. I am crazy about it." And in discussing Max Weber's *Invocation* (the piece in his collection that gave him "the most pleasure"), he pointed out that the painting's "distortion increases its feeling and adds to the de-sign," adding, "technically . . . it is a composition of triangles, and in it there is a strict absence of line, only color against color." Merle Armitage, a friend and prominent art collector in his own right, praised Gershwin's "discernment" in acquiring the better and rarer work of Derain, Pascin, Utrillo, and others.[14]

In a 1937 essay, *Vanity Fair* editor Frank Crowninshield further ob-served, "Among the modern painters whose works George Gershwin col-lected so prodigally and knowingly, he found his spirit in the most ex-act accord with that of George Rouault. He responded particularly to the Frenchman's breathtaking power; the almost barbaric cadences that infused his canvases. 'Oh,' he used to exclaim, 'if only I could put Rouault into music!'" Botkin confirmed, "The work of Rouault was especially close to him and he was constantly enthralled by the life and spirit that animated his work." In view of the strong Christian iconography in

Rouault's work, this identification seems somewhat unexpected, though not when one considers the painter's intense colors and folklike imagery; or perhaps the fact, too, that many of Rouault's clown and Christ heads resembled Gershwin's own visage.[15]

In his final years, Gershwin took a special interest in Armitage's collection of Paul Klee. "He studied some of my Klee water colors with a magnifying glass one day," recalled Armitage, "then drew back and said, 'What am I doing! My music would not stand up under that kind of scrutiny.'" Armitage presented Gershwin with a watercolor by Klee as well as a lithograph by Arthur B. Davies, an American artist both men admired. (In the decades after his death, the Gershwin estate sold or donated much of his collection—both the Metropolitan Museum of Art and the Museum of Modern Art received a few choice works—though some acquisitions remain in family hands.)[16]

About the same time that Gershwin began collecting art, he started drawing and painting more seriously as well. Indeed, these activities were interrelated, as *Arts & Decoration* explained: "It is a moot question in Mr. Gershwin's mind whether he collects the moderns because he wants to learn to paint; or whether he wants to learn to paint in order to better understand the moderns." With only a few lessons from Botkin, he started producing dozens of pen-and-ink drawings, watercolors, and oils. According to Crowninshield, he regarded his music and his artwork "as almost interchangeable phenomena. They sprang he felt, from the same Freudian elements in him." Gershwin further believed that he had the talent to succeed as an artist, and by the mid-1930s, painting had become not so much a diversion from music as a rival activity that threatened to gain the upper hand.[17]

Gershwin drew and painted landscapes and still lifes, but mostly portraits, including two self-portraits—the whimsical *Self-Portrait in an Opera Hat* (1932) and the more somber *Self-Portrait in a Checkered Sweater* (1936)—along with portraits of William Daly (1929), Charles Martin Loeffler (1929), Botkin (1932), his grandmother (1930), grandfather (1933), father (1933), mother (1933), a black girl (1933), DuBose Heyward (1934), Diego Rivera (1936), Emily Paley (1936), Arnold Schoenberg (1937), Jerome Kern (1937), and others. He based many of these portraits on photographs that he had taken himself, though he used one by Edward Weston for his portrait of Schoenberg. "George never prettied up things," Botkin said in discussing his portrait of Kern in particular. "You notice the tie, the collar. He gave it plenty of verve."[18]

That both the Schoenberg and the Kern portraits became familiar representations of their subjects evidenced Gershwin's real achievement in this area. Shana Alexander, whose mother, Cecelia Ager, sat for Gershwin, provided additional testimony to his abilities as a portraitist: confronted as a child with Gershwin's portrait of her mother "heavily lined in muddy purples and greens" after the manner of Rouault, Alexander was relieved to learn that Alexander Woollcott had dismissed Gershwin's paintings as "god-awful"; but she later marveled at how Gershwin "had been able to look into the future and see the middle-aged woman inside the jazzy ex-Coed who was posing for him." Meanwhile, a major exhibition of Gershwin's original work at New York's Marie Harriman Gallery in late 1937 brought critical recognition of their "undeniable quality," with some reviews singling out the watercolors, the line drawings, and the self-portraits for special praise.[19]

Gershwin's painterly technique apparently derived from such masters as Cézanne and Kokoschka. However, his utter directness and playful humor proved less like many of the Europeans he so admired, or an American like Arthur Dove (1880–1946)—whose ebulliently abstract Gershwin-inspired paintings of 1927 included *George Gershwin—Rhapsody in Blue, Part I; George Gershwin—Rhapsody in Blue, Part II;* and *I'll Build a Stairway to Paradise—Gershwin*—than those contemporary artists with ties to folk art and popular illustration, such as Charles Alston and other members of the Harlem Renaissance, or the Mexican Miguel Covarrubias, who produced his own *Rhapsody in Blue* in 1927.[20]

This sensibility naturally drew him to the Mexican muralists, and when spending some weeks in Mexico with his psychiatrist, Gregory Zilboorg, in late 1935, he sought out local artists, attending a gathering at the home of Estrella Elizago on his second night in Mexico City with Miguel Covarrubias, Roberto Montenegro, and Diego Rivera. "We had a perfectly swell time," he wrote to Ira, "Dr. Zilboorg being particularly amusing." In the days that followed, Rivera showed Gershwin his work at the National Palace, while Gershwin made a colored-pencil sketch of Rivera's head (signed by the sitter, "Encantado de poser para George, Diego Rivera"). "Mexico is more wonderful than I expected it would be, full of surprises," George wrote Ira from Cuernavaca after touring Mexico City and Taxco, before departing from the port city of Mazatlán. On returning to New York he painted, in the style of Rivera, Emily Paley wearing a Mexican costume selected by Frida Kahlo.[21]

While in Mexico, Gershwin also met painter David Alfaro Siqueiros, and the two became friends after the latter arrived in New York in early 1936 to direct the Siqueiros Experimental Workshop, an atelier that produced such agitprop as floats for New York's May Day parade and poster portraits of the Communist Party's presidential and vice presidential candidates for a rally at Madison Square Garden. The workshop depended on private patronage, and Gershwin proved a generous benefactor. "We developed an extraordinary camaraderie," Siqueiros recalled in his memoirs, "and I believe that our exchange of ideas about the relations of painting and orchestral composition was reciprocally useful." Gershwin's purchases of various paintings, including *Two Little Mexican Girls, Self-Portrait with Mirror, Niña Madre,* and the commissioned *George in an Imaginary Concert Hall,* helped Siqueiros prepare for an exhibition in December 1936.[22]

A large canvas five by seven and a half feet, *George in an Imaginary Concert Hall* (1936) depicts the composer performing before a full-capacity crowd in an enormous theater, a "theater of the masses," as Siqueiros described it to Gershwin's delight. Siqueiros, who waggishly described Gershwin as the greatest "nuisance" *(pedigüeño)* he had ever known, had to bring increasingly larger canvases to the composer's apartment as the latter changed his mind about exactly what he wanted; at first he requested just a head portrait, then a full-length portrait, and then a portrait of himself performing in a theater, with mini-portraits of friends and family in the first two rows of the theater. Gershwin mostly provided photographs of the subjects—thus far identified as family members Morris and Rose, Ira and Leonore, Arthur, Frances and Leopold, Leopold Godowsky Sr., and Henry Botkin, and friends William Daly, Max Dreyfus, Oscar Levant, Lou and Emily Paley, Mabel Schirmer, Kay Swift, and Gregory Zilboorg—though Rose at least sat for the painter. Siqueiros recalled that after he completed the painting, he and Gershwin celebrated with a banquet at the Waldorf Astoria for thirty women and themselves, "a bacchanal in which our masculine impotence was inarguably proved . . . since we began by not knowing in which direction to head. Almost trembling, George Gershwin said to me, 'There have never been in the history of the world two flies more drowned in honey than we.'" As a final request, Gershwin asked that Siqueiros add his own portrait to the gallery, and the painter, "in violation of the safety codes of the theater," duly found some room for his head "in a corner just beside lights of the kind that burn hotter than a gas stove." (In 1961 Ira Gershwin bequeathed this painting to the Ransom Center at the University of Texas, where it arrived in 1997.)[23]

Gershwin's activities as an art collector and painter naturally shed light on his music. Botkin, for instance, observed resemblances between "the linear counterpoint of a Gershwin composition" and "the linear factors of an arrangement by Picasso or Kandinsky," noting, too, a special rapport between Gershwin's work and that of Max Weber. Merle Armitage's description of one of Gershwin's watercolors—"It seems to have been rendered with a childish, primitive violence and yet possesses an opulence of beauty"—seemed apropos of his music as well. In 1929 Gershwin drew his own typically ingenuous connection by citing the use of modern garments in the religious iconography of the ancient Greeks, Raphael, and Rembrandt with that "element of the contemporaneous" in his own music (and that of Mozart and Beethoven).[24]

Ira, who began painting seriously about the same time George did, worked in a style that, while more cartoonish than George's, featured remarkable similarities, right down to the preferred palette of rusts, teals, and grays. And although Ira's unflattering self-portrait *My Body* (1932), in which he appears potbellied in underwear, seemingly parodies George's *Self-Portrait in an Opera Hat,* these two paintings at the same time have a good deal in common—in technique, in style, and even in their whimsy. As the one area in which both men worked, their paintings most readily illustrate the similarities that undergirded their collaborative efforts.[25]

In his later years, Gershwin avidly took up photography as well, shooting numerous pictures of family and close friends. Often experimental in their use of lighting and perspective, these photographs reveal a Rembrandt-like preoccupation with illuminating faces against dark, indistinct backgrounds. Characteristically enough, Gershwin utilized time-exposure features in order to take photographs of himself.

While nowhere as bookish as Ira, Gershwin also shared to a degree his brother's literary interests, which tended toward British writers. While in London in 1924, he wrote to Ira that he hoped to purchase sets of the writings of philosopher Herbert Spencer and novelist Joseph Conrad. A 1928 profile cited his envy of the first-edition collections of Buddy De-Sylva and Jerome Kern and his fondness for the work of George Bernard Shaw and Max Beerbohm, two ironic stylists. In the same year he stopped by Sylvia Beach's legendary bookstore in Paris and purchased a signed copy of James Joyce's *Ulysses.* Although Carl Van Vechten denied that Gershwin was a "perceptive reader of literature," the composer at least acquired an impressive library. Calling on Gershwin at his apartment in the 1930s, Irving Kolodin observed books ranging from Ernest Hemingway, Aldous Huxley, and Virginia Woolf to an autographed copy of Rudy Vallee's *Vagabond Lover;* another visitor espied editions of Kant, Schopenhauer, Dostoyevsky, Nietzsche, and Proust. He apparently had some friendly contact with Amy Lowell, in his own words, "the great New England poet and seer." John Harkins further reported that he maintained an "intimate correspondence" with John Galsworthy, while pianist Lester Donahue observed the composer in Carmel discussing poetry with Robinson Jeffers "as intelligently as his favorite music."[26]

Kay Swift remembered that Gershwin "was interested in *every* subject, not just music and art. If he saw a lovely plant sitting on the table— he had a thing about flowers—he would want to know everything about it: what it was called, in what kind of soil it grew best, how often to add water, if there was a good book he could read on the subject. He approached life that way—he had a universal interest that was rare." On another occasion she recalled, "Anything he wanted to learn, he hit with a terrific sock. He just tore into it."[27]

As opposed to Ira, who barely learned to drive, Gershwin's interests extended to cars. At one point, he owned a Mercedes "painted the snappiest of greens," and in later years, a Buick. He also appreciated fine apparel. Even as a boy he dressed smartly, with "high stiff collars" and a "shirt with cuffs," as Yip Harburg recalled. As an adult, he became a veritable fashion plate, sporting custom-made English suits, spats, golfing outfits, riding outfits, tennis outfits. A 1926 photograph of Gershwin surrounded by numerous friends reveals him as the nattiest dresser, his double-breasted pinstripe jacket and polka-dotted tie a notable contrast to Ira's casual V-necked sweater and bow tie. Oscar Levant wryly remarked the grandeur of Gershwin's wardrobe, including his "repertory of tropical beach robes of almost Oriental splendor" and the "ducal fur-trimmed overcoat" that gave him "the appearance of a perpetual guest conductor."[28]

Gershwin's distinctively urbane charm complemented his refined appearance, including his slender, manicured fingers. "His manner," recalled Dimitri Tiomkin, "was courteous; this, I was to find, was invariable. He was one of those who take pleasure in courtesy for its own sake." "His voice was soft," observed Isaac Goldberg, "and it had a way, even in declarative sentences, of rising in a question-like curve. He had a gentle manner."[29]

Despite or perhaps because of Gershwin's elegant dress and graceful manners, Goldberg, in his seminal biography, seemed compelled to emphasize his manly attributes—"wholesome," "thoroughly masculine," not the "fluttery, effeminate" type, nothing "lily" about him—in a way that, while perhaps defensive, underscored the complexity of his subject. For reminiscences of Gershwin pointed to a figure both self-centered and generous, naive and perceptive, melancholy and cheerful, callous and sensitive, intemperate and restrained, promiscuous and prudish, outgoing and shy. "He was a very complicated person," recalled Anne Brown, who created the role of Bess in *Porgy and Bess,* as mentioned earlier. "He had so many different sides. And if one was sensitive one could sense this conflict, so to speak, in his behavior."[30]

For example, although Gershwin loved company—he seemed ever surrounded by friends and family—his valet Paul Mueller, among others, emphasized an emotional reticence that seems to have been characteristic of the Gershwin family as a whole. Irving Caesar described him—at least away from the piano—as "diffident" and "passive," not only with women, but even in professional matters: "He wouldn't project himself as I did when we were together to try to sell something [a song]. . . . He was just a little bit withdrawn." Ethel Merman similarly noted, "There was an aloofness—not rudeness, but an aloofness—about him. I think basically he was shy more than anything else. He adored me. I know that. But from afar."[31]

Another contradiction lay in what Bennett Cerf called Gershwin's "monumental but strangely unobjectionable conceit." Recalled Tiomkin:

> With company at a restaurant, he'd walk in first, with a gracious air, as a king might, taking the first place as his royal prerogative. At a party where eminent pianists were present he'd go to the piano and play all evening, never thinking of making way for anyone else. He had a supreme self-confidence that may sound egotistical; but it was always accompanied by his courtesy and charm. He thought it acceptable to all, and it was.

"He was just plain dazzled by the spectacle of his own career," explained Behrman; "his unaffected delight in it was somewhat astonishing but it was also amusing and refreshing." Bennett Cerf liked telling how, on driving "rather recklessly" to a football game, he was cautioned by the composer, "For God's sake, be careful! You've got Gershwin in the car!"[32]

Friends were not always so amused, as when he told Harry Ruby, "I couldn't afford to take a chance on my hands the way you do. But then your hands don't matter so much." But Ruby later reflected, "He was, of course, right." Gershwin's friends more than tolerated his egoism because, paradoxically enough, he appeared so modest. "In spite of the self-certainty of his own uniqueness," remembered Harold Arlen, "I always saw a questioning look—which to me meant humility. His greatness lay not only in his dynamic talent, drive and sureness, but in that questioning look." He struck most observers, including Igor Stravinsky, as honest and unspoiled, and intent on pleasing others.[33]

In their satiric play about lost ideals, *Merrily We Roll Along* (1934), George S. Kaufman and Moss Hart tapped this quality of "unobjectionable conceit" in an apparent caricature of Gershwin pointedly named Sam Frankl. At one point Frankl, a pianist at the start of his career, responds to entertainment agent Sid Kramer's admiration of Berlin and Kern by saying,

> *Frankl:* Those old hacks. They were washed up ten years ago, only they don't know it. Listen—when they write the history of American music they're only going to mention one song writer. Sam Frankl.
>
> *Sid:* Sam Frankl? Who's that?
>
> *Frankl:* Me.
>
> *Sid (a trifle stunned):* Oh! Well, it doesn't do a young fellow any harm to feel that way.
>
> *Frankl:* What do you mean feel that way. I *know.* Why should I be modest? I'm a genius. It's got nothing to do with me—I just am. Say, I sit down in the morning and what comes out of that piano frightens me sometimes. It's tremendous. Berlin, Kern, Friml—don't make me laugh! Listen to this one. This is Frankl.

Espied at a performance of the show, Gershwin seemed, according to one Broadway columnist, "embarrassed now and then." But the play did not offend him. On the contrary, he told Isaac Goldberg, "I'm the only normal person in the show!" In any case, his "conceit" became an accepted source of teasing within his inner circle, as indicated by his friendship with Kaufman and Hart.[34]

Along with his "unobjectionable conceit," commentators most often singled out what many perceived as his childlike nature. "If I . . . could have but one adjective for George Gershwin," stated Alexander Woollcott, "that adjective would be 'ingenuous.'" Describing Gershwin as "boyish," S. N. Behrman noted that when he played golf, "He ran from hole to hole. He was like a young colt." Both Arthur Kober and Robert Payne depicted him as a figure of eternal youthfulness who never grew up. Kitty Carlisle referred, somewhat along these lines, to "something terribly vulnerable about him," a need for approval that made people feel "very protective about him." Vernon Duke (along with others) made the natural connection between his youthfulness and his music, writing,

"George was American youth itself, and his music was the voice of Young America."[35]

Such observations contrasted with portrayals of Gershwin as sage and mature. Rouben Mamoulian faced this seeming disparity head-on:

> George was like a child. He had a child's innocence and imagination. . . . Yet at times he was like a patriarch. I would look at him and all but see a long white beard and a staff in his hand. This would usually happen whenever a group of people around him argued violently about something. George would smile and look at them as though they were little children. . . . The simple gaiety of a child and the clear serenity of the old were the two extremities of George's character. In between there was much of him that was neither simple nor clear, nor perhaps as happy. . . . He was a complicated, nervous product of our age. There was in him an intricate and restless combination of intellectual and emotional forces.

S. N. Behrman, who some years before Woollcott popularized the notion of Gershwin as "ingenuous," at the same time thought this epithet "a condescension with which articulate people often indulge themselves when speaking of the less articulate," and wondered whether the composer's response to his mother's caution against his playing the piano too much at parties—"You see, the trouble is, when I don't play, I don't have a good time"—signaled "ingenuousness or sophistication."[36]

Gershwin's friends often alluded to another duality: his capacity for great joy, on the one hand, and a tendency toward moodiness on the other. "Thinking over the people I have known," wrote Behrman, "it strikes me that George stands almost alone among them for possessing an almost nonexistent quality: the quality of joy." Kay Swift similarly mentioned the "joyous delight in whatever he was doing," and Tiomkin remembered him once saying, "I'm the happiest man in the world. I get paid so much for what I want to do most of all." At the same time, many detected a disconsolate side, one that Gershwin associated with his Russian heritage ("Here I am, just a sad Russian again," he would tell Swift). "Deep in the being of George Gershwin was a map of all the human suffering of the world," wrote Armitage. "Anyone who knew him could not have missed that characteristic feature." In his brooding bronze bust of the composer (1929), Isamu Noguchi brought some such "feature" (described by the sculptor as "the thoughtfulness of a rich and sensitive nature") to the fore.[37]

In his unpublished play *Let Me Hear the Melody!* (1951), set in Hollywood, Behrman provided, by way of the character of composer Vincent Bendix, probably the richest literary portrayal of Gershwin, considerably more so than the caricature drawn by Kaufman and Hart, or the thumbnail sketch (via the persona of Harry Hirsch) found in Edmund Wilson's *I Thought of Daisy* (1929), though one still not fully rounded. Behrman in particular drew on the composer's years in the mid-1930s, dramatizing an encounter between Gershwin and film producer Sam Goldwyn (here represented by the character Sig Ratchett) that provides both the play's title and its central metaphor (Behrman also apparently modeled Vincent's love for the actress Esme Smith on Gershwin's infatuation with Paulette Goddard). When asked by the play's hero, playwright Nolan Sayre, what he hopes to write about when he returns to New York, Bendix even echoes remarks Gershwin once made to Behrman: "About suffering. I think a lot about that. About people suffering. I think about young girls sitting on fire-escapes outside cold-water flats on hot summer nights, dreaming of happiness, dreaming of love. People dying without telling some person they love that they love them. All that." Vincent emerges as at once wisely discerning and sweetly naive, a symbol of light amid the corruption and vulgarity of Hollywood. "You are the most enviable man in the world," another character, Manny Korvin, tells him, "because you have talent without the complications that go with talent."[38]

Gershwin, of course, had his "complications," as Anne Brown and Rouben Mamoulian pointed out, and as reflected by an excess of nervous energy. He frequently stretched his neck and jaw (described by some as a "tic"), compulsively chewed on pipes and cigars, and had the habit, noted by one reporter, of punctuating his words with "occasional staccato beats of his left hand, tightened at such times about the bowl of his ever-present briar pipe momentarily removed from his mouth." Stravinsky remembered him as "very nervously energetic," and Swift mentioned in particular his "vivacious, quick walk." Henry Cowell similarly recalled, "He was always in a terrible hurry. . . . There was tension in his music and in his voice; he was always scurrying to get the words out, always hurrying to finish one thing and get on with the next."[39]

Gershwin's enormous drive presumably contributed to his chronic gastrointestinal problems, including indigestion, constipation, and cramps; that he first remembered the onset of these digestive troubles in conjunction with the 1922 premiere of his opera *Blue Monday Blues*, and that he accordingly spoke of his having a "composer's stomach," would suggest as much. In any case, he became fairly abstemious about what he ate. And as far as alcohol was concerned, he drank only the occasional glass of beer or wine. In the 1930s he also curtailed his smoking habits, including his beloved cigars. Goldberg described all this as Gershwin's "health-complex," writing, "He has a weakness for dietary novelties, and at times will pick his way through a meal with the daintiness of the princess who could feel the pea beneath seven layers of bed-sheets." Oscar Levant described a typical Gershwin menu as consisting of "gruel (and such variants as oatmeal and farina), . . . zwieback, melba toast (only on festive occasions), Ry-krisp, Swedish bread and rusk. The 'pièce de résistance' was stewed fruit or, when he was in a gluttonous mood, apple sauce." Gershwin also took agar-agar, an Asian gelatin product with mild laxative effects. Frances Gershwin recalled, too, that he "brought vegetables into our house because my mother just never paid any attention to these things. He became very conscious of food and what was good for one." Gershwin's diet was not as strict as all that, however. Frances herself spoke of his "passion" for ice cream; and Kay Halle recalled that she would often bring him salami and brown bread as a late-night snack while he was working on *Porgy and Bess*. Yet another source reported that Gershwin's friends howled when they heard about his presumed care with food, saying, "He eats almost everything."[40]

Gershwin's "composer's stomach" was no doubt one factor prompting him into psychoanalysis with Gregory Zilboorg in 1934. Moreover, he could not decide whether to marry the recently divorced Kay Swift, who went to Zilboorg herself and who encouraged him to do likewise. But Gershwin more generally saw psychotherapy in terms of his personal and artistic growth, telling one reporter, "I'm a great debunker. I'm always searching for the truth. Psychology is like taking a college course. People who can't face themselves can never go on. I want to know myself so I can know others. I'm interested in one thing—life. I want to find its spark of truth, and have it come through my music." In 1958 Zilboorg himself stated, "I am one of those who believe that you can help artists to develop their creative capacities."[41]

Gershwin stayed in therapy for about a year and a half (from the spring of 1934 to the fall of 1935), seeing Zilboorg as often as five times a week. And he remained good friends with the psychiatrist, traveling with him to Mexico at the end of 1935, as mentioned, and seeking his advice still later. Zilboorg's continued role as a mentor of sorts came through in a 1936 letter to "Goish" in which he wrote, "It was good to know that you had not started working yet, for that meant to me that all is in the future and 'the future' is the most conspicuous birth mark of youth. There was a time when it had a birthright on it, but Hitler took it away—der Ostasiatischer Schweinehund!"[42]

Born into a Jewish family in Kiev in 1890, Zilboorg served in the medical corps of the Russian army in 1915 and 1916 and graduated from the Psychoneurological Institute of Petrograd in 1917, during which year he worked for the Kerensky government. He left Russia after the Bolshevik revolution, arriving in 1919 in New York, where he obtained a medical degree from Columbia University in 1926. After some years on staff at Bloomingdale Hospital, he established a private practice in 1931. A brilliant and somewhat eccentric man (he converted progressively from socialism to Quakerism to Catholicism), his writings included highly respected publications on psychology (including extensive research on suicide) as well as a popular translation of Leonid Andreyev's play *He Who Gets Slapped*. One observer described him as "a kind of man little known and less appreciated in this country: the rounded intellectual, idealistic and cynical at once, a professional man with a strong political sense, thoroughly cultured," as someone who "maintained a high theoretical disdain for money, but enjoyed a high income." (When Rouben Mamoulian asked Gershwin how much Zilboorg charged, he answered, "He finds out how much you make and then charges you more than you can afford!" Moss Hart reportedly paid him the astronomical fee of one hundred dollars for an hourlong session, while Gershwin's bills for 1935 topped three thousand dollars.) Lillian Hellman, his patient for seven years, observed, "He was an old-fashioned Socialist who hated inherited wealth as undeserved, and many of his patients were people like that."[43]

Zilboorg attracted as clients not only such members of the arts community as Hart and Hellman, but some wellborn men with liberal leanings, including Swift's husband, James Warburg; his cousin Edward Warburg; Marshall Field III; and Ralph Ingersoll. Zilboorg apparently fostered the social consciences of the latter group, which led to his portrayal in the press as the Svengali of the well-heeled American left, especially after Field and Ingersoll began publishing the alternative newspaper *PM*.[44]

Oscar Levant took a characteristically bemused attitude toward Gershwin's sessions with Zilboorg, writing, "This was a wholly unnecessary adventure, for it proved him to be enthusiastically unneurotic." On the other hand, Gershwin's sister, Frances, observed a greater generosity after he began therapy. Moreover, his contact with Zilboorg possibly made him more socially aware as well. True, many artists moved markedly toward the left in the early 1930s. And Gershwin had revealed an interest in progressive musical education as early as 1929, when he attended a recital of music composed by children attending the Emanuel Sisterhood of Personal Service on East 82nd Street. But, coincidentally or not, he seemingly showed increasing sensitivity to social matters soon after starting therapy. In July 1934, for instance, he wrote to his friend

Emily Paley, "Henry [Botkin], Paul [Mueller] & myself discuss our two favorite subjects, Hitler's Germany and God's women." And in a September 1934 letter to the *New York Times,* he solicited contributions to the Henry Street Settlement Music School, a music program that targeted New York's poor and immigrant children.[45]

Two months later, he publicly welcomed not only the repeal of Prohibition but also the American recognition of the Soviet Union, though he remained nonideological about both matters, claiming simply that legalizing alcohol would be good for music, and that formal relations with the Soviet Union would allow both countries to reap economic benefits. (Concerning the latter, he added that he was "personally delighted because I always wanted to go there.") And whereas Isaac Goldberg reported in 1931 that Gershwin thought politics "a bore," on the composer's return from a trip with Zilboorg to Mexico in 1935 he told reporters, "I am going to interest myself in politics, and it is true that in Mexico I talked a great deal with Diego Rivera, and with his radical friends, who discussed at length their doctrines and their intentions." Even before leaving Mexico, Gershwin used, albeit tongue in cheek, the phrase *capitalistic luxuries* in a letter to Ira.[46]

Furthermore, Gershwin surely realized in 1936 that he was helping to underwrite the radical Siqueiros Workshop. He even acquired one Siqueiros painting titled *Proletarian Victim* (1933). (Zilboorg also assisted the Siqueiros Workshop by purchasing some of the painter's work.) While such actions did not necessarily betoken Communist sympathies (Gershwin, who publicly supported Al Smith in the 1928 presidential election, was reportedly a lifelong Democrat), it at least suggested support for the anti-fascist Popular Front. Indeed, Gershwin participated in an anti-Nazi rally in the fall of 1936, and during the same years affiliated himself with the left-wing Film and Photo League. Moreover, his and Ira's Hollywood home became a center of liberal political activity, with Leonore's "labor causes" including a June 1937 tea for the imprisoned and apparently framed labor leader Thomas Mooney. Had he lived longer, Gershwin might have addressed some of these concerns in his work, for some jottings made in his sketchbook at the very end of his life—"Suite / comments / working class / Idle rich / intolerance / children / Fear / Nature"—point in that direction. In any case, his liberalism posthumously provoked the ire of anti-Communist demagogue Senator Joseph McCarthy, who in 1953 deemed his music "subversive," though contrary to some reports, the State Department did not actually ban his music from official American libraries around the world.[47]

However helpful and stimulating psychotherapy might have been for Gershwin, many commentators have disparaged Zilboorg on account of those unorthodox practices that occasionally earned him censure from his peers, including socializing with patients and speaking openly of their problems. Drawing an analogy with Stalin, Hellman herself wrote, "After he [Zilboorg] died it took me a long time to believe the ugliness I was hearing. I guess people who mesmerize other people die absolutely on the day they die—the magic is gone." Behrman took a particularly dim view of the "boorish" Zilboorg—explicitly in his memoirs, and less directly in the aforementioned play *Let Me Hear the Melody!* (to the extent that Vincent Bendix represents Gershwin). At one point in the play, Vincent tells his friend Nolan Sayre that he was "fairly happy" until his psychiatrist reminded him that he knew neither French nor history; Nolan responds by declaring the psychiatrist "an unmitigated ass." In another exchange, Vincent seems something of a pathetic dupe:

> Vincent *(going easily into his case-history):* I never could fall in love. It worried me. It worried me terribly. I went to my psychoanalyst about it. *(Nolan finds Vincent's simplicity touching. He watches him)*
> Nolan: And what did *he* say?
> Vincent: He said it was—an "emotional deficiency." "Arrested development emotionally." "Emotional in-fan-til-ism." *(Vincent is not really at home with these phrases but he repeats them with conscious accuracy)*[48]

Although Behrman presumably had in mind Gershwin during his final months in Hollywood, the composer's correspondence during this period reveals a more articulate and knowing figure than that suggested by the character of Vincent Bendix. Pleased with his Beverly Hills home, he found California more rewarding than he had in the past, as he explained to Julia Van Norman in November 1936:

> Hollywood has grown up since our last visit and has actually got something to offer besides a sun and an ocean and interesting scenery. It's getting some brains. I was delighted to find in many instances a point of view that was progressive and searching in places that formerly thought only of money. They are buying talent now where formerly they bought women and men who could boast roman noses and bedroom eyes. It is promising. Of course it still contains yes-men, charlatans, phonies, career-women, show-offs, cheats, stupid executives, neurotics by the yard, and disappointed stars.

A few months later, in April, he expressed even greater satisfaction to Norman about his time in Hollywood: "I've learned & felt more in 8 months out here than I thought possible for me. Of course the break with the East had a lot to do with it, but Hollywood is in itself capable of many of the most interesting twists & turns. Right now I am having a swell time. I suppose it's the old pendulum swinging back on the famous law of compensation paying some dividends on former costly pains. I am not trying to figure out what it is however. I accept it." And Oscar Levant noted, along these lines, "I must say that up until the six months preceding George Gershwin's death, life for him was just one big, wild, marvelous dream come true."[49]

At the same time, no fewer than four friends described Gershwin as "unhappy" during his final months: Harold Arlen, who found him "often unhappy and uneasy"; George Pallay, who similarly thought him "unhappy and a bit moody" and "critical of things, people and events"; Sigmund Spaeth, who stated, "George was not happy in Hollywood"; and Alexander Steinert, who remembered Gershwin saying, "I am thirty-eight, famous, and rich, but profoundly unhappy. Why?" Although by this point he was experiencing severe headaches caused by—unbeknownst to all—a brain tumor, many of his friends simply attributed his unhappiness to his working conditions in Hollywood or to his unrequited love for Paulette Goddard, to the point of wondering whether he was having a nervous breakdown (though some further suspected that his headaches were related to his use of an anti-balding device involving a metal suction cup placed on the scalp). Certainly composing three films in one year had been exhausting, as he made clear in his resigned, but hopeful correspondence with Mabel Schirmer. Moreover, Hollywood encouraged a psychological explanation for all physical ills, according to Behrman, who wrote, "Hollywood was so preempted by the psychoanalysts that it was inconceivable that any ailment could on occasion be physical. . . . Whatever was wrong with you must be a mental aberration due to some disappointment connected with the film industry."[50]

In fact, in the course of his last six months, Gershwin's physical health had been progressively deteriorating—surely the main reason for his growing despondency. He had complained of smelling burning rubber for some time, and during appearances with the Los Angeles Symphony in February, he experienced a blackout, accompanied by the perception of a foul scent, at the very end of the slow movement of the Concerto in F. After consulting with Zilboorg by phone, he had a medical checkup in late February; no problems were detected, but throughout the spring he experienced, especially in the mornings and during moments of nervousness or tension, disagreeable olfactory hallucinations, headaches, and dizzy spells, including another blackout while sitting in a barber shop in April.[51]

As late as May 27, Gershwin told his sister that he was in "good" health, but in early June, his headaches and vertigo worsened. He duly consulted a psychoanalyst recommended by Zilboorg, Ernest Simmel, who immediately referred him to an internist, Gabriel Segall, who examined him on June 9. "Of late I haven't been feeling particularly well," Gershwin wrote to his mother the following day, but he assured her that the situation was not serious. Indeed, an electrocardiogram, urinalysis, blood work, and other tests revealed no abnormalities. But Segall recommended that he consult a neurologist, Eugene Ziskind, who examined him on June 20, and who observed an impaired sense of smell in Gershwin's right nasal passage (hyposmia) as well as an oversensitivity to light (photophobia). Gershwin entered Cedars of Lebanon Hospital on June 23 for further study, but X-rays, an ocular fundiscopic examination, a Wassermann test, a roentgenogram of the skull, and other tests proved inconclusive. Eager to return to work and reluctant to undergo another procedure, Gershwin decided against a lumbar puncture, and he was released from the hospital on June 26 with the diagnosis "most likely hysteria." The doctors presumably thought a lumbar puncture could help determine, among other possibilities, the presence of a brain tumor, though on his release, Gershwin allegedly told Oscar Levant, with a laugh, that a brain tumor "had been ruled out."[52]

After returning home from the hospital Gershwin, though under daily medical care, declined precipitously. His motor coordination worsened— he stumbled on stairs, dropped objects, spilled liquids, and had trouble using a fork and playing the piano—and grew increasingly listless, in part because of the phenobarbital administered to help relieve his everworsening headaches, which occasionally knocked him to the ground in pain. On July 4, after about a week at home, Gershwin, attended by Paul Mueller and a male nurse, Paul Levy, relocated to the quiet of Yip Harburg's empty house. About this time, he experienced two epileptic seizures known as automatisms: he tried to push Mueller out of a moving car on the way to his psychiatrist; and he smeared a box of chocolates, a gift from Leonore, over his body.[53]

In the evening on July 9, Gershwin fell into a coma and was rushed to Cedars of Lebanon, never again to regain consciousness. Segall and Ziskind, along with a young neurosurgeon, Carl Rand, examined him, and on the afternoon of July 10 a spinal tap was administered, showing evidence of a brain tumor. In an attempt to fly in one or another famous neurosurgeon from the East Coast, Leonore telephoned Emil Mosbacher in New York, who in turn called Boston's Harvey Cushing, widely regarded as the country's greatest neurosurgeon; retired from surgery, Cushing recommended another renowned brain surgeon, Walter Dandy of Johns Hopkins. Through a call to the White House from Los Angeles, George Pallay arranged for the navy to bring Dandy, then yachting in Chesapeake Bay, to shore. But the urgency of the situation demanded immediate intervention, so a neurosurgeon from the University of California Medical School, Howard Naffziger, flew in from Lake Tahoe to operate (with Rand's assistance) during the early morning hours of July 11. Ira and Leonore, along with Oscar Levant, George Pallay, and other friends, awaited the results.

The operation lasted five hours, with an hour and a half required just to locate—by way of ventriculography—a tumor in the right temporal lobe. The surgeons removed a gliomatous cyst as well as a deeply imbedded tumor nodule subsequently diagnosed as a glioblastoma multiforme. About six in the morning, family and friends returned home, to be notified by phone later that morning that Gershwin had died at 10:35 A.M., some five hours after the completed operation. "I do not see what more you could have done for Mr. Gershwin," Walter Dandy wrote to Gabriel Segall. "It was just one of those fulminating tumors." Had Gershwin survived the operation, he most likely would have experienced some paralysis; but in any event, the tumor presumably would have grown back quickly, causing more pain and, within months, death. "I think the outcome is much the best for himself," opined Dandy, "for a man as brilliant as he with a recurring tumor would have been terrible; it would have been a slow death."[54]

In discussions of Gershwin's misdiagnosis over the years, blame has been apportioned especially to his psychiatrists, in particular Gregory Zilboorg, as well as to such friends and family members as Moss Hart and Leonore Gershwin, who maintained virtually to the very end that Gershwin's symptoms were psychogenic (as late as July 10, the day before Gershwin died, Richard Rodgers wrote to his wife that he had heard—presumably from Hart—that Gershwin had had "a complete mental collapse"). But Gershwin's physicians, including his neurologist, seem most culpable in this regard. Granted, his doctors had relatively primitive diagnostic tools at their disposal, including no access to an electroencephalogram (EEG), which would have determined the physical nature of his symptoms. And Gershwin himself refused a spinal tap. Still, it seems hard to believe that it took a coma to convince the medical community that Gershwin, with all his debilitating symptoms, was physically ill.[55]

Gershwin's physicians may have misjudged his medical condition even after his death. In 1982 Swedish neurosurgeon Bengt Ljunggren, while concluding that ultimately nothing could have been done to save Gershwin's life, suggested as a root cause for his chronic gastrointestinal problems a low-grade astrocytoma of many years that degenerated into a fulminating glioblastoma only in its final phase. Neurologist Allen Silverstein, writing in 1995, was skeptical; among other things, he thought that Ljunggren relied too heavily on unsubstantiated claims that Gershwin suffered from nausea. But noting a recollection by Mitch Miller that in January 1934, while on tour with Gershwin, the latter imagined smelling burning garbage, pathologist Gregory Sloop argued in 2001 that the composer would not have experienced such a hallucination this early had he had a glioblastoma as opposed to a more benign pilocytic astrocytoma; and thus suggested, like Ljunggren, that this astrocytoma, perhaps in conjunction with other factors, could have been the source of Gershwin's stomach problems. Examining photomicrographs of the composer's tumor, Sloop further found no evidence of a glioblastoma, leading him to conclude that the tumor never degenerated, and that Gershwin would have had a reasonably good prognosis had the doctors been able to operate before he succumbed to a coma.[56]

Gershwin's body was sent east by train, and funeral services were held simultaneously on July 15 at Temple Emanu-El in Manhattan and Temple B'nai B'rith (now the Wilshire Boulevard Temple) in Los Angeles. Ira arrived in New York by plane, "white as a sheet," as Vernon Duke recalled, and "groggy after an overdose of sleeping pills." Nearly 3,500 people jammed into Emanu-El to pay their respects, and another thousand waited outside in the drizzling rain. The honorary pallbearers, headed by Governor Herbert H. Lehman and Mayor Fiorello La Guardia, included the former mayor, Jimmy Walker, as well as dozens of other eminent figures, including George M. Cohan, Walter Damrosch, Vernon Duke, W. C. Handy, Josef Hofmann, George S. Kaufman, and Paul Whiteman. Rabbi Nathan Perilman conducted the service, which included selections by Bach, Handel, Beethoven, and Schumann, along with readings of Psalms 90 and 120, while Rabbi Stephen S. Wise delivered a short eulogy, stating in part that Gershwin "was America's folkish musician, drawing his nature from the breath of American folk life and all its ways. . . . There are countries in Central Europe which would have flung out this Jew. America welcomed him and he repaid America by singing the songs of America's soul with the gusto of a child, with a filial tenderness of a son." In Los Angeles, Rabbi Edgar Magnin led the service and Oscar Hammerstein delivered a eulogy; Richard Rodgers reported to his wife that the service was "quite simple," and that Hammerstein spoke "beautifully," but that Magnin "gave the worst exhibition of bad taste and stupidity I've ever encountered. Its one advantage was that instead of making people weep it made them furious." Gershwin was buried in a family plot in Mount Hope Cemetery, Hastings-on-Hudson, shortly thereafter converted into a family mausoleum built by his mother.[57]

On August 9, 1937, a memorial concert was held in New York's Lewisohn Stadium, which for some years had been associated with Gershwin's music. A record crowd of more than twenty thousand people crammed into the arena to hear an all-Gershwin concert that included Ferde Grofé and Alexander Smallens alternately leading the New York Philharmonic in various concert works, Ethel Merman singing some of the composer's songs, and cast members from the original production of *Porgy and Bess* performing selections from the opera. Governor Lehman and Mayor La Guardia attended the concert, as did family members and such musicians as Irving Berlin, Walter Damrosch, Jerome Kern, and Sigmund Romberg. Just prior to the concert's second half, the entire audience rose in silent tribute. Wrote one reviewer: "The evening was, needless to say, one of unremitting pleasure; but one left the stadium thinking how little this harrassed [sic] world could afford to lose a voice of such captivating esprit, such natural wit, such abundant potentiality."[58]

An estimated twenty-six thousand gathered a month later, on September 8, at the Hollywood Bowl for another memorial concert in the composer's honor, this one broadcast live around the world. The concert featured Fred Astaire, Al Jolson, Oscar Levant, and others associated with Gershwin as well as Otto Klemperer leading the Los Angeles Philharmonic Orchestra in an orchestral transcription of the second of the *Three Preludes*. George Jessel's invocation, expressed in his eulogy, "And may it be His will that we shall meet here year after year and again hear the great American music of George Gershwin," for many years was answered in the form of near-annual Gershwin Nights at the Bowl.[59]

Part Two

WORK

Chapter Twelve

From "Ragging the Traumerei" (ca. 1913) to *The Capitol Revue* (1919)

Gershwin wrote his first known composition, a song titled "Ragging the Traumerei," in 1912 or ("more probably," says Ira) 1913. He would have been about fourteen or fifteen at the time and just beginning his lessons with Charles Hambitzer. The friend who provided the words, Leonard Praskins (1896–1968), used "Preston" as a pseudonym, just as Gershwin substituted a *w* for a *v* in his own name.[1]

"Ragging the Traumerei," only the music of which survives, makes an appropriate debut, because the idea of jazzing up classical music—in this case, "Träumerei" ("Reverie"), the famous daydreaming movement from Robert Schumann's *Scenes from Childhood* (1838)—casts a long shadow on the composer's career. Indeed, the "ragging" of classical music, which enjoyed considerable vogue during the 1910s, provides a clear foundation and context for Gershwin's development and aesthetic. Here, his decision to rag a particularly introspective piece highlights the essential irony and irreverence of this whole phenomenon.

Though somewhat ungainly, "Ragging the Traumerei" suggests nonetheless an innate feeling for harmony and counterpoint. The music shows some ingenuity, too, in using Schumann's principal melody as the main theme for both the song's chorus and its verse, anticipating the notable integration of verse and chorus that would come to distinguish Gershwin's mature songwriting. Meanwhile, the chorus's idiosyncratic forty-nine-bar form exemplifies an early tendency toward asymmetric phrase lengths. The spoof is gentle—Gershwin's idea of "ragging" involves not much more than smoothing out Schumann's tune to fit an oompah bass—but it features, for all that, a characteristic whimsy.

Gershwin wrote other numbers with Praskins, including "Since I

Found You," whose composition bedeviled the young composer, as discussed earlier. Although "Since I Found You" (which probably dates from
about the same time as "Ragging the Traumerei") appears lost, its main
theme—as played by pianist Milton Rettenberg—surfaced as part of a
1936 children's radio show about the composer's youth written and narrated by Ireene Wicker. As reproduced by Rettenberg, this lovely phrase,
with its characteristic drooping thirds, has a vaguely Irish American lilt.
No other collaborations by Gershwin and Praskins survive, though the
two worked together as late as 1917.[2]

In 1914 Gershwin composed *Tango* for piano, which also remains lost,
though a fragment, again played by Milton Rettenberg, similarly survives
on the aforementioned 1936 radio broadcast. Gershwin made his known
debut as a composer and pianist (as George Gershvin) playing this somewhat raggy tango on March 21, 1914, as part of an evening's entertainment at the Christodora House, a settlement house on the Lower East
Side. Sponsored by City College's Finley Club (Ira—still Isidore Gershvin—
served on the arrangements committee), the event also featured Gershwin accompanying one Charles Rose on a set of songs. In 1931 Isaac Goldberg reported, "George remembers the piece [*Tango*] perfectly, and
smilingly plays it for you when he is in the mood. It is conventional and
harmless enough, and bears testimony to assimilative rather than to creative powers." In later years, Gershwin never seemed particularly close
to the tango—a 1920 song written with Ira, "Something Peculiar," even
pooh-poohed the Argentine dance in contrast to jazz—but tango-like elements continued to appear in his work, often somewhat disguised, as in
"Bess, You Is My Woman" from *Porgy and Bess*. Presumably thinking of
the *Tango*'s main rhythmic idea, Ira also made an unexpected but revealing
comparison between that early piano piece and "Stiff Upper Lip" (1937).[3]

During his formative years, Gershwin composed some other works
for piano, according to music critic Sigmund Spaeth, who about 1916
attended a private dinner in order to hear Gershwin, then a "young pianist with concert ambitions," perform some "stock recital pieces" as
well as his own music, including "a Toccata and a Novelette of the standard Conservatory type." But after hearing some of his popular music,
Spaeth advised Gershwin to stick to that "for a while" and save his "serious work for some time later." This unique reminiscence helps support
the idea that Gershwin entertained lofty ambitions from an early age.[4]

Gershwin's first complete surviving instrumental composition, *Rialto
Ripples* (1916), a piano rag (as its subtitle states) composed in collaboration with Will Donaldson (a colleague at Remick, not to be confused

with songwriter Walter Donaldson), is closer to "Ragging the Traumerei" than to any "standard Conservatory type" (*Rialto* refers to the slang word for Broadway, *ripples* to the music's piano figuration). Remick published the piece in 1917—the only time the firm issued a work of Gershwin's during his time there—and the composer may have collaborated with Donaldson in order to help assure publication. Little is known about the music's genesis, except that in September 1916, prior to its publication, Gershwin cut a freely elaborated roll of the piece.

Impressively driving and vibrant, *Rialto Ripples* remains Gershwin's earliest work still in the repertoire. In rondo form, the principal A-minor strain looks back to Grieg's piano concerto in the same key, enough to suggest some intentional ragging; the two contrasting episodes are in a lighter F major, but the whole, framed by some intense writing in a minor mode, makes an ambivalent impression—an early instance of Gershwin's inimitable blending of humor and pathos. Notwithstanding Isaac Goldberg's criticism of the piece as failing "even remotely" to suggest the "restless spirit that eleven years later would dictate the [composer's] Jazz Préludes," certain aspects of the score, including its opening triplet figure, anticipate particularly the third prelude, casting light on that movement's ragtime origins. Moreover, as evidenced by the 1916 roll, Gershwin played the piece in a fast cut-time and freely dotted the eighth notes, whereas more recent renditions have tended to be more deliberate, thus obscuring the "restless spirit" that eluded Goldberg as well. The music, incidentally, eventually served as the basis of a Jack Newlon song, "Oriental Blues" (1933), which became widely known in the 1950s as comedian Ernie Kovacs's theme music and also surfaced in the film *Red Dragon* (2002).[5]

In 1916, while still working at Remick, Gershwin collaborated with another friend, Murray Roth, on some songs, including "A Voice of Love [indeciph.]" (a small fragment of which survives), "My Runaway Girl" (lost), and "When You Want 'Em, You Can't Get 'Em, When You've Got 'Em, You Don't Want 'Em," the last said to be the longest song title in Tin Pan Alley history. Remick declined to publish any of Gershwin's songs during his three years there, a source of ongoing disappointment; but after hearing him sing "When You Want 'Em" on a visit to the publishing house, vaudeville headliner Sophie Tucker (1887–1966) recommended the song to composer-publisher Harry Von Tilzer, who subsequently brought it out. Gershwin made only five dollars from the song, but it was a publication, his first.[6]

Isaac Goldberg fairly characterized "When You Want 'Em," which falls in the tradition of "Alexander's Ragtime Band," as "Berlinish with a dash of Kern." Walter Rimler, for his part, noted that the twenty-bar chorus moves suddenly to the minor submediant at the words "When you lose 'em / you forget 'em"; such bittersweet modulations—though here somewhat stilted—would become a Gershwin trademark. The song's appeal to Sophie Tucker, the self-styled "last of the red-hot mamas," seems readily apparent, though whether she ever performed the song remains unknown (though Tucker maintained a connection with Gershwin, recording "The Man I Love" in 1928 with Ted Shapiro and his orchestra). Meanwhile, the sheet-music cover of "When You Want 'Em" depicted a fashionable lady holding eleven diminutive male figures in formal wear each by his own string. This ironic image of female empowerment seems related to Gershwin's early championship by Tucker, Vivienne Segal, and Nora Bayes—all strongly independent women and Jewish as well.[7]

Before Gershwin and Roth went their separate ways (the latter to Hollywood, where he became a director and film executive), they auditioned "My Runaway Girl" for the Shubert organization (operated by brothers Lee and Jacob) in the hope that they might want it for one of their Winter Garden revues, such as the *Passing Shows,* a series of annual revues launched in 1912 along the lines of the *Ziegfeld Follies.* The young songwriters presumably thought specifically of a Winter Garden revue for "My Runaway Girl" because that theater, a large space on the corner of Broadway and West 50th Street that sat more than fifteen hundred people, featured a runway that jutted out into the audience down which chorus girls could saunter. After hearing his music, a representative for the Shuberts arranged for Gershwin to audition for Sigmund Romberg, who, with lyricist Harold Atteridge, had recently begun supervising the scores for the *Passing Shows.*[8]

Romberg decided to acquire "My Runaway Girl" for the *Passing Show of 1916,* though as part of their agreement, Gershwin and Roth were to share credit and royalties with Romberg and Atteridge, an accepted Broadway practice of the time. Romberg further selected another tune that Gershwin played for him and arranged for Atteridge to provide the lyrics, with himself again taking credit as co-composer, though the extent of his contribution remains dubious. The resultant effort, "Making of a Girl," marked the young composer's known debut on Broadway and initiated his ties with the musical revue, a genre with which he would remain closely associated for nearly a decade.[9]

From humble beginnings in the late nineteenth century, when the summer months brought travesties of popular Broadway shows from the previous season, the revue by the 1910s had become a major theatrical form in its own right, in large part thanks to the extraordinary success of Florenz Ziegfeld and his annual series of *Follies*. Inaugurated in 1907 and inspired by Paris's Folies-Bergère, the *Ziegfeld Follies* showcased musical numbers, comedy skits, and beautiful chorus girls lavishly attired. Other producers, like the Shuberts, responded with annual editions of their own, and soon Broadway was awash with revues all year round, many featuring the country's best light theatrical talent. The humor was typically satirical and topical, as the idea of an annual revue might suggest, and could get somewhat bawdy, which—combined with chorus girls in various stages of undress—often made these entertainments subject to censorship, especially outside of New York.

Although revues sometimes featured one person's music, their scores more typically contained the work of several composers. In either case, in the 1910s and early 1920s, when the revue was at its height, the form generated many of the popular song hits of the day, so much so that during these years, Irving Berlin, among others, devoted the bulk of his energies to the genre. For an aspiring theater composer like Gershwin, the revue offered invaluable experience and exposure.

The *Passing Show of 1916* opened on June 22 at the Winter Garden, where it ran for 140 performances, about standard for a big revue of the mid-teens. It featured comedian Ed Wynn in various sketches and, most spectacularly, a simulation of a cavalry charge that brought the first act to a dashing conclusion. Most of the music was composed by Romberg and Otto Motzan, whose jazzy numbers, like "Ragtime Calisthenics," no doubt helped keep the evening lively, though the interpolation of "Pretty Baby" (music, Tony Jackson and Egbert Van Alstyne; lyrics, Gus Kahn), introduced some months earlier in another Shubert revue, proved the evening's biggest hit, at least in part because the song, wrote *Variety*, was plugged throughout the show "to a monotonous point."[10]

Whether Romberg used "My Runaway Girl" remains undetermined, but "Making of a Girl"—published as such by G. Schirmer, but apparently the same song alternatively cited in programs as "How to Make a Pretty Face" or "How to Make a Pretty Girl"—was sung by Dolly Hackett and the chorus, in a comic dressmaking scene capped by a parade of chorus girls. (A surviving draft of this scene offers a taste of the humor of these revues: comedian Jack Boyle, as a tailor, Monsieur Tapan, asks a customer if she'd like to see a "gown that's very smart," to which the customer replies, "I've seen a hundred gowns and I haven't seen one yet that had any intelligence.") Presumably used to accompany sauntering chorus girls, the song featured the suave promenade style, tinged with romantic yearning, that achieved an apogee of sorts a few years later with Berlin's "A Pretty Girl Is Like a Melody" (1919) and that Gershwin years later had fun mocking in "Blue, Blue, Blue" (1933). Though not enhanced by Atteridge's workaday recitation of clothing apparel, Gershwin's melody, aided by insistent syncopations, had a distinctive sweep, as if a waltz were somehow embedded into its duple metrical structure, an impulse that would stay with the composer—and serve him well—for the rest of his career. Gershwin delivered what was needed and expected, but in an individual way.[11]

By 1916 Gershwin had also begun writing songs with Irving Caesar (1895–1996), his most important collaborator—along with his friend Lou Paley and his brother Ira—during these journeyman years. A figure of brusque vitality, Caesar, a tunesmith in his own right, had grown up on the Lower East Side, and like Ira had graduated from Townsend Harris Hall and briefly attended City College. In late 1915 he sailed to Europe with the Henry Ford Peace Ship, an abortive attempt to negotiate the end of hostilities in Europe. On his return to the States, he worked for a short time as a mechanic in a Ford plant but eventually established a career as a lyricist, working with Gershwin in the late 1910s and then, most notably, with Vincent Youmans in the 1920s. As a lyricist he had the common touch, often invigorated by an appealing giddiness, as in his Youmans collaboration, "Tea for Two," whose famous dummy lyric—"Picture you upon my knee, / just tea for two and two for tea, / just me for you and you for me alone"—had an almost dadaesque quality akin to Gertrude Stein.

Caesar possibly met Ira in high school, but in any case, he came to know George on visits to Remick in the mid-teens. One of their earliest collaborations, "When the Armies Disband" (lost), no doubt reflected Caesar's pacifist ideals, apparently shared by Gershwin. Although the song bears a copyright date of October 21, 1916, Caesar recalled that he had written the song in 1915 with Gershwin and fellow lyricist Alfred ("Al") Bryan (who also wrote the words for the 1915 pacifist hit "I Didn't Raise My Boy to Be a Soldier"), and that he sang it for Henry Ford during the peace ship initiative. Gershwin and Caesar collaborated on other numbers since lost, including two songs reconstructed decades later based on Caesar's recollection of their melodies: "Since You've Been Gone Away," a somewhat playful torch song; and "Good Little Tune," whose lyric anticipated "Fascinating Rhythm." Caesar, who in 1964 made a demonstration tape of the second based on a transcription of the music by Leonard Bernstein, proudly asserted in 1983, "'Good Little Tune' is one of the best songs George or I or most songwriters ever wrote," though he praised Gershwin's talents over his own.[12]

Vivienne Segal's successful launching of two other Gershwin-Caesar songs, "You-oo Just You" and "There's More to the Kiss Than the X-X-X," in late 1917 led not only to Gershwin's association with Harms, as discussed earlier, but to the incorporation of both songs into shows, and to their publication as well: "You-oo Just You" with Gershwin's former employer, Remick, in 1918, and for which Gershwin and Caesar each were excited to receive $250 ("We would have given them $500 to have the song published," said Caesar); and "There's More to the Kiss Than the X-X-X" with Harms in 1919 (also published as "There's More to the Kiss Than the Sound").[13]

"You-oo Just You," a whimsical love song addressed to "the most wonderful gal in Dixie," comes just shy of minstrelsy and represents part of a long series of lyrics about the mythic South (including the best-known Gershwin-Caesar number, "Swanee") that marked Caesar's career through the fittingly titled "Is It True What They Say about Dixie?" (1936). The chorus, at once romantic and bluesy, unfolds a truncated *aaba* form of twenty-one bars. For its part, "There's More to the Kiss Than the X-X-X" (the *x*'s standing for three puckering sounds, hence the alternate title) features some inimitable Caesar lunacy, matched here by a Victor Herbert–like exuberance on Gershwin's part. At one point, the accompaniment simulates a long kiss by way of eight quick chords (mostly augmented sixth-chords) that descend chromatically, a foreshadowing of that innovative marriage of vigorous rhythm and rich harmony that would come to characterize Gershwin's mature style.

During these early years, Gershwin also collaborated with his friend Lou Paley, composing, among other songs, the patriotic "We're Six Little Nieces of Our Uncle Sam" (late 1917 or early 1918); the lightly romantic "Something about Love" (ca. 1918, published 1919); the plaintive "Beautiful Bird" (with Ira as co-lyricist, ca. 1918, only the lead sheet and lyrics of which survive); and the sweetly romantic "A Corner of Heaven with You" (1918; revised in the early 1920s as "The Hurdy-Gurdy Man," with new lyrics by Paley and Ira). "We're Six Little Nieces," a "sextette" described by Ira in his diary as "surefire," stands out for its suave harmonies (including a progression that looks ahead to one of Gershwin's last songs, "Things Are Looking Up"), its orientalisms (Gershwin and Paley presumably had "Three Little Maids" from *The Mikado* in mind), and its quotations of "Dixie," "The Star-Spangled Banner," "Yankee Doodle," "Over There," and "The Marseillaise" (anticipating "Wintergreen for President" from *Of Thee I Sing*). As for "Beautiful Bird," Ira hoped that it might turn out "to be a 2nd 'Poor Butterfly'"—a reference to Raymond Hubbell's blockbuster hit of 1916 (lyrics, John Golden).[14]

By the spring of 1917, Ira had begun writing lyrics—including a wedding spoof, "You May Throw All the Rice You Desire (but Please, Friends, Throw No Shoes)"—and in December of that year he and George collaborated on a number, since lost, titled "You Are Not the Girl." Their earliest surviving collaboration, "The Real American Folk Song (Is a Rag)" (1918), also became Ira's first song to make it to Broadway (1919), though it was not published until 1959 and won widespread popularity only after Ella Fitzgerald recorded it that year, more than four decades after its composition.

The song resembles a manifesto of sorts: its verse, to George's siciliana-like melody, evokes various European folk musics; its vest expresses a preference for the American vernacular; and its chorus claims ragtime as "the real American folk song." Ira even wrote on an early draft of the lyric, "Too much like an essay." But whatever the song's shortcomings, it auspiciously showed Ira as marvelously attuned to his brother's music. Could any of Gershwin's other collaborators have so neatly fitted the song's punchy rhythms with a line like, "For it's inoculated / With a syncopated / Sort of meter, / Sweeter / Than a classic strain; / Boy! You can't remain / Still and quiet— / For it's a riot!"? Or consider Ira's characteristic sensitivity to the song's harmonic structure, as in the way the line, "The critics called it a joke song, but now / They've changed their tune and they like it somehow," mirrors the modulation from C major to A♭ major, the words *but now* appearing exactly at the harmonic pivot point.[15]

Gershwin wrote another of his best early songs, "Some Wonderful Sort of Someone" (1918), not with Ira but with a Harms staff lyricist, Schuyler Green. Its *aaba* chorus—which gently coils around a few pitches, modulates up a step for the second phrase, and blossoms into a more forceful bridge section, reserving its highest notes, however, for the last few bars—reveals particular ingenuity. Isaac Goldberg thought that the song, along with "You-oo, Just You," adumbrated "the humor, the gracility, the colloquialness of Gershwin's melodic line," while Alec Wilder found it "extremely inventive, though not in the manner of his later, characteristic style." Max Dreyfus astutely selected the song as Harms's first Gershwin publication.[16]

A few of these early Gershwin songs—in particular, the published ones—were interpolated into one show or another, sometimes in the midst of a Broadway run. Indeed, the relationship between stage use and publication was synergetic: interpolated unpublished songs became candidates for publication, while published songs lent themselves to interpolation. Theaters sometimes sold the hit songs of a particular show in their lobbies, and the shows themselves plugged certain favored songs by repeating them as encores or reprises and frequently by having the singer's name or picture on the cover of the sheet music. As mentioned, Max Dreyfus was particularly adept at exploiting such practices. Of course, inclusion into a show depended on a particular number's stageworthiness, and in their manifest theatricality, the songs Gershwin composed during this period largely seem to have been written with an eye toward the stage, notwithstanding Alec Wilder's contention that only a few of them "bear the character of theater music."[17]

In any case, following the *Passing Show of 1916,* Gershwin's music appeared in two shows from 1918: Raymond Hitchcock's *Hitchy-Koo of 1918,* which opened June 6 at the Globe (now the Lunt-Fontanne) and featured "You-oo Just You"; and Nora Bayes's *Ladies First* (originally *Look Who's Here*), which included "Something about Love," "Some Wonderful Sort of Someone," and "The Real American Folksong" on its tryout tour, and at least the last after opening on October 24 at the Broadhurst.[18]

The annual *Hitchy-Koo* revues (1917–1920), whose title punned their producer's nickname ("Hitchy") with baby talk, aimed for a certain intimate sophistication. For the 1919 edition, the young Cole Porter furnished songs. Although the 1918 edition credited its score to composer Raymond Hubbell and lyricist Glen McDonough, the show's content changed frequently in the course of its run of sixty-eight performances, and by its last week it was largely featuring the songs of Harold Orlob. In creating his *Hitchy-Koo* revues, Hitchcock announced that he wanted to express the "restlessness of American life" and "the quality best described as 'Zippiness.'" He surely had the right composer with Gershwin, if not the zippiest song with "You-oo Just You." On the other hand, the number might have exuded a certain sly wit if performed, as is thought, by the show's star, Irene Bordoni (1895–1953), the Corsican-born chanteuse known for her provocative stage presence.[19]

Ladies First was the Harry B. Smith–A. Baldwin Sloane musical comedy that Gershwin had toured with prior to its opening on Broadway, where it enjoyed 164 performances, notwithstanding lukewarm reviews in the press. Based on Charlie Hoyt's farce *A Contented Woman*, the show pitted a suffragette, Betty Burt (Bayes), against her fiancé and political opponent, Benton Homes (Irving Fisher), in the context of a mayoral election. On tour, Bayes sang "Some Wonderful Sort of Someone," Irving Fisher sang "Something about Love," and Hal Forde (who played Bayes's brother, Larry Burt) sang "The Real American Folksong." However, only the last song apparently made it to Broadway, as performed by Forde's replacement, Charles Olcott.[20]

In late 1918 Gershwin for the first time became the featured composer of a show of his own, *Half-Past Eight*, a revue that closed out of town after a few performances in Syracuse, New York. It was the idea of Edward B. Perkins, a Columbia University graduate and aspiring producer, to bring *Half-Past Eight*—a 1916 London revue with a score by English composer Paul Rubens—to Broadway. Perkins reconceived the show as a vehicle for Welsh opera singer Sybil Vane (who had appeared in the original London production); Parisian singer Ruby Loraine; and various comedians, dancers, and musicians, including members of New York's Clef Club Jazz Band; but primarily for famed vaudevillian Joe Cook (1890–1959). Born Joseph Lopez, Cook was one of the great headliners of the period, the most "perfect" of them all, according to Gilbert Seldes, who described him as "very wise and slightly mad." Cook's signature routine consisted of a convoluted explanation of why he would not imitate four Hawaiians playing the ukulele. "After that," wrote Seldes, "literally nothing matters. He might be with Alice in Wonderland or at a dada ballet or with the terribly logical clowns of Shakespeare. I think that Chaplin would savour his humours."[21]

On Max Dreyfus's recommendation, Perkins commissioned a new score from Gershwin, who provided at least five numbers: "Cupid," apparently performed by the Clef Club Jazz Band; "Hong Kong," sung by Loraine; "Little Sunbeam" and "Kisses," both sung by Vane; and "Half-Past Eight," used as incidental music. With some assistance from Ira, Perkins provided the lyrics under the pseudonym Fred Caryll, though judging from the identically titled song from Gershwin's subsequent *La-La-Lucille!* (1919), "Kisses" might well have been a retitled version of "There's More to the Kiss Than the X-X-X" (lyrics, Caesar). Considering that the show's sundry entertainers performed their own music as well, little of the original Rubens score probably survived the transplantation.[22]

None of the Gershwin score (aside from "Kisses," assuming it's the same song as "There's More to the Kiss") was ever published; but the music—if not the words—of "Cupid," "Hong Kong," "Little Sunbeam," and "Half-Past Eight" survives in manuscript. This extant music—some of it surprisingly modern and swank—reveals growing boldness and ambitiousness on Gershwin's part, as evident by the parallel ninth chords that introduce "Little Sunbeam" (marked by Gershwin "Debussian vamp") or the sudden move from D major to F major in the verse to "Half-Past Eight." Meanwhile, "Hong Kong" looks ahead to "Limehouse Nights" and other Gershwin chinoiserie.[23]

Half-Past Eight proved a straightforward two-act variety show, with Cook, Loraine, Vane, and others having their separate routines, the Clef Club band providing opening and closing medleys, and Cook performing a "jazz dance" with the band in the finale. Advertising Cook as "America's Foremost Specialty Comedian," Vane as the "Wee Welsh Prima Donna," Loraine as a "Parisian Favorite De Luxe," and the Clef Club Jazz Band as "Twenty Expert Syncopaters—All Spades!" the show opened on Monday, December 9, at half-past eight, in a performance sponsored by the local Loyal Order of Moose. Gershwin attended the dress rehearsal and the first few performances.[24]

Variety gave the show a scathing review, complete with a headline that blared, "$2 Show Not Worth War Tax," a reference to the forty-cent "war tax" added to a two-dollar ticket (for a premium seat: tickets could be had for fifty cents, or even twenty-five cents at matinees). The audience apparently expected a "girly show," and a few even hissed at the final curtain because of the lack of chorus girls. (Gershwin had attempted to forestall such a response by encouraging Perkins to have some of the comedians, disguised by parasols, pose as chorines, a deception that allegedly misfired when three of the umbrellas failed to open, though a review in the Syracuse *Post-Standard* actually commended the show's "Chinese Parasol Girls" as an attractive foil to Ruby Loraine.) *Variety* further reproached this "vaudeville sketch" for having little to do with its successful British original. However, the *Post-Standard* opined that with "a little pruning" the revue promised to be a "vaudeville de luxe," and that it was "well-received" by its large audience. Neither said much about the music, the *Post-Standard* not even mentioning Gershwin by name, a typical oversight in reviews of musical shows from this period.[25]

At one performance during the revue's first (and only) week, Gershwin— "in a blue suit and unshaven," as he told Isaac Goldberg—had to extemporize at the piano to cover a scene change after one of the acts refused to go on because they had not been paid. Recalled Gershwin: "I said, 'What will I do?' He [Perkins] said, 'Play some of your hits.' I should have loved to have played my hits—except that I didn't have any. But out I walked on the stage to a very small and innocent audience, and made up a medley right on the spot of some of my tunes. The audience must have thought it very queer. I finished my bit and walked off—without a hand!" The show obviously had cash-flow problems, and it folded the following Saturday after the unpaid cast members refused to show up for the 2:30 matinee. The rest of the tour was canceled. Gershwin at least walked away with the "thrill" of seeing his name on a marquee and a growing portfolio of songs to draw from in the months ahead.[26]

The next year, 1919, proved a turning point in Gershwin's career. In the course of that year, he successfully launched his first Broadway musical *(La-La-Lucille!)* and revue *(Morris Gest's Midnight Whirl)*, and supplied another three shows (*Good Morning, Judge, The Lady in Red,* and the *Capitol Revue*) with music that included his earliest hit songs, "I Was So Young (You Were So Beautiful)" and "Swanee."

Good Morning, Judge, which opened on February 6 at the Shubert, featured two Gershwin-Caesar songs: "There's More to the Kiss" and a more recent effort, "I Am So Young and You Are So Beautiful," for which Caesar collaborated on the lyric with Al Bryan. An adaptation of the British hit musical *The Boy* (1917)—which in turn was based on Arthur Pinero's farce *The Magistrate*—the show involved a nineteen-year-old, Hughie Cavanagh (Charles King), who pretends to be fourteen in order to help his mother hide her age (of thirty-one) from his magistrate stepfather; this naturally leads to complications when stepfather and son go out on the town. The few interpolations by Gershwin and others notwithstanding, *Good Morning, Judge* kept its original score (with music by Lionel Monckton and Howard Talbot) largely intact. Charles King sang "I Am So Young" with his sister Mollie in the role of Joy Chatterton, the object of Hughie's affection.

The show enjoyed 140 performances on Broadway and then a successful road tour, with Allen Kearns taking over the Charles King role. As is often the case with interpolators, especially obscure ones, Gershwin received no credit for his songs, though one review intriguingly alluded to "several numbers" composed by "some unknown native genius of syncopation" that "possibly appealed more to the audience" than the tuneful Monckton-Talbot melodies. At any event, "I Am So Young," widely singled out by the critics, became the hit of the show, which translated into sheet-music sales and increased name recognition.[27]

"I Am So Young"—published as "I Was So Young (You Were So

Beautiful)"—became, in fact, Gershwin's first popular success, what Caesar later described as "a hit, of sorts." The music's refinement and sweep presages, as David Schiff notes, the *Rhapsody in Blue,* ennobling a rather sentimental lyric described by Caesar as "quite off the beaten path for that period." Among other felicities, the vest anticipates the twenty-two-bar *abab* chorus's main theme, which appears reharmonized at its reprise to permit a poignant modulation to a minor mode. Gershwin's colleagues quickly came to admire such attention to detail.[28]

The Lady in Red, a vehicle for vaudevillian Adele Rowland (1883–1971), opened on May 12, 1919, at the Lyric. The score of this American adaptation of the German operetta *Die Dame in Rot* (1911) included original music by Robert Winterberg, newly lyricized by Anne Caldwell, as well as interpolations by Kern, Walter Donaldson, and Gershwin, the latter represented by two songs that had previously appeared on the road in *Look Who's Here:* "Something about Love" (lyric, Paley) and "Some Wonderful Sort of Someone" (lyric, Green). The *Times* described the show, which flopped after forty-eight performances, as "being concerned with an artist and the girl of his dreams." One critic thought "Something about Love," which Rowland performed as a duet with Donald Mac-Donald, to contain the score's "best lyric." That Paley was developing into an accomplished lyricist was further suggested by the fact that a few years later, Ira asked to adapt the music and words of a phrase, "he loves and she loves," imbedded in the coda of "Something about Love," as the basis for one of his own collaborations with George, a borrowing to which Paley graciously assented.[29]

Some two weeks after *The Lady in Red* opened, Gershwin enjoyed a far more significant milestone with the May 26 premiere of his first book musical, *La-La-Lucille!* It also proved the first musical comedy for Alex Aarons (1891–1943), its young producer—or rather assistant producer, for his father, Alfred, an established Broadway manager and composer, took primary responsibility for the show, as evidenced by the program, which named him as sole producer. One imagines that the senior Aarons considered the project a kind of training ground for his son, who itched to quit the retail clothing business in which he was then employed and try his own hand at producing musicals.

Introduced to Alex Aarons by Arthur Jackson, the show's co-lyricist, Gershwin later reflected that it "was very brave" of Aarons to hire him, considering that he was "quite inexperienced at the time, never having written a complete score." But a collaboration between the two seemed inevitable. Aarons wanted to produce smart musicals for the Jazz Age (he would advertise *La-La-Lucille!* as "a new, up-to-the-minute musical comedy of class and distinction"), and Gershwin fitted the bill. After *La-La-Lucille!* Aarons, in association with Vinton Freedley, would produce another six Gershwin musicals.[30]

La-La-Lucille! also marked the start of an important association between Gershwin and another young New Yorker, B. G. ("Buddy") De-Sylva (1895–1950), who cowrote the show's lyrics with Jackson (aside from a few songs that entailed various contributions from Ira, Irving Caesar, and Lou Paley). Over the next few years, DeSylva would write or cowrite the lyrics for a number of Gershwin shows, and work, more-over, with other composers on such hits as "Look for the Silver Lining" (1920), "April Showers" (1921), "California, Here I Come" (1924), and "If You Knew Susie" (1925) before collaborating with lyricist Lew Brown and composer Ray Henderson on some of the most popular musicals of the late 1920s. As for the show's book, the Aaronses engaged Arthur Jackson's older brother, Fred (1886–1953), at the relative beginnings of his playwriting career as well. Accordingly, this was a rather young team for a Broadway musical.

Gershwin signed a contract with DeSylva, Arthur Jackson, and Alex Aarons on March 5, guaranteeing him 1.5 percent of the show's weekly gross proceeds. The contract also specified a due date of April 1, which gave him about three weeks to complete the score. A clause in the contract specified that any interpolation would require the permission of the said parties, a condition that Gershwin would attempt to institute for all his musical comedies.

La-La-Lucille! takes place in New York over the course of one day. Johnathon Jaynes (J. Clarence Harvey) and his daughter, Lucille Jaynes Smith (Janet Velie), a former juggling team (the Juggling Jayneses), and Lucille's struggling dentist-husband, John Smith (John E. Hazzard), reside in a modest New York apartment. Hounded by bill collectors ("Kindly Pay Us"), John and Lucille tell the Japanese super, Oyama, of their difficulties ("When You Live in a Furnished Flat"). Though well-born, John has been disinherited for marrying a vaudevillian. He and Lucille desire finer things, but are content as long as they have each other ("The Best of Everything"). Learning that John's aunt Roberta, of Boston, has died, leaving him two million dollars on the condition that he divorce his wife, John and Lucille reaffirm their wedding vows ("From Now On"); but friends convince them to stage a divorce, collect the money, and then remarry ("Money, Money, Money!"). Lucille and her father recall their former life on the stage ("Tee-Oodle-Um-Bum-Bo"), and John leaves for a hotel with Fanny, Oyama's Irish wife (Eleanor Daniels), to fake a tryst so that they'll have grounds for divorce ("Finale").

Act 2 opens at the bridal suite of the Hotel Philadelphia ("Hotel Life"). Britton Hughes (Lorin Raker) and his newlywed Peggy (Helen Clark) have eloped because the latter's disapproving father, Colonel Marrion (Stanley H. Forde), of Norfolk, Virginia, suspects that Britton's a fortune hunter. Ensconced in their rooms, they enjoy a romantic moment ("Oo, How I Love to Be Loved by You"; lyrics, Paley). As various characters come and go, including a jealous Oyama looking for his wife, Peggy offers her views on love ("It's Great to Be in Love"). Lucille, stumbling across her husband and Peggy together, accuses John of infidelity ("Finale").

In the third act, also set in the bridal suite, Peggy attempts to set things right by writing a note to Britton ("Kisses," apparently a retitled version of "There's More to the Kiss Than the X-X-X"; lyrics, Caesar), who is comforted by Lucille ("Somehow It Seldom Comes True"). Colonel Marrion is caught in a compromising situation with Lucille (reprise of "Tee-Oodle-Um-Bum-Bo"), an embarrassment used by his daughter Peggy to her advantage. John and Lucille, finally reconciled ("The Ten Commandments of Love"), decide not to divorce after all, on which they learn that Aunt Roberta, still alive, was only testing the strength of their affection and that the money is still theirs. The various couples more or less happily reunite ("Finale," including reprises of "From Now On" and "Tee-Oodle-Um-Bum-Bo").

Two additional songs were dropped during tryouts: "The Love of a Wife," a comedy number for some of the married men, complete with the punch line "Oh, the love of a wife is a wonderful thing / But it's something that a husband never gets"; and "Kitchenette" (also known as "Our Little Kitchenette"; lyrics, Ira and DeSylva), a charming celebration of domestic life for Britton and Peggy. Based on a lyric Ira had written the previous summer, the latter song—which represented as good an imitation of Kern and Wodehouse as might be imagined—was especially clever, with Ira's hand particularly felt in such verses as "I will practice day and night and learn / To wield a wicked frying pan, / Most anything, by trying, man—can do. / I will learn to make the complicated dish / That's known as succotash; / And then we'll try our luck at hash—and stew." (Gershwin hoped to include "Kitchenette" in a subsequent show, *Sweet Little Devil*, as a duet for Joyce and Tom, but to no avail.)

After the show opened, Gershwin, DeSylva, and Jackson replaced "Oo, How I Love to Be Loved" with the more lilting "Nobody but You," and "Money, Money, Money!" with "It's Hard to Tell" (the music of which appears lost). Still more changes were made for the show's national tour in 1920, though these primarily concerned interpolations of songs by other composers. Harms published no less than eight songs from the show—"The Best of Everything," "The Love of a Wife," "Oo, How I Love to Be Loved," "Somehow It Seldom Comes True," "From Now On," "Nobody but You," "Tee-Oodle-Um-Bum-Bo," and "There's More to the Kiss"—with Gershwin cutting rolls of the last four.

One of the novelties of *La-La-Lucille!* was in adapting to the musical stage the kind of bedroom sex farce that dominated Broadway during and just after World War I, as exemplified by the plays of Avery Hopwood. Fred Jackson himself had written straight sex farces, including *A Full House* (1915), *Losing Eloise* (1917, later retitled *The Naughty Wife*), and *Your Money or Your Wife,* the play on which *Lucille* apparently was based. This new musical was even subtitled "a farce with music." At the same time, *Lucille* faced in its own way the subjects of money, marriage, and a woman's place in society, a heightened concern as the nation approached passage of the Nineteenth Amendment (1920) giving women the vote. Typical for its time, the show expressed some ambivalence about the so-called new woman, even if Lucille clearly poses a challenge to the New England matriarchy of Aunt Roberta, much as Peggy does to the southern patriarchy of Colonel Marrion.

Accommodating the requisite presence of chorus girls within the context of a domestic farce set exclusively in the small spaces of a furnished flat and a bridal suite, without a picnic ground or country club in view, proved problematic. Fred Jackson did what he could, such as having the chorus appear as bill collectors at the top of the first act. Similarly, a minor character—a French vamp named Mademoiselle Victorine—appeared throughout the show largely in order to spotlight the dance talents of Marjorie Bentley. A few reviewers alluded to the "difficulties" occasioned by this unusual blend of boudoir farce and musical comedy, but at least as far as John Corbin of the *New York Times* was concerned, "they have been in the main overcome."[31]

Gershwin wrote an appropriately smart score that revealed not only the kind of harmonic sophistication noted previously in his work but a growing rhythmic finesse as well, including distinctive use of syncopation: not startling disruptions within a phrase, as typically found in ragtime, but smoother, more speechlike phrases—Goldberg's "colloquialness"—that avoided accented downbeats and clear metrical patterns. Such rhythmic ingenuity, especially in conjunction with the music's bluesy harmonies, lent the score a jazzy ambience and marked the beginnings of a style that would climax years later in a song like "I Got Rhythm," whose main theme eschewed downbeats almost entirely. At the same time, perhaps in compensation, Gershwin largely left behind—for the time being—the irregular phrase lengths of his earliest songs.

The score also unveiled Gershwin's talents as a musical dramatist, as in the subtle but palpable distinction between the amiable "From Now On" for the reminiscing Smiths and the more ardently romantic "Nobody but You" for the newlyweds. "The Best of Everything" and "Tee-Oodle-Um-Bum-Bo" showed, for their part, a fine comic flair, while "Somehow It Seldom Comes True," one of those wistful ballads about lost ideals that became a second-act musical-comedy convention, established a standard for later theater composers. Indeed, despite its only middling success, *La-La-Lucille!* had an immediate impact on other composers, if we can judge from Jerome Kern's delightful "Whip-Poor-Will," composed later in 1919 (significantly, with Buddy DeSylva), a song seemingly cognizant of "From Now On." Gershwin himself remained fond of the score, arranging "Nobody but You" for his 1932 *Song-Book* and featuring some of the music on one of his 1934 radio broadcasts, at which time he stated, with apparent satisfaction, "Neither the lyricists nor myself were over-sentimental."[32]

Orchestrations survive for at least four songs from the show, one by Frank Saddler and three by his disciple, Maurice DePackh. Written for two flutes, oboe, two clarinets, bassoon, horn, two trumpets, trombone, strings, cimbalon (a Hungarian zither), and a large percussion battery (timpani, bass drum, snare drum, Indian drum, cowbell, bells, cymbals, wood block, tambourine, triangle, glockenspiel, and xylophone), these orchestrations show scrupulous attention to details of color and attack. In "Money, Money, Money!" for example, DePackh has the cymbals play a roll, triple pianissimo, with the "light end of S. D. [snare drum] sticks near edge." Such care and refinement help explain DePackh's dismay at the perceived decline in Broadway's orchestral standards in the course of the 1920s.[33]

Following a Boston tryout, *La-La-Lucille!* premiered on May 26 at the new Henry Miller's Theatre on West 43rd. Herbert Gresham directed, Julian Alfred staged the dances, the Robert Law Studios provided the sets, and Charles Previn conducted the orchestra and a small chorus of sixteen women. Critics in both Boston and New York exuberantly received the work as "lots of fun" and "amusing," indeed, as one of the best musicals of the season. "From the rise of the curtain to its final drop," stated one review, "this comedy is cram full of riotous action." Some commented further on its broad, absurd, sometimes vulgar qualities, epitomized by John Corbin's description of the show as "the incarnation of jazz." John Hazzard, the best-known cast member, and Eleanor Daniels elicited special praise, as did Marjorie Bentley, who in "Money, Money, Money!" according to one review, "danced with the chorus in a way that can only be described as a stampede."[34]

Critics also agreed that the music was "spirited," "original," "enticing," "pleasant," and, for the most part, "tuneful" and "melodious." "There was pretty music by someone named George Gershwin," reported Percy Hammond in Boston. "Tee-Oodle-Um-Bum-Bo" proved a popular favorite, even stopping the show. But whereas the *New York World* thought the music "the most entertaining part of the piece," the *New York Globe* complained that the music, though "tuneful," retarded the action "of what is really an otherwise swift moving farce. Musical comedy is always conventional, but it requires deftness of no mean order to weave songs into farce so that the doing does not show." Still, Gershwin had a successful musical comedy to his credit.

La-La-Lucille!—which closed on August 19 after 104 performances—presumably would have played longer but for a strike by Actor's Equity begun on August 7 (and not resolved until September 6). Although none of the songs really caught on, in the fall of 1919 the Carl Fenton Orchestra (also known as the Walter "Gus" Haenschen Orchestra) and the Van Eps Banta Trio (including banjoist Fred Van Eps and pianist Frank Banta) both recorded medleys from the musical. By melding a few of the tunes into an energetic one-step, these recordings demonstrated the music's connection with the social dancing of the arriving Jazz Age. Tellingly, decades later, in an attempt to evoke a bit of 1920s playfulness for the show *Cabaret* (1966), John Kander wrote a tune, "Two Ladies," not at all unlike "Tee-Oodle-Um-Bum-Bo."[35]

On October 24, two new Gershwin songs, "Swanee" and "Come to the Moon," appeared in the *Demi Tasse Revue,* part of the *Capitol Revue,* a show produced and choreographed by Ziegfeld associate Ned Wayburn for the opening of what was advertised as the "largest theatre in the world," the Capitol, a lavish movie palace with a seating capacity of about 5,300 located at Broadway and West 51st Street. The theater's four-hour gala inauguration entailed organ music, a newsreel, motion-picture shorts, musical selections by the Arthur Pryor Band and others, the *Demi Tasse Revue,* and, finally, a showing of the Douglas Fairbanks film *His Majesty, the American.*

The *New York Times* described the *Demi Tasse* as "a show in itself," deeming some of its scenes "noteworthy, even as compared with Broadway's best." The revue featured singers Lucille Chalfant and Paul Frawley; comedian Jim Toney; and "vamptress" Mae West, singing and shimmying her way through "Oh, What a Moanin' Man." Gershwin's "Swanee" (lyrics, Caesar) was introduced midway through the show by a little-known singer named Muriel De Forrest, while "Come to the Moon" (lyrics, Paley and Wayburn) provided the spectacular finale, with "The Man in the Moon" (Frawley) and "The Girl in the Moon" (Chalfant) supported by a female chorus of thirty "Twinkling Stars" (including a very young Jeanette MacDonald) and a smaller male chorus of eight "Moon Boys," a dazzling finish that employed two revolving and illuminated spiral stairways "loaded with twinkling 'star-girls.'"[36]

Gershwin wrote "Swanee" with Irving Caesar in 1919 not specifically for this revue, but in response to a popular one-step by Oliver Wallace and Harold Weeks, "Hindustan," part of a trend for Middle Eastern and central Asian exotica that included such contemporary hits as "My Sahara Rose" and "Afghanistan" and that eventually gave rise to Rudolph Valentino's sheik films and Sigmund Romberg's *Desert Song*. "Why don't we write an American one-step?" suggested Caesar, apparently meaning that they write a one-step (with its vigorous striding rhythm) like "Hindustan," but with a mythic American setting—"Swanee"—as opposed to an Asian one. They thus conflated two popular Tin Pan Alley tropes, Araby and Dixieland, presumably with some intent to parody Stephen Foster's "Old Folks at Home" ("Way down upon de Swanee ribber"). "We had never been south of fourteenth street when we wrote 'Swanee,'" Caesar stated (somewhat exaggeratedly) in 1954. "After the song became a hit, we took a trip down south and took a look at the Sewanee River. Very romantic, muddy little river. Very nice, nothing against it, but it's a good thing we wrote the song first and used our imagination." "The word [*Swanee*] fascinated me," recalled Gershwin, who remembered completing the song in his apartment with Caesar in about an hour. As they finished composing the number, Morris Gershwin interrupted his card game to join in with a comb wrapped in tissue paper, sounding like a kazoo. As discussed earlier, Ned Wayburn first encountered the song hearing Gershwin play it at a rehearsal of the *Ziegfeld Midnight Frolic*.[37]

"Swanee" owes more to "Hindustan" than is generally realized. Like "Hindustan," it opens, in a minor mode, with a verse of yearning set against a pastoral background, Wallace and Week's purplish lyric, with its images of nightingales and tingling harp strings, transformed into Caesar's more daffy ode to Dixie: "The birds are singing, / It is songtime— / The banjos strummin' soft and low." Meanwhile, the verse's modal harmonies probably have as much to do with Tin Pan Alley's stylized orientalism as with, as often mentioned, traditional Jewish music. In both songs, the chorus moves to the parallel major, with long notes enunciating their eponymous dream places—Hindustan and Swanee—followed by a rush of faster notes. These far-off utopias are populated by different love objects—the beloved, in "Hindustan," as opposed to "mammy" and the "old folks" in "Swanee"—but the imaginary place itself takes center stage, as suggested by their titles.

Although Alec Wilder and others have dismissed "Swanee" as "a manufactured song," an uncharacteristic effort "without any distinction," the comparison with "Hindustan" underscores, aside from its ironic intentions, the music's great novelty, including a steely rhythmic drive that outstrips any popular song of its time, one in excess of Berlin's comparable "Alexander's Ragtime Band" or Muir's "Waiting for the Robert E. Lee," and one in its own way never surpassed by the composer himself. The musical phrase "How I love you, / How I love you" implies in particular the overarching influence of machinery, perhaps trains, as do similar gestures in the *Rhapsody in Blue*. Steven Gilbert, meanwhile, observes such niceties as Gershwin's adept use of a unifying motive of three consecutive semitones in both the melody line and the accompanying voices.[38]

"Swanee" also contains, somewhat uncharacteristically, a "trio" at the end of the chorus, a section related to the extended codas of other Gershwin songs of the period, though here more self-contained. The term *trio* could justify either ending with this music or returning back to the chorus proper, as most performances over the years have done, including a 1920 Canadian release by the Fred Van Eps Quartet with Gershwin at the piano. On the other hand, the composer's 1920 piano roll of the song, which concludes with the trio, makes a compelling case for progressing from the urgency of the verse to the cheerfulness of the chorus to the final joke of the trio.[39]

This final joke includes the punch line, "I love the old folks at home," with its reference, in both word and tone, to the end of Foster's "Old Folks at Home" (1851). The punch line had been set up all along, not only by Caesar's paean to Swanee, but by the chorus's main theme, which, as Gilbert shows, paraphrases the opening melody of "Old Folks." Throughout the song, Caesar reinforces the connection with minstrelsy by using words like *Dixie* and *mammy*, but as with "Alexander's Ragtime Band," it's by no means clear that the protagonist is black, an ambiguity that no doubt registers part of the song's originality. The relation to minstrelsy is certainly ironic; the singer, unlike Foster's, is plainly not "sad and dreary," nor longing for the old plantation or death in his mother's arms. In the song's early days, performers (including Gershwin) compounded the parody—and elaborated the song's pastoral connotations—by punning another "sentimental Ethiopian ballad" of the 1850s, Septimus Winner's "Listen to the Mockingbird" (1855).[40]

Such nostalgic overtones only heightened the song's ironic celebration of the moment and its almost manic determination for joy ("I'll be happy, I'll be happy"). At the same time, those rare performances of the song as a ballad—as by KT Sullivan and Mark Nadler (1999)—revealed the pathos underpinning its relentless vigor (and its connection to the "Andantino" of the *Rhapsody in Blue*). In Gershwin's own estimation, the song contained, in any case, both elements: "I am happy to be told that the romance of that land [the 'Southland'] is felt in it, and that at the same time the spirit and energy of our United States is present. We are not all business or all romance, but a combination of the two, and real American music should represent these two characteristics which I tried to unite in 'Swanee' and make represent the soul of this country." As such, "Swanee," which probably more than any other music signaled the start of the Roaring Twenties, also helped elucidate Gershwin's self-identity as a "modern romantic."[41]

"Come to the Moon" evoked its own myth, but in more conventional *Follies* terms: a trip to the moon, a visit to "Spoonland," where "earthly troubles vanish like bubbles." The fetching melody—which offers an example of Gershwin's "gracility," to use Goldberg's expression, more than his "humor" or "colloquialness"—occasionally remembers a piece that might have been its original inspiration, Schubert's "Marche Militaire," op. 51, no. 1. Gershwin at least thought the song worthy enough to revise it as "All over Town" for his 1923 revue *The Rainbow*.

Neither the *Times* nor *Variety* mentioned Gershwin in its coverage of the *Capitol Revue*, though the former cited Dave Stamper and a few other composers on the program. It seems that "Swanee" (as opposed to "Come to the Moon," with its "twinkling stars" and "moon boys") in particular failed to make much of an impression, though an arrangement of the song for theater orchestra, possibly dating from late 1919, by Robert Russell Bennett—the distinguished orchestrator's first Gershwin score—referred to this "one-step" as "The Capitol Theatre Success." But whatever popularity the song enjoyed in the fall of 1919 hardly anticipated the extraordinary good fortune that followed its adoption by Al Jolson at the end of that year.[42]

Born Asa Yoelson, Jolson (1886?–1950), the son of a Lithuanian cantor, arrived in the States about age eight and grew up in poverty in Washington, D.C. He began singing in the streets for pennies as a child, and worked his way up through burlesque, minstrel shows, and vaudeville as a singer and comedian, emerging in the early 1910s as the most celebrated American entertainer of the time, a position he held over the next two decades. In 1920, the year he recorded "Swanee," he could command as much as one thousand dollars for a single appearance.[43]

Jolson's singing, which absorbed aspects of Jewish, Irish, and black vocal traditions, also proved the single greatest influence in the development of the modern musical-comedy voice. He did much of his most memorable work in blackface, according to one biographer, who argued that the "medium" allowed him to show "an *élan* on the Broadway stage no other performer—black or white—would dare exhibit." His enormous vitality depended in part on his singing around beats in ways not entirely unlike jazz musicians. In 1924 Gilbert Seldes described him as "possessed," as a "daemon," as (along with Fanny Brice) "all we have of the Great God Pan," as a figure more redolent of religious revivals and prizefights than of his rivals on the stage. Jolson ushered in the era of sound film with *The Jazz Singer* (1927) and the even bigger success, *The Singing Fool* (1928), but in the course of the 1930s, his great appeal diminished significantly, notwithstanding a keen but short-lived revival of interest spurred by the film biographies *The Jolson Story* (1946) and *Jolson Sings Again* (1949).[44]

Gershwin initially met Jolson during the Atlantic City tryout of *La-La-Lucille!* in April 1919, no doubt through the show's lyricist, Buddy DeSylva, a close friend of the singer's. That December, on a visit to a popular brothel in the company of DeSylva and Caesar, Gershwin played "Swanee" for Jolson, who subsequently incorporated it into his latest revue, *Sinbad*, a star vehicle that had opened in New York on February 10, 1918, but had been touring the country since March 1919, as it would through June 1921. Over the course of the show's long run, Jolson frequently tinkered with its original score, which included, as its biggest hit, another song about Dixie, composer Jean Schwartz's "Rock-a-Bye Your Baby with a Dixie Melody." The show featured a set of specialty songs near the end of the second act that in particular provided a convenient opportunity for Jolson to introduce new numbers.[45]

Jolson interpolated "Swanee" during the December 22–January 3 run of *Sinbad* at the Crescent Theatre in Brooklyn, and by the end of January the song had become, according to advertisements, "the most sensational vocal, instrumental and dance-number released for professional use in months." Meanwhile, Jolson recorded the song on January 8, and on February 20, about the time that this recording was released (complete with the singer's hallmark birdsong imitations), Harms took out a full two-page ad in *Variety,* once again touting "Swanee" as a "sensational song success." Touring in *Sinbad,* Jolson sang the song (no doubt in blackface) in scores of cities around the country and Canada, from Wheeling, West Virginia, to Missoula, Montana. Dance orchestras widely recorded the tune as well. Within a year, the song had topped sheet-music sales of a million copies and the Jolson recording, two million, bringing celebrity and riches to its authors. "Swanee" would remain the biggest-selling song of Gershwin's career.[46]

Gilbert Seldes recalled firsthand the impact of Jolson performing "Swanee":

> To have heard Al Jolson sing this song is to have had one of the few great experiences which the minor arts are capable of giving; to have heard it without feeling something obscure and powerful and rich with a separate life of its own coming into being, it—I should say it is not to be alive. . . . In the absurd black-face which is so little negroid that it goes well with diversions in Yiddish accents, Jolson created image after image of longing, and his existence through the song was wholly in *its* rhythm. Five years later [i.e., in the mid-1920s] I heard Jolson in a second-rate show, before an audience listless or hostile, sing this outdated and forgotten song, and create again, for each of us seated before him, the same image—and saw also the tremendous leap in vitality and happiness which took possession of the audience as he sang it. It was marvelous.

Jolson's later performances of the song—as heard in the 1945 Gershwin biopic and in the 1946 Jolson biopic—seemed to capture this dynamism better than the original 1920 release. In any case, aside from Judy Garland, who proclaimed her ties to Jolson (and Gershwin) by making "Swanee" one of her own theme songs (as she did, too, by naming one of her daughters after another Gershwin song popularized by Jolson, "Liza"), the song remained so identified with Jolson, even after his death, that its meaning and significance lay largely in terms of the singer's career; whereas its association with both Gershwin and jazz, white-hot in the early 1920s, dimmed within just a few years.[47]

Chapter Thirteen

From *Morris Gest's Midnight Whirl* (1919)
to *The Perfect Fool* (1921)

Toward the end of 1919, during the same week that Jolson first introduced "Swanee" into *Sinbad,* Morris Gest, a leading producer, launched *Morris Gest's Midnight Whirl,* Gershwin's first revue to appear on Broadway. An after-hours revue comparable to the *Ziegfeld Midnight Frolic,* the show opened on December 27 at the Century Grove on the roof of the Century Theatre, located at West 63rd and Broadway, and starred singers Bernard Granville, Helen Shipman, and Annette Bade; dancer and male impersonator Bessie McCoy Davis; comedian and female impersonator James Watts; and, reported *Variety,* "the usual alluring bunch" of "corphyees [*sic*]." Joseph Urban—the brilliant Viennese-born designer affiliated with both the Metropolitan Opera and the *Ziegfeld Follies*—created the scenery; Buddy DeSylva and John Henry Mears, the manager of the Century Grove, cowrote the book; and Gershwin, DeSylva, and Mears collaborated on the score, though the authorship of a few songs remains uncertain, and some of the performers interpolated various other numbers.[1]

The show started at 11:30 "for happiness, nightly," as one advertisement read. In the first act, Shipman and Granville sang "I'll Show You a Wonderful World"; Granville performed "The League of Nations Depends on Beautiful Clothes" as the chorus modeled fashions; Bade sang "Doughnuts" while the chorus sold doughnuts to the audience in order to help raise money for the Salvation Army; Watts presented a comic routine; Shipman and Granville again joined forces for "Poppyland"; Davis sang and danced to "Limehouse Nights" dressed as a Chinese man; and Watts parodied a Michel Fokine ballet. Following an intermission during which the audience could dance, Bade sang "Let Cutie Cut Your Cuticle" while the chorus gave manicures to patrons; Shipman performed "Baby Dolls" as the chorus imitated mechanical dolls (the "bit," stated *Variety,* that "seemed to please the house better than any of the others"); and Davis, Joseph Bennett, and Edward Richards performed "East Indian Maid." The revue closed after sixty-eight performances and then, revamped, toured Boston and Philadelphia, followed by ten weeks in Chicago.

Like such previous Gest productions as *Chu Chin Chow* (1917) and *The Rose of China* (1919), the *Midnight Whirl* tapped the current vogue for chinoiserie, and Gershwin duly provided some numbers along those lines, notably "Limehouse Nights" and "Poppyland," the show's two songs published by Harms, both with striking cover designs poised at that juncture between Art Nouveau and Art Deco. "Limehouse Nights" took its title from Thomas Burke's collection of tales (1917) further popularized in 1919 by *Broken Blossoms,* D. W. Griffith's film adaptation of the book's first story, "The Chink and the Child." Set in the Limehouse waterfront district of London, an area populated by sailors, dock workers, and Chinese immigrants, "The Chink and the Child" concerns an abused English girl whose barbarous pugilist-father brutally murders her after learning of her friendship with a sensitive Chinese poet (in the Griffith film, a devout Buddhist).

Gershwin's first oriental piece actually published (he had already composed "Hong Kong" and had recorded, for that matter, "Chinese Blues"), "Limehouse Nights" belongs to a subgenre of the Jazz Age musical revue, this one with Chinatowns and opium dens standing in for Harlem and gin joints, a trend that included the 1922 hit "Limehouse Blues" (Philip Braham, music; Douglas Furber, lyrics). Here, in "Limehouse Nights," "dreamers" can forget "the world of care" amid "the lantern lights" and gliding "hoppies." Onstage, chorus girls danced to the music—which features such stock oriental gestures as secondal harmonies and staccato basses—with opium pipes. The theme of narcoticized escape also informs the elegant "Poppyland," which stands in relation to "Limehouse Nights" as "Come to the Moon" does to "Swanee."[2]

Whereas the *Times* declared the *Midnight Whirl* "among the most lavish" of those revues "which have yet been turned out for the edification of those who refuse to go home when the play is over," *Variety* thought Gest's two previous Century Grove revues "better entertainments." The latter article also named "Limehouse Nights" as the show's "prettiest melody," but, like most other reviews, had little to say about the music other than that it was written by George Gershwin. Some, including the

Times, neglected to say this much. One notice opined simply that the music was "well suited to midnight entertainment." Still, the score must have made an impression; "Poppyland," "Limehouse Nights," "Let Cutie Cut Your Cuticle," and "Baby Dolls" all reappeared in a 1921 summer revue, *The Broadway Whirl,* that opened on June 8, 1921, and ran for eighty-five performances at the Times Square and then the Selwyn Theatres.[3]

Although Gershwin's involvement with Broadway had become by this point nearly all-consuming, as the decade came to a close he composed a few things not intended for any production. Early in 1919, for instance, he entered a patriotic song contest sponsored by the Hearst Corporation and judged by a panel composed of Irving Berlin, John Philip Sousa, singer John McCormack, lyricist-producer John Golden, and conductor Josef Stransky. Gershwin's entry, "O Land of Mine, America," with a favored Kern lyricist, Herbert Reynolds (as mentioned, the nom de plume of Michael E. Rourke), became one of fifteen songs selected for publication and appeared anonymously in the March 2 edition of the *New York American.* All the finalists received cash awards, and although Gershwin did not capture the remarkable first-place prize of two thousand dollars, he won a hundred dollars, the contest's smallest award. Gershwin's effort contained a spirited verse, marked "Marziale," evocative of traditional bugle calls, and a more hymnlike refrain reminiscent of "America the Beautiful." Edward Jablonski deemed its melody the "most uninspired" of Gershwin's career. Extended to a bombastic six-minute arrangement for chorus and orchestra, the song received a world premiere recording of sorts in 1998 by Erich Kunzel and the Cincinnati Pops Orchestra.[4]

In 1919 Gershwin also recorded his *Novelette in Fourths* for piano, presumably written that year. In contrast to his other rolls of the period, Gershwin's fluctuating tempos (he marked a surviving but undated draft of the piece "Tempo Rubato") clearly mark the work as something other than dance music. The music combines the parallel fourths and syncopated rhythms associated with novelty piano (and here also suggesting a bit of chinoiserie) with the refined sonorities and rich harmonies—including parallel movement of the "Tristan chord"—of the Romantic novelette. As found in the aforementioned manuscript, the piece is in *ABA* form, but as recorded by Gershwin, the work has an additional interlude to form an *ABACA* design.[5]

Warner Brothers published the *Novelette* in 1996 in an edition that raises one of the most vexing problems facing the study of Gershwin: the absence of critical editions—a problem that especially concerns his instrumental music, as Harms was rather faithful in its publications of the songs (for which the original Gershwin manuscript may not survive in any case). The corruptions here are fairly minor, but telling nonetheless, beginning with the title, *Prelude (Novellette in Fourths)*, as opposed to *Novelette in Fourths* (with one *l*). Moreover, the published edition inconsistently adds, deletes, and changes dynamic, tempo, and accent markings, and at times even pitches, in the process depriving the piece of some of its charm. Fortunately, some more reliable editions of Gershwin's music can be found.[6]

Gershwin wrote another instrumental work in 1919, or perhaps 1920: *Lullaby,* a short piece for string quartet that survives, however, only in a reduced piano score. "As a quartet," recalled Ira, "it was played in the next several months at a number of private musicales of his many musician friends before—sometimes after—they'd get down to the more serious business of classical quartets and quintets. I attended three of these intimate sessions and could see and hear that 'Lullaby' was invariably welcomed." The music remained on the shelf until, at Ira's invitation, harmonica player Larry Adler performed an arrangement of the work for harmonica and strings in the early 1960s. *Lullaby* received its first public performance as a string quartet by the Juilliard String Quartet at the Library of Congress on October 29, 1967. Since then, the work has been widely performed not only by string quartets but by pianists, string orchestras and, in an arrangement by José Serebrier, chamber orchestras as well.[7]

The music puts forth a principal strain, "dolce" (in D major); a transition, "semplice" (beginning in B minor and modulating to G major); a subsidiary melody, "dolcissimo" (in G major); and a return, "con forza," to the main theme (in D major). This *ABA* design, with its most songful tune reserved for the "dolcissimo" middle section, looks ahead to Gershwin's larger concert works, including his two rhapsodies. The music further displays the composer's invariably good workmanship, including the use of an initial syncopated motive to unify various melodies and countermelodies.

Lullaby also remains noteworthy for its blend of features derived from Debussy and popular music, the latter including not only some syncopated figures related to ragtime, but the piece's very structure: the first theme area duplicates an *aaba* popular song form, the second theme area, an *abab* song form. Pianist Herbie Hancock and his co-arranger, Robert Sadin, demonstrated the music's congeniality as a launching pad for some jazz musings in their recorded tribute, *Gershwin's World* (1998). However, for all its historical interest, the score is rather uneventful, its lovely coda notwithstanding. Ira's description of the piece as "charming and kind" seems about right.

Possibly about this time, Gershwin wrote another movement for string quartet, titled *A Piece for Four Strings,* of which only a bit of the viola part apparently survives. This extant fragment—a lilting, slightly raggy melody in duple meter—offers a tantalizing reminder of the many Gershwin pieces that have disappeared over the years.[8]

Following "Swanee," Gershwin continued to collaborate with Irving Caesar intermittently through 1923. In 1920 the two published "Yan-Kee," an oriental number along the lines of "Limehouse Nights," though here Japanese rather than Chinese, and, like "Poor Butterfly," yet another parody of the Madame Butterfly story, with the Butterfly figure singing a sort of tongue-in-cheek blues in the refrain, marked "slow with unaffected simplicity." As in other Gershwin-Caesar travesties (including "Swanee"), the combination of the satirical and the fantastic—including some adventurous harmonies appearing under the cover of japonaiserie—creates a certain tension that looks ahead to Gershwin's opera *Blue Monday Blues* (1922), and that Marion Harris nicely captured in her 1920 recording of the song, accompanied by gong and oboe for some additional color.

Gershwin also worked with both Caesar and Ira on a few songs for a show, *Dere Mabel,* that closed out of town after touring the East Coast in February and March 1920. Based on a series of books by Edward Streeter, including an epistolary novel of the same name (1918) about an amiably dumb soldier overseas, this three-act musical adaptation concerned gullible Private Bill Smith, who returns home a celebrated war hero but encounters some comedown before returning to his old job as a clerk in Philopolis. To the score by composer Rosamund Hodges and lyricist John Hodges (working with Streeter himself), producer Marc Klaw interpolated four Gershwin numbers: "Back Home," "I Don't Know Why," "I Want to Be Wanted by You," and "We're Pals," the first with lyrics by Ira, the other three with lyrics by Caesar.

The only surviving song of these four, "We're Pals," was performed onstage by a disillusioned Bill (Louis Bennison), who "talked" the number to his dog, Harold. Faithful dogs, at least since Foster's "Old Dog Tray" (1853), had long inhabited the world of popular song, though Caesar put his own wry spin on the matter, as evident from the title. For his part, Gershwin produced a melody of lovely breadth—"slow with great expression"—that he might have referred to as Brahmsian, though appropriately marked by a wide-eyed innocence that distinguishes it from, say, "Love Walked In." *Variety,* in its Boston review, thought the scene "one of the prettiest touches of the entire show." "There wasn't a dry eye in the house," recalled Caesar decades later. Although Gershwin's other songs from the show disappeared, as mentioned, Caesar, in a taped interview from 1983, sang for posterity the refrain of the jaunty "I Don't Know Why (When I Dance with You)," originally performed by Elizabeth Hines in the role of Gwendolyn Pettygrew.[9]

Shortly thereafter, another Gershwin song—the raggy "Oo, How I Love to Be Loved by You" (lyrics, Paley), which had been dropped from *La-La-Lucille!*—was interpolated into a revue, *The Ed Wynn Carnival,* possibly thanks to Ned Wayburn, the show's director. A revered vaudevillian known for his fluttery stage presence and fanciful props, Wynn (born Isaiah Edwin Leopold, 1886–1966), whose career spanned more than sixty years, had been blacklisted in some quarters because of his leadership of the Actor's Equity strike of 1919, and had responded by creating his own single-star vehicles such as this *Carnival,* which opened on April 5, 1920, at the New Amsterdam, and for which Wynn wrote some of the music and lyrics himself (the show later moved to the Selwyn Theatre, where it closed after 150 performances). Gershwin is said to have admired Wynn, and his participation in this and a succeeding Wynn revue, *The Perfect Fool* (1921), suggests that the admiration was mutual.

With *George White's Scandals of 1920,* which premiered on June 7 at the Globe, Broadway heard a complete new Gershwin score, the composer's first since the *Midnight Whirl.* Collaborating on this show with lyricist Arthur Jackson, Gershwin would continue to supply music for another four editions of the *Scandals,* right through 1924, by which time his name had become widely linked with White's.

George White (born Weitz, 1890–1968) grew up in New York and worked his way up through burlesque, joining the *Ziegfeld Follies* as a dancer in 1911. He remained in the *Follies* as a secondary principal in dance specialty numbers, often partnering Ann Pennington (1893–1971), an alluring and diminutive Ziegfeld dancer known for her long blond tresses and dimpled knees, who shimmied, shook, hulaed, and tapped her way to stardom after joining the *Follies* in 1913. A snazzy pair, White and Pennington forged a largely forgotten link between the Castles and the Astaires, though ultimately White's main contribution was as a producer.

In 1919 White left Ziegfeld to start his own series of revues, the *Scandals,* which ran successfully throughout the 1920s and beyond, proving the most formidable of those annual editions—including the *Passing Shows,* the *Greenwich Village Follies,* and the *Earl Carroll Vanities*—that rivaled the *Follies.* As his first major coup, White induced Pennington to leave Ziegfeld by promising her star billing. He also began presenting arguably the best music for any revue in town, signing up Gershwin in the early 1920s and then the team of DeSylva, Brown, and Henderson for the editions from 1925 through 1928. Ethan Mordden claims that White, who had "the keenest ear" of all the revue producers, hired Gershwin on the strength of "Swanee," but it is just as likely that he engaged him because of their mutual friendship with Arthur Jackson, who had cowritten the lyrics to both *La-La-Lucille!* and the *Scandals of 1919;* and because of the excellent work Gershwin had done on the *Midnight Whirl.*[10]

White's collaboration with Gershwin was part of a larger striving for an especially smart and modern type of entertainment. He advanced these objectives through the use of whites, grays, and blacks rather than the soft pastels of the *Follies;* leather, metallic, and synthetic materials in contrast to the furs and chiffon favored by Ziegfeld; small, lively dancers as opposed to the statuesque Ziegfeld girls; and such targets for satire as Prohibition and the Russian revolution. "The difference was probably one of degree not kind," concludes Gerald Bordman, "yet it helped give the *Scandals* their steely, cynical, sixty-mile-an-hour jazz-age tone." Ziegfeld himself realized the necessity of keeping up with White, as in his decision to hire Erté (Romain de Tirtoff, 1892–1990) to design costumes for the *Follies* after the Art Deco designer established a close affiliation with the *Scandals* in 1922.[11]

The *Scandals of 1920,* which had a book by White and Andy Rice, starred Pennington, comedian Lou Holtz, singers Lloyd Garrett and Lester O'Keefe, dancer La Sylphe, and White himself, who appeared briefly in the second-act finale. White staged the show with William Collier, Herbert Ward designed the sets, Frank Saddler provided the orchestrations, and Alfred Newman conducted the orchestra.

The show's musical numbers included "My Lady," sung by O'Keefe for the obligatory fashion show; "Everybody Swat the Profiteer," performed by a group of chorus girls, some of whom had their bare legs painted to simulate lace stockings; "On My Mind the Whole Night

Long," sung by Lloyd Garrett as yet another group of chorus girls appeared in green, orange, black, and blue paint (body painting apparently being one of the show's themes); the "Scandal Walk," sung and danced by Pennington and the chorus following a parody of William Jennings Bryan; "Come on and Kiss Me" (published as "Tum on and Tiss Me") for Pennington and the chorus dressed as "tiss me" dolls; "I Love the Old Songs" (published as "The Songs of Long Ago"), sung by O'Keefe; and "Idle Dreams," sung by Garrett, with Pennington as featured dancer. Gershwin also seems to have written his "Mexican Dance" for the show's satirical sketch about the Mexican revolution, presumably the segment identified in the program as "A Mexican Cigarette Dance."[12]

"Idle Dreams," about a Chinese boy's love for his "idol" (danced by Pennington), received the most lavish staging, including a set that contained a Chinese shrine atop rocks simulating carved jade. Such splendor helped make "Idle Dreams" the show's only number to attain even mild popularity, though Harms published all of the above-mentioned songs except "Everybody Swat the Profiteer." Gershwin's score was, as has often been pointed out, hardly his best; some of the verses, with their suave modulations, were more interesting than the choruses, in a way a point in Gershwin's favor, but not really a recommendation. But at the least, the score featured an able and elegant handling of the show's eclectic needs.

"The Songs of Long Ago" epitomized this tendency toward pastiche. As indicated in the published score, the song's refrain could be "sung or played simultaneously" with the choruses from "Home Sweet Home" and "Silver Threads among the Gold" (an original cast recording introduces another two old tunes into the melee, as may have been done onstage, and concludes with all four melodies superimposed with Gershwin's new one, creating a babel of sound that looks ahead to some of the composer's later preoccupations). Whereas the song's verse expresses longing for "the songs of long ago" rather than "the raggy kind they write today," the ensuing chorus incongruously evokes the "songs of long ago" in the despised "raggy blue" style. As a whole, the number recalls Irving Berlin's "Play a Simple Melody" (1914), but Gershwin's actual quoting of tunes and the peculiarity of having the nostalgic protagonist sing a raggy fox-trot make a different impression.[13]

The jaunty "Scandal Walk" proved, however, the show's most characteristic number, what with its original harmonic palette (including much alternating between the tonic, E♭ major, and a B-major-seventh harmony) and its chromatic main theme suggesting a ragging of Debussy's *Afternoon of a Faun.* (Some smaller-note figuration in the sheet music further indicated the relative textural richness of Gershwin's theater music.) "On My Mind" merits special mention as well, for along with "Yan-Kee" it remains one of Gershwin's first known blues. An oddly truncated number, its compressed length (its introduction, verse, and chorus total twenty-eight measures) and its static tonality enhance those bluesy qualities imparted by its blue notes and triplet rhythms. Though derivative, the music presages a distinct line in Gershwin's output that culminates with *Porgy and Bess.*

"On My Mind" no doubt reinforced connections between the *Scandals of 1920* and jazz, an association commonly made, often bemusedly, in the press, who considered the show a significant advance over the *Scandals* of the previous year. Some reviews also noted with interest the presence in the pit of the peppy nineteen-year-old Alfred Newman (later a notable film composer). While few had much to say about the music itself, the *Clipper* was exuberant in its praise: "The score which George Gershwin has composed for the show . . . is easily one of the most tuneful now being played on Broadway. Its colorful melodies and piquant jazz strains will not fail of popular rendition in the various cafes and places where orchestras hold forth." And S. Jay Kaufman, in the *Globe,* even wondered, presciently enough, if the score (along with that for *La-La-Lucille!*) did not signal the arrival of an operatic composer. "We have discovered an elusive, unforgettable, pleasing melody in all he has written," wrote Kaufman. "And then he is young. Because he has written only light music thus far does not mean that he cannot do something serious." Whatever the show's shortcomings (*Variety* thought it "could well stand another lively song number or two"), the *1920 Scandals* ran for a solid 134 performances and enjoyed a particularly vigorous life on the road, closing October 1921.[14]

Early in 1920 George and Ira wrote a song, "Waiting for the Sun to Come Out," for *The Sweetheart Shop,* then enjoying a smash pre-Broadway tour. The Gershwins had heard that the show, for which Anne Caldwell had written the book and lyrics and Hugo Felix the score, wanted a new number for its lead ingenue, Helen Ford, and they quickly composed this particular song because, as Ira later explained, musical comedies of the period "called for at least one Pollyanna song in a show." George persuaded Ira to adopt a pseudonym, lest management think twice about such an incestuous collaboration, and Ira settled on Arthur Francis, a pen name derived from the names of his youngest siblings, which he would use until 1924. The show's coproducer, Edgar MacGregor (1879–1957), purchased the number for $250, and by March the song was in.[15]

The Sweetheart Shop opened at New York's Knickerbocker Theatre on August 31, 1920, to mixed reviews, and closed after fifty-five performances, hardly the success it seemed headed for. Its story involved a matchmaking agency—the titular sweetheart shop—that guarantees its marriage contracts for the length of one year. "Waiting for the Sun to Come Out" was sung in the second act by the young romantic leads, Natalie Blythe (Helen Ford) and Julian Lorimer (Joseph Lertora), supported by the male chorus. Critics unanimously cited the song as one of the best in the show, while *Variety* described Ford, who would later star in some Rodgers and Hart musicals, as having a "sweet, well trained voice which ought to gain power with the seasons." The *Times* reported that "lobby gossip," if not the program, credited Gershwin with the music to "Waiting for the Sun to Come Out," an indication that by the summer of 1920—thanks above all to "Swanee"—he had become a known entity.[16]

Although "Waiting for the Sun to Come Out," which became George and Ira's first published song together, offered less proof than "The Real American Folksong" of their potential as a team, its modest success on the stage and in sheet-music and record sales (which brought them more than a thousand dollars each) must have encouraged future collaboration. The song also revealed Gershwin's growing penchant for modally inflected harmonies. The verse's last four measures, for instance, unfold a rather unusual progression (from a D-dominant-seventh to an E-minor to a G-dominant-seventh to a C-dominant-seventh chord), by which point the tonal direction has become so uncertain that the return of the F-major tonic at the start of the chorus sounds, appropriate to its text, sweetly comforting—all the more so as the melody begins on the mild dissonance of the sixth. Gershwin plainly was following Kern's lead in infusing some harmonic novelty into popular stage music, even if he came short in this Pollyanna song of creating a masterpiece of the genre like Kern's "Look for the Silver Lining" (also 1920). Meanwhile, the reappearance of the verse's unconventional chord progression, as described above, in a comparable spot in the chorus gave further evidence of Gershwin's skill at unifying a song's separate parts into an integral whole.

About the time *The Sweetheart Shop* opened, in late August, George

White asked Gershwin and Arthur Jackson to help doctor a revue on the road, namely, George LeMaire's *Broadway Brevities of 1920* (music, Archie Gottler; lyrics, Blair Treynor). A former *Follies* comedian, LeMaire was, like White, a Ziegfeld renegade who apparently hoped to establish his own series of revues, but the *Brevities,* which premiered at the Winter Garden on September 29, after a detour in Philadelphia for additional polishing, generated no sequel. Heywood Broun wrote a blistering review in the *Tribune,* describing the show as "the worst" he had ever seen, as a repository of "last year's dirty stories" and sheer "stupidity." Deeming the show "unusually dull even for the Winter Garden," *Theatre Magazine* similarly thought its humor "on a par with the number two burlesque shows." But a number of other notices were actually good to fair, and the show ran for 105 performances, no doubt thanks to the appeal of its leading comedians, the Jewish Eddie Cantor—a childhood friend of the Gershwins—and the black Bert Williams. It did good business on the road as well, though in Providence the "amusement inspector" on the police force declared it one of the "rawest" shows of the season and (not all that unusual for the time) demanded cuts and other modifications, including having the chorus girls wear "fleshings."[17]

Gershwin composed at least four songs used at one time or another in the show: three with Arthur Jackson ("I'm a Dancing Fool," "Lu Lu," and "Snow Flakes"), and one with Irving Caesar ("Spanish Love"). Harms published all but "I'm a Dancing Fool," illustrating their covers with Arabian-inspired designs in the style of Erté. Edith Hallor and Hal Van Rensellear performed "Spanish Love" in a scene set in a square in Spain, and "Snow Flakes" in the Swiss panorama featured in the finale to act 1, while in the second act William Sully sang "I'm a Dancing Fool" on the roof garden of a modern apartment and Edith Hallor sang "Lu Lu" ("Never was another gal like Lu Lu") on the famous Winter Garden runway. These varied numbers allowed Gershwin to explore a range of international styles, with the cuckoo-clock charm of "Snow Flakes" later adapted for the more masterful "Swiss Miss" from *Lady, Be Good!*[18]

Some of the reviews singled out one or another of these Gershwin songs as among the evening's best ("Spanish Love" even reappeared in John Murray Anderson's *The Greenwich Village Follies of 1923*). The *Herald* further thought Van Rensellear "a tenor with a very agreeable voice and unusually pleasant personality"; but the critics took a dim view of Hallor, who in the course of the run was replaced by Isabel Mohr, possibly so that Hallor could join the cast of Ray Goetz's revue *Piccadilly to Broadway.*[19]

Gershwin himself became involved in the latter production, which, its title notwithstanding, never made it to either Piccadilly or Broadway. Opening on September 27 in Atlantic City, the show floundered under different titles and in various theaters from Boston to Detroit, including a week in Brooklyn, before expiring on the road toward the end of the year. The show's producer, composer-lyricist Ray Goetz (1886–1954, the brother of Irving Berlin's first wife, Dorothy), collaborated on the music with veteran lyricist Glen MacDonough, but apparently felt the need in tryout to enliven the score with some younger talent, turning to such members of the Gershwin circle as George and Ira, Vincent Youmans, and William Daly.

Gershwin supplied three numbers: "Baby Blues" and "On the Brim of Her Old-Fashioned Bonnet" (both with lyrics by Goetz), and "Something Peculiar" (lyrics, Lou Paley and Ira). Only four measures of "Baby Blues" seem to have survived, enough to suggest that the music toyed with a nursery idiom. "Her Old-Fashioned Bonnet" essentially vanished as well, although an extant orchestration by Maurice DePackh reveals that the music, far from old-fashioned, was rather jazzy. "Something Peculiar," the score's only extant Gershwin song, commends jazz over the tango; the music alternates American and Latin idioms, the latter evoked in a trio that begins "Las chiquitas están barrachas [*sic*] / Con la música de los Yankees" ("The girls are drunk / on American music"). The Gershwins must have liked this number, for they considered adapting it for *Lady, Be Good!* (1924) and *Girl Crazy* (1930), both of which flirted with Mexican idioms.[20]

Anna Wheaton, one of the stars of *Piccadilly,* sang all three Gershwin songs, joined in "Something Peculiar" by costars Johnny Dooley and British comic Harvey Morris. Covering the show in Brooklyn, *Variety* commended "Her Old-Fashioned Bonnet," sung in a hat shop, as "one corking number," and "Baby Blues" as having a "snappy lyric" and a "catching melody." But apparently neither this infusion of songwriting talent nor an all-star cast that included Helen Broderick and Clifton Webb could save the show, which, wrote *Variety,* needed "a lot of fixing."[21]

However, remnants of *Piccadilly,* including "Baby Blues" and "Her Old-Fashioned Bonnet," resurfaced on Broadway, along with another lost Gershwin-Goetz number, "Futuristic Melody," as part of an entirely new revue, *Snapshots of 1921.* Premiering on June 2, 1921, at the Selwyn Theatre, recently built by the show's coproducers, Edgar and Arch Selwyn, *Snapshots* starred DeWolf Hopper, Lew Fields, and Nora Bayes (who quit the show after six weeks, leaving the producers two weeks to regroup before opening again for another two weeks, for a total of sixty performances). Delyle Alda sang "Her Old-Fashioned Bonnet" accompanied by chorus girls; Gilda Gray and a group of children performed "Baby Blues"; and an ensemble of principals introduced "Futuristic Melody." The papers more or less approved of the show's funmaking, notwithstanding a mention in the *New York Times* of its containing "little or nothing for the adult intelligence" and one in *Variety* complaining of "boresome periods of blank stupidity." Expectations for musical revues obviously did not run very high.[22]

Throughout 1921 Gershwin continued to write songs seemingly independent of any show, including the breezy love song "Phoebe," one of his final collaborations with Lou Paley, here once again cowriting the lyric with Ira. With other lyricists, Gershwin also published "Swanee Rose" (also known as "Dixie Rose"; lyrics, Caesar and DeSylva), "Tomalé (I'm Hot for You)" (lyrics, DeSylva), and "In the Heart of a Geisha (Nippo San of Japan)" (lyrics, Fred Fisher), all three of which brought Gershwin closer to Tin Pan Alley than was his wont. Jolson sang both of the DeSylva-Gershwin songs, introducing the lively but rather trite "Swanee Rose"—a patent attempt by all concerned to capitalize on the success of "Swanee"—into *Sinbad* early in the year. "Tomalé," a tango number whose chorus derived from Gershwin's "Mexican Dance," satirized *Carmen* in its playful lyric about the singer's love for a Spanish dancer, Tomalé, and his plot to destroy his rival, the toreador Cholly. Meanwhile, "In the Heart," like the earlier "Yan-Kee," parodied the Madame Butterfly story, though here in his one collaboration with the venerable German-born songsmith and publisher Fred Fisher (whose biggest hit, "Chicago," followed in 1922), Gershwin largely dispensed with orientalisms, writing rather a straightforward raggy number—appropriately enough, as an American man, not his beloved Japanese geisha, Nippo San, narrates the story. Ira Gershwin, who later had no recollection of the number, wondered how his brother managed to publish a song with Fred Fisher while under contract to Harms.[23]

On February 21, 1921, *Blue Eyes,* a musical with some Gershwin interpolations (not to be confused with the 1928 Jerome Kern musical of the same name), premiered at the Casino Theatre. With a book by LeRoy Clemons and Leon Gordon about a struggling Greenwich Village artist mistaken for a count by his Great Neck girlfriend, *Blue Eyes* proved a not unusual mishmash of musical comedy and vaudeville, with come-

dian Lew Fields, the star of the show, working in his own comic routines
and Mollie King, his costar (and the "blue eyes" of the title), performing some imitations of her own toward the end of the evening. The critics were clearly wearying of this sort of entertainment. *Theatre Magazine* specifically stated that *Irene* (1919; music, Harry Tierney) and *Sally*
(1920; music, Jerome Kern) had set standards, obviously not met by *Blue
Eyes,* for "a new order of humor and story and entertainer—not to mention music." The public must have agreed, for the show folded after forty-
eight performances.[24]

Blue Eyes featured a new Gershwin song, "Wanting You" (lyrics, Caesar), sung in the second act by a secondary romantic couple, Kitty Hig-
gins (Delyle Alda) and her comic boyfriend, Dawson Ripley (Andrew
Tombes), and then reprised in the finale. Mollie King also interpolated
(possibly with her leading man, Ray Raymond) the Gershwin song "I
Am So Young" that she and her brother Charles had successfully introduced two years earlier in *Good Morning, Judge.* Gershwin and Caesar
received credit in the program for "Wanting You," suggesting their growing clout, but *Variety* and the *Times* limited their remarks about the music to the score proper (by I. B. Kornblum and Z. Myers).[25]

In early 1921 producer Edgar MacGregor, who a year earlier had obtained "Waiting for the Sun to Come Out" for *The Sweetheart Shop,* asked
the same team of Gershwin and Arthur Francis to provide the score for
a new musical, *A Dangerous Maid,* to a script by Charles W. Bell adapted
from the author's 1918 play *The Dislocated Husband.* By this point, Mac-
Gregor knew that Arthur Francis was none other than Ira Gershwin, and
"was resigned," wrote Ira, "to my being George's brother." *A Dangerous Maid* would prove George's second book musical and his first full
score of any sort with Ira.[26]

A Dangerous Maid—like *La-La-Lucille!*—was conceived as a three-
act farce with music; the show was even subtitled a "music-play." And
like Fred Jackson (who wrote the book for *La-La-Lucille!*) Charles Bell
was best known for a bedroom farce, *Parlor, Bedroom and Bath* (with
Mark Swan, 1917). Moreover, both *La-La-Lucille!* and *A Dangerous
Maid* concerned female entertainers—an ex-juggler and an ex-chorus girl,
respectively—who marry into society. MacGregor presumably was aware
of these resemblances when he decided to contract the still relatively green
Gershwin.

A Dangerous Maid remains the only Gershwin musical without a
known surviving book. However, programs and reviews, along with the

script to *The Dislocated Husband,* permit some reconstruction of the show's basic plot. Elsie Crofton (Juliette Day), a sweet and bright former chorus girl of eighteen, has left the stage to elope with Harry Hammond (Creighton Hale), the spoiled but good-hearted son of a major government contractor. Harry's parents, Philip and Eleanor (Frederic Burt and Amelia Bingham), and his sister Margery (Juanita Fletcher) and her fiancé, Fred Blakely (Vinton Freedley), appalled at the marriage, have interrupted the honeymoon by arranging for Harry to leave for a family construction site, while Elsie, the "dangerous maid" of the title, stays at their summer home, the temporary shelter as well for friends of the family Alfie and Anne Westford (Arthur Shaw and Ada Meade).

While pretending to welcome Elsie into the family, the Hammonds scheme to break up the marriage by exposing her in a compromising position with an all-too-willing Fred. Meanwhile, the shrewish Anne harbors her own prejudices against Elsie. When Elsie realizes what's afoot, she hatches a plot of her own by playing the gay coquette (to the dismay of her husband, at home on a visit) and winning Philip, Fred, and Alfie over to her side. This only further enrages Eleanor, Margery, and Anne, until Elsie exposes their duplicity, at which point all are more or less reconciled.

A Dangerous Maid debuted in Atlantic City on March 21, 1921, in a production designed by the Robert Law Studios and staged by MacGregor (assisted by Eddie Leonard and, for the musical numbers, Julian Alfred), under the musical direction of Harold Vicars. Referring to the show as an "experiment," *Variety* gave it a positive review: "The spirit of the piece is the plea of youth for happiness. . . . The difference from the average musical comedy model consists mostly in the way the drama of the plot is sustained, the musical numbers and dances not being permitted to obtrude irrelevantly upon the main scheme of conveying a human story of love and sentiment." The large premiere audience, *Variety* further reported, "applauded its sentiment, laughed at its lines and in the main approved the cast."[27]

As *A Dangerous Maid* moved on to Wilmington, Baltimore, Washington, and Pittsburgh, it continued to meet with warm critical and popular response. "A laughing, sympathetic and wildly applauding audience proclaimed *A Dangerous Maid* . . . to be a great hit," reported the *Wilmington Morning News.* Critics admired the work's fast pace and its wholesome comedy, and welcomed, too, the novelty of having a chorus composed of eight of Elsie's theater friends, a touch that presumably added to the show's verisimilitude. Many reviews also found the music charming and catchy, though the Baltimore papers seemed less impressed, one opining that the music, though of "pleasing tunefulness," lacked "distinction." Another stated, "George Gershwin's music is nothing to rave about."[28]

In the course of the tour, MacGregor hired Vivienne Segal to replace Juliette Day; and perhaps in response to a Pittsburgh critic who complained that the title was misleading, as the heroine was more "demure" than "dangerous" (this reviewer found the local first-nighter who appeared with her ears "entirely exposed" more daring than the show's heroine), MacGregor decided to retitle the show *Elsie*. But after closing in Pittsburgh on April 16, MacGregor—who seems to have run into money problems—announced that he was recalling the work for revisions in the score and expressed his intention of sending the musical back out again in a month or so, possibly with a still different title. The show finally did make it to Broadway as *Elsie,* but not until two years later, in April 1923, and with an entirely new score by the team of Noble Sissle and Eubie Blake, supplemented by numbers by Alma Sanders and Monte Carlo. This reincarnation, which featured some of the show's original cast members, including Frederic Burt, who re-created the role of Philip Hammond, and Vinton Freedley, who this time played the part of Harry Hammond, flopped after forty performances, but remains historically significant as an unusual instance of black songwriters writing a musical comedy about white characters.[29]

Why MacGregor jettisoned the original score remains a mystery. In any case, the show became one of the rare Gershwin musicals that never made it to Broadway. With five years in the business, George must have been all the more impressed to find Ira, essentially a novice, land on his feet later in the same season with *Two Little Girls in Blue,* a collaboration with composers Vincent Youmans and Paul Lannin that opened in New York on May 3, 1921, and not only ran a respectable 135 performances but yielded the delightful "Oh Me! Oh My!"—the first major success for both Ira and Youmans. Meanwhile, some of the *Dangerous Maid* score disappeared, though a few of the fine Frank Saddler orchestrations managed to survive.

Harms fortunately published most of the show's songs, including two solos for Elsie (the romantic waltz "Just to Know You Are Mine" and the ballad "Some Rain Must Fall"); two duets for Elsie and Fred (the lighthearted tribute to country living "The Simple Life" and the high-spirited "Dancing Shoes"); and two choruses for Elsie's chorus-girl friends, including Teddy, Toots, Babe, and Bunny ("Boy Wanted" and

"The Sirens," the latter published only in revised form as "Four Little Sirens" from the 1924 musical *Primrose*). Of the unpublished songs introduced in Atlantic City—"Anything for You" (sung by Blakely and Margery) and "True Love" (sung by Elsie, Blakely, and Margery)—only the former survives.

The score was something of a mixed brew stylistically, with "The Sirens" evocative of Gilbert and Sullivan and "Just to Know You Are Mine" reminiscent of Lehár (Gershwin may have sensed the triumphant return of Viennese operetta in the course of 1921, following a six-year hiatus), not to mention the familiar echoes of Kern and Berlin. The more original "Boy Wanted," whose remarkable main theme floats pentatonically over the range of an octave, as if untethered to any meter, proved particularly successful, especially after Ella Fitzgerald recorded it in 1959 with new words written for her by Ira, though Michael Feinstein's 1996 recording of "Anything for You" might yet help establish that song as well.

If still somewhat eclectic, the score's wit and refinement signaled not only another step forward for Gershwin, but also Ira's emergence as an outstanding lyricist. Philip Furia mentions in particular the "light-verse flair" of some of the songs, including such inventive triple rhymes as "[ad]vertisement" and "flirt is meant" (in "Boy Wanted") and "[per]petual" and "get you all" (in "The Sirens"). Granted, Furia notes as well the presence of some hackneyed phrases, clichéd rhymes, and awkward word inversions; but such criticism makes most sense placed against standards that Ira himself set in his later work. In the context of their time, the lyrics are a marvel, impressive not only in their wit but in their ability to shape character and situation, so that the numbers emerge as dramatic vignettes, with verses effectively preparing choruses, comparable to the way recitative and aria function in opera. In "Some Rain Must Fall," for instance, Elsie muses on her innocent childhood in the verse before turning to her present resignation in the chorus; and in "The Simple Life" she thinks back to her "gay and giddy" life along "the Gay White Way" in the verse before declaiming her love for country life in the chorus. "Boy Wanted" takes a similar tack: the verse explains that the women have taken out personal ads, but the refrain provides the specifics that incisively capture, in each of the song's four choruses, each girl's fantasies, from Teddy's "He must be able to dance. / He must make life a romance," to Bunny's "The movies he must avoid, / He'll know his Nietzsche and Freud." Meanwhile, the description of "Some Rain Must Fall" as a "standard pollyanna weather song" remains debatable, too, considering the absence of any silver linings or rays of sunshine in the text, whose dark-ness seems all the more heightened by the haunting chromaticism in the melody.[30]

After *A Dangerous Maid,* Gershwin, working again with Arthur Jackson, composed the score for the *1921 Scandals,* which opened at the Liberty Theatre on July 11. The show, which had a book by White and Arthur "Bugs" Baer and ran for ninety-seven performances, featured dancer Ann Pennington, comics Lou Holtz and Lester Allen, and singers Lloyd Gar-rett, Victoria Herbert, and Charles King, as well as newcomer Tess Gardella, who stole the show performing the blues and "mammy songs" in blackface under the name Aunt Jemima (and who would later play Queenie in Kern's *Show Boat*). White, assisted by John Meehan, directed; Herbert Ward designed the sets; and Alfred Newman once again con-ducted the orchestra.

Some of the show's bigger production numbers concerned the sea, which served as a unifying theme, including a tableau depicting a battle-ship moving through the locks of the Panama Canal ("Where East Meets West," sung by King and Herbert); a Flying Dutchman scene, complete with phantom ship moored to a rock ("Drifting Along with the Tide," sung by Garrett and Herbert); and a South Sea Island extravaganza ("South Sea Isles," sung by King and danced by Pennington, wiggling in a grass skirt). Gershwin and Jackson wrote at least two other songs for this nineteen-scene revue: the lightly romantic "She's Just a Baby" for Pennington and the humorous "I Love You" for the young Harry Rose, accompanied by women representing foreign lands.[31]

Harms published all five of these Gershwin-Jackson numbers, as well as a piano reduction of the show's overture, arranged by Robert Russell Bennett. Whereas the sheet music for the *Scandals of 1920* had portrayed someone like George White peeping through a keyhole at someone like Ann Pennington at a dressing table, the similarly provocative Junius Cravens cover design for the current *Scandals* depicted a placid Eve ac-cepting an apple from a dangerous-looking serpent in an ornate Eden conceived along the lines of Aubrey Beardsley.

Gershwin and Jackson prepared as well an extensive opening num-ber, some of whose music—though not the text—survives. This scene featured a giant head of Mrs. Grundy (the fictional character who since the late eighteenth century had represented conventional public opinion, and a figure one review referred to as the "patron saint" of the *Scandals*), from whose mouth emerged figures representing "Divorce," "Style," and

"Modesty," with satirical commentary by a chorus of "Scandalmongers." Combining recitative, song, and chorus and traversing various meter and key signatures, the extant music stands as a reminder that many of Gershwin's more elaborate efforts for the popular stage—including overtures, choruses, and finales—were rarely published and frequently discarded; and that knowing only the solo songs of a Gershwin show means a limited understanding of their scores as a whole.[32]

The reviews of the *1921 Scandals* likened the show's scenic beauty to the *Follies* but parted ways over the material itself, some finding it vapid and eccentric, others clever and amusing. As for the music, although the *Times* and the *World* seemed unimpressed, the *Tribune* lauded Gershwin's melodies as "colorful" and "exquisite," and the *American* described the score as "graceful" and "above the average of the sticky and treacley stuff that adheres to most of our musical shows." Moreover, in the wake of its critique of the show as "mediocre," the *Sun* published a lengthy letter from a dissenting reader who, comparing Gershwin to Herbert and Friml, wrote, "Gershwin gave us our thrill. It is true, his 'Scandals' music is not wonderful—it is perhaps not by any means his best—but in nearly every number there was something different, a twist of harmony here and there to make one sit up and take notice."[33]

"South Sea Isles" and "Drifting Along with the Tide" especially delighted listeners. The former engages a familiar South Seas idiom but bears the distinctive touch of Gershwin's other dream worlds: like "Swanee" and "Limehouse Nights," the minor mode of its verse frames the major mode of its chorus; like "Come to the Moon" and "Poppyland," the refrain is utterly smooth, its elegance enhanced by a melody constructed almost entirely of sighing appoggiaturas.

The more remarkable "Drifting Along with the Tide," which depicts the "restless and wide" ocean in its verse and the lovelorn singer's "drifting along with the tide" in its chorus, features the sort of word-painting more associated with art song than with popular theater music. The music's adventurousness extends to its harmonic structure: the verse of this G-major song opens in E major, the better to suggest the "restless and wide" ocean, and arrives, in the middle of its refrain, at B major, again to dramatic effect. Alec Wilder acknowledged that the song, though not "great," signaled "musical ambition" and a "desire to burst out of the restrictions imposed by song writing conventions." Although Wilder scorned these kinds of lavish *Follies*-type production numbers to the point of wondering whether Gershwin could ever have taken them seriously, they apparently provided, as here, an opportunity to experiment before the large public in ways not available otherwise.[34]

"Drifting Along with the Tide" demonstrates another aspect of many of Gershwin's songs: their effectiveness at widely differing tempos. Here, the cut-time signature suggests a moderate fox-trot tempo, and in his piano roll of the song Gershwin plays the music at a rather quick pace; but the refrain is marked "slowly," and a performance of the song by, say, Bobby Short reveals how convincing the music sounds in a rather slow two. While characteristic of much popular music of the time, such elasticity of tempo proved perhaps especially pronounced in Gershwin's case. With "Someone to Watch Over Me," the Gershwins themselves realized that they had a ballad on their hands only after George perchance played the song, originally intended as an up-tempo number, slowly; with "I've Got a Crush on You," that discovery fell to others.

As for the rest of the score to the *1921 Scandals*, "She's Just a Baby," a rather coy celebration of women, and "Where East Meets West," a romanticized commemoration of free passage through the Panama Canal, pale in comparison; but "I Love You," a sweetly humorous song with a touch of Offenbach about it, stands out for its remarkable economy; nearly the entire melodic line utilizes a stepwise descending three-note motive. Although Gershwin had displayed a similar tautness in some earlier refrains, like "Nobody but You" and "Some Rain Must Fall," this song takes such restraint to new levels in response to the number's comic intentions; much as the singer needs only three words, "I love you," he needs just the simplest of motives.

Some four months after the *1921 Scandals*, two Gershwin songs— "My Log-Cabin Home" and "No One Else but That Girl of Mine"— appeared in the Ed Wynn vehicle *The Perfect Fool*, which opened at Cohan's Theatre on November 7, 1921. The show—for which Wynn largely wrote the book, lyrics, and music—enjoyed a long run of 275 performances, followed by an extended tour. Its success led Wynn to adopt "the perfect fool" as his sobriquet. *Variety* loathed the show both in tryout and on Broadway, but the reviews were generally favorable, the *Herald* calling it "for no other reason than that Wynn is the main figure in it . . . the funniest show in town." At some point during its run, the show interpolated "My Log-Cabin Home" (lyrics, Caesar and DeSylva), a marchlike song about the South as an idyllic refuge from city life, complete with a reference to Dan Emmett's "Dixie" in the piano part; and the similarly exuberant "No One Else but That Girl of Mine" (lyrics, Caesar), advertised as a "fox trot song." As in other Gershwin songs from these years, the verse to "No One Else" boldly moves from minor—here, the unusual key of E♭ minor no less—to major. Gershwin and Caesar liked this latter number well enough to recast it as "That American Boy of Mine" for *The Dancing Girl* (1923). But neither of the songs for *The Perfect Fool* proved particularly successful, and as 1921 came to an end Gershwin, though clearly a songwriter of skill and verve, had yet fully to find his stride.[35]

Chapter Fourteen

From *The French Doll* to *Our Nell* (1922)

𝒪n February 20, 1922, two shows opened on Broadway—*The French Doll* at the Lyceum and *For Goodness Sake* at the Lyric—that featured some new songs by Gershwin. Adapted by A. E. Thomas from the French of Paul Armont and Marcel Gerbidon, produced by Ray Goetz, and staged by W. H. Gilmore, *The French Doll* involved the attempts of an impoverished French American aristocrat, Baron Mazulier (Edouard Durand), to find a wealthy husband for his attractive daughter, Georgine (Irene Bordoni, the "French doll" of the title), and her eventual choice of an older millionaire over a handsome young engineer. Advertised as a play with music, the show, which ran for 120 performances, had only two songs, both performed by its star (and Goetz's wife), Bordoni: "When Eyes Meet Eyes, When Lips Meet Lips" by Gus Edwards and Will Cobb, and "Do It Again" by Gershwin and Buddy DeSylva.

In 1934 Gershwin recounted the latter's genesis: "I was in the office of Max Dreyfus, my publisher, one day when Buddy DeSylva walked in. DeSylva said jokingly to me, 'George, let's write a hit!' I matched him by saying, 'O.K.!' I sat down at the piano, and began playing a theme which I was composing on the spot. . . . Buddy listened for a few minutes and then began chanting this title—'Oh, Do It Again!,' which he had just fitted to my theme." After Gershwin played the completed song at a party at Jules Glaenzer's, "Irene Bordoni, with a true Gallic flourish, rushed across the room and cried, 'I mus' have that song! It's for me!' Needless to say, Irene got what she wanted."[1]

A perfect vehicle for the French coquette, this sweetly seductive song blended, as one commentator put it, "sentiment and humor" with a main theme that once again evoked Debussy's *Faun* and that exhibited a new rhythmic flexibility on Gershwin's part, including trenchant use of triplet rhythms. Exuding considerable sophistication (one critic thought it "of a truly boulevard order"), the song brought Gershwin and DeSylva into close proximity with Cole Porter, who also wrote for Bordoni.[2]

"Do It Again" brought down the house. "The star's lips, puckered in provocative style, worked havoc with an admiring audience," reported one review (a year later, *Vanity Fair* remembered how "Do It Again" made Bordoni "roll her eyes at the rate of two hundred revolutions per minute"), while the *Mirror* thought the number "alone worth the price of admission." The rare complaint that the song had "something of taw-driness in its fibre" was itself revealing. Alice Delysia similarly scored a hit with the number, slightly retitled as "Please Do It Again," in the 1922 London revue *Mayfair and Montmartre,* and recorded it in 1933. Meanwhile, a 1922 recording by the Paul Whiteman Orchestra took the music to the top of the charts, helping to initiate an auspicious association between the bandleader and Gershwin. The most successful of all Gershwin's collaborations with DeSylva as sole lyricist, "Do It Again" was also one of his first truly characteristic songs, though he more fully realized the tune's potential in his arrangement of the melody in his 1932 *Song-Book.*[3]

"Do It Again" remained a winning vehicle for various chanteuses, including Marilyn Monroe, whose performance of the song in early 1952 for thousands of marines stationed at Camp Pendleton, in Southern California, caused a near riot. "Marilyn left no doubt to what the title pronoun referred," writes one commentator, "delivering a sexual summons complete with little moans of longing and pleasure as she invited someone to 'Come and get it, you won't regret it.'" (Monroe's 1953 release of the song helped secure her the role of Lorelei Lee in the film *Gentlemen Prefer Blondes,* which in turn catapulted her to stardom.) Still later interpreters of the song—such as Judy Garland in her legendary Carnegie Hall concert (1961, with a rewritten verse and revised lyrics) and Marti Webb in her recorded Gershwin tribute (1987), though not Carol Channing in the movie musical *Thoroughly Modern Millie* (1967)—similarly shaped the song into rather explicit psychosexual vignettes, Garland's version intimating an evening of casual sex. DeSylva and Gershwin clearly had more ironic intentions in mind, but the lyric, with its string of "no"s and "oh"s, and the melody, with its sensuous curves, could easily be made to suggest sexual intercourse. The BBC even deemed the number "restricted" in 1950 and permitted a broadcast of the song by Dinah Kaye in 1960 only after a panel determined that her interpretation "would not offend anyone." Some of Gershwin's songs with Ira (such as "Do, Do, Do") similarly could sound lewd if, as Ira wrote, "leeringly inflected in husky tones by anyone sexy."[4]

Like *The French Doll, For Goodness Sake* involved friendly associates: producer Alex Aarons, bookwriter Fred Jackson, lyricist Arthur Jackson, and composers William Daly and Paul Lannin. Yet another Jackson farce, this one concerned a couple, Perry Reynolds (John E. Hazzard) and his wife, Vivian (Marjorie Gateson), who, as usual in such farces, suspect each other of infidelity. Reynolds feigns death by drowning, while Vivian hatches a counterplot that brings all to a happy resolution. The phony Count Spinagio (Charles Judels) and two younger romantic couples—Marjorie Leeds (Helen Ford) and Jefferson Dangerfield (Vinton Freedley), as well as Suzanne Hayden and Teddy Lawrence (Adele and Fred Astaire)—rounded out the cast.

Both Daly and Lannin were primarily conductors and orchestrators, and Aarons may have engaged them on the recommendation of Gershwin, whom Aarons originally hoped would write the whole score. That competing projects prevented this came as a particular disappointment to Fred Astaire (1899–1987). Born Frederick Austerlitz (his father was Austrian), Fred and his sister Adele (1897–1981) left their native Omaha with their mother in 1905 for New York in order to pursue careers as a juvenile dance team in vaudeville. A tunesmith and ragtime pianist himself, the young Fred enjoyed spending time at music publishers, including Remick, where he met Gershwin in the mid-teens. "We struck up a friendship at once," recalled Astaire. "He was amused by my piano playing and often made me play for him. I had a sort of knocked-out slap left hand technique and the beat pleased him. He'd often stop me and say, 'Wait a minute, Freddie, do that one again.'" Gershwin expressed the hope that one day he might write a musical for Fred and Adele.[5]

That show was still a few years away. For the one at hand, George and Ira composed three songs: the lilting "All to Myself" (sung by Suzanne and Teddy), the suave "Someone" (sung by Marjorie and Jefferson), and the charming "Tra-La-La" (sung by Perry, Vivian, and Count Spinagio). The last-named song was dropped before the Broadway opening, but decades later, Ira took advantage of its obscurity by reviving it with new words under the title "Tra-La-La (This Time It's Really Love)" as a duet for the love-smitten Jerry Mulligan (Gene Kelly) and his cynical friend Adam Cook (Oscar Levant) in the MGM musical *An American in Paris* (1951). Although Kelly performed the number—sounding impressively fresh for 1951—with his inimitable bonhomie, one missed the fine integration of the earlier lyric—which concerned singing away one's troubles, not falling in love—with Gershwin's gaily folkish music.[6]

For Goodness Sake, which ran for 103 performances, grabbed the critics as bright and sophisticated, a welcome respite, opined the *Sun,* from yet another Cinderella story: "*For Goodness Sake* has a plot, heart interest, suspense—nay, anguish! Impossible, you say, for a musical show? Not at all. Go to the Lyric and see for yourself." The show proved a particular triumph for the little-known Astaires, who, added the *Sun,* "had the Jersey commuters looking anxiously at their watches, as they stopped the show half a dozen times." Over the next ten years, right up through Adele's engagement to Lord Charles Cavendish and her subsequent retirement from the stage in March 1932, the Astaires would establish themselves as the most successful dance team in the history of the American musical theater, though Adele garnered the lion's share of praise—so much so that critics wondered whether Fred, an unlikely romantic lead, could manage on his own. "Such words as enchanting, delicious, captivating did not seem like tired adjectives from a Hollywood pressbook when applied to her [Adele]," recalled P. G. Wodehouse and Guy Bolton, who thought that her retirement left "a gap that can never be filled," adding, tongue-in-cheek, "Fred struggled on without her for a while, but finally threw his hand in and disappeared. There is a rumor that he turned up in Hollywood. It was the best the poor chap could hope for after losing his brilliant sister."[7]

When Sir Alfred Butt decided to bring *For Goodness Sake* to London in the spring of 1923, Aarons arranged for the Astaires to join the cast, realizing that the show's success depended on them. For this West End production, renamed *Stop Flirting,* Gershwin was represented not only by "All to Myself" (revised as "All by Myself") and "Someone," but by a new opening chorus; by the big hit from the *Scandals of 1922,* "(I'll Build a) Stairway to Paradise" (sung by all six principals, including the Astaires); and by two songs from *La-La-Lucille!*—"The Best of Everything" (for the actors playing Marjorie Leeds and Jefferson, now Geoffrey, Dangerfield) and "It's Great to Be in Love" (for the three female leads). The show opened at the Shaftesbury on May 30 and ran (at various theaters) for a whopping 418 performances, helping to inaugurate a new period in British theatrical life that held Gershwin and the Astaires in the highest esteem.

Meanwhile, singer Georgie Price introduced Gershwin's "Yankee Doodle Blues" (lyrics, Caesar and DeSylva) in the *Spice of 1922,* a revue that lasted eighty-five performances after opening on July 6. The show lived up to its name by pushing the limits of nudity and risqué humor on the so-called legitimate stage—baiting the censors was part of the fun— and "Yankee Doodle Blues" fitted the prevailing mood. The song's three distinct sections comprise a bluesy verse that introduces the theme of the homesick American abroad; a chorus that, in anticipation of Woody Guthrie, declares, "There's no land so grand as my land, / from California to Manhattan isle"; and a final patter that satirizes the poor American's experiences in various European countries: altogether, an affectionate sendup of American pride and know-nothingness.[8]

"Yankee Doodle Blues" became one of Gershwin's relatively few early hits, with more than ten recordings in 1922 alone, including ones by Isham Jones, Vincent Lopez, and Van and Schenck. It also appeared as the signature theme for the dark social satire *Processional* (1924) by John Howard Lawson, who thought the music to express "the crudeness and naïve vulgarity found in the play." The song, which resurfaced in the biopic *Rhapsody in Blue* (1945; sung by Hazel Scott) and in another Hollywood film, *I'll Get By* (1950; sung by June Haver), remained a lifelong favorite with such vaudevillians as George Burns, and in time proved a congenial vehicle for the team of singer Joan Morris and pianist-composer William Bolcom as well. From the standpoint of Gershwin's development, the music holds considerable interest, for its irrepressible verve looks ahead to the *Rhapsody;* its ironic nostalgia, to *An American in Paris;* and its affable mockery, to *Of Thee I Sing.*[9]

About the same time, Gershwin wrote, this time with Ira, another satire, namely, "Mischa, Jascha, Toscha, Sascha," the aforementioned good-natured roast of four prominent Russian-Jewish violinists then living in New York: Mischa Elman, Jascha Heifetz, Toscha Seidel, and Sascha Jacobsen. Ira recalled that he liked the sound of their names and wrote the song with George simply for their own amusement and that of their friends, including the forenamed violinists. "Popular with musicians and instrumentalists at informal musicales," wrote Ira, "this opus surely must have been one of the best-known unpublished and non-commercial hits of the Twenties." Ira ingeniously rhymed "sour" and "Auer" (after the legendary violin teacher Leopold Auer) and "hits" and "Fritz" (in reference to another famous violinist, Fritz Kreisler), and humorously alluded to the Jewish backgrounds of all four violinists in the quatrain, "We're not highbrows, we're not low-brows, / Anyone can see. / You don't have to use a chart / To see we're He-brows from the start." George contributed to the merriment by evoking étude-like figuration and open-fifth tuning, and by parodying that chestnut of the violin recital, *Humoresque*. Published in 1932, the song was first recorded in 1938 in a swing arrangement with the Modernaires and the Paul Whiteman Orchestra.[10]

Gershwin wrote his third *Scandals* score, the *Scandals of 1922*, mostly with DeSylva, who had succeeded Jackson as George White's in-house lyricist, though Ray Goetz and Ira worked with DeSylva on some of the lyrics as well. The show, which had a book by White, W. C. Fields, and Andy Rice, opened on August 28, 1922, and starred, in addition to White and Fields, comedian-dancers Lester Allen and Winnie Lightner; singers Richard Bold, John ("Jack") McGowan, Pearl Regay, and Coletta Ryan; a dance team, the Argentinas; and Paul Whiteman and his Palais Royal Orchestra, who jazzed symphonic works by Schubert and Beethoven before joining in the act 1 finale. George White staged the show, Erté created some of the costumes, Herbert Ward and John Wenger designed the scenery, and Max Steiner directed the orchestra.

In the first act, McGowan sang "Cinderelatives" (lyrics, DeSylva), a satire on the popular Cinderella shows of the early 1920s, complete with a processional of such stage characters as Irene and Sally; Lester Allen clowned his way through the ditty "She Hangs Out in Our Alley" (published as "Oh, What She Hangs Out"; lyrics, DeSylva), supported by the Girls on the Clothes Line; Coletta Ryan sang a lovely "valse lente," "Across the Sea" (lyrics, DeSylva and Goetz), against an elaborate sea tableau; and joined by Richard Bold, she also introduced "I Found a Four Leaf Clover" (lyrics, DeSylva), fairly described by Ira as "an obvious concession to the popular ear" (which helped make it one of the evening's favorites). The act closed with "(I'll Build a) Stairway to Paradise" (lyrics, DeSylva and Ira), a big production number sung by the ensemble against another of White's striking black-and-white sets, with chorus girls dressed in black patent leather ascending a white double staircase amid a forest of glossy black patent-leather palm trees. When the curtain rose for an encore, the girls stripped off their gowns to reveal skimpy lingerie, leaving some of the first-night audience gasping for fear that they were witnessing a mishap onstage. (The first act's third scene, in which Lightner played a flapper and Charles Wilkens, her admirer, may also have featured the Gershwin-DeSylva song "The Flapper," perhaps as a dance routine.)[11]

The second act opened with a short one-act opera, *Blue Monday Blues* (libretto, DeSylva), dropped after opening night. The ensuing musical numbers included "Argentina" (lyrics, DeSylva), a dramatic bolero, sung by McGowan and danced by the Argentinas, who performed a sort of Spanish Apache dance; "I Can't Tell Where They're From When They Dance" (lyrics, DeSylva and Ira), sung and danced by White himself; "Just a Tiny Cup of Tea" (lyrics, DeSylva), sung by Pearl Regay and Richard Bold, and accompanied onstage by various Tea Girls; and the mock-lovelorn "Where Is the Man of My Dreams?" (lyrics, DeSylva), sung and danced by Winnie Lightner and members of the company. Harms published all five Gershwin songs from the first act and "Argentina" and "Where Is the Man of My Dreams?" from the second.

The score overall revealed impressive technical command, and some of the numbers—especially "Where Is the Man of my Dreams?"—showed a deepening musical humor as well. But the daring and brilliance of "(I'll Build a) Stairway to Paradise," rendered with such panache by the Whiteman band that years later Gershwin referred to the performance as "one of those 'thrills' that come once in a lifetime," set this song apart from the others. The song's verse takes aim at "preachers" who censor dancing, arguing that "the steps of gladness" can take one to "Heaven" and "Paradise." The bluesy chorus presents the dancing song itself, its joyous determination reminiscent of such earlier Gershwin songs as "Swanee." David Schiff notes a resemblance between the music and black songwriter Chris Smith's popular "Ballin' the Jack" (1913), but this comparison only highlights Gershwin's skill and originality.[12]

The verse alone is extraordinary, a twenty-four-measure trip around the tonal universe, slipping and sliding through various keys—each a symbolic step upward to paradise—until it finally arrives at the chorus's dominant harmony, a thrilling preparation to the high-stepping chorus, with its dramatic octave leaps and its prominent blue notes. Meanwhile, Gershwin unified verse and chorus not only by the use of dotted rhythms but by stepwise chromatic gestures that point to one of the composer's most notable accomplishments: the use of extended chromaticism for the purposes of ironic humor. And judging by their smash 1922 recording of the song, the Whiteman band further enlivened matters by providing some piquant sounds, climaxing in an animated final chorus that approached New Orleans jazz.

Blue Monday Blues—or *Blue Monday* as Gershwin titled the piece in his short score and as it later became known—represented another kind of landmark: a one-act opera, lasting about twenty minutes, for six black characters and chorus. In 1931 Gershwin recalled that he and DeSylva "discussed for some time the possibilities of writing an opera for colored people" and that White agreed to try out the idea for the

Scandals a mere two or three weeks before the show opened in New Haven on August 21.[13]

White may have been more than acquiescent. He was aware of the sensational success of the all-black musical *Shuffle Along* (1921; music, Eubie Blake; lyrics, Noble Sissle), to the point that he planned his own sequel to the show (and did, in fact, produce in 1923 a notable successor, *Runnin' Wild,* with music by James P. Johnson and lyrics by Cecil Mack). Indeed, the big-voiced cast of *Shuffle Along,* which included Gertrude Saunders (later replaced by Florence Mills), Sissle himself, and no less than Josephine Baker and Paul Robeson in the chorus, may have helped steer Gershwin toward "the possibilities of writing an opera for colored people."[14]

Gershwin further recollected that he and DeSylva wrote the entire "one-act vaudeville opera" in five days. William Vodery, who had helped arrange *Shuffle Along,* orchestrated the work (subtitling it "Opera Ala Afro-American" in his score), and the piece was staged with white principals from the *Scandals* cast performing in dark makeup. (That some of the *Scandals* regulars could perform this music bespeaks the operatic abilities—borne out by recordings—of featured Broadway singers during this period; the high notes of the leading lady, Coletta Ryan, even impressed one reviewer as having the power of such operatic sopranos as Geraldine Farrar and Maria Jeritza.) Gershwin's condensed version and Vodery's orchestral score, both without words, survive to this day, but DeSylva's original text was lost so quickly that when Paul Whiteman decided to revive the work in 1925, DeSylva needed to reconstruct the libretto, writing to Gershwin, "I was unable to remember bits of it and re-wrote it as best I could." This 1925 version accordingly became the basic source for the opera's text.[15]

Blue Monday Blues takes place in a basement bar in the area near 135th Street and Lenox Avenue in Harlem about nine-thirty in the evening. A prologue sung in front of the curtain informs the audience that they are about to see "a colored tragedy enacted in operatic style," one, as in "the white man's opera," whose "theme will be Love, Hate, Passion and Jealousy!" (In the original production, the opera's villain, Walter, sang the prologue, while in the 1925 version De Sylva, who changed Walter's name to Tom, assigned the prologue to the hero, Joe, as have subsequent versions of the work.) As the curtain rises, the owner of the bar, Mike (Arthur Brooks), polishes glasses and orders his employee, Sam (Lester Allen), to sweep up ("Blue Monday Blues"). The saloon's pianist, called Cokey-Lou in reference to his cocaine use (Roger Little), and its gruff entertainer, Walter (John McGowan), arrive. Vi (Coletta Ryan) enters looking for her boyfriend, Joe ("Has One of You Seen Joe?"—also known as "Has Anyone Seen My Joe?"). After repulsing Walter's advances with a gun, she leaves in search of Joe (reprise of "Blue Monday Blues").

Joe (Richard Bold), a gambler, enters with news that he is going to use his craps-game winnings in order to go south and visit his mother, whom he has not seen for a long time ("I'm Goin' South in the Mornin'," followed by "Mother Mine"), but is reluctant to tell the suspicious Vi about his plans. As patrons enter, Vi reaffirms her love for Joe ("I Love but You, My Joe"). Walter knavishly informs Vi that the telegram Joe's expecting is from another woman. When the telegram arrives and Joe refuses to hand it over to Vi, she fatally shoots him in a jealous rage. Reading the telegram, Vi discovers that it's from Joe's sister, who has written to say that their mother has been dead for three years. The dying Joe grants Vi forgiveness (reprise of "Mother Mine").

Described by Wayne Shirley as "freeze-dried *Pagliacci*," *Blue Monday Blues* patently adapted aspects of that popular 1892 opera by Ruggero Leoncavallo, including an opening prologue that announces a tale of love and jealousy; a plot set against the background of vulgar entertainment; and a character who, repulsed by the heroine, extracts a bloody revenge. At the same time, John Andrew Johnson notes how the opera's setting and story look ahead to *Porgy and Bess*. *Blue Monday Blues* thus forms a link between *Pagliacci* and *Porgy*.[16]

Meanwhile, the score remains impressive in its own right; for whatever his debts to Chopin and others, the composer of the *Rhapsody in Blue* and *Porgy and Bess* emerges in this work for the first time, like a bolt from the blue. Apparently all Gershwin needed was an extended venue, because nothing he had ever attempted before, including the *Lullaby* (the source, incidentally, for the main theme for Vi's arioso), offered him this kind of scope. The work provided Gershwin an opportunity to shape song, recitative, pantomime, dance, and melodrama into a compelling whole, one distinguished by a fine sense of dramatic pacing, including a firm handling of counterpoint and modulation. Moreover, its boozy atmosphere—which might be compared to Milhaud's *Creation of the World* and even Berg's *Wozzeck,* both completed the following year (1923)—and various details, like the ominous countermelody for the final return of "Blue Monday Blues," hummed by the chorus (a gesture that echoes Bizet and Puccini), signal the arrival of a born opera composer.

The work's few early performances elicited highly divergent opinions. "Although Mr. White or any of his confreres may not be aware of it," stated one New Haven critic, "they will have done one thing which will, or ought to, go down in history; they have given us the first real American opera." Both the *New York Evening Telegram* and the *New York Evening Post* similarly thought *Blue Monday Blues* "by far" the best thing in the show. Others reacted quite negatively, with Charles Darnston penning a particularly scornful critique for the *New York World*: "Then followed 'Blue Monday Blues,' the most dismal, stupid and incredible blackface sketch that has probably ever been perpetrated. In it a dusky soprano fatally killed her gambling man. She should have shot all her associates the moment they appeared and then turned the pistol on herself." A number of other papers complained that the work "dragged interminably" and suggested that White omit the piece, especially since the revue lasted nearly three and a half hours. Although the received wisdom states that White withdrew the opera after its Broadway opening because, in Gershwin's seminal telling, "the audience was too depressed by the tragic ending to get into the mood of the lighter stuff that followed," the fact that the show was overlong no doubt played a part as well.[17]

Indeed, none of the papers complained about the opera's tragic ending. On the contrary, the work's tone proved altogether elusive. Minstrel shows, vaudeville, and revues had long parodied Italian opera—the aforesaid *Spice of 1922*, which premiered a bit earlier in the season, featured a parody of *Tosca*—and *Blue Monday Blues* clearly partook of this tradition, as one might expect considering its venue. But critics widely found the work's intentions hard to gauge, variously referring to it as a "colored grand opera," a "ragtime opera," a "tragedy of colored folks," a "black-face sketch," and a "blackface scene" (and in 1925, as a "jazz opera," an "operetta," and an "old hokum vaudeville skit"). Gershwin himself alternatively called it a "vaudeville opera," a "nigger opera," and an "opera for colored people," while Whiteman, who advertised the work as a "one-act jazz opera," subtitled it "a glorified mammy song." In one of the longer reviews, the *Evening Telegram* tellingly contrasted the work with typical operatic burlesques: "Instead of the broad, rough misrenderings of grand opera such as James Watts presents, the company is revealed as negro characters in a saloon proceeding gravely through such happenings as we might expect in *Pagliacci* or *Cavalleria Rusticana*." The singers, continued the *Telegram*, intoned their arias "very seriously. . . . It is all done in the excessive manner of the grand opera singers and is a delicious bit of musical fun." That such grave happenings and serious singing could add up to "a delicious bit of musical fun" suggests that at least this unidentified critic discerned some essential irony. But most reviews, whether positive or not, could not agree on how to receive the piece, one paper stating, "it is not successful from any angle—comedy, burlesque, opera or tragedy." This unsure reception presaged *Porgy and Bess* as much as the work itself did.[18]

Paul Whiteman, in any case, liked the piece well enough to feature it in two performances (on December 29, 1925, and January 1, 1926) at Carnegie Hall, here billed on a program titled Second Experiment in Modern Music (the first had occasioned the premiere of the *Rhapsody in Blue*), the score arranged for jazz orchestra by Ferde Grofé, as opposed to Vodery's more classical instrumentation. Al Jolson's first wife, Blossom Seeley (Vi), and Charles Hart (Joe) starred in a cast under James Gleason's direction. On his own initiative, but with the apparent consent of Gershwin and DeSylva, Whiteman retitled the "one-act jazz opera" *135th Street*. As Gershwin was by this time the famous composer of the *Rhapsody* and the venue was the prestigious Carnegie Hall, a number of prominent critics attended with no small interest. Whereas music critic Oscar Thompson dismissed the piece "as a crude and half-amateur parody on the worst features of the lyric drama," literary critic Edmund Wilson found it "impossible to tell whether 135th Street is to be taken as a tragedy or burlesque," noting that the music aimed "at a certain dignity," though he thought the fusion of jazz and opera ultimately "mechanical and unsatisfactory," and that "more musical drama" was to be found in Aaron Copland's "untitled and unannotated *Music for the Theatre* than in the whole of Gershwin's drama."[19]

Music critics Olin Downes, Samuel Chotzinoff, and Henry Osgood responded more appreciatively. Downes did not even attempt to reconcile the music with the drama, in which he found only the stuff of vaudeville accompanied by music that contained "not only some good melodies, but certain genuinely dramatic passages"; he simply considered himself lucky that he got to hear the music rehearsed by the band alone. Chotzinoff, who similarly regarded the drama as crude and naive, wrote, "But consider Mr. Gershwin's genius. He has taken the whole thing as Gospel and set it [to] music of real sincerity and 135th Street is a little tragedy that keeps you on the edge of your seat for the entire 25 minutes of its duration." Chotzinoff especially liked the way Gershwin was able to use jazz elements to "express the negro characters" and "give point to the things they are saying." Osgood, for his part, thought that Gershwin's "effective and distinctly dramatic" score "demonstrated the possibilities of jazz as legitimate operatic material when handled with imagination."[20]

Such sympathy did not keep the work from falling into obscurity, though it reemerged with surprising prominence in the 1945 film version of Gershwin's life, including an extended excerpt longer than that for *Porgy and Bess*. Hollywood biopics traditionally traded in noble failure, and *Blue Monday Blues* could be made to suit that need; the filmmakers dramatized the opera's reception by contrasting the formally attired white audience squirming in their seats with two black ushers in the rear of the theater moved to tears by the work on stage.[21]

This exaggerated depiction of the work's Broadway reception (many viewers clearly liked the piece) proved only one of many distortions. The sequence—though still impressive in its own way—placed the opera in the wrong show (the 1924 *Scandals*); put Paul Whiteman (as opposed to Max Steiner) in the pit; featured stylized sets and costumes (in contrast to the simple realism that made such a striking contrast to George White's Tea Girls and patent-leather fronds); and debased the music through some overripe rescoring and even rewriting. More understandably, the filmmakers excised the word *nigger,* which appears a few times in the original version, including "Mother Mine," in which Joe wonders if he's just a "sentimental nigger."

Such sanitization continued when on March 29, 1953, CBS television broadcast the opera as *135th Street* as part of its *Omnibus* series. Produced by Gershwin's friend William Spier, funded by the Ford Foundation, and prepared by George Bassman, who freely adapted both the music and the text, the cast starred Etta Warren (Vi) and Rawn Spearman (Joe), and featured jazz vocalist Jimmy Rushing (Sam). Adapting a strategy from the 1945 film, Mike, rather than state such commands as "Sweep on, you lazy nigger!" merely echoes Sam's lines, thereby diluting the dramatic tension of the original. Similar concerns ostensibly led *Omnibus* to change the pianist's name from Cokey-Lou to Sweet Pea, which, among other things, obscured the humor of the music seemingly intended to depict a cocaine-snorting pantomime (beginning at rehearsal 14 in the Bassman score).

Later renditions of the work (as either *135th Street* or *Blue Monday*), including recordings conducted by Skitch Henderson, Gregg Smith, Marin Alsop, Erich Kunzel, and Marc Andreae, varied in their music, text, and scoring. Whereas most of these performances relied on Bassman's 1953 edition, Kunzel consulted the original Gershwin and Vodery manuscripts and brought forth a version particularly faithful to the composer's intentions, including reinstatement of an ensemble number near the end that was usually cut.

Whatever its limitations, *Blues Monday Blues* gave, at least to those relatively few who heard it, some indication of Gershwin's ambitions and abilities. Regardless of whether this included concert pianist Beryl Rubinstein (1898–1952), his familiarity with the 1922 *Scandals* generally, along with some unspecified piano pieces by Gershwin that he somehow obtained and some exposure to the composer's "great charm" and "magnetic personality," resulted in the first significant public recognition for the composer. In a September 1922 article titled "Pianist, Playing Role of Columbus, Makes Another American Discovery," Rubinstein astonished a newspaper interviewer by declaring that he had discovered in Gershwin "a real American genius-composer" with "the fire of originality," one whose "style and seriousness" distinguished him from "the popular musical school." Rubinstein further predicted, "I really believe that America will at no distant day honor this young man for his talent and his seriousness and that when we speak of American composers George Gershwin's name will be prominent in the list." In 1939 Rubinstein, who directed the Cleveland Institute of Music from 1924 to his death, modestly stated, regarding this amazing prophecy, "Gershwin's songs then stuck out from the muck of that period so prominently that you couldn't fail to notice them if you were in the least interested in our music."[22]

Gershwin's next show, *Our Nell* (1922), offered—not unlike *Blue Monday Blues*—the novel spectacle of a jazzy melodrama, though set in New England rather than Harlem. Originally conceived by Ray Goetz, the show ultimately was produced by Ed Davidow and Rufus LeMaire, with a book by A. E. Thomas, a veteran playwright, and Brian Hooker, a professor of English literature who would score his greatest success as the librettist for *The Vagabond King* (1925; music, Rudolf Friml). Gershwin and William Daly, working singly and together, wrote the music, and Hooker supplied the lyrics.

In the tradition of Denman Thompson's vastly popular *The Old Homestead* (1886), *Our Nell* takes place in rural New England (in the town of Hensfoot Corners) and involves a farm at risk. As act 1 opens, Grandpa Joshua Holcombe (Frank Mayne) and his daughter Malvina (Mrs. Jimmie Barry), the local postmistress, are found in front of the family farm, awaiting the homecoming of his granddaughter and her niece, Helen Ford, the Nell of the title (Eva Clark), who has just left her job in New York as a secretary in a bucket shop—that is, a fraudulent brokerage house. Malvina's fiancé, Peleg Doolittle (Jimmy Barry), the local constable, is on the lookout for a wanted perpetrator of grand larceny (the two-thousand-dollar reward would allow him to marry Malvina) and kicks up his heels with the boys ("Gol-Durn!"). Mortimer Bayne (John Merkyl), a slick New Yorker on shady business, assumes the mortgage for the Holcombe farm from a local deacon, Calvin Sheldrake (Guy Nichols), after hearing that Helen's grandfather owns the property. He also finds himself intrigued by the local farm girls ("Innocent Ingenue Baby").[23]

Helen arrives home ("Old New England Home"), where she encounters her old sweetheart, Grandpa's farmhand Frank Hart (Thomas Conkey). Chris Deming (Olin Howland) and his girlfriend (and Peleg's niece), Myrtle Angeline Weems (Emma Haig), look forward to the upcoming county fair ("The Cooney County Fair"). Peleg, Malvina, Chris, Angeline, and the deacon ponder modern romantic mores ("Names I Love to Hear," originally "The Custody of the Child"), and Helen tells Frank that they must part ("By and By"). Because she had unwittingly served as an accomplice to Mortimer and because he now holds the mortgage on her grandfather's farm, she regretfully agrees to marry him, feebly resisting his kiss as the curtain falls ("Finale").

Act 2 opens on Helen and Mortimer's wedding night as the town celebrates in the Holcombe barn ("Madrigal" and "We Go to Church on Sunday"). Chris envisions settling down with Angeline ("Walking Home with Angeline"). Clara Rogers (Lora Sonderson), a former chorus girl, finds herself stranded in Hensfoot Corners after her car breaks down and introduces herself to the townsfolk ("Oh, You Lady!"). Peleg and Malvina, discovering that Mortimer is none other than the wanted larcenist, anticipate their married life ("Little Villages"). After swearing undying love with Frank ("Meet Me in Dreamland"), Helen reluctantly marries Mortimer ("Barn Dance"). However, the marriage is quickly annulled when Clara discloses that she and Mortimer are already married, with children at home. Threatening to hand Mortimer over to the authorities, Peleg demands the mortgage and an additional ten thousand dollars. Reunited with Frank, Helen draws the moral, "honesty is the best policy" ("Finale").

The show opened on December 4, 1922, in what the *Times* called the "lofty" Nora Bayes, previously known as Lew Fields' 44th Street Roof Garden, a rather intimate space perched on top of the 44th Street Theatre. W. H. Gilmore and Edgar MacGregor directed, Julian Mitchell staged the ensembles, the Robert Law Studios designed the sets, and the Bayer-Schumacher Company created the costumes. Charles Sieger presided over the orchestra and the small chorus of eleven "rustic maidens" and six "farm boys."

As with *Blue Monday Blues,* audiences had trouble—though not as much—deciphering the tone of *Our Nell.* Clearly the show satirized the speech and manners of New England "rubes" and "hicks," but such humor had long been a feature of the so-called hick melodrama. Moreover, the actors, especially Clark in the role of Nell, played the drama straight. During out-of-town tryouts in Stamford and Hartford, Connecticut, audiences attending the show—then titled *Hayseed, or The Villain Still Pursued Her*—didn't realize they were being kidded until well into the first act. The producers attempted to clarify their intentions going into New York by calling the newly titled show "a musical mellowdrayma" and by having the house manager announce, just before the curtain went up, that the performance was being given for the benefit of the Punxsutawney Firemen's Marching and Chowder Association.[24]

Still, virtually every New York review commented on the elusiveness of the satire, some claiming that the work was initially conceived as a straight melodrama. The *American* wrote of the show's "solemn foolery," its "dry wit," and its "ideally dutiful cast" full of comedians who never smile, all neatly supported by songs like "The Cooney County Fair," which had "as fine a sneer in E major as has been jotted down since Moussorgsky," and "We Go to Church on Sunday," which closed with an "exquisitely naughty 'Amen' right from a Back Bay hymnal." The *Clipper,* describing the work as *The Old Homestead* "on a marathon jazz jag," noted that the cast essayed their roles "with all seriousness, having their tongues in their cheek at the same time," and the *Globe* similarly complimented the cast on maintaining "an excellent air of ingenuousness."[25]

"The result," wrote the *Telegraph,* "is an uproariously funny series of situations, witty lines, clever lyrics and character drawings that satirize the rural melodrama without ever verging into the realms of burlesque." Only rarely did a paper, like the *Sun,* complain that the humor was not broad enough. The *Telegram,* meanwhile, pointed out that the show not only satirized the hick melodrama but had "a sly little laugh at the Broadway musical comedy as developed in 'Irene,' 'Sally,' 'The Gingham Girl' and other specimens of the pseudo-pastoral musical play." However, the unusual combination of melodrama and parody that so delighted the critics failed to engage the public, and the show closed after only forty performances. Gershwin, who had invested in the production, lost $3,800.[26]

Aside from the show's four published songs—"Innocent Ingenue Baby" (Daly and Gershwin), "Old New England Home" (Daly), "By and

By" (Gershwin), and "Walking Home with Angeline" (Gershwin)—and one unpublished one—"Little Villages" (Daly and Gershwin)—all of the music from *Our Nell* seems to have disappeared, making it unlikely that we'll ever get to hear the sneering "Cooney County Fair" or the naughty "We Go to Church on Sunday." But such descriptions help us better understand the humor underlying the sentimentality of Daly's "Old New England Home" and Gershwin's "By and By."

The two songs that audiences and critics liked best, "Innocent Ingenue Baby" and "Walking Home with Angeline," fortunately survive. The delightfully suave "Innocent Ingenue Baby," marked "delicately," reveals Mortimer to be an heir to Don Giovanni, while the sweetly old-fashioned "Walking Home with Angeline," which at once honors and parodies small-town America, befits the more innocent Chris (the latter song, perhaps not coincidentally, shares its title with a 1902 British hit song by John C. Rundback). "Little Villages," largely a patter-recitation of Amerindian-sounding New England towns, is more frankly satirical, somewhat along the lines of the Wodehouse-Kern song "Bungalow in Quogue."

Our Nell confirmed certain traits associated with Gershwin's emerging dramatic work, as already suggested by his musical farces and his vaudeville opera. First, it proved somewhat experimental (the words *novel* and *novelty* appeared frequently in the show's notices) and serious in its dramatic aims. "Even the chorus was subordinated to the book, probably a record for musical comedy," noted the *Times,* though that was what critics had said about *A Dangerous Maid* as well. Relatedly, it subtly mixed sentiment and satire, with jazz and blues inflections often used to make an ironic point. And finally, it neatly limned details of character and place. Here, given the story's rural New England setting, the music engaged a country idiom twenty years before *Oklahoma!* famously pioneered this vein on the Broadway stage. Had the rest of the score, including the "Cooney County Fair" and the "Barn Dance," survived, we would know more about this aspect of the work. Still, the similarities and differences between the slightly daffy "Walking Home with Angeline" and the more quaint "Surrey with the Fringe on Top" remain telling.

Chapter Fifteen

From *The Sunshine Trail*
to *Sweet Little Devil* (1923)

*F*ollowing *Our Nell,* Gershwin ventured again into the realm of satirical Americana when in 1923 he provided music for the western comedy picture *The Sunshine Trail,* produced by Thomas H. Ince, directed by James W. Horne, and starring Douglas MacLean, a leading silent-film comedian reminiscent of the better-remembered Harold Lloyd. The screenplay, written by Bradley King after a William Wallace Cook story, told the picaresque story of a guileless idealist, James Henry MacTavish (MacLean), who leaves the Wild West to return to his home in the East with the intention of scattering "seeds of kindness." Along the way, he assumes responsibility for an abandoned child, Bangs (Muriel Frances Dana), inadvertently abets and then foils a pair of crooks, and, on his arrival home, is at first vilified and then lionized by the local citizenry. "From start to finish," stated *Variety,* "the picture satirizes and burlesques the Pollyanna theme."[1]

Ince might have commissioned Gershwin because of resemblances between the film and *Our Nell.* In any case, the composer, here working with Ira, created a song, "The Sunshine Trail," somewhat like "Walking Home with Angeline," though its principal motive of an octave leap and falling third for the titular phrase emits a more western flavor, one that anticipates the similarly titled "Happy Trails" (1950) composed by the singing cowgirl, Dale Evans. Moreover, the song—which, as Walter Rimler points out, owes a debt to Kern's "They Didn't Believe Me"—has greater pathos than "Walking Home with Angeline" and deserves comparison, in this respect, with Charlie Chaplin's film music. "The Sunshine Trail" was published in conjunction with the film's April 25 opening, the sheet music's cover depicting MacLean holding Dana, while in the distance a stylized sun, with rays like spotlights, rises behind the old homestead.[2]

In early 1923 Gershwin also wrote some numbers, as he had at the very start of his career, for a Sigmund Romberg–Harold Atteridge revue produced by the Shuberts at the Winter Garden, namely, *The Dancing Girl,* which played for 142 performances after opening on January 24, and which starred comedians Lou Holtz and Marie Dressler and famed Spanish dancer Trini, as well as the world's lightweight boxing champion, Benny Leonard, in the unexpected role of a vaudevillian. The *Evening Telegram* described it as "Broadway's latest, biggest, funniest, and girliest offering."[3]

Gershwin probably joined this enterprise through the intervention of Irving Caesar, who cowrote many of show's lyrics with Atteridge. Gershwin and Caesar not only rewrote "No One Else but That Girl of Mine" as "That American Boy of Mine," but together with Atteridge created three new numbers, all long forgotten: "Cuddle Up," "Pango Pango," and "Why Am I Sad?" Sally Fields, a burlesque star making her musical-comedy debut, introduced "That American Boy of Mine" and, attired in a hula costume, "Pango Pango"; Kitty Doner, a popular male impersonator, sang "Cuddle Up" with her siblings, Rose and Teddy Doner; and Irish tenor Tom Burke stopped the show with "Why Am I Sad?"[4]

Meanwhile, Gershwin's music had begun to make its away across the Atlantic. On June 16, 1920, Albert de Courville, the producer of a series of Hippodrome revues in the West End modeled after the *Ziegfeld Follies,* opened a new show, *Jig-Saw!* (described by *The Stage* as "an English salad with American dressing"), that included "Poppyland," "Limehouse Nights," and "Swanee," which the popular Laddie Cliff performed in a "plantation scene." The British public quickly succumbed to "Swanee." "You can't get away from it," reported one London correspondent in January 1921. "Every night, everywhere, 'Swanee' has been played for months and months, with no sign of exhausting its popularity." On March 9, 1922, de Courville's rival, Charles B. Cochran, launched a revue at the New Oxford, *Mayfair and Montmartre,* that similarly featured some Gershwin songs, including "Do It Again," "She's Just a Baby," and "South Sea Isles," the last sung by Nellie Taylor with a chorus, writes a recent commentator, "as hula-like as London could make it." De Courville, in turn, lured a Gershwin described by Isaac Goldberg as "eager for foreign laurels and broadening travel" to write an original revue for the West

End with a relatively generous offer of $1,500 along with round-trip passage from New York to London.[5]

Leaving the States soon after the opening of *The Dancing Girl*, Gershwin arrived in London on February 17, 1923, a mere four days before the new show went into rehearsal, and a little over six weeks before its delayed opening at the Empire Theatre on April 3. "Writing the Scandals in a month," he wrote Ira, "will seem an eternity compared to the time allotted us [him and Clifford Grey] to write what will probably be called 'Silver Linings.'" He at least found encouragement in his reception abroad: by the customs official who recognized him as the composer of "Swanee"; by the reporter who made him "feel like I was Kern or somebody"; and by the polite taxi drivers, so different from New York's cabbies.[6]

For this revue, which came to be titled *The Rainbow*, de Courville paired Gershwin with lyricist Clifford Grey (1887–1941), whose transatlantic career resembled that of P. G. Wodehouse (and who became, incidentally, an Olympic bobsled gold medalist in 1928 and 1932). During his sojourns in New York in the 1920s, Grey worked on Kern's *Sally* (1920) and Youmans's *Hit the Deck!* (1927), for which he and Leo Robin provided the words to "Hallelujah." De Courville, who presumably considered Grey a good mediator between Gershwin and the British public, coauthored the revue's book with Noel Scott and famed thriller novelist Edgar Wallace, who wrote a number of revues for de Courville during these years. "No revue, at any rate no successful revue, bears any resemblance to the revue as it is at first suggested by the enthusiastic author," said Wallace of such undertakings. "A revue is built up step by step and almost line by line as the rehearsals proceed."[7]

Gershwin brought with him some songs for possible use, including "Yankee Doodle Blues." Grey further recycled "Innocent Ingenue Baby" as "Innocent Lonesome Blue Baby" (*ingenue* being a less familiar term in Britain), and totally reconceived "Come to the Moon" as a song for roustabouts, "All over Town." Chappell advertised thirteen songs associated with (though perhaps not all used in) the show—"All over Town," "Any Little Tune," "Eastern Moon" (also known as "Beneath the Eastern Moon"), "Give Me My Mammy," "Good-Night, My Dear," "Innocent Lonesome Blue Baby," "In the Rain," "Moonlight in Versailles," "Oh! Nina," "Strut Lady with Me," "Sunday in London Town," "Sweetheart (I'm So Glad That I Met You)," and "Yankee Doodle Blues"—and apparently published (in rather careless editions compared to those of Harms) all of these but "Any Little Tune" and "Give Me My Mammy."

(The last, though commonly attributed to Gershwin, surely was the same 1921 Walter Donaldson–Buddy DeSylva tune sung by Al Jolson in *Bombo,* while the authorship of "Any Little Tune" and the one unadvertised number listed in the program, "Wake 'Em Up"—though both presumably by Gershwin—remains unsubstantiated as well.) Whether "Give Me My Mammy"—or, for that matter, "All over Town," "Sunday in London Town," or "Yankee Doodle Blues"—even made its way into the show also remains uncertain, but Grace Hayes, described by the *Daily Mail* as "an American comedienne with a fascinating impertinence," had her own set in the second act in which, say, "Yankee Doodle Blues" might have appeared.[8]

The score fulfilled requirements similar to those for contemporary Broadway revues, from music for lavish tableaux of Versailles ("Moonlight in Versailles") and Indochina ("Eastern Moon") to the requisite romantic ballad ("Good-Night, My Dear"), Pollyanna number ("In the Rain"), blues ("Midnight Blues"), comic ditty ("Oh! Nina"), and so forth. Nonetheless, commentators have found this "strangely insipid" score among Gershwin's "most insignificant." Even at the time, the British critics—for whom Gershwin's name still meant little—found the music unexceptional. On balance, the music does seem somewhat bland compared to the composer's scores for the *Scandals,* though it's not clear whether this resulted from haste or, as Isaac Goldberg surmised, a deliberate attempt on Gershwin's part to tone down his work for the West End. The score surely attempted to accommodate British taste (soon after his arrival in London, Gershwin observed that "America is years ahead of England theatrically both in wealth of material and money"), with some songs reminiscent of such local composers as Paul Rubens. This quick adaptation on Gershwin's part would have been thoroughly characteristic; already one day after his arrival in London, he used such expressions as "ol boy," "trot along," and "heaps and heaps" in a letter to Ira.[9]

In any case, the revue contained at least a few numbers—including the vigorous one-step "Strut Lady with Me" and probably its finest song, the delightful "Sweetheart"—comparable to Gershwin's better songs from this period. Among other niceties, the latter contains a string of diminished chords that links the chorus's two halves, and an ending that completes the upward scale that conjoins its verse to the chorus. (George and Ira plainly recognized the music's distinction, for they recast it with new words as "Baby!" for the 1925 show *Tell Me More.*) Both "Strut Lady with Me" and "Sweetheart" also exploit a technique that would characterize Gershwin's jazziest music of the 1920s: the use of short, repeated rhythmic patterns that clash with the principal meter.

The Rainbow featured a transatlantic cast: the British performers included Alec Kellaway, Fred A. Leslie, Elsie Mayfair, Lola Raine, Stephanie Stephens, and, stealing the show, Lawrence Tiller's Sixteen Empire Girls; the Americans included Grace Hayes, Earl Rickard, the Fayre Four Sisters (a group of concertina players for whom Gershwin and Grey wrote "Oh! Nina," about the concertina-playing Nina), and black cast members from the Broadway production of James P. Johnson's musical *Plantation Days,* represented here by a half-hour excerpt from that show. Allan K. Foster staged the dances and Kennedy Russell directed the orchestra and the chorus of thirty-eight women and twelve men.

The first act included "Wake 'Em Up" (sung by Leslie and the chorus), "Sweetheart" (sung by Raine and Kellaway, with the Empire Girls), "Good-Night, My Dear" (sung by Stephens), "Any Little Tune" (sung by Mayfair), and, for the finale, "Moonlight in Versailles" (sung by Hayes, with Ted Grant and Frances Wing dancing a pavane). The second act presented "In the Rain" (sung by Leslie and Stephens, with the Empire Girls), "Innocent Lonesome Blue Baby" (sung by Stephens and Kellaway), "Eastern Moon" (sung by Raine, with Elaine Lettor in what one review called "a curious Oriental dance"), "Midnight Blues" (sung by Raine, with the Empire Girls), "Oh! Nina" (sung by Earl Rickards, the Fayre Four, and the chorus), and, for the finale, "Strut Lady with Me" (sung by Hayes).

Despite the tight time schedule and some backstage quarreling between de Courville and Sir Alfred Butt, managing director of the Empire, *The Rainbow* opened to fairly good reviews and, reported the London *Times,* "an enthusiastic reception." The papers thought the comedy weak and the music loud, but applauded its quick pace and scenic beauty. Playing twice daily, the show ran for 113 performances.[10]

The revue also garnered some notoriety for a "contretemps" that occurred during curtain calls at the premiere. As the actors came out onstage, British comedian Jack Edge stepped forward to complain that although he had been hired as a principal player, he was given little to do. "The curtain was hastily dropped and a hand through the centre opening seized Edge by the neck and yanked him out of sight," reported *Variety.* "The curtain was raised again and the audience had a glimpse of a stage hand carrying out the struggling Edge." Although Edge, contrary to later tellings, never expressed anti-American sentiments per se, his speech apparently implied as much, and when de Courville stepped in front of the curtain to apologize, though cheered in the main, he was also harangued with such complaints as "Why don't you give English artists a chance?" and "Send the niggers back." A cable to the *New York Times* suggested that the whole thing had been staged by people "who had come prepared to raise the color issue."[11]

A fortissimo playing of "God Save the King" brought the ruckus to an end, and Edge was immediately fired from the production; but in the ensuing weeks, management made things difficult for the American cast members: they shortened their acts, cut their salaries, and finally, in early May, told them to leave. However, none of this could slow the progress of American musical theater on the London stage, and when Fred and Adele Astaire brought more Gershwin to the West End later in the season with *Stop Flirting,* the country wholeheartedly capitulated.[12]

While the composer was still in London, *Vanity Fair* published in its April 1923 issue a one-page portrait gallery of the "Kings of Tin Pan Alley" that featured pictures and thumbnail descriptions of Gershwin and nine other composers who each had sold more than a million copies "of his best song," in Gershwin's case, "Swanee" and "Do It Again." This article, titled "Our Popular Song Writers," helped solidify Gershwin's standing alongside Berlin, Romberg, and others.[13]

Returning in May, the increasingly famous Gershwin collaborated on the *1923 Scandals,* primarily with DeSylva, but also with lyricists Ray Goetz and Ballard MacDonald. This latest edition starred comedians Lester Allen, Johnny Dooley, Winnie Lightner, and Tom Patricola; singers Delyle (here, DeLyle) Alda, Beulah Berson, Richard Bold, Helen Hudson, and Olive Vaughn; and as the year's featured jazz band, Charles Dornberger's Orchestra. Producer-director George White cowrote the book with William K. Wells, Herbert Ward served as art director, Cora McGeachy and Erté designed the costumes, and Charles Drury led the orchestra.

As in previous *Scandals,* White used the first-act finale to score his primary satirical point, here taking on Prohibition in a number ("Throw Her in High!") that pitted "reformers" in blue against "liberals" in red, the latter including chorus girls impersonating wine, beer, cocaine, opium, morphine, and other intoxicants. However, the talk of the show proved to be the Folies-Bergère–inspired "living curtain," decorated with six nude chorus girls barely covered by leaves and golden branches, that descended at intermission, leaving audience members wondering whether the girls had spent the entire first act suspended high above the stage. All

Top: George Gershwin, ca. 1908.
(Courtesy of the Ira and Leonore Gershwin Trusts.)

Bottom: Gershwin in Atlantic City, ca. 1916.
(Courtesy of the Ira and Leonore Gershwin Trusts.)

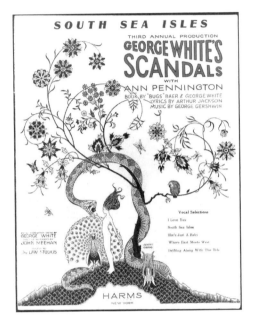

Above left: "Swanee" (1919).
(Courtesy of the Ira and Leonore Gershwin Trusts.)

Above right: "South Sea Isles"
from the *Scandals of 1921.*
(Courtesy of the Ira and Leonore Gershwin Trusts.)

Opposite top: Gershwin, ca. 1920.
(World Wide Photos. Library of Congress, box 103/II-9.)

Opposite bottom: Gershwin, ca. 1924.
(White Studio. Library of Congress, box 103/II-3.)

Top: transition to and opening measures of the "Andantino moderato" from the composer's short score for *Rhapsody in Blue*, 1924 ("J.B" indicates "jazz band").
(Courtesy of the Ira and Leonore Gershwin Trusts.)

Bottom: Paul Whiteman and his Palais Royal Orchestra, ca. 1924.
(Courtesy of the Ira and Leonore Gershwin Trusts.)

Top: In *Primrose* (London, 1924), Toby (Leslie Henson) and the ensemble look on as Pinkie (Heather Thatcher) faints in the arms of Hilary (Percy Heming). (Courtesy of the Ira and Leonore Gershwin Trusts.)

Bottom: Lou Holtz and Florence Auer in *Tell Me More*, 1924. (White Studio. Courtesy of the Ira and Leonore Gershwin Trusts.)

Opposite top: Gershwin with Walter Damrosch,
the composer-conductor who commissioned and
premiered the Concerto in F, 1925.
(Private collection of Brian and Sidney Urquhart.)

Opposite bottom: Queenie Smith
and Allen Kearns in *Tip-Toes*, 1925.
(Courtesy of the Ira and Leonore Gershwin Trusts.)

Above: Tessa Kosta (*center*) and
ensemble in *Song of the Flame*, 1925.
(White Studio. Museum of the City of New York.)

Above: George (*reclining in front*) and friends at Belmar, New Jersey, June 1926. *Left to right, front row:* Marjorie Paley, Morris Strunsky, Elsie Payson, Howard Dietz, Cecelia Hayes, Arthur Caesar, Emily Paley, Phil Charig, Leonore Gershwin, Ira Gershwin, George Backer, Harold Goldman. *Second row:* Cecelia Ager, Mrs. Bela Blau, Mischa Levitzki, Henrietta Malkiel Poynter, Jim Englander, Anita Keen. *Third row:* Milton Ager, Lou Paley, Bela Blau, S. N. Behrman, Mrs. Arthur Caesar, English Strunsky, Harold Keyserling, Barney Paley. Standing at far right: Albert Strunsky.

(deTartas, Bradley Beach. Courtesy of the Ira and Leonore Gershwin Trusts.)

Opposite top (left to right): Leonore Strunsky (later Gershwin), Ira Gershwin, and Emily Paley, ca. 1925.

(Courtesy of the Ira and Leonore Gershwin Trusts.)

Opposite bottom: Alex Aarons and Gershwin, 1926.

(Keystone View Co., New York. Courtesy of the Ira and Leonore Gershwin Trusts.)

Above: Betty Compton, Adele Astaire,
Gertrude McDonald, and Fred Astaire in *Funny Face,* 1927.
(Courtesy of the Ira and Leonore Gershwin Trusts.)

Opposite top: Gershwin *(seated)* with *Rosalie*
stars Jack Donahue and Marilyn Miller, co-composer
Sigmund Romberg, and producer Florenz Ziegfeld, 1927.
(United Press. Courtesy of the Ira and Leonore Gershwin Trusts.)

Opposite bottom: Marilyn Miller as *Rosalie,*
1927; inscribed "To George, Best love, Marilyn."
(Library of Congress, box 107/VI-4.)

Franz Lehár and Gershwin in Vienna, 1928.

Alban Berg. Signed "[To] Mr. George Gershwin in fond
remembrance," May 5, 1928, and inscribed with a
quotation from his *Lyric Suite*.

Above: Gertrude Lawrence and Gershwin, 1928.
(Courtesy of the Ira and Leonore Gershwin Trusts.)

Opposite top (from left): Lou Clayton, Eddie Jackson,
Ruby Keeler, and Jimmy Durante in *Show Girl*, 1929.
(White Studio. Courtesy of the Ira and Leonore Gershwin Trusts.)

Opposite bottom (from left): Richard Rodgers, Justine Jonston,
George Gershwin, and Jules Glaenzer as the Marx Brothers at a
costume party given by the society hostess Elsa Maxwell in 1929.
(Courtesy of the Ira and Leonore Gershwin Trusts.)

Top: Gershwin's penthouse
apartment on Riverside Drive, 1929.
(Courtesy of the Ira and Leonore Gershwin
Trusts.)

Bottom: Portrait of George Gershwin,
bronze bust by Isamu Noguchi, 1929.
(Library of Congress, box 108/19.)

agreed in any case that the curtain helped the *Scandals* live up to its name.[14]

Gershwin wrote an unusually large score for this edition, including songs for a mechanical doll sequence ("Little Scandal Doll"; lyrics, DeSylva, Goetz, and MacDonald; introduced by Vaughn), a jewelry shop scene ("There Is Nothing Too Good for You"; lyrics, DeSylva and Goetz; introduced by Bold and Hudson), a specialty comedy number ("Katinka"; lyrics, DeSylva, Goetz, and MacDonald; introduced by Lester Allen), a hula dance ("Lo-La-Lo"; lyrics, DeSylva; introduced by Bold, Patricola, and Vaughn) and a corresponding travesty ("On the Beach at How've-You-Been"; lyrics, DeSylva; introduced by Hudson), a Versailles tableau ("You and I [in Old Versailles]"; co-composed with Jack Green, the brother of composer Louis Gruenberg; lyrics, DeSylva; introduced by Berson), a living rose dance ("The Life of a Rose"; lyrics, DeSylva; introduced by Bold and dancer Marga Waldron), a comedy number about the love of a canary for a goldfish ("Let's Be Lonesome Together"; lyrics, DeSylva and Goetz; introduced by Bold and Berson), an illusionary mirror dance ("Look in the Looking Glass"; lyrics, DeSylva, Goetz, and MacDonald; introduced by Hudson and the London Palace Girls), the aforementioned anti-Prohibition extravaganza ("Throw Her in High!" lyrics, DeSylva and Goetz; introduced by Allen and Lightner), a number for a Pullman Smoker scene ("Where Is She?" lyrics, DeSylva; introduced by a vocal quartet, the Tip Top Four), and a jazzy second-act finale ("Laugh Your Cares Away"; lyrics, DeSylva, Goetz, and MacDonald; introduced by the entire company accompanied by the Dornberger band). The Tip Top Four and Helen Hudson also performed another Gershwin song ("Garden of Love"; lyrics, DeSylva) after the *Scandals* went on tour.

The show, which also included some music by James F. Hanley and Harry Carroll, opened on June 18, 1923, at the Globe amid controversy, as four days earlier the Shuberts had rushed a *Passing Show* into the Winter Garden that featured some similar scenic ideas, including a living-rose pantomime. White registered his protest not only with the press—his "outrage" made the headlines of the June 21 edition of *Variety*—but in the show itself, which had some comedians speak the couplet "Our whole show was stolen by Lee and Jake [Shubert] / We're the only things that he didn't take." The press agreed in any case that the *Scandals*—which tallied 168 performances, fifty more than the *Passing Show*—was the better of the two revues.

Audiences and critics were especially impressed with the jewelry-shop scene, in which chorus girls represented jewels against a backdrop of black velvet; Julia West opined that this tableau surpassed "in delicate beauty and imagination anything I've ever seen on the stage." In general, the revue won high marks for its visual splendor, as opposed to its comedy, which struck many as inane. "These 'Scandals' for one thousand reasons and another will breed a habit," wrote James Whittaker. "By the end of the first act you have ceased to think of your troubles. By the end of the second you have ceased to think at all." Still, Allen and Patricola came in for widespread acclaim, if not necessarily Lightner, the redheaded Irish American vaudevillian whose "zip-zowie-up-and-at-'em style" would garner unqualified praise only in the wake of the following year's *Scandals,* in which she sang "Somebody Loves Me."[15]

For all its large compass, the Gershwin score elicited little comment. The *Evening Journal* inauspiciously identified the ditty "Lo-La-Lo" as the revue's best number, while *Variety* even more inauspiciously singled out a James Hanley interpolation as the "hit song" of the show. The *Evening World* simply complained that the singers "were loud and usually off the key." None of the show's songs attained any real popularity. Still, commentators have perhaps dismissed the score too hastily. Even if subservient to the show's splendid stage pictures, such numbers as "Let's Be Lonesome Together," "The Life of the Rose," and "There Is Nothing Too Good for You" have an attractive elegance. And although Gershwin's ever-sharpening irony increasingly needed his brother's wit as a proper foil, DeSylva seems to have caught the spirit of "Where Is She?"—a playful lament that might be described as barbershop blues.[16]

Following the *Scandals,* Gershwin wrote a few songs for another two shows, *Little Miss Bluebeard* and the *Nifties of 1923.* Like *The French Doll,* the former was essentially a farce with a few songs for its leading lady, Irene Bordoni—a "song-play" as it was advertised. Adapted by Avery Hopwood from a Hungarian comedy by Gabor Dregely, the story revolved around a French girl, Colette (Bordoni), who pretends to be married as part of a scheme to get bachelor Larry Charters (Bruce McRae) to propose to her. The show opened at the Lyceum on August 28, 1923, to good reviews; Bordoni captivated the critics, English comic Eric Blore won honors in a featured role, and the show ran for 175 performances, though *Theatre Magazine* and others complained (notwithstanding the fact that Bordoni appeared much of the time dressed in either a negligee or pajamas) that the production had curbed the show's "obviously intended naughtiness, in order not to shock the moral sensibilities of its American public."[17]

Plainly hoping to repeat the success of "Do It Again," Gershwin and DeSylva wrote the similarly coquettish "I Won't Say I Will, but I Won't Say I Won't." This time, however, DeSylva collaborated on the lyrics with Ira, whose hand could be felt in a couplet like "Although my glance like ice is—/How I warm up in a crisis!" not only because of its ingenious rhyme but because of its inverted word order ("like ice is" as opposed to "is like ice"). Philip Furia thought that Ira's penchant for word inversion marred some of his finest lyrics, and even the deeply appreciative Ned Rorem carped a little at "And so all else above" from "The Man I Love"; but such constructions—presumably derived in part from classic British poetry, Yiddish syntax, and American slang—arguably project a distinctive whimsy.[18]

In 1923 Bordoni recorded "I Won't Say I Will" (which *Variety* praised as "happily in tune" with her "personality") in her appealingly coy, speechlike manner. Both of Gershwin's Bordoni songs later proved congenial vehicles as well for Sarah Vaughan, who included them in her Gershwin songbook (1957). For added sensuality, Vaughan took both songs at rather slow tempos but hewed closely to the music as written, as she was wont to do in this celebrated anthology.[19]

The *Nifties of 1923,* a revue produced by Charles B. Dillingham, opened on September 25, 1923, at the Fulton. Advertised, contra Ziegfeld, as "Glorifying American Clean Humor," the show managed only forty-seven performances, despite an all-star cast headed by William Collier and Sam Bernard and some significant talent in the wings. "There is no disputing the fact that the humor is clean or that it is American," pronounced *Theatre Magazine,* "but the fact remains that it is not very funny."[20]

Gershwin's songs for the show included the wistful "At Half Past Seven" (lyrics, DeSylva), introduced by Hazel Dawn and Joe Schenck, and the winsome "Nashville Nightingale" (lyrics, Caesar), possibly introduced by Jane Greene. Another song apparently intended for the show, "Dancing Mad," a spirited, bluesy number along the lines of "Stairway to Paradise," never made it to Broadway and for many years was presumed lost, though a manuscript copy turned up in Secaucus.

As many more people would have recognized in 1923 than today, the title "Nashville Nightingale" alluded to the epithet "Swedish nightingale" applied to Jenny Lind, the soprano whose 1850–1851 American tour proved a watershed in the nation's cultural life. Caesar's Nashville nightingale, in contrast, is a black blues singer in Tennessee, a "darktown Tetrazzini," a reference to yet another operatic soprano, Italian

Luisa Tetrazzini. The verse explains, somewhat like "Stairway to Paradise," that the singer from Nashville has usurped the "darktown preachers and the bible teachers," and that "the good church people all desert the steeple / When she starts to serenade." In the chorus, the public pleads that she "sing a little song," including some of her "do-do-di-do-di-do."

Typical of Caesar, the song trades in Dixie imagery, though here entertaining the popular notion of the blues as a surrogate form of religious consolation and the blues singer as a kind of spiritual leader. The lyric moreover reveals a number of nice details, including the incorporation of nonsense scat syllables and plenty of jingly rhymes, such as the play of *nightingale, scale, wail,* and *fail* in the chorus's second phrase. If Caesar falls back on the hackneyed rhymes of *moon, tune,* and *croon* at the song's end, that is part of the joke. Gershwin's music, awash with blue notes from start to finish (the verse begins, melodically, on a flatted seventh and the song concludes with an added flatted seventh in the piano part), matches Caesar's snazzy wit. Nearly every measure features loose, infectious syncopations, neatly offset by that part of the verse which mentions the deserted churches, where the rhythms straighten out and the music moves into minor modes (with some phrygian inflections for added churchliness). This song, their last together, probably represents their finest collaboration, making Caesar's disappointment at losing Gershwin to Ira all the more understandable.

"At Half Past Seven" and "Nashville Nightingale" may have been introduced into *Nifties* after its Broadway premiere; the opening-night program does not list them, nor are they mentioned in any of the first-night reviews. In any event, some of the time's jazzier white artists quickly got wind of the latter. Marion Harris recorded it late in 1923, and the California Ramblers, Joseph C. Smith's Orchestra, and Fred Waring's Pennsylvanians, among others, produced their own recorded versions in 1924. And yet "Nashville Nightingale" slipped just as quickly into obscurity. Some knowledge of it would have helped round out Alec Wilder's discussion of Gershwin's early output. At the same time, Bobby Short's rendition of the song in *Ben Bagley's George Gershwin Revisited* no doubt made it some new friends.

Gershwin finished the year with a show for a young producer, Laurence Schwab (1893–1951), a Harvard graduate whose first Broadway musical, *The Gingham Girl* (1922), had been a smash hit. Max Dreyfus steered Schwab toward Gershwin and bookwriter Frank Mandel (1884–1958) for this new venture. Schwab and Mandel cowrote the book, and Gershwin and DeSylva worked together on the score. Eventually called *Sweet Little Devil*, the show was directed by Edgar MacGregor and choreographed by Sammy Lee (1890–1968), whose remarkable career had been launched, in part, by *The Gingham Girl*. The team of Schwab, Mandel, and MacGregor would become one of the dominant forces in musical comedy of the 1920s, though primarily in conjunction with Youmans and Romberg, not Gershwin. Likewise on his way to succeeding Ned Wayburn as the decade's foremost Broadway choreographer, Lee, in contrast, would work closely with Gershwin in the years ahead, as well as with Schwab and just about everyone else in musical comedy.

Sweet Little Devil proved in large part a vehicle for Constance Binney, who had charmed Broadway audiences in Kern's *Oh, Lady! Lady!!* (1918) before becoming a movie star. The cast also featured the brother-sister vaudeville team of William Wayne and Ruth Warren, who, though originally considered too vulgar for such a high-toned production, succeeded in stopping the show with their dance routines. Lee Simonson designed the sets, and Ivan Rudisill led the chorus of seventeen women and nine men as well as an orchestra of, by one count, twenty-one players. Originally titled *My Dear Lady*, the show played in Boston and Providence as *The Perfect Lady* before opening in New York on January 21, 1924, as *Sweet Little Devil.*

Like *The Gingham Girl* (and *Our Nell*, for that matter), the three-act *Sweet Little Devil* celebrates the triumph of rustic innocence over urban corruption. Virginia Araminta Culpepper (Constance Binney), a young girl from Virginia, has come to New York to live with her cousin, *Follies* chorus girl Joyce West (Marjorie Gateson), in her Riverside Drive rooftop apartment, where Joyce, her friends, and her maid, Rena (Rae Bowdin) proclaim their need for better working conditions ("Strike, Strike, Strike!"). Joyce's financial situation has not profited any from her involvement in various schemes hatched by her press agent, Sam Wilson (Franklyn Ardell). Joyce's wisecracking chum May Rourke (Ruth Warren), who's trying to collect money from the estate of her deceased ex-husband, John Cappadilipo, has money problems of her own.

An aspiring author of romance stories, Virginia finds herself torn between the propriety of her father, a southern college professor, and the daring of her mother, a Parisian dancer formerly of the Folies-Bergère ("Virginia"). When Joyce shows no interest in a fan letter from a handsome but poor engineer working in Peru, Tom Nesbitt (Irving Beebe), who wrote the letter in response to some publicity hype about Joyce being "the perfect lady," Virginia initiates a correspondence with Tom in her stead, leading to a long-distance romance between the two ("Someone Believes in You").

On the verge of wealth thanks to his invention of a new kind of railroad switch, Tom asks his pal, Fred Carrington (William Wayne), to become his business partner. The two men arrive in New York to collect their first payment, a check for forty thousand dollars; because in the past Fred has had trouble with the law, he assumes the identity of the dead John Cappadilipo. While calling on Joyce, Tom spars with Virginia, who confesses her difficulties with men ("System"). Realizing that Tom stands to become rich, Joyce now takes an interest in him. Meanwhile, May demands alimony from her "husband" (Fred, posing as John), and the two find themselves attracted to each other ("The Jijibo"). As Joyce and the others gaily depart for an evening on the town, Virginia, thinking that she has lost her love, remains tearfully alone ("Finale," including a reprise of "Someone Believes in You").

As act 2 opens, Joyce's friends carouse in her apartment ("Quite a Party") and Fred and May declare their affection ("Under a One-Man Top"). Virginia resolves to become more of a flirt ("Flirtation Ballet," including a reprise of "Virginia"). May and Joyce accept the proposals of Fred and Tom, respectively, and all four contemplate the pitfalls of marriage ("The Matrimonial Handicap"). Knowing that Joyce's intentions are essentially mercenary, Virginia, with Rena's assistance, intercepts Tom's check from New York Central and forges a letter stating that the company has decided against adopting his invention, news that leaves Tom and Fred crestfallen. Virginia consoles Tom and the two imagine what it might be like to be in love with each other ("Just Supposing"). Fred shows his determination not to let his troubles get the better of him ("Hey! Hey! Let 'Er Go!"). After Joyce admits to Tom that she was only interested in his money, he angrily carries her off with him back to Peru. Determined to be more her mother's daughter, Virginia leaves for Peru with Sam ("Finale," including a reprise of "Hey! Hey!").

Act 3 opens on a fiesta day in remote Sierra Notre, Peru ("Rosita," published as "Pepita"). Tom tells Fred that he really loves Virginia, not Joyce. Virginia and Tom confess their love; but after Virginia admits her ruse and returns the check to Tom, he leaves, miffed ("The Same Old Story"). Sam, May, and Rena ponder the peculiarities of their own country ("Hooray for the U.S.A.!"). Fred and May reconcile, and Joyce, who decides to marry Sam, reveals to Tom that Virginia, not she, had been his romantic correspondent, leaving Tom and Virginia happily reconciled ("Finale," including a reprise of "Virginia").

Sweet Little Devil garnered excellent notices in Boston and Providence and overwhelmingly good reviews in New York, where it played for 120 performances at the Astor Theatre (soon to become a movie palace). Notwithstanding the story's improbabilities, many critics found the plot compelling in a novel sort of way. One review further thought that the show's "blithe liveliness" lived up to its advertisement as "the gayest of musical comedies," while another praised its raillery as "refreshing in its freedom from conventional boisterousness." However, others thought the show's humor "flat" and "vulgar," if they found any at all.[21]

Binney, upon whose shoulders the show rested, received almost universal acclaim, with phrases like "winsome charm," "puffball personality," and "infinite grace," along with "sylph," "fairy," and "elfin" turning up in nearly every review. "No more convincing or engaging personality now invests our musical comedy stage," declared the *Evening Telegram*. Primarily a dancer by training and early vocation, Binney's dancing appealed more than her singing, which was judged feeble, at times even inaudible. "She has everything a musical comedy prima donna could ask for except a singing voice," the *Sun* wryly noted. "But she is bewitching enough to make you forget her singing voice until she sings the next song." On opening night, Binney, who gladly returned to the movies after this engagement, modestly sent to Gershwin the following message on a calling card: "SWEET is the music you only can write / LITTLE the voice that attempts it to render / DEVIL take that, if the critics tonight / Will take their opinion of you from the sender." But the musical was, in any case, primarily a dance show—Michel Fokine even helped stage the "Flirtation Ballet"—and it was largely on the strength of its dancing that the show succeeded as well as it did. And Binney's singing actually found some admirers. Burns Mantle, in the *Daily News,* for instance, wrote that she sang as well as her "small voice" permitted, while the *Boston Evening Transcript* reported that her renditions of "Virginia" and "Someone Believes in You" were "many times rapturously encored."[22]

Although the reviews widely identified these two songs as the show's best, they did not generally consider the score one of the work's major assets. This was especially so among the New York critics, who tended to describe the music in passing as "agreeable" or "tuneful," or less appreciatively as "acceptable" and "average." The Boston and Providence critics seemed more attuned. One Boston review in particular admired the music of the "invaluable" Gershwin in rather unprecedented ways, pointing out that the composer not only had supplied the dancers with "artful syncopations" and "polite jazz," and the singers with "light and reticent and pleasing" sentiment, but that the show's humor owed much to his ability to be "as quick at a turn of wit as at a turn of dissonance. Not usually in American musical plays of the hour is the composer so pervadingly the life of the party." Another Boston paper wrote, "Like the story, the music is dramatic, with the emphasis always on the humor of cross-purposes," an intriguing observation that pointed to the inherent irony of Gershwin's work. And a Providence paper thought the music the best thing in the show, noting that although the score "cannot be called tuneful in the sense that it is easily absorbed and whistled on the way out . . . every song and dance has its special and striking message in rhythm and syncopation which makes it unusually delightful to listen to." These Boston and Providence critics—a few clearly impressed with Eva Gauthier's recent association with Gershwin—apparently tried harder than their New York colleagues.[23]

The score, which teetered at the brink of Gershwin's mature style, at the least exhibited both refinement and originality. "Virginia" had a particularly unusual main theme comprised of three-note motives separated by rests on the downbeat; Gershwin had explored similar ideas before (as in the bridge from "Nashville Nightingale"), but to structure an entire song—and a theme song, no less—around such a syncopated idea showed real daring. "The Jijibo," the novelty dance number, contained some tricky syncopations as well, but also featured a tolling counterpoint in the tenor range that forewarned similar gestures in the *Rhapsody* and *Primrose.* Marked "slow with sentiment," the stately "Someone Believes in You" embodied an emerging line in Gershwin's work that would continue with the "Andantino" from the *Rhapsody* and take final expression with "Love Walked In." "Under a One-Man Top," an homage to the open road, amusingly evoked an automobile ride, including some beeps—some years before *An American in Paris*—at the words "We'll thank our Lord,/Henry Ford." "Hey! Hey! Let 'Er Go" exemplified the kind of rousing anthem that would come to characterize the twenties at its most roaring, and that would prove one of Gershwin's fortes in particular: an eager determination to banish gloom and care, to "wear a smile" and "be the life of the crowd." For "Pepita," Gershwin and DeSylva recycled the chorus from their 1921 song "Tomalé," but added a different verse that more effectively prepared the refrain, which itself received a new, more folklike setting.

One number dropped during tryouts but reinstated for the post-Broadway tour (and eventually performed as well by Cyril Ritchard and Madge Elliott in London's 1926 *Midnight Follies* at the Hotel Metropole), "You're Mighty Lucky" (also known as "My Little Ducky"), merits special comment. In this comedy song, Sam and Joyce tell each other how "lucky" they are "to get a guy/girl like me" by enumerating their famous paramours in separate refrains—Sam's reflecting his kind of sleazy charm, Joyce's, her chorus-girl allure—that eventually appear simultaneously. The music demonstrated not only the composer's contrapuntal abilities but an understanding—long before *Porgy and Bess*—of the dramatic potential of the duet medium.[24]

As a whole, the score to *Sweet Little Devil* remains especially noteworthy for its rhythmic vitality, in particular, its skillful alternation of syncopated and nonsyncopated ideas both within and between the various eight-measure phrases. Along with some blatant blue notes, this "new quality of joyous rhythm," as Lester Donahue remembered the music, arguably makes the score more recognizably Gershwinesque than the composer's earlier ones. And yet Gershwin's theatrical pieces through 1923 lacked some of the brilliance and verve of those written after the *Rhapsody in Blue*. Although the *Rhapsody* clearly reflected Gershwin's activities on Broadway, that work in turn helped set the stage for his mature musical comedies.[25]

Chapter Sixteen

The *Rhapsody in Blue* (1924)

*A*bout the time that *Sweet Little Devil* went into rehearsal, Gershwin started work on a composition—soon to be known around the world as the *Rhapsody in Blue*—for Paul Whiteman and his Palais Royal Orchestra, a piece that would prove an important milestone in terms of not only the composer's career but American music in general.

Paul Whiteman (1890–1967) grew up in Denver, where his father was superintendent of music in the public schools and where his mother sang in choral societies. For a while, he played viola with the Denver Symphony Orchestra and the San Francisco Symphony Orchestra. After his release from the navy as bandmaster in 1918, he led dance bands in San Francisco and then in Los Angeles, where Ferde Grofé (1892–1972), a violist with the Los Angeles Symphony, joined him as pianist and arranger. After Whiteman and his band, which at this point numbered about nine players, moved to Atlantic City in the spring of 1920, they recorded some highly successful pressings for Victor, including Grofé's arrangement of the John Schonberger tune "Whispering," a release that sold more than a million copies. That fall, Whiteman and his orchestra began playing in a swank New York restaurant, the Palais Royal, which lent its name to the band, by now the most popular in the country.

The Palais Royal Orchestra, which Gershwin heard with some regularity, averaged about twelve musicians, often violin, three reeds, two trumpets, trombone, tuba, banjo, piano, drums, and, by 1924, vocalist. However, a number of band members played a variety of instruments; in addition to the expected doublings—a pianist, for instance, on celesta, or a trumpeter on flügelhorn—a double bass might play tuba or a violinist, accordion, all depending on the abilities of the individual players. And Whiteman clearly prized versatility. A 1922 photo of the Palais Royal Orchestra shows the band's three reed players with easy access to more than fifteen woodwind instruments.[1]

The Palais Royal personnel were not only unusually versatile, but highly accomplished, as Whiteman was able to lure some of his musicians away from prestigious symphony positions in part by offering them upwards of $250 per week, about four times the salary that many orchestras paid. Grofé and other arrangers exploited the band's virtuosity by employing a kaleidoscopic range of unusual colors, as already evidenced by an early hit like "Whispering." Whiteman—a large man whose rotund figure, thinning hair, pencil moustache, and pixieish manner found a screen double in the less elegant Oliver Hardy—led his band with a good deal of rhythmic gusto, but it was the polish and ingenuity of the band's sonorities that particularly impressed many of its admirers, including Maurice Ravel and Duke Ellington.[2]

Whiteman's attention to color led him to experiment with cello, French horn, harp, and other instruments beyond the scope of most dance bands. However, his emphasis on composed arrangements limited opportunities for improvisation, and although some gifted white jazz musicians made their way into his band over the years (including trumpeter Bix Beiderbecke), others in the group had lesser abilities in that area. But although the use of quasi-orchestral scoring distinguished the Whiteman organization from smaller "hot" bands, its timbral effects, rhythmic lilt, and repertoire plainly marked the group as a jazz ensemble. True, many later commentators balked at describing Whiteman as a jazz artist of any sort; but most experts have been reluctant to dismiss this onetime "king of jazz" altogether, such as Gunther Schuller, whose study of early jazz treated the bandleader to an appreciative footnote.[3]

Whiteman set his sights elsewhere in any case, his admiration for improvising jazz musicians notwithstanding. In 1922 he became one of the first jazz bands featured on the stage of a Broadway musical when he stopped that year's *Scandals* performing Gershwin's "(I'll Build a) Stairway to Paradise." And in 1923 he enjoyed a similar success in a West End revue, *Brighter London,* which premiered on March 28, just days before the opening of Gershwin's London revue *The Rainbow.* If audiences would listen to the band on Broadway and the West End, he reasoned, then the concert stage was just a short step away. On hearing Eva Gauthier and Gershwin perform some popular songs at Aeolian Hall on November 1, 1923, and learning about an impending concert by his archrival Vincent Lopez, Whiteman scheduled his own Aeolian Hall concert, advertised as "An Experiment in Modern Music." Held on the afternoon of Lincoln's Birthday, February 12, 1924, this concert occasioned the premiere of Gershwin's *Rhapsody in Blue* for jazz band and piano, with the composer the featured soloist. By this time, Whiteman aspired to turn the American dance band into something like a symphony orchestra, at least in prestige—to make, as Henry Osgood and others put it during these years, "an honest woman out of jazz." ("I never questioned her honesty," Whiteman remarked in 1927. "I simply thought she needed a new dress.")[4]

The enormous success of his Aeolian Hall recital encouraged Whiteman to give more concerts, including seven more Experiments (the last in 1938). He also began performing regularly on radio, and in the late forties and fifties he made some television appearances as well. He expanded his band to twenty-three players for the first Experiment largely by adding violins and French horns; and although he needed to economize during the early years of the Depression, he continued to maintain on average between twenty-five and thirty musicians in the decades following. During these later years he commissioned and performed compositions by, among others, John Alden Carpenter, Ferde Grofé, Leo Sowerby, Roy Harris, Duke Ellington, Aaron Copland, and even Igor Stravinsky; whatever his importance to jazz history, he played a decisive role in the development of "symphonic jazz," a distinctively jazzy type of orchestral music.

Gershwin prepared a two-piano fair copy of the *Rhapsody*, which Grofé subsequently scored, completing the orchestration—aside from some of the solo piano part, which did not need to be notated at this point—on February 4, 1924. Grofé assumed responsibility for the orchestration not only because of time constraints but because the Whiteman Orchestra consisted of, in Gershwin's own words, "a unique combination" of instruments, so much so that even seasoned orchestrators often deferred to Grofé. Gershwin nonetheless provided for Grofé an "orchestral sketch, in which many of the orchestral colors were indicated."[5]

Gershwin's short score bears the date January 7, 1924, which apparently marks the starting date of composition; not only would its placement at the top of the manuscript suggest as much, but as is often told, Gershwin forgot about his promise to write a work for Whiteman until he read about his forthcoming "jazz concerto" in the *New York Herald* on January 4, and it seems inconceivable that even he could compose the *Rhapsody* in four days. In light of Gershwin's statement, "I don't believe that the rhapsody took more than three weeks to write, on and off," commentators accordingly have concluded that he wrote the piece in the three weeks between January 7 and about January 28, shortly before he left for Boston for a concert with Eva Gauthier. Grofé's recollection of daily trips to the Gershwin household throughout January to collect pages to orchestrate bolsters this assumption.[6]

However, Gershwin's seminal account intimates an earlier starting date:

> Suddenly an idea occurred to me. There had been so much chatter about the limitations of jazz. . . . Jazz, they said, had to be in strict time. It had to cling to dance rhythms. I resolved, if possible, to kill that misconception with one sturdy blow. Inspired by this aim, I set to work composing with unwonted rapidity. No set plan was in my mind—no structure to which my music would conform. The rhapsody, as you see, began as a purpose, not a plan.
>
> At this stage of the piece I was summoned to Boston for the première of *Sweet Little Devil.* I had already done some work on the rhapsody. It was on the train, with its steely rhythms, its rattle-ty-bang that is often so stimulating to a composer. . . . And there I suddenly heard—and even saw on paper—the complete construction of the rhapsody, from beginning to end. No new themes came to me, but I worked on the thematic material already in my mind, and tried to conceive the composition as a whole. I heard it as a sort of musical kaleidoscope of America—of our vast melting pot, of our unduplicated national pep, of our blues, our metropolitan madness. By the time I reached Boston I had a definite *plot* of the piece, as distinguished from its actual substance.
>
> As for the middle theme, it came upon me suddenly, as my music sometimes does. It was at the home of a friend, just after I got back to Gotham. . . . Well, there I was, rattling away [at the piano] without a thought of rhapsodies in blue or any other color. All at once I heard myself playing a theme that must have been haunting me inside, seeking outlet. No sooner had it oozed out of my fingers than I knew I had found it. . . . A week after my return from Boston I completed the *Rhapsody in Blue.*

This recollection suggests that Gershwin embarked on the piece before leaving for the December 20 Boston premiere of *Sweet Little Devil;* planned out the work's basic "plot" on the trip to Boston; devised the middle "Andantino" theme soon after returning to New York in, presumably, late December; and completed the work a week later, which would make January 7 a possible completion—not starting—date.[7]

But such a conclusion fails to account for his reported reaction to the January 4 *Herald* article, and jars as well with the reminiscences of Ira, Whiteman, and Grofé. Very possibly, Gershwin worked on the piece throughout December and into January, and then, jolted by the newspaper article, began actually notating the score on January 7. This helps explain Grofé's daily trips to the Gershwin home, because it seems unlikely that Gershwin could have provided the work piecemeal unless he had a clear idea of the composition as a whole; and it accords as well with the nature of the reduced score, which proceeds confidently from page to page without much hesitation. Whether Gershwin's "three weeks" or, depending on the source, "ten days" would apply to the time spent notating as opposed to creating the work is not clear; but in any case, he seems to have composed the work and prepared a piano reduction over the two-month period from December 1923 through January 1924; and if, as is generally believed, Whiteman initially broached the idea in the wake of Gauthier's November 1 recital, Gershwin may have started thinking about the piece even earlier.[8]

Gershwin's account also challenges assertions by Grofé that the composer had written the famous "Andantino" theme five or six years prior; that he thought it "too trite, too sentimental" for the *Rhapsody;* and that he decided to incorporate it only at Ira's and Grofé's urging. The theme's organic relationship with the rest of the work supports Gershwin's differing claim that he created the "Andantino" in the midst of the compositional process, not years earlier; but Grofé and Ira may well have played some significant role in encouraging its inclusion in any case.[9]

Gershwin originally intended to call the piece *American Rhapsody,* but Ira, inspired by the titles of such James McNeill Whistler paintings as *Nocturne in Blue and Silver* and *Symphony in White,* suggested instead *Rhapsody in Blue.* (Ira possibly viewed Whistler's work—as perhaps did George—at an exhibit at the St. Botolph Club that coincided with the Boston tryouts of *Sweet Little Devil.*) The title neatly suggested that "blue" was a sort of key, a brilliant inspiration on Ira's part, for the work can almost be said to have been written in the key of blue. Although the music begins and ends in a sort of B♭ major and traverses a variety of other tonal centers in the course of its sixteen minutes, Gershwin makes such continuous use of blue notes that the terms *major* and *minor* seem inadequate. A comparison might be made with Béla Bartók's employment of Eastern European modes in the creation of his unique style. Because of the work's relatively consonant and lush surface, such tonal daring and originality might easily be missed or minimized; Ira's title plumbs deeper than casual remarks about the music's use of blues and jazz, as if that were merely an ornamental phenomenon.[10]

The work's closeness to the blues may further elude listeners who think of the genre in terms of twelve-bar folk blues; for during these years, the blues had a separate existence as a moderately fast, rhythmically vibrant urban dance music, often in sixteen-measure or thirty-two-measure *aaba* or *abab* song form, though typically sharing with folk blues some telltale stylistic traits. Gershwin himself had written some songs along these lines, and to whatever extent he then appreciated the difference between folk and popular blues, he was apparently thinking more of the latter.

Many of the themes go so far as to evoke popular *aaba* or *abab* song forms, but the hackneyed criticism of the *Rhapsody*—or any of Gershwin's concert works—as a loose collection of catchy tunes has been effectively contravened in recent years by a number of experts. John Warthen Struble even stood the received wisdom on its head, arguing that, like the symphonies of Beethoven, though even more like the rhapsodies of Liszt and Brahms, the *Rhapsody* succeeds not because of its tunes—deemed "rather pedestrian as melody writing goes"—but because of "the way that the composer handles those themes." Discussing in particular the *Rhapsody* and *An American in Paris*, Lawrence Starr similarly pointed out that their themes not only made "rather unsatisfactory pop tunes" but did not even fit the "loosened" definition of a tune as a "clear, balanced, finished" melody. "A search for 'tunes,'" concluded Starr, "leads not to small, isolated, closed structures but to rich, open-ended melodic ideas clearly designed for development over large spans of time."[11]

At two spots in the *Rhapsody*, Gershwin does put forth rounded themes, but these serve special purposes. In the first instance (at rehearsal 9), the melody in question stands out from the work's other melodic materials, in that it has an unusually singsong profile, and it appears this one time only, like a popular ditty embedded within a whirlwind of other materials, a strategy that anticipates Gershwin's quotation of "La Mattchiche" in *An American in Paris*. The second instance of a more self-contained melody occurs at a point (two after rehearsal 39) where the completion of a theme heard many times in the course of the piece satisfies climactic intentions.

The *Rhapsody* evokes, within the tradition of the piano concerto as represented by Liszt, Tchaikovsky, and others, not only the blues but quite generally the sounds of New York: the hurdy-gurdies of the Lower East Side, the calliopes of Coney Island, the player pianos of Harlem, the chugging of trains leaving Grand Central Station, the noisy construction of midtown skyscrapers, and so forth. The broad range of these allusions—exploited in the *Rhapsody in Blue* sequence as found in the film *Fantasia 2000*—goes far in explaining the music's American profile, and, in particular, its mirroring of what Ann Douglas, in her book about New York in the 1920s, calls "Mongrel Manhattan."[12]

Notwithstanding this wide stylistic reach (including some suggestions of Hispanic music in the final "Agitato" section), the work's melodic material reveals an extraordinary unity, one limited not just to the principal themes but to bass lines, middle voices, and even solo passagework. Steven Gilbert published a particularly thorough study of such "motivic interrelatedness," including a "thematic digest" that shows "just how motivically tight the Rhapsody really is." Arthur Maisel similarly marveled that a work that appears so improvisational should contain such "highly refined means of integration," and pointed, for example, to the ways in which the "Andantino" theme functions as a "recomposition" of the opening melody. And David Schiff illuminated the deft manner in which Gershwin has the pianist and the orchestra share materials: "From its first entry, the piano displays a habit of sneaking in mid-phrase and then moving toward its own statement of a theme—an effective dramatic gesture."[13]

In its own way, the work forms a compressed four-movement symphony or sonata, with an interconnected first movement, scherzo, slow movement, and finale. Gershwin apparently took his cue in this regard from such celebrated precedents as Schubert's *Wanderer Fantasy* and Liszt's Piano Sonata in B Minor. Admittedly, the use of the same or highly related materials throughout all four sections obscures the work's schematic design. But the composer's intentions seem fairly evident: each section has its own time signature and tempo indication ("Molto moderato," "Con moto," "Andantino moderato," and "Agitato e misterioso"); each ensuing section is prepared by a fermata or rest as well as by some chromatic sequencing; and each section but one progresses tonally by thirds (from B♭ to G, from G to E, from E to F♯, and from F♯ back to B♭). And although the toccatalike music that opens the "Agitato" might not necessarily seem like the start of a finale, Gershwin actually wrote "Finale" at this point in his reduced score; tellingly, the finale of the Concerto in F begins with a similar idea. The resultant form may not be structurally perfect; one senses at times a sort of inspired groping, and Gershwin's later concert music would show greater command. The scherzo section, which has been subjected to cuts over the years, seems particularly meandering (not that the cuts help—on the contrary). But the subtlety of the work's form serves the complexity of its ideas and the power of its expression.

Grofé scored the piece for an expanded Palais Royal orchestra consisting of, as mentioned, twenty-three musicians (not counting the soloist): three reeds (doubling on numerous instruments), two French horns, two trumpets (doubling on flügelhorn), two trombones (doubling on euphonium and bass trombone), eight violins (one doubling on accordion), two string basses (one doubling on tuba), banjo, percussion, celesta, and accompanying piano. Since Grofé completed the orchestration on February 4, that would have allowed about a week for rehearsal.[14]

A comparison of the original reduced score (which includes some crossed-out passages) and the full score for jazz band reveals that Grofé scrupulously honored Gershwin's intentions, impressively so, considering the speed at which everyone was working. Granted, Grofé took some liberties with dynamics and accent markings (for example, Gershwin wanted the opening clarinet melody accompanied by very quiet harmonies: triple pianissimo, not pianissimo, let alone mezzo forte, as found in still later versions), nor did he bother with Gershwin's fingerings; but he stayed extremely close to the notes and rhythms, and heeded orchestral suggestions as well, including Gershwin's marked indications for cymbal crashes (though at least one of these—the crash on the beat just prior to the "Con moto" at rehearsal 14—was subsequently deleted). The reduced score, incidentally, casts doubt on the story that Gershwin rewrote the four-bar transition to the "Andantino" in response to suggestions made by Victor Herbert during a rehearsal of the work, as the alleged changes can be found in this original manuscript. Some evidence suggests that Herbert might simply have advised Gershwin to lengthen the rolled chord just prior to the "Andantino."[15]

With a didactic impulse perhaps inherited from his father, Whiteman conceived of the February 12 concert as a lesson in jazz and its varied uses and even hired a narrator, W. C. E. Ernst, to introduce each work. The program opened with a re-creation of the Original Dixieland Jazz Band's famous recording of Nick LaRocca's "Livery Stable Blues" (1917) in an attempt to burlesque jazz's crude early days (though the point was lost on the audience, who simply thought this a rollicking good way to start the program). The first half continued with stylish arrangements of popular songs, a set in which pianist Zez Confrey played some of his own music, a potpourri of Russian melodies, and "semi-symphonic" treatments of songs by Irving Berlin. The second half included classical and semiclassical favorites, including MacDowell's "To a Wild Rose" and Friml's "Chansonette" (later known as "Donkey Serenade"), along with two commissioned works: Victor Herbert's *Suite of Serenades*, in four short movements, which the composer himself had scored for the Whiteman band; and the Gershwin *Rhapsody*. The concert concluded with the most famous of Elgar's *Pomp and Circumstance* marches, as if conferring on jazz itself, finally graduated, a diploma.

Whiteman realized he had something special with the *Rhapsody*, and set his good publicity instincts in motion. Among other things, he invited some esteemed New York critics, including John Tasker Howard, Leonard Liebling, Henry Osgood, Pitts Sanborn, Gilbert Seldes, and Carl Van Vechten, to attend a February 5 run-through of the work at the Palais Royal. Gershwin was still so unknown in the classical-music world that his name meant nothing to either Liebling or Sanborn; but after hearing the piece through twice, Liebling allowed Whiteman to send box seats to some of "the big guns in the highbrow musical racket" and to say that he, Liebling, suggested as much. This ploy—and no doubt others— worked. The attendees at that February 12 concert, which started at three on a snowy afternoon, included composers Ernest Bloch, Serge Rakhmaninov, and John Philip Sousa; conductors Walter Damrosch, Willem Mengelberg, Josef Stransky, and Leopold Stokowski; violinists Mischa Elman, Jascha Heifetz, and Fritz Kreisler; singers Amelita Galli-Curci, Mary Garden, Alma Gluck, and John McCormack; pianist Leopold Godowsky; and actress Gertrude Lawrence.[16]

Most people presumably came to the concert to hear Whiteman, not Gershwin, but come they did in any case. Aeolian Hall was packed to the rafters on the day of the concert; hundreds had to be sent away. The Whiteman publicity machine obviously had done its work; but the time was right, too, for the interest in finding some common space for concert music and jazz was intense in early 1924. "It was a strange audience out in front," Whiteman recalled. "Vaudevillians, concert managers come to have a look at the novelty, Tin Pan Alleyites, composers, symphony and opera stars, flappers, cake-eaters, all mixed up higgledy-piggledy." Issuing complimentary tickets and publishing a fancy program had its downside— Whiteman lost seven thousand dollars on the day—but he could absorb the loss, and in the long run the concert proved a shrewd investment.[17]

One popular myth surrounding this concert states that the audience grew bored and restive until, near the breaking point, the *Rhapsody* brought down the house. Although many palpably thrilled to the opening measures of the *Rhapsody*, as clarinetist Ross Gorman, with the composer's blessing, transformed the work's original ascending scale into a stupefying glissando, the crowd had been enjoying the concert all along. Whiteman's recollection—"The audience listened attentively to everything and applauded whole-heartedly from the first moment"—is confirmed by the critics, who reported enthusiastic applause after every number. The *Tribune* referred to the concert as "an uproarious success," while *Theatre Magazine* described the afternoon as "the most stimulating event of the musical season," adding, "Mr. Whiteman's jazz concert was often vulgar, but it was never dull."[18]

Listeners especially welcomed the concert as a refreshing change of pace from, in the words of the *Post,* "the tame and pallid aspect which Aeolian Hall, that temple of classical music, usually bears." As the Whiteman band growled, squawked, wa-waed, and whinnied amid oriental screens and colored lights, the critics reveled in the sheer audacity of the event. The reviewer for the *Sun* "ached" to dance "up and down the aisles." For his part, Olin Downes, writing in the *Times,* admired in particular the band's spontaneity onstage, so unlike "an army going through ordered manoeuvres," so much more like the "abandon" of "the American negro," an abandon that reminded him of a maxim he had once heard: "an Englishman entered a place as if he were its master, whereas an American entered as if he didn't care who in blazes the master might be."[19]

Although the audience responded warmly to Herbert's masterful *Suite* (his final work), the *Rhapsody* did prove the big hit of the afternoon. The sold-out house greeted it with "tumultuous applause" and demanded three curtain calls, the *Times* observing "many a hardened concertgoer excited with the sensation of a new talent finding its voice," one "likely to say something personally and racially important to the world." The work made a deep impression on the band members themselves, as Whiteman saxophonist Donald Clark recalled: "When we swung into the E-major ["Andantino"] theme, I could see some tears mingled with the sweat on almost every musician's face—the emotional impact was that great." As for the critics, they were largely appreciative, some enthusiastically so. In her review for the *Nation,* for example, Henrietta Straus spoke of "the spectacle of an American boy playing with extraordinary ease an original composition of terrific rhythmical difficulty and of individual power and beauty, and winning immediate recognition for his achievement."[20]

The critical consensus, as represented not only by Straus and Downes, but by Henry Finck *(Evening Post),* Gilbert Gabriel *(Sun),* W. J. Henderson *(Herald),* Deems Taylor *(World),* and Grenville Vernon *(Theatre Magazine),* as well as *Variety* and *Billboard,* further deemed the work lively, melodic, colorful, and full of originality and promise, if somewhat precarious in form. Some even declared it a model for contemporary American music. Even those who took a more critical stance, such as Lawrence Gilman and Pitts Sanborn, found things to admire. At the least these early critics, realizing that the piece's relation to popular music was oblique, did not allow such considerations to prevent a direct communication with the work.[21]

Encouraged by such a cordial reception, Whiteman embarked on a busy concert schedule, performing the piece to highly appreciative audiences in 1924 and 1925—variously with Gershwin, Milton Rettenberg, and Harry Perrella—in dozens of American and Canadian cities from Boston and Ottawa to Waco and Phoenix, often in theaters and halls filled to capacity. Gershwin's 1924 engagements with Whiteman included those at Aeolian Hall on March 7 (at which the fifteen-year-old Elliott Carter reportedly first heard the work); at Philadelphia's Academy of Music on April 13 and November 27; at Carnegie Hall on April 21 and November 14; and at Boston's Symphony Hall on December 4. Gershwin and Whiteman also recorded the *Rhapsody* on Victor's high-toned Blue label in June 1924, obviously a historically important recording, even if hacked up to fit onto two sides of a twelve-inch 78 rpm waxing.[22]

However, by 1926 Gershwin had become dissatisfied with Whiteman's conducting of the score. After attending a performance of the piece while in London that spring, he complained to Robert Schirmer that Whiteman had "murdered" the work "by playing it in a lot of crazy tempi that were nothing at all like the original performances." Adele Astaire confirmed his concerns, writing from London, "Paul Whiteman's band is an awful disappointment. No one likes it here, at all. And what a rendition of your glorious 'Rhapsody in Blue'! It's a crime to allow him to do it! I've never heard anything so 'lousy'. . . . I wouldn't let him ruin anymore of your work if I were you, babe." When Gershwin arrived at Liederkranz Hall to record the piece with the Whiteman band a second time on April 21, 1927, Whiteman at the last minute handed the baton over to Victor music chief Nathaniel Shilkret after he and Gershwin failed to come to an agreement about tempos, a problem exacerbated by the positioning of the piano vis-à-vis the conductor and the orchestra. This less-raucous 1927 electrical recording for a slightly expanded group took the same unfortunate cuts as the 1924 acoustic recording, but both releases, whatever their limitations, enjoyed the kind of success usually reserved only for the most popular songs—the former sold more than a million copies—and incalculably abetted the music's dissemination and fame.[23]

In the course of the 1920s, as the *Rhapsody* embarked on its remarkable career as perhaps the best-known concert work of the twentieth century, cheered on by the likes of writer Gilbert Seldes and composer Charles Martin Loeffler, it also met resistance from some critics. In 1928 Edward Robinson, for example, opined, "In the entire *Rhapsody* there is no tonal sense, no balance and arrangement of idea and phrase, no development worth calling such, no coordination of structure, no harmonic or contrapuntal solidity, no subtlety of emotion and thought, if there is any at all." And in 1929 Paul Rosenfeld stated, "The *Rhapsody in Blue* is circus-music, pre-eminent in the sphere of tinsel and fustian. In daylight, nonetheless, it stands vaporous with its second-hand ideas and ecstasies; its old-fashioned lisztian ornament and brutal, calculated effects, not so much music, as jazz dolled up." But most commentators regarded the *Rhapsody* as at least a benchmark achievement.[24]

The music also fired the imagination of some leading literary figures, including F. Scott Fitzgerald (1896–1940), who alluded to the work in his celebrated novel *The Great Gatsby* (1925), and even more explicitly in an earlier draft, titled *Trimalchio* (1924). In that draft's third chapter, at a party at which Nick Carraway first meets his neighbor and host, Jay Gatsby, the latter requests that the hired jazz orchestra play a piece called the *Jazz History of the World* by one Vladimir Epstein (in the published version, Vladimir Tostoff). The names are fictional and the story takes place in 1922, not 1924, but much else points to the *Rhapsody*, including the composer's Russian-Jewish name, the "gigantic orchestra leader," the performance of the piece "at Carnegie Hall last May," and the "fifteen minutes" playing time. In *Gatsby*, Nick's observation of his host distracts him from the music, but in *Trimalchio*, he describes the work as follows:

> It started out with a weird, spinning sound, mostly from the cornets. Then there would be a series of interruptive notes which colored everything that came after them until before you knew it they became the theme and new discords were opposed outside. But just as you'd get used to the new discord one of the old themes would drop back in, this time as a discord, until you'd get a weird sense that it was a preposterous cycle after all. Long after the piece was over it went on and on in my head—whenever I think of that summer I can hear it yet.
>
> It left me restless. . . . When the 'Jazz History of the World' was over girls were putting their heads on men's shoulders in a puppyish, convivial way, girls were swooning backward playfully into men's arms, even into groups knowing that someone would arrest their falls—but no one swooned backward on Gatsby.

What the music might mean to Gatsby can only be surmised, but something surely related to the pain and rapture of his dreams. In any case, the work's symbolic presence here intimates some profound affinities between Fitzgerald and Gershwin analogous to those between Hemingway and Copland.[25]

Another esteemed writer, William Saroyan (1908–1981), who thought the piece "one of the most purely American musical achievements of all time," penned a short rhapsody of his own (1963) that, echoing Gershwin's own remarks, placed the work in the context not only of New York but of all America:

> The *Rhapsody in Blue* is an American in New York City; at the same time it is an American in any city of the United States. It is also an American in a small town, on a farm, at work in a factory, in a mine or a mill, a forest or a field, working on the railroad or on the building of a highway. It is an American remembering and making plans for the future: dreaming. It is earnest, not sophisticated. There is great loneliness and love in it. Those who were young when they first heard the *Rhapsody in Blue* are still deeply moved by it, and those who are now young believe the *Rhapsody* speaks both to and for them as no other music in the world does.

Like Fitzgerald and no doubt countless others, Saroyan heard in the *Rhapsody* something akin to the American dream.[26]

In 1925 Russian-born pianist Dimitri Tiomkin (1894–1979) persuaded his new bride, Austrian-born choreographer Albertina Rasch (1891–1967), to stage the piece as a ballet at the New York Hippodrome, with himself at the piano. Tiomkin, who thought the *Rhapsody* "the masterpiece of American popular music," had studied with Alexander Glazounov and Ferruccio Busoni before coming to America in 1924 in order to accompany Rasch on the vaudeville circuit (Rasch, who had worked with Émile Jaques-Dalcroze and Mary Wigman, had been active in opera and vaudeville in America since the 1910s). For her *Rhapsody* ballet, Rasch fused classical and popular steps in groundbreaking ways that anticipated her ensuing work on Broadway and in Hollywood, as well as efforts by George Balanchine and Agnes de Mille that superseded her own. Gershwin attended a rehearsal of the ballet, but disappointed Tiomkin by taking less interest in his interpretation of the music than in playing a few passages at the piano himself and in getting his photograph taken with some of the dancers. Only later did Tiomkin come to appreciate the charm and graciousness underlying Gershwin's "supreme self-confidence."[27]

Gershwin gave the first British performance of the *Rhapsody* in Lon-

don with the Savoy Orpheans' Orchestra under the direction of Debroy
Somers on a June 15, 1925, broadcast by BBC radio from the Savoy Hotel. The Orpheans subsequently launched the British concert premiere
of the work at Queen's Hall on October 28, 1925, with the prominent
English pianist-composer Billy Mayerl, and programmed the piece a few
weeks later on December 9 with another popular pianist, Billy Thorburn.
Paul Whiteman's successful 1926 European tour, in which he played the
Rhapsody across England and Scotland as well as in Vienna, Berlin, Amsterdam, and Paris, helped further the music's global sweep. The same
year, a British revue, *The Midnight Follies* at the Hotel Metropole, presented the work as, in Robert Schirmer's words, "a splendid ballet—a
Greek classic idea—nymphs and satyrs, Pan etc., all the costumes and
lighting in bright blue." Other notable European performances included
a somewhat makeshift but well-received rendition in Paris at the Mo-
gador Theater on March 31, 1928, by duo-pianists Jean Wiéner and Clé-
ment Doucet with the Pasdeloup Orchestra under Rhené-Baton. The Pasdeloup repeated the work at the Champs-Elysées Theater a few weeks
later, on April 16, in conjunction with yet another ballet, *La Rapsodie
en Bleu,* choreographed by British-born dancer Anton Dolin for the Nemchinova Dolin Ballet Company. "I didn't quite grasp the story," confessed
Ira, who attended the ballet with George, "but it was a sort of tussle between classical music, as toe-danced by Vera Nemchinova, and Jazz, as
portrayed by Dolin. Who won I don't know—but I imagine Jazz."[28]

The European and especially the French press greeted the *Rhapsody*
with open arms. Even the august English critic Ernest Newman, whose
denunciations of "jazz" stirred controversy across America, described
the *Rhapsody* as "a creditable first attempt to do something bigger than
jazz," and its composer as "a gifted young man with an enviable facility in producing catchy, piquant, pungent tunes." King Carol II of Romania evidenced the work's international success by publicly praising it
in 1931 as "particularly good, not only musically, but because Gershwin seems to have captured something typically American."[29]

Hugo Leichtentritt also recalled "the enthusiasm awakened" by Gershwin and the *Rhapsody* in Berlin following its 1926 premiere there, so
much so that during the Hitler years the Nazis had difficulty suppress-
ing it. As late as 1937 the music could be heard with some regularity at
the Scala, a large music hall in Berlin, and even during the war, Luft-
waffe fighters petitioned—in vain—that a government-sponsored radio
dance band broadcast the work. (This repressed German fondness for
Gershwin informed both Joshua Sobol's 1984 play *Ghetto* and Hershey

Felder's 1998 one-man show *Sing! A Musical Journey*, the latter based in part on the experiences of a Jewish inmate at Auschwitz, Helmuth Spryczer, who survived the camp by whistling themes from the *Rhapsody* for his captors, and for whom the piece prophetically captured "the sounds of dying people and trains.") After the war, the piece maintained its appeal in Germany, not least to composer Heinz Werner Zimmermann, who thought its "predominantly rhythmical approach" to offer something felt missing "in the German music of Reger, Richard Strauss, and Hindemith," and who recalled, "For the first time in my life, I found myself thinking about a new music characterized by rhythmic innovation."[30]

Back home, Whiteman continued to play the work both with and without Gershwin, including an abridged performance featuring pianist Roy Bargy in a Universal film revue, *King of Jazz* (1930), that showcased the Whiteman Orchestra. Produced by Carl Laemmle and directed by John Murray Anderson (of *Greenwich Village Follies* fame), this Technicolor picture, one of the most expensive of its time, cost more than $1.5 million, including fifty thousand dollars paid out to Gershwin and Harms simply for the use of the *Rhapsody*. (The rest of the score, composed mostly by Milton Ager and Jack Yellen, was largely workaday, though performed by a talented cast, including Bing Crosby in his film debut.) Originally planned as a ballet, the *Rhapsody* segment alternated shots of the Whiteman band perched upon a gargantuan piano, attended by men seated at the instrument's gigantic keyboard going through the motions, with that of Bargy at his own normal-size piano surrounded by elegant showgirls (the sequence innovatively created the illusion of blue, a color not yet obtainable by the Technicolor process, by mixing greens and reds against a gray background).[31]

The film premiered on April 20, 1930, at the Criterion Theatre in Los Angeles, and opened in New York on May 2 at the Roxy Theater, a fairly new motion-picture palace situated at 50th Street and Seventh Avenue that seated more than six thousand. For the first week of the run, Whiteman and Gershwin performed the *Rhapsody*—in a shortened arrangement by the composer for the combined forces of the Whiteman Orchestra, the Roxy Orchestra, and the Roxy Chorus—as part of an accompanying stage show that played five times daily between showings of the film. "You can hear a pin drop in the Roxy when George Gershwin comes upon the stage," reported the *Evening World*, who thought the film "one of the snappiest Broadway movie bills in weeks and weeks." That such music critics as W. J. Henderson and Leonard Liebling reviewed the stage show—which they both very much liked—testified to its perceived significance.[32]

In the course of the film's opening week, Gershwin performed the *Rhapsody* more than thirty times. "I got a lame back, sore fingers & tired arms doing it," he wrote to Rosamond Walling, "but it was great fun. In fact they [Roxy management] asked me to stay another week & I accepted. It's the piano concerto [in F] this week. When I got paid for my first week I proudly showed my check around as I felt it was the first money I ever really earned." In an article for the *Sun,* published a few days earlier, Gershwin admitted that the *Rhapsody* could "mean almost anything to anybody," adding,

> But it is all New York, all America. It is a picnic party in Brooklyn or a dark-skinned girl singing and shouting her blues in a Harlem cabaret. I try to depict a scene, a New York crowd. And it's vulgar. It's full of vulgarisms. That's what gives it weight. I never tried to prettify it as most composers do. . . .
> I feel the answer, the recognition, coming from the audience as the music goes. Gee! but it's hard to play, just the same. I don't set myself up as a pianist, although I'll bet I can play that piece better than anybody you can name. But what I have to do! I have to practice ten minutes before I go on. That's to get my fingers limber. And it's so hard. It's a most difficult thing to play. When I begin I keep asking myself: "Shall I ever get through without a mistake?" I am nervous, too.[33]

Unfortunately, *King of Jazz* arrived at a time of declining interest in film musicals and did poorly at the box office, losing hundreds of thousands of dollars (though bookings of the film abroad, along with a 1933 reissue at home, allowed Universal eventually to recoup its investment). Gershwin remained at the Roxy for a second week, but the theater discharged the Whiteman band after a week and shortened the film's run from three weeks to two. In 1936 a fragment of the *Rhapsody* appeared in another opulent Hollywood extravaganza, *The Great Ziegfeld* (directed by Robert Z. Leonard), while an abridged performance of the work (with conductor Ray Heindorf and pianist Oscar Levant dubbing for Paul Whiteman and Robert Alda, respectively) furnished a dramatic high point to the Warner Brothers 1945 biopic. But the music garnered even greater worldwide attention decades later when Los Angeles surpassed such apotheosized treatments of the *Rhapsody* by having eighty-four pianists perform the piece on the occasion of the 1984 summer Olympics.[34]

In 1925 Harms published a two-piano reduction of the work that differed somewhat from the original score, including a few small deletions, mostly within the solo part. Gershwin seems to have initiated these revisions or at least sanctioned them, and on balance they helped tighten the work, though some interesting things went by the wayside, including some double-note writing for piano and a passage that helped link the "Andantino" and "Agitato" sections. This two-piano version became the basis for the *Rhapsody* as it became known. Taking advantage of the capabilities of piano-roll technology, Gershwin recorded this two-piano version in 1925 (released in two parts, 1925 and 1927), a spirited performance that constitutes the composer's most complete and in some ways most authoritative rendering of the work. In 1927 he also electrically recorded just the "Andantino"—referred to as the "Andante"—with, by necessity, a fabricated ending.

In 1926 Grofé prepared a version of the work for solo piano and chamber orchestra for more general concert, theater, and radio purposes. He duly added violas and cellos, expanded the reed section from three to eight players (flute, oboe, two clarinets, bassoon, two alto saxophones, and tenor saxophone), made do with one less trombone, and eliminated the tuba and celesta parts. However, as the work became popular with symphony orchestras, Warner Brothers, which had acquired the property, issued yet another Grofé orchestration, this one edited by Frank Campbell-Watson for publication in 1942, and scored for a still larger ensemble of two flutes, two oboes, two clarinets, bass clarinet, two bassoons, three horns, three trumpets, three trombones, tuba, timpani, percussion, and strings, with the "almost optional" addition of three saxophones and banjo. This version quickly eclipsed Grofé's earlier two and remains by far the most familiar of the three. (An earlier version for symphony orchestra allegedly prepared during Gershwin's lifetime featured an instrumentation similar to the 1942 score, but with the addition of English horn.)[35]

A modified and abridged version for solo piano by Herman Wasserman (1924) became extremely popular as well, not only with amateurs but with such virtuosi as Vladimir Horowitz, who thought Gershwin "the greatest American composer," and who in 1930 reported his enjoyment of the *Rhapsody* at home. In later years, André Watts (1976), Marco Fumo (1994), and Sara Davis Buechner (2005) released recordings of the work for solo piano, as did Eric Himy (2004) in a version that featured the uncut original short score. Meanwhile, such two-piano teams as José and Amparo Iturbi, Frances Veri and Michael Jamanis, and Katia and Marielle Labèque also recorded the piece.

Numerous other renditions were undertaken, including yet another Grofé transcription, this one for concert band without solo piano (1938). In 1928 the outstanding Mexican composer Silvestre Revueltas prepared his own version of the work for a motion-picture pit band in Mobile, Alabama (in a letter to his colleague Carlos Chávez, Revueltas, who dismissed his arrangement as "virtually worthless," reported that the music was received as "something extremely modern with very strange harmonies"). Producer Lew Leslie featured choral treatments of the work—perhaps the same—in two of his all-black revues from the 1930s: *Rhapsody in Black* (1931), where it was performed by various soloists along with Cecil Mack's Choir; and the ill-fated *Blackbirds of 1939,* where J. Rosamond Johnson's Choir had the honors.[36]

Other versions included one broadcast over the radio by accordionist Cornell Smelser and the Ohman-Arden Orchestra (1931), and those recorded commercially by Borah Minnevitch and His Harmonica Rascals (1933) and Liberace and the Warner Brothers Symphony Orchestra (1965). In 1970 Gershon Kingsley (born Ksinski, 1923), released a particularly intriguing arrangement for electronic keyboard synthesizer (played by himself) and piano (played by Leonid Hambro) on an album alternatively called *Gershwin: Alive & Well & Underground* and *Switched-On Gershwin.* Kingsley's concept of the work as a piece of cosmic honky-tonk was of its time, but his kaleidoscopic soundscape fulfilled Whiteman's vision in unique ways.[37]

Jazz bands and pianists—including musicians as diverse as Leroy Smith (1928), Glenn Miller (1942), Duke Ellington (1960), Earl Hines (1973), and Marcus Roberts (1996)—also took up at least a tune or two from the piece in some fashion or other. Countless other composers and improvising musicians similarly alluded to a phrase or snippet from the work, as Gershwin himself would quote a phrase of "Dixie" or "Old Folks," thus providing the music with a wealth of meanings and associations, though suffice to say often involving its status as a symbol of the Jazz Age.

Meanwhile, the many recordings of the work for piano and symphony orchestra included those by Malcolm Binns with Kenneth Alwyn; Alexander Cattarino with Bystrik Režucha; Michel Camilo with Ernest Martínez Izquierdo, Ivan Davis with Lorin Maazel; Misha Dichter both with Neville Marriner and John Williams; Philippe Entremont with Eugene Ormandy; David Golub with Mitch Miller; Jenö Jando with Janos Sandor; Werner Haas with Edo de Waart; Kamil Hala with Libor Pesek; Lydian Jardon with Jean-Paul Penin; Julius Katchen variously with István Kertész, Mantovani, and Artur Rodzinski; Oscar Levant with Eugene Ormandy; Eugene List variously with Samuel Adler, Howard Hanson, and Erich Kunzel; Louis Lortie with Charles Dutoit; Teodor Moussov with Pancho Vladigerov; Leonard Pennario with Felix Slatkin; André Previn both with André Kostelanetz and on his own; Jesús María Sanromá both with Arthur Fiedler and William Steinberg; Howard Shelley with Yan Pascal Tortelier; Jeffrey Siegel with Leonard Slatkin; Siegfried Stöckigt under Kurt Masur; David Syme with Herrera de la Fuente; Gabriel Tacchino with Lawrence Foster; Alec Templeton with André Kostelanetz; Alexis Weissenberg with Seiji Ozawa; Earl Wild both with Arturo Toscanini and Arthur Fiedler; Alexander Zwassman with Gennady Rozhdestvensky; as well as by conductor-pianists Leonard Bernstein, Stanley Black, Morton Gould, and Wayne Marshall. That the *Rhapsody* could engage such outstanding musicians as these and, moreover, yield so many diverse interpretations stood as testimony to Gershwin's achievement.

This rich performance history makes it all the more impressive that Gershwin's own performances from the 1920s remain in many ways unsurpassed. In a 1942 review of a performance of the *Rhapsody* by Earl Wild and the NBC Symphony (including Benny Goodman on clarinet) under Toscanini, Virgil Thomson alluded to Gershwin's distinction in this regard. Noting that the work, "a modern classic," remained "beautiful and gay" despite "tough treatment from lots of people," including the performers under review, Thomson wrote, "George played it straight, kept the rhythm going, even in the passages of free recitation, which he treated as comments on the more animated parts, not as interruptions of them. He didn't moon around, and he didn't get brutal."[38]

Most recordings of the *Rhapsody* have used Grofé's 1942 score in its entirety, though a few, including Bernstein's with the New York Philharmonic (1959) and the Los Angeles Philharmonic (1983), made cuts that arguably undermined the work's structural integrity. American pianist Julius Katchen's rendition with Hungarian-born Kertész (along with Morton Gould's, one of the best on record) demonstrated that one did not have to be American to realize the work superbly; French pianist Gabriel Tacchino made the same point in his recording with Lawrence Foster and the Orchestre Philharmonique de Monte-Carlo.

The late twentieth century witnessed a revival of interest in Grofé's 1924 version, published by Warner Brothers in a commemorative facsimile edition in 1987. Michael Tilson Thomas helped pioneer this development with a 1976 recording that superimposed a performance by the Columbia Jazz Band with a version of Gershwin's 1925 piano roll of the piece edited by Marc Goodman. Thomas went on to record the music with jazz band twice more, but with himself at the piano, accompanied once by members of the Los Angeles Philharmonic and once by the New World Symphony. Other recent recordings using the original 1924 instrumentation included those by Ivan Davis under Maurice Peress, Peter Donahue under Simon Rattle, Joanna MacGregor under Carl Davis, Georges Rabol under Jean-Luc Fillon, Alicia Zizzo under Michael Charry, and James Levine with members of the Chicago Symphony Orchestra. These varied performances more or less adhered to the original manuscript score, with both Peress and Charry (the latter more so than the former) restoring some of the passages deleted from the 1925 edition (though neither reinstated the link between the "Andantino" and the "Agitato"). The Peress recording also proved particularly faithful to performance styles of the 1920s, while the excellent Levine and Rattle-Donahue releases stood out for their vigor and wit. These recordings made the 1942 symphonic arrangement, with its largely wasted contingent of saxophones, seem bloated in comparison, as did the premiere recording of Grofé's 1926 version for theater orchestra by pianist Michael Boriskin with Jonathan Sheffer and the Eos Orchestra (1998).[39]

Over the years, performers tended to take the head motive of the "Andantino" and, in some instances, the "Con moto" themes at notably slower rates than found in recordings from the 1920s. This slowing down of the two-measure head motive of the "Andantino" theme was accompanied by a speeding up, usually at twice the speed, of the balance of the phrase; so that, in such performances, the opening eight-measure phrase of the "Andantino" in essence comprised a five-measure phrase (two measures in common time, plus the remaining six measures in cut-time), while the six-measure consequent phrase unfolded in four measures (of common time). This practice, in place since the late 1930s, became so standard that of all the aforementioned modern recordings, only Peress's preserved the temporal values as written (as did a 1996 recording by Carlos Barbosa-Lima and the Sofia Soloists in a somewhat free arrangement of the work for guitar and orchestra). Even Michael Tilson Thomas's recording with Gershwin's roll valiantly strove to accommodate this tradition. "Oddly enough," comments David Schiff, "the most famous melody in twentieth-century concert music is never played as written," though he views this phenomenon sympathetically, asserting that the theme otherwise sounds "sluggish to our ears."[40]

However, the music as written sounds "sluggish" only when the head motive is taken a good deal slower than the "Andantino moderato" specified. Gershwin's score and his four commercial recordings make his intentions perfectly clear: he wants the first phrase of the theme taken rather straight, but at each entrance of the piano during the second statement of the theme, he wants some speeding ahead in the course of the phrase, and then a return to the tempo—or some possible broadening—with each recurrence of the head motive. In short, he wants rubato, not the mechanical two-to-one ratio that has become the accepted practice, a practice that not only weakens the structure of the "Andantino" section but undercuts the correspondences between the "Andantino" theme and its later appearances in the final "Allegro."

A further performance issue involves the degree to which one might, so to speak, jazz up the work. Orchestral and jazz-band players have generally and rather successfully aimed to reproduce some of the coloristic novelties associated with the Paul Whiteman Orchestra, without which the music loses much of its charm and humor. But neither Gershwin nor the Whiteman players saw the need for dramatically changing the rhythms as written, for instance, automatically to dot strings of straight eighth notes; and those attempts to do so tend to coarsen a piece that, by its composer's admission, employed jazz "almost incidentally."[41]

Yet another question concerns the extent to which the score forms an integral whole. In one of his "imaginary conversations," "Why Don't You Run Upstairs and Write a Nice Gershwin Tune?" (1955), Leonard Bernstein argued that the *Rhapsody* is "not a real composition in the sense that whatever happens in it must seem inevitable, or even pretty inevitable. You can cut out parts of it without affecting the whole in any way except to make it shorter. . . . You can make cuts within a section, or add new cadenzas, or play it with any combination of instruments or on the piano alone; it can be a five-minute piece or a six-minute piece, or a twelve-minute piece. . . . It's still the *Rhapsody in Blue.*" Asking himself why, then, he played the work so often, he responded, "Each man kills the thing he loves." This ambivalence informed Bernstein's abridged 1959 recording of the work, perhaps the best-known performance of the piece in the later twentieth century, though so slow and mannered as to be virtually a caricature of itself (as was his 1983 recording with the Los Angeles Philharmonic).[42]

Bernstein's remarks provided some framework for a helpful published guide to the work (1997) by David Schiff, who similarly views the piece as an open-ended work whose "identity" remains "unstable." If so, this reflects not only the wide range of approaches that have attended the music from its very beginnings, but also the lack of a critical edition of the score. Otherwise, there seems no reason to think of the *Rhapsody* as anything less than a "real composition"; its performance challenges appear comparable to those of many other notated works with complex histories. That the music has appeared in so many guises speaks to its resilience, but need not dissuade us from trying to understand its composer's intentions better.[43]

Chapter Seventeen

The *Scandals of 1924, Primrose,* and *Lady, Be Good!* (1924)

*T*he *Scandals of 1924* was Gershwin's last Broadway revue. George White, who coauthored the book with William K. Wells, directed the show; DeSylva wrote the lyrics (with some help from Ballard MacDonald); G. A. Weidhaas supervised the art direction; Erté designed the costumes and curtains; William Daly conducted the orchestra; Maurice DePackh furnished the orchestrations; and James Hanley provided additional music. The show, which featured comedian Will Mahoney in addition to such *Scandals* favorites as Lester Allen, Richard Bold, Helen Hudson, Winnie Lightner, Tom Patricola, and Olive Vaughn, opened on June 30, 1924, at the Apollo Theatre on West 42nd Street and chalked up 198 performances.

Instead of an opening ensemble number, the show more unusually began with a song for the Williams Sisters, in which the duo pretended to chide the audience for coming late and having "Just Missed the Opening Chorus." "The only trouble," remarked Robert Benchley in his review, "is that most of the audience will really believe that they *have* missed the opening, as most of the audience *will* have come in late." The other musical numbers that followed, interspersed with comedy skits, included "I'm Going Back," a satire on Al Jolson's mammy songs, sung by Will Mahoney in partial blackface; "I Need a Garden," resurrected from the previous year's touring *Scandals* and once again sung by the show's "prima donna," Helen Hudson (whose high C, wrote one critic, made "the back drop tremble"), here accompanied by a quartet, the Elm City Four, and dancer Alice Weaver; "Night Time in Araby," sung by Richard Bold, with an Arabian dance performed by the De Marcos, a dance team, and accompanied by a Sheik Orchestra featured periodically throughout the show; "Somebody Loves Me," sung by Winnie Lightner, accompanied by male characters and actors from stage and screen, with Tom Patricola playing the child movie star Jackie Coogan; "Year after Year," sung by Hudson and Bold in a lavish staging that depicted a couple's married years by curtains suggesting lace, silver, gold, and diamonds; and "Tune In (to J.O.Y.)," also sung by Lightner in an elaborate finale that targeted artistic censorship, and that climaxed in a Charleston performed by the chorus.[1]

The second act contained "Mah Jongg," an oriental number for Bold about the eponymous maiden and her two lovers, Chow and Pung; "Black and White March," an instrumental interlude (ostensibly composed by Vernon Duke) for some of the chorus girls; "Lovers of Art," performed by the Elm City Four in a scene that featured special lighting—the Samoiloff Light Effects, named after its inventor, Adrian Samoiloff—which gave bathing beauties the appearance of nude sculptures; "Rose of Madrid," sung by Bold and danced by the chorus; "I Love You, My Darling," introduced by Mahoney; and "Kongo Kate," sung by Lightner in a production number that also featured Patricola as a "Congo Nutt."

Although the show's four unpublished songs—"Just Missed the Opening Chorus," "I'm Going Back," "Lovers of Art," and "I Love You, My Darling"—appear to be lost, a few other unpublished manuscripts associated with the show—whether ultimately used or not—survive, though mostly without their lyrics: an opening set piece that possibly includes "Just Missed the Opening Chorus," a song titled "Hollywood," music from the act 1 finale leading up to "Tune In (to J.O.Y.)," an operatic parody titled "Sneeze," and the "Black and White March." Some of Gershwin's sketches for the "Kongo Kate" dance, along with a scored arrangement by DePackh, also survive.

The score displayed, essentially for a final time, Gershwin's skillful handling of revue demands, from the various Arabian, Chinese, Spanish, and African production numbers to the satiric ribaldry of "Somebody Loves Me" and the chorus-girl promenading of "I Need a Garden." Still, for all its relative sophistication, the music, bounded by largely conventional dramatic ideas, seemed rather uninspired and at times commonplace. In his review of the show, Benchley wondered, tellingly enough, if the revue genre hadn't wandered so far from its roots in travesty that it required George M. Cohan to stage a show "burlesquing the Follies, the Music Box, the Scandals and the rest." And Alec Wilder could only conclude from "I Need a Garden" that Gershwin wrote the song "under duress," and that he and DeSylva "perpetrated a jape for a florid production number which must have bored them both to extinction." The more novel "Tune In (to J.O.Y.)" at least has historical interest as Gershwin's first Charleston.[2]

The show's best song, "Somebody Loves Me," became its one hit. Although DeSylva and MacDonald shared credit for the lyrics, Gershwin suggested that the latter was the song's principal lyricist. "Ballard was a typical colorful popular song writer of the first rank," he recalled. "He said, 'George, let's write a song that will be simple and yet strong enough to catch on and be a big hit.'" Gershwin had written a similarly whimsical plaint for the *1922 Scandals*, "Where Is the Man of My Dreams?"— also introduced by Winnie Lightner—and would go on to write others. This song's verse, described by Wilder as "novel" and "provocative," hovers between G major and a modal E minor, reflecting the contrast between the comfort of believing "somebody loves me" and the "regret" of not knowing "who." Such tensions spill over into the G-major chorus, with similar uncertainties evoked by blue notes as well as by a touching modulation to a minor mode. In the patter section, the singer muses on such "perfect lovers" as Romeo, Antony, comedian Harold Lloyd, film cowboy William S. Hart ("oh, girls, what a chassis"), and, as mentioned, Jackie Coogan (to whom she'll sing this song "as soon as he is grown up").[3]

"Somebody Loves Me," which helped launch Lightner's career, quickly attracted popular and jazz musicians, including the Paul Whiteman Orchestra, whose 1924 recording topped the charts for five weeks. The music proved especially amenable to varied tempos. In her 1924 recording, Isabella Patricola sang it at a moderate pace, though in the second chorus, her brother Tom entered at a faster, more swinging gait, to which she joined in for a third chorus. Over the years most musicians, including Aileen Stanley (1924), Fletcher Henderson (1930), Adrian Rollini (1934), Eddie Condon (1944), Bud Powell (1950), and Oscar Peterson (1952), tended toward Tom Patricola's moderately fast tempo, though others, like Benny Goodman (1936), Kiri Te Kanawa (1987), and Judy Blazer (1998), took a more measured pace; Bing Crosby (1939), Peggy Lee (as sung in the 1955 film *Pete Kelly's Blues*), and Meat Loaf (1998) even rendered it as a ballad, while still others, such as Benny Carter (1937) and Earl Hines (1973), hazarded rather fast tempos. For her part, Lena Horne (as sung in the 1944 film *Broadway Rhythm*), began the song as a ballad, but later picked up the tempo. These variances hinted at those quintessential ambiguities of the Jazz Age, its heartache and its roar, embodied in the song itself. Judy Blazer's version merits special attention for its use of the rarely heard patter as well as the original DePackh scoring (both discovered in Secaucus in 1982).[4]

The critics gave the *Scandals of 1924* high marks, praising especially the comedy of Lightner, Mahoney, and Patricola, as well as the show's scenic beauty, which included, wrote the *Times*, "large quantities of gorgeous costumes, much of them on the girls of the chorus from the neck up and the shoes down." Benchley opined that with this edition, which ran longer than any of the others to date, White had finally overtaken Ziegfeld. However, the show's emphasis on burlesque and spectacle tended to overwhelm its musical interest, and, notwithstanding the success of the *Rhapsody* earlier in the season, few of the reviews even mentioned Gershwin by name, though *Billboard* deemed the score the composer's best yet. Gershwin was fast outgrowing the genre's limits in any case, and even if he and White had not had the financial disagreements that reportedly precipitated their breakup, it was probably only a matter of time before he would have left the *Scandals*.[5]

Meanwhile, Gershwin continued his association with Alex Aarons, who in the early 1920s entered into a partnership with Vinton Freedley (1891–1969), a fellow Philadelphian who had gone to Groton and Harvard, where he played football and wrote music for the Hasty Pudding shows. Beginning with Victor Herbert's *Oui Madame* (1920), which closed out of town, Aarons and Freedley began coproducing shows, even as the latter appeared as a juvenile lead in musical comedies, including Gershwin's *A Dangerous Maid* (1921). The team of Aarons and Freedley lasted through Gershwin's final Broadway musical, *Pardon My English* (1933). After this, Freedley, unlike Aarons, enjoyed some success producing his own shows, including a few Cole Porter hits. Aarons and Freedley generally put up most of the money for their shows, along with such select backers as banker Otto Kahn and Mayor James ("Jimmy") J. Walker, whose investments, remembered Ethel Merman, would arrive in an envelope "stuffed with thousand-dollar bills."[6]

Aarons and Freedley made a piquant pair. They were both stylish young men—the "best-dressed" managers in the business, recalled Guy Bolton and P. G. Wodehouse—but whereas Freedley was, in the words of Robert Russell Bennett, "suave and quite dignified at all times," Aarons was excitable and known to spend opening nights throwing up in the bathroom. Bennett reports that after one dress rehearsal, Aarons told the company, "Ladies and Gentlemen, I have just seen your dress rehearsal and I want to say that I have never before seen such a disgraceful performance in all my life. You all stink!" But beneath Aarons's "blunt surface," he was "pretty friendly and understanding," recalled Bennett, who preferred dealing with him than with Freedley, who was all "steel and ice."[7]

Aarons and Freedley signed up George and Ira for a new musical for Fred and Adele Astaire; but they also arranged for Gershwin to travel first to London to write a show for George Grossmith (1874–1935), a British actor-writer-producer who, with J. A. E. Malone, had produced a string of successful musicals at London's Winter Garden Theatre (and whose father, George Grossmith Sr., had originated some legendary comic baritone roles for Gilbert and Sullivan). Grossmith and Malone realized the efficacy of tapping American talent (they had Kern write the music for their two preceding Winter Garden shows, *The Cabaret Girl* [1922] and *The Beauty Prize* [1923]), and they now turned their sights toward Gershwin. For this new show—originally called *The Clinging Vine,* though later retitled *Primrose*—the producers also engaged bookwriter Guy Bolton, then known for his work with Kern, but later associated with the Gershwins as well.

Of mixed British American heritage, Bolton (1882–1979) was one of the most successful and prolific musical-comedy bookwriters in the period 1915 to 1945, writing or more often cowriting the scripts for more than fifty musicals. As discussed earlier, along with Jerome Kern and his lifelong friend P. G. Wodehouse, he helped establish the foundation for the modern musical comedy in the 1910s. In the 1930s he largely left Broadway for the West End, where (as opposed to New York) his kind of farcical humor retained the favor of audiences (his one Broadway show of the time, *Anything Goes,* was largely rewritten by Russel Crouse and Howard Lindsay). Derisive of postwar trends, he lost his former prominence after 1945 but remained active, including cowriting with Wodehouse a memoir, *Bring on the Girls!* (1953), which took a fondly ironic view of the theatrical world in which they had both flourished. In the same year Wodehouse, who admired Bolton's worldliness, told a friend, "Guy and I clicked from the start like Damon and Pythias. . . . He is one of the nicest chaps I ever met and the supreme worker of all time." Ira, too, thought Bolton "very nice," but admitted that he never felt "at ease with him."[8]

Basing his scenario for *Primrose* on a story by Fred Jackson, Bolton wrote the script under Grossmith's supervision. For the lyrics, Grossmith hired the young and essentially untried Desmond Carter (1895–1939), who established himself with this show as one of England's foremost lyricists. Gershwin arrived in early July, armed with some sketches and songs, two weeks before rehearsals were set to begin. He expressed optimism about the show "because the book seems so good," and was pleased to learn that there would be an orchestra of thirty musicians, "which," he wrote Ira, "makes it just grand." He also found Carter a "nice quiet chap" as well as a talented lyricist.[9]

Gershwin and Carter adapted a number of older songs, all with lyrics by Ira: "The Sirens" (as "Four Sirens We") and "Boy Wanted" from *A Dangerous Maid* (1921); "Some Faraway Someone" (the music, in turn, derived from the Gershwin-DeSylva song "At Half Past Seven," introduced in the *Nifties of 1923*); and "Isn't It Wonderful," "Wait a Bit, Susie," and "Naughty Baby," all of whose origins remain obscure (though an April 19, 1922, date on Gershwin's orchestration of the last-named suggests its year of composition). This contribution on Ira's part gained him, back in New York, credit as the show's co-lyricist.[10]

As *Primrose* opens, some partygoers from London, picnicking at Little Ferry-on-Thames, praise the delights of the countryside ("Opening Chorus"). Nearby lie both the estate of Sir Barnaby Falls (Guy Fane) and the houseboat in which the popular novelist Hilary Vane (Percy Heming) lives, attended by his valet. Sir Barnaby has arranged for his nephew, Freddie (Claude Hulbert), to marry his ward, Joan (Margery Hicklin), though both are reluctant, as, among other things, Freddie is in love with the parson's daughter, May Rooker (Vera Lennox), who's more attuned to his passion for golf ("Till I Meet Someone Like You"). Joan dreams of her romantic ideal ("Isn't It Wonderful"), while the hard-boiled Hilary savors his rural retreat ("This Is the Life for a Man").

Hilary's aristocratic friend, the foppish Toby Mopham (pronounced "MOP-um") (Leslie Henson), arrives from London. Finding himself engaged to a social-climbing purveyor of beauty products, Pinkie Peach, also known as Madame Frazeline (Heather Thatcher), Toby has invited Pinkie to lunch with Hilary in the hope that the novelist will somehow extricate him from this entanglement ("When Toby Is Out of Town"). Meanwhile, Joan hopes that Hilary's current novel, about a Miss Primrose in a situation like her own, might offer a solution to her own predicament. As she and Hilary grow closer ("Some Far-Away Someone"), Pinkie and her brother, Michael (Thomas Weguelin), disguised as a chauffeur, encounter Toby, whose distinguished family name Pinkie aspires to assume ("The Mophams"). During lunch, Pinkie misinterprets Hilary's intentions and faints in his arms, only to be discovered by a happy Toby (as this gives him a pretext to break off his engagement with Pinkie) and an unhappy Joan. As the visitors depart, a distraught Hilary remains alone ("Finale").

Act 2 takes place on July 14 at the Hotel Splendide in Le Bouquet, a seaside resort in France. A flower girl sells roses ("Look at My Roses"), a Turk offers coffee ("Cafe Bwana, Cafe Noir"), and four girls enter in bathing attire ("Four Little Sirens We"). Joan and Freddie imagine living in separate homes after they marry ("Berkeley Square and Kew"). Pinkie arrives, having opened a beauty salon in the hotel ("Boy Wanted"). Hilary and Joan resume their flirtation ("Wait a Bit, Susie"). Hilary suggests that Toby impersonate the medium Professor Pahoveleski and intimidate Sir Barnaby by predicting disaster for Joan and Freddie should they marry ("Isn't It Terrible What They Did to Mary Queen of Scots"). Joan takes Pinkie's advice to become a Jazz Age vamp in order to ensure Hilary's affection ("Naughty Baby"). Toby's formidable mother, Lady Sophia (Muriel Barnby)—accompanied by her maid, Pritchard (Sylvia Hawkes)—exposes Toby's disguise, while Joan's new persona offends Hilary. As Joan and Hilary rue their situation, Bastille Day celebrations proceed apace ("Finale").

Act 3 is set at the Mopham home. Lady Sophia has allowed Pinkie to convert the place into a nightspot, the Vauxhall Club, which presents a ballet danced by Pan and three nymphs ("Ballet"; when Pan removes his mask during a curtain call, he turns out to be none other than Toby, giving the illusion that he danced in the ballet). Pinkie voices her determination to enjoy night's pleasures ("I Make Hay While the Moon Shines"), while Lady Sophia, who has gone a bit wild under Pinkie's influence, sends Toby packing ("That New-Fangled Mother of Mine," added after the premiere). Hilary arrives as the dashing Beau Brummel ("Beau Brummel"), Joan as the Primrose Girl. Toby crashes the party disguised as a policeman and forces a happy resolution amid general rejoicing ("Finale," including a reprise of "I Make Hay While the Moon Shines").

An exercise in the carnivalesque, *Primrose* unfolds against a background of communal merriment. In the very opening number, the chorus praises Pan, who reappears toward the end in a ballet, his identity merged with Toby's. And the plot's resolution depends as much on revelry as on Sir Barnaby's decision to renounce his feudal superstitions and patriarchal authority (which he does only at gunpoint at the very end). The reviews detected in all this the guiding hand of Grossmith, whose Winter Garden musicals represented a high-water mark in British theatrical life at the time. Bolton and Grossmith "may have found the germ of an idea there [in the book]," stated the *Era*, "but the new musical com-

edy at the Winter Garden is founded upon much firmer ground really—
Mr. Grossmith's many years' experience of musical comedy."[11]

Like many contemporaneous American musicals, *Primrose* manifested
some anxiety about the modern woman and her "newfangled" ways—
a concern even Joan shares, though not Freddie, who's happy to find a
girl who likes golf as much as he, and certainly not Pinkie, the new woman
personified. But despite being a hilariously vulgar social climber, Pinkie,
whose entrepreneurial savvy and personal vitality save the aristocratic
Mophams from destitution and sterility, proves in the end a sympathetic
figure.

Gershwin wrote a score British enough in profile that at least one reviewer assumed he was English. "I have inserted several numbers in 6/8
time," he told the London *Standard*, "because the English are a 6/8 nation. The Americans are a 4/4 nation and their music is essentially the
fox-trot. But the English, who are used to good lyrics, like the 6/8 rhythm,
which approaches most closely to ordinary speech, and makes it possible to hear all the words." As with *The Rainbow,* the score furthermore
found room for melodies redolent of Paul Rubens and Lionel Monckton, whose 1909 hit "Moonstruck" allegedly served as a model for "I
Make Hay While the Moon Shines," though perhaps more in its sentiment than in any musical particulars. Such strategies, which anticipated
those employed years later by Frederick Loewe in *My Fair Lady* (1956),
no doubt drew on Gershwin's Anglophilia, the work's ironic tone
notwithstanding. Guy Bolton reported that during auditions for the
show, Sylvia Hawkes, at the start of her celebrated career, sang, for want
of anything more appropriate, "God Save the King," at which point
Gershwin "rose and stood at attention," prompting the others to follow suit.[12]

As for the music composed prior to the show, Gershwin naturally selected songs that suited this prevailing tone, such as the Sullivan-inspired
"Four Little Sirens" and the Kernlike "Some Far-Away Someone,"
though he wisely included others that more distinctively featured his wit
and vitality, including the radiant "Isn't It Wonderful," the suave "Boy
Wanted," the charming "Wait a Bit, Susie," and the jazzy "Naughty
Baby." Noël Coward, who loved the score, found the contrast among
the various numbers "extraordinary." Decades later, another British observer, James Ross Moore, finding little authentically English about the
music, observed that "in the show's best songs, there is always a point
where briskness eases and the melodic line becomes languorously saxo-
phonic: Gershwin songs."[13]

For the first time in the composer's career, Harms (and its British affiliate, Chappell) published a piano-vocal score of one of his shows nearly in its entirety, providing a rare opportunity to view a full Gershwin theatrical score of the period, from such choral numbers as the lovely waltz "Look at My Roses" to such novelties as the Turkish number "Cafe Bwana, Cafe Noir." Suffice it to say, some of this music probably would have otherwise simply disappeared. This published score also preserves a valuable record of Gershwin's youthful handling of the finale form. Although common practice dictated that songs be reprised in the finale with new words, a convention honored here, Gershwin shaped these fragments into a dramatic whole, including transitional passages that accompany the action and underscore the dialogue, so that the themes appear somewhat like leitmotives. Though short and unassuming, the lovely Pan ballet, for its part, features an intriguing blend of popular and classical elements, including a harmonic daring worthy of the *Rhapsody*.[14]

Primrose received a sumptuous mounting, with an ensemble of twelve principals and a chorus of twenty-five women and ten men. Grossmith, who cast two of London's finest comedic talents, Leslie Henson and Heather Thatcher, in the parts of Toby and Pinkie, had planned on playing Hilary himself, but deferred to Gershwin's request for a stronger voice and hired an operatic baritone, Percy Heming, for the role. The fairly comprehensive original cast recording—another rarity in Gershwin's career—reveals that none of the principals besides Heming had much vocal prowess, however. Some of the cast, including Thatcher and Claude Hulbert, tended rather to sing-speak their way through their numbers. Grossmith directed the show, Laddie Cliff and Carl Hyson staged the dances, Dyta Morena choreographed the ballet, Joseph and Phil Harker created the scenery, Comelli designed the costumes, and John Ansell led the orchestra. Gershwin himself helped prepare the orchestrations, including those for "Berkeley Square and Kew," "Isn't It Wonderful," and "Naughty Baby."

The last-named score, which comprises an introduction, a verse, and three full choruses (including a dance arrangement), holds particular significance because, with its date of 1922, it remains Gershwin's earliest extant orchestration. Written for flute, oboe, two clarinets in B♭, bassoon, French horn in F, two trumpets in B♭, percussion, and strings, the scoring exhibits craft and imagination, including changing colors that delineate and articulate both smaller phrases and the larger structure. This arrangement, which also reveals careful attention to accents and dynamics (including a triple-pianissimo snare-drum roll), documents

Gershwin's ability to orchestrate—at least for a show pit band—almost two full years prior to the *Rhapsody*.

Primrose opened on September 11, 1924, to critical and popular acclaim (though on opening night a few in the gallery booed the librettists, perhaps because the third act dragged on till twenty to midnight). A number of reviews thought it the best yet of the Winter Garden shows, which was tantamount to declaring it the crème de la crème of British musicals of the period. The critics—one of whom took Ira for Gershwin's sister, a blooper that occasionally surfaced in the British press—varied in their assessment of the book but were virtually unanimous in praise of Gershwin's music, Carter's lyrics, and the production as a whole, especially the performances of Henson and Thatcher and the beauty of the costumes. "London will want to see 'Primrose' for its fashions alone," stated the *Daily Graphic*.[15]

Distinguished critic Edward Shanks even opined that the Winter Garden musicals had taken on the earmarks of a classic tradition that had reached an apogee with *Primrose*, fulfilling the promise of the Gaiety shows of George Edwardes:

> Inconsequence and improvisation are its essential qualities, but a calculated inconsequence and only an air of improvisation. The plot seems unnecessary and too slender to be worth thinking of. Why think of it? Why not throw it on one side and have a revue instead? But the plot is always there: it is the cord on which these beads are strung, and a good many of the comic effects are produced simply by reference to it. . . . It has music of a more distinctive character than most pieces of its sort. The various episodes are introduced in the right sequence and given at the right lengths. The cast is well chosen and well balanced. There is about it all an undoubted feeling of harmony and proportion; and for its moment it is classical.

Shanks also agreed that the musical showed Henson at his best: "He was always obviously a genius: now he is a great artist as well."[16]

Primrose closed in April 1925 after 255 performances, only to be replaced at the Winter Garden by another Gershwin musical, *Tell Me More*. The production probably would have run even longer had not Thatcher left the show during the course of its run. Aarons and Freedley considered bringing the show to Broadway with Basil Durant and Kendall Lee, but decided that it would not have the same appeal for American audiences. As a result, while some of the show's songs, notably "Wait a Bit, Susie," enjoyed some popularity in Britain, none of these numbers made much of a dent in the States until Ella Fitzgerald recorded "Boy Wanted" (1959) and Michele Pawk performed "Naughty Baby" in *Crazy for You* (1992).

However, as with many successful West End productions, *Primrose* traveled to Australia, arriving in Melbourne on April 11 and Sydney on August 29, 1925. Produced by Australia's premier theatrical agency, J. C. Williamson Ltd, this down-under version of *Primrose* interpolated for its leading lady, Maude Fane, "Somebody Loves Me," described by one review as "a dainty rhythmic composition with a haunting refrain." The critics liked the production but seemed unimpressed with the score, which one paper thought "bright without being particularly distinctive." *Primrose* proved the first of a number of Gershwin shows to make their way to Sydney and Melbourne, including *Tell Me More* (in 1926), *Tip-Toes* (in 1927), and *Funny Face* (in 1931).[17]

For all its subsequent obscurity, *Primrose* remains one of the best preserved of the Gershwin musicals, thanks to its published vocal-piano score and original cast recording, as well as to surviving scripts, photographs, and orchestrations. Taking advantage of some of these materials, the Library of Congress presented the show's American premiere (in a revised concert format) with Cris Groenendaal (Hilary), Rebecca Luker (Joan), John Sinclair (Toby), and Kim Criswell (Pinkie) under the direction of John McGlinn on May 15, 1987. The critics responded uncertainly to this Gershwin score for the London stage, though the *New York Post* claimed that "the melodic genius of Gershwin, an unmistakable blend of sprightliness and warmth," provided "a thoroughly idiosyncratic charm" to the score's "British flavor."[18]

On December 2, 2003, Musicals Tonight! launched a more fully staged revival at New York's 14th Street Y. Advertised as the show's North American premiere, the work's charm survived the threadbare production and largely amateur cast. "Enough comes across to make you see what the work could be, in the hands of knowing professionals, as part of a living tradition," concluded Michael Feingold in his review for the *Village Voice*.[19]

While in London, Gershwin met with Alex Aarons, Guy Bolton, and Fred Astaire about a Broadway musical for the fall, tentatively called *Black-Eyed Susan*. George and Ira completed the score over the summer, and inspired by one of the songs, "Oh, Lady, Be Good!" Aarons and coproducer Vinton Freedley renamed the piece *Lady, Be Good!* The show proved not only Gershwin's first big musical-comedy hit, but also one of the quintessential American theatrical works of the 1920s.

This breakthrough owed much to Aarons and Freedley and the artists they assembled, including not only the Gershwins but bookwriters Guy

Bolton and Fred Thompson (1884–1949); set designer Norman Bel Geddes; choreographer Sammy Lee; British director Felix Edwardes (who had staged *Stop Flirting* in the West End); a cast that featured, besides the Astaires, wisecracking comedian Walter Catlett and popular singer Cliff "Ukelele Ike" Edwards (both of whom remain best known, coincidentally, for their work on Walt Disney's animated 1940 feature *Pinocchio:* Catlett as the voice of Honest John, singing "Hi-diddle-dee," and Edwards as the voice of Jiminy Cricket, singing "When You Wish upon a Star"); and, in the pit, Phil Ohman and Victor Arden, a duo-piano team so appealing that audiences lingered after the show to listen to them.

The Astaires proved particularly crucial, as the show revolved around them; but Fred Thompson deserves special consideration as well for no other reason than that he went on to cowrite the books for another four Gershwin musicals—*Tell Me More* (1925), *Tip-Toes* (1925), *Funny Face* (1927), and *Treasure Girl* (1928)—thus playing a role in Gershwin's career comparable to that of Guy Bolton, with whom he also collaborated on *Tip-Toes.* Thompson's career ran parallel to Bolton's, from his early study of architecture to his transatlantic vocation as a musical-comedy librettist. Before arriving in New York in 1924, however, Thompson worked exclusively on the West End, where he successfully adapted French and English farces to the musical-comedy stage. In that sense, he succeeded Fred Jackson, the author of *La-La-Lucille!* (1919) and *For Goodness Sake* (1922), as a favored Alex Aarons farceur, thereby strengthening Gershwin's connection to European farce.

Act 1 of *Lady, Be Good!* opens in front of the Trevor home in Beacon Hill, Rhode Island. Unemployed Dick Trevor (Fred Astaire) and his sister, Susie (Adele Astaire), have been evicted from their house by wealthy socialite Josephine Vanderwater (Jayne Auburn), who hopes that this will force Dick to marry her. Susie meets a hobo, Jack Robinson (Alan Edwards), who's returning home from Mexico (where rumor has it he was murdered) unaware that he has inherited his wealthy uncle's estate. Dick asks his attorney, slick J. Watterson ("Watty") Watkins (Walter Catlett), for assistance; although Dick loves Shirley Vernon (Kathlene Martyn), he considers marrying Jo so that he can support Susie. Brother and sister resolve in any case to stay cheerful ("Hang On to Me").

That night the famished Trevors arrive at the Vanderwater garden party, where guests are enjoying themselves ("A Wonderful Party"), the girls reeling in boys on strings of colored ribbon ("End of a String"). Jo's friend Daisy (Patricia Clark) and her boyfriend, Bertie Bassett (Gerald Oliver Smith), also out of work, profess their mutual affection ("We're

Here Because"). Watty flirtatiously tells Jo how to catch a man. The entertainer, Jeff White (Cliff Edwards), arrives ("Fascinating Rhythm"), as does Jack, who shares a tender moment with Susie ("So Am I").

Pedro Manuel Estrada (Bryan Lycan), a hot-tempered Mexican who alleges that his sister Juanita married the presumably deceased Jack in Mexico, threatens Watty, whom he has hired to collect his sister's share of the Robinson estate. Needing someone to impersonate Juanita in order to secure her claim, Watty turns to Susie, who declines, despite Watty's offer that they split his hundred-thousand-dollar commission ("Oh, Lady, Be Good!"). Jo announces her engagement to Dick, and Susie, aware of her brother's motives, resolves to accept Watty's offer and impersonate Juanita after all. As the Trevors quarrel, the party explodes in pandemonium ("Finale").

Act 2 takes place three days later. As people congregate at the Robinson Hotel in Eastern Harbor, Connecticut ("Weather Man" and "Rainy Afternoon Girls," later replaced by "Linger in the Lobby"), Dick and Shirley ponder their troubles ("The Half of It, Dearie, Blues"). Susie enters as Juanita ("Juanita"). Bertie, who has obtained a position as a hotel detective through Daisy's intervention, arrests and handcuffs Watty for fraud, but Jack, playing along with the deception, states, to Susie's surprise, that the woman claiming to be Señora Robinson (that is, Susie) is indeed his wife (reprise of "So Am I").

At a party that night at the Eastern Harbor Yacht Club, Bertie and Watty arrive handcuffed, the former having misplaced the key. Jeff White once again entertains ("Little Jazz Bird" and other specialty numbers for Cliff Edwards, including his own "Insufficient Sweetie") and the partygoers dance ("Carnival Time"). Dick tells Susie that he has broken his engagement with Jo and has found work, while Susie, in Swiss costume, announces her own job as a yodeler ("Swiss Miss"). Susie accepts a proposal of marriage from Jack, who has inherited his family's millions, and all four couples—Susie and Jack, Dick and Shirley, Daisy and Bertie, and Jo and Watty—announce their forthcoming marriages ("Finale").

The Gershwins wrote at least eight additional songs for the show, most of which were dropped in rehearsal or during the Philadelphia tryout. However, Harms published one of these, "The Man I Love," a song so strong that financier Otto Kahn invested ten thousand dollars in the show on the strength of it. Adele Astaire introduced this "numberette" at the Philadelphia world premiere following an act 1 opening chorus, "Seeing Dickie Home" (also later cut), and reprised it with Alan Edwards and the ensemble toward the end of the second act. As Ira recalled, Astaire "sang the song charmingly and to an appreciative hand. But sweetness and simplicity in style do not make for the vociferous applause given dancing duets and novelty numbers. So, after a week, 'The Man I Love' was withdrawn. Actually the show was in good shape and the elimination required no replacement, as the show was a bit long anyway." Disappointed by the song's "lukewarm reception," Gershwin's "spirits rose shortly after" when Lady Edwina Mountbatten asked for a copy of the music to take back with her to London, where the song became a favorite with dance bands. Meanwhile, the Gershwins unsuccessfully attempted to find other uses for the number on the Broadway stage: first, at producer Edgar Selwyn's insistence, in *Strike Up the Band* (1927), which closed out of town; and then, at producer Florenz Ziegfeld's urging, in *Rosalie* (1928), which dropped the number in rehearsal. Nonetheless, by 1928, thanks especially to a hit recording by Marion Harris (1927) and public performances by Helen Morgan (described by Gershwin as "that remarkable personality"), the song had become one of Gershwin's most popular, and it would remain a favorite of many instrumentalists and singers, including Billie Holiday and Barbra Streisand.[20]

"The Man I Love" also garnered more critical praise than practically any other Gershwin song. Paul Rosenfeld called it "a moving and beautiful expression of a simple human feeling, akin to that in Schubert's 'Gretchen am Spinnrade,' only less definitely tragic." Wilfrid Mellers deemed it "the most moving pop song of our time." And Deena Rosenberg viewed it as a turning point that brought the Gershwins to "the edge of modernity." These and other commentators especially admired the way the words and music mirrored each other. Mellers, for example, pointed to the contrast between the verse, with its evocation of moon-drenched dreams, and the chorus, which "loses the innocence and becomes all yearning." The chorus itself embodies a tension between, on the one hand, the simplicity of its insistent motives and slow-moving harmonies—the score states, "molto semplice e dolce" ("very simple and sweet")—and, on the other, the rhythmic gasps and wailing blue notes in the melody and the drooping chromaticism in the accompaniment.[21]

Such subtleties may have undermined the song's effectiveness onstage, in particular in a show like *Lady, Be Good!* with its emphasis on manic movement and fast-paced dialogue. Similar reasons may have deterred the use of another marvelous song—"Will You Remember Me?"—a moving duet for Susie and Jack replaced by the more blithely tuneful "So Am I." Surely few musical comedies could be said to be so animated; especially in its early years, but even over time, critics typically described the show as "madcap," "daft," "batty," "demented," "lunatic," "nutty," "hysterical," "giddy," "blissfully idiotic," "wonderfully inane," and "charmingly absurd." Such lunacy, which marked the show a key work of the 1920s, also looked ahead to Hollywood's screwball comedies of the 1930s, including the Astaire-Rogers musicals.[22]

Relatedly, with this show, Gershwin truly found his comic voice, one that depended in large part on certain incongruities—the way, for instance, straightforward melodies rubbed up against chromatic harmonies and snappy syncopations, giving the whole an air of mock innocence. Moreover, the composer's characteristic penchant for satire—manifested in this show by its treatment of jazz ("Fascinating Rhythm"), wedding music (act-one finale), the blues ("The Half of It, Dearie, Blues"), Mexican dance ("Juanita"), and the polka ("Swiss Miss")—assumed here an extra edge and brilliance.

The music's wit also found its perfect match in Ira's playful lyrics, as in "We're Here Because," in which the simpering Bertie—who in both name and personality recalls Wodehouse's popular Bertie Wooster—exclaims, "And so if you'll permit me, darling, I'd be overjoyed / To psychoanalyze the question à la Freud. / We're here, we're here, we're here because / I love you and because you love me"; or "Fascinating Rhythm," in which the singer addresses the "persistent" rhythm that "pit-a-pats" through his brain by stating, "What a mess you're making! / The neighbors want to know / Why I'm always shaking / Just like a flivver" (*flivver* being twenties slang for an old jalopy); or "Swiss Miss," in which the snazzy appropriation of Alpine clichés neatly complements the music's ironic tone: "And then beneath her balcony / He used to stand around and try to make a hit with her, / And he would yodel, 'O lay, O lee!' / That's the Swiss idea of melody." Meanwhile, the appropriation of the stage talk of famed female impersonator Bert Savoy (1888–1923) for "The Half of It Dearie, Blues" no doubt enhanced the music's bittersweet humor.

Originally titled "Syncopated City," "Fascinating Rhythm" became paradigmatic not only of a certain side of Gershwin's work but of the Jazz Age itself. Both the low-down verse, with its insistent blue notes (a mirror image of "The Man I Love"), and the explosive chorus, with its dizzying polyrhythms, charted new territory. Describing the number in 1927 as "rhythmically not only the most fascinating but the most original jazz song yet composed," Aaron Copland rebarred the music to show how the tune and its accompaniment created clashing meters. True, Zez Confrey, among others, had already explored similar polymetrical textures, as had Gershwin himself in "The Jijibo" and other songs. But whereas such earlier uses typically involved the juxtaposition of two regular metrical patterns, this song upped the ante, as Copland showed, by having the melody further suggest changing meters—making finding a rhyme scheme a challenging business for Ira.[23]

At the same time, the score contained a sort of hidden pathos, sometimes achieved—as in "Fascinating Rhythm," "So Am I," and "Oh, Lady, Be Good!"—by having the verses open in a minor mode. More generally, the various numbers often evoked some tender sentiment by briefly alighting on a minor harmony, a blue note, or a sighing gesture, accompanied by some appropriate lyric, as in Dick's "Don't be downhearted" in "Hang On to Me," or Susie's "Will you sigh?" in "So Am I."[24]

Moreover, although "Fascinating Rhythm" helped establish the show's reputation as the work that finally severed musical comedy from operetta, the score maintained a delicacy that placed it still in the tradition of Kern. This aspect would have been even more evident had the romantic waltz for Shirley, "Evening Star," made it into the show. Even so, some early reviews tellingly referred to the music as "dainty" and "elfin." The choruses seem particularly so, all the better to delineate the New England gentry who provide the comedy's milieu. "The End of a String" and "Linger in the Lobby," for instance, feature an almost rococo quality, enhanced by such lyrics as "I very much fear, the first cavalier / Can win this lady fair"—delightfully graceful choruses that provide an effective foil to the rollicking antics of the solo numbers. But even "Little Jazz Bird," with its polished chromatic bass lines, sports a smart elegance. The original orchestrations (by Robert Russell Bennett, Stephen Jones, and Paul Lannin, among others) suited such refinement better than later, brassier ones. Bennett himself described Jones's orchestrations as "the daintiest things you could imagine."[25]

At the same time, the musical plainly represented something novel. It had, wrote Fred Astaire, "a new look to it, a flow, and also a new sound. . . . This was no hackneyed ordinary musical comedy. It was slick and tongue-in-cheek, a definite departure in concept and design." The Astaires nurtured such originality, much as it served their talents. The "Dearie, Blues," for instance, allowed Fred to experiment as a soloist; "Juanita" permitted Adele to burlesque a Mexican dance; and "Fascinating Rhythm" allowed both a chance to stage what Gershwin remembered as a "miraculous dance." Moreover, "Swiss Miss" was an ideal vehicle for the kind of runaround gallop with which they had brought down the house in *For Goodness Sake,* and that years later Fred still utilized (with Gracie Allen) in the Gershwin film musical *A Damsel in Distress.*[26]

Lady, Be Good! debuted in Philadelphia on November 17 and had its Broadway premiere at the Liberty on December 1, Paul Lannin conducting the orchestra and a chorus of twenty-five women and twelve men. Although the reviews agreed that the show was a lot of fun, many thought that the Astaires carried the evening. The *Sun* even titled its review "The Return of the Astaires." Most reviews dwelled especially on the "impish" and "bewitching" Adele, the *Times* titling its review "Adele Astaire Fascinates in Tuneful 'Lady, Be Good!'" and *Variety* frankly ranking Fred "below his sister in personality and versatility." In any case, the show made the Astaires musical-comedy stars of the first magnitude, and Adele recalled the New York opening as the thrill of a lifetime.[27]

The critics also singled out Walter Catlett's "Ed Wynnian" comedy, Norman Bel Geddes's "stunning" sets, and Gershwin's "charming" and "brilliant" music, which elicited particularly warm praise from Alexander Woollcott, who after confessing to having "seldom enjoyed a musical comedy" as much as this one, described the score as "brisk, inventive, gay, nervous, delightful." Indeed, the show established Gershwin as one of Broadway's foremost composers of musical comedies.

The show garnered an impressive 330 performances at the 1,054–seat Liberty Theatre on West 42nd Street, followed by a limited East Coast tour in the fall of 1925, which enjoyed greater critical than financial success. The Boston reviews were particularly good. "The charm of the Astaires (either one)," wrote the *Boston Transcript*, "is that they might have taken to the stage only last week, so fresh seems their outlook, so naive their manner, and so easy and headlong their enthusiasm," adding, "The fact that Mr. Fred Astaire cannot or doesn't pop out his lines like a hardened comedian, but that he turns them still a bit awkwardly and a bit boyishly, with a funny little ducking of the head and a sort of sidelong glance, is a remarkable asset which he has always preserved." Music critic Philip Hale thought the whole show a joy, describing Gershwin's music as "melodious, seductively and inspiringly rhythmed, now pretty without being mushy, now exciting without too much blare and din." He had appreciative words, too, for the show's story: "This comedy is not strung together as an excuse for the appearance of two leading dancers, a leading comedian, and a bevy of pretty girls. . . . Other characters in the play have their parts and are not merely feeders."[28]

In the spring of 1926 Aarons and Freedley, in association with Sir Alfred Butt, brought *Lady, Be Good!* to England, where it played for two weeks in Liverpool before premiering in London on April 14 at the Empire Theatre. The indispensable Astaires re-created their Broadway roles, but the rest of the company was new, including George Vollaire (Jack), Irene Russell (Shirley), Ewart Scott (Bertie), Glori Beaumont (Daisy), American comedian William Kent (Watty), and jazz guitarist Buddy Lee, here playing ukulele (Jeff). Jacques Heuvel led the orchestra, with pianists Jacques Fray and Mario Braggiotti taking the place of the Ohman-Arden duo. Aarons and Freedley also supervised some changes in the show itself in order to accommodate British taste. "Londoners want their measure of novelty," they explained shortly after the show opened, "but they will not tolerate anything revolutionary in the theatre."[29]

Gershwin traveled to England to help prepare this London production, working with lyricist Desmond Carter on two new numbers: an opening chorus, "Buy a Little Button," and a duet for the Astaires, "I'd Rather Charleston." "Buy a Little Button" appeared in a prologue possibly appended because British audiences preferred a more conventional opening, but also to save latecomers from missing the Astaires' entrance. "Like George Gershwin," explained the producers, "the Astaires have a large London society following, and as these people come to the theatre even later than they do in New York, we felt it would be better to hold off the entrance of our stars until the house was in." For its part, "I'd Rather Charleston," performed after "Linger in the Lobby" at the top of the second act, reflected the current Charleston craze. This delightful song, in which Dick tries to drum some sense into Susie, who only wants to Charleston, incisively caught the personal dynamics of Fred and Adele. About this time, the Astaires presented to Gershwin a signed photograph of themselves, in which Adele wrote, "To George—whom I admire more than anyone in the world," and Fred wrote, "Adele said it for me."[30]

The London production received a more mixed critical reception than the New York show had—even those who did not simply reject it as a sign of American imbecility wondered if it might be a little overly energetic, one critic asking, "Are we on the verge of some strange cataclysm of civilisation?"—but the spectacle of the Astaires singing and dancing to Gershwin enthralled audiences. Recalling the opening night, Gershwin stated, "The cheering for the Astaires was the closest thing to a football game I've ever heard in the theatre. If anyone ever thought the English lack enthusiasm he should have been there that night." A huge popular success, the show ran for 326 performances before touring England, Wales, and Scotland.[31]

Lady Be, Good! also enjoyed the patronage of British royalty, including

Edward, Prince of Wales (later Edward VIII), who attended numerous performances and whose brothers—Albert, Duke of York (later George VI), and Prince George (killed in World War II)—on one occasion joined him in a box. On August 9, 1926, even King George V and Queen Mary made one of their rare excursions to the theater to see the show, their presence marked by a special program. The Prince of Wales insisted on attending the last performance on January 22, 1927—the last performance, too, for the Empire itself, about to be torn down—at which a heckler who cried out, "Why have we got to stand this American stuff all the while? Surely we can have some English songs and artists on the last night of the Empire," was shouted down by the audience.[32]

In 1924 Pathé recorded Cliff Edwards singing "Fascinating Rhythm," "Oh, Lady, Be Good!" and "Insufficient Sweetie," and Brunswick recorded the Arden-Ohman duo playing the "Entr'acte" with the Carl Fenton Orchestra. Then in 1926 English Columbia recorded William Kent singing "Oh, Lady, Be Good!" with the Empire Theatre Orchestra and the Astaires performing a number of the show's songs, some with the Empire Theatre Orchestra, others with Gershwin at the piano. In 1977 the Smithsonian Institution gathered all these recordings and some others into a helpful compendium of the show's early performance history.[33]

By the 1930s, two songs—"Fascinating Rhythm" and "Oh, Lady, Be Good!"—had overshadowed the show itself and even Adele if not Fred Astaire. Both numbers became especially popular with such fine jazz musicians as Benny Goodman and Count Basie. A rather lackluster motion picture directed by Norman Z. McLeod and produced by Arthur Freed, *Lady Be Good* (1941), featured these two songs as well. The story of a married songwriting team, composer Eddie Crane (Robert Young) and lyricist Dixie Donegan (Ann Sothern), the film had virtually nothing to do with the original musical except as a kind of cryptobiography of George and Ira (John McGowan, one of the film's writers, had worked closely with the Gershwins on Broadway), with the Robert Young character drawing on the legend of Gershwin as a composer torn between grand ambitions and his allegedly truer, more unassuming self.

In later years, *Lady, Be Good!* enjoyed a number of successful revivals, including those at London's Saville Theatre (1968), Connecticut's Goodspeed Opera House (1974 and 1987), London's Open Air Theatre (1992), Ontario's Shaw Festival (1994), and New York's Musicals Tonight! (2003). In 1978 National Public Radio also broadcast an abridged version arranged by Lehman Engel, who directed the Belgian Radio Orchestra and Chorus in a leaden performance of the piece. The 1987 production at the Goodspeed, for its part, made notable use of some recent finds as well as a restored script by Tommy Krasker that conflated four separate scripts (dating from 1924 to 1963, the last a revision by Guy Bolton himself). This historically informed version became the basis, too, for a 1992 recording of the complete score produced by Krasker and John McClure and released on the Elektra Nonesuch label, though the disappearance of much of the show's material, especially many of the orchestrations and dance arrangements, precluded a truly authentic restoration.[34]

The critics generally welcomed these revivals, notwithstanding a few dismissive notices, such as one of the Open Air production that worried about the show's "blatantly escapist" attitude about homelessness and poverty. Reviewing the 1974 Goodspeed performance, the *Christian Science Monitor,* for instance, deemed the show "as lively, tuneful and care-dispelling as ever it was" and "a nonstop musical delight." And the Open Air production, nominated for an Olivier Award for best musical revival, left the *Guardian* "nostalgic for the days when the genre [the Broadway musical] had lightness, gaiety and insouciance: of the era, in fact, before musical comedy turned into musical tragedy." Although the revival at the Shaw Festival fell short of John Lahr's expectations ("Musicals shouldn't, and perhaps can't, be done on a beer budget"), he observed nonetheless that the work progressed compellingly from "punishing alienation" to "a kind of redemption, holding out the promise of delight, not disintegration." And *Back Stage* thought that even the modestly staged reading by Musicals Tonight! proved that the show was "still entertaining after nearly 80 years." Such responses belied the notion of the Gershwin shows of the 1920s as essentially exanimate.[35]

A British touring production (1956), starring Sonnie Hale as Watty, elicited a particularly eloquent appreciation from a British musicologist known for his writings on Mahler and Britten, Donald Mitchell, who admitted attending the show at the Golders Green Hippodrome three times in the space of a week:

> There is ample in "Lady be Good" to engage the serious musician's attention, not least the highly original invention and organization of the most popular "hits," and the masterful ease with which Gershwin varies his tunes and builds them up into extended ensembles, danced and sung by soloists and chorus. No amount of repetition, it seems, can exhaust the oddly haunting impact of his leading themes. . . . I doubt if this production

of "Lady be Good" was wholly authentic, but it did nothing to obscure and much to reveal Gershwin's specific genius and above all his unmistakable musical character, the strangest combination of intense vitality and incurable nostalgia, both exuberantly gregarious and intolerably lonely. His talent was strictly singular, and his music suggests that he was aware of the fact. But it is just his music's acute self-awareness that enables it to transcend the fabulous, ephemeral myth that "Lady be Good" celebrates with such zest.[36]

Chapter Eighteen

Short Story, Tell Me More,
and the Concerto in F (1925)

*L*ate in 1924, violinist Samuel Dushkin (1891–1976) asked Gershwin for a piece that he could play in recital. Born in Poland, Dushkin had grown up in New York, where he studied with Leopold Auer and Fritz Kreisler. Keenly interested in contemporary music, he would eventually commission and premiere works by, among others, Copland, Martinů, Schumann, and Stravinsky, with whom he concertized extensively in the 1930s.

In collaboration with Dushkin, who at the least helped arrange the violin part, Gershwin composed in early 1925 a brief piece for violin and piano, *Short Story.* Dushkin recalled that he himself selected the two piano pieces that served as the basis for this work: the *Novelette in Fourths* (1919), discussed earlier, and a vignette, dated August 30, 1923, titled *Sixteen Bars without a Name,* marked (like the *Novelette*) "Tempo Rubato" and dedicated "to my much admired friend Beryl Rubinstein." Although received opinion generally considers *Sixteen Bars* (variously called "Rubato," "Prelude," and "Novelette in G Major") yet another novelette, Dushkin referred to the piece as a prelude, which accords with Gershwin's stated intention of producing a set of preludes during these years. In any case, the modest *Sixteen Bars,* in *aaba* song form, contains an expressive main theme full of savory dissonances (accompanied by harmonies that anticipate "Liza") and a contrasting bridge section in minor that coils around the same five adjacent chromatic pitches, making the return to the leaping main theme all the more effective.[1]

Gershwin shaped the new violin piece into an *ABA* design, with *A* derived from the *Sixteen Bars; B,* the two statements of the main episode from the *Novelette;* and the reprise of *A,* only the first phrase of *Sixteen*

Bars. He also fleshed out the music to suit the expanded instrumentation better, and added transitions to help stitch the whole together. No doubt pleased with the result, he presented copies of the piece to pianist friends Josepha Rosanska and Beryl Rubinstein.[2]

Dushkin and Gershwin premiered *Short Story* on February 8, 1925, at New York's University Club, and the piece was published the same year by the German firm of Schott, with whom Dushkin enjoyed a close association. In 1945 Associated Music published a revised version of the work edited by Dushkin, who made mostly minor alterations, such as added trills. However, he expanded the five-measure wisp of a return into an eleven-measure reprise, including a new coda that lingers on a modal cadence and echoes the middle section, thereby providing some extra bravura while helping to unify the two disparate pieces on which the work was based, though at some sacrifice to the whimsical charm of the original ending.

Although Dushkin recorded the piece in 1928 with pianist Max Pirani and periodically performed it throughout his life, the work never really caught on—surprisingly so, given the music's attractiveness and its composer's popularity. *Short Story* found a niche in the repertoire nonetheless as a light character piece, with releases by such internationally renowned violinists as Gerhard Taschner (1954), Leila Josefowicz (1999), and David Frühwirth (2004). Meanwhile, in 1985 Michael Tilson Thomas recorded an expanded "reconstruction" of the work for solo piano.

During the winter of 1925, Gershwin collaborated with Buddy DeSylva and Ira on a musical comedy, *Tell Me More* (originally with an exclamation mark), for Alex Aarons's father, Alfred. The senior Aarons apparently conceived the show as a vehicle for comedian Lou Holtz (1893–1980), who in his younger days had performed in blackface in the style of his friend Al Jolson, but who by the early 1920s had developed a distinctively Jewish-American humor that, while curtailing his national popularity, made him a favorite among New York audiences and such younger comedians as Milton Berle and George Jessel. Gershwin, who had worked with Holtz on a few previous shows, adored the great comedians of his era and presumably welcomed the opportunity to collaborate with an actor whose "antics" and "gusto" in this particular musical would reduce critic Alexander Woollcott "to the point of howling with laughter."[3]

Alfred Aarons also retained Fred Thompson, who had coauthored

Lady, Be Good! But with Guy Bolton otherwise occupied, he hired as cowriter William K. Wells, who had helped write the scripts for two previous *Scandals*. Considering that a number of the production's key collaborators—including Holtz, Gershwin, DeSylva, and Wells—had been associated with the *Scandals*, Aarons probably intended the show to be somewhat in that spirit, as suggested, too, by its advertisement as "a spring musical comedy" and even by its title, with its overtones of gossip and scandal. Other aspects of the show—including its incorporation of specialty dancers and novelty songs (including Holtz's best-known routine, a parody of "O Sole Mio" recorded in 1923 as "Oh Sole, Oh Me!") and its satirical take on the period's Cinderella musicals—similarly bespoke a connection with the *Scandals*.[4]

With Thompson, the Gershwins, and choreographer Sammy Lee participating, *Tell Me More* continued along the lines of *Lady, Be Good!* as well. Both shows paired, on the one hand, a disenfranchised society girl with the man of her dreams, and on the other, an outlandish comedian with a haughty debutante. Before coming into New York, Aarons reportedly decided that its tryout name, *My Fair Lady*, derived from one of the show's songs, evoked such similarities a little too strongly, and renamed the show accordingly. (In 1956, Lerner and Loewe, aware of this rejected title, claimed it as their own for their greatest success.)

Act 1 of *Tell Me More* opens at the Three Arts Ball at Manhattan's Sutton Hall ("Kickin' the Clouds Away," instrumental). Billy Van De Leur (Andrew Tombes), who adopted the alias Billy Smith while out in Wyoming, has taken a fancy to Bonnie Reeves (Emma Haig); he is dressed as Charles II, she as Little Bo Peep. Meanwhile, Billy's friend, wealthy sportsman Kenneth Dennison (Alexander Gray), is drawn to Peggy Van De Leur (Phyllis Cleveland), disguised as Pierrette; little does he know that she is Billy's half-sister, Margaret. After Ken and Peggy flirt ("Tell Me More!"), the latter departs, leaving behind her mask, the marked property of the Maison Elise, a fashionable millinery on Fifth Avenue where she and Bonnie work (she as a salesgirl, Bonnie as a model); though well-born, the orphaned Peggy has fallen on hard times. She's also estranged from her half-brother, with whom she quarreled after their father's death.

The next day, the clerks and models of Maison Elise show up for work ("Shopgirls and Mannequins"). Monty Sipkin (Lou Holtz), the apparently Jewish head salesman, proudly asserts his dubious charms ("Mr. and Mrs. Sipkin"). The store's fashionable clientele enters: first the haughty Mrs. Pennyweather (Florence Auer), then some debutantes, including Monty's paramour, Jane Wallace (Esther Howard), a friend of Peggy's from their school days ("When the Debbies Go By"). Jane invites Peggy to her summer home in Viewport, New Hampshire, but Peggy proudly declines. In search of his Pierrette, Ken visits Maison Elise, accompanied by Billy. As Billy wanders off, Kenneth finds Peggy, and the two vow to spend lots of time together after his return from Viewport ("Three Times a Day").

Meanwhile, Jane accepts Monty's proposal of marriage. Knowing that it won't be easy for Jane's parents, the upper-crust George and Mrs. Wallace (Maud Andrew), to accept a sales clerk as a son-in-law, the two ponder the heartache of love ("Why Do I Love You?"). Billy, still unaware that his half-sister works in the shop, continues to court Bonnie ("How Can I Win You Now?").

In order to remain close to her fiancé, Jane suggests that Monty pose as Peggy's half-brother, Billy, and that the two of them join her in Viewport. Peggy agrees in the hope of seeing Ken again. Jane reminds Monty that Billy had been educated at Oxford and asks him to act British in front of her mother. Monty, Jane, and Billy are determinedly optimistic ("Kickin' the Clouds Away"), though they proceed on shaky ground as Monty, thinking that Jane has asked him to act Yiddish, not British, greets Mrs. Wallace with a barrage of Yiddish ("Finale").

The second act opens with strolling summer vacationers at the Balsams resort in Viewport ("Love Is in the Air"). As Jane nervously awaits the arrival of her father, the young men flatter her with their attentions ("My Fair Lady"). Dressed in a wildly checkered costume in imitation of a sporty Brit, Monty, posing as Billy, recalls his home on the Delicatessen River in his ancestral Sardinia ("In Sardinia"). Peggy and Ken resume their romance (reprise of "Tell Me More!"), while Bonnie and Billy agree that they need each other ("Baby!"). Unable to pay his hotel bill, Monty takes a job as a hotel waiter. The news that Ken is allegedly engaged to another girl leaves Peggy distraught, while on learning that Peggy is in Viewport with a man only purporting to be her brother, Ken jumps to the wrong conclusion ("Finaletto").

In the act's brief second scene, Mr. Wallace meets his daughter's fiancé, now working alongside two black waiters (Willie Covan and Leonard Ruffin) ("The Poetry of Motion"). As the next scene opens, set in the gardens of the hotel, Bonnie and the girls entertain the guests ("Ukulele Lorelei"), as does Monty ("Oh, So 'La' Mi"). Billy and Bonnie arrive, newly married, and Peggy and Ken are happily reconciled—as are brother and sister Billy and Peggy, whose paths finally cross ("Finale").

As with Gershwin's other musical comedies of the period, *Tell Me More* celebrates the triumph of young love over all else, here including the relative novelty of a Jewish-gentile romance, one that makes room for the nervous heartache of the show's theme song, "Why Do I Love You?" One wonders if the creators had in mind the much-publicized travails of Irving Berlin and Ellin Mackay, who married in early 1926. Still, most critics thought the book generally undistinguished and unoriginal; said Woollcott in an otherwise glowing review: "I never saw a musical comedy book that mattered less."[5]

Whatever the limitations of the script, the show occasioned a particularly lovely score from the Gershwins: two suave love songs for Ken and Peggy, "Tell Me More!" and "Three Times a Day"; the ironic lament for Monty and Jane, "Why Do I Love You?"; two lively numbers for Billy and Bonnie, "How Can I Win You Now?" and "Baby!"; the snappy fox-trot "Kickin' the Clouds Away"; the charming "Ukulele Lorelei"; and two hilarious solos for Monty, "Mr. and Mrs. Sipkin" and "In Sardinia," the former in the style of a music-hall jig, the latter, of a German *Ländler* (and a sly gloss on the Jerome Kern–Clifford Grey song "The Schnitza Komisski" from the 1920 show *Sally*).

These last two comedy songs especially allowed Ira (working with De-Sylva) welcome scope, for some of his "niftier-lyric'd" songs had been cut from *Lady, Be Good!* "Mr. and Mrs. Sipkin" satirized class pretensions with an esprit worthy of W. S. Gilbert ("My line of conversation/ Delights an eager nation,/ For it is styled/ On Oscar Wilde/ And Mr. Bernard Shaw"), while "In Sardinia" proved an amusing send-up of Heidelbergian nostalgia ("All the folks there in their mayonnaise dressin'/ Are free of earthly woes./ Oh! To live and to die/ While the herring swim by,/ Where the Delicatessen flows"). Such wit elicited favorable comparisons with Wodehouse, one critic finding Ira and DeSylva to have "out-Wodehoused Wodehouse" with the rhyme "spiritual" and "hear it you will" in "Kickin' the Clouds Away."[6]

The music, for its part, exhibited an impressive delicacy and restraint—even compared to the "dainty" and "elfin" *Lady, Be Good!*—with Gershwin employing his familiar strategy of writing tuneful melodies prepared by more chromatic verses and supported by stylish harmonies, prompting Burns Mantle in his review for the *Daily News* to describe him as "the Debussy of the modern syncopaters, being given to weird harmonies and fascinating discords." Burns apparently had in mind something like the spiky chromatic introduction to "Shopgirls and Mannequins," but such subtle and sometimes dazzling framing of diatonic melodies even characterizes Monty's two ditties, with Gershwin's sophisticated handling of stock vaudevillian idioms affording a special delight.[7]

The music also proved particularly vivacious, its lively dance rhythms further enlivened by punchy syncopations, apropos of a show that was—later claims to the contrary—as energetic as *Lady, Be Good!* One review even reported that *Tell Me More* moved "at a more rapid pace" than the "elegant" and "gracile" *Lady, Be Good!* though another thought that the two shows had "the same whirlwind rapidity of pace." The choruses, meanwhile, were noteworthy for not only their charm but their dramatic aptness as well, with "Shopgirls and Mannequins" portraying the frazzled store clerks preparing to open shop; "When the Debbies Go By" depicting the arrival of the lordly debutantes; "Love Is in the Air" evoking the romantic hopes of the summer vacationers; and "My Fair Lady" capturing the determination of Jane's ardent suitors.[8]

John Harwood directed the show, Sammy Lee, as mentioned, staged the dances, Charles LeMaire created the costumes, Walter Harvey designed the sets, and Max Steiner conducted the orchestra and the chorus of seventeen women and eight men. Following its world premiere in Atlantic City on April 6, the show opened in New York on April 13 at the Gaiety Theatre on West 46th, an elegant theater with a shallow stage and seating capacity for 787. The Gaiety, which rarely hosted musical comedies, may well have helped determine the show's intimacy from the start; but in any case, its small size no doubt enhanced what one reviewer described as the work's "kid-glove quality; its persistent drawingroomness, its grace and its charm."[9]

Despite excellent reviews and limited seating, however, *Tell Me More* closed after a modest one hundred performances. One problem was that aside from Holtz, who gave, perhaps, the performance of his career, and Tombes, a *Follies* favorite (though apparently underutilized here, perhaps because he joined the show a mere two weeks before the Atlantic City opening), the principal cast members seemed merely serviceable. Rather, the reviews singled out Lee's choreography and the work of the five specialty dancers: Dorothy Wilson and Mary Jane whirling in "jazz ecstasy" in "Kickin' the Clouds Away," Vivian Glenn kicking above her head in "My Fair Lady," and Covan and Ruffin performing a buck-andwing routine in "The Poetry of Motion." The *Herald-Tribune* even headed its review, with reference to Wilson and Jane, "Two Small Bacchantes Are Hit of 'Tell Me More.'"[10]

The critics agreed that the real star of the show was in any case Gershwin, a notable achievement in an age when reviews usually paid musical-comedy composers scant if any notice. Now, James P. Sinnott, whose review began, "It is never a hardship to me to spend an evening listening to the music of George Gershwin," deemed the cast unworthy of the music. A number of other notices similarly mentioned Gershwin right off the bat, including those in the *Times*, which praised the score as "lovely"; the *Sun*, which greeted the music as "the life" of the show; and the *Commonweal*, which declared its composer "within the limits of jazz . . . something of a genius." Such appreciative attention presumably owed a debt to Gershwin's heightened visibility in the wake of the *Rhapsody in Blue* and *Lady, Be Good!* but no doubt evidenced as well the real merits of this particular score.[11]

On May 26, 1925, a little over a month after *Tell Me More* opened in New York, George Grossmith and J. A. E. Malone mounted the show in London's Winter Garden Theatre, where it followed on the heels of the departing *Primrose*. Gershwin hurried overseas to help prepare the production, which featured a stronger and better-known cast than in New York, including Leslie Henson and Heather Thatcher (both of whom had also starred in *Primrose*) as Monty and Jane, accomplished singer Elsa Macfarlane as Peggy, and Claude Hulbert (another *Primrose* star) and Vera Lennox as Billy and Bonnie, with a chorus of twenty-eight.

Gershwin wrote a few new numbers for this London production, all introduced in the second act: a song for Peggy, "Love, I Never Knew" (lyrics, Desmond Carter), that showcased Macfarlane's voice; a duet for Monty and Jane, "Murderous Monty (and Light-Fingered Jane)" (lyrics, Carter) that replaced "In Sardinia," which had been dropped during the New York run ("Murderous Monty" featured—for a Gershwin song—an uncharacteristically black humor, filled with satirical British references); and a duet for Monty and Billy, "Have You Heard" (lyrics, Claude Hulbert), that substituted for the soft-shoe number for Covan and Ruffin, "The Poetry of Motion." Because British audiences had already heard an earlier incarnation of "Baby!" in *The Rainbow* (1923), Gershwin rewrote the music, keeping the basic rhythms and harmonies intact but changing the melody, which made the London rewrite sound like a variation of its New York equivalent (as can be heard on a recent recording of the score, which ingeniously employs both versions).[12]

Otherwise, the London version stayed close to the Broadway original (leaving *Variety* to brood over the spectacle of Henson impersonating an Englishman). The local papers generally deemed the piece "a pleasant evening" and "a thoroughly jolly entertainment," the London *Times* praising the plot as "cunningly put together" and the book as "often quite witty," not to mention the "always haunting" Gershwin tunes. Considering, too, the London success of *Lady, Be Good!* (also cowritten by Fred Thompson), it may be that Thompson's humor played better with British than American audiences; but one imagines that it was primarily the superiority of the English cast that allowed the London production of *Tell Me More* to run up 262 performances, 162 more than in New York.[13]

Yet another production of *Tell Me More* starring Margery Hicklin and Leyland Hodgson opened at Melbourne's Theatre Royal on July 17, 1926, Gershwin's first Broadway musical to appear in Australia *(Primrose,* which had arrived there the year before, had been written for the West End). Australian productions of Broadway musicals during this period generally followed along the lines of their British intermediaries, but with some further alterations as deemed necessary. In this case, "Murderous Monty" was cut, while "Paddlin' Madeline Home," a hit by American songwriter Harry Woods, and other numbers were added. The show, which later transferred to Melbourne's His Majesty's Theatre before moving on to Sydney, was greeted as lively entertainment, with "plenty of 'go' and 'punch.'"[14]

Although a few of the songs from *Tell Me More* enjoyed ephemeral popularity with dance bands, the show produced no enduring standard, and the score fell quickly into obscurity and was eventually disparaged as inferior. Fortunately, many of the unpublished numbers, long presumed lost, surfaced in Secaucus in 1982, permitting Tommy Krasker to restore nearly the entire score for New World Records (2001). However, since no orchestrations from the show survived—even the names of the orchestrators remain unknown—and money was tight, Krasker had the dependable Russell Warner score the work for a seven-piece ensemble. Such reduced forces naturally deprived the music of some glamour. Even so, the New World recording revealed this long-maligned score to be one of captivating charm. Discussing this release (which included the restored *Tip-Toes* as well) for *Fanfare,* James Camner pronounced it one of the "most outstanding" of his reviewing career, stating, "Playing it for the first time was like stepping out onto a cloud."[15]

On April 17, 1925, a few days after *Tell Me More* opened on Broadway, Gershwin signed a contract to compose a work for piano and orchestra, titled for the moment the *New York Concerto,* for Walter Damrosch and the New York Symphony Society. The contract specified a total of seven performances: two in New York, for which Gershwin was to receive five hundred dollars, and five additional performances at three hundred dollars each. In fact, Gershwin would perform the work six, not seven, times with the New York Symphony: in New York on December 3 and 4, 1925, and then in Washington, D.C. (December 8), Baltimore (December 9), Philadelphia (December 10), and Brooklyn (January 16, 1926). Gershwin's fee, though modest in the context of the popular-music business, was respectable enough for an orchestral commission, especially for a virtually untried orchestral composer and from an arts organization on its last legs.

Aside from his patronage of Gershwin, Walter Damrosch (1862–1950) is probably best remembered as the avuncular radio host of NBC's *Music Appreciation Hour,* or perhaps less kindly as the conductor who chose not to play Ives's music and who, after premiering a work of Copland's, made a jocular remark about its young composer. This hardly does him justice. The son of Jewish conductor Leopold Damrosch and his gentile singer-wife, Helene, both of whom arrived in New York from Germany with their young children in the 1870s, Walter followed in his father's footsteps as conductor at the Metropolitan Opera and, intermittently from 1885 to 1928, the New York Symphony Orchestra. An accomplished composer himself, he conducted a good deal of contemporary music, giving the American premiere of his friend Mahler's Fourth Symphony and performing new works by Elgar, Debussy, Strauss, Stravinsky, and Milhaud as well as such Americans as George Chadwick, Charles Martin Loeffler, Daniel Gregory Mason, John Alden Carpenter, Deems Taylor, and, as mentioned, Copland and Gershwin. This patronage made the New York Symphony a more adventurous ensemble than its great rival, the New York Philharmonic, whose takeover of the symphony in 1928 spelled a setback for modern music in New York. "He has played more new music during the past quarter century, probably," wrote Deems Taylor in 1927, "than all his New York contemporaries put together; and as a rule has played it better." This achievement was somewhat obscured by his unwavering loyalty to the German musical tradition of Bach through Wagner, as expressed in his radio show of the 1930s.[16]

Damrosch's commission of a Gershwin piano concerto came about thanks in part to the conductor's daughter, Alice, who invited Gershwin to various family functions. But the *Rhapsody in Blue,* which Damrosch heard in rehearsal and at the premiere, proved the decisive factor. In discussions of Gershwin, Damrosch used rhetoric like Paul Whiteman's— Gershwin was the "knight" who had lifted "Lady Jazz" to a level of respectability, the "prince who has taken Cinderella by the hand and openly proclaimed her a princess to the astonished world"—but he did not share Whiteman's kind of interest in jazz, however defined. Damrosch essentially viewed Gershwin in the context of the great tradition, and may well have viewed him as a successor to John Alden Carpenter, whose *Skyscrapers* (1924) he deemed, after performing it on radio in 1931, "the outstanding American symphonic work of our times."[17]

Gershwin offered his own rather defiant reasons for accepting the commission: "Many persons had thought that the *Rhapsody* was only a happy accident. Well, I went out, for one thing, to show them that there was plenty more where that had come from. I made up my mind to do a piece of absolute music. The *Rhapsody*, as its title implied, was a blues impression. The Concerto would be unrelated to any program." Tellingly, he ultimately rejected the title *New York Concerto* for the more abstract Concerto in F, though at the same time, the work apparently incorporated some material from a scrapped project whose working titles, *Black Belt* and *Harlem Serenade*, suggested a descriptive piece about Harlem.[18]

While in Europe during the spring of 1925 and then in New York and New Hampshire in the early summer, Gershwin sketched out several themes, along with some ideas on how they might appear in the course of the piece: in what key, for instance, or separated by what "interlude." Taking advantage of an offer by pianist Ernest Hutcheson to cabin in Chautauqua, the site of a summer music festival in western New York, he started serious work on the concerto in late July.

Gershwin had reasons besides the summer heat to leave New York for Chautauqua. Already finding "growing public interest in his movements, his past, his plans" something of a "nuisance," on July 20, 1925, shortly before leaving the city, he became the first composer to appear on the cover of *Time* magazine, the newsweekly founded in 1923. Such recognition brought enviable publicity but no doubt further distractions to Gershwin as well as to Ira, represented in the featured article, titled "Gershwin Bros.," with his own photograph and blurb. The article itself basically recycled an only slightly shorter column that had appeared in *Time* in May, one that had discussed the composer with some bemusement and had announced the big news of a work for Damrosch. This June feature similarly referred to its subject somewhat waggishly as a "famed jazzbo," but nonetheless expressed genuine interest in the forthcoming concerto, which, it reported, was to be "more serious than the Rhapsody, unconventional but in strict form."[19]

Gershwin completed the first movement of the concerto by the end of

August, the second movement sometime in September, and the last movement by the end of the month, and essentially finished the orchestration on November 10. He later confirmed that it took him "three months to compose this Concerto, and one month to orchestrate it" (though this does not include earlier sketching).[20]

As with the *Rhapsody,* Gershwin seems to have worked the piece out largely in his head and at the piano before committing himself to paper; the neat fluency of the condensed two-piano score, along with other evidence, suggests as much, though as he proceeded to orchestrate the music he made a few cuts. Moreover, in both the reduced and the orchestral manuscript scores (the latter published in facsimile in 1987), Gershwin left a few passages for the piano unnotated, as he had in his manuscript to the *Rhapsody.*

The first published version of the work—a 1927 arrangement for two pianos—provided these solo passages in full but also featured, in addition to some minor changes, material that had been moved around some, as well as a few additional cuts, most notably large chunks excised from both the first movement (starting at ten before rehearsal 8) and the second movement (at rehearsal 8). Though probably made in part on the recommendations of Damrosch and William Daly shortly before the premiere, Gershwin surely authorized these revisions. Charles Schwartz later argued that the cuts "strengthened" the work by "eliminating superfluous material," but at the same time, some arguably undermined the work's formal intentions; thanks to one cut in the first movement (at rehearsal 28), for instance, the music lands rather joltingly on a G♭-major triad (in second position) rather than a D♭-major triad as originally planned. In any case, the discussion that follows refers, unless otherwise indicated, to the 1927 publication—the version, too, that provided the basis for the first published edition of the orchestral score, edited by Frank Campbell-Watson (1942).[21]

Steven Gilbert and others have referred to the work's first movement ("Allegro") as a "modified sonata form," but, lacking a readily observable binary or ternary design, such a description seems tenuous. Gershwin's claim about having to buy "four or five books on musical structure" to learn about concerto form was somewhat tongue-in-cheek; he clearly had no intention of conforming to any standard formal procedure. In his own words he employed, in the first movement, a series of ideas, including an underlying "Charleston rhythm," meant to represent "the young, enthusiastic spirit of American life," as well as a "principal theme" stated initially by the bassoon (the pentatonic, dotted-rhythm melody at measure 9) and a "second theme" introduced by the piano (the syncopated melody at rehearsal 4).[22]

This use of two primary themes, each with its own profile, represents, it is true, a decided link with especially Romantic sonata form, as do other aspects of the movement, such as some of its dramatic gestures, including a "grandioso" recapitulation of the second theme (and, in classic sonata fashion, a fourth higher than before, though still not in the tonic key, since the second theme is not initially presented in the dominant). Some of the movement's opening ideas also return just prior to and after this restatement of the second theme, but as material leading up to and away from this theme, not as points of arrival in themselves; the movement's opening timpani motive reappears in something like its original guise only at the conclusion of the last movement. Moreover, Gershwin does not so much develop his ideas as juxtapose and transform them, so that the movement in some ways seems closer to variation than sonata form. As with the *Rhapsody*, these transformations are subtle, as in the neat convergence of the three principal ideas—the Charleston rhythm, the bassoon theme, and the piano theme—at the triple-fortissimo passage (at rehearsal 36) that helps bring the movement to its close. Perhaps the phrase *rhapsodic sonata form* describes the music's unique design somewhat more accurately.

The movement also has something of the tone-poem about it, especially in view of its picturesque qualities. Gershwin's ambition to write a piece of "absolute music" apparently involved style—in particular, the abstracted use of popular music—more than content, for the movement evokes a scenario not unlike that of *An American in Paris*. The opening section (in F, as announced by the work's title) suggests the great American metropolis (John Warthen Struble writes that this opening "can certainly be heard as some of the most startlingly evocative 'New York' music ever written"); and the next section, with its entering piano theme, the lonely individual. The music subsequently turns humorous (at rehearsal 14), romantic (at rehearsal 20, and in the same key—E major—as the "Andantino" from the *Rhapsody*), agitated (at rehearsal 22), and cheerful (at sixteen after rehearsal 25, music somewhat Latin in profile), followed by a climactic return of the melancholy piano theme (at rehearsal 29) and a coda (starting at rehearsal 31) that encapsulates the whole.[23]

Gershwin described the slow movement ("Andante con moto," originally "Adagio") as "almost Mozartian in its simplicity" and as having "a poetic, nocturnal tone. It utilizes the atmosphere of what has come to be referred to as the American blues, but in a purer form than that in which they are usually treated." The music unfolds an *ABACA* rondo form whose main theme, introduced by solo trumpet and wind choir in counterpoint, evokes the blues. Reversing its role in the first movement, the piano initiates, not a pensive episode, but a witty dialogue largely carried out between the soloist and the strings *(B)*. The ensuing *C* interlude, with its magnificent big tune, constitutes the heart of the movement, if not the entire concerto; as with the first movement's romantic episode, as well as the *Rhapsody*'s "Andantino," its prevailing E-major tonality contrasts poetically with the larger tonal context (here D♭, as opposed to B♭ in the *Rhapsody* and F in the first movement). Gershwin's formal intentions might have been clearer had he retained the longer middle *A* section, as put forth in the condensed manuscript but not carried over to his orchestral score. On the other hand, he imagined early on the abrupt and extremely truncated return of *A* that brings the movement to a close (precedence for this unusual gesture—the reprise as coda—can be found in his *Short Story* for violin and piano, composed earlier in the year).[24]

For the finale ("Allegro agitato"), Gershwin provided some virtuosic dash by adapting, as its main theme, a toccatalike prelude for piano (which might be called, in deference to its tonal center, Prelude in G) that he had written the previous January. This finale also opens in G but quickly moves, on the entrance of the soloist, to F, the movement's primary key and the one in which it concludes. Gilbert offers good reasons for viewing the G tonality of the opening section as both a transition from the slow movement and a preparation for the arrival of the principal tonality, including the presence of an F-major key signature at the very start of the movement.[25]

Gershwin described this finale as "an orgy of rhythms, starting violently and keeping to the same pace throughout." As part of the excitement, the movement periodically changes meters, with triple meters often interrupting the dominant cut-time. Like the "Andante con moto," this movement is essentially in rondo form, its episodes largely composed of reminiscences of themes from the preceding movements. The music accordingly can be outlined as *ABACADAEABA*, with *A* the toccata theme; *B*, the piano theme from the first movement (the first time transformed, the second time in its first-movement "grandioso" guise); *C*, a new jazzy theme put forth by the trumpet and strings (at rehearsal 7); *D*, the romantic melody from the slow movement; and *E*, that same movement's whimsical theme. However, the new jazzy theme, *C*, takes on a life of its own, intruding on nearly all the other episodes and thus obscuring the rondo format—so much so that, on another level, the movement fundamentally involves a tussle between the jazzy theme and the main toccata idea, one that further translates into a conflict between a minor mode (toccata theme) and a bluesy major mode (jazzy theme), brilliantly resolved in the work's final measures.[26]

Even more than the *Rhapsody*, the work evokes nineteenth-century concerto traditions, not only in such formal gestures as its cyclic finale but more generally in its grandiloquence. Gershwin may have had in mind especially some of his beloved Russian concertos, though a few chromatic passages more decidedly recall César Franck, whose *Symphonic Variations* can be seen as something of a progenitor. Had Gershwin lived to write the symphony he spoke about in his final years, he might have written more music like this, but he generally retreated from such grandiosity. In this respect, the alternately tender and humorous "Andante," singled out by many critics as the work's high point, remains the most characteristic of the work's three movements. Still, the Concerto in F succeeded, as Gershwin had hoped, in moving toward a more abstract use of the vernacular.

The concerto also brought to the fore Gershwin's long-standing inclination toward pentatonicism. Associating the pentatonic scale with the "Indian and the unadulterated Black," the composer himself cited the concerto in this context: "In my songs and in my pieces for symphony orchestra I've naturally made plentiful use of the five-note scale. Off-hand, you'll find an obvious example in the refrain of 'Clap Yo' Hands,' from *Oh, Kay!* [1926] and in one of the early themes of my *Concerto in F.*" That "Clap Yo' Hands" exhibits metrical dislocations of a sort found in the concerto, and that the score to *Oh, Kay!* reveals a harmonic sophistication related to the concerto as well, suggests further that Gershwin's concert pieces not only drew on but helped nourish his work in the theater.[27]

Gershwin scored the concerto for piccolo, two flutes, two clarinets, English horn, two clarinets, bass clarinet, two bassoons, four horns, three trumpets, three trombones, tuba, timpani, percussion, strings, and solo piano. Even while writing the two-piano version, he thought at least somewhat in orchestral terms, jotting down a few instrumental indications, though surely imagining much more in his head. At one point he drafted a trial orchestration of the work's opening pages, which he submitted to Damrosch and, apparently, to his friend William Daly, both of whom offered a few suggestions. Gershwin then proceeded to orchestrate the whole not only in a competent manner, but with flair and imagination, including vivid use of wood block, slap stick, bells, xylophone, and other percussion instruments.

Indeed, even here in his first major orchestral work, Gershwin's scoring reveals a distinctive inventiveness, with arresting—and certainly varied—sounds throughout. Consider, in the first movement, the duet for piano and violas doubled by English horn (at rehearsal 5); in the second movement, the very opening, with its muted trumpet (using a Derby mute, as opposed to the harmon mute used by Grofé in the *Rhapsody*) accompanied by three clarinets in close harmony (a passage rescored, at the movement's end, for flute and piano); and in the third movement, the duet for xylophone and piano (at rehearsal 18). The contrast between these chamberlike sonorities and the work's more fully scored passages helps define not only the music's formal structure, but also something of its highly individual character.

Prior to the work's premiere, producer Charles Dillingham gave Gershwin use of the Globe Theatre for a private run-through, at which the composer played the solo part accompanied by fifty-five musicians, hired at his own expense, under the direction of William Daly. Gershwin presumably made those aforementioned cuts in the score following this tryout, which Damrosch, Hutcheson, and others attended. As for the published 1942 orchestral score, editor Frank Campbell-Watson, according to Wayne Shirley, did "a good job with the standards of a commercially oriented publishing company," his main fault being "overfussiness," including numerous additions of staccati, slurs, and other markings.[28]

Gershwin gave the first public performance of the Concerto in F with the New York Symphony under Damrosch on Thursday afternoon December 3 at Carnegie Hall, the final offering on a program that also included Gluck's Overture to *Iphigenia in Aulis,* Glazounov's Symphony no. 5, and Henri Rabaud's *Suite Anglaise* no. 1. Damrosch naturally wanted to end with the program's most anticipated piece, one that brought in a full house, including many theater and jazz aficionados who might otherwise have had some qualms about sitting through a Glazounov symphony; but at least one critic felt that placing the concerto at the conclusion of an exhausting program did the work something of a disservice. The audience in any case greeted the work enthusiastically, even if, as one skeptical observer noted, Gershwin received more applause before playing the piece than afterward. Morton Gould, who attended the concert, described the audience response that rainy afternoon as "thunderous. All around me people marveled at the originality and strength of the work."[29]

The concerto arrived at the height of interest in the use of jazz in serious contexts, but except for the occasional commentator who found the whole idea of a "jazz concerto," as the work was commonly called, a "degradation," the use of the vernacular in itself proved of minor concern. Not that the appropriation of jazz in a concert setting had lost its piquancy; but critical attention focused rather on whether this new piece represented an advance over the *Rhapsody,* and here opinions varied widely.[30]

Many reviews praised the work. "The truth is that George Gershwin is a genius," wrote Samuel Chotzinoff in the *World.* " . . . He alone actually expresses us. He is the present, with all its audacity, impertinence, its feverish delight in its motion, its lapses into rhythmically exotic melancholy." "The fact is that here is a work that has something to say, even if that something is occasionally said rather crudely," stated the *Courier.* "Don't let anybody kid you out of it, children," added the *New Yorker.* "George Gershwin's piano concerto is about the most important new work that has been aired in this hamlet of ours in many somethings, and when we say 'important,' we're not using a nicenellie for 'dull.'" Even musicologist Carl Engel, head of the Music Division at the Library of Congress, described the work in *Musical Quarterly* as, for all its weaknesses, "courageous" and "creditable," writing, "The merit and the promise of this composition lie in the portions that are distinctly poetical; in the orchestral coloring, that is often piquant without ever being offensive; but chiefly in the general tenor, which is unquestionably new of a newness to be found nowhere except in these United States."

Others thought the work a step backward. The *Herald-Tribune*'s Lawrence Gilman, for instance, held that in writing a symphonic work, Gershwin wound up producing something "conventional," "trite," and "polite." "We wanted . . . to hear a young American composer talking confidently, bravely, irrepressively [*sic*], of himself," said Gilman. "Instead we heard a facile and anxiously conformist youth talking the stale platitudes of the symphonic concert hall." Oscar Thompson, in *Musical America,* similarly felt that Gershwin "sacrificed vigor and directness of utterance and became much more self-conscious and artificial than in the *Rhapsody.*" B. H. Haggin, in the *Nation,* argued that only the work's slow movement succeeded because "distinctively symphonic movements" needed to be "based on symphonic material," while Olin Downes in the *Times* likewise claimed that Gershwin lacked the "instinct" and "technical endowment" to write a work of "symphonic dimensions." Over the next few years, however, some of these more doubtful critics tempered their initial impressions. Gilman grudgingly admitted that the music might be here to stay; Downes found it more substantial than he had at first; and Charles Buchanan totally reversed himself in an article for *Outlook* titled "Gershwin and Musical Snobbery."[31]

Gershwin continued to perform the concerto for the rest of his life, including performances with Fritz Reiner and the Cincinnati Symphony Orchestra in March 1927; William Daly and the Chicago Symphony in June 1933; the Leo Reisman Orchestra in eighteen different cities in early 1934; Daly and the Pittsburgh Symphony Society in November 1934; Alexander Smallens and the Philadelphia Orchestra in January 1936; Hans Kindler and the National Symphony Orchestra in February 1936; Vladimir Golschmann and the St. Louis Symphony Orchestra in March 1936; Arthur Fiedler and the Boston Pops in May 1936; Basil Cameron and the Seattle Symphony in December 1936; both Pierre Monteux and the San Francisco Symphony, and Victor Kolar and the Detroit Symphony, in January 1937; and Alexander Smallens and the Los Angeles Symphony in February 1937, not to mention performances with the New York Philharmonic at Lewisohn Stadium. The sold-out Pittsburgh performance, incidentally, marked the end of that city's statute—in place since 1794—prohibiting concerts on Sundays; commented Gershwin, as he personally sold the first Sunday ticket to a local businessman for fifty dollars: "Although I like blue music, I can't say I'm very fond of Blue Laws." The first of his two 1937 performances with the Los Angeles Symphony, meanwhile, occasioned a buffet-supper reception at the Trocadero attended by dozens of celebrities, including Irving Berlin, Frank Capra, Moss Hart, Miriam Hopkins, Otto Klemperer, Ernest Lubitsch, Cole Porter, and Jimmy Stewart.[32]

As the concerto traveled coast to coast, it met largely with approbation. After the highly successful Cincinnati premiere, Reiner remarked, "I think a good deal of his [Gershwin's] music and of his remarkable ability as a pianist. His compositions are very inspired and original." Herman Devries of the *Chicago American* proved particularly enthusiastic: "Nothing quite like his Concerto in F has ever been heard in the symphonic world, and if it is not the very essence of Americanism, I do not know my profession or the art it serves." And one Pittsburgh critic stated, "A master of structure, his Concerto in F contains much that at once is grandiloquently expressive and musically interesting, even though other elements therein might shock the purists."[33]

At the same time, unfavorable assessments appeared as well. In Los Angeles, for instance, Richard Saunders wrote, "Little if any of Gershwin's music is likely to outlive its composer, for it is superficial and popular in an almost exact parallel to that of [Sigismond] Thalberg, who was equally popular in his day." Other critics, including such distinguished figures as Paul Rosenfeld, Herbert Elwell, Virgil Thomson, and Frederick Jacobi, also rendered rather severe judgments. Actually, Rosenfeld, who initially panned the piece, later deemed it "the juiciest and most entertaining of Gershwin's concert works," and its second movement "charming and atmospheric," though he found, in the end, that its attractive parts failed to add up and that, like all of Gershwin's ambitious compositions, it offered "an undiscriminating public" only "sensuous gratification" as opposed to a vision of reality; that it was "on the whole good circus music." Elwell claimed that the music paid "the most servile obeisance to a form with which it has nothing in common, and results in nothing but tiresome and aimless pose and gesture." Thomson suggested that its "timid and respectable charm" could not disguise its lack of professionalism and depth. And Jacobi similarly thought Gershwin "helpless in his attempts to carry along—to spin out—his ideas," adding that the concerto's "charming material is marred, for some of us, by the lack of skill, the lack of modesty with which it is presented." Rosenfeld, Elwell, Thomson, and Jacobi all preferred the show tunes, thus helping to establish an elite critical tradition that rated the composer's theater music above his concert work.[34]

Whatever the merits of such negative criticisms, some apparently failed to consider the score closely. How else to explain the remarks about the unrelatedness of the work's material, when the music contained so rich a network of thematic correspondences; or those about Gershwin's crude handling of classical form, when the forms were so personally conceived? "What the critics then and often later failed to see," Morton Gould observed, "was that Gershwin's unorthodoxy was inherent in his musical outlook, and was a major virtue of his genius. Perhaps his mistake was in tagging his works with traditional labels."[35]

The Concerto in F received its European premiere at the Paris Opera on May 29, 1928, with Dimitri Tiomkin playing the work under Vladimir Golschmann and his orchestra. Interviewed shortly before this performance, Tiomkin described the work as "an actual transcription of American life, manners and thought. It is the most splendid expression of youthful vitality and optimism." Gershwin, who attended the premiere with Ira, thought Tiomkin's performance—as well as his efforts on behalf of the piece—"wonderful," though Ira privately noted that although Golschmann "was fine," Tiomkin "might have been better." In any case, the concert, which also featured Tiomkin playing Liszt's Second Piano

Concerto and Golschmann conducting Copland's *Cortège macabre,* proved a triumph for both Gershwin and Tiomkin. For one reviewer, the concerto even offered some consolation for having to endure the Copland, actually generally well received, but here described as "a barbarous, exasperating chant, in which the instruments howl instead of playing." An eminent French critic, Emile Vuillermoz, thought that the concerto "made even the most distrustful musicians realize that jazz, after having renewed the technique of dancing, might perfectly well exert a deep and beneficent influence in the most exalted spheres," and that the work's highly individual absorption of classical styles revealed "a deep knowledge of European musical literature." Hearing that Gershwin had come to France to study counterpoint, Vuillermoz, himself a student of Fauré and a friend of Debussy's and Ravel's, expressed the hope that such studies not compromise his distinctive "ingenuousness and harmonic feeling." "Gershwin has the good fortune to possess a rich, individual harmonic sense," stated Vuillermoz. "Let him take good care not to lose this precious originality."[36]

On September 8, 1932, Europe again heard the concerto when Fritz Reiner and pianist Harry Kaufman performed its last two movements at an all-American concert sponsored by the Venice International Festival of Contemporary Music, whose audience made the rare gesture of demanding that the orchestra encore the finale. The *Gazzetta di Venezia* found the piece a relief from the monotony of the rest of the program, detecting in its "humor" and "robust yet bizarre sentiment" an "almost reckless, amoral personality," but one "healthy in a distinct American sense" and "in harmony with the spiritual attitude of the people it represents."[37]

In the fall of 1928 the Paul Whiteman Orchestra released an abridged version of the work arranged by Ferde Grofé and conducted only in part by Whiteman (William Daly presided over some retake sessions), with Roy Bargy, who had joined the band in early 1928, at the piano and either Bix Beiderbecke or, more probably, Charlie Margulis featured on the second-movement trumpet solo. This recording remains an intriguing artifact, not only because it apparently preserves some record of Daly's Gershwin, but because Grofé's lean scoring (reportedly disliked by Gershwin) accentuates the music's connection with Milhaud and Copland. Whiteman and Bargy also featured the concerto on the band's third Modern American Music Concert at Carnegie Hall on October 7, 1928, and performed it thereafter on numerous occasions. Although Whiteman never had anything like the success with the concerto that he had with the *Rhapsody,* audiences welcomed a 1987 revival of this arrangement performed by pianist Russell Sherman and the Orchestra of St. Luke's under Gunther Schuller.[38]

Even in its original guise, the Concerto in F never really established itself during Gershwin's lifetime, no doubt the main reason he never recorded it commercially, though he occasionally played abridged arrangements of the work on the radio in the 1930s. These performances are somewhat slapdash, but Gershwin, who plays along with the orchestra during rests in the solo part, as Mozart might have, renders the music with enormous élan.

After Gershwin's death, the Concerto in F entered the international repertoire. Byron Janis even made it a centerpiece of his triumphant goodwill tour of the Soviet Union in 1960. Meanwhile, the work's discography included performances by, among others, pianist Oscar Levant with no less than three conductors, namely, Toscanini, Kostelanetz, and Charles Previn; Malcolm Binns with Kenneth Alwyn; Michael Boriskin with Jonathan Sheffer; Michel Camilo with Ernest Martínez Izquierdo; Alexander Cattarino with Bystrik Režucha; Peter Donahue with Simon Rattle; Philippe Entremont with Eugene Ormandy; the composer's nephew, Leopold Godowsky III, with José Serebrier; David Golub with Mitch Miller; Isador Goodman with Patrick Thomas; Hélène Grimaud with David Zinman; Werner Haas with Edo de Waart; Loren Hollander with James Levine; Josef Jelinek with Paul Brazda; Julius Katchen with Mantovani; Alain Lefèvre with Yoav Talmi; Eugene List alternately with Samuel Adler and Howard Hanson; Joanna MacGregor with Carl Davis; Peter Nero with Arthur Fiedler; Garrick Ohlsson with Michael Tilson Thomas; Piotr Pechersky with Kirill Kondrashin; André Previn alternately with Kostelanetz and on his own; Michael Rische with Wayne Marshall; Pascal Rogé with Bertrand de Billy; Howard Shelley with Yan Pascal Tortelier; Jeffrey Siegel with Leonard Slatkin; David Syme with Herrera de la Fuente; Roberto Szidon with Edward Downes; Gabriel Tacchino with Lawrence Foster; Alec Templeton with Thor Johnson; Janis Vakarelis with Henry Lewis; Earl Wild with Arthur Fiedler; and Morton Gould, Andrew Litton, and Wayne Marshall, each conducting from the piano. The critical consensus holds the Wild-Fiedler 1961 RCA release in especially high regard, though the Gould recording rivals it in authority and charm. The other recordings had their attractions as well, from the drama of Levant (especially under Toscanini) and the elegance of Entremont to the sharp-edged intensity of Wayne Marshall and the poetic grace of Joanna MacGregor.

In 1955 the Bill Finegan–Eddie Sauter Orchestra—a kind of Paul

Whiteman Orchestra of the 1950s—released its own miniature version of the Concerto in F for jazz band as arranged by Finegan, who had similarly created a three-minute distillation of the *Rhapsody* for Glenn Miller (recorded in 1942). In a study of these Finegan arrangements, Evan Rapport argues that such labels as "concert jazz" marginalized both Gershwin's and Finegan's work, which could be seen, rather, "as part of an American music tradition that encompasses a diverse array of musicians interested in working with a range of materials, and not as hybrids of references to autonomous styles." The Finegan-Sauter version of the concerto also underscored Gershwin's amenability to the cool-jazz trends of the 1950s, a point made in other ways by renditions of Gershwin songs by such jazz artists as Chet Baker, Chris Connor, Stan Getz, Gerry Mulligan, Thelonious Monk, and George Shearing.[39]

As with the *Rhapsody* and *An American in Paris*, the Concerto in F also attracted dancers. In May 1930, choreographer Gertrude Kurath (1903–1992), an eventual expert on Amerindian dance, launched a ballet to the Whiteman recording at Yale University. In preparation, Kurath visited Gershwin at his Riverside Drive penthouse, where the composer amiably accompanied her and, pleased with her "ritualistic interpretation," offered "constructive suggestions." Kurath intended the dance to be a stylized fusion of jazz and experimental movement and a study of "space areas and levels," but recalled that some spectators read it as "a development from conflict to harmony of the sexes."[40]

In the early 1980s Billy Wilson (1935–1994) choreographed the music as *Concerto in F* (1981) for Alvin Ailey, and Jerome Robbins (1918–1998), as *Gershwin Concerto* (1982), for the New York City Ballet. Both works combined aspects of period dance and ballet movement, and both heeded the music's more introspective qualities, Robbins even identifying one of his ballet's themes as that of "urban loneliness." Anna Kisselgoff called Robbins's "brilliant ballet" a "tour de force," while Jennifer Dunning, also in the *Times*, described the "slightly elegiac" Wilson work, as danced in 1994 by the Dance Theatre of Harlem, as "a lusciously pretty and expert evocation of youth."[41]

In a more critical review of these ballets, Arlene Croce argued that the impulse to choreograph Gershwin's symphonic works was essentially misguided. "Gershwin isn't seeing dances in his 'Rhapsody in Blue' and 'An American in Paris' or in his piano concerto. The fact that choreographers persistently attempt this music testifies to its power of kinetic suggestion, but the ballets invariably fail, because Gershwin's kinetic powers are focussed in unstageable visions. . . . Neither choreographer

[Wilson nor Robbins] is able to contrive a substitute for Gershwin's construct—the panorama that he shows us in such concrete scenic and dramatic detail that if he had any visual accompaniment in mind it was surely the motion picture, in which images can be intercut with a comparable velocity." Accordingly, Balanchine had the good sense to use the composer's show tunes for his own Gershwin ballet, *Who Cares?* (1970), for "it was in the songs that Gershwin most intensely visualized his idea of dance." At the same time, Gershwin's sister, Frances, felt that all three ballets came up short (although she liked the Wilson ballet best) because their choreographers simply lacked the requisite "verve" and "humor."[42]

In any event, whereas Copland, whose *Cortège macabre* earned scant notice from a Parisian public bedazzled by the concerto, emerged a particularly crucial figure in the development of American modern dance, Gershwin, who alas never fulfilled his dream of writing a full-length ballet, remained primarily a composer of the lyric stage.

Chapter Nineteen

Tip-Toes and *Song of the Flame* (1925)

In the fall of 1925 the successful creators of *Lady, Be Good!*—the Gershwin brothers, bookwriters Fred Thompson and Guy Bolton, and producers Aarons and Freedley—launched a new musical, *Tip-Toes*. The show was designed especially for Queenie Smith (1898–1978), the diminutive ballet dancer who had left the corps of the Metropolitan Opera in order to pursue a career in musical comedy, and who had only recently achieved celebrity, thanks to a star turn in Kern's *Sitting Pretty* (1924). *Tip-Toes* would represent the pinnacle of her stage career, though she subsequently enjoyed some success in Hollywood, where she played Ellie in the 1936 film version of *Show Boat*.

Tip-Toes takes place in Florida at the height of the 1925 real-estate boom. At the Palm Beach station, real-estate brokers, awaiting the train from New York, voice their enthusiasm for the sunshine state ("Waiting for the Train"). A young, affluent married couple, Rollo and Sylvia Metcalf (Robert Halliday and Jeanette MacDonald), affectionately tease each other ("Nice Baby! [Come to Papa!]"). Sylvia leaves to prepare for an impending visit from her brother, glue magnate Steve Burton (Allen Kearns), who, though heir to their grandfather's millions, lives simply in a small town in Maine. Rollo remains to await the arrival of the Komical Kayes, a vaudeville team hired to entertain at a reception for Steve. As Rollo momentarily follows the attractive Peggy Schuyler (Amy Revere) offstage, Al Kaye (Andrew Tombes) and Uncle Henry ("Hen") Kaye (Harry K. Watson Jr.) enter, with "Tip-Toes" Kaye (Queenie Smith) stowed away in a trunk. Rollo recognizes Tip-Toes as a flirtation from his past and, fearing exposure, offers the Kayes a thousand dollars to go back where they came from. The Kayes accept, and Tip-Toes returns to Rollo a photo of the two of them on donkeys at Coney Island.

Rather than leave town, however, Al and Hen decide to use the money to buy new clothes for Tip-Toes and pass her off as a debutante, Roberta Calhoun Van Rennsalaer, in the hope that she might marry a Florida millionaire and thereby gain financial security for them all. Tip-Toes warily agrees to the scheme, but dreams of marrying for love ("Looking for a Boy"). A plainly dressed Steve Burton appears, and he and Tip-Toes are immediately attracted to each other (reprise of "Looking for a Boy").

That night, local society gathers around the gaming tables at the Palm Beach Surf Club ("Lady Luck"). Sylvia has engaged two women, Binnie Oakland (Gertrude McDonald) and Denise Marshall (Lovey Lee), to teach the reluctant Steve some social skills ("When Do We Dance?"). The Kayes arrive, posing as members of society ("These Charming People"). Steve embraces Tip-Toes in a kissing game, and the two confess their mutual attraction ("That Certain Feeling"). Binnie and Denise, meanwhile, invite Al to the local Blue's Cafe ("Sweet and Low-Down"). Before Tip-Toes manages to reveal her true identity to Steve, she falls victim to amnesia as the result of a car accident. Al convinces Tip-Toes that she's a rich debutante; Sylvia discovers the incriminating photograph of Tip-Toes and Rollo; Rollo, under threat of disclosure by Al and Hen, goes along with the charade; and Tip-Toes accepts Steve's invitation to a party the following night on a rented yacht ("Finale").

The second act begins that next night, as the crew of the yacht welcomes Tip-Toes on board ("Our Little Captain"). Steve and Tip-Toes enjoy a moment together (reprise of "Looking for a Boy") and join in the general merriment ("It's a Great Little World!"). However, after Steve learns from Rollo about Tip-Toes's past as a vaudevillian, he accuses her of deceit; this confrontation awakens her memory, and she confesses all. Steve, for his part, claims that he is actually broke. As the others depart the yacht, Tip-Toes remains on board with Steve as proof of her devotion ("Nightie-Night").

The next day, after Tip-Toes performs at the Everglades Inn to pay for the bill she incurred there when she thought she was rich ("Tip-Toes"), she accepts a marriage proposal from Steve, who admits that he made up the story about being poor only to test her. All—not least Al and Hen—celebrate the happy outcome ("Finale").

As a romantic farce about lovers who have to overcome differences in social status, *Tip-Toes* echoed a number of previous Gershwin musicals. But this comedy of gold digging among the Palm Beach elite took a more mocking view of the ambitions of the nouveau riche and the pretensions of the upper classes, a view immediately established in the opening choruses about real-estate speculation and casino gambling, and epit-omized by the posturings of the Komical Kayes in "These Charming People."

At the same time, the show struck an unusually innocent or rather mock-innocent tone, with Tip-Toes especially maintaining a charming naïveté. Even at the play's end, she remarks, on receiving a diamond en-gagement ring, "Look how it sparkles! Isn't it marvelous what they do with imitation jewelry now-a-days?" Steve is just as ingenuous—he asks, in the show's last spoken line, "Gee, but I was dumb, wasn't I?"—and their union signals the triumph of unaffected simplicity over money and position. Sylvia and Rollo are in their own way childlike, and Al and Hen, as schemers go, are pretty guileless as well. No parental figure or social snob appears as an adversary. The play's predominant mood, with its game of pig in a poke, its impatience with social etiquette, and its pa-jama party for two, is one of capricious youth.[1]

Gershwin appropriately composed perhaps the most sweetly exuber-ant score of his career, including the most insouciant of fox-trots ("That Certain Feeling"), gavottes ("These Charming People"), chanteys ("Our Little Captain"), one-steps ("It's a Great Little World!"), and lullabies ("Nightie-Night"). Ira responded with particularly childlike lyrics, from the baby talk in "Nice Baby!" to the playful alliteration of "Tip-Toes" to the whimsical rhymes of "That Certain Feeling." Even a number of the song titles themselves—including "Nice Baby!" "Our Little Captain," "It's a Great Little World!" and "Nightie-Night"—evoked the nursery.

In creating so charming a show, the creators no doubt had in mind Queenie Smith and the Kern-Wodehouse musical *Sitting Pretty*, with which she had established her name, and whose "Bongo on the Congo" served Ira as a model for "These Charming People." But whereas *Sitting Pretty* essentially represented a reformulated Princess Theatre musical, *Tip-Toes* was more clearly a work of the mid-twenties, with a score, more to the point, by the Gershwins, its innocence underpinned by strains of melancholy and anxiety, as in those touching shifts to the minor mode in "Looking for a Boy" and "Nightie-Night" that suggest real heartache and loneliness. A certain restlessness and verve—as found in "Waiting for the Train," "When Do We Dance?" and "It's a Great Little World!" not to mention "Sweet and Low-Down"—in particular distinguished the score from the classic poise of Kern and Wodehouse.[2]

Ira further thought his lyrics to represent "some development in crafts-manship," including a first-act finale that "carried plot action for four or five minutes." This achievement involved Ira's growing sensitivity to musical form and rhetoric. In "Looking for a Boy," for instance, at that point in the verse when the music modulates to a minor mode, Tip-Toes reflects on her current unhappiness; conversely, as the music moves from minor to major in the bridge section of the chorus, she imagines her "tale of woe" dispersed by her dream lover's "Hello!" In "That Certain Feeling," to take another example, the words "I hit the ceiling" neatly accompany a big leap in the chorus's first phrase; when the music later reaches its highest note, the lyric arrives at its own climax: "Now we're together." Such subtleties, while found in Ira's earlier work, abound here.[3]

Aarons and Freedley provided a first-rate production. John Harwood directed, Sammy Lee and Earl Lindsay created the snazzy dances, John Wenger painted the smartly stylized sets, Kiviette (Yetta Kiviat) designed the elegant costumes, and duo-pianists Victor Arden and Phil Ohman enlivened the orchestra, conducted by William Daly. Queenie Smith was paired not with the usual bland juvenile but with Allen Kearns (1893–1956), the wry Canadian-born vaudevillian who, recalled Ira, stood "only a couple of mites taller" than his tiny leading lady and whose ingratiating stage presence charmed men and women alike. Andrew Tombes and Harry Watson Jr., two gifted "low comedians" of a kind best remembered through the work of W. C. Fields, provided some expert slapstick (in 1953 Ira remembered Watson as "one of the greatest comics I ever saw"), while Gertrude McDonald, Lovey Lee, and Amy Revere, in minor roles, supplied additional dance talent, as did the chorus of twenty-four women and twelve men.[4]

Meanwhile, the secondary romantic couple, Robert Halliday and Jeanette MacDonald, offered more cultivated voices. Both artists would subsequently attain their greatest success in operetta: Halliday in the Romberg operettas of the late 1920s, MacDonald in a series of Hollywood operettas from the 1930s and 1940s. Ira remembered MacDonald as not quite right, however, for musical comedy, and at least one of her numbers—a planned duet with Halliday titled "We"—was dropped early on. Audiences sensed that she was underused, but her "ingratiating" beauty made an impression nonetheless.[5]

Tip-Toes premiered in Washington, D.C., on November 24, 1925, and played in Newark, Philadelphia, and Baltimore before opening on Broadway. During this tryout period, the second act proved particularly troublesome, with four of its numbers—"Harlem River Chanty," "Harbor of Dreams," "Gather Ye Rosebuds," and "Dancing Hour"—dropped after Washington, and two new songs—first, "Life's Too Short to Be Blue," and eventually, "It's a Great Little World!"—added to replace "Gather

Ye Rosebuds." Among the dropped songs, "Harlem River Chanty," a second-act opener for Uncle Hen and the sailors—a jig that bespoke the Gershwins' abiding affection for *H.M.S. Pinafore*—survives, as does the harmonically adventurous "Gather Ye Rosebuds."[6]

Tip-Toes opened in New York on December 28 at the Liberty, where it followed on the heels of *Lady, Be Good!* Gershwin's skyrocketing fame raised expectations to a high pitch and, contrary to assertions about the star-driven nature of the twenties musical comedy, theatergoers turned out in droves mainly to hear the composer's latest, as the *Herald-Tribune* stated explicitly: "It was a hopeful and expectant audience that swarmed last night into the Liberty Theater—not because Queenie Smith was to whirl about on her toes, nor because Andrew Tombes was to rub his hands together and talk in that quick, funny way of his, or because Mr. Aarons and Mr. Freedley were the producers. They were, in fact, minor considerations. The major consideration was that George Gershwin wrote the music." The *Times* similarly attributed the "large and prominent" first-night crowd to Gershwin.[7]

Nor were hopes disappointed. The *Times* sniffed a bit at the material, but otherwise the press admired virtually every aspect of the show, Alexander Woollcott stating that he would need "the literary style of the City Directory to distribute all the bouquets that are due to those who compounded this festivity." As with Edward Shanks's response to *Primrose*, critics agreed that although the show broke no new ground, it represented a perfection of sorts; in the words of *Vogue,* it utilized "all the possibilities of the material." Woollcott again proved particularly eloquent in his praise of Gershwin's "pretty, rebel, infectious" music, which he thought his best yet for the theater: "It was, of course, Gershwin's evening, so sweet and sassy are the melodies he has poured out for this 'Tip-Toes,' so fresh and unstinted the gay, young flood of his invention." The critics discerned a number of potential song hits, including "Sweet and Low-Down" (performed at one point in the show with the chorus playing kazoo-trombones), but tended to overlook the number that over time became the show's most popular, "That Certain Feeling."[8]

Tip-Toes also brought Ira his first major recognition. Woollcott even warned readers from bestowing all the wreaths on George, "for it is his elder brother, Ira Gershwin, who writes the lyrics which helped George Gershwin's tunes in their journey across the land." The critics not only relished the inventive wit of Ira's lyrics—often singling out "These Charming People," whose rhyming of "blokes pass" and "faux pas," and "enjoy it" and "Detroit," seemed worthy of Wodehouse—but their ability to project across the footlights. After seeing the show, fellow lyricist Lorenz Hart wrote a note expressing his own admiration to Ira (whom he had not yet met): "Your lyrics . . . gave me as much pleasure as Mr. George Gershwin's music, and the utterly charming performance of Miss Queenie Smith. I have heard none so good this many a day. . . . It is a great pleasure to live at a time when light amusement in this country is at last losing its brutally cretin aspect. Such delicacies as your jingles prove that songs can be both popular and intelligent." Ira in turn told George that he thought this letter "swell," explaining that Hart was someone "about whose lyrics everybody is talking."[9]

Tip-Toes ran for 194 performances in New York—decades later, playwright Jerome Chodorov remembered this, his first musical, as "dazzling" and "unbelievable"—and then undertook a national tour with a cast headed by Smith and Richard Keene. Meanwhile, on July 5, 1926, another production starring Ona Munson (Tip-Toes), Eddie Buzzell (Steve), Eddie Nelson (Al), and Charles Howard (Hen) gave the West Coast premiere at San Francisco's Curran Theatre. A. F. Gillaspey of the *Bulletin* declared the musical an "unqualified success" that profited, above all, from "the clever handiwork of George Gershwin," while George C. Warren of the *Chronicle* had special praise as well for Munson, comparing her to a wood nymph who expresses "her love of life and movement by dancing."[10]

Some weeks later, on August 13, 1926, the show debuted in London's West End with two members of the original cast—Allen Kearns and Lovey Lee—joined by a mixed British-American troupe, the Americans including Dorothy Dixon (Tip-Toes) and John Kirby (Hen), the British including Laddie Cliff (Al), Evan Thomas (Rollo), and Vera Bryer (Sylvia). The London *Times* enthusiastically greeted the show—which contained two new numbers presumably by Gershwin: "Pig in a Poke," sung by Steve and Tip-Toes in the first act, and "At the Party," a second-act opening chorus—as the best musical comedy since the arrival the previous year of *No, No, Nanette* (1925), another show involving the corrupting power of money. As with Gershwin's two previous musicals with Fred Thompson, the *Times* was better disposed toward the book than most American papers: "There is a good story, well told, with plenty of telling lines, and, above all, there is abundant humour throughout." The London cast recorded highlights of the show for Columbia, leaving behind a vital account of this production along with some record of the tweakings that accompanied a transplanted musical comedy from this era.[11]

Tip-Toes, which enjoyed 182 performances at London's Winter Garden Theatre, never achieved the spectacular international success of *No, No, Nanette,* let alone the smash Friml and Romberg operettas; but over the next three years it played far and wide, including Australia, where it arrived at Sydney's Her Majesty's Theatre on May 7, 1927, before moving on to Melbourne's Theatre Royal on August 13, 1927. One particularly disenchanted Sydney viewer thought the show "a hideous example of the eternal Americanisation of everything. . . . With the true American spirit desperate efforts are made to atone for lack of artistic quality with wildly spectacular effects." But the Australian press generally liked the show, notwithstanding a weak leading lady in Sydney and a score that seemed to make little impression other than "cheerfully spontaneous and superficial" and "more subdued than much of the American sound of the period."[12]

Tip-Toes also appeared in Montreal in 1928, and, most unusually, in translation at Paris's Folies-Wagram in 1929. Produced by Edmond Roze, the latter production opened on April 27, with the celebrated Loulou Hégoburu as Tip-Toes and Adrien Lamy, interpolating "The Man I Love" as "La femme que j'aimais," as Steve Burton. Writing in *Le Figaro,* P. B. Gheusi lauded the opulent staging, the straightforward plot, and Hégoburu's "delectable" and "touching" performance; but it was Gershwin, "the most favored of contemporary musicians," who earned his greatest praise. "He deserves his success," wrote Gheusi (in a notice that also included a review of George Auric's operetta *Sans façons*), "for he knows how to compose and orchestrate, and he has an inspired talent worthy of Puccini or Massenet. He likewise understands the resources and the dangers of the latest developments in stage music and he makes the most of that. Auric, a musician with a brilliant future, would not be wasting his time to go and listen to him."[13]

Tip-Toes received less attention in later years, but in 1978 it was successfully revived by the Goodspeed Opera, since 1963 a leading venue for classic as well as new musical comedy. Produced by Michael Price, directed by Sue Lawless, and choreographed by Dan Siretta, this revival adhered closely to the original material then available, notwithstanding the incorporation of "Why Do I Love You?" (from *Tell Me More*) as a second-act song for Sylvia. Georgia Engel—the actress familiar to television audiences as Georgette on the *Mary Tyler Moore Show*—costarred with Russ Thacker.

Premiering on April 11, 1978, this revival ran two months at the Goodspeed Opera House in East Haddam, Connecticut, and then toured, including two weeks beginning March 21, 1979, at the Brooklyn Academy's Helen Carey Playhouse, giving a number of New York critics an opportunity to assess the work (sometimes twice). While the reviews disagreed over the merits of the book (some found it amusing, some dreadful, some simply inconsequential), most welcomed the show as "dazzling" and "totally adorable," "lovable," "delectable," "entirely infectious," and "exhilarating," Mel Gussow opining that the score reaffirmed Gershwin's place as "the premier theater composer of his time" (though John Simon, who detested the show, thought that most of the Gershwin songs ranged "from serviceable to useless").[14]

The Gershwin cache discovered in 1982 yielded a particularly lucky find as regarded *Tip-Toes:* the original (though uncredited) orchestrations for most of the show. This enabled Rob Fisher and associates, with the help of historic recordings, to reconstruct a full orchestral score, premiered as such in an acclaimed concert version of the work at New York's Weill Recital Hall on May 13, 1998, as part of the Gershwin centennial celebrations. The excellent cast, headed by Emily Loesser and Andy Taylor, subsequently recorded the work under Fisher's direction for New World Records, a release that offered further proof that the original orchestrations for Gershwin's shows nicely complemented the music's refinement and charm.[15]

While working on *Tip-Toes,* Gershwin also collaborated with composer Herbert Stothart and bookwriter-lyricists Oscar Hammerstein and Otto Harbach on an operetta, *Song of the Flame.* Characterized by more operatic singing than found in musical comedy, operetta had been rather moribund since World War I; but during the fall of 1924, two new exemplars—Rudolf Friml's *Rose-Marie* (co-composed with Stothart; book and lyrics, Hammerstein and Harbach), produced by Arthur Hammerstein, and Sigmund Romberg's *The Student Prince in Heidelberg* (book and lyrics, Dorothy Donnelly), produced by J. J. Shubert—enjoyed phenomenal success, outperforming any musical comedy of the time. By 1925 Oscar Hammerstein could assert, "There has been no change in theatrical fashion so swift and complete as that which has taken place since *Rose-Marie.*"[16]

Grandson and namesake of the famed opera impresario, son of theater manager William Hammerstein, and nephew of producer Arthur Hammerstein, Oscar Hammerstein II (1895–1960), true to family tradition, played a decisive role in this resurgence of operetta. He began his remarkable career primarily working with Stothart. After nudging Vincent Youmans toward operetta with *Wildflower* (1923) and bringing

Friml back to his operetta roots with *Rose-Marie*, he worked extensively with Romberg, Kern, and Rodgers, steering all three in the direction of operetta as well, in the process collaborating on an impressive number of hits, including Kern's *Sunny* (1925) and *Show Boat* (1927), Romberg's *Desert Song* (1926) and *The New Moon* (1928), and a popular series of works with Rodgers from *Oklahoma!* (1943) to *The Sound of Music* (1959).

For Hammerstein, the reemergence of operetta marked a welcome return to the cohesive singing play—as opposed to both the "smart musical farce" of the mid-teens and the "intimate musical comedy" of the early twenties. But if Hammerstein and his like-minded colleagues sought to bring back the "good old singing" of prewar operetta, the new operetta, as represented by *Rose-Marie* and *The Student Prince*, contained some distinctive features as well, including an emphasis on spectacle and melodrama (including a murder in the former and a doomed love affair in the latter) and some incorporation of musical-comedy styles and forms. Calling this subgenre "Broadway operetta," Richard Traubner has suggested that its "full-blooded" romanticism marked a response to the "close-up intimacy and spectacular passion" of the silent screen.[17]

In the wake of *Rose-Marie*, Arthur and Oscar Hammerstein, along with Harbach and Stothart, planned another show with Friml, this time with a Russian setting; but after Friml, reportedly reluctant to have to share credit again with Stothart, pulled out, Arthur Hammerstein hired Gershwin to cowrite the score. Hammerstein similarly had paired the trusted Stothart not only with Friml for *Rose-Marie*, but before that with Vincent Youmans for *Wildflower*. Meanwhile, Stothart had worked on no less than seven shows with Oscar Hammerstein (often partnered with Harbach) in the early 1920s. Gershwin was thus joining an experienced team who, working closely together, had successfully contrived the return of operetta to Broadway.[18]

Except for Oscar Hammerstein, only a few years Gershwin's senior, they were also a relatively older group. Arthur Hammerstein (1872–1955) and Otto Harbach (1873–1963) had established their careers in the early 1910s working together with Friml on some successful operettas. Born in Milwaukee, Stothart (1885–1949) started out in the Midwest, but by the 1920s he had moved to New York and become Arthur Hammerstein's favorite conductor-composer. In the musicals that Stothart cowrote with Youmans, Friml, and—as it turned out—Gershwin, he and his collaborators worked independently as well as together, though the nature of these joint ventures remains murky. Stothart never wrote a hit song by himself (he cowrote his best-known number, "I Wanna Be Loved by You," with Bert Kalmar and Harry Ruby); his principal talent was as a conductor and arranger, and as a composer of incidental music. In the 1930s he settled in Hollywood, where until his death in 1949 he scored and conducted films for MGM, in the process earning numerous Academy Award nominations, winning an Oscar in 1939 for *The Wizard of Oz* (which featured songs by Harold Arlen and Yip Harburg).[19]

Oscar Hammerstein sketched out the plot for *Song of the Flame* in Paris in early 1925. Later the same year, while cowriting the script, Harbach discussed the process of creating a book for the Broadway musical stage with *Theatre Magazine*. Bookwriters, he explained, first needed to create "a scenario which unfolds the story from beginning to end, introduces all the characters and discloses their relation to each other and interweaves all the plot-strands." They then had to decide where to introduce musical numbers and to what dramatic purpose in order to ensure variety and "climactic order." However, he advised that they write the dialogue only after the score was complete. Once a show went into rehearsal, he continued, the delicate balance of music, drama, and dance, along with the inevitable limitations of the cast, invariably meant extensive rewriting, sometimes requiring bookwriters "to rebuild the entire act structure." Ultimately, musical comedy and operetta demanded "romance, gaiety, glamour," for "mere glitter and tinsel will not suffice. . . . However fanciful the story, however fantastic the treatment, there must be an underlying reality closer to the human heart than realism—or the audience will not *care*." For a Broadway librettist, Harbach sounded an unusually earnest note in this essay, but the methods and ideals outlined here resembled those of Gershwin's bookwriting collaborators in general.[20]

Set against the background of the Russian revolution and its aftermath, *Song of the Flame* features a large cast of principals divided more or less into serious and comic characters. The former include Aniuta (known as "the Flame"), a washerwoman whose revolutionary call for a liberated Russia has made her a national heroine; her beloved Prince Vladimir ("Volodya") Kazanov, an officer in the White army; Konstantin Danilov, an opportunistic revolutionary in love with Aniuta; and Natasha, a Tartar firebrand in love with Konstantin. The more comic characters include Volodya's rakish uncle, Count Boris Kazanov; the foreman of the Kazanov estate, Nicholas Simkov; and two peasant girls, Grusha and Nadya, smitten with Nicholas.

The first act opens with a prologue set on a crowded street in Moscow in March 1917. After Konstantin (Greek Evans) joins the people in a lament ("Far Away"), he angers them by ridiculing their support of the Kerensky government. Aniuta (Tessa Kosta) comes to his defense with a rousing march ("Song of the Flame"). The police disperse the crowd and arrest Konstantin.

Later that year, in October, on a canal tributary of the Volga by the Kazanov summer palace, the local peasants, including Grusha (Dorothy Mackaye), lightheartedly complain about a woman's lot ("Woman's Work Is Never Done"). Grusha and her strapping boyfriend, Nicholas (Hugh Cameron), tease each other ("Great Big Bear"). Volodya (Guy Robertson), about to rejoin the White army, and Aniuta signal each other from afar ("The Signal") and promise fidelity ("Cossack Love Song").

Konstantin, now a commissar for the local Soviet, suggests that he and Boris (Bernard Gorcey) divide the Kazanov jewels between them rather than allow them to be confiscated by the Russian government. Natasha (Phoebe Brune) tries to intimidate Konstantin ("Tartar!"), but the latter remains enamored of Aniuta ("You May Wander Away"). That night, at one of the gates of the Kazanov palace, Volodya thwarts Boris's attempt to transfer the jewels to Konstantin. Outside Aniuta's lodging, she and Volodya reaffirm their love, while Natasha offers to help Konstantin obtain the jewels. A restive crowd gathers, and although Aniuta urges calm, Konstantin incites the mob to attack the Kazanovs ("Finaletto," including a reprise of "Song of the Flame").

At the Kazanov palace, where a drunken revel is under way, Boris and his friends intend to have their way with Grusha, who has become drunk ("Vodka"); but before harm comes to her, Konstantin and the mob arrive. As the act ends, the romance between Aniuta and Volodya seems threatened as the former finds the latter in what only appears to be a compromising situation with Nadya (Ula Sharon); and Volodya, to his dismay, learns of Aniuta's identity as the Flame ("Finale").

The second act opens two years later, on New Year's Eve 1919, in Grusha's room at her boardinghouse in Paris's Latin Quarter. She, Nicholas, and Boris work for Konstantin, who owns a Russian restaurant in Montmartre, the Cafe des Caucasiens, which he purchased with the Kazanov jewels stolen two years earlier, though he uses an unwitting Nicholas as a front man. Grusha cannot decide between Nicholas and Boris ("I Want Two Husbands"). Having unjustly served time for the theft of the jewels, Aniuta arrives in Paris, hoping for a reconciliation with Volodya ("Midnight Bells"), though Konstantin still wants her for himself (reprise of "You May Wander Away").

Outside the Cafe des Caucasiens, an impoverished Volodya hopes to expose Konstantin and reunite with Aniuta (reprise of "Cossack Love Song"). In the cafe's samovar room, exiled Russians recall their native land (the ballet "The First Blossom" and assorted folk songs). The avengers, a White-Russian vigilante group, expose and intimidate Konstantin. Grusha chooses a vindicated Nicholas as her husband, while Aniuta and Volodya, his wealth restored, resolve to return to Russia and fight for the people ("Finale Ultimo").

Hammerstein and Harbach patently modeled their story along the lines of *Rose-Marie,* with a similar love quadrangle, and with exotic Russian and Tartar elements substituting for mythic French Canadian and Indian ones. Even the names of the heroines (The Flame/La Flamme) resembled each other, as did some of the song titles ("Cossack Love Song"/"Indian Love Song"). However, adapting the Russian revolution as the subject of an operetta required special dexterity, notwithstanding the precedent of such works as Charles Lecocq's *La fille de Madame Angot* (1872) and Franz von Suppé's *Fatinitza* (1876). (In subsequent years, with *South Pacific* and *The Sound of Music,* Hammerstein pursued the idea of framing Broadway musicals within the context of modern cataclysmic events.) The authors' solution was to intertwine two separate stories: a melodrama with strong shades of verismo opera centered on the principal love quadrangle, and a farce structured around the Grusha-Nicholas-Boris subplot. Boris's satirical commentary especially provided some comic relief. About the Communist takeover of Petrograd, for instance, he complains, "They'll take everything," to which Volodya says, "Rubbish," and Boris responds, "They'll take the rubbish too." (Nicholas, however, received one of the biggest laughs of the evening for a gag, presumably inspired by the 1925 Scopes trial, that played on the words *evolution* and *revolution:* "Nicky, do you believe in evolution?" asks Konstantin, to which Nicholas answers, "I don't think we'll ever live to see it.")[21]

The work's stance vis-à-vis the Russian revolution proved as ambivalent as that of then current American foreign policy toward the Soviet Union, a policy marked by nonrecognition of the government on the one hand and humanitarian aid and business ventures on the other. The show depicts the Russian aristocracy as largely decadent and exploitative and bestows considerable sympathy on Aniuta, whose "Song of the Flame" is heard repeatedly, either sung or as incidental music. At the same time, the musical's villain, Konstantin, is a Communist, and its hero, Volodya, a counterrevolutionary. In short, the show implies the desirability of social reform, but not of the Bolshevik variety.

A few of the show's numbers—"Far Away," "Song of the Flame,"

"Cossack Love Song," "Vodka," and the ballet "The First Blossom"—
were credited to both Gershwin and Stothart. (Yet another alleged collaboration, the love duet "You Are You," was dropped before the New
York opening in favor of "Cossack Love Song.") In addition, Gershwin
independently wrote the music for "Women's Work Is Never Done," "The
Signal," and "Midnight Bells," while Stothart contributed "Great Big
Bear," "Tartar!" "You May Wander Away," and "I Want Two Husbands."

Some of the songs—including the stirring "Song of the Flame" and
the amusing "Vodka"—revealed a marked Slavic profile, though to what
extent either Gershwin or Stothart drew on or consulted actual folk or
popular Russian music remains unknown. At the least, they seem to have
adapted the main theme of "Song of the Flame" from the Russian folk
song "Kazbeck," and that of "Cossack Love Song" from the Russian song
"Minka," or perhaps its Ukrainian cognate, "You Deceived Me" ("Ty zh
mene pidmanula"). "Far Away" also apparently derived from Russian
folk music. Gershwin gleaned some inspiration as well from his knowledge of Eastern European concert music, with "Women's Work Is Never
Done" borrowing frankly from Bedřich Smetana's tone-poem *Vltava*.
Moreover, the show's very opening contained unmetered chanting related to the music of the Russian Orthodox church.[22]

Gershwin's music reflected the work's dramatic needs in other ways,
with "The Signal," for instance, emitting a courtly quality appropriate
to the aristocratic Volodya, and "Midnight Bells" creating a poignant
mood for the uncertain Aniuta in Paris on New Year's Eve. In contrast,
Stothart provided some of the work's more generic songs—including a
lively dance number, "Great Big Bear" and a lilting waltz, adapted from
Weber, "You May Wander Away"—suggesting that Arthur Hammerstein
engaged Gershwin not so much to give the work some Jazz Age pep, as
one might suppose, as to help provide some romantic atmosphere and
dramatic integrity. The overall result was a dignified and at times lovely
score: operettaish, to be sure, but distinct from the more sentimental ones
of Friml and Romberg. Still, *Song of the Flame* was hardly an ideal vehicle for Gershwin, whose characteristic wit could be heard only sporadically, as in the boozy "Vodka," complete with musical hiccups.

Song of the Flame also occasioned Gershwin's first full-scale collaboration with arranger-orchestrator Robert Russell Bennett (1894–1981),
who had previously scored *Wildflower* and *Rose-Marie* for Arthur Hammerstein and assisted on the orchestrations for *Lady, Be Good!* as well.
(Bennett had wanted to collaborate with Gershwin at least as early as
March 1920, when he praised the composer for having written the "snap-

piest" songs of the past year.) A well-trained musician who would spend the years 1926–1929 studying intermittently with Nadia Boulanger in Paris, Bennett wrote many chamber and orchestral works of his own, but had his greatest success as the orchestrator of literally hundreds of stage and film musicals between 1920 and 1975. After *Song of the Flame,* he orchestrated a number of other shows for Gershwin, whose serious work he valued highly.[23]

Bennett later recalled that during these years, Gershwin's fans had "turned his head, in fact turned it so far around that it was on straight again. He was still full of youthful fun that protected him from being a social liability." For his part, Oscar Hammerstein—according to his biographer—thought Gershwin "conceited and cocky," but "extraordinarily talented and rather sweet" and "not difficult to work with." The show's prima donna, Tessa Kosta, confirmed that Gershwin "was very attractive, easy to work with, and cooperative in every way."[24]

Arthur Hammerstein originally wanted Mary Ellis, the original Rose-Marie, to play Aniuta, but Kosta proved a suitable alternative. One of the leading operetta stars of the 1910s and 1920s—earlier in 1925 she had starred in a Broadway revival of Gilbert and Sullivan's *Princess Ida*—Chicago-born Kosta (1893–1981) was a dark beauty who possessed a lovely soprano voice, if not the most accomplished acting abilities. Hammerstein at first cast two little-known performers—Allan Rogers and Edmund Burke—as Volodya and Konstantin, but during the tryout period replaced them with more familiar names: the handsome Guy Robertson, a baritone who had played the male leads in both *Wildflower* and the touring company of *Rose-Marie;* and another baritone, Greek Evans, who had created the role of Doctor Engel in *The Student Prince,* introducing the song "Golden Days" on the Broadway stage.

Flush with the profits from *Rose-Marie,* Hammerstein spent about $250,000 on what would be the most lavish production of Gershwin's Broadway career. He commissioned Joseph Urban to design the ornate, towering sets and Mark Mooring to create the richly textured costumes. He further engaged, in addition to an eleven-man chorus, the fifty-two-member Russian Art Choir, a mixed chorus featured at various times throughout the show, including a cappella renditions of Russian folk songs arranged by its director, Alexander Fine, in the Cafe des Caucasiens scene. The same scene's ballet, "The First Blossom" (described in the program as "symbolic of Russia's long winter of adversity and the arrival of the first blossom of victorious ideals"), also showcased forty-two women from the American Ballet. The program book advertised the show as "a romantic opera" with "Tessa Kosta and a distinguished company of 200," which, counting the fifty-odd-piece orchestra over which Stothart presided, may not have been an exaggeration.

Song of the Flame premiered in Wilmington on December 10 and moved on to Washington, D.C., and Baltimore before opening in New York on December 30 at the 44th Street Theatre, the spacious 1,463–seat auditorium best known for its operetta productions but also remembered today for housing the premiere of Virgil Thomson's opera, *Four Saints in Three Acts,* in 1934. The bejeweled first-night audience was as opulent as the production, with a top ticket, by one account, going for a very expensive eleven dollars. Even so, the show opened amid speculation about how much money Hammerstein could hope to recoup; the orchestra alone cost about four thousand dollars in weekly salaries.

Fortunately, from Wilmington, Washington, and Baltimore to New York and Boston, where the show played after 219 performances on Broadway, the reviews were rapturous. Audiences were "dazzled" and "awed" by this "magnificent," "sumptuous," "stupendous," and "resplendent" production, further described as "a spectacle that beggars description" *(Wilmington Evening Journal),* "one of those productions that you dream about but seldom see" (Larry Barretto in the *Bookman*), "a colossal and gorgeously spectacular production" (Walter Winchell in the *Evening Graphic*), "one of the seven wonders of the modern world" (Robert Coleman in the *Mirror*), and "a perfect thing" (Burns Mantle in the *Daily News*).[25]

Though perhaps most impressed with the sets, the costumes, and (especially in Boston) the Russian Art Choir, the critics cheered every aspect of the production but the "ponderous," "weighty," "trashy," "flimsy," and "hopeless" script. The critics accordingly appreciated the show to the extent that they could view the story as mere scaffolding for what the *Baltimore Sun* called a "super-pageant." Only rarely did a review, like George Jean Nathan's in *Judge,* opine that "the libretto is so poor that the virtues of the entertainment have a tough time battling against it."

Nor did critics find the connection with the Russian revolution particularly troubling, though Brooks Atkinson in the *Times* at least raised an eyebrow, writing, "to fashion a romantic theme upon a frightful social gestation, is perhaps not the quintessence of literary propriety." On the contrary, a number of reviews thought the show marked by "good taste," while Alan Dale wryly regarded the setting as a welcome change of pace from the French revolution, "which has been so overused that there have been rumors to the effect that it was really enacted for the sake of the stages of various countries." "After all," concluded the *Boston Transcript*, "it is the prerogative of operettas to sugar coat life beyond recognition."

The critics had little to say about the score, in part no doubt because the monumental production so overwhelmed the music, but perhaps also because of the uncertainty regarding the precise nature of the collaboration, left unspecified by the program. (A few reviews wrongly assumed that Gershwin had composed the more lighthearted numbers, Stothart the more romantic ones.) Most remarks about the music centered on issues of authenticity, the *Evening World* commenting, "Besides real Slavic music sung by Russians, the Anglo-Saxon songs of Mr. Gershwin and Mr. Stothart, sung by the Anglo-Saxon voices of Miss Kosta and her troupe seem somehow slender." But the critics widely admired what the *Wilmington Evening Journal* called the score's "Tschaikowsky-like splendor," while the *Boston Transcript* reasoned, "Russian folk-song and color, strained through the conventions of Viennese operetta and enlivened by frequent incursions of American jazz may bear only a slight resemblance to Mussorgsky; but they do provide acceptable diversion of a pseudo-slavic sort."[26]

In 1926 the Victor Light Opera Company recorded both "Song of the Flame" and "Cossack Love Song," helping to popularize these two numbers. But the show's viability clearly depended on its sumptuous production values, mitigating against revivals of the work. In 1930, however, Warner Brothers–First National released a Technicolor motion-picture version with the same title, directed by Alan Crosland, with the musical numbers staged by Jack Haskell. Now thought to be lost, the film starred the attractive team of soprano Bernice Claire and baritone Alexander Gray as Aniuta and Volodya, with Wallace Beery as Konstantin and Metropolitan Opera mezzo-soprano Alice Gentle as Natasha.

As had already become standard Hollywood procedure, First National not only altered the show's story but replaced original songs with new numbers composed by in-house composers. Richard Barrios states that the studios justified the latter custom by citing the need to offset a score's familiarity with new material, but adds, "the more dominant reason was that the most resolutely mediocre new song would bring more profit to a studio-owned outfit than a preexisting one over which the studio had no dominion." In this particular instance, First National, which featured only three numbers from the show ("Song of the Flame," "Cossack Love Song," and "You May Wander Away"), introduced new songs by, for the most part, composer Harry Akst and lyricist Grant Clarke (Gershwin thought Akst, who wrote "Dinah," "Baby Face," and other hit songs, "one of the cleverest men in Tin Pan Alley").[27]

The reviews described this movie adaptation, which enjoyed only a modest success, as "extravagantly unreal, entirely out of the tradition of naturalistic cinema," with "scenes of wild disorder, of mobs rushing through streets and across the countryside at night, torches flaming, men and women shouting and singing." The *Commonweal* further thought the film "a stirring picture of the early days of the Russian revolution," but *Life* missed the charm of the original show, while *Photoplay* regarded the whole idea of "comic-opera bolshevists" as "silly."[28]

In 1934 Warner Brothers released a more abbreviated film version, *The Flame Song,* which once again starred Bernice Claire but otherwise comprised a different cast, including Greek Evans in the role he had created on Broadway, Konstantin. Directed by Joseph Henabery, this Vitaphone "Broadway Brevity" short, which survives, altered the Hammerstein-Harbach story line even more completely than had the 1930 version; the references to the Russian revolution expunged, the newly conceived plot concerned rival royal factions in the mythical country of Florestan. *The Flame Song* featured only "Song of the Flame" and "Cossack Love Song" from the original score, though it used some other tunes from the show as background music, as may well have been the case with the 1930 feature film.

Song of the Flame was not Gershwin's first musical adapted for film, only the first to have sound. Indeed, four Gershwin musicals had already made it to the silver screen: *La La Lucille* (1920), a Universal production directed by its two leading men, Eddie Lyons (as John) and Lee Moran (as Britton); *Tip Toes* (1927), a British National production directed by Herbert Wilcox and featuring a cast headed by no less than Dorothy Gish (as Tip-Toes), Will Rogers (as Hen), and Nelson Keys (as Al); *Lady Be Good* (1928), a First National production directed by Richard Wallace and starring Jack Mulhall and Dorothy Mackaill; and *Oh, Kay!* (1928), a First National production directed by Mervyn LeRoy and starring one of the era's most popular actresses, Colleen Moore (as Lady Kay).[29]

As with later sound adaptations, these silent Gershwin film musicals adhered only loosely to the plots of their Broadway counterparts. Reviewing *Oh, Kay!* the *Times* noted, "As is invariably the case in the transferring of a musical comedy story to the screen, the film version of 'Oh, Kay' is longer and sillier than the original." But film critics expected such pictures to reflect the low humor widely associated with musical comedy, and duly treated them with forbearance unless impossibly inane, as seems to have been the case with *Tip Toes*. Even so, the popular adaptation of musical comedies to the silent screen belies the common notion that the twenties Broadway musical lacked a certain dramatic viability, and further suggests the ongoing dialogue between motion pictures and musical comedies that operated from their coeval beginnings.[30]

Theater musicians—whether pit bands, pianists, or organists—often accompanied these silent-film musicals with selections from the original score, to the point that a Chicago showing of *The Student Prince* (1927) featured a small chorus singing the songs. Reviews typically paid scant attention to the music (which, after all, was likely to change from theater to theater), making it difficult to generalize about such practices. However, extant cue sheets for *Lady Be Good* and *Oh, Kay!*—the former compiled by James C. Bradford, the latter by Eugene Conte—are enough alike to suggest some common practice: out of their nearly fifty musical cues (each averaging about a minute or two in length), both cue sheets include only three songs (sometimes repeated) from their original shows; most of the material derived rather from other popular and light classical scores, with a Victor Herbert melody providing the main theme for *Lady Be Good*.[31]

Moreover, neither Bradford nor Conte made any apparent effort to correlate the Gershwin tunes with their original dramatic contexts, though a comment by *Variety* in its review of *Oh, Kay!*—"For a picture it follows the show very closely as the organist peals off the tunes from the musical"—suggests that more scrupulous underscoring might have occurred. Still, most playings of these films presumably would have featured at least some of the show's big hits. Moviegoers sometimes had the opportunity to purchase sheet music from the show in theater lobbies as well. In such ways, the silent-film Gershwin musicals—only some of which are known to survive—no doubt aided in the early dissemination of the composer's music.[32]

Chapter Twenty

Oh, Kay! and Other Works (1926)

In marked contrast to 1925, Gershwin produced only one major work in 1926, the musical comedy *Oh, Kay!*—though in the course of the year he also launched his *Five Preludes* for piano and wrote "That Lost Barber Shop Chord" for the show *Americana*.

A two-act revue written by J. P. McEvoy with assistance from Morrie Ryskind, *Americana* starred Lew Brice (Fanny Brice's brother) and Roy Atwell, with a featured spot for Helen Morgan. Opening on July 26 at the small Belmont Theatre on 48th Street, the show, which ran for 224 performances, satirized American life, including an after-dinner speech at a Rotary Club and an awkward attempt by a father to talk to his son about sex; it also took aim at opera ("Cavalier Americana") as well as Shakespeare by way of Romberg ("The Student Prince of Denmark"). Critics welcomed the show as refreshingly clever—a "revue of ideas," as the *Times* headline stated—and recognized, in this new type of smart and intimate entertainment, the influence of André Charlot, the French producer who had recently transferred two of his successful West End revues to Broadway as the *Charlot's Revues* of 1924 and 1926 (which actually opened in late 1925). (Both *Charlot*s brought American recognition to their stars—Canadian Beatrice Lillie and British Gertrude Lawrence and Jack Buchanan—and helped popularize the work of Noël Coward as well.)[1]

Composers Con Conrad and Henry Souvaine, collaborating with McEvoy, wrote most of the score to *Americana*, but the congenial group of the Gershwins, Ryskind, and Phil Charig, working in varied permutations, made additional contributions. Gershwin's one song for the show, "That Lost Barber Shop Chord" (lyrics, Ira), performed by five black singers, parodied Arthur Sullivan's popular "The Lost Chord" (to a poem by Adelaide Proctor). In place of an organist seeking in vain for an idly struck chord that had brought "perfect peace," a bootblack (Louis Lazarin) tries to recapture a harmony heard sung by a vocal quartet in a Harlem barbershop (the Pan-American Quartette) that had transported him to "Kingdom Come." The song's verse depicts (with the help of some chromatically rising triads) the thrill of discovery, while the chorus (at one point marked by some Eastern-sounding augmented seconds) be-musedly mourns paradise lost. Although Harms published the music for solo voice, not vocal quartet, the piano accompaniment implies various barbershop-type harmonies.

Gershwin never again attempted anything so explicitly geared to bar-bershop singing. In this instance, he may have been inspired by the Rev-elers, whose work he admired, and who produced a number of hit record-ings in 1926. At the same time, the song's text intimates that he had African American quartets in mind as well. Although barbershop quar-tets enjoyed a certain amount of whimsical self-referentiality—as wit-ness Lewis F. Muir's "Play That Barbershop Chord" (1910; lyrics, Ballard MacDonald and William Tracey)—Gershwin's effort may have been too ironic to establish itself in the repertoire. The song proved, nonetheless, one of the high points of *Americana,* its subtle harmonic vocabulary sporting a sophistication no doubt related to general theatrical trends.[2]

Gershwin wrote his next show for Gertrude Lawrence (1898–1952), the previously mentioned English actress who had made a splash on Broad-way in the *Charlot's Revues,* though this new work—eventually titled *Oh, Kay!*—would truly launch her career. One of the period's few musical-comedy stars equally successful on both sides of the Atlantic, Lawrence was admired for, among other things, her charm onstage and her skill in playing roles across the social spectrum. Reviewing the *1926 Charlot's Revue,* Alexander Woollcott wrote, "She dances with magical lightness and her voice is true and clear; the personification of style and sophisti-cation, she can also convulse an audience with a bit of cockney horse-play or bring tears to its eyes with a sentimental ballad. She is the ideal star." Guy Bolton similarly spoke of her ability "to bring off that sure fire combination of the tear and the laugh with the artistry of Chaplin," whom Lawrence revered.[3]

For critic Harold Clurman, Lawrence embodied London's "smart set" of the 1920s, that nexus of aristocrats and theater people associated as well with Noël Coward, a friend of Lawrence's since childhood: "It was the time of self-congratulatory flippancy, giddy pleasure in believing in nothing but prickly sensation, and appreciation of one's own appreciation of the dash and swish of it all. Bad manners took on the sheen of the best. Accompanying all this was an undertone of smart music, titillatingly sentimental, champagne induced, as in a wild party where even the knell of doom becomes transposed to a beguiling tinkle." During this time Lawrence, though married, pursued love affairs in both New York and London, and was known for enjoying a good time and a drink. Following *Oh, Kay!* she starred in another Gershwin show, *Treasure Girl* (1928), and went on to create the roles of Amanda in *Private Lives* (1931), Liza Elliott in *Lady in the Dark* (1941), and Anna Leonowens in *The King and I* (1951).[4]

Oh, Kay!—produced by Aarons and Freedley and called, at various stages, *Mayfair, Miss Mayfair,* and *Cheerio!*—had a book by Guy Bolton and P. G. Wodehouse and a score by the Gershwins, assisted by Howard Dietz. Bolton and Wodehouse—who had cowritten the books to most of Kern's Princess Theatre shows, a series evoked even by the title of this new comedy, whose plot in particular recalled that for *Oh, Boy!* (1917)—took credit for spearheading this collaboration with Lawrence; but other sources report that the actress herself chose an offer from Aarons and Freedley over Ziegfeld because of their connection with Gershwin.[5]

Lawrence and Gershwin had been friends since meeting each other through Jules Glaenzer in late 1923. Some months later, Lawrence attended the premiere of the *Rhapsody in Blue* and a reception afterward at Condé Nast's, at which Gershwin arrived late, his hands, as she recalled, bandaged from the strain of the concert. When Gershwin arrived in London in 1928 for the West End production of *Oh, Kay!* Lawrence accompanied him to his fittings for suits on Savile Row and his shopping expeditions to buy shirts and ties at Hawes and Curtis's and hats at Schott's. "But he never lost his head size," she remarked. In her memoirs, she further described Gershwin as "a great man," as someone who helped raise money for charities and visited the stately homes of England, but remained a "serious, hard-working young man," sentiments reflected in a familiar photograph of the two, with Lawrence looking up admiringly at the composer. The Gershwins, for their part, greatly appreciated "Gertie's" talent, Ira finding her "enchanting" onstage, though he never developed the same warm rapport with her as did his brother.[6]

Perhaps in response to her association with revue, Bolton and Wodehouse, who worked on the show over the summer, conceived the whole as "a series of block comedy scenes tied together by a plot," as sketches each ending with "laughs and a final twist." They also decided to make bootlegging their theme. The Eighteenth Amendment, ratified in 1919, had long been good for a gag, and a strong strain of anti-Prohibitionism had run through many of Gershwin's shows over the years, especially the *Scandals*. But the dire consequences of the Volstead Act—indiscriminate arrests, contempt for the law, deaths from poisoned alcohol, and the growth of organized crime and gang warfare as well as government graft and corruption—had begun to take their toll, prompting congressional hearings in April 1926. Bolton and Wodehouse apparently felt that the hypocrisy surrounding Prohibition could stand a good send-up, one, moreover, apropos of Lawrence's talents and sensibilities; they also may have intended the show as a parody of William Anthony McGuire's successful melodrama *Twelve Miles Out* (1925), whose setting and even story line they seem to have adopted with satiric intent.[7]

Aarons and Freedley also cast, as Lawrence's vis-à-vis, Oscar Shaw (1887–1967), a dapper entertainer who had been in a number of the Princess shows and who was, recalled Wodehouse in 1960, "the best singing, dancing, light comedy juvenile of that epoch—or, in my opinion, of any since." For Shorty McGee, the main comic role, Bolton and Wodehouse wanted Victor Moore (1876–1962), a vaudevillian whose credits included playing the popular character Shorty McCabe (the inspiration, apparently, for the name of this new character). Aarons and Freedley warily agreed to the idea—"Moore's diffident style, his querulous whine, his fatuous, blundering garrulity, were lost on the two Beau Brummels who were presenting the show," recalled Bolton and Wodehouse—but were so impressed with the comedian's "staggering triumph" in *Oh, Kay!* that they went on to feature him in another five productions, three of them Gershwin musicals.[8]

The producers also requested that Bolton and Wodehouse create parts for two young actresses, Constance Carpenter and Mayor Jimmy Walker's girlfriend, Betty Compton, whose credits included an appearance in *Americana*. Elected mayor in 1925, Walker was friendly with Aarons and Freedley, in whose office at the New Amsterdam Theatre he reportedly told Bolton and Wodehouse, "With the Lawrence dame, the Gershwin score and you two gentlemen, *Oh, Kay* can't miss. All it needs is a nice little part for Betty." Bolton and Wodehouse presumably derived the name of the show's romantic male lead, Jimmy Winter, from New York's "gay" and "amusing" new mayor.[9]

While working on the score, Ira spent six weeks at Mt. Sinai Hospital following an emergency appendectomy. On his release he was so far behind that, depending on the source, either he accepted his friend Howard Dietz's offer to assist on the lyrics, or else he and George sought out Dietz because the journeyman lyricist—still a year away from his celebrated partnership with composer Arthur Schwartz—would be, in Dietz's words, "less demanding of both credit and money" than an established figure like Wodehouse. In any case, Dietz helped write the lyrics for some of the show's songs, including "Heaven on Earth," "Oh, Kay!" and possibly "Clap Yo' Hands," and came up with the title for another, "Someone to Watch Over Me"—an inspired stroke, as the phrase *watch over* neatly fitted Gershwin's downward leap of an octave. Ira offered Dietz a fair enough share of the royalties for "Heaven on Earth" and "Oh, Kay!" but as the proceeds for these two songs came to naught, he subsequently suggested canceling their financial arrangement in order to avoid bothersome paperwork. Dietz retained some bitterness about this, but stated nonetheless, "I was very proud to work with the great Gershwin, and I would have done it for nothing, which I did."[10]

Act 1 of *Oh, Kay!* opens in Jimmy Winter's summer home in Beachampton, Long Island, as some of his girlfriends, including Molly Morse (Betty Compton) and Mae (Constance Carpenter), prepare for his arrival ("The Woman's Touch"). During his absence and without his knowledge, some rumrunners living on a yacht offshore—including the Duke of Durham, a ne'er-do-well English aristocrat (Gerald Oliver Smith); his sister, Lady Kay (Gertrude Lawrence); and two assistants, Larry Potter (Harland Dixon) and Shorty McGee (Victor Moore)—have used the house's cellar to store bootlegged stock. The twins Phillippa ("Phil") and Dolly Ruxton (Marion and Madeleine Fairbanks), also friends of Jimmy, have their eye on the titled duke, but Larry suggests himself as an attractive alternative ("Don't Ask!"). Jimmy and his wife, Constance Appleton (Sascha Beaumont), just married, arrive and Shorty, having scared off a new butler and maid earlier in the day, poses as the butler in order to keep watch over the cellar. When Constance learns that her marriage is null and void because Jimmy's former wife has refused to grant an annulment, she storms off, leaving Jimmy to the care of his girlfriends ("Dear Little Girl").

Later that night, Kay steals into Jimmy's home after a shoot-out with Jansen, a revenue officer (Harry T. Shannon). Jimmy recognizes Kay as the girl in a motorboat who the previous summer had come to his rescue when he nearly drowned, and the two muse on the circumstances that have reunited them ("Maybe"). When Jansen enters looking for Kay, she impersonates Jimmy's new wife and finds that she must spend the night in his home.

As the second scene opens the next morning, the duke anxiously seeks the missing Kay, while Larry assumes an optimistic attitude ("Clap Yo' Hands"). Jimmy and Kay once again pose as newlyweds before a suspicious Jansen ("Do, Do, Do"). When Constance and her father, Judge Appleton (Frank Gardiner), appear, Kay pretends to be the butler's wife, Jane the maid. As word of a successful annulment arrives, Constance and the judge urge a wedding that afternoon to avoid a scandal, while Kay, realizing that Jimmy and Constance do not love each other, resolves to prevent the marriage ("Finale").

The second act opens later that day, with wedding preparations in full swing ("Bride and Groom"). As Dolly makes headway with the duke, Larry flirts with Phil ("Fidgety Feet"). Kay yearns for a man of her own ("Someone to Watch Over Me"). Despite a disastrous lunch with Shorty and Kay (as butler and maid) serving Constance and the judge, Jimmy retains his good spirits ("Heaven on Earth"). Jansen interrupts the wedding ceremony and arrests Jimmy on smuggling charges as Constance and the judge withdraw, appalled. Thrown into the cellar, Jimmy, Kay, and the duke make their escape.

That evening, a party of friends at the Indian Inlet Inn enthusiastically greets Kay ("Oh, Kay!"). Jansen reveals himself as a rival bootlegger, Captain Blackbird; outwitted by Larry and Shorty, he threatens to expose Kay as an illegal alien, but Jansen is once again foiled as he learns that Jimmy and Kay were married earlier in the day ("Finale").[11]

Though basically a farce, the show was also something of a satire, its main targets including Prohibition and American self-righteousness. "Say, do you know WHY I joined the Revenue Service?" Jansen asks Jimmy, who replies, "I know—don't tell me, the stuff got too expensive to buy." The judge, meanwhile, has built his career on "fearlessly" announcing the need for "keeping up the birth rate." The musical number most clearly conceived along these lines, a trio for the duke, Larry, and Shorty titled "When Our Ship Comes Sailing In," was dropped during tryouts, but the story's mockery found expression in other songs, such as "Bride and Groom."[12]

Meanwhile, the show's romantic comedy proved unusually adult, with a hero, after all, who is married to two women at the start of the play and who marries a third before the final curtain, yet who also finds time to flirt with a veritable harem of girlfriends. The heroine, meanwhile, is tough enough to rescue a man at sea and shoot it out with a supposed officer of the law. When Jimmy asks Kay if she's concerned about losing her reputation by staying with him overnight, she replies, "I'd sooner lose that than my freedom! Do you think the rest of your wives would mind very much?"[13]

The Gershwins complemented the book's tone by creating a score, distinct from the mock-innocence of *Tell Me More* or the playfulness of *Tip-Toes*, that ranged from the resigned poignancy of "Someone to Watch Over Me" and "Maybe" to the sophisticated charm of "Dear Little Girl" and "Do, Do, Do," with the title alone of Kay's duet with Shorty, "Ain't It Romantic?" (dropped during tryouts), suggesting a bemused attitude about love. Gershwin's harmonic language correspondingly featured a new depth and complexity, including suave harmonic progressions and mild but pervasive dissonances on stressed notes. The refrain of "Someone to Watch Over Me," for instance, made striking use of parallel diminished chords, with the main theme's long notes (in the first phrase, the notes accompanying the words *see, he, be,* and *watch*) boldly sounding a tritone about the bass. "To my way of thinking," stated Gershwin a few years later, "it isn't the fellow with all sorts of complicated chords up his sleeve who will capture the new audiences. It's the man with a musical vocabulary, so to speak, of simple tonic and dominants—chords built upon the first and fifth notes of the scale, respectively—but who will be able, with these fundamental harmonies, to introduce the vital change, the little twist, which will make the harmonic structure sound rich despite the simple means. It's the old case of much-in-little, and much *with* little."[14]

Moreover, some songs were a bit experimental in their rhythm and phrasing. The refrain of "Bride and Groom," for instance, contained seven-measure phrases, something of a novelty for the period, while "The Woman's Touch" and "When Our Ship Comes Sailing In" made trenchant use of irregular phrases in a way not seen since the composer's apprenticeship songs. For its part, "Clap Yo' Hands" suggested changing meters; in Gershwin's words, he interrupted its "fox-trot" rhythm with "a typical waltz rhythm."[15]

The connection between "Clap Yo' Hands" and the African American spiritual deserves special notice. Deeming the song the "earliest of the Big Four get-happy religious numbers from Broadway musicals" (the other three being Vincent Youmans's "Hallelujah," Harold Arlen's "Get Happy," and Cole Porter's "Blow, Gabriel, Blow"), Wayne Shirley noted "that this kind of show-biz religion showed up on both sides of the color line," citing Bessie Smith's recordings of "On Revival Day" and "Moan,

You Moaners." Although Shirley considered the "religious choruses" of *Porgy and Bess* to be "quite another matter," it may not have been entirely coincidental that during this show's rehearsal period, Gershwin read DuBose Heyward's novel *Porgy* and began thinking about adapting it as an opera.[16]

The placement of some of the songs proved unusually problematic, in part because the show's original prologue—which opened with the chorus taking a moonlight swim (the delightful "The Moon Is on the Sea"), proceeded to a scene for the Ruxton twins and Larry, identified here as belonging to the F.F.F., the "First Families of Flatbush" ("Don't Ask!"), and concluded with Kay's expressed hopes to meet Jimmy once again (an early draft specified "The Man I Love" or an "equivalent," which turned out to be "Someone to Watch Over Me," though the latter began life as a fast dance number à la "Fidgety Feet")—was cut on the road. The show accordingly dropped "The Moon Is on the Sea" (along with the penultimate number, "Ding-Dong-Dell," among others already mentioned), placed "Don't Ask!" in the first act proper, and moved "Someone to Watch Over Me" to the second act, where Kay's longing to find Jimmy now seemed rather after-the-fact (though Bolton and Wodehouse did what they could by casting some ambiguity on Kay's romantic aspirations at this point).[17]

"Do, Do, Do" presented just the opposite problem, a love duet for Jimmy and Kay that arrived too early. Bolton and Wodehouse proposed that either Jimmy and Constance sing the number, or else it be moved to the second act; but after these suggestions met with resistance, they had the bright idea of leaving Jansen onstage to spy on the number through a window, making the song something of a ruse. Wodehouse took Ira to task for such alleged indifference to dramatic propriety. "He [Ira] had no notion of getting a situation and fitting a lyric to it," Wodehouse wrote to Bolton in 1973, "he just turned up with a bundle of lyrics like 'Do, Do, Do' and 'Clap Your Hands' [*sic*] and expected you to fit the book to them, which you did miraculously. He improved a lot later on." In the case of "Clap Yo' Hands," a swinging dance number, Bolton and Wodehouse framed the song with a plea from the ensemble not to have to hear this cheerful "mammy song."[18]

Oh, Kay! had its world premiere in Philadelphia on October 18, 1926. Inspired by Lawrence's use of a Pierrot doll as a prop in her rendition of Noël Coward's "Parisian Pierrot," Gershwin purchased a Raggedy Ann doll in a local toy store for her to use in "Someone to Watch Over Me," which she did to touching effect. More hilariously, during one of the

Philadelphia performances, Betty Compton's dog wandered onstage during the singing of "Do, Do, Do," causing such laughter from the audience that the show stopped dead in its tracks.[19]

Directed by John Harwood, choreographed by Sammy Lee, and designed by John Wenger, *Oh, Kay!* journeyed on to Newark, where it opened November 1, and arrived on Broadway at the Imperial Theatre on November 8, 1926, with William Daly presiding over an orchestra that featured duo-pianists Phil Ohman and Victor Arden, and a chorus of thirty-three women and thirteen men. The show received overwhelmingly good reviews, a few calling it the best musical comedy of the year. Gertrude Lawrence recalled, "The piece had lots of humor and that indefinable something which can only be described as spirit." Even the few critics who quibbled about certain aspects of the show strongly recommended it, including future screenwriter Charles Brackett, who, however, disparaged the work of the Gershwins in his *New Yorker* review, a point of view rarely encountered in the popular press (and especially surprising given the enthusiasm for the Gershwins among the *New Yorker* staff, including its founder and editor, Harold Ross).[20]

The reviews generally singled out Lawrence (whom one paper described as "suavely gleeful" and "politely indiscreet," with a voice that was "softly enticing" and eyes that had "that provocative touch of world-weariness"); Harland Dixon (whose acrobatic dancing with the Fairbanks Twins wowed); and the Gershwin score (variously deemed "dainty" and "a marvel of its kind"). But the critics liked the entire show, including the performances of Victor Moore and Oscar Shaw. "Like a Sears-Roebuck catalogue," stated the *Telegram*, "'Oh, Kay' has everything."[21]

It was not only the excellence of the separate parts that impressed critics, but their compelling integration. Brooks Atkinson, whose notice for the *Times* began, "Musical comedy seldom proves more intensely delightful than 'Oh, Kay,'" was explicit in this regard: "Usually it is sufficient to credit as sponsors only the authors and the composer. But the distinction of 'Oh, Kay!' is its excellent blending of all the creative arts of musical entertainment—the arts of staging no less than those of composing and designing. For half the enjoyment of the new musical play comes from the dancing, the comic pantomime and the drilling of a large company."

After 256 performances on Broadway, *Oh, Kay!* opened in the West End at His Majesty's Theatre on September 21, 1927. Lawrence appeared with a new cast headed by Harold French (Jimmy), John Kirby (Shorty), and Claude Hulbert (the duke). The last-named role—one of those "silly ass" parts, like Bertie Bassett in *Lady, Be Good!*—was expanded to replace Larry Potter as the main male dance lead. Wodehouse helped anglicize the lyrics and otherwise adapt the show to British sensibilities, including changing the duke's title to Datchet so as not to offend the house of Durham.

London clamored to see the local girl who had taken Broadway by storm, and hundreds spent two days queued up in front of His Majesty's Theatre in order to get tickets for opening night. Nor did Lawrence disappoint: "She is wistful and absurd, graceful and doltish, fascinating and elegantly grotesque just as the whim seems to seize her," reported the London *Times*. The production as a whole did not fare as well, the *Times* arguing that a satire of Prohibition was inevitably "both more intelligible and more stirring to an American than to an English audience." Nor were French and Hulbert particularly suited to the demands of the score (which the *Times* further thought "commonplace"). But the show managed a solid 214 performances, nonetheless. Attending this production in March 1928, Ira expressed his satisfaction, even if "Gertie *did* clown too much."[22]

Meanwhile, in the fall of 1927, a production starring Julia Sanderson and Frank Crumit toured the East Coast, while another starring Elsie Janis and John Roche enjoyed runs in Los Angeles and San Francisco, where the *Examiner* commended the show's "genial and wicked flavor" as "up-to-date" (and where Janis's understudy, Katherine Kidd, stepped in on opening night). Crumit and Sanderson—the latter regarded by Gershwin as "the best" of all the period's great stars—also brought the show back to New York in early 1928 for sixteen performances at the Century Theatre.[23]

Although *Oh, Kay!* produced only one major hit song, "Someone to Watch Over Me," the show itself proved more durable than most Gershwin musicals, with numerous stagings over the years. In 1936 the work, translated into Swedish, even made its way to the Stora Teatern in Gothenberg, where it opened on November 2; starring Hilde Nyblom as Lady Kay, the production featured sets by Poul Kanneworff, who later designed and directed the European premiere (1943) of *Porgy and Bess*. For a production at the East 74th Street Theatre that premiered on April 16, 1960, Bolton and Wodehouse themselves revised the show, altering the book and interpolating songs from *Primrose* and other Gershwin musicals; more surprisingly, Wodehouse also rewrote many of Ira's original lyrics, thereby offering a unique means for comparing the two men's work. The New York press widely extolled this off-Broadway venture, starring Marti

Stevens and David Daniels, for treating the material with taste, an apparent novelty for revivals of twenties musicals during this period.[24]

Still later revivals, including those at Hollywood's Las Palmas Theatre (1964), London's Westminster Theatre (1974), the Kennedy Center (1978), and the Chichester Festival Theatre (1984), similarly revamped the show, while in 1989 the Goodspeed Opera Company, in a coproduction with Michigan's Birmingham Theater, entirely reconceived the piece. Employing an all-black cast, choreographer Dan Siretta and bookwriter James Racheff placed the action in Harlem in the 1920s, with Lady Kay now Kay Jones, a nightclub singer. Racheff adhered to the basic story outline and even recycled much of the dialogue, but among other changes, the choruses "The Woman's Touch" and "Bride and Groom" were dropped, presumably as too inapropos, as opposed to, say, "Clap Yo' Hands," which inspired this concept in the first place. The production, which premiered at the Goodspeed House on October 20, 1989, and starred Ron Richardson and Pamela Isaacs, proved both a critical and a popular success, though the show clearly sacrificed some of the charm of the original for flashy dancing and rowdy comedy, and at least some critics found the performances "mediocre" and the book "crass."[25]

The following year producer David Merrick, nearing the end of his prolific career, adapted the same version for Broadway, interpolating a lovely unpublished Gershwin song, "Ask Me Again," and engaging a new but still all-black cast that starred Brian Mitchell and Angela Teek, the latter a *Star Search* discovery. Fitted with elaborate sets and a sound so amplified that even a sympathetic reviewer like Edith Oliver complained that many of the words were "lost or crushed in the damnable din," the show opened at the Richard Rodgers Theater on November 1, 1990, to mixed but generally good reviews. Clive Barnes *(Post)* thought the production "surprisingly terrific"; Oliver *(New Yorker)* deemed it "one of the most joyous . . . to be seen locally in years"; and John Simon *(New York)* wrote that hearing the Gershwin score "in a, however doctored, dramatic context is a pleasure no concern for authenticity can undermine." At the same time, nearly everyone objected to Teek's high-powered rendition of "Someone to Watch Over Me," and the more negative reviews included a particularly scathing one in the *Times* by Frank Rich, who thought that the show contained "eye-popping gags and stereotypes . . . less redolent of the Cotton Club than of 'Amos 'n' Andy.'" (Merrick, in response, managed one of his last coups: an advertisement in the *Times*, designed to embarrass Rich, that slipped by the editor's desk.) The show folded after only seventy-seven performances, and although Merrick brought it back to Broadway with yet another cast in early April 1991, after two weeks of poorly attended previews at the Lunt-Fontanne Theater it closed for good.[26]

A few years later, the Gershwin estate commissioned playwright Joseph DiPietro to prepare another version of *Oh, Kay!* "My charge," stated DiPietro, who had written the script and lyrics to the droll off-Broadway musical *I Love You, You're Perfect, Now Change* (1996), "was to take whatever I felt like from the book and run with it—and use pretty much any Gershwin song." The estate presumably had in mind the success of such previous shows as *My One and Only* (1983), inspired by *Funny Face*, and *Crazy for You* (1992), loosely based on *Girl Crazy*. DiPietro actually hewed closer to the original book than had these other shows, but used less of the original score: only three songs. Moreover, DiPietro's choice of music—which included two utterly unknown numbers that had been cut from earlier musicals ("Will You Remember Me?" from *Lady, Be Good!* and "Demon Rum" from *The Shocking Miss Pilgrim*)—went far afield even by the standards of those earlier pastiches.[27]

The new show, titled *They All Laughed!* (and after its initial run retitled *Heaven on Earth*), opened on June 29, 2001, at the Goodspeed Opera. Director Christopher Ashley, music director Michael O'Flaherty, and a cast that starred James Ludwig and Marla Schaffel brought home an entertaining evening, but some critics raised questions about the whole enterprise, the *Times* observing that the current trend toward creating shows based on such free appropriation of a composer's catalog made "a musical theater maven suspect that recycling is replacing art." Christopher Arnott, in the *New Haven Advocate,* similarly wrote, "The misguided implication of *They All Laughed* is that good Gershwin songs are interchangeable, not bound to a book or to a Broadway era or to the gifts of specific entertainers," and lamented that the satirical spirit of the original show had been reworked into a "cartoon fantasy-land." Such pastiches at least made one all the more appreciative of the way the original score helped delineate the likes of Jimmy Winter, Lady Kay, and Larry Potter of Flatbush.[28]

Cast recordings of *Oh, Kay!* included a rather soporific studio album produced by Goddard Lieberson and conducted by Lehman Engel, featuring Barbara Ruick and Jack Cassidy (1957); a cast album of the aforementioned off-Broadway revival starring Marti Stevens and David Daniels, with Dorothea Freitag leading a tiny pit band (1960); and a Roxbury recording with Dawn Upshaw and Kurt Ollmann in the principal roles and Eric Stern conducting the Orchestra of St. Luke's (1995). Although this last release, unlike some other Roxbury cast albums, could not feature the original orchestrations (as hardly any survived), it proved nevertheless the best and most faithful recording of the show to date, with Upshaw delivering a particularly fine performance as Lady Kay. Fortunately, Gertrude Lawrence, in her own recordings of "Someone to Watch Over Me" and "Do, Do, Do," left behind an account of that special elegance and humor that, at their best, characterized Gershwin's musical comedies in their own time.

On December 4, 1926, Gershwin gave the first performance of his *Five Preludes* for piano in the grand ballroom of the Roosevelt Hotel at East 45th Street and Madison Avenue as part of a recital with contralto Marguerite d'Alvarez. The program also featured d'Alvarez in a selection of French and Spanish songs, with Edward Hart at the piano, and a set of Kern and Gershwin songs, with Gershwin at the piano; and Gershwin, accompanied by Isidore Gorn, in two-piano arrangements of the *Rhapsody* and (as an encore) the last movement of the Concerto in F.

Born in England of Peruvian French parentage, d'Alvarez (1886–1953) had a successful operatic career—including memorable performances as Carmen and Amneris—before becoming primarily a song recitalist in the 1920s. As with Eva Gauthier, Carl Van Vechten helped facilitate her friendship with Gershwin, with whom she socialized as early as 1924; soprano Mary Ellis recalled small gatherings in that year attended by both Gershwin and d'Alvarez, whom she described as "rather like a Velasquez duenna to us all."[29]

This particular concert at the Roosevelt arose in response to a heated public debate about jazz at the Town Hall Club on May 6, 1926, between d'Alvarez and the Reverend John Roach Straton, pastor of the Calvary Baptist Church. Whereas Straton thought that jazz—which he deemed "the music of the savage, intellectual and spiritual debauchery, utter degradation"—should be outlawed, d'Alvarez, visibly upset, professed her love for jazz, saying, "When I die, play George Gershwin's *Rhapsody in Blue* at my funeral." Gershwin, who attended the debate, subsequently agreed to collaborate with d'Alvarez on a "very dignified and sedate program" that would show that jazz could be "of sound musical value and worthy of a place on any sober and dignified program."[30]

In his study of the Gershwin preludes, Robert Wyatt describes the ensuing d'Alvarez concert as "just another gimmick, similar to Paul Whiteman's 'Experiment in Modern Music' and Eva Gauthier's 'Recital of Ancient and Modern Music for Voice,' designed to entice jazz-crazed audiences into the recital hall," and at least as far as Gershwin was concerned, the event certainly had its self-serving side; except for one song by Kern, all the "jazz" represented on the program was his own. But as evident from Straton's remarks, attacks against jazz—which often invoked Gershwin—could get nasty, and artists like d'Alvarez risked ridicule and contempt in their public support for such music.[31]

Gershwin had been composing piano preludes for some time, and in March 1925 Van Vechten even referred to a forthcoming set of twenty-four preludes, in the tradition of Bach, Chopin, and Debussy. But the exact makeup of the *Five Preludes* introduced in December 1926—further complicated by accompanying press coverage advertising six preludes—remains somewhat uncertain.[32]

Wyatt narrows down the choices to seven: the two pieces—*Novelette in Fourths* (1919) and *Sixteen Bars without a Name* (1923)—that Gershwin had combined as *Short Story* for violin and piano (1925); the Prelude in G (1925) that served as the main theme of the Concerto in F's finale; the *Three Preludes* published by New World Music in 1927 (the Prelude in B♭, the Prelude in C♯, and the Prelude in E♭); and a short piece from 1924, only a fragment of which survives: music that Gershwin apparently considered for use in the aborted *Harlem Serenade* but eventually played as a prelude, at least according to Kay Swift. (In 1936 Gershwin, assisted by Ira, adapted this music as a song, "Sleepless Night," published posthumously as a piano piece under the same title, with a still later edition of the piece appearing in 1987 that conflated the 1924 fragment and the 1936 song; Wyatt and others accordingly referred to the original 1924 fragment as *Sleepless Night*.)[33]

Although the *Five Preludes* no doubt included the three published preludes, which two pieces filled out the set? Wyatt eliminates the Prelude in G for the reason that the music already appeared on the program as part of the Concerto in F. He further infers from the concert's many reviews that one of the preludes may well have combined, like *Short Story,* the *Novelette* and *Sixteen Bars,* which could possibly explain the conflicting references to five versus six preludes (Gershwin initially might have intended to introduce these two pieces separately, only later deciding to shape them into one movement, as he had done before). That would leave *Sleepless Night* as a possible fifth prelude. Of course, the *Five Preludes* may have contained some other music unidentified by Wyatt or anyone else; but at this point the evidence suggests a group consisting of the *Three Preludes, Sleepless Night,* and the solo piano equivalent of *Short Story.*

Wyatt further deduces from newspaper accounts a possible order for the *Five Preludes* (the Prelude in E♭, Prelude in C♯, *Short Story, Sleepless Night,* and the Prelude in B♭), though he concedes that the second and fourth pieces may have been reversed. Knowing the content and order of these pieces, among other things, would help us better decipher the music's critical reception in New York and subsequently in Buffalo and Boston, where Gershwin repeated the *Five Preludes* in concerts with d'Alvarez on December 15, 1926, and January 18, 1927, respectively. Assuming Wyatt to be right, Paul Rosenfeld, for instance, would have had the music to *Short Story* in mind when he described the third prelude as "the most ingratiating of the set."[34]

These piano pieces form a diverse lot stylistically. The Prelude in E♭ contains features reminiscent of Debussy's "Golliwog's Cakewalk," though its passionate middle section lies more in the way of Brahms. Described by Gershwin as a "sort of blue lullaby," the Prelude in C♯ looks ahead to "Summertime"; Heinrich Schwab further observed the music's kinship to such W. C. Handy songs as "Aunt Hagar's Children Blues," while others have commented on its connection to Chopin's Prelude in A Minor, if not its comparable resemblance to Stravinsky's "Lullaby" from *The Firebird. Short Story,* as discussed earlier, contrasts bittersweet lyricism with jazzy whimsy. *Sleepless Night* shares with the more doleful Prelude in C♯ a particular closeness to the blues. And the Prelude in B♭ has a rather Hispanic profile; according to Kay Swift, Gershwin referred to the piece as his "Spanish" prelude.[35]

At the same time the preludes share, in a manner unprecedented for Gershwin, a formal concision enhanced by lean textures and spiky counterpoint—a tautness underscored by Gershwin and Oscar Levant in their sharp-edged recordings of the *Three Preludes.* Such progress almost wholly eluded contemporary critics, who generally thought the preludes "trifling" and "sketchy," a "polite" companion to the livelier *Rhapsody.* In this context, the *Christian Science Monitor*'s Carleton Sprague Smith, who marveled especially at the "amazing simplicity, yet widened scope" of the fourth prelude, showed uncommon insight in declaring the preludes "a clear advance in the composer's abilities." A similarly thoughtful review in the *New York Evening Post* declared at least two of the preludes "as fine as anything he [Gershwin] has done in the idiom of modern American music, which bears no deep or vital relation to jazz, although it is still called by that somewhat doubtful name."[36]

Although the *Evening World* reported that Gershwin intended the *Five Preludes* to form part of a larger collection to be called *The Melting Pot,* Gershwin published only the *Three Preludes* in 1927, dedicating the set to his friend William Daly. A copyist's manuscript of these preludes survives, as do two earlier manuscripts of the Prelude in E♭ in Gershwin's own hand: a preliminary version, marked "Agitato," and a later version revised for publication that matches the copyist's score. The 1927 published edition adhered fairly scrupulously to the copyist's manuscripts, making only a few minor changes, presumably at the composer's discretion. In contrast, Alicia Zizzo's more recent edition of the preludes proved less satisfactory, particularly so regarding the Prelude in E♭, which combined features from all existing manuscripts.[37]

The *Three Preludes* became a cornerstone of the American solo piano repertoire, with recordings by a wide range of pianists (most of whom played the second prelude much more slowly than did Gershwin). In addition, the music enjoyed success in various transcriptions and arrangements, especially one for violin and piano by the outstanding Russian American violinist Jascha Heifetz. A personal friend of Gershwin's, Heifetz enjoyed dancing to his songs and playing them on the accordion and the piano. After his hopes for a violin concerto were dashed by Gershwin's death, Heifetz decided to transcribe the preludes (1938–1939). Though essentially faithful to the original pieces, he added a few countermelodies of his own—revealing that Gershwin inspired flights of fancy in more than jazz musicians, a point made again in Heifetz's similarly successful arrangement of selections from *Porgy and Bess*. The Heifetz arrangements of the preludes were taken up by many outstanding violinists, including Russians Leonid Kogan, Igor Bezrodny, and Vladimir Spiakov; Americans Joshua Bell, Leila Josefowicz, and Miriam Kramer; and Israeli Gil Shaham, thereby bringing Gershwin close to the heart of the great tradition in unique ways—a phenomenon demonstrated, too, by recorded arrangements of these preludes by flutist Jean-Pierre Rampal (with piano and synthesizer; 1985) and cellists Yo-Yo Ma (with pianist Jeffrey Kahane; 1993) and Terry King (with pianist John Jensen; 2000).[38]

Other transcriptions of the preludes included those by Gregory Stone for orchestra (recorded by Arthur Fiedler and the Boston Pops in 1979) and two pianos (recorded by, among others, Aglika Genova and Liuben Dimitrov in 2003), as well as one for jazz band by Nelson Riddle released in conjunction with Ella Fitzgerald's *George and Ira Gershwin Song Book* (1959). Moreover, on the occasion of a Gershwin memorial concert at the Hollywood Bowl in 1937, the esteemed Otto Klemperer and the Los Angeles Philharmonic performed film composer David Broekman's arrangement of the Prelude in C♯, which Klemperer rendered in a dirgelike manner sober enough, no doubt, to appease even the Reverend Straton. After Klemperer arrived in Los Angeles in 1935, a refugee from the Nazis, Arnold Schoenberg and Oscar Levant had both urged him to conduct Gershwin, who, Klemperer agreed, had "real talent." But when Levant brought the composer to lunch, Klemperer found him "ein frecher Hund" ("cheeky"), supercilious, and, finally, "very, very arrogant"; although he programmed the Concerto in F, he handed over the baton to Alexander Smallens for the actual performance (Gershwin's own choice had been Fritz Reiner). Still, in 1969 Klemperer declared that of American composers—including Copland, who failed to impress him— "the composer who was important was Gershwin."[39]

Although the *Three Preludes* were, aside from the *Song-Book* (1932), Gershwin's last solo piano pieces issued during his lifetime, after his death his estate released some occasional music—mostly songs—as piano pieces, in either printed or recorded form, and often with titles devised by Ira. Some of these pieces were adaptations of songs or incidental music from musical comedies, including *Merry Andrew* (from *Rosalie*), *Impromptu in Two Keys* (from *East Is West*), *Two Waltzes in C* (from *Pardon My English*), and *Promenade* (from *Shall We Dance*). Others derived from sketches catalogued and compiled by Kay Swift, including the thirty-two-bar refrain *Violin Piece* (Melody no. 40; 1929); the little waltz *Three-Quarter Blues* (Melody no. 32; 1930); and the fragment *For Lily Pons* (Melody no. 79; undated). Gershwin may have intended at least the first two of these melodies as songs, but his estate released them as piano pieces with titles suggested by Ira, who labeled Melody no. 40 *Violin Piece* in honor of his brother's friendship with Max Rosen, Melody no. 32 *Three-Quarter Blues* in reference to its musical style (though Gershwin's original sketch bore the title "French Waltz"), and Melody no. 79 *For Lily Pons*, on the hunch that Gershwin had composed the music in the 1930s for the French soprano of that name (1898–1976).

The *Impromptu in Two Keys*—adapted from the song "Yellow Blues" from the aborted musical *East Is West*—merits comment on account of its bold dissonance, here inspired by Chinese music. Gershwin labeled his 1929 sketch of the music "two keys," but Ira's title is somewhat misleading nonetheless; for although the piece flirts with bitonality, the clashing triads, all periodically resolved at cadential points, basically elaborate the blues scale. The even more original *For Lily Pons*, with its floridly chromatic accompaniment, offers for its part a glimpse into some of Gershwin's most intimate thoughts. Appending a brief conclusion of his own, Michael Tilson Thomas adapted and recorded *For Lily Pons* as a solo piano piece (1985); and in 1983 he and the Chicago Symphony gave the world premiere of an orchestral version, *Nocturne for Lily Pons,* arranged by Arthur Morton. On the aforementioned 1985 release, Thomas also included his own arrangement of the haunting *Violin Piece,* while Richard Glazier (1995) recorded a more elaborate version of the same music by Sylvia Rabinof published in 1997 as *Gershwin Melody no. 40* ("Concert Transcription"). Such attention to incomplete jottings and rough sketches evidenced the high regard in which musicians held even the odd nooks and crannies of Gershwin's output.[40]

Chapter Twenty-One

Strike Up the Band and *Funny Face* (1927)

In 1927 George and Ira collaborated with producer Edgar Selwyn and playwright George S. Kaufman—two of Broadway's most eminent figures—on the musical comedy *Strike Up the Band,* which made it all the more surprising that the show proved—at least at first—one of Gershwin's biggest flops.

Edgar Selwyn (born Simon, 1875–1944) grew up poor in towns across the United States and Canada. Arriving in New York as a young man, he worked his way up on Broadway and by the early 1910s had established himself as a successful writer, director, and producer. He began making films as well, and in 1916 he cofounded with Samuel Goldfish the Goldwyn motion picture company—its name an amalgam of their two surnames—though he left the company in 1919. Selwyn and his younger brother Arch also managed various Broadway theaters, and in the late 1910s they built their own three-theater complex—comprising the Selwyn, the Times Square, and the Apollo—on 42nd Street. Gershwin described Selwyn as "one of the best liked men in the theatrical profession."[1]

George S. Kaufman (1889–1961), for his part, arrived in New York from Pittsburgh, establishing a reputation in the course of the 1910s and 1920s as a drama critic, playwright, director, and town wit (along with ·Robert Benchley, Ring Lardner, Dorothy Parker, Alexander Woollcott, and others, he regularly traded quips over lunch at the Algonquin Hotel's famed Round Table). At the time of this initial collaboration with Gershwin, Kaufman's greatest successes—including *You Can't Take It with You* (1936) and *The Man Who Came to Dinner* (1939), two comedies coauthored with Moss Hart—still lay ahead, but he had already written a series of popular farces with Marc Connelly in the early 1920s and a successful play on his own, *The Butter and Egg Man* (1925).[2]

In addition, he had written the books for three musicals: *Helen of Troy, New York* (1923), *Be Yourself* (1924), and *The Cocoanuts* (1925). (*Be Yourself* occasioned his first collaboration with Ira Gershwin, who finally dispensed with his pseudonym, Arthur Francis, for this show with composer Lewis Gensler; while the more successful *Cocoanuts,* with a score by Irving Berlin, brought overnight stardom to the Marx Brothers.) Kaufman would continue to write musical-comedy books throughout his career, including shows for Gershwin (*Strike Up the Band, Of Thee I Sing,* and *Let 'Em Eat Cake*) and other leading Broadway composers. He generally wrote his plays and librettos with others; though a great humorist, he apparently needed coauthors to help lend his work a certain emotional warmth.

For all his success with musical comedy, Kaufman never felt quite at home with the genre. In a 1938 article, "Music to My Ears," he explained that he needed to hear a song many times before he could appreciate its intentions and "possibilities"—"Broadly speaking, I should say that I never like a song the first time I hear it"—thus making it difficult for him to offer guidance, let alone enthusiasm, about musical matters. (Ira wrote that although Kaufman did not "hate" music, "even in musicals he regarded music as a necessary evil.") And notwithstanding his admiration for "the acrobatic ingenuity" of Lorenz Hart and Ira Gershwin, Kaufman's "idea of a lyricist" remained W. S. Gilbert: "At least Sir William never advanced the theory that trouble is just a bubble." Regarding his work with Berlin, Gershwin, Richard Rodgers, and Arthur Schwartz, he added, "Without exception, they have been delightful and considerate collaborators—fond of their music, of course, but keenly sympathetic to the problems of the book writer. In the main, I should say that their concern over the book has been far greater than mine over the music." Kaufman also felt that he failed to provide "real musical opportunity" to his composers because his shows "never have been primarily romantic, and the composer has thus been psychologically handicapped from the beginning. It is probably the reason that there never has been a real song hit in any show with which I have been connected." Here Kaufman sold himself short, because in fact his shows did generate song hits, including Schwartz's "Dancing in the Dark" from *The Band Wagon* (1931).[3]

The origins of *Strike Up the Band* remain somewhat vague, but apparently Selwyn heard in 1926 that Kaufman was at work on an antiwar satire and proposed to produce it as a musical with a score by the

Gershwins. "We can all be grateful to Edgar Selwyn," remarked Morrie Ryskind, who later rewrote the script, "for having the foresight to match their [the Gershwins'] genius with that of George Kaufman's." The Gershwins were delighted at the prospect of working with Kaufman, whom they considered "the funniest and most intelligent playwright in America." Kaufman and the Gershwins met periodically in 1926 and 1927 to plan out the show, sometimes with Selwyn. Working largely from Kaufman's scenario, the Gershwins wrote much of the score during the spring of 1927 at Chumleigh Farm, a suburban retreat in Westchester, New York, and completed most of it by June, about the same time that Kaufman finished the script, one of the relatively few written on his own.[4]

Kaufman's interest in writing an antiwar satire owed something to his friendship with Ryskind (1895–1985), the New York–born journalist and playwright who, though uncredited, helped write *The Cocoanuts;* while a student at Columbia in the mid-teens, Ryskind gained notoriety as an outspoken opponent of American involvement in World War I and remained vehemently antimilitaristic throughout the 1920s. At the same time, other American dramatists had begun raising questions with regard to war, including Maxwell Anderson and Laurence Stallings in *What Price Glory?* (1924) and—though still in the wings—George Brooks and Walter Lister in *Spread Eagle* (1927). Kaufman had long satirized the American scene himself, and this current send-up of business's unwholesome alliance with the military would remind critics in particular of his 1924 comedy, *Beggar on Horseback*. However, none of this minimizes the daring and originality Kaufman and the Gershwins showed in tackling the country's military-industrial complex as the subject for a musical comedy.

Act 1 opens in the factory showroom of the Horace J. Fletcher American Cheese Company in Hurray, Connecticut. (Horace Fletcher, who died in 1919, was an actual businessman, whose nutritional theories on the dietary benefits of slowly chewing food made him a national icon and earned him the presidency of the Health and Efficiency League of America.) At the start of their day, the factory workers greet foreman Timothy Harper (Max Hoffmann Jr.), manager C. Edgar Sloane (Robert Bentley), and owner Horace J. Fletcher himself (Herbert Corthell) ("Fletcher's American Cheese Choral Society"). Pleased that Congress has levied a 50 percent tariff on imported cheese, Fletcher agrees to allow the unctuous Sloane to marry his daughter, Joan (Vivian Hart). While Mrs. Draper (Edna May Oliver), an overbearing widow, tells Fletcher about one of her charitable schemes (giving country children the opportunity to breathe city air), her wisecracking daughter, Anne (Dorothea James), and Timothy wonder why they had to wait until the ripe old ages of seventeen and twenty-one, respectively, to fall in love ("Seventeen and Twenty-One").

Joan complains to her father about a local journalist, Jim Townsend (Roger Pryor), who has described her in a recent column as a "little social snob." Jim conducts an interview with Fletcher, who finds the reporter's lack of ambition, as compared to his own, quite un-American ("A Typical Self-Made American"). Admitting to Joan that he publicly teased her in order to get her attention, Jim hopes to charm her now ("Meadow Serenade"). After the sleuthing George Spelvin (Jimmy Savo) makes a mysterious appearance, Colonel Holmes (Lew Hearn), advisor to the President of the United States, arrives. Before the assembled workers, he attributes his success to his never saying anything ("A Man of High Degree" and "The Unofficial Spokesman"). In view of Switzerland's decision to challenge America's cheese tariff on behalf of its own cheese industry, Fletcher privately offers to bankroll a war against the country, and Holmes assents in the hope of securing another book publication. (Kaufman presumably modeled Holmes after Woodrow Wilson's Texan political advisor, E. M. "Colonel" Holmes, who during these years published his papers in four volumes, though the character recalled Calvin Coolidge as well.)

A few weeks later, citizens gather outside Fletcher's home ("Patriotic Rally," including "Three Cheers for the Union" and "This Could Go On for Years"). Having never particularly liked cheese, Jim views the growing war fever skeptically, though Joan feels that the man she loves should be proud to fight for a cheese as fine as her father's ("The Man I Love"). A soused Mrs. Draper flirts with Fletcher, himself widowed (reprise of "Seventeen and Twenty-One"). Spelvin leads the crowd in a "patriotic exercise" ("Yankee Doodle Rhythm"). After tasting Fletcher's milk, Jim, a former dairyman, accuses the company of using Grade-B milk in its cheese; Joan voices her distress, and the fickle mob throws its support behind Fletcher and Sloane against Jim ("Finaletto Act I"). Timothy, now an army captain, leads a dress parade as Congress declares war and Fletcher announces Joan's engagement to Sloane ("Strike Up the Band").

Act 2 opens "somewhere in Switzerland" as American soldiers knit sweaters for their loved ones back home ("Oh, This Is Such a Lovely War"). All the principals are on hand, including Fletcher, now the war's Brigadier-Chairman of the Board of Directors. Jim, assigned to kitchen duty, and Joan have come to an impasse in their relationship ("Hoping That Someday You'd Care"). As Mrs. Draper won't allow her daughter to marry before she herself does, Anne falsely tells Holmes that her mother is worth millions in the hope that the colonel might marry her; she also observes Timothy and the soldiers in their daily drill ("Military Dancing Drill"). Learning about Mrs. Draper's alleged fortune, Fletcher competes with Holmes for her affection ("How About a Man?"). Jim accuses Sloane of cutting the buttons off the American soldiers' uniforms; but before Fletcher can incarcerate Jim for insubordination, the Americans win the war, thanks, explains Spelvin, to a scheme of Jim's. As the crowd declares Jim a war hero and Fletcher and Holmes learn that Mrs. Draper has no fortune after all, Joan and Anne lament their romantic difficulties ("Finaletto, Act II").

On a boat headed back to the States, the soldiers (including featured tenor Morton Downey) look forward to their return ("Homeward Bound"/"The Girl I Love"), while Fletcher and Mrs. Draper fall into each other's arms. Back home, amid general rejoicing ("The War That Ended War"), Fletcher praises Jim, who, after revealing that Spelvin is an American secret agent and that Sloane is actually Colonel Herman Edelweiss of the Swiss secret service, makes Fletcher promise to devise "an international league in which all cheeses will be equal." As Jim and Joan, Mrs. Draper and Fletcher, and Timothy and Anne embrace, Holmes (who learns that Spelvin is his long-lost son) announces that he has to leave for Washington, explaining that Russia has issued a complaint about an American caviar tariff. Fletcher, who has investments in caviar, calls for resolute and immediate action (reprise of "Strike Up the Band").

Kaufman's book clearly addressed not so much the horror of war—the war itself is brief and ludicrous—as the intolerance, paranoia, hypocrisy, self-serving moralizing, and exaggerated patriotism on the home front. To this end, the script subverted theatrical representations of war, including the military epic, the spy melodrama, the sentimental pacifist drama, and the patriotic pageant, so that it operated on one level as a burlesque, not unlike other kinds of sketches found in musical revues and comedies of the period, including *The Cocoanuts*. Laurence Maslon even argued that its absurdist humor owed a debt to the Marx Brothers, and one can easily imagine, as he does, Harpo and Chico "divvying up and expanding" the role of Spelvin, or Margaret Dumont playing Mrs. Draper.[5]

The Gershwins similarly employed various archetypes—the solemn hymn, the patriotic march, the recited pledge, the military drill, the folk song, the romantic waltz—to satiric effect, partly through poetic wit and partly through incongruities between text and music. But the score's humor took shape in purely musical ways as well, via the surprising note, the mocking gesture, the sly allusion, or the unforeseen touch of levity. In all this, the Gershwins, while maintaining their distinctive whimsy, patently modeled their work after Gilbert and Sullivan; this would be by far their most Gilbert-and-Sullivanish score, including unusually frequent use of 6/8 meters and choral echoes.

The parodistic nature of the enterprise also encouraged the Gershwins to write uncharacteristically long ensembles that advanced the action in a quasi-operatic manner, most notably the two finalettos. Both of these episodes, which include fluid changes of key and tempo, occur at those moments in the story when Jim reveals his startling discoveries—in the first, that Fletcher uses adulterated milk; in the second, that Sloan has been cutting off uniform buttons—and their operatic pretensions heighten the absurdity of the melodrama. Even the work's shorter, more autonomous numbers put forth adventurous shapes that helped enhance the satire; only a few conformed to standard popular song forms, and fewer still that dance bands or popular singers could reasonably be expected to take up. The Gershwins plainly showed considerable integrity with respect to Kaufman's dramatic intentions.

At the same time, the Gershwins were not always in sync with Kaufman's acid touch, here untempered by any collaborator. For example, "Seventeen and Twenty-One," the gently mocking opening number for Anne and Timothy, seemed somewhat at odds with Kaufman's depiction of especially Anne as mercilessly callow. Similarly, the poignant "Homeward Bound" departed somewhat from the spirit of the book. The Gershwins more closely mirrored Kaufman's tone in such choral numbers as "Fletcher's American Cheese Choral Society," "Oh, This Is Such a Lovely War," and "Strike Up the Band," with its sardonic quatrain, "We're in a bigger, better war / For your patriotic pastime. / We don't know what we're fighting for—/ But we didn't know the last time!" The latter number, which Kaufman considered "the best song in any show of mine," in particular cost Gershwin considerable effort.[6]

Over the years, this 1927 version of *Strike Up the Band* gained the reputation as one of the outstanding book musicals of its time and an early example of the so-called integrated musical comedy. Certainly its script was more sophisticated than that of a typical musical comedy of the 1920s, with its low puns and broad slapstick (though Kaufman co-opted such traditions); and the score's extended set pieces marked for Gershwin yet another step toward *Of Thee I Sing* and *Porgy and Bess*. But the various songs and ensembles largely arose as they did in Gershwin's other musical comedies. The show even had one dubious interpolation, namely, "The Man I Love," a song seemingly unsuited for high satire, though included here at Selwyn's urging.

Moreover, the book had its own limitations; the plot lacked tension, and its characters, motivation. Recalling this initial collaboration with Gershwin, Kaufman himself regretted that he "failed to provide a better book on that occasion—a composer of musical comedy is so horribly dependent on the quality of the book." And for all its brilliance, the music tellingly lacked some of the vivacity and charm of Gershwin's best theater scores. (Some years later, Kaufman was mistaken for Gershwin by a backer of the show, who asked why it hadn't been a success. Reported Kaufman: "I have always flattered myself that I made the only possible answer. I said, 'Kaufman gave me a lousy book.'")[7]

The show debuted at Reade's Broadway Theatre in Long Branch, New Jersey, on August 29, 1927, before moving to a more extended tryout run at the Shubert Theatre in Philadelphia starting September 5. The cast included Herbert Corthell (Fletcher), Lew Hearn (Holmes), Edna May Oliver (Mrs. Draper), Vivian Hart (Joan), Roger Pryor (Jim), Dorothea James (Anne), Max Hoffmann Jr. (Timothy), Robert Bentley (Sloane), and Jimmy Savo (Spelvin), one of the legendary pantomimists of the American stage. R. H. Burnside directed, John Boyle staged the dances, Norman Bel Geddes designed the sets, and conductor William Daly presided over a large orchestra, supplemented by a brass band (the Waco Orchestra) and a chorus of thirty-six women (including the eight Estelle Liebling Singers) and twenty-four men.

Some of the reviews complained that the book dragged and that the cast seemed overwhelmed by the score's demands; a few further found the material inimical to the genre. "If the sprightly music and charming girls were somewhat coldly received," stated the *Philadelphia Evening Bulletin*, "Mr. Kauffman [*sic*] may blame himself for attempting to write sharply satirical drama in terms of a musical comedy." Still, many critics enjoyed the show's wit and originality. The *Philadelphia Inquirer*, which assumed that audiences "expecting to see just another musical comedy must have had the surprise of their lives," was particularly enthusiastic, describing the work as "a rollicking show, a veritable geyser of spontaneous comedy, a refreshing (if somewhat reminiscent) addition to George Gershwin's arch and individual musical output, and a thoroughly refreshing departure from routine." And although *Vari-*

ety predicted more of a succès d'estime than a popular hit, they expected that the show would "cause a furore" among New York's intelligentsia.[8]

Over the next two weeks, however, things went awry. As the authors struggled with the second act, Oliver and Hearn left the show—Blanche Ring and Florenz Ames came in for them—and Savo also gave notice, while Corthell, who Kaufman felt was miscast, was briefly replaced by Edwin Robbins and then rehired. Meanwhile, attendance dwindled dramatically. After two weeks in Philadelphia and losses in the tens of thousands of dollars, the show closed. At one of the final performances, Ira, who noted two elegantly dressed men entering the theater, said to Kaufman, "That must be Gilbert and Sullivan coming to fix the show," to which Kaufman responded, "Why don't you put jokes like that in your lyrics?"[9]

Selwyn hoped to return with a new cast and revised book in as little as eight weeks, but the show needed a more thorough overhaul. George and Ira agreed to take another crack at it, but Kaufman demurred, suggesting rather that Morrie Ryskind rewrite the book, with both credited as coauthors. Ryskind had known the Gershwins from his high school days at Townsend Harris Hall, where Ira, a fellow Savoyard, succeeded him as editor of the school paper. In later years, Ryskind affectionately remembered the "brilliant musical cyclone, George, and his equally brilliant although far less cyclonic brother, Ira," stating, "For me, it was their music, far more than anyone else's, that made the New York of the time such a vibrant city."[10]

As the Gershwins revamped the score, Ryskind finished one revision of the script in December 1928, complete except for a short final scene. He ingeniously recast the entire war sequence as Fletcher's dream: the cheese magnate collapses in his office early in act 1, imagines all the events from the arrival of Colonel Holmes on, and awakens, near the end of the second act, after he has pronounced Jim a hero; the dream reconciles Fletcher to Joan's marriage to Jim (who are now in love from the start), a narrative frame consciously derived from Dickens's *A Christmas Carol*. By the time of this 1928 script, the Gershwins had replaced the duet for Anne and Timothy, "Seventeen and Twenty-One," with "I Mean to Say," and had written a new act 1 duet, "If I Became the President," for Mrs. Draper and Holmes.[11]

About a year later, in November 1929, Ryskind completed another revision that reinstated some previously excised passages from the 1927 script but deviated further from the original, largely because by this time Selwyn had decided to showcase the vaudeville team of Bobby Clark and Paul McCullough, with the idea of casting Clark as Colonel Holmes.

Ryskind accordingly devised a new composite role for McCullough: a Marine sidekick of the colonel, Gideon, who assumes some of Spelvin's functions as well; as Holmes and Gideon only appear, as such, in the dream sequence, Ryskind also created double roles for Clark and McCullough as Jim's assistants. Moreover, the new book changed Fletcher from a cheese to a chocolate manufacturer, and merrily concluded with a triple wedding for Joan and Jim, Anne and Timothy, and Mrs. Draper and Fletcher, though it left the mordant ending, with Fletcher's protest against Russia, largely intact.

Besides "I Mean to Say" and "If I Became the President," the Gershwins added an act 1 duet (to replace "Meadow Serenade") for Joan and Jim as they anticipate married life: "Soon" (its verse derived from "Hoping That Someday You'd Care," now also dropped, and its chorus adapted from a melody from the first-act finaletto); two duets for Anne and Timothy, the first-act "Hangin' Around with You" and the second-act "I Want to Be a War Bride" (though the song—introduced as a solo for Fletcher's secretary, Myra Meade, played by Ethel Kenyon—was dropped within weeks of the Broadway opening); a second-act number for Holmes, Gideon, and the chorus girls, "Mademoiselle in New Rochelle"; an act 2 quartet for Holmes, Gideon, Fletcher, and Mrs. Draper (now named Grace), "How about a Boy Like Me?" (which replaced "How about a Man?"); and a new "Opening, Act II" for chorus that incorporated "Military Dancing Drill." Moreover, the show rescued "I've Got a Crush on You" from an intervening flop, *Treasure Girl,* as a second-act duet for Anne and Timothy; and "Ring-a-Ding-a-Ding-Dong Dell," a chorus that had been cut from the 1927 version. Gershwin furthermore provided new incidental music, including some dream music. The Gershwins retained much else from the original score, including most of the choruses, but dispensed with "The Man I Love," "Yankee Doodle Rhythm," and "Homeward Bound" in addition to the dropped numbers already mentioned.[12]

The received wisdom has tended to disparage the revised *Strike Up the Band* as a concession to popular taste. Ryskind himself confessed that he tried to make the show "palatable without losing the bite, and I'm afraid that I failed in my effort. The show did become a hit, but the bite, of necessity, was one of wobbly dentures." Ryskind surely created a more conventional show; but at the same time, the characters emerged more fully drawn, and the narrative more sharply defined, highlighting Kaufman's need for cowriters.[13]

The new book also inspired a stronger score. "I Mean to Say" and

"Hangin' Around with You" brought the characters of Anne and Timothy—she, the saucy flapper, he, the tentative lover—to life; "Soon" gave the romance of Joan and Jim some tender sentiment; "If I Became the President" came as close to the spirit of Gilbert and Sullivan as anything in the 1927 score; and "Mademoiselle in New Rochelle," with its amusing allusions to Sousa, provided some raucous fun nicely in keeping with the play's tone. The new score, in short, was livelier, funnier, and in some ways truer to Kaufman's original vision than the earlier one; one recent dismissal of the score's revisions as "mostly unnecessary" underestimated the Gershwins' capacity for self-criticism.[14]

The revised *Strike Up the Band* arrived in Boston on December 25, 1929, in New Haven on January 6, 1930, and then at the Times Square Theatre in New York on January 14. Alexander Leftwich directed, George Hale staged the dances, Raymond Sovey designed the sets, and Charles Le Maire, the costumes. In addition to Clark and McCullough, the cast featured Dudley Clements (Fletcher), Blanche Ring (Grace Draper), Margaret Schilling (Joan), Jerry Goff (Jim), Doris Carson (Anne), Gordon Smith (Timothy), Robert Bentley (Sloane), and specialty dancer Joyce Coles. Hilding Anderson led the orchestra, supplemented not with a brass band as before but rather with trumpeter Red Nichols and members of his band, variously including such excellent jazz musicians as trumpeters Ruby Weinstein and Charlie Teagarden, reed players Jimmy Dorsey, Benny Goodman, Charles "Pee Wee" Russell, and Irving "Babe" Russin, drummer Gene Krupa, and trombonists Glenn Miller and possibly Tommy Dorsey. For the Broadway opening, Gershwin conducted the show himself as he had in Boston, to the delight of such spectators as Robert Littell, who wrote, "[I]t was almost impossible to keep one's eyes off Mr. Gershwin, in the world's largest white tie and boutonniere, having as good a time as any one in the audience. You could see him—and sometimes hear him—singing along with the chorus, and every once in a while a certain pursing of the lips indicated that he was no longer singing but whistling."[15]

Although the critics thought that the second act still needed tightening, they overall liked the show, which they considered a worthy rival to Cole Porter's *Fifty Million Frenchmen,* playing down the street at the Lyric. The comic antics of Bobby Clark and the vivacious dancing of Doris Carson elicited special praise. A few notices seemed to find the Gershwin score overly complex—"After all," stated Brooks Atkinson in the *Times,* "the scores for musical comedy should be simple and frankly popular at times"—but most welcomed its ambitions, particularly Charles Darnton in the *Evening World:* "His [Gershwin's] score had sparkle, gleam, surprise, such music as Broadway doesn't get with its customary moon songs. It was different, original, distinguished. You listened to it with the pleasure which might come from a voice in the wilderness, creating melodies of freshness and charm, melodies to shame the old tin-pan tunes." Many notices also thought the lyrics Ira's best to date. "If they [the lyrics] were printed in a book," wrote Ralph Barton in *Life*, "I should buy it and find something more than the accident of alphabetical arrangement in the fact that it would be placed on my shelves next to the works of W. S. Gilbert."[16]

As for the show itself, opinions varied. Bernard C. Clausen, writing in the *Christian Century*, praised this "masterpiece of satire" for having the potential to exorcise war through laughter. *America*, on the other hand, while agreeing that Gershwin's music could "make one forget any lapses in taste," fretted that the work might offend. A handful of critiques, including those by Richard Lockridge *(Sun)*, Richard Watts Jr. *(Herald-Tribune)*, and Richard Dana Skinner *(Commonweal)*, further questioned the compatibility of political satire with, in Skinner's phrase, the "quasi-realism" of musical comedy. Musical comedy, wrote Watts, "can provide, to a high degree, the gay madness of burlesque, but it stumbles when it attempts to offer the more cerebral quality of satire." These critics accordingly thought that the framing device of a dream compromised the work's integrity, but it's not clear that they would have found the 1927 version any less problematic. In any case, Watts regarded his reservations as largely academic, and the show, indeed, enjoyed 191 performances on Broadway, an excellent run for a challenging theater piece in the early days of the Depression.

New World Music even published a complete piano-vocal score, Gershwin's first since *Primrose* (1924). In 1936 Ira adapted the title song—the show's one hit, at least until "I've Got a Crush on You" caught on in the 1940s—as "Strike Up the Band for U.C.L.A.," and then in 1940, in response to a changed political climate, rewrote the part of the original song's verse quoted above to read, "We hope there'll be no other war, / But if we are forced into one— / the Flag that we'll be fighting for / Is the Red and White and Blue one!" That same year, the song—now with all references to war expunged—appeared at the climax of a Busby Berkeley production number from the MGM film *Strike Up the Band*, starring Judy Garland and Mickey Rooney, that otherwise had nothing to do with the stage musical of the same name. (Later performances of "Strike Up the Band" by such jazz musicians as Charlie Parker and Oscar Peterson more fully captured the song's ironic humor.)

Meanwhile, as some of the music from the 1927 score disappeared and the script for the 1930 version seemed to have vanished as well, revivals of either stage version for decades became a virtual impossibility. However, the 1982 Secaucus discovery of some musical materials presumed lost, along with growing curiosity about the original Kaufman book, prompted renewed interest in the 1927 show. In 1984 composer-conductor Eric Salzman presided over a "tribute" to that version in Philadelphia by conflating the 1927 and 1930 scores in conjunction with the original Kaufman book. Tommy Krasker undertook a more faithful restoration for a 1988 production by Pasadena's California Music Theater. This exacting labor of love—which reconstructed the lost "Meadow Serenade" by fusing the song's chorus, as recalled by Kay Swift in the 1940s, to a newly composed verse by Burton Lane—provided the basis not only for this show but for a production by the Goodspeed Opera (1995) and for concert presentations by City Center's Encores! (1998), the Barbican Centre's Lost Musicals (1998), and the touring Curtain Up! (2002), as well as a Roxbury recording issued on Elektra Nonesuch (1991) and a handsome vocal score prepared and edited by Steven D. Bowen (1998).[17]

Reviews of the Philadelphia, Pasadena, and East Haddam revivals admired the score but found the Kaufman book incoherent and plodding. The *Orange County Register* observed that the script "sometimes lurches lumpily from song to song" and that the satire was "only intermittently on target, the narrative line uncomfortably embracing the songs," while *Theater Week* noted that the book failed to develop "the obligatory emotions" of the two young couples. Tellingly, these were precisely some of the problems that Ryskind and the Gershwins successfully redressed in their 1930 revision.[18]

One reason for the preoccupation with the original show concerned the near-invisibility of the Ryskind script; but in addition, the daring early version plainly appealed to late-twentieth-century sensibilities. Moreover, whereas Kaufman's reputation maintained itself, Ryskind's grew clouded as he became increasingly associated with the political right, including testimony given against the Hollywood Ten. In any case, the underrated revised version deserves reevaluation, perhaps even an airing, in which case both the 1928 and 1929 Ryskind scripts might be consulted, as the latter played heavily to the particular talents of Clark and McCullough.

With their next musical, *Funny Face* (1927), the Gershwins proceeded on more familiar though, as it turned out, no less shaky ground. An

Aarons and Freedley production, the work was written for the Astaires, who had finished their long run abroad with *Lady, Be Good!* and were eager to return to Broadway in a new Gershwin show. *Lady, Be Good!* coauthors Fred Thompson and Guy Bolton sketched out the scenario, but an overextended Bolton suggested that for the script—at this point titled *Smarty*—Thompson collaborate with actor, drama critic, and humorist Robert Benchley (1899–1945). Edgar MacGregor directed, Bobby Connolly staged the dances, John Wenger created the sets, Kiviette designed the costumes, Robert Russell Bennett and Gershwin orchestrated the score, and Alfred Newman directed the chorus of thirty-eight women and twenty-four men, and an orchestra that once again featured pianists Victor Arden and Phil Ohman.

The musical went into rehearsal after Labor Day and, according to Astaire, arrived in Philadelphia, two days prior to its announced October 10 world premiere, a "mess." After two days of intense rehearsal, including a dress that went past three in the morning, the opening was postponed by one day. When the show debuted on October 11, the audience received the work politely, but the company knew it was in trouble. "Gosh, how can I criticize other people's shows from now on?" Benchley famously remarked, while Richard Rodgers, who attended the premiere, wrote to his wife, "God will have to do miracles if it's to be fixed." As the show floundered in Philadelphia—"we were awful," recalled Astaire—and as attendance fell off, the situation no doubt gave the Gershwins, in light of their recent debacle in Philadelphia with *Strike Up the Band,* an ominous feeling of déjà vu.[19]

Aarons and Freedley were determined to get the show into shape, however. As the company moved from Philadelphia to Washington, D.C. (opening October 31) to Atlantic City (opening November 7) to an extra week in Wilmington (opening November 14), the show underwent continuous alteration. Paul Gerard Smith arrived to doctor the book, ultimately receiving credit as coauthor in place of Benchley, who bowed out. Among other cast changes, Allen Kearns arrived from England to replace juvenile lead Stanley Ridges, and Victor Moore and Earl Hampton were brought in to enlarge the comedy. Such extensive revisions meant enormous work for everyone, including the Gershwins, who by the time the show rolled into New York had prepared about twenty-five numbers—almost all new—for a show that ultimately used about half that. "We were on the road six weeks," stated Ira, "and everyone concerned with the show worked day and night, recasting, rewriting, rehearsing, recriminating—of rejoicing, there was none." The *New York*

Times further reported that "almost enough scenery and costumes were discarded to outfit another musical show." Even in Wilmington, the last stop before New York, nearly every performance involved some adjustment or other, such as reordering the material, though Astaire recalled that by this point the show, now titled *Funny Face,* was "running smoothly" and "seemed better." Gershwin remembered in particular a Thursday night performance in which "just as though a miracle had happened, the show suddenly looked great."[20]

The show's first act opens in the home of Jimmy Reeves (Fred Astaire), who has guardianship over his foster-parents' three natural daughters, Dora (Betty Compton), June (Gertrude McDonald), and Frankie (Adele Astaire). Dora and June are throwing a party in honor of Jimmy's birthday ("Birthday Party"). The guests include Dora's boyfriend, Dugsie Gibbs (William Kent) ("Once"). Because Frankie, an inveterate liar, has penned slanders about Jimmy in her diary, he has confiscated the book and placed it in an envelope in his safe. Frankie, who wants her diary back, tries to ingratiate herself with Jimmy ("Funny Face"), who advises his pals to keep cool with women ("High Hat").

Frankie persuades famed aviator and sportsman Peter Thurston (Allen Kearns) to break into Jimmy's safe and retrieve her diary that night, alleging that it contains papers she has been forced to sign; as Peter agrees, the two grow closer ("He Loves and She Loves"). Meanwhile, Jimmy humors Dora by placing her bracelets in an envelope in the same safe. Two thieves, Chester (Earl Hampton) and his bungling sidekick, Herbert (Victor Moore), break into the safe and abscond with the envelope containing the diary. As Frankie distracts Jimmy ("Let's Kiss and Make Up"), Peter and Dugsie steal the envelope containing the bracelets ("Finale").

The second act opens with a swim party at the Canoe Inn at Lake Wapatog, New Jersey ("In the Swim"). Pursued by both the thieves and the police, Peter, Frankie, and Dugsie assume the identities of an invalid, a nurse, and a doctor expected at the inn. Peter and Frankie's romance takes wing ("'S Wonderful"), while Dugsie flirts with some girls ("Tell the Doc"). As Dora plots to blackmail Peter into marrying her, Jimmy assures June of his affections ("What Am I Going to Do?"—better known as "My One and Only"). After the police discover the bracelets on Peter, Frankie thwarts Dora's scheme by falsely announcing that she married Peter that very morning.

Pretending to be married, Frankie and Peter arrive at the Paymore Hotel in Atlantic City, followed by the armed thieves, Jimmy, Dugsie, and the police. As all converge in their hotel room, chaos ensues. At the police station, the sergeant calls out the riot squad and discovers a party under way (including a reprise of some music from the show, "Sing a Little Song," performed by Arden and Ohman, the Ritz Quartette, and a small chorus; and perhaps here, too, the dance number "Blue Hullabaloo," introduced by Dora and June and dropped in the course of the run).

At the Two Million Dollar Pier (reprise of "What Am I Going to Do?"), Jimmy confronts Frankie, who explains that she's not married, but only engaged to Peter. As for Jimmy's accusation that she's "stark staring mad," she responds, "Why not? Everybody is cuckoo, these days. The dumber you talk, the more intelligent everyone thinks you are" ("The Babbitt and the Bromide"). As Dugsie and Dora reunite, Jimmy, who drops charges against Chester and Herbert on receiving the diary, happily permits Frankie to marry Peter ("Finale").[21]

In preparing the score, the Gershwins adapted at least two discarded songs from previous musicals: "Once" from *Tell Me More* and "The Moon Is on the Sea" (now "In the Swim") from *Oh, Kay!* Otherwise, the music—as best we can tell, for a handful of the numbers are lost—largely seems to have been original to this show. Because of the amount of material eventually dropped during tryouts, however, the Gershwins understandably recycled at least four cut numbers in their next musical, *Rosalie* (1928), most notably "How Long Has This Been Going On?" (originally intended for Frankie and Peter). Other unused songs similarly turned up in later works, including the jaunty "The World Is Mine" (for Jimmy, June, and Dora) as "Toddlin' Along" in the *Nine Fifteen Revue* (1930, where, as sung by Nan Blackstone, a so-called coon shouter, it proved one of the show's few bright spots); and the bridge to the plucky "Are You Dancing?" (apparently for June and Chester) as part of "I'm a Poached Egg" for the picture *Kiss Me, Stupid* (1964).[22]

The history of yet another dropped song, "Your Eyes! Your Smile!" (for Peter and Frankie, also called "Those Eyes!"), proved particularly convoluted. Gershwin recycled the song's verse—itself derived from the chorus of "Yan-Kee" (1920)—as the verse for "You Started It" from *Delicious* (1930); and adopted the first phrase of its *abab* chorus for the verse of "Oh Gee!–Oh Joy!" from *Rosalie* (1927), and its second phrase, more literally, for the parallel phrase in the chorus of "You've Got What Gets Me" from the film version of *Girl Crazy* (1932). For all his fecundity, Gershwin plainly sought to make the most of his ideas once formulated. The connection with "Yan-Kee," meanwhile, demonstrated the enduring presence of Asian-related elements in his work.

As for the discarded choruses, "Aviator," which originally opened the show, evoked the hoopla surrounding Charles Lindbergh's transatlantic crossing; as the spectators express concern over Peter on his trial flight, their anxiety reflected by short, irregular phrases, the reporters are all business, their music including clipped tone clusters. Another dropped chorus, "Finest of the Finest," a second-act number intended for an ensemble of policemen, recalled the stouthearted choruses of Friml and Romberg, an example of Gershwin's penchant for intertwining social satire and artistic parody.

The retention of these choruses—or the charming "When You're Single," an act 1 comedy number for Dugsie, cut during tryouts—would have given the score greater variety; but the show—even more than *Lady, Be Good!*—plainly aimed first and foremost to showcase the Astaires. That these two shows (as well as Gershwin's two movie musicals for Fred) occasioned a strikingly large percentage of Gershwin's biggest song hits suggests that the Astaires drew from the composer not only a high level of inspiration but a certain kind of songwriting. Tellingly, the *Funny Face* songs that involved one or the other of the Astaires—"Funny Face," "He Loves and She Loves," "High Hat," "'S Wonderful," "Let's Kiss and Make Up," "My One and Only," and "The Babbitt and the Bromide"—similarly feature catchy rhythms and short phrases, a combination that suited both the Astaires' dancing abilities and their vocal limitations, and that presumably helped foster the special success of these songs as well. At the same time, such traits characterize the score as a whole (for example, "When You're Single" makes extraordinary use of simple two-note motives), offering further evidence that Gershwin conceived of his shows as unified entities.

Within these confines, the score for *Funny Face* contained a fair degree of diversity nonetheless. The solo numbers for Jimmy, for instance, included both the nonchalant "High Hat" (Astaire made his first adult appearance in top hat and tails in this number, backed by a male chorus similarly attired) and the anxious "My One and Only" (which provided a superb vehicle for Astaire's tap-dancing). The duets for Jimmy and Frankie similarly ranged from the lilting "Funny Face," with its ironic echoes of the revue promenade; to the sprightly "Let's Kiss and Make Up," with its subtle suggestions of changing duple and triple meters; to the comical "The Babbitt and the Bromide," a polkalike number that—like "Swiss Miss" from *Lady, Be Good!*—afforded the Astaires an opportunity to stage one of their celebrated trots.

The duets for Frankie and Peter—"He Loves and She Loves" and "'S

Wonderful"—offered some contrasting romantic sentiment. But whereas the former—one of Gershwin's most glorious melodies—featured big, expressive leaps, the latter—a clear descendant of "So Am I" from *Lady, Be Good!*—put forth a melody line of astonishing economy, marked by singsong motives; the artfulness of the harmony and counterpoint lay so hidden as to be practically invisible (and did not, in any case, compensate for the tune's "monotony," according to Alec Wilder). "'S Wonderful" nevertheless became a special favorite among jazz instrumentalists, who apparently appreciated its melodic charm, its smart harmonic structure, and its general atmosphere of knowing whimsy; Benny Goodman, Eddie Condon, Coleman Hawkins, Artie Shaw, Count Basie, and Dizzy Gillespie were only a few of the many fine jazz musicians who released versions of the tune.[23]

Funny Face—like *Lady, Be Good!*—had a few comedy numbers as well, notably "Tell the Doc," an early satire of psychoanalysis, and "The Babbitt and the Bromide," a parody of American small-talk. (The terms *babbitt,* signifying a smug businessman, and *bromide,* meaning a tiresome bore, derived from two works of American literature: a 1922 novel by Sinclair Lewis, *Babbitt,* and a 1906 publication by humorist Gelett Burgess, *Are You a Bromide?* As for the phrase *olive oil,* also found in the song, Michael Feinstein quoted Ira as saying, "Olive oil was what we used to say in the '20s instead of au revoir.") George and Ira conceived "The Babbitt and the Bromide" to be delivered by Fred and Adele in deadpan unison, but did not object when the Astaires decided to alternate the phrases of the chorus in simulation of a conversation (an approach duplicated by Fred Astaire and Gene Kelly in the 1946 MGM film *Ziegfeld Follies*).[24]

Funny Face premiered on Broadway on November 22, 1927, at Aarons and Freedley's new Alvin Theatre (renamed the Neil Simon in 1983) on West 52nd Street, its name an amalgam of the two producers' given names, Alex and Vinton. With its red brick Georgian facade, its 1,362–seat auditorium decorated in gold trim and pastel shades of blue, gray, and lavender, and its stylish smoking lounge, the theater "exuded a sort of repressed opulence," reported the *New York American.*[25]

After its frantic six weeks on the road, the show opened to surprisingly unanimous acclaim. *Variety* pronounced it "a smash," and the *Commonweal,* "one of the season's joys." Other notices similarly praised the show as "chic," "smart," "glamorous," "racy," "droll," and "neat and refined." The press singled out the Astaires as scoring "the most brilliant triumph of their career," but expressed admiration as well for the comedic talents of William Kent and Victor Moore, the handsome sets of John Wenger, indeed, all aspects of the production except for the "flat" and "stale" book (prompting considerable speculation on the possible contributions of Robert Benchley, who, reviewing the show himself for *Life* magazine, described Astaire's dancing in "My One and Only" as "one of the most thrilling dramatic events in town, which includes Max Reinhardt's spectacle"). The critics also noted the effective use of the much-maligned male chorus as dapper party guests in the first act and as policemen in the second.[26]

While admiring the score's tunefulness, many critics failed to grasp its distinction, however. *Vogue* even suggested that the "commonplace" tunes "might have been written by any of half a dozen ballad smiths." On the other hand, Gilbert Gabriel, in the *Sun*, enthused over those "arch and sprightly" songs that had "such rhythms and counter rhythms as carry the tune straight down into the nether regions of your spine," while Alexander Woollcott in the *World* once again showed deep appreciation for another "clever, sparkling, teasing" Gershwin score. "I do not know whether Gershwin was born into this world to write rhythms for Fred Astaire's feet," wrote Woollcott, "or whether Astaire was born into the world to show how the Gershwin music should really be danced. But surely they were written in the same key, these two."

Funny Face's run of 244 performances at the Alvin nearly matched that of *Oh, Kay!* and exceeded that of *Tip-Toes* and *Song of the Flame,* though still paled beside that of Rodgers and Hart's *A Connecticut Yankee,* Romberg's *My Maryland,* and Youmans's *Hit the Deck!*—let alone DeSylva, Brown, and Henderson's *Good News* and Kern's *Show Boat,* both of which passed the five hundred mark. The show had a slightly better run in the West End, where it opened at the Prince's Theatre on November 8, 1928, and subsequently moved to the Winter Garden on January 28, 1929, for a total of 263 performances, the Astaires appearing with a British cast featuring Leslie Henson (Dugsie) and Sydney Howard (Herbert). This Felix Edwardes production replaced "Once" with a new Gershwin song, "Look at the Damn Thing Now"; and (sometime after the show had moved into the Winter Garden) "He Loves and She Loves" with a Joseph Meyer–Roger Wolfe Kahn interpolation, "Imagination" (not to be confused with the later Jimmy Van Heusen hit of the same name). The London *Times* reserved its biggest plaudits for Henson, but approvingly described Adele as "a heroine of musical comedy who amusingly mocks her kind," and thought Fred "as agile, as cool, and as brilliant on his feet as ever." Once again the

Astaires, joined by a few other cast members, recorded some of the show's numbers for Columbia; this included Fred, in an extraordinary tour de force, tap-dancing his way through "My One and Only," apparently accompanied by the show's duo-pianists, Jacques Fray and Mario Braggiotti. [27]

Funny Face also played successfully in Sydney, where it opened at the St. James Theatre on May 23, 1931, with Janette Gilmore (Frankie), Len Rich (Jimmy), Charley Sylber (Dugsie), and Jim Gerald (Herbert). This well-received production restored both "Once" and "He Loves and She Loves" but adapted the apparently inscrutable "The Babbitt and the Bromide" as "The Rabbit and the Bromide." [28]

During the Broadway run of *Funny Face,* the Astaires took some screen tests for Paramount Pictures, who considered adapting the show as a movie musical. Paramount initially decided against the idea—the Astaires themselves thought that they "looked awful" on film—but the Associated British Pictures Corporation acquired the rights and released a 1936 film version, *She Knew What She Wanted,* that starred Betty Ann Davies (Frankie) and Claude Dampier (Jimmy) under the direction of Thomas Bentley. The picture, which hewed fairly closely to the original Fred Thompson story, but with Peter Thurston (Fred Conyngham) now a dance-band conductor as opposed to an aviator, featured five songs from the show: "Funny Face," "Let's Kiss and Make Up," "My One and Only," "'S Wonderful," and "Tell the Doc" (the last-named as an instrumental). One reviewer thought the film's heroine "as completely amoral as it is possible to conceive" and "much of the humour" to depend "on the intoxication of the characters," but deemed the performance of Albert Burdon (who played Dugsie) "genuinely funny," and the settings "lavish." [29]

In 1957 Paramount Pictures finally released its own film adaptation of the show, also titled *Funny Face.* This project began with producer-composer Roger Edens's decision to adapt a script by Leonard Gershe as a film musical that would feature Audrey Hepburn as Jo Stockton, an intellectual bookstore clerk turned model; and Fred Astaire as Dick Avery, a fashion photographer. Inspired by the script's references to Jo's "funny face," Edens and Gershe (after complex negotiations with MGM, Paramount, and Warner Brothers) grafted some of the *Funny Face* score (fleshed out by other Gershwin songs as well as a few numbers written by Edens and Gershe) into the Gershe story. [30]

Directed by Stanley Donen, the film used four popular songs from the original show ("Funny Face," "Let's Kiss and Make Up," and "He Loves and She Loves" as solos for Astaire, and "'S Wonderful" as a duet for

Astaire and Hepburn) along with a song that had been cut during try-outs ("How Long Has This Been Going On?" as a solo for Hepburn) and a song from *Oh, Kay!* ("Clap Yo' Hands" as a duet for Astaire and costar Kay Thompson, who played Maggie Prescott, a brassy fashion-magazine editor). The picture enjoyed the supporting expertise of or-chestrator Conrad Salinger and conductor Adolph Deutsch, but Astaire was past his prime vocally, while the undubbed Hepburn really had not much of a singing voice to begin with. Moreover, Edens and Gershe tin-kered with some of the lyrics to their detriment; and the redesigned con-texts for the songs tended to undermine their humor (the Edens-Gershe numbers worked better in this respect, in that they more effectively com-plemented the film's tone and narrative).

The film received excellent notices, nonetheless. Arthur Knight, in the *Saturday Review,* even deemed it "one of the best [film] musicals" since Donan's *Singin' in the Rain* and *Seven Brides for Seven Brothers.* Hep-burn in particular dazzled the critics. At the same time, Philip Roth in the *New Republic* sounded a more skeptical note, writing that Hepburn represented "a new kind of heroine not only because she speaks of Sartre and Tolstoy but because her moral stance, in its hyper-innocence, is so novel for musical comedy," an observation that helped chart the differ-ence between the film and the original show, with its lovably impudent heroine.[31]

Among stage revivals, a successful 1973 production by Buffalo's Studio Arena featured a new book by Neal Du Brock subsequently adopted by the rental agency Tams-Witmark. This version—in which Frankie's diary reveals that she is secretly in love with Jimmy (a newly devised character, Jimmy's fiancée, June Hampton, winds up with aviator Peter Thurston)—seems to have encouraged the misconception that the musical originally cast the Astaires as a romantic couple. Meanwhile, the Goodspeed Opera launched its own, more authentic revival of the work in 1981 to a revised book by Alfred Uhry; Clive Barnes in the *New York Post* commended this production as possessing "the charm of sim-ple masquerade."[32]

The revival that became the 1983 Broadway hit *My One and Only* had a more involved genesis. A brainchild of producer Bernie Carragher, the show initially brought together dancer-choreographer Tommy Tune, director Peter Sellars, bookwriter Tim Mayer, and musical director Craig Smith with the intention of faithfully reviving the *Funny Face* score but reworking the book entirely. Discussing the musical in the context of Rus-sian constructivism and Stravinsky's *Oedipus Rex* (also 1927), Sellars won over Ira and Leonore. Tommy Tune and English model Twiggy, who had costarred in Ken Russell's film version of the musical spoof *The Boy Friend* (1971), were cast as the romantic leads; and Paramount Theatre Productions committed millions of dollars to the venture, eventually titled *My One and Only* after a song from the original score.[33]

As rehearsals began in late 1982, the production fell apart. Whereas Sellars and Mayer aspired to Brechtian satire, Tune and the producers aimed for a more commercial entertainment, with the result that, as one observer noted, "Tune's glitz and Sellars's grit began to cancel each other." Moreover, Smith's commitment to musical authenticity, including nonamplified sound, worried the producers. Before opening in Boston on February 8 at the Colonial Theatre, Sellars and Smith were fired, and Tune took responsibility for the direction, assisted by co-choreographer Thommie Walsh and an uncredited Mike Nichols, while Jack Lee stepped in to supervise the musical arrangements and orchestrations.[34]

After a disastrous Boston premiere—described by *Variety* as "a disjointed, directionless jumble"—even more extensive changes were made. Tune, with the reluctant consent of the Gershwin estate, replaced some of the *Funny Face* score with numbers from other Gershwin shows; and a new bookwriter, Peter Stone, extensively retooled the book about aviator Billy Buck Chandler (Tune) and his love for swimming star Edythe Herbert (Twiggy). From the original score, Tune and Stone retained seven songs: "Funny Face," "High Hat," "He Loves and She Loves," "In the Swim," "'S Wonderful," "My One and Only," and the excised "How Long Has This Been Going On?" However, aside from its aviator hero (reconceived as a country boy from Texas) and its 1927 setting, the plot and characters had little to do with the original. Rather, the work unfolded more along the lines of *Nine* (which Tune had directed in 1982), that is, as a fast-paced series of numbers briefly punctuated by text. By the time the show arrived in New York, its backers had spent about four million dollars.[35]

My One and Only opened in New York at the St. James Theatre on May 1, 1983, to good reviews; the cinematic staging, Adrianne Lobel's sets, and the performances of Twiggy and Tune impressed audiences, but above all, the Gershwin songs carried the day. Described by *Variety* as "one of the most successful salvage efforts in recent Broadway history," the musical received nine Tony award nominations, ran for 767 performances on Broadway, and toured extensively across the country with Sandy Duncan in the Edythe Herbert role, alternately partnered with Tune and her husband, Don Correia. In 1985 the show traveled to Tokyo and

Osaka, while in 2002 it finally arrived in London, where, as in New York, the critics largely welcomed it as campy escapist entertainment.[36]

Meanwhile, with the support of Leonore Gershwin and in conjunction with Minneapolis's Guthrie Theater, director Peter Sellars pursued his original idea of finding a more exalted dramatic vehicle for Gershwin by interpolating sixteen songs from various musicals (though none from *Funny Face*) for a 1984 show, *Hang On to Me*, adapted from Maxim Gorky's 1904 play *Summerfolk*. "It is incomprehensible that they [Gershwin's songs] have always been seen in a dramatic context that barely comes up to their ankles," explained Sellars, "and never in a situation that prods them to reveal their secrets. If our evening at the Guthrie does anything, I would like to think that it brings Ira out from under the shadow of his brother George—that suddenly these very great words are permitted to mean things, and we can feel them figuratively or very, very literally." As for the connection with Gorky, Sellars cited a "pervasive melancholy" that distinguished the Gershwins from other Broadway composers—"George and Ira are at their best when they are trying to cheer themselves out of a depression"—and musical director Craig Smith similarly wrote that "a particular melancholy 'Russianness' in the Gershwin material suggested to us the combination of Gershwin and Gorky. In a sense this union or merging is a triumph of content over style." Reviewing the over-four-hour show for the *Wall Street Journal*, Sylviane Gold was dubious: "And it wasn't that the Gershwins didn't need the Gorky, or that the Gorky didn't need the Gershwins. It was that neither needed Peter Sellars."[37]

By glaring at each other, so to speak, from opposite ends of a dramatic continuum—described by Sellars as "the forces of Brecht vs. the forces of *The Pajama Game*"—*Hang On to Me* and *My One and Only* exemplified the ambiguity of Gershwin's achievement, the latter celebrating his giddiness, the former exploring his lower depths. But in their shared urge to divorce Gershwin's songs from their intended theatrical contexts, both shows similarly demonstrated the difficulties of accommodating the composer's musical-comedy scores to late-twentieth-century expectations and sensibilities.[38]

Chapter Twenty-Two

Rosalie and *Treasure Girl* (1928)

$\mathcal{L}$ess than two months after *Funny Face* debuted in New York, producer Florenz Ziegfeld launched a new show, *Rosalie,* with music by Gershwin and Sigmund Romberg, and lyrics by Ira and P. G. Wodehouse. Ziegfeld was at his height when he approached Gershwin in 1927 about writing something for Marilyn Miller and Jack Donahue; though still mounting the annual series of *Follies* that had made him a household name, he had become increasingly involved in musical comedy, his credits including such blockbuster successes as Jerome Kern's *Sally* (1920), Harry Tierney's *Rio Rita* (1927), and a new work by Kern that would open at the end of the year, *Show Boat.*

The notion of a collaboration between Gershwin and Romberg, the composer of such operettas as *The Student Prince* and *Desert Song,* bemused commentators from the start—Alexander Woollcott expected next to see a novel cowritten by Ernest Hemingway and best-selling minister-author Harold Bell Wright—but Gershwin had already written an operetta, *Song of the Flame* (1925), with Herbert Stothart, while Romberg, for his part, had much experience with jazzier forms of musical theater. Moreover, as *Rio Rita* and *Show Boat* demonstrated, Ziegfeld was forging his own kind of musical theater, which combined elements of musical comedy and operetta. Even more to the point, this new show involved a romance between an American cadet and a Graustarkian princess. Having Gershwin and Romberg collaborate on the music made especial sense in this context, while generating a certain newsworthiness as well.[1]

Marilyn Miller and Jack Donahue were among Broadway's most popular entertainers. A dainty blonde, Miller (1898–1936) had danced her way to stardom in the *Follies of 1918* and *Sally;* though by some accounts an indifferent singer and actress, she proved irresistible onstage, especially in roles that featured her dancing. Ziegfeld's wife, actress Billie Burke, thought that Miller symbolized "the grace and joy" that her husband "reached for in everything he staged," while film historian Richard Barrios considers her work in the film version of *Sally* (1929) to represent "probably the most eloquent dance on film until the rise of Fred Astaire." Gershwin, who had befriended Miller while working as a rehearsal pianist for the 1918 *Follies,* himself stated in the early 1930s, "Since Marilyn Miller, we have not had a great star." Gangly tap-dancer Jack Donahue (1892?–1930) similarly had achieved fame in the *Follies,* though this self-described "hoofer" was basically a vaudeville headliner. When Miller and Donahue partnered in Kern's *Sunny* (1925), critics compared them to the Astaires.[2]

For his own Miller-Donahue vehicle, Ziegfeld chose a story by William Anthony McGuire, his favorite bookwriter, though a heavy drinker and notoriously unreliable. Inspired by a widely publicized monthlong tour of America in 1926 by Queen Marie, Princess Ileana, and Prince Nicolas of Romania—which included a stop at West Point—and Charles Lindbergh's 1927 transatlantic flight, McGuire concocted a scenario involving a Balkan princess who falls in love with a West Point cadet. After lining up Gershwin and Romberg for the score, Ziegfeld (who named the heroine Rosalie, after his mother) approached Guy Bolton about collaborating with McGuire on the book, and suggested further that P. G. Wodehouse work on the lyrics, prompting the following exchange between Bolton and Ziegfeld, as recalled by the former:

> "How can he? You're getting Gershwin. He'll only work with Ira."
> "I'm having Romberg as well. He knows Rumania. He's been there. Plum [Wodehouse] knows Europe too. It's a good combination."
> "Two book writers, two lyric writers, two composers?'
> "Why not?"
> "It's all right if you can pay for it."
> "If I can't pay for things, I don't pay for them."

"This simple axiom," added Bolton, "summed up the principle on which all Ziegfeld undertakings were based."[3]

At the end of July Gershwin tried extricating himself from the venture because, as he explained to Ziegfeld, his new musical for the Astaires had been postponed, and now both shows were scheduled to begin rehearsals in the fall. "This is particularly unfortunate for me," wrote

Gershwin, "as I so admire Marilyn Miller and Jack Donahue and would like so much to write for them." But in a telegram dispatched immediately, Ziegfeld pleaded, "However after your promise to me and under the circumstances don't you think George that you could give me three or four numbers for the Marilyn Miller Jack Donahue play which we could specially advertise and protect you in every way as Marilyn is so very anxious to have something from you to dance to and to sing to and as you promised me you would do the show." Gershwin duly proceeded with the show.[4]

In two acts divided into eleven scenes, *Rosalie* opens in a palace square in the fictitious kingdom of Romanza, where spectators anxiously await the landing of Lieutenant Richard Fay (Oliver McLennan), a West Point cadet and aviator ("Here They Are"). Among the crowd are two Americans: former champion prizefighter Michael O'Brien (Clarence Oliver) and his daughter, Mary (Bobbe Arnst), whose boyfriend—another West Point cadet, Dick's irrepressible pal Bill Delroy (Jack Donahue)—is (or so Mary thinks) accompanying Dick on this heroic flight ("Show Me the Town").

King Cyril of Romanza (Frank Morgan), who prefers affairs with women to those of state, reluctantly agrees to accompany his imperious queen (Margaret Dale) and his lovely daughter, Princess Rosalie (Marilyn Miller), on a trip to the States in order to help secure an American loan. The queen also intends Rosalie to marry the prim Captain Carl Rabisco (Halford Young), whose wealthy father, Prince Rabisco (A. P. Kaye), has assisted the royal family financially. Dick and Bill arrive (separately, for Bill, afraid of flying, has traveled over sea and land); the former has come to Romanza to keep a date with a peasant girl (actually, Princess Rosalie) whom he had met the preceding year at a masquerade ball in Paris. After Rosalie and a regiment of hussars make their rounds ("Entrance of the Hussars" and "Hussar March"), she and Dick declare their love ("Say So!"); but when Dick discovers Rosalie's true identity, he angrily departs for home ("Finaletto").

En route to America on the SS *Isle de France*, Rosalie and Bill comfort each other ("Let Me Be a Friend to You"). Meanwhile, Dick has been promoted to the rank of captain ("West Point Bugle"). On the terrace at West Point, the cadets welcome the royal entourage ("West Point March"). Dick resumes his romance with Rosalie, who shares her elation with Bill ("Oh Gee!–Oh Joy!"). After Dick confronts the queen, however, Rosalie sadly agrees to marry Carl in order to protect Dick from a court-martial ("Kingdom of Dreams"). Proclaiming the betrothal of Rosalie and Carl, the queen orders the princess to spend the remaining time at West Point on board ship ("Finale").

The second act opens at a dance in the ballroom at West Point ("Opening Valse"). Mary praises American music ("New York Serenade") and Cyril flirts with the girls ("The King Can Do No Wrong"). As Bill and Mary reconcile ("Ev'rybody Knows I Love Somebody"), Rosalie enters disguised in a cadet uniform smuggled to her by Bill ("Follow the Drum").[5]

Alone on Lover's Lane, Mary ponders her affection for Bill ("How Long Has This Been Going On?"). Rosalie hides in Bill's quarters; before retiring, she and Bill perform their regulation exercises ("Setting-Up Exercises"). Realizing that only royal obligations stand between them, Dick and Rosalie accept Bill's suggestion that they return to Romanza and spark a revolution that would force Cyril's abdication (reprise of "Oh Gee!–Oh Joy!"). At the Ex-Kings' Club in Paris, former European monarchs gather (perhaps "At the Ex-Kings' Club" or "Tho' Today We Are Flunkeys Merely"), and Rosalie and a corps de ballet entertain ("The Ballet of Flowers"). Cyril happily announces both his abdication and the engagement of Dick and Rosalie ("Finale").[6]

Even by the standards of 1920s musical comedy, the show's book was rather far-fetched, from the idea of a West Point cadet flying across the Atlantic in order to keep a date with a presumed Balkan peasant girl to that of the two fomenting a coup d'état so that they can marry. But such mythic elements only highlighted the story's basic concern with clashing American and European values, a classic theme that struck close to home for Ziegfeld, whose first wife, Anna Held, was Parisian, and whose second wife, Billie Burke, had grown up in London. A few months after *Rosalie* opened, Gershwin himself allegedly embarked on an affair with a French countess as he continued work on his orchestral study of French-American contrasts, *An American in Paris*.

Far from the "three or four numbers" requested by Ziegfeld, George and Ira prepared at least seventeen numbers and a possible three or four more—not all used, naturally. For at least eight of these, Gershwin revamped earlier tunes, going as far back as "When the Mites Go By" (lyrics, Clifford Grey) from an unproduced musical, *Flying Island* (1922), for the chorus "When Cadets Parade"; and "Wait a Bit, Susie" from *Primrose* (1924), outfitted with a less-winning lyric for a song for Dick and Rosalie, "Beautiful Gypsy." He also recycled or adapted discarded songs from *Lady, Be Good!* ("The Man I Love"), *Oh, Kay!* ("Show Me the Town"), and *Strike Up the Band* ("Yankee Doodle Rhythm"), along with four numbers originally intended for *Funny Face:* "Dance Alone with

You" (as "Ev'rybody Knows I Love Somebody"), "When the Right One Comes Along" (as "Say So!"), "How Long Has This Been Going On?" and "Setting-Up Exercises."

Gershwin and Romberg possibly collaborated on at least one song, "Under the Furlough Moon," but generally worked apart—more so, it seems, than Gershwin did with Stothart on *Song of the Flame*. In contrast, Ira and Wodehouse cowrote a number of lyrics, including those for "Hussar March," "Say So!" "Oh Gee!–Oh Joy!" and "The King Can Do No Wrong." Of those numbers that seem to have made it to Broadway—aside from the finales, which involved the work of all four collaborators—Gershwin wrote the music for "Show Me the Town," "Say So!" "Let Me Be a Friend to You" (the music apparently lost), "Oh Gee!–Oh Joy!" "New York Serenade," "Ev'rybody Knows I Love Somebody," "Follow the Drum," "How Long Has This Been Going On?" "Setting-Up Exercises," and "At the Ex-Kings' Club," while Romberg wrote the music for "Here They Are," "Entrance of Hussars," "Hussar March," "West Point Bugle," "West Point March," "Kingdom of Dreams," "Opening Valse," "The King Can Do No Wrong," "Tho' Today We Are Flunkeys Merely," and "Ballet of Flowers" (based on "Kingdom of Dreams"). The show accordingly contained, again excluding finales, about twenty numbers split evenly between the two composers, making the work truly a joint enterprise. ("Beautiful Gypsy" and "Rosalie," another duet by Gershwin for Dick and Rosalie, were introduced during the tryout period and published, but dropped prior to the Broadway premiere.)

Ziegfeld presumably wanted Gershwin to write the songs for the American characters and Romberg, those for the Romanzans; and furthermore, to have Gershwin write the dance numbers and duets and Romberg, the choruses. This apparent strategy could not be maintained strictly—as witness Romberg's choruses for the West Point cadets or Gershwin's dances for Rosalie—but was carried forward enough to help underscore the theme of cultural difference, manifest immediately in the opening scene, in which Romberg's quasi-Slavic "Here They Are" rubs elbows with Mary's delightfully jazzy "Show Me the Town."

In a few numbers, such as the discarded title song, Gershwin vaguely evoked an operetta idiom himself, but most of his songs proved characteristic, as one might imagine from the origins of much of the score. This was entirely apropos: the cast featured primarily dancers and singers with vaudeville and musical-comedy backgrounds, and the show itself was essentially a musical comedy with some operetta trappings. Of course, Gershwin's musical-comedy style was itself hardly monolithic, and if

"Show Me the Town," "New York Serenade," "Ev'rybody Knows I Love Somebody," "Follow the Drum," and "Oh Gee!–Oh Joy!"—with their pentatonic motives repeated in shifting metrical contexts—reflected his infectiously breezy side, "Say So!" and "How Long Has This Been Going On?" struck a more romantic note. These two songs—the first a moderately paced fox-trot, the second a slow ballad—were particularly masterful and, in their own way, daring, with "Say So!" featuring a theme full of unusual rests and syncopated accents that required from Ira and Wodehouse a matching telegraphic style of their own ("Say So! / Say you love me; / None above me / In your heart. / Pining—I'll be pining till you do!") and "How Long Has This Been Going On?"—a bittersweet study of sexual awakening—containing lush harmonies colored by blue notes, the whole rigorously unified by classic sighing gestures. As a whole, Gershwin's music for *Rosalie* displayed a sedate elegance distinct from his more boisterous scores, and congruent with the show's sheet-music cover illustration depicting Miller as a stylish, modern princess.

"Setting-Up Exercises," for its part, looked back to Debussy's "Golliwog's Cakewalk" (1908) and ahead to Gershwin's "Walking the Dog" from *Shall We Dance* (1937). William Daly's original orchestration might even eventually earn for this charming piece something of the success of *Promenade* (as "Walking the Dog" became known). An abbreviated and somewhat corrupt arrangement of the music for piano was published in 1974 as *Merry Andrew,* and as such won no lesser advocates than pianist-composers William Bolcom and Richard Rodney Bennett.

Ziegfeld lavishly spent close to $150,000 on the show. Prior to rehearsals, he hired a sixty-man orchestra just to play through the score for a large group of friends and employees, a needlessly extravagant gesture, opined his press agent. The show's supporting cast included the handsome Australian tenor Oliver McLennan (Dick), the sprightly ingenue Bobbe Arnst (Mary), the droll Frank Morgan (Cyril), and the regal Margaret Dale (the queen). Set designer Joseph Urban and costumer John W. Harkrider devised elaborate stage pictures ranging from a public square in Romanza to a West Point ballroom to a Paris nightclub. Seymour Felix staged the work, assisted by Michel Fokine, who choreographed the second-act ballet. Oscar Bradley directed from the pit and an impressive number of leading orchestrators—Hilding Anderson, William Daly, Maurice DePackh, Emil Gerstenberger, Hans Spialek, and Max Steiner—scored the music. A chorus of sixty-four, supplemented by the eight Estelle Liebling Singers, filled out the stage.[7]

The show opened at Boston's spacious Colonial Theater on December 8, 1927. Bostonians were eager to see two popular stars in Ziegfeld's latest extravaganza—with a score by Romberg and Gershwin, no less—and advance sales were brisk, even at a relatively expensive $5.50 a ticket, making the musical, according to the *Globe*, the "biggest 'money' opening" at a Boston theater. The show came into town long—it began at eight and ended close to midnight—and Ziegfeld (as he had done with *Show Boat*) asked the first-night crowd to be judicious in their applause so that they might better know what to cut before opening in New York. But the audience applauded throughout the evening, including some of Urban's set designs; the mere entrances of Donahue and Miller stopped the show for a few minutes. The critics loved the piece as well, and *Rosalie* enjoyed a highly successful Boston run for two and a half weeks, with, noted one review, demand for orchestra seats "on a par with grade A Scotch."[8]

Trimmed by about half an hour, the show opened in New York on January 10, 1928, at the New Amsterdam Theatre on 42nd Street, the large Art Nouveau showcase for the *Follies*. The production dazzled the critics, beginning with a newly designed curtain ornamented with ermine tails and jeweled crowns. "Mr. Ziegfeld again departs from the beaten track in musical comedy production," reported the *Mirror*, "and the result is a thrilling, engrossing, cyclonic entertainment, freighted with beauty and surprises." Alexander Woollcott more wryly reported in the *World*,

> There comes a time once in every two or three years when the vast stage of that playhouse [the New Amsterdam] begins to show signs of a deep and familiar agitation. Down in the orchestra pit the violins chitter with excitement and the brasses blare. The spotlights turn white with expectation. Fifty beautiful girls in simple peasant costumes of satin and chiffon rush pellmell onto the stage, all squealing simple peasant outcries of "Here she comes!" Fifty hussars in a fatigue uniform of ivory white and tomato bisque march on in column [*sic*] of fours and kneel to express an emotion too strong for words. The lights swing to the gateway at the back and settle there. The house holds its breath. And on walks Marilyn Miller.

Some thought that the musical even surpassed *Rio Rita* and *Show Boat* as Ziegfeld's finest accomplishment to date—though *Variety*, which complained about the $6.60 top ticket, thought those shows a better value. Every aspect of the production evoked accolades, especially Donahue's performance, but also the book, widely admired for its humor. *Arts & Decoration* called *Rosalie* "modern musical comedy at its peak," and

Mayor Jimmy Walker, who attended the premiere, predicted that it would run for two years.[9]

Since the program book, for the most part, cited the composer of each number, reviewers were better able to evaluate the contributions of the show's two composers than had been the case with the Gershwin-Stothart operetta, *Song of the Flame*. Romberg's choruses accordingly received their due, but Gershwin's music earned the lion's share of praise. "Brother Romberg has written his usual thunderous choruses which you enjoy while they are being roared at you and forget by the time you reach the lobby," wrote Woollcott. "Brother Gershwin has written at least two jaunty songs which follow you further up the street." By "two jaunty songs" Woollcott probably meant "Say So!" and "Oh Gee!–Oh Joy!" both widely singled out by the critics. Ironically, the number best remembered today, "How Long Has This Been Going On?" received hardly any special notice, perhaps because, as the *New Republic* reported, Arnst's "semi-conversational technique and her useful, but unbeautiful voice" obscured its "real beauty."

Rosalie enjoyed 327 performances and would prove, aside from *Lady, Be Good!* and *Of Thee I Sing*, the longest-running Broadway musical of Gershwin's career. Popular recording artists Johnny Johnson, Sam Lanin, and Ben Selvin quickly released recordings of "Say So!" and "Oh Gee!–Oh Joy!" whereas not until Lee Wiley and Peggy Lee recorded "How Long Has This Been Going On?" in 1939 and 1941, respectively, did that song catch on, eventually entering the repertoires of Rosemary Clooney, Chris Connor, Ella Fitzgerald, Judy Garland, Johnny Hartman, Dinah Shore, Sarah Vaughan, and scores of others. Meanwhile, "Say So!" and "Oh Gee!–Oh Joy!" lost their former popularity, though recordings of the former by Joan Morris–Max Morath, and the latter by both Bobby Short and Sylvia McNair–Hal Cazalet, evidenced their continued appeal.

In 1930 MGM hired Wodehouse to adapt *Rosalie* as a musical film for Marion Davies, but the project was eventually abandoned, at least in part because of declining interest in movie musicals, but perhaps, too, because of Davies's reported "indifference" to the material. In 1936, however, after musical films had come back into vogue, the studio once again retained Wodehouse to prepare a film adaptation, though the original bookwriter, William McGuire, now the film's producer, eventually rewrote the script himself. MGM commissioned a new score from Cole Porter, which seems inexplicable, though a 1936 letter from Wodehouse to Bolton intimates the studio's thinking: "*Rosalie* always was a pretty good bet, as was shown by the fact that it ran a year in New York with a score without a hit tune in it, purely on the strength of its comedy."[10]

Directed by W. S. Van Dyke, *Rosalie* (1937) starred Nelson Eddy and Eleanor Powell along with Frank Morgan, re-creating his Broadway role, and Ray Bolger in the Donahue part. The story stayed close to its Broadway source, including some incorporation of the original dialogue, documenting the viability, if not necessarily quality, of the early musical-comedy book. Porter's score featured the lovely "In the Still of the Night," Albertina Rasch staged some elaborate dances, and no expense was spared, but the two-hour spectacle, though a success at the box office, proved a critical failure, a "smash flop," in the words of the *New Yorker.* The picture's attempt to re-create some Ziegfeldian glamour at least shed light on the original show, as did some of the individual performances (explicitly in the case of Morgan, though more indirectly with Powell and Bolger, the decade's answer to Miller and Donahue). Ziegfeld never lived, incidentally, to see the picture; neither did Gershwin, Miller, or Donahue, all three of whom died tragically young in their thirties (Donahue by his own hand). Some years later, a film biography of Marilyn Miller, *Look for the Silver Lining* (1949), finally brought one of the hits of the original score—"Oh Gee!–Oh Joy!"—to the silver screen.[11]

As a stage work, *Rosalie* remained for some decades a staple among provincial theaters specializing in operetta, such as the Paper Mill Playhouse in Milburn, New Jersey (1946, 1948), the Moonlight Opera Company of Atlanta (1947), and the St. Louis Municipal Opera, where no fewer than six productions between 1938 and 1960 regularly drew upwards of ten thousand attendees at a single performance. These revivals featured revised books and scores, usually including interpolations from the Cole Porter film, while following the basic story line. They also generally won good notices. As late as 1960 the St. Louis *Globe-Democrat,* for instance, found the show "still good entertainment," in spite of its "dated" plot. On the other hand, New York's drama critics were "stupefied" by an apparently dreadful revival by Theater under the Stars in Central Park in 1957. "After being rained out on Monday night, the Central Park version of 'Rosalie' finally unveiled itself last evening," stated Walter Kerr in the *Herald-Tribune.* "What we need is more rain."[12]

After 1960, *Rosalie* increasingly vanished from public view just as some of the jazzier Gershwin musicals began appearing with greater frequency. But the New Amsterdam Theatre Company staged a particularly successful concert reading of the work at New York's Town Hall in April 1983 that starred Marianne Tatum (Rosalie), Richard Muenz (Dick),

Alexandra Korey (Mary), Russ Thacker (Bill), and George S. Irving (Cyril), under the musical direction of Evans Haile, and that included not only the full score with, for the most part, the original orchestrations, but also four dropped numbers: "Beautiful Gypsy," "Rosalie," "The Man I Love," and "Yankee Doodle Rhythm." In his review for the *New York Times,* Stephen Holden ironically singled out the last two numbers as among the score's "strongest," but Ziegfeld and his associates knew their business, and one can imagine how all four excised songs might have slowed down the drama. In any case, even without these interpolations, the score had enough of Gershwin's humor and Romberg's dash, enhanced by a charming story and delightful lyrics, to merit continued revival.[13]

Much as Aarons and Freedley produced two Gershwin shows for the Astaires in close succession, so they followed *Oh, Kay!* with another Gershwin brothers show for Gertrude Lawrence, *Treasure Girl* (originally called *Tally Ho*). For the book they engaged Fred Thompson, who had collaborated with the Gershwins on three previous musicals, and Vincent Lawrence (ca. 1890–1946), a young playwright whose credits included some successful comedies, including *Two Fellows and a Girl* (1923).

Treasure Girl opens at the beachfront home of real-estate agent Mortimer ("Morty") Grimes (Ferris Hartman), where a nocturnal pirate beach party is in progress ("Skull and Bones"). Nat McNally (Clifton Webb), though ostensibly engaged to Morty's daughter, Mary (Gertrude McDonald), flirts with Polly Tees (Mary Hay) ("I've Got a Crush on You"). Morty explains to his manager, Neil Forrester (Paul Frawley), that he has invited over a hundred people to search for twenty thousand dollars hidden on his property as part of a promotional scheme. Nat's British cousin, Ann Wainwright (Gertrude Lawrence), chances upon Neil, her former lover ("Oh, So Nice"). Nat's plans to marry Polly are contingent on his borrowing money from Ann, but she is as broke as he is; a process server, Larry Hopkins (Walter Catlett), even accosts her with a summons for money owed. All the guests dash off after Morty announces the treasure hunt ("According to Mister Grimes").

Ann, Nat, and Polly agree to look for the treasure together and invite Larry to join them ("A-Hunting We Will Go"). The first stage of the hunt brings the guests to the countrified business office of Morty's realty, where Neil presides with his assistant, Bunce ("Place in the Country"). Nat and Polly express their mutual affection ("K-ra-zy for You"), while Neil and Ann agree that their love affair is over ("I Don't Think I'll Fall in Love

Today"). Larry and the ensemble recount their good fortune ("Got a Rainbow"). In order to search the grounds for the treasure, Ann entices Neil away by pretending to have romantic feelings for him ("Feeling I'm Falling"). As Ann finds a chart indicating the location of the treasure on nearby Alligator Island, Neil discovers her deception ("Finale").

As the second act opens, the treasure seekers arrive on Alligator Island to continue the hunt ("Treasure Island"). Nat and Polly confront love's heartaches ("What Causes That?"), while Neil and Ann rekindle their romance (reprise of "Feeling I'm Falling" in some performances). Coming closer to discovering the money, Ann and Nat exult in life's simple pleasures ("What Are We Here For?"). After some gangsters, including "Slug" Bullard and his first mate, frighten almost everyone away, Neil and Ann find themselves stranded alone on the island; as Neil exacts his revenge by treating Ann roughly, she responds in kind, until he leaves her alone to fend for herself.[14]

Although Ann finds the treasure, she returns home depressed and lonely ("Where's the Boy? Here's the Girl!"). Neil intends to leave for Mexico, but Ann announces their engagement, and the two join Nat and Polly in celebrating their impending marriages ("Finale").

The book—which proved the show's downfall—was less complicated than that of most Gershwin musicals but also less focused, with some of the characters—including the key comic role, Larry Hopkins—seemingly disconnected from the main plot and its resolution. True, the script featured a smart, caustic tone, anticipating the likes of *Pal Joey* by more than a decade—Ira himself referred to "some excellent dialogue by Vincent Lawrence"—but such acerbity proved unflattering to Lawrence, who flourished in parts of greater grace and charm, and who made matters worse by joking her way through the role. "The probable reason for the demise of [*Treasure Girl*]," recalled Ira, "was that Gertrude Lawrence . . . was here cast as one so avid for money and position that she even double-crossed her favorite young man. Not even [Gertrude] could overcome the, shall we say, bitchiness of the role." The script that provided the preceding synopsis, "corrected to December 17, 1928," by stage director Sam Fischer (who had stage-managed *Tip-Toes* and *Funny Face* as well), may have tried to soften Ann's part somewhat by, for instance, having her reluctantly betray Neil only at the pleading of Nat and Polly; if so, such revisions were too little, too late.[15]

The book at least drew from the Gershwins a particularly sophisticated score, one that occasionally reflected the show's pirate theme, as in the lively "rum tum tum" opening chorus, "Skull and Bones," with its jig rhythms; the similarly jiglike "A-Hunting We Will Go," with its quotation of the popular ditty of the same name; and "Dead Men Tell No Tales," a darkly colored solo for the first mate, eventually dropped, that humorously reconceived the modern gangster as buccaneer. But the pirate-inspired numbers—which no doubt put the Gershwins in mind of Gilbert and Sullivan's *Pirates of Penzance*—merely provided background color for the score proper, which contained at its core six duets, three for Neil and Ann ("Feeling I'm Falling," "Oh, So Nice!" and "I Don't Think I'll Fall in Love Today") and three for Nat and Polly ("I've Got a Crush on You," "K-ra-zy for You," and "What Causes That?").

These duets similarly trace the vagaries of love and romance, but those for Neil and Ann naturally are more urbane than those for Nat and Polly. "I Don't Think I'll Fall in Love Today" even sports a Noël Coward–like savoir faire, though with a personality of its own, established at once in the introduction as the triadic melody clashes dissonantly with a series of descending chromatic triads. "Feeling I'm Falling" likewise features a refined though playful elegance. For its part, "Oh, So Nice!" recalls such earlier Gershwin songs as "Clap Yo' Hands" and "Let's Kiss and Make Up" in its intended "effort to get the effect of a Viennese waltz in fox-trot time," though the technique appears here with unprecedented suavity, involving subtle metrical shifts throughout its main theme (which otherwise resembles Richard Strauss's "Ohne mich" from *Der Rosen-kavalier*), and inspiring from Ira an unusual rhyme scheme that enhances the melody's intricate structure.[16]

The three snazzy duets for Nat and Polly entail more vigorous syncopation. "What Causes That?" is most remarkable in this respect, with its long strings of syncopated notes on the same pitch, a comically high-strung counterpart to the melancholy theme from the opening movement of the Concerto in F. Ira's streetwise lyrics for these duets, as suggested even by their titles, nicely complement their rhythmic verve. Like "'S Wonderful," though something of its opposite (in its use of expansions as opposed to contractions), "K-ra-zy for You" features the additional novelty of slangy pronunciations, including those for *crazy* ("k-ra-zy"), *glad* ("ga-lad"), and *craving* ("k-raving"), the last ingeniously paired with *caresses*.

Filling out the score are "What Are We Here For?" the kind of buoyant duet, like "Oh Gee!–Oh Joy!" that the Gershwins occasionally wrote for their leading lady and principal male comic; "Got a Rainbow," a lively Pollyanna number; and "Where's the Boy?"—a haunting second-act ballad whose main theme brilliantly develops, along the lines of "So Am I" and "'S Wonderful," a simple three-note motive, though the song more closely resembles, at least in tone, "Someone to Watch Over Me" (also written for Lawrence).

Treasure Girl premiered in Philadelphia on October 15, 1928, and opened on Broadway at the Alvin on November 8, 1928. Bertram Harrison directed; Bobby Connolly staged the dances; Joseph Urban designed the sets; Kiviette created the costumes; Alfred Newman led the orchestra, which included pianists Victor Arden and Phil Ohman; and William Daly supervised the orchestrations. Beside Lawrence, the cast featured Clifton Webb (Nat), one of Broadway's most graceful musical-comedy leading men (and later to become one of Hollywood's most waspish character actors); Mary Hay (Polly), who earlier had partnered with Webb in *Sunny;* Paul Frawley (Neil), another *Sunny* star, and one remembered by Ginger Rogers as having "a strong singing voice and a definite masculine appeal" (Frawley's brother William, incidentally, played Fred Mertz on the television show *I Love Lucy*); Walter Catlett (Larry), the comedian who had scored such a success in *Lady, Be Good!* and who, like Webb, would move on to a successful Hollywood career; and a chorus of forty-one women and twenty-five men.[17]

The reviews were dismal. The critics acknowledged that the sets and costumes were colorful, the chorus, vivacious, and the lyrics, catchy. And although some found Gershwin's "abstruse" music less than "contagious"—tellingly, many singled out for praise the tuneful but not particularly original "Got a Rainbow"—both Brooks Atkinson in the *Times* and Francis Bellamy in the *Outlook* thought at least some of the music among his best. Lawrence herself recalled that "Where's the Boy?" "went over big." "Gershwin has never seemed to us more melodious, whimsical and haunting," wrote Bellamy, even if, aside from Lawrence and Frawley, none of the cast members appeared, noted Atkinson, "up to the task of singing appreciatively in the vein that suits Mr. Gershwin's music best."[18]

Even so, neither the production nor the music could redeem the book, described by *Billboard* as "vapid, humorless and absolutely inane," with dialogue, added the *New Yorker,* that was "hopelessly, remorselessly dull." Robert Benchley, writing in *Life,* actually thought the lines no "worse than in most shows of this kind . . . but they obtrude themselves more and seem worse, and there is a general atmosphere of a lost cause about the whole thing which depresses the cast as well as the audience." "'Treasure Girl' simply isn't much fun," concluded the *Evening World.*

St. John Ervine suspected that the show might close before his notice went to print, while others thought that the talent assembled, even if largely wasted, would guarantee a respectable run anyway. They were overly optimistic. *Treasure Girl* closed after sixty-eight performances, leaving Ira Gershwin to observe some years later, "some songwriters to the contrary, numbers alone do not make a show." None of the show's songs had much success on their own either, at least for a while. Even "I've Got a Crush on You" did not gain wide popularity until 1939, when Lee Wiley recorded it as a ballad rather than as an "Allegretto giocoso" dance number, an approach that subsequently established itself as standard among a wide range of recording artists, from Frank Sinatra and Bill Henderson to Linda Ronstadt and Carly Simon.[19]

Over the years, a few knowing singers nonetheless unearthed some of *Treasure Girl*'s forgotten gems. Louise Carlyle recorded "Where's the Boy?" (1954); Betty Comden, no less than six songs from the show (1963); Bobby Short, "Feeling I'm Falling," "K-ra-zy for You," and "I've Got a Crush on You," the last up-tempo, as originally conceived (1973); and Joan Morris and Max Morath, "Feeling I'm Falling" and "I Don't Think I'll Fall in Love Today" (1977). Short sacrificed some of the charm of "K-ra-zy for You" by omitting its verse, in which admissions of poetic deficiencies as compared to Byron and Swinburne ("I cannot spill passion / In highfalutin' fashion") serve as a preparation for the chorus as the singer's poetic best ("Let me give you the low-down: / I'm k-ra-zy for you"). This particular song enjoyed further attention with the arrival of *Crazy for You* on Broadway in 1992, as did "What Causes That?" which went from almost complete obscurity to become the surprise hit of the show.

Chapter Twenty-Three

An American in Paris (1928)
and *East Is West* (1929)

*A*fter spending a week in Paris in April 1926, Gershwin sent his hosts, Robert and Mabel Schirmer, a thank-you postcard dated April 11 inscribed with two musical quotes: the opening of the "Andantino" from the *Rhapsody in Blue,* and a melodic fragment marked "Very Parisienne" and labeled "An American in Paris." In January 1928, as he began work in earnest on an "orchestral ballet" titled *An American in Paris,* he returned to the latter snippet. At first, he was not sure how to develop the music—"as I was not a Frenchman, I knew that I was about as far as I could get with it"—but pondering the matter in his home on 103rd Street, the sight of the Hudson River provided the necessary inspiration, as he explained in 1929:

> I love that river and I thought how often I had been homesick for a sight of it, and then the idea struck me—an American in Paris, homesickness, the blues. So there you are. I thought of a walk on the Champs Elysées, of the honking taxi, of passing a building which I believed was a church but which Deems Taylor, who wrote the program notes, says is the salon. There are episodes on the left bank, and then come the blues—thinking of home, perhaps the Hudson. There is a meeting with a friend, and after a second fit of blues [a] decision that in Paris one may as well do as the Parisians do.

In the same year, he again referred to his "love" for the Hudson in a letter to Rosamond Walling: "The Hudson River and the sunsets over the Palisades, the little tug boats and the ocean liners, the funny looking phut-phut-phutters, the graceful birds and the imitating aeroplanes—an ever-changing picture."[1]

In March 1928 Gershwin left for Europe, where he hoped to complete this new work—and possibly a second rhapsody for piano and orchestra—by the time he returned in midsummer. After arriving in France, he even contemplated spending a whole year there to compose and study, but in the end he stayed in Europe only the three months, from mid-March to mid-June as originally planned.[2]

While abroad, he made progress on the piece, trying out some of the music on April 6 for Vernon Duke, who, noted Ira in his diary, argued that Gershwin "was 1928 in his musical comedies and in most of his concert music but in latter [*An American in Paris*] he allowed himself to become somewhat saccharine in spots." Gershwin also played "quite a large portion" of the work for publisher Richard Simon, who described its slow theme to his brother, Alfred, on May 2 as "'The Man I Love' backed off the boards by several kilometers." Simon also referred to a possible May 25 premiere in Paris, but this clearly was premature. "George was getting along nicely with the *American in Paris*," observed Ira on May 22.[3]

Perhaps inspired by Varèse or Antheil, or by Frederick Shepherd Converse's use of a Ford automobile horn in his most famous piece, *Flivver Ten Million: A Joyous Epic* (1927), Gershwin decided to incorporate the sound of taxi horns into this new work; and before departing Paris, he and Mabel Schirmer went shopping for taxi horns among the automobile shops along the Avenue de la Grande Armée. "We went to every shop we could find to look for taxi horns," recalled Schirmer. "He wanted horns that could sound certain notes." When duo-pianists Jacques Fray and Mario Braggiotti visited Gershwin at his hotel, they espied about twenty taxi horns lying about, as Braggiotti later recalled:

> "Oh," he [Gershwin] said, "you're looking at these horns. Well, in the opening section of *An American in Paris* I would like to get the traffic sound of the Place de la Concorde during the rush hour, and I'd like to see if it works. I've written the first two pages of the opening. Jacques, you take this horn—this is in A flat. Mario, you take this—it's in F sharp. Now, I'll sit down and play, and when I go this way with my head, you go 'quack, quack, quack' like that in that rhythm."
>
> So we took the horns, and there we stood, nervous and excited, and for the first time we heard the opening bars of *An American in Paris*—a lanky American walking down the Champs-Elysées. He [Gershwin] captured the atmosphere, the feeling, the movement, the rhythm so perfectly.[4]

While still in Europe, Gershwin agreed to let Walter Damrosch—to whom he had granted the right of first refusal in appreciation of that conductor's commission of the Concerto in F—introduce the work that coming season with the recently merged New York Philharmonic–Symphony Society. Leopold Stokowski also expressed interest in premiering the piece, as did Sergey Diaghilev, who, according to Léonide Massine, "enjoyed the sophisticated nostalgia of Gershwin's music"; but Gershwin's promise to Damrosch precluded these other possibilities.[5]

On returning home, Gershwin completed a sketch score of the work—written in two to four staves—on August 1 and, a few weeks later, a two-piano version that included some ideas regarding orchestration. Receiving word on November 5 from Damrosch that the premiere was scheduled for December 13, he finished the orchestration of this "tone poem for orchestra," as the title page read, on November 28 in the guest quarters at Bydale, James Warburg and Kay Swift's country home in Greenwich, Connecticut. He subsequently stated that he had no idea "how much work I was in for" when he began this "rhapsody" back in January: "I intended to write just a song and dance number, but the music assumed increasingly more extensive proportions as I went on."[6]

In August Gershwin discussed the piece, here called "a rhapsodic ballet," in some detail with *Musical America:*

> This new piece, really a rhapsodic ballet, is written very freely and is the most modern music I've yet attempted. . . .
> The opening part will be developed in typical French style, in the manner of Debussy and the Six, though the themes are all original. My purpose here is to portray the impressions of an American visitor in Paris as he strolls about the city, listens to the various street noises, and absorbs the French atmosphere.
> As in my other orchestral compositions, I've not endeavored to present any definite scenes in this music. . . . The rhapsody is programmatic only in a general impressionistic way, so that the individual listener can read into the music such episodes as his imagination pictures for him. . . .
> The opening gay section . . . is followed by a rich 'blues' with a strong rhythmic undercurrent. Our American friend, perhaps after strolling into a café, and having a few drinks, has suddenly succumbed to a spasm of homesickness. The harmony here is both more intense and simple than in the preceding pages. This 'blues' rises to a climax followed by a coda in which the spirit of the music returns to the vivacity and bubbling exuberance of the opening part with its impressions of Paris. Apparently the homesick American, having left the café and reached the open air, has downed his spell of the blues and once again is an alert spectator of Parisian life. At the conclusion, the street noises and French atmosphere are triumphant.[7]

On one of his 1934 radio shows, Gershwin also provided this helpful summary:

> This piece describes an American's visit to the gay and beautiful city of
> Paris. We see him sauntering down the Champs Elysées, walking stick
> in hand, tilted straw hat, drinking in the sights, and other things as well.
> We see the effect of the French wine, which makes him homesick for
> America. And that's where the blue begins. I mean the blues begin. He
> finally emerges from his stupor to realize once again that he is in the gay
> city of Paree, listening to the taxi-horns, the noise of the boulevards, and
> the music of the can-can, and thinking, "Home is swell! But after all, this
> is Paris—so let's go!"[8]

Such commentary would have made perfectly fine program notes, but
for some reason, Gershwin asked or permitted his colleague, Deems Taylor, whose "judgement" he admired, to write a more extended narrative
for the New York Philharmonic's program book. Basing his program on
"Mr. Gershwin's own version of the succession of events, augmented
by a few details supplied by the helpful commentator and—as yet—
unrepudiated by the composer," Taylor at one point even begged to differ with the composer: "Both themes are now discussed at some length
by the instruments, until our tourist happens to pass—something. The
composer thought it might be a church, while the commentator held out
for the Grand Palais, where the salon holds forth." Some symphony patrons took offense at the note's barely disguised allusions to prostitution
in its reference to an "unhallowed" episode in which "a solo violin approaches our hero (in the soprano register) and addresses him in the most
charming broken English"; and to its reference to Prohibition in the aside
"—and by the way, whatever became of that lad Volstead?" But in any
event, for all its importance, Taylor's note (possibly influenced by John
Alden Carpenter's program to *Adventures in a Perambulator,* a work
often cited in early discussions of *An American in Paris*) cannot be considered definitive.[9]

An American in Paris comprises five sections, each with its own principal theme or themes, which once stated, however, reappear throughout the piece. The first section, "Allegretto grazioso," presents the work's
two main themes: an opening sauntering theme ("semplice"), articulated
by a taxi motive (including taxi-horn beeps) and a brief quote of the popular 1905 Charles Borel-Clerc song, "La Mattchiche" (of possible Brazilian derivation, this tune, also known as "La Maxixe" and "La Sorella,"
was parodied in the States as "My ma gave me a nickel, to buy a pickle");
and a humorous theme ("con umore") introduced by the clarinets in their

upper register. This opening section also puts forth a subsidiary idea that uses triplet rhythms (as at rehearsal 20).[10]

The sauntering and humorous themes (often referred to as the first and second "walking themes") are linked by a short flute solo that Gershwin possibly intended as an alcoholic counterpart to the presumed cocaine pantomime from *Blue Monday Blues;* an early sketch of the humorous theme tellingly bears the word *Drunk.* This might explain the humorous theme's dissonant leaps, which seem amusingly inebriated. But an air of intoxication informs this entire section as it does much of the piece (Gershwin himself spoke of his hero "drinking in the sights, and other things as well")—so much so that the work, as Taylor intimated, can be read in part as a repudiation of Prohibition. At the same time, depictions of tipsiness constituted a time-weathered comic tradition.

The second section, "Subito con brio," conforms to that part of the Taylor narrative in which the American arrives at the Left Bank. A new theme ("marcato"), introduced by the violins and trombone—sometimes called the third "walking theme"—and its percussive setting evoke a noisier and more frenetic depiction of street activity than found earlier.

The third section, "Andante ma con ritmo deciso," introduces the American's "blues" and "spasm of homesickness." This section's main theme ("expressivo"), first stated by solo trumpet with felt crown, reveals a kinship not only with the slow movement of the Concerto in F but with Bach's famous "Air." This Bachian allusion—which tenuously places the work in the context of the time's neoclassical trends—assumes even more tangibility with the string response that answers this melody (at three before rehearsal 47) and the walking bass that later supports it (at rehearsal 50).

The fourth section, "Allegro," a continued expression of homesickness, opens with a faster twelve-bar blues theme (initially put forth by two trumpets), described by Taylor and succeeding commentators as a Charleston but more accurately referred to by the composer as "a second fit of blues." A return of the sauntering theme ("Moderato con grazia") marks the start of the fifth section, which corresponds, in Gershwin's telling, to the American's reaching "open air" and becoming once again an "alert spectator of Parisian life."

All five sections arrive at climaxes—the first two marked "Con fuoco," the last three marked "Grandioso"—shortly before their conclusions. Moreover, each section starts in its own key and moves to a new key at its climax, with the resulting tonal design (F–E♭, E–A♭, B♭–A, D–C, and A–F) as colorful as its profusion of tuneful melodies and piquant sonorities. The three "Grandioso" moments feature broad statements of the slow blues, with the second of these—that is, the climax of the fourth section—forming the apex of the entire work.

After their respective climaxes, each section—with the natural exception of the last—subsides into transitional material. The first three of these transitions are marked "Calmato," while the fourth concludes with two measures of "Adagio." The first "Calmato," the longest of these bridge passages, presents a transformed version of the sauntering theme in the English horn, against soft, lush chords in the strings (related to the triplet idea), that represents Gershwin's church (and Taylor's Grand Palais). The second "Calmato" introduces a dialogue between the solo violin and the English horn (later solo viola) that presumably constitutes Taylor's "unhallowed" episode, but perhaps as well Gershwin's "meeting with a friend," though the composer's 1929 note suggests that this "meeting" occurs during, not prior to, the blues music. In any case, this second "Calmato"—"unhallowed" or not—seems to trigger the blues, thus providing the linchpin on which the narrative hangs.

The work's five sections basically form a large *ABA* structure: the first *A* (comprising the first two sections) depicting the American "drinking in the sights, and other things" of Paris; the *B* episode (comprising sections three and four), his homesickness; and the return of *A* (section five), his cheerful resignation. In the tradition of *Short Story* and some other pieces, the relatively brief reprise of *A* serves as both recapitulation and coda; Gershwin obviously liked such asymmetrical structures. That the earlier *B* episode includes two sections of widely varying mood provides additional formal ambiguity, leading some analysts to suggest other schematic interpretations of the work.[11]

During an early stage of composition, Gershwin sketched out an encapsulated program that offers additional insight into his intentions: "sees girl/meets girl/back to 2/4—strolling, flirtation/into cafe/mix love theme with 2/4/conversation leading to slow blues." How these ideas may have informed the finished tone-poem is hard to say, but they can be made to fit the initial *A* material, with the "meets girl" segment possibly corresponding to the section later identified by Gershwin as "passing a building." In any case, these sketched jottings imply that the music has a full-blown romantic subtext. The piece can even be read as a kind of self-portrait, its personality—variously debonair, energetic, melancholy, and ironic—strongly reminiscent of the composer's own. No other piece by Gershwin seems quite so confessional.[12]

On yet another level, the piece represents a study in the differences between the music of France and that of America. The *A* parts, representing Paris, largely feature duple meters, singsong rhythms, diatonic melodies, and the sounds of oboe, English horn, and taxi horns; while the *B* episode, representing New York, tends more toward 4/4 meters, syncopated rhythms, bluesy melodies, and the sounds of trumpet, saxophone, and snare drum. However, the work reveals a unified and individual voice from beginning to end, notwithstanding the composer's acknowledged debts to Debussy and *les Six*. Moreover, the concluding *A* provides a grand synthesis, most notably the final "Grandioso," which neatly juxtaposes a statement of the slow blues theme with a countermelody that features both the humorous theme and the first three—albeit elongated—notes of the sauntering theme.

Such contrapuntal ingenuity can be found throughout the work, which largely unfolds via the manipulation of key motives; Steven Gilbert thought the absence of generic material not only unprecedented but unique in Gershwin's career. The piece certainly makes extensive use of layering, retrograde, augmentation, diminution, thematic transformation, invertible counterpoint, contrary motion, and other contrapuntal techniques—all the better to convey a sense of bustling Parisian life. The taxi music (at rehearsal 4), for instance, involves a repeated six-note motive played by the flutes and xylophone accompanied by the same motive repeated in augmentation in the bassoons and lower strings, along with a melody in the oboe corresponding to the flute countermelody heard at the very start of the piece. In another passage (at rehearsal 21), this taxi motive appears for two measures juxtaposed with the triplet idea and the strolling theme in augmentation, followed by two bars that simultaneously state the sauntering theme, the sauntering theme in augmentation, and the humorous theme. Similarly, the humorous theme, the "marcato" theme, and the opening flute countermelody join together at one point (rehearsal 34), as do the sauntering theme, the humorous theme, and the triplet idea at another (rehearsal 41). Such contrapuntal dexterity seems in keeping with a musician who, on completing the sketch score, named Bach, Mozart, Wagner, and Stravinsky as his favorite composers.[13]

The work's harmonic and rhythmic resourcefulness complements its contrapuntal flair. In one especially intriguing passage (at nine after rehearsal 63), Gershwin progressively lops off the last note of a nine-note motive until reaching a two-note fragment, which subsequently serves as a polyrhythmic accompaniment to the slow blues theme. The work generally reveals a new and commanding rhythmic flexibility that often involves changes of tempo, and far more occasionally, as in the first "Calmato," changing meters as well.

Gershwin scored the piece for piccolo, two flutes, two oboes, English horn, two clarinets, bass clarinet, two bassoons, alto, tenor, and baritone saxophones (all doubling on soprano saxophone), four horns, three trumpets, three trombones, tuba, timpani, percussion (snare drum, cymbal, bass drum, triangle, bells, xylophone, wood block, small and large tom tom, and four taxi horns, each with its own pitch), celesta, and strings. The predominantly brilliant and rich orchestration, sometimes bordering on the brash, enhances the work's expressive power while posing real challenges as well, as shaping so many details into an elegant whole requires considerable conductorial skill.

As Gershwin progressed from sketch score to two-piano score to orchestral score, he made hardly any cuts. The two-piano and orchestral manuscripts are particularly alike in this respect, except for one short cut made in the latter (at seven after rehearsal 72). However, after completing his orchestral score, he made another four cuts, some quite substantial: one toward the end of the *B* episode (at rehearsal 66); one just prior to the return of *A* (ten after rehearsal 68); and two within the final *A* itself (at rehearsal 70 and at rehearsal 72). The cut in the *B* episode proved especially salutary, as it eliminated a large buildup to yet another climactic statement of the slow blues theme. And the two cuts in the reprise tightened the structure as well. On the other hand, the cut just before the return of *A* less happily resulted in a disconcerting tonal jolt at a crucial juncture. As in Gershwin's earlier concert works, cuts were made—at his own or someone else's initiative—without any special stitching, a process that usually worked well enough, though in some instances arguably less so.

The sketch score, meanwhile, contained some material that never made it to either the two-piano or the orchestral stage. One of these passages, with its simple triads moving stepwise in shifting metrical contexts (music similar to that leading up to rehearsal 76), highlighted the score's indebtedness to Stravinsky's *Petrushka*, evidenced as well by echoes of that ballet's "Petrushka chord" (at rehearsal 43) and its trained-bear interlude (the flute solo at five after rehearsal 12). That Gershwin would have had this personal favorite in mind while writing his own "orchestral ballet" hardly surprises, though in many ways, such gestures (including, too, the poignant moment at rehearsal 40, with its delicate secondal harmonies) more decidedly recall John Alden Carpenter—including the

Chicago composer's own Stravinskian ballet, *Skyscrapers* (1924)—than they do Stravinsky himself.

Walter Damrosch conducted the work's premiere with the New York Philharmonic–Symphony Society at Carnegie Hall on December 13. The concert featured Franck's Symphony in D in its first half and presented the Gershwin piece, sandwiched between Guillaume Lekeu's *Adagio for Strings* and Wagner's "Magic Fire Scene" from *Die Walküre,* after intermission. The large audience greeted the piece, reported Edward Cushing in the *Brooklyn Daily Eagle,* "with a demonstration of enthusiasm impressively genuine in contrast to the conventional applause which new music, good and bad, ordinarily arouses." Gershwin, who, according to one review, "smiled, chortled or laughed aloud as the work was being played," responded appreciatively with as many as a dozen bows from his box, though privately he expressed some dismay over Damrosch's too-leisurely approach.[14]

At a postconcert reception hosted by Jules Glaenzer, Gershwin was presented with a large silver humidor purchased and inscribed by his friends, including Damrosch, Irving Berlin, Georges Carpentier, Edsel Ford, Otto Kahn, Jascha Heifetz, Gertrude Lawrence, Lady Edwina Mountbatten, Condé Nast, Cole Porter, Francis Poulenc, Richard Rodgers, and Paul Whiteman. On this occasion, Kahn—a prominent banker and philanthropist—hailed Gershwin as one of the leaders of a young generation of Americans "groping to find the way for a franker and fuller life than that of its progenitors." But claiming that this generation lacked the "deep anguish, besetting care and heart-searching tribulations, which mark the history of older peoples, except only the epic tragedy of the Civil War," he accordingly wished for Gershwin "an experience—not too prolonged—of that driving storm and stress of the emotions, of that solitary wrestling with your own soul, of that aloofness, for a while, from the actions and distractions of the everyday world, which are the most effective ingredients for the deepening and mellowing and the complete development, energizing and revealment, of an artist's inner being and spiritual powers."[15]

Kahn's remarks made an impression, and excerpts quickly circulated in newspapers around the country. A fuller statement, "George Gershwin and American Youth," appeared as well in *Musical Courier,* whose editor, however, countered by asking, "Are not . . . aggressive optimism and freedom from the mournful introspectiveness of the European nations, the very keynotes of American character, life, and art? . . . If Gershwin is not composing great music, he surely is creating original music.

It copies nothing European, and admittedly speaks to his compatriots with a message which the majority of them have no difficulty in understanding and to which they respond with fullest fervor and feeling." A story also made the rounds that Florenz Ziegfeld, currently working with Gershwin on various projects, responded to Kahn's speech by saying, "Believe me, he'll suffer plenty."[16]

Meanwhile, *An American in Paris* received some excellent reviews. Many critics deemed the work better crafted, less pretentious, in short, a marked advance over the Concerto in F. And while a number of notices criticized the piece as somewhat faulty in structure and banal in content, such concerns did not prevent most from finding the work "merry," "amusing," "clever," "attractive," "appealing," "contagious," and "fresh, spirited, buoyant." The *Herald-Tribune*'s Lawrence Gilman, who had been highly critical of the Concerto, now found Gershwin's music—"with its gusto and naivete, its tang of a new and urgent world, engaging, urgent, unpredictable"—heartening. And the *Times*'s Olin Downes, while still concerned about formal deficiencies, perceived "combined melodic fragments with genuinely contrapuntal results."[17]

Not everyone was so approving, however. While admitting that the work was "clever whoopee," Oscar Thompson, writing in the *Evening Post,* considered such "wisecracking Broadway entertainment" unfit for the exalted company of Franck, Wagner, and even Lekeu: "To conceive of a symphony audience listening to it with any degree of pleasure or patience twenty years from now, when whoopee is no longer even a word, is another matter." Herbert Peyser, in the *New York Telegram,* penned an even harsher review, stating, "To one pair of ears Mr. Gershwin's latest effusion turned out to be nauseous, clap-trap, so dull, patchy, thin, vulgar, longwinded and inane that the average 'movie' audience would probably be bored by it into open remonstrance. . . . Even as honest jazz the whole cheap and silly affair seemed pitiably futile and inept."

The work's few naysayers hardly deterred the many conductors eager to take up the piece. Gershwin traveled to Cincinnati to attend its midwestern premiere on March 1, 1929, by Fritz Reiner and the Cincinnati Symphony Orchestra, a performance he deemed "incomparably superior" to that of the New York Philharmonic. During rehearsals, reported the *Cincinnati Times-Star,* "Gershwin stood on the conductor's platform beside Reiner and, as the latter directed the work, Gershwin, overflowing with enthusiasm, joined in. . . . It was a rare picture—a dancing young composer, smoking a pipe, swaying his body, tapping his feet to the floor in dance time and waving his hands to different parts of the orchestra."

Discussing the work with the *Cincinnati Post,* Gershwin commented, perhaps with Kahn's remarks in mind, "It's not a Beethoven symphony, you know. . . . It's a humorous piece, nothing solemn about it. It's not intended to draw tears. If it pleases symphony audiences as a light, jolly piece, a series of impressions musically expressed, it succeeds."[18]

As discussed earlier, Gershwin made his own conducting debut performing the piece with the New York Philharmonic at Lewisohn Stadium on August 29, 1929. Other 1929 performances included those by Artur Rodzinski and the Los Angeles Philharmonic, Alfredo Casella and the Boston Pops, Frank Laird Waller and the Milwaukee Philharmonic, and Henry Hadley and the Manhattan Symphony Orchestra. The work made its way to Europe as well; in July 1931 it concluded a concert of the International Society for Contemporary Music in London that also featured Anton Webern's Symphony. Everywhere the piece traveled, audiences cheered its arrival.

The music also appeared in print in a variety of forms. New World Music published a solo piano transcription (including small notes on a third staff) by William Daly in 1929 and an orchestral score in 1930, revised by Frank Campbell-Watson after Gershwin's death (most notably, Campbell-Watson reorchestrated the remarkably raucous chorus of three soprano saxophones at rehearsal 63). In 1944 New World also brought out a fine two-piano arrangement, edited by Gregory Stone, that conformed to the published orchestral score without attempting to transcribe every note; unfortunately, this publication was later withdrawn in favor of a more crudely edited 1986 two-piano edition that at least offered the novelty of the restored cuts, indicated by brackets. And in 1987 Warner Brothers published a facsimile edition of the original orchestral manuscript with helpful notes by Jeff Sultanof.

Nathaniel Shilkret and the Victor Symphony gave the radio premiere of the work on January 30, 1929, and recorded it for Victor a few days later on February 4. This Victor pressing, which preserves the sounds of the taxi horns used at the premiere, remains a favorite among aficionados, and for good reason: Shilkret conducts the work with exceptional verve and humor, imbuing the slow blues with a droll mock-pathos (the small celesta part, apparently played by Gershwin, who sometimes rolls the blocked chords, appears in full, statements to the contrary notwithstanding). Unfortunately, this release took a few small cuts and was marred further by some uneven orchestral playing.[19]

The first uncut recording of the piece arrived shortly after with Frank Milne's arranged roll for reproducing piano (1933). Although Milne allegedly created the roll on his own, the Aeolian American Corporation released it as performed by "Milne and Leith" in order to give the impression of two players. Whether Milne, who had long worked closely with Gershwin, consulted the composer, as seems probable, the resultant roll—described by Artis Wodehouse as "one of the most impressive and powerful roll performances of the era"—remains compelling for its keen sense of pacing and architecture.[20]

An American in Paris subsequently became one of the most performed and recorded orchestral works of the twentieth century, with radio broadcasts and commercial releases conducted by Maurice Abravanel, Kenneth Alwyn, Leonard Bernstein, Ricardo Chailly, Carl Davis, Charles Dutoit, Arthur Fiedler, Lawrence Foster, Morton Gould, André Kostelanetz, Erich Kunzel, James Levine, Henry Lewis, Lorin Maazel, Neville Marriner, Wayne Marshall, Kurt Masur, Eduardo Mata, John Mauceri, Mitch Miller, Zubin Mehta, Eugene Ormandy, Seiji Ozawa, Libor Pesek, André Previn, Artur Rodzinski, Gunther Schuller, Gerard Schwarz, Felix Slatkin, Leonard Slatkin, William Steinberg, Michael Tilson Thomas, Arturo Toscanini, and John Williams, among others. Over time a few questionable mannerisms attached themselves to the score. Many conductors, for instance, began slowing the tempo of the blues section, typically adding, at the risk of throwing the work's form off kilter, a minute or two to the length of the piece. Some also had the trumpets dot or swing the fast blues theme. And especially in recent years, it became de rigueur for the winds to smudge their final blue note four bars from the end. Still, the work's popularity with so many first-rank conductors and orchestras assured the kind of high performance standard rarely afforded an American orchestral composition.

The recorded legacy also revealed a fair uniformity of interpretation, though Toscanini's recording with the NBC Symphony Orchestra (1945) stood out for its attention to detail, Bernstein's with the RCA Victor Symphony Orchestra (1947) for its flair, Dorati's with the Minneapolis Symphony Orchestra (1957) for its finesse, and Fiedler's with the Boston Pops (1960) for its sonic splendor. Similar virtues distinguished Rodzinski's pioneering release with the New York Philharmonic (ca. 1945) and, among more recent airings, Carl Davis's performance with the London Symphony Orchestra (1991), James Levine's with the Chicago Symphony (1993), and Michael Tilson Thomas's with the San Francisco Symphony (1998).[21]

Among various recorded arrangements of the work, including one by the New York Banjo Ensemble (1982) and another by flutist Jean-Pierre

Rampal with members of the Los Angeles Philharmonic (1985), those by the Paul Whiteman Orchestra, including a 1934 performance with Charlie Teagarden playing first trumpet, held special historical interest. The premiere recording of the uncut two-piano version by Katia and Marielle Labèque (1984), renditions of Daly's solo piano version by Mark Anderson (1999) and Frank Braley (2004), and freer arrangements for solo piano by Jack Gibbons (1993) and Eric Himy (2004) also merited notice.

In 1929 Albertina Rasch choreographed an abridged version of the piece for the Gershwin musical *Show Girl*. And in 1936 Chicagoan Ruth Page, who had earlier choreographed Gershwin's *Three Preludes,* adapted the tone-poem as a ballet, *Americans in Paris,* for herself and Paul Draper (she revised the dance in 1950 as *Les Américains à Paris* for herself and Bentley Stone, though she did not think that the music represented "Gershwin at his best"). However, the work received far wider exposure as the featured ballet of a 1951 MGM film, *An American in Paris.* The movie was conceived by producer Arthur Freed, who knew the Gershwins from his own songwriting days and retained a close friendship with Ira. Using the Gershwin tone-poem as a springboard, Freed imagined a musical about two young American artists in Paris—a painter and his composer sidekick—modeled after Gershwin and David Diamond. As Freed recalled, MGM paid the Gershwin estate about three hundred thousand dollars for the use of *An American in Paris* and various songs as needed, and an additional fifty thousand to Ira for his help selecting songs and revising lyrics. Freed further assembled a talented team that included director Vincente Minnelli, choreographer Gene Kelly, screenwriter Alan Jay Lerner, musical directors Johnny Green and Saul Chaplin, and orchestrator Conrad Salinger.[22]

The picture concerns a romance between an American painter, Jerry Mulligan (Gene Kelly), and a French girl, Lise Bouvier (Leslie Caron), each of whom has rival obligations: Jerry to his wealthy American patron, Milo Roberts (Nina Foch); and Lise to the music-hall entertainer who took care of her during the war, Henri Baurel (Georges Guetary). A struggling composer, Adam Cook (Oscar Levant), offers sardonic commentary from the sidelines. The action, originally planned to take place in the 1920s, was moved up to the present, a change that may have fostered some of the film's anachronisms, including its preoccupation (presumably suggested by Gershwin's art collection) with post-Impressionist painting.

Kelly, Chaplin, and Minnelli regularly met at Ira's home to peruse the

Gershwin catalog for songs to complement the story, eventually settling on "By Strauss," "I Got Rhythm," "Tra-La-La" (with new lyrics), "Stairway to Paradise," "Love Is Here to Stay," and "'S Wonderful," with the *American in Paris* ballet providing the picture's climax (two other numbers, "But Not for Me" and, to Kelly's special disappointment, "I've Got a Crush on You," were cut from the film). The movie also staged an abridged finale to the Concerto in F as Adam's reverie, much as it devised *An American in Paris* as Jerry's fantasy, one that encapsulates his feelings about Paris. In addition, the film used various other Gershwin tunes along with material from the tone-poem as background music—sometimes quite knowingly, too, as at the mention of the Left Bank in the film's opening voice-over, at which point the music from *An American in Paris* identified by Deems Taylor as representing the Left Bank can be heard.[23]

Johnny Green and Saul Chaplin took pride in orchestrator Conrad Salinger's training under André Gédalge, the quality of the MGM orchestra, and their own dedication to Gershwin's work; and the arrangements of the Gershwin songs were no doubt distinguished by Hollywood standards, as was the orchestral playing throughout. But the revised scoring for *An American in Paris* trivialized the piece, even if Green thought that Gershwin's alleged deficiencies as an orchestrator (in particular, his "compulsive" doublings), along with recording exigencies of the 1950s (including lack of rehearsal time), necessitated such changes. Nor did the filmmakers show any hesitation about thoroughly reordering and rearranging the music, or adding trite filler material. Such alterations severely undermined the piece's integrity, however well they served the ballet's choreographic and visual needs.[24]

Premiering in New York on October 4, 1951, the film garnered enormous acclaim. Nominated for Academy Awards for best picture, director, story and screenplay, color cinematography, color art direction, film editing, scoring of a musical picture, and color costume design, it won all but those for director and film editing, with Kelly and Freed receiving special honorary awards from the Academy the same year as well. "Number for number, no film musical can rival *An American in Paris* for musical integrity, visual style, and performance energy," wrote Gerald Mast in 1987, apparently overlooking the bastardized treatment of its featured orchestral work. But the film's success no doubt encouraged many viewers to listen to the actual Gershwin tone-poem, in which case, even if memories of the movie clouded the score's irony, they at least would be hearing the real thing.[25]

On May 4, 2005, the New York City Ballet unveiled a new *American in Paris* ballet devised by young British choreographer Christopher Wheeldon, whose career, like that of many Gershwin choreographers, had traversed both Broadway and more serious dance venues. As a fantasy of 1950s Paris in which an American painter-hero (Damian Woetzel) romances and loses a French gamine (Jennifer Ringer) against a colorful background of gendarmes, tourists, street toughs, a bike racer, and so forth, the work adapted Kelly's narrative frame, but in its own way, including a more classically balletic vocabulary enhanced by Adrianne Lobel's cubist-inspired drops. Moreover, Wheeldon and music director Andrea Quinn used the full Campbell-Watson score, supplemented by a short piano prelude (derived from some of the transitional material just prior to the slow blues) in which the hero puts some finishing touches on the scenery, thereby intimating that the score proper is, on some level, his own work; and that he, at least metaphorically, represents the composer.

The critics, including Jack Anderson *(Times)* and Joan Acocella *(New Yorker)*, greeted the large production, which featured three soloists and a corps of twenty-eight, as genial and exuberant, if somewhat slight. Anderson recalled that the movie ended more happily, with Kelly and Caron in each other's arms; but the film's ballet sequence actually had concluded similarly with a sense of loss and nostalgia—feelings the tone-poem seemed to inspire perhaps above all others.[26]

In November 1926 the Gershwins announced that they were at work on a musical version of Samuel Shipman and John. B. Hymer's stage hit, *East Is West* (1918). A contract with William Harris Jr. (who had produced the original show) calling for production to begin on or before January 1, 1928, was drawn in May 1927, but the project never materialized. Then, in the spring of 1928—after the Gershwins, citing prior obligations, declined an invitation from Ziegfeld to write a score for Eddie Cantor for the fall—that producer suggested an adaptation of *East Is West* for the following spring. How Ziegfeld became involved with this property remains unclear, but in any case, this proposed adaptation, which also never came to fruition, was to have had a book by William Anthony McGuire, who had cowritten the script to the Gershwins' previous Ziegfeld musical, *Rosalie*. Ziegfeld reportedly planned on a cast that would have starred Ed Wynn, along with Bobbe Arnst, Kathryn Hereford, Barbara Newberry, and Oscar Shaw, though Ira recalled that the show was to feature Marilyn Miller and the team of Bobby Clark and Paul McCullough.[27]

In late 1928 and early 1929, George and Ira enthusiastically busied themselves with the show, at one point called *Ming Toy*, after the play's heroine. As of January 19, however, they still had not received a book from McGuire even though the show was set to go into rehearsal in only a few weeks' time. They were still waiting for a script in February, though they presumably had at least the original play and a story line at hand. In any event, they completed a fair amount of the score—apparently much of the first act and some of the second—before Ziegfeld decided to suspend work on the show and adapt instead J. P. McEvoy's novel *Show Girl* as his next Gershwin musical.[28]

A takeoff on the Madame Butterfly story, *East Is West* involves an amiable and well-to-do American bachelor, Billy Benson, who, while in China, rescues the charming Ming Toy from being sold as a "sing-song girl" by arranging for her to come to his native San Francisco. Already well-disposed toward the West, Ming Toy, eventually taken into the Benson home, becomes the all-American flapper, winking at men, dancing the shimmy, and shaking cocktails. Although Billy and Ming Toy fall in love and want to marry, Billy's parents, fearing social ostracism, demand an end to the affair until they discover that Ming Toy was abducted at birth from an American missionary-scholar and his Spanish wife, at which point they give their consent to the happy couple.

At its core, the play pits the views of Billy's father, who argues for a "racial determination as relentless as the laws of the Universe," against those of Billy's Chinese friend, Lo Sang Kee, who states, "In the infinite . . . whence all things come, there is no East, there is no West. West is East, and East is West." Although the authors fundamentally sympathize with the latter perspective (voiced also by Billy's sister, Mildred, which makes the conflict somewhat generational), the argument for "racial determinism" does seem to triumph, considering that the Bensons assent to the marriage only after learning about Ming Toy's biological lineage. Still, Ming Toy, on hearing that her father was "one of the most distinguished scholars in America," has the last word, telling Mr. Benson, "That don't make me better Ming Toy. I have no objection to you."[29]

Straight comedies and melodramas about mixed marriages regularly appeared in New York during this time, clearly a preoccupation in a city that had recently experienced a massive influx of immigrants from all over; the biggest hit of the decade was *Abie's Irish Rose* (1922), a romantic comedy about the marriage of a Jewish boy and a Catholic girl. Such themes eventually found their way as well onto the musical-comedy stage, whose stories typically concerned conflicts of class, not of race or religion. Friml's *Rose-Marie* (1924) and its half-Indian heroine proved a watershed in this regard. Even Gershwin's *Tell Me More* (1925) featured a Jewish-gentile romance. By 1927, musical shows involving ethnic conflict had become a virtual subgenre, what with, in that year alone, the Harry Tierney–Joseph McCarthy musical *Rio Rita* (American hero/ Mexican heroine); the Emmerich Kálmán–Herbert Stothart–Robert Stolz "music drama" *Golden Dawn* (American/African); no less than two Sigmund Romberg shows along these lines, *Cherry Blossoms* (American/ Japanese) and *My Princess* (Italian/American); and Jerome Kern's *Show Boat* (white/black)—not to mention the talking picture *The Jazz Singer* (Jewish/gentile).

Ziegfeld, who produced both *Rio Rita* and *Show Boat,* was patently inclined in this direction, perhaps because of its potential eroticism. He followed up those two shows in 1928 with *Rosalie,* in which cultural if not racial differences per se complicated the gulf separating the American West Point cadet and his Romanzan princess; and *Whoopee,* which interwove two stories of cultural conflict, one involving a white American heroine and her half-Indian lover, the other concerning a Jew in an alien American West. *East Is West* offered yet another variation on this theme, one that could accommodate some sumptuous chinoiserie as well (the original 1918 show had a celebrated opening set that included an elaborate junk docked on the Yangtze—an obvious attraction to the producer of *Show Boat*).

Such trends surely reflected, too, a national climate marked by the passage of the 1924 Second Quota Law and the growing power of the Ku Klux Klan; and the fact that many of the creators of these musicals (though not Ziegfeld) were Jewish or immigrants or both would suggest an intended plea for tolerance, as can be inferred from the shows themselves, though they were somewhat ambiguous in this regard. *Rose-Marie, Show Boat,* and *Whoopee,* for instance, skirted the issue to an extent by making the racial other a "half-breed," while the resolutions of *Golden Dawn* and *Whoopee,* like the projected *East Is West,* hinged on the discovery that the outsider was, at least biologically, an insider. Moreover, any lighthearted treatment of black-white miscegenation seemed particularly beyond the pale; only as a doomed couple in a melodramatic subplot could an interracial couple make their way into *Show Boat.* Still, whatever their biases, these shows assumed a relatively progressive attitude for the times.

In this particular case, Gershwin presumably welcomed the opportunity as well to revisit the kinds of Chinese-inspired styles that he had cultivated at the start of his career, both as a pianist—including a recording of Robert Hood Bowers's popular "Chinese Lullaby," from the original *East Is West,* for Welte-Mignon in 1919—and as the composer of such songs as "Limehouse Nights" (1919) and "Mah-Jongg" (1924). The play's fairly short prologue, set in China, was apparently to be expanded to permit greater scope for local color, though the general plan was to add straightforward musical-comedy numbers to the mix, as had been the case with *Rosalie.* "Most of the *East Is West* music had Oriental overtones," recalled Ira, "but there were several musical-comedy numbers," including "Embraceable You," probably intended as a duet for Billy and Ming Toy.[30]

In addition to "Embraceable You," no less than ten lyrics (not all complete) survive, as does some music (primarily refrains) for at least eight of them: "In the Mandarin's Orchid Garden," "I Speak English Now," "Yellow Blues," "Under the Cinnamon Tree," "Lady of the Moon," "Sing-Song Girl," "Vo-de-o-do," and "We Are Visitors Here." These songs share certain pentatonic and modal gestures that help convey their "Oriental overtones," but they employ other orientalisms as well. "I Speak English Now" and "Vo-de-o-do," for instance, feature jaunty repeated notes, while "Yellow Blues" and "Under the Cinnamon Tree" contain lively staccato basses, with the latter also including flurries of parallel fourths. Moreover, many of the tunes tend to double back on themselves in stereotypical Chinese fashion, as in the up-and-down traceries of "Lady of the Moon." Even "Embraceable You" appears to have some oriental features, such as recitative-like repetitions on a single pitch (as in the refrain's "Come to papa, Come to papa, do!").[31]

The unusual nature of this project mitigated against later uses of this material once Ziegfeld canceled the show, though the Gershwins managed to salvage "Embraceable You" as well as some other material, including "Lady of the Moon" as "I Just Looked at You" for *Show Girl* (subsequently dropped and lost), and then, further retooled, as "Blah, Blah, Blah" for the film *Delicious.* Moreover, they adapted a section from "We Are Visitors Here"—a melody, somewhat along the lines of the *Mikado*'s "If you want to know who we are," originally intended for a quartet of mandarins looking for singsong girls—as a patter interlude for "Love Is Sweeping the Country" from *Of Thee I Sing.*[32]

In addition, Harms published "In the Mandarin's Orchid Garden" (earlier called "Lonely Buttercup") as an independent concert song in 1930, with an ornate illustration of orchids on its cover. A song about a "poor little buttercup" in a Chinese orchid garden, this touching parable about sexual isolation (though not without its humor, including a playful ending) brings to a peak a string of songs by Gershwin written somewhat in the shadow of "Poor Butterfly"; but the music's oriental elements—the pentatonic melodies, modal harmonies, staccato basses, and so forth—are here masterfully subsumed into a refined and personal whole. The song proved distinctive in other respects, including its form: three strophic stanzas that comprise an *ABA* design, though the last *A*, rather than marking a literal repeat, contains a varied piano part. Many consider the work as close to an art song as Gershwin ever wrote, in part because of the marvelous word painting in the accompaniment, including vivid depictions of buzzing bees and the sighing buttercup. At the same time the song, still highly theatrical, falls in the tradition of some narrative ballads of the lyric stage, with the word *love* even calling for an operatic "tenuto"; Ira recalled that the number "was to be sung by a Sing-Song Girl at one side of the stage—as a vocal accompaniment to a Chinese ballet on full stage." Yet another sensitive song, "Till Then," published independently by Harms in 1933, may also have been originally intended for *East Is West*, possibly as a love duet. Ira's lyric, which includes the phrase "Till East is West," would suggest as much, while the musical style seems generally congruent with the other planned numbers from the show.[33]

Some circumstantial evidence—including sketches that only recently have surfaced—suggest that Gershwin adapted other materials associated with *East Is West* for such later efforts as "Liza" from *Show Girl* (1929); "If I Became the President" from the revised *Strike Up the Band* (1930); "Bronco Busters" from *Girl Crazy* (1930); "No Tickee, No Washee" from *Pardon My English* (1933); and "I Wants to Stay Here" from *Porgy and Bess* (1935). Gershwin possibly meant the music posthumously released as *Violin Piece* (Melody no. 40) for use in this show as well. Moreover, he seems to have derived the "Introduction" to *Porgy and Bess* (or at least its general contours) from some opening music for this Chinese operetta (which would help explain Todd Duncan's initial reaction to the first few pages of *Porgy* as "all this chopsticks").[34]

Two other songs—"Ask Me Again" and "I Got Rhythm"—apparently postdate *East Is West* (Gershwin sketched out their main themes in September 1929 and July 1930, respectively), but they, too, suggest the operetta's lingering impact. Concerning "I Got Rhythm," Isaac Goldberg recalled, it is true, a slowed-down version of the song "scheduled, if I remember correctly, for *Treasure Girl*"; but in light of his uncertainty and the closeness in time between *Treasure Girl* and *East Is West*, Goldberg may simply have confused the two shows. Indeed, "I Got Rhythm" sounds like a compressed version of "Liza," whose opening gesture appears among the *East Is West* sketches. The use of temple blocks in the scoring of "I Got Rhythm" in *Girl Crazy* and the Chinese section in *Variations on "I Got Rhythm"* further support such connections, underlining—as in the case of the aforementioned music from *Porgy and Bess*—the surprising extent to which Chinese music, real and imagined, influenced Gershwin.[35]

Similarly, Ira vaguely remembered "Ask Me Again" as intended for *Girl Crazy,* which seems plausible; but the nascent inspiration occurred months earlier in the aftermath of the aborted operetta. And again the tune, which features a pentatonic fragment that turns in on itself, seems akin to the music written for *East Is West.* Thought by Ira the finest of his unpublished songs, "Ask Me Again" finally saw the light of day when Brian Mitchell introduced it in David Merrick's 1990 production of *Oh, Kay!* Rosemary Clooney and Michael Feinstein subsequently recorded the song as well, suggesting the belated arrival of another, though verseless, Gershwin standard.[36]

According to Ira, Ziegfeld shelved *East Is West* because it would have been too costly to mount—about three times more expensive than *Show Girl.* But such subtle numbers as "In the Mandarin's Orchid Garden," "Sing-Song Girl," and "Yellow Blues" could not have provided much encouragement; the show clearly would have been not only expensive but risky. In any case, Ziegfeld held out hopes for a 1929 mounting, though as relations between him and the Gershwins deteriorated over *Show Girl,* the *New York Times* reported in August that Vincent Youmans, not Gershwin, would provide the score. Ziegfeld further contacted P. G. Wodehouse about writing the lyrics. But as the year unfolded, between competition from film and radio and the eventual stock market crash, any such prospect became increasingly unrealistic. *East Is West* might have been one of Ziegfeld's final triumphs; as things turned out, its collapse signaled the end of an era.[37]

Chapter Twenty-Four

Show Girl and *The Dybbuk* (1929)

$\mathscr{I}$n the spring of 1929, George and Ira temporarily—or so they thought—set aside *East Is West* in order to write another musical for Ziegfeld, *Show Girl*, after J. P. McEvoy's popular 1928 novel of the same name. Ira later recalled, "In his hypnotically persuasive manner (always great charm until a contract was signed), Ziegfeld managed to have us postpone the operetta and start on *Show Girl*."[1]

A largely epistolary novel, McEvoy's *Show Girl* revolves around Dixie Dugan, an aspiring eighteen-year-old singer whose involvements with four suitors—sweet salesman Denny Kerrigan, tempestuous tango dancer Alvarez Romana, Wall Street sugar daddy Jack Milton, and hard-boiled journalist-playwright Jimmy Doyle—catapult her, through a madcap sequence of events, to stardom on the Broadway stage. Although her ideal beau would combine aspects of all four boyfriends, Dixie ultimately chooses Jimmy (Irish like herself and presumably a stand-in for the author).[2]

In the tradition of McEvoy's theatrical work (including the revue *Americana*, for which the Gershwins had written "That Lost Barber Shop Chord"), the novel satirizes American culture from greeting-card platitudes to congressional politics, here with an emphasis on the self-serving ties between tabloid journalism and the entertainment industry. Ziegfeld, who appears in the book along with Jimmy Durante and other real-life celebrities, must have been able to laugh at himself, as McEvoy, who worked closely with the producer, surely realized.

First National quickly turned the novel into a film of the same name (1928) starring popular ingenue Alice White, the success of which inspired a sequel, *Show Girl in Hollywood* (1930). These pictures formed part of a deluge of backstage film musicals, beginning with *The Jazz Singer*

(1927) and climaxing in 1929 with dozens of others, most notably MGM's *Broadway Melody*, the first musical to win an Academy Award for best picture. "So persistent is the vogue for movies of backstage life," commented the *New Yorker* in June 1929, "so continuous the presentation of the gallantries, loves and idylls of scene-shifters and ballet ladies, that we begin to long for something as esoteric as the true romance of an accountant." Ziegfeld was more than aware of this trend; he helped supervise—and appeared in—the backstage film musical *Glorifying the American Girl* (1929), with a script coauthored by McEvoy. His decision to launch *Show Girl* in the summer of 1929 accordingly reflected the growing influence of Hollywood on Broadway.[3]

Richard Barrios has suggested various reasons for the popularity of backstage musical pictures of the late 1920s, including the notion that they represented "glossy repackagings of the Protestant work ethic," though McEvoy's novel arguably parodied as much as exemplified the genre. In any case, by the middle of 1930 and the deepening of the Depression, the vogue for such vehicles had run its course, though the backstager—both with and without music—remained particularly congenial to the film medium, with its penchant for realism; and after a hiatus of a few years, Hollywood resumed making backstage musicals, adjusted to a changed social climate, with enormous success.[4]

Possibly inspired by the novel's mention of Durante, Ziegfeld decided to have *Show Girl* feature the team of Lou Clayton, Eddie Jackson, and Jimmy Durante, a vaudeville act. All three comedians were native New Yorkers, though Durante (1893–1980)—whose large nose inspired his nickname, "Schnozzola"—was Italian, whereas Clayton and Jackson were Jewish. "We was a team," recalled Jackson. "Lou did the dancing, Jimmy played piano and told jokes. I sang and strutted." Their integration into the main plot of *Show Girl* would prove tenuous, but that was not the kind of problem that overly concerned Ziegfeld.[5]

For the part of Dixie Dugan, Ziegfeld at first considered Bobbe Arnst, but eventually cast Ruby Keeler (1909–1993), a nineteen-year-old dancer who had worked her way up through various speakeasies associated with hostess Texas Guinan to become a chorus girl in some big Broadway shows, including Ziegfeld's *Whoopee* (1928). Like the character of Dixie, Keeler was a feisty Irish New Yorker (though born in Canada) whose moderate abilities, writes Barrios, were enhanced by "an artless projection of total innocence and vulnerability," and who achieved considerable notoriety from the men in her life, including her first husband, Al Jolson, whom she married in the fall of 1928. Dixie Dugan would be

Keeler's first major role—and a star turn in a Ziegfeld musical, no less—an ascendancy that echoed Dixie's own amazing success and that helped underscore those self-referential qualities that made *Show Girl* seem, to Ethan Mordden, so Pirandellian.[6]

In 1934 Gershwin described the show as "the greatest rush job I've ever had on a score." Anxious about the Ziegfeld Theatre being left dark by the closing of *Show Boat* in early May 1929, Ziegfeld scheduled rehearsals for April 20, even though bookwriter William Anthony McGuire and the Gershwins had only begun to work on the material. When Gershwin told Ziegfeld that he couldn't possibly write an entire score within a few weeks, the latter said, "Why sure you can—just dig down in the trunk and pull out a couple of hits." Meanwhile, Ira welcomed Ziegfeld's request that he work with Gus Kahn, "because *Show Girl* had to be done quickly to make a much too soon opening date." By the time rehearsals began, only some of the book and part of the score were complete. "Genial Bill McGuire apparently wasn't worrying much about a deadline on this one," recalled Ira, "and loved listening to anything new we played him. And 'You never can tell. Maybe I'll get a good idea for a scene from one of the songs.'" The last scene was rehearsed on the train to tryouts in Boston. "As you can imagine," remarked Gershwin, "it was all pretty hectic."[7]

The script, especially as it evolved over time, lost much of the charm of the original novel. With the need to accommodate various Durante routines and other musical set-pieces, McGuire found little opportunity to explore Dixie's romantic relationships, depriving the story of some of its intrigue (concurrently, a number of duets were cut before the New York opening). And although some of the book's satirical tone survived, much of it disappeared under the weight of the show's lavish apparatus. "It was too bad," concluded Isaac Goldberg, "for McEvoy's book had the makings of a good take-off on the modern sweetie and modern salesmanship."[8]

Time constraints notwithstanding, Gershwin did not take Ziegfeld's advice and simply "dig down in the trunk," but, on the contrary, wrote about twenty-five mostly new songs for the show (often for imaginary spots, given the lateness of the script). In addition, he prepared various instrumental selections, notably an arrangement of *An American in Paris* (which included the song "Home Blues"). Meanwhile, Clayton, Jackson, and Durante interpolated songs mostly composed by Durante; Duke Ellington and his Cotton Club Orchestra (listed in the program as "Duke Ellington's Band") played their own numbers; and popular singer Nick

Lucas performed a set of songs as well. "Everything considered," remarked Ira, "I wouldn't be surprised if *Show Girl* set a record for sparseness of dialogue in a musical."[9]

The show opens with the final scene of an imaginary Ziegfeld production, a Civil War operetta titled *Magnolias,* set on Colonel Witherby's Virginia estate in 1863. Virginia (Barbara Newberry), Witherby's daughter, is celebrating her eighteenth birthday ("Happy Birthday"), attended by a black servant, Sombre Eyes (Jimmy Durante). The guests look forward to church the following day ("My Sunday Fella"), and Steve and Robert, rivals for Virginia's affections, engage in a duel ("Tell Me, What Has Happened?"). As Steve and Virginia happily unite, the curtain falls ("How Could I Forget?").

Backstage after the show, Ziegfeld expresses his disappointment with the performance. Snozzle (Durante), the theater's property manager as well as the understudy for the role of Sombre Eyes, threatens to quit ("Can Broadway Do Without Me?"; music and lyrics, Durante). Alvarez Romano (Joseph Macaulay), the son of the president of "Costaragua," dances a tango ("Lolita"). Dixie Dugan (Ruby Keeler), an aspiring actress, auditions for the stage manager, Roy Collins; as Snozzle accompanies her at the piano, Jimmy Doyle (Frank McHugh), a journalist-playwright, joins in ("Do What You Do!"). Snozzle coaches Dixie after she fails to land a part (reprise of "Do What You Do!"). Sunshine (Newberry), the actress who plays Virginia in *Magnolias,* invites Dixie to a party at the penthouse of her wealthy friend, John Milton (Austin Fairman), and Jimmy and Dixie discover that they live near each other on Flatbush Avenue in Brooklyn. After Snozzle and his crew—including the carpenter, Gypsy (Lou Clayton), and the electrician, Deacon (Eddie Jackson)—fool about ("Spain"; music, Isham Jones; lyrics, Kahn), Sunshine and the girls rehearse a number ("One Man").[10]

At the Western Union desk in a hotel in Trenton, New Jersey, Dixie's boyfriend, traveling greeting-card salesman Denny Kerrigan (Eddie Foy Jr.), encouraged by a young woman, Bobby (Kathryn Hereford), expresses his love for Dixie in a telegram ("So Are You!"). Meanwhile, at the party at John Milton's, Dixie and her friends make fun of another girl, Sylvia ("I Must Be Home by Twelve O'Clock"). As Alvarez romances Dixie, he turns on the radio only to hear Denny on the air (reprise of "So Are You!"). Rudy (Nick Lucas), one of the party guests, entertains with a selection of various numbers. Back in Brooklyn, Jimmy tells Mrs. Dugan that he has contracted a show with Ziegfeld in which he hopes to find a role for Dixie. Snozzle, who lives in the area as well, instructs Jimmy in the art of romancing women. Dixie contemplates going off with John, but decides otherwise on hearing Jimmy's voice (reprise of "Do What You Do!").

At Manhattan's Club Caprice, Duke Ellington's band accompanies both the chorus girls in a plume dance ("Black and White"; music unknown, though according to one script, Ray Henderson's "Alabamy Bound") and the Albertina Rasch Dancers ("African Daisies"; music unknown, though possibly by Ellington). Various principals have come to hear Dixie's debut at the club, where Snozzle, Gypsy, and Deacon are also performing ("(I'm) Jimmy, the Well Dressed Man"; music and lyrics, Durante). Dixie's appearance in a much-anticipated number interrupts the escalating tensions among her four suitors ("Harlem Serenade").

The second act opens with the premiere of a new *Ziegfeld Follies* with music by Gershwin and a book by Jimmy Doyle, and which includes the ballet *An American in Paris* (performed by the Albertina Rasch Dancers, with "Home Blues" sung by Alvarez). During intermission, Jimmy and Dixie, both nervous about the show, quarrel, while Snozzle enumerates New York's many attractions ("Broadway, My Street"; lyrics, Sidney Skolsky; music, Durante) and relates encounters with a homosexual and a westerner ("So I Ups to Him"; music and lyrics, Durante). The *Follies* resumes with a minstrel scene that includes a song for Deacon in front of the curtain ("Follow the Minstrel Band"), and, as the curtain rises, a production number for Dixie, assisted by Rudy ("Liza").[11]

In her dressing room after the show, Dixie, a triumphant success, eagerly awaits Jimmy; when he fails to appear, she decides to leave with Denny rather than Alvarez or John. But on her way out she meets Jimmy, with whom she shares a remembrance (reprise of "Do What You Do!") while Denny follows Sunshine offstage. As Dixie and Jimmy leave the theater together, the ensemble bids them a fond farewell ("Finale").

As indicated above, Durante interpolated the Isham Jones–Gus Kahn song "Spain" (1924), as well as a few of his own numbers, including "Can Broadway Do Without Me?" (1928), "(I'm) Jimmy, the Well Dressed Man" (1928), "Broadway, My Street" (1929), and "So I Ups to Him" (1929), songs that resembled such ragtime hits as Hughie Cannon's "Bill Bailey, Won't You Please Come Home?" (1902), a Durante signature tune. The program did not identify the music performed by singer-guitarist Nick Lucas (1897–1982), the "crooning troubadour" best remembered today for the guitar and guitar pick named after him, but one review mentioned his singing Nacio Herb Brown's 1929 hit, "Singin' in the Rain." He also possibly sang Joe Burke's "Tip-Toe thru the

Tulips" (1929), which he recorded in early May (a hit release that decades later inspired Tiny Tim's popular 1968 single).[12]

By the time of the New York premiere, the score included thirteen numbers by Gershwin, all with lyrics cowritten by Ira and Gus Kahn: "Happy Birthday," "My Sunday Fella," "Tell Me What Has Happened?" "How Could I Forget?" "Lolita," "Do What You Do!" "One Man," "So Are You!" "I Must Be Home by Twelve O'Clock," "Harlem Serenade," "Home Blues," "Follow the Minstrel Band," and "Liza." In the tradition of the backstage musical, most of these numbers functioned diegetically, that is, as actual songs within the dramatic narrative.

Harms published five of these numbers—"Do What You Do!" "I Must Be Home by Twelve O'Clock," "Harlem Serenade," "Liza," and "So Are You!"—along with a song dropped prior to the New York opening, "Feeling Sentimental." Gershwin wrote another five extant songs that never made it to Broadway: "Adored One," "At Mrs. Simpkin's Finishing School," "Somebody Stole My Heart Away," "Tonight's the Night," and, though its authorship remains a bit uncertain, "I Couldn't Be Good." Lyrics for yet five more songs, including "I Just Looked at You" (based on "Lady of the Moon"), also survive.

The show's varied stage settings called for a wide range of musical styles, and Gershwin duly took stock of Jerome Kern for the Civil War operetta, Duke Ellington for the nightclub episode, and perhaps Irving Berlin for the *Follies* parody. With regard to "Liza," the centerpiece of the last-named scene, Ziegfeld specifically told Gershwin, "I would like to have a minstrel number in the second act with one hundred beautiful girls seated on steps that cover the entire stage."[13]

"Liza" not only transcended such eclecticism to become one of Gershwin's best-known numbers, but epitomized ways in which the composer imposed his individual voice on the show's diverse needs. In the tradition of American minstrelsy, the chorus opens with a pentatonic motive supported by shuffling dotted rhythms ("Liza, Liza, skies are gray"); but the harmonies, supported by a rising chromatic bass line, provide a distinctive elegance. Similarly, the breezy verse ("Moon shinin' on the river") contains modal shadings that sensitively color the Stephen Foster–like ambience.

Though less known, "Do What You Do!" and "I Must Be Home by Twelve O'Clock" are also masterful examples of their kind. The former, one of Gershwin's most alluring melodies, serves at first as audition material, but then as a love theme for Dixie and Jimmy, almost single-handedly carrying the burden of the show's romantic interest. "I Must Be

Home by Twelve O'Clock," for its part, is a comic gem, the verse ridiculing the girl who "keeps on saying, 'I gotta go home!'" and the chorus presenting the "speech" she's always making, including a whimsical depiction of the girl's scattered thoughts. Among the unused songs, "Feeling Sentimental," a duet earmarked for Alvarez and Dixie, attained some currency thanks to its early publication, whereas "Tonight's the Night" and "Somebody Stole My Heart Away" emerged from obscurity only with the Broadway show *Crazy for You* (1992) and Michael Feinstein's recording *Nice Work If You Can Get It* (1996), respectively.

For the *American in Paris* ballet, Gershwin prepared a slightly abridged, fifteen-minute version of the score. The show's program book offered a thumbnail scenario—"Being the musical description of an American's experience in Paris. Our hero, adrift in the City of Light, swings through traffic, into a night of freedom and gaiety, with girls, wine, and song. His thoughts then turn to Home, and he dreams of the noisy, cheerful Charleston"—and designated its scenes as "La Rue St. Lazare," "Le Bar Americain" (including the "Home Blues" song), and "Le Rêve de l'Amerique." These three scenes presumably corresponded to the score's exposition, slow blues section, and fast blues section. The chorus of "Home Blues," meanwhile, featured the work's slow blues theme, but only the lyrics—not the music—of its verse survive.

Zeke Colvan directed the show, John Harkrider designed the costumes, Joseph Urban created the sets, and William Daly directed the orchestra. The secondary players included Barbara Newberry (Sunshine), who had joined the cast of *Show Boat* as Ellie in early 1929; Joseph Macaulay (Alvarez), an accomplished Gilbert and Sullivan baritone (some felt that he was underutilized here); and Frank McHugh (Jimmy) and Eddie Foy Jr. (Denny), both of whom would have notable film careers as character actors. Albertina Rasch choreographed the "African Daisies" and the *American in Paris* ballets, both danced by her own troupe of sixteen female dancers, with ballerina Harriet Hoctor soloing in the latter. Otherwise, Bobby Connolly directed the dances, which used another ensemble of thirty-seven dancers. With an additional seventeen showgirls, this brought the total number of dancers and chorus members to no less than seventy women—and no men.

Ziegfeld's decision to showcase the Cotton Club Orchestra not only brought welcome attention to Duke Ellington but represented yet another step toward the racial integration of Broadway. Employing the band cost an extra fifteen hundred dollars a week—an extravagance, Ziegfeld admitted, though he defended himself, calling the Ellington band "the finest exponent of syncopated music in existence. Irving Berlin went mad about them, and some of the best exponents of modern music who have heard them during rehearsal almost jumped out of their seats with excitement over their extraordinary harmonies and exciting rhythms." Elevated at the back of the stage, the band, featured in the Club Caprice scene, performed at least four numbers: the "Black and White" dance, the "African Daisies" ballet, "(I'm) Jimmy, the Well Dressed Man," and "Harlem Serenade." The received wisdom states that the band (which played late-night sessions at the Cotton Club after evening performances) left at intermission, but the evidence suggests otherwise, including a review that mentions its participation in the *American in Paris* ballet, not to mention trumpeter Freddie Jenkins's recollection that the group was "on stage during the whole performance," a claim supported by his vivid remembrance of Al Jolson singing "Liza" near the end of the show.[14]

Jolson began singing "Liza" during rehearsals in order to help ease his young wife's nerves, though as might be expected, he also felt some rapport with the song, which he recorded later that year. At the Boston premiere at the Colonial on June 24, he surprised both the cast and the audience by jumping up from his third-row seat on the aisle to sing "Liza" during Keeler's dance, a ploy apparently devised by Ziegfeld and Jolson to help boost interest in the show. (Ziegfeld also exploited the Jolson marriage by headlining Keeler as Ruby Keeler Jolson.) Jolson continued to sing "Liza" throughout the Boston tryout run as well as for the first week in New York (Arthur Gershwin recalled that he sang "Ruby, Ruby"— not "Liza, Liza"—"skies are gray"), a somewhat notorious incident in the annals of Broadway, as many have interpreted the move as an attempt on Jolson's part to steal his wife's thunder, though the person he truly upstaged was singer Nick Lucas, who left the production some weeks after it opened. In any case, Gershwin apparently brooked no complaint, as the caper helped draw attention to the song.[15]

Show Girl received enthusiastic notices in Boston but met with very mixed reviews in New York, where it opened at the Ziegfeld Theatre on July 2. On the one hand, such estimable critics as Percy Hammond in the *Herald-Tribune* and Gilbert Seldes in the *New Republic* considered the show one of Ziegfeld's very best, a deft transcription of the McEvoy novel into theatrical terms. Wrote Seldes:

> The stamp of the book remains even when the plot has been reduced to the terms of revue. When Ziegfeld tried a similar project, reducing Edna Ferber's *Show Boat* to a musical show, he fell to pieces, creating a dull and preten-

tious work which was saved by the supremely fine music of Jerome Kern. In *Show Girl,* Ziegfeld is back in his own field, revue, and although Gershwin's music let him down a little, he could call on the experts whose work he can himself correct. The comedy, the dancing, the staging, and the welding of all the elements into a unified whole, are all a tribute to a master hand.

However, most critics thought the show rambling and incoherent, even if good entertainment in spots.[16]

A consensus about the show's relative strengths and weaknesses emerged, nonetheless. Critics agreed, for instance, that the Urban sets—especially the nighttime Paris tableau for the *American in Paris* ballet—and the Harkrider costumes represented the show's chief assets. ("Pictorially this is Ziegfeld at his best," wrote *Billboard*'s Wilfred Riley, who otherwise thought the show "a distinct disappointment.") Keeler was found charming, regardless of whether she had the qualities to carry a show (though not a few opined that her limitations—her tentativeness, her reedy voice—suited the character of Dixie Dugan); and Durante was deemed funny, though some questioned the appropriateness of his vaudevillian shtick to a book musical. (The show, incidentally, helped make stars of both; *Time* magazine even had to report on the pronunciation of Durante's name.)

Most reviews also found Gershwin's music "distinctly under par" and "only fair," "the work," wrote Richard Dana Skinner in the *Commonweal,* "of a tired man or else of a lazy man." True, between the show's pastiche requirements (including the operetta parody, which, though handsomely done, seemed to serve little purpose other than to confuse many viewers) and its many interpolations, Gershwin had little room to maneuver. Even so, the critics underestimated such songs as "Do What You Do!" and "Liza."

Although the press exuberantly praised the work of Albertina Rasch and Harriet Hoctor, the only serious consideration of the *American in Paris* ballet—John Mason Brown's in the *New York Evening Post*—described it as "effective and charming," but lacking "the wit" and "the humanity" of Gershwin's music, and little helped by the "painful lyric" of the "Home Blues" song and the sumptuousness of the decor. "Everything is there," concluded Brown, "except simplicity, which seems to be the hardest of all things to get in our overlavish theatre, and a novelty worthy of Mr. Gershwin's score." Isaac Goldberg confirmed, "The style of the ballet and that of the abbreviated tone-poem were at all odds."[17]

On July 22 Keeler left the show for undisclosed health reasons and was replaced at first by her understudy, Doris Carson, and then by Dorothy Stone. Like her costar Eddie Foy Jr., Stone had previously performed mostly with her family in vaudeville (her father was famed comedian Fred Stone), but she proved highly capable in this featured role, her August 7 debut prompting ovations throughout the evening. "Her dancing and personality seemed to inject a new vigor into the proceedings at the Ziegfeld Theatre," reported the *Times*. Gilbert Gabriel, in the *Sun*, further suggested that by now having a leading lady who could "carry her songs . . . there'll be no trouble discovering that *Show Girl* is really and freely full of hit tunes."[18]

By this time, Ziegfeld and the Gershwins had had a falling-out. Ziegfeld liked his composers and lyricists on hand to revise shows after opening night; two months after *Rosalie* opened, for instance, he telegrammed Gershwin, "What we need is a hit number. Something they will whistle in the street. Then we will have a *Show Boat* in *Rosalie*." (The remark about the need for whistling material underscored the surprisingly widespread perception of Gershwin as the creator of somewhat tuneless music, to the point that in early 1930, Abbe Niles published a defense of the composer titled "Putting Gershwin to the Whistling Test.") The Gershwins were team players, but they had written many unused songs for *Show Girl*, and probably had had enough. In any case, Ziegfeld's lawyer wrote to Gershwin on July 25 that "although repeated demands have been made upon you to be present at rehearsals and fix the music of *Show Girl*, which you have agreed to do, you have failed to do the same, making it necessary for Mr. Ziegfeld to call in others to do your work," and that this was to be done at Gershwin's expense (the rationale, presumably, for Ziegfeld's subsequent halt of royalty payments). Gershwin in turn began legal proceedings against Ziegfeld. On October 10 Gershwin wrote to Rosamond Walling, "Ziegfeld (the rat) sent for me. On arriving in his office he immediately threw both arms around me & only my great strength kept him from kissing me. He informed me he was so sorry we had a disagreement & was anxious to make up—send me a check for back royalties—& be friends. I consented but as yet no check has arrived. Funny guy heh?"[19]

To add insult to injury, Ziegfeld publicly trumpeted in early August that he had engaged Vincent Youmans to help doctor the music. Indeed, concurrent with Stone's joining the show, he interpolated an early Youmans song, "Mississippi Dry," sung by the black Jubilee Singers, into the *Magnolias* scene, though that was about it. More provocatively, he announced that Youmans had agreed to compose the score for *East Is*

West, a turn of events that probably soured relations between the Gershwins and Youmans as well. However, not only did Youmans, too, face a cancellation of *East Is West* after he had begun work on the score, but his 1930 show for Ziegfeld, *Smiles,* occasioned a replay of the same kind of conflicts that had plagued Gershwin and the famous producer. Youmans "might have spared himself the anguish," remarks Gerald Bordman, had he paid Gershwin more heed.[20]

As some critics predicted, *Show Girl,* which ran a disappointing 111 performances, was not a smash hit. But it was not a flop either. Many of the reviews, as noted, were positive, sometimes extremely so, and the show probably would have enjoyed a longer run had not the opulent production, which closed on October 5, collided with a deteriorating financial climate. *Whoopee,* which opened in late 1928, would remain Ziegfeld's last big success.

Meanwhile, popular singers Lew Conrad (accompanied by the Leo Reisman band) and Smith Ballew (with the Ipana Troubadors) both recorded "Liza" in 1929, as did Jolson. Jazz musicians soon made the song their own as well. In 1930 Duke Ellington's band used it as the finale for a set that opened the revue *An Evening with Maurice Chevalier.* By 1934, recordings of the song by the Fletcher Henderson and Jimmy Noone orchestras, as well as by pianist Art Tatum, had established "Liza" as an up-tempo swing standard, usually performed without its verse, and generally at a much faster tempo than that favored by the song's early crooners.

Subsequent years witnessed jazz recordings of the song from Benny Goodman and Teddy Wilson to Sonny Stitt and Thelonious Monk, including an inventive two-piano rendition by Chick Corea and Herbie Hancock. Jazz artists patently enjoyed the stylish arc of the refrain's main theme, not to mention the delicious blue note at the end of the bridge section (at the mention of "Parson Brown"). By looking back to Harriet Beecher Stowe's Eliza, who boldly crosses an icy river to join her fugitive husband, and ahead to the fantasies of Corea and Hancock and beyond, Gershwin's minstrel parody proved as interesting culturally as musically.

On September 30, 1929, Gershwin signed a contract with the general manager of the Metropolitan Opera, Giulio Gatti-Casazza, to write an opera based on *The Dybbuk,* a play by Shloyme Zanvl Rappoport (1863–1920), better known by his pen name, Szymon Ansky. The agreement called for a completed orchestral score by April 1, 1931, and promised a minimum of four performances at $250 per performance.[21]

News of a Gershwin commission by the Met quickly broke in newspapers from coast to coast. "The announcement has of course thrilled the majority of Mr. Gatti's subscribers, Mr. Kahn, myself and the many patient souls who continually pray for the great American opera," wrote Samuel Chotzinoff in the *New York World*. Gershwin proposed to collaborate with Henry Ahlsberg, who had prepared the English translation of *The Dybbuk* for the 1925–1926 New York Neighborhood Playhouse production that the composer had found so inspiring, and that had starred his friend, Mary Ellis. He further announced his intention to leave for "an obscure corner of Europe" in the spring of 1930 in order to work on the opera and study Jewish music abroad (plans that anticipated his sojourn on Folly Island while writing *Porgy and Bess*).[22]

A Russian collector and writer of Yiddish folktales, Ansky originally wrote *The Dybbuk* in Russian in 1914 but prepared a Yiddish version as well, which the Vilna Troupe premiered in Warsaw in 1920 shortly after the author's death. Based on a Hasidic folktale, *The Dybbuk* takes place in a Jewish shtetl in the Pale of Settlement and concerns a young couple, Chanon and Leah, betrothed even before their birth. However, Leah's prosperous father will not allow them to marry because Chanon is a poor student. Reduced to practicing evil rites, Chanon dies and enters his beloved's spirit as a dybbuk, or migrant soul. After a failed exorcism, Leah also dies so that her soul can merge with Chanon's.

Following its 1920 premiere, performances of the play in Yiddish, Hebrew, and English enjoyed success around the world. Although its many stagings, which typically featured a score by Joel Engel based on Jewish folk music, encompassed varying dramatic sensibilities, audiences widely found the work mesmerizing. Critic Harold Clurman, who thought the Neighborhood Playhouse production one of the most memorable of his long career, wrote, "The play was viewed as a kind of phantasmagoria of a past civilization, a world beautiful in its depth of feeling but condemned for its practical organization." Gershwin, for his part, remarked, "It is the mysticism in it that fascinated me. It was a great thing for me." Gilbert Seldes's observation, in his rather critical review of the Neighborhood Playhouse production, that "all the changes in voice were so operatic" further helped explain Gershwin's attraction to the play as an operatic vehicle.[23]

Still, the choice was an unexpected one, Gershwin himself stating, "*The Dybbuk*, a sombre and mystical play, would not by any means be a jazz opera, and the fact that it would be different from any previous work [of mine] is one of its attractions." Perhaps the Yiddish plays he had seen in Europe the previous year had helped reinforce his long-standing attraction to Jewish theater. And was it merely coincidental that Aaron Copland's 1928 piano trio, *Vitebsk (Study on a Jewish Theme),* inspired by *The Dybbuk* and based on a theme from the Engel score, had premiered in February 1929 at a League of Composers concert in New York? Gershwin was known to attend such events, and this one included Schoenberg's Second String Quartet, a work that would have attracted him in particular. Tellingly, his friend Vernon Duke cited *Vitebsk* as one of those rare Copland pieces for which he'd be "ready to split my palms applauding." The Copland trio at least could have set Gershwin thinking about working with the *Dybbuk* story, perhaps even suggesting ways in which a jazz background could inform such a project.[24]

Ira recalled that George discussed the opera "a good deal and even wrote two or three mood-theme developments." However, by the end of December 1929, he essentially had to abandon the idea, as the rights for the play's operatic adaptation had already been granted to an Italian composer, Lodovico Rocca. Hearing Gershwin play some of the projected work (of which no known sketches survive), Isaac Goldberg spoke of "a slow lilt" that "gradually assumed a hieratic character, swinging in drowsy dignity above a drone," turning the room into "a synagogue" with "the indistinct prayer of those to whom prayer has become a routine such as any other." The music then "came to life as a Khassidic dance." Discerning some connection with African American song and dance, Goldberg added that Gershwin had become "increasingly conscious of the similarity between the folk song of the Negro and of the Polish pietists," an observation that recalls Emily Paley's comment, "George saw blacks and Jews as being the same in relation to the rest of society."[25]

With *The Dybbuk* detained over copyright issues, Gershwin considered other operatic possibilities, as he told Goldberg in late 1929. Whatever he wrote, he stated, it would not involve a Native American subject, alluding to the vogue for Indianist operas earlier in the century. Nor would it fall in the tradition of Verdi or Wagner:

> I'd rather make my own mistakes—break my own paths. I've been thinking for a long time of an operatic book involving the mixed population of our country. New York is not only an American city: it is a meeting-place, a rendezvous of the nations. I'd like to catch the rhythms of these interfusing peoples,—to show them clashing and blending. I'd like especially to blend the humor of it with the tragedy of it. Temperamentally I cannot enter with full sympathy into the exploitation of glorified "mushy" themes. I rec-

ognize, of course, that the highest musical expression must consider the ecstasies: but all heart and no head produce a soft, fibreless sort of music. I should want in however grand an opera, to find the head well in control of the heart.

And so, whatever else I may produce in the way of a serious opera, I shall not be content until I have managed to experiment satisfactorily with a libretto free of the conventional sentimentality that makes even the noble heroines and heroes secretly ridiculous to the very crowds that applaud them.

By February 1930 these ideas had evolved into plans for an orchestral suite that, reported one journalist, would "depict life in New York in its various and most interesting phases," including "the noise and life of the Ghetto [presumably, the Lower East Side], Chinatown, Little Italy, Harlem (at 135th Street), [and] Forty-second Street."[26]

Throughout early 1930, Gershwin also spoke about setting Lincoln's Gettysburg address for soloist and chorus, imagining the soloist (perhaps Lawrence Tibbett) solemnly intoning the words, and the chorus responding with indistinct murmurs, "Until at last, with the glorious finale of the Address itself, the chorus companions the voice of Lincoln in a climactic outburst." Gershwin never wrote a melting-pot opera or suite or a setting of the Gettysburg address—much as he never wrote the Frankie and Johnny symphonic work he had spoken about some years prior—but some of these preoccupations made their way into later ventures, nonetheless.[27]

Chapter Twenty-Five

Girl Crazy (1930)

The Gershwins spent the summer and early fall of 1930 working on another musical for Aarons and Freedley, *Girl Crazy*, to a book cowritten by Guy Bolton and John McGowan (1894–1977). Although McGowan had begun his career as an actor (he had introduced two Gershwin songs in the 1922 *Scandals*), by this time he had become a successful producer, director, and author as well, penning both a straight comedy, *Express Baggage* (1927), and a musical comedy, *Flying High* (1930).

Girl Crazy takes place in Custerville, Arizona, founded 1841—a dusty town that regularly kills off its sheriffs—and proclaims, "This lonely little village boasts of the fact there have been no women within its limits for over fifty years. The one and original woman was shot and killed in a quarrel over her. Thirty men were injured in this skirmish." As the act opens, the town's cowpunchers relax with a crossword puzzle while a quartet of cowboys (The Foursome) pass the time with a song ("Bidin' My Time"). As one of the cowboys prepares to find a wife, the others tease him ("The Lonesome Cowboy"). Danny Churchill (Allen Kearns) arrives from New York by a taxi driven by cabbie Gieber Goldfarb (Willie Howard), his fare coming to $742.30. A "girl crazy" playboy, Danny has been sent west by his father, who hopes that two years on the family's remote Buzzards Ranch in Custerville will reform him. As ruffian Lank Sanders (Carlton Macy), his sidekick Pete (Clyde Veaux), the sentimental Jake Howell (Lew Parker), and some other locals descend on Gieber for allegedly murdering their last sheriff, Danny comes to his rescue. A conversation with Molly Gray (Ginger Rogers), the local postmistress, gives Danny the idea of turning Buzzards Ranch into a dude ranch with women, alcohol, and gambling. Unimpressed with Danny,

Molly declines his advances ("Could You Use Me?" followed by a reprise of "Bidin' My Time").[1]

At the remodeled dude ranch, visiting city girls ("dudeens") gush over the manly cowboys ("Bronco Busters"). Gieber, Jake, and Patsy West (Nell Roy), a telephone operator who fancies Gieber, now work for Danny, who neglects his former girlfriend, Tess Parker (Olive Brady), in favor of Molly. Kate Fothergill (Ethel Merman), a saloon singer of the "Diamond Lil type," and her gambler husband, Slick (William Kent), arrive from San Francisco, whose praises Patsy extols ("Barbary Coast"). Danny proposes to Molly ("Embraceable You").

Danny's old rival, Sam Mason (Donald Foster), arrives from New York as well. When Lank threatens to run for sheriff and close down the dude ranch, which threatens his own gambling operation, Danny and Slick talk Gieber into running for sheriff ("Finaletto," also known as "Goldfarb! That's I'm!" followed by a reprise of "Bidin' My Time"). A fixed election assures Gieber's victory.

On the night of the opening of the ranch's Forty-Niner barroom, Danny and Molly, dressed in the fashions of 1849, ponder whether they should live in New York or Arizona (reprise of "Embraceable You"), and Frisco Kate entertains ("Sam and Delilah"). Sam, who wins six thousand dollars gambling, romances Molly, while Gieber, pursued by Lank and Pete, takes Patsy's advice to disguise himself as an Indian. Caught flirting with some girls, Slick appeases a forgiving Kate ("I Got Rhythm"). Slick mistakes a college-educated Indian, Eagle Rock (Chief Rivers), for Gieber, who enters acting the part of a stage Indian; Eagle Rock plays along, and he and Gieber exit speaking Yiddish. When Danny attempts to force Molly to accompany him to the races in San Luz, Mexico, she draws a gun on him and leaves with Sam ("Finale").

The second act opens at the Hotel Los Palmas in San Luz ("Land of the Gay Caballero"). The principals arrive, including Lank and Pete, both in pursuit of Sam's winnings. Realizing that Sam's the wrong man for her, Molly expresses her sorrows to Gieber, who cheers her up with impersonations ("But Not for Me"). Slick once again flirts with some girls ("Treat Me Rough"). After a drunken Sam tries to molest Molly, Lank and Pete accost and rob him, though suspicion falls on Danny. Kate muses on her marriage to Slick ("Boy! What Love Has Done to Me!").

Danny makes his escape as Gieber, encountering Lank and Pete, disguises himself as a woman. Molly happily returns home ("When It's Cactus Time in Arizona"), as does Gieber, who has been awarded five thousand dollars for securing the arrests of Lank and Pete. As Danny, in western wear, and Molly, in eastern clothes, are reconciled, Gieber urges (in an allusion to the time Broadway shows typically let out), "Go on—marry him, Molly. It is 11:15 now" ("Finale").

A burlesque of the western (including, perhaps, one of the most successful films of 1929, Raoul Walsh's *In Old Arizona*), the Bolton-McGowan book poked fun not only at the predictable eleven-fifteen curtain but at cardboard western villains and stage Indians. Although such parody was of a kind familiar enough—the received wisdom considers *Girl Crazy* a "retreat" from the more daring *Strike Up the Band*—the show at the same time had some novel features, including some political humor that looked ahead to *Of Thee I Sing*. "Folks I want you to know," says Gieber in his campaign speech, "I am for the people—I never stole a dollar from anyone in my life—I'm only asking you to give me the chance." Danny's arrival at Custerville could even be read as a metaphor for the Depression, with "Bidin' My Time," as Alisa Roost suggests, a response to the passivity of the Hoover administration. Other aspects of the musical—Kate and Slick's need for employment, Danny's hopping a freight to escape the authorities—also marked the show as a work of the early thirties.[2]

Relatedly, the show—as some recent commentators have pointed out—engaged some topical cultural issues. Roost, for instance, argues that "Bronco Busters"—not to mention Gieber's extensive cross-dressing—satirized stereotyped gender roles in ways that reflected some emerging gay sensibility or awareness. Andrea Most emphasizes the musical's constructions of ethnic and racial—in particular, Jewish and Indian—otherness as a means of asserting a place for minorities within the nation's power structure. For his part, Ethan Mordden finds the act 1 finale, though "old-hat in structure," surprisingly "arresting" dramatically: "Most musical comedies of the era manufactured the Boy Loses Girl plot suspense; this show features Girl robbing Boy of his Manhood. . . . Has something so brutal, so—really—suspenseful actually occurred in this farrago?"[3]

Ultimately, McGowan felt that he and Bolton failed to do Gershwin "justice," but they provided at least a colorful cast of characters. "We've come to liven the place up," Slick tells Patsy, who answers, "If we were any livelier, we'd be dead." "Wonder why I fell for you?" Frisco Kate asks Slick, who responds, "Yes, you were so exclusive, too—only went with sailors. I remember at the time I met you, you were going with the Pacific fleet." The modest charm of the story was such that more than two decades later, Anne Coulter Martens, Newt Mitzman, and William

Dalzell adapted the script as a straight comedy for the high school dramatic trade.[4]

Whatever its strengths and shortcomings, the book inspired one of Gershwin's most memorable scores. The setting surely played an important part in this regard, considering that the music drew on a variety of western idioms. "Bidin' My Time," for instance, parodied the kind of "cowboy" or "hillbilly" music popularized by Jimmie Rodgers and the Carter Family in the late 1920s, its folklike qualities underscored by its clipped form (and enhanced in the original production by having The Foursome toot on the harmonica, mouth-harp, ocarina, and tin flute); the song's verse tellingly contrasted such Tin Pan Alley favorites as "Tip-Toe thru the Tulips" and "Singin' in the Rain" with the cowboy's preferred music, lingo, and sentiment.

"The Lonesome Cowboy," "Bronco Busters," and "When It's Cactus Time in Arizona" similarly evoked cowboy and rodeo musics, while "Land of the Gay Caballero" tipped its hat to Mexico, as did, in its own way, "Could You Use Me?" What may have fired Gershwin's imagination—folk song collections or singers, the nascent country-music business, western films and Wild West shows, the composer's cross-country travels—remains uncertain, but he clearly made the West his own, including a characteristic whimsy that found resonance in Ira's words: "It's wonderful to breeze around; / They seem to have real trees around," the visiting city girls sing in "Bronco Busters," the cowboys later adding, "We pack a wallop—We never doll up / Our pants have never been creased."

The score further located some common ground between urban jazz and western honky-tonk in such numbers as "Barbary Coast," "Sam and Delilah," "Boy! What Love Has Done to Me!" and "I Got Rhythm," whose swinging rhythms intimated a larger change in the jazz world related to western influence. One early review revealingly described "Sam and Delilah," a retelling of the biblical tale as a western Frankie and Johnny story, as "a sort of mixture of Wild West, Negro spirituals and Broadway 'blues'" (and incidentally noted that the chorus "droned their accompaniment, and in the high spots raised their arms and their voices much after the manner of the Negro chorus in [the play] *Porgy*"). Meanwhile, "But Not for Me," a wry anti-Pollyanna song, fitted the show's general setting and tone as well. In these different ways, *Girl Crazy* helped mark the start of a new era, anticipating the western-inspired music of Ferde Grofé, Aaron Copland, Richard Rodgers, and others.[5]

A few numbers—significantly, those associated with Danny or Gieber—offered some contrast, in particular, the urbane duet "Embraceable You," originally written for *East Is West*. And Gieber's comedy number "Gold-farb! That's I'm!" parodied George M. Cohan's "Harrigan" (1907), some of its humor involving the substitution of a Jewish name for an Irish one and a corresponding change from "that's me" to "that's I'm." All in all, however, the music's prevailing western tone struck a distinctive note.

At the same time, the score revealed characteristic originality and refinement. In the case of its two most popular songs—"Embraceable You" and "I Got Rhythm"—this involved a striking avoidance of melodic downbeats, giving the former, in the tradition of "Virginia" and "Boy Wanted," something of its lilt, and the latter something of its zing. Such complexity posed special challenges for Ira, who, after considerable thought, fitted "I Got Rhythm" with a series of unrhymed two-foot lines, regularly capped off with the question, "Who could ask for anything more?" As for "Embraceable You," he matched the syncopated four-note motive concluding nearly every line of the chorus with a series of four-syllable rhymes, yielding such rhymes as "tipsy in me" and "gypsy in me," and "glorify love" and "'(En)core!' if I love."

Ira's masterful lyrics for the show as a whole helped to consolidate his preeminence. The *Nation*, for instance, observed, "As in *Strike Up the Band*, Ira Gershwin has demonstrated that he is the most skilful versifier writing for the American stage. There is a deftness and a wit to his lyrics that make them worthy complements to his brother's music." At the same time, his parodic humor—as in "When It's Cactus Time in Arizona"—sometimes eluded his listeners.[6]

Girl Crazy starred Ginger Rogers (Molly), Allen Kearns (Danny), and Willie Howard (Gieber). Aarons and Freedley originally wanted Bert Lahr for the lead comic role, but when Lahr, though under an alleged contractual obligation, refused to leave *Flying High*, the producers instead cast Howard (1886–1949), a vaudevillian known for his Jewish humor (he and his brother Eugene had recently headlined the Palace as "Two Hebrew Humorists Who Hail from Harlem"). Meanwhile, Kearns had played similar juvenile leads in a number of musicals, including *Tip-Toes* and *Funny Face*.[7]

In contrast, nineteen-year-old Ginger Rogers had only just won wide public attention for her appearances in the show *Top Speed* (1929) and the film *Young Man of Manhattan* (1930), in which she sang "I Got 'It' (but It Don't Do Me No Good)" and popularized the phrase "Cigarette me, big boy. Well, light it!" When she auditioned for *Girl Crazy*, she was surprised to find Gershwin at the piano, and impressed that he could "switch keys in the twinkling of an eye to accommodate any singer."

Rogers's western roots may have helped land her the part of Molly Gray, but she represented in general a new type of wisecracking heroine, as epitomized, too, by film comedienne Jean Harlow, who, like Rogers, was born in Missouri in 1911.[8]

Aarons and Freedley also signed up featured players Ethel Merman (Kate), William Kent (Slick), and Nell Roy (Patsy); specialty dancers Eunice Healy and the team of Antonio and Renee DeMarco; and a chorus of thirty women and sixteen men. Kent had garnered considerable acclaim for a similar role, that of Dugsie Gibbs, in *Funny Face;* but Ethel Merman, making her Broadway debut, wound up stealing the show.

Although she had left her job as a stenographer in her native Queens only a few months earlier, twenty-one-year-old Merman (born Zimmermann, 1908–1984) was not quite the unknown that legend would suggest. She had already appeared at such popular nightspots as Manhattan's Les Ambassadeurs, Valley Stream's Pavillon Royal, and Brooklyn's Paramount Theatre, and had even signed with Warner Brothers, singing the song "Sockety-Sock" dressed in animal skins for the musical short *The Cave Club,* shot at Warner's Avenue J studio in Brooklyn. She had, it is true, minimal stage experience, but that was not Aarons and Freedley's main concern; they were looking primarily for a vocalist who could carry the three Gershwin songs earmarked for Frisco Kate—"Sam and Delilah," "I Got Rhythm," and "Boy! What Love Has Done for Me!"—and help compensate for the cast's lack of a strong vocal presence. After catching Merman's act at the Paramount, Freedley invited the young singer to audition for Gershwin.[9]

At Gershwin's apartment, Merman sang some "swing numbers I'd been doing in night clubs and vaudeville," after which the composer played Kate's three songs from the show. Recalled Merman:

> It was the first time I'd met George Gershwin, and if I may say so without seeming sacrilegious, to me it was like meeting God. Imagine the great Gershwin sitting down and playing his songs for Ethel Agnes Zimmermann, of Astoria, Long Island. No wonder I was tongue-tied.
>
> When he played "I Got Rhythm," he told me, "If there's anything about this you don't like, I'll be happy to change it." There was nothing about that song I didn't like. But that's the kind of guy he was. I'll never forget it.

Though hired for $375 a week, less than half of Rogers's salary, Merman "felt lucky" to get the part. "I wasn't worrying about anybody else," she stated. "I just wanted to make a hit."[10]

As the show went into rehearsal, McGowan and the Gershwins grew increasingly appreciative of the clarity of Merman's diction, the brassiness of her timbre, and the sheer strength of her projection. Moreover, when McGowan heard how well she read her few lines, he expanded her part into, wrote Merman, "quite a brash comedy character." Gershwin, for his part, appreciated her fidelity to his intentions, saying that "he was glad to have somebody sing his songs the way he'd written them" (he later presented her with a photograph of himself, inscribed, "A lucky composer is he who has you singing his songs"). And Ira, confessing his clumsiness in placing the words *kootch* and *hooch* on long notes in "Sam and Delilah," observed, "I got away with it, thanks to Merman's ability to sustain any note any human or humane length of time. Few singers could give you 'koo' for seven beats (it runs into the next bar, like intermission people) and come through with a terrifically convincing 'tch' at the end." Kate's three songs so suited Merman that it seemed as if the Gershwins had written them specifically for her, whereas, on the contrary, they helped shape her stage persona. "I Got Rhythm" even became her signature theme, to the point that she titled one of her memoirs *Who Could Ask for Anything More.*[11]

From the successful revival of *Strike Up the Band,* Aarons and Freedley engaged Alexander Leftwich to direct, George Hale to stage the dances, and trumpeter Red Nichols to help man the orchestra, which again included the likes of Jimmy Dorsey, Benny Goodman, Gene Krupa, Glenn Miller, and Charlie and Jack Teagarden. Robert Russell Bennett worked with Gershwin on the orchestrations, many of which survive to reveal that Broadway's evolving sound, in some contrast to the more delicate sonorities of the 1920s, paralleled popular dance-band trends in its emphasis on saxophones and trumpets—a development related not only to the hiring of the forenamed jazz musicians (Glenn Miller might even have helped prepare some of the arrangements), but also to Gershwin's music itself. Earl Busby led the orchestra, including pianist—and future Hollywood producer—Roger Edens, though for some saloon atmosphere, Merman's regular pianist, Al Siegel, appeared onstage for "Sam and Delilah."[12]

Kiviette created the costumes, and a young member of the Yale faculty, Donald Oenslager, designed the sets, including an abstract portal inspired by Native American pottery in neutral colors that framed the vibrant sets depicting Custerville, Buzzards Ranch, and the Hotel Los Palmas. "Vinton Freedley, a producer of impeccable taste, blanched when I confided I would like to paint all these scenes in an arbitrary palette of vermilion, purple, yellow, and juniper green, with saddle brown and white adobe against pointilliste skies of yellow and cerulean blue," wrote Oenslager. "That was when I discovered he was color-blind! Only when I explained we would introduce to the contemporary musical stage the brilliant intensities of the Southwest, as well as the local color of *Girl Crazy*'s giddy shenanigans, was his faith in my sense of color restored."[13]

Unhappy with some of the staging, Aarons and Freedley also asked Fred Astaire to help polish a few dances, including "Embraceable You." Rehearsing the number in the theater's foyer, Astaire and Rogers danced together for the first time, a meeting that marked the beginning of one of the era's great dance partnerships. In its story about a suave man-about-town who courts a strongly independent woman, the musical itself anticipated the Astaire-Rogers film musicals of the 1930s.[14]

Girl Crazy had its world premiere in Philadelphia on September 29, 1930, and opened in New York at the Alvin Theatre on October 14, 1930, a performance best remembered for launching Merman's celebrated career. Within moments of her first song—"Sam and Delilah"—the audience started screaming (Merman supposed something had fallen onto the stage from the loft, or perhaps her garter had snapped). During her next number, "I Got Rhythm," pandemonium again erupted, especially during the second chorus, when she belted out long notes against the melody in the orchestra; the audience demanded encore after encore, and in later years, as Merman recalled, "even intelligent" people remembered her performance of the song as a "high point in the theater." "Although this young woman was appearing for the first time on any stage," wrote Ira, "her assurance, timing, and delivery, both as comedienne and singer—with a no-nonsense voice that could reach not only standees but ticket-takers in the lobby—convinced the opening-night audience that it was witnessing the discovery of a new star." During intermission, Gershwin, who conducted the premiere, visited Merman's dressing room in the rafters to tell her, "Don't ever let anybody give you a singing lesson. It'll ruin you."[15]

The show won excellent notices, notwithstanding a few dissenters, such as the *New York Times,* which thought it only so-so, and *Billboard,* which utterly disliked it. "After I had begun to think that I should never see a real musical show again—nothing but overripe operettas—along comes *Girl Crazy,* one of the best in years, to take its place at the top of the list," wrote Gilbert Seldes in the *Evening Graphic.* "I am overcome with gratitude." "It is difficult to discover any flaws in this musical comedy gem," agreed Stephen Rathbun in the *Sun.* The show proved a particular success for the Gershwins as well as for Merman and Willie

Howard (whose imitations of Eddie Cantor, Maurice Chevalier, George Jessel, Al Jolson, and Will Rogers delighted audiences).[16]

As with *Treasure Girl,* Gilbert Seldes and Percy Hammond thought the music particularly impressive. Seldes thanked Gershwin "for a delightful score, for several superb individual numbers, for preserving his gifts, for getting better every year, and for the tone of the whole show," while Hammond, in the *Herald-Tribune,* wrote, "The score, by George Gershwin, the sole aristocrat of the Broadway tune-business, is a fine accompaniment to the sprightly ritual, now tough, then tender, here surprising, there expected, and always blessed by the composer's irresistible originality." But in this instance, Seldes and Hammond were by no means alone. "Over and above everything," opined *Theatre Magazine,* "is the music of Gershwin—the songs, the finales, the never-ending bubbling of pure joyousness that emanates from the orchestra, and the vitality that is something esoteric, but which every Gershwin show seems to have in abundance." The *American* similarly thought the score "gorgeous," the *Telegram,* "zestful and imaginative," and the *Evening Post,* "so uniformly tuneful that it is hard to select outstanding numbers without reeling off the entire song list in the back of the program." Critical appreciation of the score presumably would have run even deeper had Rogers and Kearns been stronger singers, considering that the excellence of their numbers, including "Embraceable You" and "But Not for Me," escaped most auditors.

Because Al Siegel experienced health problems during the run of the show, Roger Edens began playing piano onstage as well as in the pit, thereby initiating an important professional relationship with Merman. Periodically Gershwin himself would turn up in the pit—at Wednesday matinees, as Merman recalled—and play the piano for some of the show's numbers. "The cast was always elated when they knew that George was in the pit," recalled Rogers; "there was a special zest when we performed *with* and *for* our composer."[17]

In the wake of her great success, Merman received a large raise and began singing after hours at the posh Central Park Casino, where cafe society gathered to hear pianist Eddy Duchin and the Leo Reisman Orchestra, and where Astaire and Rogers now occasionally went dancing after the show. Gershwin hoped to collaborate with Merman on another musical, but as the latter recalled, "nothing materialized. The producers never found a libretto that appealed to George and contained what he considered a suitable role for me. One project was undertaken but never completed."[18]

Willie Howard's departure from the show, a summer heat wave, and stifling economic conditions conspired to shorten the show's run, but even so, *Girl Crazy* enjoyed 272 performances on Broadway, grossing more than a million dollars. The show never made it to the West End, as Aarons and Freedley had hoped, nor did it have a national tour, but it played successfully in San Francisco and Chicago.

In 1931 RKO-Radio Pictures acquired the rights to *Girl Crazy*. Because of the low ebb of interest in film musicals, the studio toyed with the idea of a nonmusical adaptation, but decided in the end not only to use a large chunk of the score—including "Bidin' My Time," "I Got Rhythm," and "But Not for Me" as songs, and "Barbary Coast" and "Land of the Gay Caballero" as background music—but to commission, for two thousand dollars, a new song by the Gershwins, "You've Got What Gets Me." Released in March 1932, RKO's *Girl Crazy* featured the popular team of Bert Wheeler (essentially in the role of Gieber, though reconceived as an Irishman, Jimmy Deegan) and Robert Woolsey (as Slick), two comedians who had established themselves as a duo on Broadway in *Rio Rita* (1927).

Coproduced by William LeBaron and David O. Selznick and directed by William Seiter, the film starred, besides Wheeler and Woolsey, Eddie Quillan (Danny), Arline Judge (Molly), and Dorothy Lee (Patsy). Herman Mankiewicz, a friend of the Gershwins, adapted the story, and Tim Whelan and others created the screenplay. The studio shot the film in less than a month, but after the wrap, Selznick hired Norman Taurog to direct two weeks of retakes, which added more than two hundred thousand dollars to the film's original budget of about three hundred thousand. Quillan later claimed that, if anything, the reshoot only exacerbated the film's shortcomings—which included staging "But Not for Me" as a shouting match between him and Judge. "The whole thing was lousy, as far as I can remember," stated Lee.[19]

The picture at least occasioned the delightful "You've Got What Gets Me," adapted in part from an unused song from *Funny Face* and performed by Wheeler and Lee with charm, undermined, however, by the film's penchant for slapstick. As such, the movie won a few favorable reviews, including one in the *New York Times*, though *Variety* thought the film "too silly," adding, "The picture bunch wants its plots, menaces and romances straight, sans any Gershwinesque fol-de-rol."[20]

In 1943 MGM released its own *Girl Crazy*, giving director Taurog another go at the material. Produced by Arthur Freed and written by Fred Finklehoffe, the film reformulated the show as a Mickey Rooney–Judy

Garland musical, with Rooney's Danny Churchill more college lothario than city playboy, and Garland's Ginger (no longer Molly) Gray more dutiful granddaughter than sassy cowgirl. Danny's sent west not to spend time at the family ranch but to attend all-male Cody College; though at first alienated from both the town and the college, he falls in love with Ginger, the dean's granddaughter, and together they save the school from folding by initiating an annual rodeo to boost student enrollment.

The picture made extensive use of the original score, with six numbers sung and another six used as background music—that is, all of the songs except for "Goldfarb! That's I'm!" More gratuitously, the Tommy Dorsey Orchestra not only appeared in the rather stilted "I Got Rhythm" finale, staged by Busby Berkeley, but performed a swing arrangement of "Fascinating Rhythm," with Rooney at the piano. Still, with Garland holding forth on five songs, stylishly arranged by Conrad Salinger, the picture proved one of the more musically satisfying film adaptations of a Gershwin show. Garland's poignant rendition of "But Not for Me" even seems to have popularized that song, as suggested by *Time* magazine's 1943 description of the tune as "new." A recent assessment of the movie—widely considered the best of all the Rooney-Garland films—further considers "Could You Use Me?" as "easily the best number they did in any of their nine pictures together."[21]

In 1965 MGM released an even more juvenile version of *Girl Crazy* titled *When the Boys Meet the Girls*. Produced by Sam Katzman and directed by Alvin Ganzer, the film, which starred Connie Francis and Harve Presnell, along with cameo appearances by Louis Armstrong, Herman's Hermits, Liberace, and Sam the Sham and the Pharaohs, combined various aspects of the previous *Girl Crazy* adaptations in its plot concerning playboy Danny Churchill (Presnell), who enters Cody College in Nevada to escape a predatory showgirl (Sue Anne Langdon), and who falls in love with the local postmistress, Ginger Gray (Francis), whose crumbling home he saves by turning it into a dude ranch for Reno divorcees. The filmmakers plausibly supposed a Connie Francis vehicle the sixties equivalent of a Rooney-Garland film, though as *Time* observed, "The brains behind *The Boys* . . . seem to confuse updating with downgrading." The picture certainly had little of the charm of the 1943 film, let alone the wit of the 1930 original.[22]

While the film's featured musicians performed a motley assortment of interpolated numbers, five Gershwin songs helped tie the narrative together: "Treat Me Rough" (sung by Langdon), "Embraceable You" (sung by Presnell and reprised by Francis), "Bidin' My Time" (sung by Herman's Hermits), "I Got Rhythm" (sung by the ensemble), and "But Not for Me" (sung by Francis and Presnell). With the exception of Louis Armstrong, whose concluding performance of "I Got Rhythm" virtually redeemed the entire enterprise, the cast, however effective in the more contemporary songs, seemed largely ill-suited to the original score, with Herman (apparently confusing "Bidin' My Time" with his hit single, "I'm Henry the Eighth, I Am") obliviously changing Ira's rhyme of *time/I'm* to *time/I am*. "If the music of the Gershwin brothers can survive a terrible little musical such as *When the Boys Meet the Girls*," wrote the *Times,* "chances are it could outlast atomic annihilation."

Meanwhile, *Girl Crazy* held the stage in numerous revivals, including those at the Paper Mill Playhouse in Milburn, New Jersey (1947), the Greek Theater in Los Angeles (1949), the Starlight Theater in Kansas City (1954), the Westbury Music Fair on Long Island (1960), the Goodspeed Opera House in Connecticut (1971), the Equity Liberty Theatre in New York (1986), and the Guildhall School of Music in London (1987), as well as a concert reading with narration at Alice Tully Hall as part of Lincoln Center's Composers' Showcase series (1990). The reception of these revivals tended toward the delirious—"an evening of such pure, unadulterated pleasure as to be almost guilt-inducing," wrote Rodney Milnes about the Guildhall production—though the Lincoln Center concert presentation apparently misfired: "To work—then and for the audiences of today—such shows need idiomatic musical and theatrical verve," stated John Rockwell in the *Times,* "which are by no means yet extinct, but also the theatrical context that dialogue and staging provide, a context from which the songs can naturally arise."[23]

The enduring success of *Girl Crazy* encouraged New World Music to publish a vocal score in 1954. Moreover, in 1960 Guy Bolton prepared a revised version of the book for the Westbury Music Fair production. Among other changes, Danny became the former star of a television western, *Cowpoke;* Kate took on a larger presence as Molly's rival; and the roles of Gieber and Slick were conflated into the figure of Kate's ex-husband, Hungarian pianist Zoli. Bolton also interpolated some songs from other Gershwin shows. The result, less rollicking than the original, never caught on, nor did its change of an ironic but potentially offensive lyric in "Bronco Busters" (from "On Western prairies we shoot the fairies" to "On Western acres we shoot the fakers").

All these revivals took liberties with the score, as did the only recording that for many years even approached cast-album status: Columbia's 1951 studio release featuring Mary Martin and conducted by Lehman

Engel, an overarranged rendering whose dramatic integrity was foiled by having the same soloists perform songs intended for varying characters. Fortunately, much of the show's original material—including the orchestrations—survived, making it possible for the Gershwin estate to oversee an unusually authentic recording of the score, released by Elektra Nonesuch in conjunction with Roxbury Records in 1990, that featured Judy Blazer (Molly), David Carroll (Danny), Lorna Luft (Kate), and Frank Gorshin (Gieber), under the baton of John Mauceri.

Shortly after this Elektra Nonesuch release, a free adaptation of *Girl Crazy* titled *Crazy for You* (1992) established itself as the most successful Gershwin show of the century, surpassing the similarly conceived *My One and Only* (1983), based on *Funny Face*. Produced by Elizabeth Williams and Roger Horchow (whose parents had entertained Gershwin at their Cincinnati home in 1934), the show had a book by Ken Ludwig that drew on a number of previous *Girl Crazy* adaptations, though shaped by a tone reminiscent of the playwright's successful farce, *Lend Me a Tenor* (1985). Set in the 1930s, the plot revolves around the scion of a New York banking family, Bobby Child (Harry Groener), who is sent to the mining town of Deadrock, Nevada, in order to foreclose on a dilapidated theater owned by the father of postmistress Polly Baker (Jodi Benson). Disguising himself as Broadway impresario Bela Zangler, Bobby decides to launch a show in Deadrock, and although the arrival of his New York girlfriend, Irene Roth (Michele Pawk), and the real Zangler (Bruce Adler) creates complications, he wins Polly, saves the theater, and fulfills his dream of dancing in a show. Besides bits and pieces from Gershwin's instrumental work, the musical used eighteen songs culled from various musicals, including six from *Girl Crazy* ("Bidin' My Time," "Bronco Busters," "Could You Use Me?" "Embraceable You," "I Got Rhythm," and "But Not for Me"); the rest of the score featured some familiar tunes along with such delightful obscurities as "Tonight's the Night," "What Causes That?" and "Naughty Baby."[24]

Williams and Horchow assembled an expert team, including director Mike Ockrent, choreographer Susan Stroman, scenic designer Robin Wagner, costume designer William Ivey Long, arranger Peter Howard, orchestrator William David Brohn, and music director Paul Gemignani. Ultimately costing more than eight million dollars, the show came into its Washington tryout overlong, but opened at New York's Shubert Theater on February 19, 1992, to excellent reviews, including one in the *Times* by Frank Rich, who wondered if the "riotously entertaining show" heralded "a second coming" that might "grab the musical back from the

British." A number of critics thought the leads lackluster, but the show nonetheless walked away with the Tony award, the Drama Desk Award, and the Outer Critics' Circle Award for best musical of the year, and closed on January 7, 1996, after 1,622 performances (though it took 700 performances for it to recoup its investment). Within a year of its opening, *Crazy for You* began a worldwide sweep, beginning in Tokyo and London, where it won the 1993 Laurence Olivier Award for best new musical, before moving on to theaters from Helsinki and Sydney to Budapest and Mexico City.[25]

The show made a star of Stroman, whose choreography, with its innovative adaptation of period dance styles, also won the Tony, Drama Desk, Outer Critics' Circle, and Laurence Olivier Awards. "Short of George Balanchine's 'Who Cares?' at the New York City Ballet," wrote Rich, "I have not seen a more imaginative choreographic response to the Gershwins onstage." Stroman's kind of historical awareness informed other aspects of the production, including the arrangements and orchestrations, which knowingly updated older approaches and helped demonstrate the music's continued stageworthiness.[26]

Still, the show remained fundamentally a pastiche, including a score whose stylistic incongruities diluted the overarching local color of the original score. Moreover, the show often placed the Gershwin songs in contrived dramatic contexts, with numbers sometimes stitched together in medley fashion, and verses dropped as a matter of course. The *Village Voice* even identified as the show's "main problem" the fact that "the Gershwin brothers took pains to write very carefully shaped songs, the effect of which is lost when they're diced up as musical succotash," while the *London Observer* wrote, "The elisions between dialogue and song are not always convincing."[27]

The show's stylistic and formal weaknesses underscored a perceived lack of content. "It has no content," David Richards bluntly stated in another *Times* review, "other than performers performing." Certainly, the show's basic story had accrued different meanings over the years; whereas the original *Girl Crazy* dealt with a couple learning to love and trust each other, the 1943 film centered rather on the hero's becoming a productive citizen, a tradition of which *Crazy for You* partook, though modernized in its emphasis on historical preservation and urban renewal. "Great tunes are fine, and *Crazy for You* has them," wrote William Henry in *Time* magazine. "But it takes great words, great stories and above all great feelings to make a great show."

A number of songs from *Girl Crazy* enjoyed notable success independent of any production. "Bidin' My Time," "Embraceable You," and "I Got Rhythm" quickly gained wide currency, as did, in later years, "Boy! What Love Has Done to Me!" and "But Not for Me." "Embraceable You" became a particular favorite with singers and instrumentalists, including saxophonist Charlie Parker, whose 1947 recording became famous for its extensive use of a motive only obliquely related to the title tune. But "I Got Rhythm" surpassed all these numbers not only in terms of sheer popularity but because of its special importance to jazz history.[28]

Musicians began performing and recording "I Got Rhythm" in the weeks and months following the show's premiere, a trend that continued unabated throughout the 1930s and 1940s. As early as 1930, Kate Smith and Ethel Waters recorded the song, as did a number of dance orchestras. Louis Armstrong's brilliant 1931 recording, with pianist Fats Waller and others, "sped the song on its way toward jazz standard status," according to Will Friedwald. Each passing year brought more recordings, including one by the Casa Loma Orchestra (1933) described by Friedwald as "fantastic." The year 1937 alone witnessed recordings of the song by Benny Goodman, Jimmy Dorsey, Lionel Hampton, Glenn Miller, Django Reinhardt, and Dicky Wells, among others. Some of the performers who helped popularize the tune—including Goodman, Miller, and Gene Krupa—had played in the original Broadway production, a shared background that perhaps aided the music's dissemination; but the song early on became associated as well with musicians who had no connection with the show, including violinist Stéphane Grapelli and pianist Art Tatum.[29]

Discussions of the song have traditionally focused on its harmonic structure, including chord progressions that, in the manner of the Harlem stride pianists, cycle about energetically. But the harmony frames the melody, which similarly swings back and forth, calling for some counterweight of driving beats, including strong downbeats, which musicians have often supplied in the form of riffs, brief repeated gestures that can both anchor and launch the melody. The combination of looseness and drive nicely met the needs of such new dances as the Lindy Hop (named after Charles Lindbergh) and the jitterbug. Indeed, the song proved a veritable anthem of the new swing era.[30]

Raymond Knapp further viewed the song as "an embodiment of a new sensibility that places music and specifically rhythm (and even more specifically jazz rhythm) at the center of what matters in American life." In this respect, "I Got Rhythm" deserved comparison with an earlier

Gershwin landmark, "Fascinating Rhythm," though in that song, rhythm has the "unhappy" protagonist "shaking . . . like a flivver," whereas here, rhythm has become associated with "starlight" and "sweet dreams," leaving the singer "happy" and "chipper." William Austin, meanwhile, suggested that both songs helped introduce the word *rhythm* into common parlance.[31]

From the time Ethel Merman pitted sustained notes against the song's melody—and perhaps popularized the verbal interpolation "hangin' 'round my front and back door" in place of Ira's simpler "'round my door"—musicians and arrangers plainly feel the urge to let loose with the tune, perhaps in part because of its enormous energy. Ethel Waters, anticipating Ella Fitzgerald and others, embellished the melody with some marvelous scat singing, and even Kate Smith jazzed up the second chorus of her 1930 release. By the time of Fats Waller's riveting 1935 recording, the song had become a testing ground for virtuosity at the highest levels.

Simultaneously, jazz musicians began to create new tunes, with their own titles, that appropriated the song's basic structure and provided new but related springboards for improvisation. Martin Williams cites Sidney Bechet's "Shag" (1932) as perhaps the earliest instance of this practice. Later examples include such jazz classics as Lester Young's "Lester Leaps In" (1939), Duke Ellington's "Cotton Tail" (1940), Count Basie's "Blow Top" (1940), Coleman Hawkins's "Chant of the Groove" (1940), and a number of Charlie Parker tunes, some cowritten with Dizzy Gillespie, such as "Shaw 'Nuff" (1945) and "Anthropology" (1946).[32]

According to Gillespie, these parodies arose in response to the practice of varying the song's harmonic progression with substitute chords, which in turn suggested new melodies. Max Roach, for his part, claimed that they represented a "revolutionary" way to balance audience expectations with financial and artistic autonomy. In any case, these nonexplicit variations on "I Got Rhythm" became so widespread—Gillespie imagined that there were "about ten million" of such tunes—that the practice acquired its own name, *rhythm-changes*. For musicologists Richard Crawford and Scott DeVeaux, the tradition of rhythm-changes could even be compared to the blues. As the aforementioned examples suggest, rhythm-changes proved particularly decisive in facilitating the transition from swing to bebop in the 1940s, though this subgenre maintained its appeal in the 1950s and beyond to such varied jazz musicians as Miles Davis, J. J. Johnson, Thelonious Monk, Sonny Rollins, and Sonny Stitt.[33]

Although commentators commonly define rhythm-changes as variations on a set harmonic progression (often in B♭ major, the key of the song's published sheet music), a survey of representative examples suggests other factors at work. A number of rhythm-changes, for example, retained remnants of Gershwin's original melody. Jazz musicians probably remembered something of Ira's words as well, even if it were only the idea of having "rhythm."[34]

Chapter Twenty-Six

Delicious and the *Second Rhapsody* (1931)

*O*n Gershwin's return from Europe in August 1928, the press announced that he had signed with Winfield Sheehan of Fox Studios for $100,000 to write a Hollywood musical to be directed by Frank Borzage. "At first skeptical about the possibilities of the talking movies," stated the *New York Evening Post,* "Gershwin then made a careful study of the new medium and finally decided that it constituted a good vehicle for jazz and other forms of modern music." These reports proved premature, but two years later, on April 10, 1930, the Gershwins indeed signed with Fox to write a musical for which George would receive $70,000 and Ira, $30,000 (plus first-class round-trip travel for both from New York to Los Angeles).[1]

So large a fee for fourteen weeks of work was hardly typical for a composer—enlisting Gershwin was considered a "notable victory" for Fox—but indicative nonetheless of the imposing salaries commanded by leading songwriters during the brief period between the rise of the movie musical in 1927 and its temporary decline in 1930. Fox, for example, paid DeSylva, Brown, and Henderson $150,000 for their work on *Sunny Side Up* (1929). Such salaries attracted composers to Hollywood in droves. True, most songwriters could no longer collect a percentage of the box-office gross, as they did on Broadway, but they could expect much larger royalties; a moderately successful Hollywood song could generate sheet-music and record sales not in the tens of thousands, as with an average Broadway song, but in the hundreds of thousands. Meanwhile, with the popularity of musical films in full swing, the combination of box-office receipts and music and record sales spelled large profits for the studios, particularly if they owned the rights to the music; hence their willingness to pay well for leading songwriters and their penchant for acquiring New York's established music publishing houses.[2]

Fox engaged Guy Bolton, long associated with the composer, to write the screenplay for the Gershwin musical, and by May 1930 it had contracted Sonya Levien to work on the script as well. An attorney by training, Russian-born Levien (1895–1960) would have a prolific career spanning four decades as a story writer in Hollywood, authoring dozens of films for Fox and later MGM, including the Gershwin biopic *Rhapsody in Blue* (1945) as well as *Interrupted Melody* (1955), for which she won an Academy Award. Meanwhile, the estimable Frank Borzage was still slated to direct.[3]

In February, while still in New York, Gershwin expressed some concerns about the film medium: "The talkies are marvelous, but I don't think they have as yet achieved any sort of perfection in combining music and motion pictures and dialogue. I think they are very fine, but as a whole I have not as yet seen a perfect talkie." But he remained hopeful, with one source reporting in April that "while he admits that in picture work there must be a compromise between art and commerce, he regards the screen as the greatest of all mediums through which culture may be brought to the multitude." After arriving in Hollywood in early November 1930, he further declared that he was approaching his new assignment "in a humble state of mind," saying, "I go to work for the talkies like any other amateur, for I know very little about them. I am not a film fan, a movie addict, neither am I crazy about shows."[4]

For this prestige musical, Fox lined up two of its most popular stars, Janet Gaynor and Charles Farrell. The petite Gaynor (1906–1984) had rocketed to fame near the end of the silent-movie era, thanks largely to three films—F. W. Murnau's *Sunrise* (1927) and Borzage's *Seventh Heaven* (1927) and *Street Angel* (1928)—that together won her the first Academy Award for best actress (1929), and that established her reputation in particular for portraying vulnerable and mistreated women. In the two Borzage films, Gaynor also found in Charles Farrell (1901–1990) an attractive romantic foil. The pair—dubbed "America's favorite sweethearts"—successfully made the transition to sound, revealing with *Sunny Side Up* (1929) that they even could carry a musical. "Her [Gaynor's] winsome untrained way with song and dance added new dimensions to the waif appeal cultivated in her silent romances and helped to solidify her position as one of the biggest draws in the business," notes Richard Barrios, who further observes that while Farrell's "nasal voice" undermined the "uniquely innocent virility" he projected in his silent films, "in musicals, where Gaynor bore the main load, he made do with appearance and amiability and accumulated spectator goodwill." After their last film together, *Change of Heart* (1934), their careers waned, notwithstanding Gaynor's Academy Award nomination for one of her last films, *A Star Is Born* (1937), and Farrell's reemergence on radio and television in the early 1950s as the father in the series *My Little Margie*.[5]

Fox also enlisted one of its leading comedians, El Brendel (1891–1964), who was best known for his comic Swedish dialect (though he was of German Irish descent), and whose long career encompassed vaudeville, film, radio, and television (he also played a father on a 1950s situation comedy, namely, *I Married Joan*). In supporting roles, the studio cast Virginia Cherrill (late of Chaplin's *City Lights*), Raul Roulien, Manya Roberti, and Mischa Auer, the maternal grandson of the great Russian violinist Leopold Auer, whose surname he adopted. By the time the Gershwins arrived in Hollywood in November, Fox had also decided to have David Butler, not Borzage, direct the film. An artist of lesser stature, Butler (1894–1979) was nonetheless a competent director who had directed Gaynor and Farrell in *Sunny Side Up,* and who, writes Barrios, "ended up making a career out of light-headed fare: vehicles for Shirley Temple, Bob Hope, Doris Day."[6]

Once in California, Gershwin found himself besieged by dinner invitations, as he wrote to Ethel Merman on November 17:

> And always the same routine. First cocktails, then picture talk. Dinner is served starting with soup which is immediately followed by picture talk. Then fried fish or lobster that came on Newburg immediately followed by some more picture talk. Then a delicious steak with picture talk and onions. That continues until after dessert and then demi-tasse is served in the living room and then the butler leans over a little and says, "I'll tell you what's wrong with those musical talkies." One listens. Perhaps he is right about it after all, who knows?

After a while, he found it necessary to disconnect the telephone and bar the door of his bungalow at Fox's Movietone City in order to get his work done, though he apparently had a running start on the project, for as early as the previous April he and Ira had completed the title song, "Delishious." In the end, he found it preferable just to work at home in Beverly Hills, while for relaxation he swam, hiked, played tennis and golf, and whiled away some pleasant hours at the Malibu residence of Buddy DeSylva and the Santa Monica home of actress Aileen Pringle.[7]

Gershwin's most demanding task was to compose a piece for piano and orchestra, the "New York Rhapsody," that would serve as the background music for the film's climactic sequence. After spending an initial seven weeks on the film score as a whole, he devoted his remaining seven weeks specifically to this undertaking (Gershwin later stated that Ira liked California better than he did because "he didn't work so hard"). Hugo Friedhofer (1901–1981), at the beginnings of his career as a leading film orchestrator and composer, assisted with the scoring, which Gershwin completed after his return to New York. Gershwin then sent his orchestrated pages back to Friedhofer, who helped ready the music for recording later in the year, eliminating those orchestral "superfluities" that he attributed to the composer's "extreme pianist feeling." Gershwin hoped to return to Hollywood over the summer to help participate in the final production—"I wish to God I could be there to see it [the picture] made and possibly help a little," he wrote Pringle in August—but such intentions came to naught. Fox's musical director, Samuel Kaylin, presumably supervised the recorded score, which featured the brilliant pianist Marvine Maazel (who also had a minor role in the film).[8]

The "New York Rhapsody" proved a novelty by Hollywood standards: composed months prior to the actual filming, it provided the music around which a cinematic episode would take shape (thereby also giving the composer time to orchestrate the music); and it constituted a work so self-contained that it could be adapted for concert purposes, which Gershwin did under various working titles, including *New York Rhapsody, Manhattan Rhapsody, Rhapsody in Rivets,* and, finally, *Second Rhapsody.* However, the filmmakers ultimately cut the piece from about fifteen to about seven minutes in length. Moreover, fearful that "the music would be distracting to the action," the studio shrouded the piece by recording the work with the piano at the rear of the orchestra, and by overdubbing prominent sound effects.[9]

Delicious opens amid a transatlantic voyage to New York. On board are wealthy sportsman Larry Beaumont (Charles Farrell), his valet, Jansen (El Brendel), his girlfriend, Diana Van Bergh (Virginia Cherrill), Diana's mother (Olive Tell), and, below in steerage, immigrants to the United States, including a Scottish girl, Heather Gordon (Janet Gaynor), and a Russian family, including pianist-composer Sascha (Raul Roulien), his sister Olga (Manya Roberti), and his brothers, violinist Mischa (Mischa Auer) and cellist Toscha (Marvine Maazel). Jansen and Olga flirt with each other, while Heather sparks the romantic interest of both Larry and Sascha, who composes a song inspired by her speech mannerisms ("Delishious"). On the night before arriving in New York, Heather dreams of a glorious reception in the New World ("Dream Sequence").

However, Heather is refused entry at Ellis Island and ordered to re-turn to Scotland. Dodging the authorities, she hides in a horse-box that makes its way to Larry's country home, where Jansen puts her up for the night ("Somebody from Somewhere"). Heather subsequently takes refuge in Manhattan with Sascha and his family, who work her into their act at a Russian cafe ("Katinkitschka"). Though in love with Larry, Heather agrees to marry Sascha when she learns that Larry's engaged to Diana. On Heather and Sascha's wedding day, Jansen devises lyrics to a tune of Toscha's ("Blah, Blah, Blah").

Hearing that Larry has been injured in a polo accident, Heather rushes to his side, but Diana reports her to immigration. Heather flees to Sascha, who now grasps the impossibility of their marriage, and who plays for her portions of his recently completed "New York Rhapsody." Mean-while, Jansen and Olga agree to wed. On the run, an exhausted Heather wanders through the crowded streets of Manhattan, winding up on the quays by the waterfront; dissuaded from suicide by an old woman, she surrenders to the police ("New York Rhapsody"). Learning of Diana's treachery, Larry catches the boat taking Heather back to Europe and pro-poses to her on board.

In the background of this sober musical film hovers the growing lim-its on immigration initiated by the 1924 National Origins Act and fully implemented by 1929, a context that comes to the fore when Heather finds her application rejected because her American uncle lacks the means to support her; the irony of Heather's situation is heightened not only by her unrealistic dreams but by the Irish, Greek, and Jewish sur-names of the immigration officials. Actually, a Scot generally would have been far more welcome than immigrants from outside Western Europe, like Sascha and his family (who apparently are gentile, not Jewish, Rus-sians). But one seeming intention of the film—and Fox, the studio of director John Ford, often showed concern for the travails of society's underdogs—was to evoke sympathy for immigrants, even illegal aliens like Heather.[10]

Produced at a time of deep skepticism about the movie musical, the film was careful not to try the public's patience. Farrell is left out of the music entirely, and except for the modest "Katinkitschka" number (staged by an uncredited Seymour Felix), none of the principals dance. Moreover, most of the songs appear with the seen presence of accom-panying instruments: Sascha and Jansen sing "Delishious" and "Blah, Blah, Blah" to just a piano accompaniment; Heather intones "Somebody from Somewhere" primarily to the strains of a music box; and the Russian players perform "Katinkitschka" accompanied by a cafe orchestra. Similarly, most of the film's other musical cues—folk songs sung on board ship, party music at the Beaumont home, a rendering of "Somebody from Somewhere" heard over the radio—show or intimate a recognizable source. (The party scene, incidentally, uses "You Started It," a delightful song composed by the Gershwins for the film but never used as such; played by a dance band, the music—whose source in this instance remains out of sight—appears first in its original fox-trot guise and somewhat later as a waltz.)[11]

Aside from some brief underscoring at the start and end of the picture, the "Dream Sequence" and the "New York Rhapsody" constitute the only notable exceptions to such realistic use of music. With regards to the former, the dream framework clearly permitted greater latitude; while Heather's precarious mental state provided a similarly extenuating context for the "Rhapsody."Moreover, Sascha's authorship of the *Rhapsody* allows one to hear the music as his, not Gershwin's, an illusion furthered by having Sascha, Mischa, and Toscha's playing of the piece segue into the orchestral version. (Had the picture retained the screenplay's idea of superimposing Heather's dazed walk with footage of the piano trio, this impression would have been all the stronger.)[12]

After returning to New York in late February 1931, Gershwin made a few public remarks in conformity with the film's cautious use of music. "Hollywood is learning that music must not interfere with the story, but help it," he stated. "The directors are slowly learning that if a picture's locale is a desert, it is ridiculous to have a full orchestra burst forth at intervals during the picture." Or so it seemed in 1931. As with so many other films from the early 1930s, this austere approach to movie scoring— notwithstanding the happy indulgence of the "Dream Sequence" and the "New York Rhapsody"—seems overly circumspect by later standards. On the other hand, the spartan sound track makes, say, Sascha's piano playing all the more visceral.[13]

The music accommodates the film's realistic intentions in other ways. Both the tender "Somebody from Somewhere" and the humorous "Katinkitschka" are folklike enough to fit the characters of Heather and the Russians, respectively; this includes unusually abbreviated choruses that are more like traditional refrains than typical musical-comedy choruses, and lyrics that likewise reflect folk traditions. "Blah, Blah, Blah" relatedly—and in its own way, daringly—mocks popular-music clichés. That a Russian immigrant, not yet off the boat, would pen a song like "Delishious" perhaps strains credulity, but the implied identification of

Sascha with Gershwin assumes, especially as the film progresses, its own intriguing resonance. All of the score's numbers have, moreover, an intimacy that suits the film's untrained voices. Gershwin himself enjoyed singing "Delishious" at gatherings at his home as well as another song he and Ira hoped to introduce into the Russian cafe scene, namely, "Mischa, Jascha, Toscha, Sascha"—a song that obviously supplied the names of some of the Russian characters nonetheless.[14]

This concern for realism extends to the "New York Rhapsody," whose representational meanings Sascha, sitting at the piano, decodes for Heather: "It begins like we all see the city first. The great towers almost in the clouds [he plays a passage beginning at measure 7]. Down below in the long furrows—human seeds trying to grow to the light [rehearsal 1] . . . and noise [rehearsal 3]. Rivetters—drumming your ear from every side [two after rehearsal 7]. And this is the night motif—night silencing the rivets [rehearsal 5]." The one major theme not discussed is the "Sostenuto e con moto" melody at the work's very heart; but as that music first appears as an accompaniment to Sascha's poignant question to Heather, "But you come back?" the film patently associates it with his unrequited love. David Butler had his own complementary ideas about the music, including images seemingly inspired by Murnau. In any event, the music seems essentially preoccupied, as its title suggests, with fashioning a cityscape of New York.[15]

The "Dream Sequence," for its part, lampoons the hype associated with the American "melting pot." After reporters from various dailies conduct the most superficial of interviews with Heather, a chorus of Uncle Sams, an imaginary Mr. Ellis of Ellis Island, and finally a wiggling Statue of Liberty welcome her to the "melting pot," a clear send-up of immigration policy. Of all the film's numbers, this one most closely approximated Gershwin's theater music, anticipating especially *Of Thee I Sing* in its evocation of various ceremonial styles, but with enough unusual inflections to signal satiric intentions, including a tongue-in-cheek reference to the composer's own "'S Wonderful."

Delicious was released on December 3, 1931, though it opened in a number of cities on Christmas Day, including New York, where a large crowd thronged the Roxy Theater for the premiere. The reviews widely regarded the picture as family entertainment in keeping with the season; the *Times* reported that it seemed to appeal especially to children. Critical opinion itself proved mixed, particularly with regard to the music. The *Film Daily,* for instance, thought the picture "greatly enhanced by the musical background," and the *Motion Picture Herald* deemed the "Rhapsody" "one of the finest, if not the finest, musical composition originally conceived for motion pictures." On the other hand, *Cinema* thought the "eccentric and aggressive" music the "precise antithesis" of the film's "conventional sentimentality," while the *New York Herald-Tribune* detected nothing in the score "much beyond the commonplace." The *World-Telegram* singled out the "Dream Sequence" as "something divinely insane," but similarly found the score "far from distinguished." "Gershwin is said to have written the music involved," wrote the *Outlook and Independent,* "but you'd never know it." Gershwin himself wrote to Aileen Pringle on December 31, "I was very disappointed in the picture we wrote. . . . It could have been so swell but imagination in producing it & cutting it was lacking. However in spite of that it will come near breaking the all time record at Roxy's. They expect to do $130,000 this week."[16]

In one of the more authoritative reassessments of the film, Richard Barrios writes that although the "Dream" and "Rhapsody" sequences inspired Butler to work "way above his norm," Gershwin's departure from Hollywood in early 1931 constituted a serious blow to the project as a whole: "Without his [Gershwin's] presence, the Fox creed took over, and as with most films of its year *Delicious* is unduly heavy, the work of filmmakers who defeated the technical limitations of sound yet remained artistically pent up." Having arrived in Hollywood at an inauspicious moment, Gershwin understandably waited five years before embarking on another film. Still, his pioneering effort, though widely overlooked, deserves to be remembered not only for its own sake but for the light it sheds on the *Second Rhapsody.*[17]

The *Second Rhapsody* conveniently satisfied a request by conductor Serge Koussevitzky (1874–1951) for a new work to perform with the Boston Symphony Orchestra. Born into a Russian-Jewish family, Koussevitzky, a virtuoso double-bassist, first married a ballet dancer and then, in 1905, a wealthy heiress whose fortune allowed him to pursue a conducting career, one in which he emerged an important champion of new music, first in his native Russia, then in his adopted Paris, and finally in the States, where he assumed the directorship of the Boston Symphony in the fall of 1924. A dynamic figure on the podium and an unstinting friend of many living composers, he made the Boston Symphony Orchestra for more than two decades an international center for new music. In the fall of 1930, Gershwin himself wrote to Clarissa Lorenz (the wife of Conrad Aiken) of his admiration for Koussevitzky: "He is the kind of conductor that American composers have needed for years."[18]

Although Koussevitzky championed dozens of American composers—including some associated with jazz, such as Carpenter and Copland—his interest in Gershwin seemed lukewarm compared to such colleagues as, say, Fritz Reiner or Artur Rodzinski. During his long tenure with the Boston Symphony (1924–1949), he gave only four performances of Gershwin's music: three of the *Second Rhapsody* in 1932 and one of the Concerto in F, with Abram Chasins at the piano, as part of a festival of American music in 1939, two years after the composer's death. He never conducted the *Rhapsody in Blue* or *An American in Paris;* as with the New York Philharmonic, the Boston Symphony relegated these pieces to its Pops concerts, where Alfredo Casella and later Arthur Fiedler and John Williams presided over the music. (Not until André Previn performed the *Rhapsody* in 1997 and James Levine conducted *An American in Paris* and the Concerto in F in 2005 did the Boston Symphony program any of these works on a subscription concert.)

Nonetheless, after hearing from Vernon Duke that Gershwin hoped that Koussevitzky might conduct some of his music, the latter wrote to Gershwin (in his broken English) on October 28, 1929, "I will gladly do it, but, first of all, may I ask you to compose a piece special for the Boston Orchestra? Next season is the 50th Anniversary of the Boston Symphony Orchestra and we would much appreciate if you write a piece for this occasion." This was a rare honor. Among American composers, Koussevitzky requested jubilee pieces only from Harvard's Edward Burlingame Hill and the Eastman School's Howard Hanson, along with Carpenter and Copland; the foreign invitees included Hindemith, Honegger, Prokofiev, Ravel, Respighi, Roussel, and Stravinsky. Gershwin immediately answered Koussevitzky that he was "very much honored" to be asked to "compose something special for your magnificent orchestra," but regretfully turned down the invitation, citing plans to work on an opera *(The Dybbuk)*. However, he kept the offer in mind, and Fox's commission of the "New York Rhapsody" for *Delicious* soon enough provided a ready work.[19]

Gershwin drafted the piece in condensed form in California, as mentioned, and completed the orchestration in New York on May 23, 1931. The orchestral score deleted a few passages from the piano draft but added a few as well, including a six-measure introduction for the piano soloist and, prompted by a suggestion from his old teacher Edward Kilenyi, an extra six measures at the very end. That this new coda—if not the new introduction—appeared in *Delicious* suggests, along with other evidence, that the filmmakers had access to the music in this finished form, even if they used only about half the material.[20]

On June 26, the parts copied, Gershwin recorded the work, conducting from the piano fifty-six studio musicians of the National Broadcasting Company before a group of friends that included Max Dreyfus, the work's dedicatee, and Lou and Emily Paley. "For two and a half hours I conducted and listened to this California brain child," he wrote to Aileen Pringle on June 30, "and I'm writing to tell you I like the result. And I'm sure you would also, as almost every part of it came through as I expected. Of course I've done many things to it since you heard it but I'm sure you would approve of the changes. The N.B.C. very generously recorded the rehearsal on a Victor record so that I can listen to it over and over again and then make any possible changes I care to." This recording, though unpolished, remains an important document, revealing, for instance, that Gershwin conceived the work's middle portion as slower than commonly performed. He eventually decided on two small cuts of two and four measures (at rehearsal 3 and rehearsal 39), though the latter cut presumably postdated the 1932 two-piano score (which still contains these four measures).[21]

Like the *Rhapsody in Blue* and *An American in Paris,* the *Second Rhapsody* essentially unfolds a three-part form with fast outer sections (here centered in F) and a slower middle section (here centered in A). After a brief cadenza for the piano that opens with a fragment of the main theme in the bass, and a vamp for orchestra, the principal theme arrives, initially put forth by the oboes and first trumpet. This theme, marked "sharply," features hammered repeated notes that form a bluesy melody—the "rivets" idea that inspired the working title *Rhapsody in Rivets.* Gershwin often claimed that aside from the rivets theme, the work had no programmatic intentions, though he at least must have been aware of the dramatic context in which the music would be used in the film.

Though reminiscent of both the Concerto in F and John Alden Carpenter's *Skyscrapers* (warmly praised by Gershwin in the summer of 1931) in its evocation of a great American metropolis, the *Second Rhapsody* establishes its own character from the start. Part of this distinctiveness derives from the main theme's syncopated groupings of three and four eighth notes, which, combined with the percussive repeated notes and the trumpet sonority, lend the music a Latin quality, an association that at times becomes even more explicit (as at rehearsal 13). Tellingly, the music looks forward to such later efforts as the *Cuban Overture* and the song "Just Another Rhumba." This Latin element, which reflects the changing face of New York itself, helps mark the *Second Rhapsody* as a work of its time.[22]

The opening section also contains a secondary theme, first stated by the piano (seven after rehearsal 4), that transforms the rivets theme into a more lyrical melody (described by Sascha in *Delicious* as the work's "night motif") that moves continuously off the beat, like the secondary theme—also introduced by the soloist—in the first movement of the Concerto in F. This new mood plausibly signifies the lonely person amid the noisy city, a tension at the heart of other Gershwin works.

The last major theme, set forth at the start of the middle section and marked "Sostenuto e con moto" and "expressively" in the score, has long been a favorite among Gershwin aficionados; Robert Russell Bennett thought it "the best tune Gershwin ever wrote . . . a grand, grand tune." Though occasionally sighing downward by octave, the melody essentially climbs upward by step, synthesizing the rivets and night motives into a theme of poignant longing; its cadential tag, meanwhile, sounds like a minor version of "Old Folks at Home." This theme periodically arrives at a subsidiary idea, a noble, anthemlike melody, marked "fervently" in the score. Does this middle section represent the American dream as opposed to the urban noise and loneliness evoked earlier—or, for that matter, the slick promises of the film's "Dream Sequence"? Had Gershwin written his Lincoln piece, it might well have contained music similar to this "fervent" passage.[23]

The work's final section supports such readings. For while this music, like the return in *An American in Paris,* functions as combined finale, recapitulation, and coda (and here cadenza as well), it opens with the rivets theme in the guise of a march. What this march might denote is hard to say, but clearly not some great triumph; it is more like an uncertain fear or hope. Even the final resolution (beginning at rehearsal 46) has an uneasy undercurrent, one appropriate to the cinematic situation at hand: Heather's surrender to the police.

In comparison to Gershwin's earlier instrumental works, the *Second Rhapsody* shows greater restraint, evident immediately as the soloist, over a pedal-point in the bass, successively repeats a three-note motive in the right hand accompanied by a similar one in contrary motion in the left. Such exhaustive use of limited materials informs the entire work, whose major melodic argument, even in passagework and cadenzas, largely derives from the principal themes as discussed above. Such rigor risks monotony, but Gershwin moves things along with characteristic panache, including exciting buildups that occasionally arrive at unexpected destinations. Nor is there anything restrained about what Steven Gilbert calls the music's "contrapuntal layering," that is, its superimposition of the main melodic thread with complex countermelodies and accompanimental figures, even if such subsidiary material itself derives from the work's principal motives.

Meanwhile, the work's harmonic language reaches, for its composer, new heights of elaboration, with striking dissonant counterpoint, rich six- and seven-note chords, and fast-moving chromatic progressions. The music further samples such unusual sonorities as secondal and quartal harmonies as well as polychords that comprise separate triads a second, a third, and a tritone away, bringing the composer in range of Prokofiev and even Bartók, though the influence of Debussy remains paramount. One particularly striking chord, composed of a fourth and a tritone and heard as an accompaniment to both the night motif (see especially four before rehearsal 6) and the rivets theme (at rehearsal 17), returns so prominently at the end of the work that it might be considered one of the piece's signature harmonies. For its part, the final statement of the expressive theme (at rehearsal 43), marked "grandly," stands out for its bold harmonization.

Gershwin scored the *Second Rhapsody* for piccolo, two flutes, two oboes, English horn, two clarinets, bass clarinet, two bassoons, four horns, three trumpets, two trombones, bass trombone, tuba, percussion, harp, strings, and solo piano. He used the latter not in a full-blown virtuoso capacity but rather as a privileged member of the orchestra, a treatment appropriate to the work's use as background film music and underscored by its title, *Second Rhapsody for Orchestra with Piano*. At the same time, the solo part contains some dazzling writing, while the scoring as a whole—which Michael Tilson Thomas thought in some ways similar to that of Olivier Messiaen—is brightly dynamic, with soaring lines for trumpet and French horn, prominent percussion solos, and a fair amount of busywork for everyone, though not without its more subdued moments. Throughout, the work shows resourcefulness and imagination in its choice of colors—at one point (ten after rehearsal 10), the score calls for three flutes doubled by three solo violins playing harmonics, all pianissimo—and the music's alternately raucous and suave sonorities form an indispensable part of its basic character.[24]

At the time of the June run-through, Gershwin expected that either Toscanini or Stokowski would premiere the piece, but he promised Fox in any case that he would not introduce the work until after the release of *Delicious* on December 3. The very next day, Gershwin (having failed, presumably, to secure an offer from Toscanini or Stokowski) telegraphed Koussevitzky to say, in essence, that he was about to leave for Boston with a new show *(Of Thee I Sing)* and while there, would the Boston Symphony be interested in premiering his new *Rhapsody* before he had to return for the show's Broadway opening at the end of December? Such a proposal says much about the fast pace of Gershwin's life—and about the flexibility of orchestral programming during this period. Koussevitzky responded with no small alacrity of his own, scheduling performances of the piece, with Gershwin as soloist, for January 29 and 30 in Boston, followed by a performance at New York's Carnegie Hall a few days later, on February 5.[25]

The arrival of a new Gershwin rhapsody—almost eight years after the *Rhapsody in Blue*—naturally sparked great interest, and on January 19, ten days before the premiere, news about the piece appeared in newspapers all over the country. "In the picture [*Delicious*] a composer comes to the United States," Gershwin explained, "and I decided to write some music which would express the composer's emotional reaction to New York." He further described the work's "middle theme" as having a "broad, flowing movement which strikes me as almost religious in effect"—he wanted "merely to write a broad, flowing melody, the same as Bach, Brahms or Wagner have done," he stated elsewhere—but more enigmatically he referred to the work as having "but four movements," as opposed to the *Rhapsody in Blue,* which he described as "a pot pouri of a number of themes, written hurriedly for a set event" (a work he also described, in yet another context, as less "serious" and more "sentimental" than this new rhapsody). Aside from the idiosyncratic use of the term *movements,* the mention of four sections, unless an error, contradicts the widespread perception of the work as tripartite. Perhaps Gershwin viewed the whimsical section following the prominent timpani solo (beginning at rehearsal 13) as constituting a separate scherzo, in which case he might have intended the piece to encompass a classic if compressed four-movement structure, a formal approach for which the *Rhapsody in Blue* actually provided a precedent.[26]

At rehearsals with the Boston Symphony beginning the Tuesday prior to the Friday night premiere, Gershwin unabashedly offered suggestions to members of the orchestra, in particular, the percussion section. Far from taking offense, Koussevitzky was charmed by the composer, whom he described as "a very modest young man with a great talent." "It [the *Second Rhapsody*] is a masterful orchestration—finished—complete," he further pronounced. "It is not jazz—it is symphonic—a new development that has come from jazz. Very interesting. The boy's talent does not stop with composition—his talent to orchestrate is what amazed me.

He understands orchestration. Has been studying it." For his part, Gershwin praised the symphony players for their sight-reading abilities and Koussevitzky for knowing the score "inside out." "You know, he [Koussevitzky] brings out things, and makes them sound like a million dollars, that I hardly knew were there," he told Isaac Goldberg. "You know, he does things with pianissimos that I had not suspected. I guess I have never had a chance to know about pianissimos very well."[27]

In both Boston and New York, the *Second Rhapsody* preceded Scriabin's *Poem of Ecstasy* on the second half of the program (in Boston, Koussevitzky programmed Deems Taylor's *Through the Looking-Glass* on the first half, whereas in New York he played Prokofiev's *Classical Symphony* and, in memory of the recently deceased Vincent d'Indy, that composer's *Istar*). At the world premiere, Gershwin, who had had trouble sleeping for some days prior, had an attack of nerves at the start of the piece, which might have contributed to a performance that struck some critics as stiff, the *Boston Globe* regretting the orchestra's failure to "catch" the work's "rhythmic swing." However, by the second night the performance, reported the *Boston Evening Transcript*, "ran freer; caught at last the rhythmic impetus, the hard, bright tone, the seemingly slapdash progress intrinsic in such a music and essential to it." The audience, cordial at the premiere, was accordingly that much more appreciative. By the time of the New York premiere, the playing was even more spirited, and the reception, still warmer. Wrote the *Times:* "Koussevitzky . . . led the orchestra as earnestly as if he had been introducing a new symphony by a Roussel or a Miascovsky, and patiently labored to obtain from the players the last ounce of their energy."[28]

Most reviews were rather reserved with regard to the piece, however. Some even questioned whether a work like this belonged in a concert hall. More thoughtfully, two eminent critics—H. T. Parker in the *Boston Evening Transcript* and Olin Downes in the *Times*—voiced what would become a standard assessment of the work: that the score was more mature but less inspired than the earlier rhapsody. Parker, who attended both Boston performances, wrote (in his first review) that Gershwin "proceeded cautiously; took thought, as it seemed, of every measure and every tone; was sedulous with each accent, each shading. . . . This Second Rhapsody seemed tempered and in degree denatured by reflection and manipulation. It sounded over-often from the study-table and the piano-rack. . . . In sum Mr. Gershwin waxes in craftsmanship but at the cost of earlier and irresistible élan."

Many critics, including Paul Rosenfeld *(Boston Globe),* Philip Hale

(Boston Herald), Moses Smith *(Boston Evening American)*, and W. J. Henderson *(New York Sun)*, seemed more appreciative, notwithstanding reservations of their own. "Now and then the expression becomes unduly sentimental or bombastic," opined Smith (who would publish a biography of Koussevitzky in 1947). "But this is the exception: for the most part Gershwin displays the taste, the intellectual command of the artist." For his part, Rosenfeld welcomed the work's "vulgarity" as "genuine," and found, moreover, its "creative imagination" to reveal "more than a touch of sheer genius"; as with the superiority of Whitman's "barbaric yawps" to the "gentilities" of Longfellow and MacDowell, such "vulgarity" made the Deems Taylor work on the same program "pallid in its rather calculated prettiness."

On the other hand, in the weeks and months following the premiere, the piece received some particularly negative reviews from Marc Blitzstein *(Modern Music)*, Marshall Kernochan *(Outlook)*, and B. H. Haggin *(Nation)*. Blitzstein opined that the piece, though more "pretentious" than the *Rhapsody in Blue*, exhibited "the same 'war-horse' pianisms of Liszt; the same evidence of thinking from one four-measure phrase to another, of enough breath for the broad melodies, and too little for the patch-work-padding; the same excessive climaxes; and the same talent for easy, and extremely catchy tunes." Kernochan simply thought the work "trite," "blatant," and "humdrum." For his part, Haggin, who aside from the slow theme similarly found the piece "almost painfully dull," claimed that the work demonstrated the "false notion" that "American music must refer to the American scene by using as material the industrial noises that are supposed to be peculiar to America." The work's connection with "industrial noises" at least amused the *World-Telegram*, which printed a cartoon inspired by the rhapsody on the theme of industrial noise as music.[29]

In late January, Gershwin turned down an offer from Koussevitzky to tour—unpaid—with the piece. "This would be impossible as I would have to give up several things to go," he explained. However, he again performed the work with Albert Coates and the New York Philharmonic before a record-breaking crowd at Lewisohn Stadium on August 16, 1932, though the music, overshadowed by the still newer *Rumba* (later *Cuban Overture*), attracted little comment. Some months later, on March 20, 1933, Hamilton Harty conducted the British premiere with pianist Solomon Cutner and the London Symphony Orchestra. Meanwhile, on November 4, 1932, Paul Whiteman introduced an abridged version arranged by Ferde Grofé at the fourth Experiment in Modern

American Music at Carnegie Hall with Roy Bargy at the piano (and both Gershwin and Rakhmaninov in the audience); but as with the Coates performance, critical attention focused elsewhere, in this case on Dana Suesse's new *Concerto in Three Rhythms*. Fortunately, in 1938 Whiteman and the impressive Bargy recorded this brashly energetic arrangement.[30]

Oscar Levant also championed the piece, recording it under Morton Gould in 1949. But the work was slow to establish itself. Although New World Music quickly brought out a two-piano version (1932), an orchestral score did not appear until 1953, when New World published a version, under the supervision of Frank Campbell-Watson, arranged by composer Robert McBride (b. 1911).

McBride restored the four-measure cut and otherwise revamped the score, adding some notes to help fill in perceived holes, deleting others to help reduce alleged clutter, and changing slurs as well as dynamic and accent markings. Above all, he extensively reorchestrated the music, extending or eliminating doublings, removing certain orchestral effects and introducing others, and redistributing material—all of which tended to effect a lighter and more polished sound. Although a casual listener would not necessarily notice much discrepancy between the two versions, the net difference was substantial nonetheless, far more so than in the case of Campbell-Watson's merely fussy editions of Gershwin's previous orchestral pieces.

The reason for this extensive overhaul remains unclear. Gershwin's original score was hardly inept; on the contrary, Koussevitzky, as mentioned, declared the orchestration "masterful," as did the distinguished composer Charles Martin Loeffler, who attended the work's Boston rehearsals. Moreover, New World Music had felt no such compulsion to reorchestrate Gershwin's earlier and arguably less assured orchestral works. Campbell-Watson's 1953 justification seems dubious, to say the least: "The score [of the *Second Rhapsody*] was not completely finished. It was temporary and in its existing form there were but few pianists and orchestras close enough to the work to negotiate the hurdles offered by many structural barbed wire fences." That the work had gone unpublished for so many years probably simply emboldened Campbell-Watson. At least New World Music frankly admitted that the work had been "arranged," as opposed to "edited" or "revised," even though this probably fueled the notion that Gershwin was an incapable orchestrator (a sentiment reportedly held by Campbell-Watson).[31]

The McBride arrangement became in any case the only available version of the piece for decades and the one found on all commercial recordings of the work between Levant's 1949 release and Michael Tilson Thomas's revival of the original orchestration in 1985 (and some even later), including those of Teodor Moussov under Pancho Vladigerov, Christina Ortiz under André Previn, Leonard Pennario under Alfred Newman, Howard Shelley under Yan Pascal Tortelier, Jeffrey Siegel under Leonard Slatkin, and Ralph Votapek under Arthur Fiedler. In the wake of Thomas's landmark release with the Los Angeles Philharmonic, for which he both played piano and conducted, the original score came into current use, as found in recordings by pianist-conductor Wayne Marshall (1995), Michael Boriskin under Jonathan Sheffer (1998), Stewart Goodyear under Erich Kunzel (1998), and a second by Michael Tilson Thomas, this time with the San Francisco Orchestra (1998).

Meanwhile, Gershwin's 1931 studio recording, which included a cadenza not found in the 1932 two-piano score, may have encouraged Goodyear and Thomas (in his second recording) to venture cadenzas and embellishments of their own. Such practices seemed not only to gainsay claims of authenticity but to endanger the work's complex architecture and misconstrue the piano's understated role. Still, the general excellence of the more recent releases—including Wayne Marshall's bracing performance—suggested (notwithstanding the fine idiomatic swing of the Newman-Pennario release) that the McBride arrangement, rather than further the work's cause, possibly hindered its wider acceptance.

If the *Second Rhapsody* has attained heightened prominence in recent years, it still remains disappointingly unfamiliar in the context of Gershwin's most ambitious instrumental works. This hardly surprises: the work's brittle themes, dissonant harmonies, prickly colors, and sober tone present real challenges for performers and listeners alike. But the work remains a compelling one, not only because it represents, as often mentioned, a technical advance for Gershwin, but also because it speaks a more mature and individual language, one that would receive still fuller expression in *Porgy and Bess* and other late works.

Chapter Twenty-Seven

Of Thee I Sing (1931)

*D*iscussing the origins of *Of Thee I Sing*, Morrie Ryskind recalled that, during preparations for the revised *Strike Up the Band* (1930), producer Edgar Selwyn insisted that he, Ryskind, cut a provocative scene from Kaufman's original 1927 script; and that at the show's triumphant premiere in Boston, Selwyn remarked to Ryskind and Kaufman, alluding to the eliminated scene, "What difference could it have made anyway?" "Had Edgar not asked that question," stated Ryskind, "I seriously doubt that George [S. Kaufman]—who was basically apolitical—would have taken any more ventures into political satire. Because he was a man who expressed very few emotions, George said nothing at the time, but I sensed, correctly as events were to prove, that a challenge had been issued which George had accepted." That very evening, Kaufman and Ryskind resolved to produce a show "the way that we wanted it done even if we had to put it up with our own money."[1]

After some months of deliberation, Kaufman and Ryskind sketched out a satire of an American presidential election in which the country's two principal parties would vie for the best national anthem, only to find that the two songs had "the merest shade of difference between them." Tentatively titled *Tweedle-Dee*, the show naturally called for musical treatment, and the two playwrights approached the Gershwins. "It sounds grand," said Gershwin. "I'll write two national anthems and we'll sing each against the other for a first act finale. It'll be a great contrapuntal lark"—to which Kaufman replied, "I'll take your word for it."[2]

Kaufman and Ryskind realized that the story lacked some romantic interest and revamped the plot so that love, rather than music, would become the central focus of the campaign; though as a commentator later observed, "They never lost their original intention . . . of debunking the smug hypocrisy, the charlatanism, the essential absurdity of much that passes for political thought and action in these States." Before the Gershwins left for Hollywood in November 1930, Kaufman and Ryskind completed a fourteen-page scenario of the show, now called *Of Thee I Sing*. The Gershwins liked the story, and in their spare hours in California they started work on a number for the French ambassador, "The Illegitimate Daughter," as well as what Ira described as the "anthemy campaign title song." In the meantime, Kaufman sent the scenario to producer and theater owner Sam Harris, on vacation in Florida, with a note attached saying, "Of course, you'll never produce this, but I thought you'd like to read it."[3]

One of Broadway's most respected producers, Sam H. Harris (1872–1941) had a career that spanned the century's first four decades. In conjunction with George M. Cohan, then with Irving Berlin, and eventually with Harry Ruby, Gershwin, Porter, Rodgers, and Weill, he played a particularly decisive role in the development of the musical comedy. By late 1930 he had already worked extensively with Kaufman as well, having produced the latter's two Marx Brothers musicals, *The Cocoanuts* (1925; music and lyrics, Berlin) and *Animal Crackers* (with Morrie Ryskind, 1928; lyrics, Bert Kalmar; music, Ruby), as well as two of his straight comedies, *June Moon* (with Ring Lardner, 1929) and *Once in a Lifetime* (with Moss Hart, 1930).

After reading the scenario, Harris equivocally wired back, "It's certainly different," but decided to produce the show in any case. "Here was something startlingly different," he explained in 1932, "and if there is one thing I have been sold on for two or three years it is that the theater to live must produce novelties. It must break with the past completely." This declaration squarely placed *Of Thee I Sing* in the context of the social upheaval wrought by the Depression.[4]

Meeting sporadically throughout July and August 1931, Kaufman and Ryskind completed a 135–page script by the end of the summer. The Gershwins worked in tandem, finishing the score in the early fall in preparation for rehearsals in November. In contrast to their typical working procedure, Ira wrote many of the lyrics ("the greater proportion," according to the *Boston Globe*) before George wrote the music. Years later, Ryskind claimed that he and Kaufman in turn based some of their dialogue on the lyrics, but some evidence suggests the opposite as well, including two song titles, "Of Thee I Sing" and "Love Is Sweeping the

Country," as well as a line from the latter—"There never was so much love!"—apparently derived from the original scenario.[5]

Even before Kaufman and Ryskind heard the finished score, Gershwin was performing some of the music at parties, which made both playwrights nervous, Ryskind commenting, "Revivals aren't going so well this season, you know." For his part, Kaufman fantasized about a "new device," requiring the services of eight men, that would keep "composers away from the piano until after the show is produced," and further proposed an Olympics race for twelve composers to see who could reach a piano first.[6]

The show's first act opens in "any city in America" with a torchlight parade in support of John P. Wintergreen for president, the crowd displaying such signs as "Vote for Prosperity and See What You Get" and "Wintergreen—A Man's Man's Man." In a shabby hotel room, the National Campaign Committee—including representatives of Irish and Jewish constituencies, namely, Francis X. Gilhooley (Harold Moffet) and Louis Lippman (Sam Mann); newspaper mogul Matthew Arnold Fulton (Dudley Clements); and Senators Robert E. Lyons of the South (George E. Mack) and Carver Crockett Jones of the West (Edward H. Robins)—celebrate their party's nomination of Wintergreen (William Gaxton), though they have trouble remembering the name of the vice presidential candidate, Alexander Throttlebottom (Victor Moore). Taking his cue from a chambermaid, Fulton decides that love should be the theme of the presidential campaign and commands Wintergreen "to fall in love with a typical American girl!"[7]

At a bathing-beauty contest in Atlantic City to select a possible First Lady, newspaper photographers flirt with the contestants ("Who Is the Lucky Girl to Be?"/"The Dimple on My Knee"/"Because, Because"). Anxious about marrying someone he doesn't know and desiring a homemaker rather than a beauty queen, Wintergreen sets his sights on Fulton's young assistant, Mary Turner (Lois Moran), who makes delicious corn muffins. Although the National Campaign Committee initially crowns "the fairest flower of the South," Diana Devereaux (Grace Brinkley), as the first-place winner, after John confesses his love for Mary (and the committee has the opportunity to sample her corn muffins), all agree that she's the more suitable mate ("Finaletto," including "Never Was There a Girl So Fair" and "Some Girls Can Bake a Pie").

At the final rally of the presidential campaign in Madison Square Garden (decked out with such banners as "Woo with Wintergreen" and "Lovers! Vote for John and Mary"), Sam Jenkins (George Murphy) and

Miss Benson (June O'Dea), assistants to John and Mary, celebrate a nation transformed by love ("Love Is Sweeping the Country"). Senator Jones addresses the crowd as two wrestlers, Vladimir Vidovitch and Yussef Yussevitch, vie for the world wrestling championship; and Fulton tells the audience, "We do not talk to you about war debts or wheat or immigration—we appeal to your hearts, not your intelligence." As he has done elsewhere on the campaign trail, John proposes to Mary, who agrees to marry him if he's elected president ("Of Thee I Sing").[8]

On election night a newsreel projects the faces of famous Americans, including George Washington, Patrick Henry, Babe Ruth, and the Marx Brothers, along with bulletins stating absurd polling results, finally announcing Wintergreen's victory (underscoring of "Wintergreen for President" and "Of Thee I Sing"). On the steps of the Capitol on inauguration day, the Supreme Court justices simultaneously swear in Wintergreen and perform John and Mary's wedding ceremony; Diana delivers a summons for breach of promise; and faced with having to decide between Mary's corn muffins and Diana's demand for justice, the court decides in favor of the former ("Finale," including "Entrance of Supreme Court Justices," "A Kiss for Cinderella," "I Was the Most Beautiful Blossom," and reprises of "Some Girls Can Bake a Pie" and "Of Thee I Sing").

The second act opens in the Wintergreen White House, as the secretaries, including Jenkins and Miss Benson, arrive for work ("Hello, Good Morning"). Throttlebottom enters as part of a group of sightseers. Lippman, Gilhooley, and Fulton—now the secretaries of agriculture, the navy, and state, respectively—share the concerns of Senators Lyons and Carver about growing national sympathy for Diana Devereaux, a predicament the Wintergreens address by showing a defiant front before reporters ("Who Cares?"). To win public support, John resolves to sing on a radio show and Mary decides to bake corn muffins for the unemployed.

The French ambassador (Florenz Ames), backed by a guard of French soldiers, demands satisfaction for Diana, who, it turns out, is "the illegitimate daughter / Of an illegitimate son / Of an illegitimate nephew / Of Napoléon." When Wintergreen refuses to resign, the committee resolves to impeach him; left alone, John and Mary console each other ("Finaletto," including "Garçon, S'il Vous Plaît," "Entrance of French Ambassador," "The Illegitimate Daughter," reprise of "Because, Because," "We'll Impeach Him," and reprise of "Who Cares?").

As the senators convene in chamber ("The Senatorial Roll Call") and begin impeachment hearings, Diana takes the stand; but on learning that Mary is to have a baby, the Senate acquits the president, as no precedent exists for impeaching an expectant father; Wintergreen happily notes, "Posterity is just around the corner" ("Finaletto," including "Impeachment Proceeding," reprise of "Garçon, S'il Vous Plaît," reprise of "The Illegitimate Daughter," "Jilted," reprise of "Senatorial Roll Call," "I'm About to Be a Mother," and "Posterity Is Just Around the Corner"). The French ambassador insists that Wintergreen award a depopulated France the baby in compensation for his having jilted Diana, but the American public defends its president, now that he's about to become a father.

As the delivery day arrives, curiosity runs high about the sex of the child, Senator Carver noting, "Out on the prairie / For baby boy or girl they are keen, / But they want nothing in between" ("Trumpeter, Blow Your Golden Horn"). The Supreme Court announces—or rather, determines—the arrival of a boy, then a twin girl. The French ambassador threatens war, but Wintergreen resolves the conflict by awarding Diana to Throttlebottom, citing the constitutional article that has the vice president assume the obligations that a president cannot fulfill ("Finale," including "On That Matter, No One Budges" and reprise of "Of Thee I Sing").

Within a few years of the show's opening, Alfred Knopf (1932), Victor Gollancz (1933), and Samuel French (1935) published slightly different versions of the libretto. Discussing the script's evolution from scenario to typescript to these three published versions, Wayne Schneider observes a trend toward "simplicity and compression" as well as "a softening of satiric tone," including increasingly sympathetic portrayals of Wintergreen as gullible rather than "oily" and "knavish," and Throttlebottom as naive rather than "sly" and "almost villainous." As for the music, Schneider reports a characteristic fidelity between Gershwin's condensed manuscripts and the published piano-vocal score (1932), but observes "added counter-melodies and filigree" in the orchestrations.[9]

In the original scenario, Kaufman and Ryskind wrote, "Throughout all this, we never say whether this is the Democratic or the Republican Party—it is both, in fact. The members don't know which they are— they are willing to be anything to win. They probably decide to be Republicans on Mondays, Wednesdays, and Fridays, and Democrats on the other days." However, the slogan "Vote for Prosperity and See What You Get"—as well as the song "Posterity Is Just Around the Corner"—clearly ridiculed the famous remark attributed to sitting Republican president Herbert Hoover, "Prosperity is just around the corner." Moreover, one reviewer thought that Victor Moore's portrayal of Throttlebottom suggested "something of the Cal Coolidge back-country sourness and something of the Herb Hoover appealing fat babyhood." At the same time, the scenario identified Gilhooley as a member of Tammany, Lippman as representing "the Jewish vote," and Wintergreen as inspired by Mayor Jimmy Walker—indicating that the authors had local Democratic politics in mind as well. (In 1932 both Kaufman and Ryskind apparently voted for the Socialist presidential candidate, Norman Thomas, while the Gershwins presumably supported Franklin D. Roosevelt, at whose White House George performed in late 1934.)[10]

Although commentators have traditionally viewed *Of Thee I Sing* as a political satire—Casper Nannes, for instance, called the work an "angry satire" that pointed "sharp, cold fingers at the American dream"—the show proved in equal measure a romantic comedy. Indeed, the intertwining of the political and the romantic—from John's courtship of Mary to the pairing of Throttlebottom and Devereaux—helped smooth over those discrepancies between musical comedy and political satire that had afflicted at least the original *Strike Up the Band*. More than simply a pragmatic solution, such Brechtian allegorizing suggested that the pretensions and absurdities of our personal lives and those of the body politic reflect one another and that political reform requires examination of our social and cultural mores and vice versa.[11]

The Gershwins correspondingly blended the romantic and the satirical in ways that surpassed anything they had previously attempted along these lines, an achievement epitomized by the title number, which marvelously operates as at once a love song and a patriotic hymn. "Love Is Sweeping the Country," "I Was the Most Beautiful Blossom," and "Jilted" similarly evoked a kind of sentimental or even maudlin gushing in order to parody public posturing and affectation.

The score's romantic inclinations even imbued the book with some unforeseen poignancy. "A Kiss for Cinderella" and "Who Cares?" for instance revealed an unexpected tenderness when taken at slower tempos, as occurred in the course of the show. Ira recalled that the slow reprise of "Who Cares?" proved a particularly "touching" moment, one that reduced audience members to tears, prompting Kaufman to ask Gershwin, "What's the matter with them? Don't they know we're kidding love?" to which Gershwin reportedly said, "You're doing nothing of the kind. You may *think* you're kidding love—but when Wintergreen faces impeachment to stand by the girl he married, that's *championing* love. And the audience realizes it even if you don't." Meanwhile, Ira easily adapted the satirical "Love Is Sweeping the Country" as "Adlai's Sweeping the Country" for Adlai Stevenson's 1952 presidential campaign, much as he had revised "Strike Up the Band" for the UCLA football team.[12]

At the same time, the Gershwins employed irony, exaggeration, and incongruity—what Isaac Goldberg, reviewing the show, called the "sort of audible eye-winking at which George Gershwin is expert"—at almost every turn. Some of the humor derived from conjoining a breezy musical-comedy style with such mundane activities as a newspaper photo shoot and White House office work (Ira explained further that "A Kiss for Cinderella" was "a take-off on the bachelor-farewell type of song, best exemplified by John Golden and Ivan Caryll's 'Good-bye, Girls, I'm Through,'" from their 1914 show *Chin-Chin*). Similarly, Wintergreen's praise of Mary has something of the radio jingle about it ("Some Girls Can Bake a Pie"); the French ambassador's outraged speech takes the form of a rather sprightly Gallic march ("The Illegitimate Daughter"); Mary announces her pregnancy to the strains of a Viennese-style waltz ("I'm About to Be a Mother"); and Wintergreen reacts to the news of his impending fatherhood in music "a la salvation army," that is, in the manner of a Salvation Army band ("Posterity"). (Kaufman, who directed the show, heightened the latter song's zaniness, with its elisions of "oom-pah" and "posterity," by having the senators whip out tambourines during the number.)[13]

In addition, Gershwin sardonically quoted some familiar melodies. The opening chorus, for instance, contrasts snippets of five favorite tunes associated with early twentieth-century electioneering and especially New York's corrupt Tammany machine—Sousa's "Stars and Stripes Forever" (1897), Gus Edwards's "Tammany" (1905), James Blake and Charles Lawlor's "The Sidewalks of New York" (1894), Theodore Morse's "Hail, Hail, the Gang's All Here" (1917), and Theodore Metz's "There'll Be a Hot Time in the Old Town Tonight" (1896)—with a fanfare-like refrain in minor that evokes Yiddish music, a peculiar foil to tunes associated with Irish New York, but one that helps underscore the chorus's single quatrain: "Wintergreen for President! / Wintergreen for President! / He's the man the people choose; / Loves the Irish and the Jews." (At Ira's suggestion, Gershwin derived this refrain from the number "Trumpets of Belgravia," from an aborted musical titled *The Big Charade*.)[14]

"Trumpeter, Blow Your Golden Horn" similarly alternates its principal theme with quotations of "The Farmer in the Dell" (for the secretary of agriculture), "The Sailor's Hornpipe" (for the secretary of the navy), Percy Wenrich's "Rainbow" (for Senator Carver), and Foster's "The Old Folks at Home" (for Senator Lyons). For its part, the chorus "Garçon, S'il Vous Plaît" opens with a bit of Gershwin's own *An Amer-*

ican in Paris and concludes with a snippet of "The Marseillaise." And the first-act finale contains a slyly chromatic setting of Wagner's wedding march from *Lohengrin*. The score references a number of other styles (the accompaniment to "Garçon, S'il Vous Plaît," for instance, unabashedly appropriates the first of Poulenc's *Trois mouvements perpetuelles*) and on a certain level functions as operatic parody.

The music further displays something of the advanced harmonic language found in the *Second Rhapsody*, completed that same year, as evidenced by its conspicuous use of dissonant chords and unusual scales. Other adventurous gestures include a repeating modal refrain for the chattering crowd ("There's none but Mary Turner / Could ever be his mate"), a whistling chorus ("Hello, Good Morning"), and—not dissuaded by the dropped idea of two competing national anthems—some striking counterpoint, including one number that combines two separate choruses ("Who Is the Lucky Girl to Be?").

The work's structure arguably represents its most original feature, however. As opposed to traditional musical comedy with its rather predictable pacing of song and dialogue, scenes that have no music at all alternate with those that have ten continuous minutes of music or more, and that at their most elaborate combine recitatives, ariosos, songs, choruses, and dances. Only five of the show's numbers—"Wintergreen for President," "Love Is Sweeping the Country," "Of Thee I Sing," "Hello, Good Morning," and "The Senatorial Roll Call"—appear autonomously, with the score's compactness further enhanced by the use of unifying motives and recurring themes.

The most complex musical scenes include the two finales as well as the first-act finaletto and two second-act finalettos. The dramatic arc of three of these scenes—"As the Chairman of the Committee," the first-act finale, and "Impeachment Proceeding"—similarly involves a revelation that disrupts the action at a climactic point; in all three instances, the intruder commands, "Stop!" (a convention that naturally becomes more contrived with each new appearance). All five of these extended scenes reveal a masterful command of dramatic pacing, with the relatively seamless first-act finaletto being particularly impressive. In comparison, some of the later ensembles seem more patchwork, partly because they reprise so much material, including the song "Of Thee I Sing!" which concludes not only the first-act finaletto but the first- and second-act finales as well. Even so, all of these ensembles effectively drive the action forward.[15]

The show's distinctive tone and architecture proved rather uncategorizable; part political satire, part comic opera, it hardly fit the classic mold of either operetta or musical comedy. Perhaps more precedence could be found in the "Dream Sequence" of Gershwin's movie musical *Delicious* than in any of his theatrical work, suggesting the influence of the motion pictures on more than just the act 1 newsreel sequence. The show proved, in any case, an experimental work of musical theater, with few antecedents or, for that matter, immediate descendants other than the show's sequel, *Let 'Em Eat Cake*.

The overture was similarly novel. Gershwin had already been moving away from medley-type overtures in favor of something more integrated, but this one put forth only two complete tunes: "Who Cares?" (stated twice, the second time slower, as in the show proper) and, at the very end, "Of Thee I Sing." In contrast, three other melodies ("Wintergreen for President," "Because, Because," and "I Was the Most Beautiful Blossom") appear in fragmentary form as introductory or transitional material, or as contrapuntal support to one of the main tunes. Moreover, the music periodically states the head motive to "Of Thee I Sing" in anticipation of that tune's climactic arrival. "There is method here," concludes Wayne Schneider in his essay on Gershwin's overtures of the 1930s, "not a casual stringing together of songs; there is, in short, *composition*."[16]

Ira neatly contributed to the show's giddy humor by penning some delightfully inane verse and ludicrous rhymes. He incorporated some Yiddish expressions as well. At one point, the Supreme Court justices proclaim, "We're the A.K.s who give the O.K.s!" ("A.K." being then-popular Jewish-American shorthand for *alter kaker*, Yiddish for "old fart"). In addition, some of the pidgin French chorus, "Garçon, S'il Vous Plaît," concealed Yiddish phrases, including the macaronic couplet "Papah, pooh, pooh, pooh! / À vous tout dir vay à vous?" which comprised not only the three spits ("pooh, pooh, pooh") thought by Jewish superstition to ward off bad luck, but also a Frenchified elaboration of "Vus tut dir vey" ("What's hurting you?" in Yiddish).

Kaufman, who as mentioned directed the show, chose dapper William Gaxton (born Arturo Antonio Gaxiola, 1890–1963) to play Wintergreen. Gaxton had worked primarily in vaudeville until Rodgers's *A Connecticut Yankee* (1927) and Porter's *Fifty Million Frenchmen* (1929) established him as Broadway's foremost musical-comedy male lead, a reputation only enhanced by this show. Lois Moran (1908–1990), a dancer and film star whose short-lived career, soon to end, had peaked with the silent film *Stella Dallas* (1925), played Mary Turner (Moran remained, incidentally, an inspiration to F. Scott Fitzgerald, who modeled the character of Rosemary Hoyt from his 1934 novel, *Tender Is the Night,* after her). For the role of Throttlebottom, Kaufman and Ryskind originally had in mind someone along the lines of William Danforth, a well-known Savoyard, but decided ultimately on Victor Moore, the hapless comic who had enjoyed such success in *Oh, Kay!* and *Funny Face.* The combination of the "rakish" Gaxton and the "fumbling-bumbling" Moore, paired together for the first time, proved classic, and the two, whom Ryskind later regarded as the Broadway equivalent of Bing Crosby and Bob Hope, went on to costar in *Let 'Em Eat Cake* (1933), Porter's *Anything Goes* (1934) and *Leave It to Me* (1938), and Berlin's *Louisiana Purchase* (1940). Alfred Simon, the show's rehearsal pianist, recalled its three stars as

> remarkably like the characters they played. William Gaxton, somewhat brash but affable, was a fine choice for the breezy Wintergreen. Lois Moran was a total delight as Mary. Most inspired of all was the casting of Victor Moore as Alexander Throttlebottom. Moore, a timid, top-heavy, lovable man, with a tentative manner, would arrive at the theater even on the sunniest days with an umbrella in hand. After taking off his coat and hat, he would walk to the edge of the stage, bend down slowly, and carefully place the umbrella near the footlights.[17]

Kaufman further cast Grace Brinkley as Diana Devereaux, June O'Dea as Miss Benson, and George Murphy as Sam Jenkins. In his memoirs, Murphy (1902–1992), who following a successful film career served in the Senate (1965–1971), recollected Gershwin's kindness at his audition; Kaufman's emphasis on timing and textual fidelity; O'Dea's forbearance over jokes about her fiancé, Yankee legend Lefty Gomez; Gaxton and Moran's attempts to upstage each other; and his own problems with a drummer in the pit.[18]

Jo Mielziner created the sets; Charles LeMaire designed the costumes; George Hale directed the dances; Robert Russell Bennett, William Daly, and Gershwin did the orchestrations; and Charles Previn directed the pit band and the chorus of twenty-five women and fifteen men. Gershwin had collaborated with all these artists before save Mielziner (1901–1976), whose designs for Elmer Rice's *Street Scene* (1929) had only recently catapulted him to the front ranks of his profession. For this new show, the first of more than fifty musical comedies, Mielziner created some striking scenic and lighting effects that, according to reviews, skillfully conveyed "a feeling of crowds and hazy distances" and "the shoddiness of the political environment."[19]

Rehearsals went remarkably smoothly. "The trials, intrigues, and storms that attend practically every Broadway musical during its preparation were notably absent," remembered Simon. Gershwin, who was "more proud" of the show than of any other he had thus far written, described it as "one of those rare shows in which everything clicked just right." Other than solving an intractable staging problem, Sam Harris, to everyone's relief, refrained from interfering. "If he [Harris] had faith in you," recalled George Murphy, "he hired you. And if he hired you, he left you alone." The production's only "serious row" involved Kaufman's dislike of the title song's "martial" overtones and its opening line, "Of thee I sing, baby" (which, according to Ryskind, he considered "undignified"); in July 1931, he wrote to the Gershwins that he favored a "straight love song," but the songwriters, with Ryskind's support, stood firm.[20]

The show opened at Boston's Majestic Theatre on December 8, 1931, amid some trepidation about the local censors. Such concerns proved needless. The show was probably less provocative than even the revised version of *Strike Up the Band,* which had played so successfully in Boston. Besides, the censors largely watched for sexual improprieties, and at least in that respect the work was far less daring than the average burlesque show. The *Boston Herald* even ran an editorial praising the production as "wholesome stuff" that featured "hardly a trace of objectionable sexuality."[21]

The Boston critics immediately recognized the show as a landmark. "It is a long and brave step upward in the progress of such pieces from a characterless and threadbare convention to a lively reflection of our life and comment upon it," wrote H. T. Parker in the *Evening Transcript.* And Katharine Lyons stated in the *Traveler,* "After the manner of the immortal Gilbert and Sullivan operas the story projects itself through every line of lyrics and every bar of music. In this alone 'Of Thee I Sing' transcends all other musical comedies that have come this way in many years." Even the *Christian Science Monitor,* which complained of "various coarsenesses" redolent of "a lower type of musical comedy," found the evening "hugely amusing."[22]

The main problem was that the show, which ran about three hours and fifteen minutes, was too long. "Please make all possible musical cuts," wrote Kaufman to Gershwin a few days after the Boston premiere. "I shall continue to cut the book, even where it is fairly good, because the show is between 30 and 40 minutes too long. 'On that point nobody budges' is sung entirely too often. The rearrangement of the first act finale should get at least two minutes out of it." Kaufman also suggested omitting some of Hale's dances, including "every so-called 'hot' step," which he considered "all baloney. Never saved or helped a show yet, and everybody is sick and tired of it." Gershwin duly cut the verse to "Of Thee I Sing" and presumably eliminated other material as well.[23]

On revisiting the musical near the end of its Boston run, Parker, though gratified to find that the work had been shortened, expressed concern that a new wisecracking associated with Gaxton's performance threatened to undermine the show's integrity and, as the article's subheader stated, "dull its edge." Still, the Gershwin score remained a marvel: "Never before has Mr. Gershwin written a music that so continuously expresses the text, characters the personages, sharpens the pervading humor. Seldom has he been more fertile with apt device. One more piece now affirms him the distinctive composer of our musical pieces."[24]

The show opened in New York on December 26, 1931, at the lovely 859–seat Music Box Theatre built by Irving Berlin and Sam Harris in 1921, with Gershwin conducting the premiere as he had in Boston. The "glittering" first-night crowd included former presidential candidate Al Smith, who was visibly amused by the show; Mayor Jimmy Walker, who, delighted by Gaxton's "deliciously accurate imitation" of his "platform manner," laughed "uproariously" from his seat in the second row; and philanthropist Otto Kahn, who cried "Bravo!" at the final curtain. Judith Anderson, Ethel Barrymore, Irving Berlin, Ina Claire, Lillian Gish, Samuel Goldwyn, Florenz Ziegfeld, and other luminaries from stage and screen also attended.[25]

As in Boston, some of the more appreciative critics thought the work a watershed, and words like "classic," "event," and "milestone," sometimes capitalized, appeared in a number of reviews. "Let me tell you, my children," wrote Benjamin DeCasseres in *Arts and Decoration,* "this political musical farce is an Event in the annals of the American stage." "Whatever it is," confirmed E. B. White in the *New Yorker,* "it is a Step Forward, as anybody feels who has seen the show." Gilbert Gabriel, in the *New York American,* spoke of "a new date in stage history," while Robert Garland, in the *New York World-Telegram,* described the show as "an event in the history of the American theatre I must remember to tell my grandchildren that I was present at its opening."[26]

It was not so much the show's general excellence that precipitated such remarks—on the contrary, many critics quibbled over various aspects of the show, and a few even panned it—as its unprecedented reconfiguring of the musical-comedy genre. Traditionally, critics generally evaluated musical comedy on the basis of the individual performances, the sets and costumes, the music and dancing, and lastly the book and lyrics, more or less in that order. Here, although the cast, and especially Victor Moore, won kudos from the press (John Mason Brown's review in the *Evening Post* described Moore's "wistfully pathetic" performance "as one of the most unforgettable characterizations of recent years"), critical attention focused first and foremost on the book and the score. This shift of emphasis clearly showed Kaufman's guiding hand, though it required as well the assistance of Morrie Ryskind, the support of the Gershwins, and the benign noninterference of Sam Harris.

The experiment succeeded because the satire struck a responsive chord. *Vogue* thought the show an exposé of "our naïveté and our sentimentality"; the *Commonweal,* an attack on "the self-worship which leads mass psychology." In his aforementioned review, DeCasseres wrote that the work lampooned the "mush, gush and slush, lungs, lunacy and larceny, punk, junk and bunk, bluff, bull and blah, hokum, hooey and hooliganism with which we are fed every day and in the midst of which we live and move and have our being—such as it is! . . . And we Americans in the audience roar, chortle, wheeze, shout, howl and whistle our approval at every shot that is taken at the whole political game in this country from the rise of the curtain until its fall." Such a reception, noted the *Nation,* drew on "anger in the air . . . which suggests that its [the audience's] rage might be ominous if it were not, for the moment, released through laughter."

Some critics in this context compared the musical to Aristophanes, while a follow-up review by DeCasseres in late 1932 found some unremarked common ground with *Show Boat:*

> The colossal success of these two musical plays proves to me that the Public is both old-fashioned and new-fashioned; both satiric and sentimental; both centripetal and centrifugal; both hokum-lovers and hokum-slitters. That "Of Thee I Sing" and "Show Boat" can run equally side by side—and will run and run for many a day—is a powerful light on what the Public wants—which is simply this: Give them something that is first class and it makes very little difference what the subject matter is; *but it must mirror something that is vitally theirs.*[27]

At the same time, many reviews, as mentioned, considered the show flawed, with much of the criticism leveled, ironically enough, at the book, which some thought clichéd and labored. As with the original *Strike Up the Band,* a few critics further perceived, for all the show's later reputation as an example of the well-integrated musical, a problematic fusing of script and score. "Its music and chorus are not fully blended with the book," wrote Brooks Atkinson in the *Times*. "The Gilbert and Sullivan type of humor somehow fails to adapt itself to the burleycue traditions that underlie the American musical comedy," added Malcolm Cowley in the *New Republic*. Francis Fergusson's review for the *Bookman* wished that the authors had looked more to seventeenth-century farce than to Gilbert and Sullivan, finding the former "so much nearer, in many ways, to the best in our sense of the comic!" Robert Benchley, writing a review for the *New Yorker* on the heels of E. B. White's positive notice for the same journal, was particularly "disappointed" with the show, which he ultimately ranked "far below" *Strike Up the Band*. And although Marc Blitzstein, writing in *Modern Music*, found the "breeziness, genial insanity and undercurrent of intelligence" in both *Of Thee I Sing* and Berlin's *Face the Music* "welcome and inspiring," he thought the latter superior in all ways but the music, finding the Kaufman-Ryskind satire "heavily-paced, driving home a single theme—which is perhaps one reason why it is more popular."[28]

In contrast, the show proved a complete triumph for the Gershwins, notwithstanding a few critics who found it hard to warm up to such a sardonic score (including Blitzstein, who expressed some concern that the composer, in his "misguided attempt to approach 'art,'" forfeited the stylistic unity of his earlier work). "Whether it is satire, wit, doggerel or fantasy," wrote Atkinson, "Mr. Gershwin pours music out in full mea-sure, and in many voices. Although the book is lively, Mr. Gershwin is exuberant. He has not only ideas but enthusiasm. He amplifies the show." Percy Hammond, in the *Herald-Tribune*, similarly wrote, "The mantle of Mr. Kaufman's occasionally monotonous frivolity is embroidered with some of George Gershwin's most azure music." Nearly every review also praised Ira's lyrics, sometimes excerpted at length in the press. A num-ber of critics drew favorable comparisons between the Gershwins and Gilbert and Sullivan, especially *Iolanthe* and *The Mikado*, both of which the Civic Light Opera Company had presented on Broadway earlier in the year; though a few, like Atkinson, also noted the gulf between "the humorous elegances of Gilbert and the idyllic melodies of Sullivan" with this "nerve-twanging" work. In Gershwin's own estimation, he and Ira drew inspiration as much from Mozart's *Don Giovanni* as from *H.M.S. Pinafore*.[29]

Although the satire, for all its irreverence, struck most critics as ami-able, it offended Bishop William Manning, who proposed a resolution, adopted by the France-American Society in early February 1932, that the authors delete or revise certain lines considered objectionable, including a joke about France's tardiness in paying its war debt. Kaufman reacted by saying, "I'll be glad to drop the lines out if Bishop Manning will write a couple for me which will get the same big laughs."[30]

On May 3, 1932, the *New York Times* announced that Columbia University's School of Journalism had awarded Kaufman, Ryskind, and Ira Gershwin the Pulitzer Prize for the best American play of 1931. The decision came as a surprise; not only did insiders expect the prize to go to Eugene O'Neill's *Mourning Becomes Electra* or perhaps Robert E. Sherwood's *Reunion in Vienna* or Philip Barry's *The Animal Kingdom*, but the drama award had never before been given to a "musical play." The Pulitzer board, which had no way to recognize Gershwin's contribution, explained, "Not only is it [the show] coherent and well knit enough to class as a play, aside from the music, but it is a biting and true satire on American politics and the public attitude toward them. Its effect on the stage promises to be very considerable, because musical plays are always popular and by injecting genuine satire and point into them a very large public is reached." Such recognition validated the show's literary merit, which had already been endorsed by Knopf's publication of the libretto in April (for which Kaufman cut those lyrics he considered extraneous or repetitive).[31]

The award prompted a good deal of commentary. Some critics, including Burns Mantle in the *Daily News*, recognized the folly of awarding the prize exclusive of the music. Brooks Atkinson thought, moreover, that the show was too flawed to receive the Pulitzer in a season that included one of the better plays of Philip Barry, who had yet to win the prize. But whatever the response to Pulitzer board member Walter Prichard Eaton's learned argument that the work was indeed a "play," critical opinion largely supported the decision as "both bold and wise."[32]

The three authors divided equally (short of a penny) the one-thousand-dollar prize. Ira at first considered turning down the award unless his brother was included. "That was the only time George ever got angry at me," he later told Michael Feinstein. "He insisted that I *had* to take the Pulitzer." Still, as a gesture of protest, for many years he hung the certificate in his bathroom.[33]

More controversy attended *Of Thee I Sing* when, on August 8, 1932, a New York–born playwright living in Paris, Walter Lowenfels, sued the authors, publishers, and theater owners associated with the show for plagiarizing his 1929 "operatic tragedy" *U.S.A. with Music*, written in collaboration with composer George Antheil—a play that, though unproduced, had made the rounds and wound up in Ryskind's possession. In order to avoid a trial, the opposing parties agreed to submit the two librettos to the presiding judge, John Munro Woolsey (who in late 1933 famously deemed James Joyce's *Ulysses* "non-pornographic"). On December 28, 1932, Woolsey granted the defendants' motion to dismiss, claiming that, whatever the resemblances between the two plays, the "bitter" Lowenfels libretto differed so much from the "good-natured" Kaufman-Ryskind-Gershwin book as to protect the latter from copyright infringement; and ordering Lowenfels to pay $3,500 in attorney fees and smaller amounts to some of the defendants. But this judgment only settled matters of legal trespassing, not artistic borrowing, and Edmund Wilson, for one, remained convinced that *Of Thee I Sing* owed a debt to Lowenfels.[34]

The show's great success raised the stakes of the lawsuit all the more; for although skeptics had predicted that the musical would fail to attract women and the proverbial tired businessman, *Of Thee I Sing* ran first at the Music Box and then, beginning in the fall season, at the 1,429–seat 46th Street Theatre at full or near-full capacity for over a year, grossing between $24,000 and $30,000 a week, or about $1.5 million by the end of its first year, an excellent showing for a production that had cost $88,000. Fortunately, the Gershwins had decided to join Kaufman and Harris as principal backers, with George purchasing 10 percent of the show, and Ira (with money borrowed from George), 5 percent.[35]

By the time *Of Thee I Sing* closed on January 14, 1933, about a half million people had seen the show in New York alone. (In the course of the run, the show's topicality prompted certain revisions; after "Silent Cal" Coolidge died in early January 1933, for instance, Ryskind deleted the first-act line "And call up Coolidge and tell him I want a thousand words on love tomorrow morning!") In December 1932, the *Times* noted some of the public figures who had attended the show, including attorney and executive Owen D. Young (who had seen it four times), New York Senator Robert F. Wagner, New Jersey Governor A. Harry Moore, and presidential candidate Franklin D. Roosevelt, who afterward sent Gaxton an autographed photograph inscribed to "President Wintergreen (nee Gaxton) in memory of a delightful evening in the theatre." The show proved Gershwin's biggest Broadway hit and one of the decade's great blockbusters, its 441 performances not surpassed until the arrival of Harold Rome's revue *Pins and Needles* in 1937. The phrase "Of thee I sing, baby," even served as a popular greeting during these years, while in 1932 B. Altman's department store launched an "Of Thee I Sing" aftershave and cologne. Moreover, the young Leroy Anderson's arrangement of "Wintergreen for President" (1932) for the Harvard band—which ingeniously substituted Gershwin's quoted melodies with popular college tunes—became one of that university's most beloved fight songs.[36]

Even during the show's initial Broadway run, a production of *Of Thee I Sing* starring Oscar Shaw (John Wintergreen); Harriette Lake, soon to be known as Ann Sothern (Mary Turner); Donald Meek (Throttlebottom); and Betty Allen (Diana Devereaux) successfully toured the country. Starting out in Detroit on September 12, 1932, the tour lasted eight months, winding up in San Francisco and Los Angeles. Meanwhile, after the Broadway production closed, the original cast toured the East Coast for a few months. An ensemble drawn from both casts (including Gaxton, Lake, Moore, and Allen) returned to Broadway on May 15, 1933, for another thirty-two performances at the Imperial Theatre, closing on June 10.

Although an abridged version of the show enjoyed limited engagements at Jones Beach and Randall's Island in 1937, with John Cherry, Diana Gaylen, Jack Sheehan, and Vivienne Segal, the first major revival had to wait until 1952. Kaufman had hoped to restage the work throughout the 1940s, and Hollywood geared up for its own 1944 version, which would have starred Jack Benny as Wintergreen and Fred Allen as Throttlebottom; but the war years proved inhospitable to its satirical thrusts, especially given France's role as an ally. Moreover, growing political differences between Kaufman and Ryskind made collaboration increasingly problematic. But much as the work originated during an election year following a long Republican reign, so it seemed apropos to reintroduce the show after two decades of Democratic governance. Kaufman duly managed to mount the work on Broadway during the 1952 election year, but failed in his attempt to sell the material to Paramount as a vehicle for Bing Crosby and Bob Hope, whom he thought "very right for it."[37]

For this 1952 production, Kaufman, assisted by Ryskind and Ira, modified the show by updating lines and lyrics considered dated (in the case of "Posterity," Ira rewrote the entire lyric as "The President Is Going to Be a Daddy") and by interpolating "Mine" from the work's sequel, *Let 'Em Eat Cake*. The show opened on May 5, 1952, at the Ziegfeld Theatre, with Jack Carson (Wintergreen), Betty Oakes (Mary), Paul Hartman (Throttlebottom), Lenore Lonergan (Diana Devereaux), and Florenz Ames (the French ambassador), the only original cast member. Kaufman once again directed, but with some help from Abe Burrows, who had written the book to *Guys and Dolls* (1950), which Kaufman had also directed. Don Walker reorchestrated and rearranged the music, and Maurice Levine led the orchestra. A cast album on Capitol Records followed later in the year.

The reviews of the show were mixed, with some critics finding it delightful, if only moderately so, and others finding it creaky, if amusing in spots. The more negative notices commonly criticized the book, though some took larger issue with the production. Harold Clurman, writing for *Theatre Arts,* for instance, deemed the cast "too serious for the play's exuberant nonsense. Everyone acts as if he knew better, which makes the comedy strained and unnatural." The critics agreed on at least two things: the score remained as impressive as ever, and modernizing the book was a mistake. "The patches," concluded John Mason Brown in the *Saturday Review,* "only call attention to its age." The show closed after seventy-two performances.[38]

A more successful revival starring Hal Holden and directed with flair by Marvin Gordon opened off-Broadway, first at the Master Theater in 1968 and then, after a hiatus, at the Heritage Theater in 1969. Although Clive Barnes objected to the book as "deplorable and dull," most critics liked the show. Ross Wetzsteon of the *Village Voice,* for example, wrote that the production captured "that unique tone of American musical comedy at its best—a kind of subtle and joyous vulgarity perfectly mirroring the American spirit of generosity and banality, openness and naivete, democratic populism and bourgeois triviality. If 'Of Thee I Sing' were our national anthem, maybe we'd feel less ambiguous about standing." Even Barnes admitted that, as far as the score was concerned, "the Gershwins may still be out on their own ahead of the field in the American musical theater." An abridged version for television fared less well; starring Carroll O'Connor, Cloris Leachman, Jack Gilford, and Michele Lee, the ninety-minute production, which aired on CBS on October 24, 1972, and whose score, issued by Columbia Records, featured new musical arrangements by Peter Matz, received only lukewarm response.[39]

In 1984 some of the work's original orchestrations, discovered in a storeroom of publisher Samuel French, allowed John McGlinn and Russell Warner, under the auspices of the Gershwin estate, to reconstruct a more authentic edition that provided the basis for a staged reading of the work at the Brooklyn Academy of Music in 1987 with Larry Kert, Maureen McGovern, Jack Gilford, and Paige O'Hara in the principal roles; a narration by Maurice Levine read by Gilford; and Michael Tilson Thomas conducting the Orchestra of St. Luke's. Paired with a staged revival of *Let 'Em Eat Cake,* this production played from March 18 to

March 29 to critical and popular acclaim, and yielded the best of the cast albums of the work to date.[40]

The New York Gilbert and Sullivan Players, under the direction of Albert Bergeret, similarly used the restored edition for a three-week run of the show that opened at Symphony Space on March 29, 1990. Starring Keith Jurosko and Kate Egan, this revival, though a bit rough around the edges, was perhaps better received than any since the 1930s. "Heard as the Gershwins wrote it," wrote Bill Zakariasen in the *New York Daily News,* "'Of Thee I Sing' is still hilariously trenchant musical comedy." The production's success suggested the advantages of approaching the work with integrity—including the use of the original orchestrations—and of employing performers at home with sophisticated musical satire.[41]

The Gershwin centennial prompted additional stagings, including a touring show by Opera North (1998) that starred William Dazeley, Margaret Preece, Steven Beard, and Kim Criswell; a mounting at the Macau Festival (1998) with a Portuguese cast supported by a Chinese chorus and orchestra; and a Bridewell Theatre production (1999) that was advertised as the work's London premiere. As often observed, the events leading up to President Clinton's 1999 impeachment trial provided a surprising topicality. "The audience," reported Martin Dreyer about the Opera North production, "was still laughing on its way out."[42]

The George Bush–John Kerry presidential campaign also provided some impetus for revivals of the work, including one by the Paper Mill Playhouse in Milburn, New Jersey. Directed by Tina Landau, choreographed by Joey Pizzi, and starring Ron Bohmer, Garrett Long, Wally Dunn, and Sarah Knowlton under the musical direction of Tom Helm, the show opened on September 8, 2004. An accomplished director and playwright, Landau stated that she was attracted to the material—which she described as "wacky, jagged, deeply witty and satiric and sharp"—because it offered a broadening perspective of "our social selves, our historical selves, our political selves."[43]

A number of reviews thought otherwise, finding the work little more than "okay," a "curio" that was "only a must for musical theater aficionados who rarely get to see it." Neil Genzlinger in the *Times* penned a particularly harsh notice that deemed the production, in essence, a waste of money, and the piece a "lumbering 1931 dinosaur . . . that should have stayed in the dustbin." However, the majority of critics welcomed the show as drolly if gently satiric. "I wondered whether it might be hopelessly dated," commented Terry Teachout in the *Wall Street Journal.* "The answer is that it's dated, but not even slightly hopeless." "'Of Thee I Sing' has endured," wrote Howard Kissel in the *Daily News*, "because its satire is infused with an unmistakable affection for the dizziness of our political life. You laugh at the jokes, but as the music of the richly harmonized final chorus swells, you find yourself wiping away a tear."[44]

Two years later, New York City Center's Encores! helped salvage a lackluster musical comedy season with an even more acclaimed staged concert version of the show as adapted by David Ives, directed by John Rando, choreographed by Randy Skinner, and conducted by Paul Gemignani. Opening on May 11, 2006, this "sublime" and "sumptuous" revival, with its "terrific cast" headed by Victor Garber, Jennifer Laura Thompson, Jefferson Mays, and Jenny Powers, received rave reviews from Charles Isherwood *(Times)*, Clive Barnes *(Post)*, and various online commentators. Known primarily for his performance in the monodrama *I Am My Own Wife* (2003), Mays especially delighted and surprised critics with his masterful portrayal of Throttlebottom, even if the notion of a feeble vice president seemed, in the age of Dick Cheney, wide of the mark. As with other recent revivals, the occasional detractor wondered how such a frothy book could have won a Pulitzer Prize; but even in 1931, critics widely appreciated that the show was, as Isherwood observed, "borne aloft on the buoyancy of George Gershwin's music and Ira Gershwin's intricate, often hilarious lyrics."[45]

The score's continued appeal made the Pulitzer board's overlooking of Gershwin that much more indefensible, especially considering that the committee began to award the prize to composers of musical comedies beginning in 1944 with a special award to Rodgers for *Oklahoma!* and then in 1950 with a bona fide drama award to Rodgers for *South Pacific*. (Nor did Gershwin ever have an opportunity to win the Pulitzer Prize in music, which was not instituted until 1943.) On the occasion of the composer's centennial in 1998, the Pulitzer board made amends by awarding Gershwin a special citation posthumously—a rare gesture, but one that prompted a similar award the following year in honor of Duke Ellington on his hundredth birthday.

Chapter Twenty-Eight

George Gershwin's Song-Book (1932)

During the summer of 1928, publisher Bennett Cerf approached Gershwin about putting out a limited edition of some of his music with Random House (which Cerf had founded the previous year). "Nothing could please me more," replied Gershwin, who pursued with Cerf the idea of publishing either a concert work or a song anthology. Nothing along these lines immediately materialized, though in 1930 Isaac Goldberg reported that Gershwin had a "cherished project . . . to be cleared off his desk," a collection of sixteen of his songs that would alternate their original sheet-music versions with "an arrangement that records them exactly as he plays them." Finally, in 1932, Random House published *George Gershwin's Song-Book* (dedicated to Kay Swift), which contained eighteen songs organized more or less chronologically: "Swanee," "Nobody but You," "(I'll Build a) Stairway to Paradise," "Do It Again," "Fascinating Rhythm," "Oh, Lady, Be Good!" "Somebody Loves Me," "Sweet and Low-Down," "That Certain Feeling," "The Man I Love," "Clap Yo' Hands," "Do, Do, Do," "My One and Only," "'S Wonderful," "Strike Up the Band," "Liza," "I Got Rhythm," and "Who Cares?" A limited edition of three hundred copies, signed by the composer and the book's illustrator, Constantin Alajalov, also included a bonus insert of "Mischa, Yascha, Toscha, Sascha." [1]

In the book's introduction, Gershwin wrote,

> Sheet music, as ordinarily printed for mass sales, is arranged with an eye to simplicity. The publishers cannot be blamed for getting out simplified versions of songs, since the majority of the purchasers of popular music are little girls with little hands, who have not progressed very far in their study of the piano. . . . Playing my songs as frequently as I do at private parties, I

have naturally been led to compose numerous variations upon them, and to indulge the desire for complication and variety that every composer feels when he manipulates the same material over and over again. It was this habit of mine that led to the original suggestion to publish a group of songs not only in the simplified arrangements that the public knew, but also in the variations that I had devised.

The jest about "little girls" aside, Gershwin neglected to say that published songs obviously needed to serve singers, whereas the *Song-Book* arrangements were intended primarily for pianists.[2]

In the same introduction, Gershwin also paid homage, as discussed earlier, to some outstanding ragtime pianists, though his own arrangements resemble ragtime less than they do the smaller piano pieces of, say, Prokofiev or Poulenc; or rather, they carve out their own space between these varied repertoires. At the same time, although the pieces are extremely brief—each arrangement dispenses with the song's verse and puts forth only one chorus, aside from "Liza" and "I Got Rhythm," which have two—they offer a fair degree of variety, as suggested by such diverse tempo headings as "Capriciously," "Liltingly," "Plaintively," "Spirited," and "With agitation."

Random House published each number with an accompanying drawing by Constantin Alajalov (1900–1987), a Russian-born artist who arrived in New York in 1923 and who brought his cubist propensities to bear on his work as an illustrator, including his many cover designs for the *New Yorker* and the *Saturday Evening Post*. "No attempt was made [by Alajalov] to be faithful to the music or lyrics," noted Samuel Kootz in his own preface to the *Song-Book*, "but rather to savor their source and inspiration, which, inevitably, prompted the light, satirical vein of the illustrator." The drawings are indeed highly ironic ("Nobody but You" depicts a man serenading a harem of women, and "Swanee" portrays a sailor in blackface entertaining a tribe of Eskimos), with a few employing one of Alajalov's signature tropes: an ecstatic or displeased woman with a befuddled or apprehensive male. On some level, all the illustrations comment on the Gershwins and their world, with the cartoon for "Who Cares?"—a portrait of Gershwin painting himself at the piano—parodying the composer's own art. Gershwin, for his part, opined that Alajalov's "splendid drawings" captured "the spirit of the songs."[3]

The *Song-Book* received excellent reviews from Newman Levy in the *Herald-Tribune* and Carl Engel in *Musical Quarterly*. "We believe we are not only gratifying a personal predilection," wrote Engel, "but rendering a service to all historians and musicologists by calling to their attention a publication which might have escaped their notice." Arguing that the collection represented Gershwin at his most appealing, Engel further stated, "His workmanship is clean. Melodic phrases come to him not in long sweeps; and their shortness adds to their racy tang. . . . Rhythm, under his fingers, becomes pliant, ambiguous, elusive, stirring." Levy similarly found the *Song-Book* "a more striking illustration of his [Gershwin's] unusual gifts" than his "pretentious" orchestral music: "They have a charm, freshness and originality, without that tendency to overornamentation, which is often but an expression of musical naivete."[4]

In 1941 Simon and Schuster issued an edition of the *Song-Book* revised by Herman Wasserman, with some added fingerings, accents, and dynamic markings, and with some octaves reduced to a single pitch. About 1950 pianist Leonid Hambro recorded the entire set, as did in later years Richard Rodney Bennett, Frank Braley, Angela Brownridge, William Bolcom, Mario-Ratko Delorko, Peter Donahue, Clive Lythgoe, Midori Matsuya, Leonard Pennario, and Frances Veri (with Joanna MacGregor recording sixteen of the songs, André Watts, thirteen, and Mark Anderson, ten). These recordings revealed the collection to be adaptable to a wide range of approaches—from the capriciously romantic to the stylishly modern. The music also became a focus for theses by Steven Robert Chicural (1989) and Geoffrey J. Haydon (1992) that dealt in part with the presence of Jewish and French traits, respectively, in Gershwin's music.[5]

In 1987 and 1995 Warner Brothers published additional Gershwin song arrangements, not as he notated them, but as he recorded them on phonograph discs and hand-played rolls, respectively. The former collection included six titles recorded in 1926 and 1928 as transcribed by pianist-scholar Artis Wodehouse (b. 1946), who spent hundreds of hours on this particular project but acknowledged that the poor fidelity of early recording technology and the "jazz-oriented" nature of Gershwin's performance style precluded truly definitive results. As for the second volume, an optical reader converted some of Gershwin's rolls into computer files, subsequently transcribed by George Litterst into musical notation, and edited and arranged alternatively for one or two pianos by Wodehouse.[6]

These disc and roll transcriptions—though lacking the restraint and subtlety of the *Song-Book* arrangements—at least provided expanded options for pianists to perform the Gershwin songs more or less as the composer played them. Artis Wodehouse herself performed three of her disc transcriptions at a 1987 recital at Merkin Concert Hall; Will Crutchfield, reviewing the concert for the *Times,* thought her renditions "slower and lighter than Gershwin's, without his driving brilliance but with an appealing breezy charm." Richard Dowling subsequently recorded all of these disc and roll transcriptions (2001) and Sara Davis Buechner, a selection (2005); their performances similarly threw Gershwin's playing in some relief.[7]

Other musicians published their own arrangements of the Gershwin songs for piano. Although in 1928 noted Australian American composer Percy Grainger (1882–1961) declared Gershwin, in contrast to John Alden Carpenter, "far from being anything like genuine American music," in the course of the 1940s he expressed his newfound admiration with settings for solo piano of "The Man I Love" and "Love Walked In" (published in 1944 and 1946, respectively)—though the former essentially plagiarized Gershwin's *Song-Book* version of the tune. Gregory Stone's two-piano arrangements of "The Man I Love," "Fascinating Rhythm," "Embraceable You," and "Strike Up the Band!" (published by Harms between 1941 and 1946) proved more distinctive. Born Grigori Stonien in Odessa, Stone (1900–1991), who like Alajalov arrived in New York in 1923, was a highly respected pianist, conductor, and arranger (in 1944, Warner Brothers published his excellent two-piano transcriptions of *An American in Paris* and the *Cuban Overture*). In their admixture of Russian and American elements, Stone's arrangements exemplified that special affinity Russians often felt for Gershwin. In 1975 duo-pianists Ralph Grierson and Artie Kane released a recording of these paraphrases, along with Stone's two-piano transcriptions of *An American in Paris* and the *Three Preludes,* plus arrangements of other Gershwin songs by J. Louis Merkur and Henry Levine.[8]

In the 1950s pianist Earl Wild (b. 1915), a master of keyboard transcriptions of the Romantic era, started arranging Gershwin songs, and in 1975, after completing the last of the bunch—"Fascinatin' [*sic*] Rhythm"—he revised and published them as *Seven Virtuoso Etudes on Themes of Gershwin.* Aside from "Embraceable You," all seven songs overlapped with those used by Gershwin in his *Song-Book,* from which Wild occasionally quoted. Wild recorded this dazzling compilation (1976 and, less brilliantly, 1989), as did pianists Richard Dowling (2001) and Eric Himy (six of the seven, 2004).[9]

However, of all the published piano arrangements, two large cycles by Michael Finnissy (b. 1946)—*Gershwin Arrangements* (1975–1988) and *More Gershwin* (1989–1990, revised 1998)—proved the most remarkable. Even the selection of songs—which tended, especially in the second set, toward obscure numbers from the early 1920s, some more popular in Britain than in the States—was unusual; of those songs found in Gershwin's *Song-Book*, Finnissy chose the two least likely to attract modern improvising pianists: "Swanee" and "Nobody but You." One of the preeminent British composers of his generation, Finnissy was known— as in his *Verdi Transcriptions*—for creating complex structures in response to preexisting materials; but his use here of the term *arrangement* denoted a special explicitness. Indeed, he employed the Gershwin melodies (including verses) fairly literally, though often fragmented and reordered, and sometimes elongated to the point that they functioned like cantus firmi. But although Finnissy's harmonic palette had a richness and delicacy like Gershwin's, he set these melodies against densely chromatic and often contradictory counterpoint. This approach strongly echoed Ives, a major influence (though for these arrangements, Finnissy had Schoenberg and Berg more in mind). So dramatic a meeting between Ives and Gershwin—that much more striking in view of the music's British provenance—itself warranted attention.[10]

Finnissy, who as a child heard Gershwin's tunes over the radio and on the family phonograph, explained that these arrangements "developed as part of an evolving discourse on popular culture. . . . Jerome Kern or Irving Berlin would have done equally well, the point being to explore an era—1918 to 1939—that apparently redefined society, and in which jazz and modernism variously evolved in response to facism [*sic*] and capitalism, but via that most intimate and everyday of sentimental/romantic emotions." The first seven songs of the first set, he further wrote, "document a love affair—from tentative, if hopeful, beginnings to mournful ending." Some knowledge of both the words and the music of the original Gershwin songs aided in elucidating Finnissy's intentions; but in any case, the strength of the Gershwin melodies—along with the playfulness and wistfulness they evidently inspired—helped establish this music as among Finnissy's most popular, with masterful recordings by Ian Pace (2000) and Nicolas Hodges (2004).[11]

Scores of recording artists, aided by the advent of long-playing records, produced songbooks of their own. Lee Wiley, Bing Crosby, and Ella Fitzgerald helped pioneer this trend with their Gershwin collections from 1939–1940, 1949, and 1950, respectively (with Fitzgerald issuing two more songbooks, in 1959 and 1983). Subsequent performers— popular, jazz, and classical alike—who also released collections of Gershwin songs included, among singers, George Byron, Chris Connor,

Michael Feinstein, Wilhelmenia Fernandez, Judy Garland, Isabelle Ganz, Frances Gershwin, Glad, Mary Cleere Haran, Barbara Hendricks, Ruthie Henshall, Hildegarde, Julie Hill, the Honey Dreamers, Julia Migenes Johnson, Prudence Johnson, Jack Jones, Linn Maxwell Keller, Dorothy Kirsten, Susannah McCorkle, Maureen McGovern, Sylvia McNair, Joan Morris, Marni Nixon, the Pontarddulais Choir, Rita Reys, Benjamin Sears, Dinah Shore, Bobby Short, Carol Sloane, Kiri Te Kanawa, Sarah Vaughan, Marti Webb, Ronny Whyte and Travis Hudson, and Julie Wilson; and among conductors and instrumentalists, John Arpin, Winifred Atwell, Juraj Bartos, George Bassman, the Berkeley Square Society Band, Stanley Black, Ran Blake, the Ruby Braff and George Barnes Quartet, Billy Butterfield, the Canadian Brass Quintet, Eddie Condon, Barbara Carroll, Bill Charlap, Chick Corea, Frank Cracksfield, Buddy DeFranco and Oscar Peterson, Eddy Duchin, Dick Farney, Frederick Fennell, George Feyer, Erroll Garner, Dave Grusin, Earl Hines, Johnny Hodges, Dick Hyman and Tom Pletcher, Jack Jezzro, André Kostelanetz, Adam Makowicz, Shelly Manne, Liz Magnes, Yehudi Menuhin and Stéphane Grappelli, Mitch Miller, the New York Banjo Ensemble, 101 Strings, Eric Parkin, Joe Pass, Oscar Peterson, André Previn, the Quartet de Clarinets, Jean-Pierre Rampal, Marcus Roberts, Spike Robinson, Charlie Shavers, Zoot Sims, the Sir Roland Hanna Quartet, Lenny Solomon, Claude Thornhill, Allen Toussaint, the Trio Chizhik, Armando Trovajoli, Joe Venuti, Roger Williams, the World's Greatest Jazz Band, George Wright, and Teddy Wilson. The songs selected by Gershwin for his own *Song-Book*—with the exception of "Nobody but You"—formed part of the basic repertoire for these many songbooks, with musicians generally gravitating toward the same material, notwithstanding the periodic appearance of novelties, as in the "thirteen rediscoveries" performed by Barbara Cook, Anthony Perkins, Bobby Short, and Elaine Stritch on the album *Ben Bagley's George Gershwin Revisited,* or the three songbooks released by Gershwin authority Michael Feinstein (1987, 1996, and 1998). Along with various published anthologies of Gershwin songs, including those issued by Simon and Schuster (1960), the *New York Times* (1973), Hal Leonard (1992), and Warner Brothers (1998), the recorded songbooks helped canonize about sixty titles from an output of many hundreds.[12]

Of the vocal songbooks, those by Sarah Vaughan (1924–1990) with (primarily) arranger-conductor Hal Mooney (1957) and by Ella Fitzgerald (1917–1996) with arranger-conductor Nelson Riddle (1959) enjoyed outstanding success. Few other such recordings, moreover, approached their sheer scale, in particular the Fitzgerald release, which involved fifty-nine songs recorded over an eight-month period. Norman Granz, Fitzgerald's manager and the founder of Verve records, supervised this enormous undertaking; he not only selected the material but helped plan the arrangements (with Ira revising some of the lyrics especially for Fitzgerald). The deluxe five-album boxed set, which featured commissioned artwork by Bernard Buffet and an expanded-play seven-inch bonus recording offering some purely instrumental transcriptions, climbed to twelfth place on *Billboard*'s popular-music charts, selling more than a hundred thousand copies within two months of its release, an impressive feat for a recording that cost as much as $25.98.[13]

Neither the Vaughan nor the Fitzgerald songbook escaped criticism, however. Ira, for example, thought that Vaughan used too many "vocal tricks," while Stuart Nicholson found the Fitzgerald release (though widely regarded as her best songbook) marred by haste. Michael Feinstein further objected to some of Nelson Riddle's arrangements, whose "1950s ethic," added Charles Hamm, robbed the music "of all vitality and rhythmic life." But both songbooks remained benchmarks of their kind, not superseded by such later all-Gershwin albums as Vaughan's Grammy-winning recording with Michael Tilson Thomas and the Los Angeles Philharmonic (1982) and a release by Fitzgerald with André Previn at the piano (1983).[14]

Among other recorded songbooks, *Menuhin and Grappelli Play Gershwin* (1988) merited notice for its unusual pairing of an esteemed classical violinist (Yehudi Menuhin) and a brilliant jazz violinist (Stéphane Grappelli)—thereby dramatizing tensions inherent in the music itself. Along these lines, *Gershwin the Klezmer* (1999), featuring the Minnesota Klezmer Band, explored the confluence of Yiddish and African American elements in the composer's work; while in *Moroccan Moods of Gershwin* (1995), Israeli pianist Liz Magnes juxtaposed Gershwin tunes with traditional Moroccan and Ethiopian melodies.

As for the numerous recorded anthologies with varied artists, *The Glory of Gershwin* (1994) unusually featured some prominent rock musicians. Producer-arranger-conductor George Martin, who conceived this recording in honor of the eightieth birthday of Larry Adler, the harmonica player long associated with the Gershwins, engaged a roster of popular singers (Oleta Adams, Kate Bush, Cher, Elvis Costello, Peter Gabriel, Elton John, Jon Bon Jovi, Meat Loaf, Sinéad O'Connor, Robert Palmer, Carly Simon, Lisa Stansfield, and Sting) along with jazz saxophonist Courtney Pine and actress Issy Van Randwyck to collaborate with Adler on a Gershwin song of their choosing in jazzy orchestral settings. The results underscored some of the challenges in adapting rock styles to Gershwin's work, but Sting nicely mined the humor in "Nice Work If You Can Get It," and Costello brought a distinctive vulnerability to "But Not for Me." Rock crooner Rod Stewart similarly made effective use of some Gershwin songs, including "Embraceable You," in his series of "great American songbook" recordings.

British pianist Jack Gibbons's four-disc anthology, *The Authentic George Gershwin*—released individually in the 1990s and as a boxed set in 2004—dwarfed all other Gershwin songbooks, if one could call so monumental a compilation of songs, occasional pieces, and concert works arranged for solo piano a songbook. The 1982 winner of the Newport International Competition for Young Pianists, Gibbons (b. 1962) discovered Gershwin in 1988 "quite by accident" while studying the Concerto in F, and he immediately began playing and transcribing his music, including his rolls and electrical recordings. (When Gibbons later discovered Artis Wodehouse's published roll transcriptions, he was "surprised at the large number of inaccuracies in her transcriptions, mostly in the form of inaccurate harmonies and even melody notes, as well as the selection and distribution of notes within chords.") His epic survey of Gershwin's oeuvre from "Swanee" (1919) to "Love Is Here to Stay" (1937) drew on an extensive array of piano rolls, phonograph recordings, scores, arrangements, and sound tracks. Regarding Gershwin as "one of the greatest minds in twentieth-century classical music" and a composer of personal importance comparable only to Bach, Chopin, and Elgar, Gibbons also performed his Gershwin transcriptions in live performance, including annual all-Gershwin concerts at London's Queen Elizabeth Hall initiated in 1990.[15]

The Gershwin songbook had other uses. Warner Brothers, for instance, structured its film biography of the composer, *Rhapsody in Blue* (1945), around an assortment of Gershwin songs (and orchestral works). Howard Barnes, in his review, even referred to the picture as "an anthology of wonderful tunes" and "an expansive, sonorous and syncopated song fest." Produced by Jesse L. Lasky and directed by Irving Rapper, the film starred Robert Alda (Gershwin), Morris Carnovsky (Morris), Rosemary DeCamp (Rose), Herbert Rudley (Ira), and Joan Leslie (dubbed by Sally Sweetland) and Alexis Smith as two fictional girlfriends (Julie Adams and Christine Gilbert). Howard Koch and Elliot Paul wrote the screenplay after a story by Sonya Levien based on a draft by Clifford Odets, who in turn had taken over from screenwriters Robert Rossen and Katherine Scolar.[16]

Ray Heindorf, soon to head music at Warners, worked five months compiling and arranging the individual numbers, while Max Steiner scored some of the background music. Conducted by Leo F. Forbstein, the sound track used twenty songs (excluding operatic excerpts), though only "Swanee" was rendered with complete verse and chorus. Twelve of the twenty overlapped with those from the *Song-Book*.[17]

The film's earlier sequences—as Gershwin pounds out "When You Want 'Em" in a Remick cubicle, and Al Jolson introduces "Swanee" to a thrilled audience—presented some of these numbers in relatively authentic contexts. But the songs mostly appeared with little reference to real shows or collaborators or anything else that might interfere with its wartime-inspired agenda of presenting Gershwin as the composer of music that "personified America."

Many critics derided the film as trite and implausible. "Ah, the memories it brought back!" wrote George S. Kaufman in a humor piece for the *New Yorker*. "That night when the Rhapsody had its first hearing, when George rushed from the concert platform straight to the bedside of his dying music teacher, dear Professor Frank! It was I who buttoned his greatcoat about him on that historic occasion, I who whispered into his ear, 'Mind the snow, George.' (I was a little hurt that this was left out of the picture.)" Even James Agee, who found the picture "sympathetic," thought that Alda, "though any amount better cast than there was any law-of-averages reason to hope for," lacked "the obsessiveness, the elegance, and the power to persuade you that he is a man of great ability which would have made him fully adequate as Gershwin." At least one notice further argued that the songs, though widely considered the film's saving grace, were "dulled considerably by performances that are supposedly styled to a period in the twenties or early thirties but are diluted by a pretty, immaculate, lush, modern movie manner of singing, make-up and stage decor, the most destructive element being the hundred-piece Phil Spitalny–like orchestral accompaniment." But for all that, Heindorf and Steiner received an Academy Award nomination for best score, and the film's success at the box office no doubt helped further the popularity of its familiar songs.[18]

Director Woody Allen (b. 1935) made even more famous use of more than a dozen Gershwin songs, along with the *Rhapsody*, to help shape his motion picture *Manhattan* (1979). Allen not only derived seminal inspiration for this homage to his native city from Gershwin's work (including Michael Tilson Thomas's 1976 release of some musical-comedy overtures, as arranged by Don Rose), but actually created some sequences around the music. "I was shooting scenes deliberately to put to music that I knew beforehand," stated Allen. "I played those records every single day as soon as I got up in the morning. I played them on the way to work, and listened to them over and over."[19]

The film identified Gershwin with Manhattan from the start, not only through its montage of city images accompanied by the *Rhapsody* but by a voice-over of the protagonist's novel in progress: "Chapter one. He adored New York City. He idolized it all out of proportion. No, make that, he romanticized it all out of proportion. Better. To him, no matter what the season was, this was still a town that existed in black and white and pulsated to the great tunes of George Gershwin." This sentiment manifested itself variously throughout the picture, but as with so many pictorial representations of Gershwin, the New York skyline—images of which framed the film—proved quintessential.

Meanwhile, choreographers devised dances around the Gershwin songbook. In 1940 Léonide Massine (1896–1979)—who had staged Satie's *Parade,* Falla's *The Three-Cornered Hat,* and Stravinsky's *Pulcinella* for Diaghilev—launched *The New Yorker* for the Ballets Russes de Monte Carlo to a score composed of Gershwin songs and excerpted concert works arranged by film composer David Raksin. Massine worked with Ira on the score and collaborated with Rea Irwin on its scenario—inspired by *New Yorker* cartoon characters by Peter Arno, William Steig, and others—about New York cafe society. "I much enjoyed transposing the extravagances and absurdities of New York society life into brisk, syncopated dance rhythms," recalled Massine, who thought "the only suitable composer for this work would be George Gershwin, whose music had the right quality of New York sophistication." The critics concluded that the ballet missed its mark, but nonetheless praised the work of Frederic Franklin and Nathalie Krassovska, as well as Massine's own "grotesquely humorous" performance as Arno's Timid Man.[20]

In 1964, at conductor André Kostelanetz's suggestion, Ira sent George Balanchine (1904–1983) fourteen unpublished Gershwin songs that the lyricist hoped might serve as the basis of another Gershwin ballet. Although this proposal came to naught, it presumably set Balanchine thinking along these lines, for in 1970 he created a dance for the New York City Ballet—*Who Cares?*—based on seventeen published Gershwin songs (fifteen of which appear in the *Song-Book,* enough to suggest that the choreographer had that 1932 collection in mind). Balanchine personally knew Gershwin, whose death prevented a planned collaboration for the film *The Goldwyn Follies* (1938), and many consequently viewed this new work as fulfilling the promise of a Balanchine-Gershwin ballet.[21]

Created for an ensemble of fifteen women and five men (including soloists Karin von Aroldingen, Patricia McBride, Marnee Morris, and Jacques d'Amboise), *Who Cares?* premiered at Lincoln Center's State Theatre on February 5, 1970. Composer-arranger Hershy Kay (1919–1981) prepared the orchestrations, Karinska designed the costumes, and Robert Irving supervised the music, which featured pianist Gordon Boelzner and a recording of Gershwin himself playing "Clap Yo' Hands." Aside from the central pas de deux, "The Man I Love," danced by McBride and d'Amboise, most critics initially panned the ballet as "ill-conceived," "immoderately empty," "slipshod," and "pompous." But as Kay completed the orchestrations (at the premiere, the orchestra played only two of the numbers), Jo Mielziner redesigned the scenery, Balanchine cut "Clap Yo' Hands," Ben Benson created new costumes, and the dancers performed with greater verve and assurance, the work was received more favorably.[22]

By 1983 *New York Times* dance critic Anna Kisselgoff could declare *Who Cares?* a "fabulous ballet," attributing its new success ("the normally reserved audience went wild") to the dazzling Benson costumes and a sexier cast, including premier danseur Sean Lavery, "who could be mistaken for a gigolo, albeit of the nice-boy variety." And in contrast to those earlier critics who thought the ballet oddly academic, Kisselgoff wrote, "It is Mr. Balanchine's tour de force to reach so deeply into popular music that he brings out its essence." Later reviews by Jack Anderson and Jennifer Dunning similarly deemed the work attractively ebullient.[23]

On May 15, 1998, the Martha Graham Dance Company, under the artistic directorship of Ronald Protas, premiered its own Gershwin dance, *But Not for Me*, choreographed by Susan Stroman, best known for her work on Broadway, including *Crazy for You* (1992), as earlier discussed. Arranger Glen Kelly shaped the refrains of eight popular Gershwin songs—"But Not for Me," "'S Wonderful," "They Can't Take That Away from Me," "They All Laughed," "Liza," "Nice Work If You Can Get It," "Strike Up the Band," and "The Man I Love"—into a seven-part fantasia, with some of the tunes interwoven throughout, especially "But Not for Me," the score's idée fixe. "The piece is about being alone in New York," Stroman told the Graham company. "Sleeping alone in New York and wishing you were not alone." Each of the work's five male and five female dancers, dressed in silk pajamas and accompanied by his or her own pillow, imagines dream lovers, recalling Gershwin's stated intention of wanting "to write for young girls sitting on fire escapes on hot summer nights in New York and dreaming of love." The dance originally ended with one woman (Katharine Crockett) center stage, alone and forlorn; but a revised version, which premiered at New York's Joyce Theater in 1999, concluded more whimsically with the same figure enfolded by a male dancer (Martin Lofsnes) who emerges from under a pile of pillows.[24]

The enlistment of Broadway talent—including not only Gershwin, Stroman, and Kelly but orchestrator Doug Besterman and conductor Paul Gemignani—by the august Graham Company at first glance seemed a bit curious, but Stroman's choreography actually incorporated some Graham-like movements and Kelly's arrangements often came as close to Copland (whose *Appalachian Spring* was a company signature piece) as to Gershwin. Stroman further reasoned, "I know the Graham technique is loved across the world and the only really contemporary composer who also transcends all boundaries is Gershwin." Some critics dismissed the piece as so much fluff, but others welcomed the experiment; alluding to its "personal and universal" emotions, Lisa Traiger in the *Washington Post* wrote, "*But Not for Me* is not a Graham piece, but one that follows her."[25]

Choreographer Michael Smuin (b. 1938), whose many credits included directing the television special *Ira Gershwin at 100: A Celebration at Carnegie Hall* (1997), took a more eclectic approach in his songbook ballet, *Dancin' with Gershwin,* for the Smuin Ballet, based in San Francisco. Premiering on May 9, 2001, to generally good reviews, this two-act dance utilized movements and costumes (the latter by Willa Kim) alternatively associated with ballet, musical comedy, and vaudeville, against a similarly diverse recorded score that featured Gershwin's music—again, mostly songs—performed by singers ranging from Al Jolson to Peter Gabriel. Reviewing a performance at the Joyce Theater in 2003, Jack Anderson thought that the work might have been pruned some, but admired its exuberance. In 2005 the company duly returned to New York with a shortened version of the ballet, which Gia Kourlas, also in the *Times,* more critically found comparable to "an Americana floor show at a Catskills hotel."[26]

In the wake of the popular revue *Jacques Brel Is Alive and Well and Living in Paris* (1968), staged presentations of the Gershwin songbook began appearing with greater frequency as well. Some of these traded in nostalgia, such as Bert Convy's Gershwin "musicade" *Do It Again!* which opened on February 18, 1971, at New York's Promenade Theatre, and whose cast of five included Margaret Whiting and Clifton Davis. Noting with mixed feelings that the audience applauded the "opening phrases of its favorite numbers," Clive Barnes thought the show "so corny that I am surprised that they don't give spare box-tops for bargain-price silverware with the tickets."[27]

On January 17, 1972, NBC's *Bell System Family Theatre* subsequently aired a ninety-minute television special, *'S Wonderful, 'S Marvelous, 'S Gershwin,* starring Fred Astaire, Larry Kert, Ethel Merman, Leslie Uggams, and others, including Jack Lemmon, who not only narrated producer Martin Charnin's text but performed some of the songs. "Gershwin knocks me out, always has, maybe because his music was influenced by the blues," Lemmon stated at the time. "I've always dug that music—the wild, physically moving kind of thing." Daybreak Records released an abbreviated cast album of the show, which won five Emmys, including one for "outstanding single program."[28]

In November of the same year, the *Lawrence Welk Show*—one of television's longest-running variety shows (1955–1981)—presented "Gershwin," the first of its three Gershwin retrospectives, later followed by "The Great Gershwin" (1976) and "Salute to Gershwin" (1980, currently marketed as "Tribute to Gershwin"). Each of these hourlong episodes presented about eighteen separate numbers, mostly songs, but also extremely abridged versions of the *Rhapsody* (1972, 1976) and *An American in Paris* (1980), the latter danced by Bobby (Burgess) and Elaine (Balden)—all interspersed at intervals with commercials for Geritol, Sominex, Poligrip, and other products aimed at the program's aging but enthusiastic audience. Because Welk (1903–1992) repeated many of the same numbers from show to show (though in new arrangements and with different artists), he ultimately used only twenty-five songs, a repertoire that could be said to constitute the core Gershwin canon as it emerged during these years. Welk and his "musical family" performed these numbers—diverse enough to serve varied needs, including "champagne music" for the dancing audience—with a good deal of trademark squareness, but a performance of "Mine" by Dick Dale, Gail Farrell, and Mary Lou Metzger (1972), though largely defanged, introduced an unexpected note of Brechtian irony, while a rendition of "Oh, Lady, Be Good!" (1980) gave trombonist Bob Havens and the band an opportunity to let loose.[29]

A 1973 revue with Cayce Blanchard, Ed Dixon, Glen Mure, and Martha Williford under the direction of Christopher Alden explored some less-familiar Gershwin songs. Playing initially at the Yale Cabaret as *A*

Gershwin Celebration and then at the Manhattan Theatre Club as *Gershwin!* the show, according to Richard Shepard in the *Times*, revealed "a constancy of taste preserved in our youth who, it was feared, might have given all that up." *By George!*—a 1974 revue mounted in a church on the Upper West Side by the Intense Family—also received favorable notices. In 1976 the same title served a Gershwin revue at Canada's Charlottetown Festival mounted in honor of the American bicentennial.[30]

A number of other revues appeared in various New York venues, including *Fascinatin' Gershwin* (1986) at Don't Tell Mama, and yet another show titled *'S Wonderful, 'S Marvelous, 'S Gershwin* (1992), at Rainbow and Stars. One of the more recent, *The Gershwins' Fascinating Rhythm*, produced by Mark Lamos and Mel Marvin, aimed to update twenty-seven songs by way of rock-influenced scoring and sexually provocative staging. Debuting in Hartford in 1997, the production traveled to Tucson, Phoenix, and Las Vegas before opening with a cast of ten at Broadway's Longacre Theatre on April 21, 1999. The critics deemed this "homogenized pop-rock-disco show" an "abomination," and the revue closed after seventeen performances.[31]

Hershey Felder, playing some of the more recognizable songs and concert works at the piano, had far greater success with *George Gershwin Alone* (1999), a biographical monodrama in the tradition of Hal Holbrook's *Mark Twain Tonight!* and William Luce's *The Belle of Amherst*. Born in 1968 in Montreal the son of Holocaust survivors, Felder began his career as a concert pianist and composer and eventually started acting and writing as well. The husband of former Canadian prime minister Kim Campbell, Felder had already made use of Gershwin's music in his 1998 play *Sing! A Musical Journey* when he gained permission from the Gershwin estate to develop a one-man show based on the composer's life. First presented at Steinway Hall in New York on June 30, 1999, *George Gershwin Alone*, directed by Joel Zwick, played in Los Angeles for a number of months in 2000 before traveling to various cities around the world, including New York, where it debuted at the Helen Hayes Theater on April 30, 2001, and London, where it premiered at the Duchess Theatre on February 17, 2004. By 2005 Felder had performed the work more than fifteen hundred times.

Opening with a portrait of Gershwin at the piano toward the end of his life, the show unfolded largely as a series of reminiscences, concluding with a performance of the *Rhapsody,* followed by a sing-along in which audience members could request their favorite Gershwin tunes. Felder, who resembled Gershwin in appearance, described the shape of his script, modeled after the *Rhapsody,* as "chunks strung together with energy," articulated by "pivotal points" in the composer's life. Somewhat in the tradition of Hollywood's *Rhapsody in Blue,* Felder took liberties with the facts in order to dramatize Gershwin as a misunderstood genius, but in contrast to the patriotic impulse behind the 1945 biopic, he identified as its "driving dramatic force" the composer's "vulnerability" and "neediness." Audiences enjoyed Felder's charm as well as the opportunity to learn something about the composer's life and to sing the refrains of such songs as "Embraceable You" en masse. "By the end, the show has become something of a shrine, a work of reverence and gratitude," wrote the *Times*'s Bruce Weber, who drew a not uncommon analogy between Gershwin and Mozart (a figure mythicized along similar lines).[32]

On November 10, 2000, a few months before *George Gershwin Alone* arrived at the Helen Hayes, a saucier Gershwin revue, *American Rhapsody,* opened off-Broadway at the Triad on the Upper West Side. The show's stars, chanteuse KT Sullivan and singer-pianist Mark Nadler, took a freewheeling approach to the material, constructing exuberant and sometimes surreal medleys that occasionally satirized the whole concept of the composer revue, as in their "Mega-Medley" of thirty-eight songs and concert pieces (one for each year of Gershwin's life). But their treatment of the Gershwin oeuvre proved perhaps truer to the spirit of the composer's work and life than did many of the more reverent tributes. Stephen Holden expressed reservations about the show, but both David Finkle and Michael Feingold of the *Village Voice* thought it a delight, as did the Manhattan Association of Cabarets and Clubs (MAC), which voted it the best revue of 2001. The cast album (1999) revealed, in any case, that the uses of the Gershwin songbook remained as varied as those of many of the individual songs themselves.[33]

Chapter Twenty-Nine

The *Cuban Overture* (1932)
and *Pardon My English* (1933)

*I*n February 1932 Gershwin took a two-week vacation in Havana with some friends, including Bennett Cerf, Adam Gimbel, Everett Jacobs, Emil Mosbacher, and Daniel H. Silberberg. Staying at the Hotel Almendares, he golfed, sunbathed, and nightclubbed; visited the races a few times; went to one party hosted by J. P. McEvoy and another given by Howard Hughes; and attended a dance recital by Ruth Page, who extemporaneously danced to the second of the *Three Preludes* in his honor. "I spent two hysterical weeks in Havana where no sleep was had," he wrote to George Pallay, "but the quantity and the quality of fun made up for that. . . . Cuba was most interesting to me, especially for its small dance orchestras, who play [the] most intricate rhythms most naturally. I hope to go back every winter, if it is possible, as the warm climate seems to be just the thing my system requires for relaxing purposes."[1]

By this time, Havana had become a popular tourist resort known for its hotels and gambling; but Gershwin traveled there specifically to hear music, according to the *Havana Post:* "The siren call of Cuban music with its odd rhythms and plaintive melodies has lured George Gershwin . . . to Havana, in search for new inspiration." Gershwin was hardly alone in his interest in Cuban music. In the wake of a 1930 recording of "The Peanut Vendor" ("El Manisero," composed in 1928 by a Cuban, Moisés Simons) by Don Azpiaza and his Havana Casino Orchestra, Americans had become enamored with Cuban music and the rumba in particular, a vogue abetted by Spanish-born bandleader Xavier Cugat, who began performing at the Waldorf-Astoria in 1930; and by the MGM musical *Cuban Love Song* (1931), which featured Ernesto Lecuona's band. Gershwin himself frequented the Waldorf's elegant Sert Room (named after its murals by José Maria Sert) in order to hear Cugat, who recalled his friendship with "the immortal" Gershwin in his autobiography, *Rumba Is My Life:*

> Deep in thought, he [Gershwin] would listen to my band as if he were making mental notes. Which indeed he was. . . . Several times he invited the boys in the band and me to his Riverside Drive apartment. There, as we had done before with Cole Porter, we would have a jam session, with George sitting at the piano, alternating with my own pianist, Nilo Menendez, a talented composer who did, among other hits, "Green Eyes."

Cugat also appreciated Gershwin's intervention with hotel management to secure him some vacation time.[2]

The rumba was a relatively tame adaptation of the Afro-Cuban *son,* which in the course of the 1920s had overtaken the more genteel *danzón* as Cuba's most popular dance, thanks to the work of such groups as Ignacio Piñeiro and his Sexteto Habanero (later, with added trumpet, the Septeto Nacional). Though tailored to American fashion, the rumba nonetheless represented a notable cultural watershed: the first significant absorption of Afro-Cuban music into the nation's musical mainstream, anticipating the popularity of the conga, the mambo, and other dances. Among other traits, the rumba had a distinctive rhythmic lilt, enhanced by a tendency toward alternating harmonies that rocked back and forth in a compelling way. Moreover, like the *son,* the rumba featured not a single drum set but a percussion ensemble that variously included maracas, cowbells, bongos, conga drums, claves (wooden sticks), and guiros (scraped gourds). Americans danced the rumba essentially by adding looser hip movements to the basic patterns of the fox-trot.

While in Cuba, Gershwin heard such leading local bands as the Palau Brothers, who played nightly at the Almendares, and the Castro Brothers. On his second night there, an itinerant group of musicians, hired by his friend Henry Ittleson, serenaded him outside his lodgings at four in the morning—to the dismay of some of the hotel's patrons. Bennett Cerf recalled this serenading group as comprising sixteen musicians, but Gershwin's mention of "small dance orchestras" suggests some encounters as well with six- or seven-piece *son* ensembles, which often included two vocalists (often doubling on maracas and claves), *tres* (a Cuban guitar), guitar, double bass, bongos, and sometimes trumpet, and whose polyrhythmic complexities had to be toned down to suit the taste of upper-class Cubans. Gershwin, in fact, heard the Sexteto Habanero at the McEvoy gathering, though whether this represented his first encounter with Piñeiro remains uncertain; for according to common lore, he also heard—and transcribed themes of—the great Cuban bandleader on visits to Havana's CMCJ radio station.[3]

Returning to New York with a collection of Cuban percussion instruments, Gershwin composed an orchestral piece inspired by his experiences in Havana, in particular, the music-making of street musicians. Leaving behind ample sketches that suggest a newly deliberate frame of mind, he completed a condensed draft, in mostly three to four staves, in July, and orchestrated the whole in early August. He finished the score, initially titled *Rumba,* on August 9, a mere week before its first performance by eminent British conductor Albert Coates and the New York Philharmonic at Lewisohn Stadium on the sixteenth at the orchestra's first all-Gershwin concert.[4]

Gershwin changed the work's title to *Cuban Overture* prior to a repeat performance on November 1, with the composer leading an ensemble of two hundred unemployed players, the Musicians Symphony, at a benefit concert for the orchestra at the Metropolitan Opera that featured an all-Gershwin second half. The title *Rumba,* he explained, had misled listeners into expecting something like "The Peanut Vendor," whereas *Cuban Overture* gave "a more just idea of the character and intent of the music." He even referred to the work as a "symphonic ouverture."[5]

Like most of Gershwin's orchestral works, the *Cuban Overture* consists of a single movement with fast outer sections *(A)* and a slow middle section *(B).* Its design especially resembles the *Second Rhapsody* in that both have two distinct but related themes in their *A* sections (in the *Cuban Overture,* this includes the spectacular main theme, marked both "warmly" and "espressivo," and a subsidiary theme in minor, similarly marked "expressively"); a contrasting melody, based on the principal theme, put forth in the *B* section (here marked "plaintively," and introduced by the oboe); and a cadenza connecting the *A* and *B* sections (here played by the clarinet, not the piano).

Reflecting popular rumba practices, the piece opens with an introduction and a vamp that prepares the main theme. ("It is customary to start a rumba with a short introduction followed by a vamp," wrote Cugat, adding, "The nonmelodic group does not enter until the vamp.") The work's introduction also states (initially at measure 6) a fragment from Ignacio Piñeiro's popular *son* "Echale Salsita" (1929), a song said to have popularized the term *salsa.* On one level, this snippet provides some local color, like the quotation of "La Mattchiche" in *An American in Paris;* but in the course of the piece, it assumes a more integral function as a motive in its own right (occasionally accompanied by an inverted or augmented version of itself), an idea that may have been inspired by Don Azpiaza's use of the tune in his recording of "The Peanut Vendor."[6]

The work contains other intriguing details. For instance, the introduction develops, along with the "Echale Salsita" fragments, bits and pieces of the *A* section's two principal themes in anticipation of their eventual arrival; that the overture to *Of Thee I Sing* offers more precedence for this technique than do any of Gershwin's symphonic compositions helps document the relatedness of his theatrical and concert work. The concluding *A* section, which Gershwin labels "stretto" (in its nonfugal meaning as a fast conclusion), reveals a kindred procedure: the music begins with fragments of the principal material, reserving a full-blown return for the work's end, followed only by a brief coda.[7]

The music also reveals a heightened interest in various contrapuntal techniques. In the first *A* section, Gershwin uses, in his own words, a three-part "polyphonic episode" that twice serves as a transition to principal thematic material. In these episodes, the two upper voices—one derived from the principal theme, the other anticipating the plaintive *B* theme—appear in invertible counterpoint. Even more striking, the entire *B* section largely consists of three canons (perhaps inspired by the vocal duets of the traditional Cuban *son*), each rounded off with refrainlike commentary, the last of which also contains a climactic fourfold repetition of the canon's opening phrase, referred to by Gershwin as an "ostinato."

Gershwin spoke of writing these canons "in a polytonal manner" (by *polytonal,* he ostensibly meant that the canon and its underlying harmonies—not the individual voices of the canon—were in separate keys). Passages that can be described as polytonal or bitonal actually occur throughout the work, including the transitional episodes in the first *A* section and, even more explicitly, the restatements of the "Echale Salsita" fragment in the final *A* section. In view of the music's rumba context, these polytonal passages emit a flavor redolent of—and possibly influenced by—Darius Milhaud's Brazilian-inspired music. The work also boldly mixes modes and exploits other harmonic ambiguities, though the music sooner or later cadences onto some expected or unexpected simple triad; this includes the last of the three canons, a winding episode that represents one of Gershwin's most daring ventures.

More noticeably novel, the work—which Gershwin scored for piccolo, two flutes, two oboes, English horn, two clarinets, bass clarinet, two bassoons, contrabassoon, four horns, three trumpets, three trombones, tuba, timpani, percussion, and strings—calls for four Cuban percussion instruments: bongos, gourd, maracas, and claves (called "Cuban sticks" by Gershwin), in addition to such standard percussion instruments as snare drum, bass drum, cymbals, bells, and xylophone. Gershwin highlighted the Cuban instruments not only by using them prominently, but also by specifying their placement "right in front of the conductor's stand." Meanwhile, his polyrhythmic writing for these percussion instruments offers additional evidence that he gleaned inspiration from native Cuban ensembles as well as from Azpiaza and Cugat. He might have learned something, too, from Cuba's art-music composers, including Alejandro Caturla, who himself had written an *Obertura Cubana* in 1927—revised, ironically enough, as *Rumba* in 1931, but retitled *Obertura Cubana* in 1938, perhaps in response to Gershwin's *Cuban Overture*, which Caturla heard Nicolas Slonimsky conduct in Havana in 1933.[8]

Some of the more atypical aspects of the *Cuban Overture*—the presence of canon and polytonality, the adventurous orchestration, even the reference to such terms as *ostinato* and *stretto*—also point to the influence of Joseph Schillinger, with whom Gershwin had begun lessons earlier in 1932. But the composer had long shown an inclination toward the kind of compositional rigor found here, which, combined with the work's absorption of folk sources, bespoke yet another resemblance to Milhaud as well as to Bartók (the work's middle section might even be likened to Bartók's so-called night music). The piece similarly invites comparison with the Latin-inspired works of Aaron Copland, including *El Salón México* (1936) and, perhaps more to the point, *Danzón Cubano* (1942). Steven Gilbert, for instance, described *El Salón México* as a work of "similar character" if less "technical complexity" than the *Cuban Overture*, though one might say, rather, that they are complex in different ways.[9]

Gershwin came close, incidentally, to composing a Mexican work of his own. In the fall of 1935, as mentioned earlier, he vacationed in Mexico (with Gregory Zilboorg, his former psychiatrist; Marshall Field III, of the department store family; and Edward Warburg, who in 1933 cofounded the American Ballet with Lincoln Kirstein) with the thought that he might compose something based on native materials. On his return, however, he expressed disappointment with Mexican music, commenting specifically on the difficulty of finding "Indian music," a frustration he shared with Warburg, who "hoped to learn something of Aztec and Indian traditions." Perhaps Gershwin and Warburg had in mind the possibility of an "Aztec" ballet. In any event, Gershwin surely would have taken considerable interest in *El Salón México*—Copland's first popular success—had he lived to hear the work.[10]

A packed house of seventeen thousand at Lewisohn Stadium might not have provided ideal conditions for grasping the likes of a polytonal canon, but the audience responded enthusiastically to the premiere of the *Cuban Overture,* as listeners did to its repeat performance at the Met. The reviews were largely perfunctory, however. Howard Taubman in the *New York Times,* for instance, dismissed the work as "merely old Gershwin in recognizable form." On the other hand, Pitts Sanborn in the *World-Telegram* admired the music's "rich sonorities" and "fascinating" rhythms, and although he found a few passages "dull," he opined that with some "condensation and tightening" the piece might rival Ravel's *Bolero* (deemed its "inferior in musical body"). And in a preview of the concert at the Met, Olin Downes knowingly observed that the work's materials "have been treated in ways which depart from anything he [Gershwin] has done in earlier scores."[11]

In 1938 Paul Whiteman released a lively version of the piece for jazz band, freely arranged as a piano concertino (with Rosa Linda the featured soloist), though his subsequent recordings of the piece (including one from 1954) proved more faithful to the original score. Other arrangements included one by Greig McRitchie for pianist Leonard Pennario and the Hollywood Bowl Orchestra under Alfred Newman that, like Whiteman's various releases, strove for wider commercial appeal; and a hipper version by Philippe Selve for the Jazzogène Big Band under Jean-Luc Fillon (1992).

Meanwhile, the original version received hundreds of performances, including recordings presided over by Edo de Waart, Charles Dutoit, Arthur Fiedler, Howard Hanson, André Kostelanetz, Erich Kunzel, James Levine, Andrew Litton, Lorin Maazel, Wayne Marshall, Kurt Masur, Eduardo Mata, Zubin Mehta, Vaclav Neumann, André Previn, and Leonard Slatkin. Even these expert conductors, however, had variable success with the troublesome contrapuntal passages for woodwinds. Most recordings also tended to take the outer sections slightly faster and the middle section slightly slower than Gershwin's metronome markings specified; but Andrew Litton's recording with the Dallas Symphony made a convincing case for taking the middle section at an even slower tempo, one that made it easier for the ear to absorb the music's intricate harmonic progressions. Litton also pioneered the restoration of a few concluding bars cut from the composer's manuscript score, published in facsimile in 1987.

After the great success of *Girl Crazy,* the Gershwins "patiently" waited for Alex Aarons and Vinton Freedley to provide a script for another show. "But they seem incapable of finding one," complained Gershwin to Sonya Levien in the summer of 1931. "They are really quite stupid about books." Finally, over the following summer, Aarons engaged the Gershwins and librettists Morrie Ryskind and Herbert Fields to write a new musical comedy—eventually called *Pardon My English*—for debonair English music-hall star Jack Buchanan, who like Gertrude Lawrence had scored a hit on Broadway with the *Charlot's Revues.*[12]

Of a prominent theatrical family, Fields (1897–1958) had written the books to various musicals, including *A Connecticut Yankee* (1927) and *Fifty Million Frenchmen* (1929). He and Ryskind developed the premise of an aristocratic Englishman with a split personality, his baser self the proprietor of a German speakeasy—an idea possibly suggested by Rouben Mamoulian's 1932 film *Dr. Jekyll and Mr. Hyde* (the script alludes to the Robert Louis Stevenson novel in explaining the protagonist's "dual identity").[13]

Convinced that Buchanan was more suited to an intimate revue than to the kind of show afoot, Vinton Freedley initially disassociated himself from the project. But when a cash-strapped Aarons found himself financially overextended, Freedley told him, according to Ethel Merman, "I'll take over. You go lie down somewhere. You need it." The Gershwins had reservations of their own, but proceeded out of a sense of gratitude to Aarons, as Ira recalled:

> *Pardon My English* was a headache from start to finish. . . . I disliked enormously the central notion of the project—duo-personality or schizophrenia or whatever the protagonist's aberration was supposed to be; so why toil and moil on something we didn't want or need? However, loyalty to producer Aarons, who was broke and who told us if we didn't do the score his potential backers would back out, induced us to go ahead.

Though originally slated to direct the show, Ernst Lubitsch begged off three weeks prior to rehearsals. Ultimately, Freedley took charge of the staging, assisted by George S. Kaufman, who helped rehearse a few scenes, and choreographer George Hale, who had staged the dances for Gershwin's most recent shows. The apprehensions of Freedley and the Gershwins proved increasingly well founded, and although Aarons announced a Broadway opening in October, the show did not even begin tryouts until December 2, when it had its world premiere at Philadelphia's Garrick Theatre.[14]

In addition to Buchanan, the Philadelphia cast featured Jack Pearl (born Pearlman), one of the last of the so-called Dutch comedians (as radio's Baron von Munchhausen, Pearl amused audiences by responding, "Vas *you* dere, Sharlie?" to doubts about the veracity of his tales); Polish-born platinum blonde Lyda Roberti (parodied by Ginger Rogers as "Sharvenka" in *The Gay Divorcee*); and the alluring Ona Munson (known then for her stage work, though best remembered today for her role as the good-hearted prostitute Belle Watling in *Gone with the Wind*). John Wenger created the sets, Robert Ten Eyck Stevenson designed the costumes, and Robert Russell Bennett, William Daly, and Adolph Deutsch orchestrated the score. On opening night, Gershwin directed the orchestra and large chorus of thirty women, twenty-one men, and six "Schuhpladlers."[15]

The first act of the Philadelphia version opens on a street in Dresden, as passersby seek a local speakeasy, 21 ("Fatherland, Mother of the Band"). The action moves to the bar's quaintly German interior, where American tourists can order wine and beer as well as soft drinks—the latter prohibited in Germany. Golo (Jack Buchanan), a bootlegger (of soft drinks), runs the bar assisted by his gang, including his henchman, Katz (Manart Kippen), and his moll, Gita (Lyda Roberti). Gita entertains the crowd ("The Lorelei"), and Golo pays tribute to the waltz ("In Three-Quarter Time"). Learning that Dresden's police commissioner, Bauer (Jack Pearl), plans to raid the town's speakeasies, Golo dispatches Gita and the rest of the gang. An English visitor, Richard Carter (Gerald Oliver Smith), takes Golo for Michael Bramleigh, an aristocratic British friend injured during the war. As Golo departs, Bauer and the police raid the joint.

That evening, the town celebrates the commissioner's birthday outside his home ("Dancing in the Streets"). Within, the commissioner's daughter Ilse (Ona Munson) and maid Magda (Ruth Urban), along with various friends, offer congratulations. After Bauer leaves, Golo—a casualty in an automobile accident—arrives unconscious and awakens in a state of amnesia. Richard identifies him as Michael Bramleigh, and a doctor, Adolph Steiner (Royal Dana Tracy), suggests that he remain in Ilse's care. Michael and Ilse quickly fall in love ("Isn't It a Pity?").

At Steiner's office, six psychiatrists—doctors Freud, Jung, Adler, Adler, Jung, and Freud—warn Michael against head injuries ("Freud and Jung and Adler" and possibly "He's Oversexed!" and "Watch Your

Head"). A month later, Michael and Ilse, now engaged, hold a rendezvous, while Gita attempts to seduce Bauer. On getting hit on the head, Michael reverts to his Golo personality.

In the cellar of his speakeasy, Golo and his gang plan to retaliate for Bauer's raid by stealing Ilse's wedding gifts and kidnapping her for ransom. Golo and Gita resume their romance ("Luckiest Man in the World"). Meanwhile, Ilse attempts to cheer up her father ("So What?"), who orders his assistant, Schultz (Cliff Hall), and six policemen to guard the presents ("The Dresden Northwest Mounted"). As the gangsters steal the wedding gifts, Ilse surprises Golo by suggesting that they elope. That night, in a bridal suite at a Loschwitz inn, Golo beds his—or rather Michael's—fiancée ("Tonight").

As the second act opens, the wedding guests, unhappy about the elopement, raid Bauer's house in compensation for their stolen presents ("No Tickee, No Washee"). Meanwhile, Ilse has been abducted by Katz and Golo has reverted to his Michael persona. Michael learns from Gita (who assumes he's Golo) the address of the American Bar where the gang's holding Ilse. Gita once again vamps Bauer ("My Cousin in Milwaukee"), but the commissioner orders her arrest. At the American Bar, Michael tips off the police about Ilse's whereabouts and buys time by joining in the festivities ("I've Got to Be There"). As both Gita and Ilse confront Michael, the police arrive; during the ensuing melee, Michael's knocked senseless ("Finaletto" and reprise of "The Dresden Northwest Mounted"). After regaining consciousness, he recognizes neither Ilse nor Gita; but when Ilse hits him on the head, he turns to her with outstretched arms and the two embrace ("Finale: He's Not Himself").

The Fields-Ryskind libretto resembled a number of previous Gershwin musicals in many of its particulars, including its ploy of amnesia induced by a car accident *(Tip-Toes)* and its chorus of bumbling police *(Funny Face)*. Moreover, its absurdist elements strongly evoked *Of Thee I Sing*, with the roles of Michael, Ilse, Bauer, and Gita more or less recalling those of John Wintergreen, Mary Turner, Alexander Throttlebottom, and Diana Devereaux from the earlier Ryskind show. On the other hand, the dual-identity premise represented a newfangled twist on a comic tradition that stretched as far back as Plautus's *Menaechmi*, though the authors established no real tension between the hero and his alter ego, nor did they take consistent advantage of the story's potential for humorous mistaken identities. Even the title—a play on the popular expression "pardon my French"—seemed to serve no purpose other than to prepare the audience for some fractured English and raw humor.

Gershwin nonetheless provided this zany book with some music of near-operatic grandeur, creating a score that, while it largely lacked the extended ensembles found in *Strike Up the Band* and *Of Thee I Sing*, otherwise surpassed his previous shows in terms of sheer musical complexity. Moreover, certain musical Germanisms—mostly found in the music for the Bauers and their friends—gave the score a unique stylistic profile, including not only individual takes on the German polka, waltz, and *Ländler*, but traces of the German art-music tradition, with knowing glances in the direction of Carl Maria von Weber's *Der Freischütz* and Richard Strauss's *Der Rosenkavalier*, and even a parody, in the second-act finale, of Mendelssohn's "Spring Song." At the same time, the score found room for a wide range of American styles, including yet another parody of Friml, "Dresden Northwest Mounted." All these varied allusions served the show's overarching tone, an unusual blend of German gemütlichkeit, Weimar decadence, and American sass.

Gershwin further attempted to create somewhat different worlds for Golo and Michael, thus helping to dramatize the theme of dual personality; but the music as a whole lacked the comedic brilliance of his best show scores. The book simply failed to define moments in the action that required musical explication and development, so the numbers by and large proved ancillary to the action, always theatrical, but rarely truly dramatic. Moreover, as with *Song of the Flame*, the play's foreign setting and characters, though ostensibly welcomed by the composer as a nice change of pace, inhibited his special ability as a commentator on the American scene.

The score's most characteristic songs included the three that became best known: Michael and Ilse's lovely if wry duet "Isn't It a Pity?" and Gita's two racy solos, "My Cousin in Milwaukee" and "The Lorelei." (Another distinctive number, the beguiling fox-trot "Luckiest Man in the World," never caught on, possibly because of its offbeat lyric.) Cognizant of Roberti's trademark guttural speech, Ira prominently featured aspirated syllables in both of her numbers: "hey! ho-de-ho! hi-de-hi" in "The Lorelei" (whose coda quotes, with a wink, Friedrich Silcher's 1838 setting of Heinrich Heine's "Die Lorelei") and repetitions of "how" and "hot" in "My Cousin in Milwaukee." For the latter, he also possibly had in mind not just Milwaukee's large Polish community but specifically the chanteuse Hildegarde, who hailed from that Wisconsin city.[16]

Although the Philadelphia reviews largely thought the show—described as "a decorative but amazingly drowsy music play" by the *Evening Bulletin*—derailed by a perplexing and humorless book, reaction to the score varied. The *Inquirer,* for instance, found the "difficult" music "consistently enjoyable," the *Evening Public Ledger* even claiming that Gershwin had "unbent a little from the cryptogrammic music of 'Of Thee I Sing' and other of his recent shows," while the *Bulletin* deemed the music "intricate, unappealing, and obviously very difficult to sing" and the lyrics "not as bright as they should be." *Variety,* disappointed with the score as well, reminded readers, however, that "all Gershwin's scores are deceptive and have a way of developing sensational song hits for dance floors and jazz orchestras when least expected."[17]

The show plainly needed work. Among other problems, the principal role—as Freedley had feared—proved uncongenial to Buchanan. As Aarons and Freedley supervised extensive rewrites, Ryskind, annoyed by their meddling, quit the show, and Fields took sole credit for the book—an action considered highly courageous. Meanwhile, Ona Munson withdrew from the show after Philadelphia as well.[18]

The producers postponed a planned late December opening in New York in favor of a short run (starting December 26) at Brooklyn's Majestic Theatre, where Roberta Robinson replaced Munson, followed by another week (starting January 2) at Newark's Broad Street Theatre. During this leg of the tour, Buchanan also gave notice, agreeing to buy himself out of his contract for, as Ira recalled, about twenty thousand dollars. Meanwhile, the producers hired John McGowan (who had coauthored *Girl Crazy*) to help doctor the book. The new script deleted the characters of Katz and eventually Dr. Steiner; cast Harry T. Shannon as a new sidekick for Golo, a thug named McCarthy; and interpolated parts for dancers Carl Randall and Barbara Newberry as an American dance team—Johnny Stewart and Gerry Martin—traveling abroad.[19]

The Gershwins composed new duets for Gita and Golo ("Pardon My English") and Gita and Bauer ("Where You Go, I Go"), adapted "Watch Your Head" as the refrain of a wedding chorus ("Hail the Happy Couple"), recycled "No Tickee, No Washee" into a revamped act 1 finale ("What Sort of Wedding Is This"), and turned "Luckiest Man in the World" into a solo for Michael. The two duets in particular seemed aimed at widening the score's appeal, though neither proved all that successful (the Cole Porterish "Pardon My English," like "Hail the Happy Couple," apparently did not even make it to Broadway). Meanwhile, the deletion of Dr. Steiner necessitated the removal of the delightfully absurd "Freud and Jung and Adler."

Although the show otherwise retained most of the score, many of the songs appeared in new dramatic contexts, as the revised script involved perhaps the most extensive rewrite in Gershwin's Broadway career. Fields essentially dispensed with the satire on Prohibition, a topic made increasingly moot by a newly elected Congress set to repeal the Eighteenth Amendment. Moreover, he jettisoned the split-personality premise and reconceived Michael as a kleptomaniac, his disorder the result of an airplane crash.[20]

The newly overhauled show received surprisingly good reviews, even raves, after opening January 9 at the Colonial Theatre in Boston. The *Globe,* for instance, declared it "one of the funniest and breeziest musical comedies thus far presented here this season," while the *Traveler* wrote, "Of all the tongue-twisting, toe-tapping, eye-and-ear pleasing musical comedies that have sent up whoops of laughter from Boston boards, not one has been any merrier, any brighter, any more tuneful than 'Pardon My English.' . . . This show has everything." Isaac Goldberg in the *Evening Transcript* more guardedly described the musical as a "tug-of-war" in which "low-comedy" triumphed over "satire," and thus a work not to be taken too seriously: "Enter the theater properly adjusted to harmless impropriety and be assured of plenty of low laughter, which has, especially these days, its tonic qualities." The critics especially liked the performances of Pearl, Roberti, and Buchanan, Goldberg noting that the latter, "evidently a high favorite in Boston, long familiar on the screen, stopped the show with his dancing, his very pardonable English, his suave smile and more-than-a-soupçon of a supposedly extinct matinee idolatry."[21]

More trouble awaited, however. In the midst of the Boston run, Buchanan left the show and was replaced by the less-magnetic George Givot, a comedian known for his Greek American dialect (as in, years later, his portrayal of the restaurateur Tony in Walt Disney's *Lady and the Tramp*). Meanwhile, Aarons and Freedley—until the former simply collapsed from nervous exhaustion—replaced Roberta Robinson with, at first, Peggy Cartwright and then, just before the New York opening at the Majestic Theatre on January 20, Josephine Huston. Throughout this almost unimaginable chaos, the production relied increasingly on the draw of Jack Pearl, and by the time the musical rolled into New York, it had become very much Pearl's show, complete with top billing. On opening night, Gershwin, suffering from a cold, led the band, which included clarinetist Artie Shaw, in the overture, but otherwise left the conducting to Earl Busby, who had succeeded the show's tryout conductor, Adolph Deutsch. Ira, also nursing a cold, later recalled, "A bad cold and a lukewarm audience had me home by nine thirty."[22]

The New York premiere drew some of the worst notices of Gershwin's career, with critics widely deeming the work "tedious," "lifeless," "old-fashioned," "routine," "silly," "complicated," a "bore," and a "shambles." "*Pardon My English* spends more time in a coma than any musical comedy can afford," wrote Richard Lockridge in the *Sun*. "It is by long odds the dullest, heaviest and most tiresome musical in town," agreed Cy Caldwell in the *New Outlook*. The reviews especially assailed the book, but most also thought the production, though polished in the Aarons-Freedley manner, workaday; the cast—aside from Pearl and Roberti—unexceptional; and the score, second-drawer (a verdict surely not helped by the show's "desperate want of a single singing voice").[23]

The enormous disparity between the show's reception in New York and in Boston suggests that Buchanan's departure and other last-minute alterations severely debilitated the production. In any case, Aarons and Freedley did what they could. They lowered ticket prices and, within weeks of opening night, replaced Givot with Joseph Santley, a stage actor who later became a prominent film director. But the show managed only forty-six performances, closing on February 27, 1933, the day of the Reichstag fire. Robert Kimball contends that bootlegger-producer Waxey Gordon strong-armed the Shuberts into closing *Pardon My English* prematurely in order to get his show, *Strike Me Pink*, into the Majestic. Other commentators have suggested that contemporaneous events in Germany, including Hitler's appointment as chancellor on January 30, a mere ten days after the work opened, tarnished the show's appeal by making its German setting "disturbing" to audiences. However, none of the show's reviews gave even an inkling of such sensitivities (although they admittedly predated Hitler's chancellorship). On the contrary, *Variety* thought that, aside from a few dances, "no one would know but the setting was New York or Chicago or Paris." And Gilbert Gabriel in the *American* referred to the work's "Swiss-German atmosphere" as "this year's substitute for Harlem." Indeed, Kern's *Music in the Air*, which opened November 8, 1932, and which was set in Bavaria, proved, at 342 performances, the biggest musical-comedy hit of the season.[24]

Or did the audience simply fail to read the show as a parody of German fascism, as John Andrew Johnson has suggested? While working on *Let 'Em Eat Cake* later in the year, Ira in fact rewrote some of "In Three-Quarter Time" as a "Song for [a] Nazi Musical Comedy," one in which "Hitler puts [a] ban on 'Negro' music and calls for the return of the waltz," and that, even more chillingly, included the lines "Opponents we griddle / We cut up the Yiddle / In 3/4 time." But whether the creators of

Pardon My English had Hitler in mind—as opposed to long-standing traditions lampooning Germans as lovers of beer and liverwurst, philosophy and the waltz, spiced, perhaps, with a dash of Brecht and Weill—remains at the least inconclusive.[25]

Although *Pardon My English* folded quickly, "The Lorelei," "My Cousin in Milwaukee," and "Isn't It a Pity?" enjoyed enduring success, as mentioned. Eddy Duchin and his Central Park Casino Orchestra recorded "My Cousin in Milwaukee" even before the show opened in New York, with Gertrude Niesen imitating Lyda Roberti. Less than two months later, pianist-vocalist Ramona Davies and a few members of the Paul Whiteman Orchestra, including trumpeter Bunny Berigan, recorded the same song in a faster rendition that established the music's connection to new swing styles.[26]

Meanwhile, Gershwin and Kay Swift enjoyed playing "Tonight" as a two-piano piece, appropriately enough considering that this ambitious duet superimposed a chromatically winding waltz for Michael (derived from a July 28, 1923, sketch titled "Invitation to the Waltz: Something Else Again" and marked "Waltz: Vienese" [*sic*]) with a soaring countermelody for Ilse. In 1971, Warner Brothers published a version of this music for solo piano arranged by Saul Chaplin. Retitled *Two Waltzes in C* by Ira in order to avoid confusion with "Tonight" from *West Side Story,* this arrangement—which, like the original duet, contains four sections: an introduction, Michael's waltz, Ilse's waltz, and the two waltzes combined—entered the repertoire of a number of solo pianists. Meanwhile, some two-piano teams, like that of Frances Veri and Michael Jamanis and that of Katia and Marielle Labèque, performed two-piano arrangements of the music as well.

In 1982 the entire score for *Pardon My English,* long forgotten, was discovered in Secaucus, with nearly all of the original orchestrations intact. Conductor John McGlinn aired these numbers in concert on a double bill with the score to *Primrose* at the Library of Congress on May 15, 1987, with Cris Groenendaal (Michael), Rebecca Luker (Ilse), Jack Dabdoub (Bauer), and Kim Criswell (Gita). The critics were impressed. Tim Page, in *Newsday,* thought the piece "sheer ecstasy. . . . The melodies are tough, visceral, creative and irresistible; the lyrics are often hilarious." And Dale Harris, in the *New York Post,* imagined that the score probably sounded "more dazzling today than it did in 1933, when the American musical looked as though it would go on forever."[27]

Working with the Secaucus and other materials, Tommy Krasker and Russell Warner completed a performing edition of the work in 1993 that came closer to the Philadelphia version than the New York one but constituted yet another variant, including a rewritten overture. Elektra Nonesuch issued a recording of this revised score the following year, with William Katt (Michael), Michelle Nicastro (Ilse), John Cullum (Bauer), and Arnetia Walker (Gita) under the baton of Eric Stern—a watershed achievement, though marred by some uneven performances. In 1997 Warner Brothers published a complete vocal score, edited by Steven Bowen, that roughly conformed to the Krasker edition but contained other materials as well, including the original overture and the duet "Pardon My English," a number Ira allegedly disliked on account of its lyric.

On March 25, 2004, Encores! launched a staged reading of the show at New York's City Center directed by Gary Griffen, choreographed by Rob Ashford, and starring Brian d'Arcy James (Michael), Jennifer Laura Thompson (Ilse, renamed Frieda, as in an early draft of the script), Rob Bartlett (Bauer), and Emily Skinner (Gita) under the musical direction of Rob Fisher, who used the original orchestrations, which he thought enhanced the music's looniness. Unaware of the existence of the revised script, concert adapter David Ives—who described the show as "A Connecticut Yankee in the Weimar Republic" (a reference to Field's 1927 adaptation of the Twain novel for Rodgers and Hart)—structured the show around the Philadelphia book, but he rearranged the order of the songs and incorporated numbers introduced later in the run, including "Where You Go, I Go" and "Pardon My English." He also reconceived Michael as a former globe-trotting secret agent and created a romantic subplot by expanding the roles of Magda and Richard Carter, who performed the duet "Luckiest Man in the World."[28]

Donald Lyons in the *New York Post* opined that the musical should have been "safely left to molder," but Ben Brantley in the *Times* thought the performance a "mirage of a pleasure palace" with "therapeutic benefits beyond the reach of any analyst's couch." Ethan Mordden, who liked the production as well, commented, "It's amazing how well *Pardon My English* played in 2004, considering its stunted history."[29]

The Encores! revival led to more fully staged productions, the first of which arrived at Houston's small Main Street Theater on December 28, 2005. The local critics thought the show unable to rise above its "ridiculous" and "ludicrous" book, even as spruced up by Ives and deftly realized by such cast members as David La Duca (Bauer) and Catherine Kahl (Frieda). Still, Houston audiences, like those at New York's City Center, seemed to find this droll and wacky musical comedy a delight.[30]

Chapter Thirty

Let 'Em Eat Cake (1933) and
Variations on "I Got Rhythm" (1934)

In late 1932, as George S. Kaufman and Morrie Ryskind considered writing a sequel to *Of Thee I Sing*, Kaufman's wife, Beatrice, suggested picking up the story with John P. Wintergreen's reelection campaign following his first term as president. Kaufman and Ryskind liked the idea; the latter already had demonstrated the satire's continued viability by way of his 1932 book, *The Diary of an Ex-President*. After securing the support of some of the principals associated with *Of Thee I Sing*—including the Gershwins, producer Sam Harris, and some of the lead actors—they started work on the show in early 1933, announcing its title, *Let 'Em Eat Cake*, in April.[1]

Kaufman and Ryskind drafted two scenarios, each including suggested spots for songs, and finished the first act in New York in late May and the concluding act in Atlantic City in June, the entire script taking them less than five weeks. The Gershwins presumably completed most of the score prior to the start of rehearsals on August 15. In contrast to *Of Thee I Sing*, they reportedly reverted to their standard working procedure of Ira providing a title or lead line but otherwise waiting until the music had been composed before writing the words. Kaufman and Ryskind apparently had some input into the lyrics as well.[2]

William Gaxton, Victor Moore, and Lois Moran re-created the roles of John P. Wintergreen, Alexander Throttlebottom, and Mary Wintergreen; and Dudley Clements, George Mack, Harold Moffet, and Edward H. Robins once again played members of the Wintergreen entourage. Kaufman and Ryskind eliminated some of the earlier musical's characters—including Diana Devereaux, the French ambassador, Sam Jenkins, and Miss Benson—though they cast Florenz Ames, the original French ambassador, in the new role of General Adam Snookfield. George Murphy, who had played Jenkins, similarly hoped to be cast as the radical agitator Kruger, but that part went to Philip Loeb. (Loeb's satiric portrait of Kruger made it all the more sadly ironic that anti-Communist zealotry ended his career—which included his portrayal of Jake on the popular radio and television serial *The Goldbergs*—driving him to suicide in 1955.)[3]

Let 'Em Eat Cake premiered at Boston's Shubert Theatre on October 2, 1933. Kaufman directed, Eugene Von Grona and Ned McGurn staged the dances, John Booth and Kiviette created the costumes, Albert R. Johnson designed the sets, Edward "Eddie" Powell did the orchestrations, and William Daly conducted the orchestra and chorus of twenty-six women and thirty-two men—a rare instance of a Gershwin chorus with more men than women. Some of this talent represented a newly emerging generation, including Von Grona, who would found the American Negro Ballet in 1937; Johnson, who established himself as a leading scenic designer with two Irving Berlin shows, *Face the Music* (1932) and *As Thousands Cheer* (1933); and Powell, who for many years served Twentieth Century–Fox as one of its premier orchestrators.

The Boston premiere proved one of the most eagerly awaited events in memory, with a pair of opening-night orchestra tickets fetching as much as $17.50. The first-night audience included not only various eminent Bostonians—including the city's colorful mayor, James M. Curley, who recognized the authors after the show, and composer Charles Martin Loeffler, prominently ensconced in a box—but also an estimated two hundred visitors from New York. The show garnered an enthusiastic reception, with the header for Edward H. Crosby's *Boston Post* review reading, "One of Best Shows Ever Seen in Hub." Helen Eager in the *Traveler* described the musical as "a brilliant successor to its famous predecessor" and reported that the "smart audience ate every crumb with enthusiastic relish," while H. T. Parker's review for the *Evening Transcript* praised every aspect of the production, including the book: "They [Kaufman and Ryskind] have made 'Let 'Em Eat Cake,' like its predecessor, a musical play for an intelligent American audience that knows its ways about the American world. They have sunk deeper the old shibboleths, conventions, sentimentalities." As for the score, the *Globe* admired its "genuine musical value," while Parker thought it showed Gershwin at the top of his form: "through no recent musical play or symphonic piece has he [Gershwin] marched so resourceful, rich and alert. . . . He can turn his phrases, rhythms and harmonies to humorsome or satirical purpose."[4]

Still, the critics thought the show overlong, with too many dull patches, and the authors extensively reworked the material over the next few weeks. According to Parker, these revisions, which successfully made the work "more direct," shortened the piece from about three and a half to less than three hours, so that the show let out about eleven rather than close to midnight. "Uneasy Manhattanese," commented Parker, "will not arrive belatedly at dancing or supper parties." The show arrived at New York's Imperial Theatre on October 21 with, among other changes, a new ending.[5]

Act 1 opens with two concurrent nighttime rallies, one for the incumbent president, John P. Wintergreen, and the other for his challenger, John P. Tweedledee ("Tweedledee for President"). On election night, the president's inner circle—General Adam Snookfield (Florenz Ames), his mistress Trixie Flynn (Grace Worth), Secretary of the Navy Francis X. Gilhooley (Harold Moffet), Secretary of Agriculture Louis Lippman (Abe Reynolds), Senator Carver Jones (Edward H. Robins), Senator Robert E. Lyons (George E. Mack), newspaper tycoon Matthew Arnold Fulton (Dudley Clements), and their wives—join Wintergreen (William Gaxton) and First Lady Mary (Lois Moran) at the White House. Although Wintergreen asks the Supreme Court to overturn the election—won by Tweedledee by a landslide—the nine justices refuse, leaving John and his associates concerned about future employment; this includes vice president Alexander Throttlebottom (Victor Moore), who has to pay alimony to Diana Devereaux. After the assembled wives admire John's blue shirt, sewn by Mary, the Wintergreen gang decides to go into the garment business and produce "Maryblue shirts."

As passersby stroll by the Wintergreen shirt company in Manhattan's Union Square, a rabble-rouser, Kruger, harangues the crowd from his soapbox ("Union Square"/"Down with Everyone Who's Up"). With shirt sales languishing, Wintergreen decides to foment a blue-shirt revolution on the model of Mussolini's black shirts and Hitler's brown shirts. As business subsequently prospers, Throttlebottom happily anticipates a revolution, while John credits Mary for his success ("Shirts by Millions"/"Comes the Revolution"/"Mine"). Even Kruger has joined the blue shirts, while Mary attracts female social climbers to the cause ("Climb Up the Social Ladder"). As a member of the conservative Union League Club, the general at first withholds his support, but Throttlebottom invades the club's inner sanctum ("The Union League," originally titled "Cloistered from the Noisy City") and wins over its members by evoking the invading armies of George III (reprise of "Comes the Revolution").

Wintergreen and the general plan a coup d'état, and their supporters start their march on Washington ("On and On and On"). On the lawn of the White House on July 4, the general reviews his troops; the revolutionaries interrupt a speech by Tweedledee (Richard Temple); Tweedledee and Wintergreen put their rival cases before the army; Mary exhorts the soldiers to choose her husband, a father of two, over a "selfish, old bach'lor" like Tweedledee; Tweedledee promises each soldier a dollar a day, while Wintergreen offers them the war debts ("if we collect 'em"); and, finally, the army arrests Tweedledee, silences Kruger (who has turned against the blue shirts), and, accompanied by a display of fireworks, declares Wintergreen dictator of the proletariat ("Finale," including "I've Brushed My Teeth," "The Double Dummy Drill," a reprise of "On and On and On," "The General's Gone to a Party," "All the Mothers of the Nation," "There's Something We're Worried About," and "Let 'Em Eat Cake").

As the second act opens, the workers at the Blue House—formerly the White House—praise the color blue ("Blue, Blue, Blue"), and Wintergreen enters in dictatorial glory ("Who's the Greatest?"). Having banned lawyers, he appoints the nine Supreme Court justices the country's official baseball team, with Throttlebottom as umpire. When nine members of the League of Nations refuse to pay their war debts, Wintergreen proposes a baseball game between the league and the justices to settle the matter ("Finaletto," including "No *Comprenez,* No *Capish,* No *Versteh!*" "Why Speak of Money?" and a reprise of "Who's the Greatest?"). The game follows (baseball scene, including "No Better Way to Start a Case" and "Up and at 'Em").

After the league wins, Kruger and the army place Throttlebottom on trial for calling a foul ball fair and sentence him, Wintergreen, and their cronies to death for treason; Mary says her farewells to John; and Kruger, assuming the dictatorship, promises the crowd caviar (tribunal scene, including "That's What He Did!" "I Know a Foul Ball," "Throttle Throttlebottom," "A Hell of a Fix," a reprise of "Down with Everyone Who's Up," "It Isn't What You Did," reprise of "Mine," and "Let 'Em Eat Caviar").

Execution day arrives ("Hanging Throttlebottom in the Morning"). Trixie has taken up with Kruger ("First Lady and First Gent," cut during rehearsals). Mary and the other wives of the condemned men avert the scheduled executions by guillotine by displaying the latest fashions from Paris; forced to wear the same blue blouse by the state, the female spectators insist on Kruger's overthrow, and, goaded on by Trixie, the army removes him; Wintergreen goes into the dress business with Lipp-man and Kruger; Tweedledee accepts the presidency of Cuba; and as Tweedledee cannot remember his own vice president, Throttlebottom becomes the nation's new president ("Finale," including a reprise of "Blue, Blue, Blue" and an unspecified reprise, possibly "Of Thee I Sing" or "Let 'Em Eat Cake").[6]

The Kaufman-Ryskind book remains one of the most unusual in the history of the American musical: a caustic satire of the American body politic—including politicians, the army, the Supreme Court, the Union League, the Daughters of the American Revolution, radicals, Fascists, businessmen, radio, newspapers, movies, the fashion industry, and baseball—all in the form of a fantasy (some years prior to Sinclair Lewis's *It Can't Happen Here* of 1935) about a totalitarian America. The libretto spares no sacred cows; discussing the Founding Fathers, Wintergreen states, "They were tired of paying taxes to England, so what did he [Washington] offer them? He said, You fellows stick with me and you can pay your taxes to America instead! And they're still doing it!" ("Not Charley Mitchell," responds Lippman, alluding to the notorious banker who stood trial for tax evasion in 1934.)[7]

Kaufman and Ryskind had scored similar points—especially regarding the stupidity and venality of politicians—in *Of Thee I Sing*, but this satire assumed a darker edge; when Mary attempts a ploy used in *Of Thee I Sing* to save her husband, Kruger interrupts, saying, "You can't get away with that again! That was all right four years ago, but it doesn't go with the Army!"—an outburst that underscores the distance between the two shows wrought by deepening poverty and unemployment, the collapsed hopes of collecting billions of dollars in war debts, the Bonus Army's march on Washington, and the rise of Hitler. (Two days after the show opened on Broadway, Ira published a "book review" of Hitler's *Mein Kampf* in the *Herald-Tribune* that read, "Of Germany / And her many / —Well,—minds, / None's littler / Than Hitler, / One finds.") Nor did *Let 'Em Eat Cake* have the sort of romantic story line found in *Of Thee I Sing*; Gershwin himself expressed concern over the lack of "love interest" in this "entirely new kind of show." (In an early scenario, Kaufman and Ryskind included a romantic subplot involving Throttlebottom and Kruger's scheming daughter, Cleo, but eventually eliminated the latter character in favor of Trixie.) At the same time, the script ends somewhat optimistically with the triumph of American democracy, even if such survival depends on the vagaries of female consumers and lecherous soldiers—and even though the presidency falls to a bumbling nitwit.[8]

For this "entirely new kind of show," Gershwin wrote the most acerbic musical-comedy score of his career, its vocal lines and harmonies often spiked with pungent dissonance. Moreover, he came closer than ever to comic opera, writing extended musical scenes whose mix of recitative, arioso, song, and chorus exceeded in formal complexity anything he had attempted hitherto. With their rapidly changing moods and keys, these ensembles disguised the work's tunefulness for some listeners, but they enhanced the drama by bringing the action to a frenzy of dizzying absurdity. Sketches show that Gershwin originally intended even some of the show's shorter numbers, such as "Climb Up the Social Ladder" and "Union League Club," as part of more extended ensembles, according to Wayne Schneider, who writes, "His [Gershwin's] artistic aspirations [in *Let 'Em Eat Cake*] were clearly operatic, in the sense of continuous music-drama."[9]

Relatedly, the score made particularly ironic use of musical-comedy conventions: the soft-shoe chorus "Union Square," for instance, frames the strident "Down with Everyone Who's Up"; the ballad "Mine" has a patter that sardonically comments on the song's sentimentality; in "Blue, Blue, Blue," the revolutionary workers, after a strangely hypnotic verse, sing in the tones of a chorus-girl promenade; and in "Why Speak of Money?" the League of Nations diplomats launch into a playful chorus-boy romp. The show very possibly excised "First Lady and First Gent," one of its breezier songs (to judge from the surviving music), partly because it jarred with the work's sardonic tone. In any case, New World Music published a mere five songs from the show: "Blue, Blue, Blue," "Let 'Em Eat Cake," "Mine," "On and On and On," and "Union Square." And of these, only "Mine" achieved some popularity, and then more as a novelty item—as in the 1944 Bing Crosby–Judy Garland recording—than as a popular standard (though over the years, the song also attracted jazz musicians, including clarinetist Buddy DeFranco, who in 1954 recorded a brilliant set of variations on the tune, with pianist Sonny Clark assuming the countermelody).

Gershwin generally enlarged the work's parodistic dimensions by canvassing a variety of musical styles, as evidenced by the pseudo-Handelian "Union League," the Savoyard-inspired "I Brushed My Teeth," the faux-operatic "All the Mothers of the Nation," the militantly marchlike "Let 'Em Eat Cake" (whose main motive recalls the "rat-a-tat-tat" of artillery), the Yiddish-inflected "No *Comprenez*," and the mock-maudlin "I Know a Foul Ball" (described by the composer as a "burlesque ballad"). The score evoked folk idioms as well: Jewish *freylekhs* ("Down with Everyone Who's Up"), children's ditties ("Shirts by Millions"), limericks ("There's Something We're Worried About"), Romanian dance music ("Throttle Throttlebottom"), and African American blues ("Hanging Throttlebottom in the Morning"). Placed especially in the context of the work's operatic features, these folklike allusions pointed ahead to Gershwin's next stage work, *Porgy and Bess.*

The music's textural richness complemented its formal daring and stylistic breadth. Gershwin had exploited some of the score's more elaborate contrapuntal techniques, such as the simultaneous juxtaposition of separate tunes or choruses, in earlier shows, but they appear here with unprecedented verve. The intricate "Tweedledee for President," for instance, puts forth two discrete choruses—the "Wintergreen for President" chorus that had opened *Of Thee I Sing* (including snippets of "Stars and Stripes Forever," "Tammany," "The Sidewalks of New York," "Hail, Hail the Gang's All Here," and "There'll Be a Hot Time in the Old Town Tonight") and a newly composed chorus for the Tweedledee supporters that includes bits of Dan Emmett's "Dixie" (1860), "The Battle Hymn of the Republic" (possibly by William Steffe, ca. 1855), the Philip Phile–Joseph Hopkinson patriotic song "Hail Columbia" (1798), and George M. Cohan's "Over There" (1917)—and then combines them, so that not only the distinct choruses but the various quotes clash, creating a kind of Ivesian soundscape.

The short choral prologue that opens "Who's the Greatest?" constitutes another novel achievement, one clearly influenced by Gershwin's work with Joseph Schillinger: the accompanying voices unfold augmentations and diminutions of the principal melody's basic rhythm. In its context here, the device, which might be called a rhythmic canon, suggests the uniformity of totalitarian thought, though Gershwin would make other uses of the technique in *Porgy and Bess.*

Gershwin placed the work's contrapuntal adventurousness in the context of its satirical intentions:

> I've written most of the music for this show contrapuntally, and it is that very insistence on the sharpness of a form that gives my music the acid touch it has—which paints the words of the lyrics, and is in keeping with the satire of the piece. At least, I feel it is the counterpoint which helps me do what I am trying to do. I know that it is only contrapuntal writing of the best sort which completely satisfies me in listening to music. I feel that Bach will still live when every one later than Bach has been centuries forgotten—because there is the logic and the wit and the solidity of scientific form in everything he wrote.

As for musical humor, Gershwin elaborated as follows:

> Humor in music is a peculiarly transient thing. It is the quality least seldom found in it. There have been musicians who could write amusingly, but we don't remember them for their comedy. The wit and humor of Mozart is not what we adore in his music. The comedy that Haydn could write into a score—even Beethoven's comedy we seldom give a thought to, except as throwing a touchingly human sidelight on the work of a master.
>
> We moderns like our humor, in music, as part of an expressed thought. It must 'go with words.' For that sort of thing I believe I have a special gift. My sense of humor seems to lie in that direction.

He further claimed that his humor ran "in channels" and that there were times when he was "just not funny at all," adding, "I daresay there is no one whose humor is all-extensive."[10]

The show's reception in New York was more mixed than in Boston. With the notable exception of the *Herald-Tribune*'s Percy Hammond, who thought the musical a "funnier, prettier and crueller conspiracy against Washington, D.C., than was its parent," the critics generally deemed it less successful—and certainly less fun—than *Of Thee I Sing*. Such comparisons made it difficult for reviewers to assess the show on its own terms, as John Mason Brown pointed out in the *Evening Post*: "[*Let 'Em Eat Cake*] is handicapped by its predecessor in much the same way that a bright enough boy is by being the son of a too brilliant father."[11]

Criticism focused mostly on the book, which many thought "strained" and "bitter." Later commentators would remember in particular Brooks Atkinson's remark in the *Times*—"Their [Kaufman and Ryskind's] hatreds have triumphed over their sense of humor"—but this sentiment proved widespread. Gilbert Gabriel in the *American*, for instance, observed a disturbing "nervousness" which, he thought, rarely touched "that note of relief, of relaxment, of untroubled glee, which even the most brilliantly wrathy travesty sometimes needs." The guillotine scene, though it provided welcome scope for Victor Moore's drollery, especially disturbed viewers, in part because Moore imbued his role with such winning pathos. "Torture in a musical comedy is out of place," pronounced *Stage*.

Although the *Commonweal*'s Richard Dana Skinner dismissed such charges of "bitterness" ("It is savage, if you like, in the manner of most of the effective satires of history. It is relentless in its exposure of sham and mediocrity and inconsistency and stupid sentimentality"), he voiced a more nuanced concern: "The real trouble with this sequel is that it directs its satire away from familiar facts to a Graustarkian myth of the future. Everything in 'Of Thee I Sing' smacked of familiar fact. The new play is all a game of 'let's suppose,' and thereby loses the tang of cartooned reality." A few other critics similarly considered an imaginary American dictatorship as extrinsic to the country's "temperament" *(Variety)* and "mind" *(Stage)*.

The reviews also expressed dissatisfaction with the music. As with the script, no one denied its technical mastery, but many found the score, with the exception of "Mine," tuneless, academic, and, in the words of *Billboard*'s Eugene Burr, "thin and attenuated in its self-conscious attempt to be modernistic, possessing the same hardness and sharp angles as modernistic furniture." The drama desks—which by custom reviewed musical comedies—had been struggling for some time to grasp Gershwin's music, but this latest score tipped the scales decisively, as a few critics themselves acknowledged. "For all I know," wrote John Anderson in the *Evening Journal,* "[the music] may be great stuff, but you can't wet a whistle with it, or take it out for dancing in the streets." The *Catholic World* wondered if "a musical critic should have been in our seat." And Gilbert Gabriel ventured the suspicion that Gershwin "dedicated it [the score] to his fellow composers rather than to the public." Such a response signaled the work's singular ambitions as well as Gershwin's general distinction among popular theater composers.

These caveats about the script and score notwithstanding, the show actually received, contrary to the received wisdom, rather good reviews. True, a few critics panned the show as "verbose, unfunny, unwieldy" *(Variety)* and "bitter, cheerless, annoying" *(New Outlook),* but most regarded it as highly entertaining, singling out for special praise the sets and costumes (which featured a wide palette of blues from cerulean to indigo), the choreography (which reminded one viewer of the German expressionist dancer Mary Wigman), the lyrics (widely thought to represent some of Ira's best work to date), and the cast (especially Victor Moore). As mentioned, Percy Hammond proved particularly enthusiastic about this "keen, wholesome and lovely" work, but the show also received high marks from such varied critics as Brooks Atkinson ("a first-rate job of music show-making"), Eugene Burr ("a definitely enjoyable and satirical tunefest that is far above the Broadway average"), Gilbert Gabriel ("a generously good time all told"), Joseph Wood Krutch ("vastly amusing"), and Richard Lockridge ("Few musical comedies you will see are better"). A few notices even looked forward to a third installment, perhaps a musical comedy about a Throttlebottom presidency.

And yet the word on the street quickly turned sour. On October 30 *Time* magazine exaggeratedly described the show's opening-night reception as marked by "an embarrassing dearth of applause. Critics and spectators went out grumbling that the nation's great musicomedy quadrivirate had lain down on the job, had served up a poorly warmed-over dish," including "tedious" lyrics that "often appear to be simply slovenly, lazy work." Hammond and Atkinson publicly refuted such "rumors," the latter reminding readers that the mood on opening night had been "festive" and that the work had come across as "bristling with wit and charged with immense vitality." (Irving Berlin was so impressed with the show that he traded Kaufman a percentage of *As Thousands Cheer* for a matching percentage of this new show—no doubt to his subsequent regret.) Hiram Motherwell, the editor of *Stage,* also rose to defend the score as "dramatic rather than lyric. It is endlessly imaginative in pointing up the action in the long, concerted numbers, and has much more right to be called operatic than have most of the America-made operas that have been composed for the Metropolitan." He even suggested that Leopold Stokowski program "Tweedledee for President" under the title *Fantasia Politica.* "Mr. Gershwin is a maker of music who knows the intricacies of musical science as well as most in America," concluded Motherwell, "and in addition has a robust joy in making it."[12]

But despite such advocacy, the show managed only ninety performances and a modest road tour, not enough to make it a commercial success, though respectable enough in light of its daring and originality. In his memoirs, Ryskind looked back at the show with some satisfaction: "from this effort I learned that that terrible malady of show business known as sequelitis can be overcome by bold and imaginative writing." Gershwin, for his part, thought the work to represent his "claim to legitimacy."[13]

Let 'Em Eat Cake in any case became a work more talked about than known, and by the time Warner Brothers and the Gershwin estate decided to resuscitate the score in the 1970s, not only the orchestrations but some of the piano score had been lost, including the number "Let 'Em Eat Caviar." Warner Brothers consequently asked arranger Don Rose to reconstruct portions of the score as well as to orchestrate the whole, which made possible a 1978 revival at the Berkshire Theatre Festival and a 1981 concert version at the University of Miami. Reviewing the underrehearsed Berkshire Theatre production for the *Village Voice,* Terry Curtis Fox nonetheless hailed the work as "a lost American masterpiece, with one of Gershwin's greatest scores."[14]

Meanwhile, scholarly opinion proved none too encouraging. Kaufman biographers Howard Teichmann (1972), Scott Meredith (1974), and Malcolm Goldstein (1979), for instance, took a dim view of the piece. Teichmann thought the story "complex and confusing" and the satire "undisciplined and bitter," while Goldstein opined that Gershwin's music "offered relatively minor support" to a script whose "failure of invention" was "noticeable on every page of the printed text." In a particularly exhaustive study of the work (1985), musicologist Wayne Schneider more pointedly criticized the score for its "rambling" and "banal" melodies, "studied" and "vapid" recitatives, "bland" reminiscences of Gilbert and Sullivan, and "seeming lack of creative zest." Schneider further argued that Gershwin sacrificed the architectural coherence of traditional musical comedy without achieving the cohesiveness of operatic discourse.[15]

In the late 1980s John McGlinn, assisted by Kay Swift, prepared a new piano-vocal score that initiated a new era in the work's history. (Swift, who thought the score "much the best music Gershwin wrote right up to 'Porgy and Bess'" and "definitely ahead of its time," reconstructed from memory "Comes the Revolution" and created new versions of "The Union League" and "First Lady and First Gent" based on surviving lead sheets.) As orchestrated by Russell Warner, the McGlinn edition was unveiled in a staged reading (on a double bill with *Of Thee I Sing*) at the Brooklyn Academy of Music on March 18, 1987, with Larry Kert (Wintergreen), Maureen McGovern (Mary), and Jack Gilford (Throttlebottom) under the baton of Michael Tilson Thomas, who declared on the occasion, "'Let 'Em Eat Cake' has operatic dimensions. . . . The score is so deep and rich that it is impossible to comprehend fully with just one hearing."[16]

A few reviewers, like Clive Barnes of the *New York Post*, seemed decidedly underwhelmed, but this Brooklyn Academy performance, which provided the basis for a CBS recording the same year, greatly enhanced the work's reputation. "If any American made greater strides than George Gershwin did between writing 'Of Thee I Sing' in 1931 and 'Let 'Em Eat Cake,' its sequel in 1933," wrote Howard Kissel in the *Daily News*, "it could only have been George Gershwin between 'Let 'Em Eat Cake' and 'Porgy and Bess' a mere two years later." Writing for *Ovation*, David Patrick Stearns thought that the music's "lean, pungent style" revealed "Gershwin at his most progressive," with some of the "through-composed scenes" pointing "straight ahead to Bernstein and Sondheim." And reviewing a similar concert presentation of these two Gershwin shows in June 2005 (with Stephen Bogardus and Lisa Vroman as John and Mary, and Michael Tilson Thomas leading the San Francisco Symphony), Joshua Kosman of the *San Francisco Chronicle* deemed *Let 'Em Eat Cake* "a darker and far more interesting concoction" than its Pulitzer Prize–winning predecessor.[17]

Let 'Em Eat Cake remains one of Gershwin's most underappreciated works, nonetheless, for the description of the piece as a "flop" that "alienated audiences" pays too much attention to a few negative remarks and the show's disappointing run. Granted, the show lost money and unnerved some viewers, but many critics regarded it as a brilliantly crafted entertainment, a worthy successor to *Of Thee I Sing*, and a step forward in the direction of a vital national opera. The time seems ripe for a reappraisal of the show, one that might also explore ways in which the work anticipated not only *Porgy and Bess* but the musical-theater pieces composed later in the decade by Marc Blitzstein and others.[18]

To celebrate the tenth anniversary of the *Rhapsody in Blue,* Gershwin and Harry Askins, the theater manager who had introduced him to Max Dreyfus in 1917, launched an extensive 1934 road tour featuring the composer and the Leo Reisman Orchestra performing not only the *Rhapsody* but a new work composed specifically for the occasion, the *Variations on "I Got Rhythm"* for piano and orchestra.

Like Whiteman, Leo Reisman (1897–1961) was classically trained—he had studied violin at the New England Conservatory—and early in life juggled careers as an orchestral musician (he joined the Baltimore Symphony Orchestra at age eighteen) and a bandleader (he typically led bands with his violin in hand, though sometimes from the piano). Based in the 1920s at the Hotel Brunswick in his native Boston and in the 1930s at the Central Park Casino and the Waldorf-Astoria in New York, the Reisman Orchestra emerged as one of the premier tea-dance orchestras of the time, widely admired for its sophistication and refinement.

Reisman's bands varied in size from small combos to ensembles exceeding thirty pieces, with musicians including such notables as white trumpeter Max Kaminsky and black trumpeters Johnny Dunn and Bubber Miley; pianists Nat Brandwynne and Eddy Duchin; and vocalists Harold Arlen and Lee Wiley. For the Gershwin tour, Reisman assembled a pickup group of about thirty-five players—billed as the Reisman Symphonic Orchestra—whose makeup can be more or less deduced by the instrumentation of the *Variations:* flute (doubling on piccolo), oboe (doubling on English horn), bassoon, two alto saxophones (both doubling on clarinet), tenor saxophone (doubling on clarinet), baritone saxophone (doubling on bass clarinet), three horns, three trumpets, two trombones, tuba, percussion, piano, and strings. Notwithstanding the presence of saxophones, this particular ensemble resembled something closer to a conventional chamber orchestra than, say, the Whiteman band that had introduced the *Rhapsody,* though it was still understaffed for presenting such works on the touring program as the Concerto in F and *An American in Paris.*

Gershwin composed the *Variations* mostly while in Florida in December 1933, and he completed the orchestration in New York on January 6, 1934, a week before its premiere. Dedicated to Ira, the work is light even by Gershwin's standards, a nine-minute occasional piece for a touring society band, but not without its many points of interest.

Although Gershwin referred to the initial presentation of the tune as the first variation and the last variation as the finale, one might more conventionally describe the work as containing the "I Got Rhythm" theme (that is, its *aaba* chorus) and six variations, framed by an introduction and a coda. The introduction largely explores the tune's principal four-note motive (which generates the song as a whole), followed by a "Moderato" statement of the theme proper by the solo piano in a version—described by Gershwin as "simple"—reminiscent of its *Song-Book* arrangement.[19]

The first variation, also "Moderato," puts forth the theme primarily in the orchestra against a chromatic perpetual motion in the piano that forms, in Gershwin's words, "a very complicated rhythmic pattern." The second variation, "Allegretto"—a slow waltz that pits the tune in long notes against sighing figuration—recalls Jean Sibelius's popular *Valse Triste* (1903) as well as Gershwin's own "Across the Sea" ("Valse lente") from the 1922 *Scandals.* The next variation, "Allegretto giocoso," attempts to "imitate Chinese flutes played out of tune, as they always are" by way of some passages in which the pianist's right hand plays only the white keys and the left hand, only the black.[20]

The fourth variation, "Andantino," alternates sedate pandiatonic (or, as Gershwin writes, "modal") passages with sections "in Jazz style," thereby compressing to a nutshell a duality that informs *An American in Paris.* The fifth variation, "Allegro"—described by the composer as "hot"—features a basso ostinato derived from the theme's principal four-note motive, which also appears in the piano part in simultaneous contrary motion, "on the theory," remarked Gershwin, "you shouldn't let one hand know what the other hand is doing." The final variation, "Allegro," continues this "hot" mood, including similar use of contrary motion in the piano part at the fortissimo climax ("resoluto"). A brief coda, "Maestoso moderato," containing chiming quartal sonorities in the piano, brings the whole to a spirited close.

Although none of the variations exactly duplicates the original theme's thirty-four-bar design, they generally conform to its *aaba* shape, with the notable exception of the waltzlike "Allegretto," which seems forged out of two expanded versions of the final *a* phrase. The Chinese variation, for its part, ingeniously expands the first *a* phrase to the point that the second *a* phrase sounds like the possible start of a new variation. Similarly, the fifth variation eschews the final *a* phrase in order to elide more smoothly into the final variation and thus propel the work toward its conclusion. With their differences in mood, tempo, and key, these variations might be described as character variations, though the theme and first variation form a block, as do the last two variations, thus providing some archlike symmetry. The work overall reveals an impressive tautness, and any assessment of Gershwin's formal abilities would benefit from some consideration of this little-known piece.

The variations themselves, meanwhile, are picturesque in ways familiar to Gershwin, to the point of suggesting the projected New York "melting-pot" piece he spoke about during these years; for on a certain level the work seems a Gershwinesque reading of the industrial metropolis (first variation), "young girls sitting on fire escapes on hot summer nights in New York and dreaming of love" (second variation), Chinatown (third variation), Harlem (fourth variation), and some after-hours club, perhaps with a Cuban band (fifth and sixth variations).[21]

At the same time, the music reveals a distinctly abstruse side related to the composer's studies with Joseph Schillinger. Only numerical diagrams can clearly explain, for instance, the mathematical manipulations represented in just the first eight measures, described by Steven Gilbert as involving "the successive expansion of a motive by successively larger coefficients," in this case, an "expansion" that "successively multiplies the note-to-note intervals of the 'I Got Rhythm' motive by coefficients of 1, 2, and 3 in the original rhythm, then by 5, 3, 2, and 1 in even sixteenths." The rest of the work makes similarly imaginative use of the tune's main four-note motive as a source for harmony, figuration, canon, and so forth, with the resultant interplay between the picturesque and the abstract adding to the music's charm.[22]

Prior to the start of the road tour, Reisman broke his hip in a car accident, and Charles Previn stepped in to take over. An established conductor of Broadway shows (including Gershwin's *La-La-Lucille!* and *Of Thee I Sing*), Previn (1888–1973) would spend much of his later career in Hollywood, where he headed the music department at Universal Pictures from 1936 to 1944, winning an Oscar in 1937 for *One Hundred Men and a Girl.* The touring musicians, meanwhile, included the accomplished jazz clarinetist and alto saxophonist Benny Kanter; oboist Mitch Miller, eventually a well-known conductor in his own right; and string players who later had esteemed careers as orchestral musicians, including violinists John Corigliano Sr. and Harry Glickman and cellist Harry Fuchs. One review noted the general prominence of Jewish and Italian names among the band members.

The tour also featured Georgia-born tenor James Melton (1904–1961), who in 1927 joined the Revelers (a popular vocal group admired by Gershwin) and who enjoyed success as a soloist on the radio and in pictures as well. A handsome man with an ingratiating stage presence, Melton had a relatively small but lovely voice, and in subsequent years, while maintaining his career as a popular recitalist, he distinguished himself on the operatic stage, making his 1942 debut at the Metropolitan Opera as Tamino in *The Magic Flute* under the baton of Bruno Walter.

The touring program varied only slightly from city to city. The first half included the Concerto in F, a set of Gershwin show tunes for the orchestra, a set of western songs for Melton (Oscar J. Fox's "Hills of Home," David Guion's "Home on the Range," Carson Robison's "Carry Me Back to the Lone Prairie," and as an encore Billy Hill's "The Last Round-Up"), and the *Rhapsody in Blue.* After intermission came *An American in Paris,* a set of southern songs for Melton ("Sometimes I Feel Like a Motherless Child," arranged by Frank Black; Jacques Wolfe's "Gwine to Heb'n" and "Short'nin' Bread"; and as an encore Lily Strickland's "Mah Lindy Lou"), the *Variations,* a set of Gershwin show tunes for piano and orchestra, and as an encore some additional Gershwin songs performed by Melton with the composer at the piano. Gershwin also played the piano in the Concerto in F, the *Rhapsody,* the *Variations,* and the second set of show tunes, while pianist Edward Horne accompanied Melton in the other song sets.

Gershwin no doubt countenanced the western and southern folk or folklike numbers partly in response to an itinerary that took the band as far west as Sioux Falls and Omaha and as far south as St. Louis and Louisville. But their inclusion also bespoke shifting artistic trends, as reflected by Gershwin's own comments about the "best music" of the day coming from "folk-sources." These western and southern songs—

and their performance by Melton—presumably bore some relation to Gershwin's work in progress, the "folk opera" *Porgy and Bess* (some of whose numbers Melton would later record).[23]

Starting at Boston's Symphony Hall on January 13 and ending at the Brooklyn Academy of Music on February 10, Gershwin and the orchestra performed in twenty-eight cities in the course of twenty-nine days, covering enormous ground over the country's northeastern quadrant: after Boston, they trekked through New England and upstate New York to Toronto, farther west through Michigan, Illinois, Wisconsin, Minnesota, and South Dakota, and southward through Iowa and Missouri before turning east again through Indiana, Kentucky, Ohio, Pennsylvania, Washington, D.C., and Virginia, and returning to New York. The band traveled by train—"like a circus train," recalled Mitch Miller—at least a few hours every day, though sometimes all day; for especially long distances, they left town after a concert and boarded a sleeper. Gershwin's valet Paul Mueller joined the tour in order to look after the musical instruments as well as to give the composer a daily massage and keep his many female fans at bay. Miller recalled that Gershwin "was always sweet" and "never raised his voice," but "did not fraternize with the musicians" and was hard to read: "Gershwin had a poker face. It was impossible to judge his reactions. He never looked exultant or distressed."[24]

The band played mostly at large civic auditoriums (though in Syracuse, Madison, and Omaha they performed at local high schools), and generally attracted large crowds, some even sold out (Serge Rakhmaninov, who completed his own variations for piano and orchestra later in the year—the *Variations on a Theme of Paganini*—attended the Detroit performance). One paper declared the tour "a financial success" and hinted at a one-week run on Broadway; but according to later sources, the tour actually lost money, leaving Gershwin five thousand dollars in the red. Gershwin blamed the deficit on too many bookings in smaller towns, but for all that he declared the tour a "fine artistic success" and "an arduous and exciting trip" that left "many pleasant memories of Cities I had not visited before."[25]

The tour garnered excellent notices. Reviewing the Sunday matinee kickoff at Boston's Symphony Hall, one paper suggested that if the performances lacked something of the "finesse" of Arthur Fiedler and the Boston Pops, "It is likely that Mr. Gershwin's larger pieces have never been played with more elan than . . . under Mr. Previn's vigilant and energetic direction." The Toronto reviews were particularly appreciative. "Beauty there certainly is," wrote Lawrence Mason in the *Toronto Globe*, "and novelty, and modernity, and revolt from restraint, and aggressive individuality, and bacchanalian banishment of care." "Gershwin's music had two vital elements of art—truth and intelligence," commented Pearl McCarthy in the *Toronto Mail.* "Besides that, it was great fun." Previn, who conducted without a baton, won acclaim for his "hypnotic hands," and Melton, for his "glorious" if somewhat "colorless" voice. Gershwin's accompaniment of Melton drew special praise: "You do not often hear such perfect rapport between composer and interpreter in consonance," wrote one Milwaukee paper.[26]

Although the concert program specified the *Variations* as "new," surprisingly few reviews took any special note of the work. One Kansas City review even erroneously reported that those who attended the concert to see "whether he [Gershwin] had anything new to say . . . were somewhat disappointed, we suspect, when the program failed to include anything later than his tone poem, 'An American in Paris.'" But a few discriminating critics—including Herbert Elwell in the *Cleveland Plain Dealer* and Clarence Boykin in the *Richmond Times-Dispatch*—actually expressed a special preference for the *Variations,* which Elwell rated second only to the *Rhapsody,* "for it displays," he wrote, "great ingenuity in saying the same thing in different ways." Boykin thought, too, that the *Variations* "revealed the most notable of the Gershwinisms—'hot' rhythm in lavish display, minor chords on brilliant parade, leaping tempo in the manner of the revues," while another review remarked that the work "employed some variations that did not occur to Mozart or Beethoven."

New World Music initially published only a two-piano reduction of the work, and then, after Gershwin's death, a highly doctored full score for a more conventional symphony orchestra—this one "revised" by William C. Schoenfeld under the supervision of the inevitable Frank Campbell-Watson, who argued, "To the purists, let it be pointed out that an insistence on the original instrumental scheme would, aside from woefully stifling performance value, result in an archaic audition totally at variance with the stature of the music involved."[27]

Schoenfeld did more than just reorchestrate the piece, however. He added such phrases as "not too strictly in tempo" and "with metronomic precision," changed tempo and metronome markings, and altered articulation signs and instrumental effects. In the waltz variation, for instance, he ill-advisedly dispensed with the pizzicati that initiate the string glissandi. Charles Schwartz's claim that the published score closely followed Gershwin's intentions consequently threw his assessment of the music as "extremely shallow" into question. On the other hand, Edward Jablonski's assertion that the Schoenfeld edition "smothered" the music's "wit and charm" may have overstated the matter.[28]

A number of distinguished pianists performed and recorded the *Variations* over the years. Gershwin himself played a slightly abridged version with characteristic finesse on his radio show on April 30, 1934, with a studio orchestra presumably under the direction of Louis Katzman. Recordings of full-orchestra versions, meanwhile, included those by pianists Michael Boriskin with Jonathan Sheffer, Morton Gould with Artur Rodzinski, Werner Haas with Edo de Waart, Oscar Levant with Morton Gould, Alan Marks with Hans-Dieter Baum, Wayne Marshall (conducting from the keyboard), David Parkhouse with Bernard Herrmann, Leonard Pennario with Alfred Newman, Howard Shelley with Yan Pascal Tortelier, Jeffrey Siegel with Leonard Slatkin, David Syme with Herrera de la Fuente, William Tritt with Erich Kunzel, Alexis Weissenberg with Seiji Ozawa, and Earl Wild with Arthur Fiedler, the last a performance of particular vitality. Pancho Vladigerov (1899–1978), the preeminent Bulgarian composer of his time, also conducted the piece with pianist Teodor Moussov on a release that featured Gershwin's two rhapsodies as well.

In 1995 jazz pianist Marcus Roberts (b. 1963), blind since childhood, recorded his own version of the work with members of the Orchestra of St. Luke's and the Lincoln Center Jazz Orchestra under Robert Sadin. Like his interpretations of the *Rhapsody in Blue* and James P. Johnson's *Yamekraw* on the same release, Roberts intriguingly alternated excerpts from the original (often rescored and embellished) with freely improvised passages. "I wanted to create a modern dialogue with the entire history of American jazz piano," wrote Roberts in his liner notes, thereby explaining the music's allusions to Thelonious Monk and Erroll Garner.[29]

Meanwhile, Morton Gould wrote his own variations, *I Got Rhythm*, for an ensemble similar to that used by Gershwin, though without a featured soloist; and William David Brohn composed both an arrangement of the tune—also entitled *I Got Rhythm* (1997)—for violinist Joshua Bell and a more conventional symphony orchestra, and a longer set of variations, *I Got Variations* (1999), for the Verdehr Trio (violin, clarinet, piano)—a piece framed with references to Gershwin's *Variations*. However, even as Warner Brothers released facsimile editions of most of Gershwin's other major instrumental scores, and conductors championed the original versions of the two rhapsodies, the *Variations*, in its intended guise for piano and symphonic dance band, remained largely unknown and unavailable.

Chapter Thirty-One

Porgy and Bess (1935)

*A*sked about his ambitions in 1920, Gershwin stated, "Operettas that represent the life and spirit of this country are decidedly my aim. After that may come opera, but I want all my work to have the one element of appealing to the great majority of our people." He subsequently wrote a short one-act opera, *Blue Monday Blues*, for the *Scandals* in 1922, as discussed earlier, but as interest in "jazz opera"—understood at the time as precisely the sort of thing he might write—quickened in the mid-1920s, expectations for a full-fledged opera intensified accordingly.[1]

Discussing jazz opera himself in the spring of 1925, Gershwin declared the "home life" American "school of drama" too "drab and dull" for something so potentially rhythmic and lyrical:

> I think it [jazz opera] should be a Negro opera, almost a Negro 'Scheherazade.' Negro, because it is not incongruous for a Negro to live jazz. It would not be absurd on the stage. The mood could change from ecstasy to lyricism plausibly because the Negro has so much of both in his nature. The book, I think, should be an imaginative, whimsical thing, like a Carl Van Vechten story; and I would like to see him write the libretto.
>
> That type of opera could not, I am afraid, be done at the Metropolitan [Opera]. It is a typically opéra comique venture. I would like to see it open an opéra comique on Broadway. I would like to see it put on with a Negro cast. Artists trained in the old tradition could not sing such music, but Negro singers could. It would be a sensation as well as an innovation.

Gershwin acknowledged that John Howard Lawson's recent satire, *Processional: A Jazz Symphony of American Life* (1925), had made effective use of popular music, but he contended nonetheless that jazz opera would benefit from "a more picturesque and a less topical libretto."[2]

Throughout the remainder of 1925, Gershwin occasionally voiced his intention of writing an opera for African American singers, adding that Carl Van Vechten was helping him find a "suitable libretto." "I shall certainly write an opera," he stated in the fall. "I shall write it for niggers. Blacks sing beautifully. They are always singing; they have it in their blood. They have jazz in their blood, too, and I have no doubt that they will be able to do full justice to a jazz opera. . . . I do not think there will be undue difficulty about finding principals for the solo parts. There will probably also be a nigger orchestra." Gershwin realized that audiences might not care for such "new forms of jazz composition," arguing, "The ear does not take readily to new sounds, yet wonderful progress has been made in the last hundred years. Stravinsky seems weird to some people to-day, but the time may come when Stravinsky will be regarded as out of date."[3]

In the summer of 1926 Gershwin read, allegedly in one spellbound sitting, a book given to him by Lou and Emily Paley, namely, DuBose Heyward's 1925 novel, *Porgy*, and contacted the author about adapting it as an opera. A tale of black Charlestonians at the turn of the century with, as Gershwin later noted, "dramatic intensity in addition to humor," the book clearly met his requirements for an operatic story as outlined above. When Gershwin and Heyward, busy with tryouts (for *Strike Up the Band* and the stage version of *Porgy*, respectively), found themselves in Atlantic City in November 1927, they met to discuss the idea. "My first impression of my collaborator," Heyward later wrote, "remains with me and is singularly vivid. A young man of enormous physical and emotional vitality, who possessed the faculty of seeing himself quite impersonally and realistically, and who knew exactly what he wanted and where he was going. This characteristic put him beyond both modesty and conceit. About himself he would merely mention certain facts, aspirations, failings. They were usually right."[4]

Gershwin decided to defer a possible collaboration to some later date, for among other things, he wanted to study more before undertaking an opera. Meanwhile, the vogue for jazz opera ran its course, and by the time Gershwin was commissioned to write an opera for the Met in 1929, he opted to adapt Szymon Ansky's *The Dybbuk*. But he remained in touch with Heyward, and in March 1932, after *The Dybbuk* fell through because Gershwin had been unable to acquire the rights, the two finally resolved to adapt *Porgy*. The project, which could now be considered as much a "folk" as a "jazz" opera, occupied both men for about two years, from the fall of 1933 to its Broadway premiere as *Porgy and Bess* on October 10, 1935.

Edwin DuBose Heyward (1885–1940) was born in Charleston into an old southern family of English and French descent; one colonial ancestor, Thomas Heyward, had signed the Declaration of Independence, while the name DuBose pointed to his Huguenot ancestry. While he was still a toddler, his father died in a mill accident, and he grew up in an impoverished home, leaving school at age fourteen (even earlier than Gershwin) to take a series of odd jobs, some of which, including cotton checker for a shipping company, put him in close contact with black workers. During these adolescent years, he suffered bouts of polio, typhoid, and pleurisy, and he grew intrigued with the seeming contrast between the healthy vitality of Charleston's black population and not only his own frail constitution, including an upper torso permanently weakened by polio, but the cultural sterility of the town's white residents.[5]

By 1908 Heyward had established himself successfully in the insurance and real-estate business, but he pursued literature as a sideline, writing poems, plays, and short stories somewhat comparable to those of Jack London and Bret Harte. Meanwhile, his mother Jane pursued her own career as a folklorist specializing in Gullah ("Geechee"), the indigenous African American culture of coastal South Carolina and Georgia (the word *Gullah* represented a possible corruption of Angola or the west African tribe the Gola). Under the influence of his mother and such local writers as John Bennett and Hervey Allen, Heyward began exploring regional themes and dialects himself, while the Poetry Society of South Carolina, which he cofounded in 1920, and summers at the MacDowell Colony in the early 1920s helped introduce him to wider currents. His emerging poetry marked him as a kind of Edwin Arlington Robinson of the Carolinas.

At the MacDowell Colony, Heyward met Ohio-born playwright Dorothy Hartzell Kuhns (1890–1961), whom he married in 1923 and who persuaded him to devote himself full-time to writing. He attained nationwide fame with the 1925 publication of his first novel, *Porgy;* written in a unique style that combined standard English for the narration and Gullah mixed with other African American dialects for the dialogue, the book won kudos for its unusually sympathetic and vivid portrayal of a black community, even by black readers who, better than many white critics, could gauge its shortcomings. Heyward, who with Dorothy later adapted *Porgy* for the stage, continued to write other novels and plays, but these proved less memorable, and he died primarily known as the author of *Porgy* in its various guises, especially the opera.

Heyward took his seminal inspiration for *Porgy* from a lame black beggar and vendor of peanut cakes, Samuel Smalls (known in Charleston as "Goat Sammy"), who transported himself by way of an inverted soapbox pulled by a goat, and who, Heyward learned to his surprise, had been held on two aggravated assault charges for attempting to shoot a woman. Struck by the dichotomy between the "crushed, serio-comic figure" and the "tremendous moments" of "passion, hate, despair" implied by his criminal record, Heyward re-created Smalls as the novel's protagonist—initially called Porgo, apparently after an African wooden doll that figured in one of his mother's Gullah stories, but just before publication renamed Porgy, allegedly after the local fish. (Heyward surely knew the fishmonger cry "Porgy in the Summer-time," as found in Harriette Kershaw Leiding's 1910 pamphlet on Charleston street cries, though he probably had in mind as well Captain Porgy, the protagonist of Charleston author William Gilmore Simms's popular 1854 novel, *Woodcraft.*) For the book's setting, Heyward essentially superimposed a three-story brick tenement populated by blacks, Cabbage Row (so called because of the vegetables sold there), located near his Charleston home, onto the city's waterfront to create the fictional Catfish Row.[6]

Porgy, the novel, takes place in the early twentieth century over a seven-month period from April through October. Porgy, a crippled beggar living in Catfish Row, relies on his friend Peter to get around. Other residents of the row include Robbins and his devoutly Christian wife, Serena; Maria, the tough proprietess of the tenement's cookshop; and a fisherman, Jake, his wife, Clara, and their infant boy. During a game of craps, the muscular stevedore Crown kills Robbins in a brawl and escapes to Kittiwar Island (in the play and opera, Kittiwah; officially, Kiawah). Peter gets sent to jail as a witness to the murder, and Porgy by necessity acquires a goat cart. Crown's lover, Bess, appears, gaunt, drunk, and famished, and takes refuge with Porgy. The octoroon dandy Sporting Life, a cocaine peddler who has worked as a waiter in New York, arrives on the scene as well.

White attorney Alan Archdale helps secure Peter's release and protects a black lawyer, Simon Frasier, from indictment for fraud for granting illegal divorces. Lured into taking cocaine from Sporting Life, Bess is incarcerated for disturbing the peace; on her release she falls ill, but recovers. At a picnic on Kittiwar Island, Crown waylays and seduces Bess. Jake perishes in a hurricane, as does Clara, who leaves her baby with Bess. When Crown breaks into Porgy's room at night in pursuit of Bess, Porgy kills him. Summoned by the coroner to identify Crown's body, a frightened Porgy refuses and is put in jail for contempt of court. Returning to Catfish Row, Porgy learns from Maria that in his absence, a gang of stevedores has abducted Bess, and that Serena has taken custody of Clara's child. In the "hard, satirical radiance" and "irony" of the "morning sunlight," Maria sees that Porgy has turned old: "The early tension that had characterized him, the mellow mood that he had known for one eventful summer, both had gone."[7]

The aspect of the novel that initially earned the most praise—its portrayal of Charleston's blacks—became over time its most controversial feature. For although Heyward overcame the cruder stereotypes associated with literary depictions of blacks, the book nonetheless presented the residents of Catfish Row as noble primitives in some ways superior to but still fundamentally different from the white members of the community. This perspective took more explicit expression in such essays by the author as "And Once Again—the Negro" (1923) and "The Negro in the Low-Country" (1931). The former piece, for instance, held premarital cohabitation and the retention of a woman's maiden name after marriage as enviable aspects of black social life—as well as of white bohemia (Heyward's interest in such unconventional living arrangements emerged in Porgy by way of the Lawyer Frasier episode). "Are they an aeon behind," he asked, "or an aeon ahead of us?" The 1931 article took a similarly romantic view regarding African American traditions to the point of waxing nostalgic over the "beautiful and tender and enriching" relationships "that existed between master and servant" in the antebellum period (a sentiment that underscored the Archdale-Peter relationship in Porgy); though threatened by mass immigration to the cities and the accompanying forces of modernity, this culture (viewed by Heyward as particularly American, because ties with the African homeland had been so torn asunder) could still be heard in the black music of the Low Country: "We can still hear the Negro singing the songs of his own creation. We can see him hale, vigorous, and glad under the sun by day, and at night surrounded by wide, still fields and moon-drenched marshes. We watch him with his family, his unquestioning belief in a personal God, his spontaneous abandonment to emotion, his faith in his simple destiny."[8]

Notwithstanding all this, Porgy presumed that such cultural differences were not only atavistic but imposed by a cruel system that needed little excuse for, say, incarcerating a helpless Peter. As such, the book's reputation as socially uncritical warrants reconsideration. Relatedly, the author's implied approval of Porgy's murderous act seems more understandable in light not only of Crown's violent history but of the town's capricious and racist judicial system.

Meanwhile, the novel's similarities to *Blue Monday Blues* help explain Gershwin's receptivity: both were melodramatic tales, told with humor and pathos, about a black underclass; Porgy, Bess, Crown, Maria, and Sporting Life could even be seen as not-too-distant southern cousins to Joe, Vi, Tom, Mike, and Cokey-Lou. Gershwin must have appreciated as well the prominent role that music played in the novel, with its dirges, chants, spirituals, lullabies, and chanteys. Heyward himself spoke of the story's preoccupation with "rhythm," a word that appears frequently in the novel, and a phenomenon that the author, in his introduction to the story's stage adaptation, referred to as "the secret law" of black culture.[9]

In 1926 Dorothy Heyward, with some assistance from her husband, adapted *Porgy* for the stage, a version mounted the following year by New York's Theatre Guild, which would eventually produce the opera as well. An outgrowth of the Washington Square Players (founded 1915), the Theatre Guild was established in 1919 to promote serious and sometimes experimental plays. According to Walter Pritchard Evans's early history of the company (1929), the guild prided itself on its "intellectual appeal" but remained determined to "pay its own way" in order to assure "vital touch with the public." Run by a board of six directors (referred to by Evans as a "revolutionary theatrical soviet"), the guild produced in the course of the 1920s on average six plays a year, including the work of such Europeans as Ferenc Molnár, Luigi Pirandello, and its "patron saint," G. B. Shaw, as well as such Americans as S. N. Behrman, Sidney Howard, and Eugene O'Neill. By the time *Porgy* opened the company's tenth season on October 1, 1927, the guild, from modest beginnings, could boast a core group of distinguished actors (including Lynn Fontanne, Alfred Lunt, and Edward G. Robinson); a subscriber base of more than twenty-five thousand, and a similar number of subscribers in six other cities; and concurrent productions in various theaters, including its own Guild Theatre (now the Virginia Theatre), a 914-seat space on West 52nd Street that opened its doors in April 1925.[10]

Porgy proved one of the guild's greatest successes of the 1920s, garnering 217 performances on Broadway, another 137 performances on a return engagement in 1928 following a national tour, and a successful London run in 1929. Set designer Cleon Throckmorton's slightly askew replica of a Charleston tenement brought down the house; and director Rouben Mamoulian (1898–1987)—an Armenian American immigrant from Tbilisi, Georgia, who had studied with Konstantin Stanislavsky and Eugene Vakhtangov in Moscow and was best known at this point for his opera productions (1923–1925) at Rochester's Eastman Theater—

thrilled audiences with those innovative and carefully choreographed stage movements and lighting and sound effects that would come to distinguish his work in Hollywood. Preeminent Austrian director Max Reinhardt, in New York at the time, declared the production one of his "great experiences in the theatre."[11]

Equally impressive and historically important besides was its mostly black cast of sixty-six, including twenty-two principals. No American play had ever offered such a prestigious venue for so many black actors and singers. "In *Porgy*," wrote James Weldon Johnson in his classic study *Black Manhattan* (1930), "the Negro performer removed all doubts as to his ability to do acting that requires thoughtful interpretation and intelligent skill. Here was more than the achievement of one or two individuals who might be set down as exceptions. Here was a large company giving a first-rate, even performance, with eight or ten reaching a high mark."[12]

The play placed the action in the present as opposed to the early twentieth century, and conflated and rearranged some of the book's episodes, but overall hewed closely to the original, differing most notably in its ending: instead of being abducted, Bess departs Charleston for New York, followed by Porgy in his goat cart, a still rather pathetic though more optimistic conclusion. The Heywards also more extensively dramatized some of the characters—they shaped Bess, for instance, into a more conflicted figure, and Sporting (now Sportin') Life into a more conniving one—and introduced some comic relief through Lawyer Frasier (now Frazier) and the new character of Lily Holmes, Peter's wife. The play was more prosaic than the novel—the Heywards watered down the dialect in the interest of comprehensibility—but the production compensated by way of improvised bits by some of the actors, as well as through vibrant color, movement, and music, including the featured participation of the Jenkins Orphanage Band from Charleston. "The play carried conviction through its sincere simplicity," Johnson wrote. "But it did not run along on a monotonous level; at times it rose to heights of ecstasy and tragedy; and always it was suffused with Negro humour."[13]

This dramatic adaptation, which Gershwin thought "the most outstanding play that I know, about the colored people," confirmed his feelings about the material's potential as an opera; and in March 1932, as mentioned, he contacted Heyward about going forward with an operatic version. After his experience with *The Dybbuk,* he understandably inquired immediately about the "operatic rights," and on learning in May that they were "free and clear," planned several rereadings of the book over the summer "to see what ideas I can evolve as to how it should be done."[14]

Gershwin proposed no definite timetable, however, and in September 1932 Heyward, increasingly eager to get started, notified him that Al Jolson, who had played Porgy in a radio adaptation of the play and who had acquired the story's motion-picture rights as well, was now interested in starring in a musical *Porgy*. Feeling the pinch of the Depression, Heyward wondered whether Gershwin would consider working with Jolson, or else allow such a project to proceed independently. Gershwin wrote back, "The sort of thing that I should have in mind for *Porgy* is a much more serious thing than Jolson could ever do." But he refused to stand in the way of a Jolson *Porgy*, in part because he realized that Heyward needed the money and that an opera would take time. "Of course," he explained, "I would not attempt to write music to your play until I had all the themes and musical devices worked out for such an undertaking. It would be more a labor of love than anything." Responded Heyward, "Please let me tell you that I think your attitude in this matter is simply splendid. It makes me all the more eager to work with you some day, some time, before we wake up and find ourselves in our dotage." (The Jolson proposal came to naught, perhaps because Jerome Kern and Oscar Hammerstein, with whom the singer hoped to collaborate, had moved on to other projects.)[15]

Gershwin at least could inform Heyward that Herman Shumlin (at the start of his notable career) had expressed interest in producing the work. About this time, Otto Kahn also offered to mount it at the Met, even offering Gershwin a five-thousand-dollar bonus for the privilege. "George was of course greatly flattered and did consider it for a time," recalled Ira, "but finally felt that for the Met to acquire an all-Negro cast to be available six to eight performances a season, was not too practical a project." In October 1933 Gershwin and Heyward at last signed with the Theatre Guild, thanks to the exertions of the company's business manager, Warren Munsell, described by guild executive Theresa Helburn as "a staff of strength, a good businessman, and the most serene and understanding of colleagues. He was also a first-class fighter." Munsell's business savvy no doubt helped overcome widespread reservations, for notwithstanding three editions of *The Garrick Gaieties*, the guild—which initially hoped to present the work in its 1934–1935 season—had never undertaken anything as ambitious or expensive as an opera. Then again, the guild had little idea of how ambitious and expensive this work would actually prove.[16]

Although Gershwin had hoped to begin serious work on the opera in 1933—and met with Heyward a few times in New York in the course of the year toward that end—progress proved, especially from Heyward's perspective, painfully slow. Even after the October 1933 premiere of *Let 'Em Eat Cake* and the receipt of the libretto's first scene the following month, Gershwin wrote to Heyward, as he had some eighteen months earlier, "I want to do a great deal of thinking about the thing and the gathering in of thematic material before the actual writing begins." By late December he had made progress with the first scene; but by this time he also had the distraction of an upcoming tour with the Leo Reisman band, including the commission of a new work for piano and orchestra, which made it difficult for him to give much attention to the piece until the tour ended on February 10, 1934. From that date until its October 1935 premiere, however, he devoted nearly all of his time to the opera, notwithstanding his hosting a 1934 radio show that helped sustain him financially (Gershwin would say that were it not for the show's sponsor, a chewing-gum laxative called Feen-a-Mint, he could not have written the opera). "I am skipping around—writing a bit here and a bit there," Gershwin wrote Heyward on March 8, 1934. "It doesn't go too fast but that doesn't worry me as I think it is all going to work out very well."[17]

On his way to Palm Beach, Florida, in early December 1933, and then on his return in early January, Gershwin spent a few days with Heyward in Charleston; and for a few weeks in April 1934 Heyward stayed with Gershwin in New York. Otherwise, the two, to their mutual disappointment, worked long-distance from November 1933 to mid-June 1934, Gershwin tied down to his radio show, Heyward reluctant to leave home. Scene by scene, Heyward mailed the libretto, along with some suggestions for musical treatment, to Gershwin, who made his own cuts and revisions as deemed necessary.

A major point of contention emerged virtually at the start, when Heyward told Gershwin that he felt "that all dialogue should be spoken," and that he imagined a "new treatment" in which the orchestra would play throughout, with singing seamlessly emerging from speech and pantomime. But Gershwin remained committed to sung recitative, aside from some occasional use of unaccompanied inflected speech (involving pitches with x's rather than note heads), especially for the few minor white characters. This appropriation of German speechsong *(Sprechgesang)* suggested the influence of Schoenberg and Berg, but its presence here drew primarily on Gershwin's perception of whites as "more unemotional, dull, and drab" than blacks, and possibly as well on a passage in the Heyward novel that accompanies Archdale's entrance: "The court [in Catfish Row] had been full of the many-colored sounds that accompanied its evening life. Now, gradually the noise shrunk, seeming to withdraw into itself. All knew what it meant. A white man had entered. The protective curtain of silence which the negro draws about his life when the Caucasian intrudes hung almost tangibly in the air." True, Gershwin employed speechsong for the opera's black characters as well (as in Maria's solo, "I Hates Yo' Struttin' Style"), but—in distinction to the white characters—usually with musical accompaniment.[18]

Heyward established a natural flow between song and recitative in any case, basing many of his lyrics on lines from the novel and the play. Because of difficulties imposed by working so far apart, and because Heyward felt somewhat uneasy about some of the more humorous and romantic moments, he and Gershwin agreed to have Ira write or cowrite some lyrics and generally facilitate their collaboration. Accordingly, whereas Gershwin generally set Heyward's words to music, for Ira he provided music to versify. Porgy's second-act aria, "I Got Plenty o' Nuttin'," represented an exception, as Heyward, after hearing Gershwin play the tune in New York in April, requested the opportunity to put words to the melody. Armed with the opening line, invented by Ira, and a dummy verse, he completed the lyric on his own; Ira subsequently revised the text, claiming the end result "a 50–50 collaborative effort." The two writers similarly cowrote the duets "Bess, You Is My Woman" and "I Wants to Stay Here."[19]

Otherwise, Ira primarily created the lyrics for "Oh, I Can't Sit Down," "I Ain' Got No Shame," "It Ain't Necessarily So," "Oh, Hev'nly Father," "A Red Headed Woman," "There's a Boat Dat's Leavin' Soon for New York," and "Oh, Bess, Oh Where's My Bess," while Heyward wrote virtually everything else, including "Summertime." The score and program, making no such distinctions, somewhat misleadingly credited Heyward with the "libretto" (meaning the recitatives) and Heyward and Ira as coauthors of the "lyrics" (meaning the set pieces for the soloists and chorus). In contrast, some knowing listeners appreciated the varied contributions of both men; for instance, Stephen Sondheim—never a great Ira Gershwin admirer—pointedly singled out Heyward's work on the opera as including the "best lyrics ever written, I think, for the musical stage. They are true poetry, but the music doesn't overblow them, only enriches them, and they enrich the music, too. 'My Man's Gone Now.' 'Summertime.' Genuinely poetic."[20]

Heyward and Ira agreed to split the royalties on publishing income derived from the opera, with each getting 25 percent to the composer's 50 percent. "George had, not only a great respect for you, but also a deep affection," wrote Ira to Heyward after Gershwin's death, "and I assure you, though I believe you must have known, I felt the same way about you and considered it a great honor to be associated with you, however small my contribution." Given that the play, which provided the basic framework for the libretto, had been in good measure the work of Dorothy Heyward, her contribution to the opera, though not always acknowledged, proved considerable as well.[21]

In preparation for his few days in Charleston in December 1933 and January 1934, Gershwin wrote to Heyward, "I would like to see the town and hear some spirituals and perhaps go to a colored cafe or two if there are any." Once in Charleston, he explored under Heyward's guidance local black music, delighting especially in the cries of the city's pushcart vendors (which may well have reminded him of life on the Lower East Side). He was also "particularly impressed" with the "primitiveness" of some church services, including an "experience service" at Charleston's Macedonia church at which a woman sang a spiritual that began, "Oh, Dr. Jesus." (On a visit to Charleston after Gershwin's death, Kay Swift met a Macedonia church member who recalled that the composer "had come often to sing with them and that he always spoke to them when he came.") Gershwin was struck as well by "the artistry of the [city's] architecture, the warmth of coloring on the stones of the old buildings. . . . Everything combines to give the place a beauty only found perhaps in some Old World city such as Paris."[22]

However, whatever music Gershwin heard on this trip hardly sufficed, in the opinion of Heyward, who had some real familiarity with black folk traditions, as evident not only from his literary work but from his participation in Charleston's Society for the Preservation of Spirituals, founded in late 1922. "You really haven't scratched the surface of the native material yet," he wrote to Gershwin on February 6, 1934. "This secular stuff, for instance." After completing a season of radio shows in May, Gershwin duly spent about five weeks from mid-June to late July in the Carolinas, partly in order to work closely with Heyward, but also to investigate further the region's music.[23]

Gershwin stayed mostly on Folly Island about ten miles from Charleston, where the Heywards (who by this time resided much of the year at their Hendersonville home in the mountains of North Carolina) maintained a summer cottage, Follywood. Accompanied by his cousin, Henry Botkin, and his valet, Paul Mueller, he rented a four-room beachfront cottage (since destroyed by a hurricane) directly opposite the Heyward home on the island's ocean side, Folly Beach; owned by a local doctor, Charles Tamsberg, this beach house had no clothes closets, hot water, or telephone (though Gershwin, to his surprise, discovered a Jewish delicatessen on the island). During his time there, Gershwin apparently hired some domestics as well. "The place itself is very different from anything I've seen or lived in before & appeals to the primitive man in me," he wrote to Emily Paley. "We go around with practically nothing on, shave only every other day (we do have some visitors, you know), eat out on our porch not more than 30 feet from the ocean at high tide, sit out at night gazing at the stars, smoking our pipes."[24]

Gershwin brought in an upright piano from Charleston and made progress on the opera, meeting with Heyward every afternoon in order to get the first act into shape; but he found time as well for swimming, golf, painting, and studying marine life, including sea turtles and beach crabs. He also traveled the area, attending recitals and church services. He heard, for instance, a white group associated with the Society for the Preservation of Spirituals perform "sperrituals" at the home of James Hagood in Charleston (one of the singers, Harriet Simons, delighted to hear Gershwin play portions of the opera on this occasion, described the composer to writer John Bennett as "simple, unpretentious, attractive and intensely interesting"), and some black singers at the home of Edings Whaley Wilson in Rockville on Wadmalaw Island. "James Island with its large population of primitive Gullah Negroes lay adjacent," recalled Heyward, "and furnished us with a laboratory in which to test our theories, as well as an inexhaustible source of folk material." For Gershwin, this immersion in black southern life seemed "more like a homecoming than an exploration," according to Heyward, who recalled that one night "at a Negro meeting on a remote sea-island, George started 'shouting' with them, and eventually to their huge delight stole the show from their champion 'shouter.'" (Gershwin told Anne Brown that after the shouting ended, an elderly man clapped him on the back and said, "By God, you can sure beat out them rhythms, boy. I'm over seventy years old and I ain't never seen no po' little white man take off and fly like you. You could be my own son.")[25]

On his way back to New York, Gershwin also spent some time in Hendersonville, where he and Heyward attended an evening meeting of black Holy Rollers in a makeshift cabin. As they were about to enter, remembered Heyward, Gershwin "caught my arm and held me. The sound that had arrested him was one to which, through long familiarity, I attached no special importance. But now, listening to it with him, and noticing his excitement, I began to catch its extraordinary quality. It consisted of perhaps a dozen voices raised in loud rhythmic prayer. The odd thing about it was that while each had started at a different time, upon a different theme, they formed a clearly defined rhythmic pattern, and that this, with the actual words lost, and the inevitable pounding of the rhythm, produced an effect almost terrifying in its primitive intensity." In November Gershwin wrote to Heyward that he had included in the opera's storm scene a section "with six different prayers sung simultaneously. This has somewhat the effect we heard in Hendersonville as we stood outside the Holy Rollers Church."[26]

Gershwin more or less completed a condensed score in January 1935, frequently describing the opera in progress as both the most difficult and the most rewarding endeavor of his career, and eagerly playing excerpts for S. N. Behrman, Morton Gould, Theresa Helburn, Richard Rodgers, Sigmund Spaeth, Deems Taylor, and others. Meanwhile, he had started the immense job of orchestrating the opera in September 1934, assaying some preliminary results with the WJZ studio orchestra that fall during the second and last season of his radio show. Staying with Emil Mosbacher in Palm Beach in the winter of 1935, he began orchestrating in earnest, writing to Ira in February that the job proceeded slowly, "there being millions of notes to write." After working throughout the spring and summer, he completed the full score on September 2, about a month before the opera's Boston opening. In the process, he further tried out some of his ideas on a Hammond electronic organ (first marketed in mid-1935).[27]

While orchestrating the music, Gershwin revised the work somewhat. Most notably, he removed a 137–measure scene between Bess and Serena early in the third act that contained a brief confrontation between the two women, including an arioso for Bess in which she states her claim to raise Clara's child; and a lovely duet for Bess and Serena, "Lonely Boy," a rocking lullaby in 6/8 featuring parallel thirds in the vocal lines, which dramatizes not only their reconciliation (already implied by Serena's prayer, "Oh, Doctor Jesus") but Bess's personal growth. Wayne Shirley, who brought attention to this "suppressed" music in the 1970s and helped arrange for its first public airing in 1980, suggested that Gershwin cut the music because, among other reasons, he more succinctly fulfilled similar dramatic goals with Bess's singing of Clara's lullaby in the same scene (an idea adapted from the stage play). Still, the cut left behind a palpably missing set piece, throwing the scene's architecture somewhat off-balance.[28]

Aside from this cut scene, the short score provided the basis for both the published piano-vocal score and the orchestral score. Gershwin and Heyward planned on titling the work *Porgy,* but the guild feared that the public would confuse the opera for the play; so Heyward, citing such works as *Tristan and Isolde, Samson and Delilah,* and *Pelléas and Mélisande,* suggested *Porgy and Bess.* "Of course," agreed Gershwin, "it's right in the operatic tradition."[29]

Whereas the novel takes place at the turn of the century, and the play in "the present" (that is, 1927), the opera takes place in "the recent past" (plausibly 1927 as well), though the premiere program gave the "time" as "the present" (that is, 1935). On a summer's night in Catfish Row, a black tenement in Charleston, couples dance to the piano playing of Jasbo Brown ("Jasbo Brown Blues"). Clara (Abbie Mitchell, soprano) cradles her infant boy ("Summertime"). Some local men—including Clara's husband, Jake, a fisherman who captains the *Sea Gull* (Edward Matthews, baritone); Sportin' Life, a dope peddler visiting from New York (John W. Bubbles, tenor); Mingo (Ford L. Buck, tenor); and Robbins (Henry Davis, tenor)—prepare for a Saturday night craps game, to the dismay of Robbins's pious wife, Serena (Ruby Elzy, soprano). Jake attempts to soothe his baby ("A Woman Is a Sometime Thing"). Peter, an elderly honey vendor (Gus Simons, tenor) married to Lily Holmes (Helen Dowdy, mezzo-soprano), returns home to Catfish Row ("Here Come de Honey Man"), as does the crippled beggar Porgy (Todd Duncan, bass-baritone). As the brawny stevedore Crown (Warren Coleman, baritone) and his lover, Bess (Anne Wiggins Brown, soprano) approach, Jake teasingly notes that Porgy's fond of Bess; but Porgy replies that women take no interest in him ("They Pass By Singin'"). Crown joins the craps game, as does Porgy ("Oh Little Stars"). A fight breaks out between Robbins and Crown, who kills the former with a cotton hook. As Crown flees, Bess seeks refuge in vain with the formidable cookshop keeper, Maria (Georgette Harvey, contralto), before slipping into Porgy's room.

In Serena's room the following night (act 1, scene 2), friends—including Porgy and Bess, who arrive as a couple—mourn the death of Robbins ("Gone, Gone, Gone") and try to raise money for his burial ("Overflow"). Under questioning by a white detective and policeman, Peter discloses that Crown killed Robbins and is hauled off to jail as a witness. The bereaved Serena expresses her grief ("My Man's Gone Now"). Although the collection falls short, an undertaker agrees to bury Robbins after Serena promises to pay him back. Bess leads all in a jubilant spiritual ("Leavin' for the Promise' Lan'").

The second act opens one month later, as Jake and his men prepare for a fishing expedition ("It Take a Long Pull to Get There"). Porgy, still living with Bess, rejoices in his newfound happiness ("I Got Plenty o' Nuttin'"), and Maria reproaches Sportin' Life ("I Hates Yo' Struttin' Style"). A quack lawyer, Simon Frazier (J. Rosamond Johnson, baritone), issues Bess a divorce from Crown, though the fact that they'd never been married presents an admitted "complication." Alan Archdale, a white attorney (George Lessey, spoken role), reports that because Peter's family once belonged to his own, he'll arrange for Peter's release from jail. Porgy reacts to a hovering buzzard with superstitious dread ("Buzzard Song"). Porgy and Bess declare their love ("Bess, You Is My Woman") before the latter leaves with the others for a picnic on Kittiwah Island ("Oh, I Can't Sit Down").

On Kittiwah (act 2, scene 2), the ensemble carouses ("Pagan Dance" and "I Ain' Got No Shame") and Sportin' Life takes a skeptical look at religion ("It Ain't Necessarily So"). After Serena chastises the revelers ("Shame on All You Sinners") and the group starts for home, Crown emerges from the thickets and entraps Bess ("What You Want wid Bess?"). In Catfish Row a week later (act 2, scene 3), Jake and his crew set forth despite some threatening weather (reprise of "It Take a Long Pull to Get There"). Serena prays for Bess, who days earlier had returned from Kittiwah in a state of delirium ("Oh, Doctor Jesus," also known as "Time and Time Again"). The Strawberry Woman (Helen Dowdy), Peter, and the Crab Man (Ray Yeates) sell their goods ("Strawberry Woman," reprise of "Here Come de Honey Man," and "Crab Man"). After recovering, Bess asks Porgy to protect her from Crown, who has threatened to claim her soon ("I Wants to Stay Here," also known as "I Loves You, Porgy"). A hurricane approaches.[30]

Taking shelter in Serena's room from the raging storm (act 2, scene 4), the gathered assembly prays, while Clara comforts her baby ("Oh, Hev'nly Father," "Oh, de Lawd Shake de Heavens," reprise of "Summertime," "Oh, Dere's Somebody Knockin' at de Do'"). Crown enters and mocks Porgy and the others ("A Red Headed Woman"). Espying Jake's overturned boat in the harbor, Clara rushes out, leaving her baby in Bess's care, and Crown chases after her (reprise of "Oh, Hev'nly Father").

The next night in Catfish Row (act 3, scene 1), the residents mourn Clara, Jake, Crown, and others presumed lost in the storm ("Clara, Clara") as Bess cares for Clara's baby (reprise of "Summertime"). As Crown, who in fact has survived, approaches Porgy's dwelling, the latter kills him. The following afternoon (act 3, scene 2), the police ask Porgy to identify Crown's body; scared at the prospect of seeing Crown's corpse, he refuses and is removed to jail. Sportin' Life takes advantage of Porgy's absence by luring Bess with drugs and the promise of the "high life" in New York ("There's a Boat Dat's Leavin' Soon for New York"). One week later (act 3, scene 3), as familiar routine—men sleeping, sweeping, hammering, and sawing—returns to Catfish Row (pantomime and "Good Mornin', Sistuh!"), Porgy, freed from jail, discovers that Bess has gone ("Oh, Bess, Oh Where's My Bess?"). On hearing that she has left for New York, he resolves to find her and departs with his goat cart ("Oh Lawd, I'm On My Way").

Although a number of commentators over the years have criticized the opera, above all, for engaging racial stereotypes, the work's colorful characters seem more broadly drawn—sometimes verging on caricature, in the tradition of humorous folktales—than stereotypes per se. The work's blend of satire and melodrama even lends a certain incongruity to the work, one that helps explain the kinds of audience uncertainties—such as whether to laugh or cry—that attended the opera from its beginnings. Gershwin's music surely provides a depth to the characters beyond that of the novel or play, infusing even such minor characters as Mingo, Robbins, Peter, and the street vendors with a touching humanity. If "I Got Plenty o' Nuttin'" evokes American minstrelsy, the song needs to be not only considered as an ironic rebuke to Jake's stated intention of making enough money to provide a college education for his son, but also placed in the larger framework of Porgy's vulnerability as expressed in "They Pass By Singin'," "Buzzard Song," and "Oh, Bess, Oh Where's My Bess?" (Concerning "I Got Plenty o' Nuttin'," Todd Duncan recalled Gershwin saying, "This is a bitter song and you have to sing it with tongue-in-cheek; you have to sing it smiling all the time. Because what you're doing is making fun of us. You're making fun of people who make money and to whom power and position is very important.")[31]

Granted, Porgy can be violent and superstitious; Bess, fickle and dissolute; Serena, self-righteous; Maria, unbending; Peter, ineffectual; Frazier, underhanded. Jake, in his eagerness to provide for his family, makes one fatal mistake; and Clara, overcome by her love for him, makes another. But for all their imperfections, these characters are in their distinct ways dignified and lovable, and by the work's end, Porgy in particular attains a sort of heroic grandeur. Even Sportin' Life and Crown are figures of some ambivalence; the former, though a mischievous trickster, has greater wit than anyone else in the opera, while the latter, more brutish than malevolent, bravely attempts to rescue Clara. The opera shows scorn only to the white police, and even they are limned with an ironic hand.

Moreover, the main characters belong to a larger community that it-self takes center stage, a group victimized within by substance abuse, violence, quackery, and superstition, and without by racism, injustice, and nature, yet still hopeful and inspiring in its compassion and faith. Such admired operatic predecessors as *Boris Godunov* and *Die Meis-tersinger von Nürnberg* offered (at least in some of their more public scenes) precedent for such preoccupations, much as *Porgy* anticipated—and influenced—*Peter Grimes, Street Scene,* and *Dialogues of the Car-melites.* But Gershwin's alternately satiric and tragic portrayal of a provin-cial community on the threshold of modernity assumes its own flavor, with the conflict of sin versus salvation taking special prominence throughout. Considering that nearly all of the principals either die or leave (and Porgy's departure is a kind of death, or perhaps rebirth, one that fulfills the prophecy stated early in the opera: "One of these mornin's you goin' rise up singin'"), the survival of this community remains—along with Porgy's ability to overcome his humiliation and loneliness through his unconditional love for Bess—the story's ultimate triumph. The whole opera is like a prayer or rite, each act concluding in a state of commu-nal supplication or exaltation; even the craps game begins with an in-vocation that reflects on man's transience.[32]

The dramatic centrality of the community manifests itself most obvi-ously in the prominence of the chorus, who not only have a large num-ber of featured spots but also join in on most solo numbers as well (though not "A Red Headed Woman" or "There's a Boat Dat's Leavin' Soon for New York," both of which represent somewhat alien worlds). Moreover, the characters never confide their private thoughts; we see them only as they see one another, even in ensembles (a fundamental difference be-tween "Oh, Bess, Oh Where's My Bess?" and the final trio from *Der Rosenkavalier,* with which it has been compared). This emphasis on pub-lic as opposed to private space gives the work a unique cast that suggests aspects of oratorio, pageant, and revue, and that places the opera in the context of twentieth-century trends, including Brecht's epic theater.

In other respects, the work, with its knowing and impressive if some-what rambunctious amalgam of song, recitative, chorus, and instrumental sections, falls largely within the tradition of both number opera, as rep-resented by Bizet and Verdi, and the more throughcomposed works of Mussorgsky and Wagner—a formal approach that recalls Puccini espe-cially. Perhaps distracted by the opera's catchier arias, commentators have tended to overlook this aspect of the work, marked by dynamic fluctuations of tempo and tonal center (from an opening in a bluesy B to a conclusion in E). Consider, for example, the scene between Bess and Crown on Kittiwah, as Bess first discovers Crown ("Moderato" in G♯ and C); Crown describes his desolation, details his plans, and ridicules Porgy (a modulatory "Andantino expressivo," "Moderato animato," and "Allegro," leading to a "Moderato con moto" in A♭); Bess explains that she's "livin' decent" now (continuation of the "Moderato con moto," but in C); Crown threatens Bess ("Allegro vivace," arriving in B♭); Bess pleads for understanding ("Sostenuto a piacere" in E); Crown taunts her ("Subito allegro" in E); Bess attempts to reason with Crown ("What you want wid Bess?") ("Moderato sempre ritmato" in B); and Crown seduces Bess (a modulatory "Allegro," followed by a "Moderato robusto" in G and a modulatory "Animato) and triumphs ("Maestoso ben ritmato" in B, followed by a modulatory "Vivace" and "Allegro" and a concluding "Con moto ben ritmato" in D). This dramatic encounter, constructed almost entirely from manipulations of Crown's leitmotive, traverses the tritone (from G♯ to D) with a style of its own, but its formal organization seems essentially Pucciniesque.

Relatedly, even though the work dispenses with traditional soliloquizing, one finds, again along the lines of Puccini, heightened recitatives and little ariosos throughout—some of which are prominent enough to warrant special mention in the synopsis above, as well as in many programs—that seamlessly emerge from the larger fabric and that help develop character and drive the action. A number of the more developed ariosos—Porgy's "They Pass By Singin'" and "Gawd got plenty of money for de saucer," Sportin' Life's "Picnics is alright for these small town niggers," Serena's "Shame on All You Sinners" and "Oh, Doctor Jesus," Bess's "It's like dis, Crown," Crown's "If Gawd want to kill me," and the street-vendor cries—constitute some of the most arresting passages of the entire score. Even some brief lines—for example, Bess's "Robbins, have one to the Gawd fearin' ladies" or Peter's "De white folks put me in"—are in their own way as memorable as any of the work's big tunes. When asked about his favorite parts of the opera, William Warfield, a famous Porgy, cited just such recitatives. The opera's compelling melodic flow and plasticity accordingly make the familiar debate over the merits of the work's songs versus its recitatives somewhat academic.[33]

In the tradition of nineteenth-century opera, the work also extensively employs leitmotives to help shape and inflect the drama, including a jagged motive (act 1, one after 22) and a downward cascading gesture (act 1, two before 23) that depict the craps game (and that were probably inspired by the shaking and rolling of dice); a "risoluto" theme (act 1, 30) and an "espressivo" melody (act 1, 34) associated with life on Catfish Row; a theme for Robbins (act 1, 40); a bluesy melody that portrays Porgy, including a chromatic tag possibly meant to illustrate his handicap (act 1, 70); an aggressive, syncopated theme designating Crown (act 1, two before 84); a melody that accompanies good luck (act 1, 105); a motive (cognate to the aforesaid cascading gesture) signifying "happy dust," that is, cocaine (act 1, three before 110); and a theme related in various ways to fate or doom (first heard in the bass at the conclusion of the "Buzzard Song" in act 2, three after 81—though, like many of these leitmotifs, it is derived from material found in the opening prelude and "Jasbo Brown Blues"). In addition, the opera makes comparable use of the opening phrases of "Summertime," "Here Come de Honey Man," "My Man's Gone Now," "Bess, You Is My Woman," and "It Ain't Necessarily So" to signify Clara's baby, Peter, Serena, Bess, and Sportin' Life, respectively. Gershwin may even have based some of these songs on leitmotives, rather than vice versa; but in any case, the opera's leitmotives weave their way through the work's recitatives, ariosos, songs, and instrumental sections alike.[34]

Some passages too large, or gestures too amorphous, perhaps, to be called leitmotives similarly course through the work, including the pentatonic "Introduction," whose bustling rhythms frame not only the first act but the entire opera; Porgy's arioso, "They Pass By Singin'," which provides a trenchant climax to the end of the first scene; and a certain harmonic progression in "Gone, Gone, Gone" (first heard in act 1 at four before 165) used to denote fear and piety. Moreover, Gershwin reprises some songs, including "A Woman Is a Sometime Thing," "It Take a Long Pull to Get There," and, more extensively, "Summertime"—a penchant that, while not unknown to the operatic and oratorio repertoire, reveals, like the recapitulation of a number of prominent themes as the work nears its end, the modest residue of musical-comedy practices. But all these repetitions serve dramatic purposes; in the case of "A Woman Is a Sometime Thing," originally sung by Jake as a lighthearted lullaby to his baby, the song becomes, in the hands of Porgy and Bess, not only something of a taunt to Robbins and Serena, thereby raising tensions, but a forewarning of their own ill-fated relationship.

Gershwin treats all this basic material with characteristic flair and imagination. For example, at the top of the second act's third scene, the expressive Catfish Row theme appears transformed in a new setting that evokes, at first, the start of a new day, and shortly after, the deceptive calm of the harbor. The opera also makes notable use of the fate theme, sometimes simply as an animating rhythm, but more subtly in the bass lines for Serena's "Shame on All Ye Sinners," Crown's "A Red Headed Woman," and the storm scene's final chorus, where repeated augmented statements of the melody help bring the act to a dramatic close. Or consider the melding of the jagged craps game and Crown motives to form a fugue subject in the fight scenes; the forewarnings of "I Got Plenty o' Nuttin'" in "Oh Little Stars"; the use of Robbins's theme as a ground bass (for the first-act passacaglia that begins at 145); or the inverted and retrograde treatment of Porgy's music that accompanies his return to Catfish Row (in act 3 at two before 132). And this does not begin to suggest the interrelatedness among the score's various motives themselves.[35]

The work's thoughtful motivic integrity helps impart an impressive, almost symphonic tautness that belies the work's reputation as simply a musical comedy with sung dialogue. The opera's larger three-act design even resembles those ternary forms—consisting of a relatively brief exposition, an extended development, and an abbreviated recapitulation-finale—characteristic of many of Gershwin's instrumental pieces. Studying the work's sketches and other materials, John Andrew Johnson determined that Gershwin planned out the work's larger shape in advance, including consideration of the opera's tonal design. "In the typescript libretto," says Johnson, "Gershwin literally outlines the musical shape of the whole work, and the labels he places on many of his other sketches show him thinking in terms of the seams of the work's overall form, along with the role of his characters."[36]

The work demonstrates deft command in other ways, such as its skilled choral writing, which tends to alternate six-part textures for religious and somber sentiments with, in stark contrast, simple unisons for more carefree moments; and which generally avoids large leaps and extreme registers, reserving the latter for moments like the very end, when a high, sustained B in the sopranos on the word *Lawd* helps bring the opera to a thrilling climax. The work's orchestration, meanwhile, takes the familiar discussion of Gershwin's abilities in this area far beyond the matter of mere competence. The instrumentation itself is for the most part traditional—two flutes (one doubling on piccolo), two oboes (including English horn), three clarinets (two doubling on alto saxophone), bass clarinet (doubling on tenor saxophone), bassoon, three horns, three trumpets, two trombones, tuba, percussion, banjo, piano, and strings (along with some sparing use of onstage piano and band)—but the actual scor-

ing matches the power and charm of the music itself, including prominent and inventive use of piano. Moreover, in the course of the opera,
Gershwin regularly varies the orchestral sound, thus highlighting the impression of the work, on a certain level, as a series of picturesque vignettes.
Compare, for instance, the diverse scoring for the folkish "I Got Plenty
o' Nuttin'"; the romantic "Bess, You Is My Woman"; the percussive "Pagan Dance"; the bluesy "A Red Headed Woman"; the Broadwayish
"There's a Boat Dat's Leavin' Soon for New York"; and the bandlike
"Oh, I Can't Sit Down," for which he took a cue from the 1927 production and supplemented the pit orchestra with an eleven-piece onstage
band. (Gershwin's music for this band, bound in his orchestral manuscript at the end of the scene in which it appears, was omitted from the
performance material prepared after his death, and apparently went un-
played from 1936—or perhaps from the West Coast revival of 1938—
to the semi-staged Nashville revival of 2006.) [37]

The orchestration also generally exhibits a newfound economy—a phenomenon Vernon Duke attributed to the influence of Joseph Schillinger,
as earlier mentioned—and if some passages are still somewhat heavily
scored, others, such as the third act's opening dirge, are elegantly luminous. Gershwin's contemporaneous activities as a painter no doubt intensified the work's concern for color, as expressed in the form of innumerable orchestral details, such as Bess's "It's like dis, Crown," with its
poignant accompaniment of three clarinets and bass clarinet, articulated
by strings; or, at the other extreme, the dazzling tutti writing for the storm
scene. The music possesses a complementary harmonic richness, thanks
in large part to the use of varied modal resources, including certain pentatonic, minor, chromatic, blues, and whole-tone passages that help delineate the characters of Peter, Crown, Sportin' Life, Porgy, and Frazier,
respectively; and a sophisticated harmonic vocabulary, including a six-
note chord, stacked by fourths, that depicts the chimes of St. Michael's.[38]

Similarly, the opera uses varied textural ideas, including fugue (in act
1 at 127 and in act 3 at 22), passacaglia (in act 1 at rehearsal 145, neatly
balancing the preceding fugue), and canon (in the brief chorus "Crown
cockeyed drunk" in act 1 at 116, and the "Overflow" chorus at 173),
along with such novelties as vocal glissandi (in "My Man's Gone Now")
and complex polyrhythms, both measured (in "Pagan Dance") and unmeasured (in "Oh, Hev'nly Father"). As in other late Gershwin works,
the opera also shows a marked proclivity for augmentation and diminution, sometimes simultaneously, as in "Leavin' for the Promise' Lan',"
where the superimposition of three rhythmic versions of the same melody

(at 219) suggests both religious rapture and mechanical movement; and other times in alternation, as in "Good Mornin', Sistuh!" where such differences distinguish the adults from the children. Finally, the score periodically makes almost hypnotic use of repetition, as in the recurring two-measure idea in the "Jasbo Brown Blues" chorus and the tonally static rhythmic canon in "Leavin' for the Promise' Lan'." The more adventurous of these textures, while related to Gullah folk music, at the same time anticipate the aleatoric and minimalist trends of the late twentieth century—an achievement in keeping with Gershwin's interests and sensibilities, but one that nonetheless has escaped the notice of historians of experimental music.

For all its stylistic range and technical breadth, the opera conveys a remarkable unity and in many ways seems less eclectic than some of Gershwin's shorter musical-comedy scores. "Oh, I Can't Sit Down" borrows the same Poulenc bass used in *An American in Paris;* "Good Mornin', Sistuh!" takes a leaf or two from the *Cuban Overture;* and some passages variously echo Debussy, Puccini, Kern, Stravinsky, Berg, and others. Gershwin himself stated, "If I can be original, not in every note, only in 25 percent of the work, that will be enough." But the opera essentially sounds like nothing else, not even, as sometimes claimed, Gershwin's own musical comedies; indeed, the music—even Sportin' Life's two solo numbers, which for dramatic reasons evoke Broadway—seems a world removed from the fox-trots, waltzes, and ballads found in the composer's musical-comedy scores.[39]

The opera's distinctive absorption of African American oratory and music underpins its great individuality, including allusions to a wide range of black popular music from W. C. Handy (whose "Aunt Hagar's Children" apparently provided the prototype for Porgy's theme) to Cab Calloway (who seems to have influenced Sportin' Life's music); and black folk music, from street cries and children's ditties to, above all, the Negro spiritual, which informs not only many of the opera's songs and choruses but its recitatives as well.[40]

Gershwin's familiarity with the Negro spiritual remains largely undocumented, but at the least he had heard Paul Robeson sing spirituals and no doubt encountered other spiritual and gospel vocalists through their wide dissemination via recording and eventually radio and film. In addition, he owned various anthologies of spirituals, including those edited by George Shackley (for the 1927 *Porgy*) and Clarence Cameron White *(Forty Negro Spirituals),* and he probably also knew the two books of Negro spirituals published by the Johnson brothers and the arrangements of spirituals by Hall Johnson for the Broadway production of *The Green Pastures*. Similarities between "I Ain' Got No Shame" and the spiritual "Det' Ain't Yuh Got No Shame," as found in *The Carolina Low-Country*—a 1931 publication that included an essay by Heyward—suggests some acquaintance with that volume as well. And as discussed, he investigated folk spirituals firsthand during his visits to the Carolinas. But at any rate, he made the Negro spiritual his own. In a 1935 article for the *New York Times*, he himself spoke of the work as a "folk opera," of trying to make his recitatives "as close to the Negro inflection in speech as possible," of using a text that came "naturally from the Negro," of writing his own "spirituals and folksongs," and of early on deciding "against the use of original folk material because I wanted the music to be all of one piece."[41]

Although Gershwin's ability to evoke the Negro spiritual in his own terms particularly impressed American listeners of the time (who generally knew that repertoire better than later audiences), it remains one of the score's most impressive features, as evident by some comparison of "Sometimes I Feel Like a Motherless Child" and "St. Louis Blues" with "Summertime"; "Go Down, Moses" with "Oh, de Lawd Shake de Heavens"; "Oh, Dere's Somebody Knockin' at de Do'" (variously titled) with the same-named chorus in the opera; "Lonesome Grabe Yahd" with "Clara, Clara"; and "Ah'm On Mah Way" with "Oh Lawd, I'm On My Way." (Among other details, Gershwin rewrote the main theme of "Oh, Dere's Somebody Knockin'" to include repeated notes, all the better to evoke actual knocking.) Admittedly, the opera's general style bears some resemblance to the forenamed collections of spirituals, especially that by Clarence Cameron White, as well as to more commercial arrangements of black folk tunes, like those by Jacques Wolfe and Lily Strickland featured on the Reisman tour; but Gershwin, in his rhythmic vitality and textural complexity, went much deeper in the direction of both African American folk practices and the European classics.[42]

Elizabeth Sohler argues further that Gershwin specifically adapted traditions distinctive to Gullah culture, pointing to wailing gestures in "Gone, Gone, Gone"; the ad libitum employment of combs, bones, washboard, and washtub in the "Pagan Dance" (as indicated in the piano-vocal score); the heterophonic textures in "Oh, Hev'nly Father"; and the second-act street cries. Moreover, he plainly adopted the melody for "Strawberry Woman" as found in the aforementioned publication about Charleston street cries by Harriet Kershaw Leiding.[43]

The scoring of "Pagan Dance" may have also owed something to Asadata Dafora's surprise hit of 1935, *Kykunkor, or the Witch Woman,* which opened in a small New York loft on May 6 but moved to larger spaces in response to widespread critical acclaim. Dafora (1890–1965), who was born in Sierra Leone and educated in Europe, and who settled in New York in 1929, wrote the music and lyrics for this "Native African Opera," as the work was advertised, and apparently choreographed it as well. Contemporary descriptions of this "ritual drama"—with its stylized depiction of an African marriage ceremony, its scoring for an orchestra of eight drums, and its blend of Western and non-Western elements—bring to mind Stravinsky's *Les noces,* though its climactic exorcism also suggests some point of contact with *The Dybbuk* (as well as with *Porgy,* for Serena's prayer is a sort of exorcism), helping to explain the work's appeal to Gershwin, who reportedly attended several performances and attempted to procure some of its drums for his own opera.[44]

At the same time, Gershwin clearly had the tradition of European opera in mind as well, even referring to the work in July 1935 as his "first grand opera." Oscar Levant reports that while writing the piece, Gershwin "referred constantly to the score of *Die Meistersinger* as a guide to the plotting of the choral parts and for general precepts in vocal writing." Wayne Shirley more specifically identified the "fight fugue" from *Die Meistersinger* as the model for the opera's own two fight fugues, and further observed that reconfigurations of the "Tristan chord" yielded the principal harmonies of "Summertime." Gershwin himself drew a caricature of Wagner along with the phrase, "rhythmic figure on top a la Wagner," on a sketch of the work's finale, "Oh Lawd, I'm On My Way"; and he told Rouben Mamoulian, apropos of the difficulty of playing the score at the piano, "Can you play Wagner on the piano? Well, this is just like Wagner!" Moreover, while working on the piece in July 1934, he stated, "The production will be a serious attempt to put into operatic form a purely American theme. If I am successful it will resemble a combination of the drama and romance of *Carmen* with the beauty of *Meistersinger.*"[45]

In his opinion, *Carmen* additionally provided, along with Verdi's operas and Friedrich von Flotow's *Martha* (which appropriated "The Last Rose of Summer"), precedent for the incorporation of "song hits" into the operatic form. The connection with especially *Carmen* seemed evident enough, and commentators accordingly likened Gershwin's evocation of black Charleston to Bizet's imagined Spain—as well as to Puccini's imagined Japan. But such analogies seem inexact, as Gershwin from his youth had been familiar with various African American musics and, moreover, had studied firsthand the folkways of the Gullahs. Moreover, he spoke of the opera not only in terms of the Negro "race" but of "American life" and "American expression," claiming to have achieved "an American flavor in the melodies," and saying of the story itself, "First of all, it is American, and I believe that American music should be based on American material." As early as 1920, Gershwin himself had intimated some criticism of Puccini's more exotic efforts when he stated that the Italian, like Tchaikovsky, had failed to "represent" his native country when he "wrote in styles of other lands."[46]

Although Gershwin's equation of black folklore with "American life" evokes thorny issues, *Porgy and Bess* deserves comparison in this sense with, say, Mussorgsky as much as with Bizet and Puccini. Indeed, when Irving Kolodin asked him what opera "loomed largest" in his "eye" as he set about writing his own, Gershwin mentioned, above all, *Boris Godunov,* saying that he intended to make comparable use of folk styles, and citing that opera and *Carmen* as the two he most admired. In addition, Mussorgsky's "Song of the Flea" apparently served as a model for "Buzzard Song." Meanwhile, as discussed earlier, Gershwin absorbed various aspects of Alban Berg's *Wozzeck* as well.[47]

For all its indebtedness to the great tradition, *Porgy and Bess* seems a relatively modest work. Its use of popular dialects and musical idioms and its congeniality to improvisation and varied vocal styles mark it—to use the composer's own term—a "folk opera." At the same time, its distinctive pacing, which might be compared with film, constitutes an innovation of sorts, and its sheer verve makes many other operas sound tepid in comparison. Moreover, its vulgarities not only serve the drama but speak to a legitimate desire, long articulated by the composer, to create a popular American opera. The work further evidences Gershwin's superb abilities as a musical dramatist, including terrific handling of elaborate ensembles. Above all, perhaps, *Porgy and Bess* shows its author to be deeply humane in his sensitive understanding of the weakness and resilience, the haplessness and dignity, of an oppressed but tight-knit group. Better than anything else he ever wrote, the work reveals Gershwin as not only a brilliant artist, but a great and complex one.

Chapter Thirty-Two

The First Production of *Porgy and Bess*

In late 1934 Gershwin presented to the Theatre Guild a list of possible stage directors for *Porgy and Bess,* including Heyward's apparent first choice, John Houseman, the young writer-director who earlier in the year had staged the premiere of Virgil Thomson's opera *Four Saints in Three Acts.* But the guild ultimately engaged Rouben Mamoulian, who not only had directed the stage version of *Porgy* but had wide experience with opera. "They [the guild] feel that he knows more about music than any other producer," Gershwin explained to Heyward, "and might do a beautiful thing with the musicalization of the book. They feel that John Houseman might be somewhat inexperienced to handle so huge a task." Heyward had his doubts—he disapproved of some vulgarities in Mamoulian's direction of *Porgy*—yet had little choice but to acquiesce. Mamoulian himself was reluctant to interrupt a lucrative Hollywood career to stage a new opera, but after hearing George and Ira sing and play through the piece at the former's apartment ("sometimes I think that in a way that was the best performance of it I ever heard," Mamoulian would later write), and after some wrangling over his contract, he agreed to direct the work.[1]

For musical director, Gershwin selected Alexander Smallens (1889–1972), a Russian-born conductor who had grown up in New York and who, in the course of his association with the Chicago Opera (1919–1923) and the Philadelphia Civic Opera (1924–1931), became known for his work in contemporary opera (he gave the American premieres of Prokofiev's *The Love for Three Oranges* in 1921 and Strauss's *Ariadne auf Naxos* in 1928). As assistant conductor for the Philadelphia Orchestra (1927–1934), he remained involved with opera, leading the first American performance of Stravinsky's *Mavra* in 1934. In that year, at the behest of Virgil Thomson, who admired Smallens's "lively understanding" of his music, he conducted the world premiere of *Four Saints*.[2]

As previously discussed, in 1935 Gershwin also recruited young composer-pianist Alexander Steinert to help coach the singers. Gershwin knew Steinert primarily from the Russian Opera, a company that, under various names, presented in the early 1930s an extraordinary array of operas by Mussorgsky, Tchaikovsky, Rimsky-Korsakov, and others, performed in the original Russian at various venues, including the Earl Carroll Theatre, the Mecca Temple, and Lewisohn Stadium (the company also helped launch the American premiere of Shostakovich's *Lady Macbeth of Mtsensk* in early 1935). Steinert not only coached but also conducted for the Russian Opera, including the American premiere of Alexander Tcherepnin's *Ol-Ol* (1925, rev. 1930) on February 8, 1934. This association presumably brought him into contact with Smallens, who conducted *Boris* and *Prince Igor* for the Russian Opera in the course of 1935. In any case, the presence of Russian opera on Broadway surely had some bearing on the creation and realization of *Porgy and Bess*.[3]

Although Heyward arrived in New York for auditions in April 1935, Gershwin took primary responsibility for casting the work, scouring dozens of theaters and nightclubs for black singers. For the part of Porgy alone, he listened to about a hundred baritones. A wide network of friends and associates, including J. Rosamond Johnson and Robert Wachsman, who had helped assemble the black chorus featured in Harold Arlen's "Stormy Weather" revue at Radio City (1933), assisted in this exhaustive search.[4]

Both Gershwin and Heyward imagined Paul Robeson—who for six weeks in 1928 had played Crown on Broadway—for the role of Porgy. Gershwin also wanted Cab Calloway for Sportin' Life, at least according to Calloway, who contended that he turned down the offer because he was too busy performing at the Cotton Club (though other sources report that Gershwin wanted John Bubbles for that role from the start). And there was some talk about casting Ethel Waters. However, these stars were either too expensive or unavailable; Robeson, for instance, was abroad for much of 1934 and 1935.[5]

Still, the eventual cast did contain some familiar names from vaudeville and Broadway, including J. Rosamond Johnson (Lawyer Frazier); Georgette Harvey (Maria, a role she had created on Broadway in 1927); and the song-and-dance team of Buck and Bubbles: Ford Lee "Buck" Washington (Mingo) and John W. "Bubbles" Sublett (Sportin' Life). The other principals, all to varying degrees less known—Anne Brown

(Bess), Warren Coleman (Crown), Todd Duncan (Porgy), Ruby Elzy (Serena), Edward Matthews (Jake), and Abbie Mitchell (Clara)—had more operatic backgrounds. Mitchell, who had studied privately with Harry Burleigh in New York and Jean de Reszke in Paris, was the most established of the latter group, having already made her mark in both opera and musical comedy. Reviewing her performance as Santuzza in a mostly black performance of *Cavalleria rusticana* mounted by the Aeolian Opera at the Mecca Temple in 1934, the *Times* reported that she sang "with passionate feeling and with a true understanding of Mascagni's style." (Described by Edwin D. Johnson as "an artist of the highest sort," Mitchell was married to Gershwin's old friend Will Marion Cook.)[6]

The others were just coming into their own. Born in Newark and raised in Boston, where he studied at the New England Conservatory, Warren Coleman had gained critical recognition only lately for his starring role as an unscrupulous ex-convict in Paul Green's "symphonic play of the Negro people," *Roll, Sweet Chariot* (1934), yet another precursor to *Porgy and Bess*. Similarly, Edward Matthews, a native of Ossining, New York, who had received both bachelor's and master's degrees from Fisk University (where he sang with the Jubilee Singers), had recently won acclaim for his performance as St. Ignatius in *Four Saints* (1934).[7]

Ruby Pearl Elzy, for her part, attended Ohio State University and Juilliard, where she studied with Lucia Dunham. By the time she graduated with a certificate of maturity from Juilliard in 1934, she had begun to gain notice as a song recitalist—a *Times* review of a 1937 Town Hall program, which included Negro spirituals as well as selections by Gluck, Rameau, and Brahms, would praise her "innate sense of the dramatic"—though she remained perhaps best known as Paul Robeson's costar in the 1933 film version of *The Emperor Jones*. Heyward, who had written the screenplay for this O'Neill adaptation, recommended her to Gershwin as a possible Clara, but the composer ultimately cast the Mississippi-born singer—the only principal from the Deep South—as Serena.[8]

Born in Danville, Kentucky, Todd Duncan (1903–1998), who held a bachelor's degree from Butler University and a master's degree from Columbia University, had been on the faculty at Howard University since 1931. He, too, had made something of a name for himself in New York in 1934 with his performance as a "sonorous-voiced" Alfio in the aforementioned production of *Cavalleria rusticana*. Duncan was as wary of this new opera by Gershwin, whom he regarded "as being Tin Pan Alley and something beneath me," as the composer was of casting a university professor, notwithstanding Duncan's endorsement by both Abbie Mitchell and music critic Olin Downes. But at a December 1934 audition at his apartment, Gershwin apparently offered Duncan the role of Porgy after hearing him twice (the second time so that the composer, at the piano, could watch his face) sing eight or twelve measures of "Lungi dal caro bene" by Antonio Secchi (1761–1833). "In my opinion he is the closest thing to a colored Lawrence Tibbett I have ever heard," Gershwin wrote Heyward, in reference to the outstanding white American baritone known not only for some classic operatic roles but for his performances in new operas by Gruenberg, Hanson, Krenek, and Taylor, as well as for his work in radio and film. "He is about six feet tall and very well proportioned with a rich booming voice. He would make a superb Crown and, I think, just as good a Porgy."[9]

Duncan, still unsure, agreed to return a week later to hear George and Ira play and sing through the opera at the piano before a small group. As Gershwin began, Duncan initially thought, "All this chopsticks—it sounds awful," and muttered to his wife, "This stinks." But, recalled Duncan, "the more they played, the more beautiful I thought the music was. By the time twenty minutes or a half hour had passed I just thought I was in heaven. These beautiful melodies in this new idiom—it was something I had never heard. I just couldn't get enough of it. . . . Well, they finally finished, and when he ended with 'I'm on My Way,' I was crying. I was weeping." (He later told Ned Rorem, "I literally wept for what this Jew was able to express for the Negro.") After Duncan accepted the role, Gershwin reportedly completed the opera with the bass-baritone in mind.[10]

Anne Brown (b. 1912), the youngest principal, had grown up a doctor's daughter in Baltimore, where she attended Peabody. She continued her education at Juilliard, where, like Elzy, she studied with Lucia Dunham and graduated with a certificate of maturity in 1934. Reading about Gershwin's forthcoming opera in the newspapers, she wrote to the composer, who subsequently arranged an audition. At their first meeting, after Gershwin accompanied her in Schubert, Brahms, Massenet, and "The Man I Love," she became defensive when he requested a spiritual. "Why is it that you people always expect black singers to sing spirituals?" she asked him. "He just looked at me," Brown later recalled. "He didn't say anything or do anything at all; he didn't appear angry or disturbed. But I saw that he understood my reaction. And as soon as I saw that, my whole attitude just melted away and I wanted more than anything else to sing a spiritual for this man." She accordingly sang "City Called Heaven" without accompaniment, after which the two hugged.[11]

Brown subsequently served Gershwin as, in her own words, a "guinea pig," frequently visiting his apartment to try out the opera's voice parts and join him for lunch. (Brown also recalled that Gershwin "would sometimes, once or twice, invite me into his bed. Of course, I never went there.") Hoping perhaps for a small role, she was astounded when he offered her the part of Bess and pleased when he decided, at her urging, to have the character reprise "Summertime" in the last act. Brown's light-colored complexion—she often passed for white—made her an unexpected choice for Bess, and led, further, to some tensions with darker-skinned cast members, though Gershwin defended his decision, saying, "I don't see why my Bess shouldn't be café au lait."[12]

For the all-important chorus, Gershwin selected the Eva Jessye Choir. Born in Coffeyville, Kansas, Jessye (1895–1992) had attended Western University in her native state and Langston University in Oklahoma, and had taught school before establishing a professional chorus in New York in the 1920s and consolidating her credentials as a choral director with King Vidor's film *Hallelujah* (1929) and Thomson's *Four Saints* (1934). Her extensive involvement with black folk music—including the publication of two collections of spirituals (1927 and 1931) and, even more specifically, her interest in South Carolina's black culture, sparked by a recent tour there—made her that much more suited for this particular assignment. At their audition, remembered Jessye, her choir sang the spiritual "Plenty Good Room" and "danced all over the stage," at which point Gershwin "jumped up and shouted: 'That's it! That's what I want!'" Jessye usually worked with choruses of about twenty musicians, but for this production she assembled a larger group of seventeen women and twenty-four men.[13]

While nearly all of the principals had more extensive formal schooling than Gershwin—Duncan and Jessye, as mentioned, had even taught at the college level, as would Matthews eventually—few, aside perhaps from Jessye, possessed his knowledge of Gullah traditions; and he "often astonished the company," as Steinert recalled, "by showing them how to interpret their parts authentically." (In January 1935 Gershwin traveled with Duncan to Charleston in order to further the latter's familiarity with the regional dialect.) He also inspired a warm affection from the cast members, as suggested above by Brown's recollection of their first meeting. Duncan similarly spoke of Gershwin as a "wonderful man whom I came to love and revere," and seemed touched that, on their trip to Charleston, the composer wanted to board with him at the home of a black doctor (an arrangement prohibited by custom) rather than stay at a segregated hotel; said Duncan, Gershwin "didn't have any of that [prejudice] in him." Anne Brown, for her part, observed that whereas Mamoulian, Smallens, and the other "influential members of the troupe" never socialized with her or Duncan, Gershwin "would come to my house, come to our parties." And Buck and Bubbles sent him a telegram on opening night that he particularly liked: "May the curtain fall with the bang of success for you as the sun rises in the sunshine of your smile."[14]

The principals admired the opera as well as its composer. Brown, for instance, thought that the music used "a lot of impulses and themes and musical harmonies" of "black people," but in ways that were "his [Gershwin's] own" and "very American." She further defended the work to her father, who thought it contained "the old clichés of [black] people—dope peddlers, near-prostitutes; he especially didn't like his daughter showing her legs and all that. I thought that DuBose Heyward and Gershwin had simply taken a part of life in Catfish Row, South Carolina, and rendered it superbly." In later years, she herself directed the opera in various cities in Norway and France, including a staging for the Norwegian Opera in 1967, and observed, "If you consider all the operas written by Mascagni, Puccini or Verdi—they all in fact are about mankind, the tragedy and problems of man and so on. Those are always the operas that are the most popular ones, and Gershwin's opera was concerned with humanity."[15]

The other cast members felt similarly. Duncan recalled in particular one rehearsal at which Elzy's "Oh, Doctor Jesus" brought the proceedings to a standstill, until Gershwin appeared from the back of the theater: "He [Gershwin] simply could not stand it. He knew then, that he had put down on paper accurately and truthfully something from the depth of soul of a South Carolina Negro woman who feels the need of help and carries her troubles to her God." Meanwhile, Jessye, who had thought the original play "a splendid thing for the Negro," asserted that Gershwin "had written in things that sounded just right, like our people," and that the opera expressed "our inheritance, our own lives," in contrast to *Four Saints*, which represented "something foreign to our nature completely."[16]

J. Rosamond Johnson, who congratulated Gershwin as "the Abraham Lincoln of Negro music" following the work's premiere, was particularly explicit in this regard, stating that even if the opera was not, like the *Rhapsody in Blue,* "one hundred per cent Negroid" in its "musical idioms," still "at least eighty percent" was (the "remaining twenty per cent" he attributed to "twists and turns characteristic of the American Indian with a slight persuasion of cowboy ditties and mountain airs"). He predicted further that the work would endure as "a monument to the cultural aims of Negro art" and a "fountain of inspiration." "Some may differ at great length from his unusual style," wrote Johnson, "but nevertheless the example and magnitude of this young man's musical exposition and development of folklore, emanating from street cries, blues and plantation songs of the Negro, will prove itself a beacon light to those who are brave enough to stray from the 'web-worn' standards of the great masters of Europe."[17]

For these original cast members, the opera remained one of the glories of their professional lives. True, with the notable exception of Ruby Elzy (whose portrait Gershwin painted in 1936, and who died tragically young at age thirty-five), most enjoyed long and fruitful careers, including Duncan, who helped integrate opera when in 1945 he starred in productions of *Pagliacci* and *Carmen* at the New York City Opera; and Jessye, whose later work included an affiliation with Martin Luther King Jr. Moreover, Duncan, Johnson, and Helen Dowdy (the original Lily Holmes and Strawberry Woman) reunited on Broadway in Vernon Duke's *Cabin in the Sky* (1940), as did Duncan, Coleman, and Harvey in Kurt Weill's *Lost in the Stars* (1949). But they remained primarily associated with *Porgy.* At the same time, these performers presumably would have had more extensive careers had they enjoyed the opportunities available to white singers. "Fed up with racial prejudice," Brown even immigrated to Norway in 1948 after marrying a Norwegian journalist; in 1998, musing that if she had been born twenty years later she might have sung at the Metropolitan Opera or marched for civil rights, she added, "Of course, I would not have met Mr. Gershwin and that would have been a shame."[18]

Although the company never collaborated on an original cast album per se, a series of historic broadcasts and recordings—including excerpts from an early run-through (July 19, 1935, conducted by Gershwin), a Hollywood Bowl memorial concert (1937, the *Porgy* excerpts conducted by Steinert), two commercial recordings of highlights (1940 and 1942, conducted by Smallens), a radio broadcast of excerpts from the Cheryl Crawford revival (1942, conducted by Alfred Wallenstein), a near-complete recording of the opera (1951, conducted by Lehman Engel), and a later recording of highlights (1963, conducted by Skitch Henderson)—

taken together preserve some performances by all the original principals as well as the Eva Jessye Choir.[19]

Granted, these recordings provide only a rough idea of what audiences actually heard in 1935 (Coleman and Bubbles, for instance, had to wait until 1951 and 1963, respectively, to record Crown and Sportin' Life—and then with conductors other than Smallens). Nonetheless, the recorded legacy reveals that the original cast delivered dramatically riveting and musically accomplished performances, establishing many practices, moreover, that became part of a living oral tradition. Duncan captured with special adroitness the score's distinctive blend of operatic grandeur and folklike spontaneity—never more so, perhaps, than in the memorial broadcast, which caught some of the principals, singing live at a packed Hollywood Bowl in the immediate aftermath of Gershwin's death, at an especially intense moment. These various recordings further document Brown's vulnerable Bess, Coleman's ominous Crown, Bubbles's seductive Sportin' Life, Elzy's dignified Serena, Matthews's robust Jake, Mitchell's sensitive Clara, Johnson's hilarious Frazier, and the verve and skill of the Eva Jessye Choir, which sounded spectacular, even when humming. (Mitchell, incidentally, sang "Summertime" without the interpolated final high note and downward glissando of later interpreters.)[20]

In preparation for the premiere, the cast coached daily with Steinert through July and August 1935, at the end of which Smallens and Mamoulian began supervising rehearsals on the stage of the Guild Theatre. Irving Kolodin, who attended one such rehearsal, stressed the integrity with which everyone approached the work, citing as an example Mamoulian's command to the chorus, "Don't stand around like a chorus—break the formality of it all. . . . You don't move forward because *I* want you to—you move closer because *you* want to hear what they are saying." Meanwhile, Duncan, who performed his role on his knees, gave careful thought to singing in this awkward position in order to maximize his projection.[21]

In later years, some of the company offered reminiscences of Gershwin in rehearsal. Jessye remembered that he would sit in the back rows cracking and eating peanuts: "George didn't interfere during rehearsals; he let us do what we knew how to do." He surely countenanced the extensive extemporizing among cast members that, as surviving prompt books reveal, far exceeded those occasional ad libs indicated in the vocal score. Brown even marveled that he "never objected to changes in his music," and that he allowed, for instance, Smallens to take tempos faster than his own, or Elzy to embroider "Oh, Doctor Jesus" with "all sorts of ornamentation." Recalling that Gershwin would attend rehearsals for an hour or two each day, and would make notes and talk privately with Mamoulian, Smallens, and the cast members, Duncan confirmed that he was "very, very easy-going," and, moreover, could be "enthusiastic and exuberant" when "you did something interesting with his score." At the same time, added Duncan, "he could be equally resentful when you missed the point. How quickly he would stop you, if you had sung a wrong note; particularly, would be disturbed if you could not sense a rhythmic pattern or an off-beat pulsation which he had so carefully calculated. That would draw him to the footlights like a ball from a cannon." However, when Smallens insisted that Mamoulian fire Bubbles, whose unreliability exasperated the entire company (Brown remembered that he "smoked marijuana all the time and gave it to some of the girls in the chorus"), Gershwin defended the vaudevillian, saying, "You can't do that. Why, he's—he's the black Toscanini!" Duncan recollected that Gershwin himself taught Bubbles "to dance his part; taught him everything—all the notes, all the rhythms, all the cues—with his feet. It was brilliant."[22]

Russian-born designer Sergei Soudeikine based the opera's sets on Cleon Throckmorton's memorable designs for the 1927 stage production, and the guild further hired a rather ample orchestra of forty-five musicians or so (that is, about double the size of a typical Broadway pit band of the time, though still smaller than that called for by the score, with one less clarinet, horn, and trumpet, and no tuba), along with the eleven onstage band musicians billed as the "Charleston Orphans' Band." As in the earlier stage version, and like many to come, the production made some use of a goat as well. Originally budgeted at forty thousand dollars, the production ultimately cost a daunting (for an organization like the guild) seventy thousand dollars or so; but the company's board members and associates helped by investing in the show, as did Gershwin (at four thousand dollars) as well as Ira and Heyward (at two thousand dollars each).[23]

Billed as an "American folk-opera," *Porgy and Bess* had its world premiere on September 30, 1935, at Boston's Colonial Theater, where it played for one week. The capacity first-night audience cheered, whistled, and bravoed through the first scene; and although such enthusiasm waned somewhat in the course of the evening, Gershwin, Mamoulian, and Smallens—along with the company—received a rousing standing ovation at the end. The critics praised the production and generally concurred that the "beautiful," "magnificent," and "exciting" Gershwin score signaled an important step toward a distinctly American opera. At the same time, they seemed more impressed than thoroughly won over, with some, like the drama critic of the *Boston Post,* Elliot Norton, deferring judgment on the basis of a single hearing.[24]

The music critic for the *Post,* Warren Storey Smith, further voiced two objections that would shadow the work's future reception. First, he thought the score's "sophisticated atmosphere and idiom" unsuited to the characters; and second, he questioned the opera's lapses—as in "Bess, You Is My Woman"—into the composer's "best musical comedy manner." For Smith, the latter concern represented not only a stylistic but an aesthetic problem, as suggested by a comment that uncannily echoed the reception of *Blue Monday Blues:* "More than once last evening the spectators, becoming confused as to the real nature of the piece, did not know whether they were to laugh or cry." Grace May Stutsman in *Musical America* had reservations of her own, finding the work "enormously noisy" and lacking "intrinsically valuable music."[25]

Although the opera lasted about four hours, hardly any review complained about the work's length, notwithstanding George Holland's suggestion in the *Boston Evening American* of a cut of perhaps fifteen minutes, and Eleanor Hughes's reference in the *Boston Herald* to a "superabundance of material and a certain repetition of mood." Nonetheless, Gershwin, Mamoulian, and Smallens agreed that they needed to shorten the work before opening in New York. They had already excised some material from the piano-vocal score (published months earlier) for the Boston premiere, including the initial "Oh, Hev'nly Father" along with some of the "Jasbo Brown Blues" and the third-act pantomime. (The cutting of the latter plainly involved more than just time considerations, for Mamoulian replaced this music with "Occupational Humoresque," a sequence adapted from the stage play in which a series of noises depicting morning in Catfish Row—snores, sweeping brooms, pounding hammers, and so forth—converge into a "symphony of sounds.") But now they trimmed the work even more dramatically, making dozens of minor cuts throughout, shortening various set pieces and instrumental episodes, and eliminating some sections entirely, including "I Hates Yo' Struttin' Style," "Buzzard Song," "I Ain't Got No Shame," and "Shame on All You Sinners." Although the opera would remain in some flux in the days leading up to the New York premiere and beyond, these cuts shortened the opera by at least an additional thirty minutes, bringing it closer to three hours.[26]

In 1987 Charles Hamm, a noted scholar, argued that since Gershwin sanctioned these cuts, the New York version should be considered some-what definitive—a perspective that found some justification in Mamoulian's remark that Gershwin "never hesitated to make cuts that were necessary." Mamoulian also mentioned, in this context, that after a rehearsal on his birthday on October 8, 1935, two days before the opera premiered in New York, Gershwin presented him with a sheet of paper with some excised bars of music (presumably from the "Jasbo Brown Blues"), inscribed, "Here Rouben is a little birthday present for you—the 'cut' piano music. George Gershwin."[27]

However, Gershwin clearly assented to at least some of the cuts because of concerns about the cast's endurance in the face of a grueling run; without making one such cut, he wrote Ira, "You won't have a Porgy by the time we reach New York. No one can sing that much, eight performances a week." Nor was Gershwin as sanguine about the cuts as Mamoulian suggested. On the contrary, Duncan stated, "He [Gershwin] was upset in Boston. . . . George didn't want one beautiful blessed note cut. He and Mamoulian and Smallens walked in the Boston Common all night long [after the premiere], fighting and fussing and talking about it." Kay Swift, who had sat through the Boston premiere in tears because of the cuts already taken in the score, similarly recalled, according to one source, that the cuts "were anathema to Gershwin" and that "he may have been too conciliatory, a little too easily manipulated." Meanwhile, Mamoulian's biographer, Mark Spergel, opines that some of the cuts reflected the director's own shortcomings, whether his inability to stage a certain instrumental episode or, with regard to "Buzzard Song," his characteristic determination "to keep the Quixotic Porgy forever dreaming, safely distanced from any suffering or awareness." In short, Gershwin cut the work largely in deference to its famous director and in response to the exigencies imposed by a Broadway run. The published vocal-piano score accordingly can be considered a basic, authoritative frame of reference, notwithstanding a few minor deviations that emerged in the course of the orchestration.[28]

That Gershwin, in his few remaining years, never showed any intention to revise this published vocal score perhaps argues for its authority as well. More to the point, how he could have considered the Broadway version to be anything more than a quick fix remains hard to imagine; for, notwithstanding those commentators who have deemed them salutary, the cuts deprived the opera not only of some wonderful music but of a good deal of dramatic and musical integrity. For instance, the decision to omit most of "Jasbo Brown Blues" and have "Summertime" essentially follow the short orchestral "Introduction" not only sacrificed some telling background atmosphere and the introduction of a few germinal motives (including a gesture, "Doo-da," that neatly morphs into "Summertime"), but compromised the scene's tonal coherence: whereas the original score outlines an E-minor triad on a deep structural level as it advances from the "Introduction" (in B) to "Jasbo Brown Blues" (in E and then G) and on to "Summertime" (in B), the edited score rather lumpishly moves from one B-centered section to another.[29]

Admittedly, some of the cuts proved less structurally awkward, such as the removal of Maria's "I Hates Yo' Struttin' Style," although one thereby had no way of identifying the transition to the subsequent scene as deriving from the cut song. But other cuts seemed even worse, including those dismembered sections such as "I Wants to Stay Here," "Oh, Bess, Oh Where's My Bess?" and the two fugues that tended to trivialize the composer's intentions. Overall, the cuts made an already briskly paced work marked by abrupt tonal jolts that much more breathless and jagged.

Still, as Gershwin understood, no single cast could possibly manage eight performances of the complete opera a week. Moreover, he and Mamoulian no doubt realized that Broadway audiences had different expectations from, say, those for the Metropolitan Opera. And in fact, a number of New York critics thought the revised second act still too long, prompting about ten minutes of additional cuts after the show debuted on Broadway. The version unveiled in New York clearly fell short of ideal, but it represented a viable alternative under the circumstances.

Porgy and Bess opened at the Alvin Theatre on October 10, 1935. A host of artistic luminaries attended, including Joan Crawford, Edna Ferber, Kirsten Flagstad, Katharine Hepburn, Fritz Kreisler, and Robert E. Sherwood. George and Ira sat at the rear of the theater with Kay Swift. The house erupted into thunderous applause at various times throughout the evening, with "I Got Plenty o' Nuttin'" stopping the show, though Smallens resisted taking an encore. By the end, many spectators were moved to tears, and the audience called back the cast, along with Gershwin and Smallens, for about seven curtain calls. The evening—the most glorious in Gershwin's career—ended with a reception for more than four hundred people at the penthouse apartment of publisher Condé Nast.[30]

Because both drama and music desks of many newspapers and journals covered the event, an especially large number of reviews appeared in the days and weeks following the New York premiere. Over the years, a selective reading of only a few of these reviews—notably those by Brooks Atkinson and Olin Downes in the *New York Times,* Virgil Thomson in *Modern Music,* and Paul Rosenfeld in a 1936 collection of essays—has left the erroneous impression that the work was poorly received. In fact, whatever their reservations, the great majority of both drama and music critics loved the piece, which they widely deemed not only Gershwin's finest achievement to date but the best American opera ever written, and a milestone in the development of a national opera. They widely praised the intelligibility of the text, the way the music enhanced the drama, and the score's sincerity, freshness, and gusto. "This is the sort of thing that Pulitzer Prizes are not good enough for," wrote Arthur Pollock in the *Brooklyn Daily Eagle* (presumably in reference to *Of Thee I Sing*).[31]

And although the label "folk-opera" mystified some, including those who associated the term with Smetana's *The Bartered Bride,* very few aside from Rosenfeld, who described the work as "an aggrandized musical show," had any doubts about the work's pedigree, even if some thought it lacked the flow and intensity of opera's greatest masterpieces. "A few minutes after the curtain rises on *Porgy and Bess,*" wrote Marcia Davenport in *Stage,* "the secure realization overtakes the listener that he is hearing an opera. . . . Gershwin has not feared to lay down the work on the general lines of the soundest operas ever conceived; plot borne out by natural and realistic dialogue in music, songs that rise from the foundation and illuminate it." Grenville Vernon, in the *Commonweal,* called the work "a true music-drama." Even Thomson, who famously stated, "Gershwin does not even know what an opera is," immediately added, "and yet *Porgy and Bess* is an opera and it has power and vigor. Hence it is a more important event in America's artistic life than anything American the Met has ever done." Only a few critics, such as Downes and the *Post*'s Samuel Chotzinoff, showed concern about the work's ties to musical comedy. Rather, questions of stylistic propriety seemed largely restricted to the influence of Puccini, as perceived especially in "Bess, You Is My Woman" (perhaps the opera's least-admired set piece, though few went as far as Lawrence Gilman, who called the duet "sure-fire rubbish" in an otherwise respectful review for the *Herald-Tribune*).

The most contentious aspect of the work concerned the score's recitatives—a debate complicated by the fact that a number of drama critics, including Brooks Atkinson, clearly didn't like the kinds of parlando writing associated with opera. ("I suspect that if you are fond of opera you will be fond of 'Porgy and Bess,'" wrote Percy Hammond in the *Herald-Tribune,* "and that if you prefer your drama undefiled by music you will not care for what Mr. Gershwin has done to 'Porgy.'") But

Top: The Gershwin family in
1929. *Left to right:* George,
Rose, Arthur, Morris, and Ira.
(Courtesy of the Ira and Leonore
Gershwin Trusts.)

Bottom: Leopold Godowsky
Jr. and Frances Gershwin
Godowsky, 1930.
(Courtesy of the Ira and Leonore
Gershwin Trusts.)

Top: The chorus from *Strike Up the Band*, 1930,
flanked by Paul McCullough (*left*) and Bobby Clark.

(Courtesy of the Ira and Leonore Gershwin Trusts.)

Bottom: Ethel Merman and chorus in *Girl Crazy*, 1930.

(White Studio. Courtesy of the Ira and Leonore Gershwin Trusts.)

George and Ira with playwright-screenwriter
Guy Bolton (*center*) in Hollywood, ca. 1930.

Top: Ira and George with George S. Kaufman (*bottom left*) and Morrie Ryskind, ca. 1931.
(White Studio. Courtesy of the Ira and Leonore Gershwin Trusts.)

Bottom: Janet Gaynor and the chorus from *Delicious*, 1931.
(Hal Phyfe. Courtesy of the Ira and Leonore Gershwin Trusts.)

Left to right: Oscar Levant, Allan Lincoln Langley,
Gershwin, Robert Russell Bennett, Fritz Reiner, Deems Taylor,
and William Daly at Lewisohn Stadium, 1931.

Top: Lois Moran and William Gaxton (*center*) in *Of Thee I Sing*, 1931.
(White Studio. Courtesy of the Ira and Leonore Gershwin Trusts.)

Opposite top (from far left): Victor Moore, Grace Brinkley, William Gaxton, and Lois Moran with cast members from *Of Thee I Sing*, 1931.
(White Studio. Courtesy of the Ira and Leonore Gershwin Trusts.)

Opposite bottom: Gershwin and Serge Koussevitzky, the composer-conductor who premiered the *Second Rhapsody*, in 1932.
(Courtesy of the Ira and Leonore Gershwin Trusts.)

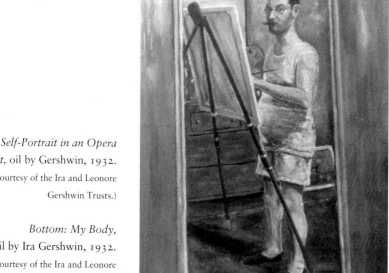

*Top: Self-Portrait in an Opera
Hat,* oil by Gershwin, 1932.
(Courtesy of the Ira and Leonore
Gershwin Trusts.)

Bottom: My Body,
oil by Ira Gershwin, 1932.
(Courtesy of the Ira and Leonore
Gershwin Trusts.)

Top: Radio program publicity photo for *Music by Gershwin*, 1934.

Bottom: My Studio—Folly Beach, watercolor by Gershwin, 1934.

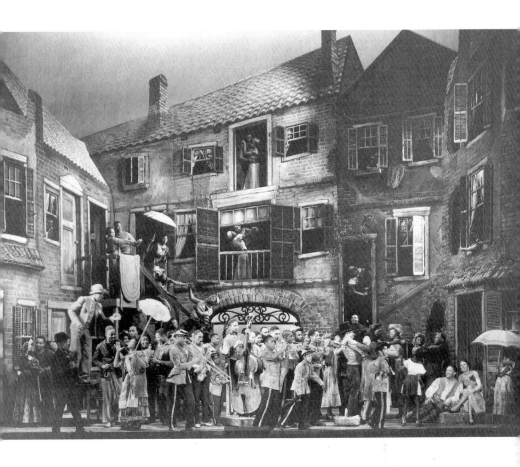

Opposite top: George and Ira with DuBose Heyward. *On the left:* "Dear Ira—As long as we're all autographing, I'd like to write what it is hard to say—that I'm very proud of you. With love, George. 'Porgy and Bess' Boston." *On the right:* "For my lyric twin, Ira, with admiration and every good wish from DuBose. Boston. Sept. 30, 1935."
(Vandamm Studio, New York. Courtesy of the Ira and Leonore Gershwin Trusts.)

Opposite bottom: David Alfaro Siqueiros with his oil *George in an Imaginary Concert Hall*, 1936. (Photo by Gershwin. Courtesy of the Ira and Leonore Gershwin Trusts.)

Above: Porgy and Bess, with Georgette Harvey (*far left*), John Bubbles
(*on chair*), and Todd Duncan and Anne Brown (*seated at doorway, far right*), 1935.
(Vandamm Studio, New York. Courtesy of the Ira and Leonore Gershwin Trusts.)

Top: Kay Swift, 1936.
(Gershwin. Courtesy of the Ira and Leonore Gershwin Trusts.)

Bottom: Gershwin with Irving Berlin, 1936. (Photo by Gershwin
[time exposure]. Courtesy of the Ira and Leonore Gershwin Trusts.)

Shall We Dance publicity photo, 1937.

Top: Ira and George in Beverly Hills, 1937.
(Rex Hardy Jr. [*Time*]. Courtesy of the Ira and Leonore Gershwin Trusts.)

Bottom: Ginger Rogers and Fred Astaire in *Shall We Dance*, 1937.
(Courtesy of the Ira and Leonore Gershwin Trusts.)

Top: George with his mother, Rose, in Beverly Hills, 1937.
(Courtesy of the Ira and Leonore Gershwin Trusts.)

Bottom: Portrait of Jerome Kern, oil by Gershwin, 1937.
(Keystone Photo. Courtesy of the Ira and Leonore Gershwin Trusts.)

Gershwin with his *Portrait of Arnold Schoenberg*, 1937. (Keystone Photo.
Courtesy of the Ira and Leonore Gershwin Trusts.)

a few music critics criticized the recitatives as well. Both Chotzinoff and Thomson thought the opera would have been better off with more spoken dialogue, the latter citing the example of Beethoven's *Fidelio*. "His [Gershwin's] prose declamation is all exaggerated leaps and unimportant accents," wrote Thomson. "It is vocally uneasy and dramatically cumbersome." On the other hand, Irving Kolodin stated, "The declamatory writing in Gershwin's opera is one of his most impressive accomplishments, for its adherence to the characteristics of the persons in the drama, for the excellent sense of word values. After close contact with the score, one recalls salient passages in the dialogue almost as readily as the more freely melodic sections."

Although most reviews opined that the opera enriched a widely admired play about a black southern community, few actually commented on its relation to African American life. Grenville Vernon, one exception, stated in *Commonweal*, "The music is always honest, and never bears that mark of moral degradation which white composers are only too prone to show in depicting the Negro." "He has written a message for the people of Broadway, and he has written it brilliantly," opined W. J. Henderson in a follow-up review for the *Sun*. "It is not grand opera; it is not folk opera; it is not pure Negro; but it is Gershwin talking to the crowd in his own way. And that is a very persuasive way."

Virgil Thomson, by contrast, decried the work's "fake folk-lore," writing that the opera, in contrast to Hall Johnson's music for *Green Pastures* and *Run, Little Chillun*, "has about the same relation to Negro life as it is really lived and sung as have *Swanee River* and *Mighty lak' a rose*." ("Folk-lore subjects recounted by an outsider are only valid as long as the folk in question is unable to speak for itself," added Thomson, "which is certainly not true of the American Negro in 1935.") Even the admiring Kolodin wondered whether the opera's contrapuntal contrivances were not "precocious for the negroes of *Porgy and Bess*" and "wholly foreign to the situation." Rosenfeld more critically wrote that the opera's individual numbers failed to "communicate a reality, either the rich, authentic quality of the Negro or the experience of Porgy the pathetic cripple who unexpectedly gets his woman and rejoices and suffers with her and then at last loses her, or of Bess, the weak victim of the flesh and the devil. It would seem as if Gershwin knew chiefly stage Negroes and that he very incompletely felt the drama of the two protagonists."

Even fewer critics, in this or any other context, alluded to Gershwin's Jewish background. However, Stark Young in the *New Republic* found "a certain monotony in the music" more "Oriental" than "Negro," while

Thomas B. Dash in *Women's Wear Daily* observed at times a "fugacious note of the Hebraic." John Mason Brown in the *Post* simply thought it wondrous that a collaboration of a Jewish composer and lyricist, a Russian director and set designer, a white southern librettist, and a black cast should produce "the most American opera that has yet been seen or heard."

The reviews parted ways most, perhaps, over Mamoulian's direction. Some found it brilliant and inspired—and a welcome change from the wooden stagings at the Met—while others thought it fussy and mechanical. In contrast, virtually no one had anything but accolades for Smallens's conducting—he conducted, wrote Gilman, "like a house-afire"— or for the cast, with the principal exceptions of Bubbles, whose droll performance delighted most, but not all; and Brown, whom some thought overly genteel. (Brown herself admitted that she must have been "a very schoolgirlish Bess," but explained that she always thought of Bess as more "earthy" than "sexy," stating, "I don't think that Bess really could stand to be lonely. Those characteristics were the ones I thought of rather than her being a flirt or a slut or anything of that kind.") Duncan's "beautiful, poignant performance" and Elzy's "amazing picture of grief and woe" garnered special acclaim. And the cast as a whole—though condescendingly described in a very few reviews as "talented Ethiopians" and even "darkies"—drew praise for its fine ensemble work.[32]

Porgy and Bess ran for 124 performances, an impressive showing for a new opera in the midst of the Depression—hardly the failure one would imagine from later accounts. With top ticket prices at $4.40 (later reduced to $3.30), the opera managed for a time to bring in about $24,000 a week, but when receipts dropped below $20,000, the box office could not cover the show's considerable expenses—especially its large orchestra— and the production closed in the red. However, for the Gershwins and Heyward, the popularity of some of the songs quickly offset the loss of their initial investment.[33]

After closing in January 1936, the opera, with a reduced cast and a thirty-piece orchestra headed by Steinert, toured five cities over a two-month period: Philadelphia (opening January 27), Pittsburgh (February 10), Chicago (February 17), Detroit (March 9), and Washington, D.C. (March 16). When Duncan and Brown insisted that Washington's National Theatre suspend its whites-only policy so that, among other things, their friends and family could attend the performance, theater management proposed reserving matinees for blacks or restricting seating for blacks to the balcony. But the cast held firm and the theater eventually agreed to integrate the house (a short-lived triumph, as the theater otherwise maintained a policy of segregation until the 1950s).[34]

In the course of the tour, audiences and critics in Philadelphia seemed a little more aloof, those in Detroit more consistently enthusiastic; but generally, critical reception proved, as in Boston and New York, overwhelmingly positive, notwithstanding some quibbling about the recitatives and certain numbers. The reviews deemed the work "masterful," "vital," "poignant," "humorous," and, time and again, "thrilling" and "moving." "It has broad melodic sweep, tenderness and understanding for the drama of Catfish Row," wrote Robert Pollak in the *Chicago Daily Times*. Again, too, critics regarded the work as the "first step to genuinely American opera," in the words of legendary soprano Mary Garden, who attended a performance in Chicago. Alice Eversman, in the *Washington Evening Star*, went further, deeming its realism and spontaneity to mark an advance in opera generally. A number of others made the related observation that the work appealed to people who did not ordinarily like opera.[35]

By this point, some reviews had appeared in the black press as well, including those by Carl Diton *(New York Amsterdam News)*, Hall Johnson *(Opportunity)*, Ralph Matthews *(Afro-American)*, and Rob Roy *(Chicago Defender)*. Diton, an esteemed composer-pianist, liked the "well-sounding score"—he concluded his review by advancing "the sincerest hope that George Gershwin's 'Porgy and Bess' may never die!"—but noted the "vocal fatigue of every character hardly without exception," and wondered "what heights this creation may reach after the younger principals have matured both vocally and histrionically in the years to come." Johnson, Matthews, and Roy expressed concern rather over the music, deemed "twangy" by Matthews and relatively "stiff" and "artificial" by Johnson. Roy wished at times that J. Rosamond Johnson had written the music, while Matthews missed the "sonorous incantations" of Hall Johnson's own scores. Still, Johnson conceded that Gershwin was "as free to write about Negroes in his own way as any other composer to write about anything else," and like Roy and Matthews—and in stark contrast to Diton—thought that the brilliant cast helped compensate for perceived shortcomings in the music and the direction. "I am now certain that I do like it and that it is a good show," decided Johnson after attending four performances. Roy, for his part, hoped that all Chicago would have the opportunity to view the work "at least once" before the production left town.[36]

Gershwin was awarded the David Bispham Memorial Medal for *Porgy and Bess* in 1937. The work no doubt played some part in his election to honorary membership to the St. Cecilia Academy of Music in Rome the same year as well. In any event, the opera's early reception, even among some of its severest critics, augured well for its continued success, and Gershwin had every reason to be pleased and proud.[37]

Chapter Thirty-Three

Porgy and Bess in Revival

$\mathcal{L}$ess than a year after Gershwin's death, Merle Armitage launched the first revival of *Porgy and Bess*. Directed by Rouben Mamoulian, Frances Herriott, and Burton McEvilly, with scenery and costumes designed by Armitage himself, the production, led by Alexander Steinert, featured many of the original principals, along with Jack Carr (Crown) and Avon Long (Sportin' Life). After premiering in Pasadena, California, on February 3, 1938, the production appeared the following night in Los Angeles at the Philharmonic Auditorium, the standing-room-only audience (which included film stars John Barrymore, Charles Boyer, Joan Crawford, and Marlene Dietrich) cheering this crowning achievement of a composer Angelenos had come to think of as their own. A concluding tribute to Gershwin by Mamoulian, followed by an encore of "Oh Lawd, I'm On My Way," only heightened the evening's drama. The critics liked the work, too. "Dramatically, it is a turbulent, tragic, humorous and human portrait of a group of colored people who lived, loved, wept, laughed, sang and danced to the fullest extent of their being," wrote Harry Mines in the *Los Angeles Daily News*. After eleven performances in Los Angeles, the opera enjoyed a well-received three-week run at San Francisco's Curran Theatre; but the great Southern California flood of March 3, which paralyzed the state, prevented planned visits to other cities, and the tour ended prematurely.[1]

Cheryl Crawford had better luck with her 1941 revival of the work. A native of Akron, Ohio, Crawford (1902–1986) had worked in the 1920s with the Theatre Guild (for which she had helped stage-manage the original *Porgy* and supervise its London run) and had codirected the Group Theatre in the 1930s. In the early 1940s she began producing her own stock shows at New Jersey's Maplewood Theatre, where she mounted a revised *Porgy and Bess* for a week in October 1941. "For me," she said, talking about her affection for Gershwin, "his music and Ira's lyrics are real 'Amurrican,' hard, tough, joyful, bold, cheerful, affirmative, never self-pitying, never sentimental. The beat is relentless." The production's warm reception enabled Crawford and her principal investor, attorney John Wildberg, to find some interested backers (including Rose Gershwin) and bring the show to Broadway's Majestic Theatre, by arrangement with Lee Shubert.[2]

Crawford reunited many of the original principals, including Duncan, Brown, Coleman, Elzy, Matthews, Harvey, Johnson, and Dowdy, though Avon Long took the part of Sportin' Life, as in California, and Harriet Jackson played Clara. Robert Ross directed, Herbert Andrews designed the sets, Eva Jessye prepared the chorus, and Alexander Smallens led a reduced orchestra of twenty-seven. Crawford and Smallens shortened the piece considerably, saving a good deal of time by converting much of the sung recitative—which Crawford thought "out of keeping with the black milieu"—into spoken dialogue, though they occasionally retained the accompanying music as underscoring. They also agreed on some new cuts, including reconceiving "Oh, Bess, Oh Where's My Bess?" as an abbreviated solo for Porgy. Conversely, at the top of act 3, they added an exchange between Maria and Serena from act 4 of the 1927 play. All in all, they reduced the opera to about a two-and-a-half-hour show.[3]

The production opened in Boston on December 29, 1941, and in New York on January 22, 1942, to raves. Helen Eager in the *Boston Traveler* called it "one of the richest theatrical experiences of a lifetime"; Robert Lawrence in the *New York Herald-Tribune* thought it "one of the finest performances of opera it has ever been my good luck to see and hear"; and Wolcott Gibbs in the *New Yorker* declared it "practically perfect." Brooks Atkinson of the *Times* still found the score "overwrought," but all who had attended the 1935 premiere—and many of the reviewers had—deemed this new version a significant improvement over the original. Certainly, the Crawford production enjoyed greater success than that of the Theatre Guild: 286 performances on Broadway, followed by a tour of forty-seven American cities and Toronto, as well as return engagements in New York at the 44th Street Theatre (starting September 13, 1943) and City Center (starting February 28, 1944).[4]

On May 7, 1942, the cast gathered at the studio of WOR radio in midtown Manhattan to record a still shorter, hourlong version of the opera, prepared by Jean Dalrymple, for the Mutual Broadcasting System. The first in a series of radio broadcasts of American operas with conductor Alfred Wallenstein and the WOR orchestra, this broadcast remains as close to a complete original cast recording as exists, even though Avon Long, Jack Carr (filling in for Warren Coleman), and Harriet Jackson (who interpolated the now-common high note and downward glissando in "Summertime") had not appeared in the original 1935 production. (As in other radio performances of the time, concerns regarding religious propriety presumably prompted the change of lyric, in "It Ain't Necessarily So," from "De t'ings dat you li'ble / To read in de Bible" to "The things that your preacher / is likely to teach ya.")

In the course of the run, Etta Moten, Alma Hubbard, and William Franklin replaced Brown, Elzy, and Duncan, respectively. When Moten refused to sing the word *nigger,* a word that Crawford already seems largely to have expunged from the show, Ira revised her part accordingly. Over the next ten years, he totally eliminated the word from the text, replacing it with such terms as *tin horns, dummy, low-life, suckers, buzzard,* and *baby* (somewhat to the regret of Eva Jessye, who remembered Brown's delivery of the line "Take that stuff [cocaine] away, nigger!" as having a "gut-bucket quality" that "just wrenched your heart"). Otherwise, Ira defended the libretto's slang and dialect: "All that was required was a suggestion of regional flavor; and if the artist preferred—for personal literacy or racial righteousness—to enunciate any words formally rather than colloquially, that was all right . . . but I do believe that a few recording artists and other well-intentioned persons are nice-nellying it a bit when they at times insist on elevating dialect grammar to Johnsonian heights."[5]

Critics widely assumed that the Crawford production owed its success to its overhaul of the work's recitatives, but they overlooked a number of other factors, including the audience's newly acquired familiarity with many of the songs, thanks to their wide exposure on radio; the long experience of the principals (including Brown, who now helped to make "Bess, You Is My Woman" a high point); a lighter directorial touch; and cheaper ticket prices, including a top of $2.75. Gershwin's demise played a part as well, or so thought Brooks Atkinson, who observed, "when a composer stops writing new music, his old music has a better chance to become appreciated." Moreover, as an opera now described by Virgil Thomson, who attended the Maplewood premiere, as one Americans "might well be proud to honor and happy to love," the work, in its depiction of a bygone America, suited wartime sensibilities. Indeed, yet another shorter version of the work—described as "90 minutes of all-

American melody, mirth and melodrama"—launched in 1944 by the USO Camp Shows delighted the country's uniformed men and women.[6]

In any case, many reviews rashly concluded that this "classic" opera, now often referred to as an "operetta," was a failure as originally conceived, not only because it had been drastically rewritten to its apparent advantage but because some of its most operatic moments seemed to miss the mark dramatically. "As an opera composer, Gershwin could make the pulse of his listener tingle but he could not make the heart throb," wrote Robert Lawrence, who in a follow-up piece declared that "judged by theatrical standards," the work was "a complete success," but "weighed by the standards of opera it fails because it lacks an articulated musical approach." Louis Kronenberger similarly stated in *P.M.*, "It is as something a little less than opera, though decidedly more than even the best musical comedy, that *Porgy and Bess* really triumphs." No one ventured the thought that perhaps the work seemed "something a little less than opera" because it had been presented that way. Thomson, who reaffirmed his conviction that Gershwin's "childlike sincerity" had transformed "a piece of phony white folklore about Negro life in Charleston" into something "beautiful," at least regarded the new version as appropriate for the moment: "Without being entirely certain from one hearing whether all these excisions, instrumental and textual, are exactly the right ones to have made and whether perhaps even more of them might be desirable, I approve heartily their having been made at all. It seems to me that that kind of correction, carried out by a skillful musician who knew the composer well and respected his genius, is exactly what the work needs right now."[7]

In the wake of the Crawford revival, the Danish Royal Opera launched the work's European premiere—as *Porgy og Bess*—in a Danish translation by Holger Bech. Opening at the King's Theater on March 27, 1943, in Nazi-occupied Copenhagen, the all-white cast (in dark makeup) starred Einar Nørby (Porgy), Else Brems (Bess), Henry Skjær (Crown), Margherita Flor (Serena), and Poul Wiedemann (Sportin' Life) under the baton of Johan Hye-Knudsen. Poul Kanneworff designed the sets and directed, and Niels Bjørn Larsen staged the dances. Kanneworff and Larsen, who decided to mount the opera after seeing the Crawford production in New York, had trouble securing the music, but they managed to have a film of the score sent to Denmark. (One Danish paper reported that the opera's director, Cai Hegermann-Lindencrone, had obtained a score prior to this, but that his wife had used the pages to make hair rollers.)[8]

The premiere, attended by Queen Alexandrine, Prince Frederik, and Princess Ingrid, took place amid rather remarkable circumstances. Although the Germans had occupied neutral Denmark since the spring of 1940, Hitler allowed the country an unusual degree of autonomy, in part because he regarded Danes as fellow Aryans, and in part because of Germany's need for Danish agricultural products. Still, as a "Negeroper" (as Danes widely referred to the work) by a Jewish composer, the opera epitomized the kind of art outlawed by the Nazis as degenerate. The production accordingly was an act of provocation, and reflected—and perhaps emboldened—a national mood that later in the year would lead to the heroic rescue of most of the country's small Jewish population.

The reviews of the opera gave little direct evidence of such sensibilities, however. Georg Wiinblad of the left-wing *Social-Demokraten* made one observation—"Negroes in the ghetto are poor, both in sorrow as in happiness: *they stick together*. They comprise one big brotherhood"— that no doubt carried political overtones. And Frithiof Rolsted, writing in the pro-Nazi *Fædrelandet* ("Fatherland"), accused the company of pandering to a "Communist-Jewish mob" by launching such a trivial and outmoded work, whose moments of beauty could hardly disguise its inauthenticity; an "outrage," declared Rolsted, especially when the company could have chosen, say, a neglected Danish opera. But most reviews more simply regarded the piece, somewhat along the lines of Puccini, as a vibrant and neatly crafted work, whose music transcended the banality of its story (Gershwin "knows his stuff," observed Erik Abrahamsen). And although some opined that the opera ultimately needed black performers, not a few thought this production proof that the work could be played successfully by a white cast. Even Rolsted thought Nørby's performance worthy of Paul Robeson.[9]

Karl Werner Best, the SS officer acting as the Reich's plenipotentiary, lodged a protest with Denmark's prime minister, Erik Scavenius, but the production proved a hit with the public and enjoyed a full run of eighteen performances, reportedly attracting young people who might not otherwise have gone to the opera. However, the company managed only four performances of the work in the spring of 1944 before an anonymous bomb threat forced them to suspend the production. Danish radio allegedly took advantage of the music's popularity nonetheless by playing "It Ain't Necessarily So" alongside broadcasts of Nazi propaganda. During the immediate postwar period, the Danish Royal Opera revived the work every year right through its 1952–1953 season, while other productions, again in translation and with white casts, appeared in Moscow (1945), Zürich (1945), Gothenburg (1948), and Stockholm (1949).[10]

In 1951 Columbia Records and producer Goddard Lieberson released the first near-complete recording of the opera, with Lawrence Winters (Porgy), Camilla Williams (Bess), Inez Matthews (Serena), and such veterans as Warren Coleman (Crown), Avon Long (Sportin' Life), and J. Rosamond Johnson (Lawyer Frazier), under the direction of Lehman Engel. Engel prepared his own version that approximated the 1935 premiere, though he reinstated the "Buzzard Song" and some other cuts. Irving Kolodin thought the recording an improvement over earlier ones, but its hectic patchwork and understated performances compromised its effectiveness. Virgil Thomson—without pondering any possible connection—approvingly referred to this version as "corrected by cuttings similar to those used in the theater," while criticizing the opera as "episodic." This release at least gave some impetus to a new production launched by Robert Breen and Blevins Davis that, within five short years, would take *Porgy and Bess* to scores of cities around the world.[11]

Robert Breen (1914–1990) was a director, actor, and producer dedicated to promoting American art internationally. In the 1940s, while serving as executive secretary of ANTA (American National Theatre and Academy), a forerunner of the National Endowment for the Arts, he initiated a professional association with Blevins Davis, a wealthy benefactor. After arranging various European tours, including one of the American Ballet (1950), the two men formed a nonprofit corporation, Everyman Opera, with the express purpose of sending *Porgy and Bess* abroad.

The project was timely. Freed from the Nazis, continental Europe had become particularly receptive to jazz and other forms of previously verboten American art. Moreover, this particular work could counter Communist propaganda about race relations in the States—or so Breen and Davis argued—by presenting an accomplished black cast in a work that sympathetically portrayed blacks—an argument that, abetted by Davis's personal friendship with President Harry Truman, helped clinch some State Department support. "*Porgy and Bess* was sent to Europe by the State Department to show that we were included in society," remarked Martha Flowers, one of Breen's eventual Besses. The State Department might also have been mindful of local prejudice against black troops in occupied Austria and Germany, as well as of the anti-Semitism that only recently had banned the Gershwins from areas controlled by Hitler.[12]

Breen and Davis recruited a wealth of talent, doubled up on various roles so as not to overtax the principals. The leading cast included William

Warfield (Porgy), Leontyne Price (Bess), John McCurry (Crown), Helen Thigpen (Serena), Cab Calloway (Sportin' Life), Joseph James (Jake), Helen Colbert (Clara), Georgia Burke (Maria), and, from the original cast, Helen Dowdy (Lily/Strawberry Woman) and Ray Yeates (Crab Man), both of whose street cries had been electrifying audiences since 1935.

Warfield and Price were only at the beginning of their celebrated careers, though the former had recently won plaudits for his 1950 Town Hall debut recital and his performance as Joe in the 1951 film remake of *Show Boat*. In contrast, the twenty-five-year-old Price, a Mississippi native fresh out of Juilliard, was virtually unknown; Breen and Davis first heard her as Alice Ford in a school production of *Falstaff.* "Being Bess was already half of me, I mean, most of me anyway," she stated years later. "I don't mean the character itself, I mean being wonderfully black. . . . It's like, here I am, isn't it terrific?" Though perhaps lacking the poignancy of Duncan and Brown, Warfield and Price, who recorded operatic selections under Skitch Henderson in 1963, made a winning pair, and their interpretations—Warfield's, dignified and forthright; Price's, earthy and irrepressible—decisively shaped midcentury perceptions of the opera, while establishing high vocal standards for the roles. (Warfield and Price, incidentally, first met each other in rehearsal and married before the production went abroad, so that Europeans saw newlyweds perform the title roles.)[13]

No longer the headliner he had once been, Cab Calloway (1907–1994) jumped at the chance to play Sportin' Life. As suggested by the recording of the opera's 1959 film version (in which he substituted for Sammy Davis Jr., who for contractual reasons could not participate in the released sound track), he brought considerable vocal nuance and heft to the role, even if—at least at that point—he could not manage the high B♭ at the end of "There's a Boat Dat's Leavin' Soon for New York." (Calloway continued to sing the music well into his eighties, including his final recording, a cantor-flavored "It Ain't Necessarily So" taped in 1993 for a compilation of selections from the opera conducted by Erich Kunzel.) The hulking John McCurry, standing six feet six inches, made an imposing Crown. Wolfgang Roth designed the dazzling sets, including a Catfish Row inspired by Soudeikine, but more colorful; and Jed Mace produced the equally eye-popping costumes, including a flaming-red dress and boa for Bess. Once again, Eva Jessye directed the chorus and Alexander Smallens conducted the orchestra.

Unable to secure an acceptable director, Breen, assisted by Ella Gerber, assumed that responsibility himself, producing an entirely new three-act version of the work, one that incorporated some cuts from earlier productions but added some previously unstaged material from the original score, including "I Ain't Got No Shame" and "Buzzard Song." Breen also rearranged materials, especially in act 3, including placing "Good Mornin', Sistuh!" at the top of scene 2, and "Buzzard Song" in scene 3 (thus necessitating a change of lyrics from "An' Porgy's young again" to "An' Porgy's home again").[14]

Limiting the production to only two sets (for Catfish Row and Kittiwah Island), Breen largely avoided set changes between scenes, thus gaining extra time for the newly restored material while achieving unprecedented momentum. In addition, he created a sensation with his rather lurid staging of Porgy's murder of Crown, and, more notoriously, an erotic seduction scene that had Crown sensuously fondle Bess and Bess rip off Crown's shirt. "Bobby Breen was a marvelously inventive director," recalled Warfield. "Bouncy and boyish and bursting with fresh ideas, he was always looking for a new highlight to accentuate—and where the libretto lacked them, he would make them up. A quirky bit of business, a slang expression that seemed to fit, a gesture or facial expression that might underline the dialogue—he'd try anything on for size, and just as easily remove it a few days later as he tried still newer director's tricks." Breen also encouraged the cast members to project the "essential flavor" of Catfish Row, telling them with regard to his own Irish background, as his wife Wilva remembered, "If I were cast in any Irish folk play, I would come up with all the richness of the Irish countryside, all the local color . . . and I would revel in it." Commented Martha Flowers: "I was always amazed that he was not put among the great stage directors of all time. No one had ever done *Porgy and Bess* that way before, with the subtleties, the touches that were so natural and beautiful. . . . And he staged it in such a way that audiences abroad, not knowing the language, nor having the libretto, clearly understood what was going on at all times."[15]

The Breen-Davis production opened in Dallas at the State Fair Auditorium on June 9, 1952, and toured three other American cities (a planned engagement at the Met fell through) before leaving for Vienna, Berlin, London, and Paris. Cab Calloway could not make the Dallas premiere, which seemed hampered as well by an initial stiffness on the part of Warfield and Thigpen—John Rosenfield in the *Saturday Review* complained that the production was "curiously de-Africanized"—but the production proved an immediate hit, and as it traveled to Chicago, Pittsburgh, and Washington, D.C. (where President Truman, cabinet members, military officials, and ambassadors attended the August 6 gala premiere), it won virtually nothing but plaudits. Price especially wowed the critics, but what most impressed was that the production, compared with those of the Theatre Guild and Cheryl Crawford, offered, in Jay Carmody's words, "at last the perfect blend of drama and music." "Hundreds of brief miniatures of beauty, of tragic power, stand out in the mind," wrote Paul Hume in the *Washington Post* after a second viewing, "but as they stand against a background of complete blending of the elements of a marvelous show." At the same time, critics had widely divergent opinions about Cab Calloway; a few disliked his mannered stage presence, though many more thought him superb and in some instances, the best thing about the production. At the very least, he stopped the show with "It Ain't Necessarily So."[16]

The idea of presenting the work abroad under government auspices proved—aside from the unimpeachable advantages of showcasing a distinguished black cast—more controversial. The *Pittsburgh Courier,* for instance, published an editorial that strenuously objected to State Department support, declaring the work a "raw, throbbing musical drama" that revealed "depraved members of the colored minority in America engaged in its stereotyped role. . . . It is a vehicle of shame, sorrow and disgust." Some commentators, black and white alike, agreed, but the opera won overwhelming support, again across racial lines, an attitude that seemed vindicated by the work's huge success abroad. Warfield recalled that the cast and most leaders in the black community felt that the opera was

> a celebration of our culture, and not an exploitation of it. The work didn't snigger at African-Americans. It ennobled the characters it depicted. . . . Almost without exception the reviewers in Europe recognized *Porgy and Bess* for what it was—a story of triumph, not degradation, despite our very real problems. By merging white and black perceptions, in its writing and in its performance, the folk opera transcended purely racial orientation and achieved that universality that characterized other world masterpieces rooted in German or Italian or other ethnic themes.

"If we begin to be more concerned about the impressions our culture makes than about the truth of what our culture is," wrote Brooks Atkinson in the *Times,* "we are drawing close to the totalitarian point of view."[17]

The production opened in Vienna at the Volksoper on September 7 and in Berlin at the Titania Palast on September 18 to great acclaim. At the end of the opera, the first-night audiences in both cities erupted into cheers and applause that lasted close to a half-hour, with fourteen curtain calls counted in Vienna, twenty-one in Berlin. The many thoughtful notices showed nothing but deep respect for the work and the production alike, including Smallens's idiomatic direction of the Volksoper and RIAS (Radio im Amerikanischen Sektor) orchestras (which averaged about twenty more players than the usual thirty-five or so employed in the States). The common American concerns about the verisimilitude of the drama and the quality of the recitatives simply failed to surface; the critics—including such formidable names as Max Graf and Friedrich Torberg in Vienna, and Werner Oehlmann and H. H. Stuckenschmidt in Berlin—widely regarded *Porgy* as a uniquely realistic, brilliantly crafted, and emotionally gripping work of musical theater. Although Kurt Westphal acknowledged the opera's eclectic origins, he argued that the concept of "kitsch" failed to apply "because the music is so obviously suited to what transpires onstage." Even Dezsö Hajas of Vienna's Communist *Der Abend* found the performance so captivating as to make it "almost possible to forget the propaganda intention which surely had been the true reason for this guest performance."[18]

In an attempt to contextualize the piece as a "jazzoper" or a "volksoper," these reviews often drew comparisons with other works. However, most made distinctions as well, arguing that Gershwin did not so much accommodate folk music (as did Smetana), jazz (as did Ernst Krenek and Kurt Weill), and modern life (as did Alban Berg or Gian-Carlo Menotti) as create a new kind of opera that emerged directly from folk music, jazz, and modern life, an achievement that gave the work its hyperrealism, and that was abetted, some also claimed, by its African American story and cast. In this respect, the Austrian and German critics showed themselves more attuned to Gershwin's intentions than many of their American counterparts.[19]

In London, where the production opened at the Stoll Theatre on October 9, audiences once again cheered, and a number of notices declared the work "brilliant," "dynamic," "terrific," and "completely shattering." As in Vienna and Berlin, some also made admiring comparisons with *Wozzeck* (the *Scotsman* ranked the opera alongside *Wozzeck*, *Mathis der Maler,* and *The Threepenny Opera* as "one of the four significant operas written between the two Great Wars"), while others applauded the work's uniqueness ("Gershwin was a law unto himself," concluded *John o' London's Weekly*). At the same time, more like the American press, a number of even positive reviews criticized the work's recitatives, its "sprawling" and "untidy" structure, its "thin" and "patchy" orchestration, and its "unrelenting" vitality. A remark by eminent drama critic Kenneth Tynan epitomized such ambivalence: "I would not respect anyone who loved all of it, but I will tolerate no one who does not travel miles to see it." In a more severe review, Mosco Carner, a Puccini authority, stated, "I was neither shattered nor deeply touched by it, merely entertained but that in a high degree. . . . Almost throughout the opera you feel the hand of an amateur gifted and sincere but sadly lacking in *savoir faire*. Nor does the general level of the score let you forget for long that its author was the uncrowned king of Tin Pan Alley obsessed with a pathetic ambition to write 'straight' music."[20]

Perhaps owing in part to such mixed notices, British attendance flagged, and after a disappointing three-month run the Breen-Davis production arrived earlier than expected at the Théâtre de l'Empire in Paris, where the opera opened on February 16, 1953. The glittering first-night audience, reported Nicole Hirsch in *Le Soir,* could not praise the work highly enough; writer Jean Kessel, actor Jean Marais, and Princess Marie Blanche de Polignac declared the opera "heavenly, sensational, overwhelming, extraordinary, stupendous," while writer Lise Deharme and composers Francis Poulenc and Joseph Kosma (the Hungarian-born film composer best known for his 1947 song "Autumn Leaves") praised its "purity" and "power." The critics commented especially on the work's naturalness, which Emile Vuillermoz found "dazzling" and "extraordinary," and which Claude Baignères thought more truthful than any documentary, writing, "Gershwin has torn down the wall against which so many composers have hit their heads." René Demesnil compared the opera's subtext, described as the "anguish of the oppressed crushed by fate as well as by man's cruelty," to Mussorgsky and even Dostoyevsky, a connection he attributed to the composer's Russian roots. Baignères similarly noted resemblances to Mussorgsky, as well as to Debussy, Stravinsky, and Charpentier, though he added, "no music could be newer, more original, more direct or more effective." On hand for the occasion, American composer Ned Rorem described the production as "the big event of the year" and a "success fou."[21]

The tour's artistic and diplomatic success—President Eisenhower commended the company as "making a real contribution to the kind of understanding between peoples that alone can bring mutual respect and trust," while Eleanor Roosevelt voiced her support as well—helped extend its life. After an eight-month run at New York's Ziegfeld Theatre (March–November 1953), Breen and Davis launched a second North American tour, including sixteen American cities as well as Toronto and Montreal (December 1953–September 1954); a tour of Europe and the Middle East, including cities in Italy, France, Yugoslavia, Egypt, Greece,

Israel, Morocco, Spain, Switzerland, and Belgium (September 1954–June 1955); a Latin American tour, including cities in Brazil, Uruguay, Argentina, Chile, Peru, Colombia, Venezuela, Panama, and Mexico (July–October 1955); and a third European tour, including cities in Belgium, Germany, the Soviet Union, Poland, Czechoslovakia, Holland, Norway, and Denmark (November 1955–June 1956). With a troupe of about seventy, the show was expensive, but Breen managed to keep it afloat thanks to Davis's fund-raising efforts (including personal loans), fitful government support, and, in the most surprising coup, some assistance from the Soviet government, which helped bring the opera to Leningrad and Moscow. By the time the tour wrapped up in Amsterdam on June 3, 1956, Smallens estimated that he had conducted the work more than three thousand times.[22]

On its return from its first European tour in 1953, the production initially retained more or less the same cast, with the notable exception of Warfield, who had scheduling conflicts and was replaced by his principal alternative, LeVern Hutcherson, among others (though not Lawrence Tibbett, whose ten guest appearances scheduled for July and August had to be canceled after the baritone contracted food poisoning). Breen, who traveled extensively with the company, further enlivened the show by, among other things, having characters frequently open and close shutters and pop out of windows, reminding one spectator of the last act of *Der Rosenkavalier.* Over the summer, he additionally quickened the pace by presenting the opera in two acts, thereby saving a second fifteen-minute interval and shortening the show to about two and a half hours. Warfield could barely recognize it when he attended a performance late in its New York run.[23]

The opera's opening at the Ziegfeld on March 9, 1953, constituted yet another milestone in its reception history. All the more prepared to love the work thanks to its well-publicized international success, the first-night audience burst forth with cheers—one observer, catching a later performance, "never heard such shouts of approbation, such sheer bedlam of delight"—while for virtually all critics, the production vindicated the composer's original vision and confirmed the work's status as a great American opera. "It is a major work of art," declared Brooks Atkinson in the *Times,* "a tumultuous evocation of life among some high-spirited, poignant, admirable human beings. It is all Gershwin and it is gold."[24]

The production made a particularly deep impression on the young Stephen Sondheim (b. 1930), at the beginning of his career as one of the preeminent American musical dramatists of his generation. In later years, he would even cite the opera as his "favorite musical." "I always find *Porgy* moving, and I always find it surprising and inventive, and I'm always jealous of it," he stated in 2000. "I've always wished that I had written it." Speaking generally of his attraction to Gershwin and Harold Arlen, Sondheim—who based one of his most memorable songs, "Losing My Mind" (from *Follies*), on "The Man I Love"—further remarked in 2002, "I could wallow in *Porgy and Bess,* the chords alone." In his study of Sondheim's stylistic development, Steve Swayne located certain aspects of the opera, including the quartal sonorities of "My Man's Gone Now" and the polytextual complexities of "Oh, Hev'nly Father," thought especially influential.[25]

As the Breen-Davis production toured the continent, American and Canadian audiences and critics responded enthusiastically. "Not that *Porgy and Bess* emerged very much like an opera as we know that form," wrote Herbert Whittaker in the *Toronto Globe and Mail,* "but rather as we would like to know it—a complete fusion of drama and music, with a miraculously equal stress on both." Tellingly, the more quibbling reviews in New York and elsewhere largely took issue with the production as opposed to the work. Some missed Todd Duncan, John Bubbles, or Ruby Elzy (though many thought John McCurry the best Crown to date), and a number found the direction too busy (George Jean Nathan wrote that in attempting to convey the work's "primitive emotion," Breen succeeded "in conveying what is only primitive theatre"). The show also sparked some minor controversy in Los Angeles when the management of the Philharmonic Auditorium (owned by the Temple Baptist Church) requested, in vain, that Breen tone down the seduction scene.[26]

At the same time, the work itself encountered some negative criticism. In a review pointedly titled "A Major Musical," drama critic Eric Bentley, for instance, wrote, "Heyward and Gershwin created a world, not an action; an idyll, not a drama; a series of numbers, not a tragic or comic whole." Some writers—including jazz critic Vic Bellerby and writer Verna Arvey—took issue with the opera's representation of African Americans. James Hicks, the noted black journalist for Baltimore's *Afro-American,* was particularly outspoken in this regard, condemning the current revival as "the most insulting, the most libelous, the most degrading act that could possibly be perpetrated against colored Americans of modern time" (taken to task for such remarks by members of the touring company, Hicks unapologetically wrote five years later, "I still think 'Porgy' stinks—even though, it does give some jobs to Negro show folks"). And while two writers for the African American *Chicago Defender* claimed

that the work offered a "faithful portrayal of Negro life," they disagreed
about its possible effects on "race relations"; Dean Gordon Hancock
thought that the opera played into the hands of "reactionary white elements," whereas George Daniels opined that such "meaningless bla-bla"
insulted the intelligence of the work's global audience.[27]

Such occasional protests notwithstanding, the Breen-Davis production—
even without Price, who left to pursue more glamorous opportunities—
went from triumph to triumph. Even in Leningrad, where the absence
of programs on opening night made it difficult for attendants to understand dramatic details, and where, as in Moscow, the public generally
reacted warily to moments of perceived lewdness, audiences responded
with standing ovations. The work's success in such operatic bastions as
La Fenice in Venice and especially La Scala in Milan (where Gloria Davy
and Leslie Scott sang the title roles at the February 22, 1955, premiere)
afforded distinct satisfactions, while the performances behind the Iron
Curtain held special cultural significance, as opening nights in particular were gala affairs attended by high-ranking government personnel and
military brass. In Moscow in early 1956, for instance, state leaders Niko-
lai Bulganin, Andrei Gromyko, Nikita Khrushchev, and Vyacheslav
Molotov attended the opera, as did contralto Larisa Avdeyeva and composer Aram Khachaturian.[28]

Ostensibly in preparation for these Russian performances, Khatcha-
turian published a tribute to Gershwin only a few months earlier in which
he extolled not only the composer's "wealth of beautiful vocal and instrumental melodies (always original and always in good taste)," but also
"his ability to absorb, subtly perceive and critically select all the best that
existed in the musical life of America in the twenties and thirties." Having seen the opera's 1945 Moscow premiere, and now reviewing the score,
Khachaturian praised both the work's solo numbers and the "impressive mass choruses, written with great polyphonic skill and a fine sense
of folk color." He further expressed the hope that "a closer acquaintance
with the music of George Gershwin and other talented American composers, as well as the performance of Soviet music in America, will greatly
contribute to the establishment of genuinely friendly relations between
the Soviet and American peoples and serve to strengthen mutual confidence
and respect."[29]

The opera's critical reception on these later European tours proved
as favorable as before. In Italy, Rubens Tedeschi declared it "a masterwork of the lyric theatre," while Riccardo Malipiero praised its rein-
vention of the genre, an accomplishment he associated with its Amer-

ican provenance: "Gershwin didn't have a tradition to defend, a civilization to explain, a crisis to resolve; he had to write an opera, with his own means, with his own longings, with his own passion." Some Communist critics proved more equivocal, with the Czech press, for instance, publishing pieces by Josef Kotek and Norbert Fryd that raised the familiar concern that, even if the Heywards and Gershwins clearly viewed the "painful position" of the American Negro, they knew neither "the causes of the situation" nor "how such horror may be wiped off the earth." Still, the overwhelmingly positive response to the opera in the Soviet bloc led some Americans, like author Eleanor Wheeler, to reevaluate the work.[30]

Before leaving on its second European tour, Everyman Opera recruited, as its principal dancer (featured in the picnic scene), a six-foot-tall cabaret singer, Maya Angelou, later a popular writer and poet. Remaining with the production through Rome, Angelou later recounted her experiences with the company ("the greatest party of my life," as she recalled) at some length in her 1976 memoir, *Singin' and Swingin' and Gettin' Merry Like Christmas*. Deeply moved by the opera, she assumed that "in the course of time the play would become stale to me and I would become partially indifferent to its pathos. Over the next year, however, I found myself more touched by the tale and more and more impressed by the singers and actors who told it." Angelou maintained her affection for the opera, stating in a 1997 documentary, "*Porgy and Bess* is a truth, 'tis a human truth. Take the beauty that is inherent in it and exalt it and cherish it and be made taller and better and freer by it, with gratitude for it."[31]

Traveling with the company to Leningrad, Truman Capote penned a more sardonic backstage account, one, however, that focused not so much on cast members as on various American and Russian ancillaries. Originally published in the *New Yorker* and then revised as *The Muses Are Heard,* Capote's report had little to say about the production either, other than to place it in the context of Soviet propaganda and to furnish a nuanced analysis of the tenuous Leningrad premiere. But overhearing some young people singing tunes from the opera after one performance, he noted that, thus "stimulated into new visions," this embrace by the young represented, compared to all the surrounding hype, "a victory of finer significance, one that would mature and matter." Not only did the music remain popular in Russia, but stagings of the work quickly proliferated throughout the Soviet republics, including a 1961 underground performance by some Moscow drama students. In 1965 the Soviets even produced their own vocal score of the opera in translation, *Porgi i Bess.*[32]

Back home, opera companies neglected the work, in part because of the logistical problems involved in hiring a mostly black cast. But on March 31, 1962, the New York City Opera launched a new production of the Breen-Davis version. Directed by William Ball, conducted by Julius Rudel, and starring Lawrence Winters and Leesa Foster, the production had slipped through the back door, so to speak, via the company's sister organization, Jean Dalrymple's New York City Center Light Opera Company, which had mounted a similar production in 1961, also conducted by Rudel, though with William Warfield and Irving Barnes alternating as Porgy, and Leesa Foster and Martha Flowers alternating as Bess. Warfield and Barnes returned to perform the work under Rudel for the Light Opera in 1964, but now with John Fearnley directing, and with Veronica Tyler and Barbara Smith Conrad alternating as Bess. The following year, Ella Gerber restaged the work for the City Opera with new sets and costumes, and with Andrew Frierson and Joyce Bryant in the title roles under the baton of Dean Ryan. All four productions were held at City Center, the Moorish-style theater on West 55th Street that housed the City Opera before its move to Lincoln Center.[33]

These City Center productions, which ran from six to sixteen performances, arrived amid signs of growing uneasiness about the work, especially on racial grounds. True, Howard Taubman and John Ardoin both liked the 1961 Light Opera production, which for the former caught the "rapture and jubilation" that Gershwin had "poured into" the piece, and for the latter confirmed the work as "an opera in the best sense of the word," one that could "hold its head high among 20th-century opera." And Raymond Ericson, reviewing the 1962 City Opera premiere, similarly spoke of the piece as "an important work in the American lyric theatre, more viable than most other serious contemporary American operas." But a *New Yorker* review of the same performance by Winthrop Sargeant argued that the drama, while "viable," seemed "to involve a good many stereotypes of plot and character and to present a picture of Negro life that is gradually becoming almost as dated as 'Uncle Tom's Cabin.' The necessity of singing synthetic spirituals, the romanticizing of the Negro as either a sexually supercharged animal or an oily crook or a good, infinitely pitiable masochist are all part of this picture. . . . The music, moreover, is Broadway music—music that reflects what Broadway thinks the Negro should feel, not what his own musical expression shows him to feel." Crown's seduction of Bess contained "raucous music that might have been written for a bump-and-grind routine in a burlesque house." In the end, the opera remained a "bastard product."[34]

In his 1965 review for the *Times*, Harold Schonberg more completely savaged the work as "mawkish," "sentimental," "awkward," and "stilted," writing, "All I can say is that it is a wonder that anybody can take it seriously. It is not a good opera. It is not a good anything . . . and in light of recent developments, it is embarrassing. 'Porgy and Bess' contains as many stereotypes in its way as 'Uncle Tom's Cabin.'" Although similar opinions had been expressed over the years, their appearance in the *New Yorker* and the *Times* suggested that such attitudes had become more entrenched. Indeed, interest in the work seemed to decline nationwide. The City Opera would wait thirty-five years before performing it again, and although the opera made its way to Charleston in 1970 and helped that city, on the occasion of its three hundredth anniversary, toward integration—"You saw people with handkerchiefs out and you just knew that something had happened that was supposed to have happened. I tell you, it was a great experience," recalled that production's Crown, Kent Byas—a 1975 performance by the Los Angeles Civic Light Opera drew only lukewarm response.[35]

During this period of national eclipse, the opera maintained a strong presence overseas. In 1965, for example, the New Zealand Opera company and director Ella Gerber launched a celebrated staging starring Inia ("Happy") Te Wiata (1915–1971), the outstanding Maori bass-baritone who had created the role of Dansker in Benjamin Britten's *Billy Budd* (1951). Using a largely Maori cast, this production—which broke box-office records in New Zealand and later toured Australia as well—resulted in broadened opportunities for Maori actors and singers. George Henare's participation in the opera, for instance, marked the start of his distinguished career, which included many years as a lead player with Auckland's Mercury Theatre. The production also proved a watershed for actor-producer-director Don Selwyn, a notable champion of Maori drama. By opening doors to minority artists, *Porgy and Bess* played a part in New Zealand society comparable to its role in the States.[36]

Other theaters around the world staged their own versions of the work for enthusiastic audiences. In Tallinn a production starring the beloved Estonian singer George Ots sold out, while in Tel Aviv a performance with Te Wiata left the Israeli audience dancing and clapping down the aisles. And in the early 1970s the Swiss Theatre Touring Company brought the piece to dozens of cities in Europe. "There's no doubt about it," stated James Helme Sutcliffe in a review of a 1970 performance by East Berlin's Komische Oper: "*Porgy and Bess* is still the only American opera that meets all the difficult requirements of that genre."[37]

Directed by Götz Friedrich, the latter production used a translation by Horst Seeger, and—aside from Cullen Maiden (Porgy) and Carolyn Smith-Meyer (Bess)—a white cast (including popular cabaret singer Manfred Krug as Sportin' Life), with the opera's white characters in whiteface and dark glasses so as to distinguish them from the rest of the players. In Friedrich's own view, as put forth in two essays (1969 and 1970), the work—better regarded by Europeans as a "folk" than a "Negro" opera—essentially concerned the hardships and strivings of an oppressed class, with Porgy a proletarian hero, the "promised land" a symbol for freedom, and Kittiwah Island a throwback to memories of an ancestral home. Set designer Reinhart Zimmermann's portrayal of Catfish Row as a real slum (as opposed to the quaintly stylized sets usually seen) helped underscore this Marxist view of the work, which a close associate of Friedrich's described as "absolutely one of his favorite operas." When Friedrich remounted the opera for the Theater des Westens in West Berlin, first in 1988 and again in 1989, 1991, and 1993, he met the Gershwin estate's demands that he use a black cast singing in English. But he affirmed his distinctive reading of the opera through the presence of a stone-like figure, representing Abraham Lincoln, perched onstage under an American flag; and through set designs (by Hans Schavernoch) that turned Catfish Row into a Harlem-style tenement and Kittiwah Island into a fantasy jungle landscape of blue-green tubes.[38]

During the 1960s and early 1970s, critical opinion mirrored the gap between the opera's reception at home and abroad. On the national front, for instance, Harold Cruse's *The Crisis of the Negro Intellectual* (1967) condemned the opera as "the most perfect symbol" of white and especially Jewish theft, exploitation, and control of black creative talent; dismissed the score as "a rather pedestrian blend of imitation-Puccini and imitation–South Carolina–Negro folk music"; and called for a permanent ban of the work "by all Negro performers in the United States." Other American writers, especially in the black community, voiced strong—if not quite so disdainful—criticisms as well. In 1963, for example, Tim Dennison Sr., while crediting Gershwin for making "a significant contribution towards carrying out Dvořák's heartening prediction" that a distinctive American music would take root from Negro melodies, felt that a black composer would be more temperamentally suited to fulfill this vision, and lambasted especially the opera's libretto as "altogether derogatory to the American Negro, and extremely out of line with his present ambitions." And in 1967 Loften Mitchell repudiated the opera as the work of people "who didn't know anything about Negroes."[39]

Other American scholars of the time voiced similar concerns. Whereas Gilbert Chase, in *America's Music* (1955), had spoken at respectful length about the opera's "vitality," "validity," and "stature," William Austin, in *Music in the 20th Century* (1966), reported that at least for some listeners, the work's "incredible characters and pretentious tragic plot made it inferior to Gershwin's best musical comedies," an assessment seconded by H. Wiley Hitchcock in the first edition of *Music in the United States* (1969). And Richard Crawford, citing mostly disapproving critics in a 1972 article about the work as "a symbol of cultural collision," concluded that the opera, though redeemed by black performers, was nonetheless in "jeopardy" of "survival."[40]

In contrast, European intellectuals seemed, as Louis Biancolli pointed out in 1965, more ready "to accept Gershwin's genius on his own terms." In his landmark book on American music, *Music in a New Found Land* (1966), British critic and composer Wilfrid Mellers devoted nothing less than an entire chapter to the opera, which the author viewed, somewhat like Friedrich, as fundamentally a parable about the struggle between, on the one hand, alienation, corruption, commerce, and modern urban life, and on the other, preindustrial harmony and innocence—a struggle whose reconciliation lay in the "personal fulfillment and togetherness that Porgy and Bess seek" and in the hopeful vision of New York as a promised land. As such, the opera, argued Mellers, transcended its racial aspects, "which is why it is of no consequence that the book offers a synthetic picture of Negro life." Mellers further claimed for the work "immense" if only "potential" historical significance in its ability to encompass, like the operas of Mozart and Verdi, "a social act, an entertainment, and a human experience with unexpectedly disturbing implications."[41]

The American bicentennial marked a new era in the work's history. In early 1976 Lorin Maazel and the Cleveland Orchestra released the first recording of the complete opera on the Decca-London label with Leona Mitchell and Jamaican-born Willard White heading a fine cast that also included McHenry Boatwright (Crown), Florence Quivar (Serena), François Clemmons (Sportin' Life), and Barbara Hendricks (Clara). Decca executive Ray Minshull recalled that the project—which he described as "one of the most difficult and complicated planning operations I can remember"—gained some incentive when plans for a Leonard Bernstein recording of the work fell through in 1975. Whatever its limitations, the recording, which won a first-place spot on *Billboard*'s classical-music chart as well as a Grammy Award, made a historic case for the unabridged score. Maazel himself stated on the occasion, "Gershwin's compassion for individuals is Verdian, his comprehension of them, Mozartean. His grasp of folk-spirit is as firm and subtle as Moussorgsky's, his melodic inventiveness rivals Bellini's, ingenious and innovative are his compositional techniques."[42]

William Youngren, who deemed Maazel's conducting "marked by a pervasive impersonality and rhythmic deadness," thought it "absurd to put Gershwin in a class with Mozart and Verdi," but he credited the recording nonetheless with helping him reach the "unexpected but firm conviction that *Porgy and Bess* is not only Gershwin's finest work but is also a fine opera, better than most both musically and dramatically." And although composer-critic Eric Salzman, in *Stereo Review,* similarly wished that the performance had greater "crispness, clarity, and punch," he, too, thought that the release demonstrated that the work was "really a grand *grand* opera, . . . a fine, moving, epic-dramatic work on a really large and powerful scale," and "a deeply human document of human passions in a strong social setting."[43]

Then on July 1, 1976, the Houston Grand Opera launched the most complete version of the opera to that date. Coproduced by Sherwin Goldman, who dreamed of a complete *Porgy* onstage, and HGO, whose venturesome director, David Gockley, had mounted Scott Joplin's *Treemonisha* (as realized by Gunther Schuller) in 1975, this new production had a rotating cast that included Donnie Ray Albert (Porgy), Clamma Dale (Bess), Andrew Smith (Crown), Wilma Shakesnider (Serena), and Larry Marshall (Sportin' Life). Jack O'Brien directed, Robert Randolph created the sets, and Nancy Potts designed the costumes. In order to keep the opera under three hours and avoid costly overtime, conductor John DeMain made a few dozen cuts throughout the score and squeezed the material into two acts, as had become customary. However, RCA recorded the opera in its entirety for its 1976 cast album (which won a Grammy Award as well as France's Grand Prix du Disque).[44]

Over the next two years, HGO brought this production to dozens of cities in the States, Canada, and Europe, including sixteen weeks in the fall of 1976 at the Uris Theatre (since 1983, the Gershwin) on Broadway (where it won the Tony award for "most innovative" revival and another five Tony nominations) and six weeks in the winter of 1977 at the Palais des Congrès in Paris (where Donnie Ray Albert partnered with Wilhelmenia Fernandez, who later starred in the 1981 French film *Diva*). The enthusiasm that greeted the opera at each turn recalled the success of the Breen-Davis production, with the critics—although they agreed that Clamma Dale was a sensational Bess—lavishing special praise on the work itself, deemed "the single great American opera" by Douglas Watt in the *New York Daily News,* and possibly "the greatest of all verismo operas" by Julius Novick in the *Village Voice.* Jack Kroll in *Newsweek* drew analogies with Fitzgerald and Hemingway ("it's poetry written on greenbacks"); Clive Barnes in the *New York Times* was reminded "strongly, in every way, of the operas of Janáček"; and Walter Kerr, also in the *Times,* wondered if any straight American play offered anything like it: "There's got to be an equivalent, at the top; there's got to be."[45]

The production also prompted some revisionist thinking about the work. A number of reviews, for instance, found the opera's long-disputed recitatives not only to contain, as Alan Rich wrote in *New York,* "passages of enormous skill and subtlety," but to represent, as Martin Gottfried stated in the *New York Post,* "a considerable improvement on traditional recitative." Similarly, the work's blend of operatic and musical-comedy styles seemed more impressive than problematic: "The fact that so many of the set pieces are essentially enrichments and extensions of the American popular song idiom of the day," stated Douglas Watt, "is not only a completely natural and cheering outgrowth of the musical-comedy world in which Gershwin had long been a master; it is also precisely in keeping with the idiom, American folk opera." The virtues of this particular production presumably aided such reassessment, but presenting the opera whole—or nearly so—plainly helped as well.[46]

More than ever before, critics also expressed admiration for the work's humanity, as in Irving Lowens's claim in the *Washington Star* that the production underlined the "universal aspects of the story" and the "basic human dignity" of the inhabitants of Catfish Row, "not their Negritude." Such assertions—though in line with long-held views of many black cast members—reflected not only a changed social temper from the 1960s, but also director O'Brien's conviction that *Porgy* "was not a put-down of blacks, written by whites, but a moving story about people who happen to be black. I was determined to tell the truth about the show as I felt it, in terms of how it dealt with love, jealousy, death and adversity. What a revelation! The company went with me all the way." At the same time, Todd Duncan, attending a performance in Washington, commented, "Every single move is just right. It is so Negro."[47]

The newly emerging critical consensus surrounding the HGO production found scholarly expression in Lawrence Starr's paper, "Toward a Reevaluation of Gershwin's Porgy and Bess," delivered in 1978 and published in 1984. Starr, who attended a performance at the Uris, praised the opera's universal message, its cohesive structure, and its splendid recitatives. "Little jewels of melody were revealed on virtually every page of the score," he wrote. " . . . It is as if the recitative in the opera is potential song, a musical language that grows into song with considerable ease and smoothness whenever the drama renders it appropriate or necessary."[48]

Not all spectators were so convinced, however. Harold Schonberg once again delivered a blistering attack in the *Times,* describing the work as "fake," "distasteful," "awkward," "pretentious," "commercial, slick and sentimental," and even less commendable than such "junk" as the *Rhapsody in Blue* and *An American in Paris.* And in response to Starr's 1978 paper, Richard Crawford, reluctant to privilege a score thought "technically suspect," argued that the opera's success depended on the "universal familiarity" of its famous "tunes," writing, "*Porgy and Bess* succeeds and endures perhaps less because it harnesses the standard technical machinery of composition than because Gershwin could deliver musically when he needed to." But Schonberg admitted his a "minority report," while Crawford addressed an academic community assumed to be "uneasy" with Gershwin's more ambitions work.[49]

In 1983 the HGO and Goldman, this time in conjunction with New York's Radio City Music Hall, once again brought the work to various North American cities. Based on the 1976 production, this revival featured a number of new singers under the baton of C. William Harwood as well as lavishly redesigned sets by Douglas W. Schmidt (including a Kittiwah Island illuminated by an enormous tropical sun) big enough to fill out the large venues slated for the tour, including Radio City, with its nearly six thousand seats and its stage (at 144 feet) almost one third larger than that of the Metropolitan Opera. This "mega-version," as critic John Von Rhein termed it, displayed *Porgy* in a somewhat new light as grand public entertainment and spectacle. The amplification proved only variably successful—as it had at the Uris in 1976—but the production garnered raves nonetheless, and moreover attracted, as Leonore Gershwin had hoped, a new black audience for the work. Walter Kerr, reviewing the opera at Radio City, thrilled to the act 1 fight scene as it unfolded against a Catfish Row the size of a city block, but more than that, argued that the production disclosed the work's operatic essence: "If it were taken as some sort of Broadway musical, the audience would expect to hear it, every word; it would also very likely demand enough intimacy to see faces and to form personal attachments. Here it has clearly opted for something else: for the rise and fall of the musical structure, the melodic cross-breeding, the surges and retreats of sound that make an ultimate shape of their own. These things *can* be heard. Since they combine to create a masterpiece, hearing them bathe an entire auditorium is in itself quite enough."[50]

In honor of the fiftieth anniversary of Gershwin's death and the tenth anniversary of the 1976 production, HGO and Goldman remounted this revival for a 1986–1987 world tour innovatively cosponsored by a consortium of American opera companies, including the Greater Miami Opera, whose black director, Willie Anthony Waters, defended the work as "a period piece." Donnie Ray Albert, not seen in the 1983 tour, recreated the role of Porgy, now paired with one of that production's Besses, Henrietta Davis. After playing in seventeen American cities, the production traveled to stages around the world, including Paris's Théâtre du Châtelet, Munich's Deutsches Theater, and, eventually in 1991, Tokyo's Bunkamura Theater.[51]

Meanwhile, the Metropolitan Opera finally staged America's best-known opera in 1985 on the occasion of the work's fiftieth anniversary. From the beginning of his association with the company, conductor James Levine (b. 1943) had wanted to perform the piece, but the expense of a large black cast, the success of the Uris Theatre and Radio City revivals, and lingering doubts about the work's pedigree had stymied such ambitions. But now, among other developments, a growing roster of black singers in the company, combined with new contractual arrangements with the Met chorus, made such an enterprise economically feasible (though the production still cost a hefty eight hundred thousand dollars).

The Met scheduled sixteen performances for the winter of 1985. The premiere cast included Simon Estes (Porgy), Grace Bumbry (Bess), Gregg Baker (Crown), Florence Quivar (Serena), and Charles Williams (Sportin' Life), with popular actor Larry Storch playing the detective, as he had at Radio City. Nathaniel Merrill, the director, and Robert O'Hearn, the set and costume designer—two standbys of an earlier Met regime—collaborated with choreographer Arthur Mitchell and the Dance Theatre of Harlem. Presiding over sixty-five instrumentalists (including onstage pianist and six-piece stage band) and a seventy-person chorus (prepared by David Stivender and Lloyd Walser), James Levine presented the work—for the first time in its history—completely uncut and with two intermissions, which brought the total performance time to about four hours.

In interviews leading up to the premiere, the key participants made connections between the work and the standard operatic repertoire.

Levine, for instance, found its "psychological and social milieu" as "involving" as that for *Don Giovanni* or *Boris Godunov,* saying, "Gershwin was the first composer since Mozart to successfully combine classical and popular idioms. He also dared to write a long opera, and judging from how the dress rehearsal went, every note of it works. It is certainly the greatest *first* opera ever written." Simon Estes declared the piece "worthy of the masterpieces of Verdi and Wagner," and the role of Porgy, along with those of the Flying Dutchman and Wotan, the most challenging in his large repertoire. Bumbry, somewhat contemptuous at first, experienced a "complete turnaround," declaring the music "fabulous" and the part of Bess comparable in different ways to La Gioconda and Salome. From a director's standpoint, Merrill thought it "perhaps the most complicated opera of all—like the first act of 'Carmen' played four times over."[52]

The opera premiered on February 6, with Estes not on his knees, as customary, but on crutches, the result of a leg injury incurred during rehearsal. The standing-room-only audience—to the Met's surprise, all sixteen performances sold out in advance—responded with a standing ovation, but the critics overall were less pleased. Almost all of the reviews at least welcomed the opera's appearance at the Met, with Jack Viertel in the *Los Angeles Herald-Examiner* breathing "a sigh of relief that *Porgy and Bess* has arrived, not at its destination, but at least at a point of no return." And most of the critics had kind words as well for some of the principals, especially Gregg Baker. But many thought the direction gimmicky, the sets and costumes overdone, the conducting ponderous, and the soloists overpowered by the orchestra, with Estes a rather blank Porgy and Bumbry unconvincing as Bess. "Miss Bumbry played not so much Bess," wrote Andrew Porter in the *New Yorker,* "as a world-famous diva attacking the role with undisciplined, even vulgar, relish." ("Where is the Vuitton tote? you wonder as she swivels off to Harlem in the last act," commented Manuela Hoelterhoff in the *Wall Street Journal.*) Such lapses allegedly decided the Gershwin estate against permission for a televised broadcast.[53]

This production also raised the question of whether an uncut version showed the work to best advantage. *New York* magazine's John Simon concurred with a remark, uttered by playwright Harvey Fierstein during intermission, that "it just goes to show that even the greatest talent can benefit from the blue pencil." And Andrew Porter, who had concluded, in the wake of a 1979 Indiana University Opera Theater production, that the work constituted "a coherent whole," was now no longer so sure: "It seemed badly in need of cutting—though perhaps all it needs is a lighter, keener, more imaginative touch in the execution." On the other hand, Joseph McClellan of the *Washington Post* could find no dull spots; and in an essay published soon after the Met premiere, composer Ned Rorem—who placed Gershwin in the company of Mozart, Poulenc, and Britten as one of those few "blessed" composers whose gifts were both lyrical (like Schubert) and dramatic (like Verdi)—argued for the "integrity" of the opera's "overall construction" as "first-rate in quality," with "scarcely an uninspired or superfluous minute."[54]

Considering the general unintelligibility of the words, some reviews, mindful that Gershwin had composed the opera for a Broadway house, wondered, too, whether the Met, with its thirty-eight hundred seats, was simply too big for the piece. But no one recommended amplification. On the contrary, Frank Rich in the *Times* suggested that Broadway producers attend a performance so that they "might rediscover what their own shows have lost since the invention of the amplifier."[55]

The production further brought to the fore some discussion—both in a featured article by Donal Henahan in the *Times* and in a *Washington Post* editorial—about the Gershwin estate's proviso that the opera be performed by a black cast. Pointing to the growing practice of racially mixed casts in opera, Henahan especially wondered why, in this particular case, companies should be so bound by racial considerations. The matter clearly was not a simple one. Trevor Nunn, who directed the work for Glyndebourne in 1986, stated point-blank that the work was "unperformable by people who are not black." And Roberta Alexander, Bumbry's principal alternate at the Met, similarly thought that the opera lost its "dynamic" when performed by a white cast, recalling in particular a Dutch performance in which she "couldn't see the place where they were as being realistic." On the other hand, M. Owen Lee recalled a production in Germany with a mostly white cast that "moved" him more than any other he had seen, and Steven Ledbetter similarly remembered a compelling performance by a white cast in Budapest.[56]

The Met production made a better impression with Alexander, who, like Bumbry, came to appreciate the opera only after learning her part; in a follow-up review for the *Village Voice*, Leighton Kerner deemed her the best Bess since Leontyne Price. But even Alexander and Estes failed to impress the critics the way some earlier pairings had. Subsequent performances at the Met during its 1985–1986, 1989–1990, and 1990–1991 seasons introduced other principals and conductors, as well as new direction and choreography, but critical response remained muted.[57]

The Glyndebourne Festival—known for its intimate 831-seat opera house (since expanded) in rural Sussex, its unusual repertoire, its exacting standards, and its high ticket prices and extended dinner interval—achieved a far more resounding success with its complete airing in 1986, conducted by Simon Rattle and directed by Trevor Nunn. Rattle (b. 1955), then director of the City of Birmingham Symphony Orchestra and regular guest conductor at Glyndebourne, had grown up loving Gershwin, thanks in part to his father, an amateur jazz pianist. His repertoire in due course would include not only *Porgy*—which he regarded as "one of the twentieth century's most neglected operas," and which he had already performed in concert in 1976, 1977, and 1984 (all with Willard White as Porgy)—but the *Rhapsody in Blue,* the Concerto in F, *An American in Paris,* the *Cuban Overture,* and even such novelties as *Promenade* and the posthumous *For Lily Pons* (arranged for orchestra). Nunn (b. 1940), nearing the end of his long tenure as director of the Royal Shakespeare Company, had directed the premieres of such blockbuster musicals as *Cats* (1981) and *Les Misérables* (1985). Rattle and Nunn had collaborated on Mozart's *Idomeneo* for Glyndebourne in 1985, and they welcomed the opportunity to work together next on *Porgy.*[58]

Glyndebourne assembled a superb cast, including Willard White (Porgy), Cynthia Haymon (Bess), Gregg Baker (Crown), Cynthia Clarey (Serena), Damon Evans (Sportin' Life), Harolyn Blackwell (Clara), Bruce Hubbard (Jake), and Marietta Simpson (Maria), along with an international chorus that included blacks from the States, the Caribbean, Europe, and Africa. John Gunter supervised the sets; Sue Blane, the costumes; David Hersey, the lighting; and Charles Augins, the choreography. But most extraordinary was the musical and stage direction. Rattle, leading the London Philharmonic Orchestra, conducted the work (as evident from his 1989 recording of this production) with unprecedented clarity and drive. Even M. Owen Lee, who objected to some interpretative decisions, found Rattle's performance—in comparison to the two previous recordings of the complete opera—"more dramatically compelling" than Maazel's and "more musicianly" than DeMain's (though John Steane, in a considered overview of the opera's recorded history, expressed a general preference for Maazel over both Rattle and DeMain).[59]

Taking his cue from the original novel, Nunn, meanwhile, brought out the opera's darker side, with Bess a tragic victim of drug abuse, and Sportin' Life a devious troublemaker. Moreover, he sharpened Porgy's trajectory from bitter anger to noble triumph, partly by stripping away, in his own words, the "general quality of bright Technicolor lovableness" associated with the opera. "I've got rid of all that rubbish of people waving at him [Porgy] as if he's the most popular guy in town," said Nunn, who rejected the goat cart as "Disneyesque" and had Porgy walk with crutches. Tapping the finale's suggestions of transfiguration, Nunn further had Porgy cast aside his crutches as he departs Catfish Row.[60]

Regarding this final curtain, Rodney Milnes appreciatively wrote some years afterward, "Porgy . . . walks slowly, unaided, not just in pursuit of Bess, but also out into the light as the confining walls of Catfish Row part before him as surely as if they were the Red Sea—Porgy as Moses, leader of the people. . . . It is a moment of Janáčekian, not to say, Biblical uplift and release. Of course events in South Africa were in everyone's mind in 1986, as they are today, and the Nunn metaphor must surely help heal sensibilities wounded throughout the opera's history." In contrast, Andrew Clements of the *Musical Times* thought this ending overly sentimental, while Michael John White of the *Independent* found the "too earnest" production generally in need of some "stylish schmaltz." But both the 1986 run, which premiered on July 5, and its 1987 revival met with enormous critical and popular acclaim, handily refuting the notion that the Met production faltered because it presented the opera uncut. Nicholas Kenyon declared the occasion "an unqualified triumph" and "one of the most thrilling, moving and indeed surprising evenings you could hope to experience in an opera house." For Wilfrid Mellers, the performance reinforced his long-standing admiration for the opera, which he was now tempted to call "one of the handful of great operas created in this century." Even Paul Griffiths, an advocate for more modernist styles, found himself convinced that "this opera has something vital it wants to say."[61]

In 1987 Damon Evans, the production's Sportin' Life, recounted the Glyndebourne experience from the perspective of the cast members, including their initial ambivalence about the piece itself (sardonically dubbed "Pork 'n Beans," in reference to the work as a source of steady employment for black singers) and their concern about working under the direction of white Englishmen. But he and his colleagues found themselves won over by the integrity of the production, to the point that while rehearsing "Clara, Clara," Cynthia Clarey was so moved that she ran from the room in tears. "She was so caught up in the reality we were creating," wrote Evans, "that the power and magic of the piece could not be denied." In the end, the production differed significantly from any other that Evans had known. "Gone were the unconsciously racist minstrel show traditions of American theatre. . . . This British production of an American classic brought the opera to its full glory. Only a few Americans have realised it as yet, but at Glyndebourne last summer, *Porgy and Bess* finally came of age."[62]

Nunn subsequently fitted the production for Covent Garden with an almost identical cast under the direction of Andrew Litton (1992); and adapted it further (with Yves Baigneres) as a home video (1993), with the mostly original cast lip-synching to the Rattle recording. (Nunn had originally hoped to interest Hollywood in the production but could not find a willing producer, one executive telling him, "It's like this. It's an all-black cast, which means no white people will go and see it. It's written by a white guy, which means no black people will go and see it. And it's an opera which means *no one* will go and see it.") The video, which omitted "Buzzard Song" and the third-act pantomime, had its shortcomings, but at least it provided a good introduction to the opera to an audience hardly confined to the seating at Glyndebourne.[63]

The Glyndebourne production inspired Houston's David Gockley to "take another crack" at *Porgy,* which he did in 1995, once again in collaboration with other opera companies. The involvement of black director Hope Clarke—whose credentials included cochoreographing *Jelly's Last Jam* on Broadway in 1992 and directing *Porgy* for the New York–based Opera Ebony in 1993—proved particularly newsworthy. Kenneth Foy designed the sets, and Judy Dearing, the costumes. Opening in Houston on January 27, with the burly Alvy Powell and the somber Marquita Lister in the title roles under John DeMain, the production eventually toured not only the States but Milan, Paris, and three Japanese cities (Tokyo, Nagoya, and Osaka).[64]

Clarke—who had Porgy appear part of the time on a self-drawn cart, part of the time on a single crutch—hoped to revitalize the opera by, among other things, accentuating its connection with Gullah culture; she interpolated a dance, accompanied by onstage percussion, in the picnic scene, and added a drum obbligato during Serena's "Oh, Doctor Jesus." On the whole, however, the production proved somewhat conventional, while the use of amplified sound (in some venues) and the introduction of surtitles, which a number of spectators found bothersome, possibly encouraged some careless diction as well. Within some months of the tour, Gockley brought in another black director, Tazewell Thompson, and choreographer, Julie Arenal, to help tweak the staging.

As the production traveled around the globe, it provoked some negative reviews, but some favorable ones as well, both at home—David

Patrick Stearns of *USA Today* thought it more "authentic" than the "stagey" Glyndebourne video—and especially abroad, where audiences at the Bastille and La Scala welcomed the opera with standing ovations, and where the critics, whatever their reservations, praised both the production and the work. Giorgio Gualerzi, for instance, declared *Porgy* "not only the definitive American opera, but also a unique case in 20th-century music-theatre," while distinguished French writer Pierre-Petit deemed the piece—along with *Pelléas, Turandot,* and *Wozzeck*—one of the most important operas of the century.[65]

That the French took *Porgy* particularly seriously was evident from the Bastille's lavish program book, which contained a translation of the libretto by Annette Bouju as well as essays on the opera by Claude Carrière, Pascal Huynh, and novelist Etienne Barilier, who concluded that Gershwin's wide artistic range served a "pure and simple affirmation of life." Bouju's translation had first appeared some years earlier in an even more imposing publication, *George Gershwin: Rhapsodie à Catfish Row,* edited by Alain Duault and released in conjunction with the 1987 performance at the Châtelet. This earlier guide included commentary by Denis Jeambar, Laurine Quetin, Alain Lacombe, Catherine Lépront, and Pierre Babin, along with a detailed analysis of the work by composer Christophe Maudot. Such thoughtful French writings, amplified by full-length studies of Gershwin by André Gauthier (1973), Lacombe (1980), Eric Lipmann (1981), and Jeambar (1982), rivaled contemporary American critical discourse about the opera, represented by a lively history of the work by Hollis Alpert (1990); informed essays by Charles Hamm (1987), Joseph Swain (1990), Deena Rosenberg (1991), Geoffrey Block (1997), and Raymond Knapp (2005); theses by Elizabeth Sohler (1995) and John Andrew Johnson (1996); and an educational film sponsored by the University of Michigan (1997) that featured helpful remarks by a number of black musicians and critics, including social historian Darlene Clark Hine, who stated, "*Porgy and Bess* should be valued for the window it affords us on an earlier time when black men and women, against a background largely absent of overwhelming white power, still struggled to love each other, to build a community, to sustain heroic even transcendent identities."[66]

After a long absence, the New York City Opera, with Sherwin Goldman now at the company's helm, revived the work in March 2000 and 2002, capped by a telecast that aired on PBS on March 20, 2002. This production—with its costumes by Nancy Potts, sets by Douglas Schmidt, staging by Tazewell Thompson and Julie Arenal, and musical direction by John DeMain—proved a further reconfiguration of previous HGO mountings. Alvy Powell (Porgy), Marquita Lister (Bess), and Angela Simpson (Serena) from Houston's 1995 production reappeared as well, though now joined by Timothy Robert Blevins (Crown), Dwayne Clark (Sportin' Life), Anita Johnson (Clara), Kenneth Floyd (Jake), and Sabrina Elayne Carten (Maria). This stolid presentation won respectful reviews in the *New York Times* by both Bernard Holland (2000) and Anthony Tommasini (2002), though the time arguably had come for new approaches to the work, including some reconsideration of the heavily abridged score. In a preview piece for the *Times*, David Schiff at least gave long-overdue attention to the merits of the Heyward libretto, a development that ironically arrived as opera companies, prompted by legal concerns of the Gershwin estate, began billing the work as "The Gershwins' *Porgy and Bess*."[67]

In celebration of its fiftieth anniversary in 2005, the Washington National Opera presented its own two-act version of the opera. British conductor Wayne Marshall, a renowned Gershwin interpreter, presided over the double cast, headed by Gordon Hawkins and Kevin Short (Porgy); Indira Mahajan and Morenike Fadayomi (Bess); Terry Cook and Lester Lynch (Crown); Angela Simpson and Dara Rahming (Serena); and Jermaine Smith (Sportin' Life). Directed by American-born Francesca Zambello, this particular staging took a notably sober approach to the material, notwithstanding its rather flamboyant portrayal of Bess. "The piece often gets sugar-coated," explained Zambello, "but it's dark—it's about drugs, abuse, crime, violence, and all these things that continue to plague our culture because of poverty and prejudice. Everyone in Catfish Row is in some way imprisoned by this situation." Peter Davison's industrial-looking set, based on a fish cannery (and thus suggesting some correspondence between the opera and John Steinbeck's 1945 novella, *Cannery Row*), and Natasha Katz's steely lighting designs underscored this basic metaphor of incarceration, while Paul Tazewell's fifties-inspired costumes—including a tight orange satin dress for Bess—similarly provided a gritty contemporaneity. The final tableau, in which the rear wall of the set opened to reveal a bright orange sky, reinforced the impression of Porgy's final departure as essentially a release from prison.[68]

Opening on October 29, the production—which contained, in addition to many customary cuts, a few popular embellishments, including cadenzas for Bess in "Leavin' For The Promise' Lan'" and Serena in "Oh, Doctor Jesus"—garnered high praise from the critics, who especially admired its dramatic force. "In the end," wrote Tim Smith in *Opera News*, "this Catfish Row became an unmistakable symbol for the larger containment of one race, one class, by another. But it was also very much a place where a genuine community could thrive and take comfort in the smallest pleasures." Bruno Marolo, writing in the leftist Italian daily, *l'Unità*, found, too, that the Hurricane Katrina debacle earlier in the year gave special resonance to the hurricane scene. ("To speak of hurricanes in the environs of the White House," wrote Marolo, "is like speaking about rope in the home of a hanged man.") On November 6, a crowd of about 13,000 thronged to the National Mall on an unseasonably warm day to watch a matinee performance simulcast on a huge video screen; and on November 12, National Public Radio broadcast another afternoon performance.[69]

By this time, *Porgy and Bess* had become something of a global cottage industry, with two ongoing productions, both initiated in the early 1990s. The first, managed by impresario Peter Klein, began touring in 1992, and within a ten-year period visited more than four hundred mostly smaller cities in the United States and Great Britain, but also such far-flung destinations as Montevideo (1992), Auckland (1997), Cairo (2000), and Beijing (2001). The other, led by American-born German conductor William Barkhymer, similarly traveled extensively after its 1993 debut, primarily on the European continent, though it arrived in Tokyo in 2004. Meanwhile, director Trevor Nunn adapted the opera as a book musical for the West End (2006), with new orchestrations by Don Sebesky and some dance and incidental music by Gareth Valentine.

Its great success notwithstanding, *Porgy and Bess* remained a misunderstood work, with the general public and even scholars often regarding it as something other than a real opera. But this represented only the most glaring of a number of misconceptions, partly the result of difficulties that made productions of the work—though still the most frequently seen American opera by far—actually something of a rarity, with unabridged stagings virtually nonexistent. As a result, perception of the opera often took shape around some familiarity with Gershwin's other work, or around one or another of the opera's popular tunes, whereas the composer really never wrote anything else like *Porgy*, nor do the songs taken out of context reveal all that much about the true nature of the piece.[70]

A proper understanding of *Porgy and Bess* depends above all on some familiarity with the original three-act score, for the commonly abridged performances, squeezed into two acts, give a distorted sense of the work's range, pacing, and architecture. Moreover, the opera needs productions equally responsive to its musical and its dramatic needs, with respect for both its grand ambitions and its modest charm. As with the *Rhapsody,* the music's appeal has made any approach viable; but a mature appreciation of the work's full stature remains an ongoing project for performers, scholars, and audiences alike.

Chapter Thirty-Four

Porgy and Bess on Disc, Film, and the Concert Stage

$\mathscr{D}$uring the original Broadway run of *Porgy and Bess,* Gershwin prepared a five-movement orchestral suite (1935–1936) from the opera (titled *Catfish Row* by Ira in 1958) about twenty-five minutes in length: "Catfish Row" ("Introduction," "Jasbo Brown Blues," "Summertime," and some of the craps-game music), "Porgy Sings" ("I Got Plenty o' Nuttin'" and "Bess, You Is My Woman"), "Fugue" (the fight music from act 3, scene 1), "Hurricane" (the calm opening and stormy conclusion of act 2, scene 3), and "Good Morning, Brother" (the act-3, scene-3 pantomime, "Good Mornin', Sistuh!" and "Oh Lawd, I'm On My Way"). Gershwin allegedly hoped in this way to salvage some of the music cut from the Theatre Guild production; though more to the point, perhaps, he prepared the Suite—most of whose music actually appeared in the guild version—with an eye to the work's purely instrumental sections, the better to make the transition to a symphonic setting.

Alexander Smallens and the Philadelphia Orchestra presented the world premiere of the Suite—which used the same instrumentation as the opera—on January 21, 1936, in Philadelphia, where it met the same kind of mixed response as attended the arrival of the opera there one week later. In the months that followed, however, as Gershwin conducted the work with the National (February 9), St. Louis (March 1), Boston (May 7), Chicago (July 25), Seattle (December 15), San Francisco (January 15, 16, and 17, 1937), and Detroit (January 20, 1937) symphony orchestras, the Suite elicited more consistently favorable response, with one Washington, D.C., critic deeming it "lively, tuneful, serious and tragic."[1]

After Gershwin's death, the work was temporarily superseded by more lushly scored suites, most notably, Robert Russell Bennett's *Porgy and*

Bess: A Symphonic Picture. But following a somewhat shaky world-pre-
miere recording by Maurice Abravanel and the Utah Symphony in 1959
(André Kostelanetz and his orchestra had recorded only excerpts in the
1940s), the Suite made a comeback, eventually yielding distinguished
recordings by Erich Kunzel and the Cincinnati Pops, James Levine and
the Chicago Symphony Orchestra, Seiji Ozawa and the Berlin Philharmonic, Leonard Slatkin and the St. Louis Symphony, and Mariusz Smolij
and the Sinfonia Varsovia. Still, the music's poetry remained somewhat
elusive when shorn of its theatrical context.[2]

In 1942, in the wake of Cheryl Crawford's revival of the opera, a somewhat reluctant Robert Russell Bennett undertook, at the behest of conductor Fritz Reiner and publisher Max Dreyfus, a one-movement orchestral suite exactly twenty-four minutes in length so as to fit two 78
rpm discs. As suggested by the work's title, *Porgy and Bess: A Symphonic
Picture*, Bennett hoped to write something more symphonic than the medley mapped out by Reiner, but he more or less complied with the conductor's specifications. Opening with a pastiche of some of the opera's
quieter moments, including the street-vendor cries and the third-act dirge,
the piece proceeded with excerpts arranged more or less in chronological order, including the "Introduction," "Summertime," "I Got Plenty
o' Nuttin'," the storm music (optional), "Bess, You Is My Woman," "Oh,
I Can't Sit Down," "There's a Boat Dat's Leavin' Soon for New York,"
"It Ain't Necessarily So," and "Oh Lawd, I'm On My Way."[3]

Bennett scored his suite for a larger orchestra than Gershwin's, including an extra flute, oboe, bassoon, horn, and trombone, as well as
two harps and an additional contingent of three saxophones (though he
dispensed with the piano). While taking stock of the work's original
orchestration, Bennett created—thanks only in part to the enriched
instrumentation—a glossier sound that altered somewhat the music's basic character. Moreover, he not only supplied the needed transitions between the big tunes but arranged some of the set numbers themselves,
including a swing version of "I Got Plenty o' Nuttin'" that arrived, not
in the expected key of G, but amid a sudden shift to E—a sort of thrill
not particularly in keeping with the original work. Bennett even rewrote
the opera's ending, though this gratuitous gesture helped define and assert his essential contribution to the work at hand.[4]

Fritz Reiner and the Pittsburgh Symphony premiered the *Symphonic
Picture* on February 5, 1943, and the piece quickly entered the repertoire of orchestras around the world. Its impressive success—its discog-

raphy included performances by Antal Dorati, Charles Dutoit, Arthur Fiedler, André Kostelanetz, Wayne Marshall, Eduardo Mata, Artur Rodzinski, Felix Slatkin, and William Steinberg—no doubt helped to popularize the opera's most famous numbers. Bennett had less success with *Porgy and Bess: A Symphonic Synthesis* and *Porgy and Bess: Selection for Orchestra,* but these served their purpose as well. Arthur Fiedler and the Boston Pops, for instance, released the former in the mid-1950s, both on the long-playing *The Family All Together* (complete with a Norman Rockwellish album design by Wilson Smith) and on the 45 rpm *The President's Favorite Music* (with a cover photograph of Dwight and Mamie Eisenhower).

Bennett's *Symphonic Picture* was only the best known of other orchestral suites, including Morton Gould's *Porgy and Bess Suite* and Robert Farnon's *Porgy and Bess Symphonic Suite.* Both of these works presented their excerpts strictly in the order in which they appeared in the opera (aside from Gould's reversing the street-vendor cries). Gould's arrangement—smartly conceived and nicely recorded by Gould and his orchestra in 1955—offered a particularly attractive alternative to Bennett's *Symphonic Picture.* Farnon, who recorded his suite with the London Festival Orchestra in 1966, took a jazzier approach, sometimes evoking big-band styles, other times those of easy-listening ensembles like Percy Faith and His Orchestra, who released their own précis of the opera in 1959.

Porgy inspired many other instrumental transcriptions and paraphrases. In 1945 Beryl Rubinstein, who had prophesied Gershwin's ascendancy in 1922, confirmed his abiding respect by publishing Chopinesque arrangements of "Summertime," "I Got Plenty o' Nuttin'," "Bess, You Is My Woman," and "It Ain't Necessarily So" for piano, all but the last recorded by Richard Glazier as *Three Concert Transcriptions from Porgy and Bess.* Percy Grainger more ambitiously prepared a *Fantasy on Porgy and Bess* for two pianos (1950–1951), which he and W. Norman Grayson premiered at New York's Town Hall on April 21, 1951. A medley of nine of the work's tunes, the *Fantasy* enjoyed a number of performances and recordings, including releases by the Labèque sisters (Katia and Marielle) and the Contiguglia brothers (Richard and John), who in 1995 also premiered an orchestral transcription, *Fantasy on Porgy and Bess* for two pianos and orchestra (arranged by Tom Kochan, 1993). (Grainger's pianistic treatment of "I Got Plenty o' Nuttin'"—like Rubinstein's—recalled Louis Moreau Gottschalk's famous piano piece, *The Banjo.*) Earl Wild published (1976) and recorded (1989) his own, even longer *Fantasy on*

Porgy and Bess, a virtuosic patchwork of eleven numbers, including, unusually enough, "Buzzard Song."[5]

Jascha Heifetz achieved special success with his transcriptions of "Summertime," "A Woman Is a Sometime Thing," "My Man's Gone Now," "It Ain't Necessarily So," "Bess, You Is My Woman," and a "Tempo di Blues" (comprised of "Picnics is alright for these small town niggers" and "There's a Boat Dat's Leavin' Soon for New York") for violin and piano (1944). According to the violinist's daughter Josefa, these arrangements derived inspiration from an early recording of the opera's highlights by Helen Jepson and Lawrence Tibbett, though Heifetz apparently knew the score in other ways, as neither of the "Tempo di Blues" melodies appears on that album. He seemed mindful in any case of the unsung lyrics in his brilliant recordings of these pieces with pianists Emanuel Bay (1946 and 1949) and Brooks Smith (1965).[6]

As with the *Rhapsody,* arrangements for other instrumental combinations arose, including a suite for electronic keyboard synthesizer prepared and recorded by Gershon Kingsley (1970); three excerpts for flute, piano, and synthesizer recorded by flutist Jean-Pierre Rampal and associates (1985); and a suite for bassoon and string orchestra recorded by bassoonist Milan Turkovic and the Stuttgart Chamber Orchestra under Martin Sieghart (1991). The Empire Brass widely performed its own five-movement suite ("I Got Plenty o' Nuttin'," "Summertime," "My Man's Gone Now," "Bess, You Is My Woman," and "It Ain't Necessarily So") jazzily arranged for two trumpets, horn, trombone, and tuba (with a supplemental rhythm section) by Frank Denson and Jack Gale (recorded 1988).

Concert presentations of operatic highlights quickly appeared as well. Smallens led Duncan, Brown, Elzy, and twenty-eight Eva Jessye choristers in about a half-hour's worth of excerpts at an all-Gershwin concert at Lewisohn Stadium on July 9, 1936. The crowd responded with "rampant enthusiasm," but the reviews varied in their assessments, the *Brooklyn Daily Eagle* even describing the opera, in one of the harshest reviews to that date, as Gershwin's "outstanding failure, an anomalous work, neither opera nor musical comedy, pretentious, inflated and essentially third rate."[7]

An all-Gershwin program with the Los Angeles Philharmonic on February 10 and 11, 1937, arranged by Merle Armitage, similarly occasioned selections from the opera performed by Duncan, soprano Marguerite Chapman, and a sixteen-person chorus under the composer's baton. The packed and star-studded audience cheered the work, as did most critics, even if Richard Saunders concluded in the *Hollywood Citizen-News,* "Little if any of Gershwin's music is likely to outlive its composer." Soon after Gershwin's death, Duncan, Brown, and Elzy again sang excerpts at overflowing memorial concerts at Lewisohn Stadium (under Smallens) on August 9 and at the Hollywood Bowl (under Steinert) on September 8, though the latter also occasioned a poignant rendition of "Summertime" by Lily Pons. Jepson and Tibbett likewise performed some numbers from the opera in Gershwin's memory at a Carnegie Hall concert on February 20, 1938, sponsored by the American Guild of Musical Artists.[8]

Over time, Robert Russell Bennett once again attained preeminence with his forty-minute "concert version" scored for soprano, baritone, chorus, and an orchestra virtually identical to Gershwin's own except for one additional French horn. This popular suite attracted such conductors as Alexander Smallens, André Kostelanetz, Franz Allers, and Robert Bass, whose 1984 performance whetted *Times* critic Edward Rothstein's "appetite" for a full staging of the work.[9]

In the 1990s singer-conductor Bobby McFerrin (b. 1950) toured widely with his own concert version, which featured additional soloists. "In large part, I wanted to do this to honor my father and my musical childhood," stated McFerrin, whose father, opera singer Robert McFerrin Sr., had provided the singing voice for Sidney Poitier's Porgy in the opera's 1959 film version. McFerrin hoped to get orchestral musicians "to play around the bar lines, to stretch and bend," but Paul Griffiths of the *Times* thought a 1998 performance with the New York Philharmonic largely "dull," despite appealing performances by Kevin Deas and Marvis Martin in the title roles.[10]

McFerrin's championship of the work seemed especially noteworthy in light of the fact that concert presentations of the opera could occasion racial divisiveness, as an episode involving the Royal Liverpool Philharmonic demonstrated. In the hope of engaging the mostly poor black community in its midst, the Liverpool Philharmonic, scheduled to open its 1989–1990 season with highlights from the opera, planned a second performance that would combine the symphony's chorus with local black choirs. But a black Liverpool arts organization, arguing that the opera was offensive, agitated for a pamphlet to be distributed at performances that would tell the "truth" about the piece. In the end, the orchestra simply canceled the community performance. David Horn, who saw this conflict as echoing long-standing disagreements about the work, observed that neither side considered "an alternative interpretation, namely that

Porgy and Bess was concerned with a specific community in a specific time and place; that it was about the way that community handled questions of old and new, public and private, and that the community need not be read as standing for anything but itself."[11]

All in all, however, concerts featuring excerpts from the opera remained quite popular around the world. John Ferguson, the artistic director of American Voices, an organization devoted to presenting American music abroad, found concert presentations of the work enthusiastically welcomed in La Paz (2002); Valletta, Malta (2002); Hanoi (2003); and Priština, Kosovo (2004). These performances typically featured American baritone and choral conductor Ira Spaulding but sometimes regional sopranos, and always local choruses. In all of these places, Ferguson observed widespread familiarity with at least "Summertime," but he found that audiences and the participating choruses took special delight in such numbers as "Leavin' for the Promise' Lan'."[12]

On February 24, 2006, the Nashville Symphony presented a particularly noteworthy concert rendering of the work: a semi-staged reading conducted by John Mauceri that attempted to recreate the opera as heard at its 1935 Broadway premiere at the Alvin Theatre. In consultation with such authorities as Robert Kimball, Wayne Shirley, and Charles Hamm, whose scholarship helped inspire this undertaking, and assisted by Scott Dunn, Mauceri based his performing edition largely on the orchestral parts used for the original Broadway run, its first national tour, and the 1938 West Coast revival (though the necessity of employing edited rental parts precluded a completely faithful restoration). Starring Alvy Powell (Porgy), Marquita Lister (Bess), Lester Lynch (Crown), Monique McDonald (Serena), Robert Mack (Sportin' Life), and Laquita Mitchell (Clara), the performance, repeated the following night, lasted about three hours, inclusive of two hours and twenty minutes of music and two intermissions.[13]

This re-creation—recorded by Decca—contained two novelties probably not heard on stage since 1938: the onstage band music composed for the number "Oh, I Can't Sit Down," and here played by members of the Tennessee State University Band; and the "Occupational Humoresque" soundscape, directions for which survived in one of the opera's early prompt scores. Mauceri judged this 1935 version "sleek, direct and still epic in proportions. It's a much better opera this way." But the cast's veteran performers were more ambivalent. "I've done two hundred Besses, so this is interesting because it's different from what I've done before," said Lister. "But I wouldn't say it's better." Lynch, for his part, found that the omission of a passage just prior to "What You Want Wid Bess?" (from rehearsal 148 to three after 152) prevented him from more fully developing Crown's character, while Powell similarly thought the abbreviated final trio too abrupt. Certainly some of the claims in the media—that this "final vision" represented "the way he [Gershwin] wanted the opera to be done"—were highly dubious, for reasons previously discussed; but the Mauceri edition—even more than the one devised by Lehman Engel for his 1951 recording—at least allowed audiences an opportunity to hear the opera more or less as originally presented, and scholars a way to better gauge its early reception.[14]

Meanwhile, a steady stream of recorded highlights also appeared. Even within days of the premiere, Gershwin oversaw an RCA Victor four-record album of excerpts with Metropolitan Opera stars Helen Jepson and Lawrence Tibbett, along with the Eva Jessye Choir, under Smallens. Brown and the other original cast members resented this release as a typical example of white exploitation, especially as Jepson and Tibbett prepared for the recording by attending rehearsals of the opera; but the cast blamed the record company, not Gershwin. In any case, the album found Tibbett in especially fine form; in 1992 John Steane deemed his performance "among his best work for the gramophone" and "still the finest pieces of singing among the men in the whole of the opera's history on records."[15]

Subsequent recordings of operatic highlights included those featuring Anne Brown and Todd Duncan under Alexander Smallens (1940 and 1942); Anne Ziegler and Webster Booth with the Savoy Hotel Orpheans (1938); Risë Stevens and Robert Merrill under Robert Russell Bennett (1950); Helen Thigpen, Leslie Scott, and Cab Calloway under Jay Blackton (1953); Margaret Tynes and Brock Peters under Paul Belanger (ca. 1955); Leontyne Price, William Warfield, and John Bubbles under Skitch Henderson (1963); Urylee Leonardos and Valentine Pringle under Lehman Engel (ca. 1965); Martha Flowers and Irving Barnes under Lorenzo Fuller (ca. 1965); Isabelle Lucas and Lawrence Winters under Kenneth Alwyn (ca. 1965); Claudia Lindsey and Benjamin Matthews under Ettore Stratta (1980); Roberta Alexander and Simon Estes under Leonard Slatkin (1985); Roberta Alexander and Gregg Baker under Zubin Mehta (1991); Cynthia Haymon and Gordon Hawkins under Andrew Litton (1996); and Marquita Lister and Gregg Baker under Erich Kunzel (1998). Most of these recordings involved choruses as well, including the estimable Robert Shaw Chorale on the Stevens-Merrill release. That the

1935, 1938, and 1950 albums featured white soloists underscored the marginalization of black opera singers during these years. After 1950, black principals became de rigueur for all such recordings, with an occasional exception like Anna Moffo's Clara on the Leonardos-Pringle release.

Like many concert presentations, these recorded highlights proved somewhat unsatisfactory, in large part because the widespread use of only two voices—the soprano taking on three roles (Bess, Clara, and Serena), the baritone, as many as four (Porgy, Crown, Jake, and Sportin' Life)—naturally curtailed dramatic verisimilitude and variety. Moreover, few of the songs and choruses, contrary to common assumptions, were all that self-contained, making it necessary to fabricate introductions and codas, or else to start and conclude, so to speak, in midair. Still, all these releases had their points of interest, including Kunzel's restoration of the Bess-Serena scene deleted by Gershwin.

Concert and opera singers sang and recorded individual songs as well. Paul Robeson's 1938 recordings of "A Woman Is a Sometime Thing," "It Ain't Necessarily So," "It Take a Long Pull to Get There," and "Summertime" held special importance, even if none of these songs belonged to Porgy or Crown, the parts Gershwin possibly had in mind for him. As earlier mentioned, James Melton, with whom Gershwin collaborated on the Leo Reisman tour, also recorded selections from the work. Other eminent opera singers who recorded "Summertime" included Kathleen Battle, Barbara Hendricks, Kiri Te Kanawa, and Eleanor Steber, whose eloquent 1946 rendition, with Jay Blackton and the RCA Orchestra, though not particularly idiomatic, remains one of the gems of the Gershwin discography. Such accomplished choirs as the Bellefield Singers, the King's Singers, the Swingle Singers, and the Vasari Singers also recorded the song.

In 1959 Columbia Pictures released a film version of the opera—also titled *Porgy and Bess*—produced by the legendary Samuel Goldwyn (this would be his eightieth and last picture). As early as January 1937, Gershwin predicted (in a letter to Heyward) that although the studios had some trepidation about the material "on account of the color question," the opera would be filmed sooner or later "as the music is constantly being played and the enthusiasm for it is great on all sides." Over the years, the Gershwin and Heyward estates fielded dozens of inquiries and offers from leading producers—including one from Columbia's Harry Cohn for a version for Al Jolson (Porgy), Rita Hayworth (Bess), and Fred Astaire (Sportin' Life)—but Ira in particular hesitated, the "lone holdout," in fact, on a 1956 proposal by Robert Breen and Blevins Davis, who had secured a five-year film option in 1953.[16]

In 1957 Goldwyn, whose credits—since he had worked with the Gershwins on *The Goldwyn Follies* (1938)—included *Wuthering Heights* (1939), *The Little Foxes* (1941), *The Best Years of Our Lives* (1946), *Hans Christian Andersen* (1952), and *Guys and Dolls* (1955), obtained the film rights for $650,000 (against 10 percent of the gross receipts), partly by co-opting Breen (who in the interim had acquired Davis's interest) by naming him associate producer. Breen assumed that he would direct the picture, but Goldwyn, who had hoped to film the opera since attending its 1935 premiere, had no intention of entrusting such a cherished project to an untried film director, even one with extensive experience directing the work onstage. Rather, he selected (though apparently not his first choice) Rouben Mamoulian, who had distinguished himself as an opera and film director, and who had supervised the premieres of both the stage and the operatic versions of *Porgy*.[17]

Goldwyn also engaged screenwriter Richard N. Nash (known primarily for his 1954 hit play, *The Rainmaker*), set designer Oliver Smith, wardrobe designer Irene Sharaff, cinematographer Leon Shamroy (working with Technicolor and wide-screen Todd-AO projection), choreographer Hermes Pan, sound editors Fred Hynes and Gordon Sawyer, and musical director André Previn (assisted by Ken Darby). A composer, conductor, and pianist, Previn (b. 1929)—whose father's cousin, Charles Previn, had conducted some Gershwin premieres—grew up in Berlin, Paris, and Los Angeles, where he studied with Joseph Achron and Mario Castelnuovo-Tedesco; in 1946, at a tender age, he joined the music staff at MGM, orchestrating and later scoring numerous films for the studio, including *Kiss Me Kate* (1953) and *Gigi* (1958), for which he won an Oscar.[18]

Goldwyn advertised the film as an "opera," but the picture, which lasted just under two and a half hours (with an intermission following Crown's seduction of Bess, as in many two-act versions of the work), more closely resembled a movie musical, with songs and choruses (though a good many of these, by Hollywood standards, and with some snippets of recitative as well) alternating with dialogue, typically underscored by music derived from the original score. However, Previn rarely adapted this underscoring verbatim, even when one might have expected him to do so, as in the two fight scenes (the fight between Crown and Robbins strangely used no music whatsoever); presumably the filmmakers felt that Gershwin's fugal fight music belonged in the opera house, not the movie theater. In any case, Previn's reworking of the music distinguished the film from the Crawford production, which sometimes synchronized spoken dialogue with corresponding music from the original score.

Concern in the black community about how the picture might affect the civil rights movement, then reaching critical mass, complicated the making of the film. The NAACP eventually approved the script, but a group called the Council for the Improvement of Negro Theater Arts urged black performers to boycott the production, claiming, in a two-page advertisement in the *Hollywood Reporter,* that the Heywards had written stories in which Negroes were "given to erupting with all sort of goings-on after their day's work in the white folks' kitchen or the white folks' yard was over, like sniffing happy dust, careless love, crapshooting, drinking, topping it all off with knife play." In a television debate between Goldwyn and Lorraine Hansberry held in May 1959 shortly before the film's release, the latter, whose play *A Raisin in the Sun* (1959) had recently opened on Broadway, similarly objected "to roles which consistently depict our women as wicked and our men as weak," a quote reported some months later by Era Bell in an article for *Ebony,* "Why Negroes Don't Like 'Porgy and Bess.'" Hansberry, who admitted that she had never seen the opera, plainly misrepresented the work; but her claim that the opera represented an excursion into the "exotic" ironically found common ground with Goldwyn, who read the work, though more sympathetically, along similar lines.[19]

The racially charged atmosphere made some black stars—with the notable exception of Sammy Davis Jr., who actively campaigned for the role of Sportin' Life—wary of getting involved, notwithstanding the prestige of both Goldwyn and Mamoulian. Harry Belafonte, who had starred in the film version of *Carmen Jones* (1954), an all-black adaptation of Bizet's *Carmen,* turned down Goldwyn's offer to play Porgy, a part eventually accepted by Sidney Poitier only after an unauthorized promise from an agent—unaware that his client thought the opera "an insult to black people"—made it virtually impossible for him to do otherwise. Some of Poitier's costars, including Dorothy Dandridge (Bess), Diahann Carroll (Clara), and Pearl Bailey (Maria), had reservations of their own, Dandridge's exacerbated by the critical letters, verging on hate mail, that she received from the start. Like Poitier (with whom she had an extramarital affair while working on the film), Carroll thought the story offensive, while Bailey, who declined to wear a bandanna or go barefoot, balked at what she called the script's "dialect bit." Some of the other cast members who had long experience playing *Porgy* onstage (sometimes in big-

ger roles than here)—such as Brock Peters (Crown), Earl Jackson
(Mingo), Leslie Scott (Jake), and Helen Thigpen (Strawberry Woman)—
presumably had fewer such concerns.[20]

These veterans of the operatic stage naturally sang their own music,
as did Sammy Davis and Pearl Bailey, who performed "Oh, I Can't Sit
Down" as a solo. In contrast, Poitier, Dandridge, Carroll, and the
movie's Serena, Ruth Attaway, were dubbed by Robert McFerrin, Adele
Addison, Loulie Jean Norman, and Inez Matthews, respectively. An outstanding baritone, McFerrin became the first black man featured in an
opera at the Met when on January 27, 1955, some twenty days after Marian Anderson's historic performance there, he sang Amonasro in a production of *Aida*. Adele Addison and Inez Matthews were also highly accomplished black singers, the former associated especially with oratorio
and contemporary music, the latter (the Serena on the Lehman Engel
recording) for her work in Kurt Weill's *Lost in the Stars*, where she shared
the stage with both McFerrin and Todd Duncan. Although Goldwyn preferred that black singers dub all the voices as needed, for Carroll's double, Previn chose white soprano Loulie Jean Norman, at least in part, no
doubt, on the strength of her performance as the Strawberry Woman on
Bethlehem Records' 1956 jazz version of the opera. (Norman went on
to ghost-sing for a number of Hollywood actresses, though she remains
best known for her vocal solo in the title music to television's *Star Trek*.)

Previn recorded the sound track in six-track stereo in June 1958, highlights of which Columbia Records later released, though with Cab Calloway as Sportin' Life, as Davis's contract with Decca records prevented
his inclusion (this recording vaguely credited "the voice of Robert Mc-
Ferrin" and egregiously made no mention of Addison, Matthews, or
Norman whatsoever). The singing throughout reflected the high priority
Goldwyn and Previn placed on the intelligibility of the text, and McFerrin
and Addison delivered particularly polished performances, though they
seemed hampered by the necessity to match the spoken voices of Poitier
and Dandridge and, more generally, by Goldwyn's wariness about producing too operatic a sound. Moreover, Addison sang her duets with a
prerecorded McFerrin, which precluded a certain spontaneity. "There I
was, singing some glorious love duet and my lover wasn't even in the
building," she later remarked. "Just the conductor and I, each listening
on earphones to an orchestra that had disbanded months before."[21]

Although common lore asserts that Previn reorchestrated the score
from scratch, he in fact relied heavily, especially in the sung portions, on
the original scoring, sometimes as a template, but often rather literally

(notwithstanding a general enrichment of the orchestral texture and some thoroughly reconceived orchestrations, including the romantically embellished "Oh Lawd, I'm On My Way"). The lyrics remained largely intact as well, though the singers adapted much of the dialect to standard English pronunciation, and a few phrases apparently considered too dated or vulgar went by the wayside. The inclusion of some version of "Occupational Humoresque," employed in the original productions of both the play and the opera—and which can be heard on the Columbia sound track at the top of the cut titled "Morning; Catfish Row"—remains of particular historical interest.

In the early morning hours of July 2, a day scheduled for a full dress rehearsal, a fire on the Goldwyn lot destroyed not only costumes but the elaborate Catfish Row set, modeled by Oliver Smith after Soudeikine and estimated at about one million dollars (though covered by insurance); some suspected arson, others faulty wiring or a carelessly tossed cigarette. As the studio rebuilt the set, tensions between Goldwyn and Mamoulian escalated—the latter wanted a more realistic look to the film—and on July 27 Goldwyn fired Mamoulian (who, though paid his entire fee, waged a bitter and ultimately futile struggle for official credit) and hired in his stead Otto Preminger. A successful actor-director-producer who had immigrated to the States from his native Vienna in 1935, Preminger (1906–1986) seemed a logical replacement, as he had produced and directed *Carmen Jones*, whose all-black cast included Bailey, Carroll, Dandridge, and Peters. Moreover, he had had one of his biggest hits, *Laura* (1944), after stepping in for Mamoulian.[22]

Filming began on September 15 with an on-location shoot near Stockton, California, and ended on December 18 after about ten weeks on the Goldwyn set. Costing about $6.5 million, the film—for which neither McFerrin nor Addison received screen credit—premiered at New York's Warner Theatre on June 24, 1959, accompanied by congratulatory remarks by Ira Gershwin and Dorothy Heyward. The picture received good reviews in *Newsweek* and *Variety,* and even something close to a rave in the *Times* by Bosley Crowther, who thought that this "stunning, exciting and moving film" bid fair "to be as much a classic on the screen as it is on the stage." "'Porgy and Bess' wasn't written for the movies," wrote Crowther in a follow-up piece, "but it obviously should and could have been." In stark contrast, Robert Hatch *(Nation)*, Arthur Knight *(Saturday Review)*, and John McCarten *(New Yorker)* thought that the picture's static direction, stagey sets, deafening amplification, and flawed dubbing painfully exposed the difficulties in filming opera. "The projection process known as Todd-AO is plain misery—too large, too loud, with close-ups used as blunt instruments and voices (rarely synchronized to mouths) blaring 'stereophonically' from implausible nook-and-corners," wrote Hatch. "I sat right in the center of the Warner Theatre, presumably a good seat, and I emerged from the place after two and a half hours feeling that I had come through a rigorous test of nerve stamina with no worse after-effects than a sharp headache."[23]

Although nearly all the reviews praised Goldwyn's courage in bringing the work to the screen, and some further observed that Sammy Davis—who portrayed Sportin' Life as "the epitome of evil"—gave a new sinister spin to the character (thus establishing a precedent for later interpretations), few critics had much to say about the adaptation per se, aside from *Variety*, which noted that "some liberties with the arrangements, in the de-operatizing direction, may irritate the loyal followers of Gershwin who notice such matters." The mainstream media tended to overlook racial issues as well. *Variety*, again an exception, observed that certain viewers might resent the Lawyer Frazier scene as something "right out of the white Southern stock-in-trade of amused condescension," but added, "In the main, the desperate poverty of Catfish Row is presented sympathetically"— or perhaps too sympathetically, to judge from a review by noted black author James Baldwin. Deeming the opera "an extraordinarily vivid, good-natured, and sometimes moving show," that is, "until Mr. Preminger got his hand on it," Baldwin thought that the depiction of Catfish Row as "such a charming place to live" assuaged white "guilt about Negroes" without attacking any of "their fantasies." "I am certainly not the first person to suggest that these Negroes seem to speak to them [white Americans] of a better life—better in the sense of being more honest, more open, and more free: in a word, more sexual," he wrote. "This is [the] cruelest fantasy of all, hard to forgive. It means that Negroes are penalized, and hideously, for what the general guilty imagination makes of them." Baldwin further believed that singer Billie Holiday, who died a few days after the film opened, "would have made a splendid, if somewhat overwhelming Bess," one "closer to the original, whoever she was, of this portrait than anyone who has ever played or sung it."[24]

Goldwyn hired Kay Swift, who admired the film, to travel to various cities to help promote the picture, which won an Academy Award for best scoring of a musical picture, as well as Oscar nominations for color cinematography, color costume design, and sound. But the movie did poorly at the box office, earning back only about half its cost. *Variety* identified from the start three primary hurdles for commercial success:

"(a) the drab story, (b) the opera form, (c) the known fact that all-Negro casts usually run a hard course." Moreover, Goldwyn scaled back distribution in the South after the film became a rallying point for the desegregation of movie houses in the region.[25]

After Goldwyn's lease on the film expired in 1972, Ira and Leonore Gershwin recalled it; their nephew and executor, Michael Strunsky, explained in 1993, "My aunt didn't want it distributed. She and my uncle felt it was a Hollywoodization of the piece. We now acquire any prints we find and destroy them." Nevertheless, the estate permitted occasional screenings, including one at the 1998 Gershwin Centennial Festival held by the Institute for Studies in American Music at Brooklyn College. At that "triumphant" showing, a panel composed of three academics and journalist Margo Jefferson largely commended the picture, at least taken on its own terms. Stated film professor Foster Hirsch: "What he [Preminger] has done is to transform Gershwin's magnificent folk opera into a stately, elegant film with daringly long takes, an avoidance of close-ups, intricately composed deep focus shots, and sedate, objective camera movement. The costumes, sets, and rich, autumnal color design are appropriately stylized. Preminger's *Porgy and Bess* unfolds in a world apart."[26]

The suppression of the film naturally hindered more widespread reassessments. But the picture plainly gave only a rough sense of the original opera. For instance, the squeaky-clean sets and neatly tailored costumes (intended to represent, more like the original novel than the play or opera, Charleston circa 1912), not to mention the watered-down score and the tendency, as Diahann Carroll later complained, to portray the residents of Catfish Row as nonthreatening "lost children," devitalized the material. Dandridge, who thought that the Heyward story actually offered "an accurate picture of the harsh, terrorized lives of Negroes forced to live in ghettoes," eloquently addressed this matter in her memoirs:

> When pressure is brought against an actress, a picture, a book, anything creative, you are apt to get a vitiated, neutralized product which comes out weak, mediocre, and not believable.
> What happened was an attempt to clean up Catfish Row! An actual attempt to make life on Catfish Row look not so bad. Everyone connected with the movie embarked on a program to take the terror, fright, and oppression out of ghetto living.

The picture obscured not only the opera's darker side but much of its humor as well, with some welcome exceptions, such as Helen Thigpen's appearance as the Strawberry Woman.[27]

For all its limitations, the Goldwyn picture helped popularize a number of the work's songs, though "Summertime," "I Got Plenty o' Nuttin'," and "It Ain't Necessarily So" had enjoyed success practically from the start. The Guy Lombardo and Leo Reisman bands, for instance, recorded the latter two numbers in 1935, while Billie Holiday released "Summertime" (with Artie Shaw) in July 1936, the melody's relatively small range compressed that much more. Bing Crosby, the time's most popular singer, recorded all three songs: "I Got Plenty o' Nuttin'" and "It Ain't Necessarily So" with the Victor Young Orchestra in early 1936 (performances deemed "unexpectedly rueful" by Gary Giddins) and "Summertime" with Matty Malneck in 1938, the year, too, that the Bob Crosby band adopted the music as its theme song. The Duke Ellington Orchestra frequently played "Summertime" as well, with the first of a number of recordings dating from 1943.[28]

"Summertime," "I Got Plenty o' Nuttin'," and "It Ain't Necessarily So" attained early popularity in part because their tuneful regularity met the needs of dance bands, which typically presented them as moderately paced swing numbers. But other songs from the opera soon became popular as well. In 1942 Mabel Mercer recorded not only "Summertime" but "I Loves You, Porgy" (as the abbreviated version of "I Wants to Stay Here" generally became known) and "My Man's Gone Now," accompanied by pianist Cy Walter, who recorded another three numbers for solo piano in tandem with these releases. In 1948 Billie Holiday also recorded "I Loves You, Porgy," completing the process begun by Mercer of turning the duet into a solo song in *aaba* form, and in general setting a standard for many renditions to come, including her own (Holiday's later performances—in which she'd bring the music to a near standstill during the bridge section—increasingly assumed a tragically personal resonance). And in 1946 Frank Sinatra released a characteristically mellifluous recording of "Oh, Bess, Oh Where's My Bess?" that—though conceived by Gershwin as a trio—often appeared, both onstage and off, as a solo, in large part simply by the omission of the upper two voices.[29]

Popular medleys from the opera began to circulate as well. On a 1938 memorial radio broadcast, Jane Froman, Felix Knight, and Sonny Schuyler, with some choral assistance, sang various selections under the baton of Nathaniel Shilkret. Sinatra also performed medleys of the work over the radio, one in 1944, and another with Jane Powell and the Pied Pipers in 1947. Medleys from the opera eventually found their way onto television as well, including arrangements for a ballet sequence with Carmen DeLavallade, Claude Thompson, and Alvin Ailey (General Electric's *The Gershwin Years,* airing January 15, 1961); for Vic Damone and Judy Garland (the *Judy Garland Show,* airing November 3, 1963); and for Larry Kert, Leslie Uggams, and others, including Jack Lemmon, who sang "It Ain't Necessarily So" (the Bell System's *'S Wonderful, 'S Marvelous, 'S Gershwin,* airing January 17, 1972).

These radio and television medleys proved mere ephemera compared to jazz albums based on the opera, a virtual subgenre that arose in the late 1950s partly in response to the vogue for Broadway-themed jazz albums. These *Porgy* albums ranged from solo releases to those for large jazz band, occasionally supplemented by strings; some featured vocalists, while others were strictly instrumental. All offered a good sampling of the opera's ten or so most popular numbers, but less-known sections— "Jasbo Brown Blues," "They Pass By Singin'," "Oh, I Can't Sit Down," "Oh, Doctor Jesus," and the street-vendor cries—regularly turned up as well. The unusual and relatively lengthy shapes of most of these excerpts mitigated against the straightforward variation forms characteristic of classic jazz, and some musicians accordingly shortened and standardized certain numbers to permit just such treatment; but approaches varied considerably, yielding tracks of less than a minute to those lasting more than ten. Suffice it to say, the *Porgy* album provided a coherent framework for a good deal of experimentation.

These albums generally showed awareness—if in varying ways—of the music's dramatic context. In discussing his 1959 release, arranger Bill Potts, for instance, stated, in reference to the Gershwin score and presumably the Lehman Engel recording of the opera, "I wore out the records. And I studied that score. I listened and studied for about six weeks before I wrote the first note." Many of these albums tellingly presented the material in chronological sequence. Joe Henderson (1997) even grouped his selections by act and limited his liner notes to a synopsis of the plot. But even those that reshuffled the order of the songs often implied some kind of narrative related to the original story.[30]

One of the earliest *Porgy* albums—Bethlehem's three-record *Porgy and Bess* (1956) produced by Red Clyde—was in many ways the most ambitious and unusual of them all: a full-scale jazz version of the opera, with a script by Al Moritz (narrated by Al Collins, a popular disc jockey), arrangements by Russell Garcia, and a full roster of Bethlehem singers supported by sundry ensembles, including the Duke Ellington Orchestra, the Australian Jazz Quintet, and the Pat Moran vocal quartet, but mostly the Bethlehem Orchestra led by Garcia. The interracial cast included Mel Tormé (Porgy), Frances Faye (Bess), Johnny Hartman (Crown), George Kirby (Sportin' Life), and an utterly cool Frank Rosolino (Jake) (this version eliminated the character of Maria). The arrangements, which for the most part stayed close to the score (including a transcription of the first-act fugue), bore some of the hallmarks of the decade's jazzy film and theater scores and looked ahead, in this sense, to *West Side Story* (1957). Tormé (who in later years continued to sing medleys from the opera in his nightclub act) loathed the results, feeling that he and the others "belittled" the opera "with our polyglot styles and approaches"; but the recording nevertheless became, as Tormé acknowledged, "a cult favorite."[31]

Garcia followed this achievement with arrangements for Verve's own *Porgy and Bess,* a two-record set featuring Ella Fitzgerald and Louis Armstrong, who sang as well as played trumpet. Producer Norman Granz no doubt regarded the album as jazz's answer to the many concert versions of the work for two singers; and in their poignant rendering of "Bess, You Is My Woman," Armstrong and Fitzgerald came closer in some ways to the classic pairing of Duncan and Brown than did many opera singers, even with Armstrong improvising his way through the duet portions. But the release overall proved somewhat uneven.

The year 1958 witnessed the first purely instrumental *Porgy* albums: guitarist Mundell Lowe's *Porgy and Bess,* elegantly arranged for septet, including Art Farmer on trumpet and Ben Webster on tenor saxophone; and the most celebrated of all such recordings, arranger Gil Evans's stunning *Porgy and Bess,* with Miles Davis on trumpet and flügelhorn, supported by a band of eighteen: two flutes, two saxophones, three French horns (including Gunther Schuller), four trumpets, four trombones, tuba, bass, and drums. In their search for a follow-up vehicle to their first large-scale collaboration, *Miles Ahead* (1957), Evans and Davis found common ground in their attraction to the Gershwin score; the former had arranged selections from the work as early as 1941, while the latter developed a special interest in the material after attending performances of the opera in which his girlfriend and future wife, Frances Taylor, took part. Evans and Davis no doubt hoped to capitalize on the buzz surrounding the forthcoming Goldwyn film as well.

More than any other such album, the Evans-Davis *Porgy* brought the opera's somber subtext to the fore; even "I Got Plenty o' Nuttin'" assumed an unexpected gravity (though the album ended jauntily enough with a buoyant rendition of "There's a Boat That's Leaving Soon for New York"). Evans's collage-like arrangements also broke new ground, Davis argued, in their emphasis on melody as opposed to harmony. This Columbia release proved one of Davis's best-selling albums, while the suite itself became a prized staple of the jazz concert repertoire, first with Davis as soloist, and then, after the charts—presumed lost—were discovered in a warehouse in the late 1990s, with successors like trumpeters Jon Faddis and Lew Soloff.[32]

In conjunction with the Gershwin centennial, Hope Clarke, the choreographer who had staged various mountings of the opera, as discussed earlier, created a ballet to the Davis-Evans recording (filled out by some transitional material by Dick Hyman) for the Dallas Black Dance Theatre. This two-act *Porgy and Bess*—the first full-length dance based on the story—premiered at Washington's Kennedy Center on September 11, 1998, with the company's fourteen-person ensemble joined by guest artists LeVon Campbell (Porgy)—making full use of only one leg—and Sarita Allen (Bess). As with her stage productions of the opera, Clarke emphasized the concept of Catfish Row as a working community. She also allowed the dancers to improvise lines in undertones. The reviews were mixed; critics widely admired the dancing, but found the two-hour production somewhat ponderous and the sotto voce dialogue distracting. Still, the dance toured at home and abroad successfully and remained in the company's repertoire for a few successive seasons.[33]

In 2004 conductor Jeff Lindberg and the Chicago Jazz Orchestra released a new version of the Davis-Evans suite featuring the venerable Clark Terry (b. 1920), a former Duke Ellington trumpeter then in his eighties. "This recording was hard at times," Terry stated, "because the songs are so challenging, and because Miles already put his stamp on it. But, I love this music so much, and I love a challenge, so I wanted to take a crack at it." Lindberg transcribed the suite directly from the Davis recording, except for "I Loves You, Porgy," which he regarded as the original album's "weak link," and which Charles Harrison III rearranged for the same instrumentation plus one extra woodwind. Terry sometimes replicated Davis's improvisations, sometimes not, but in any case, his performance threw the unique daring and drama of Davis's achievement in relief. "Going from Davis to Terry is like going from Debussy to Ravel," opined Michael Ullman in a favorable review for *Fanfare*. "Terry's playing is bold, fluent, and predominantly sweet."[34]

Although the Davis-Evans suite overshadowed all other *Porgy* albums, many more followed, with 1959 a banner year thanks to the Goldwyn film. A number of these recordings even featured singers associated with the picture in one way or another, including the lively Pearl Bailey (singing some of Gershwin's show music as well); the smooth Harry Belafonte (together with the sultry Lena Horne); the elegant Diahann Carroll (stylishly supported by the André Previn Trio); and the suave Sammy Davis Jr. (accompanied by a more subdued Carmen McRae).[35]

The same year's instrumental *Porgy* albums ranged from a lyrical outing by pianist Oscar Peterson (with double bass and drums) and a whimsical release by pianist Hank Jones (with guitar, double bass, and drums) to big-band arrangements by Bill Potts *(The Jazz Soul of Porgy and Bess)* and Jim Timmens *(Porgy and Bess Revisited).* Potts's arrangements, described by André Previn as exhibiting "an ever-present aura of strength and vitality," involved a wide range of distinguished soloists, including trumpeters Art Farmer and Harry Edison, saxophonists Al Cohn and Zoot Sims, trombonists Bob Brookmeyer and Jimmy Cleveland, and pianist Bill Evans. The Timmens release, in contrast, featured only five soloists, each representing characters from the opera: Cootie Williams, trumpet (Porgy); Hilton Jefferson, alto saxophone (Bess); Rex Stewart, cornet (Sportin' Life); Pinky Williams, baritone saxophone (Jake); and Lawrence Brown, trombone (Serena and Clara). Such identification of particular instruments with specific characters naturally encouraged a rather dramatic approach to the material, including Stewart's humorous handling of the Sportin' Life numbers. This recording also stood out for its use of a classic swing style, as opposed to the bebop or cool idioms associated with most of the *Porgy* albums of this period (all five soloists had played with Duke Ellington).[36]

The *Porgy* album remained an attractive vehicle for jazz musicians after the Goldwyn film had been largely forgotten. The Modern Jazz Quartet (John Lewis, piano; Milt Jackson, vibraharp; Percy Heath, double bass; and Connie Kay, drums) brought a somewhat discursive approach to the material in an album released in 1965. Argentine Enrique Villegas and Frenchman George Rabol recorded suites for solo piano in 1968 and 1992, respectively, the former in a spiky manner reminiscent of Thelonious Monk, the latter in a jazz-classical style that echoed Gershwin's own pianism. Trumpeter Ivan Julien's arrangements for a mostly French big band (1971), with Eddy Louiss on the Hammond organ, adapted some so-called fusion elements, as did tenor saxophonist Joe Henderson's recording featuring his own septet with Tommy Flanagan on piano (1997). And Oscar Peterson released his second *Porgy* album in 1976, here playing clavichord—an instrument he had discovered only the year before, thanks to a meeting with British prime minister Edward Heath—and joined by Joe Pass on acoustic guitar, a rapturously delicate album that proved a milestone in the use of the clavichord in jazz. In the same year another accomplished duo, George Mraz on double bass and Roland Hanna on piano, issued their own understated *Porgy* album.[37]

The year 1976 also saw the release of a two-album *Porgy and Bess* with Cleo Laine and Ray Charles, accompanied by chorus and full orchestra, arranged and conducted by Frank DeVol. Produced by Norman Granz, this recording followed along the lines of his earlier Fitzgerald-Armstrong *Porgy,* with Charles, like Armstrong, in the dual role of singer and instrumentalist, here including improvisations on piano, electric piano, organ, and celesta. Like that earlier release as well, the results varied, with "Bess, You Is My Woman" a high point (unlike Armstrong, Charles sang his part more or less as written, though in his own extraordinary way).

In 1996 pianist Joe Utterback released an almost hourlong *Porgy and Bess Jazz Suite,* composed of nine of the opera's numbers, that traversed various keyboard styles—including those of Art Tatum, Bill Evans, and Maurice Ravel—with dazzling facility; Utterback subsequently adapted four of these improvisations as a *Concert Fantasy on George Gershwin's "Porgy and Bess"* (performed by pianist David Allen Wehr on a 1999 disc). Herbie Hancock's *Gershwin's World* (1998), for its part, featured a few selections from the opera, including a "Summertime" that included himself on piano, along with Joni Mitchell, voice; Stevie Wonder, harmonica; Wayne Shorter, soprano saxophone; and Ira Coleman, double bass. And in 2000 a Norwegian sextet headed by singer Magni Wentzel brought a new vigor to this tradition with their release *Porgy & Bess.*

Enough similarities could be found among the different *Porgy* albums to suggest a complex and distinctive lineage. For instance, Russell Garcia's clinking arrangement of "Here Come de Honey Man" (1956) reverberated in a number of later recordings. Similarly, Mundell Lowe's common-time version of the triple-metered "My Man's Gone Now" provided a precedent for comparable transformations. More generally, certain reharmonizations, melodic elaborations, and even ways of articulating phrases threaded their way through these various compilations. At the same time, each *Porgy* album teased out of the original score unique meanings, yielding no shortage of surprises, from Bill Potts's swing arrangement of "Clara, Clara," Hank Jones's waltzlike treatment of "My Man's Gone Now," and Ray Charles's sexually suggestive "Here Come de Honey Man" to Oscar Peterson's use (in his 1976 album) of "Strawberry Woman" as a bona fide blues and Magni Wentzel's interpretation of "There's a Boat Dat's Leavin' Soon for New York" as a metaphor for a drug trip.

Popular and jazz musicians continued to perform and record individual numbers from the opera as well, especially "Summertime," which became Gershwin's best-known song. Will Friedwald attributed its broad appeal to its "multi-faceted, poly-generic nature," and, indeed, it was performed variously as a lullaby, a blues, a ballad, a comedy song, and so forth; and, moreover, in a wide range of styles, particularly jazz, but also folk, rhythm-and-blues, country, gospel, rock, and world pop, including a recording by celebrated Beninese singer Angélique Kidjo, sung in the African language of Fon (1997). One Web site listed hundreds of musicians from around the world who recorded the song.[38]

The song's simplicity helps explain its popularity. Comprising two sixteen-measure halves that virtually mirror each other (though separated by a two-measure interlude, and prepared and completed by a brief introduction and a codetta, respectively), the melody encompasses, with the range of an octave, a purely pentatonic scale (F♯–A–B–D–E–F♯) save for two crucial arrivals on a sixth pitch (C♯) for the words *high* and *sky*. No verse or bridge disturbs its neat symmetry, which can be diagrammed as A *(aaab)* A *(aaab);* nor does the music stray very far from its tonic minor (B minor in the full score, A minor in its sheet-music version). At the same time, the song's subtleties include a sophisticated harmonic palette that enhances the tune's quiet elegance. And although all six *a* phrases begin on the same pitch and with a similar upbeat figure, none of these incipits are identical; in the song's first half, they gradually lengthen note by note, from "Summertime" to "Fish are jumpin'" to "Oh yo' daddy's rich" to, finally, "So hush, little baby," all of which gives the music a kind of improvisatory quality. Of course, the song's appeal depended not only on the music, but on Heyward's lyric and Gershwin's integration of word and tone as well.[39]

Will Friedwald observed an especially large number of recordings of the song by saxophone players, including such giants as Charlie Parker (1949), John Coltrane (1960), Sonny Rollins and Coleman Hawkins (together, 1963), and Stan Getz (1964). Parker's soaring interpretation, accompanied by strings and harp, proved particularly influential. Coltrane's similarly celebrated but more hard-hitting release, which also featured McCoy Tyner on piano, Steve Davis on bass, and Elvin Jones on drums, actually constituted, for all its complexity, a fairly straightforward set of variations, disguised as such not only by the intricacy of the melodic lines but by the interpolation of a six-bar interlude in the midst of the theme (an idea borrowed from Gershwin's own two-bar interlude) and another six-bar codetta at the chorus's end. Tyner's penchant for augmented triads further threw the song's harmonic structure off-kilter, though he often settled firmly on the song's cadential harmonies, thereby helping to anchor the whole.

Described by Friedwald as "nothing short of majestic," Getz's recording fell more along the lines of Parker, only slower; an ascending phrase at the (unsung) words "an' you'll take the sky" suggested that Getz, like many jazz instrumentalists, shaped his improvisation with the lyric in mind. Friedwald cites renditions of the song by such other saxophonists as Lee Konitz, Grover Washington, and Kenny G., but not President Bill Clinton, who performed it—better than one might expect—in a 1994 jam session at the Reduta Jazz Club in Prague with a combo of Czech musicians before an enthusiastic crowd that included Secretary of State Madeleine Albright and Czech president Václav Havel.[40]

Meanwhile, the popular singers who recorded "Summertime" were legion. In addition to those already mentioned, a sampling includes Mildred Bailey, Maxine Sullivan, Peggy Lee, Sarah Vaughan, Mahalia Jackson, Perry Como, Helen Merrill, Sam Cooke, Nina Simone, Pete Seeger, Jeanne Lee, James Brown and Martha High, Lou Rawls, the Zombies, Billy Stewart, Sonny and Cher, Janis Joplin, Willie Nelson, R.E.M., Paul McCartney, Jerry Garcia, Peter Gabriel, Al Jarreau, Sarah Brightman, Smashing Pumpkins, Booker T and the MG's, and Dionne Warwick. Although early performers, like Billie Holiday, generally took the song at (or slightly under) the "Moderato" tempo specified by Gershwin, by the 1950s singers tended toward still slower, sometimes even lugubrious tempos, as in the case with Helen Merrill (1957) and Nina Simone (1959); these "stoned-sounding versions," as Friedwald calls them, culminated in Janis Joplin's psychedelic rendition (1968), which gave the phrase "an' the cotton is high" new meaning, and which established the song as a hippie anthem (like Simone, Joplin ended the song, unusually enough, on a major triad, but on the tonic, not the mediant). Still later performances of "Summertime" helped Jenny Gear reach the finals and Fantasia Barrino capture first prize on two popular televised talent shows, *Canadian Idol* (2003) and *American Idol* (2004), respectively.

"Summertime" also attracted such gospel singers as Mahalia Jackson (1956), who underscored the song's connection to black spirituals not only by alternating it with "Sometimes I Feel Like a Motherless Child" in a six-minute medley, but by actually blending the two tunes; the song's comforting assurances thereby became a poignant hope for the "motherless child," with Jackson revising the final line to " . . . with daddy and mommy, they'll be standin' by." More like the earliest popular performers of the song, musicians like the "godfather of soul," James Brown (1962, with Martha High), Billy Stewart (1966), and Al Jarreau (1994) brought dance rhythms—though rhythm-and-blues, soul, and funk rather than swing—to bear on the music. At the same time, their renditions had an expectant quality like Mahalia Jackson's. Brown and High in particular placed the song at some junction between an idyllic past ("When the world began, it wasn't supposed to be this way," says High in a spoken introduction), an oppressive present (Brown changes the song's lyric to read, "I don't see the cotton grow very high" and "My ole daddy ain't rich"), and a brighter future ("Don't you cry," sings Brown at one point. "I don't care whether you're white, black, blue, or green, yellow, red, purple, or orange. Don't you cry. God is goin' make it better. Yeah, yeah . . . in the summertime"). At the conclusion of Jarreau's recording, in a cadenza ostensibly influenced by Stewart's own scat singing, he similarly interpolated the line, "Do you know that life could be just like, summer, summer, summertime?" This sort of tugging between despair and hope also emerged among some instrumental releases, such as one by Sun Ra (1988) that juxtaposed a playfully innocent version of the song for celesta against discordant harmonica sputterings.

Popular and jazz musicians gravitated toward other numbers from the opera as well, if not necessarily those—like "I Got Plenty o' Nuttin'" and "Bess, You Is My Woman"—that won the most applause in opera houses. "I Loves You, Porgy," for instance, proved a favorite of pianist Bill Evans, whose many renditions of the song included a melancholy one at the Village Vanguard in 1961 and a somewhat more upbeat one at the Montreux Jazz Festival in 1968 (like Ella Fitzgerald and others, Evans treated the song as an *aaba* chorus, with an extended ten-measure bridge). Pianist Keith Jarrett gave a similarly ruminative account of the song (1999). More unexpectedly, James Brown placed the song (1964) in an inverted dramatic context, as a cry—"one of the most weirdest, sorrowful, pleadin' things I've ever heard before"—from a man "beggin'" to his "girl," Porgy; arranger Sammy Lowe retained only remnants of the lyric and melody, now set against a recurring four-chord progression, with Brown declaiming at the song's conclusion, "You know what this means? This means that everything is all right. This means that they are together, that they love each other. This means that you can go on and on and on. This means that everything's all right." Diana Ross delivered her own up-tempo version at Caesar's Palace in 1974, while Barbra Streisand elided the melody with "Bess, You Is My Woman" on a 1985 release whose liner notes explained that she had wanted to sing these two songs—which she described as "two of the most beautiful melodies ever written"—for years.[41]

Much as "I Loves You, Porgy" appealed to the soulful, "It Ain't Necessarily So" attracted such hipsters as Peggy Lee, Cher, and, as earlier mentioned, Sting. Other numbers from the opera similarly found varied adherents and treatments. Bill Evans performed "My Man's Gone Now" as a slow waltz (1961); Barbra Streisand belted out "I Got Plenty o' Nuttin'" (1965); saxophonist Cannonball Adderley, accompanied by pianist Jimmy Jones, delivered a subtle reading of "Oh, Bess, Oh Where's My Bess?" (1974); singer Phoebe Snow, like Magni Wentzel after her, interpreted "There's a Boat That's Leaving Soon for New York" from a woman's perspective (1976); and Michael Feinstein sensitively refashioned the duet "Lonely Boy" as a solo (1998).

Porgy and Bess had various histories, but two primary ones: as a frequently performed stage work and as an important resource for popular and jazz artists. This double history found only vague precedent in those variations on operatic melodies by Salieri and Mozart from the eighteenth century or those paraphrases of Wagner and Verdi from the nineteenth. Nor did it find a real parallel, as intriguingly proposed by Benny Green, with the "dual life" of the Mark Twain novels "as works of art and as repositories of the best jokes and the deepest compassion." Such Gershwin works as the *Rhapsody in Blue* and *Girl Crazy* perhaps offered truer analogies, but even they paled in comparison. As the most successful American opera to date and one of the most internationally popular ever written—and one, moreover, composed for an almost all-black cast—*Porgy and Bess* held a unique position in the annals of opera; but in light of its larger life, the work seemed to constitute a phenomenon distinct from any other piece of music in the repertoire.[42]

Chapter Thirty-Five

From *Swing Is King* (1936)
to *A Damsel in Distress* (1937)

*I*n the first half of 1936, Gershwin published little new music other than a song, "King of Swing," that helped fill out an all-Gershwin revue, *Swing Is King,* at the Radio City Music Hall, the enormous Art Deco theater that opened its doors in late 1932. With Ira on vacation, Gershwin wrote the number with Albert Stillman (1906–1979), the Radio City staff lyricist who had changed his name from Silverman at Gershwin's suggestion and who would later provide the words for hits by Perry Como, Johnny Mathis, and Cher. This commission, if not the entire revue itself, probably owed something to Kay Swift, also on staff at Radio City during 1935 and 1936. Produced by Leon Leonidoff and "fashioned . . . on the current agitation for swing music," *Swing Is King*—sandwiched between a Walt Disney cartoon and a Fritz Kreisler–Dorothy Fields musical starring Grace Moore, *The King Steps Out*—premiered on May 28, 1936, and featured a "futuristic ballet," titled "Manhattan Nocturne," for Radio City's corps de ballet; the *Rhapsody in Blue,* performed by pianist Henrietta Schumann and the Music Hall Symphony Orchestra under Erno Rapee; "King of Swing," introduced by the vaudeville team of Ford Buck and John Bubbles (fresh from their appearance in *Porgy and Bess*); and another dance, "The Hall of Swing," for Radio City's precision dance ensemble, the Rockettes.[1]

In the tradition of "Alexander's Ragtime Band," "King of Swing" celebrates a presumably fictitious musician—trumpeter Smoky Johnson—who plays, however, not ragtime but "a great deal hotter / Thing that's known as Swing." Venturing into swing territory, Gershwin aimed for something "hotter" himself. In its favorable review of the show, *Variety* doubted that any of the music could be characterized as swing, but reasoned that Radio City "could scarcely be expected to unbend to the Onyx Club furnace level. Suffice that it's a dressed-up lah-de-dah version of lowdown hotcha." Alec Wilder considered the "King of Swing" "hack work," though it presumably provided an effective vehicle for Buck and Bubbles.[2]

Gershwin also collaborated with Stillman on the song "Doubting Thomas," only the chorus of which survives. Whether they wrote this song—a poignant number along the lines of "Where's the Boy? Here's the Girl!"—for Radio City remains unknown. Some sources credit Stillman with the lyrics of yet another Gershwin song, "I Won't Give Up," but in fact, Ira wrote the words; the Gershwins possibly intended this breezily insistent love song—again, only the chorus of which survives— for one of the Fred Astaire films that occupied them in 1936 and 1937.

On June 3, a few days after *Swing Is King* opened, *Variety* announced that a forthcoming revue starring Beatrice Lillie and Bert Lahr under the direction of Vincente Minnelli might, too, have a Gershwin score. Gershwin's subsequent contract with RKO Radio Pictures nixed that possibility, but Minnelli secured one Gershwin number anyway, a waltz parody titled "By Strauss" that the director had heard the composer play in an informal setting—a song in which Gershwin exaggerated "the lifts and plunges and *luftpauses* of the Viennese waltz," and which he and Ira completed at Minnelli's request on their arrival in Hollywood in August. After a number of delays, the revue, called *The Show Is On,* opened at the Winter Garden on December 26, 1936, to enthusiastic reviews, and tallied 236 performances plus an additional seventeen performances after reopening at the Winter Garden on September 18, 1937.[3]

Gracie Barrie and Robert Shafer sang "By Strauss" at the top of the second act, with Mitzi Mayfair and the ensemble dancing to the music. Neither *Variety* nor the *Times* mentioned this particular song in reviews of the show—an understandable omission considering that, as Brooks Atkinson noted, the contributing songwriters, who also included Harold Arlen, Hoagy Carmichael, Vernon Duke, Richard Rodgers, and Arthur Schwartz, "read like a roll-call of the town's bards and minnesingers." Moreover, Barrie's voice, according to *Variety,* did not "ordinarily project into the house as far as her personality."[4]

An exuberant waltz, "By Strauss" satirizes both American and Viennese popular music; the singer, tired of the "music of Broadway"— including Gershwin, who keeps "pounding on tin"—yearns for a "free 'n' easy waltz that is Viennesey." Commentators often regard the music, which neatly alludes to a bit of *Die Fledermaus,* as something of an anomaly; but the song actually represents the culmination of a long series of Viennese-style waltzes by Gershwin. Minnelli restaged the song with a revised lyric for the picture *An American in Paris* (1951), where, sung and danced by Gene Kelly and Oscar Levant, it made a more lasting impression.[5]

In the years 1933–1935, the movie musical—as represented by Warner's Busby Berkeley backstagers, RKO's Fred Astaire–Ginger Rogers musicals, MGM's Jeanette MacDonald operettas, and Twentieth Century–Fox's Shirley Temple films—made a strong comeback from its slump of the early 1930s, one abetted by advances in sound engineering and cinematography, and operating under the vigilant eye of Joseph Breen, enforcer of the Hays Office's Production Code. In early 1936, the immense labor of *Porgy and Bess* behind him, Gershwin contacted his agent, Arthur Lyons, about possibly writing a film musical of his own. Hollywood was naturally interested. Paramount floated the idea of a musical for Bing Crosby; Samuel Goldwyn, one for Eddie Cantor; and RKO's executive producer, Pandro S. Berman, an adaptation of *Strike Up the Band* for Fred Astaire or Harold Lloyd, or a picture for Astaire and Rogers.

Money proved a sticking point, however, as no studio would meet Gershwin's demand for a fee of $100,000 for sixteen weeks of work, plus a share of the film's profits. Producers explained that the Hollywood brass, to quote a June 1936 telegram from Archie Selwyn, was "afraid" that Gershwin would "only do highbrow songs" (to which Gershwin famously telegraphed back, "Incidentally rumors about highbrow music ridiculous. Am out to write hits"). More to the point, the studios— especially financially shaky ones like RKO—could no longer indulge those extravagances characteristic of the early days of sound, when Universal paid $50,000 simply for the use of the *Rhapsody in Blue*. Even Irving Berlin and Jerome Kern, the country's highest-paid composers, worked under more modest terms than those proposed by Gershwin. Berlin, for instance, had written *Top Hat* (1935) for RKO for $75,000 plus a 10 percent share of the profits, while Jerome Kern had recently signed with RKO to write *Swing Time* for $50,000 and a capped percentage of the profits.[6]

In late June the Gershwins finally came to an agreement with Pandro Berman to write an Astaire-Rogers musical for RKO for $55,000, with a possible second film optioned at $70,000, both for periods of sixteen weeks. "I think you are letting a few thousand dollars keep you from having [a] lot of fun," Berman had telegraphed to Gershwin on June 24, "and when you figure the government gets eighty percent of it do you think its [*sic*] nice to make me suffer this way." Irving Berlin also encouraged Gershwin, stating, "There is no setup in Hollywood that can compare with doing an Astaire picture, and I know you will be very happy with it."[7]

The Gershwins had shown interest in working on an Astaire-Rogers musical as early as October 1935. They had collaborated successfully with both performers on Broadway, even playing seminal roles in their careers. Now Astaire and Rogers were a celebrated dance team at their height, having appeared in a series of RKO pictures—*Flying down to Rio* (1933; music, Vincent Youmans), *The Gay Divorcee* (1934; music, Cole Porter and others), *Roberta* (1935; music, Jerome Kern), *Top Hat* (1935; music, Irving Berlin), *Follow the Fleet* (1936; music, Berlin), and, soon to be released, *Swing Time* (1936; music, Kern)—that to this day represent some of the most original and memorable film musicals ever made.[8]

Described by P. G. Wodehouse as "the first really intelligent man I have come across here [in Hollywood]—bar [Irving] Thalberg, whom he rather resembles," Pandro S. Berman (1905–1996) produced all but the first of these Astaire-Rogers films, which also tended to feature character actors Eric Blore, Edward Everett Horton, and Erik Rhodes, all three of whom lent some homosexual subtexts to the proceedings, and, writes John Clum, "were cast as foils to Astaire's lean androgyny." But the films took their essential appeal from the unique chemistry between Astaire and Rogers, who similarly projected, for all their wholesome charm, stylish elegance and saucy wit—personas not unlike Gershwin's own. They typically played professional entertainers—film, more than the stage, needed this context to help frame their extraordinary dancing—so that the series offered a blend of backstage musical and screwball comedy. Their pictures further embodied elaborate courtship rituals, in which Rogers at first resisted but eventually succumbed to Astaire, the dance used, writes Gerald Mast, to "mime the myth of modern marriage—too perfect ever to be achieved by mere mortals but a representation of the idea beneath our imperfect mortal striving." Locating their allure within the context of the Depression, J. P. Telotte adds, "In their recurring invitations to dance, they suggested that we could effectively channel our expressive energies into asserting a kind of interpersonal harmony which might, in turn, enhance the world in which we live."[9]

The new Gershwin film, initially called *Watch Your Step*, had a story by Lee Loeb and Harold Buchman, adapted by P. J. Wolfson, that ran afoul of the Production Code ("The attempt," wrote Joseph Breen, "to make comedy out of the suggestion—even though such suggestion is quite untrue—of an unmarried woman who is pregnant, is, in our judgment, highly offensive"). Armed with at least a story outline, the Gershwins started composing some of the songs in New York and, after arriving in Los Angeles on August 10, continued working as they awaited a finished screenplay. Others involved in the project included film director Mark Sandrich (1900–1945), screenwriters Ernest Pagano and Allan Scott, art directors Van Nest Polglase and Carroll Clark, costume designer Irene, cinematographer David Abel, film editor William Hamilton, dance director Hermes Pan, and musical director Nathaniel Shilkret (1895–1982), who had left RCA Victor in 1935 to pursue a career in Hollywood, replacing Max Steiner as music head at RKO in 1936.[10]

In early September Gershwin previewed Kern's *Swing Time* (directed by George Stevens), which he liked "very much," though he underestimated such numbers as "The Way You Look Tonight" and "A Fine Romance," writing to Mabel Schirmer, "Although I don't think Kern has written any outstanding song hits, I think he did a very creditable job with the music and some of it is really delightful. Of course, he never really was ideal for Astaire, and I take that into consideration." Finally, a script to the newly titled *Stepping Toes* arrived in mid-October. "The story has been altered considerably," Gershwin wrote to Schirmer, "and we like it very much." In turn, Hollywood must have appreciated the score in progress, for by late October the Gershwins had signed contracts for a second Astaire picture and a film for Samuel Goldwyn as well. George and Ira completed the score in early December, and during production in early 1937, the film was renamed *Shall We Dance* at Vincente Minnelli's suggestion.[11]

The Astaire-Rogers comedies usually featured about six or seven numbers, with story outlines and scripts often specifying spots and ideas for songs. Assisted by choreographer Hermes Pan and pianist Hal Borne, Astaire—a "trained musician" who, wrote Arlene Croce, "knew how to manipulate a composition for maximum theatrical effect"—subsequently worked out the dance arrangements in collaboration with the composer and the music director. Pandro Berman also helped supervise the music, as did his directors, including Mark Sandrich, whom Hermes Pan credited with good musical instincts and "a great appreciation for the musical *feeling* of the film." By 1936, film technology advances allowed Shilkret to prerecord numbers in a studio—rather than, less optimally, perform them on a set—making it possible for music to be played back during filming. Finally, arrangers would underscore some sequences (including the opening titles), and Astaire and Pan would dub in the sounds for the dance numbers (Pan usually dubbing for Rogers).[12]

In the case of *Shall We Dance,* the filmmakers, apparently responsive to Gershwin's special abilities, devised a scenario that also allowed for some featured instrumental sections, most notably, the "Dog Walking Sequence" ("Walking the Dog") and "Hoctor's Ballet," at least the former of which he orchestrated as well. Gershwin additionally composed some smaller and less conspicuous instrumental cues, as specified by a surviving cue sheet. However, a group of largely uncredited assistants—including Robert Russell Bennett, Maurice DePackh, Joseph ("Fud") Livingston, Edward Powell, and Herbert Spencer—prepared most of the arrangements and orchestrations, though presumably under Gershwin's supervision, as a comment by Richard Rodgers would suggest.[13]

Shall We Dance opens in Paris. The "Russian" ballet star "Petrov"— in actuality, Peter P. Peters of Philadelphia (Fred Astaire)—has become enamored with a popular American singer-dancer, Linda Keene (Ginger Rogers), after seeing her photograph and a flip-book of her dancing. Jeffrey Baird (Edward Everett Horton), a ballet impresario, finds Peter's attraction to Linda and ballroom dancing worrisome. Meanwhile, Linda, fed up with show business, decides to retire from the stage and marry a wealthy suitor, Jim Montgomery (William Brisbane), though nightclub owner Arthur Miller (Jerome Cowan) hopes she'll cure his financial woes by starring in a new revue at his club, the Roof Top.

"Petrov" introduces himself to an unimpressed Linda. After overhearing that she's about to set sail for New York, he decides to do likewise. Jeffrey approves of this decision—he wants "Petrov" to dance at the Metropolitan Opera—and obliges Peter by agreeing not to rehire the seductive Lady Denise Tarrington (Ketti Gallian), a former ballerina and wealthy divorcée infatuated with Peter; rather, he attempts to discourage Denise by falsely saying that Peter has been secretly married for a number of years.

Aboard the *Queen Anne,* as the ballet troupe rehearses, Peter enjoys a jam session with black crew members (including featured singer Dudley Dickerson) in the engine room ("Slap That Bass"). He also makes progress with Linda ("Walking the Dog"), to his great delight ("[I've Got] Beginner's Luck"). Denise mischievously notifies the crew that "Petrov" has a wife, and word spreads that he's married to Linda. After Jeffrey untruthfully tells Linda that Peter started the rumor to extricate himself from a girlfriend, she angrily leaves the ship by plane; on arriving in New York, she turns her attentions to Jim. The hotel floor manager, Cecil

Flintridge (Eric Blore), assumes along with everyone else that Peter and Linda are married and places them in adjoining suites.[14]

In order to thwart Linda's involvement with Jim, Arthur fans gossip about her marriage to "Petrov," which he hopes will lead to the "Petrovs" starring together in one of his revues. At the Roof Top, Linda agrees to perform a number ("They All Laughed") and finds herself having to dance with "Petrov" ("Balloon Ballet"). To satisfy media demand for more concrete evidence of the "Petrov" marriage, Arthur takes and distributes a photograph of a wax dummy of Linda in bed with a sleeping and unsuspecting Peter. Barraged by reporters, Peter and Linda spend the afternoon roller-skating in Central Park ("Let's Call the Whole Thing Off").

Linda decides to put the rumors to rest by marrying Peter and immediately divorcing him the next day. As she and Peter return to New York by ferry from their marriage in New Jersey, the latter wistfully looks ahead to their divorce ("They Can't Take That Away from Me"). That night, Linda discovers Denise in Peter's suite and leaves town.

After the Metropolitan Opera cancels his contract because of his notoriety, "Petrov" agrees to dance in Arthur's revue at the Roof Top. Since he can't dance with Linda, he decides to perform with her look-alikes; the revue, titled *Shall We Dance,* accordingly features not only a ballet with Harriet Hoctor ("Hoctor's Ballet") but a jazzy number with chorus girls donning masks of Linda ("Shall We Dance?"). Linda arrives on opening night to serve Peter with a summons for divorce, but touched by the show, she joins the other "Lindas" onstage. She and Peter finish the number together (reprise of "They All Laughed").

Shall We Dance differed from previous Astaire-Rogers musicals in its overriding preoccupation with the subject of high versus low art. This contest (typically won by low art) enlivened many a movie musical over the years, but it shadowed Gershwin particularly closely, perhaps because the film industry needed this handle to help understand and market the composer. Peter quickly sets the tone by displaying the taps on his ballet shoes and telling Jeffrey, "I wish we could combine the technique of the ballet with the warmth and passion of this other mood," the "other mood" variously associated with tap, jazz, and ballroom dancing.[15]

The film literally explores this high-low divide in the sequence aboard the *Queen Anne,* in which the French ballet troupe rehearses on deck while below in the engine room Peter, accompanied by black musicians and the sounds of the ship's machinery, launches into a jazz dance that has him occasionally backing away from some balletic gestures in disgust. For their part, Jeffrey and Linda are—at least at first—rather hostile to Peter's ideals, Jeffrey (representing high art) derisively calling Linda a "tap-dancing dummy," Linda (representing low art) dismissing "Petrov" as "a simpering toe-dancer." More like Peter, Arthur wants to blend ballet and jazz—though as a publicity ploy to save a financially strapped nightclub.

At the same time, Gershwin's presence only partially explains the film's preoccupation with ballet. As Arlene Croce noted—citing Bronislava Nijinska's work on *A Midsummer Night's Dream* (1935) and Agnes de Mille's on *Romeo and Juliet* (1936) in Hollywood, and George Balanchine's choreography for *On Your Toes* (1936) on Broadway—"ballet was in the air." Indeed, 1936 witnessed the founding of Lincoln Kirstein's Ballet Caravan, which in its own way accommodated the competing claims of ballet and popular dance.

Astaire and Pan, who had little expertise in ballet, duly hired choreographer Harry Losee (1901–1952)—a Ruth St. Denis and Ted Shawn alumnus later associated with the films of ice-skater Sonja Henie—for assistance, but they were still in over their heads. Losee himself had only a limited background in classical dance, and for the climactic ballet sequence he relied on Hoctor's trademark back bends. Croce wrote that the film reveals a "crippling naiveté about ballet," though she found the finale "more riotously exciting than we can believe possible." John Mueller similarly thinks moments in the finale "delivered with pungent effectiveness," but adds, "for the most part, ballet is shrugged off as pretentious and emptily decorative." The more balletic moments at least set off the freshness and vigor of the jazzier choreography, as in the finale, or in "They All Laughed," in which Peter's segue from ballet to jazz proves a decisive turning point in his relationship with Linda.[16]

In the meantime, the Gershwins provided music and lyrics of enormous charm for the film. Since they wrote—even more so than in *Lady, Be Good!* and *Funny Face*—virtually every song for Astaire, the score lacked some range and variety, but it encompassed nonetheless the snappy cool of "Slap That Bass," the delightful whimsy of "Beginner's Luck," the swinging humor of "They All Laughed," the quirky wit of "Let's Call the Whole Thing Off," the bittersweet poignancy of "They Can't Take That Away from Me," and the cheerful elegance of "Shall We Dance."

These songs further contain some shared features that distinguish them as the work of Gershwin's final year, including extended harmonies distinctively spaced, and, as Steven Gilbert notes, unusual formal and permutational devices related to his work with Joseph Schillinger. "Carefully written accompaniments," writes Gilbert, "contrapuntal bias, the thoughtful selection of key, a flirtation with quartal harmony, and the influence of Gershwin's studies with Joseph Schillinger mark the late songs in special ways." The score also displays knowing mastery of the latest popular swing styles, an achievement all the more remarkable for coming in the wake of *Porgy and Bess.*[17]

In addition to the aforementioned numbers, the Gershwins wrote two unused songs for the film: "Hi-Ho!" and "Wake Up, Brother, and Dance." "Hi-Ho!" was, as Ira recalled, "not called for in the script but an idea we had for the opening of the picture: 'Fred Astaire sees on a Paris kiosk the picture-poster of Ginger Rogers, an American girl then entertaining in Paris, and immediately feels: THIS IS SHE! He dances through the streets, extolling to everyone the beauty and virtues of this girl whom he has never met, but whose picture he sees pasted on walls and kiosks everywhere.'" Sandrich liked this sophisticated ballad, which he described, in a reference to top ticket prices on Broadway, as the "real $4.40 stuff," but Berman ultimately decided against the number as too costly. Ira published the song, largely unknown for many years, in 1967 in a version close though not utterly faithful to the surviving manuscript; perfectly suited to Astaire's ironic whimsy, the number proved nonetheless an attractive vehicle for others, including Bobby Short.[18]

As for "Wake Up, Brother, and Dance," the Gershwins originally wrote that song for the film's finale, but late in production they replaced it with "Shall We Dance?"—which not only helped plug the picture's new title but better served the needs of Astaire and Pan. "Wake Up, Brother, and Dance" actually resembles "Shall We Dance?" in a number of ways, though it has a more pronounced Latin flavor, Cuban to be sure, but possibly, as Walter Rimler suggests, Mexican as well. Gershwin published the song in early 1937 along with other numbers from the score, but he subsequently suppressed its distribution, hoping in vain to reuse it for one of his next two pictures (Ira eventually adapted the music as "Sophia" for the 1964 film *Kiss Me, Stupid*).[19]

Of the film's instrumental cues, "Walking the Dog" eventually attained independent success as a novelty piece titled *Promenade,* alternatively arranged for solo piano, orchestra, and other instrumental combinations. This delightful music accompanies a pantomime in which Linda walks her dog on deck while Peter courts her by walking a dog of his own. The music seems an instrumental counterpart to "Hi-Ho!" with whimsical outer sections filled with comical blue notes (and here, some dog barks as well) set off by a more ardent middle section, which harmonically travels widely and urgently before the return to the jovial main theme. Gershwin lightly scored this episode for a relatively small ensemble of clarinet, alto saxophone, tenor saxophone, two trumpets, trombone, percussion, two pianos, and strings, a sonority that befits the cue's playful intentions, and one, according to Oscar Levant, intended as "a private commentary on the plushy, overstuffed scoring favored by most Hollywood orchestrators."[20]

Gershwin's other instrumental cues—including the galop "French Ballet Class" at the film's very opening (immediately following Bennett's title music, which is a medley of the score that includes a bit of the *Rhapsody* at the credits for the Gershwins); the barcarole "Dance of the Waves Ballet"; the fragment accompanying Linda's initial appearance, "Ginger Rhumba"; the waltz "Graceful and Elegant"; and, most notably, "Hoctor's Ballet"—provided some additional tone and humor. A grouping of these cues might make an attractive suite.

The longest of these sequences, "Hoctor's Ballet" (or "Ballet"), comprises a dramatic introduction, a fast waltz for the female corps, a stately section for Harriet Hoctor, and an extended pas de deux for Hoctor and Astaire that concludes with a climactic instrumental reprise of "They Can't Take That Away from Me." Gershwin helped classicize the latter not only by presenting the song in a richly symphonic setting, but more subtly by creating a larger structure that anticipates and leads to its arrival. Reflecting the film's concern with high-low dichotomies, some of the ballet music reappears during the ensuing "Shall We Dance?" sequence as well, betokening some sort of rapprochement.

Although Gershwin spent a fair amount of time on the set, he felt marginalized in Hollywood as compared to Broadway, as perhaps exemplified by the torturous genesis of the film's finale (ultimately composed of "Hoctor's Ballet" and "Shall We Dance?"). After he auditioned his original ballet score for Astaire, Berman, and Sandrich (described by Robert Russell Bennett as one of Hollywood's "absolute monarchs"), the studio ordered a rewrite. "Either it [the ballet] sounded different from what they expected," recalled Shilkret, "or they could not connect the music with their flimsy idea of a story." Unfortunately, Gershwin's revised finale met with rebuff as well; Berman insisted that the ballet include "the main hit song" (presumably "They Can't Take That Away from Me"), while Astaire emphatically rejected the concluding number, "Wake Up, Brother, and Dance." Gershwin duly rewrote the finale once more, including replacing "Wake Up, Brother, and Dance" with "Shall We Dance?" as mentioned; but the studio, still displeased, asked arranger Fud Livingston to incorporate some of Astaire's own musical ideas into the ballet. Appalled by the studio's treatment of Gershwin and dismayed by Livingston's "impossible" arrangement, Shilkret boldly held up production so that he, Bennett, and Gershwin, working until three in the morning, could overhaul the sequence one last time. Some of this final version—such as the fast waltz music, which echoes the likes of Debussy's *Jeux*—suggests that Gershwin imagined something along the lines of a Ballet Russe score, a lofty ambition thwarted by a lack of sympathy on the part of his collaborators.[21]

The conventional wisdom holds that the score to *Shall We Dance* is less dramatically integrated than those of the preceding Astaire-Rogers musicals, but at the least, the music serves the narrative in one way or another. The opening ballet cues and "Slap That Bass" set forth the film's basic conflict; "Walking the Dog" and "Beginner's Luck" chart the budding friendship between Peter and Linda; "They All Laughed" advances their romance, for although Linda uses the song to taunt Peter, he subsequently appropriates the music for a dance that reveals their compatibility; "Let's Call the Whole Thing Off" dramatizes the vicissitudes of their relationship; "They Can't Take That Away from Me" expresses their growing attachment; and the final revue—including "Shall We Dance?"—resolves both personal and artistic tensions, with the reprise of "They All Laughed" taking on a double meaning, the line "They all said we never could be happy" referring to both Peter and Linda, and, by extension, to high and low art. In short, the score deftly carries the story along.

Attending a preview in Santa Barbara in early April, Gershwin thought the film a "funny farce" with "lots of laughs," but was dismayed by its treatment of some of the music. "The picture does not take advantage of the songs as well as it should," he wrote to Isaac Goldberg. "They literally threw one or two songs away without any kind of a plug. This is mainly due to the structure of the story which does not include any other singers than Fred and Ginger and the amount of singing one can stand of these two is quite limited." By "one or two songs," Gershwin presumably meant "Beginner's Luck" and "They Can't Take That Away from Me," both of which received short shrift. At the same time, Gershwin took pleasure in Astaire's recordings of the film's six songs with the Johnny Green Orchestra on the Brunswick label, and pride in Irving Berlin's and Jerome Kern's assessment of "They Can't Take That Away from Me" as a "lasting song" and "one of the best songs Ira and I have written in a long time."[22]

Released on April 30, the nearly two-hour film garnered excellent reviews, including one in the *New York Times* by Frank S. Nugent, who declared it "a zestful, prancing, sophisticated musical show" with "a grand score by George Gershwin." Some critics quibbled that the plot sometimes dragged, that Rogers was underutilized, and that the music was not as tuneful as Berlin's or Kern's; but they generally ranked the film at least on a par with the previous Astaire-Rogers films, singling out for special kudos Astaire's dancing and Blore's comedy. *Variety* liked, too, the very thing that most disappointed Gershwin, namely, the restrained use of reprises, or as they also put it, "the reluctance of the picture to force its songs down the audience's throat." Only an occasional critic, like Winston Burdett, gave the film thumbs down: "'Shall We Dance' is proof that even the best formula begins to wear thin after the seventh try."[23]

Burdett apparently had his thumb on the public's pulse. Whereas *Top Hat* had made more than $1 million, and both *Follow the Fleet* and *Swing Time* earned in excess of $800,000, *Shall We Dance* netted a far more modest $413,000. Astaire and Rogers themselves were tiring of the series and had already made plans to go it alone on their next films. Of their subsequent reunions, *Carefree* (1938) and *The Story of Vernon and Irene Castle* (1939) proved even less successful at the box office, though after the war they enjoyed one last triumph together with *The Barkleys of Broadway* (1949), in which they finally danced to "They Can't Take That Away from Me" (a performance that attained a special pathos not only in terms of the picture's dramatic narrative, but in the context of the Astaire-Rogers partnership itself).

Meanwhile, the public seemed curiously reserved about a musical score that the critics obviously loved—and whose six songs even turned up, arranged as an orchestral suite, on a concert broadcast by Italian radio in early 1938. Of eight viewers who commented on the music following a preview of the film, only two had positive responses; one viewer thought the music "mediocre," while another complained of an absence of "'tone' or apparent 'melody.'" True, "Let's Call the Whole Thing Off" and "They Can't Take That Away from Me" both made it to the *Lucky Strike Hit Parade* (later, *Your Hit Parade*), a weekly radio (and eventually television) show that featured "top ten" songs based on sales of sheet music and recordings. But the popularity of even these songs paled in comparison to that of contemporary hits by Berlin, Kern, Porter, Rodgers, Harry Warren, and dozens of lesser songwriters.[24]

Tellingly, from the wealth of songs composed for *Shall We Dance* and Gershwin's next film musical, *A Damsel in Distress*, the Academy of Motion Pictures nominated only "They Can't Take That Away from Me" for best song of 1937, and then presented the award (at a ceremony held March 10, 1938, months after Gershwin's death) to Harry Owens for "Sweet Leilani," which Bing Crosby had sung in the picture *Waikiki Wedding*. ("I'd like to say something about Harry Owens," Oscar Levant reportedly stated at the time. "His music is dead, but he lives on forever.") In late 1937 Ira asserted that he and George were "pretty proud" of a score they considered "smart" and "a little sophisticated," but wondered, "Maybe that was a mistake, to put so many smart songs in one picture." Ira needn't have been so doubtful. *Shall We Dance* remains, for all its flaws, a classic film, and every song from the picture, a treasured gem.[25]

For Astaire's next picture, RKO decided, at Gershwin's suggestion, to adapt P. G. Wodehouse's 1919 novel *A Damsel in Distress* (released as a motion picture in October 1919, with Creighton Hale and June Caprice directed by George Archainbaud; and adapted by Wodehouse and Ian Hay—the pseudonym for John Hay Beith—as a straight play in 1928). Wodehouse's novels, which the author himself characterized as "a sort of musical comedy without music," lent themselves to musical adaptation; they contained not only types and situations drawn from musical comedy, but even the equivalent of song spots, with characters nearly or actually breaking into song.[26]

As an added inducement, the hero of this particular novel, George Bevan—a modest but ambitious young composer of successful musical comedies—bore a striking resemblance to Gershwin. His name even sounded a bit like George Gershvin. Had Wodehouse written the novel a few years later, readers might reasonably have guessed that he had modeled the character after Gershwin, which remains only a distant possibility. In any case, Gershwin's Hollywood collaborators clearly welcomed vehicles that mirrored him in some fashion, as evidenced also by *Delicious* and *Shall We Dance*.[27]

The Gershwins worked on the score from mid-January to mid-May. "There wasn't one number he [Astaire] could find fault with," Gershwin wrote to his sister on May 27. "Producer Pandro Berman thinks our second score much finer than the first." Meanwhile, Ernest Pagano and S. K. Lauren worked on the script, though the studio subsequently hired Wodehouse and Pagano to rewrite the dialogue. "*A Damsel in Distress* was fun," recalled Wodehouse, "because I was working with the best director here—George Stevens—and on my own story." Shooting began in late July, soon after Gershwin's death, though Wodehouse did not com-

plete the screenplay until some weeks later. In adapting the story for Astaire, the writers recast the protagonist as an entertainer rather than a
composer. They also eliminated certain supporting characters and sub-
plots and made other alterations, while retaining the spirit of the original.[28]

Although Van Nest Polglase, Carroll Clark, and Hermes Pan worked
on this film as well, in other respects the production team differed
significantly from that of *Shall We Dance*. Most notably, the young
George Stevens (1904–1975), later celebrated for such 1950s melodramas as *A Place in the Sun* (1951) and *Giant* (1956), directed the picture.
In addition, Joseph August oversaw the cinematography; Henry Berman,
the film editing; and Victor Baravalle, the music. Remembered above all
for his affiliation with *Show Boat*, Italian-born Baravalle (1885–1939)
worked mostly as a conductor-arranger on Broadway, but he spent his
last years in Hollywood, where he supervised the music for three Astaire
pictures (*A Damsel in Distress* was the first). Robert Russell Bennett, who,
with the assistance of George Bassman, Ray Noble, Max Steiner, and
Roy Webb, arranged and orchestrated the score, remembered Baravalle
as "a rather rough-hewn character, but he had the quality as a conductor that made your instrument begin playing before you were conscious
of playing it—just as the violinist said of Stokowski."[29]

The cast proved considerably different from Astaire's earlier pictures
as well. Because of the story's largely British dramatis personae, RKO engaged English actors Constance Collier, Reginald Gardiner, and Montagu
Love, along with popular British bandleader Ray Noble. Similarly, after
considering such celebrities as Alice Faye, Katharine Hepburn, Ruby
Keeler, Ida Lupino, and British musical-comedy star Jessie Matthews for
the female lead, the studio engaged a fetching nineteen-year-old American of British parentage, Joan Fontaine, better known at this point as
the younger sister of Olivia de Havilland than for her work in some minor films. As Stevens realized, Fontaine had potential—she would become a major star in the 1940s—but she had little background in musical comedy, making her a curious partner for Astaire. On the other hand,
the role as conceived did not presume such abilities; and besides, Astaire
seemed inclined, at this stage, toward dancing on his own. Moreover,
the film neutralized the lack of a musical leading lady by drawing on the
talents of the popular vaudeville team of George Burns and Gracie Allen,
cast late in the production (the script simply called for a "vaudeville
couple").[30]

The picture takes place in Great Britain, where imperious Lady Caroline Marshmorton (Constance Collier) wants her stepson, Reggie (Ray

Noble), a jazz enthusiast, to marry her niece, Lady Alyce (Joan Fontaine), the daughter of mild-mannered Lord John Marshmorton (Montagu Love). The servants hold a sweepstakes, drawing lots on a likely husband for Alyce; the crafty chief steward, Keggs (Reginald Gardiner), makes sure he draws Reggie's name, while the rascally page Albert (Harry Watson), who knows that Alyce has fallen in love with an American while vacationing in Switzerland, opts for a wild card, "Mr. X."

Alyce slips into London to meet her American lover, but trailed by Keggs and Albert, she takes refuge in a cab occupied by a popular American entertainer, Jerry Halliday (Fred Astaire), whom Keggs and Albert assume to be her American boyfriend. As Keggs confronts Jerry, a policeman intervenes, but Jerry smoothly escapes ("I Can't Be Bothered Now"). Eager to win the sweepstakes, Albert forges a note from Alyce to Jerry in which she confesses her love to him and pleads that he rescue her. Accompanied by his press agent, George Burns (himself), and press secretary, Gracie Allen (herself), Jerry leaves for the Marshmorton ancestral manor, Totleigh Castle.

Prevented from entering the castle by Keggs, Jerry sneaks in with a group of madrigal singers ("The Jolly Tar and the Milkmaid"). Convinced that Alyce loves him, Jerry happily takes up quarters in a cottage by the castle ("Put Me to the Test"). After Alyce angrily resists Jerry's advances at an amusement park, Gracie cheers him up ("Stiff Upper Lip"). Returning home, Alyce realizes that she does, in fact, love Jerry ("Things Are Looking Up").

At a ball at the castle, the madrigal singers once again entertain ("Sing of Spring"). Having been forced to exchange his sweepstakes ticket with Keggs, Albert shifts tactics and shows Alyce a newspaper article written by George Burns that portrays Jerry as a lady-killer and Alyce as his "28th victim." Unaware of Alyce's dismay, Jerry reflects on his good fortune ("A Foggy Day [in London Town]"); now barred from the castle by Alyce, Jerry once again enters with the madrigal singers ("Nice Work If You Can Get It"). Meanwhile, Reggie proposes to Gracie. Though banned from singing opera, Keggs cannot resist an aria from Friedrich von Flotow's *Martha* after Albert gets the band to play the music ("Ah! che a voi perdoni iddio," translated into Italian from Wilhelm Friedrich's original German, and dubbed by Mario Berini).

To avoid a scandal, Lady Caroline—to Lord Marshmorton's delight—insists that Alyce wed Jerry. Gracie chooses George over Reggie, and Jerry, after resolving his differences with Alyce, gives both Keggs and Albert a swift kick in the pants (reprise of "Nice Work").

Like *Shall We Dance,* though more subtly, the film engages the theme of high versus low art; patron of a madrigal consort, Lady Caroline disapproves of jazz, the music her stepson adores, even if he's forced to oblige her preference for traditional English music. This opposition of madrigal and jazz reflects some of the story's transatlantic and generational conflicts, but hardly involves Lord Marshmorton, aside from the use of "Sing of Spring" as his signifying music, or for that matter, Alyce, who has no clear musical personality. Keggs's weakness for nineteenth-century opera, meanwhile, basically provides a weathered comic device—the undemonstrative butler giving way to passion—but forms at the same time a third spoke to the madrigal-jazz opposition.

The film treats this theme even more lightly than *Shall We Dance.* Jerry broadly subverts "The Jolly Tar," for instance, by obtrusively singing the wrong part. And in contrast to the finale to *Shall We Dance,* the high and the low simply collide toward the picture's end as the madrigal singers sit in with Reggie's dance band, and then put forth a rendition of "Nice Work" in swing style. The old order further collapses as Jerry, who has just won Alyce's hand, reprises the same song, dancing and playing drums in a thrilling display of rhythmic cacophony.

The Gershwins wrote nine numbers for the film, including an unused duet, "Pay Some Attention to Me," based on a song written about 1928. John Mueller describes the score as "probably the best ever written for an Astaire film—and, therefore, for any movie musical," opining that its "incredibly high quality . . . may well have been inspired at least in part by George Gershwin's personal identification with the moods and motivations of the hero in the novel." The score certainly had greater variety than *Shall We Dance,* most obviously by way of the two English-style numbers for mixed voices: "The Jolly Tar and the Milkmaid," a jaunty narrative in which the tar discovers that the milkmaid he attempts to marry has a husband and three children, while she learns that he already has three wives; and "Sing of Spring," an exquisite idyll that contains, nonetheless, some wayward blue notes and whimsical nonsense refrains, such as "Willy-wally-willo" and "Jug-a, jug-a, jug." Ira wrote that in "The Jolly Tar," he and George "tried for the feel of an English eighteenth-century light ballad," though the number seems more patently descended from Gilbert and Sullivan (Stephen Banfield detected as well more than a slight musical resemblance to John Ireland's song "The Bells of San Marie," published in 1919). Ira further recalled that Gershwin based "Sing of Spring" on "a short contrapuntal exercise originally called 'Back to Bach,'" though again, the music also evokes nineteenth-century British traditions—"the circumstance," commented Oscar Levant, "if not the pomp of Elgar."[31]

Some of the solo numbers recall British music as well, including "Stiff Upper Lip," described by Gershwin as a "little English comedy song." (Ira enhanced the music's Englishness with such colloquialisms as "pip-pip" and "stout fella," in part culled from the Wodehouse novel, though he learned some years later, to his surprise, that the phrase "stiff upper lip" had been coined in America.) "A Foggy Day," for all its originality, also reveals some English inflections, most obviously the allusion to Big Ben's chimes at the start of the piece, though as Allen Forte points out, this Big Ben motive ingeniously hovers in the background of the entire song, thus helping to explain its "distinctly British lilt." The other numbers, including the euphoric "I Can't Be Bothered Now," the jazzy "Put Me to the Test," the sprightly "Things Are Looking Up," the tuneful "Nice Work If You Can Get It," and the adorable "Pay Some Attention to Me," seem more typically Gershwinesque.[32]

Although these numbers contain those aforementioned features characteristic of Gershwin's late work, they reveal an even more pronounced tendency toward irregular phrase lengths. The two English ballads especially display various asymmetries, but some of the other songs lean in that direction as well, most notably, "Things Are Looking Up" and "I Can't Be Bothered Now," both of whose choruses combine eight-measure units with longer ones (10 + 10 + 8 + 8 and 8 + 10 + 8 + 12, respectively). In light of the complex structures of some of the verses as well, Gershwin seemed on the verge of significantly breaking through the formal constraints of musical-comedy song, a direction his early death left unfulfilled.

Had Gershwin lived longer, he might, too, have been able to fine-tune the score, for instance, to replace "Put Me to the Test" (apparently intended for Jerry) with another number after Stevens failed to find a spot for the song and decided to use it simply as dance music. (Ira, incidentally, recycled its lyric while working with Jerome Kern on the 1944 film *Cover Girl,* thereby providing a unique opportunity to compare a Kern and a Gershwin song with virtually the same lyric.) Nor did Gershwin compose, it seems, any of the background music, though Baravalle and his team made good use of the songs in their underscoring, often using them as leitmotives in ingenious ways. For instance, when Jerry, besieged by admiring fans, first appears, the music breaks into a short fugal passage based on the main theme of "A Foggy Day." In time, both John McGlinn (1987) and John Mauceri (1991) recorded suites drawn from the sound track.

In addition to its excellent music and expert scoring, the picture had in its favor an amusing screenplay, skilled direction, radiant cinematography, and fine sets (which earned Carroll Clark an Oscar nomination). The film also contained some brilliant dance sequences, including Astaire's spectacular final solo, which caused movie audiences to erupt in applause at its conclusion ("There could be nothing better than this," remarked Mark Van Doren in his review of the film, "either as poetry or in itself"); and two delightful trios for Astaire, Burns, and Allen: "Put Me to the Test," a droll commentary on vaudeville shtick in the form of a whisk-broom dance; and "Stiff Upper Lip," in which navigating a fun house becomes an allegory for "muddling though" life—a scene that won Hermes Pan an Academy Award for dance direction and that Ira thought comparable to the cinema of René Clair.[33]

All these strengths could compensate only so much for the uninspired pairing of Astaire and Fontaine. During production, Astaire even pleaded that the studio replace Fontaine, who nearly suffered a breakdown from all the pressure ("For me," wrote Fontaine in her memoirs, "the title [of the film] was appropriate"). Some critics, disregarding the "mostly decorative, but very sweet Fontaine," viewed the picture as proof that Astaire could star successfully in a film on his own, so to speak; but many others—not to mention the larger public—missed Ginger Rogers, and the movie became Astaire's first to lose money.[34]

At the same time, "A Foggy Day" and "Nice Work" had greater immediate success than anything from *Shall We Dance;* a number of popular musicians recorded both tunes about the time of the film's premiere at Radio City Music Hall on November 19, 1937. That both numbers appear in the film in the context of dance-band entertainment raises the question of whether such treatment helped to popularize them, or the songs lent themselves to such treatment. With its swing rhythms and its "cottage door" clichés, "Nice Work" seemed—for all its sophistication—especially pitched toward a mass audience. In any case, early recordings of that particular song, which nearly made it to number one on the *Lucky Strike Hit Parade,* included those of Astaire, Bob Crosby, Billie Holiday, and the Andrews Sisters. In later years, Rosemary Clooney, Peggy Lee, Carmen McRae, Frank Sinatra, and many others recorded the song as well.

Some of the film's other numbers enjoyed a more modest but similarly enduring success, though the irregular phrase lengths of "I Can't Be Bothered Now" and "Things Are Looking Up" may have limited their popularity. In 1976 the picture's two choruses—"The Jolly Tar" and

"Sing of Spring"—finally became available as well, and a subsequent recording of both by the Gregg Smith Singers revealed that the film had failed to do them justice, and that neither would be out of place in a concert setting. Few pieces demonstrated as well as these two choruses Gershwin's ability to spin magic in the most unexpected ways.

On October 20, 1987, in commemoration of the fiftieth anniversary of Gershwin's death, the Eastman Opera Theatre premiered a stage musical, *Reaching for the Moon,* adapted from *A Damsel in Distress.* John Mueller, a professor of film and political science at the University of Rochester, fleshed out the original score (including "Put Me to the Test" and "Pay Some Attention to Me") with ten songs from other Gershwin shows and devised a book that hewed closer to the original Wodehouse novel than had the film musical. Richard Pearlman directed, Rayburn Wright supervised the music, and Ronald Watkins (as Steve Riker) and Nancy R. Allen (as Lady Jessica) headed the all-student cast.[35]

The three-hour show received mixed reviews—Stephen Holden of the *Times,* attending the first of its six performances at Kilbourn Hall, thought that its "musical charms far outweighed its literary ones"—but Canada's Shaw Festival picked up the property and reintroduced it, with a revised book by popular playwright Norm Foster, in its 328–seat Royal George Theatre as *A Foggy Day* on May 23, 1998. Starring Jeffry Denman and Stephanie McNamara, and directed by Kelly Robinson—who thought that the show's "aspects of love" refracted "the urbanity, wit and teasing awareness of George and Ira Gershwin's art"—*A Foggy Day* proved the surprise hit of the season, and the festival accordingly remounted it the following year, this time with Larry Herbert and Glynis Ranney in the principal roles. Critics appreciated the show's charm and intimacy, free of the "elaborate stage machinery" and "electronic amplification" that had come to dominate the Broadway musical.[36]

Chapter Thirty-Six

From *The Goldwyn Follies* (1938)
to *Kiss Me, Stupid* (1964)

*N*o sooner had the Gershwins completed *A Damsel in Distress* than they started work in mid-May on the picture *The Goldwyn Follies* for Samuel Goldwyn. Goldwyn had an option for a second film as well, but as Ira had rightly predicted in December 1936, "by that time, if not before, we'll probably be fed up." Indeed, by May, Gershwin—his weariness with the film industry no doubt exacerbated by his declining health—could hardly wait to leave Hollywood, take a vacation (perhaps to Europe), and turn his attention to more serious work. That Goldwyn could be overbearing no doubt made him all the more eager to put the movies behind him.[1]

Born Shmuel Gelbfisz in Warsaw, Samuel Goldfish/Goldwyn (1879?–1974) arrived in the States in 1899 and entered the film business in 1913; as mentioned earlier, he co-founded Goldwyn Pictures in 1916, and before resigning in 1922 adopted the company name as his own (in 1924 the studio, independent of his involvement, merged to become MGM). In 1923 he established the Goldwyn Company, which for nearly four decades produced a few high-caliber and generally successful films each year, thereby providing a model for such Hollywood independents as Walt Disney and David O. Selznick.

Though a self-made businessman famous for his malapropisms, Goldwyn's association with the likes of director William Wyler and playwright Lillian Hellman helped secure for his films a certain prestige, the "Goldwyn touch." He attracted such distinguished collaborators in part because they could count on working with other estimable figures on lavishly budgeted and well-crafted films. "Sam Goldwyn's name stood for something, for quality," stated William Wyler. And he paid well, too, though the seventy-five thousand dollars he offered the Gershwins for sixteen weeks of work was only five thousand more than they had received for their second Astaire film.[2]

In the early 1930s Goldwyn began to entertain the notion of an annual series of revues along the lines of those by Florenz Ziegfeld, whom he revered and emulated. After trying in vain to interest Irving Berlin in such a project, he contracted the Gershwins when they became available, lining up as well director George Marshall (aided by an uncredited H. C. Potter), cinematographer Gregg Toland, choreographer George Balanchine, and musical director Alfred Newman, assisted by Edward Powell and David Raksin. Moreover, he decided to film the revue in Technicolor, with Natalie Kalmus, a leading expert in this area, supervising the color scheme in conjunction with art director Richard Day and costume designer Omar Kiam.[3]

Goldwyn further assembled an assortment of stars from radio (tenor Kenny Baker, comedian Phil Baker, and ventriloquist Edgar Bergen), vaudeville (Bobby Clark and the zany Ritz Brothers), ballet (Vera Zorina and William Dollar), opera (soprano Helen Jepson and tenor Charles Kullmann), and the pictures (Jerome Cowan, Andrea Leeds, and Adolphe Menjou), along with Ella Logan, a singer-actress best remembered today for creating the role of Finian's daughter in *Finian's Rainbow*. (Virginia Verrill, originally cast as the female lead, provided only the singing voice for her replacement, Andrea Leeds, then enjoying some short-lived fame in the wake of the 1937 film *Stage Door*.) In a May 12 letter to Isaac Goldberg, Gershwin wryly referred to the film as "a super, super, stupendous, colossal, moving picture extravaganza," though in a letter to his sister, Frances, he seemed genuinely intrigued by Goldwyn's decision to use Technicolor, perhaps in part because Frances's husband, Leopold Godowsky Jr., had played a notable role in the development of color photography.[4]

As the film's main attraction, Goldwyn planned a ballet choreographed by Balanchine to a score by Gershwin for the Metropolitan Opera's American Ballet. As with *Delicious*, Gershwin chose to write the songs first so as to be able to devote at least six weeks to this extended sequence, tentatively titled "Swing Symphony." He apparently hoped to use this music—again as in the case with *Delicious*—for some other purpose, perhaps as an orchestral work or as a ballet for the American Ballet or the Ballet Caravan, both cofounded by his friend Edward Warburg. Alas, he never lived to write the piece.

Because the picture's plot proved intractable, the Gershwins presumably went to work without a precise story line. In any case, by late June they had five songs readied: "I Love to Rhyme," "I Was Doing All Right," "Just Another Rhumba," "Love Is Here to Stay," and "Love Walked In." After Gershwin played some of the music for Goldwyn and his staff, the producer offered only faint praise and offended him—"one of the few occasions in my experience," recalled Oscar Levant, when Gershwin "was genuinely offended"—by asking why he didn't write "hit songs you can whistle," like Irving Berlin. "I had to live for this," Gershwin later told S. N. Behrman, "that Sam Goldwyn should say to me: 'Why don't you write hits like Irving Berlin?'" For all its indelicacy, Goldwyn's query underscored the common perception of Gershwin's songs as somewhat unmelodious by the standards of Berlin and Kern.[5]

However, Oscar Levant noted Gershwin's "resiliency" by way of the "amusement" he derived the following day at a conference with Goldwyn and Balanchine in which the two Russian-born Americans failed to understand each other's English. "It was veritably," reported Levant, "a 'Great Waltz' of accents—in which, by some remarkable divination, they established a common meeting ground based on mutual incomprehensibility." Gershwin only added to the confusion by attempting to mediate with a pidgin English of his own (Balanchine later described Gershwin's speech on that occasion as sounding like, "me Tarzan, you Jane," until Ira suggested that he "speak a little real English"). When Balanchine mentioned, as a theme for the dance, a "competition" between jazz and ballet, Goldwyn said, "That's great. *Competition!*"—"lunging at the word," wrote Levant, "as though he had at last encountered a compatible emotion." One can imagine Gershwin, though quickly deteriorating, relating this story with his customary wit and gusto.[6]

A few weeks later, Gershwin was dead. After the funeral in New York on July 15, Ira returned to Hollywood to complete work on the picture. At his suggestion, Goldwyn replaced Gershwin with Vernon Duke, whose background and abilities—his credits included a successful ballet as well as some hit songs—made him an appropriate substitute. Moreover, he and Ira had recently worked together on the *Ziegfeld Follies of 1936.*

Whether Goldwyn had earlier intended only one ballet sequence, he now envisioned two smaller ballets of about ten minutes in length each. Balanchine decided to choreograph not only an original score by Duke but also Gershwin's *An American in Paris,* to a scenario cowritten with Ira titled "Exposition." In this scenario, the hero pursues a schoolgirl throughout a large fairground, until she finally rejoins her classmates;

the hero, "seeing his cause is hopeless," departs by taxi as the fair closes. Balanchine rehearsed the ballet for about three weeks—"It was a charming and lively ballet and worked perfectly," recalled Vera Zorina—but Goldwyn scrapped the dance after attending the final rehearsal, complaining to the choreographer "that the miners in Harrisburg wouldn't understand it" and telling Zorina, in inimitable Goldwyn fashion, that the ballet had "too much ballet." According to Zorina, Goldwyn simply couldn't grasp the ballet's innovative staging, nor could he realize that Balanchine "was way ahead of the game in choreographing for the camera and not the theater." (Some years later, MGM's *An American in Paris* ostensibly drew on the "Exhibition" scenario for its own ballet based on the Gershwin tone-poem.) A "furious" Balanchine "disappeared" for a while, but he eventually returned to choreograph two Duke ballets, the "Romeo and Juliet Ballet" and the "Water Nymph Ballet" (also called "Ondine"); the former apparently evolved from Balanchine's early notion of a "competition" between jazz and ballet, here represented by the Montagues and the Capulets, respectively.[7]

Although Gershwin, as mentioned, had composed five songs for the picture, he never fully notated the verses to "I Was Doing All Right" and "Love Walked In," and neither the verse nor the complete chorus of his final song, "Love Is Here to Stay." Assisted by Ira, Levant reconstructed the chorus of the latter song from memory and helped Duke furnish the missing verses as well. Ira and Duke also collaborated on two new songs, "Spring Again" and "I'm Not Complaining," only the first of which made it into the film. As the Gershwins' joint contract had ended with George's death, Goldwyn decided to let Ira go in mid-August, some weeks earlier than specified by the original agreement. "Legally there's nothing to do," Ira wrote to his mother. "Morally, Goldwyn proved himself lacking. However, I'm not going to worry myself about it. I'm quite run down and maybe it's better that I didn't continue."[8]

Goldwyn had originally imagined the film as a "counterblast against theatre critics," but over time the movie evolved into a more conventional backstage musical, like *The Great Ziegfeld*, voted best picture of 1936 by the Motion Picture Academy. Incorporating such disparate entertainments into a coherent narrative proved problematic, however, and Goldwyn, after discarding the preliminary work of such varied writers as Lillian Hellman, Anita Loos, and Dorothy Parker, hired Ben Hecht to write the script, with Sam Perrin and Arthur Phillips creating some of the comedy routines.[9]

As the film begins, movie producer Oliver Merton (Adolphe Menjou) and his leading lady, the temperamental Russian Olga Samara (Vera Zorina), preview their latest flop and begin a new picture, *Forgotten Dance*. During a shoot in the country, Oliver overhears a local girl, Hazel Dawes (Andrea Leeds), critiquing the movie in progress as "unreal," and decides to hire her as his consultant, "Miss Humanity." ("I can buy wagon-loads of poets and dramatists," he tells her, "but I can't buy common sense. I cannot buy humanity.")

Oliver places Hazel in the care of Glory Wood (Ella Logan), the actress-girlfriend of casting director A. Basil Crane Jr. (Bobby Clark). Edgar Bergen (himself), accompanied by his dummy, Charlie McCarthy, hopes to find work with Oliver Merton, as do the Ritz Brothers (themselves). Oliver takes Hazel to observe a ballet version of *Romeo and Juliet* planned for his new film, and at her suggestion changes the ending to a happy one (the "Romeo and Juliet Ballet," with Vera Zorina and William Dollar; music, Vernon Duke). As Michael Day (Phil Baker) fusses over his one line, the film's director (Jerome Cowan) halts the production for rewrites. During auditions for a new tenor role for the picture, that of a gondolier, the Ritz Brothers storm Oliver's office ("Here Pussy, Pussy"; music and lyrics, Ray Golden and Sid Kuller).

At a local eatery, Hazel falls for the hamburger slinger, Danny Becker (Kenny Baker), after hearing him sing ("Love Walked In"). Oliver takes Hazel to the opera to hear Leona Jerome (Helen Jepson), whom he's hoping to feature in the new film (excerpts from *La Traviata* with Jepson and Charles Kullmann; music, Giuseppe Verdi; libretto, Francesco Maria Piave). Hazel and Danny begin to date (reprise of "Love Walked In") and Glory helps Danny land a spot on a radio talent show. At Hazel's request, Oliver listens to Danny over the air and decides to hire him as the gondolier ("I Was Doing All Right," sung by Logan, and "Love Is Here to Stay," sung by Baker).

During filming on the Venetian set, Leona Jerome performs a number ("Serenade"; music, Enrico Toselli; lyrics, Afredo Silvestri) as does Danny ("Spring Again"; music, Duke; lyrics, Ira). Another ballet follows ("Water Nymph Ballet," with Zorina and Dollar; music, Duke), subsequently satirized by the Ritz Brothers dressed at one point as Rhine maidens ("Serenade to a Fish"; music and lyrics, Golden and Kuller). On the verge of announcing his engagement to Hazel, Oliver discovers that Danny and Hazel are in love; Hazel agrees to marry Oliver after he threatens to fire Danny from the picture. At a cast party at Oliver's that night, Michael Day and Edgar Bergen entertain ("I Love to Rhyme"). Realizing that Danny prizes love more than his career, a chastened Oliver renounces Hazel and offers Danny a five-year contract (reprise of "Love Walked In").

The picture—with its basic theme that the simple innocence of the common man can redeem Hollywood and its moguls—was of its time, and not without its ironies, including the fact that Goldwyn spent close to two million dollars on the film. Hecht at least tried for a light touch, apparently modeling Oliver Merton on Goldwyn and his reported infatuation with Vera Zorina. Goldwyn presumably was in on the joke, pleased to be portrayed as a crusty but ultimately benevolent magnate, though the picture needed yet more mockery and wit.

The Goldwyn Follies had its world premiere in Miami on January 28, 1938. The critics generally liked the nearly two-hour film, especially the elegant "Water Nymph Ballet" and the impudent Charlie McCarthy. John Mosher in the *New Yorker* proclaimed, "Our civilization is now further enlivened by another bright musical movie," described further by Peter Galway in the *New Statesman and Nation* as "remarkably gay, witty and enjoyable." At the same time, Frank Nugent in the *New York Times* and Howard Barnes in the *Herald-Tribune* offered more critical appraisals, Nugent calling the film a "hodge-podge," even if a "superior hodge-podge, peopled almost exclusively by superior specialists," and Barnes deeming the book "extremely banal and unamusing" and the production "rather ponderous," even though "big" and "beautiful."[10]

Gershwin's music figured mostly in tangential ways. "Love Walked In" and "Love Is Here to Stay" provided the needed note of redemptive love—the former further served as the film's theme song and as Hazel's signature motive ad nauseam—but the picture made only cursory use of "I Was Doing All Right" and "I Love to Rhyme," and discarded "Just Another Rhumba" altogether. Even "Love Is Here to Stay" received glib treatment. The critics offered various opinions about the Gershwin score, but considering its near-invisibility, one wonders what they had in mind. Howard Barnes came closer than most to the mark, writing, "The Gershwin songs are scattered through the show so that they rarely give the zest to the exposition that Gershwin songs can give."[11]

Although the critics generally overlooked Duke's involvement, the movie belonged at least as much to him as to Gershwin; and the Academy of Motion Pictures very likely nominated the picture for best score of 1938 (naming musical director Alfred Newman) as much on the strength of the Duke ballets as on the Gershwin songs, none of which were among the Academy's ten nominees for best song, even though a 1938 recording of "Love Walked In" by the Sammy Kaye Orchestra topped the charts for three weeks. The picture itself proved a financial failure—it lost more than seven hundred thousand dollars—and cured Goldwyn of his ambition of becoming a second Ziegfeld.

Gershwin nevertheless enjoyed a posthumous triumph with his score to the film. "Love Walked In" and "Love Is Here to Stay" in particular became acknowledged high-water marks in the history of the American song, despite lingering questions about the quality and authenticity of their verses. However, these two songs differed significantly, with the restrained "Love Walked In" capturing the freshness of new love with hardly an accidental or syncopation to interrupt the nobility of its melody, and the wistful "Love Is Here to Stay" featuring a more bluesy palette, as jazz musicians quickly came to appreciate. If Gershwin thought of "Love Walked In" as a "Brahms strain," then "Love Is Here to Stay" exemplified his more Debussian inclinations.[12]

Gershwin's other three songs for the film are masterful in their own right and deserve to be better known. "I Was Doing All Right," somewhat reminiscent of those bittersweet love songs of Rodgers and Hart, features an evocative verse, a harmonically suave bridge, and a main theme that dips surprisingly low at what Alec Wilder describes as "a marvelous cadence, unlike any I've ever heard," and one nicely matched by Ira's refrain, "Till you came by." "I Love to Rhyme" is more insouciant, even singsong, with words, moreover, that resemble a casual dummy lyric (no pun intended, though the Gershwins presumably intended the number for Bergen and McCarthy, which would help explain its distinctive character).[13]

"Just Another Rhumba" did not surface until Ella Fitzgerald's premiere recording in 1959 and its subsequent publication. This comedy song (whose verse sounds like a Latin reworking of "Summertime") recalls "Fascinating Rhythm" in that the music—in this case not jazz, but a rumba heard in the West Indies—is wrecking the poor singer's life. However, as opposed to the riotous polyrhythms of that earlier song, Gershwin here makes a similar point by way of a complex, 128–measure structure full of interesting twists and turns, including some delightfully adventurous harmonies, propelled by a syncopated rumba bass. Ira enhanced the song's whimsy with a long list of capricious rhymes inspired by the word *rhumba,* including "throat-ah" and "(anti)dote-ah."

During his last months in Los Angeles, Gershwin considered a number of possible future projects, including a string quartet and a symphony, as well as a collaboration with Robert E. Sherwood for the Theatre

Guild that would present "a cavalcade of American history." He and Ira also approved a proposal from George S. Kaufman and Moss Hart—scrapped, however, by April 1937—for a spring 1938 show, *Curtain Going Up,* about the writing of a musical in which Kaufman, Hart, and Gershwin would appear onstage as themselves (with the more reserved Ira speaking offstage) and in which Ina Claire and Clifton Webb would star.[14]

Gershwin hoped to write more opera as well. In January 1937 he spoke of his desire to write a "cowboy opera," adding, "Indians, however, are taboo for operatic purposes. We think of Indians as hunters, not as lovers or humorists." About the same time he contacted DuBose Heyward about "another opera or operetta" (Heyward eventually turned preliminary work on a possible libretto for Gershwin into his 1939 novel, *Star Spangled Virgin,* set in the Virgin Islands). And in February Gershwin began discussions with Lynn Riggs, the author of the play *Green Grow the Lilacs* (1931, later adapted as *Oklahoma!*), about an opera set in Lamy, New Mexico, that would involve a clash between Mexicans and Americans. This interest in cowboys and Mexicans showed Gershwin headed in a direction that had begun to preoccupy Copland and other native composers; had he lived, he would presumably have contributed something vital and original to this collective engagement with the American West, over and above his score for *Girl Crazy.*[15]

No music for any of these projects seems to have survived, but Gershwin left behind sketches for scores of other pieces, mostly songs written for specific shows or for unspecified future use. Some of these sketches constitute fully realized pieces; some, complete melodies with a few or no harmonies; and still others, mere fragments. At Ira's request, Kay Swift not only catalogued most of this music but, thanks to her extraordinary recall, in some instances completed unfinished sketches on recognizing them as parts of finished songs. Additionally, she wrote down certain Gershwin melodies that either she or Ira remembered, in the end creating a numbered song file consisting of more than one hundred separate items. (Michael Feinstein substantiated her abilities in this area by noting that her 1972 reconstruction of a Gershwin song closely duplicated an original 1932 manuscript that turned up in 1982.) "There's enough good solid music for two musical shows with 20 to 25 numbers each and one or two films each using five or six songs," she announced at the end of 1938.[16]

With Swift's help, Ira made use of this cache in early 1938 by adapting some sketches as the theme song for the 1939 New York World's Fair,

"Dawn of a New Day." The fair's president—New York's former police commissioner, Grover Whalen—had commissioned the Gershwins in 1937 to write a theme song for the exposition, and after the composer's death had begun to look for a replacement when Swift (who served on the fair's entertainment committee) delivered some music that Gershwin had allegedly composed specifically for this purpose. Such claims seemed more than plausible, considering that the verse consisted of a slow anthem and the chorus, a festive march. But in fact, Swift had stitched together the music from two disparate sources: for the verse, a "Salvation Army type of tune" that Gershwin had written about 1930 for, as Ira recalled, "a show started with Ben Hecht but abandoned after three unfruitful sessions with him and producer Billy Rose" (Ira also remembered that this song began with the words "Come, Come, Come to Jesus"); and for the chorus, an unused march, "Revolution in Blue," composed for the first-act finale of *Let 'Em Eat Cake*. In keeping with the fair's theme, "The World of Tomorrow," Ira's lyric evoked "all creeds and races" meeting "with smiling faces" to fulfill the "dream" of "democracy," the phrase "world of tomorrow" appearing in the chorus.[17]

The extant "Revolution in Blue" sketch, which contains a finished melody along with a few choice harmonies, reveals that Swift wholly reconceived both the melody and the accompaniment, straightening out some novel syncopations, removing some arresting dissonance—in short, depriving the original music of much of its character. Ira and Swift no doubt felt that the ironic wit of "Revolution in Blue" would not serve this particular occasion, but claiming the revised version as Gershwin's showed, like some other posthumous publications, a certain casual attitude about matters of authorship, to say the least.

Gladys Swarthout gave the premiere of "Dawn of a New Day" at a special musical program on the fairgrounds in Queens on April 30, 1938, exactly a year prior to the fair's official opening. Hundreds of thousands attended. Soon after, Paul Whiteman broadcast the song—or at least the chorus—over the radio with the Lyn Murray Chorus in a brash arrangement by Fred Van Eps, followed by recordings the next year by the Johnny Messner Orchestra and by Horace Heidt and His Musical Knights. In a 1998 tribute to the fair by the Eos Ensemble, Michael Feinstein revived this curiosity, brightly arranged by the group's director, Jonathan Sheffer.

Aside from "Dawn of a New Day," Ira initially left the song file and other unpublished sketches alone. When in 1942 Samuel and Bella Spewack approached him, for instance, about raiding what the press called Gershwin's "ice box" for a projected show, *Birds of a Feather,* he declined, stating, "when a show or film is done with the posthumous music it ought to have a more romantic background than the one the *Bird* presents." In 1945, however, after producer William Perlberg of Twentieth Century–Fox suggested that he collaborate with either Harold Arlen or Harry Warren on a Betty Grable–Dick Haymes musical, *The Shocking Miss Pilgrim,* set in nineteenth-century Boston, and neither composer proved available, Ira—apparently recognizing this as an appropriately "romantic" vehicle—suggested that he base the score on Gershwin's unpublished melodies. No doubt encouraged by the recent success of the biopic *Rhapsody in Blue,* Perlberg announced in July 1945 a new Gershwin musical on the way.[18]

Ira once again turned to Kay Swift for assistance, and for ten weeks the two culled music from Gershwin's notebooks and other manuscripts in order to fashion a score. Ira then spent another ten weeks on the lyrics, completing the work in mid-November. He and Swift prepared ten songs: "Sweet Packard," "Changing My Tune," "Stand Up and Fight," "Aren't You Kind of Glad We Did?" "The Back Bay Polka," "One, Two, Three," "For You, For Me, For Evermore," "Demon Rum," "Tour of the Town," and "Welcome Song" (the last three unused by the filmmakers). The sources for these songs proved varied. "Demon Rum" derived from a song cut from *Funny Face* ("Blue Hullabaloo"); "The Back Bay Polka" from a Fred Astaire number for *A Damsel in Distress* ("Heigh-Ho the Merrio," reconstructed by Ira and Oscar Levant after Gershwin's death); and "Aren't You Kind of Glad We Did?" from a song from the early thirties, for no specific show, about a couple who decide to marry "despite the fact that they are practically penniless" (Ira kept some of the words and altered others, changing the lyric "from an Epithalamium of the Depression to a Mid-Victorian Colloquy"). Still others originated from sketches, including "For You, For Me, For Evermore" (initially titled by Ira and Swift, in reference to its potential, "Gold Mine"). "The music [for *The Shocking Miss Pilgrim*], outside of a few grace notes which I had to add for extra syllables, was all my brother's," Ira later wrote, though according to Michael Feinstein, Swift composed the suffragette anthem "Stand Up and Fight" (which indeed resembles "Fordyce" from *Fine and Dandy*).[19]

Director-writer George Seaton began shooting the Technicolor picture in late 1945, but because he fell ill and needed to be replaced, first by John Stahl and later by Edmund Goulding, the film did not premiere until December 31, 1946. Seaton based his screenplay on a 1941 story by

Ernest and Federica Maas; Leon Shamroy supervised the cinematography; Hermes Pan choreographed the ballroom scene; and Alfred Newman directed the music, assisted by Maurice DePackh, Charles Henderson, Arthur Morton, Edward Powell, David Raksin, Herbert Spencer, and Jack Virgil.[20]

The film opens in 1874 as Cynthia Pilgrim (Betty Grable) graduates at the top of her class from New York's Packard Business College ("Sweet Packard"). Among the country's first "typewriters," she accepts a secretarial position with the Pritchard Shipping Company in Boston. Her boss, John Pritchard (Dick Haymes), and his office manager, Saxon (Gene Lockhart), are reluctant to employ a woman, but Dick's assertive aunt Alice Pritchard (Anne Revere), a leader of the local suffrage movement, rallies on her behalf. Cynthia takes a room at a boardinghouse run by the unconventional Catherine Dennison (Elizabeth Patterson) and occupied by eccentric artists, including a poet, Leander Woolsey (Allyn Joslyn), and a composer, Herbert Jothan (Charles Kemper). Delighted with her new quarters, Cynthia reflects on her good fortune ("Changing My Tune").

John accompanies Cynthia to a suffragette meeting ("Stand Up and Fight") and then takes her out for dinner unchaperoned ("Aren't You Kind of Glad We Did?"). Cynthia becomes enamored of John (reprise of "Changing My Tune"). Invited by John's mother to dinner prior to a regiment ball, and expecting to be snubbed, she learns an insulting song about Boston from Leander and Herbert ("The Back Bay Polka"); but in the end, she finds Mrs. Pritchard (Elisabeth Risdon) charming. At the ball, John romances Cynthia ("One, Two, Three"), who subsequently attains increasing prominence as a suffragette (reprise of "Stand Up and Fight").

John proposes to Cynthia ("For You, For Me, For Evermore"), but when he presumes that she'll now quit the suffragette movement, Cynthia angrily breaks off their engagement and establishes her own Boston Academy of Typewriting. On the pretense of trying to find a secretary to replace her, John visits the school, where he and Cynthia are reconciled (reprise of "For You, For Me, For Evermore").

The picture received largely negative reviews. Bosley Crowther, for instance, deemed the show, for all its liberal trappings, "just another stenographer-boss romance." And although the critics did not gripe about getting only an occasional peek at Grable's famous "gams," as did thousands of her fans, some found it laughable that she would arrive at her modest secretarial job dressed in gorgeous Orry-Kelly gowns. For all this, the movie did well at the box office.[21]

One of the picture's most distinguished assets was surely its score, whose "peaceable charm"—as Ethan Mordden described the film itself—seems more the work of Ira than of George. Its three principal songs—"Changing My Tune," "Aren't You Kind of Glad We Did?" and "For You, For Me, For Evermore"—are all ballads: the first lilting, the second bluesy, and the third romantic, like "Love Walked In." The other numbers—"Sweet Packard," "Stand Up and Fight," "The Back Bay Polka," and "One, Two, Three"—parody the anthem, the march, the polka, and the waltz, respectively, with "The Back Bay Polka" offering especially ample scope for Ira's wit.[22]

In her recordings of the movie's three ballads (1947, partnered in the two duets by Haymes), Judy Garland more fully than Grable realized the music's potential. (Ira, who served as best man at Garland's marriage to Vincente Minnelli in 1945, had the opportunity to collaborate with Harold Arlen on a 1954 film for Garland, *A Star Is Born*.) Still, aside from "For You, For Me, For Evermore," the score made little dent, in part because the songs were too wedded to their Victorian milieu for wide commercial use. "Aren't You Kind of Glad We Did?" posed a special problem, for it could insinuate, when heard out of context, illicit sex as opposed to an unchaperoned dinner. In his published version of the song, Ira duly rewrote some of the words to suggest that the singers do nothing more than kiss, "thus making all," he explained, "morally impeccable." But the rewrite proved, he recalled, "to no avail," and "the song was banned from the air by the networks." At the same time, this very ambiguity attracted the likes of Peggy Lee, who brought a certain smoky sensuality to her recording of the song (1946).[23]

In 1964 Ira came out of retirement to lyricize some of his brother's melodies once again, this time at the request of Billy Wilder (1906–2002), the German-Jewish refugee who had written and directed some of Hollywood's best midcentury films. Together with the principal coauthor of his later years, Romanian-born I. A. L. Diamond (Itek Dommnici), Wilder planned a satire of the popular music business—eventually titled *Kiss Me, Stupid*—that would star Dean Martin in a self-parodying role and would feature three songs composed by a fictional team of aspiring songwriters: an Italian-like ditty along the lines of the Harry Warren hit "That's Amore," popularized by Martin in 1953, and two other novelty numbers. Wilder thought that Ira might be interested in working with André Previn, the film's musical director, or perhaps with Henry Mancini, like Warren a leading Italian American songwriter; but he welcomed Ira's suggestion that he dip instead into his trove of unpublished Gershwini-ana with the assistance of composer-producer Roger Edens.

Because Wilder and Diamond wanted to select spots for these three numbers only after Ira completed them, the lyricist worked—to his dis-appointment—without an outline or script. But as the songs represented the work of songwriters created prior to the action, it made sense for Wilder to see what Ira came up with and respond accordingly.[24]

In simulating the work of amateur songwriters, Ira wrote not so much bad lyrics—something he was probably incapable of doing anyway—as distinctively quirky ones. For the "That's Amore" parody, he devised a serenade to an imagined "Sophia" (a name presumably inspired by the day's leading Italian actress, Sophia Loren) that contained some charm-ing rhymes on Italian musical terms—and desserts. He also prepared a sweet ballad, "All the Livelong Day (and the Long, Long Night)," based on a few lines that dated back to the twenties (he additionally wrote an amusing dummy lyric for this tune, imagining that its fictitious composer might nervously sing this nonsensical lyric by mistake, an idea that Wilder decided against); and a humorous love number, "I'm a Poached Egg," for which he similarly returned to a metaphor that had caught his fancy at least as far back as an unused Jack Donahue song for *Rosalie* (1928), "You Know How It Is," that had never before seen the light of day: that of a "poached egg without a piece of toast." Working on the latter cat-alog song, he compiled dozens of like phrases—including "*My Fair Lady* / Without the rain in Spain"—leading Philip Furia to suggest that Ira's "longing" for George found some outlet in this outpouring of im-ages of "incompleteness."[25]

None of these numbers corresponds exactly to a complete Gershwin song. For "Sophia," Ira and Edens adapted the Latin-flavored "Wake Up, Brother, and Dance" (intended for *Shall We Dance*) as a waltz, smoothing out its syncopations as well as some of its blue notes (not that they had far to go, as the original melody implied a waltzlike rhythm within the framework of common time). Ira later explained that an early version of "Wake Up, Brother, and Dance" had reminded him "a lot of an Italian song we used to hear on the East Side when I was a kid," and he presumably felt that turning the song into a waltz heightened its Ital-ianate qualities, though even as a waltz the music still sounded Latin, only perhaps now more Spanish than Cuban (a connection obviously felt by Wilder and Previn, who gave the number the full Spanish treatment, including cries of "Olé"). Simplifying "Wake Up, Brother" made for a less interesting song, but at least it served the purpose of converting a lively dance number for Fred Astaire into a romantic serenade for Dean Martin.[26]

"I'm a Poached Egg" and "All the Livelong Day" involved more intricate patchwork. The former used (for its verse) a verse originally intended for "I Can't Be Bothered Now," (for its main theme) a melody that Ira had dictated to Kay Swift (Melody no. 105), and (for its bridge) part of a rejected song from *Funny Face* (1927), "Are You Dancing." "All the Livelong Day" similarly adapted (for its verse) the verse to a song, "Phoebe," that Gershwin had written with Lou Paley and Ira in 1921; and (for its chorus) another melody that Ira had sung for Swift (Melody no. 57), somewhat touched up by Edens with, among other things, little reminiscences of the "Phoebe" verse in the piano part.

Based on the Italian farce *L'Ora della fantasia* (1945) by Anna Bonacci, as adapted to the stage by Ketti Frings and José Ferrer as *The Dazzling Hour* (1953), *Kiss Me, Stupid* is a moral fable as well as a satire of American cultural and sexual mores. Dino (Dean Martin), a lounge singer and boozy womanizer, finishes up a Las Vegas engagement ("'S Wonderful") and leaves by car for Hollywood. On the way, he needs to detour through the remote town of Climax, Nevada, where a local church organist and piano teacher, Orville J. Spooner (Ray Walston), and an ambitious gas station attendant and would-be lyricist, Barney Millsap (Cliff Osmond), have been collaborating on songs, thus far without success ("I'm a Poached Egg"). After Dino stops for gas, Barney disconnects his car's fuel line and talks him into spending the night at Orville's home, hoping in this way to interest Dino in their songs. Barney also persuades Orville to use a woman as sexual bait, but because Orville is insanely jealous of his wife, Zelda (Felicia Farr)—who had a schoolgirl crush on Dino to boot—he picks a fight with her to get her out of the house (even though it's their fifth wedding anniversary) and hires a prostitute, Polly the Pistol (Kim Novak), who works at a local saloon, the Belly Button, to take her place.

As Dino attempts to seduce "Zelda," Orville auditions an Italian-flavored number ("Sophia") as well as a ballad that he wrote while courting his wife ("All the Livelong Day"). Meanwhile, the real Zelda gets drunk at the Belly Button and finds herself ushered into Polly's trailer to sleep it off. Back at the Spooners', as Orville grows more protective of his "wife," he throws Dino out of his house and spends the night with "Zelda." Dino makes his way to the Belly Button and to Polly's trailer, where he discovers "Polly" (actually, Zelda), who succumbs to Dino's advances while plugging her husband's music.

The next morning, Dino leaves behind a five-hundred-dollar tip for "Polly." On arriving home, Polly discovers Zelda, who gives her the five hundred dollars in exchange for her husband's marriage band; with this unexpected windfall, Polly can leave Climax and start a new life. Threatening to divorce Orville unless he overcomes his jealousy, Zelda takes him back as Dino appears on television (reprise of "Sophia"). Thus, all the principals have benefited in various ways by the events set into motion by Dino's visit, though how much Orville grasps—how, for instance, his jealousy led to his being cuckolded—remains an open question ("Kiss me, stupid," Zelda tells him as the film ends).

The three featured numbers enhance the film. "I'm a Poached Egg" establishes Orville and Barney as a sympathetic and talented, if somewhat loony, songwriting team. "Sophia" provides an ironically slick vehicle for Dino. And "All the Livelong Day" gives the picture some heart, as it not only expresses the love between Orville and Zelda but awakens Polly to the nobility of such love, a realization heightened when Orville tells Dino that this is his one song that is "not for sale." Wilder, in short, used all three songs effectively, even ingeniously staging "I'm a Poached Egg" so that one essentially hears only its main theme, thereby circumventing the number's awkward seams.

Unfortunately, the film encountered a number of setbacks along the way. Peter Sellers, originally slated to play Orville, suffered a series of heart attacks and needed to be replaced by a somewhat miscast Ray Walston. Sensing trouble brewing over its adult content, Wilder made some last-minute revisions, including toning down the lovemaking scene between Dino and Zelda; but United Artists remained apprehensive nonetheless and delegated the film's distribution to Lopert Pictures, its art-house subsidiary. The studio's fears proved well-founded; on the film's release on December 16, 1964, the Catholic Church's National Legion of Decency (now the U.S. Catholic Conference), which had recommended that the picture not be released until after the holiday season, gave it an unusually severe "C" ("condemned") rating.

In addition, critics skewered the film from coast to coast (it was better received in Europe) as "sleazy," "dirty," "tasteless," "loud-mouthed," "coarse," "smutty," and "pitifully unfunny." Joan Didion, in one of the movie's few positive reviews, wrote, "It is a profoundly affecting picture, as witnessed by the number of people who walk out on it." Between bad reviews, limited distribution, and boycotts (including one by the Christian Family Movement), the picture did poorly at the box office and quickly dropped out of sight. Some good reappraisals have appeared since, but received opinion has been slow to appreciate the film's many strengths. It seems appropriate, in any case, that Gershwin's last songs should be associated with such a sophisticated farce.[27]

Can we speak, though, of any of the posthumously lyricized songs since "Dawn of a New Day" as the work of Gershwin? What about such numbers as "All the Livelong Day" or "I'm a Poached Egg," for which Roger Edens stitched together Gershwin melodies, some of which Ira dictated to Kay Swift? Should their music be attributed to Ira for recollecting the melodies, to Swift for writing them down, to Edens for piecing them together, as well as to Gershwin, their initial source? Authorship problems aside, would Gershwin have wanted these melodies to come forward in these contexts or in these ways? In any event, the Gershwin songs arranged and versified after his death largely consist of secondhand efforts, and they remain in essence footnotes to a glorious career.

Conclusion

$\mathcal{T}$wentieth-century depictions of Gershwin tended toward one of two scenarios. The first viewed him as a childlike genius who scaled the heights without benefit of formal instruction, a modest and somewhat naive man scorned by disdainful critics and envious colleagues. The second regarded him, more darkly, as a flawed genius incapable of sustained study, but ambitious and vain and eager for critical approbation. That both stereotypes were in a number of ways diametrically opposed helped underscore their basic inadequacy: for Gershwin, it might be argued, was thoughtful and generous, if evidently self-absorbed; more tactful than not; artistically adventurous and open-minded; a little shy and reserved, but animated and extremely amiable; and widely respected not only by a large international public but by numerous colleagues, including some of the foremost composers of his time.

Ironically, one point of agreement between the two archetypal narratives—that Gershwin was unlearned—seems particularly dubious. Although he dropped out of high school to take a job plugging songs for a Tin Pan Alley music publisher, he studied extensively on his own under three brilliant musicians—Charles Hambitzer, Edward Kilenyi, and Joseph Schillinger—and worked for shorter periods with a number of others, including Rossetter Cole, Rubin Goldmark, Artur Bodanzky, Henry Cowell, and Wallingford Riegger. In the process, he acquired a good knowledge of piano, harmony, counterpoint, orchestration, conducting, and music history. And although he sometimes emphasized (and overstated) the relative informality of his musical education, he placed great value on academic work, and diligently studied music—not only art music, but popular and folk music—throughout his short life.

The supposed lack of formal musical training nourished other assumptions about the composer, including the common criticism that his larger works were deeply marred by an inadequate command of orchestration and form—a notion that unfortunately led some performers and editors to rescore and cut these works. Because extenuating circumstances led Ferde Grofé to score the *Rhapsody in Blue* (1924), and because Broadway and Hollywood composers typically collaborated with professional orchestrators, some wondered whether Gershwin could even orchestrate, whereas, in fact, he demonstrated his aptitude in that area even prior to the *Rhapsody*. As for his formal abilities—never disputed when it came to smaller forms—recent scholarship concurs that his larger works have far greater architectural subtlety and cohesion than previously assumed. But the success of his music speaks for itself, for works like *An American in Paris* or *Porgy and Bess* would not live as they do if their composer did not know his business. Moreover, in the course of his career, he made continuing and dramatic strides toward ever greater technical mastery.

Relatedly, the clichéd notion that Gershwin came from the wrong side of the tracks, that he was fundamentally a Tin Pan Alley songwriter who grew ambitious, was, at the least, simplistic. He grew up in a Jewish middle-class family on the Lower East Side and in Harlem, largely immigrant neighborhoods in which an openness to American popular music coexisted with an appreciation for both lighter and more serious kinds of European music. Gershwin's earliest musical recollections and aspirations encompassed these different repertoires; and his school-days friends, like his adult friends, had varying musical tastes, though over the years, he tellingly cultivated close friendships with figures—such as Carl Van Vechten, Vernon Duke, Oscar Levant, and Kay Swift—who shared his attachment to both popular and serious music. Considering his activities in the years 1912 and 1913—as he began his work with Hambitzer, as he started to compile his scrapbook of concert programs and articles on classical composers, and as he began to write pieces for the piano—it might be truer to say that in 1914 he arrived in Tin Pan Alley from the world of classical music. But this, too, would be an exaggeration, for he had become a good ragtime player by the early 1910s. Rather, from a young age he embraced both popular and serious music in a uniquely balanced way, much as in later years he could enthuse about a string quartet by Paul Hindemith or a song by Harold Arlen, and happily spend time with Alban Berg or with Art Tatum.

Irving Berlin proved a crucial linchpin in this respect, for Gershwin considered the composer of "Alexander's Ragtime Band" (1911) not merely a good songwriter but a brilliant craftsman whose work provided the foundation for a distinctly American music. As early as 1920, he declared Berlin "more typically American than many of those [Americans] whose works are heard in opera and concert halls." And in 1929 he further pronounced, "Berlin had shown us the way"; hence, too, his references to Berlin as the American Schubert, as "the fourth B," as a genius. Gershwin especially appreciated Berlin's ability to speak to his fellow citizens, an ideal he felt appropriate to a democratic, egalitarian society.[1]

Other Americans working in the vernacular also helped chart a path for Gershwin, including Jerome Kern, whose musical comedies forged a new form of lyric theater; W. C. Handy, whose songs helped popularize the blues; Mike Bernard and Luckey Roberts, who pioneered new pianistic idioms; and Frank Saddler and James Reese Europe, who created new orchestral sonorities. Again, for Gershwin, this collective achievement mirrored American life more profoundly and eloquently than almost anything found in the concert hall or opera house.

Early on, Gershwin decided not just to appropriate the American vernacular, but actually to work within its confines and among its accoutrements, including eventually film and radio. In the process, he brought American popular theater music to a remarkable level of refinement, so much so that he could in turn bring this transformed vernacular to bear on such classic forms as the piano prelude, the concerto, the tone-poem, and opera. To be sure, the time and place were right for such a remarkable synthesis. As mentioned, Berlin and others had laid a foundation for such an enterprise, much as many of Gershwin's contemporaries—including Cole Porter, Ferde Grofé, James P. Johnson, Zez Confrey, Vincent Youmans, Richard Rodgers, Duke Ellington, and Fats Waller—helped promote this development as well. But leaving aside the special tradition of jazz, none of these musicians made as deep or wide a mark as Gershwin, whose distinction plainly depended not only on his circumstances but on his vision and originality.

This involved Gershwin's extraordinary ability to absorb a wide spectrum of seemingly incongruous styles and materials, including the masterpieces of the classical repertoire from the English madrigalists through Stravinsky, American popular song and light opera, and vernacular musics associated with Jewish, Irish, British, Asian, Spanish, Latin, and black communities. Gershwin's assimilation of so many varied sources gave his music some of its urbane charm. But his work rose above mere pastiche; it always reflected his personality and particular point of view. Such individual use of diverse materials placed him, in his own estimation, in the tradition of Mozart and Chopin. Opinions vary over whether Gershwin deserves a place in such exalted company, or whether his achievement might better be compared to, say, Johann Strauss or Offenbach. Shortly after Gershwin's death, Arnold Schoenberg—a friend and admirer—deferred such judgments to posterity; but more than fifty years later the matter remained undecided, evidence itself of the novelty of Gershwin's accomplishment.

Gershwin occasionally grappled with such issues himself by distinguishing his music for the popular stage from his more serious work. In actuality, however, the lines were never so neatly drawn. He composed his two operas, for example, for the Broadway stage; and his *Rhapsody* (1924) and *An American in Paris* (1928) found their way into revues and musical comedies. Conversely, he derived the *Second Rhapsody* (1931), one of his most challenging concert works, virtually verbatim from a sequence for his Hollywood musical *Delicious*.

Moreover, although Gershwin's orchestral pieces and operas clearly represented his most ambitious work, his output in its entirety contained an identifiable stylistic profile featuring expressive melodies (often marked by pentatonic gestures and blue notes); vibrant, syncopated rhythms; rich and piquant harmonies; sharply etched textures and brilliant colors; and compelling forms with thrilling climaxes. Many musicians prized his popular and serious works alike, much as the full range of his music by and large proved appealing to the same audience.

Finally, in his varied work, Gershwin consistently aimed to reflect American life, to give "voice," as he put it, to the "spirit" and "soul" of the American people, and in ways accessible to the average listener. A statement made in the context of the *Rhapsody in Blue* offered a particularly good clue to his intentions: "I heard it as a sort of musical kaleidoscope of America—of our vast melting pot, of our unduplicated national pep, of our blues, our metropolitan madness."[2]

By *melting pot*, Gershwin meant the country's ethnic diversity—epitomized by the Manhattan of his youth, and reflected in his work by a wide absorption of various musical styles, as mentioned above; while by *national pep* he had in mind the nation's propensities for hard work and speed—a disposition that matched his own energetic personality and that found utterance in his music by way of vigorous rhythms, crisp accents, and dynamic chord progressions. "I'd like my compositions to be so vital that I'd be required by law to dispense sedatives with each score sold," he once said.³

Blues signified sadness and loneliness, but in an ironic way, as he made fairly explicit in *An American in Paris,* not to mention such songs as "The Half of It, Dearie, Blues." This wistful side accorded with his once telling S. N. Behrman that he "wanted to write for young girls sitting on fire escapes on hot summer nights in New York and dreaming of love"; but it also resonated with his own emotional life, often described by friends as harboring some inner melancholy. His music along these lines often featured, naturally enough, blue notes, but also falling intervals, chromatic counterpoints, and poignant modulations to minor modes.⁴

The phrase *metropolitan madness* may have betokened for Gershwin something akin to *pep* and *blues,* but perhaps also that tendency toward the ludicrous and the parodistic that underscored so much of his work. He expressed such humor—and he surely was one of the great musical humorists of his time—in part through satirical handling of various styles and conventions, but also more generally through smart twists and turns: what Isaac Goldberg neatly described as the "sort of audible eye-winking at which George Gershwin is expert," and which no doubt related to those descriptions of the man himself as "ingenuous." But Gershwin believed that his humor profited best "as part of an expressed thought," that is, when accompanied by words; and in this respect, he luckily found such fine collaborators as Irving Caesar, Buddy DeSylva, DuBose Heyward, and above all, his brother Ira, who enriched the wit of his music in manifold ways.⁵

Yet another trait, one related to his ironic humor but even more difficult to define in musical terms, involved his often-noted ability to convey a sense of joy, even ecstasy. Gershwin never discussed this aspect of his art, but some of the lyrics and even titles of his songs—"(I'll Build a) Stairway to Paradise," "Tune In (to Station J.O.Y.)," "Oh Gee!–Oh Joy!" and "Love Is Sweeping the Country," to name just a few—alluded to such preoccupations. Gershwin plausibly associated such joyfulness, in which the delights of love, music, and dance often commingled, with traditional American optimism; but in any case, such attributes emanated from his own personality as described by S. N. Behrman, who thought that among his friends, Gershwin stood "almost alone among them for possessing an almost nonexistent quality: the quality of joy"; and by Kay Swift, who noted the composer's "joyous delight in whatever he was doing."⁶

The verve and melancholy, wit and joy that distinguished Gershwin's music—along with its unassuming frankness and overwhelming charm—

could thus be seen in terms of not only his reading of an American national identity, but his unique personality as well. In any event, his music, with all its powerful emotions and novel ideas, proved to have broad universal appeal, and demonstrated, in a most spectacular fashion, the considerable extent to which a sophisticated and original twentieth-century composer could reach a worldwide public.

For all abbreviations used in the notes, see the Selected Bibliography.

1. Gershwin and His Family

1. United States Census: 1900 (Morris Greshevin, Kings County, e.d. 366, sheet 11, line 55); 1910 (Morris Gershvein, New York County, e.d. 191, sheet 187, line 10); 1920 (Morris Gershwin, New York County, e.d. 1428, sheet 14, line 65); see also 1900 census for Gershin Bruskin, 1910 census for Gersen Bruskin, and 1930 census for Abraham Wolpin. Note that some of the information reported changed over the years, including Rose's age and Morris's date of arrival in the States (listed as "1891" in 1900 and 1910, but "1893" in 1920).

2. KW, p. 2.

3. EWE, p. 2; HYL, p. 1.

4. Gershwin's birth certificate reads, "Jacob Gershwine"; FG, p. 2, suggests that Morris's brother, Aaron, first changed the family name, though the latter gave his name in the 1920 census as "Gershvin."

5. AG, p. 10; Katharan McCommon, "Gershwin, King of Jazz Composers at 26, Says Piano Made Good Boy of Him," 1924, GCLC; Ira Gershwin, letter to Henry Botkin, 2 January 1915, GCLC; SUR, p. 47. Morris apparently acquired the two Turkish baths, the St. Nicholas Baths uptown and the Lafayette Baths downtown, in 1917. The latter was a well-known meeting place for homosexuals and had been raided the year before (1916) by the police, leading to seventeen arrests; see CHA, pp. 220–221.

6. EWE, p. 1 ("always"); "Music: Gershwin Everywhere," *Time* 46, no. 2 (9 July 1945): 67 ("Poppa"); MEY, p. 16; FG, p. 6; "'A Regular Kid'—Mrs. Rose Gershwin's Warmest Tribute to Her Famous Son," *Jewish Examiner* (2 September 1938).

7. GOL, p. 52 ("He could"); KIM/G, p. 46; STE, p. 5; DUK/PP, p. 103.

8. Benjamin Welles, "Lyricist of 'The Saga of Jenny' et Al.," *New York Times* (25 May 1941), sect. 9, p. 2 ("A craftsman"); ARM/GG, pp. 180–181; DUK/PP, p. 234; as a consultant on the film, Ira could have helped coach Carnovsky and the other actors, though he apparently took a hands-off approach to such matters: see John C. Tibbetts, *Composers in the Movies: Studies in Musical Biography* (New Haven, CT: Yale University Press, 2005), p. 139.

9. ARM/GG, p. 215; ROS, p. 11; FG, p. 7; for Rose's dates, see WS, p. 13 ("She was very social. After Morris died, she had a number of boyfriends in her later years").

10. Rose Gershwin, letter to Ira Gershwin, 19 February 1935, ILGT.

11. JAB/GY, p. 32; EWE, p. 6.

12. The Zilboorg quote has been challenged by the psychiatrist's wife and

others on the grounds that psychiatrists do not routinely flaunt patient-doctor confidentiality to biographers, though it must be admitted that Zilboorg was not the most scrupulous of psychiatrists. Isaac Goldberg, "All about the Gershwins: Principally George, Incidentally Ira," *Boston Evening Transcript* (21 December 1929); Bennett Cerf, *Try and Stop Me: A Collection of Anecdotes and Stories, Mostly Humorous* (New York: Simon and Schuster, 1945), p. 211; see also BEH: "You know the extraordinary thing about her—she's so modest about me," p. 245; GOL, p. 52; KW, p. 9.

13. KIM/G, pp. 47, 215; GG to Isaac Goldberg, 30 June 1931, Houghton Library, Harvard University.

14. ARM/GG, p. 204; EWE/SGG, p. 14; EWE, p. 5; PEY; FG, p. 8.

15. "George Gershwin," *Life* (1931), GCLC.

16. Nadia Turbide, *Biographical Study of Eva Gauthier (1885–1958), First French-Canadian Singer of the Avant-Garde* (PhD diss., University of Montreal, 1986), p. 278.

17. Nelson Lansdale, "My Boy George," *Listen* (September 1945): 6–7; IC ("a very wonderful"); ARM/GG, p. 204 ("She was always"); KIM/G, p. 46; Anne Brown, interview, GGR; WYA, p. 229 ("rather arrogant"); PEY, p. 240.

18. Frances Gershwin, quoted by Alfred Simon, liner notes, *Frances Gershwin— "For George and Ira"* (Monmouth-Evergreen MES/7060, 1973).

19. Kate Wolpin, letters to GG, 1 October 1936, 9 October 1936; GG, letters to Kate Wolpin, 5 October 1936, 7 October 1936, ILGT; KW, pp. 6, 11; David Alfaro Siqueiros, *Me llamaban el coronelazo* (Mexico City: Grijalbo, 1977), pp. 299–302 (translation courtesy of Lois Zamora).

20. KW, p. 13; Ira to GG, 25 August 1924, ILGT.

21. United States Census: 1920 (Aaron Gershvin, New York County, e.d. 694, sheet 9, line 18); Nancy Gershwin (Emil's daughter), interview by the author, 2 December 2004.

22. EWE, p. 3; PEY, p. 25, JAB, p. 3; "Gershwin: Of Thee We Sing," *Brooklyn World-Telegram* (27 September 1963), including a reminiscence by Louis and Margie Taffle, presumably the children of the said Mr. Taffelstein. According to Trow's General Directories (New York: Trow, 1909 and 1910), the Gershwins lived at 255 Grand in 1909 and 253 Grand in 1910.

23. John McCauley, "Stray Notes," ILGT.

24. Igor Stravinsky with Robert Craft, "Some Composers," *Musical America* 82, no. 6 (June 1962): 6; Jerry Herman, "Stars Come Out for Dedication of Gershwin Theater," *Jewish Bulletin of Northern California Online* (2 May 1999) (for Robinson).

25. FEI, p. 55; "'A Regular Kid'" ("devout"); KW, p. 11.

26. For Irving Caesar and Yip Harburg, see Ethel Beckwith, "Gershwin Music Is Forever," [Bridgeport, CT] *Sunday Herald* (22 July 1962); OHL, p. 116 (Ohl, e-mail to the author, 31 October 2004, cites a note from Esther Tuttle that remembers Swift's 86th Street apartment as "way over between East End and York [Avenues]"); "Deposits to the account of George Gershwin" (1934–1936) lists a December 1934 ASCAP royalty check minus a donation to the Federated Jewish Charities, as well as an April 1935 deposit from Emil Mosbacher "to-

ward fund to send Mrs. Garbat's man to Palestine," which suggests some support for Zionist causes.

27. Kitty Carlisle, interview by the author, 24 March 2003; KAS, p. 125; many sources state that Gershwin was a Freemason—for example, Dan Brown's best-selling thriller, *The Da Vinci Code* (New York: Doubleday, 2003), p. 389—but his name has yet to turn up on any registry of Masons; G7 ("My people").

28. HOW, p. 170.

29. HOW, p. 257.

30. HOW, p. 257.

31. "The Ascendent Gershwin," *New York Times* (14 November 1926), GCLC; Allene Talmey, "His Father Predicted He Would Grow Up to Be a Bum," *Boston Globe* (12 January 1929); John McCauley, letter to Isaac Goldberg, 22 August 1929, ILGT; GG, letter to Isaac Goldberg, 30 June 1931, Houghton Library, Harvard University; KW, p. 5 (the Wolpins had three children: Arnold, Gerald, and Frances).

32. "Teacher, 75, Recalls Famous E. Side Grads," *New York World-Telegram and Sun* (16 March 1960); "Ira Gershwin Reveals How He and His Brother George Were Helped in Their Careers by P.S. 20—with Plenty," [P.S. 20 Alumni Association] *Chronicle* 1, no. 1 (June 1961), GCLC. Ira's brother-in-law William English Strunsky (WS, p. 2), offered another anecdote related to the genesis of "Let's Call the Whole Thing Off": in 1933, Strunsky purchased a New Jersey factory that made tomato-related products and began purchasing tomatoes from local farmers; when Ira noticed that he had changed the way he pronounced the word *tomatoes* (from "to-MAH-toes" to "to-MAY-toes"), Strunsky said, "Ira, if I said to-MAH-toes to my farmers, they wouldn't know what I was talking about," to which Ira responded, "Oh, you're just like your sister. I say EE-thur, but she has to say EYE-thur."

33. Frank Lee Donoghue, "Ira Gershwin's Home Still Glorifies George," *Los Angeles Examiner* (13 July 1959) ("poor student"); GG, letter to Julia Van Norman, 6 November 1936, GCLC; MEY, pp. 12–15.

34. GG, letter to Rosamund Waller, 24 August 1930, GCLC; Frances Gershwin, interview, GGR.

35. KIM/CLIG, p. xii.

36. FUR, pp. 3, 15, 191; Ewen, apparently erroneously, states that Ira graduated from high school in three and a half years, and entered City College in February 1914: EWE, p. 35. Ira remained a voracious reader of fiction; during a busy four months in Europe in 1928, he read a number of novelists, including Aldous Huxley, D. H. Lawrence, Edgar Wallace, and P. G. Wodehouse.

37. Entirely unlike George, Ira had little interest in jazz: FEI, p. 57; KIM/G, p. 14 ("I"); JAB/GY, p. 319; FUR, p. 191.

38. ROS, pp. 15, 19, 20; KIM/CLIG, p. xii. Ira's diaries, IGLT, reveal that he attended evening sessions at City College from the fall of 1916 through the fall of 1917, studying English, economics, history, and accounting; however, by the end of 1917, his work on the *Clipper* apparently made it impossible for him—at least temporarily—to take night classes ("If I land with the Clipper," he wrote on November 26, "won't have time to continue"). EWE, p. 37, mentions that Ira took a chemistry class at Columbia University Extension, but no documentation to that effect has surfaced thus far.

39. E. Y. Harburg et al., "Notes and Quotes from Ira's Friends," *ASCAP Today* 5, no. 3 (January 1972): 7; LEV/MA, p. 119. Harburg implies that Gilbert was Ira's favorite lyricist, whereas Levant states that it was Wodehouse: LEV/MA, p. 139. Safe to say, he admired both greatly. For more on Ira as lyricist, see FUR as well as Brad Leithauser, "Here to Stay," *New York Review of Books* 43 (17 October 1996): 35–38.

40. Lorenz Hart quoted by Zero Mostel, "Ira Gershwin," in Roddy Mc-Dowall, *Double Exposure* (New York: William Morrow, 1966), p. 59; LEV/MA, p. 140; DON, pp. 207, 209; KIM/CLIG, p. xii; Leon Lipsky, "George Gershwin: Jazz Glorifier," *American Hebrew* (27 November 1925): 59 ("wistfulness").

41. Lawrence Stewart, "The Gershwins—Words upon Music," *Ella Fitzgerald Sings the George and Ira Gershwin Song Book* (Verve 314 539 759–2, 1959, reissued 1998); ROS; FUR; Lincoln Kirstein, "Lyrics by Ira Gershwin," program notes for *Who Cares?* New York City Ballet, NYPL; Ned Rorem, "Living with Gershwin," *Opera News* (16 March 1985): 12; John O'Hara, "Critic in the Dark," *Newsweek* (3 February 1941).

42. FUR, p. 193; ARM/GG, p. 50; BEH, pp. 242–243; KIM/CLIG, p. xvi.

43. ARM/GG, p. 70; WS (including plaque, p. 23); "'Papa' Strunsky Learns No Rent Can Pay No Tax," *New York Herald-Tribune* (10 December 1934); Robert Sylvester, *No Cover Charge: A Backward Look at the Night Clubs* (New York: Dial Press, 1956), p. 246; James Boylan, *Revolutionary Lives: Anna Strunsky & William English Walling* (Amherst: University of Massachusetts Press, 1998); Andrew Sinclair, *Jack: A Biography of Jack London* (London: Weidenfeld & Nicolson, 1978).

44. LS (for Leonore's many proposals); FEI, p. 114; KW, p. 18.

45. BEH, p. 251; LEV/SI, p. 202; Maya Angelou, *Singin' and Swingin' and Gettin' Merry Like Christmas* (New York: Random House, 1976), p. 215; Truman Capote, *The Muses Are Heard* (New York: Random House, 1956), p. 136; FEI, pp. 44–45; English Strunsky, interview by the author, 16 May 2002; KW, p. 18 ("every woman").

46. FG, p. 7; AG, p. 2 ("We used"); Ronald Sullivan, "Arthur Gershwin, 81, Composer and Producer," *New York Times* (22 November 1981); FEI, p. 55.

47. DUK/PP, p. 93; KIM/G, pp. 46, 139.

48. Jeremy Nicholas, *Godowsky: The Pianists' Pianist* (Northumberland: Appian Publications, 1989), p. 89; LG.

49. EWE, p. 4; JAB, p. 118; FEI, 56; *Frances Gershwin: "For George and Ira"* (Monmouth-Evergreen MES/7060, 1973); Jo Matthews, "Artist in Midstream," *Fairfield County Fair* (1957), GCLC; for Leopold Godowsky, see Joseph Wechsberg, "Whistling in the Darkroom," *New Yorker* (10 November 1956): 61–109.

50. Ira Gershwin, letter to Rose Gershwin, 17 August 1937, GCLC; FEI, p. 76.

51. *Speak Low (When You Speak Love): The Letters of Kurt Weill and Lotte Lenya*, ed. and trans. Lys Symonette and Kim H. Kowalke (Berkeley: University of California Press, 1996), p. 416.

52. Howard Reich, "Best Gershwin Interpreters," *Chicago Tribune* (20 September 1998).

53. Alan Gershwin, "I Am George Gershwin's Illegitimate Son," *Confiden-*

tial (February 1959): 10–13, 45–46; see also Cindy Adams, "Secret Son of Gershwin Eyes His Big \$core," *New York Post* (4 January 1993).

54. Laurie Winer, "New Gershwin Biography Hits a Sour Note," *Wall Street Journal* (20 April 1993); Michael Strunsky, interview by the author, 25 August 2005 (for Ira Gershwin estate); Roberta Korus, interview by the author, 12 September 2005 (for George Gershwin estate).

2. Gershwin's Musical Education to the *Rhapsody in Blue*

1. Sam Franko, *Chords and Discords: Memoirs and Musings of an American Musician* (New York: Viking Press, 1938), pp. 127–128 (Franko alludes to selections by "Pergolesi, Gluck, Mozart, Schubert, etc.").

2. GOL, pp. 54, 58; Ada Hanifin, "Gershwin Is Bewildered by Own Fame," *San Francisco Examiner* (27 September 1930); EWE/SGG, p. 41, states that Gershwin heard the Dvořák "apparently in about 1908 or 1909," a reminder that many guesses about Gershwin are given as fact (in this case, that he was ten when he heard Rosen).

3. Peter Van der Merwe, *Roots of the Classical: The Popular Origins of Western Music* (New York: Oxford University Press, 2004); David Ewen, *All the Years of American Popular Music* (Englewood Cliffs, NJ: Prentice-Hall, 1977), has a chapter on this subject titled "The Gentle Art of Tune Lifting," pp. 447–452.

4. Hans Keller, "Rhythm: Gershwin and Stravinsky," *The Score and I. M. A. Magazine* 20 (June 1957): 25; Paul Bowles, "Zino Francescatti Gives Town Hall Violin Recital," *New York Herald-Tribune* (28 February 1945); Van der Merwe, *Roots of the Classical*, pp. 459–461.

5. GOL, pp. 58–59; AG, p. 6. Franciska Schwimmer also presents a version of this story in *Great Musicians as Children* (Garden City, NY: Doubleday, Doran, 1929), pp. 234–235; KW, p. 28.

6. "East Side Boy Wins Fame as Violinist," *New York Times* (31 December 1917); "Max Rosen Wildly Cheered at Debut," *New York Times* (13 January 1918); "Max Rosen Dies; Violinist Was 56," *New York Times* (17 December 1956); EWE/SGG, p. 24 ("any talent"); for the Hurst connection, see "Bernard Rosen," *New York Times* (5 July 1946); and Carol Dolgon-Krutolow (Max Rosen's daughter), e-mail to the author, 30 October 2004.

7. Louis Sobol, "The Voice of Broadway," *New York Evening Journal* (10 February 1934) ("to be in style"); Gershwin's aunt, Kate Wolpin, stated, "Then my sister bought a piano because George thought he ought to have one," KW, p. 3; KIM/G, p. 7 ("But the upright"); Frank Lee Donoghue, "Ira Gershwin's Home Still Glorifies George," *Los Angeles Examiner* (13 July 1959); Ethel Beckwith, "Gershwin Music Is Forever," *Sunday Herald* (22 July 1962), GCLC (for Yip Harburg). Ira typically gave the date of 1910 as the year in which the Gershwins acquired a piano, adding that George would have been about eleven or twelve; he also remembered that at the time they lived on 7th Street and Second Avenue, above Saul Birns's phonograph store. Since the Gershwins lived on Grand Street in 1909 and at least part of 1910, that might mean that they acquired a piano either before then, in 1908 or early 1909, or in late 1910 or 1911. The 1908 date better fits the recollection of one of George's first piano teachers, Mrs. Louis Greene ("Hy

Gardner Calling," *New York Herald-Tribune* [15 July 1959], GCLC), who stated that she started teaching Gershwin when he was nine years old and that he studied with her for three years. But judging from Manhattan's telephone directories, the Birns Brothers did not open their 77 Second Avenue store (though JAB/GY, p. 8, gives the Gershwin address as 91 Second Avenue) until late 1909 (Birns already had a store on East 138th Street). Meanwhile, Yip Harburg recalled that when the piano first arrived, Gershwin played "You've Got Your Mother's Big Blue Eyes," a 1913 song by Irving Berlin; but that plainly seems too late a date. All things considered, the Gershwins most likely obtained a piano in late 1910.

8. Katharan McCommon, "Gershwin, King of the Jazz Composers at 26, Says Piano Made Good Boy of Him," 1924, GCLC; Richard Kogan, interview by the author, 5 September 2005.

9. "Gershwin Bros.," *Time* 6, no. 3 (20 July 1925) (for "Miss Green"); "Hy Gardner Calling" (Greene claimed that the neighborhood teacher taught Ira as well as George, though Ira suggested that his lessons came to an end after George's demonstration at the upright); KS, p. 4 ("Mom, if").

10. GOL, pp. 59–60; ROS, p. 12; for Von Zerly's alleged but unsubstantiated composition of a *Theodore Roosevelt March*, see EWE, p. 15.

11. GOL, p. 60; an article in the Gershwin Collection about the society, "Starving for Music—and This Is the Result," *World Magazine* (27 April 1913), does not list Miller as one of the orchestra members; Walter Monfried, "Charles Hambitzer Was My Greatest Influence, Says 'Rhapsody' Writer," *Milwaukee Journal* (28 January 1931).

12. According to Edward Kilenyi, Hambitzer played viola, cello, and French horn with the Waldorf-Astoria Orchestra (NEI, p. 32), while Shilkret mentioned viola, oboe, bassoon, cello, and organ (SHI, p. 29); for Schoenberg, see EWE, p. 16, and NEI, p. 62, though Sabine Feisst, an expert on the reception of Schoenberg in the United States, has thus far been unable to confirm this: Feisst, e-mail to the author, 11 May 2001; JAB, p. 10 (for Shilkret and Schirmer).

13. There are conflicting accounts of the cause of Hambitzer's death: GOL, p. 63, and EWE, p. 17, mention tuberculosis, while PAY, p. 48, says he killed himself after his wife died of tuberculosis; Monfried, "Charles Hambitzer"; Walter Monfried, "Celebrated Milwaukee Musician's Compositions Have Disappeared," *Milwaukee Journal* (6 December 1945).

14. Charles Hambitzer Collection (Finding Aid), Music Division, Library of Congress (2002).

15. "Gershwin Versatile Composer" (ca. 1 December 1925), GCLC; Monfried, "Charles Hambitzer"; Carl Van Vechten, "George Gershwin: An American Composer Who Is Writing Notable Music in the Jazz Idiom," *Vanity Fair* 24, no. 1 (March 1925): 84; PEY, p. 31; McCommon, "Gershwin, King of the Jazz Composers" ("My technique").

16. Monfried, "Charles Hambitzer," and GOL, p. 61, duplicate this letter identically, but in other particulars their accounts of Gershwin and Hambitzer differ; it's hard to say which source is the more dependable, though such statements as Gershwin "got a job as pianist with Paul Whiteman" and was at the time studying with Nadia Boulanger throw Monfried's general reliability into question.

17. JAB, p. 10 ("He was"); SHI, p. 30.

18. JAB, p. 10 ("a lot"); "Gershwin Bros." further reports, "His [Gershwin's] first teacher [presumably Hambitzer] died when he was still torturing Chopin's preludes"; Van Vechten, "George Gershwin," p. 84; LEV/SI, p. 192; SHI, p. 30.

19. Van Vechten, "George Gershwin," p. 84; for Bach, see EWE/SGG, p. 124.

20. McCommon, "Gershwin, King of the Jazz Composers" ("very serious," "I think"); Monfried, "Charles Hambitzer"; see also GOL, p. 62: "Under Hambitzer, I first became familiar with Chopin, Liszt and Debussy" (regarding the mention of Chopin's "polkas," Gershwin possibly said or meant "polonaises").

21. EWE (1956 ed.), p. 165; see SCH, p. 303 n. 5, for Gershwin's alleged "lack of savvy" in this regard.

22. For Grieg, see PEY, p. 94; for Ravel, see EWE, p. 18; Percy Aldridge Grainger, "Foreword," *The Man I Love* (New York: G. Schirmer, 1944).

23. GOL, pp. 62 ("harmony-conscious"), 67; for a slightly different telling (with a modulation a full step higher rather than lower), see Ireene Wicker, WJZ radio broadcast (25 September 1936), courtesy of Michael Feinstein ("You are"); most sources report that Gershwin did not study harmony with Hambitzer, but Van Vechten ("George Gershwin") states that Gershwin "received his first lessons in harmony" from Hambitzer; Schwimmer, who interviewed Gershwin for her book *Great Musicians as Children,* mentions that he studied with "two other teachers" on Hambitzer's recommendation, but provides no additional information about them (p. 233).

24. NEI; Eleanor Hague, ed., *Folk Songs from Mexico and South America* (New York: H. W. Gray, 1914); Edward Kilenyi, "Arnold Schonberg's 'Harmony,'" *New Music Review* 14, nos. 6 and 7 (September and October 1915): 324–328, 360–363; idem, "The Theory of Hungarian Music," *Musical Quarterly* 5 (1919): 20–39; idem, "George Gershwin . . . as I Knew Him," *Etude* 68 (October 1950): 11–12, 64; Clif Paisley, "Edward Kilenyi Takes Local Residence," *Tallahassee Democrat* (29 May 1966); Edward Kilenyi, *Gershwiniana: Recollections and Reminiscences of Times Spent with My Student George Gershwin* (unpublished manuscript, Library of Congress). In 1966, Kilenyi retired to Tallahassee, where his son, Edward Kilenyi Jr., taught piano on the Florida State University faculty.

25. OSG, p. 174; Kilenyi, "George Gershwin"; Percy Goetschius, *The Material Used in Musical Composition* (New York: G. Schirmer, 1889, repr. 1913); Benjamin Cutter, *Harmonic Analysis* (Boston: Oliver Ditson, 1902); JAB, p. 106; NEI, p. 66.

26. Although Charles Schwartz (SCH, p. 55) points out that these later exercises do not employ augmented sixth chords and other chromatic harmonies, if Gershwin studied the Goetschius and Cutter texts as thoroughly as Kilenyi claims, he might well have also grappled with augmented chords, polychords, modal harmony, and other features of advanced harmony at some point or other.

27. JAB, p. 21; EWE, p. 114; NEI, pp. 66–71. Neimoyer also believes that two surviving free studies in "two-part Lied" (featuring the "Tristan chord") and an "eight-bar period," dated 29 January and 1 February 1923, respectively, constitute work undertaken with Kilenyi, although by this point Gershwin had already begun lessons with Goldmark.

28. NEI, pp. 73, 76, 87–99; Kilenyi, "Arnold Schonberg's 'Harmony'" (where *Stufenreichtum* is identified with Goetschius's "law of appropinquity"

[*sic*]), p. 360; Goetschius, *The Material Used in Musical Composition*, p. 234: "The ruling condition for these 'wandering harmonies,'—as far as it is possible to systematize so elusive a process,—seems to be: *That any change which results from either a whole-step or half-step progression in any or all of the parts, is permissible* (as long as it preserves a reasonable degree of consonance), by virtue of the relation of propinquity."

29. Kilenyi, "George Gershwin . . . as I Knew Him," p. 12; NEI, p. 74 ("never").

30. GG, "Figured Choral," GCLC; Wayne D. Shirley, "George Gershwin Learns to Orchestrate," *Sonneck Society Bulletin* 16 (1990): 102; LEV/SI, p. 190; NEI, p. 74.

31. Course information courtesy of Jocelyn K. Wilk, Assistant Archivist, Columbia University Archives & Columbiana Library, e-mails to the author, May 2001.

32. Ira Gershwin, letter to Benjamin Botkin, 12 January 1923, GCLC; EWE, p. 58; note also Goldberg's reference to "the early weeks with Goldmark," GOL, p. 63.

33. ARM/GG, p. 28; GG, *A George Gershwin Ms. Music Notebook* (March and April 1924), GCLC.

34. KS, p. 48; GOL, pp. 63–64; Van Vechten, "George Gershwin," p. 40.

35. G4; Ross Parmenter, "Music: Lincoln Program," *New York Times* (11 February 1960).

36. Signed photographs, GCLC; ARM/GG, pp. 171–172.

37. "Looking Backward," *Time* (11 May 1953).

38. NEI.

39. G7, p. 14.

40. GER, p. 178.

41. David Metzer, "The New York Reception of *Pierrot lunaire:* The 1923 Premiere and Its Aftermath," *Musical Quarterly* 78, no. 4 (Winter 1994): 669.

42. See SCH, p. 75, for the 1 November 1923 program; Nadia Turbide, *Biographical Study of Eva Gauthier (1885–1958), First French-Canadian Singer of the Avant-Garde* (PhD diss., University of Montreal, 1986).

43. ARM/GGML, p. 78.

44. DUK/PP, p. 90.

45. DUK/GS, p. 106; GOL, p. 63.

46. Abram Chasins, "Paradox in Blue," *Saturday Review* 37 (25 February 1956): 37–39, 64–66.

47. Carol J. Oja, *Making Music Modern: New York in the 1920s* (New York: Oxford University Press, 2000).

48. Bettina Mershon, "An Hour with George Gershwin" (December 1930), GCLC ("My serious").

3. Gershwin and the New Popular Music

1. GOL, p. 55; FUR, p. 16; ROS, p. 9.

2. Walter H. Rubsamen, "Music in the Cinema," *Arts and Architecture* 62, no. 9 (September 1945): 20–21.

3. JAB/GY, p. 69 (for "He's Gone Away"); Carl Sandburg, *The American Songbag* (New York: Harcourt Brace Jovanovich, 1927), pp. 3–7; GER, p. 159.

4. G7, p. 52B.

5. G7, p. 52B; "Gershwin Works on His First Opera," *New York Sun* (10 November 1933): "I feel close to Negro music. In Russia, the country of my ancestors, folk music always finds a response."

6. Leon Lipsky, "George Gershwin: Jazz Glorifier," *American Hebrew* (27 November 1925): 59.

7. Lazare Saminsky, *Music of the Ghetto and the Bible* (New York: Bloch, 1934), pp. 120–121; Nathan Ausubel, *A Treasury of Jewish Folklore: Stories, Traditions, Legends, Humor, Wisdom, and Folk Songs of the Jewish People* (New York: Crown Publishers, 1948), p. 654; Isaac Goldberg, "What's Jewish in Gershwin's Music?" *B'nai B'rith Magazine* (April 1936): 226.

8. William K. Zinsser, "Harold Arlen: *The Secret Music Maker*," *Harper's* (May 1960): 45 ("there was no Jewish music"); GOL, p. 41; PAY, p. 36.

9. LOG, p. 894; MEY, p. 11.

10. Mark Slobin, *Yiddish Theater in America* (New York: Garland, 1994); Irene Heskes, *The Music of Abraham Goldfaden, Father of the Yiddish Theater* (New York: Tara Publications, 1990); Mark Slobin, *Tenement Songs: Popular Music of the Jewish Immigrants* (Urbana: University of Illinois Press, 1982).

11. GER, p. 187; GOL, p. 42; KIM/G, p. 17; PAY, p. 37; SCH, 27; for Milton Thomashevsky, see "Victim of Shooting Dies after 5 Years," *New York Times* (15 May 1936).

12. Joseph Rumshinsky, *Klangen Fun Mayn Lebn (Sounds from My Life)* (New York: Biderman, 1944), p. 500; SCH/GS, p. 230 (these songs were released as "Das Pintele Yud" and "Gott Un Sein Mishpet Is Gerecht").

13. Ira Gershwin, quoted by Alan Hutchinson, "A Song-Writer Listens to Some Foreign Melodies," *Paris Comet* (July 1928), GCLC; Ira Gershwin, Diaries (12 June 1928), ILGT.

14. PAY, pp. 30, 46, 157; Saminsky, *Music of the Ghetto*, p. 122.

15. Saminsky, *Music of the Ghetto*, p. 121; SCH, pp. 28–29, 323–325 (including Secunda); Maurice Peress, *Dvořák to Duke Ellington: A Conductor Explores America's Music and Its African American Roots* (New York: Oxford University Press, 2004), p. 71; GOT, pp. 42 (for Picon), 81 (for Secunda); Max Wilk, "They Wrote Songs, Too," *Variety* (8 January 1986): 6, 239 (for Herrmann).

16. GOT (for comparison with Kern and Rodgers, see p. 47).

17. Zinsser, "Harold Arlen," p. 45 ("Hebraic influence").

18. Ashby Deering, "Brothers as Collaborators," *Morning Telegraph* (1 February 1925), GCLC.

19. Alexander Woollcott, *The Story of Irving Berlin* (New York: G. P. Putnam's Sons, 1925), p. 85; GOL, p. 82.

20. GOL, p. 80; EWE, p. 19; G4 ("the first").

21. For a summary and evaluation of the literature on "Alexander's Ragtime Band," see Charles Hamm, *Irving Berlin, Songs from the Melting Pot: The Formative Years, 1907–1914* (New York: Oxford University Press, 1997).

22. AUS, p. 331; WIL, pp. 16, 94; see also Irving Berlin (as told to Russel

Crouse), "The Composer of 'Alexander's Ragtime Band,'" *Stage* (August 1936): 80–81.

23. Hamm, *Irving Berlin*, pp. 80, 103.

24. *Jewish Influences in American Life*, vol. 3 (Dearborn, MI: Dearborn Publishing, 1921), pp. 64–87; Constant Lambert, *Music Ho! A Study of Music in Decline* (London: Faber and Faber, 1934), pp. 211–212; Michael H. Kater, *Different Drummers: Jazz in the Culture of Nazi Germany* (New York: Oxford University Press, 1992), p. 32; Henry Cowell, "American Composers," *Ohio State Educational Conference* 36, no. 3 (15 September 1931): 378; John Tasker Howard, *Our Contemporary Composers: American Music in the Twentieth Century* (New York: Thomas Y. Crowell, 1941), p. 6; see also Paul Fritz Laubenstein, "Race Values in Aframerican Music," *Musical Quarterly* (July 1930): 396; and Macdonald Smith Moore, *Yankee Blues: Musical Culture and American Identity* (Bloomington: Indiana University Press, 1985), pp. 143–144.

25. HOW, pp. 557–560; Andrea Most, *Making Americans: Jews and the Broadway Musical* (Cambridge, MA: Harvard University Press, 2003), p. 10. For some representative viewpoints on Jewish assimilation of black styles, see Goldberg, "What's Jewish in Gershwin's Music?" p. 227; HOW, p. 563; Ronald Sanders, "The American Popular Song," in *Next Year in Jerusalem: Portraits of the Jew in the Twentieth Century,* ed. Douglas Villiers (New York: Viking Press, 1976), p. 198; Stephen J. Whitfield, *In Search of American Jewish Culture* (Waltham, MA: Brandeis University Press, 1999), pp. 149–150; David Brion Davies, "Jews and Blacks in America," *New York Review of Books* (2 December 1999): 57–63; and Michael Alexander, *Jazz Age Jews* (Princeton, NJ: Princeton University Press, 2001). These critics tend to view (alleged) Jewish mimicry of African American culture sympathetically as at least liberating for the Jews involved and in some respects a helpful tool for negotiating or defusing racial conflict. Though concerned with black-white interactions rather than black-Jewish ones per se, see somewhat along these lines, W. T. Lhamon Jr., "Every Time I Wheel About I Jump Jim Crow: Cycles of Minstrel Transgression from Cool White to Vanilla Ice," in *Inside the Minstrel Mask,* ed. Annemarie Bean, James V. Hatch, and Brooks McNamara (Hanover, NH: University Press of New England for Wesleyan University Press, 1996), pp. 275–284, and the same author's *Raising Cain: Blackface Performance from Jim Crow to Hip Hop* (Cambridge, MA: Harvard University Press, 1998). Other critical traditions have been less sanguine. Even Howe and Whitfield acknowledge that opportunism played its part among Jewish entertainers, a notion taken to considerable lengths by Michael Rogin in *Blackface, White Noise: Jewish Immigrants in the Hollywood Melting Pot* (Berkeley: University of California Press, 1996), who proposes that Jews mimicked blacks not in order to assert their Jewishness or to subvert societal repression, but on the contrary, to assimilate into a racist American mainstream. Jeffrey Melnick, *A Right to Sing the Blues: African Americans, Jews, and American Popular Song* (Cambridge, MA: Harvard University Press, 1999), p. 97, furthered this argument to suggest that Jews "used Blackness to define their social status. The Jewish men involved in popular culture productions of Blackness projected racial imagery which seems concerned not only with their 'ethnic' suitability but also with the confirmation of their gender and sexual legitimacy." Melnick also contends that

the popular correspondences drawn between Jewish cantorial music and jazz fostered the "sacralization" of Jews in popular music. For yet another interpretation, one that considers black blackface as well as African American response to blackface, see Arthur Knight, *Disintegrating the Musical: Black Performance and American Musical Film* (Durham, NC: Duke University Press, 2002).

26. Daniel Hardie, *The Loudest Trumpet: Buddy Bolden and the Early History of Jazz* (iUniverse), pp. 111, 146; Alan Lomax, *Mister Jelly Roll,* 2nd ed. (Berkeley: University of California Press, 1973 [orig. 1950]), p. 143; Francis Davis, *The History of the Blues* (New York: Hyperion, 1995), p. 59; Edward A. Berlin, *Ragtime: A Musical and Culture History* (Berkeley: University of California Press, 1980), pp. 128–167.

27. Hamm, *Irving Berlin,* pp. 107–108; DOU, p. 359; Al Rose, *Eubie Blake* (New York: Schirmer Books, 1979), p. 51; Michael Freedland, *Irving Berlin* (New York: Stein and Day, 1974), pp. 32–33. The suspicion that an African American might have composed "Alexander's Ragtime Band" was itself revealing, as was Alec Wilder's discussion of Muir's "Play That Barber Shop Chord": "Both verse and chorus are so loose and relaxed that they might well have been written by a Negro. For up to this time there had been little evidence of white writers having absorbed, or having capably handled, the rhythmic materials that the Negroes had created," WIL, p. 15.

28. Reid Badger, *A Life in Ragtime: A Biography of James Reese Europe* (New York: Oxford University Press, 1995).

29. Badger, *A Life in Ragtime,* p. 117; EWE, p. 13; Edward A. Berlin, *Reflections and Research on Ragtime* (Brooklyn, NY: Brooklyn College Institute for Studies in American Music, 1987), p. 74; PEY, p. 36.

30. Gunther Schuller, *Early Jazz: Its Roots and Musical Development* (New York: Oxford University Press, 1968), pp. 248–249; Samuel B. Charters and Leonard Kunstadt, *Jazz: A History of the New York Scene* (New York: Da Capo Press, 1962, repr. 1981), p. 38; Eileen Southern, *The Music of Black Americans: A History* (New York: W. W. Norton, 1971), p. 348 ("New York").

31. Southern, *The Music of Black Americans,* pp. 347–350.

32. David Evans, "The Development of the Blues," in *The Cambridge Companion to Blues and Gospel Music,* ed. Allan Moore (Cambridge, Eng.: Cambridge University Press, 2002), pp. 20–27; Peter Muir, *Before "Crazy Blues": Commercial Blues in America 1850–1920* (PhD diss., City University of New York, 2004). Evans and Muir concur that the first published titled blues to feature a characteristic twelve-bar sequence was Antonio Maggio's instrumental "I Got the Blues" (1908).

33. W. C. Handy, *Father of the Blues: An Autobiography,* ed. Arna Bontemps (New York: Da Capo Press, 1941), pp. 137, 158; Southern, *The Music of Black Americans,* pp. 337–339.

34. Handy, *Father of the Blues,* pp. 93–99; for more on Crump, see William D. Miller, *Mr. Crump of Memphis* (Baton Rouge: Louisiana State University Press, 1964), especially pp. 101–102, 104.

35. Handy, *Father of the Blues,* p. 120; see Muir, *Before "Crazy Blues."*

36. Handy, *Father of the Blues,* pp. 143–144, 289; Abbe Niles, introduction to *Blues: an Anthology,* ed. W. C. Handy (New York: Albert and Charles Boni,

1926), p. 20; Adam Gussow, *Seems Like Murder Here: Southern Violence and the Blues Tradition* (Chicago: University of Chicago Press, 2002), pp. 70, 92; Evans, "The Development of the Blues," p. 22.

37. Handy, *Father of the Blues*, pp. 216, 287.

38. Henry Levine, "Gershwin, Handy and the Blues," *Clavier* 9, no. 7 (October 1970): 10–11; Gershwin, RB, 23 March and 11 May 1934; SPE (for Still).

39. Niles, introduction to *Blues*, pp. 15, 21; Levine, "Gershwin, Handy," pp. 10–20; for more thoughts on the subject of Gershwin and the blues, see Charles Hamm, "A Blues for the Ages," in *A Celebration of American Music: Words and Music in Honor of H. Wiley Hitchcock,* ed. Richard Crawford, R. Allen Lott, and Carol Oja (Ann Arbor: University of Michigan Press, 1990), pp. 346–355, and NEI; such music as the verse to "Oh, You Beautiful Doll" (1911) by Nat Ayer (1887–1952) headed in polyrhythmic directions as well.

40. Daniel Gregory Mason, "Stravinsky as a Symptom," *American Mercury* 4 (1925): 466.

41. Marshall Stearns and Jean Stearns, *Jazz Dance: The Story of American Vernacular Dance* (New York: Macmillan, 1968), p. 95.

42. Stearns and Stearns, *Jazz Dance,* p. 95; Woollcott, *The Story of Irving Berlin,* p. 85; Handy, *Father of the Blues,* p. 122.

43. "Mr. and Mrs. Vernon Castle's Dances for This Winter," *The Ladies' Home Journal* (Christmas 1914): 24–25; Vernon Castle and Irene Castle, *Modern Dancing* (New York: Da Capo Press, 1980), p. 47.

44. GRA, p. 164.

45. Robert P. Crease, "Jazz and Dance," in *The Cambridge Companion to Jazz,* ed. Mervyn Cooke and David Horn (Cambridge, Eng.: Cambridge University Press, 2002), pp. 69–80.

46. Ira Gershwin, letter to Max Wilk, 14 January 1971 [i.e., 1972], GCLC.

47. AST, pp. 238–239.

4. The Popular Pianist

1. "Gershwin Versatile Composer," GCLC ("could read"); GGR2; FG, p. 8 (for Rose's hopes); GG, letter to Isaac Goldberg, 30 June 1931, Houghton Library, Harvard University ("she offered").

2. David A. Jasen and Gene Jones, *The American Rag: The Story of Ragtime from Coast to Coast* (New York: Schirmer Books, 2000), p. 283.

3. Arthur Loesser, *Men, Women and Pianos: A Social History* (New York: Simon and Schuster, 1954), pp. 599–600; Arthur W. J. G. Ord-Hume, *Pianola: The History of the Self-Playing Piano* (Boston: George Allen & Unwin, 1984), p. 124; Isaac Goldberg, *Tin Pan Alley: A Chronicle of American Popular Music* (New York: Frederick Ungar, 1930), pp. 216–219.

4. GOL, p. 75.

5. KIM/G, p. 13; see Ewen's depiction of Gershwin as "a prisoner to the keyboard," EWE, p. 24; ARM/GG, p. 234 ("Every day").

6. KIM/G, pp. xxiii ("this very talented"), 23 ("much sought"); EWE, pp. 25–26. *Ofay* is slang for "white."

7. LEV/SI, p. 148; DUK/GS, p. 105; Abram Chasins, "Paradox in Blue," *Saturday Review* 37 (25 February 1956): 37–39, 64–66; Jean Wiéner, *Allegro Appassionato* (Paris: Pierre Belfond, 1978), p. 152 ("la diabolique indépendence de ses mains"); TIO, p. 135.

8. Mario Braggiotti, "Gershwin Is Here to Stay," *Etude* 71, no. 2 (February 1953): 14, 63; Braggiotti further suggested that concert pianists could profit from studying Gershwin's music, as its "blend of the sophisticated and the primitive," he argued, also informed the work of the greatest European masters. "The pianist's study of Gershwin," he concluded, "will give him truer rhythm[ic] vitality and stylistic color from which to tackle any program from Bach to Stravinsky."

9. Reiner quoted by Charles Ludwig, "Banjo, up from Georgia, Elbows Lordly 'Cello" (March 1927), GCLC; ARM/GG, p. 113; JAB/GY, p. 48; G7, p. 14.

10. Herbert Elwell, "Overflows Hall to Hear Gershwin," *Cleveland Plain Dealer* (21 January 1934); Earl Wild, interview by the author, 18 May 2005; "Two Piano Recitals for Benefit of MacDowell Foundation Given in Steinway Hall, New York," *Music Trades* (29 January 1927); G2.

11. JAB/GY, p. 48; the Victor trial recordings took place on 13 and 28 July 1920; for Gershwin's recordings with Van Eps, see Brian Rust, *The American Dance Band Discography*, vol. 2 (New Rochelle, NY: Arlington House, 1975), pp. 1852–1853; Brian Rust with Allen G. Debus, *The Complete Entertainment Discography* (New Rochelle, NY: Arlington House, 1975), p. 294, claims that Ralton played clarinet and oboe on these recordings, and identifies the banjoist as Eddie King, whereas PEY, pp. 60–61, identifies Ralton as a saxophonist and the banjoist as George King.

12. Michael Montgomery, "George Gershwin's Piano Rollography," in SCH/GS, pp. 225–253; Montgomery, in an interview by the author, 29 December 2004, revised his figure of known rolls from 141 to 140); according to Michael Feinstein (interview by the author, 24 October 2004), the rolls released in 1926 were possibly recorded in 1925.

13. Loesser, *Men, Women and Pianos*, pp. 582–586; Ord-Hume, *Pianola*.

14. ALE, p. 99; concerning the involvement in the editing process on the part of recording artists, see Richard J. Howe, "The Dumesnil Answers," *AMICA Bulletin* (July–August 2002): 152–153, and Prokofiev's contracts with the Aeolian company, both courtesy of Jeffrey Morgan.

15. Artis Wodehouse, "Tracing Gershwin's Piano Rolls," in SCH/GS, pp. 209–223; Montgomery, "George Gershwin's Piano Rollography."

16. Wodehouse, "Tracing Gershwin's Piano Rolls," p. 217; Jeffrey Morgan, letter to the author, 19 February 2005; Charles Davis Smith and Richard James Howe, *The Welte-Mignon: Its Music and Musicians* (Vestal, NY: Vestal Press, 1994).

17. Wodehouse, "Tracing Gershwin's Piano Rolls," pp. 213–214.

18. James Edward Hasse, ed., *Ragtime: Its History, Composers, and Music* (New York: Schirmer Books, 1985), p. 177; BAN.

19. Jack Gibbons, *The Authentic George Gershwin* (Sanctuary Classics 401, 2004); *Gershwin Plays Gershwin: Selections from the Piano Rolls*, ed. Artis Wodehouse (Miami: Warner Bros., 1995).

20. *Gershwin Plays Rhapsody in Blue* (Biograph 30120, 2003); *Gershwin Plays Gershwin: The Piano Rolls*, realized by Artis Wodehouse (Elektra Nonesuch 9 79287-2, 1992, 1993); *George Gershwin: The Piano Rolls*, vol. 2, realized by Artis Wodehouse (Nonesuch 79370-2, 1995); *Kickin' the Clouds Away: Gershwin at the Piano* (Klavier K 77031, 2001)—note that track 10, "Some Sunday Morning," is actually the song given for track 13, "The Land Where the Good Songs Go," and vice versa; Michael Walsh, "Gershwin, by George," *Time* (31 January 1994), courtesy of Artis Wodehouse ("the most careful"); Howard Reich, "It Ain't Necessarily George," *Chicago Tribune* (2 January 1994); Jack Gibbons, e-mail to the author, 14 May 2005; Montgomery recently sold his collection of more than one hundred Gershwin rolls to the Valley Forge Music Roll Company, Valley Forge, Pennsylvania; for a critique of the digitalization of rolls, see Jeffrey Morgan, "Digital Subversion," *AMICA Bulletin* (July–August 1998): 172–173 ("Pleasing though they may be, today's digital 'images' of reproducing piano rolls are, nonetheless, patently bogus—because they are inevitably colored by the subjective notions of those persons creating them," p. 173).

21. L. Douglas Henderson, skeptical of the authenticity of the Gershwin rolls, has inscribed his own piano rolls based on a study of the composer's electrical recordings; Wodehouse, "Tracing Gershwin's Piano Rolls," p. 218.

22. For more on this electrical recording, see SHI, p. 58.

23. Richard Dowling, liner notes, *Sweet and Low-Down* (Klavier K 11117, 2001).

24. Artis Wodehouse, "Introduction," *Gershwin's Improvisations for Solo Piano* (Miami: Warner Bros., 1987).

25. Edward Berlin, "Gershwin on Disc," *ISAM Newsletter* 28, no. 1 (Fall 1998): 5–6.

26. *Gershwin Performs Gershwin: Rare Recordings 1931–1935* (Musicmasters 5062-2-C, 1991).

27. G5.

28. Gershwin, RB, 7 October 1934.

29. For late ragtime and stride piano, see John L. Fell and Terkild Vinding, *Stride! Fats, Jimmy, Lion, Lamb, and All the Other Ticklers* (Lanham, MD: Scarecrow Press, 1999); Edward A. Berlin, *Reflections and Research on Ragtime* (Brooklyn, NY: Brooklyn College Institute for Studies in American Music, 1987); Hasse, ed., *Ragtime;* Al Rose, *Eubie Blake* (New York: Schirmer Books, 1979); Terry Waldo, *This Is Ragtime* (New York: Hawthorn Books, 1976); Willie "The Lion" Smith with George Hoefter, *Music on My Mind: The Memoirs of an American Pianist* (New York: Da Capo Press, 1975); Gunther Schuller, *Early Jazz: Its Roots and Musical Development* (New York: Oxford University Press, 1968); Rudi Blesh and Harriet Janis, *They All Played Ragtime*, 4th ed. (New York: Oak Publications, 1971 [orig. 1950]); Ed Berlin, e-mail to the author, 20 July 2004 (for Eubie Blake's revised birth date of 1887).

30. Blesh and Janis, *They All Played Ragtime*, pp. 188, 190.

31. Hasse, ed., *Ragtime*, p. 170 ("The reason"); for more information on *Yamekraw,* including its role as "a pointed African-American response to the success of Gershwin's *Rhapsody in Blue,*" see John Howland, *Between the Muses, the Masses, and the Masses: Symphonic Jazz and the Rise of American Musical*

Middlebrow, 1924–1950 (PhD diss., Stanford University, 2001); for *De Organizer,* see Stephen Kinzer, "From Oblivion to Ovation: An Opera Right out of the Harlem Renaissance," *New York Times* (28 December 2002).

32. Smith, *Music on My Mind,* p. 188.

33. Fell and Vinding, *Stride!* p. 88; "Potent Cocktail," *Newsweek* (15 June 1942): 69: "Among the exercises Gershwin was given was a little thing Roberts made up a few years before—a melodic phrase, but one which had to be hammered out at a quick staccato"; PEY, p. 40; Robert Kimball, interview by the author, 9 July 2004, recalled Roberts saying that Gershwin came to his apartment for "lessons in styling."

34. Hasse, ed., *Ragtime,* p. 177; Bernard L. Peterson Jr., *A Century of Musicals in Black and White: An Encyclopedia of Musical Stage Works by, about, or Involving African Americans* (Westport, CT: Greenwood Press, 1993), pp. 270–272.

35. Smith, *Music on My Mind,* p. 226–227.

36. For a summary of the "I Got Rhythm" controversy, including the allegations that Gershwin "stole" at least the main idea of the song from Still, see Catherine Parsons Smith, *William Grant Still: A Study in Contradictions* (Berkeley: University of California Press, 2000), pp. 136–143 (Smith imagines that Still associated the tune with blackface minstrelsy, but there's no definite evidence concerning this); ARV, p. 27. Joan Peyser emphasized such allegations in order "to convey the very real sense of rage many blacks continue to feel because they believe a language that was once theirs was expropriated from them and exploited by whites," PEY, p. 44. However, Blake seemed to reveal more bemusement than "rage," an impression confirmed by Robert Kimball, interview by the author, 9 July 2004. Meanwhile, black critic and author Stanley Crouch attributed such "attacks" to the fact that "Gershwin was Jewish, and there is an extremely complicated history fundamental to the tale of Negroes and Jews in show business"; Crouch also notes the irony that Gershwin, far from stealing, provided jazz musicians with "jumping off points for classic improvisations," and that the harmonic progression of "I Got Rhythm" in particular has "been used by so many jazz musicians that we have no idea how much larger the Gershwin fortune would be if his estate could lay claim to every use of that harmonic material": Stanley Crouch, "An Inspired Borrower of a Black Tradition," *New York Times* (30 August 1998).

37. Waldo, *This Is Ragtime,* p. 113; Terkild Vinding, "Forgotten People," *The Second Line* (May–June 1970): 330; see also Fell and Vinding, *Stride!* p. 88.

38. Lawrence Stewart, "The Gershwins—Words upon Music," *Ella Fitzgerald Sings the George and Ira Gershwin Song Book* (Verve 314 539 759-2, 1959, reissued 1998), p. 39 ("You can't").

39. Hasse, ed., *Ragtime,* pp. 169, 171; Fell and Vinding, *Stride!* p. 183.

40. Jasen and Jones, *The American Rag,* p. 261.

41. Artis Wodehouse, "Time to Remember Zez Confrey," *ISAM Newsletter* 28, no. 1 (Fall 1998): 8; Richard M. Sudhalter, *Lost Chords: White Musicians and Their Contribution to Jazz, 1915–1945* (New York: Oxford University Press, 1999), p. 801; Zez Confrey's *Modern Course in Novelty Piano Playing* (New York: Jack Mills, 1923).

42. EWE, p. 31.

43. Sudhalter, *Lost Chords*, p. 800 n. 21; Fell and Vinding, *Stride!* p. 53; for a dismissal of the "pseudo ragtime" of white pianists, see Blesh and Janis, *They All Played Ragtime*, pp. 224–225.

44. Hoagy Carmichael, *The Stardust Road & Sometimes I Wonder: The Autobiography of Hoagy Carmichael* (New York: Da Capo Press, 1999), p. 237; Martin Williams, *Jazz Heritage* (New York: Oxford University Press, 1985), p. 70; Sudhalter, *Lost Chords*, p. 801; see also James Weldon Johnson's statement that Gershwin's piano playing had some of the "feeling" of "pure Negro rhythm" in Shirley Graham, *Paul Robeson: Citizen of the World* (Westport, CT: Negro Universities Press, 1946, repr. 1971), pp. 147–148.

5. Toward a Career in the Theater

1. EWE, p. 26.

2. GOL, p. 86; Katharan McCommon, "Gershwin, King of the Jazz Composers at 26, Says Piano Made Good Boy of Him," 1924, GCLC.

3. Ira Gershwin, Diaries, ILGT (see also KIM/G, p. 96); ARM/GG, p. 175; Vera Kálmán, *Grüss mir die Süssen, die reizenden Frauen: Mein Leben mit Emmerich Kálmán* (Bayreuth: Hestia Verlag, 1966), pp. 92–94 (the author's translation of Kálmán's "Meinem grossen Freund Kalman in Verehrung. George," an inscription George presumably wrote in English); Vera states that Gershwin gave Kálmán the silver pencil with which he allegedly had written the *Rhapsody;* Marion Bussang, "Rhapsody in Gotham," *New York Post* (8 May 1940); see also Stefan Frey, *Unter Tränen Lachen: Emmerich Kálmán, eine Operettenbiografie* (Berlin: Henschel, 2003), pp. 193–194.

4. Ira Gershwin, marginalia, Oscar Straus to Ira Gershwin, 12 July 1937 (Straus's telegram of condolence read, "Deeply touched by the loss of your brother and my dear friend George Please accept my sincerest sympathy"); Gershwin, RB, 10 November 1934.

5. Gershwin, RB, 16 March 1934, 9 December 1934 ("I feel").

6. Gershwin, RB, 30 March 1934.

7. LEV/SI, p. 206.

8. SCH, p. 31; GOL, p. 81.

9. The five productions included *The Laughing Husband, The Girl from Utah, The Marriage Market, The Passing Show,* and *The Passing Show of 1914.*

10. BOR/JK, p. 171; James Kenneth Randall, *Becoming Jerome Kern: The Early Songs and Shows, 1913–1915* (PhD diss., University of Illinois at Urbana-Champaign, 2004), courtesy of the author.

11. WOD; DAV/B.

12. DAV/B, p. 76; Andrew Lamb, *150 Years of Popular Musical Theatre* (New Haven, CT: Yale University Press, 2000) (for Rubens; see also Lamb's "From *Pinafore* to Porter: United States–United Kingdom Interactions in Musical Theater, 1879–1929," *American Music* 4, no. 1 [Spring 1986]: 34–49); for more on musical traits, including vocal style, rhythm, and sound, related to the creation of the modern musical comedy, see GRA.

13. FER, p. 65.

14. Ira Gershwin, marginalia, 17 May 1966, GCLC, in which Ira further described Saddler as "a charming man, who usually wore a black woolen shirt when he came in with his work from his home in the country"; FER, pp. 287–288.

15. WOD, p. 102; KIM/G, pp. 17–18.

16. JAB/GY, p. 48.

17. GOL, pp. 87–90.

18. WOD, p. 83.

19. BOR/JK, pp. 157–158.

20. KIM/G, p. 17; WOD, pp. 83, 84.

21. BOR/AMT, p. 373.

22. WOD, p. 98.

23. William Boosey, *Fifty Years of Music* (London: E. Benn, 1931), pp. 191–192; *The Story of Francis, Day & Hunter* (London: Francis, Day & Hunter, 1952). Regarding the history of Harms and Chappell, the sources are contradictory; even the same source can give inconsistent information, as in the articles "Max Dreyfus" and "T. B. Harms" in David A. Jasen, *Tin Pan Alley: An Encyclopedia of the Golden Age of American Music* (New York: Routledge, 2003): Dreyfus joins the company as an arranger in 1898 in the former entry, and 1901 in the latter entry; a reliable study of Max Dreyfus is needed.

24. ROD, p. 75; FER, p. 11; Hans W. Heinsheimer, *Best Regards to Aida: The Defeats and Victories of a Music Man on Two Continents* (New York: Alfred A. Knopf, 1968), pp. 88–94; GG, letter to Julia Van Norman, 5 March 1929, GCLC.

25. DUK/PP, pp. 93–94; EWE (1956 ed.), p. 75 (EWE, p. 48).

26. KIM/G, p. 18.

27. JAB/GY, pp. 54–57.

28. BOR/JK, p. 177; KIM/G, p. 18. Gershwin possibly derived one of his signature gestures—three rising half-steps, as found in "Swanee"—from one of its songs, "The Big Spring Drive."

29. According to Barbara W. Grossman, Fanny Brice recalled Gershwin rehearsing the chorus for the *Ziegfeld Follies of 1910,* but this is more than improbable, as he would have been eleven at the time: Grossman, *Funny Woman: The Life and Times of Fanny Brice* (Bloomington: Indiana University Press, 1991), p. 40.

30. SCH, p. 216.

31. ZIE, pp. 62–71; Marcelle Earle with Arthur Homme Jr., *Midnight Frolic: A Ziegfeld Girl's True Story* (Basking Ridge, NJ: Twin Oaks Publishing, 1955, repr. 1980 and 1999), p. 236.

32. KIM/G, p. 24 ("to entertain").

33. GG, letter to Max Abramson, 12 September 1918, GCLC.

34. GG, letter to Abramson; LEV/SI, p. 148; GOL, pp. 93–94.

35. GG, letter to Abramson; BOR/JK, p. 175; JAB/GY, pp. 63–64 ("And here's"); LEV/MA, p. 120. In 1972 Ira, who collaborated with Kern on the film *Cover Girl,* remembered the composer as "brilliant" but "strange," stating, "I always shrugged my shoulders when Kern said something rather arbitrary": Ira Gershwin, letter to Max Wilk, 18 January 1972, GCLC.

36. JAB/GY, p. 64.

37. See KIM/G, p. 20, and JAB/GY, p. 65, for variants.

6. Gershwin among His Friends

1. Anne Pleshette Wiggins, interview by the author, 13 September 2004; "Max Abramson Dies; Publicist of Movies," *New York Times* (12 April 1956).

2. DUK/PP, p. 223; PEY, p. 277; Lawrence Stewart, "The Gershwins—Words upon Music," *Ella Fitzgerald Sings the George and Ira Gershwin Song Book* (Verve 314 539 759–2, 1959, reissued 1998), p. 54.

3. KIM/G, p. 205 ("Perhaps"); GG, letter to Mabel Schirmer, 18 October 1936, GCLC ("Why don't"); Mary Pleshette Willis, "A Friendship Saved" (letter to the editor), *New York Times* (13 September 1998); Leopold Godowsky III, interview by the author, 24 September 2004.

4. Howard Dietz, *Dancing in the Dark: Words by Howard Dietz* (New York: Quadrangle, 1974), p. 61.

5. Samuel Chotzinoff, "Jazz: A Brief History," *Vanity Fair* 20, no. 4 (June 1923): 69, 104, 106. For more on Chotzinoff, see his memoir, *Day's at the Morn* (New York: Harper & Row, 1964), which, incidentally, includes a noteworthy portrait of Mason.

6. Samuel Chotzinoff, review of the Concerto in F in the *New York World* (4 December 1925); idem, "Good Music," *Stage Magazine* (September 1935): 13–15.

7. Robert F. Gross, *S. N. Behrman: A Research and Production Sourcebook* (Westport, CT: Greenwood, 1992), pp. 6, 8; LOG, pp. 266–267. A fantasy set in Oxford in the early twentieth century, *Zuleika Dobson* is about a bewitching young woman whose arrival on campus leads to the communal suicide drowning of all the university's undergraduates. Coincidentally or not, Kurt Weill, in the wake of his collaboration with Ira Gershwin, suggested a *Zuleika Dobson* musical to Alan Jay Lerner: Ronald Taylor, *Kurt Weill: Composer in a Divided World* (Boston: Northeastern University Press, 1991), p. 320.

8. ALE, p. 11, 18–19; for an enlarged version of the photograph, along with identifications of the participants, see KIM/G, pp. 66, 68–69; GOL, p. 14; Alexander Woollcott, "George the Ingenuous," *Cosmopolitan* (November 1933): 32–33 ("I wonder," "An evening"); JAB/GY, p. 131; LEV/MA, p. 142; BEH, p. 244; KS, p. 31; KOL, p. 259.

9. Edward Lueders, *Carl Van Vechten* (New York: Twayne Publishers, 1965), p. 113; Dwight Taylor, *Joy Ride* (New York: G. P. Putnam's Sons, 1959), pp. 134–144.

10. Maurice Zolotow, *It Takes All Kinds* (New York: Random House, 1944), pp. 250–302.

11. Zolotow, *It Takes All Kinds*, p. 293.

12. Larry Adler, *It Ain't Necessarily So* (London: Collins, 1984), p. 69; Zolotow, *It Takes All Kinds*, p. 294; Benjamin Botkin to Mary Ritchey, 13 February 1924, Henry Botkin Papers, Archives of American Art, Smithsonian Institution; SCH, p. 48; see also PAY, p. 77.

13. Edward Lueders, *Carl Van Vechten and the Twenties* (Albuquerque: University of New Mexico Press, 1955), pp. 19–20; DOU, p. 544.

14. Carl Van Vechten, "The Great American Composer," *Vanity Fair* 8, no. 2 (April 1917): 75, 140.

15. Richard J. Powell, "Re/Birth of a Nation," in his *Rhapsodies in Black:*

Art of the Harlem Renaissance (Berkeley: University of California Press, 1997), p. 17; for homosexuality and the Harlem Renaissance, see Eric Garber, "A Spectacle in Color: The Lesbian and Gay Subculture of Jazz Age Harlem," in *Hidden from History: Reclaiming the Gay and Lesbian Past,* ed. Martin Bauml Duberman, Martha Vicinus, and George Chauncey Jr. (New York: New American Library, 1989), pp. 318–331.

16. DOU, p. 327; see Leon Coleman, *Carl Van Vechten and the Harlem Renaissance: A Critical Assessment* (New York: Garland Publishing, 1998).

17. Bruce Kellner, *Carl Van Vechten and the Irreverent Decades* (Norman: University of Oklahoma Press, 1968), p. 192; GOL, pp. 126–130; Carl Van Vechten, "George Gershwin: An American Composer Who Is Writing Notable Music in the Jazz Idiom," *Vanity Fair* 24, no. 1 (March 1925): 40, 78, 84; Nadia Turbide, *Biographical Study of Eva Gauthier (1885–1958), First French-Canadian Singer of the Avant-Garde* (PhD diss., University of Montreal, 1986), pp. 275–278. Gauthier chose the material—Berlin's "Alexander's Ragtime Band," Kern's "The Siren's Song," Donaldson's "Carolina in the Morning," Gershwin's "Stairway to Paradise" and "Swanee," the Gershwin-Daly "Innocent Ingenue Baby," and, as an encore, Gershwin's "Do It Again"—in consultation not only with Gershwin but with Berlin and Kern as well: Turbide, *Biographical Study,* p. 278.

18. Turbide, *Biographical Study,* pp. 279–280; "Respectablizing Jazz," *Literary Digest* (24 November 1923): 31 (for Deems Taylor).

19. H. T. Parker, "Jazz Enlarges Mme. Gauthier's Newest Harvest," *Boston Transcript* (30 January 1924).

20. Carl Van Vechten, letter to GG, 14 February 1924, GCLC; Lueders, *Carl Van Vechten,* p. 46; Van Vechten, "George Gershwin"; Carl Van Vechten, letter to GG, 7 October 1924, GCLC.

21. Lawrence Langner, *The Magic Curtain: The Story of a Life in Two Fields, Theatre and Invention by the Founder of the Theatre Guild* (New York: E. P. Dutton, 1951), p. 196; PAY, p. 79; JAB/GY, p. 25.

22. "In Dat Great Gittin' Up Mornin'" features an accompanying idea that resembles the head motive of Gershwin's "Clap Yo' Hands" from *Oh, Kay!* which premiered soon after the music's publication; J. Rosamond possibly heard Gershwin play the song, and perhaps decided to allude to it in homage. In any case, the resemblance speaks to artistic affinities between these two composers, as evident, too, from a remark J. Rosamond made in 1937: "Negro characteristics in music are blending themselves into Negroid-American idioms with the verve of motion, speeding along on a rhythmic-streamlined vehicle" (see AUS, p. 314); ARM/GG, pp. 69–70; James Weldon Johnson, telegram to Ira Gershwin, 14 July 1937, GCLC.

23. Coleman, *Carl Van Vechten,* p. 99; Eugene Levy, *James Weldon Johnson: Black Leader, Black Voice* (Chicago: University of Chicago Press, 1973), p. 318.

24. Bennett Cerf, *Try and Stop Me: A Collection of Anecdotes and Stories, Mostly Humorous* (New York: Simon and Schuster, 1945), p. 130; Edward Burns, ed., *The Letters of Gertrude Stein and Carl Van Vechten 1913–1946,* vol. 2: *1935–1946* (New York: Columbia University Press, 1986), p. 767; Harold Acton, *Memoirs of an Aesthete* (London: Methuen, 1948), pp. 146–148; Kitty

Carlisle Hart, *Kitty: An Autobiography* (New York: Doubleday, 1988), p. 70. Regarding Gershwin's performance of the opera for Stein, other sources contain conflicting information: Diana Souhami, *Gertrude and Alice* (London: Harper-Collins, 1991), writes that Gershwin played only "tunes" from the opera (p. 210); John Malcom Brinnin, *The Third Rose: Gertrude Stein and Her World* (New York: Atlantic Monthly Press, 1959), says that Gershwin played the whole score, but that Stein sat on the piano bench (p. 240); Cerf's account may well be the most accurate, because he was presumably there himself, though it's unlikely that Gershwin would have read through the entire score.

25. Osbert Sitwell, *Laughter in the Next Room* (Boston: Little, Brown, 1948), pp. 201–202.

26. Carl Rollyson, *Lillian Hellman: Her Legend and Her Legacy* (New York: St. Martin's Press, 1988), p. 45; KIM/G, p. 231.

27. LEV/SI, p. 171; Marc Gershwin, interview by the author, 25 March 2004 (for Pallay); Robert Mosbacher Jr., interview by the author, 30 November 2004.

28. ARM/GGML, pp. 113–120.

29. WS, p. 4; FEI, p. 65; KAS, p. 186; PAY, p. 81.

30. FEI, p. 65 (for Simon); ALE, p. 293 (for Ager); PEY, p. 90 ("George was"), p. 157 ("when you"); LEV/SI, p. 201.

31. PAY, p. 79 (Van Vechten); "Gershwin on American Music" (1934), GCLC ("yellow-brown"); Barry Paris, *Louise Brooks* (New York: Anchor Books, 1989), p. 68; GGR; Ira denied the story about the little waltz, LS.

32. Mary Ellis, *Those Dancing Years: An Autobiography* (London: John Murray, 1982), p. 51; KW, p. 17; PEY, pp. 90–92.

33. KIM/G, p. 138.

34. GG, letter to Rosamond Walling, 5 September 1931; KIM/G, pp. 136–139 ("Despite"); Audree Penner, "Rosamond Walling Tirana '31 was courted by George Gershwin," www.swarthmore.edu/bulletin/archive/99/mar99/profiles.html (28 December 2005). In 1932 Walling married Rifat Tirana, with whom she had three children.

35. OHL.

36. Ron Chernow, *The Warburgs: The Twentieth-Century Odyssey of a Remarkable Jewish Family* (New York: Random House, 1993), p. 316; Trader Faulkner, e-mail to the author, 24 May 2005.

37. Katharine Weber, liner notes, *Fine and Dandy* (PS Classics, 2004).

38. Chernow, *The Warburgs*, p. 333; James P. Warburg, *The Long Road Home: The Autobiography of a Maverick* (Garden City, NY: Doubleday, 1964), pp. 71–72; see also Katharine Weber, "The Memory of All That," in *A Few Thousand Words about Love*, ed. Mickey Pearlman (New York: St. Martin's Press, 1998), pp. 15–30.

39. FEI, p. 65; PEY, p. 194 ("From George"); GG, letter to Mabel Schirmer, 9 February 1937, GCLC; GGR; KW, p. 20; Kitty Carlisle, interview by the author, 24 March 2003.

40. Julia Van Norman, letter to GG, 21 July 1933; Nancy Bloomer Deussen, e-mails to the author, 4 and 5 April 2003; see also PEY, pp. 136–140, 205–207.

41. Elsa Maxwell, *R.S.V.P.: Elsa Maxwell's Own Story* (Boston: Little, Brown, 1954), pp. 197–198 (Maxwell's recollection includes some factual er-

rors, including the year in which Gershwin and the countess met); GG, letter to the Countess de Ganny, 27 July 1928, GCLC.

42. GG, letter to Aileen Pringle, 30 June 1931, GCLC.

43. GG, quoted in "Men about Women," *Vogue* (November 1934), GCLC; Sheilah Graham, "Gershwin Rhapsodic over 'Single Bliss,'" *Los Angeles Examiner* (29 September 1935), GCLC; for Swift's suppositions, see Weber, "The Memory of All That," and Doris B. Wiley, "Gershwin's Gal: It Never Got to 'Toothbrush Time,'" *Evening Bulletin* (21 July 1976).

44. KW, p. 17; Kitty Carlisle, interview by the author, 24 March 2003.

45. Hart, *Kitty*, pp. 68–69, 80; Carlisle, interview by the author.

46. ROG, pp. 181–184.

47. ARM/GGML, p. 61; LEV/MA, p. 144; Adler, *It Ain't Necessarily So*, pp. 84–86; FEI, pp. 65–66; SCH, p. 280; Carmela de León, *Ernesto Lecuona: El mastero* (Havana: Editora Musical de Cuba, 1995), p. 78 (for 1928); Adler *(It Ain't Necessarily So)* and Joan Peyser (PEY, p. 278) state that Simon accompanied Gershwin to the Philadelphia performance of *Wozzeck* in 1931; without cited sources, this claim needs further verification, as Simon apparently arrived in the States in September 1935.

48. GG, letter to Julia Van Norman, 6 November 1937, GCLC.

49. GG, letter to Mabel Schirmer, 10 May 1937, GCLC.

50. FG, p. 30; Julie Gilbert, *Opposite Attraction: The Lives of Erich Maria Remarque and Paulette Goddard* (New York: Pantheon Books, 1995), pp. 140–141; Joe Morella and Edward Z. Epstein, *Paulette: The Adventurous Life of Paulette Goddard* (New York: St. Martin's Press, 1985), pp. 54–59.

51. Isaac Goldberg, "In Memoriam: George Gershwin," *B'nai B'rith Magazine* (August–September 1937): 8; Malcolm Goldstein, *George S. Kaufman: His Life, His Theater* (New York: Oxford University Press, 1979), p. 292; MER, pp. 543, 646; Lillian Hellman, *An Unfinished Woman* (New York: Little, Brown, 1969), pp. 73–74; George Pallay, letter to Irene Gallagher, July 1937, GCLC.

52. *George Gershwin Remembered* (Facet D/CD 8100, 1987); OHL, pp. 236–237; John O'Hara, "An American in Memoriam," *Newsweek* (15 July 1940); DUK, p. 352.

7. Later Studies

1. G11, p. 30; G6, p. x. Queried by a reporter in 1925 about his forthcoming concerto ("Gershwin Versatile Composer," ca. 1 December 1925, GCLC), Gershwin implied, however, that the American composer did not need "to study too closely" traditional European forms per se: "I don't think it is necessary for one who aims to write really American music to study too closely and pattern after the fugues and other forms that were original with the old German masters. We need American forms for American music."

2. PAY, p. 83 ("I can't"); Bernard Holland, "Street-Smart Composers Turn Noise into Art," *New York Times* (11 January 2005). Another link with Varèse was suggested by the satiric dance sequence "Basal Metabolism" from the 1957 film *Funny Face*, inspired by the Gershwin musical of the same name; set in a bohemian haunt in Paris, the music (presumably by Adolph Deutsch) for this

Audrey Hepburn dance number moved easily from faux Varèse to an arrangement of Gershwin's "How Long Has This Been Going On."

3. ARM/GG, p. 199 ("enchanted"); Arbie Orenstein, ed., *A Ravel Reader: Correspondence, Articles, Interviews* (New York: Columbia University Press, 1990; repr. Minneola, NY: Dover, 2003), pp. 289, 293; for the reference to the Savoy, see Benjamin Ivry, *Maurice Ravel: A Life* (New York: Welcome Rain Publishers, 2000), p. 147.

4. Nadia Turbide, *Biographical Study of Eva Gauthier (1885–1958), First French-Canadian Singer of the Avant-Garde* (PhD diss., University of Montreal, 1986), pp. 360–361; ARM/GG, p. 199; Orenstein, ed., *A Ravel Reader*, pp. 294, 390–391; SCH, p. 43; Gerald Lavner, *Maurice Ravel* (London: Phaidon Press, 1996), p. 195, points to a motive from the Sonata that anticipates Gershwin's "I Got Rhythm" (1930), but the connection is remote and the notion of influence is accordingly far-fetched. Indeed, suggestions of "I Got Rhythm" turn up more decidedly in the Gershwinesque second theme of the first movement of the Piano Concerto in G Major, completed after "I Got Rhythm."

5. ARM/GG, p. 199. This exchange has been somewhat misreported over the years. Ewen's 1943 version (EWE/SGG, p. 125), in which Ravel asks, "Why do you want to become a second-rate Ravel when you are already a first-rate Gershwin?"—slightly modified in the biopic *Rhapsody in Blue* (1945) as "Gershwin, if you study with me, you'll only write second-rate Ravel instead of first-rate Gershwin"—became standard.

6. Orenstein, ed., *A Ravel Reader*, p. 293; Jérôme Spycket, *Nadia Boulanger*, trans. M. M. Shriver (Stuyvesant, NY: Pendragon Press, 1987), pp. 71–72, 73; Léonie Rosenstiel, *Nadia Boulanger: A Life in Music* (New York: W. W. Norton, 1982), p. 181.

7. Rosenstiel, *Nadia Boulanger*, pp. 181, 216–217; "Music," *Time* (28 February 1938) ("I had nothing"); KIM/G, p. 90 ("because he had"); Rosenstiel also notes, more controversially, that although Boulanger admired Ravel, she felt "cool" toward him and "tended to deny his requests."

8. André Gauthier, *George Gershwin* (Paris: Hachette, 1973), pp. 92–94: "mais que j'imagine mal qu'un musicien de sa qualité ait besoin de conseils. . . . Ce fut un enchantement. J'étais ébloui par sa prodigieuse technique et émerveillé de son sens mélodique, de la hardiesse de ses modulations, de ses recherches harmoniques audacieuses et souvent inattendues."

9. Igor Stravinsky and Robert Craft, *Dialogues and a Diary* (London: Faber and Faber, 1968), p. 101; ARM/GGML, p. 113.

10. ARM/GG, pp. 172–173.

11. EWE/SGG, pp. 124–126; JAB, p. 168 (for Hammond); Stravinsky and Craft, *Dialogues*, pp. 101–102.

12. Nicholas Fox Weber, *Patron Saints: Five Rebels Who Opened America to a New Art 1928–1943* (New York: Knopf, 1992), pp. 294–295 (for *Les noces* in Hartford); LEV/SI, pp. 289–290 *(Symphony of Psalms)*; GG, letter to Mabel Schirmer, 19 March 1937, GCLC ("eight pieces").

13. GIL, pp. 121, 184–185, 233 n. 20; less persuasively, Gilbert also mentions Gershwin's penchant for a certain group of four pitches, found prominently in *Petrushka*, used as well in the main motive of "I Got Rhythm" and

the opening to *Porgy and Bess* (hence Gilbert's reference to an "I Got Rhythm" tetrachord); as in similar claims of influence made on behalf of William Grant Still, such resemblances seem to point, rather, to a common pentatonic source; Hans Keller, "Rhythm: Gershwin and Stravinsky," *The Score and I.M.A. Magazine* 20 (June 1957): 19–31; perhaps Keller would say that although the suspended opening motive of the chorus to "Embraceable You" ("Embrace me") exhibits a Stravinskian aggressiveness ("Thanatos"), as it reaches the downbeat ("you sweet em*brace*able you"), the melody evokes a Schoenbergian eroticism ("Eros").

14. David Platt, "A Never Before Printed Story about Gershwin and Glazounov," *Daily Worker* (4 January 1956): 6–7. There's no indication in this firsthand account by Drozdoff that Gershwin telephoned Glazounov the next day, or that Gershwin thanked Glazounov for his candor, as often reported. Glazounov subsequently asked Drozdoff for a teacher to recommend, and Drozdoff mentioned Joseph Schillinger. Drozdoff also told Platt that on hearing some orchestral music from *Porgy and Bess* over the radio, he wondered whether it might have been by Stravinsky or perhaps Glazounov.

15. WIL/T, p. 93.

16. Winthrop Sargeant, *Geniuses, Goddesses, and People* (New York: E. P. Dutton, 1949), p. 101.

17. Howard Shanet, *Philharmonic: A History of New York's Orchestra* (Garden City, NY: Doubleday, 1975), pp. 239–244.

18. During the composer's lifetime, his music was performed at Lewisohn Stadium on July 25, 1927; July 8, 1929; August 26, 1929; August 28, 1930; August 13, 1931; August 16, 1932; and July 9, 1936. In addition, the Paul Whiteman Orchestra performed the *Rhapsody* at Lewisohn Stadium on August 4, 1933, but with Roy Bargy at the piano.

19. LEV/SI, pp. 192–193; LEV/MA, p. 121.

20. Francis D. Perkins, "Gershwin Draws Audience That Taxes Stadium," *New York Herald-Tribune* (27 August 1929); "Gershwin Conducts Own Music at Stadium," *New York Times* (27 August 1929); "15,000 Rush to Lewisohn Stadium to Hail Gershwin in Triple Role," *New York Evening Telegram* (27 August 1929); Charles D. Isaacson, "Music," *New York Telegram* (28 August 1929).

21. Grena Bennett, "Gershwin Plays and Directs Own Work at Stadium," *American* (29 August 1930); L. L. B., "Stadium Acclaims Gershwin in Jazz," *New York Telegram* (29 August 1930), NYPA; Allen Lincoln Langley, "The Gershwin Myth," *American Spectator* (December 1932): 1–2.

22. GOL, p. 247.

23. Henry Cowell, letter to David Ewen (7 December 1954), Cowell Collection, NYPL (freely transcribed in EWE, p. 114, where a probably too-early 1927 starting date for Gershwin's lessons with Cowell is given, based on this letter); Edward R. Carwithen, *Henry Cowell: Composer and Educator* (PhD diss., University of Florida, 1991), p. 54 (for a 1931 date for lessons with Cowell); SCH, p. 294 n. 26 (for Riegger).

24. Michael Hicks, *Henry Cowell, Bohemian* (Urbana: University of Illinois Press, 2002), pp. 17, 19 (Hicks reports that Anna Strunsky Walling claimed to

have saved the young Cowell's life "by extracting a handful of pebbles from his mouth as he was choking on them," p. 17); Isaac Goldberg, "Chiefly about Henry Cowell," *Disques* 2, no. 5 (July 1931): 205–208; ARM/GGML, p. 144 (for *The Banshee*).

25. *American Composers on American Music: A Symposium,* ed. Henry Cowell (New York: Frederick Ungar, 1933, repr. 1961), p. 8 ("who is the"); Henry Cowell, "American Composers," *Ohio State Educational Conference* 36, no. 3 (15 September 1931): 379; Cowell, letter to David Ewen (for *Porgy and Bess*); Henry Cowell to Nicolas Slonimsky, 6 August 1937; Carwithen, *Henry Cowell,* pp. 46, 53, 82, 93, 112.

26. Cowell, letter to David Ewen; PEY, p. 158; Carwithen, *Henry Cowell,* p. 101 ("Henry"); David Nicholls, *American Experimental Music, 1890–1940* (New York: Cambridge University Press, 1990), p. 91.

27. Cowell, letter to David Ewen.

28. Joseph Schillinger, "Author's Preface," in *Kaleidophone: New Resources of Melody and Harmony* (New York: M. Witmark, 1940), pp. 5–7; Ira Gershwin, "Gershwin on Gershwin," *Newsweek* (23 October 1944): 14; Charles Previn, "Schillinger's Influence on Film Music," *Music News* 34, no. 3 (1947): 39.

29. Ilya Levinson, *What the Triangles Have Told Me: Manifestations of "The Schillinger System of Musical Composition" in George Gershwin's "Porgy and Bess"* (PhD diss., University of Chicago, 1997); Elena Dubinets and Lou Pine, "Earle Brown and the Schillinger System of Musical Composition," annual meeting of the Society for American Music (17 February 2005).

30. Arnold Shaw, "What Is the Schillinger System?" *Music News* 34, no. 3 (1947): 37–38; see also Warren Brodsky, "Joseph Schillinger (1895–1943): Music Science Promethean," *American Music* 21, no. 1 (Spring 2003): 45–73; Henry Cowell and Sidney Cowell, "The Schillinger Case: Charting the Musical Range," and Elliott Carter, "The Schillinger Case: Fallacy of the Mechanistic Approach," both in *Modern Music* 23, no. 3 (Summer 1946): 226–230; Previn, "Schillinger's Influence," p. 39.

31. GG, letters to Zena Hanenfeldt, 13 October 1936, 8 January 1937, GCLC.

32. GIL, pp. 174–175; SCH/GS, pp. 21–34 (Shirley, "rotations"); Paul Nauert, "Theory and Practice in *Porgy and Bess:* The Gershwin-Schillinger Connection," *Musical Quarterly* 78, no. 1 (Spring 1994): 9–33.

33. Levinson, *What the Triangles Have Told Me;* William H. Rosar, "Letter to the Editor," *Musical Quarterly* 80, no. 1 (Spring 1996): 182–184; KS, p. 49.

34. DUK/GS, pp. 102–115.

35. "Inside Stuff—Music," *Variety* (4 April 1956): 49 (Ferris also claimed that Schillinger "got him [Gershwin] away from ending each song a third up or a third down, as happens in most of his popular songs"); Nauert, "Theory and Practice," p. 20; DUK/GS, p. 109.

36. GG, letter to Joseph Schillinger, 13 October 1936, cited in SCH, p. 125; "Schoenberg Scholarship Fund," *New York Times* (1 October 1933); PEY, pp. 200–201.

37. Lilly Toch, "The Orchestration of a Composer's Life," interview by Bernard Galm, ed. Lawrence Weschler (Oral History Program, University of California, Los Angeles, 1978), courtesy of Lawrence Weschler, pp. 326–327, 358a, 369–370; Ernst

Toch, signed photograph, GCLC; Diane Peacock Jezic, *The Musical Migration and Ernst Toch* (Ames: Iowa State University Press, 1989), pp. 72–73.

38. SCH, p. 125.

39. GG, letters to Mabel Schirmer, 1 September 1936, 18 September 1936, GCLC; Toch, "The Orchestration," pp. 326–330, 596 (all quotes are hers).

40. LEV/SI, pp. 186–187; ARM/GG, pp. 102–112.

41. JAB/GY, p. 264; LEV/MA, p. 129.

42. LEV/SI, p. 188.

43. LEV/SI, pp. 209–210; Kenneth H. Marcus, *Musical Metropolis: Los Angeles and the Creation of a Music Culture, 1880–1940* (New York: Palgrave Macmillan, 2004), p. 82 (enclosed disc includes Schoenberg's remarks).

44. ARM/GG, pp. 97–98.

45. Arnold Schoenberg, *Style and Idea* (New York: Philosophical Library, 1950), p. 51.

46. JAB, pp. 106 ("I can't recall"), 158 ("that George from"; this last in response to Barry Ulanov, "Gershwin Wasn't That Great," *Metronome* [August 1945]: 12, 22); Murray Schumach, "Hollywood Recall," *New York Times* (21 June 1959) (for Polynesian music).

8. Gershwin and the Great Tradition

1. ARM/GGML, p. 73.

2. "Jazz to Survive Says Gerschwin [*sic*]," *Montreal Daily Star* (6 January 1927); Hyman Sandow, "Gershwin Presents a New Work," *Musical America* 48, no. 18 (18 August 1928): 5, 12 (note that Sandow offers this list twice, mentioning Mozart only on p. 12); Hyman Sandow, "Gershwin to Write New Rhapsody," *Musical America* 47, no. 18 (18 February 1928): 5.

3. Isaac Goldberg, "As Gershwin Makes Ready His Rhapsody," *Boston Evening Transcript* (28 January 1932); KS, pp. 35, 43; LEV/SI, pp. 191–192; LEV/MA, p. 121 (Levant mentions "Schubert's C-Major Quartet," but he probably meant that composer's famed String Quintet in the same key, rather than either of Schubert's early, obscure C major string quartets; and the second theme in the quintet's first movement does bear a resemblance to "Union Square," which Levant refers to as "Two Hearts Are in Communion"). For Gershwin's relation to the great tradition, see also JOH, pp. 106–111.

4. Morris Hastings, "Gershwin Scoffs at Musical Traditions: Would Build Anew," *Boston Sunday Advertiser* (29 December 1929).

5. "Gershwin Goes Political after Chats with Rivera," *New York Post* (17 December 1935); "Gershwin on American Music" (1934), GCLC; S. J. Woolf, "Finding in Jazz the Spirit of His Age," *New York Times* (20 January 1929) ("to me"); Leon Lipsky, "George Gershwin: Jazz Glorifier," *American Hebrew* (27 November 1925): 67 ("nothing").

6. Arthur Loesser, "Loesser Discusses Gershwin's Contribution to American Music," *Cleveland Press* (4 September 1937).

7. Richard Rodney Bennett, interview by the author, 21 February 2003 (for "I Was So Young"); Michael Kennedy, *Portrait of Walton* (New York: Oxford University Press, 1989), p. 40; Stephen Lloyd, *William Walton: Muse of Fire*

(Woodbridge, Eng.: Boydell Press, 2001), p. 73; Susana Walton, *William Walton: Behind the Façade* (New York: Oxford University Press, 1988), p. 180.

8. John Longmire, *John Ireland: Portrait of a Friend* (London: John Baker, 1969), p. 51 ("That"); Muriel V. Searle, *John Ireland: The Man and His Music* (Tunbridge Wells: Midas Books, 1979), pp. 143–144 ("Ah!").

9. Donald Mitchell, ed., *Letters from a Life: The Selected Letters and Diaries of Benjamin Britten 1913–1976* (Berkeley: University of California Press, 1991), pp. 637–638; "Coates Selects 'Best in Music'; Lists 50 Composers of All Time," *New York Evening Post* (4 August 1930); Constant Lambert, *Music Ho! A Study of Music in Decline* (London: Faber and Faber, 1934), p. 223; JAB/GR, p. 122; Ian Kemp, *Tippett: The Composer and His Music* (New York: Oxford University Press, 1987), pp. 59, 92, 148, 164; Michael Tippett, *Those Twentieth Century Blues* (London: Pimlico, 1991), p. 249 ("I have since").

10. Sandow, "Gershwin Presents."

11. PEY, p. 103.

12. JAB/GY, p. 132 ("Good"); "Gershwin Meets Honegger," *Musical Leader* (26 July 1928); DUK/GS, p. 108; LEV/SI, p. 190.

13. LEV/SI, p. 189, alludes to "the Milhaud violin concerto," but in view of the fact that the First Violin Concerto had not as yet been recorded, he must have meant the *Concerto de printemps;* for Milhaud's *Creation of the World* in New York, see Carol J. Oja, *Making Music Modern: New York in the 1920s* (New York: Oxford University Press, 2000), pp. 65–66, 355; Deborah Mawer, *Darius Milhaud: Modality and Structure in Music of the 1920s* (Brookfield, VT: Ashgate, 1997), p. 163.

14. Nancy Perloff, *Art and the Everyday: Popular Entertainment and the Circle of Erik Satie* (Oxford: Clarendon Press, 1991), pp. 92–93; Samuel Brylawski kindly brought the quotation from "Swanee" to my attention.

15. EWE, p. 138.

16. DUK/PP, pp. 108, 209, 218, 233; LEV/MA, p. 141; LEV/SI, p. 190.

17. Barbara Nissman, "Gershwin Meets Prokofiev: The Hidden Connections," *Piano Today* (Winter 2005): 4–7, 45, 54–55; Sergey Prokofiev, *Dnevnik 1907–1933* (Paris: SPRKFV, 2002), pp. 629, 746 (translation courtesy of Noëlle Mann); Serge Prokofieff, "Music in America," trans. Florence Jonas, *Listen* (December 1963), GCLC; see also Sergej Prokofjew, "Das Musikalische Amerika," *Dokumente, Briefe, Erinnerungen,* ed. S. I. Schlifstein (Leipzig: Veb Deutscher Verlage für Musik, 1961), pp. 216–218.

18. DUK/PP, p. 458; Nissman, "Gershwin Meets Prokofiev"; AUS, p. 471.

19. Ira Gershwin, Diaries (24 April 1928, 25 April 1928), ILGT (see also KIM/G, p. 96); Ronald Sanders, *The Days Grow Short: The Life and Music of Kurt Weill* (New York: Holt, Rinehart and Winston, 1980), p. 101; *Speak Low (When You Speak Love): The Letters of Kurt Weill and Lotte Lenya,* ed. and trans. Lys Symonette and Kim H. Kowalke (Berkeley: University of California Press, 1996), p. 58.

20. Ronald Taylor, *Kurt Weill: Composer in a Divided World* (Boston: Northeastern University Press, 1991), pp. 84–85; GG, quoted by Alan Hutchinson, "A Song-Writer Listens to Some Foreign Melodies," *Paris Comet* (July 1928), GCLC; Michael von der Linn, "'Johnny', 'Mahagonny', and the Songs of Tin

Pan Alley," *Amerikanismus Americanism Weill: Die Suche nach kultureller Identität in der Moderne,* ed. Hermann Danuser and Hermann Gottschewski (Schliengen: Argus, 2003), pp. 160–170 (especially p. 163).

21. *Speak Low,* pp. 206–207, 227; Sanders, *The Days Grow Short,* p. 218 (for "squitchadickeh," apparently a made-up, but Yiddish-sounding, word for "squeaky"); see also JAB/GY, p. 299.

22. *Speak Low,* pp. 127, 207, 226, 240, 243, 287; Sanders, *The Days Grow Short,* pp. 219, 385; John O'Hara, "Critic in the Dark," *Newsweek* (3 February 1941); for more on *Street Scene* and *Porgy,* see Kim Kowalke, "Kurt Weill and the Quest for American Opera," in *Amerikanismus Americanism Weill.*

23. Donald Jay Grout, *A Short History of Opera* (New York: Columbia University Press, 1947), p. 515; *Kurt Weill: The Threepenny Opera,* ed. Stephen Hinton (New York: Cambridge University Press, 1990), pp. 146–147.

24. Ira Gershwin, Diaries, ILGT (see also KIM/G, p. 96); Hutchinson, "A Song-Writer Listens"; John L. Stewart, *Ernest Krenek: The Man and His Music* (Berkeley: University of California Press, 1991), p. 31.

25. EWE, p. 133; Ira Gershwin, Diaries (3 and 5 May 1928), ILGT; "Gershwin Finds Great Opera Artist," *New York Morning Telegraph* (20 June 1928).

26. Sandow, "Gershwin Presents" and "Gershwin Finds"; GG, letter to Mrs. William C. Hammer, 18 April 1931, GCLC ("thrilled"); LEV/SI, p. 189 ("deeply"); Paul Moor, "'Porgy' Comes to Germany," *High Fidelity/Musical America* 20, no. 8 (August 1970): 28–29 ("grinning").

27. Stuart Isacoff, "Fascinatin' Gershwin," *Keyboard Classics* (January–February 1984): 8 (see also p. 11); Allen Forte, "Reflections upon the Gershwin-Berg Connection," *Musical Quarterly* 83, no. 2 (Summer 1999): 150–168; Christopher Reynolds, "Why 'It Ain't Necessarily Soul': On *Porgy*'s Debts to *Wozzeck,*" annual meeting of the American Musicological Society (Seattle, 18 November 2004); Reynolds's musico-dramatic parallels include the lullabies of Clara and Marie, the seductions of Bess and Marie, the drowning of Jake and Wozzeck, as well as the use of fugue and a children's chorus.

28. JAB, p. 175; LEV/SI, p. 193.

29. Andrew Lamb, "Gershwin's Cuban Vacation," courtesy of the author; Charles W. White, *Alejandro García Caturla: A Cuban Composer in the Twentieth Century* (Lanham, MD: Scarecrow, 2003): White gives an alternate date for Lecuona's first Havana performance of the *Rhapsody,* p. 148 n. 9.

30. Benjamin Suchoff, *Guide to the Mikrokosmos of Béla Bartók,* rev. ed. (London: Boosey & Hawkes, 1970), p. 138; Marjory Irvin, "It's George, Not Jazz: Gershwin's Influence in Piano Music," *American Music Teacher* (November–December 1973): 34. In an early draft of a 1941 or 1942 lecture touching on his own use of folk musics, Bartók further stated, "I don't even shrink from [oriental (for instance, arabic) influences] and even american influences (I mean of course the jazz)": *Béla Bartók Essays,* ed. Benjamin Suchoff (London: Faber & Faber, 1976), p. 350. This essay, along with the aforementioned *Six Dances,* implies perceived ties on Bartók's part among Gershwin, Bulgarian dance rhythms, American folk music, and jazz, a complex nexus that bears on the subject of the composer's absorption of American music during his final years.

31. Ira Gershwin, letter to Gershwin, 16 February 1935, ILGT; "'Porgy' in

U.S.S.R.," *New York Times* (17 June 1945); "Ear to the West" (3 July 1954), Aaron Copland Clipping File, NYPL.

32. GG, letters to Isaac Goldberg, 11 October 1929, 22 December 1930, Houghton Library, Harvard University (although Gershwin told Goldberg in 1929 that he subscribed to *New Music,* his name has not yet surfaced among lists of subscribers in the Cowell Collection, NYPL); see also JAB/GY, p. 185.

33. G4; Gershwin made similar points in a 1920 interview with *Edison Musical Magazine,* though somewhat more crudely, with references to "the redman" and "the darky"; these earlier remarks—which struck his interlocutor as "more suited to the learned lecturer than to a composer of popular hits"—revealed his basic aesthetic to be more or less in place by this date; see "Tales of Tin Pan Alley: 'Swanee' and Its Author," *Edison Musical Magazine* (October 1920): 9.

34. Hyman Sandow, "Latest Argument about the Jazz Age," *Every Week Magazine* (29–30 August 1931), GCLC; "Fifteen Years: A Survey of American and Soviet Music," *Worker Musician* 1, no. 1 (December 1932): 3–5 (which described Carpenter and Gershwin as "clever manipulators of musical forms" who "have nothing much to say, despite their efforts to emulate Stravinsky in the American idiom"); W. C. Handy, ed., *Blues: An Anthology* (New York: Albert and Charles Boni, 1926); Howard Pollack, *Skyscraper Lullaby: The Life and Music of John Alden Carpenter* (Washington, D.C.: Smithsonian Institution Press, 1995), p. 402; for a reference to Carpenter's admiration for *Porgy and Bess,* see Cecelia Ager, "George Gershwin Thinks You Can Write Opera and Make It Tuneful," *Variety* (16 October 1935), GCLC.

35. ARV, p. 27 (at the same ICG concert, Gershwin also heard works by Marguerite Béclard d'Harcourt, Eugene Goossens, Ottorino Respighi, Vittorio Rieti, and Carl Ruggles); Catherine Parsons Smith, *William Grant Still: A Study in Contradictions* (Berkeley: University of California Press, 2000), pp. 139, 252 ("I felt all along"); SPE, pp. 114–115, 137–138.

36. Jan Swafford, *Charles Ives: A Life with Music* (New York: W. W. Norton, 1996), pp. 341, 489 n. 67; *Selected Correspondence of Charles Ives,* ed. Tom C. Owens (Berkeley: University of California Press, forthcoming), courtesy of the editor.

37. "Hans Barth Gives a Unique Recital," *New York Times* (24 February 1930); Nicolas Slonimsky, *Music since 1900* (New York: Coleman Ross, 1949); "Concert Programs for Current Week," *New York Times* (7 December 1930); according to Barth, Gershwin "felt that this Prelude should be written for quarter tones instead of half tones," letter to Bertha M. Mustain, 20 December 1954, courtesy of Michael Feinstein.

38. GG, letter to DuBose Heyward, 26 February 1934, GCLC; Steven Watson, *Prepare for Saints: Gertrude Stein, Virgil Thomson, and the Mainstreaming of American Modernism* (Berkeley: University of California Press, 1998), pp. 284, 286; "The Conning Tower," *New York Herald-Tribune* (27 February 1934) ("refreshing").

39. Howard Pollack, *Aaron Copland: The Life and Work of an Uncommon Man* (New York: Henry Holt, 1999), pp. 163–164; Elizabeth B. Crist, *Music for the Common Man: Aaron Copland during the Depression and War* (New York: Oxford University Press, 2005), p. 91.

40. Vernon Duke, *Listen Here! A Critical Essay on Music Depreciation* (New York: Ivan Obolensky, 1963), p. 54; DUK/PP, pp. 77, 90–91.

41. GG, letter to Ira Gershwin, 3 March 1926, ILGT; DUK/PP, p. 218; Duke, *Listen Here!* pp. 53–54.

42. Ellen Knight, *Charles Martin Loeffler: A Life Apart in American Music* (Urbana: University of Illinois Press, 1993); Ellen Knight, "Charles Martin Loeffler and George Gershwin: A Forgotten Friendship," *American Music* 3, no. 4 (Winter 1985): 453 (see also KS, p. 13).

43. Knight, *Charles Martin Loeffler*, p. 236.

44. Charles Martin Loeffler, letters to GG, 27 June 1927, 10 March 1928, 3 January 1932, GCLC.

45. Charles Martin Loeffler, letter to GG, 3 January 1932, GCLC.

46. DUK/PP, p. 223; "Stadium Filled as 17,000 Hear Gershwin Play," *New York Herald-Tribune* (17 August 1932), NYPA; LEV/SI, p. 151.

47. Among the many liberties the film takes, Levant appears chronologically much too early in the film; LEV/SI, pp 147, 160.

48. "Mr. Levant Discusses Mr. Gershwin," *New York Times* (8 July 1945); LEV/SI, p. 170.

49. ARM/GG, pp. 43–45.

50. LEV/SI, p. 184 (the "piano concerto" in question was presumably the *Concerto sinfonico*, which Koussevitzky premiered with the Boston Symphony Orchestra on 8 February 1935, Steinert playing the solo piano part).

51. Linda Whitesitt, *The Life and Music of George Antheil: 1900–1959* (Ann Arbor, MI: UMI Research Press, 1981), p. 112; Carol Oja, "Gershwin and American Modernists of the 1920s," *Musical Quarterly* 78, no. 4 (Winter 1994): 656.

52. George Antheil, *Bad Boy of Music* (New York: Da Capo Press, 1981), p. 179; G3 ("those compositions"); ARM/GG, pp. 115–119; George Gershwin–George Antheil correspondence, Rare Book and Manuscript Library, Columbia University.

53. ARM/GG, p. 117; GG, letter to George Antheil, 13 April 1936, Rare Book and Manuscript Library, Columbia University; FG, pp. 40–41.

54. Douglas Moore, letter to GG, 10 January 1936, Rare Book and Manuscript Library, Columbia University.

55. John McCauley, undated letter to Isaac Goldberg (ca. 1929), ILGT; David Diamond, interview by the author, 21 July 2001; Oja, "Gershwin and American Modernists," p. 661; Aaron Copland, "Contemporaries at Oxford, 1931," *Modern Music* 9, no. 1 (November–December 1931): 17–23; *Aaron Copland and His World*, ed. Carol J. Oja and Judith Tick (Princeton, NJ: Princeton University Press, 2005), p. 404 ("serious"); see also Pollack, *Aaron Copland*, pp. 163–164; Peter Dickinson (e-mail to the author, 16 July 2001) remembers Copland mentioning how "impressed" he and his friends were with the *Rhapsody in Blue*.

56. Oja, "Gershwin and American Modernists"; Alan Lincoln Langley, "The Gershwin Myth," *American Spectator* 1, no. 2 (December 1932): 1–2.

9. Gershwin and Popular Music and Jazz after 1920

1. AST, p. 266; EWE, pp. 103 ("the warmest"), 146 ("It will"); KIM/G, p. 66 ("I never"); BL, pp. 1–5; "A Young Gershwin as Role Model," *New York*

Times (7 January 1997): Burton, consciously following in Gershwin's footsteps, also left the High School of Commerce to take a job as a song plugger for Remick.

2. Maurice Zolotow, *It Takes All Kinds* (New York: Random House, 1944), p. 290.

3. MEY, p. 76; KS, p. 32.

4. DUK/PP, p. 397; BL, pp. 4, 9–10.

5. Peter Dickinson, *Marigold: The Music of Billy Mayerl* (New York: Oxford University Press, 1999), pp. 30, 58–66, 79, 120; Noël Coward, letter to Gershwin, 29 October 1924, ILGT; GG, quoted by Alan Hutchinson, "A Song-Writer Listens to Some Foreign Melodies," *Paris Comet* (July 1928), GCLC. Ira, who also attended *This Year of Grace,* admitted that it was "a great production for one man to do," and might have remembered another song from the show, "The Lorelei," for his own song so titled: Ira Gershwin, Diaries (23 March 1928), ILGT.

6. BOR/D, p. 33; MOR/MB, p. 112.

7. BOR/D, p. 94.

8. KIM/G, p. 203; LEV/SI, p. 183; Dorothy Rodgers, *My Favorite Things* (New York: Atheneum Publishers, 1964), p. 227. Although some commentators have claimed that Gershwin had followed Rodgers's work since the latter's Columbia University shows with Lorenz Hart in the early 1920s, a letter from Ira to George (1 April 1926, ILGT) suggests that the two did not really become aware of at least Hart until that date, which seems curious given the 1925 success of "Manhattan."

9. ROD, pp. 121–122; *Richard Rodgers: Letters to Dorothy,* ed. William W. Appleton (New York: New York Public Library, 1988), pp. 70, 102, 225 ("damn fools"); Alfred Simon, interview by Vivian Perlis, 10 May 1974, transcript, American Music Series, Yale University, p. 16.

10. William McBrien, *Cole Porter: A Biography* (New York: Vintage Books, 1998), p. 119; Stephen Citron, *Noel and Cole: The Sophisticates* (New York: Oxford University Press, 1993), p. 74; MEY, p. 76; KS, pp. 44, 47.

11. JOH, p. 245; MEY, p. 95; WIL, p. 253; Edward Jablonski, *Harold Arlen: Rhythm, Rainbows, and Blues* (Boston: Northeastern University Press, 1996), p. 114.

12. OHL, p. 52; Harry Evans, "Odds and Ends," *The Family Circle* (21 September 1934): 10 (Evans specifically mentions "negro harmony"); see also Richard M. Sudhalter, *Stardust Melody: The Life and Music of Hoagy Carmichael* (New York: Oxford University Press, 2002), pp. 166, 175, 180, 321; KIM/G, p. 66. Zolotow, *It Takes All Kinds,* implies that Gershwin met Carmichael before "Stardust," but it seems more likely that the two men became acquainted only after Carmichael moved to New York in the early 1930s. In his autobiography, *The Stardust Road & Sometimes I Wonder: The Autobiography of Hoagy Carmichael* (New York: Da Capo Press, 1999), p. 236, Carmichael mentions meeting Gershwin at Glaenzer's but relates a different anecdote about how Gershwin, after failing to interest the assembled guests in *Porgy and Bess,* resigned himself to yet another performance of the *Rhapsody;* the composer of "Stardust" could relate.

13. George Gershwin, interviewed by Rudy Vallee on *The Fleischmann*

Hour, 10 November 1932, *Gershwin Performs Gershwin: Rare Recordings 1931–1935* (Musicmasters 5062-2-C, 1991); BOR/JK, p. 361; ARM/GG, p. 120; Ronald Sanders, "The American Popular Song," *Next Year in Jerusalem: Portraits of the Jew in the Twentieth Century,* ed. Douglas Villiers (New York: Viking Press, 1976), p. 203.

14. RYS, p. 98 ("awe"); "Tales of Tin Pan Alley: 'Swanee' and Its Author," *Edison Musical Magazine* (October 1920): 9 ("more typically"); Charles Ludwig, "Banjo, up from Georgia, Elbows Lordly 'Cello" (March 1927), GCLC ("And to the list"); EWE, pp. 146–147; G4 (by "greatest songwriter," Gershwin presumably meant the greatest American songwriter).

15. JAB/GY, p. 102; ARM/GG, p. 78.

16. "Composer of a Thousand Songs Finds Radio Is Fast Pace-Maker," GCLC; Gershwin, RB.

17. Carl Van Vechten, "Memories of Bessie Smith," *Jazz Record* (September 1947): 7; Charles G. Shaw, *The Low-Down* (New York: Henry Holt, 1928), p. 156; Gershwin quoted by Hyman Sandow, "Latest Argument about the Jazz Age," *Every Week Magazine* (29–30 August 1931), GCLC.

18. John McCauley, "Stray Notes," ILGT ("loud"); Gershwin, RB, 25 November 1934 (for description of early jazz as "blatant and loud").

19. Joel Vance, *Fats Waller: His Life and Times* (Chicago: Contemporary Books, 1977); Maurice Waller and Anthony Calabrese, *Fats Waller* (New York: Schirmer Books, 1977), pp. 30, 144.

20. Waller and Calabrese, *Fats Waller,* pp. 136, 150; Richard Hadlock, *Jazz Masters of the Twenties* (New York: Collier Books, 1965), p. 156 ("was an attempt").

21. Dick Hyman, "George Gershwin 50 Years Later: Reevaluating His Legacy in Jazz," *Keyboard* (July 1987): 78–84 (for the Kentucky Club); Stuart Nicholson, *Reminiscing in Tempo: A Portrait of Duke Ellington* (Boston: Northeastern University Press, 1999), p. 79. John Franceschina, *Duke Ellington's Music for the Theatre* (Jefferson, NC: McFarland, 2001), p. 205 n. 10; Edward Kennedy Ellington, *Music Is My Mistress* (Garden City, NY: Doubleday, 1973), p. 77 ("invaluable").

22. "Immortal Gershwin Pays Tribute to the Duke," William Morris Agency Press Department (1946), courtesy of John Howland; LEV/SI, p. 190; Ellington, *Music Is My Mistress,* p. 106; Nicholson, *Reminiscing in Tempo,* p. 79.

23. Gunther Schuller, *Early Jazz: Its Roots and Musical Development* (New York: Oxford University Press, 1968), pp. 353–354; *The Duke Ellington Reader,* ed. Mark Tucker (New York: Oxford University Press, 1993), pp. 249–250.

24. Ellington, *Music Is My Mistress,* pp. 104–106.

25. Roger Pryor Dodge, "Negro Jazz," in his *Hot Jazz and Jazz Dance: Collected Writings, 1929–1964* (New York: Oxford University Press, 1994), pp. 3–8; *The Duke Ellington Reader,* pp. 57–65, 69–75, 114–118 (for Morrow); Constant Lambert, *Music Ho! A Study of Music in Decline* (London: Faber and Faber, 1934); see also Paul Allen Anderson, *Deep River: Music and Memory in Harlem Renaissance Thought* (Durham, NC: Duke University Press, 2001).

26. *The Duke Ellington Reader,* p. 116 n. 3; Walter van de Leur, *Something to Live For: The Music of Billy Strayhorn* (New York: Oxford University Press, 2002), pp. 16, 30.

27. Franco Fayenz, liner notes to *Earl Hines Plays George Gershwin* (Classic Jazz CJ 31, 1977).

28. LEV/SI, pp. 195–196.

29. Richard M. Sudhalter, *Lost Chords: White Musicians and Their Contribution to Jazz, 1915–1945* (New York: Oxford University Press, 1999), pp. 125, 135–136; SCH, p. 195; LEV/SI, p. 195; EWE, p. 148.

30. SCH/GS, pp. 175–206.

31. See the section "Gershwin's Writings" in the bibliography (according to Ira, Goldberg wrote the introduction to his book himself, LS).

32. GRE, p. 13 (for Bach and syncopation); G7, p. 52B ("improved"); G3.

33. G3, pp. 13–14; G9, p. 32.

34. A. Walter Kramer, "I Do Not Think Jazz 'Belongs,'" *Singing* 1, no. 9 (September 1926): 13–14; G10.

35. "Our Music Leads, Gershwin Asserts," *New York Times* (25 September 1932): 17 ("There are"); G1, p. 266 ("Basically"); "Gershwin, Prince of Jazz, Pounds Out Rhythm at Folly," *Charleston News and Courier* (19 June 1934).

36. G3, pp. 13–14.

37. GRE, p. 13 ("Europeans"); G7, p. 52B ("voice"); G1, p. 266 ("one thing"); "Jazz No Worse Than the Auto," *Montreal Herald* (6 January 1929).

38. G11, p. 30 ("superstition"); G7, p. 52B ("the voice"); G4, p. 46 ("roots deeply").

39. G11; in the same year (1925) Gershwin was even quoted as saying, "I cannot imagine a serious composer making use of jazz, but writers of jazz are already striving after the form and dignity characteristic of the high realms, and are, to some extent at any rate, succeeding," GRE, p. 13.

40. GG, quoted in "Our Music"; G11, p. 30 ("germinal state"); G1, pp. 264–265.

41. G9, p. 32; G11, p. 30 ("Indeed, when a conductor").

42. GRE, p. 14; G1, pp. 268–269.

43. AUS, pp. 162, 295, 320.

44. GRE, p. 14 (for quarter-tone pianos: "I do not think they are a success yet . . . not because of the defects of the instrument, but owing to the strangeness of the sounds"); FEI, pp. 63, 82.

45. G12. The idea of jazz or at least popular music as a kind of folk music appeared earlier, in Gershwin's 1930 introduction to Isaac Goldberg's book *Tin Pan Alley* ("Foster's tunes, which we now venerate as folk songs, were in their own day just popular songs"), but according to Ira (via Lawrence Stewart, LS), Goldberg, not Gershwin, actually wrote this introduction, which also claimed the waltz's "superiority" over dance rhythms in duple and quadruple time. In 1927 Paul Whiteman ("In Defense of Jazz and Its Makers," *New York Times Magazine* [13 March 1927]: 4) similarly spoke of jazz as "the folk music of the machine age."

46. "Gershwin on American Music" (1934), GCLC ("I want"); Ruth Ayers, "Gershwin Forgets His Rhapsody in Blue Long Enough to See Pitt Play Nebraska" (19 November 1934), GCLC ("I base"); Isabel Morse Jones, "Gershwin Analyzes Science of Rhythm," *Los Angeles Times* (2 February 1937) ("always hated").

47. GG, letter to Isaac Goldberg, 23 October 1929, Houghton Library, Harvard University; see R. W. S. Mendl, *The Appeal of Jazz* (London: Philip Allan,

1927). Mendl, incidentally, offers a brief discussion of the *Rhapsody*, along with jazz-related works by Leighton Lucas and Eric Coates, and concludes, "These compositions are to be regarded as in the nature of experiments. They are not striking works of art, but they open the door to further developments" (p. 180).

10. Working Methods

1. Ira Gershwin, "Words and Music," *New York Times* (9 November 1930).

2. ROS, p. 122 ("To me"); G6, pp. viii ("I can," "talent"), ix ("Like the pugilist"); G9, p. 32 ("Melodies"); ARM/GG, p. 239 ("I got right up").

3. "Talented Composer Gave Porgy Life and Rhythm," *News-Week* 6, no. 15 (12 October 1935): 22; Morris Hastings, "Confident George Gershwin," *The Microphone* (16 May 1936), GCLC ("It's just as"); G9, p. 32.

4. John Harkins, "George Gershwin," *Life* (August 1932): 13; KIM/G, p. 151 ("Once"); JAB, p. 285; G6, p. ix ("A beautiful").

5. G8, p. 2 ("Frequently"); G6, pp. viii–ix.

6. GER, pp. 225, 379; GOL, pp. 39, 139; Robert Wyatt, *The Piano Preludes of George Gershwin* (DMA diss., Florida State University, 1988), p. 23.

7. GOL, p. 251 ("small"); Samuel Chotzinoff, "Good Music," *Stage Magazine* (September 1935), GCLC; ARM/GG, p. 177 ("inelastic"); GGR2 ("piping"); BL, p. 7 ("nasal"); DUK/PP, p. 93; KIM/G, p. 181 ("awful"); WYA, p. 232 ("His voice"); ARM/GG, p. 239 ("to see").

8. NEI, pp. 137–144.

9. A. Walter Kramer, "I Do Not Think Jazz 'Belongs,'" *Singing* 1, no. 9 (September 1926): 13–14; G10; Alan Lincoln Langley, "The Gershwin Myth," *American Spectator* 1, no. 2 (December 1932): 1–2.

10. ARM/GG, pp. 30–31; SCH, pp. 81, 296 n. 20.

11. William King, "Gershwin Puts Dice to Music," *New York American* (31 July 1934) ("As a matter of fact," he stated, "I could have orchestrated the Rhapsody"); KS, p. 35; Dolly Dalrymple, "Pianist, Playing Role of Columbus, Makes Another American Discovery" (6 September 1922), GCLC ("Gershwin knows").

12. Virgil Thomson, "George Gershwin," *Modern Music* 13, no. 1 (November–December 1935): 18–19; for the reprint of this article see *A Virgil Thomson Reader* (Boston: Houghton Mifflin, 1981), pp. 23–27 (Thomson, as an afterthought, apparently changed "plum-pudding" to "gefiltefish," a popular Jewish appetizer); PEY, pp. 106, 164 ("messy"); see also SCH/GRB, p. 75; Maurice Peress, *Dvořák to Duke Ellington: A Conductor Explores America's Music and its African American Roots* (New York: Oxford University Press, 2004), pp. 75, 218–219; Wayne D. Shirley, "Scoring the Concerto in F: George Gershwin's First Orchestration," *American Music* 3, no. 3 (Fall 1985): 283.

13. KIM/G, p. 179.

14. WOD, pp. 36, 81; James Kenneth Randall, *Becoming Jerome Kern: The Early Songs and Shows, 1913–1915* (PhD diss., University of Illinois at Urbana-Champaign, 2004), p. 185 ("It is my opinion"); "Reformed Column Conductor and Architect Go 'Fifty-Fify,'" *Cleveland Leader* (24 June 1917); LOG, p. 498.

15. MCC, p. 150 ("In musical comedy you gain so tremendously in Act One if you can give your principal characters a *dramatic* entrance instead of just walk-

ing them on," commented Wodehouse in 1922); WOD, p. 9; Neil Simon, *Rewrites: A Memoir* (New York: Simon and Schuster, 1996), p. 44.

16. GG, letter to Isaac Goldberg, 30 June 1931, Houghton Library, Harvard University ("Ira and I are biding our time, waiting for Aarons and Freedley to deliver a book, which always seems like a difficult thing for them to do"); see also GG, letters to Mabel Schirmer, 28 October 1936, 18 September 1936, GCLC; FUR, p. 58; and see DAV/B, p. 211, for more on Guy Bolton's working method.

17. GER, p. 174.

18. Gershwin, "Words and Music."

19. GER, pp. 381–383; FUR, p. 21 (see also, for "lodgments," JAB/GY, p. 322); Murray Schumach, "17 Gershwin Songs Are to Be Released," *New York Times* (17 February 1964).

20. "Tales of Tin Pan Alley: 'Swanee' and Its Author," *Edison Musical Magazine* (October 1920): 9 ("Operettas"); Katharan McCommon, "Gershwin, King of Jazz Composers at 26, Says Piano Made Good Boy of Him," 1924, GCLC; Ashby Deering, "Brothers as Collaborators," *Morning Telegraph* (1 February 1925), GCLC; G6; G9, p. 32 ("combination"); Hyman Sandow, "Gershwin to Write New Rhapsody," *Musical America* (18 February 1928): 5; Jack Neiburg, manuscript extracts (ca. 1929), ILGT.

21. Gershwin, "Words and Music"; FEI, p. 80; ROS, p. 134 ("sublimated").

22. ROS, p. 81; RYS, p. 77.

23. GER, p. xvii; Gershwin, "Words and Music."

24. ROD, pp. 220–221; WIL, p. 217; note, however, that according to Stephen Sondheim, "Hammerstein . . . almost always wrote to well-known tunes. He just wouldn't tell Rodgers what they were. He would take operatic arias or whatever." "The Musical Theater: A Talk by Stephen Sondheim," *Dramatists Guild Quarterly* 8, no. 3 (1971): 19.

25. GER, pp. 360–361.

26. GOL, pp. 198–199; MCC, p. 128; GER, p. 360.

27. GOL, p. 192, states that Ira Gershwin did not use a lead sheet, though a 1925 source reports that he at least sometimes did: "Ira Gershwin Gives Views on Modern Lyric Writing," *Philadelphia Public Ledger* (6 December 1925); Ira Gershwin, "Which Comes First?" (25 October 1930), GCLC.

28. ARM/GG, p. 70.

29. Gershwin, "Words and Music"; see also "Ira Gershwin Gives Views."

30. GER, p. 66 ("All I"); KIM/G, p. 23 ("just to have").

31. George Gershwin, interviewed by Rudy Vallee on *The Fleischmann Hour,* 10 November 1932, *Gershwin Performs Gershwin: Rare Recordings 1931–1935* (Musicmasters 5062-2-C, 1991); DuBose Heyward, "Porgy and Bess Return on Wings of Song," *Stage* 13 (October 1935): 25–28; RYS, p. 77.

32. LEV/SI, p. 204; FEI, p. 67; GER, p. 271 ("more folksy").

33. SCH, p. 213; PEY, p. 28 ("When Ira"); GER, p. 106 ("If, once").

34. GER, p. 66 ("I like it"); GOL, pp. 201–202 ("for days"); Gershwin, "Words and Music" ("We are").

35. Isaac Goldberg, "The Gershwins—Study in Collaboration," *Jewish Ledger* (17 December 1937).

36. FUR, p. 5; PEY, p. 29.

37. FEI, pp. 162–189.

38. SCH/GS, p. 62.

39. G9, p. 32 ("no time"); G10, p. 18.

40. FER, p. 115 ("help in the form," "an undercurrent"); KIM/G, p. 40 ("attending to").

41. FER, p. 115 ("Most of"); Maurice DePackh, "A Plea for Better Orchestras" (letter to the dramatic editor), *New York Times* (3 February 1929), courtesy of George Ferencz ("help and advice"); Mark Tucker, "In Search of Will Vodery," *Black Music Research Journal* 16, no. 1 (1996): 137, 158–162.

42. Ronell quoted in PEY, p. 150; Ira Gershwin, description of photograph of William Daly, GCLC; SCH, p. 66; Rian James, untitled article (2 October 1932), GCLC ("cartoonist's"); "Rites Tomorrow for William Daly," *New York Times* (5 December 1936); "W. M. Daly Dies, Noted Musician," *Cincinnati Post,* GCLC; "William M. Daly Dies; Conductor and Composer," unattributed, GCLC; EWE, pp. 71–72; FER, p. 115.

43. LS (for Pincus); see also William Daly, letter to Gershwin, 13 September 1936, ILGT; Olin Downes, "A Program of Native Works," *New York Times* (9 August 1931) (for Daly as Gershwin's "favorite conductor"); TIO, p. 136; SCH, p. 66 ("my best friend").

44. "All-American Concert Heard by Stadium Audience," *Brooklyn Eagle* (14 August 1931), NYPA; Frances D. Perkins, "10,000 Applaud All-American List at Stadium," *New York Herald-Tribune* (14 August 1931), NYPL; H. T., "17,000 Hear Gershwin Program," *New York Times* (17 August 1932), NYPA ("particularly lively"); obituaries state that Daly died on 4 December at age forty-nine, but his Harvard transcript reveals that he was born on 1 September 1888, which would have made him forty-eight at the time of his death.

45. FER, p. 248 ("large, rotund"); JAB/GY, p. 223; William McBrien, *Cole Porter: A Biography* (New York: Vintage Books, 1998), p. 287.

46. McBrien, *Cole Porter,* p. 151; SCH, p. 361 n. 28; EWE, p. 266.

11. Gershwin the Man

1. SCH, p. 320 n. 29; see also "Gershwin Left $341,089 Estate to His Mother," *New York Herald-Tribune* (27 September 1938); HYL, p. 228; Universal Pictures Corporation, contract with George Gershwin and Harms, Inc., 3 October 1929, GCLC.

2. LEV/MA, p. 130; Isaac Goldberg, "Pocketful of Gershwiniana January, 1932," *Boston Evening Transcript* (30 January 1932).

3. An October 1921 Manhattan telephone directory reveals that the Gershwins arrived at 110th Street no later than that date; FG, p. 12; LS (for table tennis, not, as commonly reported, billiards room).

4. ARM/GG, p. 215; GG, letter to Rosamond Walling, 19 January 1929, GCLC.

5. LEV/SI, p. 181.

6. The house at 1019 North Roxbury was razed, over the objection of conservationists and Gershwin admirers, in August 2005: Martha Groves, "No Rhapsody on Roxbury," *Los Angeles Times* (12 August 2005).

7. Albert Glinsky, *Theremin: Ether Music and Espionage* (Urbana: University of Illinois Press, 2000); ARM/GG, pp. 235–247 (for Kutner); GG, letters to Rosamond Walling, 21 November 1929, 10 May 1930, GCLC; PEY, p. 284; Behrman refers to Mueller as Swedish, BEH, p. 254.

8. AG, p. 7; Frank B. Gilbreth, "Gershwin, Prince of Jazz, Pounds Out Rhythm at Folly," *Charleston News and Courier* (19 June 1934); LEV/MA, p. 129.

9. AG, p. 12 (for Miller and Donahue); Frances Gershwin, quoted by Alfred Simon, liner notes, *Frances Gershwin— "For George and Ira"* (Monmouth-Evergreen MES/7060, 1973); KS, pp 28–29.

10. GOL, pp. 11–12; Carolyn Anspacher, "From Tin Pan Alley to Top Hat Row; Still Going!" *San Francisco Chronicle* (13 January 1937) ("I'd like").

11. Hyman Sandow, "Gershwin Presents a New Work," *Musical America* 48, no. 18 (18 August 1928): 5; JAB, p. 185.

12. Dorothy Rosenthal, letter to the author, postmarked 25 June 2001 (concerning the relations between the Gershwins and the Botkins).

13. KIM/G, p. 154.

14. JAB, pp. 186, 187; "A Composer's Pictures," *Arts & Decoration* 40 (January 1934): 50.

15. Frank Crowninshield, "Introduction," *George Gershwin* (Marie Harriman Gallery, 18 December 1937–4 January 1938); ARM/GG, p. 139.

16. ARM/GGML, p. 68; JAB/GY, pp. 388–389.

17. "A Composer's Pictures," pp. 49–50; Crowninshield, "Introduction."

18. Henry Botkin, interviewed on the *Today Show* (4 June 1963), courtesy of Michael Feinstein; the dates of these paintings are perhaps in error, LS.

19. ALE, pp. 51, 52, 189; reviews of the Harriman exhibition in the *New York Times* (21 December 1937), *New York Sun* (24 December 1937), *New York Herald-Tribune* (26 December 1937), *Time* (27 December 1937), and the *New York World-Telegram* (31 December 1937) ("undeniable quality").

20. According to Donna M. Cassidy, *Painting the Musical City: Jazz and Cultural Identity in American Art, 1910–1940* (Washington, D.C.: Smithsonian Institution Press, 1997), Dove titled his *Rhapsody* paintings *Part I* and *Part II* based on the two sides of the 1924 Whiteman recording; Miguel Covarrubias, *Negro Drawings* (New York: Alfred A. Knopf, 1927).

21. GG, letters to Ira Gershwin, 23 November 1935, 2 December 1935, ILGT; see also José Barrios Sierra, "Conciertos y Recitales," *El Universal* (5 December 1935).

22. David Alfaro Siqueiros, *Me llamaban el coronelazo* (Mexico City: Grijalbo, 1977), pp. 299–302 (translation courtesy of Lois Zamora); Laurance P. Hurlburt, "The Siqueiros Experimental Workshop: New York, 1936," *Art Journal* 35, no. 3 (Spring 1976): 237–246; Philip Stein, *Siqueiros: His Life and Works* (New York: International Publishers, 1994), pp. 100–101; David Alfaro Siqueiros, letters to Gershwin, 13 October, 20 November, and 10 December 1936, ILGT.

23. Siqueiros, *Me llamaban;* Katharine Weber, "In a Painting, Gershwin Packed the House," *New York Times* (30 August 1998), sect. 2, pp. 30, 33, including identification of the known mini-portraits; for a good color reproduction, see KIM/G (note, however, that the picture's date is incorrect).

24. Henry Botkin, foreword to *The Arts Club of Chicago Exhibition of the George Gershwin Collection of Modern Paintings,* courtesy of the Arts Club of Chicago; S. J. Woolf, "Finding in Jazz the Spirit of His Age," *New York Times* (20 January 1929) ("element").

25. Ira referred to *My Body* as "Ira In His Gotkes" (Yiddish for "underwear"), LS.

26. Gershwin, letter to Ira Gershwin, 9 July 1924, ILGT; Charles G. Shaw, *The Low-Down* (New York: Henry Holt, 1928), pp. 154, 158; JAB, p. 170; JAB/GY, p. 23; KOL, p. 255; Bettina Mershon, "An Hour with George Gershwin" (December 1930), GCLC (for Kant et al.); G3 (for Amy Lowell); John Harkins, "George Gershwin," *Life* (August 1932): 15; ARM/GG, p. 177 ("as intelligently").

27. Robert Wyatt, *The Piano Preludes of George Gershwin* (DMA diss., Florida State University, 1988), p. 52 ("was interested"); ARV, p. 11 ("Anything").

28. Ira took some driving lessons "but abandoned the wheel because of the dirty looks from other drivers," LS; GG, letter to Rosamond Walling, ca. 10 February 1929, GCLC ("snappiest"); E. Y. Harburg, "Notes and Quotes from Ira's Friends," *ASCAP Today* 5, no. 3 (January 1972): 7; LEV/SI, pp. 154–155, 186.

29. TIO, p. 134; Isaac Goldberg, "In Memoriam: George Gershwin," *B'nai B'rith Magazine* (August–September 1937): 26.

30. GOL, p. 6; Goldberg, "In Memoriam," pp. 8, 26; GGR ("He was"). In an interview with Robert Wyatt (WYA, p. 236), Brown added, "And do you know the only thing that he feared? He was afraid not to be the person he was supposed to be," though in a letter to this author, 13 June 2004, she qualified these remarks, stating, "George Gershwin always wanted to live up to his *own* image of himself! I think . . . that he demanded of himself a high standard. But I never had the idea that he was *afraid* of anything."

31. PEY, p. 189; Irving Caesar, interview by Alfred Simon and Robert Kimball, American Music Series, Yale University, p. 12; Ethel Merman with George Eells, *Merman* (New York: Simon and Schuster, 1978), p. 46.

32. Bennett Cerf, "Trade Winds: In Memory of George Gershwin," *Saturday Review* 26, no. 29 (17 July 1943): 14, 16; TIO, p. 135; BEH, p. 245.

33. EWE (1956 ed.), p. 184, one of many variants of the Ruby story (worded slightly differently in EWE, p. 127); see JAB/GR, pp. 46, for two others, and 76 ("In spite"); Igor Stravinsky with Robert Craft, "Some Composers," *Musical America* 82, no. 6 (June 1962): 6.

34. George S. Kaufman and Moss Hart, *Six Plays* (New York: Modern Library, 1942), p. 196; MER, p. 489; Goldberg, "In Memoriam," p. 8.

35. Alexander Woollcott, "George the Ingenuous," *Cosmopolitan* (November 1933): 32–33, 122–123; BEH, pp. 249, 256; SUR, p. 73; PAY, p. 155; KIM/G, p. 168 ("something terribly"); DUK, p. 352.

36. ARM/GG, pp. 54–56 ("George was like"); S. N. Behrman, "Troubadour," *New Yorker* (25 May 1929): 27–29.

37. BEH, p. 245; KIM/G, p. 140 ("joyous"); TIO, p. 136; GGR ("Here I am"); ARM/GGML, p. 37 ("Deep in"); ARM/GG, p. 210 ("the thoughtfulness").

38. S. N. Behrman, *Let Me Hear the Melody!* (1951), NYPL.

39. Sandow, "Gershwin Presents," p. 12; Stravinsky, "Some Composers," p. 6; KS, p. 41; PAY, p. 84.

40. GOL, pp. 23–24; LEV/SI, p. 158 (the sentence mistakenly has "rusk" listed twice); KIM/G, pp. 47, 48, 178; "Talented Composer Gave Porgy Life and Rhythm," *News-Week* 6, no. 15 (12 October 1935): 22 ("He eats").

41. Nanette Kutner, "Radio Pays a Debt," *Radio Star* (February 1936); SCH, p. 240.

42. EWE, p. 267, reported, "Gershwin did not complete his analysis since he finally felt—as with all the other treatments physicians had been prescribing for him for years—that he was not being helped"; Gregory Zilboorg, letter to GG, 9 September 1936, GCLC.

43. "Dr. Gregory Zilboorg dies at 68; Noted Psychiatrist and Teacher," *New York Times* (18 September 1959); Stephen Becker, *Marshall Field III* (New York: Simon and Schuster, 1964), p. 135; ARM/GG, pp. 56–67; Steven Bach, *Dazzler: The Life and Times of Moss Hart* (New York: Alfred A. Knopf, 2001), p. 129; Lillian Hellman, *An Unfinished Woman* (New York: Little, Brown, 1969), p. 207.

44. Becker, *Marshall Field III*, pp. 234, 237–238; Roy Hoopes, *Ralph Ingersoll: A Biography* (New York: Atheneum, 1985), pp. 171–172 (regarding Zilboorg, Ingersoll stated, "from no other experience in my life have I felt so benefited"); Carl Rollyson, *Lillian Hellman: Her Legend and Her Legacy* (New York: St. Martin's Press, 1988), p. 157.

45. "Emanuel Play School Children Give Musicale," *New York Sun* (16 August 1929); GG, postcard to Emily Paley, 11 July 1934, GCLC; G14.

46. Ruth Ayers, "Gershwin Forgets His Rhapsody in Blue Long Enough to See Pitt Play Nebraska" (19 November 1934), GCLC; "Gershwin Goes Political after Chats with Rivera," *New York Post* (17 December 1935); GG, letter to Ira Gershwin, 2 December 1935, ILGT.

47. ROS, p. 203; GG, letter to Mabel Schirmer, 18 September 1936, GCLC (rally); Un-American Activities in California, p. 238, Gershwin FBI File, courtesy of the FBI (for Film and Photo League); GG, letter to his mother, 10 June 1937, GCLC (Gershwin refers to the labor leader as Martin, as opposed to Tom, Mooney, suggesting some vagueness about this particular issue); JAB/GY, p. 284; Frederick Kuh, "Top American Composers' Works Barred at U.S. Libraries Abroad," *Chicago Sun-Times* (26 April 1953); "'Gershwin's Music Subversive' Says Senator McCarthy," *Melody Maker* (13 June 1953); Garnett D. Horner, "Policy of Books Used Overseas Involves Authors' Reputation" (22 May 1953) and "Security Officer Drops Job of Checking Up on Authors" (23 May 1953), Gershwin FBI File.

48. Hellman, *An Unfinished Woman*, p. 207; BEH, p. 255; Behrman, *Let Me Hear the Melody!*

49. GG, letters to Julia Van Norman, 6 November 1936, 15 April 1937, GCLC; LEV/MA, p. 149.

50. KIM/G, pp. 203 (for Arlen), 205 (for Schirmer; see also JAB/GY, p. 287); George A. Pallay, letter to Irene Gallagher, July 1937, GCLC; Sigmund Spaeth, *Fifty Years with Music* (New York: Fleet Publishing, 1959), p. 242; EWE, p. 277; BEH, p. 253; see also *Yours, Plum: The Letters of P. G. Wodehouse*, ed. Frances Donaldson (London: Hutchinson, 1990), p. 66.

51. The performances of the concerto were on 10 and 11 February, and the literature disagrees over which of these two occurrences transpired on which of

the two evenings; Levant (LEV/MA, p. 145), an eyewitness, suggests that Gershwin blacked out on the tenth and had the olfactory hallucination on the eleventh, but that seems doubtful, as these symptoms presumably would have happened at the same time.

52. GG, letter to Frances Gershwin, 27 May 1937, GCLC; GG, letter to Rose Gershwin, 10 June 1937, GCLC; LEV/MA, p. 146. The medical literature on Gershwin's final illness is in some particulars contradictory; see Noah D. Fabricant, "George Gershwin's Fatal Headache," *Eye, Ear, Nose and Throat Monthly* 37 (May 1958): 332–334; Louis Carp, "George Gershwin—Illustrious American Composer: His Fatal Glioblastoma," *American Journal of Surgical Pathology* 3, no. 5 (October 1979): 473–478; Bengt Ljunggren, "The Case of George Gershwin," *Neurosurgery* 10, no. 6 (1982): 733–736; Allen Silverstein, "Neurologic History of George Gershwin," *Mount Sinai Journal of Medicine* 62, no. 3 (May 1995): 239–242; Allen Silverstein, "The Brain Tumor of George Gershwin and the Legs of Cole Porter," *Seminars in Neurology* 19, no. 1 (1999): 3–9; Gregory D. Sloop, "What Caused George Gershwin's Untimely Death?" *Journal of Medical Biography* 9 (February 2001): 28–30; Hélio A. G. Tieve et al., "As crises uncinadas de George Gershwin," *Arquivos de Neuro-Psiquiatria* 60, no. 2B (June 2002).

53. Pallay, letter to Irene Gallagher; for Leonore's alleged behavior during this time, see especially PEY.

54. Fabricant, "George Gershwin's Fatal Headache," p. 334.

55. PEY; BEH, p. 255 (is the unnamed friend mentioned at the bottom of the page Moss Hart as well?); see also Bach, *Dazzler*, p. 154 (note, however, that the altercation between Hart and Behrman, according to the latter, took place some days before Gershwin's death, not at the hospital, as Bach states); *Richard Rodgers: Letters to Dorothy*, ed. William W. Appleton (New York: New York Public Library, 1988), p. 239; Silverstein, "The Brain Tumor," p. 6.

56. Ljunggren, "The Case"; Silverstein, "Neurobiologic History"; PEY, p. 296; Sloop, "What Caused." Anne Brown, meanwhile, recalled Gershwin's complaint of a headache, the result of being hit in the head by a golf ball, around 1935, and added, "I have often wondered whether that blow by a golf ball had caused a tumor," WYA, p. 235.

57. DUK/PP, p. 352; "Gershwin Paid Final Tribute by Thousands," *New York World-Telegram* (15 July 1937); *Richard Rodgers*, p. 241 ("beautifully"); see also clippings, GCLC.

58. G. G., "Gershwin Concert Has Record Crowd," and other reviews of the August 9 memorial concert, archives, New York Philharmonic Orchestra.

59. *George Gershwin Memorial Concert* (North American Classics NAC 4001, 1998).

12. From "Ragging the Traumerei" to *The Capitol Revue*

1. Ira Gershwin, marginalia, GCLC; JAB, p. 12.

2. Ireene Wicker, WJZ radio broadcast, 25 September 1936, courtesy of Michael Feinstein; Michael Feinstein, e-mail to the author, 30 October 2004 (Gershwin wrote out the music for Rettenberg, but it was destroyed in a fire);

JAB/GY, p. 51. Praskins was very likely the same Leonard Praskins (1896–1968) who later had a notable career as a film and television scriptwriter.

3. GOL, pp. 66–67; JAB/G, p. 13; for the Finley Club program and Ira's recollection, and an unsubstantiated claim that Gershwin recorded the *Tango* with banjoist Fred Van Eps, see JAB/GY, p. 36; Christophe Maudot, *Gershwin: Porgy and Bess* (Paris: L'avant-scène opéra, 1987), p. 61, refers to the tango-like rhythm in "Bess" as a habanera rhythm, an intriguing connection in light of Gershwin's admiration for *Carmen.*

4. Sigmund Spaeth, "Spaeth Recalls Prophetic Tip to a Shy Youngster, Gershwin," *New York Herald-Tribune* (28 March 1942); Sigmund Spaeth, *Fifty Years with Music* (New York: Fleet Publishing, 1959), pp. 238–242. Gershwin composed various "novelettes" in his early years, including one he recorded in 1919, and another that survives only in fragmentary form.

5. GOL, p. 101; David A. Jasen and Trebor Jay Tichenor, *Rags and Ragtime* (New York: Seabury Press, 1978), p. 209 (for "Oriental Blues"); *Rialto Ripples* has also been arranged for a cappella SATB chorus by David Düsing (King of Prussia, PA: Theodore Presser, 2002); in the wake of Gershwin's death, Ernie Kovacs (1919–1962), apparently a great admirer, "cried for an entire night": Diana Rico, *Kovacsland: A Biography of Ernie Kovacs* (New York: Harcourt Brace Jovanovich, 1990), p. 24.

6. The title, "A Voice of Love," as written out in the surviving manuscript, actually has another word after "love," but it's indecipherable.

7. GOL, p. 85; RIM, pp. 1–2.

8. The Shuberts, who adopted the title *Passing Show* from a successful 1894 revue of the same name, produced *Passing Shows* every year from 1912 through 1924 (with the exception of 1920), and then again in 1932 and 1945.

9. Contract letter signed by George Gershwin, Murray Roth, and Sigmund Romberg, 8 March 1916, ILGT.

10. Review of the *Passing Show of 1916, Variety* (30 June 1916).

11. Draft of the *Passing Show of 1916,* Shubert Archives; NOR, p. 98, credits Dolly Hackett as singing "How to Make a Pretty Girl," but an 8 April 1917 program credits Jack Boyle; see also BLO, p. 563.

12. IC ("Good Little Tune"): Caesar sings both lost songs in this taped interview; Irving Caesar, interview by Alfred Simon and Robert Kimball, American Music Series, Yale University, p. 21; Irving Caesar, letter to Fred Astaire, 18 August 1978, courtesy of Michael Feinstein (for Leonard Bernstein).

13. IC ("We would have"); Caesar remembered writing "You-oo Just You" in 1915, stating, "that was one of the songs I was going to bring to Ford's attention"; but JAB/GY reports a copyright date of 21 October 1916.

14. JAB/GY, p. 58 ("to be"); KIM/CLIG, p. 4; "We're Six Little Nieces" must be the "sextette" that Ira refers to in his diary, KIM/G, p. 17; although the song's date is typically given as 1917, Ira's entry of 20 January 1918 suggests that the song was completed that month.

15. JAB/GY, pp. 60–61; Although Ira wrote a draft of this lyric before George began composing the music, a comparison of this draft (JAB/GY, pp. 58–59) with the finished product reveals that even here, Ira worked with and around George.

16. GOL, p. 101; WIL, pp. 124–125.

17. WIL, p. 126.

18. Although the secondary literature cites the use of only "Some Wonderful Sort of Someone" and "The Real American Folksong" in *Look Who's Here,* Gershwin, in an undated letter to Irving Caesar from Baltimore from late September 1918 (courtesy of Michael Feinstein), specifies the use of all three songs.

19. DAV/SF, p. 139.

20. Reviews of *Ladies First* in the *New York Times* (25 October 1918) and *Variety* (3 November 1918); Gershwin, undated letter to Irving Caesar; it's not clear whether Bayes ever actually performed "The Real American Folksong" in the show as opposed to private performances or concert performances; some sources report that Bayes continued to sing "Some Wonderful Sort of Someone" on Broadway, but the evidence is inconclusive; see also Lawrence Stewart, "The Gershwins—Words upon Music," *Ella Fitzgerald Sings the George and Ira Gershwin Song Book* (Verve 314 539 759–2, 1959, reissued 1998), pp. 42–43.

21. SEL, pp. 258–259.

22. Another song from late 1918—"There's Magic in the Air," with lyrics by Ira, possibly used or considered for use in this revue (GG, letter to Isaac Goldberg, 30 June 1931, Houghton Library, Harvard University, actually states that the song was used in the show, but it doesn't appear in the musical's "running order")—also turned up in *La-La-Lucille!* with new lyrics as "It's Great to Be in Love." Some sources identify "Magic in the Air" as the source for another song from *La-La-Lucille!*—"The Ten Commandments of Love"—but it does not seem likely that a single song would have provided the music for two different songs in the same show (JAB/GY, p. 66, states only that Gershwin derived "The Ten Commandments of Love" from some unnamed music from *Half-Past Eight*). Yet another song composed by the Gershwin brothers in late 1918, "If You Only Knew," provided some of the music for "Tee-Oodle-Um-Bum-Bo," also from *La-La-Lucille!* (Ira Gershwin, marginalia, GCLC).

23. Michael Feinstein, interview by the author, 10 April 2004, also identified a lost number from about this period composed with writer-actor Eddie Buzzell, "Tiny Chinee Little Girl."

24. *Half-Past Eight,* running order, GCLC; "The Playgoer," [Syracuse] *Post-Standard* (10 December 1918), courtesy of Wendy Bousfield, Syracuse University. In her set, Vane also performed an Italian aria, apparently from Verdi's *La Traviata,* though it was reported as *Il Trovatore* in the press.

25. KIM/G, p. 19; "The Playgoer."

26. GG, letter to Isaac Goldberg, 15 and 16 June 1931, Houghton Library, Harvard University.

27. "Old Pinero Farce Revived by Music," *Good Morning, Judge* clipping file, NYPL.

28. Irving Caesar, interview by Alfred Simon and Robert Kimball, American Music Series, Yale University, p. 1 ("a hit," "quite off"); SCH/GRB, p. 42.

29. "'The Lady in Red' Is Here," *New York Times* (13 May 1919); "The Lady in Red," unidentified review, GCLC.

30. Gershwin, RB, 12 March 1934.

31. John Corbin, "Drama," *New York Times* (27 May 1919).

32. Gershwin, RB, 12 March 1934.

33. Maurice DePackh, "A Plea for Better Orchestras," *New York Times* (3 February 1929), courtesy of George Ferencz. Saddler scored "The Love of a Wife" and DePackh, "Money, Money, Money!" "Our Little Kitchenette," and "The Ten Commandments of Love," GCLC. Yet another Gershwin arrangement by Saddler, "Japanese," a sprightly 2/4 version of the 6/8 chorus for "The Love of a Wife," also survives; discovered by Michael Feinstein ca. 1978 in the garage of arranger George Bassman among materials from the revue *Half-Past Eight,* the music—whose Asian gestures include some pentatonic flourishes and even a wink at *The Mikado*—might have been composed for that 1918 revue.

34. "New Musical Play a Riot of Color" ("From the rise") and "Plays and Players" ("danced with the chorus"), unidentified articles, GCLC; Percy Hammond, "'La La Lucille,'" GCLC; see also reviews of *La-La-Lucille!* in the [New York] *Daily Sun,* Charles Darnton in the *Evening World, Herald, Globe, Morning Telegraph,* John Corbin in the *Times,* Heywood Broun in the *Tribune, World* (all 27 May 1919), *Theatre Magazine* 30, no. 221 (July 1919): 16; and *La-La-Lucille!* clipping file, NYPL.

35. "*La La Lucille* Medley," Carl Fenton Orchestra (Brunswick 2012, 1919); "*La La Lucille* Medley," Van Eps Banta Trio (Emerson 503, 1919), both courtesy of Paul Charosh; while professing his great admiration for Gershwin (and Kern), Kander reported that when writing "Two Ladies," he "was inspired by listening to German vaudeville music of the 20's": John Kander, letter to the author (postmarked 13 February 2005).

36. "Capitol Theatre Opens to Throng," *New York Times* (25 October 1919); see also "Capitol," *Variety* (31 October 1919). Caesar's recollection, "Sixty girls danced to 'Swanee'; they had electric lights in their shoes," has been widely cited, though Caesar apparently confused the presentation of "Swanee" with that of "Come to the Moon."

37. *And Then I Wrote: Irving Caesar* (Coral CRL 57083, 1957) ("We had never"); Gershwin, RB, 23 February 1934 (Caesar typically claimed that he and Gershwin wrote the song "in about fifteen minutes or less"); KIM/G, p. 24 (for Wayburn; see also chapter 5).

38. WIL, p. 125; GIL, pp. 53–54.

39. For the Van Eps release, see Edward B. Moogk, *Roll Back the Years: History of Canadian Recorded Sound and Its Legacy: Genesis to 1930* (Ottawa: National Library of Canada, 1975), p. 70.

40. GIL, pp. 52–53.

41. "Tales of Tin Pan Alley: 'Swanee' and Its Author," *Edison Musical Magazine* (October 1920): 9 ("I am happy").

42. "Swanee," arranged by Robert Russell Bennett, NYPL, courtesy of John Howland; like many recordings of the song during this period, this stock arrangement juxtaposed the number's trio with the verse to Septimus Winner's "Listen to the Mockingbird"; George Ferencz, e-mail to the author, 19 January 2006 (for "Swanee" as Bennett's first Gershwin assignment).

43. "Jolson's $2,000 Highest Price Yet," *Variety* (30 April 1920).

44. GRA, pp. 21–23; Herbert G. Goldman, *Jolson: The Legend Comes to Life* (New York: Oxford University Press, 1988), p. 36 ("an *élan*"); SEL, p. 191.

45. Michael Feinstein, interview by the author, 10 April 2004 (for mention of the brothel, which Feinstein identified as run by Bessie Bloodgood, based on conversations with Irving Caesar).

46. Miles Kreuger, interview by the author, 16 July 2004 (for the Crescent Theatre, based on conversations with Irving Caesar); advertisement for "Swanee," *Variety* (24 January 1920).

47. SEL, pp. 74, 195.

13. From *Morris Gest's Midnight Whirl* to *The Perfect Fool*

1. "Midnight Whirl," *Variety* (2 January 1920) ("the usual"). As a rehearsal pianist for various Ziegfeld shows, Gershwin had probably worked with Davis, the popular "Yama Yama Girl," a Pierrot figure of ambiguous gender and sexuality; for one reading of the constructs of gender and sexuality represented by McCoy and other female Follies stars, see Linda Mizejewski, *Ziegfeld Girl: Image and Icon in Culture and Cinema* (Durham, NC: Duke University Press, 1999).

2. For some preliminary considerations of orientalism and Tin Pan Alley, see BAN; Charles Hiroshi Garrett, "Chinatown, Whose Chinatown? Defining America's Borders with Musical Orientalism," *Journal of the American Musicological Society* 57, no. 1 (Spring 2004): 119–173; and Aline Scott-Maxwell, "Oriental Exoticism in 1920s Australian Popular Music," *Perfect Beat* 3, no. 3 (July 1997): 28–57.

3. Reviews of *Midnight Whirl*, GCLC, including "'Aphrodite' Nightcap Needs Embroidery," unidentified ("well suited"); "'Midnight Whirl' Lavish," *New York Times* (29 December 1919); "Midnight Whirl," *Variety*.

4. JAB, p. 35.

5. Ryan Raul Banagale has transcribed this interlude (BAN, p. 43), and Richard Dowling, the entire roll (Boca Raton, FL: Masters Music Publications, 2005).

6. To take one detail, in measures 8 and 12, Gershwin indicates, in the manuscript, a "rallentando" (slowing down) followed by a "tenuto" (hold) on the last quarter-note; the printed edition presumes the two rallentandos (because there's an "a tempo" in measures 9 and 13), but only measure 12 indicates "rallentando," and neither measure indicates the "tenuto."

7. Ira Gershwin, preface, *Lullaby*, arranged for string orchestra (New York: New World Music, 1968).

8. GG, fragment, *A Piece for Four Strings*, courtesy of Michael Feinstein.

9. "Dere Mabel," *Variety* (19 March 1920); IC; Irving Caesar, interview by Alfred Simon and Robert Kimball, American Music Series, Yale University, pp. 19–20 ("talked," "There wasn't").

10. MOR/MB, p. 89.

11. BOR/AMR, pp. 75–76.

12. Because one section of "Mexican Dance" has the same tune as found in the chorus of Gershwin's 1921 song "Tomalé," presumably sung by Al Jolson, Ira Gershwin guessed that it may have been written for one of Jolson's Winter Garden shows: Ira Gershwin, marginalia, 14 May 1966, GCLC. But

the fact that the *Scandals* featured a Mexican scene, and that a surviving orchestration of "Mexican Dance" was scored by Frank Saddler, who orchestrated
the *Scandals of 1920,* would seem to suggest some connection with the latter
show.

13. For the notion that eclecticism and pastiche were congenial to Jewish-
American sensibilities, see Ronald Sanders, "The American Popular Song," *Next
Year in Jerusalem: Portraits of the Jew in the Twentieth Century,* ed. Douglas Villiers (New York: Viking Press, 1976), p. 202: "Pastiche is a gift of peoples who
live in culturally ambivalent situations. . . . In this vein Jewish and American culture came together with a resonance that is still being heard and will be for years
to come."

14. Reviews of the *Scandals of 1920* in the *New York Times* (8 June 1920),
New York Daily Clipper (9 June 1920), *Variety* (11 June 1920), *New York Dra-
matic Mirror* (12 June 1920); S. Jay Kaufman, "Round the Town," *New York
Globe* (1920), GCLC.

15. GER, pp. 188–189.

16. Reviews of *The Sweetheart Shop* in *Variety* (31 January 1920, 2 April
1920, 16 April 1920, 3 September 1920 ["sweet"]), *New York Times* (1 September
1920).

17. "'Broadway Brevities' Has Many Changes," *Variety* (17 September
1920); reviews of *Broadway Brevities of 1920* in the [New York] *Commercial,
Evening Telegram, Evening World, Herald, Morning World, Times,* and *Tribune*
(all 30 September 1920), *Variety* (8 October 1920), and *Theatre Magazine* 32
(December 1920): 371; "Providence Censor Cuts 'B'wy Brevities,'" *Variety* (14
January 1921) (note varied spellings of "Rensellear").

18. Some sources credit Gershwin with another number from the show, "I
Love to Dance," introduced by Teck Murdoch and others in a Times Square scene
in the first act, though the song's authorship remains uncertain; as for yet another song ascribed to Gershwin, "Love, Honor and O'Baby" (performed by Eddie Buzzell and Peggy Parker), James F. Hanley wrote the music; Joe Goodman
and Murray Roth, the lyrics.

19. Reviews of *Broadway Brevities* in the [New York] *Herald, Tribune,* and
Times.

20. Although "Something Peculiar" never made it into either of these later
shows, Ira went so far as to rewrite the original lyric as a paean not to jazz, but
to Mexican music; see KIM/CLIG, p. 9.

21. KIM/CLIG, pp. 7–10; "Piccadilly to Broadway," *Variety* (29 October
1929).

22. "'Snapshots of 1921' Rough-and-Ready Fun," *New York Times* (3 June
1921); reviews of *Snapshots* in *Variety* (29 July 1921) and *Theatre Magazine* (August 1921): 97–98; see also "'Snapshots' Ends," *Variety* (12 August 1921).

23. Ira Gershwin, letter to Melvin Parks, 29 July 1971, GCLC.

24. Review of *Blue Eyes* in *Theatre Magazine* (May 1921): 340.

25. Reviews of *Blue Eyes* in the *New York Times* (22 February 1921) and *Variety* (25 February 1921).

26. Ira Gershwin, marginalia (17 May 1966), GCLC.

27. Review of *A Dangerous Maid* in *Variety* (18 March 1921).

28. Reviews of *A Dangerous Maid* in the *Wilmington Morning News* (25 March 1921) and the [Baltimore] *Evening Sun* and *News* (both 29 March 1921).

29. Pittsburgh reviews of *A Dangerous Maid*, GCLC; "*Dangerous Maid*," *Variety* (13 April 1921); "*Dangerous Maid* Comes In," *Variety* (29 April 1921).

30. FUR, pp. 31–32.

31. The Gershwin literature attributes yet another *Scandals of 1921* song, "Mother Eve," to Gershwin and Jackson, but that was written by James F. Hanley, with words by Ballard MacDonald.

32. Kenneth MacGowan, "The New Play," *New York Globe* (12 July 1921); see also "George White's Scandals," *Atlantic City Press* (5 July 1921).

33. Reviews of *George White's Scandals of 1921* in the [New York] *American, Evening Journal, Globe, Herald, Sun, Times, Tribune*, and *World* (all 12 July 1921), and in *Variety* (15 July 1921); Stephen Rathbun, "The Broadway Theatres Are Now Having Their Quiet Summer Season" (1921), GCLC.

34. WIL, p. 126.

35. Reviews of *The Perfect Fool* in the [New York] *Times* (8 November 1921), *Herald* (9 November 1921), *Tribune* (10 November 1921), and *Variety* (21 October 1921 and 11 November 1921).

14. From *The French Doll* to *Our Nell*

1. Gershwin, RB, 14 April 1934.

2. Review of *The French Doll* in *Variety* (3 February 1922) ("sentiment"); "Irene Bordoni Is Star in Comedy with Songs," *The French Doll* clipping file, NYPL ("of a truly").

3. "Irene Bordoni," and other reviews of *The French Doll*, clipping file, NYPL; "Our Popular Song Writers," *Vanity Fair* (April 1923): 44; Charles Pike Sawyer, review of *The French Doll* in the [New York] *Mirror*, GCLC; "'The French Doll' Has Paris Touch," clipping file, NYPL.

4. Donald Spoto, *Marilyn Monroe: The Biography* (New York: HarperCollins, 1993), pp. 209–210; see also Adam Victor, *The Marilyn Encyclopedia* (Woodstock, NY: Overlook Press, 1999), p. 48; "BBC Frees Banned Song—for Teenagers," *London Evening Standard* (9 January 1960); GER, p. 262.

5. AST, p. 55.

6. "All to Myself" appears to be lost, but the music for the refrain of its British version—"All by Myself"—survives in the piano selections from *Stop Flirting*.

7. Review of *For Goodness Sake* in the *New York Sun* (22 February 1922); see also BIL, p. 52; WOD, pp. 198, 208.

8. The published version of the song by Harms in 1922 included only the verse and the chorus, while those issued the same year by Irving Berlin and Bourne included patter episodes as well; moreover, Harms's edition had Georgie Price's name on the cover, while Berlin's had a cover photo of Jolson, for whom, as Caesar remembered, the song originally was written: *And Then I Wrote: Irving Caesar* (Coral CRL 57083, 1957).

9. Henrietta Malkiel, "Scheherazade in West Virginia: Jazz Opera on Its Way," *Musical America* (25 April 1925): 3, 26 ("the crudeness").

10. GER, p. 178.

11. GER, p. 296.

12. Gershwin, RB, 9 March 1934 ("one of those"); KIM/G, p. 34; SCH/GRB, p. 44.

13. GG, letter to Isaac Goldberg, 15–16 June 1931, Houghton Library, Harvard University; see also Wayne D. Shirley, "Notes on George Gershwin's First Opera," *I. S. A. M. Newsletter* 11, no. 2 (May 1982): 8–10.

14. HYL, p. 156 (for White and *Shuffle Along*).

15. "White's 'Scandals' at the Globe," *New York Evening Telegram* (27 August 1922) (for Ryan); Buddy DeSylva, letter to GG, 25 November 1925, GCLC; for more on *Blue Monday Blues,* see Shirley, "Notes," and John Andrew Johnson, "Gershwin's Blue Monday (1922) and the Promise of Success," in SCH/GS, pp. 111–141.

16. Shirley, "Notes"; Johnson, "Gershwin's Blue Monday."

17. Reviews of *Blue Monday Blues* and *135th Street,* clipping file, NYPL and GCLC (see also Johnson, "Gershwin's Blue Monday," pp. 125–128); Shirley, "Notes," p. 10; JAB, pp. 50–51.

18. Reviews of *Blue Monday Blues,* including "White's 'Scandals' at the Globe" ("very seriously"); Johnson, "Gershwin's Blue Monday," pp. 126–127; GG, letter to Goldberg ("nigger opera"). For Gershwin's use of the word *nigger,* one might consider Randall Kennedy's discussion of Carl Van Vechten's contemporaneous use of the word: "Van Vechten, a key supporter of the Harlem Renaissance, had shown time and again that he abhorred racial prejudice, would do what he could to improve the fortunes of African Americans, and treasured his black friends. It was against this backdrop of achieved trust that [Langston] Hughes (and other black writers) rightly permitted Van Vechten to use *nigger* as so many African Americans have used it—as an ironic, shorthand spoof on the absurdity of American race relations": *Nigger: The Strange Career of a Troublesome Word* (New York: Pantheon Books, 2002), pp. 53–54.

19. RAY, pp. 119–129; reviews of *135th Street* by Oscar Thompson, *Musical America* (13 February 1926): 23, and Edmund Wilson, *New Republic* (13 January 1926): 218.

20. Reviews of *135th Street* by Olin Downes in the *New York Times* (31 December 1925), and Samuel Chotzinoff in the *New York World* (30 December 1925); OSG, pp. 183–185.

21. Johnson, "Gershwin's Blue Monday," p. 120. Regarding the film's treatment of the work, Oscar Levant reported that producer Jesse L. Lasky "felt it necessary to have a setback, a failure, for contrast and had had a very difficult time finding one": "Mr. Levant Discusses Mr. Gershwin," *New York Times* (8 July 1945); in fact, Gershwin had other setbacks and failures throughout his career.

22. Dolly Dalrymple, "Pianist, Playing Role of Columbus, Makes Another American Discovery" (6 September 1922), GCLC; EWE, p. 67.

23. The program spells the names "Mrs. Jimmie Barry" and "Jimmy Barry," as such.

24. "'Our Nell' Is Righted," *New York Telegram* (5 December 1922), and other Stamford, Hartford, and New York reviews of *Our Nell,* clipping file, NYPL and GCLC.

25. Reviews of *Our Nell* by James Whittaker in the *New York American* (6

December 1922), in the *New York Clipper* (13 December 1922), and by Kenneth MacGowan in the *New York Globe* (5 December 1922).

26. Reviews of *Our Nell* in the [New York] *Telegram, Telegraph, Times,* and *Sun* (all 5 December 1922); Ira Gershwin, letter to Benjamin Botkin, 12 January 1923, GCLC.

15. From *The Sunshine Trail* to *Sweet Little Devil*

1. Eve Golden, *Golden Images: 41 Essays on Silent Film Stars* (Jefferson, NC: McFarland, 2001), pp. 84–87; review of *The Sunshine Trail* in *Variety* (30 August 1923).

2. RIM, p. 58.

3. Reviews of *The Dancing Girl* in the *New York Evening Telegram* (25 January 1923) and *New York Clipper* (7 February 1923).

4. Review of *The Dancing Girl* in *Variety* (1 February 1923); Irving Caesar sang the refrain of "That American Boy of Mine" in a 1983 taped interview by Michael Feinstein (IC).

5. MOO, pp. 35–36 ("as hula-like"); reviews of *Jig-Saw!* in the *Times* (17 June 1920), *Era* (23 June 1920), and *Stage* (24 June 1920); "London Life Back to Normal," *New York Evening Sun* (25 January 1921) ("You can't"); GOL, p. 124 ("eager for").

6. GG, letter to Ira Gershwin, 18 February 1923, GCLC (see JAB/GY, p. 81, for facsimile).

7. Edgar Wallace, quoted in Margaret Lane, *Edgar Wallace: The Biography of a Phenomenon* (London: Hamish Hamilton, 1938), p. 218.

8. Reviews of *The Rainbow* in *Era* (11 April 1923) and *Daily Mail* (4 April 1923).

9. Reviews of *The Rainbow* in the *Daily Mail, Era, Stage,* and *Times,* (the latter two 5 April 1923); GOL, p. 126; GG, letter to Ira.

10. Review of *The Rainbow* in the *Times.*

11. Review of *The Rainbow* in *Stage* (de Courville apologized for this "contretemps"); "English Actor Creates Scene," *Variety* (5 April 1923); *New York Times* (8 April 1923).

12. "First Night Scene," *Daily Mail* (5 April 1923); "American Performances Cut in New Empire, London, Revue," *Variety* (12 April 1923); "American Artists Are Badly Treated at Empire, London," *Variety* (26 April 1923); "Americans Retiring from Empire Review," *Variety* (10 May 1923). According to MOO, p. 37, a week into the run, "the *Plantation Days* company began an entire show of their own at 5:15 and 11:15 each evening, sandwiching the main offering."

13. "Our Popular Song Writers," *Vanity Fair* (April 1923): 44.

14. Reviews of *George White's Scandals of 1923* in *Variety* (7 June and 21 June 1923), the [New York] *Evening Journal, Evening World,* and *Times* (all 19 June 1923), *New York Clipper* (27 June 1923), and *Life* (12 July 1923).

15. Julia West, "George White's 'Scandals of 1923' Is Really Gorgeous Spectacle," *Evening World* (19 June 1923); James Whittaker, "Fifth 'Scandals' Opens at Globe," *Scandals of 1923* clipping file, NYPL; Eugene Earle, "Winnie Wows 'Em!" in *The Movie Musical from Vitaphone to 42nd Street: As Reported in a*

Great Fan Magazine, ed. Miles Kreuger (New York: Dover Publications, 1975), pp. 150–151; for more on Lightner, see BAR, pp. 171, 192.

16. Reviews of *George White's Scandals of 1923* in the [New York] *Evening Journal* and *Evening World* (both 19 June 1923), *Variety* (21 June 1923).

17. Review of *Little Miss Bluebeard* in *Theatre Magazine* (October 1923): 50.

18. FUR, p. 32; Ned Rorem, "Living with Gershwin," *Opera News* (16 March 1985): 12.

19. Review of *Little Miss Bluebeard* in *Variety* (30 August 1923).

20. Review of *Nifties of 1923* in *Theatre Magazine* (November 1923): 56.

21. Reviews of *Sweet Little Devil,* GCLC (including unidentified Providence review ["blithe"]), and clipping file, NYPL; see also reviews in *Variety* (10 January and 24 January, 1924), [New York] *Evening Telegram, Herald, Times,* and *Tribune* (all 22 January 1924), [New York] *Evening Post* and *Evening World* (both 23 January 1924), [New York] *American, Sun,* and *World* (all 24 January 1924), [New York] *Daily News* (26 January 1924), *Christian Science Monitor* (31 January 1924), *Time* (4 February 1924): 12, *Life* (14 February 1924): 18, *Theatre Magazine* (March 1924): 70.

22. KIM/G, p. 35 ("SWEET"); review of *Sweet Little Devil* in the *New York Daily News; A Perfect Lady, Boston Evening Transcript* (21 December 1923).

23. Unidentified Boston and Providence reviews of *A Perfect Lady,* GCLC.

24. The verse of "You're Mighty Lucky" resurfaced in "Naughty Baby," while its lyric anticipated by about ten years "Luckiest Man in the World," from *Pardon My English* (1933).

25. ARM/GG, pp. 170–171.

16. The *Rhapsody in Blue*

1. Thomas A. DeLong, *Pops: Paul Whiteman, King of Jazz* (Piscataway, NJ: New Century Publishers, 1983).

2. Niven Busch Jr., "The Paid Piper," *New Yorker* (20 November 1926): 25–27.

3. Gunther Schuller, *Early Jazz: Its Roots and Musical Development* (New York: Oxford University Press, 1968), p. 192.

4. DeLong, *Pops,* p. 61; Paul Whiteman, "In Defense of Jazz and Its Makers," *New York Times Magazine* (13 March 1927): 22.

5. G10.

6. GOL, p. 140.

7. GOL, pp. 139–140.

8. ARM/GG; GGR2; HYL, p. 54.

9. RAY, pp. 78–79; see also Michael Feinstein, who, in an interview by the author, 10 April 2004, reported that Ira and Grofé took some credit for encouraging Gershwin's incorporation of the "Andantino" melody into the piece.

10. For a groundbreaking study of the structural use of the blues scale in *Rhapsody in Blue,* see NEI; see also, along these lines, the analysis of Milhaud's *Creation of the World* in Deborah Mawer, *Darius Milhaud: Modality and Structure in Music of the 1920s* (Brookfield, VT: Ashgate, 1997).

11. John Warthen Struble, *The History of American Classical Music: Mac-Dowell through Minimalism* (New York: Facts on File, 1995), p. 107; SCH/GS, pp. 97, 104 (for Starr); see also GIL; NEI; SCH/GRB.

12. DOU; for an early consideration of the *Rhapsody* in the context of Liszt and Tchaikovsky, see OSG, pp. 198–203.

13. GIL, pp. 57ff.; Arthur Maisel, "Talent and Technique: George Gershwin's Rhapsody in Blue," in *Trends in Schenkerian Research,* ed. Allen Cadwallader (New York: Schirmer Books, 1990), pp. 51–69; SCH/GRB, p. 27.

14. For instrumentation and a list of the personnel, see George Gershwin, *Rhapsody in Blue Commemorative Facsimile Edition,* ed. Jeff Sultanof (Miami: Warner Bros., 1987), duplicated, too, in SCH/GRB, p. 5. Some irregularities concerning this list need to be noted. First, the preface to this edition lists Gus Helleberg and Albert Armer as "tuba and string bass," but in the score, Grofé refers to the string bass and tuba part in the singular, and regularly instructs "change to tuba" or "change to string bass," suggesting a single player. Perhaps one bass player played this part throughout, while the other alternated between the two instruments. Note, too, that this list suggests that Henry Lange doubled on piano and celesta, whereas the score seems to require only one accompanying piano.

15. GOL, p. 161 (the passage in question is reproduced in KIM/G, p. 37); Maurice Peress, *Dvořák to Duke Ellington: A Conductor Explores America's Music and Its African American Roots* (New York: Oxford University Press, 2004), p. 91 (for Herbert).

16. GOL, pp. 140–142; John Tasker Howard, *Our American Music,* 3rd ed. (New York: Thomas Y. Crowell, 1954 [orig. 1929]), p. 448; Leonard Liebling, "Variations," *Musical Courier* 100, no. 20 (17 May 1930): 27; ARM/GG, p. 124.

17. Paul Whiteman and Mary Margaret McBride, *Jazz* (New York: J. H. Sears, 1926), p. 99 (*cake-eater* was twenties slang for a womanizer).

18. EWE/SGG, p. 98; Peress, *Dvořák to Duke Ellington,* p. 91 (for Gorman and the opening glissando); Whiteman and McBride, *Jazz,* p. 104; Lawrence Gilman, "Music," *New York Tribune* (13 February 1924); Grenville Vernon, "Music," *Theatre Magazine* 39, no. 5 (May 1924): 34.

19. Henry T. Finck, "Jazz Invades Aeolian Hall," *New York Evening Post* (13 February 1924); "The Heyday of the Jazzlings," *The Sun and the Globe* (13 February 1924); Olin Downes, "A Concerto of Jazz," *New York Times* (13 February 1924).

20. Downes, "A Concerto" (what Downes intended by "racially" is not clear from the article's context, but given the rhetoric of the day, he probably meant American); RAY, p. 85 ("When we"); Henrietta Straus, "Jazz and 'The Rhapsody in Blue,'" *Nation* 118 (5 March 1924): 263.

21. Whiteman and McBride, *Jazz,* pp. 106–110; JAB/GR, pp. 30–32; Downes, "A Concerto"; Gilman, "Music"; Straus, "Jazz"; Vernon, "Music"; see also W. J. Henderson, "Paul Whiteman's Concert Reveals the Rise of Jazz," *New York Herald* and Deems Taylor, "Music," *New York World* (both 13 February 1924); "Paul Whiteman's Brilliant Recital Says Jazz Craze Will Never Die," *Variety* (14 February 1924); and L. M. M., "An Experiment in Modern Music," *Billboard* (23 February 1924): 30.

22. CAR, pp. 549–554; RAY, pp. 87–110; David Schiff, in SCH/GRB, p. 104

n. 10, states that Carter attended the premiere, but in an e-mail to the author, 31 May 2005, reports that he actually attended this second performance.

23. KIM/G, p. 63 ("murdered"); Adele Astaire, letter to GG, undated (ca. 1926?), ILGT; SHI, pp. 58–59; DeLong, *Pops,* p. 116; JAB, pp. 139–140; RAY, pp. 162, 519, 579.

24. Edward Robinson, "George Gershwin: a Punster Turned Poet," *Fortnightly Musical Revue* 2, no. 1 (31 October 1928): 3–4; Paul Rosenfeld, *An Hour with American Music* (Philadelphia: J. B. Lippincott, 1929), p. 138.

25. F. Scott Fitzgerald, *Trimalchio: An Early Version of "The Great Gatsby,"* ed. James L. W. West III (New York: Cambridge University Press, 2000), pp. 33–42; idem, *The Great Gatsby,* ed. Matthew J. Bruccoli (New York: Cambridge University Press, 1991), pp. xxxvii, 33–41 (note that Fitzgerald removed the word *gigantic* from the phrase "gigantic orchestra leader").

26. William Saroyan, "Paris in an American," *Country Beautiful* (February 1963): 17–19.

27. Frank W. D. Ries, "Albertina Rasch: The Broadway Career," *Dance Chronicle* 6, no. 2 (1983): 95–137; idem, "Albertina Rasch: The Concert Career and the Concept of the American Ballet," *Dance Chronicle* 7, no. 2 (1984): 159–197; TIO, pp. 126, 128, 134.

28. For the performances by the Savoy Orpheans, see Peter Dickinson, *Marigold: The Music of Billy Mayerl* (New York: Oxford University Press, 1999), pp. 59–63; see also Andrew Youdell, "Storm Clouds: A Survey of the Film Music of Arthur Benjamin," *British Music* 18 (1996): 19, for claims that Benjamin, not Mayerl, gave this first concert presentation of the work; KIM/G, p. 64 ("a splendid ballet"); Ira Gershwin, Diaries (16 April 1928), ILGT.

29. Ernest Newman, "Summing Up Music's Case against Jazz," *New York Times* (6 March 1927) (see also "Jazz to Survive Says Gerschwin [*sic*]," *Montreal Daily Star* [6 January 1927]); "King Carol Asserts," ca. 1931, GCLC.

30. Hugo Leichtentritt, *Serge Koussevitzky: The Boston Symphony Orchestra and the New American Music* (Cambridge, MA: Harvard University Press, 1946), p. 57; DeLong, *Pops,* pp. 95–96; Michael H. Kater, *Different Drummers: Jazz in the Culture of Nazi Germany* (New York: Oxford University Press, 1992), pp. 91, 129; Hershey Felder, "Production Diary," www.georgegershwinalone.com/home/Home02.html (27 December 2005, for Spryczer); Michael J. Budds, ed., *Jazz & the Germans* (Hillsdale, NY: Pendragon Press, 2002), p. 180 (for Zimmermann).

31. BAR, pp. 181–187; RAY, pp. 233–249; John Murray Anderson, *Out without My Rubbers,* as told to and written by Hugh Abercrombie Anderson (New York: Library Publishers, 1954), pp. 122–126; Universal Pictures Corporation, contract with George Gershwin and Harms, Inc., 3 October 1929, GCLC (for original plans as a ballet); see also HIR, p. 53.

32. Review of *King of Jazz,* in the *New York Evening World* (5 May 1930); reviews of Gershwin at the Roxy, [New York] *Sun* (3 May 1930) and *American* (9 May 1930).

33. GG, letter to Rosamond Walling, 10 May 1930, GCLC; "Gershwin Plays His Rhapsody," *New York Sun* (7 May 1930).

34. RAY, p. 248; BAR, pp. 186–187; Gary Giddin, *Bing Crosby: A Pocket-*

ful of Dreams: The Early Years, 1903–1940 (New York: Little, Brown, 2001), pp. 212–213.

35. As to why Gershwin didn't rescore the work himself, David Schiff (SCH/GRB, p. 11) guesses that Grofé retained certain legal rights, while Michael Feinstein (interview by the author, 10 April 2004) suggests that he simply didn't have the time or the inclination to do so; Ray White, e-mail to the author, 26 January 2005 (for information about these later versions).

36. Joseph Edelstein, "Horowitz Calls Jazz Fun; He Even Plays It," GCLC; Silvestre Revueltas to Carlos Chávez, 20 August 1928, *Epistolario Selecto de Carlos Chávez,* ed. Gloria Carmona (Mexico City: Fondo de Cultura Económica, 1989), pp. 83–84 ("vale sombilla," "algo *modernísimo con acordes muy raros*").

37. Toni Charuhas, *The Accordion* (New York: Pietro Deiro Publications, 1955), p. 38, states that Gershwin permitted radio broadcasts of the *Rhapsody* only by Smelser, by organist Jesse Crawford, and by the Paul Whiteman Band.

38. Virgil Thomson, "It's About Time," *New York Herald-Tribune* (2 November 1942). The following year Thomson added, "I believe it to be incorrect and ineffective, when conducting the *Rhapsody in Blue,* to concentrate on climax-building at the expense of spontaneous lyricism. Efforts to make *William Tell* music out of it and Holy Grail music are equally, in my opinion, doomed to failure": "Landscape with Music," *New York Herald-Tribune* (11 July 1943).

39. Jonathan Sheffer, liner notes, *Gershwin: Complete Works for Piano and Orchestra* (Conifer Classics 75605 51342 2, 1998).

40. SCH/GRB, p. 22; see also David Schiff, "Ado over Plenty o' Nuttin'," *New York Times* (29 June 1997), in which he offers a more extensive defense for the accepted practice regarding this theme as opposed to the written score (or Gershwin's own performances).

41. G11.

42. Leonard Bernstein, *The Joy of Music* (New York: Simon and Schuster, 1959), pp. 52–62.

43. SCH/GRB, pp. 4–11.

17. The *Scandals of 1924, Primrose,* and *Lady, Be Good!*

1. Robert C. Benchley, "Mr. Ziegfeld—Meet Mr. White," *Life* 84 (31 July 1924): 18. See also reviews of *George White's Scandals of 1924* in *Variety* (25 June 1924 and 2 July 1924), [New York] *Herald-Tribune, Sun, Times,* and *World* (all 1 July 1924), Gordon Whyte, *Billboard* (12 July 1924), *Theatre Magazine* 39 (September 1924): 14; "'Scandals' Has More Humor Than Ever," clipping file, NYPL.

2. Benchley, "Mr. Ziegfeld"; WIL, p. 127.

3. Gershwin, RB, 26 February 1934 ("Ballard"); WIL, p. 128.

4. *George and Ira Gershwin: Standards & Gems* (Nonesuch 79498-2, 1998). The song appeared in other films, including *Rhapsody in Blue* (1945), as sung by Sally Sweetland, dubbing for Joan Leslie, and apparently Tom Patricola himself; *Lullaby of Broadway* (1951), as sung by Doris Day and Hal Derwin, dubbing for Gene Nelson; *Somebody Loves Me* (1952), as sung by Betty Hutton;

and *The Helen Morgan Story* (1957), as sung by Gogi Grant, dubbing for Ann Blyth.

5. Review of *Scandals of 1924* in the *New York Times;* Benchley, "Mr. Ziegfeld."

6. Ethel Merman, as told to Pete Martin, *Who Could Ask for Anything More* (New York: Doubleday, 1955), p. 90.

7. WOD, p. 233; FER, p. 114.

8. MCC, p. 127 ("Guy and I"); Ira Gershwin, Diaries (20 March 1928), ILGT.

9. JAB, pp. 79–80; GG, letters to Ira Gershwin, 22 and 25 July 1924, GCLC; on meeting Carter in 1928, Ira Gershwin described him as "charming, about 5 ft. 10; grey eyes; very soft manner," Diaries (20 March 1928), ILGT.

10. Considering that "Naughty Baby" would have suited the role of Elsie in *A Dangerous Maid,* the Gershwins may originally have prepared the song for that particular show.

11. Review of *Primrose* in *Era* (17 September 1924).

12. Review of *Primrose* in the [London] *Times* (14 September 1924) (assumption that Gershwin was English); "A Londoner's Diary," *London Standard* (6 September 1924) ("I have inserted"); for the alleged influence of Lionel Monckton, see Ethan Mordden, *One More Kiss: The Broadway Musical in the 1970s* (New York: Palgrave Macmillan, 2003), p. 80; WOD, p. 196 ("rose and stood").

13. Noël Coward, letter to Gershwin, 29 October 1924, ILGT; MOO, p. 40 ("in the show's").

14. Ira recalled that Gershwin intended the Pan ballet as a parody, Michael Feinstein, interview by the author, 10 April 2004.

15. Reviews of *Primrose* in the *Daily Express, Daily Graphic, Daily Mail, London Morning Post, Manchester Guardian, Times* (all 12 September 1924), *Sporting Life* (13 September 1924), *Era* (17 September 1924), *Stage* (18 September 1924), *Horse and Hound* and *Outlook* (both 20 September 1924); MOO, p. 40 (for Ira as George's "sister").

16. Review of *Primrose* in the *Outlook.*

17. Reviews of *Primrose* in the [Sydney] *Telegraph* (31 August 1925) and *Mail* (2 September 1925), [Melbourne] *Argus* (13 April 1925; 13 December 1926).

18. For photographs, see "Primrose," *Play Pictorial* 45 (July–December 1924): 112–130; Dale Harris, "Golden from Gershwin," *New York Post* (18 May 1987): 26; Tim Page, "The Lost Gershwins at Last," *New York Newsday* 2 (18 May 1987): 7–8.

19. Michael Feingold, "Goods and Disservices," *Village Voice* (10–16 December 2003).

20. GER, p. 5; GG, RB, 19 February 1934. Gershwin performs "The Man I Love" on a commercial release of this radio broadcast, *Gershwin Performs Gershwin: Rare Recordings 1931–1935* (Musicmasters 5062-2-C, 1991); yet another cut song, "The Bad, Bad Men"—a second-act trio for Watty, Dick, and Jeff—appeared in the Philadelphia tryout.

21. Paul Rosenfeld, "George Gershwin at Symphony Hall," *Boston Globe* (17 January 1927); MEL, pp. 388–389; ROS, p. 71. The song's lyric also proved grist for demagogic criticism of American popular music, as in S. I. Hayakawa's "Popular Songs vs. the Facts of Life," in *Mass Culture: The Popular Arts in Amer-*

ica, ed. Bernard Rosenberg and David Manning White (New York: Free Press, 1957), pp. 393–403.

22. "Will You Remember Me?" seems to have been the source, highly disguised, for part of "Linger in the Lobby."

23. Aaron Copland, "Jazz Structure and Influence," *Modern Music* 4 (January–February 1927): 9–14; GER, p. 173.

24. See ROS, p. 86, for more on this aspect of the score.

25. Reviews of *Lady, Be Good!* in the *New York Commercial* and *New York Sun* (both 2 December 1924) ("dainty," "elfin"); FER, p. 67.

26. AST, p. 128; GG, RB, 16 March 1934 ("miraculous").

27. Reviews of *Lady, Be Good!* in *Variety* (26 November 1924 ["below his sister"] and 3 December 1924), [New York] *Commercial, Sun, Telegram and Evening Mail, Times,* and *World* (all 2 December 1924), *Sun* (9 December 1924), and *Theatre Magazine* 40 (February 1925): 16; Charles G. Shaw, *The Low-Down* (New York: Henry Holt, 1928), p. 263 (for Adele's recollection); see also BIL, p. 58, and later reviews in *Canadian Magazine* 64 (July 1925): 164–166.

28. Review of *Lady, Be Good!* in the *Boston Transcript* (1 December 1925); Philip Hale, "'Lady, Be Good,' at Colonial," *Boston Herald* (1 December 1925).

29. "Musical Shows for Domestic and Foreign Trade," *New York Times* (6 June 1926), GCLC.

30. "Musical Shows" ("Like George"); Fred Astaire mistakenly gave Ira rather than Desmond Carter credit for "I'd Rather Charleston," writing that it "was one of Ira's best comic ideas suited to Adele" (AST, p. 135); liner notes, *Lady, Be Good!* Smithsonian American Musical Theater Series (New York: Columbia Records, 1977) ("To George").

31. E. A. Baughan, "Are We Dance Mad?" [London] *Daily News* (17 April 1926) ("Are we"); GG, RB, 16 March 1934.

32. AST, pp. 143–148.

33. *Lady, Be Good!* Smithsonian American Musical Theater Series.

34. *Lady, Be Good!* (New York: Elektra Nonesuch 9 79304–2/4, 1992); see Christopher Pavlakis, "'Lady, Be Good!' Revival," *Sonneck Society Bulletin* 13, no. 3 (Fall 1987): 105.

35. Jack Tinker, review of *Lady, Be Good!* in the *Daily Mail* (30 July 1992) ("blatantly"); Louis Snyder, "'Lady, Be Good!' Is Lively as Ever in Goodspeed Revival," *Christian Science Monitor* 66 (12 June 1974): 6; Claire Armistead, review of *Lady, Be Good!* in *Guardian* (1 August 1992); John Lahr, "The Theatre: City Slickers," *New Yorker* 70, no. 26 (22 and 29 August 1994): 110–112; Victor Gluck, "Lady, Be Good! in Concert," *Back Stage* (27 June 2003), courtesy of Mel Miller.

36. Donald Mitchell, "Concerts and Opera," *Musical Times* 97 (July 1956): 374–375.

18. *Short Story, Tell Me More,* and the Concerto in F

1. Samuel Dushkin, letter to Edward Jablonski, 19 January 1952, Jablonski-Stewart Collection, University of Texas.

2. Ira Gershwin contended that Dushkin arranged *Short Story* on his own: Michael Feinstein, interview by the author, 24 October 2004.

3. Alexander Woollcott, "Gershwinisms at the Gaiety," *New York Sun* (15 April 1925).

4. JAB, p. 95.

5. Fred Thompson and William K. Wells, *Tell Me More* (1925), ILGT; Woollcott, "Gershwinisms"; see also reviews of *Tell Me More* in the [New York] *Herald-Tribune, Telegram and Evening Mail, Times, World* (all 14 April 1925), *Evening World, Sun,* and *Variety* (all 15 April 1925), *Daily Mirror* (16 April 1925), *Daily News* (18 April 1925), *Amusements* (20 April 1925), *Billboard* (25 April 1925), *Daily News* (28 April 1925), *Commonweal* (27 May 1925): 80, *Life* (28 May 1925): 18, *Theatre Magazine* (July 1925): 16; GCLC.

6. KIM/G, p. 40 ("niftier"); *Daily News* (18 April).

7. Burns Mantle, "Another about Love and Then Milliners," *New York Daily News* (28 April 1925).

8. *Herald-Tribune* (14 April); unidentified review, GCLC.

9. Alan Dale, "'Tell Me More' at the Gaiety Is Inspiring Show," GCLC ("kid-glove").

10. *Herald-Tribune.* Tombes had some success in later years as a bit-part player in Hollywood, including the role of Mr. Milton in *Rhapsody in Blue.*

11. James P. Sinnott, "Easy to Hear More of 'Tell Me More,'" *New York Morning Telegraph* (14 April 1925); reviews of *Tell Me More* in the *Times, Sun,* and *Commonweal*; see also the reviews in the *World, Life,* and *Theatre Magazine.*

12. *Tell Me More* and *Tip-Toes* (New World Records 80598-2, 2001).

13. Reviews of the 1925 London production of *Tell Me More* in *Variety* (10 June 1925), *London Times*, GCLC; see also "Tell Me More!" *Play Pictorial* 47, no. 282 (26 May 1925): 33–48.

14. "Music and Drama," [Melbourne] *Argus* (19 July 1926).

15. James Camner, review of Gershwin's *Tip-Toes* and *Tell Me More, Fanfare* 25, no. 4 (March–April 2002): 119.

16. George Martin, *The Damrosch Dynasty: America's First Family of Music* (Boston: Houghton Mifflin, 1983), p. 284 ("He has played").

17. Martin, *The Damrosch Dynasty,* p. 289; "A Piano Concerto," *New York Times,* and "N.Y. Symphony Waxes Modern This Week; Gershwin Plays His Concerto," *New York Herald-Tribune* (both 29 November 1925) ("knight"); Howard Pollack, *Skyscraper Lullaby: The Life and Music of John Alden Carpenter* (Washington, D.C.: Smithsonian Institution Press, 1995), p. 243 ("the outstanding"; Damrosch furthermore described Carpenter as "among the most American of our composers," p. 118).

18. GOL, p. 205 ("Many persons").

19. "Gershwin Bros.," *Time* (20 July 1925) ("growing"); "Gershwin," *Time* (4 May 1925): 13; for a chronology of Gershwin's activities in July 1925, see SCH, p. 107.

20. KIM/G, p. 52.

21. SCH, p. 113.

22. GIL, p. 91; KIM/G, p. 52 ("four or five"; to yet another reporter he said, "I got out my books and studied up on the 'concerto' style and then wrote," suggesting that he had already owned such books: "Gershwin Versatile Composer" [ca. 29 November 1925], GCLC); "N.Y. Symphony" ("Charleston rhythm").

23. John Warthen Struble, *The History of American Classical Music: Mac-Dowell through Minimalism* (New York: Facts on File, 1995), p. 108.

24. Jessie McBride, "The New Prophet of American Music," *Washington News* (24 November 1925) ("almost Mozartian"); "N.Y. Symphony" ("a poetic").

25. GIL, p. 107.

26. "N.Y. Symphony" ("an orgy").

27. Jack Neiburg, manuscript excerpts (ca. 1929), ILGT ("In my songs").

28. Wayne D. Shirley, "The 'Trial Orchestration' of Gershwin's Concerto in F," *Notes* 39 (March 1983): 570–579; "Scoring the Concerto in F: George Gershwin's First Orchestration," *American Music* 3, no. 3 (Fall 1985): 277–298 ("a good job," p. 281); "George Gershwin Learns to Orchestrate," *Sonneck Society Bulletin* 16 (1990): 101–102 (one of the more notable alterations—changing the opening meter from 4/4 to cut-time—seems to have been made initially by Damrosch, but in any case had been incorporated by the time of the 1927 edition for two pianos).

29. Reviews of the Concerto in F in the [New York] *Evening Journal* and *Sun* (both 4 December 1925); Morton Gould, liner notes to the Gershwin Concerto in F (RCA LM-2017, 1956).

30. Reviews of the Concerto in F in the [New York] *Evening Journal, Evening World, Herald-Tribune, Sun, Telegraph, Times, World* (all 4 December 1925), *Musical Courier* (10 December 1925), *New Yorker* (12 December 1925), *Outlook* (16 December 1925), *New Republic* (23 December 1925), *Nation* (13 January 1926), *Musical America* (13 February 1926), *Musical Quarterly* (April 1926), and others, GCLC; Tim Freeze, "Toward a Reception History of Gershwin's *Concerto in F*, 1925–1937," paper delivered at the national meeting of the Society for American Music, 14 March 2004, courtesy of the author. Freeze notes that early reviews, in discussing the concerto's use of jazz, used rhetoric similar to Damrosch's including (in Freeze's words) "making an outlaw fit for society, purifying an individual through the donning of religious garb, making a flapper honest through marriage, grafting a branch onto a trunk, dressing up a doll in nice clothes, and launching a military invasion."

31. Reviews of the Concerto in F in the [New York] *Times* and *Tribune* (both 27 December 1926); Charles L. Buchanan, "Gershwin and Musical Snobbery," *Outlook* (2 February 1927).

32. "4,079 Bury Blue Law Here at Gershwin's Concert" (20 November 1934), GCLC.

33. Charles Ludwig, "Banjo, up from Georgia, Elbows Lordly 'Cello" (March 1927) ("I think"); reviews of the Concerto in F in the [Chicago] *American, Examiner, Tribune* (all 15 June 1933); Ralph Lewando, "Symphony Buries Blue Laws, Hangs Up S.R.O. at Recital," GCLC ("A master").

34. Richard D. Saunders, "Screen Celebrities Put Show on as Gershwin's Symphonic Fare Heard," [Hollywood] *Citizen-News* (11 February 1937); Paul Rosenfeld, "Musical Chronicle," *Dial* (February 1926): 173–175; idem, *An Hour with American Music* (Philadelphia: J. B. Lippincott, 1929), p. 138–139; idem, "No Chabrier," *New Republic* (4 January 1933): 217–218; idem, *Discoveries of a Music Critic* (New York: Harcourt, Brace, 1936), pp. 264–272; Herbert Elwell, "Overflows Hall to Hear Gershwin," *Cleveland Plain Dealer* (21 January

1934); Virgil Thomson, "George Gershwin," *Modern Music* 13, no. 1 (November–December 1935): 13–19; idem, *Music Right and Left* (New York: Greenwood Press, 1951), pp. 111–112; Frederick Jacobi, "The Future of Gershwin," *Modern Music* 15, no. 1 (November–December 1937): 6.

35. Gould, liner notes.

36. J. Douglas Cook, "Gershwin Music True Interpretation of American Culture, Says Tiomkin," GCLC ("an actual"); Ira Gershwin, Diaries, ILGT (29 May 1928); Louis Schneider, "Tiomkin's Concert Introduces Gershwin Composition to Paris," GCLC ("a barbarous"); Emile Vuillermoz, "Gershwin's Concerto in Paris," *Christian Science Monitor* (7 July 1928).

37. G. C., review of the Concerto in F, *Gazzetta di Venezia* (9 September 1932), GCLC (translation courtesy of Mario Inglese).

38. Thomas A. DeLong, *Pops: Paul Whiteman, King of Jazz* (Piscataway, NJ: New Century Publishers, 1983), pp. 122–123; William Youngren, "Gershwin, Part II, Concerto in F," *New Republic* (30 April 1977): 27–30; for a current appraisal of the Beiderbecke versus Margulis question, see RAY, pp. 208–210, 212.

39. Evan Rapport, "The Idea of Hybridity in the Music of Bill Finegan and George Gershwin," annual meeting of the Society for American Music, 16 March 2005.

40. Gertrude Prokosch Kurath, "George Gershwin's Concerto in F at the Yale School of Drama," *Dance Research Journal* 20, no. 1 (Summer 1988): 44–45.

41. Anna Kisselgoff, "Jerome Robbins," *New York City Ballet Program Book* (May 1982), NYPL ("urban"); idem, "City Ballet: New Robbins 'Gershwin,'" *New York Times* (4 February 1982); idem, "Dance: 'Gershwin,' by City Ballet," *New York Times* (4 February 1986); Jennifer Dunning, review of Wilson's Concerto in F in the *New York Times* (28 March 1994).

42. Arlene Croce, "Dancing," *New Yorker* 58, no. 1 (22 February 1982): 99–103 (Croce exaggerates when she writes, "Gershwin had no conception of ballet or of modern dance, which was just then beginning to be known in this country," for he had some familiarity with the work of choreographers as different as Michel Fokine, Albertina Rasch, George Balanchine, Anton Dolin, Ruth Page, and, as mentioned, Gertrude Kurath, and he very likely saw the Ballets Russes and possibly Isadora Duncan as well); FG, pp. 36–37.

19. *Tip-Toes* and *Song of the Flame*

1. Guy Bolton and Fred Thompson, *Tip-Toes* (1925), GCLC.

2. GER, p. 120.

3. GER, p. 120.

4. GER, p. 9; Ward Morehouse, "Ira Gershwin Likes That Other Coast," *New York World Telegram* (29 May 1953).

5. For "We," see EWE, p. 105 (Ira Gershwin informed Ewen, "After the first week on the road one of the songs was taken away from her [MacDonald]," but whether he meant the duet "We" or some other song is not clear; KIM/CLIG, p. 76, states that "We" was dropped during rehearsals); Edward Baron Turk, *Hollywood Diva: A Biography of Jeanette MacDonald* (Berkeley: University of California Press, 1998), p. 49 ("ingratiating").

6. According to Robert Kimball (interview by the author, 16 January 2004), "Dancing Hour" may have been an instrumental dance number as opposed to a song.

7. W. M., "'Tip-Toes,' With Gershwin Tunes, Is Frisky Show," *New York Herald-Tribune* (29 December 1925); "'Tip Toes' Here with Tunes," *New York Times* (29 December 1925).

8. "'Tip Toes' Here"; Alexander Woollcott, "Mr. Gershwin's Latest," *New York Evening World* (29 December 1925); see also reviews of *Tip-Toes* in the *Newark Star-Eagle* (1 December 1925), *Baltimore Sun* (22 December 1925), *Brooklyn Daily Eagle,* [New York] *Daily News, Evening Post, Herald-Tribune, Sun* (all 29 December 1925), *Wall Street News* (1 January 1926), *Amusements* (3 January 1926), *Billboard* (9 January 1926), *Variety* (13 January 1926), *Commonweal* 3, no. 11 (20 January 1926): 301, *Vogue* (15 February 1926).

9. Woollcott, "Mr. Gershwin's Latest"; KIM/G, p. 55 ("Your lyrics"); Ira Gershwin, letter to GG, 1 April 1926, ILGT.

10. *Broadway: The American Musical* (New York: PBS, 2004) ("dazzling"); reviews of *Tip-Toes* in the [San Francisco] *Bulletin, Call and Post,* and *Chronicle* (all 6 July 1926).

11. "'Tip-Toes' Opens in London," *New York Times* (1 September 1926); "Tip-Toes," *Play Pictorial* 296, no. 49 (June–December 1926): 70–88; review of *Tip-Toes,* [London] *Times* (1 September 1926). The London program does not specify any other composers for either "Pig in a Poke" or "At the Party."

12. Reviews of *Tip-Toes* in the [Sydney] *Daily Telegraph* and *Morning Herald* ("cheerfully") (both 9 May 1927), *Mail* (11 May 1927), *Just It* (12 May 1927): 16 ("hideous"), [Melbourne] *Argus* (15 August 1927) ("more subdued"). Thurza Rogers took over the principal lead in Melbourne.

13. Review of *Tip-Toes,* [Paris] *Figaro* (28 April 1929), translated by the author ("Elle [Hégoburu] a fait du rôle de Tip-Toes [sur la pointe des pieds] une création délicieuse, touchante. . . . A cet égard, G. Gershwin nous paraît le plus favorisé des musiciens actuels. Il mérite sa réussite. Car il sait écrire, orchestrer, avoir des trouvailles, une inspiration et un talent dignes d'un admirateur de Puccini ou de Massenet. Mais il connaît aussi les ressources, les dosages, les dangers des importations nouvelles dans le domaine des sons devant la scène et il en tire le meilleur parti. M. Auric, musicien du plus brillant avenir, peut aller l'entendre sans perdre son temps.")

14. Reviews of *Tip-Toes* by Ernest Leogrande, *New York Daily News* (2 May 1978), Rex Reed, *New York Daily News* (3 May 1978), Mel Gussow, *New York Times* (3 May 1978), Clive Barnes, *New York Post* (17 May 1978), *Variety* (24 May 1978), Martin Gottfried, *Saturday Review* 5, no. 24 (16 September 1978): 35, Clive Barnes, *New York Post,* Mel Gussow, *New York Times,* and Douglas Watt, *New York Daily News* (all 27 March 1979), John Beaufort, *Christian Science Monitor* (28 March 1979), *Variety* (4 April 1979), John Simon, *New York Magazine* (9 April 1979): 93–94; Michael Feingold, *Village Voice* (9 April 1979), and Edith Oliver and Arlene Croce, *New Yorker* 55, no. 8 (9 April 1979): 99–100, 147–153.

15. Stephen Holden, "Audacious Social Climbing in a '25 Gershwin Soufflé," *New York Times* (15 May 1998); the score, wrote Holden, "at its perkiest conveys a compressed frenzy of euphoria."

16. Oscar Hammerstein II, "Voices versus Feet," *Theatre Magazine* (May 1925): 14, 70.

17. Hammerstein, "Voices" ("smart musical"); Richard Traubner, *Operetta: A Theatrical History* (Garden City, NY: Doubleday, 1983), p. 377 ("full-blooded").

18. Hugh Fordin, *Getting to Know Him* (New York: Random House, 1977), p. 64; see also JAB, p. 115.

19. FEI, p. 174 (for Stothart's collaborations).

20. Otto A. Harbach, "The Writing of a Musical Comedy," *Theatre Magazine* (November 1925): 10, 54, 56; see also Fordin, *Getting to Know Him*, pp. 43–44.

21. I am indebted to Andrew Lamb for providing me with the Lecocq and von Suppé examples, though as Lamb points out, "such precedents dealt with distant events, and it was a bold stroke on Hammerstein's part to choose so recent an event as the Bolshevik revolution": e-mail to the author, 9 February 2005; Otto Harbach and Oscar Hammerstein II, *Song of the Flame*, I-25, II-3, GCLC.

22. GOT, p. 75; Larissa Jackson, interview by the author, 14 September 2004 (for "You Deceived Me").

23. Robert Russell Bennett, letter to GG, 23 March 1920, ILGT, courtesy of George Ferencz; FER, pp. 67, 93.

24. FER, pp. 77–78 ("turned his"); Fordin, *Getting to Know Him*, p. 64 ("conceited"); KIM/G, p. 59 ("was very attractive").

25. Reviews of *Song of the Flame* in the *Wilmington Evening Journal* (11 December 1925), [Washington] *Herald* and *Post* (both 15 December 1925), *Baltimore Sun* (22 December 1925); [New York] *Daily News, Evening Graphic, Evening Post, Evening World, Herald-Tribune, Mirror, Sun, Telegram, Times* (all 31 December 1925), *Variety* (6 January 1926), *Judge* (30 January 1926): 16, 30, *Vogue* (1 March 1926): 75, 106, *Theatre Magazine* (March 1926): 16, 18, *Bookman* (March 1926): 80–81, [Boston] *Globe, Herald, Transcript, Traveler* (30 November 1926). See also clipping file, NYPL, including review by Alan Dale.

26. See the review in *Variety,* and Frank Vreeland's review for the *Telegram* for assumptions concerning the respective contributions of Gershwin and Stothart.

27. BAR, p. 108; Gershwin, RB, 14 October 1934; see also HIR, p. 50 (Akst and Clarke wrote "Petrograd," "Liberty Song," "The Goose Hangs High," "Passing Fancy," and "One Little Drink"; Ed Ward contributed "When Love Calls").

28. Reviews of *Song of the Flame* in the *New York Times* (7 and 11 May 1930), *Variety* (14 May 1930), *Time* (19 May 1930), *Commonweal* (28 May 1930), *Life* (6 June 1930), *Photoplay* (July 1930). See BRA, pp. 185–187.

29. In addition, there were silent-film musicals based on shows for which Gershwin had composed at least some of the music, including *Miss Bluebeard* (1925) and *Stop Flirting* (1925).

30. Michael G. Garber, "Silent Film Musicals: The Exploration of an Oxymoron," paper delivered at the Third Triennial Susan Porter Memorial Symposium (Boulder, CO, 2 August 2001); Mordaunt Hall, "A Bootlegging Farce," *New York Times* (27 August 1928) ("As is"; by "longer," Hall possibly meant more

involved, for he also writes of the film's "extraneous absurdities"); review of *Tip Toes*, *Variety* (8 June 1927).

31. Garber (for *The Student Prince*); cue sheets for *Lady Be Good* and *Oh, Kay!* courtesy of Michael Feinstein; the former cue sheet uses "Fascinating Rhythm" (three times), "Oh, Lady Be Good!" (once) and "So Am I" (once); the latter uses "Oh, Kay!" (four times), "Fidgety Feet" (twice), and "Do, Do, Do" (twice); both cue sheets use Gershwin tunes for the main titles.

32. Review of *Oh, Kay!* in *Variety* (29 August 1928); the British Film Institute houses a print of *Tip Toes*, the George Eastman House, one of *Oh, Kay!*

20. *Oh, Kay!* and Other Works

1. Reviews of *Americana* in the [New York] *Evening Sun*, *Times* (27 July 1926), *Theatre Magazine* (October 1926): 16.

2. For some critical response to the song, see GER, p. 185.

3. Sheridan Morley, *Gertrude Lawrence* (New York: McGraw-Hill, 1981), p. 58 ("She dances"); WOD, p. 286.

4. LOG, p. 732.

5. WOD, p. 209; EWE, p. 116; JAB, p. 126.

6. Gertrude Lawrence, *A Star Danced* (Garden City, NY: Doubleday, Doran, 1945), pp. 132–134, 177; GER, p. 220.

7. WOD, p. 221.

8. P. G. Wodehouse, "A Nostalgic Look at 'Oh, Kay!' of '26," *New York Herald-Tribune* (10 April 1960); WOD, p. 236 ("Moore's diffident").

9. WOD, p. 233 ("With the"); Guy Bolton, "Gertie Lawrence in 'Oh, Kay,'" typescript, p. 4, GCLC ("gay").

10. GER, pp. 111–112; Howard Dietz, *Dancing in the Dark* (New York: Quadrangle, 1972), p. 74.

11. For a more complete synopsis, see Wayne D. Shirley, liner notes to *Oh, Kay!* (Washington, D.C.: Smithsonian American Musical Theater Series, R011–RCA, 1978).

12. Guy Bolton and P. G. Wodehouse, *Oh, Kay!* (New York: Tams-Witmark, 1926), pp. 1-1–14, 2-1–21.

13. Bolton and Wodehouse, *Oh, Kay!* p. 1-1–41.

14. Jack Neiburg, manuscript extracts (ca. 1929), ILGT ("To my way"). Gershwin continued, "I get a great 'kick' out of using, as bass, the simple tonic and dominant, in musical comedy songs. How do I get my variety? By introducing into the melody, or the upper harmony, an unexpected note—a note that doesn't belong to the chord—a surprise, or spice, as it were, that enlivens the whole composition. Of course, this device may be employed in the rhythms of the music, playing off accents against one another."

15. Gershwin, RB, 5 March 1934.

16. Shirley, liner notes to *Oh, Kay!*

17. Michael Feinstein, interview by the author, 10 April 2004 (for "Someone to Watch Over Me" as a fast number).

18. Bolton, "Gertie Lawrence," pp. 2–3 (for placement of "Do, Do, Do"); DON, p. 236 ("He had no").

19. *Star!*—the 1968 biopic of Gertrude Lawrence starring Julie Andrews—offered a fabricated account of the Raggedy Ann story.

20. Reviews of *Oh, Kay!* in the [New York] *Evening World, Herald-Tribune, Post, Sun, Telegram, Times,* and *World* (all 9 November 1926), *New Yorker* (20 November 1926): 33, *Vogue* (1 January 1927): 100–102; Lawrence, *A Star Danced,* p. 173.

21. Reviews of *Oh, Kay!* by Frank Vreeland in the *Telegram* ("suavely"), Stephen Rathbun in the *Sun* ("dainty"), and Percy Hammond in the *Herald-Tribune* ("a marvel").

22. Review of *Oh, Kay!* in the [London] *Times* (22 September 1927); see also Morley, *Gertrude Lawrence,* pp. 66–67; "London Theatre Fees Queue Waiting to See American Play," *New York Times* (22 September 1927); "Oh, Kay!" *Play Pictorial* 51, no. 309 (21 September 1927): 94–112; Ira Gershwin, Diaries (24 March 1928), IGLT.

23. Review of *Oh, Kay!* in the *San Francisco Examiner* (11 October 1927); Grace Davidson, "More Serious Things Replace Love Songs and Dances Now, Says Composer Gershwin," *Boston Post* (3 October 1933) ("the best").

24. Magnus Blomkvist, e-mail to the author, 8 August 2005 (the Swedish *Oh, Kay!* which managed only ten performances, had less success, however, than the 1982 Swedish premiere of *Of Thee I Sing* in Linköping, which ran for eighty performances); reviews of *Oh, Kay!* in the [New York] *Herald-Tribune, Journal-American, Mirror, Post, Times* (all 18 April 1960), *Variety* (4 May 1960).

25. Reviews of *Oh, Kay!* in the *New York Times* (22 October 1989), *Hartford Courant* (23 October 1989), *New York Times* and *Variety* (both 1 November 1989) ("crass"), *Springfield Union News* (10 November 1989) ("mediocre").

26. Reviews of *Oh, Kay!* in the [New York] *Post, Times,* and *Newsday* (all 2 November 1990), *Variety* (5 November 1990), *Wall Street Journal* (7 November 1990), *Time, New York,* and the *New Yorker* (all 12 November 1990), *Village Voice* (13 November 1990), *Christian Science Monitor* (15 November 1990). The Cotton Club was a fashionable Harlem nightclub that for a while featured Duke Ellington's band; *Amos 'n' Andy* was a highly popular midcentury radio and television show in which two white actors, Freeman Gosden and Charles Correll, played Amos and Andy, two comic black characters.

27. "Playbill On-Line's Brief Encounter, with Joe DiPietro" (26 June 2001), ILGT; see also Bonnie Goldberg, "Joe DiPietro Is in Search of the Perfect Comedy," *Middleton* [Connecticut] *Press,* ILGT.

28. Alvin Klein, "A Not-So-New Gershwin Musical," *New York Times* (12 August 2001); Christopher Arnott, "Same Old Song and Dance," *New Haven Advocate* (2–8 August 2001), ILGT.

29. Mary Ellis, *Those Dancing Years: An Autobiography* (London: John Murray, 1982), p. 51.

30. "Pastor and Singer Debate over Jazz," *New York World* (7 May 1926); "Rev. Dr. Straton Jumps on Jazz," *New York Sun* (7 May 1926); G4. D'Alvarez is often quoted as saying she wanted Gershwin's "jazz concerto played over my grave," as in ARM/GG, p. 125.

31. Robert Wyatt, *The Piano Preludes of George Gershwin* (DMA diss., Florida State University, 1988), p. 37; see also idem, "The Seven Jazz Preludes

of George Gershwin: A Historical Narrative," *American Music* 7, no. 1 (Spring 1989): 68–85.

32. Carl Van Vechten, "George Gershwin: An American Composer Who Is Writing Notable Music in the Jazz Idiom," *Vanity Fair* 24, no. 1 (March 1925): 78.

33. Wyatt, *The Piano Preludes,* p. 20.

34. Wyatt finds no evidence of a performance in Buffalo, but the GCLC contains an undated review of a performance at Buffalo's Elmwood Music Hall sponsored by the Chromatic Club, "Gershwin Wins Acclaim Here," *Buffalo Evening Times;* P. R. [Paul Rosenfeld], "George Gershwin at Symphony Hall," *Boston Globe* (17 January 1927).

35. Wyatt, *The Piano Preludes,* pp. 64–67; *Gershwin Performs Gershwin: Rare Recordings 1931–1935* (Musicmasters 5062-2-C, 1991) ("sort of blue lullaby"); Heinrich W. Schwab, "Zur Rezeption des Jazz in der komponierten Musik," *Dansk Aarbog for Musikforskning* 10 (1979): 127–178, especially 151–153.

36. For transcripts of numerous reviews of the *Five Preludes,* see Wyatt, *The Piano Preludes,* pp. 138–153; these include reviews in the [New York] *Herald-Tribune* ("polite"), *Times, World* ("trifling") (all 5 December 1926), [New York] *Evening Journal* and *Evening World* (both 6 December 1926), *New Republic* (29 December 1926), *Christian Science Monitor,* [Boston] *Evening American, Globe* ("sketchy"), *Herald, Post* (all 17 January 1927). Although the critics widely praised d'Alvarez's dramatic presence and rich voice, they disagreed over her abilities in the area of musical-comedy song; a few also criticized her intonation.

37. Whereas the manuscript to the Prelude in C♯, marked "Andante con moto e poco rubato," indicates "a tempo" at the start of the middle section, preceded by a "ritard," the published version dispenses with the ritard and offers a new tempo marking, "Largamente con moto," at the start of the key change, thus undermining the uniformity of tempo presumably desired by Gershwin—as indicated, too, by his recording of the piece (musicians generally interpret "largamente" as slower than "andante").

38. Gershwin played the Prelude in C♯ faster than commonly done (quarter note = 116 on the Rudy Vallee show on November 10, 1922), with quarter notes often prominently detached: *Gershwin Performs Gershwin;* Josefa Heifetz, liner notes, *Heifetz: Gershwin and Encores* (BMG Classics, 1994); Herbert R. Axelrod, ed., *Heifetz,* 2nd rev. ed. (Neptune City, NJ: Paganiniana Publications, 1981 [orig. 1976]), p. 518.

39. Peter Heyworth, ed., *Conversations with Klemperer* (London: Victor Gollancz, 1973), p. 70; idem, *Otto Klemperer: His Life and Times,* vol. 2: *1933–1973* (Cambridge, Eng.: Cambridge University Press, 1979), p. 79; JAB/GY, p. 275.

40. *George Gershwin: Michael Tilson Thomas* (CBS Records MK 39699, 1985); *Gershwin: Remembrance and Discovery* (Centaur CRC 2271, 1995).

21. *Strike Up the Band* and *Funny Face*

1. Gershwin, RB, 25 November 1934.

2. MER; Howard Teichmann, *George S. Kaufman: An Intimate Portrait* (New

York: Atheneum, 1972); Malcolm Goldstein, *George S. Kaufman: His Life, His Theater* (New York: Oxford University Press, 1979); Rhoda-Gale Pollack, *George S. Kaufman* (Boston: Twayne Publishers, 1988); Jeffrey D. Mason, *Wisecracks: The Farces of George S. Kaufman* (Ann Arbor, MI: UMI Research Press, 1988).

3. George S. Kaufman, "Music to My Ears," *Stage* 15 (August 1938): 27–30; Ira Gershwin, letter to Max Wilk, GCLC.

4. RYS, p. 76; MER, p. 405 ("the funniest").

5. Laurence Maslon, "George S. Kaufman: The Gloomy Dean of American Comedy," liner notes to *Strike Up the Band* (Elektra Nonesuch 79273–2, 1991).

6. Kaufman, "Music to My Ears," p. 20.

7. Kaufman, "Music to My Ears," pp. 29–30.

8. Reviews of *Strike Up the Band* in the [Philadelphia] *Evening Bulletin, Evening Public Ledger,* and *Inquirer* (all 6 September 1927), *Variety* (7 September 1927).

9. "Changed 'Band,'" *Variety* (14 September 1927); "'Band' Taken Off," *Variety* (21 September 1927); Tommy Krasker, "What Price Cheese?" liner notes to *Strike Up the Band* (Elektra Nonesuch 79273–2, 1991); JAB/GY, pp. 125–126 ("That must be").

10. "Theatre Asides," *Stage* 11, no. 3 (December 1933): 26–27; RYS, p. 76 ("brilliant").

11. RYS, p. 79 (for Dickens).

12. A synopsis of the revised *Strike Up the Band* follows: Workers at the Horace J. Fletcher Chocolate Works greet foreman Timothy Harper (Gordon Smith), manager Richard K. Sloane (Robert Bentley), and owner Horace J. Fletcher (Dudley Clements) ("Fletcher's American Chocolate Choral Society"). Exultant over passage of a 50 percent American tariff on Swiss chocolate, Fletcher regards this legislation as a personal triumph over his daughter Joan's boyfriend, muckraking journalist Jim Townshend; Fletcher would prefer that his daughter marry Sloane. Mrs. Grace Draper (Blanche Ring), a local matron who has set her sights on marrying Fletcher, enters with her sassy daughter, Anne (Doris Carson), who asks Timothy, her boyfriend, for reassurances that he loves her ("I Mean to Say"). Joan (Margaret Schilling) and Jim (Jerry Goff) arrive, as do two of Jim's investigative assistants, identified in the program as "Two Men about Town" (Bobby Clark and Paul McCullough). Jim interviews Fletcher, who prides himself on his success ("A Typical Self-Made American"). Jim and Joan look forward to married life ("Soon"). Hearing that Colonel Homes, a presidential advisor in town on a visit, has spoken with Jim and has moved to repeal the chocolate tariff, an enraged Fletcher collapses, and his doctor (Maurice Lapue) orders quiet solitude.

Fletcher's dream follows: Holmes (Bobby Clark) arrives at the chocolate factory ("A Man of High Degree" and "The Unofficial Spokesman"), accompanied by his right-hand man, a marine named Gideon (Paul McCullough). Eager to publish another memoir, Holmes accepts Fletcher's offer to pay for a war against the Swiss. The local citizenry gather for a nighttime rally at Fletcher's home ("Patriotic Rally," including "Three Cheers for the Union" and "This Could Go On for Years"). A flirtatious Mrs. Draper encourages Holmes to run for the presidency ("If I Became the President"). Jim and Joan arrive (reprise of "Soon"), as do Timothy and Anne, the latter eager to get married before the former leaves for war ("Hangin' Around with You"). After being served a glass of Fletcher's milk, Jim, familiar with dairy products, accuses the manufacturer of duplicitously using Grade-B milk in his chocolate (as in the original show, Joan expresses her displeasure with Jim, who's reviled by the crowd) ("He Knows Milk"). As Congress declares war, a disgusted Jim dons a uniform and leads all in a parade ("Strike Up the Band").

In Switzerland, American soldiers prance about with some Swiss girls ("In the Rattle of the Battle" and "Military Dancing Drill"). Jim, now a captain, accuses Sloane (now a colonel and engaged to Joan) of treason and is placed under arrest by Fletcher. As Mrs. Draper has failed to entice either Fletcher or Holmes (now both generals), Timothy suggests to Anne that they try to lure Gideon into marrying her mother by telling him that she's worth millions. Holmes and Gideon flirt with some local girls ("Mademoiselle in New Rochelle"). Fletcher, his resources dwindling, can't understand why there hasn't been a battle yet—little realizing that Sloane is sabotaging the war effort, abetted by a Swiss innkeeper, Herr Konrad (Lapue). Timothy and Anne express their mutual affection ("I've Got a Crush on You"). Presuming that Mrs. Draper is wealthy, Fletcher, Holmes, and Gideon all woo her ("How About a Boy?"). Fletcher's secretary, Myra Meade (Ethel Kenyon), dreams of marrying a soldier ("I Want to Be a War Bride"), and Holmes prepares his men for battle ("Unofficial March of General Holmes," also known as "Soldiers' March"). Jim helps win the war and unmasks Sloane as Herman Edelweiss of the Swiss secret service. As Sloane fires at Jim, Fletcher imagines that he has been shot and awakens from his sleep.

Interpreting his dream as an omen, Fletcher gives his approval to his daughter's marriage to Jim. The chorus summarizes the action ("Official Résumé"). A triple wedding—for Jim and Joan, Timothy and Anne, Fletcher and Mrs. Draper—ensues ("Ring-a-Ding-a-Ding-Dong Dell"). Hearing of Russian protests against an American tariff on caviar, Fletcher, who has just bought shares of American Caviar, calls for a resolute response (reprise of "Strike Up the Band").

The Gershwins and Ryskind—at least at the time of the revised 1929 script—seemingly intended "I Want to Be a War Bride" to be sung by Anne in the spot in which "Hangin' Around with You" eventually appeared, but the song ultimately was used in the second act as a number for Kenyon, a principal backer of the show (Ira recalled that during the second week of the New York run, Kenyon "eloped with a Hollywood director without giving notice to the management. Neither she nor song ever returned," KIM/CLIG, p. 158); "Ring-a-Ding-a-Ding-Dong Dell" first appeared during the tryouts of *Oh, Kay!* as "Ding-Dong-Dell," where it was sung by the principals near the end of the second act, but it was cut before the New York opening; for rehearsal footage of *Strike Up the Band*, see Fox Movietone (unidentified) and Hearst Metrotone (1/225) newsreels, UCLA film archive.

13. RYS, p. 79.

14. SCH, p. 186, ROS, p. 207; MOR/MB, pp. 203–204 ("mostly unnecessary").

15. Review of *Strike Up the Band* in the *New York World* (15 January 1930) ("it was almost"). For the Red Nichols personnel used in the pit, see D. Russell Connor, *The Record of a Legend: Benny Goodman* (New York: Let's Dance Corp., 1984), p. 26; Richard M. Sudhalter, "And You Should Have Heard the

Hot Stuff They Played," liner notes, *Girl Crazy* (Elektra Nonesuch 9 79250-2, 1990), pp. 51–55; and Robert L. Stockdale, *Jimmy Dorsey: A Study in Contrasts* (Lanham, MD: Scarecrow Press, 1999), p. 146.

16. Reviews of *Strike Up the Band* in the *Brooklyn Daily Eagle,* [New York] *Evening World, Herald-Tribune, Sun, Telegram, Times,* and *World* (all 15 January 1930), *Variety* and Richard Watts Jr., "Sight and Sound," *New York Herald-Tribune* (both 22 January 1930), *Billboard* (25 January 1930): 44, *New Yorker* (25 January 1930): 27–28, *Outlook* (19 January 1930): 191, *Life* (7 February 1930): 18, *New Republic* (12 February 1930): 328, *Town and Country* (15 February 1930): 44, *Nation* (19 February 1930): 226, *Theatre Magazine* (March 1930): 48, *Commonweal* (16 April 1930): 687–688, *America* (26 April 1930): 68, *Christian Century* (8 July 1931): 899–901.

17. *Strike Up the Band* (Elektra Nonesuch 79273-2, 1991); *Strike Up the Band* vocal score, prepared and edited by Steven D. Bowen (Warner Brothers Music Corporation, 1998).

18. Reviews of *Strike Up the Band* in the *Philadelphia Inquirer* (28 June 1984), *New York Times* (11 July 1984), *Los Angeles Herald-Examiner* and *Orange County Register* (both 8 August 1988), *New York Post* (8 December 1995), *Theater Week* 9, no. 20 (1995): 34–37.

19. *Richard Rodgers: Letters to Dorothy,* ed. William W. Appleton (New York: New York Public Library, 1988), p. 41; AST, p. 152–154; "Building the Successful Musical Show," *New York Times* (4 December 1927).

20. GER, p. 24; AST, p. 154; "Building the Successful"; Gershwin, RB, 20 April 1934.

21. Paul Gerard Smith and Fred Thompson, *Funny Face* (1927), ILGT, 2-4-40.

22. Review of Ruth Selwyn's *Nine Fifteen Review* in the *New York Times* (12 February 1930); for the unused songs from *Funny Face* see Robert Kimball (KIM/CLIG, pp. 108–112); however, Kimball's claim that "Are You Dancing?" was originally written for *Girl Crazy* (p. 169) seems questionable, for the names of the two characters on the lyric sheet ("June and Chesty"), and even something of the musical style itself, mark *Funny Face* as its more likely source.

23. WIL, p. 139; on the song's amenability to jazz improvisation, see C. André Barbera's commentary in SCH/GS, p. 200.

24. GER, p. 25 (for "bromide"); FEI, p. 99.

25. Review of *Funny Face* in the *New York American* (23 November 1927).

26. Reviews of *Funny Face* in the [New York] *American, Daily News, Evening World, Herald-Tribune, Sun, Times, World* (all 23 November 1927), *Variety* (30 November 1927), *Billboard* and *New Yorker* (both 3 December 1927), *Commonweal* (14 December 1927): 817, *Life* (22 December 1927): 19, *Vogue* (15 January 1928): 118, 120, *Theatre Magazine* 47, no. 323 (February 1928): 58.

27. "'Funny Face' a London Hit," *New York Times* (9 November 1928); "Funny Face," *Play Pictorial* 54, no. 324 (1929): 42–60; review of *Funny Face* in the [London] *Times* (9 November 1928).

28. "Music and Drama," *Sydney Mail* (27 May 1931).

29. E. P., review of *She Knew What She Wanted* in the *Monthly Film Bulletin of the British Film Institute* 3, no. 29 (30 May 1936), courtesy of Sally Plowright.

30. AST, p. 157 ("looked awful"); BIL, pp. 142–145; Peter Krämer, "'A Cutie

with More Than Beauty': Audrey Hepburn, the Hollywood Musical and Funny Face," in *Musicals: Hollywood and Beyond* (Portland, OR: Intellect Books, 2000), pp. 62–69.

31. Reviews of *Funny Face* in *Variety* (13 February 1957), *New York Times* (29 March 1957), *Newsweek* (1 April 1957): 106, *Time* (1 April 1957): 94, 96, *New Yorker* (6 April 1951): 77, *Saturday Review* (13 May 1957): 26, *New Republic* (10 June 1957): 122–123, *Commonweal* (5 August 1957): 16–17. See also MAS, pp. 282–287.

32. Reviews of *Funny Face* in the *Christian Science Monitor* (12 December 1973), *Variety* (15 July 1981), *New York Post* (1 August 1981).

33. FEI, pp. 150–162; Kevin Kelly, "Falling on Its Funny Face," *New York* 16, no. 9 (28 February 1983): 57–67; Don Shewey, "How 'My One and Only' Came to Broadway," *New York Times* (1 May 1983); Edwin Wilson and Trish Hall, "'My One and Only' Opens on Broadway—After Losing Its Head in Boston," *Wall Street Journal* (6 May 1983).

34. Kelly, "Falling on Its Funny Face," p. 61 ("Tune's glitz"); "Director of 'Only' Gets Hub Heave-Ho; Tune, Walsh Step In," *Variety* (February 1983): 117, 121.

35. Review of *My One and Only* in *Variety* (23 February 1983).

36. Reviews of *My One and Only* in *Variety* (4 May 1983), *New York Daily News* (8 May 1983), *New York Times* and *Village Voice* (both 10 May 1983), *Milwaukee Journal* (31 July 1983), *Vanity Fair* 46 (July 1983): 20–21, *New York Post* (7 December 1984), *Dallas Morning News* (22 December 1984), *Dallas Morning News* (28 June 1985), [Los Angeles] *Herald-Examiner* and *Times* (both 15 July 1985), *San Diego Union* (16 July 1985).

37. Peter Sellars and Craig Smith, quoted in *The Guthrie Theater Program and Magazine (Hang On to Me)*, courtesy of the Guthrie Theater; Sylviane Gold, "The Marriage of Gershwin and Gorky," *Wall Street Journal* (29 May 1984).

38. Jerry Floyd, "George and Ira Gershwin: Their Tunes Return as Fascinatin' Rhythm of the '80s," *Washington Times Magazine* (28 July 1984).

22. *Rosalie* and *Treasure Girl*

1. Alexander Woollcott, review of *Rosalie* in the *New York World* (11 January 1928); Charles Higham, *Ziegfeld* (Chicago: Henry Regnery, 1972), p. 187; Elliott Arnold, *Deep in My Heart: A Story Based on the Life of Sigmund Romberg* (New York: Duell, Sloan and Pearce, 1949), p. 365, portrays Romberg as first suggesting to Ziegfeld the idea of a collaboration between himself and Gershwin, but this source does not seem particularly reliable.

2. Warren G. Harris, *The Other Marilyn: A Biography of Marilyn Miller* (New York: Arbor House, 1985), pp. 47, 58, 133; BAR, p. 234, considers the Warner Brothers film biography of Miller, *Look for the Silver Lining* (1949), "insipid"; Gershwin quoted in Grace Davidson, "More Serious Things Replace Love Songs and Dances Now, Says Composer Gershwin," *Boston Post* (3 October 1933).

3. WOD, p. 246.

4. Gershwin, letter to Florenz Ziegfeld, 22 July 1927, and Ziegfeld, telegram to Gershwin, 23 July 1927, ILGT.

5. Both "Ev'rybody Knows I Love Somebody" and "Follow the Drum" ap-

peared both before and after the New York premiere, and though not listed on the opening-night program, at least the latter may have been performed then as well.

6. The Romberg-Wodehouse chorus "Tho' Today We Are Flunkeys Merely," found both at the Library of Congress and in the Tams-Witmark score, presumably appeared where indicated (the script mentions a number for "flunkeys" at the top of the scene), though early programs do not list the song.

7. Bernard Sobel, "Recherche du Temps Perdu," *Rosalie* clipping file, NYPL; Gershwin apparently remained friendly with Morgan in later years, drawing a colored-pencil portrait of the actor in California in 1935.

8. Reviews of *Rosalie* in the [Boston] *Globe, Evening Transcript, Traveler* (all 9 December 1927), *Variety* (14 December 1927), GCLC.

9. "The New Marilyn Miller Show," *New York Times* (18 December 1927); reviews of *Rosalie* in the [New York] *American, Evening Journal, Evening Post, Evening World, Mirror, Sun, Telegram, Times, Women's Wear,* and *World* (all 11 January 1928), *Variety* (18 January 1928), *Billboard* (21 January 1928), *New Republic* (29 February 1928): 70, *Outlook* (29 February 1928): 344, *Vogue* (1 March 1928): 114, *Arts & Decoration* (28 March 1928): 98.

10. BAR, p. 240; DON, p. 61; JAS, pp. 125, 151, 153; MCC, pp. 194, 202; "Hollywood Bulletins," *Variety* (1 October 1930) ("indifference"); "Metro's Unique Attempts to Salvage Fortunes Spent on 'Rosalie' and 'Time,'" *Variety* (19 November 1930).

11. Reviews of *Rosalie* in the [New York] *Herald-Tribune* and *Times* (both 31 December 1937), *New Yorker* (8 January 1938): 61–62.

12. Reviews of productions of *Rosalie* by the St. Louis Municipal Opera (1938, 1940, 1943, 1946, 1950, 1960), including the cited review by Margaret J. Brink in the *Globe-Democrat* (26 July 1960), courtesy of Larry Pry, Municipal Theatre Association of St. Louis; reviews of *Rosalie* in the [New York] *Herald-Tribune, Times, World-Telegram,* and *Sun* (all 26 June 1957), *Variety* (3 July 1957); see also *Rosalie* clipping file, NYPL.

13. Stephen Holden, "1928 Musical 'Rosalie' in Concert at Town Hall," *New York Times* (21 April 1983).

14. Even though "What Causes That?" does not appear in the opening-night program and was reportedly added after the Broadway premiere, a *Brooklyn Daily Eagle* review of that performance (9 November 1928) mentions the song; where it came in relation to the reprise of "Feeling I'm Falling" is not clear, however.

15. Reviews of *Treasure Girl* in the [New York] *American, Daily News, Evening Post, Evening World, Herald-Tribune, Sun, Times, World* (all 9 November 1928), *Variety* (14 November 1928), *Billboard* (17 November 1928), *New Yorker* (17 November 1928): 32–33, *Outlook* (21 November 1928): 1195, *Vogue* (22 December 1928): 82, *Life* (30 November 1928): 11, GCLC; GER, p. 37 ("some excellent"); KIM/G, p. 102 ("The probable").

16. Gershwin quoted by Bide Dudley, "The Stage," *Evening World* (12 November 1928).

17. ROD, p. 60.

18. Gertrude Lawrence, *A Star Danced* (Garden City, NY: Doubleday, Doran, 1945), p. 178; reviews of *Treasure Girl* in the *Outlook* and *Times*.

19. St. John Ervine, review of *Treasure Girl* in the *World;* GER, p. 37.

23. *An American in Paris* and *East Is West*

1. KIM/G, p. 63; S. J. Woolf, "Finding in Jazz the Spirit of His Age," *New York Times Magazine* (20 January 1929); Gershwin, letter to Rosamond Walling, 29 April 1929, GCLC.

2. Hyman Sandow, "Gershwin to Write New Rhapsody," *Musical America* 47, no. 18 (18 February 1928): 5; "New Gershwin Symphony Will Jazz Jazzy Americans Who Jazz Paris," *New York Evening World* (13 April 1928).

3. KIM/G, pp. 94, 99, 107; Ira Gershwin, Diaries (6 April, and 22 and 24 May 1928), ILGT.

4. KIM/G, p. 95.

5. Walter Damrosch, letters and telegrams to Gershwin, ILGT; W. Ward Marsh, "Ira Gershwin Tells How 'American in Paris,' Now Wonder Film, Was Written," *Cleveland Plain Dealer* (24 September 1951); Léonide Massine, *My Life in Ballet,* ed. Phyllis Hartnoll and Robert Rubens (New York: Macmillan, 1968), p. 86.

6. Hyman Sandow, "Violet Rays," *New York University Daily News* (2 October 1928).

7. Hyman Sandow, "Gershwin Presents a New Work," *Musical America* 48, no. 18 (18 August 1928): 5, 12.

8. Gershwin, RB, 9 December 1934.

9. GG, letter to DuBose Heyward, 17 December 1934, GCLC ("judgement"); Taylor's note is reproduced in full in "Variations," *Musical Courier* (20 December 1928), GCLC.

10. James J. Fuld, *The Book of World-Famous Music: Classical, Popular and Folk* (New York: Dover Publications, 1966, repr. 2000), pp. 358–359. According to some preliminary sketches, Gershwin considered the sauntering theme, the taxi motive, and the humorous theme as three principal ideas, labeled "A," "B," and "C" in his sketchbooks.

11. Gilbert, following Jablonski, views the work in four parts, similar to the scheme of five sections above, but with sections one and two making up one part; he also, incidentally, speaks of the final part as a "recapitulation-coda": GIL, p. 112.

12. KIM/CLIG, pp. 278–279 (Ira-Balanchine scenario).

13. GIL, p. 111. Many of these learned devices are not obviously displayed—on the contrary, their extent would likely surprise even educated listeners—but they repay careful study. For instance, at the climactic "Largo" seven measures before the piece's end, Gershwin juxtaposes an augmented version of the humorous theme with, at the "Più mosso," a fragment from the slow blues theme, followed by one final chord. Some conductors, however, impose a fermata and pause just before the "Più mosso," thereby sacrificing the integrity of the motive and the neat overlapping of contrasting ideas (made even clearer in Gershwin's sketch score by a line connecting the last note of the "Largo" with the first note of the "Più mosso").

14. Reviews of *An American in Paris* in the *Brooklyn Daily Eagle* (14 December 1928) ("with a demonstration"), *New York Evening Post* (14 December 1928) ("smiled"); JAB, pp. 180–181.

15. Leonard Liebling, "Banker Praises Gershwin's Newest Orchestral Work," *New York American* (23 December 1928); Otto H. Kahn, "George Gershwin and American Youth," *Musical Courier* (22 January 1929), GCLC.

16. Editor in Chief, "Variations," *Musical Courier* (3 January 1929): 31.

17. Reviews of *An American in Paris* in the [New York] *American, Evening Post, Evening World, Herald-Tribune, Sun, Telegram, Times, World* (all 14 December 1928), *Musical America, New Yorker,* and *New York Sun* (all 22 December 1928), Samuel Chotzinoff, "Concert Pitch," *Sunday World* (23 December 1928), *Outlook and Independent* (2 January 1929), *Literary Digest* (5 January 1929), *Nation* (13 February 1929); other clippings, GCLC.

18. Reviews of *An American in Paris* in the [Cincinnati] *Post* and *Times-Star* (both 1 March 1929), [Cincinnati] *Commercial Tribune, Post, Times-Star* (all 2 March 1929); for Gershwin's thoughts about Damrosch's performance, see also JAB, p. 181.

19. Shilkret related two well-known anecdotes (see, for instance, JAB, p. 183, and SHI, p. 99) concerning what's at least thought to be the recording session on the fourth. He stated that after Gershwin "kept suggesting this and that for about fifteen minutes," he told him, "George, please get lost for about one hour. This is a new work for me and the orchestra." Shilkret further recalled that at the same session, Gershwin offered to fill in for a missing celesta player, but became so enraptured and excited that he forgot to play his part. These anecdotes don't quite add up: first, the 78 rpm recording contains the celesta part in full, as mentioned; second, although Shilkret implies that neither he nor the orchestra had seen the score prior to this session, the February 4 recording date (provided that it's the correct date) followed the radio premiere by a few days. Perhaps these related events took place at the January 30 broadcast, although Gershwin's name does not appear on Shilkret's payroll for that performance (this information courtesy of Niel Shell).

20. Artis Wodehouse, liner notes, *Gershwin Plays Gershwin: The Piano Rolls* (Elektra Nonesuch 9 79287–2, 1992–1993).

21. Toscanini actually broadcast the work in both November 1943 and March 1945, with RCA releasing the latter performance in May 1945; Bernstein apparently recorded the work with the Victor Symphony Orchestra in 1947, but RCA seems to have issued this recording in 1948.

22. Ruth Page, *Page by Page,* ed. Andrew Mark Wentink (Brooklyn, NY: Dance Horizons, 1978), pp. 131–132; Donald Knox, *The Magic Factory: How MGM Made* An American in Paris (New York: Praeger, 1973), p. 43.

23. An outtake of Kelly singing "I've Got a Crush on You" can be heard on the sound track anthology *George and Ira Gershwin in Hollywood* (Turner Entertainment, 1997); the idea of having Adam play, conduct, and applaud the Concerto in F apparently derived from Levant's experiences filming the 1945 Hollywood biography of Gershwin, *Rhapsody in Blue.* "There were these guys [Robert] Alda and [Paul] Whiteman on the stage," stated Levant, "taking bows for music I myself had played and which I was applauding them for. It got very Pirandelloish": "Mr. Levant Discusses Mr. Gershwin," *New York Times* (8 July 1945).

24. Knox, *The Magic Factory,* especially p. 155.

25. MAS, p. 254.

26. Reviews of *An American in Paris* in the *New York Times* (6 May and 12 May 2005) and *New Yorker* (6 June 2005).

27. "The Ascendant Gershwin," *New York Times* (14 November 1926); GER, p. 30; KIM/CLIG, p. 138.

28. GER, p. 30; GG, letters to Rosamond Walling, 19 January 1929, ca. 10 February 1929, GCLC.

29. Samuel Shipman and John B. Hymer, *East Is West* (New York: Samuel French, 1924), pp. 57, 89, 90.

30. GER, p. 31. Presumably the show would have integrated Clark and Mc-Cullough or Ed Wynn into the drama much as McGuire worked Eddie Cantor into *Whoopee* and Jimmy Durante into *Show Girl,* though all that remains speculative.

31. KIM/CLIG, pp. 138–140; lead sheets for the refrains of "I Speak English Now" and "Vo-de-o-do" can be found in a book of "Fragments/Sketches" (1929–1931), courtesy of Michael Feinstein.

32. KIM/CLIG, p. 139; GER, pp. 304–305; for "Embraceable You," see also BAN, p. 48.

33. GER, p. 237.

34. "Fragments/Sketches"; these sketches suggest that Gershwin wrote both the verse and the chorus of "Bronco Busters" for *East Is West;* KIM/G, p. 181 ("all this").

35. GOL, p. 261.

36. Michael Feinstein, liner notes, *Nice Work If You Can Get It* (Atlantic 82833-2, 1996).

37. "Gossip of the Rialto," *New York Times* (8 August 1929); MCC, pp. 181, 454.

24. *Show Girl* and *The Dybbuk*

1. GER, p. 30.

2. J. P. McEvoy, *Show Girl* (New York: Simon and Schuster, 1928).

3. BAR, p. 212 ("So persistent").

4. BAR, p. 190; see also pp. 59–104.

5. David Bakish, *Jimmy Durante: His Show Business Career* (Jefferson, NC: McFarland, 1995); "Eddie Jackson, Longtime Friend and Partner of Jimmy Durante," *New York Times* (18 July 1980) ("We was").

6. BAR, p. 376; MOR/MB, p. 193; see also Herbert G. Goldman, *Jolson: The Legend Comes to Life* (New York: Oxford University Press, 1988).

7. GG, RB, 2 March 1934 ("greatest rush," "Why sure," "As you can imagine"); GG, letter to Rosamond Walling, 29 April 1929, GCLC; GER, p. 152.

8. GOL, p. 246.

9. GER, p. 152.

10. "Lolita" and "Spain" were apparently dropped during the New York run.

11. Students of gay culture in New York in the 1920s might find "So I Ups to Him" and responses to it, including reviews of *Show Girl* in the *Commonweal* (24 July 1929) and *Life* (30 August 1929), of interest. See also CHA, especially chaps. 1 and 2.

12. One finds slight orthographic differences between the Durante titles as listed in the program and as published or recorded.

13. GG, RB, 2 March 1934.

14. Stuart Nicholson, *Reminiscing in Tempo: A Portrait of Duke Ellington* (Boston: Northeastern University Press, 1999), pp. 95 ("on stage"), 97 ("the finest"); A. H. Lawrence, *Duke Ellington and His World: A Biography* (New York: Routledge, 2001), pp. 143–148.

15. AG, p. 11.

16. Reviews of *Show Girl* in the [Boston] *Evening American, Evening Transcript, Globe, Herald,* and *Traveler* (all 26 June 1929), [New York] *American, Evening World, Herald-Tribune, Sun, Times,* and *World* (all 3 July 1929), *New York Daily News* (4 July 1929), *New York American* (5 July 1929), *Variety* (10 July 1929), *Billboard* (13 July 1929), *Commonweal, New Republic,* and *Outlook* (all 24 July 1929), *Life* (30 August 1929), *Time,* GCLC.

17. John Mason Brown, "Two on the Aisle," *New York Evening Post* (9 September 1929); GOL, p. 245.

18. Reviews of *Show Girl,* [New York] *Times* and *Sun* (both 8 August 1929).

19. Florenz Ziegfeld, telegram to GG, 4 March 1928, ILGT; Abbe Niles, "Putting Gershwin to the Whistling Test," *Boston Evening Transcript* (8 March 1930); GG, letter to Rosamond Walling, 10 October 1929, GCLC.

20. BOR/D, p. 122; see also pp. 123–143.

21. For a copy of the contract, see SCH, p. 26; a letter from Edward Ziegler to GG, 31 October 1929, suggests that Gershwin did not sign with the company until after this date.

22. GG, letter to Rosamond Walling, 10 October; GG, letter to Isaac Goldberg, 23 October 1929, Houghton Library, Harvard University (the news, Gershwin wrote Goldberg, broke in the *Morning World*); Samuel Chotzinoff, "Concert Pitch," *New York Sunday World* (20 October 1929); "Gershwin Attuned to Write an Opera," *New York Evening Post* (16 October 1929); "George Gershwin Plans New Opera," *Los Angeles Examiner* (6 November 1929); "Gershwin to Quit Jazz for Opera," *Los Angeles Examiner* (17 October 1929); GOL, p. 274; also "Gershwin Shelves Jazz to Do Opera" and "Gershwin Plans American Opera after Good Rest," unidentified articles, GCLC.

23. LOG, pp. 212, 898; "Gershwin Plays His Rhapsody," *New York Sun* (7 May 1930); Gilbert Seldes, "The Theatre," *Dial* 80 (March 1926): 255–257.

24. "Gershwin Attuned"; DUK/PP, p. 253; Gershwin and Copland were often mentioned together during these years, as in, for example, David Ewen, "Gershwin and Copland," *Forward* (15 June 1930).

25. Ira Gershwin, letter to Merle Armitage, 20 August 1957, GCLC; Isaac Goldberg, "All about the Gershwins: Principally George, Incidentally Ira," *Boston Evening Transcript* (21 December 1929); according to an article from the *American Hebrew* hand-dated 28 February 1930, GCLC, Gershwin was still thinking about going to Europe to work on a *Dybbuk* opera as late as this; GOL, pp. 39–41; PEY, p. 132.

26. Goldberg, "All about the Gershwins"; "George Gershwin, Composer of Extraordinary Ability, Visits Resort for a Winter Vacation," *Palm Beach News* (12 February 1930).

27. Isaac Goldberg, "If Not Back to Bach, Then on to Lincoln," *Boston Evening Transcript* (10 May 1930).

25. *Girl Crazy*

1. Guy Bolton and John McGowan, *Girl Crazy* (New York: Tams-Witmark, 1930), 1–1–1.

2. Miles Kreuger, "Some Words about Girl Crazy," liner notes, *Girl Crazy* (Elektra Nonesuch 9 79250-2, 1990), p. 21; JAB, p. 201 ("retreat"); Bolton and McGowan, *Girl Crazy*, 1–5–15, 1–3–3; ROO, pp. 60–61.

3. ROO, pp. 63–65; MOR/SS, p. 220 (see also 217–221); Andrea Most, *Making Americans: Jews and the Broadway Musical* (Cambridge, MA: Harvard University Press, 2003), pp. 32–65.

4. JAB, p. 201 ("justice"); Bolton and McGowan, *Girl Crazy*, 1–2–8, 1–2–9; Anne Coulter Martens, Newt Mitzman, and William Dalzell, *Girl Crazy: A Comedy in Three Acts* (Woodstock, IL: Dramatic Publishing Company, 1954).

5. Arthur Ruhl, review of *Girl Crazy* in the *New York Herald-Tribune* (15 October 1930).

6. Newman Levy, review of *Girl Crazy* in the *Nation* 131, no. 3408 (29 October 1930): 479–480; for more on Ira's reception in 1930, see clippings, GCLC; in his review of *Girl Crazy, New York Sun* (15 October 1930), Stephen Rathbun wrote about "Cactus Time," "Although it sounded silly, perhaps it was intended to be a comic ditty. At least, one can give Ira Gershwin, the writer of the lyrics, the benefit of the doubt."

7. Kreuger, "Some Words about Girl Crazy," pp. 16–17; see also "'Flying High' Holds Bert Lahr's Services," *New York Telegram* (25 October 1930).

8. ROD, pp. 60–64, 71.

9. Many sources state Merman's year of birth as 1909; Ethel Merman, as told to Pete Martin, *Who Could Ask for Anything More* (New York: Doubleday, 1955); Ethel Merman with George Eells, *Merman* (New York: Simon and Schuster, 1978); Vinton allegedly went to hear Merman at the suggestion of Ginger Rogers's mother, Lela: ROD, p. 74, though Merman biographer Caryl Flinn believes that he did so on the recommendation of Jimmy Durante, e-mail to the author, 29 July 2005.

10. Merman, *Who Could Ask*, pp. 78–79 ("It was"); Merman, *Merman*, p. 38 (Merman claims that Rogers earned fifteen hundred dollars per week, but Rogers put the figure at a thousand, ROD, p. 71).

11. Merman, *Merman*, pp. 39 ("quite a brash"), 46 ("A lucky"); Merman, *Who Could Ask*, p. 88 ("he was glad"); GER, p. 204.

12. For the pit musicians, see GER, p. 233; Richard M. Sudhalter, "And You Should Have Heard the Hot Stuff They Played," liner notes, *Girl Crazy* (Elektra Nonesuch 9 79250-2, 1990), pp. 51–55; and Robert L. Stockdale, *Jimmy Dorsey: A Study in Contrasts* (Lanham, MD: Scarecrow Press, 1999), p. 169.

13. Donald M. Oenslager, *The Theatre of Donald Oenslager* (Middletown, CT: Wesleyan University Press, 1938), p. 41. The sets generally received high marks with the critics, with the notable exception of *Billboard*'s Rives Matthews,

who wrote, "*Girl Crazy* is an eyeful of unmatched colors, which are striking only because they knock you dead with horror and amazement. About the only picture they convey is of a paint shop after an earthquake": *Billboard* 42 (25 October 1930). For color reproductions of these sets, see the booklet accompanying *American Musicals: George Gershwin* (Alexandria, VA: Time-Life Records, 1982).

14. ROG, p. 75; AST, p. 163.

15. Merman, *Who Could Ask,* pp. 82 ("screamed and yelled"), 83 ("Don't let"); Merman, *Merman,* p. 40 ("even intelligent"); GER, p. 233.

16. Reviews of *Girl Crazy* in the *Philadelphia Public Ledg*er (30 September 1930), [New York] *American, Daily Mirror, Daily News, Evening Journal, Evening Graphic, Evening Post, Evening World,* Arthur Ruhl in the *Herald-Tribune, Sun, Times, World* (all 15 October 1930), *Billboard* and *Telegram* (both 25 October 1930), *Nation* 131, no. 3408 (29 October 1930): 479–480, Percy Hammond in the *New York Herald-Tribune* (2 November 1930), *Life* 96 (7 November 1930): 16–17, *Theatre Magazine* 52 (December 1930): 26, 64, 66, *Vogue* 76, no. 12 (8 December 1930): 136. Many of the reviews cited Howard's impersonations of Cantor, Jessel, Jolson, and Chevalier in "But Not for Me," though the *Daily Mirror* also mentioned imitations of Will Rogers.

17. Merman, *Who Could Ask,* pp. 46, 81; Merman, *Merman,* p. 46; ROD, p. 75.

18. ROG, p. 80; Merman, *Who Could Ask,* pp. 92–93; Merman, *Merman,* p. 49 ("nothing materialized").

19. BAR, pp. 352–353; Edward Watz, *Wheeler & Woolsey: The Vaudeville Comic Duo and Their Films, 1929–1937* (Jefferson, NC: McFarland, 1994), pp. 155–163; BRA, p. 302–303 ("The whole thing"); Max Steiner, letter to GG, 30 January 1932, Institute of the American Musical, courtesy of Miles Kreuger. Richard Barrios writes that Busby Berkeley assisted Taurog on the reshoot (BAR, p. 353), a claim unsubstantiated by the RKO file archives at the Institute of the American Musical, according to Miles Kreuger, interview by the author, 3 September 2003.

20. Reviews of *Girl Crazy* (1932) in the *New York Times* (25 March 1932), *Variety* (29 March 1932), *Motion Picture Herald* (2 April 1932).

21. Reviews of *Girl Crazy* (1943) in *Variety* (4 August 1943), [New York] *Morning Telegraph, Sun, Times* (all 3 December 1943), *Commonweal* 39 (17 December 1943): 233, *Time* (27 December 1943), *Video Review* 11, no. 9 (December 1990): 114, 116 ("easily"). "Treat Me Rough," "Bidin' My Time," "Could You Use Me?" "Embraceable You," "But Not for Me," and "I Got Rhythm" are the six numbers that are sung.

22. Review of *When the Boys Meet the Girls* in *Time* 87, no. 3 (21 January 1966): 80; see also reviews in *Variety* (1 December 1965), *Los Angeles Times* (25 December 1965), and the [New York] *Herald-Tribune* and *Times* (both 20 January 1966).

23. Reviews of *Girl Crazy* in *Opera* 39 (September 1988): 1140–1141, *New York Post* (20 February 1990), *New York Times* (4 March 1990).

24. Robert Kimball, "Crazy about Gershwin," liner notes, *Crazy for You* (Angel CDC 7 54618 2, 1992).

25. Bruce Weber, "On Stage, and Off," *New York Times* (3 December 1993), reviews of *Crazy for You* in *Variety* (23 December 1991), Frank Rich in the *New York Times* (20 February 1992), David Richards in the *New York Times* (1 March 1992), *Time* (2 March 1992), *Village Voice* (3 March 1992), *Newsday* (7 January 1996), [London] *Times* (4 March 1993), *Observer* (7 March 1993); see also "'Crazy' Sells Out to Japanese Auds," *Variety* (15 February 1993); "West End 'Crazy' Rakes in Raves," *Variety* (8 March 1993); "London Hit Filling 'Crazy' Coffers," *Variety* (26 April 1993).

26. See, in addition to the aforementioned reviews, Jennifer Dunning, "Crazy for Dance," *New York Times* (16 February 1992); Anna Kisselgoff, "Dance and Song Are Cheek to Cheek on Broadway," *New York Times* (5 July 1992); Mark Shenton, "Crazy for Susan," *Plays International* 8, no. 6 (1 January 1993): 10–11.

27. Although Ethan Mordden argued that the score to *Crazy for You* worked "mainly because Gershwin songs were the most generic in 20's musical comedy," most of the original *Girl Crazy* songs had, as discussed, a distinctly western flavor, even if these were largely omitted from *Crazy for You*: Ethan Mordden, "When the Go-Everywhere Song Grew Exclusive," *New York Times* (17 May 1992).

28. Gary Giddins, *Celebrating Bird: The Triumph of Charlie Parker* (New York: Beech Tree Books, 1987); Parker's famed six-note motive more obviously resembled, as Gary Giddins points out, the opening phrase of Dana Suesse's "A Table in a Corner," though many commentators have underestimated the extent to which the great saxophonist's improvisation as a whole absorbed the rhythmic structure and melodic shape, not to mention the harmonic implications, of the original Gershwin tune, including a few explicit references, such as at the words "Above all."

29. Will Friedwald, *Stardust Melodies: The Biography of Twelve of America's Most Popular Songs* (New York: Pantheon, 2002), pp. 190, 195.

30. See, for example, RIM, p. 241.

31. Raymond Knapp, *The American Musical and the Formation of National Identity* (Princeton, NJ: Princeton University Press, 2005), p. 85; William Austin, quoted by Richard Crawford, *The American Musical Landscape* (Berkeley: University of California Press, 1993), p. 219.

32. Martin Williams, *The Jazz Tradition* (New York: Oxford University Press, 1983), p. 49.

33. Dizzy Gillespie, with Al Fraser, *To Be, or Not . . . to Bop* (Garden City, NY: Doubleday, 1979), pp. 207, 209; Crawford, *The American Musical Landscape*, p. 226; Scott DeVeaux, *The Birth of Bebop: A Social and Musical History* (Berkeley: University of California Press, 1997), p. 203; Joshua Berrett and Louis G. Bourgeois III, *The Musical World of J. J. Johnson* (Lanham, MD: Scarecrow Press, 2002), pp. 67, 70, 201, 210; Woodrow Witt, *Sonny Stitt: His Life and Music* (DMA thesis, University of Houston, 2000).

34. One might roughly diagram this melodic structure as $2 + 2 + 4 / 2 + 2 + 4 / 2 + 2 + 2 + 2 / 2 + 2 + 6$ (with each single digit representing a single measure), though improvising jazz musicians often dispensed with the two-bar cadential tag; moreover, later rhythm-changes, such as those by Miles Davis ("The Theme"), Thelonious Monk ("Rhythm-a-ning"), Sonny Rollins ("No Moe"), and Sonny Stitt ("Sonny Side"), tended to construct more asymmetrical melodies by

eliding phrases; for more on uses of "I Got Rhythm," see Lawrence Michael Zbikowski, *Conceptualizing Music: Cognitive Structure, Theory, and Analysis* (New York: Oxford University Press, 2002): 203–231.

26. *Delicious* and the *Second Rhapsody*

1. "George Gershwin Accepts $100,000 Movietone Offer," *New York Evening Post* (14 August 1928); see also "Gershwin to Write for Fox Films Only," GCLC; EWE, p. 178; SCH, p. 197.

2. "Gershwin, Famous Composer, to Fox," *Hollywood Filmograph* (10 May 1930) ("notable victory"); Jerry Hoffman, "Westward the Course of Tin-Pan Alley," *The Movie Musical from Vitaphone to 42nd Street: As Reported in a Great Fan Magazine,* ed. Miles Kreuger (New York: Dover Publications, 1975).

3. "Fox to Make 72 Films in Hollywood This Year" (4 February 1930), GCLC; "Gershwin, Famous Composer."

4. "George Gershwin, Composer of Extraordinary Ability, Visits Resort for a Winter Vacation," *Palm Beach News* (12 February 1930) ("The talkies"); Regina Crewe, "Gershwin to Play His Own Work at the Roxy Theatre," *New York American* (23 April 1930) ("while he admits"); Isaac Goldberg, "About the Gershwins: To Hollywood Bound," *Boston Evening Transcript* (24 November 1930) ("in a humble").

5. BAR, pp. 139–140.

6. BAR, p. 246. Auer, who arrived in New York at age twelve, a refugee from the Russian revolution, and who studied music before turning his attention to the stage, would have a memorable film career, including a featured turn in *My Man Godfrey* (1936) that won him an Oscar nomination.

7. Ethel Merman with George Eells, *Merman* (New York: Simon and Schuster, 1978), p. 47; Crewe, "Gershwin to Play"; *David Butler,* interviewed by Irene Kahn Atkins (Metuchen, NJ: Directors Guild of America and Scarecrow Press, 1993), p. 100 (for DeSylva).

8. "Gershwin Sings Score of Praise for Hollywood," *New York Herald-Tribune* (3 March 1931) ("he didn't"); DAN, pp. 49, 51 ("superfluities"); Irene Kahn Atkins, *Source Music in Motion Pictures* (Teaneck, NJ: Fairleigh Dickinson University Press, 1983), pp. 100–108. GG, letter to Aileen Pringle, 17 August 1931; see also GG, letter to Isaac Goldberg, 29 April 1931, Houghton Library, Harvard University.

9. Atkins, *Source Music,* p. 101; see also *David Butler,* p. 100; a 1991 recording of this abridged version by Wayne Marshall and the Hollywood Bowl Orchestra under John Mauceri retains a few passages, especially in the middle section, that never made it into the film's final cut.

10. Although Sascha and his family are ostensibly Christian in the film, the screenplay contains references to their singing Yiddish as well as Russian: Guy Bolton and Sonya Levien, *Delicious* (1931), GCLC.

11. For Felix's involvement, Miles Kreuger, interview by the author, 3 September 2003; see also Seymour Felix, "The Fable of a 'Big Town' Boy in a Little City," *Hollywood Reporter* (8 December 1931); "Los Angeles Reports on 'Delicious' Dance Numbers," *Hollywood Reporter* (7 January 1932).

12. Bolton and Levien, *Delicious.*

13. "Gershwin Sings."

14. Bolton and Levien, *Delicious.*

15. Rehearsal numbers mentioned in this discussion of *Delicious* and the *Second Rhapsody* refer to the two-piano score of the *Second Rhapsody* (New York: Warner Bros., 1996).

16. Reviews of *Delicious* in the *Motion Picture Herald* 102 (12 December 1931): 35–36, *New York Herald-Tribune* (25 December 1931), [New York] *Sun, Times,* and *World-Telegram* (all 26 December 1931), *Film Daily* (27 December 1931), *Variety* (29 December 1931), *Los Angeles Examiner* (1 January 1932), *New Outlook and Independent* 160 (13 January 1932): 55, *Cinema,* GCLC; GG, letter to Aileen Pringle, 31 December 1931.

17. BAR, p. 351.

18. GG, letter to Mrs. Conrad Aiken, 2 September 1930, Sonya Levien Collection, Huntington Library.

19. Serge Koussevitzky, letter to GG, 28 October 1929, ILGT; GG, letter to Serge Koussevitzky, 31 October 1929, Koussevitzky Collection, Library of Congress.

20. Edward Kilenyi, "George Gershwin . . . as I Knew Him," *Etude* 68 (October 1950): 64.

21. GG, letter to Aileen Pringle, 30 June 1931, GCLC. Most sources cite the number as fifty-five musicians, though Gershwin writes, "I engaged 55—no it was 56 men"; see also GG, letter to Rosamond Walling, 12 July 1931.

22. Hyman Sandow, "Latest Argument about the Jazz Age," *Every Week Magazine* (29–30 August 1931), GCLC.

23. FER, p. 93.

24. Stuart Isacoff, "Fascinatin' Gershwin," *Keyboard Classics* (January–February 1984): 9.

25. GG, letter to Sonya Levien, 21 August 1931, Sonya Levien Collection, Huntington Library (for Toscanini and Stokowski); GG, telegram to Serge Koussevitzky, 4 December 1931, Koussevitzky Collection, Library of Congress.

26. Numerous 19 January 1931 articles, for example, "Gershwin Has Written Encore to His Rhapsody," [Sterling, Illinois] *Gazette,* GCLC; "As Gershwin Makes Ready His Rhapsody," *Boston Evening Transcript* (28 January 1932) ("merely to write"); Katharine Lyons, "Symphony Launches Gershwin's 'Second Rhapsody' on Friday," *Boston Traveler* (27 January 1932) ("serious").

27. Lyons, "Symphony Launches" ("a very modest"); Isaac Goldberg, "As Gershwin Makes Ready His Rhapsody," *Boston Evening Transcript* (28 January 1932); idem, "Pocketful of Gershwiniana January, 1932," *Boston Evening Transcript* (30 January 1932).

28. Reviews of the *Second Rhapsody* in the [Boston] *Evening American, Evening Transcript, Globe, Herald* (all 30 January 1932), *Christian Science Monitor* (30 January 1932), *Boston Evening Transcript* (1 February 1932), [New York] *American, Evening Journal, Evening Post, Herald-Tribune, Sun, Times, World-Telegram* (all 6 February 1932).

29. Reviews of the *Second Rhapsody* in *Outlook* 159–160, no. 6 (March 1932): 196, *Modern Music* 10, no. 3 (March–April 1932): 122, and *Nation* (Sep-

tember 1932), GCLC; "Manhattan Musicals," *New York World-Telegram* (8 February 1932).

30. GG, telegram to Serge Koussevitzky, 21 January 1932, Koussevitzky Collection, Library of Congress.

31. Goldberg, "Pocketful of Gershwiniana" (for Loeffler); Frank Campbell-Watson, "Preamble," *"I Got Rhythm" Variations* (New York: New World Music, 1953); SCH, p. 208.

27. Of Thee I Sing

1. RYS, pp. 80–81.

2. "Events Leading Up to a Congressional Record," *New York Times* (10 January 1932); along with this key source, see SCH/GG, pp. 166–172.

3. GER, pp. 331–332.

4. "Harris Tells How He Came to Produce the Pulitzer Play," *New York Herald-Tribune* (8 May 1932).

5. "Trying to Interview Gershwin Brothers," *Boston Globe* (13 December 1931); see also Percy N. Stone, "Ira Gershwin's Light Is Shining without George's Reflected Glory," *New York Herald-Tribune* (27 December 1931); RYS, p. 82; SCH/GG, p. 465; George S. Kaufman and Morrie Ryskind, "Scenario" to *Of Thee I Sing*, GCLC (the authors actually wrote, "There has never been so much love").

6. "Events Leading Up"; Malcolm Goldstein, *George S. Kaufman: His Life, His Theater* (New York: Oxford University Press, 1979), p. 200.

7. George Kaufman, Morrie Ryskind, and Ira Gershwin, *Of Thee I Sing* (New York: Knopf, 1932), p. 37.

8. Kaufman, Ryskind, and Gershwin, *Of Thee*, p. 87.

9. SCH/GG, pp. 230, 231, 250, 357, 360, 374.

10. Francis Fergusson, "A Month of the Theatre," *Bookman* (January–February 1932): 561–562 ("something of"); Kaufman and Ryskind, "Scenario"; George S. Kaufman and Morrie Ryskind, "Socratic Dialogue," *Nation* (12 April 1933): 403 (Ryskind suggests here that he voted for Thomas, though in RYS, p. 170, he even more vaguely intimates that he voted for Roosevelt); for Gershwin's appearance at the White House, see JAB/GY, pp. 284–285.

11. Casper H. Nannes, *Politics in American Drama* (Washington, D.C.: Catholic University of America Press, 1960), p. 103.

12. GER, p. 55; Gershwin and Kaufman quoted by MER, p. 441 (for a variant of this story, see WIL/T, p. 91).

13. Isaac Goldberg, "American Operetta Comes of Age," *Disques* 3, no. 1 (March 1932): 10; GER, p. 307; SCH/GG, p. 421 n. 166 ("a la").

14. Theodore and his lyricist-wife, Theodora, derived "Hail, Hail" from a chorus from Sullivan's *Pirates of Penzance,* which itself parodied the "Anvil Chorus" from Verdi's *Il trovatore.*

15. The shortest of these episodes, the second-act finale, was originally a much longer scene; see KIM/CLIG, pp. 189–191.

16. SCH/GS, p. 62.

17. RYS, p. 83 ("rakish" and "fumbling-bumbling"); KIM/G, p. 143 ("remarkably").

Notes

18. George Murphy and Victor Lasky, *Say . . . Didn't You Used to Be George Murphy?* (New York: Bartholomew House, 1970), pp. 134–144.

19. M. C. [Malcolm Cowley], "Burleycue and Whimsey," *New Republic* (13 January 1932): 243–244 ("feeling"); Brooks Atkinson, "The Play," *New York Times* (28 December 1931) ("the shoddiness"); see also Gilbert W. Gabriel, "New Offerings on Broadway Stage and Screen," *New York American* (28 December 1931); Mary C. Anderson, *Mielziner: Master of Modern Stage Design* (New York: Back Stage Books, 2001). Gershwin apparently orchestrated the second act's opening number: SCH/GG, pp. 348–357. The program, incidentally, also lists eight members of the Jack Linton Band, who apparently supplemented the orchestra proper.

20. KIM/G, pp. 144 ("The trials"), 146 ("more proud"); RYS, pp. 84–85; Murphy and Lasky, *Say*, p. 136; George Kaufman, letter to George and Ira Gershwin, 21 July 1931, GCLC.

21. "Of Thee I Sing" (editorial), *Boston Herald Sunday* (27 December 1931).

22. Reviews of *Of Thee I Sing* in the [Boston] *Evening Transcript, Globe, Herald, Post, Traveler* (all 9 December 1931), *Christian Science Monitor* (9 December 1931).

23. George Kaufman, letter to GG, 14 December 1931, ILGT. The refrain "On that point nobody budges" occurs in both "Trumpeter, Blow Your Golden Horn" and the second-act finale; Gershwin possibly took out one or more statements of this refrain.

24. H. T. P. [Parker], "Under Peril of Newfound Wisecracker," *Boston Evening Transcript* (22 December 1931).

25. Robert Garland, "Cast and Miscast," *New York World-Telegram* (28 December 1931); Murphy and Lasky, *Say*, pp. 140–141; MER, p. 438.

26. Reviews of *Of Thee I Sing* in the [New York] *Daily News, Evening Graphic, Evening Post,* Arthur Ruhl in the *Herald-Tribune, Sun* (all 28 December 1931), E. B. White in the *New Yorker* (28 December 1931): 26, 28, *New York Morning Telegraph* (29 December 1931), Percy Hammond in the *New York Herald-Tribune* and Brooks Atkinson in the *New York Times* (both 3 January 1932), *Billboard, Nation,* Robert Benchley in the *New Yorker* (all 9 January 1932), *Commonweal, Nation, Outlook and Independent* (all 13 January 1932), *Vogue* (15 February 1932): 73, 86, Benjamin DeCasseres in *Arts and Decoration* (February 1932): 39, 56, *Catholic World* (February 1932): 587–588, *Theatre Guild* (February 1932): 4, 17–20, *New York Times* (20 March 1932), *Theatre Arts Monthly* (March 1932): 196; see also Atkinson, "The Play"; Cowley, "Burleycue"; Fergusson, "A Month" (Jan.–Feb. 1932); Garland, "Cast and Miscast"; Gabriel, "New Offerings"; Goldberg, "American Operetta"; *Vanity Fair* (June 1932): 57.

27. Benjamin DeCasseres, "Midsummer Stage Gayeties," *Arts and Decoration* (September 1932): 43, 58–59.

28. Atkinson, "The Play"; Cowley, "Burleycue"; Fergusson, "A Month" (Jan.–Feb. 1932); Benchley, *New Yorker;* Marc Blitzstein, "Forecast and Review," *Modern Music* (May–June 1932): 164–169.

29. Blitzstein, "Forecast"; Atkinson, "The Play" ("Whether it is"); Hammond, *Herald-Tribune* ("The mantle"); Atkinson, *Times* ("the humorous"); GG cited by Stone, "Ira Gershwin's Light." Those minority naysayers who found the

music shrill, brassy, or unmelodic included E. B. White *(New Yorker)*, Ed Sullivan *(Evening Graphic)*, and Burns Mantle *(Daily News)*; in the end, the show proved one of the Gershwins' few collaborations in which, for a number of spectators, Ira made a stronger impression than George.

30. "Happy Birthday to 'Of Thee I Sing!'" *New York Times* (18 December 1932).

31. "Musical Play Gets the Pulitzer Award," *New York Times* (3 May 1932); George Kaufman, letter to Ira Gershwin [1932], ILGT.

32. SCH/GG, pp. 205–206; Brooks Atkinson, "Pulitzer Laurels," *New York Times* (8 May 1932); Walter Prichard Eaton, "Between Curtains," *Theatre Arts Monthly* (July 1932): 593–596; see also John Hutchens, "End of a Season," *Theatre Arts Monthly* (June 1932): 448 ("both bold"); "Applause!" *Stage* (June 1932): 5; Francis Fergusson, "A Month of the Theatre," *Bookman* (June–July 1932): 291.

33. FEI, p. 109.

34. "'Of Thee I Sing' Authors Sued as Plagiarists," *New York Herald-Tribune* (9 August 1932); Decision, Judge John Munro Woolsey, 28 December 1932, GCLC; "'Of Thee I Sing' Original," *Variety* (3 January 1932); Edmund Wilson, *The Twenties* (New York: Farrar, Straus and Giroux, 1974), p. 46; see also SCH/GG, pp. 206–213.

35. "Happy Birthday"; WIL/T, p. 91.

36. "Play Is Revised as Coolidge Dies," *New York Times* (6 January 1933); "Happy Birthday." Leroy Anderson—whose original music, including his popular orchestral miniatures, exhibited the profound influence of Gershwin—ended his career much as he had begun it, with a Gershwin arrangement: a 1974 medley of tunes from *Girl Crazy*.

37. George Kaufman, letters to Ira Gershwin, 22 January 1944, 5 September 1949, 12 September 1949, ILGT; "Morros Starting on 'Sing' May 1," *Hollywood Reporter* (1 February 1944).

38. Reviews of *Of Thee I Sing* in the [New York] *Daily Mirror* and *Times* (both 6 May 1952), *New York Daily News* (9 May 1952), *Nation* (17 May 1952): 486, *New Yorker* (17 May 1952): 87, *Newsweek* (19 May 1952): 101, *Time* (19 May 1952): 83, *Saturday Review* (24 May 1952): 30–32, *Commonweal* (30 May 1952): 196–197, *Harper's Magazine* (July 1952): 92–93, *Theatre Arts* (July 1952): 16–17, 82; see also Milton Bracker, "'Of Thee I Sing' in Modern Dress," *New York Times* (4 May 1952); Brooks Atkinson, "'Of Thee I Sing,'" *New York Times* (11 May 1952).

39. Reviews of *Of Thee I Sing* in the *New York Post* (23 October 1968), Ross Wetzsteon in the *Village Voice* (14 November 1968), [New York] *Post* and Clive Barnes in the *Times* (both 8 March 1969), *New York Morning Telegraph* (11 March 1969), *Wall Street Journal* (12 March 1969), Molly Haskell in the *Village Voice* (13 March 1969), *Billboard* (22 March 1969); SCH/GG, pp. 491–492.

40. Reviews of *Of Thee I Sing* in the *New York Post* (20 March 1987), *New York Times* (22 March 1987), *New York Daily News* (29 March 1987), *Opera* (July 1987): 765–766; see also Stephen Holden, "Two Classics by Gershwin in Brooklyn," *New York Times* (20 March 1987); David Patrick Stearns, "Let 'Em Sing Gershwin!" *Ovation* (December 1987): 12–14, 16.

41. Review of *Of Thee I Sing* in the *New York Post* (31 March 1990), *New York Daily News* and *Newsday* (both 2 April 1990), *New York Times* (3 April 1990), *Village Voice* (10 April 1990), *New York Observer* (16 April 1990), *Native* (30 April 1990); see also Allan Kozinn, "Gilbert and Sullivan Players Send an SOS to Gershwin," *New York Times* (29 March 1990).

42. Martin Dreyer, "Of Thee I Sing," *Opera* (August 1998).

43. "Wintergreen for President!" *Curtain Up!* (Fall 2004): 3–4.

44. Reviews of *Of Thee I Sing* in the [New Jersey] *Star-Ledger* (14 September 2004) ("only a must"), *Variety* (15 September 2004) ("curio"), [Bergen County] *Record* and *New York Sun* (15 September 2004), [Milburn] *Item* (16 September 2004), *New York Times* (19 September 2004), *New York Post* (20 September 2004), [Monmouth County] *Two River Times* (24 September 2004), *Wall Street Journal* and *New York Daily News* (both 1 October 2004), all courtesy of the Paper Mill Playhouse.

45. Reviews of *Of Thee I Sing* in the [New York] *Times* ("sublime," "terrific") and *Post* ("sumptuous") (both 13 May 2006).

28. George Gershwin's Song-Book

1. Bennett A. Cerf, letter to GG, 25 August 1928, and GG, letters to Bennett A. Cerf, 3 August 1928 ("Nothing could"), 18 August 1928, Rare Book and Manuscript Library, Columbia University; Isaac Goldberg, unidentified article, *Boston Evening Transcript* (ca. November 1930), GCLC; sketches suggest that Gershwin also considered including settings of "Virginia" and "But Not for Me," sketches, courtesy of Michael Feinstein.

2. G5.

3. Samuel M. Kootz, "Constantin Alajalov," *George Gershwin's Song-Book* (New York: Random House, 1932); G5.

4. Reviews of *Gershwin's Song-Book*, Carl Engel, "Views and Reviews," *Musical Quarterly* 18 (1932): 646–651, Newman Levy, "Authentic Broadway," *New York Herald-Tribune* (25 September 1932), "Books" section.

5. Steven Robert Chicural, *George Gershwin's Songbook: Influences of Jewish Music, Ragtime, and Jazz* (DMA diss., University of Kentucky, 1989); Geoffrey J. Haydon, *A Study of the Exchange of Influence between the Music of Early Twentieth Century Parisian Composers and Ragtime, Blues, and Early Jazz* (DMA diss., University of Texas at Austin, 1992).

6. *Gershwin's Improvisations for Solo Piano*, transcribed by Artis Wodehouse (Miami: Warner Bros., 1987); *Gershwin Plays Gershwin: Selections from the Piano Rolls*, ed. Artis Wodehouse (Miami: Warner Bros., 1995).

7. Will Crutchfield, "Piano: Artis Wodehouse in Gershwin," *New York Times* (3 December 1987).

8. "Grainger Says Gershwin Melody Is Not American," *Omaha Bee-News* (1 March 1928); John Bird, *Percy Grainger* (London: Faber and Faber, 1982); for an overview of some of these arrangements, see Laura W. Holleran, "Gershwin: 'S' Wonderful for Students," *Clavier* (September 1982): 27–29.

9. Both the Wild and the Dowling recordings present the seven études in orders distinct from that of the 1975 Michael Rolland David publication (Colum-

bus, OH): "Liza," "Somebody Loves Me," "The Man I Love," "Embraceable You," "Lady Be Good" [*sic*], "I Got Rhythm," and "Fascinatin' Rhythm" [*sic*].

10. Michael Finnissy, e-mail to the author, 16 June 2005.

11. Michael Finnissy, liner notes, *Gershwin Arrangements/More Gershwin* (Metier MSV CD92030, 1999 [2000]); *Gershwin* (Metronome MET CD 1063, 1999 [2004]).

12. *The George and Ira Gershwin Song Book* (New York: Simon and Schuster, 1960); *Gershwin: Years in Song* (New York: New York Times, 1973); *The Gershwin Collection* (Milwaukee: Hal Leonard, 1992); *The Songs of George and Ira Gershwin: A Centennial Celebration*, 2 vols. (Miami: Warner Brothers, 1998).

13. Geoffrey Mark Fidelman, *First Lady of Song: Ella Fitzgerald for the Record* (New York: Birch Lane Press, 1994), pp. 119–121; Peter J. Levinson, *September in the Rain: The Life of Nelson Riddle* (New York: Watson-Guptill, 2001), p. 193; the Nelson Riddle instrumental selections include a transcription of the *Three Preludes* and something called *Ambulatory Suite*, comprising "Promenade," "March of the Swiss Soldiers," and "Fidgety Feet" (the so-called "March of the Swiss Soldiers" consists of the same music as that for the "Unofficial March of General Holmes" from the revised *Strike Up the Band*—music referred to in that show's vocal score as "Soldiers' March").

14. FEI, pp. 97–98 ("vocal tricks"), 123; Stuart Nicholson, *Ella Fitzgerald: A Biography of the First Lady of Jazz* (New York: Charles Scribner's Sons, 1993), p. 185; Charles Hamm, *Putting Popular Music in Its Place* (Cambridge, Eng.: Cambridge University Press, 1995), p. 316. The Fitzgerald songbook by oversight included a song composed by Ira Gershwin with Harry Warren, "Cheerful Little Earful"; an early take of "The Lorelei" also had Fitzgerald mistakenly singing "Ja Ja" with a hard *j,* but when Ira Gershwin pointed this out to Granz, the record producer insisted on rerecording the song—at considerable expense.

15. Jack Gibbons, e-mail to the author, 14 May 2005.

16. Howard Barnes, review of *Rhapsody in Blue* in the *New York Herald-Tribune* (28 June 1945); Ray Turner and, for the concert pieces, Oscar Levant, dubbed Alda's piano playing, while various sources have credited either Sally (Mueller) Sweetland or Louanne Hogan as providing the singing voice of Joan Leslie. Although both Sweetland and Hogan had dubbed Leslie in prior films, in interviews by the author (15 January 2006), historian Miles Kreuger and Sweetland herself confirm that for this picture, the latter dubbed all of Leslie's numbers.

17. "Hollywood Turns to Gershwin," *New York Times* (16 April 1944).

18. Reviews of *Rhapsody in Blue* in the *Hollywood Reporter* and *Variety* (both 27 June 1945), [New York] *Daily News* and *Times* (both 28 June 1945), *New Yorker* (7 July 1945), *New York Times* (8 July 1945), *Newsweek, Spectator, Time* (all 9 July 1945), *Life* (16 July 1945), *Nation* (21 July 1945) ("sympathetic"), and *New Republic* (23 July 1945) ("dulled"); George S. Kaufman, "Notes for a Film Biography," *New Yorker* (11 August 1945); see also Charlotte Greenspan, "*Rhapsody in Blue*: A Study in Hollywood Hagiography," in SCH/GS, pp. 145–159; John C. Tibbetts, *Composers in the Movies: Studies in Musical Biography* (New Haven, CT: Yale University Press, 2005), pp. 138–141. Phil Spitalny led the popular all-girl "Hour of Charm" Orchestra during this period; Sherrie Tucker considers *Spitalny* a "useful adjective" to mean, among

other things, "strings and harps and elaborate production numbers": *Swing Shift: "All-Girl" Bands of the 1940s* (Durham, NC: Duke University Press, 2000), p. 71.

19. John Baxter, *Woody Allen: A Biography* (New York: Carroll & Graf, 1998), p. 272 ("I was shooting"); see also Julian Fox, *Woody: Movies from Manhattan* (Woodstock, NY: Overlook Press, 1996), p. 109; Douglas Brode, *Woody Allen: His Films and Career* (Secaucus, NJ: Citadel Press, 1985). The songs used in the film (mostly arranged by Tom Pierson for orchestra and performed by the New York Philharmonic under Zubin Mehta) included such Gershwin *Song-Book* favorites as "He Loves and She Loves" and "Strike Up the Band," along with such less-known titles as "Land of the Gay Caballero" and "Mine."

20. Léonide Massine, *My Life in Ballet,* ed. Phyllis Hartnoll and Robert Rubens (New York: Macmillan, 1968), pp. 216–217; Leslie Norton, *Léonide Massine and the 20th Century Ballet* (Jefferson, NC: McFarland, 2004), pp. 246–250; Russell Rhodes, "New York Letter," *Dancing Times* (December 1940): 122–125; Albertina Vitak, "Dance Events Reviewed," *American Dancer* (December 1940): 13. Originally cast as the House Painter, Massine assumed and expanded the role of the Timid Man in the course of the work's run.

21. Murray Schumach, "17 Gershwin Songs Are to Be Released," *New York Times* (17 February 1964); A. Scott Berg, *Goldwyn: A Biography* (New York: Alfred A. Knopf, 1989), p. 302.

22. Reviews of *Who Cares?* in the *New York Post, New York Times, Saturday Review, Time Magazine, Village Voice,* and unidentified (all 1970), clipping file, Dance Division, NYPL.

23. Reviews of *Who Cares?* in the *New York Times* (16 January 1983, 21 November 1984, 16 February 1986, 8 February 1997, 11 February 2003); see also John Percival, "Balanchine's Gershwin," [London] *Times* (12 February 1975).

24. Jennifer Dunning, "Dancing All the Way," *New York Times* (11 October 1997); Aaron Sherber, e-mails to the author, 3 and 21 July 2005; BEH, p. 256.

25. Lisa Traiger, "'Appalachian Spring': Peak Performance," *Washington Post* (16 May 1998); see also reviews by Anna Kisselgoff in the *New York Times* (18 May 1998; 5 February 1999), Jane Vranish in the *Pittsburgh Post-Gazette* (31 January 2002), and Marc Shugold in the [Denver] *Rocky Mountain News* (3 March 2000).

26. Octavio Roca, "Smuin, 'Gershwin' Perfect Pair," *San Francisco Chronicle* (10 May 2002); Jack Anderson, "Gershwin in Gloom and Sunlight, with Boundless Energy," *New York Times* (13 August 2003); Gia Kourlas, "It's One More for Sinatra as Dancers Fly to the Moon," *New York Times* (11 August 2005).

27. DAV/SF, p. 373; Clive Barnes, "Theater: The Gershwins Are Back," *New York Times* (19 February 1971).

28. Robert Berkvist, "He Sings, He Dances, He Plays Piano!" *New York Times* (16 January 1972) ("Gershwin"); for a review, see John J. O'Connor, "TV: Watching Thomas to Astaire to Hope to Bunker," *New York Times* (19 January 1972).

29. *The Lawrence Welk Show,* 2–S-10 (1972), 5–S-24 (1976), 9–S-19 (1980), courtesy of Margaret Heron and the Welk Group, Inc.; the Welk show also presented four tributes to Berlin, three to Kern and Warren, two to Porter and Rodgers, and one to Youmans and Oscar Hammerstein II.

30. Richard Shepard, "Going Out Guide," *New York Times* (20 November 1973); Steven Weisman, "Going Out Guide," *New York Times* (10 August 1974).

31. John S. Wilson, "Cabaret: One Hour of Gershwin," *New York Times* (12 January 1986); Stephen Holden, "'S Wonderful, 'S Marvelous, 'S Gershwin," *New York Times* (2 April 1992); for reviews of *The Gershwins' Fascinating Rhythm,* see Elyse Sommer, CurtainUp (online, April 1999) ("homogenized"), BOR/AMT, p. 816, Mark S. P. Turvin, Goldfish Publications (online, 15 January 1999), Peter Marks in the *New York Times* (26 April 1999), John Simon in *New York Magazine* (10 May 1999) ("abomination").

32. Hershey Felder, interview by the author, 6 January 2005 ("chunks"); Bruce Weber, "A Solo Requiem for America's Mozart," *New York Times* (1 May 2001); and other reviews, courtesy of Hershey Felder; Hershey Felder, e-mail to the author, 27 June 2004.

33. Stephen Holden, "Fizzy Cabaret-Style Toast to the Gershwins' Zaniness," *New York Times* (13 November 2000); David Finkle, "Sounds of the City," *Village Voice* (15–21 November 2000); Michael Feingold, "You Must Remember Disc," *Village Voice* (11–17 July 2001).

29. The *Cuban Overture* and *Pardon My English*

1. GG, letter to George Pallay, 8 March 1932, anonymously transcribed, ILGT; see also JAB, p. 227; "George Gershwin Havana Visitor," *Havana Post* (18 February 1932), p. 6, courtesy of Andrew Lamb (later sources, including KIM/G, p. 151, cite a "Danny Silverberg," not Silberberg; presumably he is the unidentified man in the photograph on p. 150).

2. Andrew Lamb, "Gershwin's Cuban Vacation," courtesy of the author; "George Gershwin Havana Visitor"; Xavier Cugat, *Rumba Is My Life* (New York: Didier, 1948), p. 123.

3. Bennett Cerf, *Try and Stop Me: A Collection of Anecdotes and Stories, Mostly Humorous* (New York: Simon and Schuster, 1945), pp. 214, 215, 217; Helio Orovio, *Diccionario de la música cubana* (Havana: Letras Cubanas, 1981, repr. 1992), p. 356.

4. "Gershwin 'Rumba' to Have Premiere at Stadium Tonight," *New York American* (16 August 1932).

5. "Gershwin to Lead Musicians Concert," *New York Times* (8 October 1932) ("a more just"); see also "Concert for Idle Tonight," *New York Times* (1 November 1932); George Gershwin, "Program Notes," *Cuban Overture* (Warner Bros., 1987), p. 7 ("symphonic").

6. Cugat, *Rumba,* p. 105.

7. Gershwin, "Program Notes"; also sketched outline, *Cuban Overture,* GCLC.

8. Lamb, "Gershwin's Cuban Vacation"; Charles W. White, *Alejandro García Caturla: A Cuban Composer in the Twentieth Century* (Lanham, MD: Scarecrow Press, 2003), pp. 124, 162.

9. GIL, p. 173.

10. "Gershwin Goes Political after Chats with Rivera," *New York Post* (17 December 1935).

11. Reviews of *Cuban Overture* in the [New York] *American, Herald-Tribune,*

Times, World-Telegram (all 17 August 1932), *Time* (24 August 1932), *New York American* (2 November 1932), Olin Downes, "Helping the Unemployed," *New York Times* (30 October 1932).

12. GG, letter to Sonya Levien, 21 August 1931, Sonya Levien Collection, Huntington Library.

13. Tommy Krasker, "Pardon My English: A Tale of Two Psyches," *Pardon My English* (Elektra Nonesuch, 79338-2, 1994), p. 12; Herbert Fields and Morrie Ryskind, *Pardon My English*, GCLC.

14. Ethel Merman, as told to Pete Martin, *Who Could Ask for Anything More* (New York: Doubleday, 1955), p. 101; GER, p. 325.

15. For more on Pearl and the "Dutch" comic tradition, see "Pearl Reviving 'Dutch' Comic of Early 1900s," *New York Herald-Tribune* (22 January 1933).

16. Hildegarde, who recorded and frequently sang "My Cousin in Milwaukee," allegedly claimed that the Gershwins wrote the song for her.

17. Reviews of *Pardon My English* in the [Philadelphia] *Evening Bulletin, Evening Public Ledger,* and *Inquirer* (all 3 December 1932), *Variety* (6 December 1932); see also "Three New Shows in the Tryout Cities," *New York Times* (11 December 1932).

18. RYS, p. 90.

19. GER, p. 325.

20. The revised version opens in a beer garden in Dresden ("In Three-Quarter Time"). Police lieutenant Schultz is on the lookout for a pair of thieves: Michael Bramleigh, an Englishman also known as Golo, and his Polish moll, Polly Polechefsky, known as Gita. Johnny Stewart and Gerry Martin, an American dance team, perform ("The Lorelei"). After Michael's unsavory associate, McCarthy, robs a bank, police commissioner Bauer incarcerates Stewart and Martin for the crime, and invites Michael and Gita to a party at his home the following evening in honor of his birthday ("The Dresden Northwest Mounted").

The next evening, the townspeople celebrate Bauer's birthday ("Dancing in the Streets"), while his daughter, Ilse, attempts to calm his nerves ("So What?"). Michael and Ilse meet and are drawn to each other ("Isn't It a Pity?"). Gita vamps Bauer and the entire police force ("My Cousin in Milwaukee"). At police headquarters, Michael announces to Bauer his engagement to Ilse and wins the release of Stewart and Martin. As the town prepares for the marriage of Michael and Ilse ("Fatherland, Mother of the Band"), the groom enters in high spirits ("Luckiest Man in the World"). Under threats from Gita and McCarthy, Michael and Ilse elope. McCarthy and his gang steal the wedding gifts, which the guests demand be returned, and Bauer collapses ("Finale").

Act 2 opens in an inn at Schandau on the Elbe. Ilse suggests that she and Michael stay in the bridal suite although they are not yet married ("Tonight"). Gita appears, however, and she and Ilse, both disgusted with Michael, leave together. Gita once again attempts to seduce Bauer, who tries extricating himself from her ("Where You Go, I Go"). McCarthy kidnaps Ilse and holds her for ransom in the cellar of the American Bar, where Stewart and Martin perform ("I've Got to Be There"). Michael enters with the ransom money, followed by the police; a blow on the head leaves him unconscious ("Finaletto" and a reprise of "The Dresden Northwest Mounted"). Dr. Steiner (or, in the final Broadway version, Michael's friend Richard Carver, now a doctor) guesses that if Michael, on awakening, recognizes Ilse, he will be cured of his kleptomania. Regaining his senses, Michael in fact turns to Gita, but after another bop on the head by Ilse, he embraces her in the end ("Finale: He's Not Himself").

21. Reviews of *Pardon My English* in the [Boston] *Evening Transcript, Globe, Herald,* and *Traveler* (all 10 January 1933).

22. GER, p. 325.

23. Reviews of *Pardon My English* in the [New York] *American* (Gilbert Gabriel; "desperate want"), *Evening Post, Herald-Tribune, Sun, Times, World-Telegram* (all 21 January 1933), *Brooklyn Daily Eagle* (21 January 1933), *New Yorker* (28 January 1933): 26, *Variety* (4 February 1933), *New Outlook* 161 (March 1933): 48.

24. BOR/AMT, p. 533 ("disturbing"); Stanley Green, *Broadway Musicals of the 30s* (New York: Da Capo Press, 1971), p. 79; Robert Kimball, e-mail to the author, 31 March 2004; *New York American; Variety* (6 December 1932) ("no one").

25. John Andrew Johnson, "*Pardon My English* (1933): The Gershwins on the Eve of the Third Reich," unpublished article; ROS, pp. 250–251.

26. Dwight Blocker Bowers, liner notes to *I Got Rhythm: The Music of George Gershwin* (Smithsonian Collection of Recordings, DMC 4–1247, 1995).

27. Reviews of *Pardon My English* in the *Washington Post* (16 May 1987), [New York] *Newsday* and *Post* (both 18 May 1987).

28. Rob Fisher, "Keeping Score," *Playbill: Pardon My English* (25–28 March 2004); Rob Fisher and David Ives, postperformance dialogue, 27 March 2004.

29. Reviews of *Pardon My English* in the [New York] *Post* and *Times* (both 27 March 2004); MOR/SS, pp. 51–52.

30. Everett Evans, "Pardon Labors for Its Laughs," *Houston Chronicle* (6 January 2006) ("ridiculous"); D. L. Groover and Lee Williams, "Capsule Reviews," *Houston Press* (12 January 2006) ("ludicrous").

30. *Let 'Em Eat Cake* and *Variations on "I Got Rhythm"*

1. MER, pp. 460–461; SCH/GG, pp. 543–545; Malcolm Goldstein, *George S. Kaufman: His Life, His Theater* (New York: Oxford University Press, 1979), pp. 218–220.

2. John Peter Toohey, "A Few Characteristic Lyrics from the Gershwins' New One," *New York Herald-Tribune* (5 November 1933); George S. Kaufman, letter to Ira Gershwin, 1933, GCLC.

3. George Murphy and Victor Lasky, *Say . . . Didn't You Used to Be George Murphy?* (New York: Bartholomew House, 1970), p. 149.

4. Reviews of *Let 'Em Eat Cake* in the [Boston] *Evening Transcript, Globe, Post, Traveler* (all 3 October 1933), *Christian Science Monitor* (3 October 1933).

5. H. T. Parker, "Musical Play in the Making and Re-Making," *Boston Evening Transcript* (18 October 1933); see also idem, "'Let 'Em Eat Cake' Cheered in Boston," *New York Times* (3 October 1933), and idem, "From Beans to Cake," *Boston Evening Transcript* (8 October 1933); SCH/GG, pp. 548–551. In the Boston version, John P. Tweedledee reoccupies the White House, while in the New York version, the line of succession falls to Alexander Throttlebottom.

6. See SCH/GG, p. 773, for some discussion of this unspecified reprise. Schneider reasonably imagines "Let 'Em Eat Cake" a likely candidate, though he notes that the show's musical outline indicates "Finale ultimo—Of thee I song [*sic*]." Regarding the idea of ending a new show with the title song of a previous one, he concludes, "This notion—unprecedented in American musical theater—was probably dropped, although no hard evidence supports any song over any other."

7. George S. Kaufman, Morrie Ryskind, and Ira Gershwin, *Let 'Em Eat Cake* (New York: Alfred A. Knopf, 1933), p. 75. A hereditary order of women descended from American revolutionaries, the Daughters of the American Revolution was founded in 1890 and elicited public censure in 1939 after it banned the distinguished African American contralto Marian Anderson from performing at the group's Constitution Hall. New York's similarly august Union League Club, founded in 1863, moved to its present quarters at 37th Street and Park Avenue in 1931; a current brochure proclaims the club's dedication to "national integrity, civic purpose, and gracious company" and further states, "The club has always provided its members with quiet sanctuary and relief from city traffic" ("The Tradition Continues," Union League Club brochure, courtesy of Arthur Lawrence). While the blue-shirt revolution patently satirizes fascism, the figure of Kruger remains somewhat ambiguous. As a Union Square agitator, he would seem to be a Communist or a Socialist, but when he assumes power, the army gives him a Nazi salute; moreover, he refers to himself as an "Aryan," and his name is indeed Germanic (ROO, pp. 117, 126). This implied identification of Communists with Fascists seems characteristic of Kaufman, who thought of the Democratic and Republican parties as Tweedle-dee and Tweedle-dum.

8. Ira Gershwin, "Book Review" in "The Conning Tower," *New York Herald-Tribune* (23 October 1933); JAB, p. 242 ("love interest"); George S. Kaufman and Morrie Ryskind, scenarios to *Let 'Em Eat Cake,* GCLC.

9. SCH/GG, p. 654.

10. Elizabeth Borton, "'Must Let One's Ego Flower to Do Creative Work'— Gershwin" (ca. October 1933), GCLC.

11. Reviews of *Let 'Em Eat Cake* in the [New York] *American, Evening Journal, Evening Post, Herald-Tribune,* Richard Lockridge in the *Sun, Times, World-Telegram* (all 23 October 1933), *Variety* (24 October 1933), *Time* (30 October 1933): 29–30, *Billboard* (4 November 1933), Joseph Wood Krutch in the *Nation* (8 November 1933): 548, *Commonweal* (10 November 1933): 47, *Musical Record* (November 1933): 216–219, *Theatre Arts Monthly* (July–December 1933): 921, *Catholic World* (December 1933): 338–339, *New Outlook* (December 1933): 47, *Stage* (December 1933): 9–10.

12. Percy Hammond, "The Theaters," *New York Herald-Tribune* (29 October 1933); Brooks Atkinson, "'Let 'Em Eat Cake,'" *New York Times* (12 November 1933); Hiram Motherwell, "Music in the Musicals," *Stage* (December 1933): 37–38; "More Music in the Musicals," *Stage* (January 1934): 41–42.

13. RYS, p. 90; JAB/GY, p. 200 ("claim").

14. Terry Curtis Fox, "Aced in the Berkshires," *Village Voice* (17 July 1978): 77–78; see also SCH/GG, pp. 800–801.

15. Howard Teichmann, *George S. Kaufman: An Intimate Portrait* (New York:

Atheneum, 1972), p. 65; Scott Meredith, *George S. Kaufman and His Friends* (Garden City, NY: Doubleday, 1974); Malcolm Goldstein, *George S. Kaufman: His Life, His Theater* (New York: Oxford University Press, 1979), p. 222; SCH/GG, p. 679, and pp. 608, 645, 679, 682, 702, 728, 729, 739, 752, 757, 767, 804–805.

16. Stephen Holden, "Two Classics by Gershwin in Brooklyn," *New York Times* (20 March 1987). Swift had access to a complete lead sheet for the refrain of "The Union League" but only the first strain of a lead sheet for the chorus of "First Lady and First Gent," making her reconstruction of the latter number that much more her own work.

17. Reviews of *Let 'Em Eat Cake* in the [New York] *Post* and *Daily News* (both 20 March 1987), *New York Times* (22 March 1987), *Opera* (July 1987): 765–766, *Ovation* (December 1987): 12–14, 16; Joshua Kosman, "Gershwin Salvages Rusty Re-creations," *San Francisco Chronicle* (25 June 2005).

18. JAB, p. 249.

19. For "simple" and other descriptions of the work by Gershwin, see his outline of the work, GCLC, and remarks made on a radio broadcast (RB, 30 April 1934).

20. Concerning Gershwin's "out of tune" remark, Ryan Raul Banagale writes, "When one actually listens to the recorded broadcast, his voice takes an ironic tone when he says, 'as they always are,' as if to say instead, 'as *we think* they always are,'" BAN, p. 56.

21. BEH, p. 256.

22. GIL, p. 174.

23. G12; James Melton, recording of selections from *Porgy and Bess* released by various companies under different titles, but paired with selections by Cole Porter (as in *James Melton Sings George Gershwin, Cole Porter* [Zenith L1609, 1960]).

24. PEY, pp. 216–217 (for Miller); JAB/GY, pp. 208–209.

25. "Gershwin Date" (1934), GCLC; JAB/GY, p. 207; see also EWE, pp. 214–215.

26. C. W. D., "Symphony Hall: Gershwin Concert" (1934), GCLC ("It is likely"); "Music and the Drama," *Toronto Globe* (20 January 1934); "Gershwin Provides Exhilarating Night," *Toronto Mail* (20 January 1934); C. Pannill Mead, "Gershwin, as Pianist, Wins Praise, Melton Scores Hit" (1934), GCLC ("You do not"); see also CAR, pp. 554–556.

27. Frank Campbell-Watson, "Preamble," *"I Got Rhythm" Variations* (New York: New World Music, 1953).

28. SCH, p. 315 n.14; JAB, p. 260; to his credit, Schoenfeld at least consulted, in addition to the orchestral manuscript, an original piano part with annotations apparently in the composer's hand.

29. Marcus Roberts, liner notes, *Portraits in Blue* (Sony SK 68488, 1995).

31. *Porgy and Bess*

1. "Tales of Tin Pan Alley: 'Swanee' and Its Author," *Edison Musical Magazine* (October 1920): 9.

2. Henrietta Malkiel, "Scheherazade in West Virginia: Jazz Opera on Its Way," *Musical America* (25 April 1925): 3, 26.

3. GRE, pp. 13–14 ("I shall certainly"); see also "Gershwin Versatile Composer," GCLC (ca. 1 December 1925); for Gershwin's use of the word *nigger,* see chapter 14 n. 18.

4. G13 ("dramatic intensity"); Dorothy Heyward, "Porgy's Goat," *Harpers* 215, no. 1291 (December 1957): 37–41; DuBose Heyward, "Porgy and Bess Return on Wings of Song," *Stage* 13 (October 1935): 25.

5. Frank Durham, *DuBose Heyward: The Man Who Wrote Porgy* (Port Washington, NY: Kennikat Press, 1954); Frank Durham, *DuBose Heyward's Use of Folklore in His Negro Fiction,* The Citadel Monograph Series 11 (Charleston, NC: The Citadel, 1961); William H. Slavick, *DuBose Heyward* (Boston: Twayne Publishers, 1981); James M. Hutchisson, *DuBose Heyward: A Charleston Gentleman and the World of Porgy and Bess* (Jackson: University Press of Mississippi, 2000); James M. Hutchisson, ed., *A DuBose Heyward Reader* (Athens: University of Georgia Press, 2003).

6. DuBose Heyward, "Introduction" ("The American Negro in Art"), in *Porgy: A Play in Four Acts* by Dorothy Heyward and DuBose Heyward (Garden City, NY: Doubleday, Doran, 1928), pp. ix–xxi; idem, *Porgy* (Garden City, NY: Doubleday, Doran, 1925, repr. 1953); Harlan Greene, "'The Little Shining Word': From Porgo to Porgy," *South Carolina Historical Magazine* 87, no. 1 (1986): 75–81; Harlan Greene, *Mr. Skylark: John Bennett and the Charleston Renaissance* (Athens: University of Georgia Press, 2001), pp. 198–199; Harriette Kershaw Leiding, *Street Cries of an Old Southern City* (Charleston, SC: privately printed, 1910); Wayne Shirley, letter to the author, 25 November 2004 (for *Woodcraft*). For more on Smalls, who disappeared from view shortly after the book's publication, see Greene, *Mr. Skylark,* pp. 229–230, and JOH, pp. 280ff.

7. Heyward, *Porgy,* p. 196.

8. DuBose Heyward, "And Once Again—the Negro," *Reviewer* (October 1923): 39–42; idem, "The Negro in the Low-Country," in *The Carolina Low-Country,* ed. Augustine T. Smythe, et al. (New York: Macmillan, 1931).

9. Heyward, *Porgy,* pp. 23–30 ("rhythm"); idem, "Introduction," p. x.

10. Walter Pritchard Evans, *The Theatre Guild: The First Ten Years* (Freeport, NY: Libraries Press, 1929), pp. 4, 8, 13, 85; see also Roy S. Waldau, *Vintage Years of the Theatre Guild: 1928–1939,* Cleveland, OH: Press of Case Western Reserve University, 1972).

11. Mark Spergel, *Reinventing Reality: The Art and Life of Rouben Mamoulian* (Metuchen, NJ: Scarecrow Press, 1993), p. 67 ("great experiences"); Tom Milne, *Rouben Mamoulian* (Bloomington: Indiana University Press, 1969), p. 12, quotes the director as saying, "My aim always was rhythm and poetic stylization."

12. James Weldon Johnson, *Black Manhattan* (New York: Atheneum, 1968), p. 212.

13. Johnson, *Black Manhattan,* p. 211. Note certain orthographic changes between the novel and play: for example, Sporting Life, Kittiwar, and Frasier become Sportin' Life, Kittiwah, and Frazier. The spelling for the operatic Sportin(g) Life remains especially problematic, as the libretto and published vocal score re-

tain the *g*, whereas the orchestral score and premiere playbill (and most subsequent programs) do not; this book follows common practice in referring to the operatic Sportin' Life with an apostrophe.

14. G13; GG, letter to DuBose Heyward, 29 March 1932, GCLC.

15. ALP, pp. 70–71, 74–76; GG, letters to DuBose Heyward, 29 March, 20 May, 9 September, 14 October 1932, GCLC; Heyward, letters to GG, 3 September, 17 October 1932, GCLC; Waldau, *Vintage Years,* p. 189.

16. GG, letter, 9 September; Ira Gershwin, marginalia, "Five Letters from Otto H. Kahn to George Gershwin," GCLC; Lawrence Langner, *The Magic Curtain: The Story of a Life in Two Fields, Theatre and Invention, by the Founder of the Theatre Guild* (New York: E. P. Dutton, 1951), p. 265; Theresa Helburn, *A Wayward Quest: The Autobiography of Theresa Helburn* (Boston: Little, Brown, 1960), p. 113.

17. DuBose Heyward, letter to GG, 12 November 1933, GCLC; GG, letters to Heyward, 25 November 1933, 8 March 1934, GCLC; "'Palm Beach Ideal Spot for Composers,' Says Gershwin," *Palm Beach News* (29 December 1933) (as of this interview, Gershwin had not fully made up his mind how to treat the recitative); KIM/G, p. 171 (for Feen-a-Mint).

18. DuBose Heyward, letter to GG, 12 November 1933; JAB/GY, p. 22 ("more unemotional") (this press release, dated 7 July 1934, also quoted Gershwin as saying, "I am trying to get a sensational dramatic effect. I hope to accomplish this by having the few whites in the production speak their lines while the Negroes, in answering, will sing"; however, he eventually settled on a less rigid scheme, as described above); Heyward, *Porgy,* p. 57.

19. Durham, *DuBose Heyward: The Man,* pp. 126–127; see also GER, pp. 359–360.

20. EWE, p. 220; *Broadway: The American Musical* (New York: PBS, 2004) ("best lyrics"); Stephen Sondheim, letter to the author, 8 September 2005; see also Stephen Sondheim, "Stephen Sondheim: Theater Lyrics," *Dramatists Guild Quarterly* 15, no. 3 (1978): especially 22–24.

21. Hutchisson, *DuBose Heyward,* p. 176.

22. GG, letter to DuBose Heyward, 23 November 1933, GCLC; Janet Mabie, "Rhapsody on Gershwin" (August 1935), GCLC; JOH, p. 336; KIM/G, p. 177 (see also Frank B. Gilbreth, "Gershwin, Prince of Jazz, Pounds Out Rhythm at Folly," *Charleston News and Courier* [19 June 1934] [for "Oh, Dr. Jesus"]); "George Gershwin Arrives to Plan Opera on 'Porgy,'" *Charleston News and Courier* (4 December 1933) ("primitiveness"); ARV, p. 27 ("had come"); "George Gershwin to Compose Music for Operatic Version of 'Porgy,'" GCLC ("the artistry").

23. DuBose Heyward, letter to GG, 6 February 1934, GCLC.

24. GG, letter to Ira Gershwin, June 1934, ILGT; JAB, pp. 272–273; KIM/G, pp. 174–77; see also JAB/GY, pp. 218–222; Gilbreth, "Gershwin, Prince of Jazz" (this article refers to "two servants").

25. KIM/G, p. 177; "Gershwin, Heyward Visit in Rockville," *Charleston News and Courier* (17 July 1934); John Bennett, letter to Susan Bennett, 15 July 1934, Bennett Collection, South Carolina Historical Society; Heyward,

"Porgy and Bess Return," pp. 27–28; ARM/GG, p. 39; WYA, pp. 235–236 ("By God").

26. Heyward, "Porgy and Bess Return"; GG, letter to DuBose Heyward, 5 November 1934, GCLC.

27. JAB/GY, pp. 224–226; KIM/G, pp. 178–179; JAB, pp. 278, 285; James A. Pegolotti, *Deems Taylor: A Biography* (Boston: Northeastern University Press, 2003), p. 212.

28. Wayne D. Shirley, "Porgy and Bess," *Library of Congress Quarterly Journal* 31 (1974): 97–107; idem, "Reconciliation on Catfish Row: Bess, Serena, and the Short Score of 'Porgy and Bess,'" *Library of Congress Quarterly Journal* 38 (1981): 144–165. Anne Brown stated (in WYA, p. 232) that Gershwin told her that he had "composed a trio for Lily and Serena and Maria for that spot in Act III" (presumably the same "spot" as "Lonely Boy"), but "decided to drop the trio and let you sing your favorite melody" (i.e., "Summertime"); Brown possibly misremembered this incident, in which Gershwin perhaps told her about cutting a duet for Bess and Serena; or perhaps he had, indeed, written yet another set piece—this one a trio for Lily, Serena, and Maria.

29. Heyward, "Porgy and Bess Return," p. 28.

30. The title "Pagan Dance" appears among the composer's sketches, but not in the published score or program.

31. WYA, pp. 224–225.

32. For an all-too-brief reference to Britten and *Porgy and Bess,* see Bayan Northcott, "The Search for Simplicity," [London] *Times Literary Supplement* (15 February 1980): "Peter Grimes is audibly steeped in *Porgy and Bess*—and not so much the tunesmith side of Gershwin either, but his much-criticized methods of transition, recitative and scene structure."

33. AV (for Warfield).

34. Maudet, for instance, identifies the promenade theme as a "theme of tragic destiny, of fate" ("le thème du destin tragique, de la fatalité"); the "espressivo" melody as associated with Jake, Clara, and "the simple life of Catfish Row" ("la vie simple de Catfish Row"); and Porgy's theme as symbolizing "his happiness, his triumph" ("son bonheur, son triomphe"); see pp. 31, 35.

35. See JOH, pp. 422–427, and GIL, pp. 182–207, for more on Gershwin's use of leitmotives.

36. JOH, p. 413.

37. Regarding the "African drums" called for by the score (usually rendered by tom-toms), Gershwin apparently had in mind drums that he had heard in a production of the African drama *Kykunkor* at the Chanin Auditorium in New York (see below); Wayne Shirley (e-mail to the author, 4 March 2006) reports that Gershwin scored the onstage band for clarinet, two alto saxophones, tenor saxophone, three trumpets, trombone, snare drum, bass drum, and double-bass; as for why the band parts escaped notice for so long, he writes, "The score prepared by the publishers probably was done from a set of photostats of Gershwin's orchestral score made for the use of conductors. Such a score would have had no use for an appendix containing supplementary parts: the conductor needs a single text going through from beginning to end. The photostat became the ba-

sis for the preparation of the first rental score—remember, the original manuscript was then in the possession of Gershwin's mother—and what had been an omission made for the exigencies of practical performance became an omission due to the inaccessibility of the primary source."

38. DUK/GS, pp. 102–115.

39. Irving Kolodin, "Gershwin Writes an Opera and Harlem Cheers," *Brooklyn Daily Eagle* (27 January 1935).

40. Both Hollis Alpert (ALP, pp. 96–97) and John Andrew Johnson (JOH, p. 247) cast doubt on Calloway's claim that Gershwin modeled the role of Sportin' Life on him, Alpert writing, "But Gershwin's choice for Sportin' Life was, from the beginning, the dapper John W. Bubbles"; Gershwin, of course, may well have drawn inspiration from both men. As mentioned earlier, Johnson also suggests that white composers working in black-influenced idioms may have also influenced *Porgy*, noting, for instance, similarities between "Summertime" and Harold Arlen's "Stormy Weather" (1933).

41. George Shackley, *Spiritual Songs from the Theatre Guild Production of Porgy, a Folk Play by DuBose and Dorothy Heyward* (New York: Bibo, Bloedon and Lang, 1928); Clarence Cameron White, *Forty Negro Spirituals* (Philadelphia: Theodore Presser, 1927); James Weldon Johnson and J. Rosamond Johnson, eds., *The First and Second Books of Negro Spirituals* (New York: Viking Press, 1925–1926); Hall Johnson, The *Green Pastures Spirituals* (New York: Farrar & Rinehart, 1930); *The Carolina Low-Country;* G13. For more on *Porgy*'s relation to the American vernacular, see JOH, pp. 158–265.

42. For the claim, made by one of the opera's original cast members, that "Summertime" deserves comparison sooner with "St. Louis Blues" than "Sometimes I Feel," see Irving Kolodin, "Porgy and Bess: American Opera in the Theatre," *Theatre Arts Monthly* 19, no. 11 (November 1935): 861.

43. Elizabeth Sohler, *The Influence of Gullah Culture on the Opera "Porgy and Bess"* (Master's thesis, University of Kentucky, 1995); Leiding, *Street Cries.*

44. Maureen Needham, *"Kykunkor, or the Witch Woman:* An African Opera in America, 1934," in *Dancing Many Drums: Excavations in African American Dance,* ed. Thomas F. DeFrantz (Madison: University of Wisconsin Press, 2002), pp. 233–252; ALP, p. 107.

45. "Bet on First Opera Lost by Gershwin," *New York Times* (21 July 1935) ("first grand opera"); LEV/SI, p. 190; LEV/MA, p. 126; Shirley, "Reconciliation," p. 161; Shirley, conversation with the author, 15 November 2003 (for "Tristan chord"); JOH, pp. 126–127 (for Wagner caricature); ARM/GG ("Can you play"); JAB/GY, p. 222 ("The production").

46. Nanette Kutner, "Radio Pays a Debt," *Radio Star* (February 1936), GCLC (*Carmen* as "practically a collection of song hits"); G13 (for Verdi and Bizet as composers of "song hits"); Mabie, "Rhapsody on Gershwin" (for Italian opera); "Bet on First Opera" ("an American flavor"); "Tales of Tin Pan Alley."

47. Kolodin, "Gershwin Writes" ("loomed"); Kolodin, "Porgy and Bess," p. 861; see also Mabie, "Rhapsody on Gershwin" (for Mussorgsky); for "Buzzard Song" and Mussorgsky, see chapter 32, n. 10; for more on the opera in the context of folk music see, AUS, pp. 331–332, and especially Ray Allen, "An American Folk Opera? Triangulating Folkness, Blackness, and Americanness in Gersh-

win and Heyward's *Porgy and Bess*," *Journal of American Folklore* 117, no. 465 (Summer 2004): 243–261.

32. The First Production of *Porgy and Bess*

1. GG, letter to DuBose Heyward, 17 December 1934, GCLC; Mark Spergel, *Reinventing Reality: The Art and Life of Rouben Mamoulian* (Metuchen, NJ: Scarecrow Press, 1993), p. 160, writes, contrary to Gershwin's letter, that the guild wanted Houseman and that Gershwin advocated for Mamoulian; ARM/GG, pp. 47–57.

2. Virgil Thomson, *Virgil Thomson* (New York: Da Capo Press, 1966), p. 261.

3. Beginning in 1930, and apparently subsidized by wealthy Russian émigrés, this company was variously called the Russkaya Grand Opera Company, the Russian Opera Company, and the Art of Musical Russia. *Lady Macbeth* had its American premiere in Cleveland on 31 January and its New York premiere on 5 February 1935. The interest in Russian opera during these years extended to the Metropolitan, which gave the American premiere of *Sadko* in 1930.

4. Edward Jablonski, *Harold Arlen: Rhythm, Rainbows, and Blues* (Boston: Northeastern University Press, 1996), pp. 71–72.

5. Martin Bauml Duberman, *Paul Robeson* (New York: Alfred A. Knopf, 1988), p. 193; DuBose Heyward, letters to Paul Robeson, 21 June 1934 and 19 August 1935, Howard University Library, Paul Robeson Collection (Heyward must have been rather out of the loop, as he admitted to Robeson, for he seems to have learned that the latter would not play Porgy only shortly before writing the letter of August 1935); for Calloway, see chapter 31 n. 41.

6. "'Emperor Jones' with Negro Cast," *New York Times* (11 July 1934) (*Cavalleria* appeared on a double bill with Louis Gruenberg's *The Emperor Jones*, with Bledsoe in the starring role; Thernay Georgi sang the role of Turiddu, but otherwise, the cast was black); Edwin D. Johnson, "The Jewel in Ethiope's Ear," *Opportunity* (June 1928): 166–168.

7. Brooks Atkinson, "Experiment in Epic Drama," *New York Times* (14 October 1934).

8. N. S., "Other Music," *New York Times* (11 October 1937); David E. Weaver, *Black Diva of the Thirties: The Life of Ruby Elzy* (Jackson: University Press of Mississippi, 2004), p. 84.

9. "'Emperor Jones'"; WYA, pp. 221–228, 232–233; KIM/G, pp. 179–181 (Duncan, in KIM/G, credits Olin Downes as his principal advocate, as opposed to Anne Brown, in WYA, who gives full credit to Abbie Mitchell; similarly, Duncan, in KIM/G, says "about eight bars" of "Lungi dal caro bene," as opposed to "twelve measures" in WYA); GG, letter to DuBose Heyward, 17 December 1934 (note the possible contradiction between Duncan's recollection of being offered the part of Porgy immediately, and Gershwin's statement about his making "a superb Crown and . . . just as good a Porgy").

10. KIM/G, p, 181; Ned Rorem, "Living with Gershwin," *Opera News* (16 March 1985): 16. The claim that Gershwin wrote "Oh, Bess, Oh Where's My Bess?" and "Oh Lawd, I'm On My Way" with Duncan's voice in mind—or Anne Brown's recollection that he composed "Buzzard Song" specifically af-

ter hearing Duncan sing Mussorgsky's "Song of the Flea" (WYA, p. 233)—needs to be weighed against Duncan's remembrance of hearing "Oh Lawd" at this run-through, and Gershwin's aforementioned 17 December 1934 letter to Heyward, which suggests that the composer cast Duncan only weeks before completing the short score.

11. Barry Singer, "On Hearing Her Sing, Gershwin Made 'Porgy' Porgy and Bess," *New York Times* (29 March 1998); see also James Barron with G. S. Bourdain, "Gershwin Duets," *New York Times* (23 December 1998).

12. WYA, pp. 228–236; Singer, "On Hearing"; JAB, p. 281. Some sources also claim that Gershwin, concerned about Brown's lack of stage experience, had her perform with the London touring company of Lew Leslie's latest *Blackbirds* revue, but according to Brown (letter to the author, 13 June 2004), she arranged that engagement herself.

13. KIM/G, p. 184.

14. ARM/GG, pp. 43–44 ("often astonished"); KIM/G, p. 179 ("wonderful"); WYA, p. 235 ("influential"); GER, p. 83.

15. KIM/G, p. 181; AB; Singer, "On Hearing."

16. ARM/GG, pp. 59–60; Johnson, "The Jewel in Ethiope's Ear," p. 167 ("splendid"); KIM/G, p. 184 ("had written"); Steven Watson, *Prepare for Saints: Gertrude Stein, Virgil Thomson, and the Mainstreaming of American Modernism* (Berkeley: University of California Press, 2000), p. 245 ("our inheritance").

17. ARM/GG, p. 65–71.

18. Singer, "On Hearing."

19. Regarding the 1940–1942 recordings of highlights, Decca originally released the overture and nine numbers with Brown, Duncan, and the Eva Jessye Choir, conducted by Smallens, on a four-record set (with Brown and Duncan doubling up on various parts); in 1942, during the successful Cheryl Crawford revival, Decca recorded another six numbers on a three-disc set with members of that production, including some who had been in the original production, including Brown, Duncan, Matthews, Dowdy, and Harvey, again under Smallens. In 1959 Decca released both sets on one twelve-inch LP; WOR radio broadcast, courtesy of David E. Weaver, also available through Cambria Records (Cambria CD 161, 2000).

20. For a more critical assessment, see Ethan Mordden, *A Guide to Opera Recordings* (New York: Oxford University Press, 1987), pp. 292–296.

21. Irving Kolodin, "Porgy and Bess: American Opera in the Theatre," *Theatre Arts Monthly* 19, no. 11 (November 1935): 853–865; WYA, pp. 224, 231.

22. KIM/G, pp. 181 ("very, very"), 184 ("George didn't"); WYA, pp. 223 ("to dance"), 231 ("all sorts"), 233 ("smoked"); ARM/GG, p. 61 ("enthusiastic"); JAB, p. 286 ("You can't"); for an example of ad libs indicated in the vocal score, see, for example, "Everyone on stage thanks and blesses Archdale for his kindness," *Porgy and Bess* (New York: Gershwin Publishing, 1935), p. 233.

23. Some sources alternatively put the number of pit musicians at forty-two or forty-four; note that the Alvin Theatre program lists fourteen, not eleven, members of the Charleston Orphans' Band, but one served as a drum-major and two others assisted the double-bass (and whereas the members of the Jenkins Orphanage Band used in the stage play came from Charleston, the Charleston Or-

phans' Band probably consisted of local musicians, according to Wayne Shirley, interview with the author, 5 March 2006). For an account of the use of goats in various productions of *Porgy and Bess*, see Dorothy Heyward, "Porgy's Goat," *Harpers* 215, no. 1291 (December 1957): 37–41.

24. Reviews of *Porgy and Bess* in the *Christian Science Monitor,* [Boston] *Evening American, Evening Transcript, Globe, Herald, Post, Traveler* (all 1 October 1935), *Daily Record* (2 October 1935), *Herald* (6 October 1935), *Musical America* (10 October 1935).

25. Warren Storey Smith, review of *Porgy and Bess* in the *Boston Post* (1 October 1935); Smith reiterated his concerns in "'Rhapsody' Gershwin Classic, the News of the World of Music," *Boston Post* (18 July 1937).

26. Mamoulian stated (ARM/GG, p. 52), "Porgy and Bess as performed in New York was almost forty-five minutes shorter than the original score," though by "original," he very possibly meant the already-cut Boston version.

27. Charles Hamm, "The Theatre Guild Production of *Porgy and Bess*," *Journal of the American Musicological Society* 40, no. 3 (Fall 1987): 495–532; ARM/GG, p. 52. Like so many other Gershwin anecdotes, this story has taken on a life of its own, with the composer allegedly presenting Mamoulian with reams of cut music; Miles Kreuger (interview by the author, 3 September 2003) recalled that Mamoulian had told him that Gershwin had said on this occasion, "Rouben, it's all the junk you made me take out of *Porgy and Bess*."

28. GOL, p. 325 ("You won't"; see also Steinert's recollections, ARM/GG, pp. 44–46); ARM/GG, p. 52; KIM/G, p. 181 ("He was upset"); ALP, pp. 301, 303 ("were anathema"); Eva Jessye's statement about, apparently, the Jasbo Brown music— "A lot of the gutbucket stuff he particularly liked had to be cut"— also suggested some unhappiness on Gershwin's part; Spergel, *Reinventing Reality*, p. 162.

29. JOH, pp. 474–475, has argued in favor of taking cuts in the craps-game scene, while Wayne D. Shirley, "Porgy and Bess," *Library of Congress Quarterly Journal* 31 (1974): 104, wrote that the opera "flows better" without the "Buzzard Song," and in a letter to the author (22 December 2004) defends the removal of Porgy's reprise of "A Woman Is a Sometime Thing," which, he writes, "brings the action to a halt where it should move forward"; Geoffrey Block, "Gershwin's Buzzard and Other Mythological Creatures," *Opera Quarterly* 2 (1990): 74–82, also argued that "Buzzard Song" "creates an intrusion that undermines the effect of a scene that otherwise successfully shows Porgy and Bess as fully accepted members of the Catfish Row community" (p. 79). On the other hand, "Buzzard Song" not only introduces some important musical themes developed later in the opera and generally functions as a forewarning of things to come, but represents and elucidates the triumph of Porgy's love, helping to detail what's at stake for the protagonist.

30. PEY, p. 245; OHL, p. 97. In a review of the opera, *Variety* (16 October 1935) reported that the premiere was slated to begin at 8:10, began at 8:25, and ended at 11:20; and further stated that an additional ten-minute cut would allow a playing time from 8:30 to 11:10.

31. Reviews (often music and drama) of *Porgy and Bess* in the [New York] *Daily News, Evening Journal, Herald-Tribune, Mirror, Sun, Times, World-Telegram*

(all 11 October 1935), *Brooklyn Daily Eagle* and *Women's Wear Daily* (both 11 October 1935), [New York] *American* and *Post* (both 12 October 1935), *New York Sunday News* (13 October 1935), *Variety* (16 October 1935), *Time* (21 October 1935), *Commonweal* and *Musical America* (both 25 October 1935), *Nation* and *New Republic* (both 30 October 1935), *Stage* 13, no. 2 (November 1935): 31–33; Irving Kolodin in *Theatre Arts Monthly* 19, no. 11 (November 1935): 853–65; *Modern Music* 13, no. 1 (November–December 1935): 13–19; W. J. Henderson in *New York Sun* (December 1935), GCLC; Edith J. R. Isaacs in *Theatre Arts Monthly* 19, no. 12 (December 1935): 888–902, GCLC; Paul Rosenfeld, *Discoveries of a Music Critic* (New York: Harcourt Brace, 1936).

32. WYA, pp. 230–231 ("a very"); Marcia Davenport in *Stage* held Brown largely responsible for the "staginess" of the two love duets, notwithstanding the loveliness of her voice; Stark Young, *New Republic* review ("beautiful"); Burns Mantle, *Daily News* review ("amazing picture").

33. ALP, pp. 136–137; HYL, p. 170.

34. ALP, pp. 123–124; Barron, "Gershwin Duets."

35. Reviews of *Porgy and Bess* in the [Philadelphia] *Daily News, Evening Bulletin, Evening Public Ledger, Inquirer* (all 28 January 1936), [Pittsburgh] *Press* and *Sun-Telegraph* (both 11 February 1936), [Chicago] *American, Daily Journal* ("first step"), *Daily Times, Herald, Tribune* (all 18 February 1936), [Detroit] *Evening Times* and *News* (both 10 March 1936), [Detroit] *Free Press* (11 March 1936), [Washington, D.C.] *Daily News, Evening Star, Post, Times* (all 17 March 1936).

36. Carl Diton, "Diton on the New Opera: Music Master Gives Studied Opinion on New Creation of George Gershwin," *New York Amsterdam News* (19 October 1935); reviews of *Porgy and Bess* in *Opportunity* 14, no. 1 (January 1936): 24–28 and *Chicago Defender* (both 22 February 1936); Matthews quoted by Robert Garland, "Negroes Are Critical of 'Porgy and Bess,'" *New York World-Telegram* 68 (16 January 1936): 14.

37. Henry Cowell (letter to David Ewen, 7 December 1954, Cowell Collection, NYPL) stated, regarding *Porgy and Bess,* "Gershwin took me to hear it, and was overcome with joy. He felt with greatest sincerity that it was the greatest work ever produced in this country."

33. *Porgy and Bess* in Revival

1. Merle Armitage, *Accent on America* (New York: E. Weyhe, 1944), pp. 163–166; reviews of *Porgy and Bess* in the [Los Angeles] *Daily News* (4 February 1938), *Evening Herald, Evening News, Times* (all 5 February 1938), *Times* (6 February 1938), *Saturday Night* (12 February 1938), GCLC; ARM/GGML, pp. 151–152.

2. Cheryl Crawford, *One Naked Individual: My Fifty Years in the Theatre* (New York: Bobbs-Merrill, 1977), p. 112–115.

3. Crawford, *One Naked Individual*, p. 114.

4. Reviews of *Porgy and Bess* in the [Boston] *Daily Globe, Evening American, Herald, Post, Traveler* (all 30 December 1941), [New York] *Daily News, Herald-Tribune, Journal-American, P.M., Post, Sun, Times, World-Telegram* (all 23 January 1942), *Variety* (28 January 1942), *New Yorker* (31 January 1942), *Life* (23 February 1942), *Catholic World* 154, no. 924 (March 1942): 726–727,

[Rochester] *Times-Union* (29 September 1942), *New York Times* (5 July 1942), *Variety* (15 September 1943), *New York Journal-American* (8 February 1944). For a complete itinerary of this tour, see ARM/GGML.

5. ALP, p. 169; GER, p. 83; William Warfield, in contrast, thought the expunging of the word "salutary," writing that although the word might be "appropriate and dramatically effective" in some contexts, "it would be unacceptable to give the word currency—and maybe even a stamp of approval—through loose usage for mixed audiences": Warfield with Alton Miller, *William Warfield: My Music & My Life* (Champaign, IL: Sagamore Publishing, 1991).

6. Brooks Atkinson, "Music in Catfish Row," *New York Times* (1 February 1942); Virgil Thomson, "Porgy in Maplewood," *New York Herald-Tribune* (19 October 1941); Robert Garland, "'Porgy and Bess' at Mitchel Field," *New York Journal-American* (22 September 1944).

7. Robert Lawrence, *New York Herald-Tribune* (23 January 1942); idem, "More about 'Porgy,'" *New York Herald-Tribune*, (1 February 1942), GCLC; Louis Kronenberger, *P.M.* (23 January 1942); Thomson, "Porgy in Maplewood."

8. The date of the Danish premiere is given alternatively as 23 March and 27 March 1943; EWE, pp. 249–251; "Nazis Criticize 'Porgy and Bess,'" *Chicago Defender* (17 April 1943); Geoffrey Lamb, "The Danish 'Porgy,'" *Opera* (February 1991): 169–170; Ejnar Thomsen, "Besættelse og Befrielse," in *Teatret paa Kongens Nytorv 1748–1948* (Copenhagen: Berlingske, 1948); Georg Leicht and Marianne Hallar, *Det kongelige Teaters Repertoire 1889–1975* (Ballerup: Bibliotekscentralens, 1977); Robert Neiiendam, *Den danske Nationalscene under Besættelsen* (1946), p. 231; premiere program of *Porgy og Bess*; reviews (all 28 March 1943): Erik Abrahamsen, "'Porgy og Bess' paa Det kongelige Teater," and St. Paul, "Fra Parkettet" (for the hair roller story), *Berlingske Tidende*; K. B., "Mere Italien end Amerika," *Social-Demokraten*; Sverre Forchhammer, "Neger-opera paa Det kgl," *Børsen*; Vagn Kappel, "'Porgy og Bess' paa Det kgl. Teater," *Kristelig Dagblad*; Axel Kjerulf, "Premièren i Aftes paa Gershwins' Neger-Opera," *Politiken*; Frithiof Rolsted, "En Skændsel for Det kgl. Teater," *Fædrelandet*; Nils Schiørring, "Pegeroperæn paa Det Kgl.," *National Tidende*; Georg Wiinblad, "Neger-Operæn 'Porgy og Bess'" *Social-Demokraten*; all Danish materials courtesy of Lilo Skaarup, Danish Royal Opera.

9. Wiinblad, "Neger-Operæn"; Rolsted, "En Skændsel"; Abrahamsen, "'Porgy og Bess'" ("kan sit Kram").

10. Common lore states that the Danish underground (as opposed to Danish disc jockeys) interrupted radio broadcasts by playing "It Ain't Necessarily So," but this is highly unlikely: René Peschcke-Koedt (member of the Danish underground), interview by the author, 8 February 2005; moreover, Danish disc jockeys and radio announcers were known for being slyly subversive.

11. Irving Kolodin, "Charleston Revisited," *Saturday Review* 34, no. 39 (29 September 1951): 50–51; Virgil Thomson, "Music and Musicians," *New York Herald-Tribune* (7 October 1951); Douglas Watt, "Concert Records," *New Yorker* (10 November 1951): 133–135.

12. AV (*"Porgy and Bess"*).

13. AV ("Being Bess").

14. Wayne Shirley (e-mail to the author, 30 November 2003) states that the

Breen version provided the basis for the libretto as found in Stanley Richards, ed., *Ten Great Musicals of the American Theatre*, vol. 1 (Radnor, PA: Chilton Book Company, 1973).

15. Warfield, *William Warfield*, p. 131; ALP, pp. 167 ("If I were cast"), 191 ("I was always").

16. Dallas, Chicago, Pittsburgh, and Washington, D.C., reviews of *Porgy and Bess*, GCLC; John Rosenfield, "A New 'Porgy' in Dallas," *Saturday Review* (28 June 1952), Jay Carmody, "Greatest 'Porgy and Bess' Opens in Triumph Here," *Washington Evening Star* (6 August 1952), Paul Hume, "'Porgy' Has Punch on 2d Viewing," *Washington Post* (17 August 1952). Calloway joined the cast in the midst of the Dallas run, not in Chicago, as stated in ALP, p. 167.

17. Joseph D. Bibb, "Catfish Row," *Pittsburgh Courier* (26 July 1952); Warfield, *William Warfield*, pp. 132–133; Brooks Atkinson, "Negro Folk Drama," *New York Times* (7 September 1952); see also "New Role for Porgy and Bess," *Chicago Sun-Times* (26 June 1952); Ann Marsters, "'Porgy and Bess' Becomes Reply to Red Propaganda," *Chicago Herald-Tribune* (29 June 1952); Gwynne Kuhner Brown, "A Dubious Triumph: *Porgy and Bess* as Propaganda, 1951–1956," annual meeting of the American Musicological Society (Seattle, 18 November 2004), courtesy of the author.

18. Austrian and German reviews of *Porgy and Bess*, GCLC, including Dezsö Hajas, "Porgy and Bess," *Der Abend* (8 September 1952) (translated as "Ambassador Porgy," *Newsweek* [22 September 1952]); Max Graf, "Gershwin Meisterwerk," [Vienna] *Welt Press* (9 September 1952); Friedrich Torberg, "Post Scriptum," *Wiener Kurier* (11 September 1952); Kurt Westphal, "Jubel um 'Porgy und Bess,'" *Die Berliner Abendzeitung* (18 September 1952) ("Aber das Wort 'Kitsch' kommt hier gar nicht auf, weil sich diese Musik so selbstverständlich dem, was auf der Bühne vor sich geht, einfügt"); Werner Oehlmann, "Porgy and Bess," [Berlin] *Tagesspiegel*, and H. H. Stuckenschmidt, "Die amerikanische Volksoper 'Porgy and Bess,'" *Die Neue Zeitung* (both 19 September 1952). See also John MacCormac, "'Porgy' Scores Hit at Bow in Vienna," *New York Times* (8 September 1952); review of *Porgy and Bess* in *Variety* (17 September 1952); Jack Raymond, "Berlin Loves 'Bess' as Much as 'Porgy,'" *New York Times* (18 September 1952); Don Cook, "'Porgy,' a Hit Abroad," *New York Herald-Tribune* (28 September 1952).

19. In addition to the articles cited in note 18, see especially K. M., "Begesiterungsstürme um 'Porgy und Bess,'" *Wiener Kurier* (8 September 1952); Felix Hubalek, "Porgy und Bess," [Vienna] *Arbeiter-Zeitung*, and Fritz Skorzeny, "Porgy and Bess," *Neue Wiener Tageszeitung* (both 9 September 1952); and Erwin von Mittag, "Jazz erneuert die Oper," [Vienna] *Die Presse* (13 September 1952). Hubalek made the unusual point that the work could not be considered an American folk opera until Americans fully identified with their country's black minority; but he saw Gershwin as "a great step forward on this path" ("einen grossen Schritt auf diesem Weg vorwärts").

20. British reviews of *Porgy and Bess*, GCLC, including "Porgy and Bess," *Edinburgh Scotsman* (11 October 1952) (for another comparison to *Wozzeck*, see D. C. B., "At the Opera," *Punch* [22 October 1952]), Sidney Harrison, "Trouble in Catfish Row," *John o' London's Weekly* (undated), Kenneth Tynan, "Catfish Row Sets the Heart Pounding," *London Evening Standard* (10 Octo-

ber 1952), Mosco Carner, "Porgy and Bess," *Time & Tide* (18 October 1952); see also "'Porgy and Bess' Opens in London," *New York Times* (10 October 1952); "Porgy Orgy," *Time* (20 October 1952).

21. Nicole Hirsch, "'Porgy and Bess,' l'opéra noir de Gershwin a connu le triomphe," [Paris] *Le Soir* ("Divin, sensationnel, bouleversant, extraordinaire, prodigieux," "la pureté," "la force"); Emile Vuillermoz, "'Porgy and Bess' au théâtre de l'Empire," *Paris-Presse L'Intransigeant;* Claude Baignères, "'Porgy and Bess," *Le Figaro* ("Gershwin a renversé le mur où tant de compositeurs se sont heurtés le front, il a dit, mieux encore qu'un documentaire cinématographique, la vérité. . . . Et pourtant nulle musique ne peut être plus neuve, plus originale, plus directe et plus efficace"); René Dumesnil, "'Porgy and Bess' de Gershwin," *Le Monde* (all 18 February 1953); Ned Rorem, "'Porgy' Brightens Paris, in Musical Doldrums," *New York Herald-Tribune* (17 February 1953); see also "Paris Greets Opening of 'Porgy and Bess,'" *New York Times* (17 February 1953); Emile Vuillermoz, "Lessons from Bali Dancers and Touring 'Porgy and Bess,'" *Christian Science Monitor* (7 March 1953) ("dazzling," "extraordinary").

22. Dwight D. Eisenhower, letter to Blevins Davis, 30 March 1953, GCLC; Eleanor Roosevelt, "Mrs. Roosevelt Likes New 'Porgy and Bess,'" *New York World-Telegram and Sun* (31 March 1953).

23. Warfield had hoped at least to open the Broadway run, and, as he tells it, the reluctance of Breen and Davis to meet him halfway proved not only a wrenching professional disappointment, but a precipitating factor in the collapse of his marriage to Price: Warfield, *William Warfield*, pp. 142–147; Sam Zolotow, "Tibbett Goes on July 15 as Porgy," *New York Times* (24 June 1953); "'Porgy and Bess' May Visit Japan," *New York Times* (14 July 1953); John Chapman, review of *Porgy and Bess* in the *New York Daily News* (10 March 1953) (for *Der Rosenkavalier*).

24. George Freedley, "Off Stage—and On" (unidentified and undated), GCLC ("never heard"); Brooks Atkinson, "At the Theatre," *New York Times* (10 March 1953).

25. Stephen Sondheim, letter to the author, 8 September 2005 ("favorite musical"); Steve Swayne, *How Sondheim Found His Sound* (Ann Arbor: University of Michigan Press, 2005), pp. 68–77; for more on a comparison of at least the music of "Losing My Mind" and "The Man I Love," see pp. 105–107.

26. American and Canadian reviews of *Porgy and Bess*, GCLC, including Herbert Whittaker, "Showbusiness," *Toronto Globe and Mail* (5 April 1954); George Jean Nathan, "Met Bing and Ziegfeld Band," *New York Journal-American* (12 April 1953); see also William Hawkins, "'Porgy and Bess' Again Thrill Theatergoers," *New York World-Telegram,* Walter Kerr, "Porgy and Bess," *New York Herald-Tribune,* Richard Watts Jr., "The Return of 'Porgy and Bess,'" *New York Post* (all 10 March 1953), and Harold Clurman, "Porgy and Bess," *Nation* (28 March 1953); Claudia Cassidy ("On the Aisle," *Chicago Tribune* [3 March 1954]) was one of those rare critics who generally preferred the original Mamoulian production; "Director Bars Plea to Tone Down Scenes," *Los Angeles Times* (14 July 1954); "Ministers Find 'Porgy' Hygienic," *Los Angeles Mirror* (16 July 1954).

27. Eric Bentley, "A Major Musical," *New Republic* 128 (6 April 1953):

30–31; V. L. Bellerby, "Second Thoughts on 'Porgy and Bess,'" *Jazz Journal* 6, no. 1 (January 1953): 6 (Bellerby still recommended the show as "an exhilarating, exciting experience"); in a related vein, see Rudi Blesh, *Shining Trumpets: A History of Jazz* (New York: Alfred A. Knopf, 1958), pp. 204–205; SPE, p. 28 (for Arvey's letter of 17 May 1953); James L. Hicks, "We Don't Need 'Porgy and Bess,'" [Baltimore] *Afro Magazine, Afro-American* (28 March 1953); James L. Hicks, "Theatricals," *New York Amsterdam News* (6 September 1958); Dean Gordon Hancock, "'Dangerous Propaganda' Says This Critic of Planned Tour," and George Daniels, "Amusing Art, People the World over Should See, Says Another," both in the *Chicago Defender* (17 April 1954); Hicks articles courtesy of Gwynne Kuhner Brown.

28. "'Porgy' Bows in Venice," *New York Times* (23 September 1954); "'Porgy' Is Cheered in La Scala Opening," *New York Times* (23 February 1955); "Leningrad Sees 'Porgy' Company," *New York Times* (27 December 1955); "'Porgy and Bess' Wins Ovation in Moscow," *Daily Worker* (12 January 1956); "From Catfish Row to the Kremlin," *Saturday Review* (14 January 1956): 37–38; Welles Hangen, "'Porgy and Bess' in the U.S.S.R.," *New York Times* (15 January 1956); Ollie Stewart, "An American Opera Conquers Europe," *Theatre Arts* 39, no. 10 (October 1955): 30–32, 93–94.

29. Aram Khachaturian, "Homage to George Gershwin," *Masses and Mainstream* 8, no. 11 (1955): 24–26; see also idem, "George Gershwin," *Uj zenei szemle* 6, no. 12 (December 1955): 32–33.

30. ALP, pp. 189–247 ("a masterwork," p. 205); Riccardo Malipiero, "Porgy and Bess," *La biennale di Venezia* 22 (1954): 36–38 ("Gershwin non aveva una tradizione da difendere, una civiltà da spiegare, una crisi da sistemare; aveva da scrivere un'opera, coi suoi mezzi, coi suoi desideri[,] con la sua passione"); David Platt, "Letters from Prague Reveal Divided Opinions on 'Porgy and Bess,'" *Daily Worker* (22 March 1956): 5–7 (for Wheeler; and "painful position," etc., attributed to Josef Kotek); Russian critic U. Kovalyer, like some German colleagues, suggested that the work's organic fusion of drama, music, and dance more specifically owed a debt to the "original combination of melody and movement" as found in such African American forms as ragtime and the blues: U. Kovalyer, "The Russian Critic," *Saturday Review* (14 January 1956): 38.

31. Maya Angelou, *Singin' and Swingin' and Gettin' Merry Like Christmas* (New York: Random House, 1976), pp. 126–256 ("in the course," p. 166; "the greatest," p. 247); AV ("*Porgy and Bess*"). Angelou recalled seeing Warfield as Porgy in San Francisco, an apparent inaccuracy; she also commented (somewhat negatively) on the "many male homosexuals in the company" (Angelou, *Singin'*, p. 246).

32. Truman Capote, *The Muses Are Heard* (New York: Random House, 1956), p. 178 (Capote suggested reasons for Leningrad's lukewarm reception of the work beyond the lack of programs, including assertions that the production's eroticism shocked the city's puritanical audiences, and that it had simply fallen off in quality); Osgood Caruthers, "Catfish Row a la Soviet," *New York Times* (28 May 1961).

33. Fred Grunfeld, "The Great American Opera," *Opera News* 24, no. 20 (19 March 1960): 6–9.

34. Howard Taubman, "A Rich 'Porgy,'" *New York Times* (18 May 1961);

John Ardoin, "Warfield Outstanding in Porgy and Bess," *Musical America* 81, no. 7 (July 1961): 45; Raymond Ericson, "City Opera Gives 'Porgy and Bess,'" *New York Times* (2 April 1962); Winthrop Sargeant, "Musical Events," *New Yorker* (14 April 1962): 174–176.

35. Harold Schonberg, "Once Again, 'Porgy and Bess,'" *New York Times* (6 March 1965); ALP, pp. 291–292; AV ("You saw people").

36. Beryl Te Wiata, *Inia Te Wiata: Most Happy Fella* (Auckland: Hutchinson Group, 1976, repr. 1982), pp. 179–199; Henare sang in the chorus and understudied for Sportin' Life, while Selwyn played Jim, a minor role.

37. ALP, pp. 289–291; Joseph Wechsberg, "Vienna," *Opera News* (11 December 1965): 32; "American Tour Group Stars a Maori as Porgy," *New York Times* (15 September 1966); "Revive 'Porgy & Bess' In Estonia," *Variety* (15 February 1967): 22; James Helme Sutcliffe, "East Berlin," *Opera News* (14 March 1970): 32–34 ("There's no doubt"); idem, "West Berlin," *Opera* (June 1971): 535–537; see also Paul Moor, "'Porgy' Comes to Germany," *High Fidelity/Musical America* 20, no. 8 (August 1970): 28–29.

38. Program notes, *Porgy und Bess*, Komische Oper (premiering 24 January 1970); program notes, *Porgy and Bess*, Theater des Westens (premiering 28 May 1988); Götz Friedrich, "'Porgy und Bess': Von der 'Neger'-Opera zur Volksoper"; "'Porgy und Bess' von George Gershwin: Zwanzig Notizen zu einer Aufführungskonzeption," *Musiktheater: Ansichten—Einsichten* (Berlin: Propyläen, 1986) (courtesy of the Deutsche Oper); Dolly Hauns, e-mail to the author, 28 January 2004. Friedrich apparently made some scenic changes for the 1989 production in response to objections from the Gershwin estate regarding the Kittiwah Island design.

39. Harold Cruse, *The Crisis of the Negro Intellectual* (New York: William Morrow, 1967), pp. 100–109; Tim Dennison Sr., *The American Negro and His Amazing Music* (New York: Vantage Press, 1963), pp. 45–48; Loften Mitchell, *Black Drama: The Story of the American Negro in the Theatre* (New York: Hawthorn Books, 1967), p. 120.

40. Gilbert Chase, *America's Music: From the Pilgrims to the Present* (New York: McGraw-Hill, 1955), pp. 637–640; William W. Austin, *Music in the 20th Century from Debussy through Stravinsky* (New York: W. W. Norton, 1966), pp. 502–503; H. Wiley Hitchcock, *Music in the United States: A Historical Introduction* (Englewood Cliffs, NJ: Prentice-Hall, 1969), p. 158; Richard Crawford, "It Ain't Necessarily Soul: Gershwin's 'Porgy and Bess' as a Symbol," *Yearbook for Inter-American Musical Research* 8 (1972): 17–38. Austin admitted that the opera's "tunes were splendid"; that for some listeners, its shortcomings "were outweighed by its vitality"; and that Gershwin's music in general "satisfied a widely felt need better than any other." For his part, Hitchcock wrote that *Porgy* offered "a more pretentious but hardly more artistically successful contribution [than *Of Thee I Sing*]," adding that it "relied mainly on some memorable songs." For a later assessment that emphasized the opera's perpetuation of "stereotypes," see Sam Dennison, *Scandalize My Name: Black Imagery in American Popular Music* (New York: Garland, 1982), pp. 472–473.

41. Louis Biancolli, "Gershwin Formula Died with Him," *New York World-Telegram and Sun* (8 June 1965); MEL, pp. 392–413.

42. Michael Gray, "One of These Mornings, You're Gonna Rise Up Singing: Recording Porgy and Bess," *Absolute Sound* (April 1995): 131–134 ("one of"); Eric Salzman, "Porgy & Bess: A New London Recording," *Stereo Review* (April 1976): 74–75 ("Gershwin's").

43. William Youngren, "Gershwin, Part IV," *New Republic* 176 (14 May 1977): 23–27; Salzman, "Porgy & Bess."

44. "Porgy and Bess: Musical Cuts," Archives, Houston Grand Opera.

45. Reviews of *Porgy and Bess* in the *New York Times* (27 September 1976) ("strongly"), *New York Daily News* (27 September 1976), *New York Times* (10 October 1976) ("There's got"), *Village Voice* (11 October 1976), *Newsweek* (11 October 1976). For more on Clamma Dale, see the *Newsweek* review, which quoted her as saying, "Very few singers are able to do justice to the role of Bess, because not only do you need an operatic voice and the ability to act, but you must also be constantly aware of the sensuousness of your own body without ever being slutty. Bess is sensual and sexy, but at the same time she wants to be respected by her peers. Society, even today, doesn't want to let a woman be both."

46. Reviews of *Porgy and Bess* in the [New York] *Post* and *Daily News* (both 27 September 1976), *New York* (11 October 1976).

47. Irving Lowens, "'Porgy and Bess' in Fine Revival," *Washington Star* (25 August 1976); ALP, p. 299; "D.C. Loves Houston's 'Porgy,'" *Houston Chronicle* (25 August 1976) ("Every").

48. Lawrence Starr, "Toward a Reevaluation of Gershwin's Porgy and Bess," delivered at the annual meeting of the American Musicological Society (20 October 1978); *American Music* 2 (Summer 1984): 25–37.

49. Harold C. Schonberg, "A Minority Report on 'Porgy,'" *New York Times* (17 October 1976); Richard Crawford, "Gershwin's Reputation: A Note on Porgy and Bess," *Musical Quarterly* 65 (1979): 257–264.

50. John Von Rhein, "'Porgy' Is Super on Both Ends of Stage," *Chicago Tribune* (18 February 1983); Walter Kerr, "'Porgy and Bess' Finds Its Showcase at Radio City," *New York Times* (1 May 1983); see also other reviews of the 1983 tour, Archives, Houston Grand Opera; for Leonore Gershwin, see ALP, p. 316.

51. George Heymont, "In It Together," *Opera News* (28 March 1987); Tim Smith, "'Porgy and Bess' Revival a Cooperative Effort," *Ft. Lauderdale News* (26 December 1986); see also other reviews of the 1986–1987 tour, Archives, Houston Grand Opera.

52. Joseph C. Koenenn, "A Grand Entrance for 'Porgy and Bess,'" *Newsday* (3 February 1985) ("worthy," "fabulous"); Samuel G. Freedman, "After 50 Years, 'Porgy' Comes to the Met as a Classic," *New York Times* (3 February 1985) ("psychological"); Nan Robertson, "Populating Catfish Row on the Met Opera Stage," *New York Times* (5 February 1985) ("complete"); Bill Zakariasen, "The real 'Porgy and Bess,'" *Daily News* (6 February 1985) ("Gershwin was," "perhaps the"; courtesy of the Metropolitan Opera).

53. Reviews of *Porgy and Bess* in the [New York] *Daily News, Times, Post* (all 8 February 1985), *Washington Post* (8 February 1985), *Wall Street Journal* (12 February 1985), *Newsweek, New York, Time* (all 18 February 1986), *New Yorker* (25 February 1985), *Village Voice* (26 February 1985), [New York] *Daily*

News and *Times* (both 3 March 1985), *Los Angeles Herald-Examiner* (24 March 1985); ALP, p. 327 (for television broadcast).

54. Ned Rorem, "Living with Gershwin," *Opera News* (16 March 1985): 11–18, 46. Indiana University Opera Theater produced *Porgy and Bess* in 1976 and 1979, both times with a mostly black cast.

55. Frank Rich, "In Its 'Porgy,' the Met Out-Broadways Broadway," *New York Times* (21 March 1985).

56. In 1971, for instance, Ib Hansen and Ellen Winther sang the title roles in a production at the Danish Royal Opera under Tamás Vetö; Donal Henahan, "In Opera, Race Isn't a Black or White Issue," *New York Times* (14 April 1985); Edward Rothstein, "George Gershwin's Heav'nly Lan'," *New Republic* (18 March 1985); Michael Billington, "Learning to Live on Catfish Row," *Guardian* (6 October 1992) ("unperformable"); Paul Thomason, "The Problem with Porgy and Bess," *Opera News* (August 1998): 18–22 (for Alexander); M. Owen Lee, review of *Porgy and Bess* in *Opera Quarterly* 7, no. 2 (Summer 1990): 153–156; Steven Ledbetter, interview by the author, 18 February 2005.

57. Thomason, "The Problem" (for Alexander); Leighton Kerner, "Lulu, Bess, and Others," *Village Voice* (16 April 1985); see also reviews of *Porgy and Bess* in the [New York] *Daily News* and *Times* (both 30 October 1985), *New York Times* (29 September 1989), *New York* (16 October 1989), *New York Times* (4 November 1990), *Newsday* (5 November 1990).

58. Nicholas Kenyon, *Simon Rattle: From Birmingham to Berlin* (London: Faber and Faber, 1987); *In Memoriam Lily Pons* appears to be a variant title for *Nocturne for Lily Pons,* the orchestral version of *For Lily Pons.*

59. Lee, review in *Opera Quarterly;* John Steane, "Porgy and Bess," *Opera* (October 1992): 1154–1162.

60. Joseph Lelyveld, "Briton Stirred by New 'Porgy' at Glyndebourne," *New York Times* (8 July 1986) ("general," "Disneyesque"); Billington, "Learning to Live" ("I've").

61. Rodney Milnes, "All the Things You Are," *Opera* (October 1992): 1148–1152; reviews of *Porgy and Bess* in the [London] *Daily Telegraph, Financial Times, Times* ("this opera") (all 7 July 1986), *Observer* (13 July 1986) ("an unqualified"), [Toronto] *Globe and Mail* (23 July 1986), *Times Literary Supplement* (25 July 1986) ("one of the handful"), *New York Times* (19 August 1986), *Opera* (August 1986), *Musical Times* (September 1987), [London] *Times* (7 August 1987), *Financial Times, Guardian, Independent* (all 8 August 1987) (courtesy of the Glyndebourne Festival).

62. Damon Evans (with David Ellison), "Glyndebourne Will Never Be the Same Again," *Glyndebourne Festival Programme Book* (1987) (courtesy of the Glyndebourne Festival).

63. The video's Clara and Jake—Paula Ingram and Gordon Hawkins—lip-synched to Blackwell and Hubbard, the latter of whom died young in 1991; Billington, "Learning to Live"; reviews reveal that the production, if not the video, included at least "Buzzard Song."

64. "New Production, Conducted by John DeMain and Directed by Hope Clarke, to Tour Japan in 1996" (news release), Archives, Houston Grand Opera; Rosalyn M. Story, "Hope Clarke, the First African-American to Direct Gersh-

win's Masterpiece, Casts the Work in a New Light for Houston Grand Opera," *Opera News* (21 January 1995).

65. American, French, and Italian reviews of *Porgy and Bess* (1995–1996), *USA Today* (16 February 1995), *Opera* (November 1996) ("not only"), *Le Figaro* (19 December 1996) (for Pierre-Petit), and others in the Archives, Houston Grand Opera.

66. *The Gershwins' Porgy and Bess* (Paris: Opéra Bastille, 1996) ("d'une pure et simple affirmation de la vie"); DUA; André Gauthier, *George Gershwin* (Paris: Hachette, 1973); Alain Lacombe, *George Gershwin: Une chronique de Broadway* (Paris: Francis Van de Velde, 1980); Eric Lipmann, *L'Amérique de George Gershwin* (Paris: Messine, 1981); Denis Jeambar, *George Gershwin* (Paris: Mazarine, 1982); ALP; Charles Hamm, "The Theatre Guild Production of *Porgy and Bess*," *Journal of the American Musicological Society* 40, no. 3 (Fall 1987): 495–532; Joseph P. Swain, *The Broadway Musical: A Critical and Musical Survey* (New York: Oxford University Press, 1990), pp. 51–72; ROS, pp. 263–319; Geoffrey Block, *Enchanted Evenings: The Broadway Musical from Show Boat to Sondheim* (New York: Oxford University Press, 1997), pp. 60–84; Raymond Knapp, *The American Musical and the Formation of National Identity* (Princeton, NJ: Princeton University Press, 2005), pp. 194–204; Elizabeth Sohler, *The Influence of Gullah Culture on the Opera "Porgy and Bess"* (master's thesis, University of Kentucky, 1995); JOH; AV.

67. Reviews of *Porgy and Bess* in the *New York Times* (9 March 2000 and 5 March 2002); David Schiff, "The Man Who Breathed Life into 'Porgy and Bess,'" *New York Times* (5 March 2000); see also Elysa Gardner, "We Loves You, 'Porgy,'" *USA Today* (20 March 2002).

68. Cori Ellison, "An Interview with Francesca Zambello," *Washington National Opera Playbill* (November 2005) (courtesy of the Washington National Opera).

69. Reviews of *Porgy and Bess* in the *Washington Times* and *Washington Post* (both 31 October 2005), *l'Unitá* (1 November 2005) ("Parlare di uragani nei paraggi della Casa Bianca è come parlare di corda in casa dell' impiccato"), *MetroWeekly* (3 November 2005), [Washington] *Sun* (4 November 2005), *Washington Informer* (3–9 November 2005), *Ópera Actual* (December 2005), *Opera News* 70/3 (February 2006); "Porgy and Bess Simulcast Draws Thousands," *Washington National Opera Season Book* (Spring 2006): 15–16 (courtesy of the Washington National Opera).

70. For instance, in *Camp*—a 2003 film about a musical-theater camp—a black teenager wonders why they can't put on an all-black show like *Porgy and Bess* or *Bring in 'da Noise, Bring in 'da Funk*.

34. *Porgy and Bess* on Disc, Film, and the Concert Stage

1. Reviews (1936 and 1937) of Suite from *Porgy and Bess* in the [Chicago] *Daily News, Daily Times, Evening American,* [Philadelphia] *Daily News, Public Ledger,* [San Francisco] *Chronicle, News Call-Bulletin,* [Seattle] *Post-Intelligencer, Star,* [St. Louis] *Post Dispatch, Star-Times,* [Washington, D.C.] *Star, Post, Times,* and others, GCLC.

2. RIM, pp. 448–449.

3. FER, pp. 183–184.

4. Olin Downes, "'Porgy' Fantasy," *New York Times* (15 November 1942).

5. Richard Glazier, liner notes, *Gershwin: Remembrance and Discovery* (Centaur CRC 2271, 1995).

6. Josefa Heifetz, liner notes, *Heifetz: Gershwin and Encores* (RCA 09026–61771-2, 1992).

7. Reviews of all-Gershwin concert at Lewisohn Stadium in the [New York] *American, Mirror, Sun, Times, Tribune, World-American* (all 10 July 1936), [B. H. Haggin?], *Brooklyn Daily Eagle* (10 July 1936), GCLC.

8. Reviews of all-Gershwin concert by the Los Angeles Philharmonic, *Hollywood Citizen-News,* [Los Angeles] *Examiner, Times* (all 11 February 1936), GCLC.

9. Edward Rothstein, "Concert: 'Porgy and Bess,'" *New York Times* (24 January 1984); the Bennett concert version comprises an "Introduction," "Summertime," "A Woman Is a Sometime Thing," "Gone, Gone, Gone," "Overflow," "My Man's Gone Now," "Leavin' for the Promise' Lan'," "I Got Plenty o' Nuttin'," "Bess, You Is My Woman," "Oh, I Can't Sit Down," "I Ain' Got No Shame," "It Ain't Necessarily So," "There's a Boat Dat's Leavin' Soon for New York," and "Oh Lawd, I'm On My Way."

10. Cori Ellison, "'Porgy' and the Racial Politics of Music," *New York Times* (13 December 1998) ("In large part"); Paul Griffiths, "The Folks on Catfish Row in Concert," *New York Times* (19 December 1998).

11. David Horn, "From Catfish Row to Granby Street: Contexting Meaning in Porgy and Bess," *Popular Music* 13, no. 2 (1994): 165–174; idem, "Who Loves You Porgy? The Debates Surrounding Gershwin's Musical," in *Approaches to the American Musical,* ed. Robert Lawson-Peebles (Exeter: University of Exeter Press, 1996), pp. 109–126.

12. John Ferguson, interview by the author, 2 June 2004.

13. "Nashville Symphony presents Gershwin's Lost Score: The Original 1935 Production Version of Porgy and Bess," press release, Nashville Symphony; *Nashville Symphony Concert Program: Porgy and Bess* (24 and 25 February 2006); Alan Bostick, "Symphony gives Gershwin last word on 'Porgy and Bess.'" *Tennessean* (19 February 2006); Rebecca Bain, "Porgy and Bess," *All Things Considered*, National Public Radio (24 February 2006); Wayne Shirley and Alan D. Valentine, interviews by the author, 27 February 2006 (all printed materials courtesy of the Nashville Symphony).

14. Bostick ("sleek," "I've done"); Lester Lynch, interview by the author, 18 March 2006; Alvy Powell, interview by the author, 29 March 2006; "Nashville Symphony" ("final vision"); Charles Hamm quoted on *All Things Considered* ("the way he").

15. John Steane, "Porgy and Bess," *Opera* (October 1992): 1161–1162.

16. GG, letter to DuBose Heyward, 26 January 1937, ILGT; "Ira Gershwin Opposes Filming 'Porgy' Now," *Variety* (8 February 1956); for information on the picture in general, see ALP, pp. 249–281; Loudon Wainwright, "The One-Man Gang Is in Action Again," *Life* 46, no. 7 (16 February 1959): 103–116; A. Scott Berg, *Goldwyn: A Biography* (New York: Alfred A. Knopf, 1989), pp.

478–488; Harper MacKay, "Porgy in Hollywood," *Opera News* 54, no. 9 (20 January 1990): 8–12, 46.

17. Breen stayed on for five weeks and helped coach the actors, but then quit the production; in 1963 he lost a jury verdict in a suit brought against Goldwyn for breaking a verbal agreement that they share artistic control of the film: "Bobby Breen Loses Suit to Goldwyn," *Los Angeles Herald-Examiner* (25 March 1963).

18. Martin Bookspan and Ross Yockey, *André Previn: A Biography* (Garden City, NY: Doubleday, 1981).

19. ALP, pp. 260–261 ("given to"); Jack Pitman, "Lorraine Hansberry Deplores 'Porgy,'" *Variety* (27 May 1959); Era Bell, "Why Negroes Don't Like 'Porgy and Bess,'" *Ebony* 14, no. 12 (October 1959): 50–52, 54.

20. Gary Fishgall, *Gonna Do Great Things: The Life of Sammy Davis, Jr.* (New York: Scribner, 2003), pp. 128–129; Sidney Poitier, *This Life* (New York: Alfred A. Knopf, 1980), pp. 205–224; Dorothy Dandridge and Earl Conrad, *Everything and Nothing: The Dorothy Dandridge Tragedy* (New York: Perennial, 1970, repr. 2000), pp. 199–202; Diahann Carroll, with Ross Firestone, *Diahann: An Autobiography* (Boston: Little, Brown, 1986), p. 73; Pearl Bailey, *The Raw Pearl* (New York: Harcourt Brace, 1968), pp. 76–77 ("dialect bit").

21. "Dubbing in the Voices, Also a Big Production," *Life* (15 June 1959): 79–82 ("There I was").

22. "Mystery Fire Razes Huge Goldwyn Studio," *Los Angeles Evening Mirror-News* (2 July 1958); Mark Spergel, *Reinventing Reality: The Art and Life of Rouben Mamoulian* (Metuchen, NJ: Scarecrow Press, 1993), pp. 220–228.

23. Reviews of *Porgy and Bess* in the *New York Times* (25 June 1959), *Variety* (1 July 1959), *Nation, New Yorker, Saturday Review* (all 4 July 1959), *Newsweek* (6 July 1959), *New Republic* (13 July 1959); see also Bosley Crowther, "Fitness of Folk Opera," *New York Times* (28 June 1959) ("'Porgy and Bess' wasn't written"); idem, "'Porgy and Bess' Again," *New York Times* (2 August 1959).

24. Fishgall, *Gonna Do Great Things,* p. 130 ("epitome"); James Baldwin, "On Catfish Row," *Commentary* (September 1959), reprinted in his *Price of the Ticket* (New York: St. Martin's, 1985), pp. 177–181.

25. OHL, pp. 179–180; Berg, *Goldwyn,* p. 487; ALP, pp. 279–280.

26. ALP, pp. 280–281; David Gritten, "Gershwins Were No Fans of Preminger's 'Porgy,'" *Los Angeles Times* (19 January 1993) ("My aunt"); [George Cunningham, Foster Hirsch, James Standifer, and Margo Jefferson], "Porgy and Bess—the Film," *I.S.A.M. Newsletter* (Fall 1998): 12–13.

27. AV ("lost children"); Dandridge and Conrad, *Everything and Nothing,* pp. 199–201.

28. Gary Giddins, *Bing Crosby: A Pocketful of Dreams: The Early Years, 1903–1940* (New York: Little, Brown, 2001), p. 473.

29. Walter recorded "Bess, You Is My Woman," "I Got Plenty," and "There's a Boat."

30. Dome Cerulli, "Recording the Jazz Soul of Porgy and Bess," *The Jazz Soul of Porgy and Bess* (United Artists UAL 4032, 1959).

31. Mel Tormé, *It Wasn't All Velvet* (New York: Viking, 1988), p. 185;

"'Porgy and Bess' Medley," *Mel Tormé and Friends* (Finesse Records W2X 37484, 1981).

32. Ian Carr, *Miles Davis: The Definitive Biography* (London: HarperCollins, 1998); Stephanie Stein Crease, *Gil Evans: Out of the Cool, His Life and Music* (Chicago: A Cappella Books, 2002); Jon Pareles, "Who Loves You, Porgy? Illuminating the Details," *New York Times* (23 June 2000).

33. Sarah Kaufman, "'Porgy and Bess': Feet Do the Talking," *Washington Post* (14 September 1998); Margaret Godfrey, "Dallas Dancers Interpret 'Porgy and Bess' with Eloquent Grace," *Salt Lake Tribune* (9 November 1998); Margaret Putnam, "Slow Burn," *Dallas Morning News* (2 June 2000); Jean Reynolds Page, "'Summertime' Is Here," *Dallas Morning News* (1 June 2001); LeVon Campbell, interview by the author, 24 January 2005.

34. Steven Graybow, liner notes, *Porgy & Bess* (Americana Music A 440, 2004) ("This recording"); Jeffrey Lindberg, e-mail to the author, 13 January 2005; Michael Ullman, "The Jazz Corner," *Fanfare* (January–February 2005): 279–280.

35. The Bailey and Davis albums are presumed to have been released in 1959. Some commentators were perplexed that Previn would make a *Porgy* recording with Carroll after hiring Loulie Jean Norman as her vocal double for the film, though the two voices were considerably different.

36. André Previn, "Porgy and Bess and Bill Potts," *The Jazz Soul;* for some 1959 reviews of various *Porgy* albums, see John S. Wilson, "A Wide Variety of Porgys and Besses," *New York Times* (24 May 1959); idem, "Four More Jazz Approaches to Porgy," *High Fidelity Magazine* (June 1959): 92; and Irving Kolodin, "Catfish Row and Wilshire," *Saturday Review* (13 June 1959): 52.

37. Villegas actually released two different suites on the two sides of his 1968 release; neither of the listed items on the record jacket, incidentally, mentioned "A Red Headed Woman," which appears after "It Ain's Necesseraly Now" [*sic*] on side 1, and after "I Wants to Stay Here" on side 2, *Porgy and Bess* (Trova TL-19, 1968).

38. Will Friedwald, *Stardust Melodies: The Biography of Twelve of America's Most Popular Songs* (New York: Pantheon, 2002), p. 344; http://members.lycos.nl/summertimeweb/Artists.html (27 December 2005).

39. Friedwald, *Stardust Melodies*, p. 314, reasonably preferred to view the song as A (A–B–A'–C) A (A–B–A'–C).

40. Friedwald, *Stardust Melodies*, p. 326; *Two Presidents' Jam Session* (Radegast CR 0001–2–531, 1994).

41. Alan and Marilyn Bergman, *Barbra Streisand: The Broadway Album* (CBS OCT 40092, 1985).

42. Benny Green, liner notes, *Porgy and Bess*, with Ray Charles and Cleo Laine (RCA CPL 2–1831, 1976).

35. From *Swing Is King* to *A Damsel in Distress*

1. OHL, pp. 98–99.
2. Review of *Swing Is King* in *Variety* (3 June 1936); WIL, p. 155.

3. GER, pp. 169–171.

4. Reviews of *The Show Is On* in *Variety* (11 November 1936), *New York Times* (28 December 1936), *Variety* (30 December 1936).

5. For the revised lyric, see GER, p. 171.

6. Archie Selwyn, telegram to GG, 12 June 1936, GCLC; GG, telegram to Selwyn, 22 June 1936, GCLC.

7. Pandro Berman, telegram to GG, 24 June 1936, GCLC; Irving Berlin, letter to GG, 23 June 1936, GCLC.

8. John Mueller, *Astaire Dancing* (New York: Alfred A. Knopf, 1985), p. 115.

9. DON, p. 67; John M. Clum, *Something for the Boys: Musical Theater and Gay Culture* (New York: St. Martin's Press, 1999), p. 96; MAS, p. 149; J.P. Telotte, "Dancing the Depression: Narrative Strategy in the Astaire-Rogers Films," *Journal of Popular Film and Television* 8 (Fall 1980): 23–24.

10. Bob Thomas, *Astaire: The Man, the Dancer* (New York: St. Martin's Press, 1984), p. 140 ("the attempt"); Leonard Lyons, "Lyons Den," *New York Post* (19 November 1937) (for mention of their having a script to *Shall We Dance* in New York).

11. GG, letter to Mabel Schirmer, 18 September 1936, GCLC; GG, letter to Zena Hannefeldt, 22 October 1936, GCLC.

12. Arlene Croce, *The Fred Astaire & Ginger Rogers Book* (New York: Outerbridge & Lazard, 1972), pp. 90–91; Hermes Pan, quoted by John Kobal, *People Will Talk* (New York: Auruna Press, 1986), p. 626.

13. Rodgers wrote to his wife on April 28, 1937, "The new Astaire-Rogers job [*Shall We Dance*] is generally admired, but the damn folks all hate George's score. That may be due to the fact that he orchestrated it himself": *Richard Rodgers: Letters to Dorothy*, ed. William W. Appleton (New York: New York Public Library, 1988), p. 225.

14. Croce identified the featured black singer in the engine-room scene as Mantan Moreland, but historian Miles Kreuger (interview by the author, 23 July 2004) disputes this.

15. When Jeffrey asks, "What other mood? You mean this jazz business?" Peter elusively answers, "Oh, jazz went out with the flapper. That isn't jazz." These last remarks are problematic, for jazz, of course, did not go "out with the flapper," and the film itself later associates this "other" dancing with "jazz."

16. Croce, *The Fred Astaire*, pp. 120, 142; Mueller, *Astaire Dancing*, p. 115.

17. Steven Gilbert quoted in SCH/GS, p. 68.

18. Ira Gershwin, introduction, "Hi-Ho!" (New York: Gershwin Publishing Corporation, 1967).

19. RIM, p. 358.

20. LEV/SI, p. 208.

21. GOL, p. 343; JAB/GY, p. 288; FER, pp. 155–156 ("absolute monarchs"); Croce, *The Fred Astaire*, p. 126; SHI, pp. 172–174.

22. GG, letter to Zena Hannenfeldt, 12 April 1937, GCLC; GG, letter to Julia Van Norman, 15 April 1937, GCLC; GG, letters to Isaac Goldberg, 13 April 1937, 12 May 1937, ILGT.

23. Reviews of *Shall We Dance* in the *Hollywood Reporter* (27 April 1937), *Time* (10 May 1937), *Variety* (12 May 1937), [New York] *American, Herald-*

Tribune, Times (all 14 May 1937), *Scholastic, Literary Digest, New Yorker, Newsweek* (all 15 May 1937); clipping file, NYPL (including two unidentified reviews by Winston Burdett).

24. Edizoni Curci, letter to Mr. Ganne of Chappell, GCLC (Alberto Semprini conducted the symphony orchestra of the EIAR); Mueller, *Astaire Dancing*, p. 116 ("mediocre," "tone"); Roy Hemming, *The Memory Lingers On: The Great Songwriters and Their Movie Musicals* (New York: Newmarket Press, 1986), pp. 65–66.

25. IC ("I'd like to," as quoted by Michael Feinstein); Ira Gershwin quoted by Eileen Creelman, "Pictures Plays and Players," *New York Sun* (22 December 1937). Regarding the direction, Croce (*The Fred Astaire*, pp. 51, 57) notes that Sandrich was "more gifted as a technician of musicals than as a director," identifying his "slack timing of comic dialogue" as his "major flaw."

26. P. G. Wodehouse, *A Damsel in Distress* (New York: Penguin Books, 1961 [orig. 1919]), pp. 1, 102, 113; for more on the interaction between Wodehouse's prose and his work in musical comedy, see MCC, especially pp. 135–137.

27. Benny Green, *Fred Astaire* (New York: Exeter Books, 1979), p. 86; whatever the possibility that Wodehouse had Gershwin in mind, the reference to "a summertime number" was obviously coincidental.

28. GG, letter to Frances Gershwin, 27 May 1937, GCLC; David A. Jasen, *P. G. Wodehouse: A Portrait of a Master* (New York: Continuum, 1974), pp. 155–156; DON, p. 67, 131; Mueller, *Astaire Dancing*, p. 128 (for more on the differences between the novel and the picture, see p. 129).

29. FER, p. 169.

30. MCC, p. 247.

31. Mueller, *Astaire Dancing*, pp. 127–128; GER, p. 197; Stephen Banfield, "The English 'Other' in the American Musical: *A Damsel in Distress*," unpublished paper, courtesy of the author; LEV/SI, p. 204.

32. GG, letter to Chappell & Co., 17 March 1937, GCLC; GER, pp. 157–158; Allen Forte, *The American Popular Ballad of the Golden Era, 1924–1950* (Princeton, NJ: Princeton University Press, 1995), pp. 166–171.

33. Eileen Creelman, "Picture Plays and Players," *New York Sun* (22 December 1937) (René Clair); Mark Van Doren, review of *A Damsel in Distress* in the *Nation* (18 December 1937): 697.

34. Joan Fontaine, *No Bed of Roses* (New York: William Morrow, 1978), p. 89. Reviews of *A Damsel in Distress* in *Film Daily* (20 November 1937) ("mostly decorative"), *Variety* (24 November 1937), [New York] *Herald-Tribune* and *Times* (both 25 November 1937), *Motion Picture Herald* (27 November 1937), *Life* (29 November 1937), *Commonweal* (3 December 1937): 160, *Newsweek* and *Time* (both 6 December 1937), *Literary Digest* (11 December 1937): 34.

35. Thomas Fitzpatrick, "Production!" *Rochester Review* (Winter 1987–1988): 3–8.

36. Stephen Holden, "Stage: From Gershwin, 'Reaching for the Moon,'" *New York Times* (2 November 1987); reviews of *A Foggy Day* in the *Toronto Sun* (24 May 1998), *Variety* (1–7 June 1998), *Wall Street Journal* (29 July 1998), *Chicago Tribune* (2 August 1998) ("elaborate stage"), [London] *Times* (25 August 1998); *A Foggy Day,* 1998 and 1999 program books ("aspects"), courtesy of John Mueller.

36. From *The Goldwyn Follies* to *Kiss Me, Stupid*

1. Ira Gershwin, letter to A. M. Wattenberg, 5 December 1936, GCLC.

2. A. Scott Berg, *Goldwyn: A Biography* (New York: Alfred A. Knopf, 1989), p. 267.

3. HIR, p. 145.

4. GG, letter to Isaac Goldberg, 12 May 1937, and GG, letter to Frances Gershwin, 27 May 1937, GCLC.

5. Berg, *Goldwyn*, p. 300; LEV/SI, p. 196; BEH, p. 253.

6. LEV/SI, p. 197; see also KIM/G, p. 222; KIM/CLIG, p. 278 ("me Tarzan").

7. KIM/CLIG, pp. 278–279 ("Exposition"); DUK/PP, p. 356; Vera Zorina, *Zorina* (New York: Farrar, Straus and Giroux, 1986), pp. 164–173; Berg, *Goldwyn*, p. 302.

8. JAB, p. 326; GER, p. 284; LEV/SI, p. 204; Ira Gershwin, letter to Rose Gershwin, 17 August 1937, GCLC.

9. Frank S. Nugent, "Fable of the 'Follies,'" *New York Times* (27 February 1938).

10. Reviews of *The Goldwyn Follies* in the *Hollywood Reporter* (26 January 1938), *Film Daily* (27 January 1938), *Variety* (2 February 1938), *Life* and *Time* (both 7 February 1938), *Newsweek* (14 February 1938), *Commonweal* (18 February 1938), *Literary Digest* and *New Yorker* (both 19 February 1938), [New York] *Daily Mirror* and *Daily News* (both 20 February 1938), [New York] *Herald-Tribune, Post, Times* (all 21 February 1938), *New Statesman and Nation* (19 March 1938).

11. Howard Barnes, review of *The Goldwyn Follies* in the *New York Herald-Tribune* (27 February 1938).

12. LEV/SI, p. 191 ("Brahms").

13. WIL, p. 160.

14. JAB/GY, p. 173; Steven Bach, *Dazzler: The Life and Times of Moss Hart* (New York: Alfred A. Knopf, 2001), pp. 152–154.

15. Carolyn Anspacher, "From Tin Pan Alley to Top Hat Row; Still Going!" *San Francisco Chronicle* (13 January 1937); JAB/GY, pp. 274–275.

16. FEI, pp. 176–179; "New Gershwin Music Found," unidentified (28 December 1938), GCLC.

17. "World Fair March Is Gershwin Tune," *New York Times* (24 April 1938); "Gershwin Song Will Be Anthem of World's Fair," *New York Herald-Tribune* (24 April 1938); JAB/GY, p. 318; Ira Gershwin, marginalia (24 September 1971), *Gershwin Tune Book (1933–1937)*, GCLC.

18. JAB, p. 347; "Unpublished Gershwin Tunes Bought for Grable-Haymes Film," *Los Angeles Examiner* (25 July 1945).

19. JAB, p. 327; GER, pp. 21, 70; FEI, p. 179; Michael Feinstein, interview by the author, 24 October 2004, for Levant's participation in the reconstruction of "Heigh-Ho the Merrio."

20. For more on the original Ernest and Frederica story, see Frederica Sagor Maas, *The Shocking Miss Pilgrim: A Writer in Early Hollywood* (Lexington: University Press of Kentucky, 1999), pp. 232–240.

21. Reviews of *The Shocking Miss Pilgrim* in *Variety* (1 January 1947), *Film*

Daily (2 January 1947), *Newsweek* (10 February 1947), *New York Times* (12 February 1947), *Los Angeles Times* (15 February 1947), *New York Times* (16 February 1947) ("just another"), *Commonweal* (7 February 1947), *New Republic* and *Time* (both 17 February 1947), *Holiday* (April 1947). See also Tom McGee, *Betty Grable: The Girl with the Million Dollar Legs* (Vestal, NY: Vestal Press, 1995), p. 136.

22. Ethan Mordden, *The Hollywood Studios: House Style in the Golden Age of the Movies* (New York: Alfred A. Knopf, 1988), p. 290.

23. GER, pp. 22, 262.

24. JAB/GY, pp. 321–322.

25. FUR, pp. 240–241.

26. JAB/GY, p. 322.

27. Reviews of *Kiss Me, Stupid* in *Variety* (16 December 1964), *Film Daily* (17 December 1964), *Commonweal* (18 December 1964), *Los Angeles Herald-Examiner* (19 December 1964), *New York Times* (23 December 1964), *Newsweek* (28 December 1964), *Time* (1 January 1965), *Saturday Review* (2 January 1965), *New Republic* (9 January 1965), *Village Voice* (14 January 1965), *Vogue* (1 March 1965) ("profoundly affecting"), *Christian Century* (3 February 1965), [London] *Times* (25 February 1965), *Playboy* (March 1965), *Spectator* (5 March 1965), and *Esquire* (June 1965) (*Film Daily* and *Newsweek* also liked the film); George Morris, "The Private Film of Billy Wilder," *Film Comment* (January–February 1979): 34–39.

Conclusion

1. "Tales of Tin Pan Alley: 'Swanee' and Its Author," *Edison Musical Magazine* (October 1920): 9 ("more typically"); G4 ("Berlin had").

2. GOL, p. 139.

3. Carolyn Anspacher, "From Tin Pan Alley to Top Hat Row; Still Going!" *San Francisco Chronicle* (13 January 1937).

4. BEH, p. 256.

5. Isaac Goldberg, "American Operetta Comes of Age," *Disques* 3, no. 1 (March 1932): 10; Elizabeth Borton, "'Must Let One's Ego Flower to Do Creative Work'—Gershwin" (ca. October 1933), GCLC ("as part").

6. BEH, p. 245; KIM/G, p. 140 ("joyous").

Archival Sources

GCLC. Gershwin Collection at the Library of Congress
ILGT. Ira and Leonore Gershwin Trusts
NYPA. New York Philharmonic Archives
NYPL. New York Public Library
RB. Radio Broadcasts at the Ira and Leonore Gershwin Trusts

Gershwin's Writings

G1. "The Composer in the Machine Age." In *Revolt in the Arts: A Survey of Creation, Distribution and Appreciation of Art in America,* ed. Oliver Sayler, pp. 264–269. New York: Brentano's, 1930. Reprinted in ARM/GG, pp. 225–230.

G2. "Critic Artist, Artist Critic in This Review of Concert." *New York World* (22 January 1927), p. 13.

G3. "Does Jazz Belong to Art?" *Singing* 1, no. 7 (July 1926): 13–14.

G4. "Fifty Years of American Music." *American Hebrew* (22 November 1929): 46, 110.

G5. "Introduction." *George Gershwin's Song-Book,* pp. ix–x. New York: Random House, 1932.

G6. "Introduction." *Tin Pan Alley: A Chronicle of the American Popular Music Racket,* by Isaac Goldberg, pp. vii–xi. New York: John Day, 1930.

G7. "Jazz Is the Voice of the American Soul." *Theatre Magazine* 45, no. 311 (March 1927): 14, 52B.

G8. "Making Music." *Sunday [New York] World Magazine* (4 May 1930): 2–14.

G9. "Melody Shop Formulas." *Musical Digest* 11, no. 20 (1 March 1927): 32, 64.

G10. "Mr. Gershwin Replies to Mr. Kramer." *Singing* 1, no. 10 (October 1926): 17–18.

G11. "Our New National Anthem." *Theatre Magazine* 41, no. 5 (May 1925): 30.

G12. "The Relation of Jazz to American Music." In *American Composers on American Music: A Symposium,* ed. Henry Cowell, p. 187. Palo Alto, CA: Stanford University Press, 1933.

G13. "Rhapsody in Catfish Row: Mr. Gershwin Tells the Origin and Scheme for His Music in That New Folk Opera Called 'Porgy and Bess.'" *New York Times* (20 October 1935), sect. 10, pp. 1–2. Reprinted in ARM/GG, pp. 72–77.

G14. "Talented Children Need Help" (letter to the editor). *New York Times* (22 September 1934): 14.

Selected Bibliography

General

Adler, Larry. *It Ain't Necessarily So.* London: Collins, 1984.

ALE. Alexander, Shana. *Happy Days: My Mother, My Father, My Sister & Me.* New York: Doubleday, 1995.

ALP. Alpert, Hollis. *The Story of Porgy and Bess.* New York: Alfred A. Knopf, 1990.

ARM/GGML. Armitage, Merle. *George Gershwin: Man and Legend,* with a note on the author by John Charles Thomas. New York: Duell, Sloan & Pearce, 1958.

ARM/GG. Armitage, Merle, ed. *George Gershwin.* New York: Longmans, Green, 1938.

ARV. Arvey, Verna. "George Gershwin through the Eyes of a Friend." *Opera and Concert* 13 (April 1948): 10–11, 27–28.

AST. Astaire, Fred. *Steps in Time.* New York: Harper & Bros., 1959.

AUS. Austin, William W. *"Susanna," "Jeanie," and "The Old Folks at Home": The Songs of Stephen C. Foster from His Time to Ours.* New York: Macmillan, 1975.

Bach, Steven. *Dazzler: The Life and Times of Moss Hart.* New York: Alfred A. Knopf, 2001.

BAN. Banagale, Ryan Raul. *An American in Chinatown: Asian Representation in the Music of George Gershwin.* Master's thesis, University of Washington, 2004.

BAR. Barrios, Richard. *The Birth of the Musical Film.* New York: Oxford University Press, 1995.

BEH. Behrman, S. N. *People in a Diary.* Boston: Little, Brown, 1972.

Bernstein, Leonard. "A Nice Gershwin Tune." *Atlantic Monthly* (April 1955). Reprinted in *The Joy of Music.* New York: Simon and Schuster, 1959.

BIL. Billman, Larry. *Fred Astaire: A Bio-Bibliography.* Westport, CT: Greenwood Press, 1997.

Block, Geoffrey. *Enchanted Evenings: The Broadway Musical from Show Boat to Sondheim.* New York: Oxford University Press, 1997.

BLO. Bloom, Ken. *American Song: The Complete Musical Theatre Companion.* Vol. 1. New York: Facts on File Publications, 1985.

BOR/AMR. Bordman, Gerald. *American Musical Revue: From* The Passing Show *to* Sugar Babies. New York: Oxford University Press, 1985.

BOR/AMT. Bordman, Gerald. *American Musical Theatre: A Chronicle.* 3rd ed. New York: Oxford University Press, 2001.

BOR/D. Bordman, Gerald. *Days to Be Happy, Years to Be Sad: The Life and Music of Vincent Youmans.* New York: Oxford University Press, 1982.

BOR/JK. Bordman, Gerald. *Jerome Kern: His Life and Music.* New York: Oxford University Press, 1980.

BRA. Bradley, Edwin M. *The First Hollywood Musicals: A Critical Filmography of 171 Features, 1927 through 1932.* Jefferson, NC: McFarland, 1996.

Capote, Truman. *The Muses Are Heard.* New York: Random House, 1956.

CAR. Carnovale, Norbert. *George Gershwin: A Bio-Bibliography.* Westport, CT: Greenwood Press, 2000.

Cerf, Bennett. *Try and Stop Me: A Collection of Anecdotes and Stories, Mostly Humorous.* New York: Simon and Schuster, 1945.

CHA. Chauncey, George. *Gay New York: Gender, Urban Culture, and the Making of the Gay Male World 1890–1940.* New York: Basic Books, 1994.

DAN. Danly, Linda, ed. *Hugo Friedhofer: The Best Years of His Life—A Hollywood Master of Music for the Movies.* Lanham, MD: Scarecrow Press, 1999.

DAV/B. Davis, Lee. *Bolton and Wodehouse and Kern: The Men Who Made Musical Comedy.* New York: James H. Heineman, 1993.

DAV/SF. Davis, Lee. *Scandals and Follies: The Rise and Fall of the Great Broadway Revue.* New York: Limelight Editions, 2000.

DON. Donaldson, Frances, ed. *Yours, Plum: The Letters of P. G. Wodehouse.* London: Hutchinson, 1990.

DOU. Douglas, Ann. *Terrible Honesty: Mongrel Manhattan in the 1920s.* New York: Farrar, Straus and Giroux, 1995.

DUA. Duault, Alain, ed. *George Gershwin: Rhapsodie à Catfish Row.* Paris: L'Avant-Scène Opéra, 1987.

DUK/GS. Duke, Vernon. "Gershwin, Schillinger, and Dukelsky: Some Reminiscences." *Musical Quarterly* 33, no. 1 (January 1947): 102–115.

Duke, Vernon. *Listen Here! A Critical Essay on Music Depreciation.* New York: Ivan Obolensky, 1963.

DUK/PP. Duke, Vernon. *Passport to Paris.* Boston: Little, Brown, 1955.

EWE. Ewen, David. *A Journey to Greatness: The Life and Music of George Gershwin.* New York: Henry Holt, 1956. Enlarged as *His Journey to Greatness,* 1970.

EWE/SGG. Ewen, David. *The Story of George Gershwin.* New York: Holt, Rinehart and Winston, 1943.

FEI. Feinstein, Michael. *Nice Work If You Can Get It: My Life in Rhythm and Rhyme.* New York: Hyperion, 1995.

FER. Ferencz, George J., ed. *"The Broadway Sound": The Autobiography and Selected Essays of Robert Russell Bennett.* Rochester, NY: University of Rochester Press, 1999.

Forte, Allen. *The American Popular Ballad of the Golden Era 1924–1950.* Princeton, NJ: Princeton University Press, 1995.

Friedwald, Will. *Stardust Melodies: The Biography of Twelve of America's Most Popular Songs.* New York: Pantheon, 2002.

FUR. Furia, Philip. *Ira Gershwin: The Art of the Lyricist.* New York: Oxford University Press, 1996.

GER. Gershwin, Ira. *Lyrics on Several Occasions,* with a preface by John Guare and l'envoi by Lawrence D. Stewart. New York: Limelight, 1997 (orig. 1959).

GIL. Gilbert, Steven E. *The Music of Gershwin.* New Haven, CT: Yale University Press, 1995.

GOL. Goldberg, Isaac. *George Gershwin: A Study in American Music,* supplemented by Edith Garson, with foreword and discography by Alan Dashiell. New York: Frederick Ungar, 1958 (orig. 1931).

Goldberg, Isaac. "In Memoriam: George Gershwin," *B'nai B'rith Magazine* (August–September 1937): 8–9, 26.

GOT. Gottlieb, Jack. *Funny, It Doesn't Sound Jewish: How Yiddish Songs and Synagogue Melodies Influenced Tin Pan Alley, Broadway, and Hollywood.* SUNY in association with the Library of Congress, 2004.

GRA. Grant, Mark N. *The Rise and Fall of the Broadway Musical.* Boston: Northeastern University Press, 2004.

Greenberg, Rodney. *George Gershwin.* London: Phaidon, 1998.

GRE. Greenhalgh, Herbert S. "When We Have Jazz Opera: An Interview with Mr. George Gershwin." *Musical Canada* (October 1925): 13–14.

Harburg, E. Y., et al. "Notes and Quotes from Ira's Friends." *ASCAP Today* 5, no. 3 (January 1972): 7–9.

Harkins, John. "George Gershwin." *Life* (August 1932): 13–16.

HIR. Hirschhorn, Clive. *The Hollywood Musical.* New York: Crown Publishing, 1981.

Hoogstraten, Nicholas Van. *Lost Broadway Theatres.* New York: Princeton Architectural Press, 1991, repr. 1997.

HOW. Howe, Irving. *World of Our Fathers.* New York: Harcourt Brace Jovanovich, 1976.

HYL. Hyland, William. *George Gershwin: A New Biography.* Westport, CT: Praeger, 2003.

Irvin, Marjory. "It's George, Not Jazz: Gershwin's Influence in Piano Music." *American Music Teacher* 23 (November–December 1973): 31–34.

JAB. Jablonski, Edward. *Gershwin: A Biography.* New York: Doubleday, 1987.

JAB/GR. Jablonski, Edward. *Gershwin Remembered.* Portland, OR: Amadeus, 1992.

JAB/GY. Jablonski, Edward, and Lawrence D. Stewart. *The Gershwin Years,* with an introduction by Carl Van Vechten. Garden City, NY: Doubleday, 1958, rev. ed. 1973.

JAS. Jasen, David A. *P. G. Wodehouse: A Portrait of a Master.* New York: Continuum, 1981.

JOH. Johnson, John Andrew. *Gershwin's "American Folk Opera": The Genesis, Style, and Reputation of "Porgy and Bess" (1935).* PhD diss., Harvard University, 1996.

KAS. Kashner, Sam, and Nancy Schoenberger. *A Talent for Genius: The Life and Times of Oscar Levant.* New York: Villard Books, 1994.

Keller, Hans. "Rhythm: Gershwin and Stravinsky." *The Score and I.M.A. Magazine* 20 (June 1957): 19–31.

KEN. Kendall, Alan. *George Gershwin.* New York: Universe Books, 1987.

Kilenyi, Edward. "George Gershwin . . . as I Knew Him." *Etude* 68 (October 1950): 11–12, 64.

KIM/CLIG. Kimball, Robert. *The Complete Lyrics of Ira Gershwin.* New York: Da Capo Press, 1993.

KIM/G. Kimball, Robert, and Alfred Simon. *The Gershwins,* with an introduction by Richard Rodgers. New York: Atheneum, 1973.

Knapp, Raymond. *The American Musical and the Formation of National Identity.* Princeton, NJ: Princeton University Press, 2005.

KOL. Kolodin, Irving. *The Musical Life.* New York: Alfred A. Knopf, 1958.

Krellman, Hanspeter. *George Gershwin.* Hamburg: Rowohlt, 1988.

Lamb, Andrew. *150 Years of Popular Musical Theatre.* New Haven, CT: Yale University Press, 2000.

Lawrence, Gertrude. *A Star Danced.* Garden City, NY: Doubleday, Doran, 1945.

Leithauser, Brad. "Here to Stay." *New York Review of Books* 43 (17 October 1996): 35–38.

LEV/MA. Levant, Oscar. *The Memoirs of an Amnesiac.* New York: G. P. Putnam's Sons, 1965.

LEV/SI. Levant, Oscar. *A Smattering of Ignorance.* New York: Doubleday, Doran, 1940.

Levinson, Ilya. *What the Triangles Have Told Me: Manifestations of "The Schillinger System of Musical Composition" in George Gershwin's "Porgy and Bess."* PhD diss., University of Chicago, 1997.

LOG. Loggia, Marjorie, and Glenn Young. *The Collected Works of Harold Clurman.* New York: Applause Books, 1994.

MAS. Mast, Gerald. *Can't Help Singin': The American Musical on Stage and Screen.* Woodstock, NY: Overlook Press, 1987.

MCC. McCrum, Robert. *Wodehouse: A Life.* New York: W. W. Norton, 2004.

MEL. Mellers, Wilfrid. *Music in a New Found Land: Themes and Developments in the History of American Music.* New York: Alfred A. Knopf, 1966.

MER. Meredith, Scott. *George S. Kaufman and His Friends.* Garden City, NY: Doubleday, 1974.

Merman, Ethel, as told to Pete Martin. *Who Could Ask for Anything More.* Garden City, NY: Doubleday, 1955.

MEY. Meyerson, Harold, and Ernie Harburg, with the assistance of Arthur Perlman. *Who Put the Rainbow in The Wizard of Oz?* Ann Arbor: University of Michigan Press, 1995.

MOO. Moore, James Ross. "The Gershwins in Britain." *New Theater Quarterly* 37 (February 1994): 39–43.

MOR/MB. Mordden, Ethan. *Make Believe: The Broadway Musical in the 1920s.* New York: Oxford University Press, 1997.

MOR/SS. Mordden, Ethan. *Sing for Your Supper: The Broadway Musical in the 1930s.* New York: Palgrave Macmillan, 2005.

Morrison, William. *Broadway Theatres: History and Architecture.* Mineola, NY: Dover Publications, 1999.

Most, Andrea. *Making Americans: Jews and the Broadway Musical.* Cambridge, MA: Harvard University Press, 2003.

NEI. Neimoyer, Susan E. *Rhapsody in Blue: A Culmination of George Gershwin's Early Musical Education.* PhD diss., University of Washington, 2003.

NOR. Norton, Richard C. *A Chronology of American Musical Theater.* 3 vols. New York: Oxford University Press, 2002.

OHL. Ohl, Vicki. *Fine & Dandy: The Life and Work of Kay Swift.* New Haven, CT: Yale University Press, 2004.

Oja, Carol. "Gershwin and American Modernists of the 1920s." *Musical Quarterly* 78, no. 4 (Winter 1994): 646–668.

Oja, Carol. *Making Music Modern: New York in the 1920s.* New York: Oxford University Press, 2000.

OSG. Osgood, Henry Osborne. *So This Is Jazz.* Boston: Little, Brown, 1926.

PAY. Payne, Robert. *George Gershwin.* New York: Pyramid Books, 1960.

PEY. Peyser, Joan. *The Memory of All That: The Life of George Gershwin.* New York: Simon and Schuster, 1993.

Selected Bibliography

RAY. Rayno, Don. *Paul Whiteman: Pioneer in American Music.* Vol. 1: *1890–1930.* Lanham, MD: Scarecrow Press, 2003.

RIM. Rimler, Walter. *A Gershwin Companion: A Critical Inventory and Discography, 1916–1984.* Ann Arbor, MI: Popular Culture, Ink., 1991.

ROD. Rodgers, Richard. *Musical Stages: An Autobiography.* New York: Random House, 1975.

ROG. Rogers, Ginger. *Ginger: My Story.* New York: HarperCollins, 1991.

ROO. Roost, Alisa C. *The Other Musical Theatre: Political Satire in Broadway Musicals from "Strike Up the Band" (1927) to "Anyone Can Whistle" (1964).* PhD diss., City University of New York, 2001.

ROS. Rosenberg, Deena. *Fascinating Rhythm: The Collaboration of George and Ira Gershwin.* New York: E. P. Dutton, 1991.

RYS. Ryskind, Morrie, with John H. M. Roberts. *I Shot an Elephant in My Pajamas.* Lafayette, LA: Huntington House Publishers, 1994.

SCH/GRB. Schiff, David. *Gershwin: Rhapsody in Blue.* New York: Cambridge University Press, 1997.

SCH/GG. Schneider, Wayne. *George Gershwin's Political Operettas "Of Thee I Sing" (1931) and "Let 'Em Eat Cake" (1933), and Their Role in Gershwin's Musical and Emotional Maturing.* PhD diss., Cornell University, 1985.

SCH/GS. Schneider, Wayne, ed. *The Gershwin Style: New Looks at the Music of George Gershwin.* New York: Oxford University Press, 1999.

Schwartz, Charles. *George Gershwin: A Selective Bibliography and Discography.* Detroit: College Music Society, 1974.

SCH. Schwartz, Charles. *Gershwin: His Life and Music.* Indianapolis: Bobbs Merrill, 1973.

SEL. Seldes, Gilbert. *The Seven Lively Arts.* New York: Harper & Bros., 1924.

Shaw, Charles G. *The Low-Down.* New York: Henry Holt, 1928.

SHI. Shilkret, Nathaniel. *Nathaniel Shilkret: Sixty Years in the Music Business,* ed. Niel Shell and Barbara Shilkret. Lanham, MD: Scarecrow Press, 2005.

SLI. Slide, Andrew. *The Encyclopedia of Vaudeville.* Westport, CT: Greenwood Press, 1994.

Sohler, Elizabeth. *The Influence of Gullah Culture on the Opera "Porgy and Bess."* Master's thesis, University of Kentucky, 1995.

SPE. Spencer, Jon Michael, ed. *The William Grant Still Reader: Essays on American Music.* Special issue of *Black Sacred Music: A Journal of Theomusicology* 6, no. 2 (Fall 1992).

STE. Stevenson De Santis, Florence. *Gershwin.* New York: Treves Publishing, 1987.

Stewart, Lawrence. "The Gershwins—Words upon Music." *Ella Fitzgerald Sings the George and Ira Gershwin Song Book.* Verve 314 539 759–2, 1959, reissued 1998.

Stravinsky, Igor, with Robert Craft. "Some Composers." *Musical America* 82, no. 6 (June 1962): 6, 8.

SUR. Suriano, Gregory. *Gershwin in His Time: A Biographical Scrapbook, 1919–1937.* New York: Gramercy Books, 1998.

Swain, Joseph P. *The Broadway Musical: A Critical and Musical Survey.* New York: Oxford University Press, 1990.

TIO. Tiomkin, Dimitri, and Prosper Buranelli. *Please Don't Hate Me.* Garden City, NY: Doubleday, 1959.

WIL. Wilder, Alec. *American Popular Song: The Great Innovators, 1900–1950.* New York: Oxford University Press, 1972.

WIL/T. Wilk, Max. *They're Playing Our Song.* New York: Zoetrope, 1986.

WOD. Wodehouse, P. G., and Guy Bolton. *Bring on the Girls! The Improbable Story of Our Life in Musical Comedy, with Pictures to Prove It.* New York: Simon and Schuster, 1953.

WOO. Wood, Ean. *George Gershwin: His Life & Music.* London: Sanctuary Publishing, 1996.

Woollcott, Alexander. "George the Ingenuous." *Cosmopolitan* (November 1933): 32–33, 122–123.

WYA. Wyatt, Robert, and John Andrew Johnson, eds. *The George Gershwin Reader.* New York: Oxford University Press, 2004.

ZIE. Ziegfeld, Richard, and Paulette Ziegfeld. *The Ziegfeld Touch: The Life and Times of Florenz Ziegfeld, Jr.* New York: Harry N. Abrams, 1993.

Scripts

Behrman, S. N. *Let Me Hear the Melody!* (1951). NYPL.

Bell, Charles W. *A Dislocated Husband* (1918). New York: Shubert Archives.

Bolton, Guy, and George Grossmith. *Primrose* (1924). GCLC.

Bolton, Guy, and Sonya Levien. *Delicious* (1931). GCLC.

Bolton, Guy, and John McGowan. *Girl Crazy* (1930). New York: Tams-Witmark. Rev. by Guy Bolton (1960), New York: Tams-Witmark.

Bolton, Guy, and William Anthony McGuire. *Rosalie* (1928). GCLC.

Bolton, Guy, and Fred Thompson. *Lady, Be Good!* (1924). ILGT; restored by Tommy Krasker, New York: Tams-Witmark.

Bolton, Guy, and Fred Thompson. *Tip-Toes* (1925). GCLC.

Bolton, Guy, and P. G. Wodehouse. *Oh, Kay!* (1926). ILGT; New York: Tams-Witmark.

Fields, Herbert, and Morrie Ryskind. *Pardon My English* (1932). GCLC; rev., 1932, courtesy of Michael Feinstein.

Harbach, Otto, and Oscar Hammerstein II. *Song of the Flame* (1925). GCLC.

Hooker, Brian, and A. E. Thomas. *Hayseed, or The Villain Still Pursued Her [Our Nell]* (1922). GCLC.

Jackson, Fred. *La-La-Lucille!* (1919). NYPL.

Kaufman, George S. *Strike Up the Band* (1927). NYPL; rev. by Morrie Ryskind, 1928, ILGT; rev. by Morrie Ryskind, 1929, ILGT.

Kaufman, George S., Morrie Ryskind, and Ira Gershwin. *Let 'Em Eat Cake.* New York: Alfred A. Knopf, 1933.

Kaufman, George S., Morrie Ryskind, and Ira Gershwin. *Of Thee I Sing* (1931). Scenario, 1930, GCLC; typescript, 1931, GCLC; New York: Knopf, 1932; London: Victor Gollancz, 1933; New York: Samuel French, 1935.

Lawrence, Vincent, and Fred Thompson. *Treasure Girl* (1928). GCLC (corrected to December 17, 1928, by Sam Fischer).

Ludwig, Ken. *Crazy for You* (1992). New York: Tams-Witmark.

Mandel, Frank, and Laurence Schwab. *Sweet Little Devil* (1923). GCLC.
Mayer, Tim. *My One and Only* (1983). New York: Tams-Witmark.
McEvoy, J. P., and Willliam Anthony McGuire. *Show Girl* (1929). GCLC.
Smith, Paul Gerard, and Fred Thompson. *Funny Face* (1927). ILGT; adapted by Neal Du Brock, New York: Tams-Witmark.
Thompson, Fred, and William K. Wells. *Tell Me More* (1925). ILGT.

Videography

AV. *Porgy and Bess: An American Voice.* PBS Great Performances. Ann Arbor, MI: PBS, 1997.
GGR. *George Gershwin Remembered.* London: BBC, 1987.

Taped Interviews

AB. Anne Brown, interview by Carl G. Friedner, 21 May 1987. Transcript, American Music Series, Yale University.
AG. Arthur Gershwin, interview by Robert Kimball and Alfred Simon, 30 November 1972. Transcript, American Music Series, Yale University.
BL. Burton Lane, interview by Alfred Simon, 28 September 1978. Transcript, American Music Series, Yale University.
GGR2. *George Gershwin Remembered* (Facet 8100, 1987).
FG. Frances Godowsky, interview by Vivian Perlis, 3 June 1983. Transcript, American Music Series, Yale University.
IC. Irving Caesar, interview by Michael Feinstein, 10 June 1983. Courtesy of Michael Feinstein.
KS. Kay Swift, interview by Vivian Perlis, 1 May 1975. Transcript, American Music Series, Yale University.
KW. Kate Wolpin, interview by Vivian Perlis, 30 January 1986. Transcript, American Music Series, Yale University.
LG. Leopold Godowsky II, interview by Vivian Perlis, 4 September 1970. Transcript, American Music Series, Yale University.
WS. William English Strunsky, interview by Vivian Perlis, 10 June 2000. Transcript, American Music Series, Yale University.

Marginalia

LS. Lawrence Stewart, marginalia, author's manuscript.

Index

Index

Gershwin, George *(continued)*
39, 144, 147, 158, 159, 161, 162, 168,
583, 673; as "ingenuous," 204, 205;
Irish music and, 41, 186, 220, 703;
jazz, 12, 27, 41, 52, 66, 76–80, 164–
74, 250, 253, 297, 330, 351–52, 389–
90, 761n30; Jewish music and, 36,
42–47, 173, 238, 462–63, 521, 703;
literary interests, 201–2; in London,
139, 282, 306–7, 321, 323, 326, 333;
as melodist, 98, 139, 142, 178, 633;
melting-pot and, 42, 171, 297, 391,
463–64, 488, 704; in Mexico, 146,
199, 207, 209, 538; modality and, 30,
41, 45, 46, 145, 238, 251, 288, 298,
506, 587; motion pictures, 279–80,
308–9, 374–76, 413–14, 474, 482–
89, 648, 667–83, 703, 764n29; musical education, 22–40, 118–35, 701,
702, 711–12n7; Negro spirituals and,
173–74, 383–84, 463, 563, 588–89;
notebooks, 24, 31, 34, 175, 176, 177–
78, 693; opera and, 22, 37, 38, 115,
123, 132–33, 136, 144, 145, 150,
269–75, 461–64, 554, 559, 567–95,
691, 703; operetta and, 26–27, 41,
43–45, 81–83, 140, 183, 231, 258,
331, 366–67, 374, 417, 421, 691;
orchestration, 30–33, 34, 38, 39, 40,
131, 176, 179–80, 188–90, 300–301,
324–25, 351, 438, 495, 538, 586–87,
674, 702, 704, 812n13; Paley circle
and, 96–100, 107; in Paris, 120–21,
139, 140–41, 161, 201, 432; pentatonicism, 46, 449, 587, 661, 704,
748n33; personality, 39, 195, 202–
6, 564, 705; phonograph recordings,
71–73, 172–73, 304, 441, 774n19,
767n37, 774n19; as pianist, 24–25,
61–80, 99–100; as photographer, 201;
piano rolls and, 35, 58, 62, 66–73,
76, 93, 221, 238, 261, 312, 313, 526,
720n21; politics and, 209, 504; Polynesian music and, 61, 135, 259, 285;
as possible father, 20–21; pseudonyms, 67; psychotherapy, 109, 207–
8, 744n42; radio broadcasts, 73, 83,
92, 131, 163, 193, 235, 434, 575, 703;
ragtime and, 61, 63, 68, 78–79, 226,
245, 520, 702; Remick and, 28, 31,
43, 61–63, 65, 81, 83, 159, 221, 265,
527, 701; residences, 10, 194–95;
rhythm, 46, 56, 72, 76, 122, 130, 135,
159, 170–71, 224, 225, 226, 245, 292–
93, 308, 330–31, 342, 349, 383, 428,
469, 555, 587–88, 704; romantic and
sexual life, 21, 97, 107, 108–16, 211,

420; Russian-Jewish background, 11–
12, 36, 110, 112, 122, 140, 205, 521,
605–6, 619; saxophone, 89; schools
attended, 11, 13–14; singing voice,
177; sports and athletics, 133, 134,
162, 195; stereotyped depictions of,
701–2; in Vienna, 81–82, 139; working
methods, 175–92; writings, 147–48,
169–74, 738n45, 817; Yiddish theater
and, 43–45, 462–63
Gershwin, Ira (Israel/"Izzy") (brother);
American in Paris and, 432, 443,
686–87; as artist, 196, 201; "Ask Me
Again" and, 450; on Bolton, 320;
business matters, 7, 193; in California,
158, 195, 485; collaboration/relations
with composers other than George, 20,
83, 143, 151, 153, 681, 686, 691, 693,
695, 696, 723n35; collaboration with
George (general), 8, 16–17, 92, 94,
176, 180, 184–88, 226, 288, 777, 418,
666, 705; collaboration with George
(on films), 279, 482, 667, 667, 684;
collaboration with George (on shows),
255, 321, 326, 338, 359, 395, 406,
417, 426, 445, 451, 465, 499, 540,
549; collaboration with other lyricists,
225, 228, 253, 254, 321, 338, 381,
417, 421, 453, 576; critical reception,
16, 152, 258, 329, 363–64, 405, 469,
512, 557–58, 675, 783–84n29; on
Daly, 191; on *The Dybbuk,* 463; early
life and education, 4–5, 10, 11, 14–
16, 59, 709n38; early songs, 92, 94,
225–26, 233, 246, 250, 253, 254, 258,
267, 279; *East Is West* and, 445, 448,
449; estate of, 20, 21; in Europe, 139;
on George, 13, 24, 46, 88, 145, 175,
177; George's death, 19–20, 213, 214;
on George's education, 15, 34, 129,
135; on George as possible father, 21;
Gershwin songbooks, 525; W. S. Gilbert
and, 15, 41, 86, 96, 341, 396, 400,
405, 428, 512; "Hi-Ho!" and, 673;
on Hitler, 546–47, 553; humor of, 15,
402, 407, 507; "I Got Rhythm," 469,
480, 481; "The Jolly Tar" and "Sing
of Spring," 680; literary and other
interests, 14–15, 193, 196, 201, 202,
709n36; on *Lullaby,* 246; lyrics, examples of, 226, 233, 258, 267, 330, 331,
341, 362, 400, 405, 422, 430, 468,
680, 690; marriage, 17–18, 194–95;
"The Man I Love" and, 328–29; on
Merman, 471; musical abilities and
interests, 15, 24, 41, 86, 87, 127, 132,
134, 140, 144, 146, 164–65, 188; *My*

842

Index

Designer
Victoria Kuskowski

Text
10/13 Sabon

Display
Edwardian Script, Edition Caps, Sabon

Compositor
Integrated Composition Systems

Indexer
Alexander Trotter

Printer and binder
Thomson-Shore, Inc.